The Cambridge Handbook of Material Culture Studies

Material culture studies is an interdisciplinary field that examines the relationships between people and their things: the production, history, preservation, and interpretation of objects. It draws on theory and practice from disciplines in the social sciences and humanities, such as anthropology, archaeology, history, and museum studies. Written by leading international scholars, this handbook provides a comprehensive view of developments, methodologies, and theories. It is divided into five broad themes, embracing both classic and emerging areas of research in the field. Chapters outline transformative moments in material culture scholarship, and present research from around the world, focusing on multiple material and digital media that show the scope and breadth of this exciting field. Written in an easy-to-read style, it is essential reading for students, researchers, and professionals with an interest in material culture.

LU ANN DE CUNZO is Professor of Anthropology at the University of Delaware. She is Past President of the Society for Historical Archaeology, 2009–10. Notable publications include *A Historical Archaeology of Delaware* (2004) and *Unlocking the Past* (2005).

CATHARINE DANN ROEBER is Interim Director of Academic Programs and Brock W. Jobe Associate Professor of Decorative Arts and Material Culture at Winterthur Museum, Garden & Library affiliated with the University of Delaware. She is Executive Editor for the *Winterthur Portfolio* and is Co-founder of the Consortium of Digital Decorative Arts (CODA).

CAMBRIDGE HANDBOOKS IN ANTHROPOLOGY

Genuinely broad in scope, each handbook in this series provides a complete state-of-the-field overview of a subdiscipline or major topic of anthropological study and research. Grouped into broad thematic areas, the chapters in each volume encompass the most important issues and themes within each subject, offering a coherent picture of the latest theories and findings. Together, the volumes will build into an integrated overview of the discipline in its entirety.

The Cambridge Handbook of Material Culture Studies

Edited by

Lu Ann De Cunzo
University of Delaware

Catharine Dann Roeber
Winterthur Museum, Garden & Library

CAMBRIDGE UNIVERSITY PRESS

CAMBRIDGE UNIVERSITY PRESS

Shaftesbury Road, Cambridge CB2 8EA, United Kingdom

One Liberty Plaza, 20th Floor, New York, NY 10006, USA

477 Williamstown Road, Port Melbourne, VIC 3207, Australia

314–321, 3rd Floor, Plot 3, Splendor Forum, Jasola District Centre, New Delhi – 110025, India

103 Penang Road, #05–06/07, Visioncrest Commercial, Singapore 238467

Cambridge University Press is part of Cambridge University Press & Assessment, a department of the University of Cambridge.

We share the University's mission to contribute to society through the pursuit of education, learning and research at the highest international levels of excellence.

www.cambridge.org
Information on this title: www.cambridge.org/9781108465052
DOI: 10.1017/9781108622639

© Cambridge University Press & Assessment 2022

This publication is in copyright. Subject to statutory exception and to the provisions of relevant collective licensing agreements, no reproduction of any part may take place without the written permission of Cambridge University Press & Assessment.

First published 2022
First paperback edition 2024

A catalogue record for this publication is available from the British Library

ISBN   978-1-108-47461-0   Hardback
ISBN   978-1-108-46505-2   Paperback

Cambridge University Press & Assessment has no responsibility for the persistence or accuracy of URLs for external or third-party internet websites referred to in this publication and does not guarantee that any content on such websites is, or will remain, accurate or appropriate.

To James Deetz, who opened my eyes and mind to the wonder of material culture

Lu Ann De Cunzo

Contents

List of Figures	page ix
List of Tables	xiv
List of Case Studies	xv
List of Contributors	xvi
Acknowledgments	xviii

1 Suitcases, Selfies, and the Global Environment: Material Culture, Materiality, and the New Materialism
  Lu Ann De Cunzo and Catharine Dann Roeber   1

Part I Scholarly Genealogies   25
2 Materiality   *Julian Yates*   27
3 Representation   *Sarah Wasserman*   54

Part II Relevant Pasts   75
4 Disciplinary Complicity: The University, Material Culture Studies, and Global Environmental Crisis   *Richard M. Hutchings*   77
5 Social Justice: Material Culture as a Driver of Inequality
  Claire Smith, Jordan Ralph, Cherrie De Leiuen, and Kellie Pollard   100
6 Engagement and the Politics of Authority
  Cristóbal Gnecco   128
7 War and Violence: How to Rescue a Wartime Artifact
  Bożena Shallcross   146
8 Material Culture and Heritage   *Laura McAtackney*   167
9 Material Culture and the Politics and Profession of Preservation and Representation   *Gretchen Sullivan Sorin*   190
10 Reenacting the Past   *Heather Fitzsimmons Frey and Marlis Schweitzer*   205
11 Indigenous Heritage   *Emily L. Moore*   236

Part III Engaging Across Cultures and Around the Globe — 267
12 The Matter of Cultural Exchange: China, Europe, and Early Modern Material Connections   *Anna Grasskamp* — 269
13 Migration and Material Culture   *Magdalena Naum* — 301
14 Identity and Agency   *Veronica Strang* — 327

Part IV Cultural Production and Reproduction — 355
15 Modes of Representation   *Sebnem Timur* — 357
16 Aesthetics   *Timothy Carroll* — 380
17 Objects Are Alive: Producing Animacy in the Inanimate   *Peter Roe* — 402
18 Technology   *Ludovic Coupaye* — 436

Part V Experience — 469
19 Place and Materiality   *Elijah Gaddis* — 471
20 Home and Domesticity   *Psyche Williams-Forson* — 493
21 The Materiality of Institutional Life   *Eleanor Conlin Casella and Linnea Kuglitsch* — 513
22 Material Religion   *Gretchen Buggeln* — 538

Part VI Materiality and the Digital World — 565
23 Material Cultures of the Digital   *Ryan Cordell* — 567
24 Curating the Digital: Understanding Flows of Data and Their Relations   *Natasha Chuk* — 590
25 Boundaries and Borderlands, Inclusion and Holism: Political and Relevant Material Culture Studies   *Lu Ann De Cunzo and Catharine Dann Roeber* — 623

Bibliography — 632
Index — 719

Figures

3.1 Paul Cezanne, "*Apples and Oranges*", 1900. Oil on canvas, 74 x 93 cm. Musée d'Orsay, Paris, France *page* 55
3.2 Markus Maurer, Plato's "Allegory of the Cave," published originally in Gabriele Veldkamp's *Zukunftsorientierte Gestaltung informationstechnologischer Netzwerke im Hinblick auf die Handlungsfähigkeit des Menschen* (Aachen, Germany: Verlad der Augustinus Buchhandlung, 1996) 56
3.3 Emily Dickinson, "A Great Hope Fell" envelope poem. Emily Dickinson Collection in the Amherst College Digital Collection 58
3.4 October 1953 issue of *Galaxy Science Fiction*, which featured *The Caves of Steel* by Isaac Asimov. Published by Galaxy Publishing, illustrated by Ed Emshwiller 71
4.1 This Western, scientific representation of the "total environment" includes the anthroposphere (human-built and modified environments), atmosphere (gaseous environments), biosphere (living environments), hydrosphere (water environments), and lithosphere (geological environments). Adapted from the journal *Science of the Total Environment*, www.journals.elsevier.com/science-of-the-total-environment 79
4.2 The six consequences of the modern Western school model – inequality, alienation, anxiety, consumption, addiction, and domination – collectively drive late-modern environmental destruction. Prepared by Richard Hutchings 85
5.1 The increased regulation of private space in gated communities. The entrance to the Paradise Village Grand Marina Villas gated community at the Paradise Village Resort, Nuevo Vallarta, Nayarit, Mexico. Photo: Coolcaesar

	at the English language Wikipedia (CC BY-SA 3.0 (http://creativecommons.org/licenses/by-sa/3.0/))	106
5.2	Communicating hospitality versus segregated status: community and government signs on either side of the entrance to Barunga community, Northern Territory, Australia. Photos: J. Ralph and C. Smith	110
5.3	Long grass camp, Darwin, Australia. Photo: K. Pollard	112
5.4	Comparison of roadside facilities available for tourists and Aboriginal communities immediately south of Katherine, Northern Territory, Australia.	115
5.5	Postblloku (Checkpoint) installations, Tirana, Albania. Photos: G. Jackson	116
6.1	The ruins of the church of São Miguel Arcanjo, Brazil. Photo: Cristóbal Gnecco, 2014	131
6.2	Locals making their way from Sisipampa to Pomata, southern shore of Lake Titicaca, Peru. Photo: Cristóbal Gnecco, 2015	137
7.1	Mieczysław Porębski's knife. Photo: Katarzyna Brodowska, courtesy of the artist	153
7.2	Pierre Levi's suitcase, Auschwitz-Birkenau Memorial and Museum and Shoah Memorial Museum in Paris, public domain	158
9.1	Game Room, c. 1900 with blackamoor chairs. Dr. William Seward and Lila Vanderbilt Webb House, Shelburne Farms. Courtesy of Shelburne Farms	192
9.2	Detail of chairs with blackamoor carving. Dr. William Seward and Lila Vanderbilt Webb House, Shelburne Farms. Courtesy of Shelburne Farms	193
9.3	A contemporary art installation on slavery at the Dyckman Farmhouse Museum by Peter Hoffmeister. Courtesy of Dyckman Farmhouse Museum	197
10.1	Girls trying on corsets at Heather's workshop, August 2018. Photo courtesy of Heather Fitzsimmons Frey	206
10.2	Queen Victoria and Prince Albert at the Bal Costumé of May 12, 1842. By Sir Edwin Landseer. Royal Collection Trust/© Her Majesty Queen Elizabeth II 2019	215
10.3a and b	Fancy dress costumes, from Arden Holt, *Fancy Dress Described* (1887). Courtesy of York University Libraries	217
10.4	Maud Allan as Salome, c. 1907. Courtesy of Dance Collection Danse	220
10.5	Image of two young Métis volunteers at Winter Camp. Courtesy of Fort Edmonton Park	229

11.1 Kwakwa̱ka'wakw masks confiscated by the Canadian government from Dan Cranmer's potlatch, 1921. Image PN. 12191. Courtesy of the Royal BC Museum and Archives 238
11.2 Typological display of weaving tools from various Indigenous peoples in the US National Museum, 1890. Smithsonian Institution Archives. Image # MAH-21389 239
11.3 Installation view of the exhibition "Indian Art of the United States," January 22, 1941 through April 27, 1941. The Museum of Modern Art, New York. Photographic Archive. The Museum of Modern Art Archives, ART470221 242
11.4 U'Mista Cultural Centre exhibition, Alert Bay, British Columbia, 2003. Photo: Aaron Glass. 257
12.1 Unidentified maker, *Ewer*, China, Ming dynasty, Wanli reign (1572–1620). Porcelain, painted in underglaze blue, h. 19 cm. Gilded silver mounts by Georg Berger (active c. 1547–77), Erfurt. Berlin, Staatliche Museen Preussischer Kulturbesitz, inv. no. 1889,305. Photo: bpk/Kunstgewerbemuseum, smb/Funke 270
12.2 Unidentified maker, *Carved Shell*, probably South China, before 1590. Gilded silver mounts by Bartel Jamnitzer (c. 1548–96), Nuremberg, c. 1590. Stuttgart, Landesmuseum Württemberg, inv. no. KK hellblau 10. Photo: Hendrik Zwietasch 277
12.3 Unidentified maker, *Lidded jar with gold-painted flowers on white glaze ground*, Sèvres ware, Sèvres, France, eighteenth century, h. 9.7 cm, d. 5.7, h. (lid) 3.6 cm. With inscribed wooden container by Qing imperial workshop, 1736–96. Taipei, National Palace Museum, inv. no. 015560–392–1 279
12.4 Unidentified maker, *Architectural fitting*, stoneware with turquoise-blue glaze, Yuanmingyuan, China, 1747–70, h. 34.5 cm, w. 38.0 cm, d. 23.0 cm. London, Victoria and Albert Museum, inv. no. C.382–1912 283
12.5 Unidentified maker, *A Sloop with Dutchmen and their Goods*, Guangzhou, China, 1700–50, ivory and paint, l. 16 cm. Amsterdam, Rijksmuseum, inv. no. NG-1994–12 286
13.1 What reminds me of home in Syria. Courtesy of Europeana Foundation 309
13.2 Feeling at home in a new home/Macrameul de acasa. Courtesy of Europeana Foundation 310
13.3 The taste of my whole life. Courtesy of Europeana Foundation. 315
14.1 Kunjen elders at sacred site. Photo: Veronica Strang 329
14.2 String ("dilly") bag containing goose eggs, Kowanyama. Photo: Veronica Strang 332

14.3	Stockman's Hall of Fame, Longreach, North Queensland. Photo: Veronica Strang	336
14.4	Children painted with clan designs for ceremony, Kowanyama. Photo: Veronica Strang	340
14.5	Nelson Brumby (deceased), one of the first Aboriginal rangers in Kowanyama. Photo: Veronica Strang	342
14.6	Dunbar cattle station homestead. Photo: Veronica Strang	346
14.7	Maytown historic mine site, Palmer River. Photo: Veronica Strang	347
14.8	MRWMG meeting in Kowanyama. Photo: Veronica Strang	348
15.1	A tattoo designed by the wearer to represent her identity. Photo: Sebnem Timur.	363
15.2	Statue of a homunculus in front of Feza Gürsey Science Center in Ankara, Turkey. https://bit.ly/3GbOGc7	363
15.3a and b	The AuthaGraph World Map created by Hajime Narukawa, www.authagraph.com	369
15.4	Diagrams showing the three phases of design (illustrated by the author from Shove et al. (2007))	370
15.5 and 15.6	Furniture demonstrated on the pavements by upholstery makers in Istanbul. Photos: Sebnem Timur	371
17.1	A Cashinahua warrior, Peruvian jungle, as a Bird Man in feather art. The Chonta palm lance is in the author's collection. Drawing: Author, 2018	409
17.2	The author excavating a secondary burial with partial vessels as a funerary offering at the Maisabel site, north coast Puerto Rico. Photo: Unknown student from author's field school, 1985	414
17.3a	A Shipibo effigy pot whose upper design mirrors Sky World.	417
17.3b	The lower designs represent Earth World and the Sub-Aquatic Underworld. Drawings: author, 1981	417
17.4	A Shipibo shaman, *Bahuan mëtsa* ("Like a Green Amazonian Parrot"), with his painted *tari* (cotton poncho). Photo: author, 2010	418
17.5	A tour boat in the Boston harbor with shark-mouth decoration. Photo: author, 2017	427
19.1	Confederate monuments achieved central placement in civic spaces and in cultural expression of place, as in this dedication ceremony in Tennessee, c. 1910. Dedication ceremony for Confederate Monument in Mulberry, Tennessee, Prints and Photographs Division, Library of Congress	480

19.2	"Confederate Monument, Oxford, NC." Durwood Barbour Collection of North Carolina postcards (P077), North Carolina Collection. Photographic Archives, Wilson Library, UNC-Chapel Hill	482
20.1	Kitchen with ornate stove and dishes. Irma and Paul Milstein Division of United States History, Local History and Genealogy, The New York Public Library. *The New York Public Library Digital Collections*. 1902–14. https://on.nypl.org/3lVXnQz	497
20.2	Front parlor. Courtesy of the Heurich House Museum	498
20.3	Dining room. Courtesy of the Heurich House Museum	499
20.4	Biertstube Courtesy of the Heurich House Museum	500
20.5	A musical rehearsal. Schomburg Center for Research in Black Culture, Jean Blackwell Hutson Research and Reference Division, The New York Public Library. *The New York Public Library Digital Collections*. 1914. https://on.nypl.org/3lPhYWI	510
21.1	Ross Female Factory site plan, with insert location map of Tasmania (Van Diemen's Land). Image courtesy of Eleanor Conlin Casella	519
21.2	Home economics class for women, Carlisle Indian School, Pennsylvania, c. 1900. Photograph by Frances Benjamin Johnston. Library of Congress, Prints and Photographs Division, LC-USZ62-55456	524
21.3	Pair of shanked buttons found pressed into the joints of a brick-floored privy at the Eastern Lunatic Asylum. Photo: Linnea Kuglitsch. Reproduced by permission of the Colonial Williamsburg Foundation, Department of Archaeology, Object ER2284X	529
22.1	Woman (Venus) of Willandorf. Limestone figure, representative of a woman's body. Photo: Mattias Kabel. Wikimedia Commons	542
22.2	Sofia Atlantova (b. 1981) and Oleksandr Klymenko (b. 1975). *Our Lady with the Child*, 2018. Tempera, gold leaf, and ammunition box fragments, 49 x 53 cm. Collection of the artists. Photo: Yevhen Chorny	544
22.3	Store selling head scarves in Damascus, Syria, 2010. Photo: Bernard Gagnon. Wikimedia Commons	548
22.4	Repurposed choir loft, Lake View Lutheran Church, Chicago, Illinois, 1961. Photo: Author, 2012	550
22.5	Ganesha statue, crystal. Photo: Sundar Ganesh Babu	557
23.1	A server room at CERN. Creative Commons image via Wikimedia Commons.	568

Tables

4.1	Common academic ideologies and their consequences	*page* 83
4.2	The global environmental crisis in material culture studies texts	89
15.1	David Chandler's (2002) explanation of C. S. Pierce's three modes of signs. Created by author	358
15.2	Comparisons, modes of representation. Created by author	359

Case Studies

13.1	Belongings: post-World War II migration memories and journeys	*page* 306
13.2	What reminds me of home in Syria	308
13.3	Feeling at home in a new home	310
13.4	The taste of my whole life	315
15.1	The story of zero	365
15.2	Act of mapping and politics	367
15.3	"This is Not a Pipe" versus "Banana with Duct Tape"	376
16.1	Aesthetics across genres	384
16.2	Antiphonal relations	394
22.1	The woman of Willandorf: What makes an object "religious"?	541
22.2	Ukrainian "Icons on Ammo Boxes": strategic transformations	543
22.3	Muslim head scarves: expressive and contested objects	547
22.4	Dynamic repurposing: Lake View Lutheran Church, Chicago	549
22.5	Vodou: strategies of interpretation and display	554
22.6	Ganesha and auspicious beginnings: Does the medium matter?	556

Contributors

Gretchen Townsend Buggeln, Valparaiso University, USA
Timothy Carroll, University College London, UK
Eleanor Conlin Casella, University of Tasmania, Australia
Natasha Chuk, School of Visual Arts, USA
Ryan Cordell, School of Information Sciences at the University of Illinois at Urbana-Champaign, USA
Ludovic Coupaye, University College London, UK
Catharine Dann Roeber, Winterthur Museum, Garden & Library, USA
Lu Ann De Cunzo, University of Delaware, USA
Cherrie De Leiuen, Flinders University, Australia
Heather Fitzsimmons Frey, MacEwan University Canada
Elijah Gaddis, Auburn University, USA
Cristóbal Gnecco, Universidad de Cauca, Colombia
Anna Grasskamp, St. Andrews University, UK
Richard Hutchings, Institute for Critical Heritage and Tourism, Canada
Linnea Kuglitsch, New Jersey State Park System, USA
Laura McAtackney, Aarhus University, Denmark
Emily L. Moore, Colorado State University, USA
Magdalena Naum, Aarhus University, Denmark
Kellie Pollard, Charles Darwin University, Australia
Jordan Ralph, Flinders University, Australia
Peter Roe, University of Delaware, USA
Marlis Schweitzer, York University, Canada
Bozena Shallcross, University of Chicago, USA

Claire Smith, Flinders University, Australia
Gretchen Sullivan Sorin, Cooperstown Graduate Program, SUNY, USA
Veronica Strang, Durham University, UK
Sebnem Timur, Istanbul Technical University, Turkey
Sarah Wasserman, University of Delaware, USA
Psyche Williams-Forson, University of Maryland, USA
Julian Yates, University of Delaware, USA

Acknowledgments

The editors are grateful and extend our thanks to:

- Our institutions, the Department of Anthropology, University of Delaware, and Winterthur Museum, Garden & Library, for supporting this undertaking. In anthropology, special thanks are extended to Andrea Anderson, who compiled the volume bibliography;
- The University of Delaware Center for Material Culture Studies, for a generous grant to support image publication;
- Our authors, for their outstanding scholarship, passion, engagement, and patience;
- Our patient editor at Cambridge University Press, Andrew Winnard, and Isabelle Collins;

Our families, for everything.

1

Suitcases, Selfies, and the Global Environment

Material Culture, Materiality, and the New Materialism

Lu Ann De Cunzo and Catharine Dann Roeber

> An object in possession seldom retains the same charm that it had in pursuit.
>
> Pliny the Younger

Introduction

For scholars, the category "handbook" carries certain expectations. A guide to methodology, a catalog of traditions, or an encyclopedia of ideas and people may come to mind. Public historians James Gardner and Paula Hamilton suggest that handbooks "stake a claim to [the field of study's] significance, chart its trajectories across time and space, and push its boundaries." Our goals for *The Cambridge Handbook of Material Culture Studies* build on these foundations and push against the boundaries of what a handbook can be. The "mission" of this handbook is to be inclusive and current, while offering an interdisciplinary, post-disciplinary, and even undisciplined view of developments, methodologies, and theories in the field/s of material culture. In order to accomplish these project goals, we have structured the volume around broad themes that cross disciplinary and theoretical boundaries and embrace both the classic and the emerging in material culture, materiality, and new materialism studies.

In planning this project, we identified established and emerging leaders in the field who could address both past and contemporary theory and practice as well as look toward future trends in material culture studies. Their chapters outline transformative moments in material culture scholarship and challenge and enrich existing paradigms of material culture research. This volume is neither wholly comprehensive nor a definitive roadmap for "doing" material culture. Instead, the volume provides readers with a snapshot of current approaches and a review of disciplinary contributions to material culture study. This volume gives readers a taste of the multiple ways scholars engage with material culture and guides readers to useful scholarly literature and "signature" studies.

The volume incorporates projects based in the Americas, the British Isles, Western Europe, Australia, and China. Authors represent institutions in the United States, Canada, Colombia, Australia, England, Denmark, Turkey, and Hong Kong. As a result the authors address and acknowledge differences and similarities that exist between the understanding of, framing of, and study of material culture in an international context. The project is global in scope, but Anglophone in practice and we are indebted to authors working with translators and editors when English is not their first language.

The handbook is written for an audience of students and professionals in a variety of material culture disciplines, including anthropology, the historical disciplines, and cultural studies. It is designed to serve as a central text for material culture courses, even as each chapter and section contributes to thematic and topical courses and scholarly reading lists. The breadth and depth of case studies contribute to a "functional" text for teaching and not simply a thought exercise.

What Is Material Culture Studies?

What is material culture? A list assembled from the chapters in this volume offers a provocative, comprehensive image of material culture: teaspoons; Emily Dickinson's poem-objects; the human body; the unprecedented crisis to the global environment; gated communities around the world; Qhapaq Ñan, the Andean road system; a knife used in a concentration camp by a Holocaust survivor; remains of individuals murdered during the 1994 Rwandan genocide; a late-baroque mahogany high chest; corsets; Minik, a young Greenland Inuit boy brought to the American Museum of Natural History in 1897; a *kendi*, a Chinese blue-and-white porcelain jug; migrants' suitcases, chests, backpacks, and belongings packed therein; the waters of Australia; maps; Picasso's *Nude Descending a Staircase* and a Trobriander garden in Papua New Guinea; bird feathers; a hammer; a thirty-four-foot-tall memorial statue of Confederate leader George Davis, erected in 1910 in Wilmington, North Carolina; a piano; the Ross Female Factory, a mid-nineteenth-century Tasmanian prison; a circa 30,000-year-old limestone figure from southern Austria labeled the "woman of Willendorf"; an abandoned paper mill in Hamina, Finland repurposed as a Google digital data center; and "selfies."[1]

Material culture includes objects, living and dead bodies, and parts thereof, although as author Emily Moore reminds us, many Indigenous populations, and others, find this categorization highly offensive. Buildings, landscapes, images, texts, and elements of the biosphere are all elements of material culture, but it is not limited to these categories. As Julian Yates states, "it is the involutions of substance, ideas, belief, design, and form that produce a built world." For Sebnem Timur Ogut, material culture emanates power by "embracing all the representative load of the thing/object, [while] it still remain[s] still and silent with the singular, one and only thing itself, with its iconic, indexical and symbolic qualities; its visceral, behavioral, and reflective characteristics; its mundane, material, everyday existence," even as it is being "reproduced, re-experienced, recontextualized or reenacted in different settings, contexts, scenarios" by and with any kind of agents.

Studying material culture qualities, characteristics, existences, and scenarios, Anna Grasskamp demands that we attend to "aesthetic, economic, social, political, ecological, technological, terminological, cultural, and ideological approaches and factors." Interrogating "materiality" is also required, or as Yates suggests, questioning "the winking in and out of being of our awareness of the pull things have upon us, [and] the ways in which what passes as media does more than mediate." More than objects or mass, Sarah Wasserman reminds us that material culture *represents*, and our studies pursue the material dimensions of subject-object relations even when they are opaque or available to us only *as* representations. Indeed, many authors in this volume examine meaning as the "work" of material culture.

For Peter Roe, understanding the ways people invest life in objects occupies the center of material culture study. Grasskamp points out the importance of tracing objects' "global lives," the ways both "social circumstances and the variable conditions of cultures and places connected in a global network" define their biographies. Ryan Cordell expands these focuses to include "the ways material cultures imbricate across time." For Laura McAtackney, this involves probing "our legacy from the past, what we live with today and what we pass on to future generations," our heritage. She explains that it is about the materials, practice, process, legal designation, value, the global, the national, and the individual. In sum, this volume's contributors, like archaeologist Victor Buchli, understand material culture studies as "united by an abiding concern for the materiality of cultural life and its diverse and at times conflicting vitality."[2]

We also encouraged the authors to use their essays as a platform for promoting growth and change in the field. The result is three entangled themes, threaded through the volume: the relationships between materiality and immateriality; the posthumanism of the "new materialism"; and the political nature of contemporary material culture studies. In her politically inspired critique, for example, Gretchen Sorin characterizes the study of American material culture as "more about style than substance – aesthetics than meaning." American museums are crowded with "objects in praise of great wealth" that celebrate the values of "materialism and consumption" and deny the injustices of the colonialist policies and practices that enabled the accumulation of such wealth. Cordell identifies the digital, which pierces the boundaries between the material and immaterial, as the "fastest-growing domain of material culture ... understanding and theorizing [it] is thus one of the field's most pressing mandates." Buchli has politicized this position, linking the "increasing alienability of our material world" with its increasing immateriality, and thus one of the most important challenges facing students of material culture.[3] New materialism scholars like Yates pose another challenge to material culture studies' fundamental assumption of human dominance of the material world, one with its own political implications. He asks, "What might material culture studies look like if we assumed that our objects necessarily play host to" other-than-human forms of "writing?"

People have long revered and studied the physical world, but the term and concept of material culture first appeared in the nineteenth century and expanded in use in the mid-twentieth century. It had formative stages in the nineteenth and twentieth centuries with the growth and formalization of disciplines like anthropology and history alongside the creation of museums dedicated to decorative arts, design, and the study of cultures. As Hutchings reminds us, the legacy of material culture studies' academic origins is not only intellectual, but itself has real environmental consequences as we face an era of climate crises and extirpation of flora and fauna worldwide. And as recent events underscore again, each of these traditions developed within and supported systems of exclusion and trauma for Black, Indigenous, and People of Color worldwide.

Perspectives

In this volume, we embrace multiple approaches to defining, theorizing, and doing material culture scholarship. Our aim is for readers to apprehend the scope of scholarship in the field from the perspective of proponents and critics of different traditions. We charged authors to present theoretically informed definitions of material culture and materiality; disciplinary, social, and political agendas; and methodologies. They assess the contributions, relevance, values, significance, critiques, and implications of the positions they advance in their chapters. In this volume, readers will engage with Marx, performance, embodiment-phenomenology-sensory studies, culture, communication, text, aesthetics, functionalism, structuralism, biography, postcolonial theory, structure and agency, transculturalism, and multiple imaginaries. The result is a series of essays that vary in tone, approach, and agenda, and that demonstrate well the scope and diversity of material culture studies today. All are well thought out and executed, but be prepared for a disruptive reading experience.

Moreover, in the volume, we unabashedly highlight multi-, inter-, post-disciplinary, and undisciplined approaches. In doing so, we counter the position that Dan Hicks and Mary Beaudry profess in the *Oxford Handbook of Material Culture Studies*. They introduce their handbook goals by noting that "as anthropological archaeologists, we were bothered by the idea of material culture studies as representing a new cross-disciplinary field of enquiry, rather than a place for conversation." Like them, we acknowledge that disciplinary traditions remain strong in material culture studies and share a "commitment to the value of situated, extended studies of particular items or bodies of material culture." Rather than lamenting that the value of such studies is "all too often lost in theoretical debates about material culture or materiality,"[4] we view the interplay between theory and practice as a great strength of the field. We both trained in the interdisciplinary field of American studies, which incorporated theory, method, and content from anthropology, archaeology, art history, folklore and folklife studies, history, geology, literary studies, material culture studies, preservation studies, and sociology.

In *The Material Culture Reader*, a compilation of representative work of the Material Culture Group at University College London, editor Buchli makes a compelling argument for considering material culture studies an "intervention between disciplines" rather than a discipline like history or interdiscipline like American studies. The "interstitial positions" it occupies "provide a platform for a critical engagement with materiality" and therefore with "those key materializing and transformative processes" shaping a wide range of matter, such as gender fluidity, genetic engineering, and the Internet.[5]

Others have proposed that material culture studies prototype another approach to scholarly investigations: post-disciplinarity.[6] This construct, unsurprisingly, has also been demarcated in diverse ways. Some post-disciplinary social scientists unite around their common research topics and questions aimed at understanding humans rather than around disciplines. The shared topical interests have ensured that, in contemporary practice, "good ideas, approaches and perspectives are not unique for a particular discipline."[7] Post-disciplinary social scientists seek out these "parallels in knowledge constructions" and welcome flexibility and innovation in defining objects and methods.[8] Post-disciplinarity "opens up the field to anyone and everyone who may have contributions to the study of humans and societies, both in the past and the present." Disciplinary boundaries, proponents argue, are hindrances and obstacles to learning when they "become more structures of dominance and weapons of exclusion ... These are good reasons to challenge the old hegemonies and work inter-disciplinary and post-disciplinary."[9] Archaeologist Christopher Tilley and his editorial colleagues promoted a similar post-disciplinary conception of material culture study in their *Handbook of Material Culture*. Hicks and Beaudry critiqued the approach precisely because it disregarded "disciplinary histories, allegiances, and intellectual debts."[10] They argue that it is "the complexity, mess, and diversity ... from which [disciplinary] knowledge emerges" that forms the foundation of our practice.[11]

For other archaeologists, post-disciplinary embraces the undisciplinary as well as the interdisciplinary. In their introduction to *After Ethics: Ancestral Voices and Post-disciplinary Worlds in Archaeology*, Alejandro Haber and Nick Shepherd define post-disciplinary archaeology as having multiple aims, of which knowledge production is but one. They reference archaeology as a capitalistic practice, and archaeologists' complicity in the "expansion of marketplace-like relationships" in contexts such as cultural resource management, development, and the heritage industry. They counter this unethical archaeology with "un-disciplined archaeology," characterized as "the skill of following (with the body and the soul) disconnected and dismembered threads expressed in a diversity of languages, textualities and forms of expression, including repressed histories, and spectral presences."[12]

Post-disciplinary and undisciplined scholarship expand the postcolonial critique initiated in post–World War II political activism. In support of anticolonial liberation and nationalism, the postcolonial critique unmasked the ways that colonialism and European culture are deeply implicated within each other, founded in Western thought systems on notions of the "other." This work exposed the disjunction between European Enlightenment concepts of reason and humanism and reductionist colonial deployment of "White settler male" supremacy. Self-reflexive, political, and committed to understanding power relationships, postcolonial perspectives provide the "fundamental ethical basis in examining oppression and inequality in the present."[13]

We will return to material culture studies and these disciplinary critiques in our conclusion.

Contents and Organization

Together, the contributors to this handbook present a reflective critique of geographical and disciplinary and interdisciplinary traditions and agendas of material culture studies. Their work is grounded in and informed by American studies, anthropology, archaeology, architecture, art and visual studies, art history, cultural theory, decorative arts and connoisseurship, design and design history, digital studies, folklife, geography, history, literary studies, popular culture, social studies of medicine, and sociology. Each author also introduces, applies, and critically assesses relevant theory, intellectual approaches and perspectives, sources of evidence, and methods. The contributors' work addresses materiality in the wide-ranging genres of architecture, body, costume, landscape, furnishings, information technologies, literature, tools, and visual culture.

The volume is organized into five parts: "Scholarly Genealogies," "Relevant Pasts," "Engaging Across Cultures and Around the Globe," "Cultural Production and Reproduction," "Experience," and "Materiality and the Digital World," introduced here.

Scholarly Genealogies

The two chapters in "Scholarly Genealogies" present multivocal genealogies outlining the ways scholars have vested and represented cultural ideologies and meanings in materials and bodies over time and across space. Authors approach their topics from three intellectual "places": the material, the embodied, and the represented. Julian Yates opens Part I with his musings on how "materiality" shapes current conversations in material culture studies. "Question your teaspoons," he suggests, to disclose a multiplicity of stories about tea, cutlery, opium wars, colonialism, and the world made by tea-drinking. Teaspoons and other objects do not belong to one time or place but to many. They are multiple, and in aggregates or assemblages, they produce different temporal and spatial effects. They may be subjects and objects or challenge us to reject this distinction. Informed by the new materialism and the multispecies or "ontological" turn in anthropology, Yates urges us to think of materiality as comprising objects' animal, plant, mineral, bacterial, and viral remainders that encode ways of conceiving of the products of human labor, valuing them, using them, and preserving them.

Material culture "represents" and "re-presents" people, places, other objects, taste, soundscapes, and more in meaningful ways. Sarah Wasserman selected Emily Dickinson's poem, "Perception of an Object Costs," to encapsulate representation. The absolute being of any object for Dickinson and Wasserman is lost in perception; perception, in fact, turns the object into any object. Our attempts to approach it, capture it in our gaze, or represent it on the page only push the truths of the object further away. Wasserman's work highlights the inherent tensions between thing, representation, and meaning that are central in so many of the discussions in the book.

Relevant Pasts

In Part II, eight author teams explore the implications of past practices on and for the future. An emphasis on the political and the silenced links the diverse essays from scholars in Colombia, Australia, Denmark,

Britain, Canada, and the United States. Indigeneity, inequality, environmental exploitation, war, and genocide constitute "Relevant Pasts" confronting material culture scholars, museum and heritage curators, cultural resource managers, and reenactors. Their stories emerge from a wide range of things and places, from objects as small as a knife to human bodies and the global environment and are the subject of often fiercely contested politics. In this part, authors ask who has the right to speak on whose behalf. Who has the authority to define what constitutes "heritage"? Whose stories are privileged, whose are ignored, and how is material culture complicit? In Chapter 10, Heather Fitzsimmons Frey and Marlissa Schweitzer reflect on the politics of reenactment and reenactors' investment in critiquing or sustaining received historical narratives. Acts, or more accurately, "reenacts" like donning a corset make the past physically present and "body forth" the lived experiences of others.

Can a handcrafted knife that a Holocaust survivor used in a concentration camp do the same? Bozena Shallcross (Chapter 7) reviews how scholars may incorporate material culture as they interrogate the meaning and chronology of war, peace, occupation, and Holocaust. To do so, she engages with objects that evidence the debased and brutalized existence instigated by war. She attends to the degraded system of war economy driven by human and material losses, expensive technological innovations, and civilians' simple mode of survival that generated wartime objects' overarching material and materialistic concerns. These objects were "damaged, displaced, and dispossessed even as, simultaneously, they at times represented some sense of stability, facilitating survival and suturing one's broken memory and identity." She asks how we can describe such a multivalent, yet easily destroyed, world of objects today? What are the elements that constitute a wartime artifact in a time of peace? Wherein lies its authenticity?

In Chapter 9, Gretchen Sorin considers the institutionalization and professionalization of preserving and representing the material past in the present. Museums, government agencies, preservation organizations, and various social and community groups collect, conserve, interpret, and present material culture of their own and of others' pasts. Sorin queries the "relevant past" of a late-baroque mahogany high chest in a fine art collection that was preserved for its aesthetic value and as a representation of the furnishings of elite eighteenth-century Americans. She presents the need and value of viewing the chest from different perspectives, so we can understand how one woman's high chest is another woman's oppression. The chest embodies both the wealthy woman owner and the enslaved makers of the chest. It contains the stories of the dangerous work engaged in by the enslaved harvesters of mahogany trees and the resulting technological changes that led to deforestation in the Caribbean and Central America. Discussing mahogany chairs and tables as both trees and fine furniture – commodities and luxuries – broadens the story to include the entire supply chain, linking object and environment, and opens up questions surrounding authenticity and authentication, values, meanings, authority, ownership, and stewardship.

Like Sorin, Richard Hutchings (Chapter 4) exhorts material culture scholars to accept responsibility for our complicity in silencing stories of capitalist exploitation. Targeting North American archaeologists and cultural resource managers, his analysis of the literature exposes the critical need to reflect, self-critique, and self-confront the ways our capitalist universities, institutions, and practices created and promote the unprecedented global environmental crisis we now face.

In Chapter 5, Claire Smith, Jordan Ralph, Cherrie de Leiuen, and Kellie Pollard also engage with our contemporary material world, its role in social movements, and its importance in limiting and expanding efforts for social justice. Regulation of space, use of objects to uphold or erode bias, and construction of objects as political tools are but some of the relationships outlined by scholars who position the material world as inherent to political and social actions. In places such as gated communities, the authors expose the role material culture plays in reproducing an unequal distribution of wealth, opportunities, and privileges within a society. They ponder how we can deploy material culture to promote greater equality and explore ways we can promote social justice in our practice.

Cristóbal Gnecco tackles the same questions in the colonized landscape of South America as he exposes the role of material culture in negotiations of power, in gifting, as regulatory tools, and as modes or tools of empowerment and connection or, conversely, disinheritance and disregard. In Chapter 6, he literally and figuratively follows the history of Qhapaq Ñan, the Andean road system, and the places and people it connected and disenfranchised. Now a UNESCO designated World Heritage Site, Gnecco demonstrates the opportunities heritage like Qhapaq Ñan presents as a privileged theater in which to confront issues of engagement and authority, of violence and hierarchies, of dispossession and exclusion.

The painful legacy of human remains appropriated as material heritage claim the attention of Laura McAtackney and Emily Moore. Global and cross-cultural in scope, McAtackney's Chapter 8 considers the discourses of heritage across national, ethnic, and regional traditions. Examining the remains of Rwandans murdered in the genocide of 1994 and other examples, she fashions a compelling impression of the tangle of preservation, memory, horror, denial, and "raw" authenticity wrapped up in such "dark heritage." In Chapter 11, Moore examines repatriation and Indigenous meanings, values, and uses of material heritage. She probes the global legacy of conquest that postcolonial scholarship and advocacy are challenging, and shares the story of Minik, the young Greenland Inuit boy and his father brought to the American Museum of Natural History in the 1910s to support anthropologist Franz Boas' cultural studies. Upon his father's death, the museum resorted to subterfuge to deny Minik his body for burial, and then displayed his skeleton until the 1990s. It took an exposé for the museum to finally return the skeletons to Greenland for burial. This tale exemplifies the amalgamation of colonial subjugation, paternalism, and the fight for sovereignty that saturate the objectified Indigenous body.

Engaging Across Cultures and Around the Globe
The three chapters in the Part III highlight different approaches to the movement of materials, goods, people, and ideas around the world. Examining different regions and times, the authors probe the ways that cross-cultural and global exchange, change, and difference have shaped the material world, social identifications, and human agency. Anna Grasskamp in Chapter 12 interrogates a Chinese blue-and-white porcelain jug, a *kendi*, made in China and received in Europe, a type of "transcultural" object. Analyzing the *kendi* from a multidisciplinary perspective and in its wider material, cultural, and historical contexts, she introduces readers to "transcultural" material cultural scholarship. Transcultural interpretative approaches transcend Europe-Asia interactions, and conceptualize the agency, social, and global lives, and vital materiality of objects in the diverse cultural contexts they touch.

In Chapter 13 Magdalena Naum reviews cultural exchange, change, and continuity through the lens of population movement: migration, refugees, displacement, diaspora, and the modes of transportation that brought diverse people into direct engagement with each other. She turns our attention to "translocal," sometimes "transnational," objects, the suitcases, chests, and backpacks that hold the precious belongings people take with them when they move (or are moved). Her interests lie in migrants' relationships with material objects in moments of packing, unpacking, and furnishing new homes; the impact of displacement on people's real and imaginary engagements with objects; and objects' roles in shaping identity and structuring the migration experience. Her analysis reveals the complexities and even contradictions engendered in experiences with these possessions in motion. Their physical presence and the memories surrounding them help migrants to experience a continuity of life even as their association with the past provoke painful reminders of loss. Indeed, the power of translocal and transnational objects lies in their connectivity, compensating for physical absence and maintaining social relations.

In the context of globalization, postmodernity, and transnationalism, identity, for most people, is no longer securely located in specific material environments. Yet the desire to "ground" identity in place by acting in and on the material world remains. Veronica Strang (Chapter 14) uses semiotics to understand how objects can convey messages and how messages can be inscribed on objects to carry meaning, action, and transgression. Examining water and Australian Aborigine identity, she demonstrates the ways individual and collective identity-making processes depend on conceptual and material boundaries. In and beyond Aboriginal Australia, water enculturates and socializes. It is inalienable and circulates ancestral power and life-giving force essential to the renewal of life, land, and people. Its flows are regulated in use and in identity-making, especially those constituting "otherness." Attending to the larger context and the field of action in which "objects" such as water belong reveals its use in the performance of space.

Cultural Production and Reproduction

In Part IV, four authors analyze objects, processes, imaginaries, and expressive venues involved in cultural transmission. Technology, aesthetics and art, animated objects and places, and other media of material expression and representation of human bodies and identities frame their topics. In the Chapter 15, Sebnem Timur surveys the material expression of othering, inequality, resistance, subversion, and transgression, in other words the politics of representation. Like Strang, she examines the "performance of place." Imagine the globe as a seamless structure, without borders. Consider a map without direction, hierarchy, or center. Representing political, geographical, atmospheric, seismic, social, cultural, dimensional, and directional information on a map renders it a performative act. The political is marked and reproduced through acts of mapping, so it can become an object of resistance, a way to make visible and become visible.

Coupled closely in our intellectual schema with representation is aesthetics. In Chapter 16, Timothy Carroll troubles and interrogates concepts of aesthetics and art. Referencing a range of objects from Picasso's *Nude Descending a Staircase* to an Indigenous Trobriander garden on Papua New Guinea, Carroll asks whether aesthetics is beauty, a mediator between interior and exterior worlds, the embodied experience of sensual forms, or a style and harmony of form and social practice? He proposes that aesthetics is the internal, intuitive geometries of logic and society, the means by which reality becomes sensibly apprehended. The work of material culture scholars, he contends, is ethnographically grounded research into what aesthetics does.

Anthropologist and archaeologist Peter Roe (Chapter 17) has spent almost half a century studying Indigenous peoples in South America. His work elaborates a fundamental sacred dichotomy between two grand cultic systems and their contrasting attitudes toward nature, perhaps derived from their origin biomes – the desert and the jungle, or the "West" and the "Rest." The jungle spiritual tradition revolves around the concept that objects are alive. Consider Roe's work, in part, an ethnography of aesthetics. Bird feathers offer one avenue into this cosmology. Feather color, reflectivity, bodily locus, and species of origin engender human to bird transformations and transference of energies and powers. Donning bird feathers in ritual performances, the dancer is transformed into a moving, living microcosm of the forest macrocosm.

In the concluding chapter on cultural production and reproduction, Ludovic Coupaye (Chapter 18) unpacks the multivalent category of technology. Within seemingly simple ways of doing and making, technology incorporates objects, knowledges, processes, embodied performed actions, energies, organizations, systems, and networks. It implicates perceptions of materials, memory, instrumentality and efficiency, dynamism, and the social. The dynamism of a hammer, for example, emerges at the junction between an efficacious action of percussion and the type of materials it can affect; different shapes and sizes develop from this synergy of form, material, and effects of heat, noise, and vibration.

Experience

Part V considers people's "experiences" of space, place, home, institutions, the digital, and the spiritual.

Material culture studies have long incorporated analysis of domestic environments and dynamics of home in shaping culture, rituals of power and more. Chapter 20 examines the centrality of consumption, home, and domestic environments in regulating and subverting notions of cultural and legal citizenship. Psyche Williams-Forson explains: "domesticity is a middle-class construct used by white people (especially women) to exert and uphold power structures and ideals of American exceptionalism." Contemporary scholars are developing counter-narratives of domesticity, consumption, and citizenship from the perspectives of marginalized and underrepresented people.

How is the material world affected by place? How does an urban, suburban, or rural environment shape spaces, the built environment, and the form and use of objects? Why does this matter? In Chapter 19 on "place," Elijah Gaddis explores the importance of siting and location in understanding the material world. In 1910, a thirty-four-foot-tall memorial statue of Confederate attorney general George Davis was erected in a major thoroughfare in Wilmington, North Carolina. A ritualized homage to white male supremacy performed in the dedication ceremony, the associations and meanings of the Davis statue changed over time. Assaults on it during the racial violence of the 1960s compelled the town government to relocate the statue to the new library's entrance. For Gaddis, the monument always stood for a broader symbolic spatial and social order; its relocation offered a real, material response to the violence without engaging with the underlying issues. In Wilmington, the Davis statue represents an all-encompassing symbol and material representation of the material realities expressed in the geography of the town.

Archaeologists Eleanor Casella and Linnea Kuglitsch (Chapter 21) also examine space and place, specifically those of schools, hospitals, prisons and other institutions, and the ways they shape physical experiences and act as organizational entities for many material endeavors. They ponder the constituents of a materiality of institutional life and ask why daily operations crystallize into an institutional built environment characterized by bodily discipline, deprivation, and regulation. Isolation, enclosure, surveillance, bodily mortification, coercion and re-inscription, reformative labor, and the black-market economy structured the "powered cultural landscapes" of the institutions they depict. The Ross Female Factory, a mid-nineteenth-century prison in Tasmania, for example, evidenced ritual, labor, and routine, but also inmates challenging the discipline through insubordinate actions, desires, and attitudes made material.

We often classify "religion" as an institution. Building on the work of David Hall and others, in Chapter 22 Gretchen Buggeln discusses the concept that religion is "lived," something that happens in and through material practices.[14] Religion, in other words, is *made* as well as thought, and has been for more than the 30,000 years since someone in today's Austria carved the 11 cm "woman of Willendorf" figure from a chunk of limestone. Like all material expressions of belief, the limestone figure raises questions about agency, identity, embodiment, and practice for our consideration.

Materiality and the Digital World

We conclude the volume with perhaps the newest addition to the pantheon of material culture forms: the digital. The two contributors to Part VI consider how digital forms of representation blur the boundaries between what is considered material and how digital objects and technologies alter human experiences with the material world. Their scope spans an abandoned paper mill in Finland that Google acquired for a data center to mobile phone "selfies." Without Google and other corporate data "farms," we could not create "selfies," enlisting our bodies in creating digital content that reveals, experiments with or challenges aspects of identity, character, or other individual qualities. Ryan Cordell (Chapter 23) and Natasha Chuk (Chapter 24) describe networked exchanges and the contested distinctions between public and private spaces, conditions, and/or content across them. They also consider the ways that personal privacy and the shared public of networked environments inevitably creep into each other, creating "glass bedrooms." And where, they ask, is the line between virtual and real?

Themes

True to its interdisciplinary perspective and commitment to expansive exploration of material culture, this volume supports themes that cross the volume's parts. As previously mentioned, woven or entangled throughout the handbook are three main themes we identified the relationships between materiality and immateriality; the posthumanism of the "new materialism"; and the political nature of contemporary material culture studies. Certainly, there are other linkages in theme, theory, approach, and invocations for future study that run through the various chapters. We encourage readers to draw out these and other connections to place these essays in conversation, just as these scholars do themselves at conferences, in their writing, in their teaching, and in their research.

Materiality and Immateriality

"What is material about material culture?" This central question animates this volume and material culture studies writ large. A quick answer that can be handy at a cocktail party is that material culture involves studying stuff, objects, and things. Studies of potsherds and polebarns, textiles and telephones, gardens and gritty streets all fall under the umbrella of material culture. But scholars have long acknowledged that material culture does not end with things that have mass and a physical presence in the world. Things without matter ... matter in material culture. The tension between materiality and immateriality then is a theme that arises throughout the chapters that follow.

As Chuk reminds us, "For centuries we have understood our world through objects of creation: design, ingenuity and creativity come together in various physical objects that reflect aspects of our daily life, values, desires, and innovations." Each of the studies here do consider physical things. Some authors engage with material as material, for example, the Chinese *kendi* of Grasskamp, the roads of Gnecco, or the Confederate statues of Gaddis. However, they and others move on from physical descriptions to discussions of representation/s of material and questions of what material represents. Motivations are multiple for building on foundations set by earlier scholars who studied materials, typologies, patterns, and spatial arrangements. As Chuk explains further,

> The advanced communications technologies of the past several centuries helped usher a significantly new form in the digital object,

which is partially or entirely intangible. The information age brought about a system of not only information exchange, storage and retrieval, but also new ways of thinking and being in the world, and in particular new ways of understanding materiality and our relations to objects and systems that are intangible but ever-present.

Scholars like Chuk, Cordell or others in this volume explore the ways in which not only the tools of the digital age, but new ways of "being digital" are changing our notions of how we define materiality and immateriality. Technological shifts in understanding materiality in a digital age are moving material culture studies in new directions.

Interdisciplinarity shepherded in insights from psychology, brain science, and scholars of human and animal development that make us more attuned to the material resonances and implications of emotion, senses, thoughts, and behaviors. As Sarah Wasserman suggests in relation to objects in artistic productions such as still lives or prints, "the objects *in* art and the object that *is* art always entail subjectivity and interpretation, even when they are actually 'there' before us." The act of seeing (or not) and how our brains encode the view is but one way that representation of the material becomes enacted. Some scholars of material culture have traced the move to consider things as meanings and less as materials with hesitation, suggesting that in the later twentieth century, the "strangely abstract, dematerialized quality of many material culture studies, in which things appear to disappear into spectral fields of social relations or meanings, and the complexities of materials and their change over time are not accounted for."[15] The authors of this volume and their peers in the early twenty-first century seem more at peace intellectually with the tension that emerges when we consider these relationships and boundaries between human and nonhuman things, and the formation of ideas and thoughts about them.

Technical and chemical analysis allows a view into micromateriality and can help scholars understand, or at least interrogate, much better how the tiniest elements and DNA chains may impact the becoming and unbecoming of material things or circumstances related to them. In her evocative discussion of the post–World War II era, Shallcross demonstrates how the very processes of oxidation and degradation not only reshape material forms, but also reshape the memory and understanding of historical events: "Suspended between materiality and immateriality due to processes such as rusting, decomposition, recycling, restoration, and preservation, the objects' bodies gain more agency because they play the role of reminders as vessels of the memory of the Holocaust. Yet these objects are visibly vulnerable, suspended between a violent past and the vestiges preserving the present – between materiality and immateriality." Suspended materiality also relates to the digital, "Mind-body relations are important to understanding how the digital realm is organized, managed, accessed, coordinated, and negotiated by users. Questions about how time, effort, creativity, and personhood are used and shaped by the interplay between and intermingling of the virtual body and the physical one are at the center of this relationship." Are our emotional responses to objects part of physical and chemical changes in our brains? How does this work? Are ideas really material? Many of the authors here lead us to probe deeper and explore further the shifting boundaries between materiality and immateriality in new and exciting ways.

Finally, and connected to the following theme of lived experience is an openness to varied forms of belief and motivations behind understanding the relationship between materiality and immateriality. As Roe, Moore, and other authors remind us, what one culture may value for its physical attributes and historical context may not even have a status as "material" in another culture, even if there is acknowledgment of the presence of the entity. Strang explains further:

> Discourses about indigenous connections to place have also helped to articulate ideas about cultural heritage, a concept which recognizes that the embedding of identity in places creates a legacy that is both tangible and intangible. Material heritage may be expressed through the shaping of cultural landscapes .... It may rest on visual and written records. But for "heritage" and cultural identity to be maintained it must also be accompanied by intangible legacies: social histories and memories, and specifically cultural beliefs and practices.

While we most often discuss these tensions in the context of "non-Western" people and cultures, Gaddis reminds us that we should be mindful of the different states of material thingness everywhere:

> Place calls us to think about absence and immateriality, with the paradoxes of a material culture that is once everywhere and nowhere, surrounding us and largely invisible to our visual scrutiny. This also allows for a reordering based on spatiality rather than temporality and to see the world of people and their localities as linked as much by space as by time.

The multivalent properties of objects throw a wrench in "traditional" definitions of material culture and encourage scholars to think more expansively, openly, honestly, and ethically about the material world. In doing so, something like a ceremonial mask or a feather or a statue can operate as a cultural artifact, spiritual being, a combination of both simultaneously, or an active force that moves between these categories situationally.

It is easier to understand why the tensions between materiality and immateriality have become central to discussions of material culture than to clearly define these terms or plot when these can be useful subjects. Clearly, the authors in this volume bring their own disciplinary and thematic perspectives to these issues and do not come to the same conclusions about how material culture scholars should understand these terms. However, universally, the authors implicitly suggest that both materiality and immateriality are important concepts with which to grapple. And in doing so, material culture scholarship helps break down the political, emotional, cultural, and other barriers that have previously limited participation in conversations about the material world.

Lived Experience

Anthropologists began studying the experience of non-Western "others" in the nineteenth century, to what they understand today as nefarious ends, constructing racist hierarchies supportive of colonial regimes. Today, Western museums like the British Museum or Pitt-Rivers Museum remain crowded with the material culture of those peoples' experiences (except for those recently repatriated), collected to preserve "dying cultures," as supposed expressions of the "primitive" mind. In Europe, folklore and folklife studies of nonliterate folk with rich oral and material traditions filled living history museums such as Stockholm's Skansen with the handcrafted products of "us" before industrialization. In the academy, these distinctions resolved into two disciplinary categories: the social sciences, defined by the study of populations and behaviors, and the humanities, the study of people and their histories.

American historical archaeology presents an informative example of the implications of this divide. The field still struggles with, or thrives on, depending on one's perspective, an identity crisis born of its borderland situation straddling the social sciences and humanities. On one hand, the British historical tradition of archaeology informed our practice. The arrival of British archaeologist Ivor Noël Hume at Colonial Williamsburg fortified this effort at telling the stories of people, appropriate to goals of the living history museum.[16] On the other hand, most American archaeologists trained in anthropology and the social sciences, which stressed the study of behavior rather than lived experience.

The elaboration of Marxian perspectives in 1980s' archaeology stimulated vigorous debate about agency, if not experience. The conversation centered, in part, on the question whether, and how, individuals can act in meaningful ways to institute structural, systemic change. A contextual, interpretive archaeology countered Marxian arguments that initially presented structure as predetermining behavior. Informed by phenomenology, narrative history, storytelling, and the archaeology of everyday life, this approach drew many proponents in the 1990s. At the same time, African diaspora and feminist archaeologists sought to move beyond identifying material markers of African or gender identity to understand the lived experience of enslavement, racism, and male domination. These efforts have expanded to include other underrepresented, marginalized, silenced populations.

With implications well beyond archaeology, Judith Butler's paradigm-shifting perspectives on sexuality and gender invigorated material culture scholarship on embodiment and the intersectionality of race, class, gender, sexuality, and other phenomena that contribute to oppression and acts of survivance.[17] In this volume, authors scrutinize the impact on studies of technology, religion, and place. For Coupaye, "the study of techniques starts at the level of the body itself and the ways in which people do things" because some norms are expressed only through technical activities. Buggeln establishes that contemporary scholars of religion also seek understanding of religion as "something that happens in and through material practices, something experienced and negotiated not just in words but in interactions with objects, places and other bodies." Material practices "take place," Gaddis argues, which requires thinking about "bodily making meaning amid locality."

Historians turned to the senses to further understanding of lived experience. Constance Classen, a contributor to the University of Illinois Press Studies in Sensory History, introduced her study of touch by emphasizing that "an embodied approach saves historical figures from being perceived as lifeless puppets who move across the stage of the past without any real feelings. When we allow historical figures to be of flesh and blood, we make it possible to relate to them as fellow beings and, therefore, to make meaningful comparisons between their lives and situations and our own."[18] Jonathan Reinarz, another contributor, also commends historical attention to the senses, with the novel perspectives they provide to the "corporal realm, its cultural and social locations, experiences, roles, and functions."[19]

In this volume, Frey and Schweitzer concur, but caution that "connecting to the past through living, breathing bodies is ... a complicated, time-bending project." In reenactment, a form of performance-based historiography, "bodies reach across time and space, animating imagined moments to serve research." The project has generated controversy. The validity and efficacy of the endeavor depend on seeking to understand contextualized experience, avoiding the reductionist essentialist assumption that all humans experienced and interpreted sensory perceptions in comparable ways. Writing of institutional experiences, Casella and Kuglitsch urge scholars to focus on the "sensory, experiences such as sound, textures, light, hunger, temperature, and fatigue" that impacted *all* occupants, not merely the incarcerated. Carroll develops this point as he argues for greater phenomenological emphasis and cross-cultural ethnographic approaches to the study of "aesthetics as relating to the somatic experience of sensual forms in the world." For material culture scholars who associated aesthetics with beauty, imagining imprisonment as an aesthetic experience is itself paradigm shifting.

The new materialism denotes another politicized paradigm shift, encapsulated in Jane Bennett's urgent appeal for a "cultivated, patient, sensory attentiveness to nonhuman forces operating outside and inside the human body."[20] Such micro-studies of the "embodied quotidian," Diana Coole elaborated, expose how experiences of deprivation, wasted resources, and erosion of wages "translate into diet, health, despair, pain," and compromise wellbeing.[21]

Politics of Material Culture Studies

Studies of material culture are inherently political. From relationships between individuals to overt expressions of power, politics is at play. This occurs at varied scales and in differing contexts. Several authors cite the influence of Jane Bennett's concept of "vital materiality," which she defines as the "capacity of things – edibles, commodities, storms, metals – not only to impede or block the will and designs of humans but also to act as quasi agents or forces with trajectories, propensities, or tendencies of their own."[22] Guiding her thinking is the question: "How would political responses to public problems change were we to take seriously the vitality of (nonhuman) bodies?" This "thing-power" enables objects to "manifest traces of independence or aliveness."[23] Indeed, the concept shares affinities with animism, which Roe examines in Chapter 17, "Objects are Alive." He explains, "Animism seeks to maintain equilibrium in nature by treating it as a sentient being worthy of a 'dialogue' of negotiation and adulation." In ways, the "new materialism" movement, inspired by this reconceptualization of matter and materials and "biophilosophy," represents the West's colonization and appropriation of non-Western, Indigenous cosmology.[24]

Scholars of diverse backgrounds are deploying this "new materialism" to reimagine humans' relationship with the world. At the cx Center for Interdisciplinary Studies in the Academy of Fine Arts, Munich, researchers seek to understand how the world works in order to isolate "leverage points for critical intervention" and save it from environmental collapse. The language is apocalyptic and redemptionist and pervades our media feeds: "We are at the tipping point of an environmental crisis unprecedented in human history and our very survival is dependent on saving nature." Do you recognize this one? Bernie Sanders, Mikhail Gorbachev, Pope Benedict VXI, or Francis? No, it is Leonardo di Caprio, whose voice matters to many in our celebrity aspirational cultural moment, although the others voiced similar dire sentiments.

New materialism proponents share with other politically engaged scholars a conviction that a systemic critique of capitalism is crucial.[25] Strang (see also Chapter 14) and Mark Busse, in their studies of Indigenous people's encounters with capitalist modernity, interrogate the concept of ownership and query how previously inalienable, unowned things such as water, fish, and radio frequencies become subjected to property claims under late capitalism.[26] In Chapter 21 on institutions, Casella and Kuglitsch chart an associated ideology of "improvement" that supported industrial capitalism. Harnessed to shifts in attitudes that stressed the environment's determining role in personal behavior and moral character, the ideology persuaded adherents that "the very materiality of modern society not only could, but *should*, be harnessed to exact improvement."

Roe traces the origins of this thinking to and before biblical references to human dominion over nature, which the West has treated as a "storehouse from which resources are extracted until they run out." The West's imaginary of animated objects, he argues, manifests not in plants and water, but in "living machines" such as robots actuated by artificial intelligence. Countering this paradigm, new materialists seek to reunite Western dichotomous constructs such as nature versus culture, living versus inert (or dead), and human versus nonhuman.[27] Hutchings makes the argument most stridently in his chapter, declaring that the "inequality, alienation, anxiety, consumption, addiction, and domination" driving capitalist consumer society have engendered the current environmental crisis. Indeed, he continues, North American cultural resource managers' virtual silence about the global ecological crisis has rendered us and the universities that train us complicit.

Material inequalities inhere in capitalism and colonialist hierarchies of superiority and inferiority, and Smith and colleagues guide us through the ways that inequality perpetrates social injustice. Spatial segregation promotes little interaction between people with greater and fewer economic resources, precluding opportunities to engage and understand the lived experience of others. Objects are also tools of bias, Carroll adds, when criteria for evaluating and valuing aesthetic forms is "the product of socioeconomic elite privilege." Museums have been part of the apparatus of elite white privilege and, as Wasserman observes, the "dehumanization of historically marginalized subjects," a situation slowly changing. Barbara Franco reports that in the United States, it was not until the 1990s that history museums began to share authority and ownership with communities.[28] Gnecco and McAtackney concur that power still pervades heritage matters. Sorin, in Chapter 9 on the politics of material culture practice and professions, proposes that we "consider dissolving museums that no longer have any relevance to make room for new and important histories." For Shallcross, the Holocaust stands out among these important histories, and although museums devoted to remembering the Holocaust exist, they do not suffice for us to "experience and apprehend its violence through the material connection with the dead." Objects, images, buildings, documents, and landscapes alone will remain as survivors pass away.

Museums have an ethical responsibility to preserve and interpret this "material inheritance of the tragic past."

Indigenous populations in the Americas survived a violent, tragic past, a holocaust wrought by European colonial and imperial projects, and museum collectors have been complicit. Moore's account outlines the enormous cost Indigenous peoples paid as museums built "collections through genocidal campaigns and harsh assimilation policies." Especially offensive has been the legal and anthropological classification of ancestors' human remains as "material culture," disregarding the "sanctity of Native beliefs about their dead." The terms themselves misrepresent Indigenous views: "'material' fails to capture the songs, names, and other immaterial prerogatives that are so often bound up with physical objects, and 'object' fails to recognize" that "objects are alive."

Tourism and the art market magnify these problems, Gnecco claims, reducing Indigenous culture to a "set of commodities for sale." When Indigenous people do engage heritage and the market, they face an unequal relationship, an iteration of colonization often fraught with violence. Gnecco insists that it is past time to transcend "the idea of a single world with different interpretations . . . [and] reach a more comprehensive perspective, that of many worlds and thus many conceptions . . . This is the world of materiality in its fullest, not as a naturalized realm but a constructed space where politics are always at stake." And with this we end the introduction where we began, with a call to explore, refine, and critique scholarship about the material world.

Notes

1. The objects are listed in the order the chapters from which they are drawn appear in the volume.
2. Victor Buchli, "Introduction," in Victor Buchli, ed., *Material Culture Reader* (Oxford: Berg, 2002), 1.
3. Ibid, 18.
4. Dan Hicks and Mary Beaudry, "Introduction. Material Culture Studies: A Reactionary View," in Dan Hicks and Mary Beaudry, eds., *Oxford Handbook of Material Culture Studies* (Oxford: Oxford University Press, 2010), 15.
5. Buchli, "Introduction," 13, 15.
6. Christopher Tilley, ed., *Reading Material Culture: Structuralism, Hermeneutics, and Post-structuralism* (Oxford: Basil Blackwell, 1990); Christopher Tilley, Webb Keane, Susanne Küchler, Michael Rowlands, and Patricia Spyer, eds., *Handbook of Material Culture* (London: Sage, 2006).
7. Fredrik Fahlander and Terje Oestigaard, "Introduction: Material Culture and Post-disciplinary Sciences," in Fredrik Fahlander and

Terje Oestigaard, eds., *Material Culture and Other Things: Post-disciplinary Studies in the Twenty-First Century* (Lindome: Bricoleur Press, 2004), 5.

8. Mark J. Smith, *Social Science in Question* (London: Sage, 1998), 311; Fahlander and Oestigaard, "Introduction," 7.

9. Fahlander and Oestigaard, "Introduction," 15, 7–8.

10. Dan Hicks, "The Material-Cultural Turn: Event and Effect," in Hicks and Beaudry, *Oxford Handbook of Material Culture Studies*, 92.

11. Hicks and Beaudry, "Introduction," 20.

12. Alejandro Haber and Nick Shepherd, "After Ethics: Ancestral Voices and Post-disciplinary Worlds in Archaeology: An Introduction," in Alejandro Haber and Nick Shepherd, eds., *After Ethics: Ancestral Voices and Post-disciplinary Worlds in Archaeology* (New York: Springer, 2015), 3–5.

13. Jane Lydon and Uzma Z. Rizvi, "Introduction: Postcolonialism and Archaeology," in Jane Lydon and Uzma Z. Rizvi, eds., *Handbook of Postcolonial Archaeology*, World Archaeological Congress Research Handbooks in Archaeology, Vol. 3 (Walnut Creek: Left Coast Press, 2010), 19.

14. David D. Hall, *Lived Religion in America: Toward a History of Practice* (Princeton: Princeton University Press, 1998).

15. Hicks, "The Material-Cultural Turn," 69.

16. See, for example, Ivor Noël Hume, *Here Lies Virginia: An Archaeologist's View of Colonial Life and History* (New York: Alfred A. Knopf, 1963), and Audrey Noël Hume, *The Archaeology of Martin's Hundred* (Philadelphia: University of Pennsylvania Museum of Archaeology and Anthropology, 2001) and *The Virginia Adventure: Roanoke to Jamestown* (Charlottesville: University of Virginia Press, 1994).

17. Judith Butler, *Undoing Gender* (New York: Routledge, 2004); *Gender Trouble: Feminism and the Subversion of Identity* (New York: Routledge, 1999); and *Bodies that Matter: On the Discursive Limits of "Sex"* (New York: Routledge, 1993). On survivance in postcolonial archaeology, see Stephen Silliman, "Archaeologies of Survivance and Residence: Reflections on the Historical Archaeology of Indigenous People," in Neal Ferris, Rodney Harrison, and Michael Wilcox, eds., *Rethinking Colonial Pasts Through Archaeology* (Oxford: Oxford University Press, 2014).

18. Constance Classen, *The Deepest Sense: A Cultural History of Touch*. Studies in Sensory History (Urbana: University of Illinois Press, 2012), xii.

19. Jonathan Reinarz, *Past Scents: Historical Perspectives on Smell*. Studies in Sensory History (Urbana: University of Illinois Press, 2014), 3–4.

20. Jane Bennett, *Vibrant Matter: A Political Ecology of Things* (Durham: Duke University Press, 2010).

21. Diana Coole, "New Materialism: The Ontology and Politics of Materialization," in Susanne Witzgall and Kerstin Stakemeier, eds.,

Power of Material/Politics of Materiality (Chicago: Diaphanes, distributed by University of Chicago Press, 2017), 38–9.
22. Bennett, *Vibrant Matter*, viii.
23. Ibid, xvi.
24. Susanne Witzgall and Kerstin Stakemeier, "Introduction," in Witzgall and Stakemeier, *Power of Material/Politics of Materiality*, 10; Sarah Whatmore and Steve Hinchcliffe, "Ecological Landscapes," in Hicks and Beaudry, *Oxford Handbook*, 448.
25. Coole, "New Materialism," 37–8.
26. Veronica Strang and Mark Busse, "Introduction: Ownership and Appropriation," in Veronica Strang and Marke Busse, eds., *Ownership and Appropriation*, ASA Monograph 47 (New York: Berg, 2011), 4, 10.
27. Sarah Whatmore and Steve Hinchcliffe, "Ecological Landscapes," 448.
28. Barbara Franco, "Decentralizing Culture: Public History and Communities," in James B. Gardner and Paula Hamilton, eds., *The Oxford Handbook of Public History* (Oxford: Oxford University Press, 2017), 69–70.

Part I

Scholarly Genealogies

Every current of fashion or of worldview derives its force from what is forgotten.

Walter Benjamin

2
Materiality

Julian Yates

Materiality

> Describe your street. Describe another street. Compare.
>
> Make an inventory of your pockets, of your bag. Ask yourself about the provenance, the use, what will become of each of the objects you take out.
>
> Question your tea spoons.
>
> Georges Perec, *L'Infra-ordinaire* (1973)

My aim in this chapter is to provide an overview of the theoretical and philosophical underpinning to material culture studies. Such an overview cannot pretend to be exhaustive. Instead, I have chosen to tell one particular story. I begin by posing a constitutive question about matter, the meaning of the word and its origins. The chapter then goes on to consider the legacies of phenomenology with particular attention to distinctions (or the lack thereof) between what we call "objects" and "things"; the continued urgency of Marxist-oriented commodity studies and considerations of fetishism (literal and methodological); and the contributions of actor network theory and the new materialism. I end by considering the demands made of our field by the advent of ontological or multispecies anthropology and eco-critical or environmental writing. While it has been a habit of the field to understand the word "culture" in purely anthropic terms, how might our understanding change if we were to extend the possibility of culture and so "material culture" to entities otherwise than human?

I begin, however, with a question.

Materia /Matter/Material Culture (Definitions)

If there is such a thing as material culture studies, then it would seem obvious that there is something called material culture that it is the study of. I begin by asking what is material about material culture studies?[1] If the phrasing of that question puzzles or gives you pause, then that puzzlement and pause might be for good reason. Does the word material refer to the "stuff" of material culture, to the objects fabricated by *Homo sapiens* to encode or formalize social relations that material culture studies takes as a subject? Or does the word refer, instead, to something deeper, an "essence," to what may then be considered "essential" about the field or the approach, to what really *matters*? Does my question speak, in other words, to the physicality of things or to what, by most metaphysical yardsticks, might be described as immaterial, the insubstantial stuff of ideas? Strangely, it is the immateriality of these shaping "ideas" that apparently makes them really real and so really count. More strangely still, we only come to know these immaterial ideas by way of objects, which we say enact, reflect, encode, or express them. The word material refers to phenomena (stuff) and to qualities of things that do not appear as such – – to attributes that might, in differing philosophical lexicons, be called noumena, spirit, idea, form, energy, the divine. This seeming paradox lies at the heart of the word material. Accordingly, this paradox haunts the array of approaches that we name material culture studies.

   A brief inquiry into the origins of the word reveals a to-ing and fro-ing between the apparently material and the immaterial. In English, material derives from the word "matter," whose origin lies, via French borrowing, in the Latin *materia*, which referred, as Raymond Williams informs, to building materials, most usually timber. "Thence, by extension," he offers, the word matter came to refer to "any physical substance considered generally, and, again, by extension, the substance of anything."[2] Matter, however, was to be contrasted to form or, in the theological register, spirit, or, in the philosophical register, ideas, "which it was held w[ere] required to bring matter into being." The word material contains within itself this seeming contradiction. In one sense, the word refers to that most basic of substances, the physicality and malleability of things and to our ability to transform matter into a whole host of objects that then make up a built world. But, so also, the word alludes to an understanding that all that exists does so by virtue (force) of some shaping design, idea, or form, which in and of itself is immaterial. The word material toggles back and forth between these two senses. How we understand or program this toggling will decide almost everything about what we take to be life, death, and the essence of a human person. The word materiality might be said to describe this crux or crossing. It designates a problem or, more productively, signals that the object world, that which mediates our existence, constitutes a contact zone with how we understand and take up our relation to what we call making and manufacture.³

Perhaps, as my etymologically "wooden" or infrastructural working definition of material (*materia*) suggests, it is the whole process of making worlds, and the resulting hierarchy of differently valued objects (and persons), which either trumpet their existence or seemingly disappear into the background so that they can serve as shaping forces, that material culture studies takes as its subject? Certainly, it is this infrastructural nexus between the material and immaterial that UNESCO's definition of "Tangible and Intangible Cultural Heritage" seeks to finesse as the organization thinks through the challenges (ethical, political, logistic) of what it means to "preserve" human artifacts and practices. Trading on the sense of touch, UNESCO's language toggles back and forth between definitions that key "tangible cultural heritage" to "physical artifacts produced, maintained and transmitted intergenerationally in a society" and "intangible" heritage to "the practices, representations, expressions, knowledge, skills."⁴ Though, at the risk of tautology, or to see off some Doubting Thomas who asks for the proof of touch, that list of "intangibles" accrues a subsidiary definition that includes "the instruments, objects, artifacts and cultural spaces associated therewith." Waxing dialectical, UNESCO goes on to "stipulate ... the interdependence between intangible Cultural Heritage, and tangible cultural and natural heritage, and acknowledges the role of intangible Cultural Heritage as a source of cultural diversity and a driver of sustainable development." Human persons, they conclude, are and so can and should be honored and protected as living repositories of the immaterial shaping forces that produce material cultures.

More power, I say, to UNESCO for seeking to broach the core difficulty at the heart of the word materiality. Though the supposed physicality of the sense of "touch," the lexicon of tangibility, will not quite square this circle or resolve the conceptual (and practical) difficulties. "*Noli me tangere*" [Touch me not], says the resurrected Jesus to Mary Magdalene in John 20:17 for there is more, apparently, to appearances than substance. UNESCO deploys a similar but more ecumenical lexicon of tangibility in order to acknowledge the difficulty in preserving and protecting the folding together of physical substances, shared forms, individual ideas, and finite human existences, that produces what we call culture. UNESCO understands that we might need to feel things, that knowledge and understanding sometimes requires the sense of touch. Strange stuff this matter. Objects are at once so much more and so much less than they seem.

So, the word "material" in material culture seeks to grasp the involutions of substance, ideas, belief, design, and form that produce a built world. Materiality refers to the winking in and out of being of our awareness of the pull things have upon us, the ways in which what passes as media does more than mediate, and how differently configured and timed congelations of labor, practice, time, and energy press upon us, shaping our actions, perceptions, and feelings. The word toggles back and forth between these two registers or senses and so also does the array of differing, complementary and sometimes competing approaches that orient themselves by way of the things we make. Every approach to material culture studies is, therefore, at base, a theory of matter, making, and manufacture, a theory of media, of use, and of practice – even if it claims to concern itself only with empirical objects.

If it appears that my infrastructural definition of the word material (*materia*) risks a conceptual slide into fields far beyond those usually identified as part of material culture studies, then that seems about right. Guilty as charged. One of the things that interests me is the way archaeology, anthropology, architectural history, art history, museum and preservation studies cohabit with approaches whose homes lie in science studies (science and technology studies, actor network theory); media studies more generally; translation studies; and, as I shall argue at the end of this chapter, now also critical animal studies, the emerging fields of plant studies, and ecocriticism. While material culture studies has always understood its focus to be infrastructural, focusing, that is, on aspects of our world frequently taken for granted and so un- or under-thought, the nature of our object is changing.[5] By broadening the traditionally defined fields that make up material culture studies into a much more varied series of approaches I do not mean to argue for a post-disciplinary breakdown of coherence or, for that matter, a liberation from the nitty gritty of empirical studies or historical constraints. On the contrary, I think Christopher Pinney gets things pretty much exactly right when he states that "'materiality' might be defined as that (figural) excess which cannot be encompassed by linguistic-philosophical closure."[6] By this statement he means to suggest the way objects come haunted by the sense that there is more to them than meets the eye. Any confrontation with materiality, any interaction with an object in all its density, should prove disorienting. It should lead us to question what counts as the subject of our work, the limits to our *object*, and throw into doubt categories that we had taken as givens. True to their Latin name (*ob*/against, *iacere*/to throw), objects get in the way. They multiply; trip us up; slow us down; render us a figure of fun, as they upend our handy ability to craft familiar narratives. Thus arrested, we find that we are suddenly present to an immense gathering of beings, a world of objects crafted from the remainders of differently animated animals, plants, and minerals by human persons whose labor and skill or whose suffering remains only partially legible. This altered and altering sense of the world teaches us that what we thought were *just* objects, were in fact *things*, or true to the Scandinavian origins of the word (*Þing*), an assembly or assemblies – whole polities of beings that we come into being with. And so, our object encounters return us to a host of ethical, political, and ecological questions that even as we may have always posed them (from time to time) now become urgently and captivatingly present as the basis of our field in its theoretical discussions and everyday practices.[7]

It is this confrontation with something basic to the world and to human existence that I hear partially encrypted in such questions that migrate through conversations about material culture: "Do objects have agency?" "In what sense do they have lives?" "Do animals or plants produce material culture?" Such are the kinds of conceptual vertigo or disorientation that facing matter and materiality head on should produce. "Disorientation," as Sarah Ahmed writes, "is vital," it produces energy, liveliness.[8] Not knowing demands that we heighten our feats of description; attend to the constraints of time and place; keep an eye open for different scales of temporality; for competing geographical scales; tune our senses to the object before us and so own up to the density to the aesthetic (sensory) dimension of the way in which our bodies and our disciplines record the impressions objects make upon them. Traditionally defined fields of material culture studies have grown up in response to the possibilities or difficulties generated by specific types or families of objects. The expertise these fields offer is real, important, and crucial – as are the larger questions about matter and making that they enable us to answer even as, on occasion, they presume that they have answered them already.

In what follows I tell a story about what it means to confront the strangeness of objects or things and how that strangeness enables us to open to view the processes by which worlds and infrastructures are made. I cannot pretend that this story exhausts all the possibilities. Please consider it an invitation to take up the reins and retell it in your own particular way. As a first step, let's attend to the objects you find around you and see what we may learn by doing so. As you will see, this phenomenological tradition of attending to ordinary things has a long history.

Teaspoons and Questions (Objects and Things)

"Question your tea spoons," instructs experimental writer and sometime archivist Georges Perec. Inquire into the wherewithal of your cutlery, muse on the form a fork takes, on forks themselves, to say nothing of spoons, and knives, chopsticks or all the various prostheses for eating that mediate between hand and mouth. Or, maybe, start with yourself. Empty your pockets and make an inventory; map the diverging paths, the different timelines, down which their contents take you; juxtapose; describe one street; then another; compare the two.[9] Perec is out "to found our own anthropology," an anthropology of what he calls the infra-ordinary, all those things so obvious as not to deserve much scrutiny. Indeed, he suggests that it is the fact that they seem "trivial and futile" that "makes them essential."[10] In his writings, he suggests a range of activities of observation that might attune the observer to the way our infrastructures shape existence.

Perec's call comes, so he writes, from his frustration with the way "what speaks to us, seemingly, is always the big event, the untoward, the extraordinary." Ostensibly, Perec is speaking of newspapers and the news cycle but he is also speaking of certain use-oriented traditions in phenomenology for which objects only start to matter when they break or fail to act as good instruments or tools. "Railway trains only begin to exist when they are derailed," he writes. "Airplanes," he amplifies "achieve existence only when they are hijacked."[11] These words are his own, but they might as well be those of Martin Heidegger or any of his commentators, explaining how humans rarely encounter entities "present-at-hand" (*vorhanden*), in their fullness. Instead, as Graham Harman explains, we encounter them "through 'using' them" or by "simply *counting on them*" as equipment or as a set of actions or possibilities inscribed in an infrastructure (*Gestell*) or as what Heidegger calls "readiness-to-hand" (*Zuhandenheit*). It is only when such objects break or malfunction that we take cognizance of them as such but even then, a derailed railway train or hijacked airplane, to take Perec's examples, remain technological devices whose routines have been interrupted. We tend, even then, not to encounter them as brute or dense material presences, shorn of their uses, the density of their agglomeration as matter pressing upon our senses.[12]

The *topos* of the broken tool undoubtedly counts as a privileged and powerful figure in material culture studies, but Perec worries that attending only to the failures of equipment and its uses naturalizes the way the world is and so amounts to a form of political quietism. On the contrary, infrastructures are, he thinks, every bit as strange when they work as when they break down. Indeed, remarking its failures, attending only to broken things, might even tend to inoculate us against what Perec calls "the truly intolerable, the truly inadmissible" facts of existence. "What is scandalous isn't the pit explosion, it's working in coalmines," he explains. "Social problems aren't 'a matter of concern' when there's a strike, they are intolerable twenty-four hours out of twenty-four, three hundred and sixty-five days a year." Perec worries that the routinization of our infrastructures, what he calls the "habitual," carries with it an anesthetizing force so that "we sleep through our lives in a dreamless sleep."[13] His solution is a set of instructions for a DIY phenomenology that would inquire not only into those things that break but into the very stability of those things that always seem to work or never change. Where might challenging the somnambulism of everyday life lead us?

Perec's invocation of sleep as the habituation of routine and waking as the coming-in-to-focus of the object world has a long pedigree. It dates back at least to the first century CE to a poem attributed to Virgil titled "Moretum."[14] The poem traces the experience of Simulus, a poor peasant waking and slowly coming back to sense. Simulus gets up in the dark of the early morning and is able to make his breakfast – the mess or "salad" of herbs, olive oil, and cheese he spreads on bread that gives the poem its title – by touch. When the sun rises and the light returns, all the things of the world – or his garden – get named again. The light "'lists' and so names the things in the garden, distinguishing the various crops growing there: cabbage, beets, asparagus." The dawn forces his eyes open and, as philosopher Remo Bodei observes, "the order of words and of things is reborn," almost as if objects were summoned back to the roles they play for Simulus by the rising sun.[15] Oil, cheese, and herbs agree to combine to form a spread for bread. Water agrees to slake thirst. But this agreement is never exactly total. The strangeness of waking along with the residues of habit memory ensure that we know that there is more to the objects that populate our worlds and mental habits than their apparent functionality. As Bodei tells us, this scene of waking replays in various guises in the writings of René Descartes, Immanuel Kant, Georg Wilhelm Hegel, Edmund Husserl, Sigmund Freud, Karl Marx, Martin Heidegger, Gaston Bachelard, Maurice Merleau Ponty, and more. But, as Perec's worries about the way objects seem only to attract attention when they fail, go awry, or cause catastrophes signal, at issue in this coming to consciousness of phenomena in all their density is the difficulty we have in parsing the difference between *objects* (frequently said to be forlorn, inanimate, mute) and *things* (richly networked, used, felt, sustaining).

Bodei proves helpful here again. In *The Life of Things, The Love of Things*, he takes readers on a tour of the two words' histories, citing his native Italian *cosa*, which derives from the Latin *causa* and designates less a physical entity than something so "important and engaging that it can mobilize us to defend it."[16] The word cohabits with the Latin *res* and so with notions of the *res publica*, the public thing or common cause. Things, in this sense, constitute networks or "gatherings" of significance and beings, as Martin Heidegger describes them, configurations of matter, persons, social relations that demand speech and require collective discussion.[17] Bodei curates this linkage of philosophical systems to political forms of speech from Aristotle to Hegel, indicating the way philosophical maxims such as Aristotle's *"auto to pragma"* (the thing itself) or Hegel's *"Zu den Sachen selbst"* (to the things themselves) refer not to unmediated access to the world but to a mediation (form of speech) so compelling that things appear to speak for themselves, with a primary obviousness that may be agreed upon or contested in the name of a different order of truth.[18] *Things*, in this sense, happen. They impress themselves on us; we receive their impression and are made to speak – such that they seem to speak for themselves. Things are objects shorn of their use, freed from the world of habit. Picture a work of art, your mother's shawl, your lover's pipe, *things* worth keeping, things *that* sustain. People are *things* in this sense – so are ideas.

Objects, in contrast, so the story goes, belong to a different register of more highly purified categories. "The idea of *objectum* (or in German

Gegenstand – what is before or against me) . . . implies a challenge . . . and an overpowering." The relation between subject and object figures an antagonism, a power play. How awful, then, to be an object, an obstacle, something literally thrown (the Latin *ob* + *iacere*) in the way and batted aside by the subject (you and I). Except that the story is not so neat, nor the categories so clearly marked. If a *thing* designates "a cluster of relationships in which I feel and know that I am implicated and of which I do not want to have exclusive control," then full disclosure requires that we acknowledge that the word (human) "subject" (*subiectum*) originally referred not to personhood, but to the underlying foundation or the "substrate that supports the qualities or the mutations of a material" – the impress of a situation or *thing* on the perceptual/physiological reality of human embodiment. For Descartes, credited with the birth of the individual via the self-grounding "*Cogito ergo sum*" (I think therefore I am), *subjectum* remained something immanent to a philosophical machine or project and not something to be alienated as a form of personhood in opposition to a world of objects.[19] Objects refuse to sit still and remain inanimate – especially as they tend to formalize social relations and are the product of vast inputs of resources and conglomerations of human labor. Every attempt to delineate a stable difference between object and *thing* thus tends to produce an anthropology in which we now know what is animate and not, who and what counts as "human," and who or what lives on as so much disposable life.[20] It is this kind of danger that animates the likes of Perec when he invites us to inquire into all the objects around us as part of an infrastructure of which we also are part.

Lurking in the uncertain distinction between object and thing is a salutary attempt to posit and so know the difference between ways of being, to derive stable value systems from our relations with objects, and, as Perec intuits, to establish some sort of difference between human persons and other entities whose very being is typically put to use. Tinges of melancholy at the depredations (real and important) of consumer capitalism or the deadening of sense from mass production rear their heads here. Tuning into *things* as opposed to *objects* can manifest here as something like a materialist cure for the ills of industrialized society in the West. But these fears may also signify a regressive attempt to fill in and so preserve the "human" as a viable category distinct from animal, plant, and machine, along with all those human persons not granted membership to the "human." Such appeals to authentic thingliness are thus frequently insensitive to race and gender, to the realities of embodiment, and serve to privilege a one-size-fits-all (aka straight, white, masculinist) default.[21]

Instead, as Perec offers, everyday objects, mass-produced objects, discarded and used up commodities, simulacra, even accidents and violent atrocities, are *things* just as much as more rarefied art objects or natural phenomena. You may not like them. You may not find the relations they offer sustaining. They may disturb you. But those are different questions.

There is no essential difference between a *thing* (rich, networked, complex) and an object (orphaned, forlorn, stripped of nuance). The difference between the two lies in the value relations derived from both. A derailment or a hijacking is just as much a *thing* as anything else – and acknowledging that conceptual indistinction might reveal how value cohabits with atrocity in ways that complicate everything. "There is," as we know "no document of culture which is not at the same time a document of barbarism."[22] All objects are *things*. Some provide good, which is to say sustaining and reciprocal relations; others prove abusive, contemptible, deadly. Question your teaspoons indeed. They will disclose a multiplicity of stories about tea, cutlery, opium wars, colonialism, and the world made by tea-drinking.

Fetishism (All Animism All the Time)

Of course, sometimes the brokenness is attributed not to the object/tool but to the perceiving subject. When misuse occurs at the level of practice or you are regarded as valuing the wrong thing or some thing too much, charges of fetishism may fly. In Western usage, a fetish implies "something irrationally reverenced" over and above its obvious value or "an object, nonsexual part of the body, or particular action which abnormally serves as the stimulus to, or the end in itself of, sexual desire." To have a fetish is to enter into an excessive, addictive, or otherwise dissident object relation that defies common sense and received wisdom.[23]

Even the likes of Arjun Appadurai worry about such charges in the introduction to his now classic collection of essays, *The Social Life of Things* (1986). Appadurai is rightly credited with sponsoring a mode of commodity history that traces objects as they move through a "life cycle" from making to consumption, destruction, discarding, or disaggregation. Within the collection, Igor Kopytoff's conception of a "cultural biography of things" captured the imaginations of many readers because it charts how the meaning of an object changes over time and by locale. "The biography of a car in Africa would reveal a wealth of cultural data," he writes, "the way it was acquired, how and from whom money was assembled to pay for it, the relationship of the seller to the buyer, the uses to which the car is regularly put" and so on.[24] As compelling as Kopytoff's insights are, still Appadurai worries that "following things themselves" will attract accusations of animism or fetishism. To inoculate the volume against such charges, he observes, "even though from a *theoretical* point of view human actors encode things with significance, from a methodological point of view it is things-in-motion that illuminate their human and social contexts." Accordingly, to trace the "biography" of a thing cannot "avoid a minimum level of what we might call methodological fetishism."[25] The analyst must act as if he or she were a fetishist, as if he or she were attributing agency to an object in order to untie the knot of labor, substance, and practice that holds it together. The work of tracing the trajectory of an object's becoming is reciprocal to the acts of making and manufacture, the practices of use and misuse, for which it is an occasion. Tracing the "life" of an object means treating it as if a human person to be able to perceive all the differently distributed groups of humans the object gathers as it leads its life.

What, however, some of us may ask, is so horrible about a fetish? Why would an acknowledgment that, in some shape or form, an object *matters*, has efficacy, makes things happen, be the cause of scandal? What is so embarrassing about animism? Here it is worth teasing out from Appadurai's rhetorically circumspect language the implicit conflict of viewpoints and value systems that an accusation of fetishism entails. Appadurai positions his approach as a "minimum of methodological fetishism," treating objects as if they were alive, all to let the implied skeptic know that, in fact, he and they share the same value system that, generally speaking, precludes according agency or animation to objects. Consider how different this self-aware, inoculating perspective sounds from the likes of the "patients" to whom Sigmund Freud attributes a fetish. In "Fetishism" (1927), Freud observes that most of his patients did not seek him out because of their fetish. "No doubt a fetish is recognized by its adherents as an abnormality," he writes, though "it is seldom felt by them as the symptom of an ailment accompanied by suffering."[26] On the contrary, they are "usually ... quite satisfied with it, or even praise the way in which it eases their erotic life." No uncomfortable rhetorical manoeuvring on the part of his patients. Their fetish objects provide them with a sustaining if idiosyncratic relation. Typically, shame, embarrassment, or even the notion of dissidence is not felt or acknowledged by the fetishist even if she or he conceals the object relation because it is understood not to be normative. Accusations of a pejorative fetishism come from without. Charges of fetishism are the product of incompatible value systems that parse the relation between certain configurations of matter and human persons differently. The word fetish, in this lexicon, indicates a face off or encounter of two or more divergent value systems.

In a series of ground-breaking essays, anthropologist William Pietz takes this sense of conflicting value systems as the key to the emergence of the fetish as what he calls a "concept-problem."[27] Pietz traces a value neutral or even positive genealogy of the fetish as "basically a middle-man's word" from its emergence as the "pidgin word *Fetisso*" combining Portuguese and native languages in the "cross cultural spaces of the coast of West Africa during the sixteenth and seventeenth centuries," through to its negative recasting in Enlightenment discourses and eventually in the hands of Sigmund Freud and Karl Marx in the nineteenth century.[28] The story he traces figures the "fetish" as a category of *things* with a problematic or contested relationship to rationalized modes of exchange. His genealogy demonstrates how, in all discourses, regardless of which particular *thing* is in question, the "fetish not only originated in, but remains specific to, the problematic of the social value of material objects as revealed in situations by the encounter of radically heterogeneous value systems" (West African and Portuguese; Catholic and Protestant; religious and rational; fetishistic and psychoanalytic; capitalist and Marxist).[29] Pietz goes on to demonstrate the way the fetish both enacts and scrambles anthropological desires to universalize or particularize cultural dynamics. A fetish relation is defined by four governing characteristics: an "irreducible materiality" or the non-substitutability of *this* object; "singularity and repetition ... an ordering power derived from its status as the fixation or inscription of a unique originating event"; localizing "the problem of the nonuniversality and constructedness of social value"; and "the subjection of the human body (as the material locus of action and desire) to the influence of certain significant material objects."[30] As Pietz is eager to point out, these four criteria apply equally to forms of art as they do to the ritual objects of major world religions.[31]

Pried free from its retroactive disciplining as an overinvestment or symptom that proves coterminous with the racist modeling of non-Christian peoples as "irrational," Pietz's positive estimation of the fetish enables us to understand the way the pull of the object world upon us produces a parade of objects that vie with the anchoring power of such supra or sublime objects as the Eucharist or the commodity form. The fact that the word fetish emerges as a pidgin, a word that belongs to no single language system but which is produced by two languages attempting to map one another's semantic fields, signals that it belongs to the conflicts generated as two or more different ways of valuing objects. The fetish names a confusion of categories and the inability to translate across value systems without static, noise, difficulty, as well as possibility. It designates a moment in which a concern for matter and how we understand it comes to dominate the scene. Following Pietz's genealogy, we can conclude that objects with fetish power exist in all cultures and historical moments even as the object worlds of each culture or historic moment differ and may prove incompatible. All objects are, in some shape and form, fetishes. All societies are animistic. Fetish accusations arise when not all users agree on the same definitions of matter, agency, and efficacy – when differing forms of animism collide. (See Roe, Chapter 17.)

It is easier now to make sense of Freud's pathologizing of the fetish relation and the allied deployment of "fetish" as a pathological condition by Karl Marx in his exposure of the "cell form of the commodity" in *Das Kapital*. Both writers are out to diagnose what they regard as a pathological interruption of what, otherwise, would lead to a healthy and desirable outcome: a heterosexual male subject (Freud) and a mode of relation not grounded in the routinized and occulted exploitations of capitalism (Marx). In volume one of *Kapital*, in the section on "The Fetishism of the

Commodities and the Secret Thereof," Marx famously explains that "in order... to find an analogy" to the "mysterious thing" that is a commodity, "we must have recourse to the mist-enveloped regions of the religious world" where "productions of the human brain appear as independent beings endowed with life, and [enter] ... into relation both with one another and the human race. This I call the Fetishism which attaches itself to the products of labor, as soon as they are produced as commodities."[32] Here it is worth pointing out the way Marx is out to skewer a very specific aspect of the commodity form, the way in which capitalism fetishizes something peculiarly immaterial – not the materials used to make something, nor the labor of those who make things, but the abstract exchange value that comes from the object receiving valuation from the market.

As Peter Stallybrass writes, "the fetishism of the commodity inscribes *im*materiality as the defining feature of capitalism. Thus, for Marx, *fetishism* is not the problem: the problem is the fetishism of *commodities*."[33] Extracting abstract value by occulting the labor and lived reality of making, capitalism enacts a mysterious dematerialization that for Marx amounts to theft. The shape of *Kapital* and, in particular, of some of Marx's most famous rhetorical gambits, is to make palpable the strangeness of this theft:

> It is as clear as noon-day, that man, by his industry, changes the forms of the materials furnished by Nature, in such a way as to make them useful to him. The form of wood, for instance, is altered, by making a table out of it. Yet, for all that, the table continues to be a common, every-day thing, wood. But, so soon as it steps forth as a commodity, it is changed into something transcendent. It not only stands with its feet on the ground, but in relation to all other commodities, it stands on its head, and evolves out of its wooden brain grotesque ideas far more wonderful than "table turning" ever was.[34]

Noon is the time for geometry lessons – when the sun casts no shadows. Accordingly, Marx is attempting to deliver something truly, as it is. Human beings make objects. When those objects become commodities, however, something strange happens. To capture this strangeness Marx personifies the table. He animates it; has it do a handstand; gives it a head; has it think grotesque thoughts much worse than the conning, charlatan-spiritualist "table-turn[ers]" of Marx's nineteenth century. Marx's *prosopopoeia* (the trope that means to give face to things) is, of course, itself an instance of rhetorical table turning, but one that seeks to recover to the object the occluded labor robbed from its making when it "steps forth" as a commodity for it is "human labor-power in motion, or human labor, that creates value."[35] So pathological is the orientation to matter and labor under capitalism, so irrational are its modes of valuation and representation, that Marx must produce this order of compensatory personification strategies.

Marx ends this section of *Kapital* by deploying the same trope of the speaking thing. But this time, he has commodities speak among themselves. While the table's animation marks an attempt to recover or to represent the labor capitalism steals, these commodities now voice the kinds of conversation they have among themselves. "Could commodities themselves speak," writes Marx, "they would say: 'Our use-value may be a thing that interests men. It is no part of us as objects. What, however, does belong to us as objects, is our value. Our natural intercourse as commodities proves it. In the eyes of each other we are nothing but exchange values.'"[36]

In comparison to the acrobatic, attention-seeking table of Marx's rhetorical high jinx, what commodities say amongst themselves might make for dull reading. For while Marx allows us to listen in on the commodities' rehearsal, their actual dialogue might sound more like the quasi-algebraic analysis Marx provides as to how commodities receive their value on the market:

X commodity A = y commodity B, or
X commodity A is worth y commodity B.
20 yards of linen = 1 coat, or
20 yards of linen are worth 1 coat.[37]

Still, the theatrical dimension to Marx's animations is what *matters*. His animation games mark an attempt to own the way a capitalist mode of production estranges our relation to the material world to produce a vampiric immaterialism.

On this reading of Marx, the way forward lies in reversing the pejorative, apparently commonsensical statement "that we should not treat people like things." On the contrary, as Stallybrass asks, "what have we done to things to have such contempt for them? And who can afford to have such contempt for them?"[38] Perhaps, our relations with others ought therefore to become more- rather than less-thing-like. Perhaps, a more equitable polity would route human relationships through and derive social meaning from objects. We might then take objects as *things*, gatherings, occasions, whose very process of making becomes the site of a community of production as well as consumption. Certainly, this is what Pietz hopes for when he argues on behalf of the ability of "border fetishisms," or "heterospaces," where capitalism and non-capitalism coexist to offer momentary stays or interruptions to exchange that allow something else to emerge. "Rather than adapting their cultural forms to a 'hegemonic' or global economy or 'resisting' it," he writes, "indigenous people" appropriate global commodities, transforming them back into objects in ways that defy exchange value.[39] Such "border fetishisms" stand as a witness to a productive reversal of fortune "that might be termed the social appropriation of capitalism" to produce collectives that arise on the basis of and in relation to *things*, as opposed to the dematerializing and so empty fetishism of the commodity form. Goodbye to the bad fetish of the commodity, then; hello to the good, sustaining fetish relation of the retrofitted or otherwise altered objects collectively remade by the labor of these localizing polities whose forms of sociality have become *thing*-like.[40]

But before we find ourselves too happily enchanted by our new-found or rediscovered entanglement with one another in and through and by way of things, it seems crucial to own the fact that, as Dan Hicks puts it in *The Brutish Museums*, the:

> most violent and purposeful of category mistakes, the mixing-up of humanity and things, had come to West Africa with the slave trade – the commoditisation of people on an industrial scale, the treatment of the body as if it is property. This blurring was achieved, as Igor Kopytoff has shown, through social transformations that changed the status of people by removing identity and reducing personhood, which do not simply end in the relatively short period between capture and sale but involve being "re-individualised by acquiring new statuses" ... while always remaining a "potential commodity."[41]

For Hicks, this insight marks the genesis of a mode of cultural biography that seeks to own its complicity with such genocidal violence by proceeding as "forensic death writing ... forensic because this is about understanding the truth at the scene of a crime: necrography." Necrography radicalizes the attention to occluded or stolen labor-time that Marx demands by insisting on the dehumanizing violence and suffering caused by the elaborated networks of circumatlantic slavery, colonialism, and the aftermath of these structures as subsequent generations of people live on "in the wake," as Christina Sharpe puts it.[42] That work of redescription allied to the return of stolen artifacts, the dismantling of the colonial museum, and the depathologizing of museum space itself, are ongoing projects.

Throughout this section, I have been working toward the position that the words "fact" and "fetish" result from a conflict over how to understand what counts as making – much as did object and thing in the previous section. The process of making, in other words, permits no easy separation of maker and made into finite, noncontradictory categories. This insight voices the position of sociologist Bruno Latour who has attempted to stitch fact and fetish back together as value terms produced by competing valuations derived from the process of making (the Latin verb *facere* gives us the word fact). This position that facts and fetishes are mirror images, fractured halves of a single process Latour names the ungainly "factish." Rejoining the broken pieces of this factish to constitute a "whole" does not necessarily carry any positive or reparative value. On the contrary, Latour's modeling of the factish remains exactly that, a way of modeling, an order of description, that maps a field of forces. It marks the beginning of a conversation about the limits of such an enterprise, about the ethics and politics of such descriptions, and about what it will mean for an uncertainly referential "us" to think about matter beyond or otherwise than human – as Marx's table-turning metaphors already invite us to do. Though, to follow the likes of Latour and the many, differing, approaches designated by the "new materialism" means that we shall have to rethink the human exclusivity to Marx's concept of "labor-power in motion."[43]

New Materialisms (Theories of Action)

Inspiration for this endeavor to think yet more broadly about "labor-power" comes from philosopher Michel Serres who offers ways of modeling our infrastructures as co-productions among human persons and the host of animals, plants, bacteria, viruses, and the other entities with whom we come into being. Following Serres, Latour offers what he calls a "flat ontology" in which categories of being (animal, vegetable, mineral, and so on) are not givens but are understood to derive from our acts of making, coming then to serve as inputs to our routines or rituals that keep certain versions of the world in place and prevent others from coming into being. Along with his fellow travelers in science and technology studies (STS) and what became actor network theory (ANT), Latour develops a semiotics of "actants" and "actor networks" to describe the way persons and the vast array of other entities formed aggregates or assemblages.[44] Taking Marx at his word that "all values, all commodities are only definite masses of congealed labor-time," Serres and Latour invite us to extend this understanding of labor and time in directions otherwise than human.[45]

In *The Parasite* (1982), Serres models action/events as a cybernetic or "parasitic" cascade in which the positions of subject and object, host and guest, "food" and "parasite" become a way to theorize action, events, and production in general. Trading on the multiple meanings of parasite, especially so in French, Serres explains that "the prefix *para-* means 'near,' 'next to,'" it "measures a distance. The *sitos* is the food [differently encoded forms of information]."[46] What matters is precisely this insistence on relations, the links that develop as entities switch positions, interrupting one another, oscillating between serving as subject and object as "events" unfold. As soon as one parasite installs itself as king, another chases it out, and so on, ad infinitum. Ontology, as we had known it, collapses. Parasitism as primary relation necessitates a new understanding of the human as one group of entities among many rather than as the transcendental subject of philosophy or phenomenology. To be human in such a model is to "parasite each other and live amidst parasites," ingesting other entities for food, wearing their skins for warmth, and tooling their beings into forms with which we build our worlds, which necessarily are then shot through with remainders of their being.[47]

One key concept that emerges from *The Parasite* is that of the "quasi-object" and "quasi-subject" as essentially positions in the grammar of a game or event. As an event or game unfolds differing entities who play a part in the proceedings (persons, animals, plants, and so on) shift positions and so appear, by turns, as if a subject or as if an object. It is only by attending to the process of the event or game itself that we can begin to approach and so understand the meaning of the action in question. The winner, he or she or it that is pronounced the arch-subject is he or she who comes last – the parasite who parasites all. For Serres, human history has amounted to an attempt of variously reduced groups of human animals to occupy this position and achieve mastery at the cost to their excluded fellows.[48] Mastery, however, as the word "cascade" implies, proves impossible for events always spin out of control – hence the violence of exclusion deployed to preserve the apparently superior position. Against this horrific notion of the human-as-arch-parasite, Serres advances an alternate definition of the human that as his work develops coalesces into this adage: "*errare humanum est*" (it is human to wander, to be in error, to get things wrong).[49] Error is our essential medium. Error is our home. And this knowledge, what appears in *The Parasite* as the "always already" inevitability of the random, the impossibility of permanently installing oneself at the end of the parasitic chain, of becoming the "big Subject" of post-Cartesian fantasy, provides the elements for another way of thinking matter and so describing the world that owns our debts and connections to other beings.

Bruno Latour along with fellow thinkers in STS and ANT develop the model of the quasi-object/hybrid as a fully articulated regime of description. For Latour, the choices currently available to us in social theory for describing action are inadequate for the task. We remain torn between according either the system or the user sovereignty. Instead, Latour proposes an alternative model of what occurs in the act of making:

> Whenever we make something *we* are not in command, we are slightly *overtaken* by the action: every builder knows that. Thus the paradox of constructivism is that it uses a vocabulary of *mastery* that no architect, mason, city planner, or carpenter would ever use. Are we fooled by what we do? Are we controlled, possessed, alienated? No, not always, not quite. That which overtakes us is *also*, because of our agency, because of the *clinamen* of our action, slightly overtaken, modified. Am I simply restating the dialectic? No, there is no object, no subject, no contradiction, no *Aufhebung*, no mastery, no recapitulation, no spirit, no alienation. But there are events. I never *act*; I am always slightly surprised by what I do, by the chance to mutate, to change,

and to bifurcate, the chance that I and the circumstances surrounding me offer to that which has been invited, recovered, welcomed.[50]

Latour's use of the word "clinamen," recalls the turn or swerve, theorized first by Lucretius and then by Serres, by which an event occurs – the little turbulence at the heart of things that none can master.[51] What we have taken to calling the new materialism, then, amounts to the return of the much older materialism of Lucretius and Epicurus – thinkers with whom Marx also engaged in his notebooks and thinking about matter.[52] Latour is careful also to make clear that he is not simply "restating the dialectic" – there is no "contradiction, no *Aufhebung*," no overcoming. Instead, he speaks of the "slight surprise of action" that takes hold of both person and thing, remaking all in the act of making. The human may serve as prime mover – we may speak of a setting in motion – but there is no mastery, no control, on either side. Indeed, it becomes impossible to speak simply of "sides" – for while there is a "setting into motion" that might originate with a human hand, there is no ontological priority to the person. All (persons and things) are remade in the act of making. Moreover, winking at his readers, Latour insists that he is not telling us anything that a cook or an artist or a writer does not already know. Events happen. We can speak of a setting into motion but not an author or mastery. If you burn the cake, you are a bad cook. If the cake tastes well, you are good. A good cook is only as good as their cake. We are all hybrids.

Latour seeks to capture this process of hybridization through a variety of lexicons. Most compelling has been his use of the verbal construction "make make" (*faire faire*), using "what the Greeks call the 'middle voice', the verb form that is neither active nor passive," to express the division of labor by which things we make make us make.[53] This usage dissipates the problem of control or mastery. In place of a defined "before" and "after," and an autonomous subject-maker, we have instead a series of entities (human and not) linked in a chain of making. What is important is the chain, the series of attachments that make a person into a particular historical subject or event. Questions of ontology instead become instances when the chain of making that leads to the production of a particular world or a particular subject form is forgotten or "black boxed."[54] Distinctions – "subject" and "object," for example – are understood to be an effect or outcome of a given act of making. And to be "human" means necessarily to be "attached" and so, in a certain sense, controlled by things. What is more, if this new understanding of what it means to be human as necessarily being attached requires forgoing the idea of the perfectly autonomous user and the accompanying myth of total alienation, then what Latour requires of us is a very careful thinking of which attachments lead to less alienated beings. "If it is no longer a question of opposing attachment to things to detachment [from things or techniques – but also food, biology, etc.], but instead of good and poor attachments," he writes, "then there is only one way of deciding the quality of these ties: to inquire of what they consist, what they do, how one is affected by them."[55]

It is important to understand that Latour's restatement of what happens during an act of making or an "event" as a process shared by various actors (human and otherwise) raises a series of questions. For, if the "distinction between subjects and objects is not primordial," but is merely the way in which a given situation presents itself to us, then our job as analysts is to recover "the multitudinous entities that give rise to [that] action."[56] Lowering the threshold of visibility far enough to see all the entities that constitute a particular artifact or "event" is what Latour asks us to do, and what Serres's description of the parasitic chain does. To follow Serres and Latour is to make this move and so to retell our stories and reimagine our communities as collectives of many humans and nonhuman actors. Hence the proliferation of regimes of description across disciplines that all deploy some version of an additive or assemblage model of phenomena: Donna Haraway's "cyborg," "companion," "multispecies," and kin making inquiries; Jane Bennett's vibrant or "vital materialism"; Stacy Alaimo's "transcorporeality"; Timothy Morton's burgeoning lexicon of dark ecology and hyperobjects; the "*zoë* egalitarianism" of Rosi Braidotti; and the "agential cuts" and "intra-action" of Karen Barad; the making and walking knowledges of Tim Ingold; Ian Hodder's entangled thinking; John Law's conception of sociology as "mess"; and Mel Y. Chen's conception of "animacy" – or any number of inspiring projects that seek to own the co-imbrication of beings in our acts of making.[57]

It is here with the attention to "ties" or relations between beings that material culture studies might make a yet more significant contribution as it seeks to reconcile its own object fidelities and varieties of expertise with these emerging modes of thinking matter. A strategic difference, for example, between Latour's model analysts and many of us housed in the humanities lies in the way we find ourselves oriented to our objects of study. Tuned to things past, to the fragments of chains of making longsince severed or attenuated, partially interrupted, and so to actor networks that have dropped actants as they have added new ones, we are obliged to deal with the fractured objects that result from these dropped connections. It is these texts or traces, these partial connections that we take as our points of departure. Our object remains always the archive of a practice, the remnants of something, which, by our joining, we only partially re/activate, alive to the ways the figure of the archive itself as actor network enables certain modes of joining and disables others and so makes certain worlds or prospects un/thinkable. Here it seems important to own further the way the objects configured by new materialist studies are never singular, never "one." As aggregates or assemblages, they produce different temporal and spatial effects. Objects do not belong to one time or place but to many. They are multiple.

Crucial here is Serres's sense of space and time as a crumpled or folded series of forms. "Time," writes Serres, "does not always flow according to a line ... nor according to a plan, but, rather, according to an extraordinarily complex mixture, as though it reflected stopping points, ruptures, deep wells, chimneys of thunderous acceleration, rendings, gaps."[58] The time of objects is multiple, best thought of in terms of a handkerchief. "If you spread [the handkerchief] out in order to iron it" you maximize the surface and two points seem quite distant. "Then take the same handkerchief and crumple it" and two points that seem distant "suddenly are close, even superimposed."[59] One of Serres's favorite illustrations of how this model of reversible, nonlinear time shapes our worlds is the everyday example of a "late-model car." How do we date this car? To what period does it belong? The answer runs as follows:

> the car is a disparate aggregate of scientific and technical solutions dating from different periods. One can date it component by component: this part was invented at the turn of the century, another, ten years ago, and Carnot's cycle [key to the workings of the combustion engine] is almost two hundred years old. Not to mention that the wheel dates back to Neolithic times.[60]

Add to this description the cultural time keyed to the array of media platforms that enable you to play this or that piece of music while you drive or that show a TV program or film to passengers in the back seat, and every time you get in your car you might consider yourself a quotidian time-traveler. Zooming off to the shops you might listen to music played in 1964, to a novel written in 1982, 1882, 1782, and so on. When is your car exactly? When are you and your car?

Adapting Serres's insights, Latour offers that this "disparate aggregate" is best described as a palimpsest, a string, or overlay of dates (4500 BCE, 1824 CE, 1900, 2004). The chain of time indices continues obviously, the status of the gathering or *thing* that *is* your car keeps changing as it unfolds or is performed, as it sits in your driveway and rusts or drives down the road, idles at the light, breaks down.[61] As *things* break and are discarded; as new *things* are added; as you change the radio station or the song that plays; when the car is sold or totaled; recycled or consigned to a landfill; the *thing* as aggregation or gathering changes, dropping and adding components or, in Latour's terminology "actants." According to this model, we are always able to say *when* and *where* we are. But we can do so only by owning up to the co-imbrication of beings, cultures, and places that make our being possible. Every object constitutes a waxing and waning multiplicity.

Futures (Material Culture Studies Beyond the Human?)

The story I have been telling about matter and materiality is one in which the relation between the immaterial and the material drives successive ways of conceiving of the products of human labor, valuing them, using them, and preserving them. That this story is driven by and so founded on and funded by violent exploitation of historically particular groups of human beings along with their worldviews, their metaphysics, is a constant that successive models of materiality and its limits have variously sought to address and/or disown. It is hardly a coincidence, in this regard, that the inspiration and model for Kopytoff's biography of things and for commodity history run in tandem with his thinking through and with the life cycle of enslaved persons.[62] Our conceptions of matter unfold across thresholds of sentience, animation, life, and death, in ways that have historically contradicted themselves in order to assert the racial, gendered, generational, or species privilege of a subgroup of human animals. One of the hallmarks of the last twenty years of work, in this regard, has been an attempt to provincialize still further Western categories with the aim of legitimizing all forms of human finitude or metaphysics with the aim of exposing the always troubled pronoun "we" to all the persons to whom the pronoun should refer.[63]

But how do we respond now if we accept, as Serres argues, that "we aren't the only ones to write and read ... to code, to decipher the codes of others, to understand, mutate, invent, communicate, exchange signals, process information, encounter one another ... to thus win our lives. Everything in the world does it."[64] If we now take as a given that what we call "humanity [our physiology, psyches, cultures, stories] derives," in Donna Haraway's terms, "from a spatial and temporal web of interspecies dependencies," then how should we draw the limits of our object of study?[65] What counts now as "material culture"? While studies of material culture have traditionally assumed "culture" to be an exclusively "human" production, trading on an anthropology that would delineate human animals as remarkable because they formalize social relations in and by and through objects, the recent broadening of concepts of agency and action to include objects as compeers to human subjects opens the way for a yet more capacious account of "culture." After all, a material-centered, production-oriented approach to objects has always, in practice, attended to local ecologies, questions of resources, climate, and other constraints in addition to questions of design to comprehend features of an object. The adoption of object biography, actor network models, and cognitive models that understand the way objects may serve as actants essentially paves the way for a yet broader conception of culture and so of our archive that might include animals, plants, and more as actors.

In this regard, the tensions within material culture studies as a nomadic approach that unfolds across multiple disciplines, each differently oriented to the life cycle of an object, may prove a potential source of invention and new research. In one sense, the opening up of "culture" to nonhuman entities would assuredly wrest our "objects" beyond the walls of our usual archives, museums, and rare book libraries. But, in another, it might productively intrude field sciences such as primatology, anthropology, and science and technical studies into them. This would enable us to grasp yet more fully the ways in which what we call "human" objects are and have always been constellations of animal, plant, and mineral matter in ways that exceed our agency and the social meanings we derive from them. What I am suggesting, then, amounts to more than an extension of the concept of "culture" to animals and plants and minerals. The objects of material culture studies have always had a tendency to migrate across the species barrier to primates or mammals capable of tool use, to say nothing of birds with architectural mating rituals. The field's orientation to the role of matter and technology in shaping human thought and experiences has inclined it, always, toward a deep questioning of the limits of the "human." Extending culture to other primates and charismatic mammals hovers on the edge of the discipline.[66]

What might material culture studies look like if we assumed that our objects necessarily play host to or come crowded with other-than-human forms of "writing" or marking, traces that our acts of making erase, obliterate, but also render sensible, knowable, precisely by taking so many others as a substrate for our own acts of expression? Let us imagine that our archives are full of other now fugitive or partially erased modes of inscription, coding or making that do not allow themselves to be linearized or readily processed, but which necessarily we receive by and as they press or impress themselves upon us. These other forms of "writing" haunt the objects we make, put to use, discard, and conserve. Fragments of bacteria, fungi, protists, and such dally in our archives as in our genome, rendering our bodies as well as our objects multispecies impressions. Individually and collectively, we exist as strange archives of multispecies relating, or our co-becoming with other forms of life. Accordingly, the objects "we" make must be understood to be shot through with remainders not just of other beings as material supports for our own forms of expression but with remnants or traces of their own forms of "writing" or coding.

How material culture studies responds to what we might name an unreduced "ecological" pressure to accord the benefits of culture and history to beings other than human remains to be seen. Question our teaspoons we should and we may. But, the answers we now receive, as they always have, lead us beyond a reduced conception of the human. Undoing the distinction between objects (forlorn and mundane) and *things* (rich, networked, and sustaining), as Perec hopes, opens the door to this more expansive sense of an infrastructure as necessarily shot through with animal, plant, mineral, bacterial, and viral remainders. The disciplinary openness of material culture studies, its potential indistinction from an unreduced biomedia studies to come suggests that the questions we have posed of our objects might be asked more broadly. And the answers we receive – and who and what we receive them from – might change every*thing*.

Notes

1. Please note the homage to the first sentence of Terry Eagleton, *Literary Theory: An Introduction* 2nd ed. (Minneapolis: University of Minnesota Press, 1996 [1983]), 1. Faced with the daunting subject of this chapter, I needed a voice other than my own with which to begin.
2. Raymond Williams, *Keywords: A Vocabulary of Culture and Society* (New York: Oxford University Press, 1976), 164.
3. For a very useful collection of essays that approaches the subject of material culture under the sign of "immateriality," see Daniel Miller, ed., *Materiality* (Durham: Duke University Press, 2005).
4. https://bit.ly/3Bx0L9x (accessed April 4, 2019). UNESCO's definition cites "UNESCO (2003) Convention for the safeguarding of the intangible Cultural Heritage" (Paris: UNESCO) and UNESCO (n.d.) Guidelines for the Establishment of National "Living Human Treasures" Systems (Paris: UNESCO) as key guiding documents.
5. On the infrastructural orientation of media studies, see Marshall McCluhan, *The Gutenberg Galaxy*, reprint (Toronto: University of Toronto Press, 2011). For the turn within media studies to model media much more generally as that which mediates, see Sybille Krämer, *Medium, Messenger, Translation: An Approach to Media Philosophy* (Amsterdam: Amsterdam University Press, 2015).
6. Christopher Pinney, "Things Happen: Or, From Which Moment Does That Object Come?" in Miller, *Materiality*, 266.
7. On the origin of the word thing, see Bruno Latour, "From Realpolitik to DingPolitik," in Bruno Latour and Peter Weibel, eds., *Making Things Public: Atmospheres of Democracy* (Cambridge: The MIT Press, 2005), 22–23.
8. Sarah Ahmed, *Queer Phenomenology: Orientations, Objects, Others* (Durham: Duke University Press, 2006), 157.
9. Georges Perec, *Species of Spaces and Other Pieces*, ed. and trans. John Sturrock (London: Penguin Books, 1999), 210–11.
10. Perec, *Species of Spaces*, 211.
11. Ibid, 209.
12. Graham Harman, *Tool-Being: Heidegger and the Metaphysics of Objects* (Chicago and La Salle: Open Court, 2002), 18. Heidegger's *topos* of the broken hammer in *Being and Time* provides one key inspiration for the

variety of literary approaches called "thing theory," identified most closely with the critic Bill Brown. See "Things," Bill Brown, ed., *Critical Inquiry* 28 (2001); Bill Brown, *A Sense of Things: The Object Matter of American Literature* (Chicago: University of Chicago Press, 2004) and *Other Things* (Chicago: University of Chicago Press, 2016); though other key contributions come from Susan Stewart, *On Longing: Narratives of the Miniature, the Gigantic, the Souvenir, the Collection* (Durham: Duke University Press, 1993); and Elaine Scarry, *The Body in Pain: Making and Unmaking the World* (Oxford: Oxford University Press, 1985).

13. Perec, *Species of Spaces*, 209–10.
14. Virgil, *Eclogues, Georgics, Aeneid*, H. Rushton Fairclough, trans., G. P. Goold, rev., Loeb Classical Library 64 (Cambridge: Harvard University Press, 1999–2000), 519–25.
15. Remo Bodei, *The Life of Things, The Love of Things*, trans. Murtha Baca (New York: Fordham University Press, 2015), 3. For Bodei's rendering of Virgil's poem, see 1–3.
16. Ibid, 10.
17. Martin Heidegger, *What Is a Thing?* trans. W. B. Barton Jr., Vera Deutsch, Eugene T. Gendlin (Chicago: Gateway/Henry Regnery, 1970).
18. Bodei, *The Life of Things*, 11–12.
19. For this connectionist reading of Descartes, see John Sutton, *Philosophy and Memory Traces: Descartes to Connectionism* (Cambridge: Cambridge University Press, 1998), 17–18. For this cognitive approach to the subject-object distinction see, among others, George Lakoff and Mark Johnson, *Metaphors We Live By* (Chicago: University of Chicago Press, 1980); Andy Clark, *Natural Born Cyborgs: Minds, Technologies, and the Future of Human Intelligence* (Oxford: Oxford University Press, 2003); and most recently, Lambros Malafouris, *How Things Shape the Mind: A Theory of Material Engagement* (Cambridge: The MIT Press, 2016).
20. On the production of disposable bodies as indexed to the racial necropolitics of the circumatlantic slave trade, the history of capitalism, and colonialism, see Achille Mbembe, *Necropolitics*, trans. Steven Corcoran (Durham: Duke University Press, 2019). Mbembe's work has been crucial in expanding the purchase of Michel Foucault's insights about the relation between discourses of race and species and in re-evaluating the concept of "bare life" as articulated by Giorgio Agamben in such works as *Homo Sacer: Sovereign Power and Bare Life*, trans. Daniel Heller-Roazen (Stanford: Stanford University Press, 1998).
21. For this critique of disembodied knowledge and the masculine subject, see, among others, Donna Haraway, "Situated Knowledges: The Science Question in Feminism and the Privilege of Partial Perspective," in Donna Haraway, ed., *Simians, Cyborgs, and Women: The Reinvention of Nature* (New York: Routledge, 1991), 183–201 and 248–50.

For an account of the human as a category plagued by the way "Man ... overrepresents itself as if it were the human itself," see Sylvia Wynter's "Unsettling the Coloniality of Being/Power/Truth/Freedom: Towards the Human, After Man, Its Overrepresentation – An Argument," *The New Centennial Review* 3, no. 3 (2003), 257–337, at 260.
22. Walter Benjamin, "On the Concept of History," *Walter Benjamin: Selected Writings*, Vol. 4 (1938–40), trans. Edmund Jephcott et al., eds. Howard Eiland and Michael W. Jennings (Cambridge: The Belknap Press of Harvard University Press, 2003), 392.
23. "fetish, n.". OED Online. June 2019. Oxford University Press. https://bit.ly/3nK3fMR (accessed July 2, 2019).
24. Igor Kopytoff, "The Cultural Biography of Things: Commoditization as Process," in Arjun Appadurai, ed., *The Social Life of Things: Commodities in Cultural Perspective* (Cambridge: Cambridge University Press, 1986), 67.
25. Arjun Appadurai, "Introduction: Commodities and the Politics of Value," 5.
26. Sigmund Freud, "Fetishism" (1927) in *Miscellaneous Papers, 1888–1938*, Vol. 5 of *Collected Papers* (London: Hogarth and Institute of Psycho-Analysis, 1924–50), 198–204.
27. William Pietz, "The Problem of the Fetish, I" *Res* 9 (1985), 5; "The Problem of the Fetish, II" *Res* 13 (1987), 23–45; and "The Problem of the Fetish, IIIa," *Res* 16 (1988), 105–24.
28. Pietz, "The Problem of the Fetish, I," 5; "The Problem of the Fetish, II," 23–45; and "The Problem of the Fetish, IIIa," 105–24.
29. Pietz, "The Problem of the Fetish, I," 7.
30. Ibid, 7–10.
31. In Pietz's terms, Walter Benjamin's conception of film as "liquidating" the aura of rarified art objects in his successively rewritten essay "The Work of Art in the Age of Its Technological Reproducibility," becomes an instance in examining how technological shifts alter the fetish-value of different orders of objects. Benjamin's insistence that the advent of film politicizes art derives from this sense that successive technological changes alter the "flow" of aura through our infrastructures. See Walter Benjamin, *Selected Writings*, Howard Eiland and Michael W. Jennings, eds., Vol. 3, 1935–38 (Cambridge: The Belknap Press, 2002), 101–33.
32. Karl Marx, *Das Kapital*, in Robert C. Tucker, ed., *The Marx-Engels Reader*, 2nd ed. (New York: W. W. Norton, 1978), 321.
33. Peter Stallybrass, "Marx's Coat," in Patricia Spyer, ed., *Border Fetishisms: Material Objects in Unstable Spaces* (New York: Routledge, 1998), 184–85.
34. Marx, *Das Kapital*, 319–20.
35. Ibid, 316.
36. Ibid, 328.
37. Ibid, 313.

38. Stallybrass, "Marx's Coat," 203.
39. William Pietz, "How to Grow Oranges in Norway," in Patricia Spyer, ed., *Border Fetishisms: Material Objects in Unstable Spaces* (New York: Routledge, 1998), 250.
40. For a rousing reading of Pietz as enabling us to think about forms of association routed through the object world, see Nicholas Thorburn, "Communist Objects and the Values of Printed Matter," *Social Text* 103, no. 2 (2010), 1–32. For an allied observation, see Michael Taussig's estimation that what Pietz "does for us with his genealogizing is restore certain traces and erasures and weave a spell around what is, socially speaking, at stake in making." Michael Taussig, *The Nervous System* (New York: Routledge, 1992), 118–19.
41. Dan Hicks, *The Brutish Museums: The Benin Bronzes, Colonial Violence and Cultural Restitution* (London: Pluto Press, 2020), 33–34; quoting Kopytoff, "The Cultural Biography of Things," 65.
42. Christina Sharpe, *In the Wake: On Blackness and Being* (Durham: Duke University Press, 2016).
43. On the "factish," see Bruno Latour, "Factures/Fractures" *Res* 36 (1999), 21–31 and *On the Modern Cult of the Factish Gods*, trans. Catherine Porter and Heather MacLean (Durham: Duke University Press, 2010).
44. For introductions to ANT, see John Law and John Hassard, eds., *Actor Network Theory and After* (Oxford: Blackwell, 1999) and Bruno Latour, *Reassembling the Social: An Introduction to Actor Network Theory* (Oxford: Oxford University Press, 2005).
45. Marx, *Das Kapital*, 307. Bruno Latour explicitly invokes Marx in *Pandora's Hope: Essays on the Reality of Science Studies* (Cambridge: Harvard University Press, 1999), 189. While Latour's reading of Marx remains implicit, it is tempting to suggest that he is himself a kind of nondialectical Marx, reading *Kapital* as a text on the *poetics* of the machine age, a text on making and mobility, that opens the black box of production to tell the story of the working of the capitalist state.
46. Michel Serres, *The Parasite*, trans. Lawrence R. Schehr [1982] (Minneapolis: University of Minnesota Press, 2007), 144.
47. Ibid, 10.
48. For Serres's theory of the "quasi-object" via an analysis of ball games, see *The Parasite*, 224–34 and Latour, *We Have Never Been Modern*, trans. Catherine Porter (Cambridge: Harvard University Press, 1993), 51–55.
49. Michel Serres, *The Troubadour of Knowledge*, trans. Sheila Faria Glaser, with William Paulson (Ann Arbor: The University of Michigan Press, 1997), 79.
50. Bruno Latour, *Pandora's Hope: Essays on the Reality of Science Studies* (Cambridge: Harvard University Press, 1999), 281.
51. Michel Serres, *The Birth of Physics*, trans. Jack Hawkes (Manchester: The Clinamen Press, 2000).

52. On Marx's reading of ancient philosophies of matter, see Jacques Lezra, "On the Nature of Marx's Things," in Jacques Lezra and Liza Blake, eds., *Lucretius and Modernity* (New York: Palgrave Macmillan, 2016), 125–43.
53. Bruno Latour, "Factures/Fractures," 21.
54. On black boxes and "blackboxing," see Latour, *Pandora's Hope*, 304.
55. Latour, "Factures/Fractures," 22.
56. Ibid, 26.
57. For these terms, see Donna Haraway, "The Cyborg Manifesto," in *Simians, Cyborgs and Women*, 149–81; *The Companion Species Manifesto* (Chicago: Prickly Paradigm Press, 2003); *When Species Meet* (Minneapolis: University of Minnesota Press, 2008); and *Staying with the Trouble: Making Kin in the Chthulucene* (Durham: Duke University Press, 2016); Jane Bennett, *Vibrant Matter: A Political Ecology of Things* (Durham: Duke University Press, 2010); Stacy Alaimo, *Bodily Natures: Science, Environment, and the Material Self* (Bloomington: University of Indiana Press, 2010); Timothy Morton, *Ecology without Nature: Rethinking Environmental Aesthetics* (Cambridge: Harvard University Press, 2007); *The Ecological Thought* (Cambridge: Harvard University Press, 2010); and *Hyperobjects* (Minneapolis: University of Minnesota Press, 2013); Rosi Braidotti, *The Posthuman* (London: Polity Press, 2013); Karen Barad, *Meeting the Universe Halfway: Quantum Physics and the Entanglement of Matter and Meaning* (Durham: Duke University Press, 2007); Tim Ingold, *Making: Anthropology, Archaeology, Art, and Architecture* (London: Routledge, 2013) and *The Life of Lines* (London: Routledge, 2015); Ian Hodder, *Entangled: An Archaeology of the Relationships between Humans and Things* (Oxford: Wiley Blackwell, 2012); John Law, *After Method: Mess in Social Research* (London: Routledge, 2004); Mel Y. Chen, *Animacies: Biopolitics, Racial Mattering and Queer Affect* (Durham: Duke University Press, 2012).
58. Michel Serres with Bruno Latour, *Conversations on Science, Culture, and Time*, trans. Roxanne Lapidus (Ann Arbor: The University of Michigan Press, 1990), 57.
59. Ibid, 60.
60. Ibid, 45.
61. Latour, *Pandora's Hope*, 145–73.
62. Kopytoff, "The Cultural Biography of Things," 64–65.
63. Dipesh Chakrabarty, *Provincializing Europe: Postcolonial Thought and Historical Difference* (Princeton: Princeton University Press, 2000).
64. Michel Serres, *Biogea*, trans. Randolph Burks (Minneapolis: Univocal, 2012), 171–72.
65. Haraway, *When Species Meet*, 11. See also the "ontological" or multispecies turn in anthropology: Philippe Descola, *Beyond Nature and Culture*, trans. Janet Lloyd (Chicago: University of Chicago Press, 2013 [2005]); Eben S. Kirksey and Stefan Helmreich, "The Emergence of

Multispecies Ethnography," *Cultural Anthropology* 25, no. 4 (2010), 545–76 and, less programmatically, John Hartington, Jr., *Aesop's Anthropology: A Multispecies Approach* (Minneapolis and London: University of Minnesota Press, 2014); and the collection of essays in cultural anthropology, Eben Kirksey, ed., *The Multispecies Salon* (Durham: Duke University Press, 2014).

66. Mike Hansell, *Built by Animals: The Natural History of Animal Architecture* (Oxford: Oxford University Press, 2009) and Tatyana Humle, "Material Culture in Primates," in Dan Hicks and Mary C. Beaudry, eds., *The Oxford Handbook of Material Culture Studies* (Oxford: Oxford University Press, 2010), 406–21.

3

Representation

Sarah Wasserman

In one of the most famous passages of *Capital*, Karl Marx switches from abstraction to a concrete example to explain his concept of the commodity. In the midst of describing commodities' dual nature – the disjunction between their utility as things that can be consumed and their force as agents of intangible value – Marx turns to an overturned table:

> The form of wood [*Die Form des Holzes*], for instance, is altered if a table is made out of it. Nevertheless the table continues to be wood, an ordinary, sensuous thing. But as soon as it emerges as a commodity, it changes into a thing which transcends sensuousness. It not only stands with its feet on the ground, but, in relation to all other commodities, it stands on its head, and evolves out of its wooden brain grotesque ideas, far more wonderful than if it were to begin dancing on its own free will.[1]

For Marx, the table comes alive and begins to dance when it is no longer "ordinary, sensuous" wood. When it *represents* something else – the labor that went into its making – the table grows a brain, stands upon its head, and dances. Marx's vivid image is a useful point of departure for understanding the role of representation in material culture studies because it reminds us that every object can represent something else (in this case labor) and be represented (Marx must describe the table in prose). Though cultural studies, art history, literary criticism, musicology, and other humanistic disciplines concern themselves with various kinds of objects, material culture studies attends to things in order to understand both strategies of representation: what is represented in *and* by a given object.

This essay tracks material culture studies' ongoing engagement with representation, with an eye toward methods in literary studies and their approaches to various kinds of objects. If an older, aesthetic approach to objects – say, a study of the mountains in German romantic literature – showed readers what is represented *by* objects, more recent work informed by material culture studies tells us instead what is represented *in* objects. This turn, from an aesthetic or symbolist approach to a material culture studies one, has reframed the kinds of questions scholars ask about the representation of objects. Paradoxically, material culture studies reminds us that when confronting matter, we are never free from representation. If the discipline seeks to move away from representation, it is nonetheless continually rediscovering it.

***

The term *representation* arises from multiple sources, borrowing from French and Latin and appearing for the first time in writing in the late twelfth century. During that time, the Anglo-Norman and Middle French word *representer* meant "to evoke, to recall the memory of," "to resemble, imitate," and "to depict in a painting, engraving, or sculpture."[2] In addition to these aesthetic and artistic meanings, the term has always connoted the substitution of one entity by another: the first definition given by *The Oxford English Dictionary* is "the action of standing for, or in the place of, a person, group, or thing, and related senses."[3] Representation calls forth, conjures, and makes an absent thing manifest; it also entails an act of substitution so that the object represented is displaced and replaced. In other words, representation is never presentation: through a painting, a poem, or a memory, we have an evocation of an object but never the thing itself. The word is sometimes hyphenated to stress the sense that representation entails a second or further encounter with something: the oranges in a Cézanne painting, for instance are a representation of fruit that he arranged as "models" for his still life paintings (Figure 3.1). If we

Figure 3.1 Paul Cézanne, "Apples and Oranges," 1900. Oil on canvas, 74 x 93 cm. Musée d'Orsay, Paris, France.

view the painting, we admire it because the oil brushstrokes on canvas look so much like oranges we have seen in "the real world."

But this distinction between the representation and the real has been troubled for as long as there has been representation. What happens when an image of an orange or a description of a table becomes so accurate, so lifelike, that we find it not so much a representation as the actual object depicted? One of the oldest and most famous inquiries into this aspect of representation can be found in the Greek philosopher Plato's work, *The Republic*, written around 380 BC. In a section commonly referred to as "The Allegory of the Cave," Plato, through his narrator Socrates, describes a group of people who have lived chained to the wall of a cave, facing a blank wall. These people watch shadows projected on a wall from objects that pass in front of a fire burning behind them (Figure 3.2). Socrates explains that while the shadows are the captive people's reality, the philosopher is

Figure 3.2 Markus Maurer, Plato's "Allegory of the Cave," published originally in Gabriele Veldkamp's *Zukunftsorientierte Gestaltung informationstechnologischer Netzwerke im Hinblick auf die Handlungsfähigkeit des Menschen* (Aachen, Germany: Verlad der Augustinus Buchhandlung, 1996).

like a person who has been freed from the cave and at last understands that the shadows are not reality but only an illusion projected upon a wall. The allegory illustrates that humans are forever bound to the impressions they receive through their senses. Even if these impressions are gross misrepresentations of reality, they form the only world available to humans: the human condition, according to Plato, is defined by its phenomenal relation to the world.[4] Seen in this light, representation is not ornamental or additive – it is the very essence of human experience.

This Platonian approach to things is more paradoxical than it might at first appear. Aristotle famously contends that every physical object is a compound of matter and form.[5] In this line of thought, the representation of matter must be tracked to matter itself: regardless of the contortions it may undergo, matter is understood as primally and finally physical. But following Plato's insights, the "stuff" of material culture needs instead to be understood as always, already represented. Broadly speaking, material culture studies works from the assumption that even things that seem to be "just themselves" are instances of representation. Objects can evoke multiple meanings – meanings that differ depending on observer, context, place, and time. Thus, scholars of material culture studies have developed methods for assessing these meanings, for determining what a given object at a given moment represents. But one strange consequence of this attention to objects is that even as it brings things like tables and oranges into focus, it estranges them, breaking them down into component parts, revealing that the way something looks to us may have nothing at all to do with its production or its reception in another part of the world, reminding us of the obdurate materiality of a thing that we usually overlook. In a sense, the material culture scholar often begins by exposing a familiar understanding or encounter with an object as something like one of the shadows on Plato's cave. Rigorous attention to the materiality of things helps reframe objects so that we can see them more clearly. In other words, the methods of material culture studies uncover the fact that what we might dismiss as merely "a typical orange" always congeals and conceals within it many mysteries.

One of the best accounts of the gap between object and representation is also one of the shortest: an eight-line poem by Emily Dickinson. Written around 1866, Dickinson's poem 1071, "Perception of an Object Costs," describes the fundamentally negative relationship we have to all things, insofar as we can only encounter representations of things and therefore never grasp them in their entirety:

> Perception of an object costs
> Precise the Object's loss –
> Perception in itself a Gain
> Replying to its Price –

> The Object Absolute – is nought –
> Perception sets it fair
> And then upbraids a Perfectness
> That situates so far –

The poem tells its readers that the absolute being of any object is lost the moment it is perceived. This is, in fact, what turns it into an object. Any attempt we make to approach it, to capture it in our gaze, or to represent it on the page only pushes the truths of the object further away. As in Plato, to be a perceiving subject here is to confront the endless receding of things, the self-defeating nature of our sensory attempts to know things. But this is not to say that the world is impoverished; Dickinson's negative theology allows for intensity, pathos, and beauty. The poem is an act of perception and of representation, "itself a Gain," proportional to what we have lost, so that its eight short lines are not a nihilistic lament that we can never access "The Object Absolute," but an examination of human limits and the longing they generate.

There has been considerable excitement over discovering in Dickinson some of our own recent enthusiasm for materiality; for the text's literal surface; and for the scene of writing as it is self-reflexively described in her poems. Especially since the 2013 publication of *The Gorgeous Nothings*, the first full-color facsimile edition of Dickinson's manuscripts that presents her late work as she wrote it (on scraps of envelopes), the long-standing sense of Dickinson's poems as objects has been reinforced by the materiality of her writing practice (Figure 3.3).[6] Dickinson seems to have been

Figure 3.3 Emily Dickinson, "A Great Hope Fell" envelope poem. Emily Dickinson Collection in the Amherst College Digital Collection.

aware of this drift toward the material and she complicates it from the start. Her poems, and poems more generally, are often described as objects – language compressed and crystallized until it takes on a heft, a density. But poems are simultaneously thought to be ephemeral – because they are short or intended to be spoken aloud or because they convey a kind of artlessness that makes them seem as if they were written on the fly. Dickinson's poem intuits this contradiction and extends it to objects more generally. In doing so, it suggests that all our object relations have the potential to be poetic insofar as they require us to negotiate between loss and gain, distance and intimacy, presentation and representation.

Literature has long been a privileged medium for representing objects while also thematizing the challenges of representation. Although representation is the task and terrain of many forms – from painting, sculpture, and museums themselves to theater, film, and digital media – literature highlights the fundamental strangeness of representation because it creates whole worlds for readers using only language, which seems largely immaterial. Books, of course, exist in material forms, be it on paper or a screen. But poems and stories "work" by representing unreal people, places, and things – by making them real in the reader's mind. As Susan Stewart puts it, literature draws upon "two primary functions of language – to make present what can only be experienced abstractly, and to textualize our experience and thereby make it available for interpretation and closure."[7] Indeed, the material culture of fiction – the objects represented therein – can give texture to an author's imagined world and help process abstractions like love, death, nationhood, or history. Represented objects, in other words, disclose what it is that objects represent.

In one of the landmark works of twentieth-century literary criticism, *Mimesis: The Representation of Reality in Western Literature*, the German philologist Erich Auerbach outlined the concept of "represented reality." A monumental text that sweeps from Homer to Virginia Woolf, *Mimesis* argues that representation and reality are not two separate categories but a single one. According to Auerbach, reality is always mediated through some construction; in his book he takes representative examples from literature that illustrate particular historical and cultural contexts.[8] The long arc of realist fictions that Auerbach traces begins with a distinction that helps illustrate the two functions of language that Stewart names. *Mimesis* begins with a comparison between the way the world is represented in Homer's *Odyssey* and the way it appears in the Bible. The biblical mode entails no description and no setting. Everything except the "decisive points of the narrative" is "left in obscurity." The Homeric style, however, casts characters, objects, and surroundings into bright light so that they are "uniformly illuminated" and present to readers.[9]

What happens when the foregrounding and illumination of objects discloses their secret, obscure nature? What kind of realist representation can account for the sometimes mysterious and mythic dimensions of things? As one example, take a famous scene from Theodore Dresier's naturalist novel *Sister Carrie*, published in 1900. The novel tells the story of Carrie Meeber, a country girl who moves to Chicago, becomes a mistress to men who she believes can furnish her with the glamorous city life she desires, and eventually transforms herself into a famous actress. Soon after her arrival in Chicago, Carrie must look for work. When she enters a department store to apply as a clerk, she is mesmerized by the merchandise on display: "Carrie passed along the busy aisles, much affected by the remarkable displays of trinkets, dress goods, stationery, and jewelry. Each separate counter was a show place of dazzling interest and attraction ... The dainty slippers and stockings, the delicately frilled skirts and petticoats, the laces, ribbons, hair-combs, purses, all touched her with individual desire."[10] Dreiser captures the abundance of the department store, at the time a relatively new institution – one that displayed consumer goods like artifacts in a museum to be admired, exonerated, and desired.

Dreiser represents the material culture of late-nineteenth-century Chicago in order to illustrate how objects can inspire longing and shape the subjects who encounter them. Later in the novel, Carrie's ardent desire to own fine things animates them – so much so that they seem to speak to her:

> Fine clothes to her were a vast persuasion; they spoke tenderly and Jesuitically for themselves. When she came within earshot of their pleading, desire in her bent a willing ear. The voice of the so-called inanimate! Who shall translate for us the language of the stones?
> "My dear," said the lace collar she secured from Partridge's, "I fit you beautifully; don't give me up."
> "Ah, such little feet," said the leather of the soft new shoes; "how effectively I cover them. What a pity they should ever want my aid."[11]

Fiction affords Dreiser the opportunity to breathe life into things – not just to represent the soft leather and lace of the goods that Carrie wants to own but to depict what it feels like for her to want them. Relations to these goods are part of what gives Carrie her sense of purpose. As Bill Brown says of the novel, "the power of Dreiser's description lies in the way that 'individual desire' can be understood as the claim that each individuated object has on Carrie, and on the way that such claims seem to individuate her."[12] Dreiser helps readers see the opposing vectors of production and consumption: the way that commodities represent the labor "behind" them as well as the desires ahead. The novel becomes, among other things, a place where authors "translate for us the language" of objects by representing their multiple meanings on the page.

Dreiser helps us see how representation, even as it tends toward realism, evokes what is strange or unreal about material culture. Writing about realism and the novel, Michael Sayeau notes that "realism is as much about the distance from reality as its proximity."[13] Material culture studies makes this distance clear – not only as it functions in the novel, but in all expressive culture. The objects *in* art and the object that *is* art always entail subjectivity and interpretation, even when they are actually "there" before us. So if total realism is impossible, then why do writers and artists go to such lengths to show things "as they really are?" One reason is that a faithful imitation of real life – people, landscapes, objects, and so on – is a marker of technical skill. This point goes beyond nineteenth-century realism and beyond representations of the commodity: from a whaling ship to a distant planet populated by nonhuman creatures, novels are immersive insofar as their settings and objects are vividly described.

In his well-known 1968 essay on the so-called reality effect, Roland Barthes considers these effects of representation. Reading Gustave Flaubert's short story "A Simple Heart," Barthes wonders what critics should do with textual details – the material culture of a story – that serve no function in the plot and do not seem to tell us anything profound about the characters. He is especially interested in the description that Flaubert gives of a room occupied by Madame Aubain, in which "an old piano supported, under a barometer, a pyramidal heap of boxes and cartons."[14] Barthes concludes his essay with the assertion that "[W]hen these details are reputed to *denote* the real directly, all that they do – without saying so – is *signify* it; Flaubert's barometer ... finally say[s] nothing but this: *we are the real* ... *the reality effect* is produced, the basis of that unavowed verisimilitude which forms the aesthetic of all the standard works of modernity."[15] For Barthes, the objects' lack of usefulness is precisely what makes them important. Because they have no function to the narrative, they show that the world of the story is like the world in which the reader reads, filled with things that have no immediate purpose. Sayeau astutely summarizes Barthes' argument when he says that literary realism "not only includes but revels in the inclusion of material seemingly too banal, ordinary, or useless to merit fictional inclusion."[16]

Much earlier than Barthes, the Hungarian philosopher György Lukács contemplated the role of description in literature, likewise wondering why an author might devote so much ink to seemingly useless details. In his now-classic 1936 essay, "Narrate or Describe?," Lukács distinguishes between these two modes of novelistic writing. According to Lukács, novelists narrate when they present a world in flux, riven by the forces of change in which the novelist and narrator have an interest. Narration therefore recounts action, be it interior or external. By contrast, novelists describe when they enumerate the details of a world that serve as backdrop or setting. For Lukács, these details do not matter and therefore amount to nothing more than a kind of "still life."[17] No novelist, even by Lukács's account, *only* narrates or describes; action coexists with setting, plot with detail. Literary scholars interested in material culture, especially those working with/in the new materialisms, have done much work to show how integral description's role is in making meaning – how it gives life to objects that are anything but still.

***

In this volume, Julian Yates chronicles the various strands of materialist thought that have contributed to the field of what we now call material culture studies. But a focus on representation and, in particular, on the *literary* representation of objects necessitates its own scholarly history. Although anthropologists and archaeologists have been studying material culture since at least the 1870s, it was taken up in literary and cultural studies only toward the end of the twentieth century. The key theories developed in the 1970s demonstrated that objects were more than mere props in the drama of human development; that they were in fact the physical determinants of imaginative and cultural life. Drawing heavily upon Marx's ideas of the commodity, scholars like Jean Baudrillard and Pierre Bourdieu examined the ways in which production under capital involves a projection of the human into the made world.[18] During the 1980s and 90s, however, the attention paid to things shifted as many scholars relinquished a version of Marxist ontology that insisted on the subject's constitution through production. Instead, in part through the influence of the Birmingham School of Cultural Studies, consumption became the new center of attention – the key process by which subjects entered into meaningful relations with objects and with one another. This scholarly arc is mirrored in the movement I have traced from Emily Dickinson as a producer of poem-objects to Theodore Dreiser's attention to Carrie Meeber's consumption of things. Purchase, barter, exchange, and use stole the spotlight from production as scholars grew more interested in the social functions of objects.[19]

In his introduction to the seminal volume, *The Social Life of Things: Commodities in Cultural Perspective* (1986), Arjun Appadurai insists that "commodities ... can be usefully regarded as having life histories."[20] He adds that the commodity phase of an object's "life history" does not exhaust its biography. Alongside efforts to narrate the complete histories of things, work in museum and conservation studies began to formalize ways of approaching objects outside of what might be called their "natural" social context. What is a student of material culture to do when faced with an unknown artifact – be it a canister of Civil War era gunpowder or a lava lamp – that does not disclose its function or significance? The 1982 essay, "Mind in Matter: An Introduction to Material Culture Theory and Method," by Jules David Prown laid out a method for examining and extracting cultural evidence from "mute" objects.[21] This approach, now known as the "Prownian method" entails three steps – description, deduction, and speculation – that are intended to help an observer move from observation of an object's physical properties to an understanding of its function in a particular cultural context. The Prownian method and other strategies that have emerged from the hands-on efforts of curators and conservators to acknowledge the dense network of meanings that can inhere in an artifact – what it is that objects represent.

That things should be objects of study precisely because they are objects of desire is a claim explored by Susan Stewart in 1984, in her influential book *On Longing: Narratives of the Miniature, the Gigantic, the Souvenir, the Collection*. Stewart's book made it clear that subjects come to know themselves through a number of different material relations and practices – many of which cannot be neatly aligned with Marxist theories of value, hence Stewart's use of psychoanalytic and semiotic criticism. *On Longing* also makes a compelling case for literature as a space in which some of these enigmatic relations are best described. One of the book's most significant and lasting interventions is that it not only explains how certain objects can give meaning or shape to a subject; it also shows how the narration of these objects can give form or shape to literary expression. There is, of course, a long tradition of scholarship about objects in literature: books that track swords and armor in early modern texts, the rose or the hillside in pastoral poetry, a French cookie or a lighthouse in texts of high modernism, the car or the road in mid-century American novels. But the turn largely inaugurated by Stewart's *On Longing* entails less a following of literary details and more a reckoning with the thorny work objects can perform in fiction. Returning briefly to Lukács's notions of narration and description, we might add to it by distinguishing an older model of details that are inert backdrop to action in a text from a newer concept of objects as the vehicles of social, psychological, and ecological change.

In *The Material Unconscious* (1996) and *A Sense of Things: The Object Matter of American Literature* (2003), Bill Brown explores how changes in the material culture of late nineteenth- and early twentieth-century America found their way into the literary imagination and how literature itself becomes a vehicle for giving meaning to the object world.[22] Brown's books, along with his introduction to a 2001 special issue of *Critical Inquiry* on "Things," established "thing theory" as a method for examining human-object interactions in literature and culture. Brown borrows from Heidegger's distinction between objects and things, which maintains that an object *becomes* a thing when it can no longer serve its "normal" function. When an object does not work as we expect it to, it becomes present to us in new ways. As Brown explains:

> We begin to confront the thingness of objects when they stop working for us: when the drill breaks, when the car stalls, when the window gets filthy, when their flow within the circuits of production and distribution, consumption and exhibition, has been arrested, however momentarily. The story of objects asserting themselves as things, then, is the story of a changed relationship to the human subject and thus the story of how the thing really names less an object than a particular subject-object relation.[23]

Brown's work helped illustrate how reading things in and out of literature – reading their histories, their biographies, their affective and aesthetic dimensions – could be a fruitful endeavor. In his latest book, *Other Things* (2015), Brown explains that this endeavor requires interpretation in part because meaning often exceeds or lies beneath the surface: "The arts," he writes, "seem to have a material unconscious, by which I mean (most simply) that they *register* transformations of the material world that they do not necessarily *represent* or intentionally express."[24] Brown's insight reminds us that material culture studies pursues the material dimensions of the relations between subjects and objects even when those relations are opaque or available to us only *as* representations. It offers a method that allows us to read across the spectrum of signification, attending to material transformations that are registered and refracted in various artistic forms.

Subsequent books such as Elaine Freedgood's *The Ideas in Things* (2006), John Plotz's *Portable Property* (2008), Mary Jacobus' *Romantic Things* (2012), and Matthew Mullins's *Postmodernism in Pieces* (2016) draw upon Brown's insights and expand on them within different literary fields.[25] Tracing the meanings of a thing represented in literature can lead to many places, and these scholars help readers follow their paths. The material culture of fiction is not always benign – objects can encode violence, mortality, loss, and grief. Brown's discussion of Mrs. Blackett's sewing chair in Sarah Orne Jewett's *The Country of the Pointed Furs*, Freedgood's reading of "Negro Head" tobacco in *Great Expectations*, Plotz's treatment of jewelry in Trollope's *The Eustace Diamonds*, and Mullins's study of Coke bottles in Leslie Marmon Silko's *Ceremony* are just a few instances in which scholars demonstrate the way objects make legible the regionalism, colonialism, imperialism, and racism that circulate in and around literary texts. The representation of objects can provide access to the stories that dominant narratives seek to obscure. Plot or character may do one type of work while the material culture in a given literary text does another. Claims to space, to national belonging, and political subjectivity can inhere in the welter of objects that an author depicts; so too can histories of violence. As Katherine Behar notes, there are many "histories of treating certain humans (women, people of color, and the poor) as objects." Can representations of material culture expose these histories or correct them?[26]

This issue of representation has long been considered by anthropologists, curators, and other museum professionals who investigate the political dimensions of collections and exhibits. As Emily Moore, Magdalena Naum, Gretchen Sullivan Sorin, and Veronic Strang note in their contributions to this volume, who and what is represented by which artifacts is a question with very real stakes. And many scholars have written about the dehumanization of historically marginalized subjects by drawing upon historical archives and artifacts. Jacqueline Goldsby's *A Spectacular Secret*, for instance, examines an archive of gruesome lynching photographs to show how photography structured Americans' perception of anti-Black violence before World War I. In *Slavery and the Culture of Taste*, Simon Gikandi considers a wide range of objects – from portraits and decorative arts to personal diaries – to demonstrate that during the eighteenth century, the violence and ugliness of enslavement shaped ideas of taste and high culture in Britain, the antebellum South, and the West Indies. While this body of material culture scholarship is well developed and still growing, far less writing exists on race and the representation of objects in literature. In a brief essay from 2015, Uri McMillan notes that recent work in material culture studies has frequently neglected concerns of race: "the failure to interrogate critical race studies in much of new materialist thought and the resultant and ongoing violence of such an occlusion particularly when theorizing Blackness has long required considering existential questions of life and death, the limits of humanity, and a stultifying thingness."[27] McMillan explicitly names the overwhelming whiteness of material culture studies within literary criticism. In addition to the neglect that McMillan names, the history of discipline formation has also played a role. The methodologically-oriented fields of material culture studies, book history, and, a bit later, digital humanities coalesced at the same moment when race and ethnic studies gained institutional traction in literature departments. These fields often developed in silos, so that scholars working in one area made little attempt to engage with work being done in another. As a result, material culture studies has been somewhat insular, and scholars of race using its methods did not necessarily identify with its keywords.

This separation has begun to change over the past decade, in large part due to the work by scholars working in performance studies who have written about race and material culture studies as a question of representation. In "Dances with Things: Material Culture and the Performance of Race" (2009), Robin Bernstein analyzes photographs, caricatures, and dolls, from the late nineteenth to the early twentieth century to show how racial subjectivization depends upon "dances" between people and things.[28] And Tavia Nyong'o has written about racist kitsch objects, arguing in his essay "Racial Kitsch and Black Performance" that while such objects engender shame and abjection, they may also be artifacts in practices of "oppositional curating and ownership." Reading racial kitsch objects from the nineteenth century up to Spike Lee's 2002 film *Bamboozled*, Nyong'o demonstrates that subjects can relate to kitsch in such a way that "dismantle[s] the protections of disgust."[29] Sandy Alexandre's work likewise considers how radical possibilities may exist for Black subjects in their object relations. In her 2009 essay on August Wilson's play, *The Piano Lesson*, Alexandre explores the representation of Black-owned property, asking what it means to "enlarge the historical connotations of chattel discourse for Black prosperity's sake? What would it mean to contain and thereby reduce the richness of the past to an object – to objectify the past, to itemize it, to salvage the all-too-crass chattel aspect of chattel slavery?"[30] Alexandre's attention to the piano, or more precisely, to Wilson's representation of the piano, allows her to show how the logics of ownership and property might be used to challenge the notion that "the privileges of inheritance and legacy" are the "province solely of white people."

The corrective goal of scholarship like Alexandre's describes much of the work done by curators, conservationists, archivists, and museum and memorial designers. This work asks which objects, in which configurations, might best represent the lives silenced and erased from history by systemic, racialized violence. In his influential 1991 essay, "Race Under Representation," postcolonial scholar David Lloyd argues that the concept of representation itself, tethered to the development of aesthetic culture in the late eighteenth century, "continues to regulate racial formations through the various sites of contemporary practice." Through his analysis of the epistemic violence implicit in the formation of the subject and the public sphere, Lloyd concludes that it is impossible for "the racialized individual to enter the domain of representation except as that Subject which negates difference."[31] If all representation is compromised in this way, scholars must not simply seek to correct it but look for forms which acknowledge this compromise. Saidiya Hartman's formative intervention into the limits of the archive has crystallized the difficulty and importance of this task. Archives of slavery, Hartman writes, cannot give scholars access to enslaved people, only to the violence done to them: "The archive is, in this case, a death sentence, a tomb, a display of the violated body, an inventory of property ... an asterisk in the grand narrative of history."[32] Hartman's efforts to do more than recount the violence of the archive and to put words to the lives encoded there while also respecting what cannot be known has led her to advance speculative arguments, develop new grammars, and, most of all, fashion narratives based on archival research that "tell an impossible story and to amplify the impossibility of its telling."[33] New methods in material culture studies, especially as employed in the study of literature, are poised to reckon with the painful paradox Hartman names.

This is in part because literature has the unique capacity to (re)present a lost object while also representing its loss. Unlike a physical display where an artifact or what is left of an artifact are present to the viewer, literature summons objects only through language. Material objects appear on the page as reminders of their absence, and thus literature is uniquely suited to tell stories of elision and erasure. To illustrate what I mean, I want to turn to another poem that uses objects directly to address questions of loss. Elizabeth Bishop's famous villanelle, "One Art," which appeared in her book *Geography III* in 1976, was, according to her note to an editor at *The New Yorker*, "very SAD – it makes everyone weep."[34] All the drafts of the poem are reproduced in *Edgar Allan Poe & the Juke-Box*, the collection of

Bishop's fragments and mostly unfinished poems that was published in 2006. There we see that "One Art" began as a set of notes in prose with the title "The Art of Losing Things." It mentioned at first the loss of small objects like reading-glasses and fountain pens and then went on to enumerate larger things lost, mostly places like "one peninsula and one island" and "a small-sized town," then "two whole cities ... two of the world's biggest cities" and finally a person. The finished poem follows this same movement from the mundane door keys to a watch, a house, a city, and then, at last, a loved one:

> The art of losing isn't hard to master;
> so many things seem filled with the intent
> to be lost that their loss is no disaster.
>
> Lose something every day. Accept the fluster
> of lost door keys, the hour badly spent.
> The art of losing isn't hard to master.
>
> Then practice losing farther, losing faster:
> places, and names, and where it was you meant
> to travel. None of these will bring disaster.
>
> I lost my mother's watch. And look! my last, or
> next-to-last, of three loved houses went.
> The art of losing isn't hard to master.
>
> I lost two cities, lovely ones. And, vaster,
> some realms I owned, two rivers, a continent.
> I miss them, but it wasn't a disaster.
>
> – Even losing you (the joking voice, a gesture
> I love) I shan't have lied. It's evident
> the art of losing's not too hard to master
> though it may look like (*Write* it!) like disaster.

The villanelle form at first deceives: with its rules and repetitions, it reads like a closed form that contains experience, rather than one that releases or revels in the messiness of grief. But the pathos of the poem – the way that it catches the reader off guard at the end and delivers its *coup de grâce* – depends precisely upon the strictures of the form. "*Write* it!" the poem intones, a glimpse of the violent struggle the poet feels within her strategy of measured representation. The strain of representation is made palpable by the last stanza: its halting dash, its interruptive parentheses, and emphatic punctuation deliver the full force of the poet's grief within and through the poem's formal bonds. The poem preserves, in some gestural sense, the lost objects – the watch and the rivers endure in the lines of Bishop's poem. But they do so as specters, real things that haunt the words so artfully chosen to elegize them. The art of writing, the poem suggests, *is* the art of losing: we press the things that elude us into words and phrases that capture them and capture their evasion.

"One Art" also suggests that this art is deeply gendered. In addition to a poem about grief, this is a poem about domestic life – about keys and homes and mothers. Even as she claims (former) ownership over cities, rivers, and continents, Bishop manages to evoke the daily life of a woman who is a steward of objects, as well as a daughter and a lover. The depth of feeling that the poet feels must be pushed under the service, bent into service of the poem itself, never unleashed or unfiltered. And the poem seems aware of its status as "women's writing" – work that was and was often declared ephemeral. Diaries, letters, shopping lists, household ledgers, housekeeping guides, and pamphlets about ethical and social issues name just a few of the forms frequently authored by women and deemed unworthy of archiving or "filled with the intent to be lost." The poem gives readers a language for imagining these many instances of now invisible writing as an art form – and one whose value does not depend on its material presence. In this case, representation becomes a container that holds the ghosts of lost texts alongside the vanishing objects in which their stories reside.

By representing objects that seem unworthy of representation, like the poet's lost door keys, literature reveals how even minor objects – ephemera, trash, junk, fragments, and debris – shape our lives. Drawing upon the insights of consumer historians, most notably Susan Strasser, whose *Waste and Want: A Social History of Trash* (1999) was one of the first extended forays into the topic, literary scholars also began to take trash seriously.[35] In 2004, the volume *Filth: Dirt, Disgust, and Modern Life*, edited by William A. Cohen and Ryan Johnson, includes entries that address everything from the building of sewers in nineteenth-century European metropolises to the fictional representations of laboring women and foreigners as polluting.[36] The volume makes it clear that culturally mandated categories of exclusion and repression deserve to be interrogated; the notion that what we throw out can tell us as much about our culture as what we save runs through this body of scholarship. Jani Scandura's *Down in the Dumps* (2008), for instance, performs a cultural archaeology of refuse, visiting in person and in fiction a variety of refuse sites: decrepit parts of once-glittering towns, landfills, and secret dump sites at the Pentagon.[37] Scandura's readings attest to the power that literature has to make readers see and re-see the objects and their attached narratives that are usually forgotten, hidden, and discarded.

Given the way literature can represent the unseen afterlife of things – even trash – it can help reveal the enduring impact that our material habits have not only on us but also on our surroundings. Material culture studies approaches to literary representation have thus been carried back into other forms of material culture studies, so that scholars better understand its non-verbal objects *as* representational. The expanding scale of representational material, from discrete objects to vast networks of connected things to the endangered planet itself as an object has pushed material culture studies methods toward new limits. A novel like Don DeLillo's best-seller, *Underworld* (1997), draws connections between US consumer habits, chemical warfare in Vietnam, and global strategies for waste processing by using canisters of orange juice concentrate to evoke canisters of Agent Orange. This is just one example of how representations of objects can insist that we contemplate our treatment of the object that is the earth. As Richard Hutchings discusses in his entry in this volume, material culture studies and the environmental humanities are deeply interconnected. One reason for this is that material culture studies is environmental in its drives even when it does not purport to be since it looks at the objects around us. Moreover, many of the most urgent problems of the twenty-first century reveal an entanglement between humans and things. Climate change, biotechnology, drought and famine, even war and terrorism can hardly be discussed without addressing such entanglement.

***

As literature and the arts respond to what Kate Marshall has called increasing "scalar pressures," representational strategies are being stretched to new limits. These pressures, such as the imperative to think globally about networks and systems of exchange, a growing interest in deep time, and attempts to imagine the planet or even the galaxy as *things* that can be represented, also challenge the conventions of material culture studies. How scholars respond to this challenge will determine the future of material culture studies, the way that it toggles between the cultures that it seeks to understand and the larger environment that shapes and is shaped by those cultures. Elsewhere in this volume, Richard Hutchings explores the resonance of the term environment, showing how understanding it more clearly helps us see how the natural, human, and non-human are always entwined. But writing about the particular challenge of scale, Marshall notes that "as narratives – fictional and cultural – reach for formal means to capture the newly urgent scales of cosmic and systemic sensibilities, the critical vocabularies developed in the wake of thing theory become newly important as well."[38] In addition to representing things at various stages in their "life cycles," literature has long depicted otherworldly things: alien landscapes, future technologies, stars, planets and galaxies distant from our own. Without going too deep into the rabbit hole (the black hole?) of science fiction and its particular generic capacity to imagine radically different worlds, I want to suggest that science fiction gives us a language for discussing the future of material culture studies. In his introduction to *Archaeologies of the Future*, Fredric Jameson writes that science fiction affirms "that even our wildest imaginings are all collages of experience, constructs made up of bits and pieces of the here and now." The genre thus highlights "our own mode of production" while also attempting to go beyond it, to a world whose objects are made under regimes of production different from our own.[39] Material culture studies has given us a language to look at the objects of the past and the present; it can also provide a path into the archives of the future. What things lie ahead, as our horizon of inquiry expands in both space and time?

One of the most famous and most prolific science fiction writers of the twentieth century, Isaac Asimov, began writing fiction in the 1950s that grappled with scalar concerns preoccupying scholars today. Asimov's relentless interests in outer space, robotics, and artificial intelligence make his work galactic in scope: many of his hundreds of short stories and novels consider the impact of technology on the human species in a distant future. In one of his earliest novels, *The Caves of Steel*, which was first published as a serial in *Galaxy Magazine* from October to December 1953 and then as a Doubleday hardcover in 1954, Asimov represents a world three millennia in the future. Hyperspace travel has been discovered and a few worlds close to Earth have been colonized (Figure 3.4). These fifty planets, known as the "Spacer worlds" are sparsely populated, rich in resources, and rely on robot labor. Meanwhile, Earth is overpopulated (eight billion people inhabit the planet, three times the population of the Earth at the time Asimov was writing), and strict anti-robot laws have been passed.

The "caves of steel" are enormous city complexes enclosed by huge metal domes. Each "cave" can support tens of millions of people. New York City in the novel encompasses Manhattan as well as large swaths of New Jersey; the subway system connects to malls and apartment blocks so that no one ever exits the domes. At the beginning of the novel, the narrator boasts about the feats of engineering that have made life on an overcrowded Earth possible:

> Each City became a semiautonomous unit, economically all but self-sufficient. It could roof itself in, gird itself about, burrow itself under. It became a steel cave, a tremendous, self-contained cave of steel and concrete.
>
> It could lay itself out scientifically. At the center was the enormous complex of administrative offices. In careful orientation to one another and to the whole were the large residential Sections connected and interlaced by the expressway and the local ways. Toward the outskirts were the factories, the hydroponic plants, the yeast-culture vats, the power plants. Through all the melee were the water pipes and sewage ducts, schools, prisons, and shops, power lines and communication beams.
>
> There was no doubt about it: the City was the culmination of man's mastery over the environment. Not space travel, not the fifty colonized worlds that were now so haughtily independent, but the City.

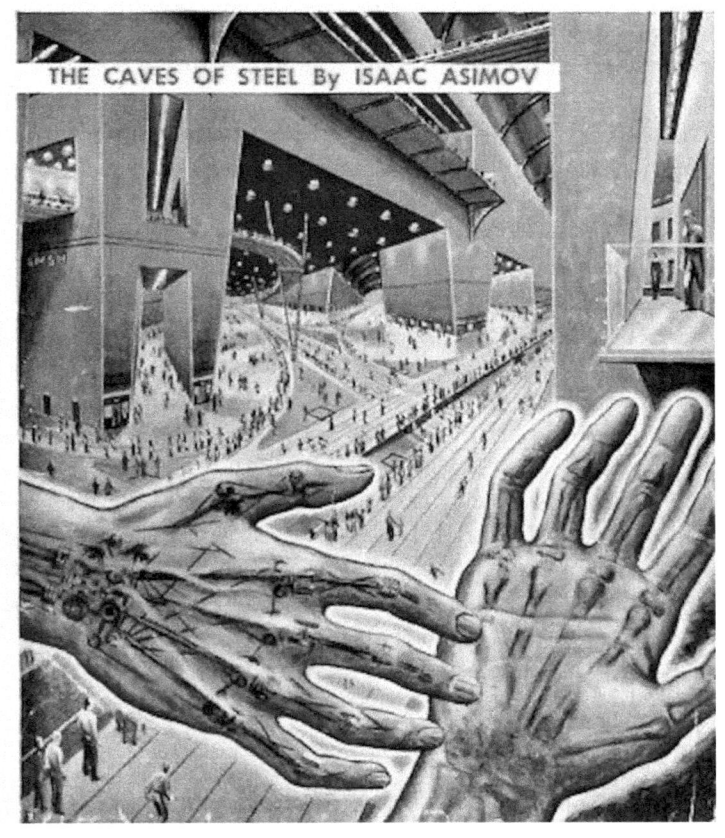

Figure 3.4 October 1953 issue of *Galaxy Science Fiction*, which featured *The Caves of Steel* by Isaac Asimov. Published by Galaxy Publishing, illustrated by Ed Emshwiller.

Practically none of Earth's population lived outside the Cities. Outside was the wilderness, the open sky that few men could face with anything like equanimity.[40]

The narrator insists that the City represents the apex of "man's mastery over the environment," but Asimov's clever phrasing here suggests otherwise. The City is "semiautonomous" – the subject of these sentences and apparent agent of its own destiny. And while it is presented as a model of efficiency and urban planning, the City also has come to dominate humans – so that "practically none" of them leave its confines. Though the gleaming walls of Asimov's steel caves may seem a far cry from the shadow-filled depths of Plato's cave, they both demonstrate the power and primacy of representation. If the Earth dwellers never venture outside the walls of their fabricated urban domes, how "real" can their City be said to be? Perhaps the sky that they can no longer bear to face is more real than the urban mazes they have constructed for themselves. Asimov's fiction, filled to the brim with infrastructural objects – hydroponic plants and sewage ducts – prompts readers to ask such questions of representation, and to interrogate their own surroundings in light of this future terrain.

Another effect of Asimov's imagined future world is to make readers question the relation it bears to their own. After all, how different really are these steel caves from cities as we know them? New York, Los Angeles, Hong Kong, Istanbul, and other sprawling metropolises might aptly be described by the same prose out of which Asimov constructs his dystopian domes. The texture of Asimov's textual world causes readers to see how fine the line between fact and fiction, or rather, between representation and reality can be. Plato's enduring lesson is that we must rely on representation because we can never encounter the world itself. In this reading, the one object that always recedes behind culture, behind the cave wall of representation is nature. Nature not only in the sense of the environment outside, but as the world before people manipulate it, things before they are altered by our existence and perception. Material culture studies names the desire to push through representation's veil and access objects themselves while knowing that it can only ever inventory the veil's matter. This is why we do not have material natural studies but instead material culture studies, a field that from the outset names the way objects come to us always and only through the prism of representation.

Notes

1. Karl Marx, *Capital: A Critique of Political Economy*, vol. 1 (London: Penguin, 1990 [1976]), 163–64.
2. "represent, v.1," *Oxford English Dictionary* Online (Oxford University Press, 2018), https://bit.ly/3jYYyxJ (accessed August 18, 2018).
3. "representation, n.1," *OED* Online, www.oed.com.udel.idm.oclc.org/view/Entry/162997 (accessed August 18, 2018).
4. Plato. *The Republic*, ed. G. R. F. Ferrari and trans. Tom Griffith (Cambridge: Cambridge University Press, 2000).
5. *Aristotle: Physics, Books I and II*, trans. William Charlton (Oxford: Clarendon Press, 1970).
6. Emily Dickinson, Marta L. Werner, and Jen Bervin, eds., *The Gorgeous Nothings* (New York: New Directions, 2013).
7. Susan Stewart, *On Longing: Narratives of the Miniature, the Gigantic, the Souvenir, the Collection* (Durham: Duke University Press, 1993), 19.

8. Erich Auerbach, *Mimesis: The Representation of Reality in Western Thought* (Princeton: Princeton University Press, 1953, 2003).
9. Auerbach, 11, 7.
10. Theodore Dreiser, *Sister Carrie* (Doubleday, 1900; New York: Penguin Books, 1981), 22.
11. Ibid, 98.
12. Bill Brown, *A Sense of Things: The Object Matter of American Literature* (Chicago: The University of Chicago Press, 2003), 33.
13. Michael Sayeau, "Realism and the Novel," in Eric Bulson, ed., *The Cambridge Companion to the Novel* (New York: Cambridge University Press, 2018), 91.
14. Quoted in Roland Barthes, "The Reality Effect," in *The Rustle of Language*, trans. Richard Howard (Oakland: University of California Press, 1989), 141.
15. Ibid, 148.
16. Sayeau, "Realism and the Novel," 92.
17. György Lukács, "Narrate or Describe?" in *Writer and Critic and Other Essays*, ed. and trans. Arthur Kahn (London: Merlin Press, 1970), 131.
18. See, for instance, Jean Baudrillard, *The System of Objects* (1968; New York: Verso, 1996) and Pierre Bourdieu, *Outline of a Theory of Practice* (New York: Cambridge University Press, 1977).
19. For examples of work with a focus on consumption and exchange, see Arjun Appadurai, *The Social Life of Things: Commodities in Cultural Perspective* (New York: Cambridge University Press, 1986), which includes Igor Kopytoff's essay "The Cultural Biography of Things: Commodification as Process;" Daniel Miller, *Material Culture and Mass Consumption* (New York: B. Blackwell, 1987) and his edited volume, *Acknowledging Consumption: A Review of New Studies* (New York: Routledge, 1995).
20. Appadurai, *The Social Life of Things*, 17.
21. Jules David Prown, "Mind in Matter: An Introduction to Material Culture Theory and Method," *Winterthur Portfolio* 17, no. 1 (Spring 1982), 1–19.
22. Bill Brown, *The Material Unconscious: American Amusement, Stephen Crane, and the Economies of Play* (Cambridge: Harvard University Press, 1996); *A Sense of Things: The Object Matter of American Literature* (Chicago: University of Chicago Press, 2003).
23. Bill Brown, "Thing Theory," *Critical Inquiry* 28, no. 1 (2001), 4.
24. Bill Brown, *Other Things* (Chicago: University of Chicago Press, 2015), 9.
25. Elaine Freedgood, *The Ideas in Things: Fugitive Meaning in the Victorian Novel* (Chicago: University of Chicago Press, 2006); John Plotz, *Portable Property: Victorian Culture on the Move* (Princeton: Princeton University Press, 2008); Mary Jacobus, *Romantic Things: A Tree, A Rock, A Cloud* (Chicago: University of Chicago Press, 2012); Matthew Mullins,

Postmodernism in Pieces: Materializing the Social in US Fiction (New York: Oxford University Press, 2016).

26. As Katherine Behar notes in "An Introduction to OOF," there are many "histories of treating certain humans (women, people of color, and the poor) as objects." One question material culture scholars consider is whether or not representations of material culture expose these histories or correct them? See *Object Oriented Feminism* (Minneapolis: Minnesota University Press, 2016), 3.

27. Uri McMillan, "Objecthood, Avatars, and the Limits of the Human," *GLQ: A Journal of Lesbian and Gay Studies* 21, nos. 2–3. (June 2015), 224. McMillan's book develops this critique of the new materialisms and offers readings of Black feminist art and performance. See *Embodied Avatars* (New York: New York University Press, 2015).

28. Robin Bernstein, "Dances with Things: Material Culture and the Performance of Race," *Social Text* 27, no. 4 (2009), 67–94.

29. Tavia Nyong'o, "Racial Kitsch and Black Performance," *The Yale Journal of Criticism* 15, no. 2 (Fall 2002), 374.

30. Sandy Alexandre, "'[The] Things What Happened with Our Family': Property and Inheritance in August Wilson's *The Piano Lesson*," *Modern Drama* 52, no. 1 (Spring 2009), 74.

31. David Lloyd, "Race Under Representation," *Oxford Literary Review* 13, no. 1/2 (1991), 63, 86.

32. Saidiya Hartman, "Venus in Two Acts," *Small Axe* 12, no. 2 (June 2008), 2.

33. Ibid, 11.

34. Quoted in Colm Tóibín, *On Elizabeth Bishop* (Princeton: Princeton University Press, 2015), 121.

35. Susan Strasser, *Waste and Want: A Social History of Trash* (New York: Henry Holt, 1999).

36. William A. Cohen and Ryan Johnson, eds., *Filth: Dirt, Disgust, and Modern Life* (Minneapolis: Minnesota University Press, 2004).

37. Jani Scandura, *Down in the Dumps: Place, Modernity, American Depression* (Durham: Duke University Press, 2008).

38. Kate Marshall, "Thing Theory at Expanded Scale," in *Thing Theory in Literary Studies*, curated by Sarah Wasserman and Patrick Moran (2018), https://stanford.io/3ECsTdh.

39. Fredric Jameson, *Archaeologies of the Future: The Desire Called Utopia and Other Science Fictions* (New York: Verso, 2005), xiii.

40. Isaac Asimov, *The Caves of Steel* (New York: Bantam Books, 1954/1991), 21.

Part II

Relevant Pasts

4

Disciplinary Complicity: The University, Material Culture Studies, and Global Environmental Crisis

Richard M. Hutchings

Introduction

> When our descendants look back from the despoiled planet that they will inherit, they will want to discover how human beings could possibly have done what we did.
>
> Bruce Alexander[1]

The modern university is the capitalist university, serving elite economic interests by disciplining students in the environmentally destructive culture of capitalism. An academic discipline embedded in the capitalist university, material culture studies is inherently complicit. Material culture studies is also complicit via cultural resource management, which is how material culture studies is most commonly practiced. Complicating matters is that material culture studies practitioners have very little to say about their role in the global environmental crisis.

In this chapter, I examine the evidence for the aforementioned claims, relying in part on reflexive environmentalism, a theoretical approach that involves critical reflection and self-confrontation.[2] I begin the chapter by introducing three core concepts: environment, global environmental crisis, and disciplinary complicity. I then examine in detail the capitalist university and my own discipline of material culture studies. While some readers may find the contents of this chapter provocative, my goal is not to incite; rather, it is to speak the truth as I see it, which I have sought to do in all my work on the subject.

Environment

The term environment is widely misunderstood, misused, and taken for granted. One source of confusion is many people consider it synonymous with "nature" and "wilderness," characterized by the absence of humans. This usage is incomplete and inaccurate, as it accounts for neither the *human social environment* nor the *total environment*.

Human social environments encompass the physical surroundings, social relationships, and cultural milieus within which groups of people function and interact:

> Components of the social environment include built infrastructure; industrial and occupational structure; labor markets; social and economic processes; wealth; social, human, and health services; power relations; government; race relations; social inequality; cultural practices; the arts; religious institutions and practices; and beliefs about place and community. The social environment subsumes many aspects of the physical environment [and] resources have been at least partially configured by human social processes. Embedded within contemporary social environments are historical social and power relations that have become institutionalized over time. Social environments can be experienced at multiple scales, often simultaneously.[3]

The environment has thus been the center of conversation since the beginning of human time. Despite this, or perhaps because of it, there is little agreement today on what the term means.

In its broadest, most inclusive usage, environments are the areas and conditions that surround. In this context, environment is synonymous with surroundings. Indeed, the word derives from the French *environ* (literally "in a circle" [en + viron]), meaning to encircle, encompass, enclose, or circumscribe. While there are many different kinds of environments (e.g., arctic, contested, cosmic, gendered, historic, idyllic, political, subterranean, temporal, urban, zoo), the total environment is theorized as the sum or aggregate of all surrounding areas, conditions, and relationships, as illustrated in Figure 4.1. Environment and total environment are akin to ecosystem and total ecosystem.

When people use the term environment today, they are likely not referring to the total environment. It is more likely they are talking about a very particular kind of environment. This is exemplified in Western scholarship where academics have gone to great lengths to delineate or "stake out" the environment. Where social scientists have historically conceived of the environment as the social milieu, natural scientists have used the word to signify "natural ecosystems independent of humans and surrounding a living being or an animal or plant

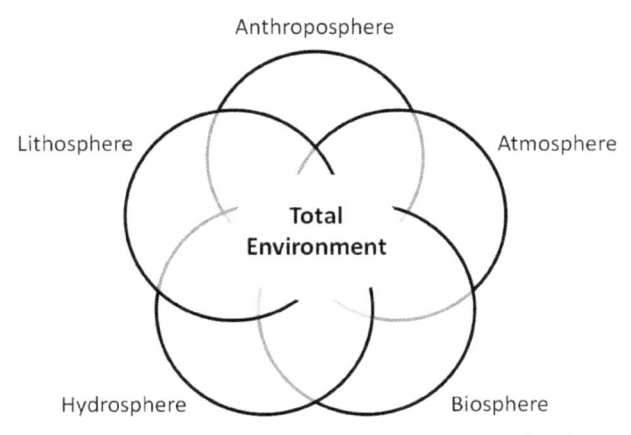

Figure 4.1 This Western, scientific representation of the "total environment" includes the anthroposphere (human-built and modified environments), atmosphere (gaseous environments), biosphere (living environments), hydrosphere (water environments), and lithosphere (geological environments). Adapted from the journal *Science of the Total Environment*, www.journals.elsevier.com/science-of-the-total-environment.

population."[4] Where the former excludes nonhuman "nature," the latter excludes human "culture."

In this chapter, I use the term environment to mean both cultural and natural, human and nonhuman worlds in their entirety. To this end, *environmental problems* are considered to be the "social aspects of natural problems" and the "natural aspects of social problems," meaning they have natural and social dimensions[5] and directly affect human health and well-being.[6]

Global Environmental Crisis

While many communities faced environmental crises in the past, the unfolding global environmental crisis is unprecedented insofar as (1) there are significantly more people on the planet today than in the past, (2) today's technologies do much greater harm much faster than in the past, (3) environments are in far worse shape than before, and (4) our current economic system – capitalism – is based on the principle of infinite or limitless growth.[7]

> The damage being done today is so widespread that it not only degrades local and regional ecologies, as in earlier civilizations, but also affects the planetary environment, threatening the existence of a majority of species on the planet, including our own. There are ... sound scientific reasons to be concerned about the current rapid degradation of the earth's environment.[8]

While extensive, the damage is quite recent, with most occurring within living memory. Most of the built environment in existence today postdates

1950, as do the most environmentally harmful technologies. Since 1970, humans have destroyed 60 percent of the planet's mammals, birds, fish, and reptiles such that "the annihilation of wildlife is now an emergency that threatens civilisation."[9] The damage is so widespread it is approaching "total," such that 87 percent of the ocean and more than 77 percent of land (excluding Antarctica) has been modified by human activities.[10]

The global environmental crisis is not a single issue, but rather a complex web of interrelated problems[11] that include climate change, ocean acidification, ozone depletion, freshwater depletion, land degradation, biodiversity loss, and chemical pollution.[12] Further, because humans are part of the total environment, the human impact of capitalism on the natural environment is recursively manifested in a wide range of human social, physical, and mental health problems.[13] These include the dislocation of people from their homelands, communities, and families[14] and the psychological effects of global climate change.[15] Capitalism interferes with the humanization process, which includes the biological production and maintenance of human beings and the cultural production and maintenance of human societies and cultures.[16]

The mainstream response to the global environmental crisis is business as usual or status quo, but there is a cost to doing nothing as environmental problems get more complex and concatenated over time, sometimes becoming unresolvable, as with climate change.[17] In this chapter, capitalism is understood to be the prime driver of the global environmental crisis.[18] More than an economic strategy, capitalism is an ideology and a culture.[19]

Disciplinary Complicity

While I have written about critical pedagogy in material culture studies before, this is the first instance I have used the term disciplinary complicity. It comes to me from Cristóbal Gnecco (see Chapter 6), who has applied the concept to archaeology in Latin and South America.[20] According to Gnecco, archaeology is a capitalist project and archaeologists are complicit in capitalist development, primarily through the practice of archaeological resource management. This chapter builds on Gnecco's work by expanding the conversation beyond the discipline of archaeology to include the wider environment and university.

Complicity refers to group involvement in an activity that is morally wrong. In this chapter, I distinguish between *institutional complicity*, which concerns the academy and university, and *disciplinary complicity*, which concerns the academic discipline. As Moghaddam points out,

> The university long ago abandoned the idea of striving to achieve complete individuals, and has instead focused on attempting to

complete itself as an institution. Through employing experts in multitudes of ever-increasing specializations [disciplines], and thus being able to call on researchers to provide expert opinion on the narrowest of topics, the university attempts to portray itself as complete. ... Rapid increases in numbers of specializations have led to a mushrooming of departments, institutes, centers and other bureaucratic units for demarcating and operating specialty territories.[21]

My point is that the academic discipline, manifested locally as the university department, is such a bureaucratic unit, and material culture studies is such a specialty territory. As a point of departure on this subject, consider that the word *discipline* refers simultaneously to (1) the practice of training people to behave in a particular way (i.e., to be compliant) by using punishment to correct noncompliance and (2) a specialized branch of knowledge studied in higher education.

The rest of this chapter moves from general (institutional complicity) to specific (disciplinary complicity), starting with the university and capitalism and ending with material culture studies and resourcism. Where the first section considers the ways the academy (re)produces capitalism thus environmental destruction, the second focuses on material culture studies and cultural resource management. I end the chapter with a discussion of compliance and complicity.

The University and Institutional Complicity

The crises of late capitalism aren't coming from outside academe: The caller is inside the house.

Andrew Seal[22]

In his groundbreaking text *Homo Academicus*, sociologist Pierre Bourdieu deconstructed the networks of power that define the French academy,[23] turning "the objectifying gaze of science onto his fellow intellectuals, whom he depicted as willing accomplices in the business of domination."[24] What Bourdieu found – and many others have since[25] – is that Western schools are not just interconnected with but fully embedded in capitalist society and culture. Moghaddam is clear: "The source of modern academic ideals is to be found in the larger society. Far from being an 'ivory tower,' the modern university is both fundamentally influenced by, and has an impact on, the rest of society."[26] This "larger society" is the culture of capitalism.[27]

A distinguishing feature of *Homo Academicus* is Bourdieu's description of "something that everybody already knows, but nobody speaks openly about,"[28] or nondiscussables.[29] Where Bourdieu's nondiscussable was seeing the university as an elite-directed sphere of power, mine is seeing the university as a driver of environmental destruction. Consequently, my case for institutional and disciplinary complicity reflects and builds on Bourdieu's observation that the academy is involved in the "business of domination."

Understanding the role of the modern university in the "domination of nature" (thus culture[30]) involves considering how capitalism influences the university, and how universities reproduce that culture. Heller examines this history in the United States post-1945, concluding that: (1) modern universities have always had a close relationship with private business;[31] (2) from the 1970s onward the influence of large corporations in university governance became "overwhelming";[32] and (3) as key loci of training, research, and economic development, "universities have become central locations within the structure of contemporary capitalism."[33]

Joel Spring studies the global impacts of the Western school model, emphasizing what he calls "hierarchical urban-consumer society."[34] He concludes that the outcome of corporate and government control of education has been "the triumph of urban-consumerism and the loss of the empathy and compassion necessary to maintain communities":

> Workers alienated from their work and each other seek solace in striving for higher incomes to spend on status and shopping. Progress up the educational ladder ... based on test performance and staff ratings is preparation for the evaluations that move workers up the corporate ladder. The link between the Western school model and economic globalization is the promise that graduation will lead to a "good" job in an urban-consumer economy.[35]

Spring identifies anthropocentrism as a central ideology driving capitalist urban-consumer society,[36] where Western schools teach that nature should serve humans and that humans are superior to nature and other animals.[37] As shown in Table 4.1, anthropocentrism is one of many Western school model ideologies that are harmful and morally suspect.

As illustrated in Figure 4.2, the six key consequences identified in Table 4.1 – inequality, alienation, anxiety, consumption, addiction, and domination – collectively drive capitalist urban-consumer society thus environmental crisis.[38] Of these, the first (inequality) and last (domination) are pivotal.

Inequality. Western schools increase socioeconomic inequalities caused by differences in school achievement and access to schooling[39] while fostering dreams of upward socioeconomic mobility and greater consumption – "Rather than opening the imagination to thoughts of better political and economic systems, the modern school sparks desires for more money and shopping."[40] Those desires result in psychosocial dislocation and alienation.[41]

Alienation. Promoting inequality through its various ideologies, Western schools create "a loss of the spiritual feelings of compassion and

Table 4.1 Common academic ideologies and their consequences

Ideology	Description	Consequences	Examples
Achievement	Belief that "success" (income, social status) is paramount and earned (merited) through hard work and education; factors such as ethnicity, class and "privilege" are downplayed in meritocracies.	Inequality, Alienation, Anxiety, Domination	Adler (2017) Berg et al. (2016) Mullaly (2010)
Anthropocentrism	Belief that "nature should serve humans and that humans are superior to other animals" (Spring 2019:17).	Inequality, Alienation, Domination	Leiss (1994) Miklós (2014) Quinn et al. (2015)
Careerism	Belief that one's career is more important than what one's company or institution does, and that achievement (i.e., "climbing the corporate ladder") is paramount (Spring 2019:3).	Inequality, Alienation, Anxiety, Addiction	Andrews (2006) Berg et al. (2016) Schmidt (2006)
Classism	Belief that an individual's lower economic or class standing is normal and the result of poor life choices and work ethic.	Inequality, Alienation, Domination	Langhout et al. (2007) Mullaly (2010)
Competition	Belief that rivalry, ranking, and hierarchy raise achievement and promote social progress.	Inequality, Alienation, Anxiety, Addiction, Domination	Bakan (2004) Berg et al. (2016)
Progress (social)	Belief that certain individuals, cultures, and societies have "developed" more or "progressed" further than others and can be ranked accordingly; ranking systems routinely "place (largely white) European, North American and Antipodean countries [i.e., Canada, United States, Australia, New Zealand] at the top, and Asian and African countries at the bottom" (Moore 2018: n.p.).	Inequality, Alienation, Anxiety, Addiction, Consumption, Domination	Berg et al. (2016) Bodley (2012a, 2012b) Leiss (1994) Moghaddam (1997)

Table 4.1 *Continued*

Ideology	Description	Consequences	Examples
Growth (economic)	Belief that economic growth is limitless and the best measure of social progress (Moore 2018).	Inequality, Alienation, Anxiety, Addiction, Consumption, Domination	Bakan (2004) Bodley (2012a, 2012b) Magdoff and Foster (2011) Ritzer (1993, 1996)
Individualism	Belief that the individual is more important than the group and that individuals are responsible for their own achievement.	Inequality, Alienation, Anxiety, Addiction, Consumption, Domination	Moghaddam (1997) Mullaly (2010)
Materialism	Belief in the values and goals associated with wealth, possessions, image, and status (Kasser 2016).	Inequality, Alienation, Consumption	Bakan (2004, 2011) Schmidt (2006) Spring (2019)
Modernization-McDonaldization	Belief that efficiency, calculability, predictability, and control are the best strategies for dealing with contemporary human problems (Hutchings 2018).	Inequality, Alienation, Anxiety, Addiction, Consumption, Domination	Hayes and Wynyard (2002) Moghaddam (1997) Ritzer (1993,1996)
Resourcism	Belief in the use of "rational planning to promote efficient development and use of all resources" (Hays 1979:2), particularly as commodities.	Alienation, Consumption, Domination	Foresman (2007) Hutchings (2017, 2018) King (2009)
Scientism	Belief in the supremacy of scientific knowledge, institutions, techniques, and experts (specialists).	Inequality, Alienation, Anxiety, Addiction, Consumption, Domination	Leiss (1994) Moghaddam (1997)
Specialization	Belief that experts and their modern knowledge and technology are superior to nonexperts and their knowledge and technology.	Inequality, Alienation, Anxiety, Addiction, Consumption, Domination	Leiss (1994) Moghaddam (1997)
Urban-Consumerism	Belief that urban, Western, globalized lifeways and worldviews, with their emphasis on urban-directed growth and consumption, are superior to the rural, local, and non-Western.	Inequality, Alienation, Anxiety, Addiction, Consumption, Domination	Meneley (2018) Bakan (2004) Spring (2019)

Table 4.1 Continued

Ideology	Description	Consequences	Examples
Work	Belief in two categories of daily activities: work and leisure, such that "energy put forth for the purpose of earning a paycheque is categorized as work, whereas energy invested in 'elective' activities is called leisure" (Schmidt 2006:2).	Inequality, Alienation, Anxiety, Addiction, Consumption, Domination	Andrews (2006) Posen (2013) Rinehart (1996)

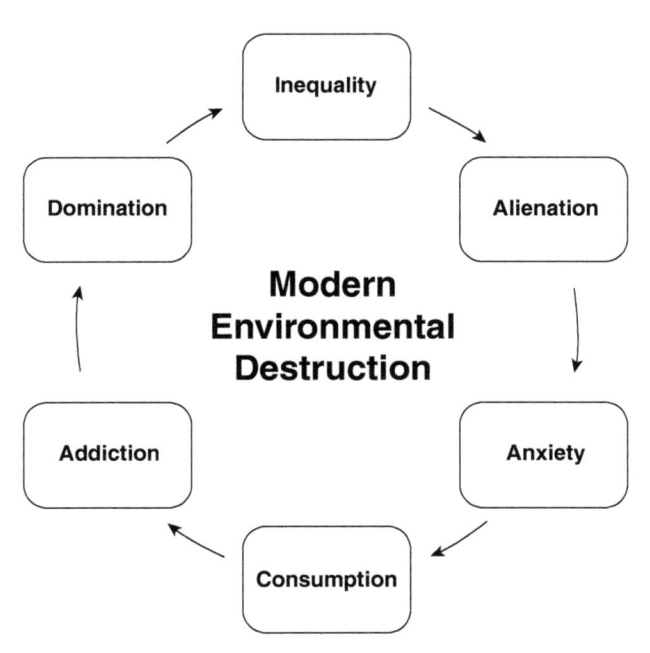

Figure 4.2 The six consequences of the modern Western school model – inequality, alienation, anxiety, consumption, addiction, and domination – collectively drive late-modern environmental destruction. Prepared by Richard Hutchings.

empathy and an increase in feelings of loneliness," making it difficult for people to maintain healthy relationships with each other and their environment.[42] People who prioritize materialistic goals and values "engage in fewer environmentally beneficial behaviors and have higher ecological footprints"; they "consume more and incur more debt, have lower-quality interpersonal relationships, treat other people in less caring ways, and have adverse educational and occupational motivation."[43]

Anxiety. In Western schools today, academic departments and faculty are expected to operate as competitive businesses; consequently, "Unprecedented levels of anxiety and stress among both academic and academic-related staff and students abound, with 'obedient' students expecting, and even demanding, hoop-jumping, box-ticking and bean-counting."[44] For the university, late-modern capitalism entails "shifts from exchange to competition, from equality to inequality," and turning faculty and students alike into "human capital."[45] The Western school model promotes competition between students, teachers, academic departments, academic disciplines, academic institutions, and states.[46] Systems of audit, assessment, and ranking are key mechanisms of late capitalism that produce high levels of anxiety and stress.[47] The Western school model contributes to alienation and anxiety by promoting rural to urban movement of people, resulting in breakdown of traditional communities and families.[48]

Consumption. Western schools promote the ideologies of consumerism and materialism. Consumerism is essential to the positive functioning of capitalism[49] and people who prioritize materialistic aims report higher levels of compulsive consumption, lower personal well-being, more physical health problems, and more ecologically destructive attitudes and behaviors; they also consume more.[50] According to Alexander, consumption is a global addiction and prime driver of global social problems, including environmental destruction; "Wasteful consumption is essential for the survival of a bloated economy. There must be affluent people to consume the products of the factories as wastefully as possible so that more can be manufactured, because corporations that do not grow must die."[51] As people are converted into consumers, they lose "the essence of ... common humanity" as it is defined in terms of a connection to commodities instead of each other and the environment.[52]

Addiction. Alienated, anxious, and disciplined in the ideologies of global free-market capitalism, the Western school model produces addicts, where addiction is defined as "overwhelming involvement with any pursuit whatsoever that is harmful to the addicted person and his or her society."[53] Most academics, for example, are addicted to work. And so, probably, will be their students. "Multiplied by millions, they form a perfect vicious cycle. They work compulsively; they consume compulsively; the gross-domestic product rises; the environment deteriorates; the poor get poorer; everyone feels more dislocated; they work *more* compulsively; they consume *more* compulsively; the gross-domestic product rises *further*."[54] Schmidt connects the ideology of work to the global environmental crisis by emphasizing how our "perverse" work ethic is not just a social problem: "The environmental tragedy of global warming, pollution and the extinction of millions of species are linked to the behaviour of our consumerist society. We are working longer and harder at decreasing the ability of our planet to sustain us, and less time at doing the work of enjoying life."[55]

Domination. Like the Western school model and Western society in general,[56] the global environmental crisis is rooted in the tortured cycle of alienation and domination.[57] This is because the Western school model's science-based view of nature is a "philosophical commitment to rational science, logical thinking, and mathematical reasoning that allow[s] nature to be known, managed, mastered, and dominated. According to Francis Bacon (1571–1626), the key conceptual author of the mastery of nature thesis, 'nature must be 'bound into service' and made a 'slave', put 'in constraint' and 'molded' by the mechanical arts."[58] Identifying the domination of nature with scientific and technological progress, Leiss maintains that "If the idea of *domination* of nature has any meaning at all, it is that ... some [people] attempt to dominate and control other [people]. The notion of a common domination of the human race over external nature is nonsensical."[59] Domination in this context is thus not about "nature" or "environment" as much as it is about inequality and the ideology of science as progress.

It is clear the university is complicit in capitalism and the global environmental crisis. The most apparent way is by reproducing capitalist ideologies through discipline.

Material Culture Studies and Disciplinary Complicity

> As schools erode the spiritual values of compassion and empathy and create populations alienated from each other, the world rushes to its own environmental destruction.
>
> Joel Spring[60]

Determining disciplinary complicity involves demonstrating it is (1) an academic discipline and (2) complicit in capitalism. Material culture studies constitutes an academic discipline insofar as it has:

- an established, rigorously delineated, highly specialized academic history with concomitant "disciplinary perspectives" and jargon;[61]
- dedicated, specialized academic journals (e.g., *Material Culture*; *Material Culture Review*; *Journal of Material Culture*);
- dedicated, specialized academic texts (e.g., *Handbook of Material Culture*; *The Oxford Handbook of Material Culture Studies*; *Cambridge University Press Handbook of Material Culture Studies*; *Material Cultures in Canada*); and
- dedicated, specialized university programs, degrees, certificates, centers, laboratories, etc.

It is difficult to imagine a case for material culture studies *not* being an academic discipline, but it would likely involve the argument that material culture studies is a theoretical field of inquiry, not an academic discipline. In addition to being flawed on numerous practical fronts (see above), any attempt to separate the intellectual "field" from the academic "discipline" is a slippery slope argument that can only be taken so far. Practically speaking, "material cultural studies" does not exist without the university and its disciplinary structure, whatever we choose to call it.

The determination that material culture studies is complicit in capitalism, thus the global environmental crisis, is based on three lines of argument:

1. Material culture studies is complicit in capitalism, thus the global environmental crisis, because it is an academic discipline, embedded theoretically and practically in the capitalist university. As an academic product, material culture studies promotes the same core ideologies as the university and is thus subject to the same critiques. If, for example, the university promotes the ideologies of capitalism and hyper-competition then material culture studies promotes the ideologies of capitalism and hyper-competition.[62]
2. Material culture studies is complicit in the global environmental crisis based on the fact it has very little to say about the global ecological crisis. In this sense, silence is consent.
3. Material culture studies is complicit in the global environmental crisis based on how it is practiced. Here, I follow Aristotelian ethics in that "we are what we repeatedly do."

Arguments two and three are examined in detail below.

Material Culture Studies in Theory

To analyze material culture studies, I consider what its practitioners say (theory) and what they do (practice). I consider what they say by examining six edited volumes on material culture studies in light of "environment" and "ecology" generally and the global environmental crisis in particular. Specifically, I reviewed each chapter and counted the number that address the global environmental crisis. I also examine each book's index for the words "environment" and "ecology." The six texts are reviewed chronologically and then summarized. The texts, which represent a total of 129 chapters, were selected because of their relevance and my familiarity with them.

The *Handbook of Material Culture* has thirty-three chapters and none focus on the global environmental crisis, although the chapter on consumption is certainly relevant. The terms environment and ecology do not appear in the handbook's eleven-page index.[63]

The Oxford Handbook of Material Culture Studies has twenty-eight chapters and none focus on the global environmental crisis. The terms environment and ecology appear numerous times in the handbook's sixteen-page index.[64]

Material Powers: Cultural Studies, History and the Material Turn has ten chapters and none focus on the global environmental crisis. The terms environment and ecology do not appear in the handbook's seven-page index.[65]

Material Cultures in Canada has fifteen chapters and none focus on the global environmental crisis. The terms environment and ecology do not appear in the handbook's thirteen-page index.[66]

The Oxford Handbook of Public Heritage Theory and Practice has twenty-seven chapters, with three that focus on the global environmental crisis.[67] The terms environment and ecology do not appear in the handbook's twenty-four page index.

Human-Centered Built Environment Heritage Preservation: Theory and Evidence-Based Practice[68] has sixteen chapters, with one that focuses on the global environmental crisis, although Kaufman's and Wells and Stiefel's chapters have some relevance.[69] The terms environment and ecology do not appear in the handbook's eleven-page index.

As shown in Table 4.2, of the 129 chapters examined, only four (3 percent) address the global environmental crisis. The terms environment and ecology do not appear in the indexes of five of the six texts. I examine what this means in my discussion later, but not before considering what material culture studies is in practice.

Table 4.2 *The global environmental crisis in material culture studies texts*

Texts examined in this chapter	Number of chapters in text	Number of chapters in text focusing on the global environmental crisis
Handbook of Material Culture (2006)	33	0
The Oxford Handbook of Material Culture Studies (2010)	28	0
Material Powers: Cultural Studies, History and the Material Turn (2010)	10	0
Material Cultures in Canada (2015)	15	0
Human-Centered Built Environment Heritage Preservation: Theory and Evidence-Based Practice (2018)	16	1
The Oxford Handbook of Public Heritage Theory and Practice (2018)	27	3
Total	129	4
Percent		3

Material Culture Studies in Practice

While much has been written about what material cultural studies is in theory, what material cultural studies practitioners do is less clear.[70] Who does material cultural studies? What do material cultural studies practitioners do?

In this section, I correlate material culture with "cultural resource" and material cultural studies with "cultural resource management." The reason for this is there is no such thing as a material culture analyst in practice. Instead, people with this specialization end up working in various sectors dealing with tangible heritage including artifacts, texts, in situ sites and landscapes. In Western schools, these are called "cultural resources" and assumed to be in need of expert management.

According to King,[71] the term cultural resource is commonly applied to:

- historic/heritage properties
- Indigenous graves and cultural items
- shipwrecks
- museum collections
- historical documents
- religious sites
- religious practices
- cultural use of natural resources
- folklife, tradition, other social institutions
- theater groups, orchestras, and other community cultural amenities.

A cultural resource is thus a component of the human social environment such that (1) every human product or construct, physical and mental, is potentially a cultural resource and (2) every intentional act upon a cultural resource is potentially cultural resource management. Who has the authority to name and manage cultural resources is a primary concern of critical heritage studies and of direct relevance to academics, as they are not only authorities themselves, but they determine through official accreditation who will be authorities in the future.[72]

The practice that most commonly identifies and is associated with material culture studies is archaeology, which focuses explicitly on material culture and built environments. Archaeologists are also the group most closely linked to cultural resource management. Therefore, understanding material culture studies in practice involves the analysis of archaeologists and cultural resource management.

Cultural resource management is a technology of government insofar as cultural resources are considered the property of the state, to be managed as such under state permit.[73] Like natural resource management, upon which cultural resource management is based, the practice is entrenched in the capitalist ideology of *resourcism*, which utilizes "rational planning to promote efficient development and use of all resources."[74]

A professional, scientific managerial elite was deeply rooted in the [early] resourcism movement. Hays says that this elite believed, "Since resource matters were basically technical in nature ... technicians, rather than legislators should deal with them." And, "Conflicts between competing resource users ... should not be dealt with" by the political process, but rather by professional resource managers coolly making "rational and scientific decisions." They had a vision of a school of resource management "guided by the ideal of efficiency and dominated by technicians."[75]

Foreman outlines the various beliefs that define the ideology of resourcism,[76] four of which are reproduced here:

- Professionalism. Trained experts are best qualified to manage resources.
- Progressivism/Optimism. Progress as a secular religion of material, informational, moral, and organizational advances is key to resourcism, as is an intensely optimistic view of the future benefits of wise management.
- Engineering. The science behind resourcism is manipulative and controlling [or "engineered"].
- Utilitarianism. Resources are here to be used to produce goods and services for humans.

Motivated by the "drive for [environmental] domination," resourcism "was and is solidly in the imperialist tradition" insofar as its goal is "to squeeze as much wealth out of the land as possible."[77] Capitalism and resourcism thus go hand in hand.

Capitalism and cultural resource management have a more direct relationship with development. In many parts of the world, developers pay for archaeology to be done in advance of their project.[78] While "management" of cultural resources might imply their protection, in practice the destruction of heritage sites is at best mitigated, at worst secured. My research demonstrated that cultural resource management had failed to protect over 75 percent of known archaeological sites from destruction.[79]

Cultural resource management assumes that state control over material culture is legitimate and that state-sanctioned, university-trained experts are authorities.[80] Cultural resource management presupposes and facilitates capitalism.[81] Working under the authority of the state and funded by developers, cultural resource management facilitates capitalism by permitting the industrial-scale clearance of material culture from the landscape to make way for economic development.[82] Insofar as material culture studies practitioners work as cultural resource managers – paid to clear material culture from the landscape so that development can proceed unimpeded – the discipline is complicit in the global environmental crisis.

The connection between the university, the state, and capitalism is well documented.[83] So, too, is the link between state heritage regimes and violence.[84] Whether or not state-sanctioned heritage workers can or want to see those connections is another matter.[85]

Compliance and Complicity

[T]he ecological crisis is a moral crisis.

Pope John Paul II[86]

Three lines of argument indicate material culture studies' complicity in the global environmental crisis. First, material culture studies is complicit in the global environmental crisis via the university. Material culture studies is embedded practically and theoretically in the capitalist university, which disciplines students – future managers and workers – in the culture of capitalism.

Second, material culture studies is complicit in the global environmental crisis via institutional silence. Material culture studies authors, most of whom are academics, have very little to say about environmental crisis. Their silence is overwhelming – 97 percent, as measured in this chapter – and problematic, as it can be interpreted as indifference or consent.

Third, material culture studies is connected to the global environmental crisis via cultural resource management. Outside the university and the museum, material culture studies is most commonly practiced as cultural resource management, a suite of state-sanctioned institutions, laws, regulations, and policies concerning the official dispensation of material culture. Rooted in the capitalist ideology of resourcism, cultural resource management is a technology of government designed to facilitate capitalist expansion, thus the environmental crisis.

In the remainder of this chapter I focus on this issue of representation and how it perpetuates a culture of compliance and complicity. I have identified three reasons why material cultural studies practitioners misrepresent their discipline:[87]

- They do not know they are misrepresenting their discipline.
- They do not believe they are misrepresenting their discipline.
- They are misrepresenting their discipline willfully to deceive others and/or themselves.

There are some good reasons why material cultural studies practitioners *might not know* they are misrepresenting their discipline. As belief systems, ideologies are largely taken for granted by their practitioners, rendering those ideologies "invisible" to them. This is why nonbelievers and outsiders are oftentimes the best observers of culture.[88]

Although rarely expressed publicly, many material cultural studies practitioners presumably *do not believe* they misrepresent their discipline. The distinguishing feature here is the existence of (1) some level of understanding by the practitioner about the problems of institutional and disciplinary complicity and (2) a rational defense they use to absolve themselves of responsibility. The simplest defense is holding up institutional or professional ethics codes as evidence of actual ethical behavior. In reality, however, ethics codes are rarely more than highly selective, self-serving aspirational documents that have little bearing on actual practice. Another common strategy employed by academics is to distance theoretical practice (academic research) from applied practice (nonacademic work) such that academics are not accountable for how the discipline is applied. In reality, of course, academics train the people responsible for environmental destruction (business leaders, politicians, lawyers, managers), providing them with expert credentials and establishing the expert philosophical/scientific basis for their work.

There is also good reason to believe that material cultural studies practitioners *misrepresent their discipline willfully* to deceive others and/or themselves. In the real world, material cultural studies practitioners – as indoctrinated believers in the culture of academia[89] – have a strong tendency to conform,[90] and expect others to conform as well.[91] In the academy, conforming involves not just believing in the discipline but actively celebrating it, a practice that invariably involves deception.

In *The Toxic University*, John Smyth asks why academics have been so compliant in acquiescing to capitalism. According to Smyth, the university has become "enveloped" in capitalism's "unquestioning embrace,"[92] with serious consequences:

> The essence, Gatto (2001:305) says, is that we have to start with the paradox: "All large bureaucracies, public or private, are psychopathic to the degree that they are well managed." What he is saying is that when the profit motive, or its ideological proxy, is the animating force (i.e., *homo economicus*), then the underlying logic is that "the pain of the moment leads inevitably to a better tomorrow for those who survive." Organizations that blindly follow this article of faith in the pursuit of profitability succeed, and they are acting rationally within their own logic, but they do so at the cost of enormous suffering and degradation – because they have no conscience.

This lack of conscience, I conclude, is the issue.

What can or should be done about the global environmental crisis in light of material culture studies and heritage management is beyond the scope of this chapter, as illustrated in recent studies of "the future" and "sustainability."[93] However, I offer two salient points of departure. The first concerns truth-telling – as Andrew Seal warns, the ideologies that destroy "aren't coming from outside the ivory tower: The caller is in the house."[94] In truth, the Western school is for many a "colonial institution designed to replicate capitalism, heteropatriarchy, white supremacy, and dispossession."[95] Material culture studies practitioners must start talking, as there can be no empathy in silence.[96]

The second point, related to the first, is that "you can't be the colonial doctor if you're the colonial disease."[97] Can universities and their disciplines heal that which they harm? Institutions and the people who work for them have a moral responsibility – to each other, to the natural world, and to the social environments we construct. Artificial boundaries between disciplines (material culture studies, archaeology) and between their applied settings (cultural resource management) fragment the total environment and prevent cause and effect from being connected. Under this framework, the global environmental crisis will continue to unfold while academics and other practitioners of material culture studies refuse to acknowledge their complicity.[98] Perhaps, then, radical change is what is required; perhaps Gatto is correct and we need to consider being "against school" altogether.[99]

Notes

1. Bruce Alexander, *The Globalization of Addiction: A Study in Poverty of the Spirit* (Oxford: Oxford University Press, 2008), 250.
2. Magnus Boström et al., "A Reflexive Look at Reflexivity in Environmental Sociology," *Environmental Sociology* 3 (2017), 6–16.
3. Elizabeth Barnett and Michele Casper, "A Definition of 'Social Environment,'" *American Journal of Public Health* 91, no. 3 (2001), 465.
4. Jean-Guy Vaillancourt, "Environment," in Robert Paehlke, ed., *Conservation and Environmentalism* (New York: Garland, 1995), 218.
5. Ibid.
6. Rachel Cooper, "Wellbeing and the Environment: An Overview", in Rachel Cooper, Elizabeth Burton, and Cary L. Cooper, eds., *Wellbeing and the Environment: A Complete Reference Guide*, Vol. 2 (New Jersey: John Wiley, 2014), 1–19.
7. Fred Magdoff and John Bellamy Foster, *What Every Environmentalist Needs to Know about Capitalism* (New York: Monthly Review Press, 2011), 12.
8. Ibid.
9. Damian Carrington, "Humanity Has Wiped Out 60% of Animal Populations since 1970, Report Finds," *Guardian*, October 30, 2018, https://bit.ly/3pZXJZt.
10. James E. Watson et al., "Protect the Last of the Wild," *Nature*, 563 (2018), 27–30.
11. Samuel Day Fassbinder, "The Literature of the Anthropocene: Four Reviews" *Capitalism Nature Socialism*, 28 (2017), 139–48.
12. Magdoff and Foster, *What Every Environmentalist Needs to Know about Capitalism*, 12–25.

13. Glenn A. Albrecht et al.,"Solastalgia: The Distress Caused by Environmental Change," *Australasian Psychiatry*, 15 (2007), Special supplement 95–98; John Coates, *Ecology and Social Work: Towards a New Paradigm* (Halifax: Fernwood, 2003).
14. Bruce Alexander, *The Globalisation of Addiction: A Study in Poverty of the Spirit* (Oxford: Oxford University Press, 2008); John H. Bodley, *Victims of Progress*, 5th ed, (Lanham: AltaMira, 2012).
15. Thomas J. Doherty and Susan Clayton, "The Psychological Impacts of Global Climate Change," *American Psychologist* 66 (2011), 265–76.
16. Bodley, *Victims of Progress*, 3–4.
17. Peter J. Balint et al., *Wicked Environmental Problems: Managing Uncertainty and Conflict* (Covelo and London: Island Press, 2011); Richard J. Lazarus, "Super Wicked Problems and Climate Change: Restraining the Present to Liberate the Future," *Cornell Law Review* 94 (2009), 1153–234.
18. John Bellamy Foster, Brett Clark, and Richard York, *The Ecological Rift: Capitalism's War on the Earth* (New York: Monthly Review, 2010); Magdoff and Foster, *What Every Environmentalist Needs to Know about Capitalism*.
19. John H. Bodley, *Anthropology and Contemporary Human Problems*, 6th ed. (Lanham: AltaMira, 2012); Richard H. Robbins, *Global Problems and the Culture of Capitalism*, 7th ed. (New York: Pearson, 2018).
20. Cristóbal Gnecco, "An Entanglement of Sorts: Archaeology, Ethics, Praxis, Multiculturalism," in Cristóbal Gnecco and Dorothy Lippert, eds., *Ethics and Archaeological Praxis* (New York: Springer, 2015), 1–17; Cristóbal Gnecco, "Development and Disciplinary Complicity: Contract Archaeology in South America under the Critical Gaze" *Annual Review of Anthropology* 47 (2018), 279–93; Cristóbal Gnecco and Patricia Ayala. "Introduction" in Cristóbal Gnecco and Patricia Ayala, eds., *Indigenous Peoples and Archaeology in Latin America* (Walnut Creek: Left Coast Press, 2011), 11–27; see also Alejandro Haber, "Archaeology and Capitalist Development: Lines of Complicity," in Cristóbal Gnecco and Dorothy Lippert, eds., *Ethics and Archaeological Praxis* (New York: Springer, 2015), 95–113.
21. Fathali M. Moghaddam, *The Specialized Society: The Plight of the Individual in an Age of Individualism* (Westport: Praeger, 1997), 33.
22. Andrew Seal "How the University Became Neoliberal," *Chronicle of Higher Education* (June 22, 2018) www.chronicle.com/article/How-the-University-Became/243622.
23. Pierre Bourdieu, *Homo Academicus*, trans. Peter Collier (Stanford: Stanford University Press, 1980).
24. Thomas Medvetz, "Bourdieu and the Sociology of Intellectual Life," in Thomas Medvetz and Jeffrey J. Sallaz, eds., *The Oxford Handbook of Pierre Bourdieu* (Oxford: Oxford University Press, 2018), 467.
25. For example: John Taylor Gatto, *Weapons of Mass Instruction: A Schoolteacher's Journey through the Dark World of Compulsory Education*

(Gabriola: New Society, 2010); Henry Heller, *The Capitalist University: The Transformations of Higher Education in the United States since 1945* (London: Pluto Press, 2016); Andrew Marzoni, "Academia is a cult," *Washington Post*, November 1, 2018, https://wapo.st/3mCFNSr; Toni Ruuska, "Reproduction of Capitalism in the 21st Century: Higher Education and Ecological Crisis" (PhD dissertation, School of Business, Aalto University, Helsinki, 2017); John Smyth, *The Toxic University: Zombie Leadership, Academic Rock Stars and Neoliberal Ideology* (London: Palgrave Macmillan, 2017); Joel Spring, *Global Impacts of the Western School Model: Corporatization, Alienation, Consumerism* (London: Routledge, 2019); Spring et al., *The Business of Education: Networks of Power and Wealth in America* (London: Routledge, 2017).
26. Moghaddam, *The Specialized Society*, 25.
27. Bodley, *Anthropology and Contemporary Human Problems*; Robbins, *Global Problems and the Culture of Capitalism*.
28. Håkan Karlsson, "Review of *Maritime Heritage in Crisis: Indigenous Landscapes and Global Ecological Breakdown* by Richard M. Hutchings," *Norwegian Archaeological Review* 50 (2017), 176.
29. Richard M. Hutchings, *Maritime Heritage in Crisis: Indigenous Landscapes and Global Ecological Breakdown* (London: Routledge, 2017); Richard M. Hutchings, "Meeting the Shadow: Resource Management and the McDonaldization of Heritage Stewardship," in Jeremy C. Wells and Barry L. Stiefel, eds., *Human-Centered Built Environment Heritage Preservation: Theory and Evidence-Based Practice* (London: Routledge, 2019), 67–87.
30. William Leiss, *The Domination of Nature* (Montreal and Kingston: McGill-Queen's University Press, 1994), originally published 1972 by George Braziller.
31. Heller, *The Capitalist University*, 2.
32. Ibid, 5.
33. Ibid, 202.
34. Spring, *Global Impacts of the Western School Model*, 136.
35. Ibid.
36. Ibid, 125.
37. Ibid, 17.
38. Alexander, *The Globalisation of Addiction*; Coates, *Ecology and Social Work*; Maike Hamann et al., "Inequality and the Biosphere," *Annual Review of Environment and Resource* 43 (2018), 61–83; Leiss, *The Domination of Nature*; Smyth, *The Toxic University*; Spring, *Global Impacts of the Western School Model*.
39. Spring, *Global Impacts of the Western School Model*, 2.
40. Ibid, 4.
41. Albrecht et al., 'Solastalgia'; Alexander, *The Globalisation of Addiction*; see also: Joel Bakan, *The Corporation: The Pathological Pursuit of Profit and*

Power (London: Penguin, 2004); Joel Bakan, *Childhood Under Siege: How Big Business Callously Targets Children* (London: Penguin, 2006).
42. Spring, *Global Impacts of the Western School Model*, 4.
43. Tim Kasser, "Materialistic Values and Goals," *Annual Review of Psychology* 67 (2016), 489, 496.
44. Karín Lesnick-Oberstein et al. (126 signatories), "Let UK Universities Do What They Do Best – Teaching and Research," *Guardian*, July 6, 2015, https://bit.ly/3EARS0A; Lawrence D. Berg et al., "Producing Anxiety in the Neoliberal University," *The Canadian Geographer* 60 (2016), 169.
45. Berg et al., "Producing Anxiety in the Neoliberal University," 168.
46. Ibid, 171.
47. Ibid, 169.
48. Spring, *Global Impacts of the Western School Model*, 6.
49. Anne Meneley, "Consumerism," *Annual Review of Anthropology* 47 (2018), 118.
50. Kasser, "Materialistic Values and Goals," 496.
51. Alexander, *The Globalisation of Addiction*, 252.
52. Magdoff and Foster, *What Every Environmentalist Needs to Know about Capitalism*, 53.
53. Alexander, *The Globalisation of Addiction*, 48; see also Spring, *Global Impacts of the Western School Model*, 4–6.
54. Alexander, *The Globalisation of Addiction*, 252.
55. Conrad Schmidt, *Workers of the World Relax: The Simple Economics of Less Industrial Work* (Conrad Schmidt: Vancouver, 2006), 6.
56. Alexander, *The Globalisation of Addiction*, 246–52.
57. Leiss, *The Domination of Nature*.
58. Hannah Wittman, "Domination of Nature," in P. Robbins, ed., *Encyclopedia of Environment and Society* (Thousand Oaks: SAGE, 2007), 480.
59. Leiss, *The Domination of Nature*, 122–23.
60. Spring, *Global Impacts of the Western School Model*, 17.
61. Hicks and Beaudry, "Introduction," 2; see also: Allen and Blair, "Material Cultures in Canada"; Layton, "Structuralism and Semiotics"; Hicks, "The Material-Cultural Turn."
62. Heller, *The Capitalist University*; Berg et al., "Producing Anxiety in the Neoliberal University."
63. Chris Tilley et al., eds., *Handbook of Material Culture* (London: SAGE, 2006); Miller, "Consumption," in Tilly et al., 341–54.
64. Dan Hicks and Mary C. Beaudry, eds., *The Oxford Handbook of Material Culture Studies* (Oxford: Oxford University Press, 2010).
65. Tony Bennett and Patrick Joyce, eds., *Material Powers: Cultural Studies, History and the Material Turn* (London: Routledge, 2010).
66. Thomas Allen and Jennifer Blair, eds., *Material Cultures in Canada* (Waterloo: Wilfrid Laurier University Press, 2015).

67. Angela M. Labrador and Neil Asher Silberman, eds., *The Oxford Handbook of Public Heritage Theory and Practice* (Oxford: Oxford University Press, 2018); Glenn A. Albrecht, "Public Heritage in the Symbiocene," in Labrador and Silberman, 355–67.; Ned Kaufman, Ned. "The Social Sciences: What Role in Conservation?" in Labrador and Silberman, 281–94; Daniel Niles, "Agricultural Heritage and Conservation," in Labrador and Silberman, 39–54.
68. Jeremy C. Wells and Barry L. Stiefel, eds., *Human-Centered Built Environment Heritage Preservation: Theory and Evidence-Based Practice* (London: Routledge, 2019).
69. Hutchings, "Meeting the Shadow"; Kaufman, "Resistance to Research"; Wells and Stiefel, "Introduction" and "Conclusion" in Wells and Stiefel, *Human-Centered Built Environment*.
70. Kaufman, "Resistance to Research"; Laurajane Smith, *Archaeological Theory and the Politics of Cultural Heritage* (London: Routledge, 2004); Wells, "Bridging the Gap"; Wells and Stiefel, "Introduction."
71. Thomas F. King, *Cultural Resource Laws and Practice* (Lanham: AltaMira, 1998), 6.
72. Smith, *Archaeological Theory*; Smith, *Uses of Heritage*; Wells, "Bridging the Gap"; Wells and Stiefel, "Introduction"; Wells and Stiefel, "Conclusion."
73. Gnecco, "Development and Disciplinary Complicity"; Tom F. King, *Whitewashing the Destruction of Our Natural and Cultural Heritage* (Walnut Creek: Left Coast Press, 2009); Hutchings, *Maritime Heritage in Crisis*; Richard M. Hutchings and Joshua Dent, "Archaeology and the Late Modern State: Introduction to the Special Issue," *Archaeologies* 13 (2017), 1–25; Richard M. Hutchings and Marina La Salle, "Archaeology as Disaster Capitalism," *International Journal of Historical Archaeology*, 19, no. 4 (2015), 699–720; Smith, *Archaeological Theory*.
74. Samuel P. Hays, *Conservation and the Gospel of Efficiency: The Progressive Conservation Movement 1890–1920* (New York: Athenaeum, 1979), 2.
75. Dave Foreman, "The Arrogance of Resourcism," *Around the Campfire* 5 (2007), www.rewilding.org/pdf/campfiremarch107.pdf.
76. Ibid.
77. Ibid.
78. Gnecco, "Development and Disciplinary Complicity."
79. Hutchings, *Maritime Heritage in Crisis*.
80. Herdis Hølleland and Joar Skrede, "What's Wrong with Heritage Experts?" *International Journal of Heritage Studies* 25 (2019), 825–36.
81. Hutchings and La Salle, "Archaeology as Disaster Capitalism."
82. Hutchings, "Meeting the Shadow."
83. LouAnn Wurst, "Should Archaeology Have a Future?" *Journal of Contemporary Archaeology* 6 (2019), 168–69.

84. Hutchings, *Maritime Heritage in Crisis*, 96–98; Nancy Lee Peluso and Michael Watts, eds., *Violent Environments* (Ithaca: Cornell University Press, 2001).
85. Cristóbal Gnecco, "A World Full of Adjectives: Sustainable Archaeology and Soothing Rhetoric," *Antiquity* 93 (2019), 1664–65; Richard M. Hutchings and Marina La Salle "Sustainable Archaeology"; Richard M. Hutchings and Marina La Salle "Like a Chicken Talking to a Duck about a Kettle of Fish," *Antiquity* 93 (2019), 1672–75.
86. Pope John Paul II, "Peace with God the Creator, Peace with All of Creation. Message of His Holiness Pope John Paul II for the Celebration of the World Day of Peace, 1 January 1990", https://bit.ly/3w7ZNQ7.
87. Richard M. Hutchings and Marina La Salle, "Why Archaeologists Misrepresent their Practice: A North American Perspective," *Journal of Contemporary Archaeology* 2 (2015), S11–17, 15.
88. Beenash Jafri, "Intellectuals Outside the Academy: Conversations with Leanne Simpson, Steven Salaita, and Alexis Pauline Gumbs" *Social Justice* 44 (2017), 119–31.
89. Andrew Marzoni, "Academia Is a Cult," *Washington Post*, November 1, 2018, https://wapo.st/3pZ9u29.
90. Dan M. Kahan et al., "Cultural Cognition of Scientific Consensus," *Journal of Risk Research* 14 (2011), 147–74.
91. Hutchings, "Meeting the Shadow."
92. Smyth, *The Toxic University*, 5.
93. Anders Högberg et al., "No Future in Archaeological Heritage Management?" *World Archaeology* 49 (2017), 639–47; Hutchings and La Salle, "Sustainable Archaeology."
94. Seal, "How the University Became Neoliberal", n.p.
95. L. Simpson, quoted in Jafri, "Intellectuals Outside the Academy," 120.
96. Jenny Kidd and Joanne Sayner, "Intersections of Silence and Empathy in Heritage Practice," *International Journal of Heritage Studies* 25 (2019), 1–4.
97. Marie Battiste, "You Can't Be the Global Doctor if You're the Colonial Disease," in Peggy Tripp and Linda Muzzin, eds., *Teaching as Activism: Equity Meets Environmentalism* (Montreal: McGill-Queen's Press, 2005), 121.
98. Richard M. Hutchings and Marina La Salle, "Endgame: Contemplating Archaeology's Demise." *Revista de Arqueologia* 34 (2021), 2–22.
99. Gatto, *Weapons of Mass Instruction*.

5

Social Justice

Material Culture as a Driver of Inequality

Claire Smith, Jordan Ralph, Kellie Pollard, and Cherrie De Leiuen

In 1832, Alexis de Tocqueville argued that injustice is perpetrated by differences in material living standards that inhibit empathy between different social strata. He contended that substantial differences in material conditions prevented the French nobility from empathizing with the sufferings of peasants, and that these material inequalities also explained why slave owners in America did not empathize with the sufferings endured by slaves.[1] More recently, Richard Wilkinson and Kate Pickett[2] have demonstrated that material inequalities can have powerful psychological effects on individuals, altering how they think, feel, and behave. They argue that when the gap between rich and poor increases, so does the tendency for people to define and value themselves and others in terms of superiority and inferiority. Within this scenario, material culture can play a role in social inclusion and exclusion and, through this, in perpetrating or challenging social injustice.

This chapter takes a post-disciplinary theoretical perspective to investigate the role of material inequalities in promoting social inclusion or exclusion and, through this, in limiting or expanding efforts for social justice. It is framed around two core concepts. Following the insights of de Tocqueville[3] and Wilkinson and Pickett,[4] the first core concept is that material inequalities perpetrate social injustice through being the material embodiment of a tendency for people to conceive of themselves and others in terms of superiority and inferiority and that this leads to a greater acceptance of inequality and social injustice.

The second concept that informs this chapter draws upon a distinction made by Stefan Gosepath[5] between unjust actions and unjust circumstances and individual and collective responsibilities. Gosepath draws a moral distinction between an injustice due to unjust treatment through an individual or collective action and an injustice due to a failure to correct unjust circumstances. He argues that:

> Equality in its prescriptive usage has, of course, a close connection with morality and justice in general and distributive justice in particular ... The predicates "just" or "unjust" are only applicable when voluntary actions implying responsibility are in question. Justice is hence primarily related to individual actions. Individual persons are the primary bearer of responsibilities (ethical individualism) ... Establishing justice of circumstances (ubiquitously and simultaneously) is beyond any given individual's capacities. Hence one has to rely on collective actions. In order to meet this moral duty, a basic order guaranteeing just circumstances must be justly created. This is an essential argument of justice in favor of establishing social institutions and fundamental state structures for political communities; with the help of such institutions and structures, individuals can collectively fulfil their responsibility in the best possible manner.[6]

Consequently, the second core concept to this chapter is investigating notions of individual and collective responsibility to address inequality. As Allan Ornstein[7] points out, "in a just society, all lives have equal value, equal opportunity and equal chances for success." For archaeologists – the only scholars whose sole focus of study is material culture – the challenge is to identify the role that material culture plays in social inclusion and exclusion and, through this, in informing social justice outcomes. In this chapter, we focus on these issues primarily in terms of the regulation of space. We consider the responsibilities of individuals as well as the collective, within an overall framework that considers the role that material culture plays in perpetuating the inequalities that characterize social justice. Several questions arise:

(1) What role does material culture play in reproducing an unequal distribution of wealth, opportunities and privileges within a society?
(2) In what ways can material culture be used to create or promote a more equal distribution of wealth, opportunities, and privileges?
(3) How can the study of material culture be used to promote social justice?

What is Social Justice?

While the term "social justice" is relatively recent, the notion of social justice is not. It is inherent in all major religious doctrines, expressed in terms of the responsibility of individuals to help those who are less fortunate – the poor, the weak, the sick, the oppressed.[8] In its current form the notion of social justice is largely framed in terms of institutional responsibility. This can be traced to John Rawls's *A Theory of Justice*, originally published in 1971, which focuses on "justice as fairness" and on recognizing that differences in life expectations are due to "deep inequalities" in economic opportunities and social conditions. Rawls argues that:

> Our topic, however, is that of social justice. For us the primary subject of justice is the basic structure of society, or more exactly, the way in which the major social institutions distribute fundamental rights and duties and determine the division of advantages from social cooperation. By major institutions I understand the political constitution and the principle economic and social arrangements ... Taken together as one scheme, the major institutions define men's [sic] rights and duties and influence their life prospects, what they can expect to be and how well they can hope to do. The basic structure is the primary subject of justice because its effects are so profound and present from the start.[9]

It is possible to distinguish two overarching approaches to social justice. The first, following the work of Rawls, defines social justice in terms of a fair and equitable distribution of resources. This imbues widely accepted definitions of social justice, such as "justice in terms of the distribution of wealth, opportunities, and privileges within a society."[10] This approach foregrounds collective rather than individual action. Sian Lea,[11] for example, draws on the *Oxford Living Dictionaries*' definition to argue that social justice often "is achieved through institutions or services that work to ensure that people can equally access the benefits of social cooperation and guard against socio-economic inequality." Such conceptions of social justice are primarily in terms of the distribution of resources within and/or between societies and are associated with an imperative to engage in acts that redress this unequal distribution of resources.

A second approach to social justice – and the one that we take in this chapter – is linked to a range of human rights issues, and foregrounds the histories, experiences, and values of different groups: "Social justice refers to reconstructing society in accordance with principles of equity, recognition, and inclusion. It involves eliminating the injustice created when differences are sorted and ranked in a hierarchy that unequally confers power, social, and economic advantages, and institutional and cultural validity to social groups based on their location in that hierarchy."[12]

This approach foregrounds social justice issues that are more clearly the purview of human rights, rather than being primarily focused on resource distribution. For example, the recognition of past injustices (truth telling) is essential to social justice efforts in colonized countries, such as Canada, South Africa, and Australia.[13] In terms of Gosepath's[14] moral distinction concerning injustices due to individual or collective action this approach to social justice is more amenable to action by an individual. For example, while it is difficult for one individual to change the economic status of another, it is within the capacity of an individual to acknowledge the injustices that another person, or group of people, has suffered. The imperative here is for individual as well as collective action.

What is Social Inclusion and Social Exclusion?

Social exclusion is defined as "exclusion from the prevailing social system and its rights and privileges, typically as a result of poverty or the fact of belonging to a minority social group."[15] It is sometimes referred to as marginalization or social marginalization. The notion of social exclusion was originally constructed as a more nuanced way of thinking about poverty and disadvantage. However, one of the recurrent critiques of the terms "social inclusion" and "social exclusion" is that they are assessed in terms of social norms, and through this process reinforce those norms and by this, paradoxically, increase social exclusion (see discussion in Peace[16]). In his analysis of ambiguities in the social exclusion literature, Andrew Fischer[17] has addressed this issue by redefining social exclusion as "structural, institutional or agentive processes of repulsion or obstruction." Fischer's definition was adopted in our study as it was shaped to draw attention to processes of disadvantage (i.e., exclusionary processes), that can occur from any social position across a social hierarchy, rather than states of deprivation (i.e., the excluded) occurring at the bottom of a social hierarchy.[18] He contends that exclusion is "a pressing concern in its own right and it should not require an overlap with poverty in order to legitimize our attention."[19] The World Health Organization also defines social exclusion as a relational concept: "Exclusion consists of dynamic, multidimensional processes driven by unequal power relationships interacting across four main dimensions – economic, political, social and cultural – and at different levels including individual, household, group, community, country, and global levels. It results in a continuum of inclusion/exclusion characterized by unequal access to resources, capabilities and rights which leads to health inequalities."[20]

There are many ways in which a person may be included or excluded from the prevailing social system. In his study of European social policy texts Robin Peace[21] identified fifty-one ways that a person could be classified in a category of the "socially excluded," ranging from the "landless peasant" (someone without land) to the "homeless" (someone without a home). In addition, he identified fifteen kinds of exclusion that are named in European social policy texts. These include social marginalization, new poverty, democratic legal/political exclusion, nonmaterial disadvantage, exclusion from the "minimal acceptable way of life," cultural exclusion (including race and gender), exclusion from family and the community, exclusion from the welfare state, long-term poverty, exclusion from mainstream political and economic life, poverty, state of deprivation, detachment from work relations, economic exclusion, and exclusion from the labor market.[22]

The usual focus of social inclusion studies is participation in mainstream activities, such as employment and the enactment of rights and privileges. This works for government policy because it can be measured. However, as Steven Davey and Sarah Gordon[23] point out, definitions of social inclusion and social exclusion that focus on participation often overlook the social dynamics that underpin participation, or failure to participate. Their study of the subjective perspectives of people who experience mental distress in New Zealand identifies subtle cases that cannot be adequately assessed under current definitions. Instead, they argue for the need to focus less on measurement and more on the social constructs involved. They contend that focusing on the "terms and conditions" of social exclusion and inclusion in order to encompass invisible phenomena, such as mental illness, brings these concepts closer to underlying social processes. This approach aligns with an analysis of the psychological effects of material inequities.

The Psychological Effects of Material Inequities

An understanding of the psychological effects of material inequities is critical to the arguments presented in this paper. For this, we draw primarily on the work of Wilkinson and Pickett, who have undertaken extensive empirical studies of the levels of equality in a society and education, health, and social outcomes. In their book *The Spirit Level*,[24] they demonstrate that societies with higher levels of equality have better outcomes for all, in areas ranging from education and employment to health and life expectancy. These concepts are investigated further in their recent book *The Inner Level*,[25] which investigates the psychological effects of material inequities. Wilkinson and Pickett argue that when the gap between rich and poor increases, so does the tendency for people to define and value themselves and others in terms of superiority and inferiority. They demonstrate a direct link between pressure on social status and elevated levels of stress hormones and show that rates of anxiety and depression are closely related to inequality, which makes status critical to an individual's wellbeing.

Inequality is not the same as poverty. Inequality is concerned with relative differences, while the latter is concerned with absolute differences. Put simply, "poverty is when people don't have very much and inequality is when some people have more than others."[26] The psychological effects of material inequities were investigated in Katherine DeCelles and Michael Norton's[27] study of on-board air rage incidents. They found that:

> Physical inequality on airplanes – that is, the presence of a first class cabin – is associated with more frequent air rage incidents in economy class. Situational inequality – boarding from the front (requiring walking through the first class cabin) versus the middle of the plane – also

significantly increases the odds of air rage in both economy and first class. We show that physical design that highlights inequality can trigger antisocial behavior on airplanes. More broadly, these results point to the importance of considering the design of environments – from airplanes to office layouts to stadium seating – in understanding both the form and emergence of antisocial behavior.[28]

These behaviors can be linked to the ways the material structure of the world impacts individual self-esteem. As James[29] points out, in societies that place a high value on the acquisition of material possessions and, through this on the esteem of others, people become vulnerable to depression, anxiety, drug abuse, and mental illness. Wilkinson and Pickett[30] argue that the wider the gap between high income and low income, the greater the importance of social hierarchy within a country. As Lyndsay Grant and Glen O'Hara[31] state, where there are large differences between people's incomes, the markers of social status – whether that be buying new smart phones or cars, traveling to exotic locations or visiting the opera – become more important. Moreover, through visually communicating status and social hierarchy, material culture feeds consumerism.

Material Inequities and the Regulation of Space

The premise of this chapter is that social injustice is driven by material inequalities and that material inequalities embody a tendency for people to define and value themselves and others in terms of superiority and inferiority. Within this scenario, what is the role of material culture in inhibiting or promoting a more equal distribution of wealth, opportunities, and privileges? One of the ways in which economic inequalities are reproduced and created is through the governance of space. The regulation of space is, *ipso facto*, aimed at including or excluding groups of people from a physical area. Sometimes, this differential access to space, with its attendant material culture, is reinforced through social exclusion, in which certain groups or individuals have severely limited access to the basic services of society, such as education, health services, and transport. The material inequalities associated with the process of inclusion/exclusion emerge from, and reinforce, the construction of people in terms of superiority and inferiority and inhibit the empathy that underwrites the pursuit of social justice.

While they can be analyzed separately there are parallel trends in the regulation of public and private spaces. Increasingly, new social orders are embedded in the governance of space. In many countries, a new urban social order is characterized by privatized security systems and consumer-policed public spaces such as malls.[32] The material embodiment of this social order ranges from the keypads and door alarms of both private and public security systems to the uniforms of security staff at shopping malls.

The underpinning concept is that of inclusion/exclusion. In both public and private spaces material inequalities emerge from, and reinforce, the vast and increasing gap between rich and poor. In this section we look at three examples of the regulation of space, at the extreme ends of the income spectrum. These are gated communities, segregated communities, and the temporary living spaces of homeless people. We also consider how the provision of, and access to, public amenities impacts upon social justice issues.

Gated Communities

One of the clearest examples of the increased regulation of private space is gated communities. These are typically housing subdivisions that are surrounded by walls, fences, and other physical barriers, and are sometimes accompanied by security guard posts at their entrance (Figure 5.1). Gates and other barriers regulate access to both private residences and public spaces such as parks, pools, and other amenities.[33] Typically, they are usually rich in amenities, designed to affirm the status of residents and their inclusion in an elite "club" and to exclude those from outside the community, though there are trends toward "affordable" gated cities. Some are designed around exclusive lifestyle amenities, such as pools and golf courses, while others focus on services for a particular social group, such as the aged.[34]

In a highly influential paper, Chris Webster, Georg Glasze, and Klaus Frantz[35] charted the growth of gated communities, not only in the United States, where the concept was embraced in the early 1970s, but also

Figure 5.1 The increased regulation of private space in gated communities. The entrance to the Paradise Village Grand Marina Villas gated community at the Paradise Village Resort, Nuevo Vallarta, Nayarit, Mexico. Photo: Coolcaesar at the English language Wikipedia (CC BY-SA 3.0 (http://creativecommons.org/licenses/by-sa/3.0/)).

internationally. They considered three interpretations for the growth of gated housing. The first interpretation, *social-spatial polarization*, emphasizes a global economic restructuring that is producing "a new class structure: a transnational elite and a growing number of economically excluded" and considers that "guarded enclaves are the places in which transnational elites organize their administration, consumption, production, leisure, education, and housing."[36] However, the authors found that this interpretation did not explain vast regional differences, such as the low incidence of gated housing in the global cities of Paris and Tokyo. In the end, they found this interpretation to be "reductionist, modernist, and Anglo-American ethnocentric." The second interpretation, *changing tastes and values*, emphasizes "an accelerated global diffusion of consumer preferences by electronic media and international migration"[37] and the capacity of international trends to transform differently, according to the context of locally specific social and environmental capital and the local values that govern interpersonal and intergroup relationships.[38] The third interpretation, *institutional evolution*, can be used to explain the consumption decisions that prompt certain groups of people to choose to live in gated communities. From this viewpoint, these communities are simply one form of more general proprietary developments that include shopping malls, retirement communities, condominiums, and science parks. Taken together, these are "a new form of territorial organisation."[39]

Globally, there is great diversity in the institutional, social, economic, and cultural contexts in which gated communities are created. In Saudi Arabia, they are large master-planned enclave developments designed to house the large community of expatriate workers, and to contain expatriate culture. This is perceived as being of benefit to those inside and outside the communities.[40] In the United States, where this phenomenon emerged, gated communities have been characterized as "Fortress America."[41] Studies of these communities have highlighted a fear of crime, including statistically rare crimes such as kidnapping, and a distrust of racial and ethnic minorities.[42] The consequences of such heightened levels of fear can be tragic. Such heightened levels of fear informed the 2012 shooting of a young Black man, Trayvon Martin, by police at a gated community in Twin Lakes, Florida. In his analysis of this shooting, Edward Blakely[43] highlighted the blurring of public and private space that occurs in gated communities and the different interpretations (and associated behaviors) that "insiders" and "outsiders" bring to this space:

> On the night he was shot, Trayvon Martin walked through an area that he may have thought was public territory. George Zimmerman, on the other hand, saw "a real suspicious guy" walking into what he probably perceived as his private domain. Because the Retreat at Twin Lakes, where the girlfriend of Martin's father lives, is surrounded by gates with controlled access, the community is not quite public and not quite private space.[44]

In addition, he draws attention to a "dangerous mindset" that is shaped by a fear of crime and an "us" and "them" mentality: "Though gates reroute traffic, they do not lower crime. Instead, in these controlled spaces, an 'us vs. them' mentality festers: Leaders of gated communities need to show that there is value to their rules by creating an external enemy – those people outside the walls."[45]

In terms of the principal subject of this chapter – the material inequities associated with social injustice – it is a small step from the "us" and "them" mentality identified by Blakely[46] to defining and valuing people in terms of superiority and inferiority that Wilkinson and Pickett[47] associated with a high tolerance for social injustice. Elena Vesselinov, Matthew Cazessus, and William Falk's[48] application of Ann Tickamyer's[49] sociological framework for incorporating space into the study of inequality is pertinent here. They found that gating increases urban inequality through reproducing existing levels of social stratification and by defining a new, permanent differentiation order in the spatial organization of cities.

While the emergence of gated communities may be linked to a democratic emphasis on individualism, this is not a global explanation. The emergence of gated communities in post-socialist countries over the last twenty years, for example, has been attributed to a range of different motivations. Gabor Hegedűs[50] argues for the pursuit of higher quality "club" goods compared to public services and links this to a post-socialist transition to a market economy and a dramatic increase in social and economic differences. Using a broad definition of "gated" he identifies 270 types of gated communities in Hungary, with a total of 96,000 residents. Not all gated communities in Hungary are strictly gated or legally separated from their environment and most provide only a few exclusive services for their residents. However, they are usually inhabited by the (upper) middle class. Hegedűs found that safety plays only a minor role in the motivations of residents to move into gated communities in Hungary and that demand is based on the desire for well-arranged modern flats and pleasant landscapes. According to a study by Lajos Boros,[51] a significant portion of the population of the city of Szeged in Hungary approves the exclusion of homeless people from living spaces in the city. In Poland, Dominika Polanska[52] interprets the emergence of gated communities as a reaction to the housing conditions that prevailed under communism. Alena Rochovská and Miriam Miláčková[53] link the growth of gated communities to increased social inequalities in post-socialist cities in their study of gated communities in Bratislava, the capital of Slovakia. The constant variable is an increase in social and economic equality.

While most gated communities are inhabited by those on high incomes, there is a trend toward "affordable" gated communities. Nicholas Arese[54] has conducted an urban ethnography of Haram City, an "affordable" gated community in Egypt that hosts both aspirational middle-class homeowners and resettled poor urban residents. Arese identifies the merging of two visions of governance: top-down – "seeing like a state" master planning – and the use of interpersonal adjudication to resolve disputes over "reasonableness" in city life – "seeing like a city." Arese contends that this melding of top-down urban planning and bottom-up dispute resolution is the "consensual" outcome of a rigged game: "Evoking both colonial Egyptian vagrancy laws and neoliberal paternalist welfare, 'seeing like a city-state' governance amounts to authoritarianism that conceals itself within custom, appearing neutral so as to plan streets, codes and inner lives at once."[55]

Segregated Communities

A comparison of gated communities, most of which are located in urban areas, with segregated communities in rural areas reveals vast differences in material living standards. This social-spatial polarization limits efforts for social justice by inhibiting empathy for the lived experiences of others, impeding communication across diverse cultural groups and minimizing access to alternative models of material lives.

Alena Rochovská and Jurina Rusnáková[56] identified spatial separation as a driver of extreme poverty in their study of poverty, segregation, and social exclusion in Roma communities in Slovakia. This study compared the living conditions of Roma communities in rural and urban areas. The authors assess the articulations between exclusion and social networks and other spheres of assets, such as formal and informal labor, state benefits, and the use of material assets. They found that segregation and distance from the municipal core usually meant poor access to kindergartens and elementary schools, fewer labor opportunities, and lower levels of health care,[57] and consequently results in low education levels, unemployment, and poor health. They link a substantially higher incidence of chronic diseases within a segregated community's population to a lack of material assets and access to infrastructure, including basic facilities, such as access to water and electricity:

> Roma inhabitants who have been integrated into the majority population usually live in poor but brick-built houses with relatively large floorage and frequently with a plot and small garden appropriate for home production. On the other hand, Roma households in segregated communities generally do not own the dwellings and plots which they occupy. Numerous segregated communities lie on a doubtful land with small dwellings built from wood or other unstable materials and with no access to infrastructure.[58]

Similar problems are faced by Aboriginal people living in remote communities in Australia, as demonstrated in our research with the communities of Barunga, Werenbun, Manyallaluk, and Beswick, which are 80, 60,

100, and 120 km, respectively, from the township of Katherine, in the Northern Territory, Australia. The economic status of these communities is grossly unequal when compared to the local township, or Australia as a whole. For example, at Barunga, the self-reported unemployment rate is 27.7 percent and the median weekly income is $248 per person. This is in comparison to an unemployment rate of 3.9 percent for Katherine Township and a medium weekly income of $938 per person. For Australia as a whole, the unemployment rate is reportedly 6.9 percent and the medium weekly income $662 per person.[59] Of the population of 363 people, 328 are Aboriginal and/or Torres Strait Islander people (89.9 percent), with the remainder being English, Scottish, or European Australians who are working in the service industries of schools, the clinic, and local shops. In Katherine, Aboriginal people comprise 19 percent of the population and they are 2.8 percent of the Australian population.[60]

In 2007, the segregated status of Aboriginal communities in the Northern Territory, Australia, was reinforced with the passing of the Northern Territory National Emergency Response Act, known as "the intervention." This segregation (and an implied suspect status for each of these communities as a whole) was visually reinforced at their entrances through signs that identified them as "prescribed areas" that are subject to "no alcohol" and "no pornography." In 2022, the signs still exist, though with the wording modified to refer to "prescribed materials" rather than pornography. The two signs on either side of the entrance to Barunga community (Figure 5.2) highlight the vast difference between how the community wishes to welcome visitors and the segregated status imposed by the government sign.

The physical challenges of living in a segregated community is captured in the response by Nell Brown, *junggayi* (traditional custodian) of Bagala

Figure 5.2 Communicating hospitality versus segregated status: community and government signs on either side of the entrance to Barunga community, Northern Territory, Australia. Photos: J. Ralph and C. Smith.

clan lands that encompass these communities, to the question: what is hard about living in community?

> Housing is hard. No support. Even if we tell that officer we got leaking pipe, but sometimes that plumber don't want to come out, or they come but don't fix it good way. Sometimes it's really hard for some people when they got leaking pipe, water on the floor. Maybe blocked toilet. That plumber has got to come from Katherine (80 km away).
> We had it before when local people were trained to do that sort of thing, but not now. The change is ... maybe they not qualified people, local people. They got *mununga* (white people) from town, qualified people. They should train Aboriginal people to do that job. They did that job before. Plumber or whatever. Like builder. These days it's real hard. Nobody listening to anyone.[61]

While this social-spatial polarization unquestionably limits efforts for social justice, it can have important positive features, such as the security that comes from having family members close (in addition to protecting segregated groups from overt bias or discrimination). Consider Nell Brown's answer to the question: what is good about living in community?

> Living with families. It's our home, it's our families. We happy to stay la [at the] community. Maybe some people don't [want to], they want to go la [at the] city, move on. Some want to stay la [at the] community for the rest of their life. Some go, but they come back. It's our own country. Most of the people were born there and grew up there and got kids of their own. They call community home.[62]

The Temporary Living Spaces of the Homeless

As the gap between rich and poor continues to rise, so does the number of people who cannot afford to maintain a home. This is a global, and increasing, problem.[63] The overregulation of public spaces used by homeless people is grounded in economic and social inequalities. Moreover, the fines that are charged to homeless people can increase these inequalities through criminalizing behaviors that transgress dominant values and exacerbating the distance from mainstream services.

The Darwin City Council in the Northern Territory, Australia, has passed a series of regulations aimed at governing the spaces used by homeless people. While these regulations ostensibly target behaviors, they are also race-based as they differentially impact Aboriginal people – over 90 percent of homeless people in Darwin are Aboriginal.[64] Many of these people have come to Darwin from remote Aboriginal communities for a specific purpose such as visiting someone in hospital. A significant proportion of them end up living in the "long grass" on the fringes of the city and the suburbs. The term "long grass" refers to the tall spear grass that grows

Figure 5.3 Long grass camp, Darwin, Australia. Photo: K. Pollard.

around Darwin. It is also a term that describes public spaces in Darwin, such as beaches, parklands, and urban bushlands. The long grass is shared space although Aboriginal and non-Aboriginal people may behave differently in these spaces (Figure 5.3).[65]

Kellie Pollard's[66] study of Aboriginal camps in the long grass demonstrates cultural continuity from the initial European colonization of Darwin in 1869 to the present. The archaeological evidence of this behavior demonstrates a cultural continuum. Aboriginal camps of the initial contact period contain evidence of the use of introduced European materials, such as huts of traditional design that are fashioned from scavenged sheet metal and cloth bags, or glass tools, such as blades, manufactured from nineteenth-century glass bottle bases. Conversely, contemporary Aboriginal camps contain material culture such as discarded clothes and personal belongings (sometimes cached), literature, sleeping materials, medicinal items, and cooking paraphernalia. The majority contain evidence of freshly gathered shellfish for eating. Collected bush foods are also a dietary staple in contemporary Aboriginal camps, including mangrove worms, crabs, fish, stingray, and turtle. Non-Aboriginal people see all of these materials as rubbish and judge them accordingly. However, one can view them as innovative, creative, and distinct cultural ways of adapting to homelessness in the long grass that connects to a history extending back nearly 140 years. For example, like other Australians, people in the long grass eat take-away foods or prepare meals. Food remains show a fusion of traditional and contemporary economies. The remains of shop-bought produce, such as tins of tuna, mussels, oysters, and sardines, can be interpreted as the extension of a bush food menu in that they are affordable and accessible. While the hunting and collecting of bush foods is a continuation of cultural practices, it is more than this. People on low incomes need to use all their skills to survive in such situations. Aboriginal people are simply activating skills that they use when they are in their communities. In contrast to perceptions of other homeless people who are "sleeping rough," "long-grassers" are applying a long cultural tradition to deal with the situation in which they find themselves.

However, the Aboriginal use of long grass spaces contravenes Northern Territory laws regulating the use of space. For example, under Darwin City Council Bylaws Regulation 103, it is an offense to camp or sleep in public places and under Regulation 99, it is an offense to erect a structure or permit a structure to encroach on a public place.[67] Kellie Pollard links the use of the long grass by Aboriginal people to individual agency, cultural continuity, and a challenging of mainstream values:

> If Aboriginal people express agency by choosing to sleep in tents, cook a meal in pots and pans on a fire, eat freshly gathered shellfish or drink alcohol, such behavior challenges mainstream values about the proper use of shared public spaces. Darwin City Council By-laws make it illegal to sleep or camp in public spaces, leave food scraps in public, or drink alcohol in areas not specifically delineated for that purpose between certain hours. Aboriginal people in the long grass do all these things and risk consequences such as fines for these transgressions.[68]

The fines imposed for transgressing these bylaws increase social and economic inequalities by criminalizing relatively innocuous behaviors that are rarely a matter of choice. Unable to access financial resources, both Aboriginal and non-Aboriginal people who are homeless can be jailed for the nonpayment of fines. As their disadvantage becomes criminalized, their capacity to improve their lives decreases and their exclusion from mainstream services increases.

The Impacts of Extreme Spatial Segregation

What are the impacts of extreme spatial segregation? Spatial polarization reproduces existing levels of social stratification and defines a new, permanent differentiation order in the spatial organization of cities;[69] reinforces an "us" and "them" mentality and a fearful, potentially dangerous, mindset;[70] and inhibits the empathy that Wilkinson and Pickett[71] identify as a driver of social justice.

If empathy is a driver of social justice, extreme spatial segregation is its enemy. By creating the conditions for minimal interaction between people who are living at different ends of the income spectrum, extreme spatial segregation diminishes the opportunities for people to communicate directly or to understand the lived experience of others. For those who are in an advantaged situation, this socio-spatial segregation enforces a tendency to "blame the victim," to demonize those who face structural disadvantages from birth. This is apparent in the statement by former prime minister of Australia, Tony Abbott, that the poor living conditions of Indigenous Australians are due to "lifestyle choices."[72] This has now become a mantra for advantaged populations living in Australian states and territories with significant Indigenous populations. It allows people who are living adjacent to massive poverty to look the other way with a clear conscience and to avoid both collective and personal responsibility to redress this situation. For those who are disadvantaged, extreme spatial segregation can feed feelings of oppression and resentment, which can lead to social unrest. In addition, by locating models of other lifestyles, with attendant material culture, at an unattainable physical distance from these populations, socio-spatial segregation inhibits the pursuit of social mobility. Reinforced by material inequalities, the failure of communication transmutes into a failure of vision that inexorably increases the gap between rich and poor.

Differences in Material Living Standards

Let us return to de Tocqueville's[73] argument that differences in material living standards inhibited the capacity of slave owners in America to understand the anguish of the enslaved or the French nobility to understand the afflictions endured by peasants. If we accept Wilkinson and Pickett's[74] argument that material inequities reinforce a tendency for people to define and value themselves and others in terms of superiority and inferiority, how does this play out in the modern world?

This vast disparity is part of a wider pattern of structural violence in northern Australia. Figure 5.4 shows the disparities between the roadside facilities that are available for tourists and for Aboriginal communities immediately south of Katherine, Northern Territory, Australia. Viewed in conjunction with other material culture in the region, these differences are most cogently explained through race. They are part of a pattern of everyday racism in which the dominant society normalizes disparities and the injured group does not have sufficient power to change the situation.[75] The manifestation in this case is that the people who use the tourism rest area accept the facilities offered to them without recognizing their privilege in relation to other social groups. Meanwhile, Aboriginal people have complained about their facilities to various government entities (the police, the health service, the local council), yet nothing has changed. The continuation of these truly abject conditions reinforces Aboriginal powerlessness, part of a feedback loop that derives from, maintains, and reinforces racially based inequality. Though the effects of structural violence can be difficult to document, it can be identified through a comparative and cumulative assessment of the material worlds of different peoples.[76]

Figure 5.4 Comparison of roadside facilities available for tourists and Aboriginal communities immediately south of Katherine, Northern Territory, Australia.

Broader Trends

The core premise of this chapter is that material inequalities perpetrate social injustice through embodying a tendency for people to conceive of themselves and others in terms of superiority and inferiority and more frequently and easily accepting social injustice. As an active component of complex social systems, material culture can reinforce social justice or social injustice. While this chapter has focused on this issue primarily in terms of the regulation of space, it is important to recognize that this is just one aspect of a much wider sphere of study. What are the broader trends?

Memorials

Memorials have a capacity to simultaneously exclude and include. This is clear in the contested public spaces associated with memorials to the Confederate dead in the United States. As Gaddis (Chapter 19) points out, for people of color these memorials create "a southern sense of place that is synonymous with whiteness and exclusion." In addition, the role of material culture in social justice can extend beyond dealing with the material inequalities that reinforce processes of inclusion/exclusion and notions of individual or group superiority and inferiority. Material culture also can engender understandings of, and empathy for, the experiences of others. Through the embodiment of stories of alternative histories, memorials can contribute to the processes of truth telling and reconciliation. Memorials can celebrate social justice movements, commemorate key events, and identify new heroes. They can confront the injustices of the past and help a nation come to terms with past cultural traumas. Cultural trauma relates to the capacity to impact upon group identity, rather than that of individuals.[77] Examples of cultural trauma are massacres, attempted genocide, and prolonged political repression.

The cultural trauma imposed by of one of the most punitive communist regimes is addressed in the Postblloku (Checkpoint) installations in Tirana, the capital of Albania. Designed by former political prisoner Fatos Lobonja and artist Ardian Isufi, these installations include a number of small concrete bunkers, the supports of a mining passageway from the notorious forced-labor camp, Spaç, and a section from the Berlin Wall, taken from Potsdamer Platz (Figure 5.5). Postblloku is a monumental work that commemorates and honors political prisoners, especially those that died while incarcerated by the government.[78] This installation reflects on totalitarian rule in a country that was as isolated in its time as North Korea is today. The installation bunker is one of an estimated 750,000 bunkers built by President Enver Hoxha during the Communist era to defend the country against an invasion that never happened. As Olia Miho[79] stated, the "imaginary enemy never came and the bunkers now stand as physical manifestations of the madness of totalitarianism." Today, the general opinion is

Figure 5.5 Postblloku (Checkpoint) installations, Tirana, Albania. Photos: G. Jackson.

that the bunkers were built as a physical reminder of the government's control over the populace and to distract people from the country's economic woes:

> The dictator's strategy was to frighten people. [He was] not for the people, not for poverty. For the government people. Just for the dictator, the Communist Party, the government. Party over everything. No religion. Party. "I am the God, everything."
>
> Imagination. [The bunkers were] never used. Everywhere. Near the border, near the sea, especially near the government offices. There are tunnels underground in Tirana's main roads. One side, the home of government officials, the other side his office. Some bunkers are small, just for two people with a gun. Others are bigger. At that time, everyone was in the military for two or three years. I worked in a bunker for one year. Bunkers are connected. Inside the bunker, one small table for the gun. Some have one, some have two.
>
> When the dictator built the bunkers he wanted the people to be scared of [an] enemy. Don't [Not to] think about the economy of Albania. The enemy was America, Australia, Italy, Russia, China, Yugoslavia. Everywhere. People had no other choice. You don't like me, you can have eight years in prison. Like [the] Stasi. The dictator was like Stalin in Russia.[80]

Throughout Eastern Europe, memorials address social justice issues relating to the social and political upheaval that followed the dissolution of the Soviet Bloc. In spelt Kyiv, Ukraine, a grassroots response to government-inflicted cultural trauma is embodied in street memorials to those who died in the Revolution of Dignity in 2014 that finally ousted President Yanukovych. The street is lined with photographs of those who died, and adorned with fresh flowers. In February 2018, a "flash mob" took place on this site, which reenacted these events.[81] While the efforts of former Soviet Bloc countries to retain their freedom have received limited press coverage in the West, over the last few years, the people in these countries are using memorials and monuments to record their struggles and as a physical prompt to reflection by national and international visitors as well as the local populace. One outcome is that younger generations understand this struggle, and are better able to protect themselves from totalitarian regimes in the future. This can be clearly seen in the responses of ordinary Ukrainian citizens to the Russian invasion of their country in 2022.[82]

Justice for the Living – and the Dead

One area in which a social justice agenda has been a major driver is that of forensic archaeology. Important work in this area has been undertaken in

Lithuania by Rimantas Jankauskas,[83] who highlighted the difficulties of identifying the victims of Nazi and communist regimes. Different but equally important issues are raised in Zoe Crossland's work[84] regarding the 9,000 people who "disappeared" under the Argentinian military government that ruled from 1976 to 1983. Ongoing investigations are being undertaken by the Argentine Forensic Anthropology Team (Equipo Argentino de Antropología Forense, EAAF), a nongovernmental, not-for-profit, scientific organization that uses forensic anthropology and archaeology to investigate human rights violations in Argentina and worldwide.[85] The capacity of archaeology to redress the injustices of the past is clear, not only in terms of allowing families to conduct appropriate burial rights for the bodies of their loved ones,[86] but also because excavated evidence from mass graves and clandestine burials provides information that is critical to the international prosecution of human rights abuses and individual criminal cases.[87] As J. P. Taavitsainen[88] stated:

> In human terms, the need for archaeological and physical-anthropological exhumation is obvious and needs no explanation. The nations, ethnic groups, families, and individuals that experienced the terror have finally been given a chance to know the fate of their lost members and loved ones and their possible places of burial and to complete the process of individual and collective grieving.[89]

The Use of Objects to Reinforce Bias

Throughout the world, objects are used to reinforce bias. Well-known examples include the objects associated with the Holocaust,[90] apartheid,[91] and the American South.[92] However, even everyday objects can be a source of bias through differential access, or differential capacities to make use of those objects. This is particularly true when using the objects requires culturally specific knowledge or physical skills that are not held by everyone. In an article on disabilities, anthropologist Michael Pearson points to the role of everyday objects in framing his child, who has trisomy 21 (also known as Down syndrome), as a "deficient existence" in a system that places extraordinary and undue emphasis on material achievements:

> Abilities such as riding a bike and driving a car – by no means universal or inherent – are widely celebrated as key milestones in the United States. They tend to represent levels of personal autonomy and independence, particularly in the type of suburban setting where I grew up. Likewise, going to college, getting a job, marriage, owning real estate – these have become benchmarks of middle-class success, empty boxes to check off in the pursuit of happiness narrowly defined as becoming wealthy and shoring up class status. This is not a recipe for wellbeing, but rather an ideology of material achievement dictated by our economic system and our cultural emphasis on

individualism ... Perceptions have changed dramatically since the 1960s, when parents and self-advocates fighting against social exclusion fuelled the growth of disability rights activism. They challenged the logic of institutionalization, demanded access to health care, pushed for inclusive education, and advocated for support systems to enable increased autonomy and independent living, struggles that resulted in major policy changes, such as the Americans with Disabilities Act of 1990. Today, people with trisomy 21 exhibit a range of abilities and increasingly lead meaningful lives in their communities. While trisomy 21 contributes to diverse developmental outcomes, many people with Down syndrome ride bikes, succeed in school, get married, find jobs, and live independently.[93]

Pearson[94] argues cogently that these labels set boundaries, that they distance and subtly dehumanize and that lurking within this language is the assumption that Down syndrome represents a deficient existence. The capacity to use material resources is one component of this discrimination. Moreover, Pearson contends that the Western cultural emphasis on individual achievement (and the material embodiments of this emphasis) can be dangerously selfish, tethered to a value system that stigmatizes entire groups of people as existing beyond arbitrary boundaries of a normalcy that is, in fact, a fiction.

Indigenous Peoples

The third question posed at the beginning of this chapter, how can the study of material culture be used to promote social justice, is considered here in terms of Indigenous archaeologies. A social justice approach is apparent in the work of many archaeologists who work with Indigenous peoples. As Claire Smith and Martin Wobst[95] point out, this is indicated in a realignment of archaeological values to suit Indigenous agendas (see, for example, Chapters 6, 11, and 14 by Gnecco, Moore, and Strang). Increasingly, Indigenous people are steering archaeological practice toward the recent past, a past that is more relevant to the Indigenous present. In many colonised countries, this has led to a shifting of archaeological research priorities from the deep and distant past to the recent and immediate past, with new projects focusing on early contact sites, such as frontier conflict,[96] missions,[97] and fringe camps.[98] By using its place as a means for sculpting cultural identities, archaeology can assist communities in achieving social justice by telling the stories they want told, while upholding normal standards of academic and ethical rigor.

In South America, a social justice agenda was embraced by Gustavo Politis, Almudena Hernando, Alfredo Gonzalez-Ruibal, and Elizabeth Beserra Coelho in their ethnoarchaeological research with the Awá, a Tupi-Guarani hunter-gatherer group from the northeast of Brazil. One of the objectives of this research "was to generate useful information that would assist the Awá to improve their living conditions and to take effective political actions in order to protect them."[99] One of the strategies to achieve this was to have all project papers translated into Portuguese so that the data and proposed interpretations were available in Brazil to support the design of protection and sustainability projects.

Wider International Trends

Over the last two decades, the United Nations has advanced the notion of social justice through several initiatives. In 2007, the United Nations declared 20 February each year to be the World Day of Social Justice. This annual event aims to promote national and global economic systems based on the principles of "justice, equity, democracy, participation, transparency, accountability and inclusion." The November 2007 resolution on the World Day of Social Justice states, "social development and social justice are indispensable for the achievement and maintenance of peace and security within and among nations and ... cannot be attained in the absence of peace and security or in the absence of respect for all human rights and fundamental freedoms."[100] The underlying principle is the importance of eradicating inequality by guaranteeing fair outcomes for all through conduits such as employment and social protection, which promote more equal access to wealth, opportunities, and privileges: "Social justice is an underlying principle for peaceful and prosperous coexistence within and among nations. We uphold the principles of social justice when we promote gender equality or the rights of indigenous peoples and migrants. We advance social justice when we remove barriers that people face because of gender, age, race, ethnicity, religion, culture or disability."[101]

Discussion

The chapter investigates the role of material culture in promoting social inclusion or exclusion and, through this, in limiting or expanding efforts for social justice. We argue that material inequalities perpetrate social injustice through embodying a tendency for people to conceive of themselves and others in terms of superiority and inferiority. This reinforces notions of social inclusion or exclusion, inhibits empathy with others, and promotes a greater acceptance of social injustice. Wilkinson and Pickett see material inequalities as building blocks that are fundamental to the construction of social inclusion or exclusion in the form of class and cultural differences: "We should perhaps regard the scale of material inequalities in a society as providing the skeleton, or framework, round which class and cultural differences are formed. Over time, crude differences in wealth gradually became overlaid by differences in clothing, aesthetic taste, education, sense of self and all the other markers of class identity."[102]

At the beginning of this chapter, we posed three questions. Our analysis has focused primarily on the first question – the role of material culture in reproducing an unequal distribution of wealth, opportunities, and privileges within society. We would argue that the answer to the second question – how material culture can play a role in promoting a more equal distribution of wealth, opportunities, and privileges – is to redress the material patterning identified in our response to the first question. As others have observed, social inclusion is simply the opposite of social exclusion. The third question that we posed – how the study of material culture can be used to promote social justice – highlights the role of archaeologists as active agents in a complex and increasingly polarized world. Several of the chapters in this volume address this issue, either directly or in response to material injustices, as in Moore's analysis (Chapter 11) of the framing of Indigenous heritage as "material culture." In our chapter, we have considered this issue largely through the lens of Indigenous archaeologies. However, these are early days. Increasingly, scholars are engaging with the role of the material world in relation to social movements and the importance of the material world in limiting and expanding efforts for social justice. The regulation of space, use of objects to reinforce bias, and the use of memorials to commemorate alternative histories are but some of the processes outlined by scholars who position the material world as more than a backdrop to social change, but as inherent to political and social actions.

Most, if not all, archaeologists would agree that material inequities visually communicate and reinforce economic inequalities – that they contribute a sense of normality to entrenched economic and social disparities.[103] In this chapter, we have taken a post-disciplinary approach to extend this by addressing the psychological effects of material inequities. As an active component of complex social systems, material culture can reinforce social justice or social injustice. It can promote an acceptance of inequality through normalizing even vast economic disparities by contributing to social constructions of "us" and "them." Conversely, it has the capacity to promote equality and social justice by visually communicating social and cultural connections between people of different economic capacities and by visually challenging the norms embedded in such disparities. As we move toward a future that promises to be increasingly polarized, we anticipate the development of a post-disciplinary theoretical perspective that focuses on relationships between material inequalities, social exclusion, and social injustice. We expect that this will become an increasingly pressing concern, for archaeologists and for all who study material culture.

Acknowledgments

The ideas presented in this paper emerge from our relationships with Indigenous people. We thank all the Australian Aboriginal communities with whom we work, particularly the Barunga community and Larrakia people in the Northern Territory, and Ngadjuri people in South Australia. Photo compilations were designed by Antoinette Hennessy. Claire Smith's views on this subject were, as ever, developed in rumination with Gary Jackson.

Notes

1. Alexis de Tocqueville, *De la Démocratie en Amérique* (*Democracy in America*) (London: Saunders and Otley, 1832).
2. Richard Wilkinson and Kate Pickett, *The Inner Level: How More Equal Societies Reduce Stress, Restore Sanity and Improve Everyone's Wellbeing* (London: Penguin, 2018).
3. De Tocqueville, *De la Démocratie en Amérique*.
4. Wilkinson and Pickett, *The Inner Level*; Richard Wilkinson and Kate Pickett, *The Spirit Level: Why More Equal Societies Almost Always Do Better* (London: Penguin, 2009).
5. Stefan Gosepath, "Equality," in Edward N. Zalta, ed., *The Stanford Encyclopedia of Philosophy* (Spring 2011). https://plato.stanford.edu/archives/spr2011/entries/equality.
6. Ibid.
7. Allan C. Ornstein, "Social Justice: History, Purpose and Meaning," *Society* 54, no. 6 (2017), 541–48.
8. Ibid.
9. John Rawls, *A Theory of Justice*, rev. ed. (Cambridge: The Belnap Press of Harvard University Press, 2009), 6–7.
10. *Oxford Living Dictionaries*, "Social Exclusion." 2019. https://en.oxforddictionaries.com/definition/social_exclusion.
11. Sian Lea, "Five Ways Human Rights Help the Fight for Social Justice," *Human Rights News, Views, News & Info*. 2017. https://bit.ly/3CQcyBh.
12. Lee Anne Bell, "Theoretical Foundations for Social Justice Education," in Maurianne Adams and Lee Anne Bell with Diane J. Goodman and Kyathi Y. Joshi, eds., *Teaching for Diversity and Social Justice*, 3rd ed. (London: Routledge, 2016), 4.
13. For example, Paulette Regan, *Unsettling the Settler Within: Indian Residential Schools, Truth Telling and Reconciliation in Canada* (Vancouver: University of British Columbia Press, 2010); Heidi Grunebaum, *Memorializing the Past: Everyday Life in South Africa after the Truth and Reconciliation Commission* (New York: Routledge, 2011); Kelly J. Butler,

Australian Stories: History, Testimony, and Memory in Contemporary Culture (New York: Routledge, 2017).
14. Gosepath, "Equality."
15. *Oxford Living Dictionaries*, 2019.
16. Robin Peace, "Social Exclusion: A Concept in Need of a Definition?" *Social Policy Journal of New Zealand* 16 (2001), 17–36.
17. A. M. Fischer, *Resolving the Theoretical Ambiguities of Social Exclusion with Reference to Polarization and Conflict.* Working paper, Development Studies Institute (London: London School of Economics and Political Science, 2008), 27. www.lse.ac.uk/internationalDevelopment/pdf/WP/WP90.pdf.
18. Fischer, *Resolving the Theoretical Ambiguities of Social Exclusion*, 1.
19. Ibid, 28.
20. World Health Organization, 2019.
21. Peace, "Social Exclusion."
22. Ibid, 22.
23. Steven Davey and Sarah Gordon, "Definitions of Social Inclusion and Social Exclusion: The Invisibility of Mental Illness and the Social Conditions of Participation," *International Journal of Culture and Mental Health* 10, no. 3 (2017), 229–37.
24. Wilkinson and Pickett, *The Spirit Level*.
25. Ibid.
26. Tim Worstall, "Poverty and Inequality are Not the Same Thing So Let's Try Not to Confuse Them," *Forbes*, March 19, 2015. https://bit.ly/3mMg4XC.
27. Katherine A. DeCelles and Michael I. Norton, "Physical and Situational Inequality on Airplanes Predicts Air Rage," *Proceedings of the National Academy of Sciences (PNAS)* 113, no. 2 (2016), 5588–91.
28. Ibid.
29. Oliver James, *Affluenza: How to be Successful and Stay Sane* (London: Vermillion, 2007).
30. Wilkinson and Pickett, *The Inner Level*.
31. Lyndsay Grant and Glen O'Hara, "*The Spirit Level* by Richard Wilkinson and Kate Pickett," *Geography*, 95, no. 3 (2010), 149–53.
32. Sally E. Merry, "Spatial Governmentality and the New Urban Social Order: Controlling Gender Violence through Law," *American Anthropologist* 103, no. 1(2010), 16–29; N. Lutfun Lata, "Counter-Space: A Study of the Spatial Politics of the Urban Poor in the Megacity of Dhaka," PhD dissertation (Queensland, University of Queensland, 2018).
33. Edward J. Blakely and Mary G. Synder, *Fortress America: Gated Communities in the United States* (Washington, DC: Brookings Institution Press, 1999).
34. Xiangming Chen, Anthony M. Orum, and Krista E. Paulsen, "Introduction," *Cities: How Place and Space Shape Human Experience*, 2nd ed. (Oxford: Wiley Blackwell, 2018), 146.

35. Chris Webster, Georg Glasze, and Klaus Frantz, "Guest Editorial," *Environment and Planning B: Planning and Design* 29 (2002), 318.
36. Ibid.
37. Arjun Appadurai, *Modernity at Large: Cultural Dimensions of Globalization* (Minneapolis and London: University of Minnesota Press, 1996).
38. Webster, Glasze, and Frantz, "Guest Editorial," 319.
39. Ibid.
40. Ibid, 317.
41. Blakely and Synder, *Fortress America*; Setha Low, *Behind the Gates: Life, Security, and the Pursuit of Happiness in Fortress America* (New York: Routledge, 2004).
42. Blakely and Synder *Fortress America*; Setha Low, "The Edge and the Center: Gated Communities and the Discourse of Urban Fear," *American Anthropologist* 103, no. 1 (2001), 45–59.
43. Edward J. Blakely, "In Gated Communities, Such As Where Trayvon Martin Died, A Dangerous Mind-Set," *The Washington Post*, April 6, 2012. https://wapo.st/31khpg7.
44. Ibid.
45. Ibid.
46. Ibid.
47. Wilkinson and Pickett, *The Inner Level*.
48. Elena Vesselinov, Matthew Cazessus, and William Falk, "Gated Communities and Spatial Inequality," *Journal of Urban Affairs* 29, no. 2 (2007), 109–27.
49. Julie Tickamyer, "Space Matters! Spatial Inequality in Future Sociology," *Contemporary Sociology* 29, no. 6 (2000), 805–13.
50. Gabor Hegedűs, "Features of Gated Communities in the Most Populous Hungarian Cities," in C. Smiegel, ed., *Forum IfL: Gated and Guarded Housing in Eastern Europe* (Leipzig: Leibniz Institute for Regional Geography, 2009), 91–99.
51. L. Boros, "But Some are Less Equal: Spatial Exclusion in Szeged," in C. Kovács, ed., *From Villages to Cyberspace – Falvaktól a Kibertérig* (Szeged: University of Szeged, Department of Economic and Human Geography, 2007), 151–60.
52. Dominika V. Polanska, "The Emergence of Gated Communities in Post-Communist Urban Context: And the Reasons for Their Increasing Popularity," *Journal of Housing and the Built Environment* 25, no. 3 (2010), 295–312.
53. Alena Rochovská and Miriam Miláčková, "Gated Communities: A New Form of Residential Areas in a Post-Socialist City," *Geographia Cassoviensis* 6 (2012), 165–75.
54. Nicholas S. Arese, "Seeing Like a City-State: Behavioral Planning and Governance in Egypt's First Affordable Gated Community," *International Journal of Urban and Regional Research* 42, no. 3 (2018), 461–82.

55. Ibid.
56. Alena Rochovská and Jurina Rusnáková, "Poverty, Segregation and Social Exclusion of Roma Communities in Slovakia," *Bulletin of Geography. Socio-Economic Series* 42 (2018), 195–210.
57. See also Marcel Horňák and Alena Rochovská, "Do Mesta Čoraz Ďalej: Dopravné Vylúčenie Obyvateľov Vidieckych obcí Gemera," *Geographia Cassoviensis* 8, no. 2 (2014), 141–49.
58. Rochovská and Rusnáková, "Poverty, Segregation and Social Exclusion."
59. Australian Bureau of Statistics, "Census Quickstats. Barunga," 2016. https://bit.ly/2ZRm3Cc.
60. Ibid.
61. Nell Brown, pers. comm. January 14, 2019.
62. Ibid.
63. Alan B. Krueger, "Inequality, Too Much of a Good Thing," in D. Grusky and S. Szelénya, eds., *The Inequality Reader. Contemporary and Foundational Readings in Race, Class and Gender* (New York: Routledge, 2018), 25–35.
64. Australian Bureau of Statistics. Census Quickstats. Barunga.
65. Kellie Pollard, Archaeology in the Long Grass: Aboriginal Fringe Camps in Darwin, Northern Territory, Australia. PhD dissertation (Flinders: Flinders University, South Australia, 2019).
66. Ibid.
67. Darwin City Council, "Darwin City Council By-Laws – Reg 103 Camping or Sleeping in Public Place," 2019. https://bit.ly/3wfgEjX.
68. Pollard, Archaeology in the Long Grass.
69. Vesselinov, Cazessus and Falk, "Gated Communities."
70. Blakely, "In Gated Communities."
71. Wilkinson and Pickett, *The Inner Level*.
72. Shalaila Medhora, "Remote Communities are 'Lifestyle Choices', Says Tony Abbott," *Guardian*, March 10, 2015. https://bit.ly/31x3UtK.
73. De Tocqueville, *De la Démocratie en Amérique*.
74. Wilkinson and Pickett, *The Inner Level*.
75. Claire Smith, Jordan Ralph, and Kellie Pollard, "The Markers of Everyday Racism in Australia," *The Conversation*. 2017. https://bit.ly/3H0WJKG.
76. Mia Mochizuki and Claire Smith, *Global Social Archaeologies: Making a Difference in a World of Strangers* (London: Routledge, 2019).
77. Jeffrey Alexander, Ron Eyerman, Bernard Giesen, Neil J. Smelser, and Piotr Sztompka, *Cultural Trauma and Collective Identity* (Berkeley and Los Angeles: University of California Press, 2004), 1.
78. Klea Vyshka, "Postbllok – Checkpoint – Communist isolation," 2019. www.spottedbylocals.com/tirana/postbllok-checkpoint.
79. Olia Miho, Concrete Cathedrals: Reinterpreting, Reoccupying, and Representing the Albanian Bunkers. Electronic Thesis or Dissertation (Cincinnati: University of Cincinnati, 2012). https://etd.ohiolink.edu/.

80. Arseni Omeri, pers. comm. September 29, 2018.
81. Ukrainian Independent Information Agency (UNIAN), "Heavenly Hundred Heroes Honored in Kyiv," February 19, 2018. https://bit.ly/2ZP7y19.
82. Claire Smith and Anna Glew "How Ukraine's personal, grassroots memorials honour individual citizens who fought for their nation." The Conversation, 22 March 2022. https://theconversation.com/how-ukraines-personal-grassroots-memorials-honour-individual-citizens-who-fought-for-their-nation-178899.
83. Rimantas Jankauskas, "Forensic Anthropology and Mortuary Archaeology in Lithuania," *Anthropologischer Anzeiger* 67, no. 4 (2009), 391–405.
84. For example Zoe Crossland, "Forensic Archaeology and the Disappeared in Argentina," *Archaeological Dialogues* 7, no. 2 (2000), 146–59; Zoe Crossland, "Of Clues and Signs: The Dead Body and Its Evidential Traces," *American Anthropologist* 111, no. 1 (2009), 69–80.
85. Equipo Argentino De Antropología Forense (EAAF), "Argentine Forensic Anthropology Team," 2017. www.eaaf.org.
86. Crossland, "Of Clues and Signs."
87. See Zoe Crossland, "Evidential Regimes of Forensic Archaeology," *Annual Review of Anthropology* 42 (2013), 121–37.
88. Jussi-Pekka Taavitsainen, "Burial Archaeology and the Soviet Era," in Claire Smith, ed., *Encyclopedia of Global Archaeology* (New York: Springer, 2014), 1048.
89. Ibid.
90. Emily Stiles, Narrative, Object, Witness: The Story of the Holocaust as Told by the Imperial War Museum, London. PhD dissertation (University of Winchester, 2016).
91. Heidi Grunebaum, *Memorializing the Past: Everyday Life in South Africa After the Truth and Reconciliation Commission* (New York: Routledge, 2011).
92. David Sears, "Symbolic Racism," in Phyllis A. Katz and Dalmas A. Taylor, eds., *Eliminating Racism*, Perspectives in Social Psychology Series (Boston: Springer, 1988), 53–84.
93. Thomas Pearson, "A Daughter's Disability and a Father's Awakening," *Sapiens*, 2019. www.sapiens.org/culture/down-syndrome-baby/.
94. Ibid.
95. Claire Smith and H. Martin Wobst, "The Next Step: An Archaeology for Social Justice," in Claire Smith and H. Martin Wobst, eds., *Indigenous Archaeologies: Decolonising Theory and Practice* (London: Routledge, 2005,) 369–71.
96. Heather Burke, Bryce Barker, Noelene Cole, Lynley A. Wallis, Elizabeth Hatte, Iain Davidson, and Kelsey Lowe, "The Queensland Native Police and Strategies of Recruitment on the Queensland Frontier, 1849–1901," *Journal of Australian Studies* 42, no. 3 (2018), 297–313; Kelsey Lowe, Noelene Cole, Heather Burke, Lynley A. Wallis, Bryce Barker,

and Elizabeth Hatte, "The Archaeological Signature of 'Ant Bed' Mound Floors in the Northern Tropics of Australia: Case Study on the Lower Laura (Boralga) Native Mounted Police Camp, Cape York Peninsula," *Journal of Archaeological Science: Reports* 19 (2018), 686–700; Pam Smith, "Frontier Conflict: Ways of Remembering Contested Landscapes," *Journal of Australian Studies* 31, no. 91 (2007), 9–23.

97. Jane Lydon, *Fantastic Dreaming: The Archaeology of an Aboriginal Mission* (Walnut Creek: AltaMira Press, 2009); Michael Morrison, Darlene McNaughton, and Claire Keating, "'Their God Is Their Belly': Moravian missionaries at the Weipa Mission (1898–1932), Cape York Peninsula," *Archaeology in Oceania* 50, no. 2 (2015), 85–104.

98. Wendy Beck and Margaret Somerville, "Conversations between Disciplines: Historical Archaeology and Oral History at Yarrawarra," *World Archaeology* 37, no. 3 (2007), 468–83.

99. Gustavo Politis, "Reflections on Contemporary Ethnoarchaeology," *Pyrenae* 46 (2014), 52.

100. United Nations, "Resolution adopted by the General Assembly on 26 November 2007. 62/10. World Day of Social Justice," 2007. http://undocs.org/A/RES/62/10.

101. United Nations, "World Day of Social Justice," 20 February 2019. www.un.org/en/events/socialjusticeday.

102. Wilkinson and Pickett, *The Spirit Level*, 28.

103. See Mark P. Leone, "Interpreting Ideology in Historical Archaeology: The William Paca Garden in Annapolis, Maryland," in Daniel Miller and Christopher Tilley, eds., *Ideology, Power and Prehistory* (Cambridge: Cambridge University Press, 1984), 25–36; Mark P. Leone, Parker Potter, and Paul Shackel, "Toward a Critical Archaeology," *Current Anthropology* 28, no. 3 (1987), 283–302; Heather D. Burke, *Meaning and Ideology in Historical Archaeology* (New York: Springer, 1999); Anne Pyburn, "Archaeology as Activism," in H. Silverman and D. Fairchild Ruggles, eds., *Cultural Heritage and Human Rights* (New York: Springer, 2007), 172–83; Jordan Ralph and Claire Smith, "'We've Got Better Things to do Than Worry about Whitefella Politics': Contemporary Indigenous Graffiti and Recent Government Interventions in Jawoyn Country," *Australian Archaeology* 78 (2014), 75–83.

6

Engagement and the Politics of Authority

Cristóbal Gnecco

The archaeological reflection on issues of materiality and power has been fruitful (as Strang demonstrates in Chapter 14), especially as it abandoned a rigid approach to engage an active perspective, in which both humans and things have agency; yet, it has been basically restricted to the past, as if it were a domain on its own whose relevance for the present is only marginal. However, if thinking about the past means thinking about today and, especially, about a reassembled future, we can see politics and social life from an entirely different angle (McAtackney pursues this in Chapter 8). In this sense, this chapter does not deal with authority and how people engage it in the past (in the way the topic has been dealt with by archaeologists) but in the present – although in relation to the past, that is, how power, hierarchies, and asymmetries circulate and are engaged by different collectives/actors in the processes of elevating specific materialities to the condition of heritage. I will center my attention on the weakest part of the heritage equation, the local communities affected by patrimonial processes, the *others* of heritage, those others routinely left out of the picture except when their presence is functionalized as suppliers of authenticity and exoticism. This chapter is about the present, then; it is about how power pervades the dealings with the temporal referent (post) modernity calls "the past" in a specific instance of its operation, that of heritage.

Power, present, materiality, authority, past, heritage, engagement, violence, dispossession. Those are the building blocks of the arguments I put forth. I deploy them in several locations across South America, relating them to two iconic heritage objects-signs: The Jesuit missions in Guarani territory and the Qhapaq Ñan, the Andean road system. This is not mere chance. In most heritage acts in the Global South a generalized process of alterization occurs; local inhabitants are converted into the archetypal Other of national times: the primitive, the premodern, the savage. This (re)conversion is fascinating and curious because it recycles the ancient roles of the national theater in the post-national scene, that the former somehow authorizes. This alterization is not minor: not only does it provide a sense of authenticity to heritage assets, sold as emblems of the really historical; it also provides the heritage consumer with the exoticism (meals, crafts, dances, healings) eagerly sought. But there is more. The alter thus constructed underpins, once again, the direction and meaning of the dominant time, still modern despite so much discussion to the contrary. (If not, then, why does the evolutionary model continue to dominate basic temporal considerations that speak of progress, novelty, improvement, changes, destinies?). The old new alter attached to heritage – an integral part, though tangential, of that baptized as "intangible heritage" two decades ago – continues to inhabit a different, non-modern time, prior to any transformation. It inhabits an arrested, cold time, a time that does not move, but that has to be constantly re-created. Therefore, if not for another reason, the alter created by the heritage act is preterized – with the invaluable help of archaeological narratives that speak of disappearance, replacement, migration, catastrophe, in short of times gone that are also, of course, other times, with all the preterize burden of the denial of coevalness that one can imagine. They are, however, also times of Others, in which case we are already talking about excessive appropriation and dispossession.

To contextualize: in the seventeenth century the Jesuits created thirty missions in the territory of the Guarani in what is now southwestern Brazil, southeastern Paraguay, and northeastern Argentina, a region known in colonial times as the "Jesuit Province of Paraguay" or "Paracuaria." The missions constituted a relatively autonomous project of civilization that had a strong and lasting influence on the life of the Guarani; they were also a referent of how the policy of nucleation and conversion promoted by Portugal and Spain should (or should not) be conducted. For various political reasons the missions were dismantled over a period of half a century and they ceased to exist by the first decades of the nineteenth century, which resulted in the dispersion and fragmentation of the Guarani that had been nucleated. The constructions of the missions, especially their imposing stone churches and other buildings, soon turned into ruins, some of which became a part of the daily landscape of the new settlers of the region, mostly European immigrants. Yet, the civilizational imprint of the missions survived unevenly in the national histories of the three countries that were created in the region after 1810. From a different perspective, that is, from the interpretation provided by quite a different ontology, the Jesuits and the missions also have a place in the memory of contemporary Guarani populations. In 1984 and 1993 the best-preserved ruins were elevated to the status of "world heritage" by UNESCO, prompting a re-signification of their meaning (this time uttered from a universal, humanistic discourse) and a collision of varied interests.

The Qhapaq Ñan, the miles-long trails that connected many locations in South America, mainly in the Andes and the Pacific coast, had an ancient pre-Hispanic origin but were converted into an efficient and well-maintained road network by the Incas. The network collapsed after the Spanish conquest and now is just a disconnected patchwork of trail stretches, some of which still serve the original function of getting people from place to place. In 2014, some surviving stretches of the Qhapaq Ñan were admitted into UNESCO's World Heritage List due to the bid made by the six countries where the network once stood (Colombia, Ecuador, Peru, Bolivia, Argentina, and Chile). Although the consecration of the Qhapaq Ñan as world heritage was unanimously celebrated by national and regional governments, the press,[1] and academia, recent years have witnessed how the heritage meaning that was accorded to it is beginning to be contested. In sum, these two heritage objects-signs are privileged theaters to describe issues of engagement and authority, of violence and hierarchies, of dispossession and exclusion.

Take One: A Film within a Film

I watch a group of Guarani youngsters watching *The Mission*, a 1986 film directed by Roland Joffé, which portrayed the so-called Guarani wars of the 1750s. They were not actually wars, but vicious massacres inflicted on Guarani resisting the order to vacate the mission in which they had been living in what had become Brazilian territory. I watch them because they have been filmed watching the film in the documentary *Tava, a casa de pedra*,[2] made by Guarani filmmakers about the significance of the missions and their ruins for current Guarani populations. A film within a film, then, and a voyeur watching two films unfolding, intertwining, telling how history is written by those who win, how it is contested by those who lost; telling how the very collectives marginalized and silenced by the authority of "heritage" engage with it, yet from a different ontology that questions its very meaning (that of "heritage") and, notably, its utter naturalization.

Seven of the mission ruins were declared world heritage a few years ago (and that universal and humanistic meaning extends to the others), but before that they were regional and national patrimonies (Figure 6.1). What has been patrimonialized in/of the missions? The general idea of civilization, to be sure, not the legacy of the societies subdued by that idea. The civilization ideal was genocidal, violent, and imposed on the indigenes because it was solidly based on the belief that it was better, superior, more advanced; it was based, that is, on the then undiscussed assumption that there were natural hierarchies articulated by racial and religious criteria. That is why in the relationship between the Jesuits and the Guarani what has counted for the most part is the place of the former, not that of the

Figure 6.1 The ruins of the church of São Miguel Arcanjo, Brazil. Photo: Cristóbal Gnecco, 2014.

latter. What has mattered most is the modernity that the Jesuits still represent. In that story (save in some academic fields) the Guarani are mute, the weakest link in the missions' narrative chain. Paraguay is a good example because after the War of the Triple Alliance (1864–70) the process was exacerbated during nation building. The place of the Jesuits (and their missions) in the nation was bitterly discussed, but not that of the Indians, who had (and have) no place in the national scene. Has that changed with the recent heritage processes to which the ruins of the missions have been subjected? Not so much, except in Brazil (for the reasons I will describe).

The presence of the Guarani in the missionary story, that story that lingers until today through patrimonialization, is obscure, opaque, and unequal, and demands to ask: why patrimonialize the ruins of the missions in the first place, such objects-signs of a project that, in any case and from wherever you look at it (with a little or a lot of empathy, with a little or a lot of contempt), was part of the conquest of America, one of the biggest genocidal enterprises in history? Why patrimonialize precisely those ruins, eloquent witnesses of the submission of the Guarani to civilization, witnesses of their reduction? Because they are part of a *good genocide*, let us say, if something so abominable can be conceived? But is that not what humanism has always done, to justify colonialism and its violence if it leads to civilization, to get these poor Indians out of their primitive, primordial condition? So yes, an object-sign that is a part of a genocidal enterprise can be patrimonialized. Moreover, it *must* be patrimonialized. And it is neither an accident nor a coincidence that this violent and unconsented act occurs through a fully androcentric-laden term: the tutelage a father exercises over his submissive children. I already noted that alterization widely occurs in heritage processes; the Other thus created is taken as a non-imputable, unconscious, feminine, infantile being.

Although the national rhetoric of Argentina, Brazil, and Paraguay is different, the supposed civilizing deed of the Jesuits in indigenous territory appears in them all as an important example, either as an idealized and bucolic model of coexistence, purely utopian, or as a peaceful way of inserting the Indians into modernity (a civilized way of civilizing, that is) getting around that it happened through religious violence. Although heritage erases the original meaning, say, of what it patrimonializes and imposes new meanings, is not in this case the UNESCO heritage narrative as humanistic as the act of civilization of the Jesuits? What brings these two humanisms together – one of the sixteenth century with another of the twenty-first century – that makes clear that humanism is the same totemic (and violent) animal in a new skin? Would not this come to resignify the act of civilization and to renew its validity, now as development (through heritage)? Since the ruins were elevated to world heritage, at the same time as the creation of the Common Market of the Southern Cone, the search for a common history and, above all, for common commodities has been notorious. The missions have not escaped that search: their utopian value became an exchange value to which development clings forcefully.

Having asked these basic questions about the heritage meaning of the missions, their present and past protagonists are exposed: the Guarani, the Jesuits, the *encomenderos*, the settlers, the colonial and republican officials, the historians and the anthropologists, the heritage agents. They intersect, these protagonists, and erase the boundaries between past and present. The missions, and their ruins, are central icons in the imaginary of the three nation-states in which they now stand because they helped to build what Rita Segato[3] called "national formations of otherness," historical regimes that created the others of the nation and, now, of the post-nation. To ask about the missions from the vantage point of those formations is to ask about the place of their others, the place of the Guarani, and to find that theirs is a rather opaque place filled in uneven ways in Argentina, Brazil, and Paraguay during the last two centuries.

The first thing that calls my attention when I ask about the place of the Guarani in the missions is the lack of consensus, not so much historical but contemporary. The canonical, and dominant, narrative about the missions was conservative, unidirectional, and static: it was an apology for what the Jesuits considered their civilizing deeds, without recognizing the indigenes' agency or even that of history. But the historiography on the Guarani of the missions has changed, and it now investigates their active role moving away from the idea of their essential passivity that accorded, until recently, the central role of the story to the Jesuits.[4] There, in that question about the agency of the Guarani in the missions, a certain new consensus begins to form. The same thing does not happen when the question moves from the ghostly character of the missionary Guarani to the utter concretion of the contemporary Guarani; in other words, when one asks about the relationship between today's Guarani, especially the Mbyá, and the Guarani of the missions, which is tantamount to asking, of course, about the relationship between the current Guarani and the missions, or their ruins. There dissent reigns, as if the real bodies (individual and, above all, social) challenge the possibility of establishing unequivocal answers. Dissension reigns because the place of the current Guarani in the missionary story is no longer just an academic issue, as in the case of historiography (still dominated by disciplinary preoccupations), but rather a political one, a matter of engagement and authority, then. This dissent can be seen by comparing the narratives about the missions and their others in the three countries.

In Brazil, the story of the missions had the Jesuits as protagonists until the 1980s, when a dramatic change resulted in transference to the Guarani due, mostly, to academic militancy, especially around the demarcation of indigenous lands. As a result, the relationship of the Mbyá with the Guarani of the missions is not a matter of discussion any longer but of documentation (in ethnographies, workshops, documentaries). Is this a new political flag, a pure conjuncture, a way of ensuring continuity in time and space and countering the version that delegitimizes the claims of the Mbyá (mostly territorial), which points out that they are newcomers? In the juridical dispute on land issues, temporal and territorial continuity matters much and being heirs of the Guarani of the missions provides rhetorical fuel to the Mbyá and their academic supporters. This does not happen in Argentina and Paraguay, where the approach to the issue is academic, not political. There, not coincidentally, regulations for the demarcation of indigenous lands are either nonexistent or not widely applied. In those two countries there is little doubt: the current Guarani are not thoroughly related to the Guarani of the missions and, therefore, their relationship with the ruins (and the memories they trigger) is rather ethereal. To put it another way: while in Brazil the issue is already clearly discursive in the other two countries it remains substantive. In Brazil it abandoned the positivistic limits of disciplinary research and the modern criteria of reality; in Argentina and Paraguay such an abandonment (such an escape) is still far from happening.

Anthropologists in Argentina and Paraguay claim not to know expressions of the Mbyá about the missions or their ruins, implying that they are not interested in them. But, if so, should not that disinterest or distance be the reason for an investigation? It would not seem possible to affirm that the Mbyá are unrelated to the Guarani of the missions, that they are not their heirs, except from the claims of truth of the modern disciplines and their monological channel of communication. In this, as in so many other things, disciplinary truths are ideologically veiled: the missionary work is celebrated (even if the emphasis falls on the Jesuits, making the Guarani inferior, poor infantile souls). At the same time, a place is denied to the contemporary Guarani, who are said to have "arrived" in the mission area not long ago (even after the Eastern Europeans who populated the region since the late nineteenth century and who have created a "missionary culture") and whose life elapses between poverty and welfare.

The differences between the three countries on this issue are also due to different and, to a certain extent, closed academic traditions. They do not know each other well, despite a certain fluidity and exchange. If the missions were a question of frontiers, not only geographic but also cultural, their academic research is another form of frontier, not because such research is positioned in the frontier – in the postcolonial sense of Anzaldúa[5] – but because it establishes rigid and quite insurmountable borders: the historians here, the anthropologists there; the Brazilians here, the Paraguayans there; as before, the Indians of the missions here, the forest Indians there. Borders between themes and also between academic traditions.

Seen from the discursive corner, not from the disciplinary one, the sharp separation between the Guarani of the missions and the contemporary Guarani has catastrophist overtones and it is a part of the reproduction of the civilized/savage dichotomy; a part of the enlightened meaning of heritage (the missionary Indians *in* the ruins, the contemporary Indians *outside* them, selling handicrafts: an insulting, shameful contrast, worthy of the heritage act, as disinterested from the fate of the new Indians as it is concerned about the fate of the old Indians); a part of academic traditions (the Indians of the missions with the historians and the current Indians with the anthropologists, without communicating vessels, each of them preserving their parcel of knowledge and, therefore, their parcel of otherness); a part, alas, of the denial of coevalness.[6] If the subject is seen from the discursive corner, then, other things begin to emerge, even in terms of ontological divergences. In the memory of the Mbyá the missionary story, but not its modern patrimonial conversion, is a firm historical source, quite relevant for their struggle for territory and self-determination.

There is a mythical place called Tava Miri of great cultural importance because it is "recognized as a work left by the ancestors of the current Mbyá-Guarani ... Tava Miri is a source of knowledge of the Mbyá because it marks their union with the gods."[7] Tava Miri keeps "a kind of 'petrified message' left to his descendants about the fact that life is made by successive challenges, that it is worthwhile to fight against death and decomposition knowing that victory is almost impossible but motivated by the idea that there is an immortality and a fullness of existence here and beyond this world."⁸ This centrality of Tava Miri is purely utopian, both as a no-place and as a horizon of possibility. What must be clear, however, is that the Mbyá do not engage with the authority of the heritage discourse from a different perspective, as if it were just an epistemological issue; they engage the ontological peculiarity of their historical narrative differently than the conception and mobilization of "heritage." Their bearing on heritage, which has not been forcefully articulated yet, is thus ontological.

The missions were utopian in a broad sense, that is, they were located nowhere – they were neither in a Western country nor in the colony, since they were worlds apart in all respects, an unanchored idea – and were, therefore, perfect mirrors of what was possible. But this utopia, as seen from Western eyes, was surgically separated from the ontology of modernity, from the relations of power it established, as if it had not been a fundamental beachhead in modernity's advance over other ontological frontiers. Maybe because of this brutal separation, the utopia of the missions eventually disappeared in thin air. The missions suffered a similar fate. The Jesuits were expelled from Portugal and Spain and their colonies and their work of conversion came to a halt, and what little remained of their buildings soon turned into ruins. Utopia was devoured by the jungle, like the ruins. It returned, let us say, to its place in nature, to the world of the primitive. But recently, after more than two centuries of twilight, utopia once again showed its face and, wonderful paradox, it did it in the hands of the contemporary Guarani, those subjects on the margins (in every sense: on the margins of history, the countryside, cities). Nothing can hide, however, that the missions were the ruin of the Guarani. Their ruins, then, are places of consolidation of the indigenous ruin, of its exaltation (tourist, national, supranational) as a project of civilization. The meaning of a ruin is imposed (because it glorifies, exalts, markets) over the meaning of another. What lingers is the imprint of the ruin as ruin: a vestige of what there was, but an unmistakable emblem of what it remains.

Take Two: Trout, Poverty, Development

Raúl Tenezaca and I climb the Culebrillas ascent, an Ecuadorian stretch of the Qhapaq Ñan. Raul goes forward, jumping nimbly on the stones. I walk behind him, tired, saving the little air of these heights. I walk through centuries of history, passing from one time to another on this road that Atahualpa and Pizarro and Bolívar walked before me and the millions of faces that history, so selective, does not remember. I walk, or so I would like to think, searching for the connection with the trails that the Incas and their ancestors made. I walk through a time that resists, does not surrender, is rebellious and difficult to pierce. I, who live thousands of miles away and come here to walk and to describe, of course, to leave my mark on this text. Raúl lives below, in a community near Achupallas. He lives on little, like almost everyone around here. Raúl has a small plot of land where he grows cereals and Andean tubers. He is building pools for trout and is thinking of a lodging for the tourists that are to come when the promise of progress that the Qhapaq Ñan conveys materializes in a few backpackers willing to make the long (and beautiful) hike to Ingapirca. Suddenly the trail he has walked all his life is more than the winding and meandering line that takes him to so many parts. The trail is no longer the trail. It now is the Qhapac Ñan. The disinherited see in it a solid promise. It now offers development, an elusive healing, although its cost can be appallingly high. Yet, it is undeniable that a marketable heritage is alluring, especially (as so often happens) when the peoples living near or at heritage site(s) or landscapes are destitute.

In situations in which deprived peoples eagerly engage heritage and the market, the relationship is uneven, an iteration of colonial times. Further, patrimonalizing the trail is violent. The politics of naming, in which it partakes, is imbricated in the politics of accumulation. Naming places as heritage is caught up in the (re)production of broader processes of fetishization that seek to obliterate modern relationships of dispossession. In Pomata, on the southern shore of Lake Titicaca, a few steps from the border of Peru with Bolivia, I asked about the Inca trail. No one knew anything. I asked about the Qhapaq Ñan. Much less. I went to the police station. They had no idea. I went to the municipality, where a man responsible for the institutional image told me that he had heard about the matter but that he did not know anything precise. Then he remembered that another official might know better. He called him. He knew better. The Inca trail, the portentous Qhapaq Ñan of UNESCO, to which he took me, is a few blocks from where we were. It is the modest trail that links Pomata with Sisipampa, on the other side of the hill, perhaps from times so old that they are no longer remembered. It is the trail used by the locals to go from one place to another (Figure 6.2). The trail, simply. Nothing about the Incas or the Qhapaq Ñan, a "nothing" that exposes the hierarchy of naming.

The politics of naming is a politics of possession (and dispossession, of course), broad and comprehensive. The trail now belongs to someone, no matter that it is as abstract as the nation or humanity. It belongs to someone because it now is a "road system" with a purpose and a destination: heritage. Naming along with owning. Restrictions on the meaning and the use of the trail: this is what the communities were informed in the "consultation" protocols that were implemented before its nomination (and that ended with papers full of agreeing signatures, obtained who knows how) and that are still being implemented, perhaps even more vociferously, now that the trail is a management object. The deleterious aspects of naming cannot be more evident than in the sense of ownership and

Figure 6.2 Locals making their way from Sisipampa to Pomata, southern shore of Lake Titicaca, Peru. Photo: Cristóbal Gnecco, 2015.

verticality of patrimonialization. To name the trail with a Quechua name does not attenuate the dispossession; it underlines it. It exacerbates the violence of naming and the material aspects of marginalization through accumulation by dispossession that, for David Harvey, includes the "commodification and privatization of land and the forceful expulsion of peasant populations ... conversion of various forms of property rights (common, collective, state, etc) into exclusive private property rights ... suppression of rights to the commons; commodification of labor power and the suppression of alternative (indigenous) forms of production and consumption."[9] The state, with its monopoly on violence and on definitions of legality, plays a crucial role in supporting and promoting these processes.

Patrimonializing the road is not as innocent as it seems or as it is widely proclaimed. Beyond the calls to identity, integration, and development lies an ontological condition: the trail as a heritage asset (i.e., as the Qhapaq Ñan) is an advance of the (post)modern occupation of territories and subjectivities that had not previously been so aggressively intervened. This ontological condition is evident in the articulation of the patrimonial process with developmental discourses, from the obvious one disseminated by heritage agents, tourism, to others much less obvious, such as extractive industry and its concomitant expansion of infrastructure.[10]

This hierarchy of obviousness suggests that tourism is a decoy that distracts analytical and political attention from where it can matter more: in uncovering deeper and harmful links between heritage and development. Not that the consequences of tourism are unimportant, of course, for they have proved to cause lasting damages to fragile community solidarities and ancient relationships; it is that tourism is much less damaging (and with impacts that can be somehow limited, if not even curtailed) than the wider ontological advance that heritage supports and legitimizes. A basic component of that advance is naturalizing the inevitability of development, of extractive industry, of their violation of natural and human rights. In line with such an advance, the heritage industry is also extractive: it does not extract traditional commodities but new ones, "heritage values," from their places of origin in networks of relationships whose importance is not only historical. It uproots "heritage" from origins, destinies, differences, and struggles of power: its historicity is thus veiled by its reification. It transforms places of memory in archaeological sites and, later, heritage sites.[11] By uprooting "heritage values" from their traditional networks of relationships, the heritage industry arranges them for their possession by the ontology of (post)modernity. Traditional semiotic dimensions are torn from social totalities, not only rhetorically but also as lived experiences. Heritage extracting resonates with a very strong echo other extractive industries and indicates their simultaneous concurrence in the scenario of development; it also points to its purely industrial nature. By extracting "heritage values" in this way, it singularizes and isolates them – giving them a new, (post)modern meaning – allowing the heritage operation.

If tourism is the lesser evil, say, the greatest evil is that the local inhabitants enter, fully, into an ontology that they had mostly seen from afar. The heritage act over the ancient Andean trails creates them as *others* and locates them out of this time, denying them coevalness; after all, they must provide the temporal authenticity that tourism demands, that is, they have to belong to a different time, the time when the trail was a trail and not a ruin, when it was the trail and not the Qhapaq Ñan. They are the inheritors not heirs of the trail, the ethnic salt that spices the patrimonial dish that tourists eat with avidity and for which they pay sometimes outrageous prices. Now their culture is a set of commodities for sale, weighed and evaluated for their consumption potential by others coming from outside only for the moment.

In the industrial transformation of the trails into the glamorous Qhapaq Ñan nostalgia plays an important role. It is a nostalgia for an earlier era (that of the Incas and their ancestors, with its powerful resonance of the authentic Andean) that has not yet lost its utopian halo, although it is diminished and has been subjected to the commodity form. That is the utopian halo that transpires the Qhapaq Ñan (and, well, its ghostly totality): truncated worlds, worlds that could have been and were not, bucolic alternatives (but also a constructed bucolic, a central issue for the tourism industry) vis-à-vis the depredations of modernity. Bucolicizing, of course, because the idealization of such a lost arcadia, such a paradise located in the Andean mountains as much as in the mist of the romantic dream, contrasts positively with the aporia of civilization. This nostalgia has undoubtedly a political potential, although no contemporary agenda claims it fully. Yet, the nostalgia described by Fredric Jameson as a basic component of (post)modernity is incompatible with "a genuine historicity" and is limited to using the past as a histrionic component of a temporal choreography restricted to the experience of the here and now.[12]

This is the nostalgia that dominates the experience of the Qhapaq Ñan and does not put the past, as Jameson would have it,[13] beyond an "aesthetic retrieval" but, rather, within the exclusive limits of such a retrieval, if by that I mean a retrieval that deliberately eludes the political as transformation. Because the power of patrimonializing is its ability to neutralize (if not to eliminate) the *real* historical meanings of the goods turned into heritage while at the same time delivering them for consumption as cultural assets in a space emptied of historicity, and I put real in italics not for alluding to the modern naturalization of the real but to its meaning prior to the patrimonial action. That is why patrimonializing can take something like the trail, which belonged to a world subjected and trampled by the Spanish conquest, but still feared as a possible horizon of insubordination, and place it in an aseptic and harmless space which tourists attend with an unprepared and innocent manner as if they were going to a Sunday party. This double operation of patrimonializing – to neutralize a certain sense of the political and to deliver to the cultural market – has been very successful worldwide. This emptying of historicity, this putting the past beyond any non-modern political enterprise, makes the heritage industry a superb ally of government policies in the era of multicultural neoliberalism and, above all, a fundamental spearhead in the (post)modern ontological crusade.

Who has the interpretive control of the Qhapaq Ñan? Anyone could say that the issue is relative because interpretations are idiosyncratic. In that sense no one could control them. But power has long hands and distinguishes between good and bad interpretations, and that distinction has been increasingly important and with more lasting consequences alongside a very clear desire of the (post)modern for filling the spaces that it had left relatively untouched, spaces located within frontiers with fragile biomes, vulnerable populations, and desired commodities, a condition of which "heritage values" partake and which, at the same time, it serves. However, although patrimonializing the trail is widely promoted and sponsored, this does not mean that it has not been challenged; several communities in Argentina and Peru have opposed it with arguments springing from territorial protection and uttered from a cultural language which, as in the case of the missions, translate into ontological differences. As a special UN rapporteur on indigenous peoples noted more generally:

> In reality, indigenous peoples do not see their heritage at all as property – that is, goods owned by an owner and used for economic gain – but in terms of individual and collective responsibility. The possession of a song, a story or medical knowledge brings with it certain responsibilities to respect human beings, animals, plants and places with which the story, song or medicine are linked, and involves maintaining a reciprocal relationship with them. For indigenous peoples, heritage is more a set of relationships than a set of economic rights. The "object" is completely meaningless without a relationship, whether it be a physical object, for example a sacred place or a ceremonial instrument, or intangible, such as a song or a story. To sell it is essentially to end the relationship.[14]

That is the point, it seems to me, the basic element in the conversion of the trail into the Qhapaq Ñan: to sell it as a heritage of humanity it is necessary to put an end to the relationships in which it participated. To sell it in the tourist market and as an important element of (post)modern ontological sovereignty the other voices that name it must be silenced.

In doing so, the authority of the heritage discourse produces a legitimized locus where those who believe and accept that discourse dwell, and which disqualifies the place of refractory peoples. The issue is frankly Manichaean: there are good fellows, those who know what heritage is and how to take care of it, those who act as its heirs, as if it were a question of property and not of meaning; those who dress in the role of their guardians, self-appointed experts who treat it as a helpless child (who must be protected and guarded), who strip it of its historical condition. And there are the bad fellows, those who do not know what it is, those who have not yet heard that the ancient Andean trail is now the Qhapaq Ñan, a world heritage asset. The good fellows are on the side of disciplinary knowledge and laws, the neat tangle of regulations that separate heritage from life and that determine what a heritage asset is, where to find it, when to set it up, how to take care of it. The bad fellows are on the side of the illegal, on the side of ignorance. They are on the outskirts of modernity. The good ones know that the trail that has become heritage means identity, progress, development; that opposing it would be as ignorant as it is foolish. The bad ones oscillate between a sustained skepticism or an aggressive radicalism and an anxious complacency, on the way to becoming good. Paraphrasing Hall, when heritage knowledge is exercised, in practice those who are "known" in a particular way are subject (subjected) to it, and those who produce it have the power to make it true, to reinforce its validity, its status as reality.[15]

Thus seen, the Qhapaq Ñan is not free: it is trapped by the discourse that created, measured, and circulated it. It is the heritage discourse, then, that turns the modest (because local) Andean trails into the Qhapaq Ñan of global announcements. But the patrimonialized trail celebrated and promoted as an emblem of identity and development hides that its meaning is controlled by the heritage apparatus and that those other voices that have stakes in the matter are not really heard; when they appear on the scene, even if their contradictory potential has been neutralized, they are only there to sanctify the disciplinary argument with their presence. It hides nasty social realities: hierarchies, inequalities, violence.[16] The story that goes from the uprising of Manco Inca and Tupac Amaru to the Taki Unquy, from José Miguel Condorcanqui to Juan Santos Atahualpa, is the story of the struggle for the restitution of the world as it was until the *pachacuti* unleashed by the Spaniards began. Chronicler Martín de Murúa translated *pachacuti* as "to turn around the land" (meaning transforming it) and "to take away and to disinherit," the inversion of order.[17] Patrimonializing the trail, with its violent accumulation by dispossession, is a continuation of the *pachacuti* by other means.

Dialectical Images and the Heritage Lure

The heritage processes enacted upon the materialities I have discussed and with which local populations diversely relate have created enduring and powerful images, most of them tied to the very old idea of civilization, today disguised as development. If I am to use the terms preferred by the temporality of modernity, I should say that those images mix past and present in very curious ways because they create things that are linked to the former but speak to the latter. How to handle this curiosity? One way is through the "dialectical images" sketched by Walter Benjamin as follows:

> It's not that what is past casts its light on what is present, or what is present casts its light on what is past; rather, image is that wherein what has been comes together in a flash with the now to form a constellation. In other words, image is dialectics at a standstill. For while the relation of the present to the past is a purely temporal, continuous one, the relation of what-has-been to the now is dialectical: is not progression but image, suddenly emergent. Only dialectical images are genuinely historical – that is, not archaic – images.[18]

Says Taussig on that regard: "History decayed into images, not stories, and it was the task of the historian to locate those images – dialectical images, Benjamin called them – which would rescue the past because of their resonance with present circumstance."

What is this shudder when the past finds the present? It has nothing to do with continuity but with juxtaposition, as Taussig noted.[19] But if this is so evident, the way the present touches the "facts" of the past with its magic wand to make them their own; if it is so evident that the past does not exist except in its relation to the present, in its indestructible articulation with the events that it requires and makes, producing something entirely new out of the encounter (dialectical, then); if, in truth, all this relationship is so obvious, what makes it so invisible, so unapparent, so spectral? What prevents some people from seeing it and continue so determinedly to treat its materiality as an issue of another time that speaks of another epoch? Because what should amaze us is not that the "things" of another epoch speak in this time but that some people refuse to admit it. On the wave of this refusal I have written this chapter about materialities of the past that are, in truth, materialities of the present.

Dialectical images in the heritage field create hardly credible (but useful) creatures because they mingle destruction with survival. The destruction of the missions and of the Andean trails and now their heritage salvation, at least of what little remains, are obvious acts in the unfolding of modern history. Between those objects-signs destroyed and those saved mediate the ruins. This makes more surprising, not least, the heritage industry's images because the relation with objects-signs turned into heritage bespeak a terrifying atemporality: it is a current experience in current objects-signs but their emotional meaning (and their value in the tourist market) is tied to the past of the Jesuits and of the Inca. That timelessness, deliberately acted upon on the patrimonial scene, neutralizes any political value and allows the hegemonic control of utopian meanings. These meanings, however, are not obliterated and fight to find wider spaces of operation and circulation. The missions and the Qhapaq Ñan dramatize the past in contemporary scenarios full of heritage significations controlled, promoted, and marketed. That timelessness is an index of the present, no longer concerned with time as much as with space. The missions and the trail are places, not times, even though their appeal (their calling) is, pretends to be, temporal.

This timelessness summons the concept of heterotopia.[20] Heterotopias are counterpoints to utopias (places without place) because they are "real places – places that do exist and that are formed in the very founding of society – which are somehow like counter-sites, a kind of effectively enacted utopia in which the real sites, all the other real sites that can be found within the culture, are simultaneously represented, contested, and inverted."[21] Heritage images as heterotopias are therefore absolutely real (so much so that the intimate, phenomenological relationship with them defines their heritage value) and absolutely unreal; the time that localizes, defines, and gives them value is a time forgone and a time of others. They juxtapose in one "real" place many places, many incompatible sites, and are linked to several dimensions of time. Thus, they are also heterochronic and (post)modern, of course, because they represent lost times that collapse (without a sense of orientation) in a single place a wide range of temporal experiences. The creation of a heterotopic place, warned Foucault, can abolish time. But these objects-signs, of course, were not heterotopic when they were trails and missions, not a heritage of humanity. That is why they are not rediscovered but created as heterotopic places where the abolition of time is decreed, yet where its enjoyment is demanded, an otherwise strange experience if it were not so frequent in (post)modernity. Their heterotopic character displays their otherness and their liberating exoticism because "their role is to create a space that is other, another real space, as perfect, as meticulous, as well arranged as ours is messy, ill constructed, and jumbled."[22]

In the real-unreal spaces that I have dealt with, the discursive authority of heritage is enacted, but not for and by itself but as a central element in the advance of the ontological frontier of (post)modernity. Heritage, therefore, is not about the past but about the present. Heritage is a lure of something bigger, more powerful, more pervasive. Thus seen, the materiality of the missions and the Andean trails (of their ruins, that is) loses its innocence: they are no longer just "things" with immanent patrimonial significances but battlefields in which different conceptions of heritage (different conceptions of the past, of time, of life) are now deployed in highly politicized settings characterized by antagonistic positions and institutions. They are rather conflictive semiotic constructions, rhetorical places where diverse actors are positioned and where a tough struggle for meaning, identity, and life unfolds. If those meanings are to be fully grasped, if the relationship between politics and wills (both individual and collective) is to be accounted for, it is necessary to go beyond the idea of a single world with different interpretations (an epistemological closure) to reach a more comprehensive perspective, that of many worlds and thus many conceptions (an ontological openness). This is the world of materiality in its fullest, not as a naturalized realm but a constructed space where politics are always at stake.

Acknowledgments

My research of the Qhapaq Ñan is funded by the Fundación de Investigaciones Arqueológicas of the Banco de la República and that of the missions, which I conduct along with Adriana Dias (Universidade Federal do Rio Grande do Sul), by Wenner-Gren, and the Conselho Nacional de Desenvolvimento Científico e Tecnológico (CNPq).

Notes

1. Pierre Losson, "The Inscription of Qhapaq Ñan on UNESCO's World Heritage List: A Comparative Perspective from the Daily Press in Six Latin American Countries," *International Journal of Heritage Studies* 23, no. 6 (2017), 521–37.
2. Patricia Ferreira, Ariel Ortega, Vincent Carelli, and Ernesto de Carvalho, *Tava, a Casa de Pedra* (Recife: Vídeo nas Aldeias, 2012).

3. Rita L. Segato, *La Nación y sus Otros: Raza, Etnicidad y Diversidad Religiosa en Tiempos de Políticas de la Identidad* (Buenos Aires: Prometeo, 2007).
4. For example, Guillermo Wilde, *Religión y Poder en las Misiones de Guaraníes* (Buenos Aires: Editorial SB, 2009); Eduardo Neumann, *Letra de Indios* (São Bernardo do Campo: Nhanduti, 2015); Graciela Chamorro, *Cuerpo Social: Historia y Etnografía de la Organización Social en los Pueblos Guaraní* (Asuncion: Tiempo de Historia, 2017).
5. Gloria Anzaldúa, *Borderlands/La Frontera: The New Mestiza* (San Francisco: Spinsters/Aunt Lute, 1987).
6. Johannes Fabian, *Time and the Other: How Anthropology Makes its Object* (New York: Columbia University Press, 1983).
7. Carlos N. de Moraes, "A Refiguração da Tava Miri São Miguel na Memória Coletiva dos Mbyá-Guarani nas Missões/RS, Brasil," PhD dissertation (Universidade Federal do Rio Grande do Sul, Porto Alegre, 2010), 15.
8. Jose C. de Souza and Jose C. Morinico, "Fantasmas das Brenhas Ressurgem nas Ruínas: Mbyá-Guaranis Relatam sua Versão Sobre as Missões e Depois Delas," in Arno Kern, Maria dos Santos, and Tau Golin, eds., *Historia Geral do Rio Grande do Sul. Volume 5, Povos Indígenas* (Passo Fundo: Méritos, 2009), 314.
9. David Harvey, *A Brief History of Neoliberalism* (Oxford: Oxford University Press, 2005), 159.
10. Marcela Díaz, *Implicaciones Patrimoniales: La Declaratoria del Qhapaq Ñan como Patrimonio Mundial* (Buenos Aires: Ediciones del Signo, 2017); Carina Jofré, "Una Mirada Crítica de los Contextos de Patrimonialización en el Contexto Megaminero," in Roberto Pellini, ed., *Arqueología Comercial: Dinero, Alienación y Anestesia* (Madrid: JAS Arqueología, 2017), 143–75.
11. Carina Jofré, "Arqueología de Contrato, Megaminería y Patrimonialización en Argentina," in Cristobal Gnecco and Adriana Dias, eds., *Crítica de la Razón Arqueológica: Arqueología de Contrato y Capitalismo* (Bogota: Instituto Colombiano de Antropología e Historia, 2017), 123–41.
12. Frederic Jameson, *Postmodernism or, the Cultural Logic of Late Capitalism* (London: Verso, 1991), 19.
13. Ibid.
14. Erica-Irene Daes, *Protección del Patrimonio de los Pueblos Indígenas* (New York: United Nations, 1999), 12.
15. Stuart Hall, "Whose Heritage? Un-settling 'The Heritage': Re-imagining the Post-nation," *Third Text* 49 (2000), 3–13.
16. Sebastian Jallade, "La Réinvention des Routes Incas: Représentations et Construction de la Mémoire au Pérou (2001–11)," *Droit et Culture* 62 (2011), 119–37.
17. Alberto Flores, *Buscando un Inca: Identidad y Utopía en los Andes* (Lima: Sur, 1987), 40.

18. Walter Benjamin, *The Arcades Project* (Cambridge: Harvard University Press, 1999), 462.
19. Michael Taussig, *My Cocaine Museum* (Chicago: University of Chicago Press, 2004), 90.
20. Michel Foucault, "Des Espaces Autres (Of Other Spaces: Utopias and Heterotopias)," *Diacritics* 16, no. 1 (1986), 22–27.
21. Ibid, 25.
22. Ibid, 26.

7

War and Violence

How to Rescue a Wartime Artifact

Bożena Shallcross

Toward a Definition of a Wartime Artifact

It would be an overstatement to say that the bare life of the last world war in Europe created the proper conditions for an unprecedented rise of crude materialism, for what had happened and what was observed at that time was a debased and brutalized form of existence. The overarching material and materialistic concerns were caused by a degraded system of war economy driven by human and material losses, expensive technological innovations of the war machine, and a greatly simplified everyday survival of civilians. The extent of these materialist constraints varied from one impoverished region to another, from ruined urban centers to the depleted countryside, but regardless of setting they had a common denominator in survival. For struggling civilians, ensuring survival required food, shelter, clothes, and some other rudimentary artifacts. Theirs was the crudest materialism in action. At the same time, they were the targets of systemic and systematic lootings as well as more spontaneous acts of wartime plunder, with these violent dispossessions only adding to the traumatic destruction of the built environment. Amid these circumstances, artifacts were damaged, displaced, dispossessed even as, simultaneously, they at times represented some sense of stability, facilitating survival and suturing one's broken memory and identity. How can we define such a multivalent, yet easily destroyed world of objects today? What are the elements that constitute a wartime artifact in a time of peace? One common aspect is indisputable at this point of my analysis: matter is constitutive of all these objects and all matter is subject to change.[1]

Given the generative matrix of diverse plans, agencies, and accidents that coproduce a wartime artifact, this brief topological exercise, which opens my interrogation, necessitates first asking a reductive question: what *does not* constitute it? Briefly, a wartime artifact is not defined only by its setting. It can be both displaced and localized: it is not necessary to find it in an attic, a basement, or a flea market, and it does not have to be picked up from a battlefield or displayed in a wartime museum, even if it usually belongs to military museums and memorials. Whether it is marked by wartime events, invented or produced during a war, used in the hinterlands or the trenches, a wartime artifact usually emerges at an intersection of traumatic events inherent in its biography as inextricably related to its human counterpart. Its formed materiality, more often than not marked by deformation and partial destruction, requires care and preservation – a demanding and costly effort often invisible to the public eye. An artifact, scarred by such forms of violence as dispossession, is still usable, as opposed to artifactual remnants that are entirely divested of their use value. The remnant's broken form factors large in this equation as it announces its disability and consequent gradual dematerialization into, if you will, a void.

The discussion will consider several specific examples of wartime artifacts: a bridge, a knife, a suitcase, and a collection of shoes; they were chosen for their link to the World War II atrocities, as well as for their swerving from typical trajectories of objectual survival. With the exception of the Warsaw bridge, I had an opportunity to perceive all of the objects discussed in this chapter firsthand, as they are, by observing and foregrounding their physicality: their texture, shape, type of material, patina, rust, fragmentation, decomposition, traces, and all other forms of diminishing materiality. In a search for authenticity, I focused on signs of natural decay and of violent tearing in the physical fabric of objects. Whether or not these processes compromise an object's integrity, they act as peculiar agents that can actually enhance the sense of original provenance, at least in revealing its material source. Accepted and respected as they are, these artifacts create a veritable atlas of testimonies that turns out to be more honest and persuasive than statistics, charts, or guidebook accounts of war's impact on the fabric of individual and social lives.

The following exploration of wartime artifacts considers several such objects, ranging from monumental infrastructure and architecture to detritus. Their provenance, especially of the small-scale private belongings that were often displaced and aged beyond recognition, is one of the more difficult genealogies to trace. Since I look at these objects through a prism of authenticity, an unsolvable tension between their original and restored condition, their neglect and care, lies at the core of my deliberations. There are several strategies for dealing with this tension in which pragmatic concerns may prevail over mnemonic symbolization, or vice versa. For example, some European World War II sites, for instance, Oradur-sur-Glane, were left in a state of ruin as a remainder-reminder of their tragic history and evidence of their community's utter trauma.[2] Conversely, other similarly ruined structures were rebuilt, out of necessity, using new construction materials, with the objects' original provenance lost and replaced by a mere or nearly perfect copy.³ Such is the case with Warsaw's Royal Castle, that was bombed by the Germans at the very beginning of the war. A network of postwar initiatives, from fundraising among American and Canadian Polonia to the arduous process of rebuilding the monumental Baroque structure, resulted in a shift of its meaning. In part also because of its altered material embodiment, the Royal Castle's inscription of World War II trauma was replaced by another symbolic inscription – of the Poles' triumphant will to remake what violence had obliterated.⁴

A reconstructive strategy can sometimes involve combining an original structure with new, deliberately modernist elements, leading to a carefully curated mix of old and new styles and spaces, an exercise in contrast often employed in postwar Germany.⁵ A somewhat similar strategy is best illustrated by Dresden's Baroque church, known as the Church of Our Lady (*Frauenkirche*); its story necessitated balancing the church's material embodiment and its evolving symbolism. After it was destroyed by the Allies' carpet bombing of the city, the German Democratic Republic (DDR) Communist regime decided to keep the church in ruins as a war memorial. Dresden citizens, however, had already begun to gather its unique sandstone elements with in the mid-1940s. These building materials were stored and protected, with some of them eventually reused when the church was rebuilt after the unification of Germany. The end result is a patchwork of temporalities tied by the architectural design. The largest remaining and deliberately unrestored part of the Church – its chancel – was incorporated in the exterior wall of the rebuilt structure like a rough cameo; the fire, smoke, and heat of the wartime bombing blackened the chancel's sandstone surface, making the war trauma starkly visible in the unavoidable juxtaposition of dark, older stones and warmly honey-hued, new stonework. The chancel was not subjected to conservation and maintenance processes so its presence could speak to its own story as marked by barbarism, trauma, and material impermanence. As far as the authenticity of the end result of the entire reconstruction is concerned, however, it was seriously compromised. The present material and visual patchwork convey the conflict inherent in the church's current meaning, which emerges from the encounter of post-1989 ideological assumptions of reconciliation and hope with the turbulent history that the reconstructed building still reflects. At the same time, because the material quality of the chancel stirs a traumatic memory,⁶ this monumental artifact of artistic and historical significance delivers to the beholder a punctum, a sudden sensation of sharp pain fused with a sensation of beauty: ultimately, *Frauenkirche* evokes sublimity.⁷

The complicated provenance and stories of war-marked artifacts require that they be looked at through a prism of a revised, nonbinary understanding of authenticity. Such perspective unifies provenance and ownership and has been at the forefront of authenticity discourse due to Walter

Benjamin's ideas presented in "The Work of Art in the Age of its Technological Reproducibility." The manner of production is at the core of Benjamin's approach, which posits that a nonmechanically produced object is endowed with a quality of an aura that "even the most perfect reproduction of a work of art" could not deliver, or evoke, to the same extent as the original.[8] Benjamin further describes authenticity as a fluctuating process anchored in temporality: "The authenticity of a thing is the quintessence of all that is transmissible in it from its origins on, ranging from its physical duration to the historical testimony relating to it."[9] Thus, authenticity implies changeability, not stasis.

I set aside Benjamin's notion that mechanically produced artworks cannot be elevated to the status of authentic works here, since this distinction was made obsolete already in the early twentieth century. The Benjaminian assumption that only handmade artifacts possess an auratic and authentic quality has been challenged by a variety of artistic developments and genres, to mention only collage, assemblage, and the readymade, all of which incorporated numerous mechanically produced, everyday objects. In discourse, the normative notion of authenticity along with the distinction between artworks and artifacts has been abolished. In order to comprehend the authenticity and agency of wartime artifacts, therefore, their nature needs to be conceived and analyzed in more nuanced and broader terms that stress their material impermanence rather than nonmechanical origin. In the same famous essay Benjamin also considered the question of tactile perception and habit. This consideration allows us to capture the illusive auratic quality in the everyday objects. This claim is of particular importance in this chapter, as I understand auratic authenticity not as an aesthetic quality, but a trait pertinent to all material things.

Looting in the War and in the Law

The question of illegal provenance and authenticity of wartime artifacts has been subject to scrutiny and ongoing discussion for several decades. The way in which the question is, or should be, approached has evolved. Historically, among concepts associated with warfare, taking the spoils was considered legitimate by victorious armies and was often celebrated by them, which further humiliated the losing side. The relief sculpted on the Arch of Titus in Rome, showing a triumphant parade carrying away the contents from the Temple in Jerusalem, including one of its golden menorahs, provides a case in point. In this broad historical context, much may seem to have improved as far as standards for the protection of property are concerned. The beginning of the twentieth century facilitated some progress with the Hague Convention of 1907, which was further aided in 1954 by the Convention for the Protection of Cultural Property in the

Event of Armed Conflict. These documents signaled a growing legal awareness of the need for protection of cultural heritage. In reality, the application of the law remains a very different and complicated story.

Looting not only destroys numerous fundamental dependencies among users and objects, but also violates their subtler, more easily overlooked intimacies among them. Spoliation demonstrates the overarching asymmetry between human subjects and their ordinary, inanimate belongings. Deprived of agency, mundane objects are relegated to a submissive relationship with their users and owners. Expensive objects such as artworks, on the other hand, destabilize this relational pattern. For one, artworks are endowed with a more multidimensional agency; valuable paintings augment the prestige of their owners during times of peace and can be used as life-saving barter in wartime.[10]

The challenge facing international humanitarian law (as laid out by the Fourth Geneva Convention and the Additional Protocols) regarding the protection of civilians and of both public and private property is serious. This law was a response to the extreme brutalities of World War II; ratified in 1949, it introduced the right of civilians to protection from all forms of violence, be it deportations, exploitative labor, torture, starvation, captivity, or plunder.

The subsequent, repeated failures of the law have had myriad multilateral reasons, but they ultimately bespeak the immense vulnerability of life and matter and the defenselessness of human beings whose bodies are deprived of basic material necessities of safety and security: clothes, shoes, walking canes, blankets, coats, gloves, and hats – items that shield civilians as much as the proverbial roof over the head.

The Warsaw Bridge

When W. G. Sebald bemoaned the unprecedented scale of devastation the Allied air raids brought upon German cities and their inhabitants in *On the Natural History of Destruction*, he did not look at other scarred parts of Europe that were ruined during German military action, or deliberately destroyed by the TN and other withdrawing German military forces.[11] Stalingrad, Rotterdam, Warsaw, and Hamburg were among the cities nearly erased in this systematic manner. The Polish capital's infrastructure and historical material legacy was left unrecognizable, with several of its neighborhoods pulverized.[12] In fact, the initial postwar plan for Warsaw's reconstruction was to abandon the old site completely and rebuild the capital from scratch in a new space. This scale of destruction, followed by the long and costly reconstruction, must demand a reevaluation of the concept of authenticity. When historical buildings or smaller artifacts are not just restored, but entirely rebuilt, the results vary extensively. The original integrity of design and materials, already seriously undermined by the wartime bombardment, is further altered by the restorative process, which can leave them looking better than ever, often picture-perfect. The new ontology that emerges along the way is more nuanced and puts into question an essentialist understanding of authenticity.

To further contextualize the interrelationship among matter, its traumatic deformation, and its erasure, a look at a specific encounter between an artist and a wartime object is in order. The artist is Tadeusz Kantor and the object a damaged bridge that used to span the banks of the Vistula river, in Warsaw. Kantor's notes, essays, and meditations, which are presented as diary entries, include a brief, poetic note dated rather imprecisely "1947, right after the war."[13] The notation describes his experience of coming across one of the many monumental elements of Warsaw's infrastructure to have been obliterated during the war. Kantor gave his note the prophetic title of "Photographic Plates of the Future":

> When I was in Warsaw, I saw a part of an iron bridge smashed by
>   a bomb.
> I was struck by the sight of its unreal/crushed-upness. . . .
> It also occurred to me that this
> Unbelievably flattened form might
> Herald the canons of post-war aesthetics.[14]

Kantor's eye registers the crushed iron structure of a bridge mutilated by bursts energy released by bomb explosions, a previously authentic and well-functioning object now altered in its previous form, function, and meaning. The mangled structure retains traces of its original shape and can still be identified as a bridge, but deciphering its original form would require using old photographs and technical drawings.

Ancient Greeks introduced the concept of form to link what they saw as unrelated and opposite notions of matter and ideas. Applying this ancient conceptualization to the image of the bridge as observed by Kantor reveals a rupture of matter, form, and idea, their unified triangle now torn asunder. Kantor's creative eye, attracted to the dramatic spectacle of disentanglement, clearly apprehended its material, functional, and formal aspects despite the fragmentation, seeing a new material presence in the contorted configuration. The sight of the nearly formless bridge was a moment of revelation for Kantor, for whom a monumental fragmentation was a fertile artistic concept.

The Polish artist focused on the interplay between the bridge's old practical usage and its new status as a useless yet sublime thing anchored in the powerful, artistically expressive effect of bombing. His minimalistic record of the experience captured as a prophetic moment for art, though devoid of the prophetic rhetoric, had a posttraumatic foundation. Kantor does not indicate how the bridge was crushed, with his wording suggesting a generalized agency – a sort of immanent evil. Rhetorically appropriating concepts of deformation and destruction, he seizes the opportunity to look past historical details and into the future without losing sight of war's affect. His prophesy, which envisions recycling damaged objects as clichéd as the titular photographic plates, is accompanied by recognition of a very different kind. The war negated the bridge's functionality as an engineered structure enabling transport and turned it into a material victim of war, one of many likewise damaged objects. This development, in turn, opens up a space that precipitates the encounter between the deformed bridge and the artist, whose reflection on the contorted matter figuratively emancipates it from both past dependencies and determinants. The narrative framing of Kantor's vision, which juts into the future, illustrates an artist's response to a war artifact that salvages it conceptually in an experimental genre mix of proto-happening with recycling instead of using it to broadcast a propagandistic antiwar message.[15]

The Warsaw bridge that Kantor encountered is long gone since its compromised structural integrity could not be repaired. With its formal design and functionality irrevocably compromised, this particular wartime artifact has retreated back to the matter it came from. This is the point in its history that asserts the role of written sources in preserving wartime artifacts, for the bridge now "exists" because of Kantor's particular reimagining of it.

A Well-Cut Knife

In putting a monumental object (a damaged Warsaw bridge) in dialogue with something small, though not miniature, namely a knife – by pitting the damaged against the whole – a certain disclosure is choreographed: its gist is that the fractured object – now perhaps a thing – reveals itself materially.[16] The function and provenance of the latter artifact is enigmatic at first (Figure 7.1). Is it a farming tool made by an anonymous hand during the Iron Age, or perhaps a stylized, yet roughhewn letter opener from Anthropologie? The item exudes simplicity on the one hand, while on the other bearing little resemblance to Iron Age metal tools. How does its materiality manifest itself? It is evident on inspection that it is made from one solid piece of metal, with the handle cleverly formed by a single cut into its halfway point. The handle end, folded for a rounded, "user-friendly" shape, is slightly worn by the user's hand; likewise, the blade end bears the trace of its sharpening and usage. The line of the blade speaks of frequent rough handling, rougher than the work of merely peeling potatoes or slicing bread. The slight spots of rust on the tool's lower part may signal a long period of disuse, the low quality of the material, or both; otherwise, it lacks obvious signs of corrosion or long-term use. The photograph's apparent artistic quality enhances the knife's auratic presence, which radiates in the photographic space almost devoid of other objects,

Figure 7.1 Mieczysław Porębski's knife. Photo: Katarzyna Brodowska, courtesy of the artist.

except for the vague outlines of books in the background. The image is centered around this one small, metal object resting on the desk's edge.

One cannot read this artifact's provenance from its surface; it bears no inscription to assist in its identification, nor is it supplied with a didactic panel. My phenomenological description of its appearance targets its texture, surface, exteriority, and matter, but does not reveal much about the knife's origin or its provenance. The object remains inaccessible, with its own secret biography, context, and matter. Tracing its provenance requires reaching for outside sources and reconstructing the network of historical events around its creation. The biography of the knife, its maker and user, including the time and place of its manufacture, form a single narrative that I compiled from multiple sources, including word-of-mouth accounts. It begins in 1944 at the KL Groß-Rosen labor camp in Lower Silesia, where Mieczysław Porębski, then a young art history student, was imprisoned for conspiratorial activities before being relocated to the main KL Sachsenhausen.[17] As the story goes, during his imprisonment he came to own a small knife cut out from an old metal barrel hoop. The knife was apparently handmade for Porębski by a Ukrainian prisoner, and it is proof of its maker's ingenious resourcefulness in recycling materials and of his manual dexterity.[18] By Porębski's admission, the knife helped him survive in one of the most brutal concentration camps. In this way, its use value was amplified by the prisoner's objective of self-preservation. As his only valuable possession, it facilitated such affordances as peeling potatoes, cutting bread, or fixing damaged things, in other words, the daily activities of a camp prisoner. Crucially, then, the knife became a practical extension of its owner. At the same time, as indispensable as it was, the tool also exposed its owner to danger since it was illegal and punishable for prisoners to own such instruments. Its transgressive meta-function meant it had to be hidden; Porębski kept it close to his body, in the fold of his striped prisoner's uniform.

The knife's paradoxical status as both a safeguard and hazardous contraband was neutralized when these functions were rendered obsolete by its owner's return to a life of relative normalcy in postwar Poland. Yet Porębski decided to keep the knife after leaving the camp and, indeed, he did not part with it for the rest of his life, despite the shift in its daily usage. With the reasons for its precarious existence, which helped its owner survive the war, the knife's survival was ensured by Porębski's protection. Their interdependence, even if viewed in entirely anthropomorphic terms, illustrates the human subject's capacity to reciprocate.

The unquestionable and permanent closeness between the owner and the object transformed into a relative closeness when the knife was openly displayed on Porębski's desk in his study. Thus, the knife made necessary by concentration camp realities became an occasional talking point for visitors and a veritable war artifact. Displayed outside a museum's formal environment and without an inscription, the knife stood out as a peculiar object with a mysterious history that needed its owner to both explain and authenticate it. It was his narrative that triggered his friend, the poet Tadeusz Różewicz, to write *The Professor's Knife*. The poem is now one of the sources, albeit incomplete, from which one can learn about the knife's place in Porębski's everyday life: a place of attachment and memory, but devoid of sentimentality. The knife appears as a topic of conversation between the poet and his professor friend, followed by an additional explanation quoted in the poem from Porębski's letter:

> Mieczysław:
> I've been thinking further about my knife,
> the one made out of a barrel hoop.
> You had to carry it in the hem of a concentration camp uniform
> since they'd confiscate things
> and one could pay dearly . . .
> So it served its purposes,
> not just utilitarian
> but far more subtle ones
> (it would be worth talking about it sometime) . . .[19]

The letter acts to authenticate the knife by confirming and explaining its origin; it provides a framing context and a kind of a singular authenticity conferred by Porębski. An authentic artifact's patina, that enigmatic or abject residue of time and a part of its biography (that in the knife's case includes traces of manual use, cleaning, and repairs, and of being held by a hand), dominates its texture and often conceals the material underneath. The knife's surface, despite being hard and nonporous, lends itself to those kinds of rusty marks, to the profane patina as defined by Shannon Lee Dawdy.[20]

Restoration acts retroactively in defying and removing such traces, in contrast to maintenance, which prevents an object's current material state from deteriorating further. There is no information about the knife having ever been restored, however. To access an artifact in its physicality requires a nonnormative understanding of authenticity that allows for changeability and which, in its focus on the material, is akin to the phenomenological approach on the one hand, while echoing Bennett's vitalist approach in *Vibrant Matter* on the other. The knife's biography, irrevocably tied to Porębski's own biography, brings it from its hiding place and illegal status out into the open, a shift into the domestic space that foregrounds its new role as a vestigial memento from afar, as well as speaks of its diminishment in, or perhaps even loss of, use value. The narrative of Porębski's knife does not follow the pattern typical for wartime artifacts, for it never changed hands from one owner to another, nor was it destroyed, or even slightly damaged. Indeed, it survived unscathed in its substance, marked only by tiny spots of rust. What do we make of the particles of rust visible on its surface? While they are, the undesirable result of the low-grade iron from which the knife was made, their presence actually confirms its authenticity and biography spanning several decades.

The knife is handmade and unique, for it bears no stamps or trademarks to indicate that it was mechanically manufactured. Its authenticity and uniqueness are not in doubt, warranted by the narrative of this artifact's provenance. Does this mean that this tool possesses an inherent aura? It does fulfill most of the defining criteria of an auratic object, with the only reservation being that a knowledge of its biography is requisite to perceive it fully. If viewed directly, without a framing Holocaust narrative, its inconspicuous appearance and reliance on a prosthetic explanation hinder its ontology of an aura-exuding artifact.

Unlike many wartime artifacts, the knife, which survived the war intact and, ultimately, also its owner Professor Porębski, all the while remaining a material metonymy for his wartime survival, does not need to be salvaged. Inherited by Jerzy Porębski, the professor's son, it speaks of heritage and continuity that may suture scars. Ensconced in family life, it is nonetheless not a neutral object; it has the mnemonic potential to cut through the everyday and to seed fear and trauma in a daily routine.[21] In the camp, the knife was a risky commodity with a potential exchange value; in today's world, it is a difficult metonymic presence: a wartime artifact that cannot be embraced entirely, or with the same dose of tenderness, as other family heirlooms. Its redeeming value belongs to the traumatic past when it helped its owner survive.

Whose Suitcase?

Wartime artifacts often exist in a precarious physical state due to passage of time, exposure to the elements, and the inferior quality of construction materials, which is sometimes further exacerbated by improper display conditions.[22] Former concentration camp sites along with piles of things they contain have been inevitably deteriorating, with certain artifacts already replaced by copies, for example, in Dachau. Authenticity has thus been aligned with ongoing efforts at the preservation, conservation, and even its opposite – replacement and simulacrum – of wartime artifacts. At this juncture, I want to consider how the drive toward authenticity of display becomes a source of a certain paradox that goes unrecognized when authenticity is not properly conceptualized. Natural processes of decay and signs of transitoriness, perceived as undesirable in certain post-Holocaust curatorial practices and discourse, call for conservation and necessitate intervention into the integrity of displayed artifacts, buildings, and the surrounding terrain. Each restorative intervention, performed for the sake of preservation, arrests deterioration and prolongs the life of things, but it also impacts their authenticity. Instead of enhancing desired authenticity, preservation changes it by producing an "idealized" retroactive effect.

Negotiating between authenticity and human intervention is a challenge for Holocaust memorials, which recognize the goal of keeping objects in their purported authentic state and the costs of such efforts. Thus, the Auschwitz Memorial and Museum website often foregrounds the value of authenticity to its mandate. In the News section from June 24, 2019, for instance, the website informs visitors that the Master Plan for Preservation, implemented in 2012, preserved the authenticity of the buildings,[23] as the long and costly first stage of renovating the oldest brick barracks was finalized. The fact that the use of new technologies, methods, and materials such as synthetic resin was a form of intervention (albeit minimal, as the website rightly claims) has some bearing on the understanding of authenticity it foregrounds.[24] One can observe, nonetheless, here a tension between preserving the historic value of the barracks and diminishing their material authenticity. The question of whether restoration invested the barracks with a new ontology was addressed in the way that underscores defiance of biological determinants: "We have created a mechanism that prevents this history from disappearing with the natural aging of buildings."[25]

The stored or displayed holdings in the former KL Auschwitz are endowed with both use and museum values. Among these objects are pieces of the victims' luggage that bear many marks of use and abuse together with actual inscriptions still visible on some of their surfaces. Altogether, several thousands of cheap cardboard suitcases, as well as some made of real or imitation leather, comprise the collection.[26] Carried by deportees from all over occupied Europe, they once contained everything deemed necessary for survival that fell within the prescribed weight limit. In the extreme situation of an environment that offered no affordances to prisoners, retaining some belongings asserted a modicum of stability and continuity with the past. Suitcases were also used for storing personal items of symbolic value. Indeed, they were vessels marked with their owners' identities, with most having personal data inscribed on lids for easier identification.[27] Brief inscriptions, hand-painted or written in chalk, or printed stickers, tags, and labels bearing the owners' names and dates of birth, can be seen on the luggage pieces; sometimes, one can spot entire addresses and identification numbers on their surface. Besides confirming an inscription's habitual function as a mark of ownership, they constitute a language of connection and interrelationality with their murdered owners and, ultimately, comprise a veritable moving anthology of the subgenre of luggage writing, so to speak. Inscriptions on the camp suitcases were "the embodiment of hope"[28] that turned out to be illusory for most, but they are nonetheless proof of provenance, past ownership and violence, and of both existence and death.

The deportees were stripped of their belongings forcefully, with their suitcases, bundles, and bags taken, opened, and searched for valuables upon arrival in the camp. One act of material violence followed another: many suitcases in Auschwitz have broken locks – visible traces of a search for valuables hidden in them and of the greed and violence that prompted their penetration and plunder.[29] As testimonies to their owners' trauma and death, these suitcases were amassed in storage rooms to represent not the spoils of war, but rather its dead victims. The suitcases on display, only a small portion of the lot, reference their owners as specters whose personal data writ large disturbs the visitors' comfort zone.[30]

To understand a wartime artifact in its combination of physical, authentic, and symbolic traits, I introduce a peculiar "revenant remnant" of a suitcase. It is a leftover in a literal sense – a survivor, to use more elevated rhetoric – for it has no lid, having lost it in unknown circumstances. Its missing lid is not the only gap in its story, as nothing is certain about the event that caused its fragmentation. This leaves fertile ground for speculation, or for forensically imagining its now lost wholeness. Through its violated thingness, the suitcase represents its owner's traumatic past and, in doing so, authenticates itself.

Violence shuttles the functionality of objects to the background, since violated and damaged objects, especially tools, cannot perform adequately, if at all. Instead they enact something else. As stated earlier: a fractured artifact reveals itself materially, displaying its interiority, its "intestines." The suitcase in question here is perpetually open to the viewers' gaze; its interior can be seen with ease, which is unusual for private luggage (Figure 7.2). This broken half-suitcase manifests its authenticity

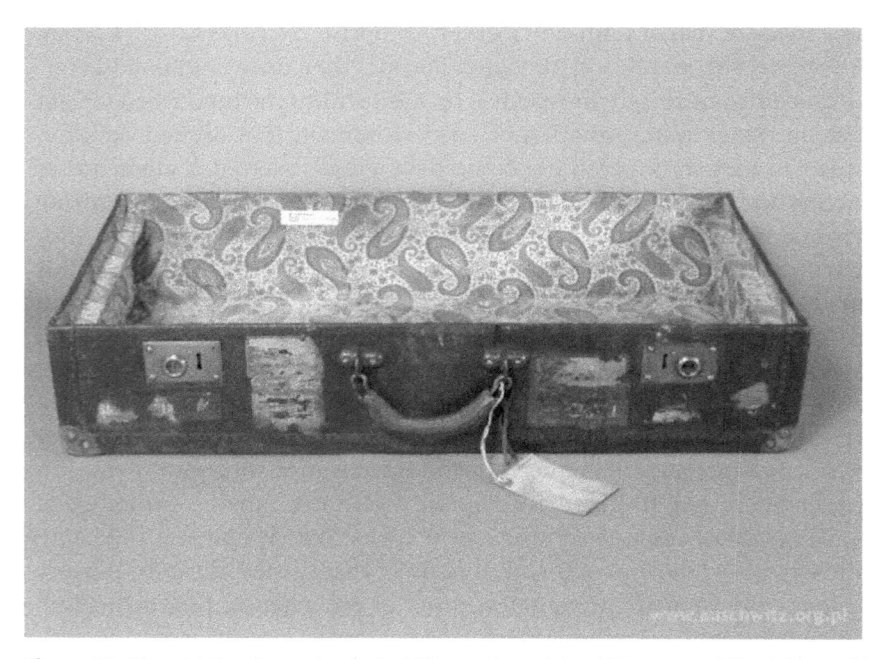

Figure 7.2 Pierre Lévi's suitcase, Auschwitz-Birkenau Memorial and Museum and Shoah Memorial Museum in Paris, public domain.

through its material remains, thus there is no need to reconstruct, or confirm, its provenance. The violence implied by its physical fragmentation – pulling and tearing – enhances the sense of its genuineness. It thus seems striking that in the numerous press reports related to the closely observed legal battle over its possession, the journalists refrained from discussing its individual, material peculiarities, as if the battered thing lacked such characteristics.[31]

The half-suitcase – or a crippled suitcase, you might say – lined with a green paisley cloth, takes the beholder aback. Clearly, its damaged, ripped open body can no longer serve as a secure container. While under normal circumstances it would be discarded, its strangely dramatic biography ensures that it continues to testify to its owner's violent demise. Unlike its owner, *la valise* was given a second chance at life when it returned to France on loan to the Shoah Museum in Paris. It was there that it had been originally produced, purchased, and used by a French Jew named Pierre Lévi. The suitcase – a mobile object *sui generis* – was part of "The Fate of Jews of France" exhibition, where it triggered a special encounter between Michel Lévi-Lelou and his daughter Claire, suddenly morphing from its obvious pitiful brokenness into something unattainable and precious. This story played out when the murdered owner's son and granddaughter visited the exhibit and took a closer look at the inscription on *la valise*. The inscription, written by Pierre's wife and Michel's mother, contained only essential information: his name, Paris address, and identification number ("48 Gruppe 10"). There could be no doubt that it belonged to Pierre Lévi, Michel's and Claire's father and grandfather, respectively, who had perished at KL Auschwitz. The inscription pulled the victim and his possession out of the dark anonymity of the concentration camp and into the presence of his family. Both the victim and his possession became personalized when the members of his family recognized the identity inscribed on the piece of luggage. Their familial gaze rendered the man, his name, nationality, ethnicity, and the city where he lived distinct. One would be hard-pressed to find a more significant instance of objectual agency than the naming of the spectral entity of Pierre Lévi and his metonymic return – via his material property – to his relatives.

According to law, like any other looted artifact, the suitcase should have been returned to the owner's descendant in defiance of the lawlessness of war and recognition of legal ownership. This is not what happened, however. Understandably, Pierre Lévi's son requested the return of *la valise*. He wished to habituate the thing as his private property within the walls of his home, where he could keep it within his eye and hand range – one may imagine, in a humidity-resistant acrylic glass box. The Auschwitz museum, its position backed by the International Auschwitz Council, was reluctant to return this eerie piece of inheritance to Lévi-Lelou, however. The next stage of the suitcase's uncanny biography can now be read in numerous court trial documents, correspondence between involved parties, and press articles.[32] Eventually, Lévi-Lelou and both the Polish and the French museums came to an agreement. According to the final verdict, the suitcase's broken body would continue to be owned by the Auschwitz museum, but it would be displayed on loan in Paris at the Mémorial de la Shoah. From the point of view of the Auschwitz museum's curators, their role is to gather, store, maintain, and protect all material shreds of the genocide and its victims. From the curatorial point of view, returning the suitcase to its rightful owner would result in the undesirable scattering of the Holocaust's extant traces that the Auschwitz museum had accumulated and protected.

Lévi-Lelou's intentions regarding the suitcase changed over time. Initially, he maintained that his wish to reclaim it was motivated by reluctance to visit Auschwitz, where his father's ashes were scattered along with those of thousands more. He did not want to endure the trauma of the experience in order to see the suitcase; he simply wanted to own the suitcase that metonymically represented both his father's life and death. His approach to reclaiming this portion of his heritage changed with the stakes of the endeavor, with the legal case for its retrieval stressing restoration and the public display of the luggage fragment at the Mémorial de la Shoah. Lévi-Lelou's final decision can be seen as either reasonable compromise or magnanimous resignation, since in giving up on possessing the only memento left from his father's existence he definitely enriched the exhibit at the Mémorial. Notably, the suitcase evolved during this process from the common understanding of a memento as a vestigial keepsake to that of a relic, yet it is completely devoid of nostalgia. The tortured materiality of an object returned to its place of origin acquires a spectral aura of a tragic relic. Thus, the battle over ownership of the suitcase can be seen as the outcome of trying to reframe it outside an institutional context, with a radical de-instituting of the artifact proving impossible; this traumatic family heirloom was not fully reclaimed. Lévi-Lelou's desire for full, at-home accessibility, the initial point of disagreement, was reversed when he relinquished his ownership and the responsibilities that come with it, although the suitcase's current location in Paris makes access much easier for him.[33]

Paradoxically, it was a museum visit that catapulted the suitcase from the typical confines of its narrative of material survival. That event foregrounded its objectual agency as forceful enough to destabilize a dominant trope in the Holocaust narrative of the irrevocability of wartime plunder and loss. Disrupting this narrative's negative closure, the story of Lévi's suitcase simultaneously reveals another, complementary layer of meaning to issues surrounding the compensatory nature of repossessions. Emancipated from its role as a container and a carrier because of a missing lid, the artifact has since been subjected to legal, restorative, and textual processes. For over half a century, it was an immobilized wreck, hiding in a collection of suitcases with no known relationship with the outside world. On its return to Paris, it became a site of mobile memory and a concrete item with power to mobilize the press to follow the controversy over its ownership. Its relationality changed again when the legal procedure for determining its rightful owner led to an agreement between the two concerned parties (Lévi's son and the public institution of Auschwitz-Birkenau Memorial and Museum): while the latter would remain its proprietor, the suitcase would stay on display in Paris. Reminiscent of an open coffin, the suitcase is a thing that no longer conceals personal belongings and will never serve as intended again. Unencrypted – only because it is a textual object – this crippled crypt reveals its ontology of a spectral receptacle of familial memory.

A Pile of Shoes

In times when the last eyewitnesses to history are passing away, original objects connected with such historical sites as Auschwitz assume ever greater significance, prompting a hierarchical shift, along with its ontological and ethical implications. The artifacts at the Auschwitz-Birkenau Memorial Museum are displayed on the premise that they belonged to camp prisoners and were part of their struggle for survival. As one online description states, "preserving the original post-camp remains is one of the most important objectives of the Museum. Conducting scientific research and educational activity at the Memorial Site is possible thanks to the protection of authentic structures and documents."[34] I do not intend to contest this authenticity in terms of the artifacts' provenance; instead, I would like to point to the specific conceptualization of authenticity in discourse pertaining to artifacts and sites of remembrance. For instance, the current conceptualization of Auschwitz or Majdanek has to do with a clear set of ontological, cultural, and historical premises that put the authenticity of artifacts and infrastructure at the center of preservation efforts due to their ethical status as witnesses to the genocide. The ethical dimension is the primary reason that even the best-intended preservation undercuts the authenticity of Holocaust artifacts.

The challenge posed by the natural process of decay and transitoriness, perceived in curatorial practice and discourse as undesirable, calls for conservation and necessitates interventions in the material integrity of displayed artifacts, buildings, and the surrounding terrain. This institutional perception depends on the notion of authenticity one embraces, as well as on the material complexity of the artifact at hand, as evidenced by the case of the Majdanek State Museum. The Majdanek camp originally served as a sorting and storage depot for Operation Reinhard, and the museum now owns the largest portion of indispensable Holocaust artifacts. The first museum of its sort in Europe, it was initially overwhelmed by the sheer mass of everyday items accumulated there.[35] The American journalist and writer Edward Snow, in describing his experience of visiting the site, pays particular attention to the diversity of the amassed shoes:

> I was most terrified and shocked not by the barracks and wire, nor by the ovens that swallowed human bodies, but by objects caringly stored on shelves that belonged to the murdered people. A storage of footwear! I will never forget their infinite diversity – from the little red shoes of a child killed for things it could not yet understand to the high-heeled shoes of some tortured woman.[36]

Indeed, there were mounds of shoes left in the camps. Their number steadily dwindled when they were left unprotected from theft and exposed to the elements, deteriorating in the rain, snow, sun, and wind.[37] It is difficult to keep leather in good condition even under normal circumstances, and the task of restoring the hardened or rotting leather in postwar Communist Poland was quite an experiment. In the 1960s, the shoes in question were treated with lanoline and some chemical substances to increase their flexibility, which actually caused some of the shoes to deteriorate further. Despite the wrong kind of restoration, these artifacts did not rot and disintegrate entirely, but stirred the matter's vitality, thus challenging the conservationists. At present, in the words of a contemporary scholar of Majdanek,

The state of the shoes varies. The decisive majority have very worn out soles and heels resulting from their intensive use by their owners (in particular, men's shoes, with numerous traces of repeated repairs and patches). Some have been deliberately torn apart in the search for treasures and banknotes, often hidden by deportees in shoes. However, there are also shoes that show no sign of damage. The shared characteristic of the collection is a specific, dark brown color. The passage of time and methods of conservation and display caused the footwear to become discolored, and only a few samples show preserved leather that is natural or painted in various colors.[38]

Usually, the discoloration is a unifying work of a patina, which in the case of Majdanek shoes originated in their exposure to the elements. Patina covers the surface and does not allow the matter to reveal itself. The shoes' discoloration in Majdanek went so far that it permanently turned victims' shoes – personal items *par excellence* – into homogenized artifacts.

At the United States Holocaust Memorial Museum in Washington, DC, the displayed shoes are on loan from Majdanek, and the American curators have to contend with the same precarious physical state of these artifacts as at Majdanek.[39] The color of the shoes displayed at both institutions has darkened, although to slightly different hues. At the Holocaust Memorial Museum in Washington, visitors can smell the shoes when passing by their display. Their uncanny odor is the result of their initial neglect and inadequate care during the 1960s along with the nature of leather; in sum, the smell bespeaks their history and precarious material state. Their maintenance has to be ongoing despite the cost, but it is worthwhile even if the shoes no longer look as they did in the 1940s, when they were ripped open in search of valuables. They are only vestiges of the shoes that belonged to that violent time; their contorted and shapeless forms demonstrate to the beholder that they can never be put to use again. Rescuing these artifacts of shared authenticity means rescuing them from their own matter and function.

Scattering Matter – Gathering Matter

As survivors pass away, the fact that objectual and material heritage gathered in museums and memorials, along with the multitude of written accounts by survivors, will be the only available remnants of the past calls for a greater ethical responsibility on the part of museums and memorials. Through the material and textual inheritance of the tragic past, we can understand and apprehend violence dealt to the dead.

Unrestored, damaged, rusting, and crumbling objects stir memory more strongly than those in good condition. There is certainly a heightened sense of drama in such artifacts. How they are perceived, however, is usually shaped by didactic panels, with the information they provide framing the nondiscursive, emotional, and ocular perception of artifacts by providing visitors with a specific interpretative lens. At sites of remembrance, such texts lead visitors to a preestablished and uniform, "ready-made" meaning, instead of allowing them to see the victims' personal belongings as they appear. As Benjamin wrote, they demand a specific kind of perception.[40] Supplementing such objects with preestablished explanations risks "silencing" them instead of creating new forms of engagement with contemporary viewers, even if they are nevertheless indispensable.

Suspended between materiality and immateriality, the present ontology of the last war's artifactual remains reveals a major pattern of the changing or diminishing materiality. In my search for nonessentialized authenticity, I focus on the signs of violent fragmentation or natural decay that are present in the physical fabric of wartime detritus, made evident by processes such as the crumbling of bricks, the formation of a patina on footwear, or such signs of aging and decay as discoloration. While these processes compromise objects' physical integrity, they also act as agents that actually amplify the sense of original provenance and historical trauma. As these processes evolve, the preference for authenticity understood as a noninterventionist faithfulness implicated in the artifacts' narrations must be relegated to the sphere of utopian anxiety.

Notes

1. My understanding of matter is thus close to the vitalist approach elaborated by Jane Bennett in *Vibrant Matter: A Political Ecology of Things* (Durham and London: Duke University Press, 2010), 52–61.
2. Oradur-sur-Glane is a village located in central France; on June 10, 1944 it was a site of a massacre by the German Waffen-SS company.
3. I do not adhere to the notion that a copy is better than an original.
4. The castle's inauthentic character ceased to bother the public since over time and with exposure to the elements, the structure acquired a certain patina that softens its once sparkling newness.
5. For instance, Nuremberg's Germanisches Nationalmuseum was installed in a fourteenth- century Carthusian monastery by incorporating modern galleries built of steel and glass.
6. I connect the notion of traumatic memory as a mental wound, as theorized by Cathy Caruth, to the concept of material transferability of trauma, while Caruth's approach stresses the tangled configuration of the unconscious and the known. See Cathy Caruth, *Unclaimed Experience: Trauma, Narrative and History* (Baltimore: Johns Hopkins University Press, 2016).

7. Roland Barthes described the notion of a punctum, present in a photographic image, as an aberrant and often subjective element that heightens and disturbs the photograph's perception; see Roland Barthes, *Camera Lucida: Reflections on Photography*, Robert Howard, trans. (New York: Hill and Wang, 1981), 25–26.
8. Walter Benjamin, "The Work of Art in the Age of its Technological Reproducibility," in Howard Eiland and Michael W. Jennings, eds., *Selected Writings Volume 3, 1938–1940*, trans. Edmund Jephcott et al. (Cambridge, MA and London: Belknap Press, 2003), 254.
9. Benjamin, "The Work of Art in the Age of its Technological Reproducibility," 254.
10. In Nazi Germany, the practice of looting and confiscating precious artworks from public museums and private collectors was officially backed by Nazi ideology. The extent of this practice has prompted debates, detective searches, police work, discoveries, and legal restitutions. In turn, these developments have led to new approaches in museum studies, putting the provenance of art at the center of scholarly attention in several major museums. For example, one Getty Research Institute initiative produced, in partnership with the Heidelberg University Library and Kunstbibliothek-Staatliche Museen zu Berlin, an online research database (German Sales Catalog) that provides access to German auction catalogs from 1930–45.
11. The acronym TN refers to a special unit called Technical Emergency Help (Technische Nothilfe).
12. This is particularly true of Warsaw's wartime ghetto area. There were three subsequent stages of Warsaw's destruction: the 1939 war campaign, the Warsaw Ghetto Uprising of 1943, and the Warsaw Uprising of 1944. Both uprisings were followed by a deliberate targeting of civilians and the built environment.
13. Tadeusz Kantor (1915–90) was a preeminent Polish theatre director, painter, set designer, and founder of the Cricot 1 and Cricot 2 theatre ensembles. Tadeusz Kantor, "Klisze przyszłości," *Metamorfozy: Teksty o latach 1934–1974*, in Pleśniarowicz Krzysztof, ed., *Pisma* vol. 1 (Wroclaw and Krakow: Księgarnia Akademicka, 2005), 97. For more on his approach to questions of materiality and the body, which were central to his theatrical-dramatic imagination, see also Magdalena Romanska, *The Post-traumatic Theatre of Grotowski and Kantor: History and the Holocaust in "Acropolis" and "The Dead Class,"* foreword by Kathleen Cioffi (London: Anthem Press, 2014).
14. Kantor, "Klisze przyszłości," 97. If not indicated otherwise, all translations are mine.
15. Such depersonalized visual statements as photographs and posters documenting monumental steel bridges and viaducts smashed by explosions were quickly employed as a persuasive propaganda tool to condemn the war and celebrate the rebuilding efforts across a liberated, postwar Europe.

16. In *Being and Time*, Martin Heidegger distinguishes between an object and a thing, the latter being broken, or out of service. One might therefore say that, in losing its usefulness, the bridge's status changed from an object to a thing.
17. KL Groß-Rosen was a sub-camp of the Sachsenhausen concentration camp.
18. Jerzy Porębski (Mieczysław Porębski's son) stated this in our e-mail correspondence from October 2018.
19. Tadeusz Różewicz, "The Professor's Knife," in *Sobbing Superpower*, trans. Joanna Trzeciak, foreword by Edward Hirsch (New York and London: W. W. Norton, 2011), 229. Tadeusz Różewicz (1921–2014) was an acclaimed Polish poet, playwright, writer, and translator.
20. Shannon Lee Dawdy, *Patina: A Profane Archaeology* (Chicago and London: The University of Chicago Press, 2016), especially see sub-chapter "A Brief History of Patina," 11–19.
21. Carol Kidron, "Breaching the Wall of Traumatic Silence: Holocaust Survivor and Descendant Person-Object Relations and the Material Transmission of the Genocidal Past," *Journal of Material Culture* 1, vol. 17 (2012), 3–21.
22. For more on the precarious ontology of artifacts, see Bożena Shallcross, *The Holocaust Object in Polish and Polish–Jewish Culture* (Bloomington and Indianapolis: Indiana University Press, 2011).
23. http://auschwitz.org/en/, News – main page.
24. As visitors read on the same page: "The entire project is carried out in compliance with the conservation philosophy of the Museum [that includes], among other things, reducing the necessary interventions to a minimum resulting from technical requirements and protecting to the maximum extent possible all preserved historical elements, while limiting aesthetic interventions and changes in the visual perception of the buildings."
25. http://auschwitz.org/en/, News – main page.
26. There are about 3,800 suitcases, out of which 2,100 bear the names of their owners.
27. As was the case with the suitcase that belonged to Else Ury, a well-known German-Jewish author of children's books who perished in Auschwitz. It was made from patent leather, elegant and adorned with solid brass hardware and an inscription on the lid. According to P. J. Grisar, it was a group of German youth who noticed the inscription, identified the owner using deportation lists, and wrote about their findings. See P. J. Grisar, "Remembering Else Ury, Famed Children's Writer and Victim of the Holocaust," *Forward*, July 17, 2019. https://bit.ly/308dx1o. Accessed September 20, 2019.
28. This phrase was coined by Dag T. Anderson in "Trusted Vagueness: The Language of Things and the Order of Incompleteness," in Bjørnar Olsen and Þóra Pétursdóttir, eds., *Ruin Memories: Materiality,*

Aesthetics and the Archaeology of the Recent Past (New York: Routledge, 2014), 33.
29. I refer to this kind of material desire as agalmatic (the Greek *agalma* means jouissance); it is a pleasure-inducing search for hidden valuables of all sorts, which under extreme conditions could mean even food. More on the agalmatic paradigm in Shallcross, *The Holocaust Object in Polish and Polish-Jewish Culture*.
30. Liliane Weissberg described the display of suitcases in Majdanek by comparing their hollow shapes to tombs that lack only the date of death. Liliane Weissberg, "In Plain Sight," Barbie Zelizer, ed., *Visual Culture and the Holocaust* (New Brunswick: Rutgers University Press, 2001), 24.
31. In this sense, the situation reflects our widespread asymmetrical approach to the object world.
32. Anne Laure Bandle, Raphael Contel, and Marc-André Renold compiled a detailed chronology and documentation of the fight over the suitcase in "Case Auschwitz Suitcase: Pierre Lévi Heirs and Auschwitz-Birkenau State Museum Oswiecim and Shoah Memorial Museum Paris." See *Platform ArThemis*, Art-Law Centre, University of Geneva, no date. https://bit.ly/3wzOrob. Accessed September 26, 2019.
33. A private home that is inaccessible to the public and lacks proper control of room temperature and humidity levels does not meet the requirements of this fragile object's conservation regime. A museum can provide the proper conservation as well as public accessibility that is limited only by opening hours and ticket prices.
34. http://auschwitz.org/en/. Auschwitz-Report-2013, 29.
35. Even today, the number of shoes in Majdanek is only approximate.
36. Edgar Snow, "Amerykanin i Anglik o Majdanku," *Rzeczpospolita* 27, 29 VIII, 1944.
37. Some documents indicate that theft occurred on a vast scale, sometimes even by the cartload. See Danuta Olesiuk, "Obuwie więźniarskie w zbiorach Państwowego Muzeum w Majdanku," *Zeszyty Majdanka* XXIV (2008), 235–62, and 245–46.
38. Olesiuk, "Obuwie więźniarskie w zbiorach Państwowego Muzeum w Majdanku," 237.
39. In the United States Holocaust Museum and Memorial, maintaining the shoes is a demanding conservation challenge, starting with the humidity and temperature control at the exhibit space through vacuuming the shoes' surface in situ and rotating a portion of shoes for a more thorough conservation. There is no interventional type of treatment of the artifacts (as per my email correspondence with the curators at the USHMM in 2012).
40. Benjamin, "The Work of Art in the Age of its Technological Reproducibility," 258.

8

Material Culture and Heritage

Laura McAtackney

Until relatively recently the concepts of heritage and material culture were treated as intimately connected. Breaking down heritage to its most basic binaries of cultural and natural heritage (and this chapter will almost exclusively focus on cultural, due to its close relationship with material culture), it was traditionally assumed that cultural heritage was a material thing that persisted into the present. This meant materials were viewed as being the starting point for how we defined heritage, how we considered it, how we legislated for it, and how we cared for it. In our contemporary world these binaries no longer hold firm, and this chapter will act to complicate our ideas about the relationship between heritage and materials. It will argue that heritage can be material as well as immaterial and that it has tangible as well as intangible qualities. In doing so, this chapter will trace the Eurocentric origins of heritage and how they have been increasingly challenged by indigenous and Global South conceptions and practices with both expected and unexpected consequences. It will note how the materials of heritage can be the old monumental things and the artifacts in "universal" museums but can also be interventions in the landscape and relatively mundane things such as lace. The "things" we call heritage are constantly in flux and this is driven by both bottom-up initiatives of communities and activists as well as top-down directives and conventions of global heritage organizations. We are currently at a particularly interesting juncture to explore and dissect the variety of relationships between material culture and heritage, especially regarding how it can differ across various scales (from the international through national down to community), in terms of legal protections, in practice as well as in academic conceptions.

As a starting point, one must look back to the construction of heritage as a concept and to the original domination of Global North, and especially Eurocentric, values that have roots in the empirical, modern, and "progressive" ideas of the European Enlightenment. These underlying assumptions set the tone for global ideas about what is considered heritage and their emphasis on material forms had been naturalized until relatively recently.[1] One only need examine the long list of international treaties that have aimed to protect, conserve, and exult the material remains of past human cultures to note the emphasis on the material and monumental. The long-established practice of assuming heritage is material culture continues to have ramifications. Martin Carver has argued that what we "value" as heritage has become self-replicating, rather than diversifying, and is often directly inspired by those things that were previously established as "of value." This resulted in the continued emphasis on the ancient, monumental, and durable.[2] One could argue that one of the earliest international treaties that was created to protect heritage was intimately connected to materials – the Hague Convention for the Protection of Cultural Property in the Event of Armed Conflict (1954).[3] In the first protocol, "cultural property" was only defined in terms of materials and the convention was primarily concerned with preventing "any form of theft, pillage or misappropriation of, and any acts of vandalism directed against, cultural property." Clearly, cultural property in 1954 was considered as self-evidently materialistic and universally acknowledged as of "great importance" and thereby required protection. Consideration of the intangible issues of meaning, and how it may change, was not a concern in early heritage discourse.

Since the 1960s, terminology used to govern "heritage" in international treaties has expanded to incorporate more flexibility and less explicitly materialist definitions of Global South and indigenous heritage. This includes the move from self-contained "sites" to more holistic "landscapes."[4] However, a major break in the implicit connection between heritage and material culture was not clearly articulated until the codification of immaterial or intangible aspects of heritage within the Australasian context with the Burra Charter starting in 1979.[5] In terms of heritage practice, the Burra Charter, and its various updates, have been viewed as an evolving document that has redefined heritage. This charter used existing international conventions as inspiration but reformulated them in ways that made sense to the Australasian context. This meant moving beyond object-oriented heritage to employ terminology such as "place," "cultural significance," and "fabric" to allow for the intangible nature of much indigenous heritage (Moore also discusses this in Chapter 11).[6] It is surely not a coincidence that in such an environment, Australian scholars have been so influential in terms of spearheading "critical heritage studies" since the early 2010s. This now global movement has presented a strong challenge to the idea that heritage and materials are somehow natural bedfellows. The work of Laurajane Smith, in particular, has been extremely influential in directing critical heritage discourse away from assuming heritage is a material thing. In her important monograph *Uses of Heritage* she argued, "There is, really, no such thing as heritage." In clarification, she argued that there is no such thing as heritage being restricted to "old, grand, monumental and aesthetically pleasing sites, buildings, places and artifacts." In its place critical heritage studies has centered the understanding that all heritage is by its very nature intangible because it is about processes of engagement, acts of communication, and the ability to make meaning in the present.[7] At the time of writing, in 2019, the ideas of Smith still hold significant sway; indeed it could be argued that her works on illuminating and then critiquing the "authorized heritage discourse" of traditional heritage have become the "authorized discourse" for critical heritage scholars. However, this interpretation is not unchallenged. In particular, the theoretically nuanced works of "new materialists," such as Þóra Pétursdóttir and Bjørnar Olsen, have increasingly asserted the centrality of materials to understanding heritage.[8]

By necessity, this chapter will be selective in terms of what it explores. It will start with an overview of definitions and terminology. For such a vast field there will be gaps and oversights, however, the aim is to explore heritage's relationship with material culture that moves beyond the texts of scholars, moves across scales, and includes the role of global organizations and heritage practitioners in shaping our ideas. In doing so, this chapter will recognize that heritage is a broad field and touches on the aligned discipline of memory studies. Alongside exploring heritage as it exists in institutions – such as museums – and in normative societies, it will also consider the roles of materials in remembering difficult pasts and how this can make heritage both a powerful force for change but also a potentially dangerous focus for attack. In terms of sources, this chapter will use a variety of case studies and will highlight the significance of national and international charters, treaties, and documents in directing, shaping, and sometimes following how we think about and manage heritage as a multifaceted, complex, and contested arena of theory, practice, and law.

Definitions

"Heritage" is a broad and generally loosely defined term that needs some unpacking, especially to allow a fuller understanding of its complicated and evolving relationship with material culture. In terms of academic discourse, heritage has been used to describe traditions, legacies, ancestries, and material remnants from the past that are considered meaningful, at least to some individuals and collectives, in the present. This means heritage can be many things. It can be about the materials,[9] it can be about practice,[10] it can be about process,[11] it can be about legal designation,[12] it can be about value,[13] it can be about the global,[14] the national,[15] the individual.[16] Heritage can be prosaically described as "things of value that we wish to keep,"[17] cynically labeled as "a commodity that nobody seems able to define, but which everybody is eager to sell"[18] or we can simply accept defeat and state it "all but defies definition."[19] In essence, it is a term that is so broadly defined that it has become a catch-all term for almost anything; as a term it has global reach and so it is seldom closely defined. Indeed, one could argue that its power resides in a lack of specific definition allowing for it to encompass many different (even contradictory) meanings, modes of practice, and theoretical standpoints. In terms of how it is understood globally, one can revert back to the carefully worded documents of international treaties, agreements, and charters to retrieve how the term "heritage" has evolved across spatial and temporal dimensions. In this respect, heritage can be articulated as material and immaterial, tangible and intangible, cultural and natural, of the past and of the present, and a mixture of all. One of the most frequently quoted definitions of heritage emphasizes its cross-temporal nature, "our legacy from the past, what we live with today and what we pass on to future generations."[20] Such definitions can be useful because they ignore debates about what heritage *actually is* to instead focus on our presumed relationship with it – that of custodians and/or protectors of something of value.

To date, heritage's most influential scale of influence has been at the level of the nation state. The role of heritage in creating and shaping the modern nation state, especially in western Europe and European settler societies, can be seen by the importance placed on heritage as material culture in defining what (and by extension whom) is included and excluded from the imaginary of this ultimate "imagined community."[21] During what Hobsbawm and Ranger have called the "age of invention" in the nineteenth century the material culture of national heritage became central to how nations defined and presented themselves both internally and externally.[22] This was not only in institutionalizing the past through the creation of national museums to house national collections, but also in terms of selecting what material culture was showcased within them. Museums have been central, alongside traditions, monuments, and ceremonies, in consciously forming the nation. Evans has argued that museums allow for the nation to be "imagined in a particular and selective style" that is powerful due to both its tangible and symbolic form.[23] In the Global North, the selecting, acquiring, and displaying of material culture as representing the nation was often supplemented through the acquisition and display of the material culture of the colonial "other." This mechanism was used not only as a means of reflecting power and mastery but also in defining the boundary between "us" and "them."

It is important to acknowledge that these boundaries continue to exist and have power. Following Divya Tolia-Kelly, we can view the traditional, Global North museums (her case study was the British Museum) through a postcolonial lens as a place of unequal power relations that continues "taxonomies and hierarchies of culture that underpin its use."[24] However, there have been notable attempts by preexisting and newly established museums to decolonialize, decentralize, and democratize their collections and role in many contemporary societies starting with the "New Museology" movement from the late 1980s.[25] This includes meaningful attempts to repatriate material culture, including through the implementation of legislation, such as NAGPRA in the USA, as well as those looted from colonials contexts that have been housed in so-called "universal museums,"[26] from many national museums in Europe. On an internal management level, there are ongoing attempts to address the implicit biases that still lurk in many museum practices, policies, and personnel in terms of inclusion and serving contemporary communities (Sorin discusses this further in Chapter 9). Furthermore, the establishment of new museums in significant locations can contribute to cementing their narratives into the national heritage discourse, such as the addition of the National Museum of the American Indian (established 1989) and Museum of African American History (opened in 2016) as part of the Smithsonian Institution and most importantly, in central Washington, DC.

Delving deeper into terminology in order to ascertain what materials constitute heritage, especially in terms of those that are acquired, accessioned, and displayed in museums, makes the term yet more difficult to pin down. What is considered "heritage" in the UK can differ greatly from Australia or Denmark or Nigeria or Singapore. This is because "heritage" at once reflects the historic connection of materials to the nation alongside their potential for continual reemergence in the contemporary. Therefore, it is in attempting to categorize the materials that we can argue that heritage is not simply a material thing because heritage is related to the values and meanings we place upon them. Following David Harvey, heritage can be considered a process that is about selecting, valuing, collecting, and curating. In terms of national heritage, there is a presumption that the most exceptional remnants of the past should be collected in order to protect and preserve them.[27] A by-product of this collecting is to reflect on the value of the past as a means of creating pride and meaning in the present. This selection process allows for the curation of a very selective memory of the national past.

The increasing acknowledgment of the politics of heritage and the subjective nature of what we decide is our heritage – and what is conveniently forgotten – has been thoughtfully critiqued by critical heritage scholars in recent years. Many have moved their lens from examining the materials of "cultural heritage" to instead dissecting the meanings placed on these materials, the role of the expert in defining them and the processes involved in "valuing" them as heritage.[28] Expanding on discussions in the introduction, Laurajane Smith has been particularly influential in articulating the hidden power of the "authorized heritage discourse" (or "AHD") of the nation – that is, those things accepted as national heritage, considered part of our identities, collected by museums, and utilized as focal points of commemoration.[29] She has argued that this AHD has acted to maintain the status quo and preexisting unequal power relations that are a feature of modern, capitalist societies. This has resulted in the materials selected to be naturalized as "our" heritage being in reality mainstream and middle-class representations of an imagined collective identity. Whereas the AHD is supposedly representing everyone, it often acts to exclude those who are marginalized, othered, or do not associate their values and experiences with the mainstream of society. If we follow those arguments then there is a need to unpack not only what we assume heritage is but the connections between the seeming immutability of material culture, on the one hand, and the potential for fluctuating meaning on the other in order to question not only what heritage is but how and why heritage is created. In this respect, there is a need to expand our definitions of heritage beyond AHD and the presentation of heritage in specially curated environments. For while heritage is often connected with a positive celebration of collective identity, and is put on display in museums as a source of pride, there are categories of heritage that connect to the darker, more difficult, and negative aspects of the past. In many cases they have been deliberately retained and curated as a form of memory practice. The next section will examine the relationship between heritage, material culture, and its role in selective remembering (and forgetting) of our more difficult pasts.

Dark Heritage, Material Culture, and Memory

One cannot discuss heritage without highlighting the role of memory. This is not simply in terms of acknowledging the growth in importance of memory studies in the humanities more broadly – and its subsequent interconnections with the aligned field of heritage – but also in considering the role of memory in how societies function. Memory is often articulated around materializations of the past intruding into the present (and subsequently becoming heritage). Memory studies has grown rapidly in importance through the 1980s and 1990s, primarily due to high-profile history versus memory disputes in historical studies and the breakdown of post–World War II and post–Cold War certainties in contemporary Global North societies.[30] Although still paying homage to many of the foundational thinkers of the discipline with its enduring focus on communal memory,[31] memory studies has developed in many directions pushing boundaries and establishing new and innovative frontiers of research. This includes incorporating the experience of forgetting, intersecting Holocaust memory with postcolonial studies, making sense of the Anthropocene, and future studies.[32]

In many ways, the study of memory is interconnected with heritage as both are broadly interdisciplinary fields that span humanities disciplines and are preoccupied with dissecting how the past-present-future are made meaningful, relate to, and constitute each other. There is also a significant crossover in memory studies and heritage in terms of their focus on how and why negative and difficult aspects of the past are retained in the present. In memory studies the overwhelming influence of studies of the Holocaust and how it is remembered – from the trauma memories of individual survivors through to the collective guilt of perpetrator societies – has ensured some of the darkest episodes of the recent past have developed and shaped the discipline (Shallcross Chapter 7).[33] In this respect, the emphasis on material culture has been an extremely important facet of understanding and exploring memory.[34] This has resulted in publications theorizing the relationship between memory and materials and led to in seminal texts in both disciplines.[35] To a lesser but still notable extent, heritage scholars have also had a long-term preoccupation with why we choose to retain aspects of difficult and dark pasts as heritage, with some of the most influential work also focusing on the Holocaust.[36] In many ways these two disciplines are intimately connected in their twin concerns with why and how we choose to remember difficult pasts and the role of contemporary politics in how this is shaped and continues to evolve.

When exploring the relationship between the difficult pasts, heritage, and material culture we need, again, to be cognizant of terminology. There remains a lack of consensus as to how we prefix the "heritage" of difficult pasts in order to differentiate it from the more normative "heritage" of pride and celebration. The term "negative heritage" was coined by Lynn Meskell in describing what she called "a conflictual site that becomes the repository of negative memory in the collective imaginary" in response to the symbolic and physical transformations of the World Trade Center after the 9/11 attacks.[37] Although the term has been used a number of times[38] it has not been established as the dominant descriptor for the wide range of heritages that could be considered "negative." Before Meskell was writing about sites of conflict and violence as heritage, J. E. Tunbridge and G. J. Ashworth coined the term "dissonant heritage" in order to highlight the contentiousness of heritage in, and of, conflict. They highlighted how different events, places, or materials can be interpreted in oppositional and even contradictory ways by the protagonists in terms of heritage.[39] Similarly, David Uzzell and Roy Ballantyne had been writing about "heritage that hurts" and their call for heritage practitioners to engage with the "hot interpretation" of conflict sites – that is, interpreting heritage sites to ensure audience engagement with their emotional impact – since the late 1980s. One of their key case studies was the changing interpretive approaches to the ruined French village of Oradour-sur-Glane, which was razed by Nazis during World War II.[40]

The term "difficult heritage" has also been used by scholars in order to explain a range of sites that vary from the darkest reaches of the Nazi German past, such as at Nuremburg, to the more ambiguously named places of "pain and shame."[41] The latter category includes overt places of conflict such as massacre sites as well as the infrastructure of structural violence such as internment camps, detention centers, and prisons.[42] Lastly, the term "dark heritage" is a relatively widely used term that has been employed to cover a wide gamut of places, events, experiences, and materials. It is difficult to pinpoint exactly when it first appeared in print, but it seems to have been inspired by, if not derived from, the more widely used "dark tourism."[43] Catherine Roberts and Philip Stone[44] have written about the crossover of the two terms in terms of "how dark tourism can construct and disperse knowledge through touristic consumption of traumascapes that, in turn, can help make contested heritage places salient and meaningful."

However, the slipperiness of these terms is evident in how this relationship can be viewed from various angles. I have discussed "dark heritage" in the context of a derelict prison in a reversal of Roberts and Stone's portrayal of the relationship between tourism and heritage. When writing about the politically loaded site of Long Kesh/Maze prison in Northern Ireland (2014), it had been presented by the media and a range of academics[45] to the public as a difficult and yet meaningful place of unofficial heritage that had not yet made the transition to a site of tourism (and indeed may never do so). This short overview of terminology is not simply to illuminate the wide range of perspectives and descriptors for this specific area of heritage studies – and to show how little agreement there is in how we describe them – but to also indicate how this form of heritage is almost universally contextualized through case studies that take material form. The close connection between material culture and difficult heritage comes from an implicit understanding that materials are authentic connections to those difficult pasts (see Shallcross's Chapter 7 as applied to Holocaust materials) and are a prerequisite to ensuring the impossibility of forgetting. In this way, the materiality of conflict, trauma, and outrage holds a special place in heritage practice and studies. While debates may ebb and flow between materialists and constructivists in Global North academies regarding the importance of material authenticity versus the construction of value that is placed on material, they do not impinge on the centrality of material remains in remembering conflict.[46]

At sites that are considered central to the memory culture of conflict and atrocities, such as Auschwitz-Birkenau, the focus on preservation of the material remains can be all-encompassing. For example, the website of Auschwitz-Birkenau makes a direct connection between the importance of the material remains of the former concentration camp and remembering. This is consciously done not only to ensure against forgetting but also to ensure the past is not repeated in the future. Its foundation emphasizes: "it is imperative that we keep the authenticity of the Auschwitz-Birkenau Memorial viable and palpable" in order to "Help us to warn humanity against itself. Do not allow history to become a deafening silence." In this respect, the primacy of the material, and anxiety about its potential loss, is overwhelming.[47] The degree that the maintenance of the original material culture of the site is a focus of its contemporary management can be seen not only in the prominence "Preservation" is given on the website but also how broad that preservationist agenda spreads. "Preservation" is broken down in categories to include a sub-tab for the conservation of the natural heritage of Auschwitz-Birkenau. The aim of the "conservation of vegetation" is "to rescue and display all the extant vestiges of the camp," including "the special arrangement of trees that was used to camouflage the mass killing facilities."[48] This holistic approach and broad understanding of the material realities of the landscape of the former concentration camp is revealing not only in its level of detail but also in the changing language between the aim of "preserving" cultural heritage and "conserving" natural heritage. This interplay between terminology highlights different implicit understandings as to the aims and limits of what we can do to maintain the material nature of cultural versus natural heritage.

The distinction between preserving and conserving may seem an important division, but one could argue that attempting to completely focus on the material form of a complicated place at a particular point in its biography is not only impossible but, in practice, it is undesirable. Regardless of how much the material form of the heritage is deemed integral to remembering, there are always choices made that ensure some materials are promoted whereas others are sidelined or even conveniently forgotten. Writing at a time before its future as heritage had been fully confirmed, Lynn Meskell's discussion on the heritage potential of the World Trade Center site saw no other potential future for the site. However, even in accepting this foregone conclusion, she opined it would require material negotiation: "Despite the potency of the WTC site, it would be unthinkable to preserve the site as it remains – it requires a complete reconfiguration including appropriate memorialization."[49] It transpired as predicted: the transformed site of the World Trade Center was designated to be heritage and in this value transition it was heavily curated in a way to allow it to make sense for those who would visit it afterwards as a site of memory.[50]

Moving away from the Global North, the long-term experience of working with the material culture of the Rwandan genocide (1994) has created its own particular material concerns. This includes having to navigate the problematic preservation needs of the ultimate material remains of genocide – human remains – due to their inclusion in heritage sites of memory. The use of human remains as central to preserving the memory of the genocide in Rwanda has a number of facets. They are viewed as appropriate material to remember the horrors of ethnic genocide while also acting to prevent attempts at genocide denial. On a more practical level, the retention of mass graves and large collections of skeletal human remains *in situ* also answers a governmental need to collectivize the human remains to prevent costly attempts to locate individual bodies while they focus on the pressing concerns of restoring civic society for the survivors.[51] The "raw" authenticity of preserving human remains has been articulated as important to local survivors and their communities but it has had mixed responses from international tourists, who often voice their culturally dictated distaste at treating human remains in ways that differ from their societies. On a more prosaic level, human remains also present long-term preservation challenges: how do you maintain a large number of skeletal remains in their current (powdered lime) form of preservation while dealing with a tropical climate and lack of significant funds?[52] Will there come a stage when the society – or sections of it – demand they are no longer on display? These are the darkest of dark questions associated with the material remains of conflict and for heritage managers there are few easy answers.

Lastly, in terms of the relationship between difficult, negative, or dark heritage and materials there is the need to engage with the delicate issue of the limitations of materials in remembering and forgetting. To facilitate sites of memory to be preserved and presented in the aftermath of conflict there exists a selection process that simultaneously ensures alternative sites – that may contain similar or different narratives – are forgotten and potentially lost. An interesting case study, explored by Mats Burström and Bernhard Gelderblom, is Bückeberg, the site of the Third Reich Harvest Festival in Germany. Bückeberg was an arena designed by Albert Speer that was dismantled after World War II and eventually housing was built alongside it for ordinary citizens. However, an extensive footprint of the arena survives in the landscape, especially the Führerweg, which is a causeway of four to five meters wide elevated as much as one meter above ground level.[53] The local desire to ignore the potential dark heritage of this place has ensured that despite federal interest in assigning it status, the local district council has argued that there is no need for a "green meadow" to be protected as heritage when housing is a more pressing issue for the locale. It was not designated as an official heritage site, and there was little willingness by the local population for it to be recognized despite the heritage of World War II eliding sites of Nazi spectacle from the national picture.[54]

Such marginal sites can be inconvenient to remember, especially because they make us recognize the active acquiescence of the wider populace to the Nazi regime; they are an ambiguous presence in the landscape and sit at the cusp of being considered "heritage." While not representing the most obvious "material culture" of Nazism, Bückeberg does retain material traces that are discreet enough to be ignored by those who wish to forget them but can also be located by those who wish to find them. Burström and Gelderblom noted that already in 2011, Bückeberg was becoming an unofficial heritage site for neo-Nazis who wished to visit the rallying sites of the Third Reich.[55] They raise questions as to what can be or should be done with such places. Must there be official recognition of materials as heritage for them to be meaningful to others and can we stop materials becoming a form of heritage if interested people decide they are? Can transformed, ignored, and forgotten materials associated with conflict be reinvigorated, even if this is not desired by those who live alongside them? How much "material" needs to survive for it to be the "material culture" of a place, structure, or event? In this context, how we define "material" is by necessity very broad and ambiguous. Clearly, the case of Bückeberg shows that the material presence may be as subtle as traces in the landscape. Whereas the decaying bones of genocide can be viewed as the most meaningful material culture of a national memorial in the "new" Rwanda. Following Laurent Olivier's argument, the "material memory" of the past that persists in the present is not always understood, explored, or lauded as such but while it remains it retains the latent ability to presence various pasts (even if they are not doing so).[56] Those materials can take many forms, but as long as such materials are not purposefully and thoroughly eradicated, they retain the potential to be "discovered" and become heritage at some future point.

The (Im)Material Nature of Heritage

On moving from the "material culture" of heritage to considering its "immaterial" nature, it is important to remember its previous centrality to conceptions of heritage and exactly why it has been challenged by both scholars and practitioners. This is especially apparent in the reconceptualization of heritage in international documents, treaties, and charters. The Australian heritage document, the Burra Charter, is often presented as one of the first major heritage documents that initiated a deviation from the Eurocentric model of prioritizing the material, monumental, and ancient. The Burra Charter, with its many updates, has been extremely influential in presenting a form of heritage management that is not solely focused on conserving materials. The current version defines heritage as explicitly including the immaterial, including a definition of place that concludes it "may have tangible and intangible dimensions." The aim of this broad definition is not solely to move beyond the monumental and static as heritage but also to allow for heritage to have a multiplicity of potential meanings and "a range of values."[57] Following the Burra Charter, there have been other international documents that have deemphasized the material, which likewise have been initiated outside of Europe. The ICOMOS/UNESCO Nara Document on Authenticity was drafted in 1994 and has had a much bigger impact than its original aim, which was to insert Japanese practices of dismantling, repairing, and reassembling wooden temples into international conservation best practice.[58] Stovel has argued that this document marked a "watershed moment" in modern conservation practices due to its putting in place a set of internationally applicable conservation principles that accepted conservation decisions were relative to the societal context rather than absolute rules.[59] This meant that the emphasis on authenticity being inherent in the materials was no longer a guiding principle of international conservation best practice. Taken together, the impact of the Burra Charter and Nara Document on international conceptions of heritage have been significant. Without these documents, one could not imagine the UNESCO Convention for the Safeguarding of the Intangible Culture Heritage being created in 2003. This convention follows and reflects the increasing influence of non-Eurocentric models of heritage practice and theory that has allowed for heritage to move beyond the material to encompass a wide range of "practices, representations, expressions, knowledge, skills."[60]

At its most basic level, the importance of the 2003 Convention can be viewed quantitatively through how many countries have ratified it. By the tenth anniversary there had been 155 ratifications, which compares favorably with the 187 ratifications of the much more established World Heritage Convention (1972). Examining the impact of this convention qualitatively reveals the factors and nuances behind its success. Starting with a direct comparison of how the 1972 World Heritage and 2003 Intangible Heritage lists compare, Janet Blake has argued that the former is a "hit-parade of outstanding examples of cultural and natural heritage," while in contrast the 2003 Convention "is intended to include representative examples ... to showcase the diversity of Intangible Cultural Heritage present around the world."[61] One could argue that this binary presentation of the two lists may be overstating the differences. In terms of origins, Hafstein has emphasized that the 2003 Convention developed from a Korean formal proposal in 1993 to establish a UNESCO system of Living Cultural Properties that, at that time, was directly modeled on the 1972 Convention in terms of selecting "treasures."[62] In practice, the convention has left negotiating room for groups, governments, and international organizations to navigate it and utilize it in ways that work for them. Blake has argued the 2003 Convention's successes are due to its ability to address the flaws of the World Heritage List – that is, it does not reify the material or promote competition – by instead emphasizing the human context of heritage.[63] However, the 2003 Convention focusing on "intangible" heritage does not mean that material culture is absent – indeed many of the listed heritages are explicitly material – but it refocuses on why the material is meaningful, and it allows for that material culture to be mutable and living. Furthermore, the removal of a competitive undertone allows for the inclusion of heritage that represents the previously unconsidered, non-elite, and marginalized forms. The repercussions of designating "intangible heritage" in this way has allowed for all member states to break from the assumption that heritage must follow traditional, European models that demand long-term preservation of large monuments created of durable materials.[64]

However, the move from "exceptional" (World Heritage List) to "representative" (Intangible Cultural Heritage) listing criteria has not necessarily freed the 2003 Convention from all the critiques of elitism and political usages. The acceptance of cultural heritage as being immaterial as well as materialistic has had repercussions on how nation states have designated, protected, and prioritized their heritage and not all of these are positive celebrations of intangible heritage. One interesting case to highlight the changing relationship between the state agencies, heritage, and intangibility is that of Ireland. Despite Ireland's long history, extensive diaspora, and vibrant material and intangible cultural heritage it has very few designations on the World Heritage List. Since becoming a signatory of the convention in 1991, Ireland has only added two sites (with seven tentative). The two listed sites are traditional "Eurocentric" entries – a collection of ancient, monumental tombs that contain the largest concentration of prehistoric, megalithic art in Europe (Brú na Bóinne) and a "unique" site of early, Christian monastic settlement located on an isolated outcrop off the west coast of Ireland in the Atlantic Ocean (Sceilg Mhichíl). Both sites were added within five years of Ireland signing the convention (1993 and 1996 respectively) and both are "traditional" – ancient, monumental, and static – material forms of Irish heritage. Since 1996 there have been no new additions to the list and five of the seven sites currently languishing on the tentative list (all in 2010) are cultural additions that reinforce the ancient and monumental.[65]

A wider view of the societal and political context in Ireland since the 1990s provides some explanation as to the less than enthusiastic participation on the World Heritage stage. One can trace a changing relationship between "Official" Ireland and heritage as material culture through a focus on two major changes since 2000: first, the major economic crisis that began in 2008 and second, the ratification of the 2003 Intangible Heritage Convention (in 2015). Since Ireland became a signatory of the Intangible List, it has been active in creating an initial inventory of thirty cultural practices that are considered the cornerstone of "intangible" heritage of Ireland.[66] The new inventory covers many aspects of Irish culture from the highly material – Limerick lace – to the almost completely intangible – Cant/Gamon, the traditional languages of Irish travelers. Three of these national "intangible heritages" have been added to the global Intangible Cultural Heritage list, including the traditional *Gaelige* sport of hurling (2018), Uilleann piping (2017), and Irish harping (2019). This highly publicized and focused engagement with the Intangible Cultural Heritage list, in comparison to the relative neglect of the World Heritage list, ties into a wider governmental policy change regarding how they engage with heritage.

Lagerqvist has argued that post-2008 economic crisis, the Irish government's policy toward heritage has been reconceptualized with heritage moving from being old material sites requiring protection to a revenue-creating resource ripe to be exploited. She has argued that this rebranding of heritage – as an economic driver of recovery – is notable in the shift in language from heritage belonging to everyone and in need of protection, to something requiring management, as "non-problematic and integrated with development."[67] One could argue this view on heritage was merely sharpened by stark economic difficulties, as there have been longstanding, heated debates in Ireland regarding how to balance development alongside protecting Ireland's traditional (archaeological) heritage. In the early 2000s there were highly public and vitriolic exchanges that followed the controversial plan to construct a new motorway close to the ancient royal site of Tara in 2003.[68] One could argue that the ongoing fall-out from the Tara dispute, and the interest in intangible cultural heritage, dovetailed at the right time in Ireland. The known implications and restrictions of managing and protecting material sites placed on the World Heritage list (see Gnecco, Chapter 6, for more detailed discussions on the implications of World Heritage status in South America) has made it less attractive to pursue in comparison to the alternative of acknowledging cultural forms and activities that are non-site specific and do not require material protection. In effect, the 2003 convention has provided an alternative means for promoting Ireland's cultural heritage on a global scale without the *material* repercussions (and the extensive management plans) of protecting sites placed on a World Heritage list.

Clearly, the tracing of the "immaterial" or intangible nature of heritage is just as complex as tracing the relationship between heritage and material nature. There has been a global turn in emphasis from fixating on the material nature of heritage to recognizing heritage is not just about conserving immutable, monumental, and elite structures as static entities for future generations. The influence of heritage practices and realities from the Global South and societies with indigenous cultures has ensured we are not simply concerned with the conservation of materials; heritage has been reconceptualized as a changeable, living expression of culture (Moore develops this argument in Chapter 11). This change of perspective is welcome but there has been little written about the potential problems that might arise from a stark turn from the material to the "intangible." As the case with Ireland has shown, it does present an opportunity for development-friendly Global North countries to enthusiastically embrace "intangible" heritage as a means of promoting national heritage globally that implicitly downplays the need to protect traditional sites. Furthermore, a perusal of the Intangible Heritage list reveals that while the 2003 Convention has moved beyond a focus on materials, there remains a strong connection to material culture that should not be completely bypassed. One of the first additions to the Intangible Heritage list– Jamaa el Fna Square in Marrakech, Morocco – has already been the subject of a number of critical assessments due to the impact of heritage tourism. This is because the lack of "safeguarding" in order to facilitate the "intangible" nature of the heritage can underplay the significance of its materiality.[69] Is it now necessary to defend the material basis of heritage?

New Materialism and Heritage

The increasingly popular writings of "new materialists" in heritage studies are articulating theoretically sophisticated cases *for* emphasizing material culture alongside refocusing the role and place of heritage in the contemporary world. In the crossover area between contemporary archaeology and critical heritage studies, there have been intriguing attempts to push back against a more general shift to the intangible. This has been especially notable from a group of "new materialists," primarily based in Northern Europe, who have written a number of widely discussed and debated papers, edited volumes, and books "in defense of things."[70] Many of these writings have emanated from Tromsø under the guidance of Bjørnar Olsen. In particular, the *Ruin Memories*, *Object Matters*, and This project was ongoing when I wrote this piece but it is now completed *Unruly Heritages* projects have produced an outpouring of nuanced and at times provocative publications and events that have articulated heritage and contemporary archaeology as disciplines with a renewed focus on materials. Þóra Pétursdóttir's *Concrete Matters* used the case study of an abandoned fish factory in Iceland to explicitly critique Laurajane Smith's focus on intangible heritage. Pétursdóttir argued that heritage management has always implicitly focused on heritage having meaning that is connected to humans, and she called for a new recognition that there are separate tangible qualities inherent in material heritage.[71] In this respect, Pétursdóttir, Olsen, and many archaeologists of a "new materialist" persuasion have directly confronted and critiqued the dominance of constructivist articulations of heritage and in so doing have reasserted the importance of its material basis.

An interesting point of departure from many of the emerging "new materialist" (Yates [Chapter 2], Fitzsimmons and Schweitzer [Chapter 10], Grasskamp [Chapter 12], and Strang [Chapter 14] also discuss "new materialism") approaches is not only the primacy of the material but a deemphasis on the relationship between heritage and humans. Rather than exulting the material by reverting to an earlier model of "heritage as material culture that we find meaningful," their object-oriented research has taken a distinctly post-human perspective. In this respect, the exploration of ruins has been an especially fruitful arena. In Olsen and Pétursdóttir's edited volume *Ruin Memories: Materialities, Aesthetics and Archaeologies of the Recent Past*, they argued for the exploration of materials and places long forgotten – that are "unwanted, outmoded or discarded" – and their research has continued to evolve and change without overemphasizing human angles.[72] These ideas have also been promoted by the geographer Caitlin Desilvey, who has argued for the "curated decay" of heritage and against the interventions of conservation and preservation management. In her recent monograph she claims "a structure that is caught up in active processes of decay and dereliction has many more potential configurations than those structures that are consolidated or conserved."[73]

These boundary-pushing and thought-provoking arguments are gaining traction in critical heritage studies and practice and in doing so reinvigorating debates within the wider field, but they have also been the subject of strong critique.[74] My own personal reservations with this complete divorce of materials from a human context is that such a perspective can result in research that is both apolitical and privileged. Ignoring the context of why things become ruins – and how those ruins can be used to facilitate the eradication of difficult heritage – can have problematic consequences in contested places and times. I have recently argued in the context of an archaeological investigation of an abandoned (and ruined) Magdalene Laundry in Ireland, "While the patina of ruination can 'look' the same, can take the same material form, create the same patterns, contain the same biological components, the reasons for otherwise functional structures to be allowed to become 'ruined' can be very different." In my experience of working with post-conflict heritage, materials are important but so too are their evolving connections to individual people and wider society, especially when they appear not to be connected.[75] To limit our engagement with the materials of heritage as being exclusively post- or non-human, can result in interesting insights, but it can also unnecessarily skew the interpretations we can make of the materials we study.

Conclusion: Materials, Heritage, and the Future

Currently, we are at an interesting point in tracing the relationship between material culture and heritage. This chapter has highlighted trajectories that are complementary, oppositional, and even contradictory in terms of how they conceive the relationship with material culture within heritage international treaties, theory, and practice. Let us conclude by going back to near the start: David Lowenthal's foundational text *The Past is a Foreign Country*. These significant early texts created heritage as a scholarly discipline with an implicit focus on material culture. Lowenthal waxed lyrically about the many material forms and facets of nostalgia and how they facilitated the misremembering of the past. However, he was also very aware that what was being sought in retaining these nostalgic materials was not simply "stuff," rather they were vehicles for individual and collective meanings. He mused, "What pleases the nostalgist is not just the relic but his own recognition of it, not so much the past itself as its supposed aspirations, less the memory of what actually was than of what was thought possible."[76] In this respect, he set the tone for how heritage studies engaged with the slippery relationship between the past and its material remnants in the present.

It was after these ideas moved outside of the Anglo-American and European academies, and particularly were expanded by those working in archaeology and heritage in Australasia and Asia, that the shift to the "intangible" nature of heritage became apparent. The influence of Laurajane Smith's *The Uses of Heritage*,[77] in particular, has ensured that a constructivist approach to heritage, which emphasizes the politics of value, has long held sway. However, it is interesting to note how quickly accepted truths can be challenged. Just when we have reached the point when there seems to be a universal acceptance of the centrality of the nonmaterial and intangible aspects of heritage, then a counter-proposition is presented and begins to gain traction. "New materialist" heritage is not simply materialistic in focus; it has often been post-human, nonhuman and object-oriented. While there have been major critiques of these standpoints, there is little doubt that they have added a much-needed critical sharpening to heritage scholarly discussions in the age of the Anthropocene. Whether the detachment from human concerns and interests will traverse from academic writing to heritage practice in any significant way in the future is yet to be seen.

In conceiving this chapter, it was important to acknowledge that heritage has different manifestations, concerns, and interests beyond those of scholars. This chapter has presented some insights into the changing relationship between heritage and material culture at various scales. At an international level, the focus on the materials of heritage was a direct repercussion of World Wars and particularly how heritage is treated during times of war (1954). This concern has evolved into promoting heritage as a vehicle of peace through the emphasis on "universal" values (1972). In more recent years, there has been a more notable impact of non-European and North American understandings of heritage in shaping global ideas of heritage. This includes the idea that conservation does not have to solely aim to maintain an original material, but could be context-specific and could incorporate change, which has had major repercussions on global heritage thinking and practice.[78] It has shown how on the national scale, countries like Ireland have moved their focus to "intangible" heritage as a means of diversifying but also to potentially avoid difficult struggles between the desire for development over the need to protect the materials of the traditional old things of heritage.

Moving into the future, we are taking tentative steps toward reconfiguring the relationship between heritage and materials. The "new materialist" emphasis on the material nature of heritage and its disconnection from human agency is a new frontier that is beginning to influence how we deal with heritage in practice today. In June 2019 it was announced that the modernist masterpiece St. Peter's Seminary in Cardross, Scotland, would not be taken into state care and instead a policy of "curated decay" was recommended by Historic Environment Scotland.[79] This decision reflected the growing influence of nonhuman conceptions of heritage but also a pragmatism in rejecting the huge cost estimated to ensure an unwanted building could be made safely accessible to the public. Such pragmatism will be increasingly employed as more and more heritage sites fall into ruin or are impacted by the increasingly noticeable impacts of climate change.

There will always be a place for materials in the theory and practice of heritage – on a practical level, we fill our museums with material culture, we memorialize with it, we make connections through it, and we require the material survivals of the past to facilitate remembering (and forgetting). However, the relationship between heritage and material culture is no longer a straightforward one, if it ever was. We can no longer take for granted that heritage and materials are intimately connected. There are increasing questions as to the need to maintain, conserve, or retain the material culture of heritage solely due to human desires and needs, but can we divorce abandoned places from humans completely? Alfredo Gonzáles-Ruibal has argued that even in the humid jungles and ruinous towns of South America, buildings that are left as ruins or reconstituted as heritage remain problematic (see also Gnecco [Chapter 6]): "this [material] memory is not less biased than its human counterpart. It is not always a humble recollection."[80] We should not underestimate the complexities and biases of what Laurent Olivier has called "material memory"[81] and while we embrace the intangible nature of heritage, or its post-human condition, we should be aware that while there are materials there will always be other meanings waiting to be found.

Notes

1. William Logan, "Globalizing Heritage: World Heritage as a Manifestation of Modernism and Challenges from the Periphery," in *Twentieth Century Heritage: Our Recent Cultural Legacy: Proceedings of the Australia ICOMOS National Conference 2001, 28 November – 1 December 2001* (University of Adelaide, Adelaide, SA, 2010), 51–57.
2. Martin Carver, "On Archaeological Value," *Antiquity* 70 (1996), 45–56.
3. The Hague Convention for the Protection of Cultural Property in the Event of Armed Conflict (1954). Article 4, Article 1.
4. Yahaya Ahmad, "The Scope and Definitions of Heritage: From Tangible to Intangible," *International Journal of Heritage Studies* 12, no. 3 (2006), 292–96.
5. ICOMOS Australia. *The Burra Charter: The Australian ICOMOS Charter for Places of Cultural Significance* (Australia ICOMOS Incorporated: Burwood, [1979], 2013), 297.https://bit.ly/3rwG0I5.

6. Ibid.
7. Laurajane Smith, *Uses of Heritage* (London: Routledge, 2006), 11.
8. Þóra Pétursdóttir, "Concrete Matters: Ruins of Modernity and the Things Called Heritage," *Journal of Social Archaeology* 13, no. 1 (2013), 31–53; Þora Pétursdóttir and Bjørnar Olsen, "Imaging Modern Decay: The Aesthetics of Ruin Photography," *Journal of Contemporary Archaeology* 1, no. 1 (2014), 7–56.
9. Pétursdóttir, "Concrete Matters."
10. Rodney Harrison, *Heritage: Critical Approaches* (London: Routledge, 2013).
11. David C. Harvey, "A History of Heritage," in Brian Graham and Peter Howard, eds., *Research Companion to Heritage and Identity* (Basingstoke: Ashgate, 2008), 19–36.
12. John Carman, *Archaeological Resource Management: An International Perspective* (Cambridge: Cambridge University Press, 2015).
13. Randy Mason, "Assessing Values in Conservation Planning: Methodological Issues and Choices," in Graham Fairclough, Rodney Harrison, John H. Jameson Jr., and John Schofield, eds., *The Heritage Reader* (London: Routledge, 2008), 99–125.
14. UNESCO "World Heritage." http://whc.unesco.org/en/about/.
15. David Lowenthal, *The Heritage Crusade and the Spoils of History* (Washington, DC: Free Press, 1996).
16. Christine Finn, *Leave Stay Home*. www.leavehomestay.com/.
17. M. Brisbane and C. Wood, *A Future for our Past* (London: English Heritage, 1996).
18. Robert Hewison, *The Heritage Industry: Britain in a Climate of Decline* (London: Methuen, 1987), 12.
19. Lowenthal, *The Heritage Crusade*, 94.
20. UNESCO "World Heritage." http://whc.unesco.org/en/about/.
21. Benedict Anderson, *Imagined Communities: Reflections on the Origin and Spread of Nationalism* (London: Verso, 2016 [1983]).
22. Eric Hobsbawm, and Terence Ranger, *The Invention of Tradition* (Cambridge: Cambridge University Press, 1983).
23. Jessica Evans, "Introduction: Nation and Representation," in Jessica Evans and David Boswell, eds., *Representing the Nation: A Reader: Histories, Heritage and Museums* (Routledge: London, 1999), 1–8.
24. Divya P. Tolia-Kelly, "(Postcolonial) Museum: Presencing the Affective Politics of 'Race' and Culture," *Sociology* 50, no. 5 (2016), 897.
25. Including Peter Vergo, ed., *The New Museology* (London: Reaktion Books, 1989).
26. Neil G. W. Curtis, "Universal Museums, Museum Objects and Repatriation: The Tangled Stories of Things," *Museum Management and Curatorship* 21, no. 2 (2006), 117–27.
27. David Harvey, "Heritage Pasts and Heritage Presents: Temporality, Meaning and the Scope of Heritage Studies," *International Journal of Heritage Studies* 7, no. 4 (2001), 319–39.

28. For example, Harrison, *Heritage*; Harvey, "A History of Heritage," 19–36; Smith, *Uses of Heritage*.
29. Smith, *Uses of Heritage*.
30. Wulf Kansteiner, "Finding Meaning in Memory: A Methodological Critique of Collective Memory Studies," *History and Theory* 41 (May 2002), 179–97; Susannah Radstone, "Memory Studies: For and Against," *Memory Studies* 1, no. 1 (2008), 31–39.
31. Including Émile Durkheim, *The Rules of Sociological Method*, trans. S. A. Solovay and H. H. Mueller (New York: Free Press 1966 [1894]); Maurice Halbwach, *On Collective Memory* (London: University of Chicago Press, 1992 [1925]).
32. Paul Connerton, *How Modernity Forgets* (Cambridge: Cambridge University Press, 2009); Michael Rothberg, *Multidirectional Memory: Remembering the Holocaust in the Age of Decolonialization* (Stanford: Stanford University Press, 2009); Stef Craps, Rick Crownshaw, Jennifer Wenzel, Rosanne Kennedy, Claire Colebrook, and Vin Nardizzi, "Memory Studies and the Anthropocene: A Roundtable," *Memory Studies* 11, no 4. (2018), 498–515; Rosalind Shaw, "Provocation: Futurizing Memory," *Fieldsights*, 5 September 2013. https://culanth.org/fieldsights/provocation-futurizing-memory.
33. Primo Levi, *The Complete Works of Primo Levi* (London: Penguin Classics, 2015); Saul Friedlander, *Memory, History and the Extermination of the Jews of Europe* (Bloomington: Indiana University Press, 1993).
34. Kansteiner, "Finding Meaning in Memory."
35. Including Pierra Nora, "Between Memory and History: Les Lieux de Mémoire," *Representations* 26 (1989), 7–24.
36. Sharon Macdonald, *Difficult Heritage: Negotiating the Nazi Past in Nuremburg and Beyond* (London: Routledge, 2010).
37. Lynn Meskell, "Negative Heritage and Past Mastering in Archaeology," *Anthropological Quarterly* 75, no. 3 (2002), 557–74.
38. Including Cornelius Holtorf, "Can Less be More? Heritage in the Age of Terrorism," *Public Archaeology* 5, no. 2 (2006), 101–09; Trinidad Rico, "Negative Heritage: The Place of Conflict in World Heritage," *Conservation and Management of Archaeological Sites* 10, no. 4 (2008), 344–52.
39. J. E. Tunbridge and G. F. Ashworth, *Dissonant Heritage: The Management of the Past as a Resource in Conflict* (Chichester: Wiley, 1996).
40. David L. Uzzell, "The Hot Interpretation of War and Conflict," in David L. Uzzell, ed., *Heritage Interpretation: Volume 1: The Natural and Built Environment* (London: Belhaven Press, 1989), 33–47; David L. Uzzell and Roy Ballantyne, "Heritage that Hurts: Interpretation in a Post-Modern World," in David Uzzel and Roy Ballantyne, eds., *Contemporary Issues in Heritage and Environmental Interpretation: Problems and Prospects* (Norwich: The Stationery Office, 1998), 152–71.
41. Macdonald, *Difficult Heritage*.

42. William Logan and Keir Reeves, eds., *Places of Pain and Shame: Dealing with "Difficult Heritage"* (London: Routledge, 2008).
43. Term coined by John Lennon, and Malcolm Foley, "Editorial: Heart of Darkness," *International Journal of Heritage Studies* 2, no. 4 (1996), 195–97; John Lennon and Malcolm Foley, *Dark Tourism: The Attraction of Death and Disaster* (London: Thomson Learning, 2000).
44. Catherine Roberts and Philip R. Stone, "Dark Tourism and Dark Heritage: Emergent Themes, Issues and Consequences," in Ian Convery, Gerard Corsane, and Peter Davis, eds., *Displaced Heritage: Responses to Disaster, Trauma and Loss* (Woodbridge: Boydell Press, 2014), 9.
45. Including Brian Graham and Sara McDowell, "Meaning in the Maze: The Heritage of Long Kesh," *Cultural Geographies* 14, no. 3 (2007), 343–68.
46. Including Siân Jones, "Negotiating Authenticity Objects and Authentic Selves: Beyond the Deconstruction of Authenticity," *Journal of Material Culture* 15, no. 2 (2010), 181–203; Holtorf, "Can Less be More?;" Cornelius Holtorf, *Archaeology is a Brand! The Meaning of Archaeology in Contemporary Popular Culture* (New York: Routledge, 2007).
47. Piotr M. A. Cywiński, Auschwitz Birkenau Foundation. www.foundation.auschwitz.org/.
48. Auschwitz-Birkenau. "Memorial and Museum Auschwitz-Birkenau: Former German Nazi Concentration and Extermination Camp/Conservation of Vegetation." http://auschwitz.org/en/museum/preservation/vegetation.
49. Meskell, "Negative Heritage," 558.
50. Joy Sather-Wagstaff, *Heritage that Hurts: Tourists in Memoryscapes of September 11* (New York: Routledge, 2016).
51. Mona Friedrich and Tony Johnston, "Beauty versus Tragedy: Thanatourism and the Memorialization of the 1994 Rwandan Genocide," *Journal of Tourism and Cultural Change* 11, no. 4 (2013), 302–20.
52. Ibid, 311–13.
53. Mats Burström and Bernhard Gelderblom Burström, "Dealing with Difficult Heritage: The Case of Bückeberg, Site of the Third Reich Harvest Festival," *Journal of Social Archaeology* 11, no. 3 (2011), 272.
54. Ibid, 278.
55. Ibid.
56. Laurent Olivier, *The Dark Abyss of Time: Archaeology and Memory* (New York: AltaMira Press, 2011).
57. Burra Charter, Article 1, Article 2; Ahmed, "Scope and Definitions of Heritage."
58. Herb Stovel, "Origins and Influences of the Nara Document on Authenticity," *APT Bulletin* 39, nos. 2/3 (2008), 9–17.

59. Ibid.
60. UNESCO Convention for the Safeguarding of the Intangible Culture Heritage (2003 [2018]), 5.
61. Janet Blake, "Seven Years of Implementing UNESCOs 2003 Intangible Heritage Convention: Honeymoon Period or the 'Seven Year Itch'?" *International Journal of Cultural Property* 21 (2014), 298.
62. Hafstein, "Intangible Heritage," 94–95.
63. Blake, "Seven Years," 299.
64. Logan, "Globalizing Heritage," 55.
65. UNESCO 1972 World Heritage Convention.
66. Connor McCrave, "30 Cultural Practices Given Official State Recognition to 'Protect and Preserve' for Future Generations," Thejournal.ie. (July 18, 2019). www.thejournal.ie/cultural-heritage-state-recognition-4729827-Jul2019.
67. M. Lagerqvist, "Reverberations of a Crisis: The Practical and Ideological Reworkings of Irish State Heritage in Economic Crisis and Austerity," *Heritage & Society* 9, no. 1 (2016), 57–75.
68. Conor Newman, "In the Way of Development: Tara, The M3 and the Celtic Tiger," in Rosie Meade and Fiona Dukelow, eds., *Defining Events: Power, Resistance and Identity in Twenty-First Century Ireland* (Manchester: Manchester University Press, 2015), 32–50.
69. Thomas Schmitt, "Jemaa al Fna Square in Marrakech: Changes to a Social Space and a UNESCO Masterpiece of the Oral and Intangible Heritage of Humanity as a Result of Global Influences," *The Arab World Geographer* 8, no. 4 (2005), 173–95.
70. Including Bjørnar Olsen, *In Defense of Things: Archaeology and the Ontology of Objects* (Lanham: AltaMira Press, 2010); Timothy Webmoor, "STS, Symmetry, Archaeology," in Paul Graves-Brown, Rodney Harrison, and Angela Piccini, eds., *The Oxford Handbook of the Archaeology of the Contemporary World* (Oxford: Oxford University Press, 2012); Christopher Witmore, "Archaeology and the New Materialisms," *Journal of Contemporary Archaeology* 1, no. 2 (2014), 203–46; Bjørnar Olsen and Þora Pétursdóttir, "Unruly Heritage: Tracing Legacies in the Anthropocene," *Arkæologisk Forum* 35 (2016), 38–45; Olsen and Pétursdóttir, *Ruin Memories*; Gavin Lucas, "Archaeology and Contemporaneity," *Archaeological Dialogues* 22, no. 1 (2015), 1–15.
71. Pétursdóttir, *Concrete Matters*.
72. Olsen and Pétursdóttir, *Ruin Memories*.
73. Caitlin DeSilvey, *Curated Decay: Heritage Beyond Saving* (Minneapolis: University of Minnesota Press, 2017).
74. See responses to Pétursdóttir and Olsen, "Imagining Modern Decay," in defense of ruin photography.
75. Laura McAtackney, "Materials and Memory: Archaeology and Heritage as Tools of Transitional Justice at a Former Magdalen Laundry," *Éire-Ireland* 55, nos. 1+2 (2020): 221–44; Laura McAtackney, *An Archaeology of*

the Troubles: *The Dark Heritage of Long Kesh/Maze* (Oxford: Oxford University Press, 2014).
76. David Lowenthal, *The Past is a Foreign Country* (Cambridge: Cambridge University Press, 1985), 8.
77. Smith, *Uses of Heritage*.
78. Nara Document, "Nara Document on Authenticity," ICOMOS, 1994.
79. Phil Miller, "No Resurrection for St Peter's: New Report Urges 'Curated Decay' for Modernist Masterpiece," *Herald* (June 28, 2019).
80. Alfredo Gonzáles-Ruibal, "Ruins of the South," in Laura McAtackney and Krysta Ryzewski, eds., *Contemporary Archaeology and the City: Creativity, Ruination and Political Action* (Oxford: Oxford University Press, 2017), 162.
81. Olivier, *Dark Abyss of Time*.

9

Material Culture and the Politics and Profession of Preservation and Representation

Gretchen Sullivan Sorin

The study of American material culture has traditionally been more about style than substance – aesthetics than meaning. The abundance of objects, museums, and particularly histories devoted to the praise of great wealth defines a culture in which materialism and consumption are prized above all other values. In some historic houses, excess, grandiosity, and greed are the prevailing qualities. Rather than critically interrogating objects and exploring their meaning and role within American culture most museums – particularly historic houses and those focusing on the decorative arts – prefer to focus on the superficial. We value the object for its aesthetic qualities alone, perhaps because to scratch beneath the surface might be less comfortable for visitors who prefer the voyeuristic experience and less comfortable for boards and donors who were the purchasers and owners of these objects. Ironically, failing to critically interrogate objects may be one reason that many museums fail miserably at reaching the broader audiences they currently profess to desire as visitors.

For example, we know that the Isaac Bell House in Newport, Rhode Island "is a fully realized experiment that visually represents the search for an American style of architecture," according to the website of the Newport Preservation Society. The 1883 McKim Meade and White designed building blends Colonial American, European, and Asian influences and reflects not only an excellent and beautiful example of the shingle style of architecture, but is also a monument to the incredible wealth that individuals of the period achieved by speculating in cotton. This was not Bell's primary home, but merely his summer cottage. Bell was a very successful cotton merchant, a fact mentioned, but not explored in any depth, as a part of the interpretation of the building. Yet, the cultivation of cotton in the United States transformed the nation's economy as well as agriculture and labor in the south. Cotton and slavery were inextricably linked and many northerners as well as southerners grew rich from speculation in this industry and used that wealth to build great houses and summer houses like the Isaac Bell House. Despite the recent and well-publicized inclusion of more complete histories at sites like Mount Vernon, Montpelier, and Monticello, many, and perhaps most of the historic house museums in the United States continue to focus on "creating exquisite spaces," as one museum described their goal.

Museum professionals for years have argued that their museums are neutral spaces, welcoming to all. Yet, an obvious and deeper analysis indicates that these public spaces cannot possibly be neutral and obviously must reflect the values of the culture in which they were created, a sentiment of late that has sparked a popular debate and now appears on t-shirts and blog posts. Started in 2017, LaTanya S. Autry, Teressa Raiford, and Mike Murawski founded the #MuseumsAreNot Neutral campaign to refute the ideas of some museum professionals that the nature of museums and the way that they present art, history, and culture is inherently neutral. Proponents of the museum as a neutral entity believe that somehow, despite the history of the way in which museums acquired their objects and the point of view of their well-meaning curators, that it is possible to create spaces and exhibitions that do not reflect a particular world view. Indeed, every aspect of our museums, their architecture, the way in which they acquire objects, the objects they acquire and those they choose not to acquire, the composition of museum boards of trustees, and the manner in which objects are displayed reflects a particular perspective. To suggest that institutions that stray from traditional approaches of display and interpretation, that tell broader more inclusive stories, or that offer a critique of museums are somehow political, while mainstream museum approaches are not, is disingenuous. Museums, like every other institution in a society relate to the way that power is held and used within that culture. Museums reflect the prevailing power structure. Our role as museum professionals is to "just tell the facts" an anonymous letter writer told me. As an historian, I wonder, WHOSE facts shall we tell?

Seema Rao, a museum consultant and author of the Brilliant Ideas Studio blog, succinctly argues, that museums do not exist in a vacuum and that everything is created within culture, thus nothing can be neutral.[1] Our institutions may not be partisan, but they are decidedly political institutions and the material culture chosen for museums is political as well. The choices that we make – the objects we choose to include in our collections, our decisions about what to preserve and what not to preserve are all grounded in the cultural baggage of our curators, directors, and board members. Moreover, the objects in our collections frequently reflect the values, taste, and judgment of curators, years, decades, even centuries ago who determined that this or that object was significant and important to be preserved. Other objects, deemed unimportant, either remain in the hands of the people who owned them or were not preserved. Our collections may have been relevant and important in a particular time period, but their meaning may change over time or we may struggle when we find that our curatorial predecessors did not preserve particular objects that we now wish we had because they would enable us to tell the stories of those whose history not been included in the official record. As museums attempt to be responsive to more diverse audiences, to be relevant to the lives of their constituents, and to focus on service to their communities, there are significant issues related to the things that museums collect – the material culture we have chosen to save – that should be considered by those who amass these collections and those who teach about objects to the next generation of museum professionals.

Objects, writes museum studies theorist Simon Knell of the University of Leicester, "are not pieces of the past, as such, but pieces of the present which have a past." The things that we have collected in our museums have stories and meanings attached to them that relate to their past histories, but they also have meaning in the present that may or may not have changed with the passage of time. The changing meaning of artifacts, the professionalization of museums, and the lack of diverse perspectives among museum professionals all contribute to the challenging nature of material culture scholarship and teaching today. Take, for example, the chairs in the game room at one historic house (Figures 9.1 and 9.2). The height of fashion in the nineteenth century, the carvings of "blackamoors"

Figure 9.1 Game Room, c. 1900 with blackamoor chairs. Dr. William Seward and Lila Vanderbilt Webb House, Shelburne Farms. Courtesy of Shelburne Farms.

Figure 9.2 Detail of chairs with blackamoor carving. Dr. William Seward and Lila Vanderbilt Webb House, Shelburne Farms. Courtesy of Shelburne Farms.

on the arms of the chairs offend many visitors today. Blackamoors became popular following the contact between the Muslim Moors of North Africa and the Europeans. While the use of Black figures in art predates slavery, owning these objects enabled wealthy families in the United States to demonstrate their good taste by purchasing expensive European decorative objects. The depictions of the blackamoors as subservient, barely clothed, candelabras, furniture, even jewelry, suggested racial conquest.[2]

Rightly concerned about visitors' reaction to the chairs, the curator struggled with the best way to interpret the artifacts, help visitors understand the environment in which they were created, and discover why these racist objects were on view in the twenty-first century. Some visitors even demanded that the objects were so offensive that they be removed from view despite their original placement in the house. How should the site talk about the owners of the objects and why they purchased the chairs? Does the continued exhibition of the chairs contribute to the notion of Black people as exotic and subservient? Are there other objects that might counter this view? As a historian of twentieth-century African American history my focus in this chapter is to raise some issues related to the problematic nature of material culture teaching with a concentration on my area of expertise, African American history, but many of these issues certainly pertain to other groups – women, working-class people, immigrants, whose history and art have been ignored or discounted, but whose stories enrich our understanding of who we are as Americans. And there are pertinent issues/questions here not only for history museums, but also museums of natural history, anthropology, art, and decorative arts.

The United States Remains an Essentially Segregated Society

From the period of European settlement and the introduction of African slaves on the American Continent, African American mobility and the organization of physical spaces has been strictly controlled. Enslaved Americans could not move about freely, for fear that they were escaping servitude and they could not gather together, even in many cases for funerals, for fear that they were fomenting a rebellion against their masters. From this early time the nation was divided into Black spaces and white spaces. White spaces constituted anyplace and everyplace that white Americans chose to inhabit or to claim for themselves. Black Americans could not enter most spaces without reason or permission. Taverns, for example, constituted a prohibited space unless an enslaved person was a server or a person entertaining the guests by playing a musical instrument. The Black codes barred slaves from such things as purchasing or drinking alcoholic beverages. The most restrictive statutes kept enslaved persons confined to the master's property and as isolated from one another as possible. In the Virginia colony, the extensive slave code required the constable to give any slave who departed from his master's grounds without permission and without a pass "twenty lashes on his bare back well layd on, and soe sent home to his said master, mistress or overseer."[3] Comparable laws existed throughout the colonies and later the states added restrictions. The Fugitive Slave Clause criminalized mobility, a basic American right, making enslaved individuals who sought their freedom by running away lawbreakers.[4]

Free African American people suffered from the restrictions placed on enslaved people and they faced many indignities when they attempted simply to move about in public. On public conveyances like stagecoaches or trains they were pushed off or into separate and inferior cars. White passengers found it acceptable to toss insults and racial epithets at Black people who attempted to occupy white spaces. Free Black people knew to avoid white spaces for fear of being attacked.

In 1919 Eugene Williams, a young Black boy swam into an area of Lake Michigan claimed as white space. White men stoned him to death in the water and he drowned, sparking a northern riot in which white people killed Black people, that resulted from the escalating fear of Black migration from the south to the north – the Great Migration. Throughout the Jim Crow era the south enforced the separation of space by law and in the north by tradition. But federal policy initiatives, not simply individual prejudices, maintained both residential and school segregation both in the past and today.[5]

How does this affect how we think about material culture? In reality, most white Americans know little about the lives, artifacts, and culture of people of color in the United States. White Americans rarely enter Black spaces, in particular, and know little about how Black people live or what material objects might be important. Sadly, this is true both in the past and today. Seventy-five percent of white Americans have entirely white social networks according to a study by the Public Religion Research Institute. They don't have any Black friends and they don't know anything about Black people, except, perhaps what they see on television. Sixty-five percent of Black Americans reported having an all-Black social network.[6] Since the baggage that curators, who are largely all white, bring to their jobs is based on their own personal experiences and biases, it is no wonder that our museums' material culture collections and the stories that we tell are often as segregated as the population. Not only diversifying museum staffs is important, but teaching all students how to approach communities and listen to the stories of people who do not look like them is essential for the success of museums in the future.

A Token of Our Affection

As museums seek to diversify their collections, and material culture professors seek to develop more inclusive curricula, they find it difficult to grasp the difference between well-meaning tokenism and real inclusion. "Anything and everything is diversity," a colleague said at a meeting recently. That is not true. To achieve real diversity in teaching material culture means addressing historically marginalized and excluded groups and seeking to include them at the same level that traditional groups are studied. It means breaking open the usual cannon and changing it which requires new scholarship as well as an open mind. It is not sufficient simply to add an article on slavery and a mention of southwestern Santos, Gees Bend quilts, or the Harlem Renaissance, amid a traditional material culture curriculum. Nor is it acceptable to offer a lecture on African American art, women's art, or Native American art in an art history class and assume that the course has been brought up to date. Such insertions represent only token and stereotypical representation. A truly inclusive curriculum involves remaking the course of study.

Abundance

We have preserved far more sterling silver epergnes adorning the dining tables of robber barons and plantation owners, showcasing great wealth, than we have preserved the objects of those who risked their lives and reputations to end slavery, promote the eight-hour workday, or the Pure Food and Drugs Act, or to further suffrage rights – all things that dramatically changed the lives of Americans and furthered our democracy. In a nation whose founding stories center on the Revolutionary War and immigration, reinforcing these values would seem a key aspect of museums' responsibility in helping Americans to understand their shared experience. Instead, many of the significant events that represent these core American values are not fully represented in our museums or collections, although they are well represented in historical scholarship.

In a similar vein, we have preserved at least 15,000 historic houses as museums, many of them great mansions. The heyday of historic houses was 1976, the bicentennial year, when Americans demonstrated a great enthusiasm for history and visited houses, battlefields, and monuments in record numbers. A plethora of historic house museums were established along the way. At least once a month we field telephone calls from concerned citizens whose first inclination when they are trying to save an old barn, house, or church is to turn it into a museum. Some historic house museums are the homes of significant political, artistic, or literary figures, or in more recent years, structures that illuminate an important and more complete but ignored aspect of our history, like the Maggie Walker site in Richmond, Virginia, the home of, as the Park Service notes, a "national activist for economic independence, educational opportunities, and civil rights, particularly on behalf of women and children in the African American community."[7] But a large proportion of them are simply the largest or oldest house in a particular community – extant only as a museum because they remained intact and because their owners were the richest families in town. Often the family, now several generations removed can no longer maintain these large buildings and donating them both preserves the family's legacy and eliminates a huge tax expense.

As museums, many of these historic houses offer only stagnant rooms of expensive antique furniture, opulent chandeliers, large family portraits and a standard "this-is-a, that-is-a tour." This is a Chippendale chair. That is a clock the family purchased in Paris.[8] Philadelphia alone hosts about 300 historic house museums, many of them open only a few hours each week. Much like the 1980s and 1990s television program hosted by Robin Leach, *Lifestyles of the Rich and Famous*, many historic house tours fulfilled our "champagne wishes and caviar dreams," as exercises in voyeurism but offer little in the way of education or community engagement except, perhaps as the local wedding venue.

The vast majority of these houses represent the wealthiest Americans and relatively few depict working-class or middle-class stories (although preserving the homes of individuals who made a mark but were not necessarily wealthy is a positive and growing trend). Many of the houses represent only a house in which a family of no particular consequence lived except perhaps for inherited wealth. It is not that these particular houses should not be preserved, but that if we used historic houses as a way of telling the story of the United States their story is a very limited one that helps to maintain one particular notion of success and achievement. If we truly want to offer enriching experiences for visitors that inspire them to civic participation and action perhaps the homes or buildings that represent the expansion or protection of democracy would make strong choices.

Some institutions have identified a need within their communities that has given renewed vigor to historic houses. The Dyckman Farmhouse Museum, the last farmhouse in Manhattan, for example, although not a large mansion, was the home of a wealthy Dutch family who owned a large portion of the upper part of the island (Figure 9.3). Once a part of a rural Dutch community, it is now the center of a large Dominican neighborhood. While visitors may still walk through some furnished rooms, the museum has dedicated itself to providing arts and science programing, a community arts space, park space, science camp, festivals, music, and literacy programs that meet the current needs of the Dominican residents and that include their history and culture. The staff worked with children to plant and care for earth boxes that contained a Native American garden, a Dutch garden, and a Dominican garden. Local contemporary art is showcased in the museum in thought-provoking

Figure 9.3 A contemporary art installation on slavery at the Dyckman Farmhouse Museum by Peter Hoffmeister. Courtesy of Dyckman Farmhouse Museum.

exhibitions. A current art exhibition, integrated into the period rooms, explores the local slave burial ground, now beneath the land on which an elementary school was built. The art is juxtaposed against a Dutch portrait and the belongings of the Dyckman family and the kitchen in which the enslaved worked.

The Whitney Plantation in New Orleans distinguishes itself through an innovative interpretive program that enables the site to attract a diverse audience that alludes other museums. The plantation focuses its interpretation on the hundreds of thousands of enslaved Africans who labored on Louisiana plantations during the eighteenth and nineteenth centuries – the only such site in Louisiana to take this approach. The world of the enslaved people is fully developed here and brings to life the slave quarters, work areas, and punishment areas using first-person narratives. Memorials and contemporary sculptures punctuate the grounds and identify the slaves by their names. Visitors to Whitney Plantation learn a broader story of Louisiana history and have the opportunity to understand plantation life in a deeper way.

Coming Too Late to the Party

Many years ago, I was asked by the Jewish Museum in New York to work with another historian to research the Gomez Mill House in Newburgh New York. The research report concluded that the house – an eighteenth-century Sephardic Jewish House – was rare and very significant, the only such extant structure in the United States. The Gomez family made their money in the fur trade and the house, in rural upstate New York, was a trading post. The men in the family traveled here from New York City with their enslaved Africans and traded with Native Americans. The research team proposed that the State of New York acquire the building and add it to the state historic site system. Sadly, the state decided that they could not take on another building. The full complement of structures acquired during the twentieth century were a considerable expense and New York could not accept responsibility for another historic site, no matter how important.

The series of historic sites acquired through the 1970s included very significant buildings such as the intact Moorish-inspired home of Hudson River painter Frederick Edwin Church and Ganondagan, the original site of a seventeenth-century Seneca Indian town. Several other sites were the historic house equivalent of big box stores – large mansions on the Hudson River. The homeowners happened to be wealthy, but their stories offer little in the way of valuable interpretation other than the praise of great wealth and lovely settings for Christmas decorations. These houses, I would argue, are of much less importance from a state or national history perspective, but are perhaps somewhat important to the local community for generating tourist dollars. There are dozens, probably hundreds, of such houses throughout the nation open to the public with a similar message while a wide variety of historic places that represent a more significant story that should not be forgotten – a story that deepens our understanding of American culture or contribute to our understanding of our diversity languishes without funding simply because there are already too many sites being preserved.

Like the New York State historic sites, many houses were gathered up at a time when the preservationists were working hard to protect the architectural heritage of the community and the creation of a museum seemed the best way to do so. Today, there are many other options to preserve historic buildings. However, it seems that once a building becomes a state site, museum status cannot change despite the fact that additional research or changing attitudes mean that other sites should be recognized as well. Sadly, recognition is offered, but the money goes to the sites who did not come late to the party. And, as in the case of New York's historic sites, local politicians step in to ensure that decisions are made based on politics and political clout. The decision to protect important historic sites does not always rest with curatorial, or preservation staff, but rather with politicians. There are many ways of protecting buildings without creating a museum and perhaps we should also consider dissolving museums that no longer have any relevance to make room for new and important institutions while finding other ways of preserving these historic buildings. Should we reevaluate the status of some historic house museums?

The Tyranny of Collections

Writer, attorney, museum administrator, and museum thought leader Stephen Weil warned about museums becoming focused on function rather than purpose. He imagined the National Toothpick Museum, an institution that does everything correctly.[9] The museum's collection is perfectly stored in a climate-controlled facility. An aggressive program of changing exhibitions and programs interprets the toothpicks and it is a well-endowed museum. While we do not know the annual visitation of the National Toothpick Museum, it is highly likely that the staff has not thought much about the public in their zeal to protect the collection. Indeed, the public are the very people from whom the collection needs to be protected. The employees are so dedicated to following all of the professional rules that they tend to forget that museums are first and foremost places of education, wonder, and contemplation for their communities. The museum fails to answer an essential question – Why should anyone care?

In the last sixty years museum work has become increasingly professional, technical, and specialized. We have written carefully constructed collections policies, but use them primarily to enable curators to turn down objects they do not want. Collecting in many instances has not been strategic and storage facilities overflow with things – often duplicates or triplicates or even dozens of the same type of artifact, whether or not the objects will ever be on exhibition or are likely to be used for research. We know precisely what types of boxes to use to store paper artifacts and the least obtrusive ways of attaching numbers to textiles. Collections care is important, and these methods will ensure the survival of museum collections for many years to come, but have we, in some cases, created a monster?

Many museum studies programs, in particular, focus almost entirely on teaching the various collections functions of the museum – registration methods, collections handling, collections care, collections ethics, collections storage, collections law, etc. Collections are paramount. And many museums face the tyranny of this professionalization focusing most of their money and their efforts on caring for the collections rather than remembering for whom they have been entrusted with these objects. We use velvet ropes to keep visitors out of rooms, cases to separate the public from even the most pedestrian objects, and we color every artifact with the same collections care brush whether rare or ubiquitous. Visitors are admonished for touching or even getting too close to objects. Sadly, we fail to differentiate between a common object that exists in many multiples and in many places. Many of these objects that might better be used as props or for teaching are cared for as if they were valuable paintings. Should museums have deaccessioning policies that permit them, with thoughtful consultation, of course, to reevaluate the material objects in their collections and dispose of some objects to replace them with others that meet current community, exhibition, and programmatic needs?

Collections are also in control when it comes to the stories that we tell. Many a curator will say, "we can't tell that story, we don't have collections that will support it." The things that have been collected sadly have enabled some museums to opt out of particular narratives that may be important to audiences and compelling when it comes to their communities, but because the objects in the storage room do not support a particular narrative, whether it is global climate change or immigration history, they feel that they can ignore the story. Objects are certainly central to museums and important in the telling of visual stories, but perhaps we need to stop empowering objects to control the narrative.[10] Although it adds time to the exhibition process, exhibition-based collecting can add collections to the museum that are more representative of the museum's varied constituencies and provide an opportunity for the museum to tell the stories for which there are no artifacts in the collection.

Toward a More Perfect Interpretation

The way that we interpret material culture reflects the aversion of many museums to controversy and the need to remove any perceived political implications from the discussion of American decorative arts and from the teaching of material culture. We fail to tell the public a complete story choosing instead to focus on design and aesthetics, both of which are valid topics, but are not the only topics for discussion. It is all about perspective – one woman's high chest is another woman's oppression. Consider this description of a mahogany bookcase from a prominent art museum, a fairly typical approach to the fine furniture owned by wealthy families:

> This very early American example incorporates many characteristics of the late Baroque style. The architectural form and strong verticality of the piece give it a striking presence, while its narrow proportions, clean lines, and high-quality woods add sophistication and refinement. The surface is enlivened by swirling veneers and inlaid designs in light and dark woods, including bands in a checkerboard pattern and five stars that create the illusion of spinning. The interior is lavishly fitted with stepped, undulating drawers; carved shells; and pigeonhole compartments that held important business and family documents.

The museum tells us the lens through which we are to look at the object and the derivation of its design. Since this is an online catalog description the institution might argue that this is everything we need to know to locate and admire the object. Or, they might say that as an art museum they are concerned only with the object as a work of art. Yet certainly we cannot truly understand this object outside of its context. As an historian this is an extremely unsatisfying description because it is so incomplete and fails to help us to truly understand the environment in which the object was produced and the consequences of its manufacture within the context of its time or of our own. A discussion of American clothing in the twenty-first century most certainly would include mention of garments manufactured within the United States and the often-discussed controversy of cheaply made clothing and sneakers fabricated by exploited children in other countries.

Harvesting the wood to make mahogany furniture was an extremely dangerous business in the eighteenth century, carried out in large measure by enslaved people, according to Jennifer Anderson's excellent book, *Mahogany: The Costs of Luxury in Early America*.[11] A fuller understanding of the dangerous work of cutting and removing mahogany trees led to changes in technology as well as to deforestation in the Caribbean and Central America. Discussing mahogany chairs and tables as both trees and fine furniture – commodities and luxuries – broadens the story to include the entire supply chain. Those people who harvested the wood, transported the wood, made and sold the furniture as well the end user become a part of the story and it deepens our understanding of this time and place. Even if the fine mahogany furniture of the eighteenth century has no meaning for some modern visitors, the story has resonance for those concerned about the environment today, as well as anyone who understands the cost to the natural world of our insatiable desires for such things as chocolate and coffee. Telling a much more nuanced and complete story, not just in the classroom, but in the museum gallery helps visitors to understand that history is complex and that what happened in the past affects what happens in the present. It is not sufficient simply for material culture scholars to research, write, and read the books that discuss controversial issues related to material objects, that information must be communicated somehow to wider audiences if we are to understand the role that material objects play in understanding history.

There are often institutional barriers that affect the acquisition of material objects in museum collections. One major art museum curator advocated on many occasions that the institution should acquire a work of art made by a Filipino artist. Barriers to the acquisition were many, including timelines for the particular project and the often long process for the acquisition of art. Yet one of the most difficult obstacles proved to be the lack of teaching about Filipino art in art history and material culture programs. There is just very little scholarship to draw on, and few curators are willing to add work with which they are unfamiliar and for which they do not have a body of literature to draw on to their Asian art collections. This is a problem not unique to Filipino art but encompasses many areas of material culture. If curators are not familiar with the subject matter they are unlikely to acquire the objects or to see them as important. This brings us full circle back to the issue of a more diverse curatorial workforce in museums, but also raises concerns about the culture of museums and the structure within which they operate that privileges some groups and excludes others.

Where Do We Go from Here?

First, we must acknowledge that the lack of material culture research and writing about certain groups affects the way that museums collect and interpret history, art history, and culture.

American material culture is interpreted by historians, folklorists, decorative arts curators, art historians, anthropologists, and geographers, both professional and amateur. Each of these groups brings their own approach to bear on our understanding of the plethora of things made by human beings. Despite this breadth of scholarship, the research that informs exhibitions and the material culture taught in graduate programs needs to expand to be more inclusive. African American museums and museums that serve specific ethnic groups provide excellent models for ways to engage with community constituents as well as how to identify the objects that tell broader American stories.

As teachers of material culture, we must look at our own biases and identities and how they affect what we teach. Taking a more inclusive approach to the material objects that are worthy of study and collection is essential if the field is to attract students from a wide variety of backgrounds.

In addition to reinvigorating stagnant historic house museums it may be necessary to create new criteria to determine the use of both current and future historic houses. The review of these structures may determine, going forward, that some of them may be best suited for adaptive reuse rather than preservation as a museum.

Most importantly, those of us who work in museums must also make the people who live in our communities a priority, not simply the objects in our collections. Building trust with these constituents, learning about their experiences, and documenting their stories will ensure a body of material culture scholarship that reflects more Americans as well as more relevant institutions.

Notes

1. Seema Rao, *Brilliant Ideas Studio*, https://bit.ly/3c0JD1G.
2. For additional work on blackamoor figures see Adrienne Childs, "Sugarboxes and Blackamoors: Ornamental Blackness in Early Meissen Porcelain," in Michael Yonen and Alden Cavenaugh, eds., *The Cultural Aesthetics of Eighteenth-Century Porcelain* (Farnham: Ashgate, 2010).
3. Hening, ed., *The Statutes at Large*, 2, 481–82, June 1680 "An Act for preventing Negroes Insurrections."
4. Article IV, Section 2, Clause 3 of the United States Constitution. "No Person held to Service or Labour in one State, under the Laws thereof, escaping into another, shall, in Consequence of any Law or Regulation therein, be discharged from such Service or Labour, but shall be delivered up on Claim of the Party to whom such Service or Labour may be due."
5. Richard Rothstein, *The Color of Law* (New York: Liveright, 2017).
6. Public Religion Research Institute, "Race, Religion and Political Affiliation of Americans' Core Social Networks," https://bit.ly/3wxjwca.
7. Museum Collections. Maggie L. Walker National Historic Site, National Park Service. www.nps.gov/museum/exhibits/maggie_walker/index.html. Accessed January 12, 2022.
8. Ruth Graham, "The Great Historic House Museum Debate," *Boston Globe*, August 10, 2014; Gerald George, "Historic House Museum Malaise: A Conference Considers What's Wrong," *History News* 57 (2002), #4; Marian Godfrey and Barbara Silberman, *Model for Historic House Museums*, Pew Charitable Trust, 2008, https://bit.ly/3D3sX5q.

9. Stephen E. Weil, *Rethinking the Museum and Other Meditations* (Washington: Smithsonian Institution Press, 1990).
10. *Peak Experience Lab*, blogpost, "Museums, Can We Stop Letting Objects Control the Narrative?" May 3, 2017. https://bit.ly/3FKdDeq.
11. Jennifer Anderson, *Mahogany: The Costs of Luxury in Early America* (Cambridge: Harvard University Press, 2012).

10
Reenacting the Past

Heather Fitzsimmons Frey and Marlis Schweitzer

Did you decide to try on one of the corsets?

Yes, I was surprised, actually, about how comfortable it was.

I felt very supported wearing it – I didn't expect that.

I couldn't really bend to the side. You know what else though, I actually always imagined that corsets were metal. I didn't realize they were fabric. That they were – they weren't so bad.

I didn't realize they were so pretty.

Yes, I tried one on. But I put it on upside down! And I didn't even know it until two other girls asked me about it.

August 2018, Institute for Dance Studies
Pop Up Research Workshop

In August 2018, a group of "girls," aged five to twenty-five, participated in a performance-based research project concerning nineteenth-century amateur at-home dance and theater as part of Heather's postdoctoral research. After playing a very silly game of forfeits and learning two dances from Florence Bell's *Fairy Tales and How to Act Them*,[1] they tried on corsets pulled from the University of Toronto Centre for Drama, Theatre, and Performance Studies costume collection (Figure 10.1). The corsets represented a hodge-podge of styles and eras: Renaissance, Elizabethan, nineteenth-century, and twenty-first-century burlesque, and given the participants' heights and ages, they certainly did not all fit to measure. But as the participants put them on, laughing as they tried to fasten them for each other, they discovered how the costumes altered the way they moved and simultaneously challenged their assumptions about the impact of wearing corsets. The probable silliness of a Victorian game of forfeits needed to accommodate girls wearing corsets; while girls discovered some of their movements were constrained, they also felt supported.

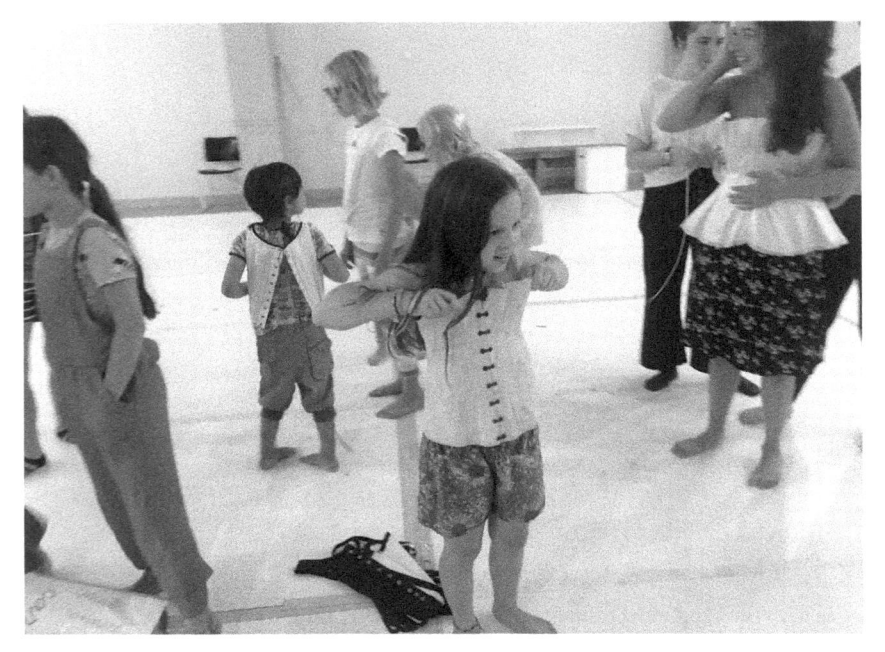

Figure 10.1 Girls trying on corsets at Heather's workshop, August 2018. Photo courtesy of Heather Fitzsimmons Frey.

As Heather's corset workshop suggests, the act of putting on a historical costume offers a uniquely embodied way to explore the past and revise preconceptions about the lived experiences of historical subjects. The research participants were surprised by the texture, malleability, and support of the corsets, not to mention the challenge of figuring out just *how* to put them on. Such discoveries became possible through the girls' engagement with the materiality of the corsets, their heightened attention to the shape and movement of their bodies, and their interactions with one another. While they remained aware of the historical distance separating them and their imagined nineteenth-century counterparts, the act of dressing in the corsets allowed them to briefly "touch time," to use Rebecca Schneider's evocative phrase,[2] to reach across past and present through what Rachel Hann describes as the "hug" of the costume.[3] While the simplest definition of *reenact* is to act out a past event, the specific actions and gestures that people make to interpret a historical moment are frequently informed by an engagement with material culture and the concerns of the temporary moment. No reenactment is apolitical or devoid of an investment in critiquing or sustaining received historical narratives. As Tommy DeFrantz and Gustavo Furtado write, "Reenactments are, above all, disturbances to the perceived linearity of time. Through corporeal repetition the past gains a ghostly simultaneity with the present and every repetition harbors the possibility of difference – that is, the possibility that the past may yet have another future."⁴ In other words, dressing up in a corset can yield new ways of thinking about the past and future.

This interest in using objects – costumes, props, makeup, and so forth – to reenact historical events and cultural experiences is part of a much larger material culture "turn" in theater and performance studies.⁵ Such a focus is perhaps unsurprising given that theater and performance studies delights in all manner of "stuff" in the interests of telling stories and pulling audiences into different worlds. What is new, however, is the way that theater and performance studies scholars have turned (or returned) to material culture to ask new questions about the past. This heightened interest can be attributed to several overlapping developments, three of which we'll briefly summarize here: (1) the uptake of new materialist frameworks; (2) the emergence of critical costume studies; and (3) a deep investment in historical reenactment as a mode of practice-based research. As might be expected, material culture studies can also benefit from an engagement with theater and performance studies, particularly where questions of costuming and historical reenactment are concerned. We hope that in bringing the two disciplines into dialogue with one another in this chapter, we can offer a fresh perspective on how material culture has influenced and continues to shape practices of re/enactment.

"New materialism" is an umbrella term first coined in the 1990s by Diana Coole and Samantha Frost to urge social sciences and humanities scholars to think differently about their relationship to the natural world. New materialist frameworks acknowledge the agency or "vibrant matter"⁶ of the nonhuman or more-than-human world and seek to disrupt the power hierarchies that privilege human subjects over animals, environments, objects, and other entities. For Coole and Frost, the new materialist project can be understood as a response to "the emergence of pressing ethical and political concerns that accompany the scientific and technological advances predicated on new scientific models of matter and, in particular, of living matter."⁷ Of course, "new materialism" is something of a misnomer in that it not only implies a strong break from "old materialism" when in fact it retains many of the latter's political aims, but also overlooks the many world cultures and religions – from the Indigenous peoples of Turtle Island to Buddhists in Asia – for whom belief in the vibrancy of all matter is a foundational tenet.⁸ The heightened emphasis on new materialist perspectives has nevertheless opened up new vistas for theater and performance studies scholars, inviting them to approach the material culture of theater and performance with different theoretical tools.

For our purposes, one of the most exciting new materialist tools can be found in Robin Bernstein's "Dances with Things: Material Culture and the Performance of Race," wherein she introduces the term "scriptive thing" to describe objects that impel the humans who encounter them to move or act in a particular way. Building on Bill Brown's "thing theory,"[9] which identifies moments when objects exceed their object status and call attention to human dependency on the material world, Bernstein investigates how some objects function like blueprints or play texts to direct human performance.[10] For example, a soft stuffed animal invites but cannot force someone to cuddle it just as a fragile ornament encourages care in handling but can do nothing to prevent human hands from dropping it. Or, to use the example of the corsets from Heather's workshop, the fabric and boning guided the girls' movements in new ways, simultaneously providing support and comfort while limiting their ability to bend sideways. In such moments, the seemingly quotidian object crosses into the realm of the "thing," asserting a kind of power independent of human thought or will. Yet while scriptive things can guide movement, they cannot determine it: as with play scripts, Bernstein writes, scriptive things "[allow] for agency and unleashing original, live variations that may not be individually predictable."[11] Bernstein's concept of the scriptive thing has gained a great deal of traction in recent years, especially among theater and performance historians looking to recover performance histories that have not been documented through writing. Whether by attending to the thingness of objects found in archives or incorporating historical objects into practice-based workshops and inviting participants to follow the scripts they find within them, historians are finding new ways to access the previously obscured repertoires of past lives.

The emergent field of critical costume studies shares a similar interest in the thing-ness of objects, past and present. Led by Rachel Hann, Donatella Barbieri, and Aoife Monks, among others, critical costume studies understands "costuming as a critical act," one that extends beyond consideration of craft, technique, and period detail to query how costumes mediate, and are in turn mediated by, broader social and cultural ideologies.[12] A critical costume studies approach is distinctly interdisciplinary, in that it recognizes costuming as "an activity that bridges a number of established disciplines: including theatre and performance, fashion, dance, fine art, cultural studies and anthropology among others."[13] At the same time, it insists on the distinctiveness of approaching costume *as* costume, as a "performance tactic"[14] concerned not only with how an individual item of clothing looks or fits but also with how and what it signifies to those who see it within the context of a performance event. In this respect, critical costume studies extends the theory of nineteenth-century scholar Thomas Carlyle who in *Sartor Resartus* (1833–34) asserted that "Matter exists spiritually, and to represent some Idea, and body it forth. Hence Clothes … are so unspeakably significant."[15] Costumes – as clothes and more than clothes – "body forth" particular ideas that often extend beyond the imagination of the individuals wearing them. For Hann, costume involves "a conscious act of showing dressing"[16] and is therefore an ideal site for exploring how bodies appear and are made legible to audiences.

Such an approach is helpful for our purposes, in that most, if not all, costuming in historical reenactment scenarios is explicitly a "conscious act of showing dressing."

Finally, theater and performance studies scholars have embraced material culture methods as they have undertaken various forms of historical reenactment. Such research is inherently physical and requires the presence of living people to do the work. Projects range from reanimating historically located performance practices referenced in existing play texts and other primary sources, to staging new performances in and around museums or living history sites, to using oral history and historical visual imagery to connect with past practices, but ultimately create something new and make fresh discoveries. It is this emphasis on the production of knowledge through performance that most distinguishes performance-based research from a more straightforward theater production (e.g., staging of *Hamlet*). Connecting to the past through living, breathing bodies is, in many ways, the complicated, time-bending project of performance-based historiography. It demands that bodies reach across time and space, animating imagined moments to serve research – and it is this aspect of the methodology that is perhaps its most controversial. Scholars claim variously that embodied inquiries and performative-research produce theater that is valid but not authentic;[17] that is made of "respectful forgeries and faithful betrayals";[18] and that foregrounds "the processes that construct history out of the past" but "blur the boundaries between historiography and dramaturgy."[19]

This chapter explores how professional and nonprofessional performers have used costuming to imagine or enact or "body forth" the past, tracing developments from the early nineteenth century to the present. We argue that costume's unique relationship to the human body makes it ideally suited to reenacting the past, in that the touch of cloth on the body can be understood as one way for contemporary performers to "touch time." In this context, we draw inspiration from Hann's "theory of hugging" to describe the relationship between costume and wearer: "The hug of a costume shapes how movement is conceived, as well as read by an observer," she writes. "To understand the event of costume is to understand how the intimate relationship of material and body sustains action through qualities of tension, texture and pliability."[20] It is the hug of the costume that activates performers' travel through time, allowing them to simultaneously occupy past and present within the semiotic realm of the performance event.

This chapter further acknowledges that how a costume functions as a mode of creation and storytelling is informed by the material conditions of a historical moment. To that end, we track some key developments over time – identifying shifts in how historical subjects/creators used material culture (specifically costume) to imagine/enact the past, while remaining attentive to the way that historical reenactments support or critique established social hierarchies and dominant ideologies. Although the history of reenactment is as old as the history of performance (e.g., one of the earliest known Greek tragedies, Aeschylus's *The Persians* [472 BCE], is essentially a reenactment of a naval defeat), we have opted to begin this chapter in the early nineteenth century, the moment when professional theater artists in England first became concerned with questions of historical accuracy in costuming. From there we move forward in time to consider a range of late nineteenth and early-twenty-first century reenactment projects. As we leap across historical periods, we continue to ask questions about identity and authenticity: who has the authority to reenact the past (and who does not)? Which bodies slip easily into costumes from the past and why (which do not)? In what ways have costumes been deployed to bring history to life? What is it about costuming, specifically, that makes it such a valuable site for considering practices of reenactment?

The allure of a costume's hug as a way to immerse oneself in a distant place and time has retained its appeal, but the discourses surrounding North American, British, and settler colonialism have altered how people interpret and imagine costumed bodies. Today, those who engage in historical reenactment continue to grapple with issues around identity, authenticity, authority, and "correctness," but as contemporary understandings of the implications of those words have shifted, the power of costumes to embrace the wearer and transport them into other spaces changes too. On the surface, the idea of "correct" and "accurate" costume may seem similar, but just as nineteenth-century beliefs about ways costumes could enhance a woman's charms were at least as important as selecting the right fabric for a dress, twenty-first century ideas about bodies directly impact what a costume can *do*. In this section, we consider how twenty-first century ideas about costume "correctness" and historical reenactment engage with other contemporary discourses connected to race, gender performance, body type, and attitudes about the *purpose* of costumed historical reenactments.

When amateurs and interpreters work and play in public or semipublic spaces, costume and costuming decisions collide the present with the past, across multiple twenty-first century reenactments and performative expressions of alternate time-spaces. From the moment a participant decides to perform "as if" they are in another time, decisions about dress drive reenactment explorations, and donning the clothing of: a space and time beyond the reenactor's own lived experiences encourages participants to use the intimate experience of what they wear, as Schneider writes, to bend time and *touch* the past. Notably, as Pravina Shukla explains, while clothing is not only "a palpable, immediate, and intimate form of material culture,"[21] the way a person dresses also offers a way to send "meaningful messages."[22] Yet, as the example of the girls experimenting with corsets demonstrates, the power of intimacy in clothing that actually touches the skin and surrounds the reenactor is such that wearers not only expect that they are sending meaningful messages to others through their historical clothing choices, but wearers also anticipate that the hug of the clothing itself may actually send meaningful messages to the wearer – messages about the time period, and the historical "reality" of that time, and also, about how a certain time and place might *feel*.

Reenactments in the Nineteenth Century

William Charles Macready's 1823 production of *King John* at Theatre Royal Covent Garden in London stands as a significant moment in theater's relationship to history and the use of costuming to stitch past to present. Of course, elaborate costuming had long been an important feature of stage productions, most notably in the eighteenth century when rival actresses used their wardrobe to appeal to audiences and managers.[23] For the most part, however, these performers were less concerned with historical accuracy than with the grandeur and costliness of their gowns. Occasionally, actor-managers would invest in historically specific costumes for productions of Shakespearean tragedies or other well-known plays from the Elizabethan era, but such productions were exceptions rather than the rule. What made *King John* so unique, then, was its full-fledged embrace of historical costuming as part of the emergent antiquarian movement.[24] Designer James Robinson Planché approached *King John* from the perspective of a historian, turning to medieval painting and statuary for inspiration, much to the delight and amazement of the Covent Garden audience. As Planché later recalled, when Macready appeared onstage as the king:

> dressed as his effigy appears in Worcester Cathedral, surrounded by his barons sheathed in mail, with cylindrical helmets and correct armorial shields, and his courtiers in long tunics and mantles of the thirteenth century, there was a roar of approbation, accompanied by four distinct rounds of applause, so general and so hearty, that the actors were astonished.[25]

The audience's enthusiasm for the meticulously detailed costuming points to a much larger cultural transformation occurring in this period. As theater historian Andrew Gibb argues in a recent study of the production, one of the key factors in *King John*'s success was the way it deployed the "historical sublime," a distinctly Romantic-era vision of history that marked a sharp division between the present, post-Napoleonic realities of a society riven by war and suffering and the (imagined) idyllic, pre-Revolutionary period when lingering medieval and Renaissance values prevailed.[26] Audiences looking for some kind of escape at the theater experienced the historical sublime when "presented with visions of that unattainable past, a past that present shocks had made sublimely remote from their own lives."[27] Put differently, seeing actors dressed in "cylindrical helmets and correct armorial shield" produced an emotional and perhaps even physiological response in audiences akin to the "period rush" that Rebecca Schneider describes in her account of Civil War reenactors, a sense of time collapsing, of one period folding over another in a brief yet intense burst of feeling.[28]

It is worth stressing the importance of costumes to the achievement of the historical sublime. For as much as *King John* animated the past in its use of scenery and stage settings, it was the costumes that inspired the "roar of approbation" from the audience. Indeed, as Richard Schoch observes, "the theatre's comparative advantage [to other art forms] in historical representation was not in scenery, but in costume."[29] Outside the theater, nineteenth-century audiences had frequent access to painted historical scenes as rendered in paintings, illustrated books, dioramas, panoramas, and other forms of visual entertainment. But only at the theater could they see living, breathing actors quite literally *wearing* the past on their bodies; as Schoch puts it, "the authority of the performance came to reside in the historically marked bodies."[30] More than other material objects, then, Planché's costumes acquired a thing-like status, prompting the opening night audience to erupt into "four distinct rounds of applause" in a seemingly spontaneous expression of surprise and pleasure as they contemplated the gap between their own time and the time represented on stage.

Curiously, despite the success of the Planché/Macready *King John*, the production did not upend theatrical practices overnight. In fact, it would take several decades for antiquarianism to take a firm hold on British production practices. Gibb attributes this delay to the time needed for other artists to acquire the same level of skill and promotional sophistication as Planché, who made effective use of the playbill and illustrated book of his costumes to educate the audience about what they were seeing. In brief, the material culture of advertising and the broader business of bookselling in and around the West End theater district were also critical to the production of the "historical sublime."[31]

Although by the 1850s, Romantic-era notions of the idealized past were shifting, theater artists retained an interest in the medieval period. This interest was fueled in large part by nationalist and increasingly imperialist interests, as Britain sought to affirm its status by reclaiming (and reenacting) a glorious past that was distinct from that of other nations, most notably its long-time rival France. For the actor-manager Charles Kean, Shakespeare offered the most appropriate vehicle for affirming British dominance and promising theatergoers exhausted by years of social and political crisis that a future founded on the traditions and values of the medieval era would prevail.[32] In particular, Kean's productions of *Richard II*, *Henry V*, and other history plays found favor with audiences of all classes, reassuring them that – as Kean claimed in an 1842 playbill essay – "the prowess of Englishmen in the early days" offered an "assurance of what they will ever do in the hour of peril."[33] For an 1855 production of *Henry VIII*, Kean brought the pomp and ceremony of the king's court to life, filling the stage with dozens of actors dressed as courtiers and participating in court masques.[34] Two years later, the actor-manager appeared as Richard II dressed in a meticulous recreation of the king's coronation robes and jewels inspired by a portrait hanging at Westminster Abbey. In both instances, it was the costumed body that carried forward the glorious, twinned image of past triumph and future glory. Although supported by other details of the mise-en-scène (i.e., backdrops, set pieces), the "actor's irreducible physical presence endowed the past with a singular material solidity."[35] And if the past was, quite literally, within reach, then it was possible to believe that a victorious future was as well.

Victorian audiences took great pleasure in watching history come to life before them on stage, but they did not limit their desire to consume the objects of the medieval past to the theater. Those eager to transport themselves back in time could partake of an assortment of spectacular reenactments, including panoramas, dioramas, and various exhibits designed for international exhibitions. For example, visitors to the 1851 International Exhibition in London could find themselves in Augustus Welby Pugin's meticulously recreated medieval court, complete with stained glass windows and Gothic architectural features.[36] This particular exhibit was so popular, in fact, that it became part of a semi-permanent exhibit at Crystal Palace at Sydenham for over a decade, where it inspired Australian colonial officials to recreate their own version for the 1866 Melbourne Intercolonial Exhibition.[37] Such exhibits assumed a thing-like influence over visitors, placing them in a fully conceived installation, complete with historically accurate lighting and architectural features that invited them to imagine themselves in a different time and place. It is no surprise to note that such elements remain critical to the success of many living history museums today,[38] not to mention consumer environments that offer temporary escape from the pressures of contemporary life in exchange for consumer labor.[39]

Yet while visitors may have experienced a thrill of historical recognition akin to "period rush" as they walked through a medieval court, they may also have felt limited by their own contemporary dress. Other forms of public spectacle, such as the 1839 Eglinton Tournament held in Ayrshire, where participants dressed in historically accurate medieval costumes, facilitated the "bodying forth" of the past, whereby the act of dressing in historical costuming contributed "to a remodeling of material form, and with it, of cultural sensibility."[40] Some participants were so eager to remake themselves in the historical mold of a medieval knight that they purchased "authentic uniforms" from a theatrical costumer who promised that each item had been "exactly copied from a portrait of medieval manuscript."[41] Whether or not these costumes lived up to their promise, the literal "hug" of medieval-inspired cloth or armor on the bodies of nineteenth-century men and women bodied forth a new experience that was strange and, for some, incredibly real.

On a smaller scale, English and settler-colonial middle- and upper-class children also found ways to experiment with medieval costuming in at-home theatricals staged during the holidays. In the story-frame of Charlotte Yonge's 1864 historical drama, *The Mice at Play*, the girls are inspired by various medieval illustrations in books they owned and find ways to adapt and retailor pieces of their own, and from their grandmother's collections of old clothes. Yonge describes, in great detail, the way the girls created medieval costumes by doing things like opening up two old dark green wool "merinos" and placing them over "white frocks," harvesting a "moth-eaten swan's down boa of grandmamma's" for "fur" for borders on pockets and sleeves, and building an enormous cone-shaped hat out of pasteboard, and covering it with a "geranium-coloured" scarf "which, by flowing down from the peak, just saved it from being an absolute fool's cap." A suit of armor was "grand work ... consisting of shiny gray lining."[42] For these young girls, the very act of creating medieval costumes – of working with pasteboard, old merinos, and "grandmamma's" boa – activates their journey into the past, giving them a kind of ownership over the journey and their place within it.[43]

Fancy dress balls, held to celebrate military victories, the Queen's birthday, or national achievements likewise invited members of the social elite to both indulge their love of the past and temporarily dwell within it by adopting the clothing and gestures of another historical moment. In fact, it was Queen Victoria herself who sparked the craze for fancy dress balls in 1842, when she and Prince Albert hosted a medieval-themed Bal Costumé at Buckingham Palace for 2,000 guests. Ostensibly held to support the local Spitalfields silk industry, the young queen also used the event to assert her royal lineage, appearing as Queen Philippa of Hainault alongside Albert as Edward III in costumes inspired by the historical royals' effigies in the catacombs of Westminster Abbey (Figure 10.2). Overseeing the design of these costumes was none other than James Robinson Planché, the man whose detailed replicas of medieval courtiers had so enraptured audiences two decades before.[44] Victoria's bid for historical accuracy does not appear to have extended to her silhouette, however, as artist Sir Edwin Landseer's commemorative painting reveals. While the fur, velvet, and golden-threaded train are appropriately medieval, the queen's cinched waist is the product of 1840s corseting practices, enhanced by voluminous layers of petticoats.[45] Such historical anachronisms do not appear to have diminished the overall effect of the costume for Victoria and her court or the ball's function as spectacular propaganda. By casting herself and Albert as medieval royalty, she performatively equated her reign with the glory of that earlier period, sending a powerful message to anyone who might question her suitability for the crown. Tellingly, the Bal Costumé was only the first of three fancy dress balls the Queen hosted; the other two

Figure 10.2 Queen Victoria and Prince Albert at the Bal Costumé of May 12, 1842. By Sir Edwin Landseer. Royal Collection Trust/© Her Majesty Queen Elizabeth II 2019

transported courtiers back to the Georgian period (1845) and the Restoration (1851), respectively, further suturing the Queen to her royal past and thereby stabilizing her reign in the present.[46]

Though fancy dress balls first gained popularity in Britain, they soon spread throughout the British colonies and found favor among settler-colonial subjects eager to demonstrate their sophistication, elegance, and knowledge of the past.[47] By dressing in historically accurate costuming, these settlers bodied forth their own position within the Empire and its glorious history. Such performances can be understood as yet another example of "intimate distance," Elizabeth Maddock Dillon's term to "describe the way in which colonial culture in the Atlantic world involved bringing communities together and sustaining them – creating intimacy – across great distances."[48] With fancy dress balls, intimacy for participants arose from the shared act of celebrating the Queen's birthday or another moment of significance to British culture as well as from the intimate, bodily act of dressing themselves in historically accurate costuming. The distances traversed through such intimate acts were both geographic and temporal.

Although the medieval period remained a popular source of inspiration, fancy dress ball revelers also modeled costumes after influences as widespread as ancient Egypt and the Elizabethan era. Significantly, whereas professional theater artists like Kean and actor-managers like Henry Irving who followed him prided themselves on the historical accuracy of the costumes in their productions, fancy dress ball revelers seem to have been more preoccupied with selecting a costume that their peers would find "correct" and appropriate for the situation. Men and women had to balance the desire for authenticity and accuracy in historical detail with their own physical appearance and personality. In the 1887 manual *Fancy dresses described: or, What to wear at fancy Balls*, author Ardern Holt advised: "It behoves those who really desire to look well to study what is individually becoming to themselves, and then to bring to bear some little care in the carrying out of the dresses they select, if they wish their costumes to be really a success. There are few occasions when a woman has a better opportunity of showing her charms to advantage than at a Fancy Ball."[49]

Here, Holt strongly urges readers (who we can assume from the volume's title were primarily, if not exclusively, women) to study themselves when selecting a costume and to first find one suited to their individuality – one that "hugged" them well, to use Hann's term – before worrying about the accuracy of specific details (Figures 10.3a and 10.3b). Echoing this advice two decades later, Mrs. Aria, author of *Costume: Fanciful, Historical and Theatrical* (1906), also urged her readers to care for their personal appearance:

> In deciding upon a costume for a fancy-dress ball, the first thought of the reveller should be to secure the becoming and the suitable, and to be successful the choice should be mainly influenced by his or her personality. I quite realize the problem to be a difficult one, since happily we have not the gift given to us to see ourselves as others see us, else should we never meet a podgy Mephistopheles bulging out of his clothes, nor an attenuated Juno, nor a dusky Desdemona, nor a buxom Puck.[50]

Victorian advice manuals also established that the wrong fancy dress choice could be dire, but the right choice could enhance a person's charms, and provided, as Cynthia Cooper put it in her discussion of the Victorian passion for fancy dress, "a reprieve from limitation on their identities," while balancing on a fine line between "ephemeral freedom and retaining integrity."[51] Indeed, in many cases, Victorian costume balls only offered an

Fig. 16.—QUEEN ELIZABETH.

Figures 10.3a and b Fancy-dress costumes, from Arden Holt, *Fancy Dress Described* (1887). Courtesy of York University Libraries.

illusion of choice. *Myra's Journal* writes, "In choosing fancy dresses for children, the complexion, figure, and even disposition of the wearer should be taken into consideration ... The choice of pretty costumes is so large and varied that it is an easy task to find one to suit any child, whether

Fig. 5.—DRESS OF CHARLES II. PERIOD.

Figures 10.3a and b (cont.)

she be fair or dark, short or tall, lively or a 'sober-sides' without doing violence to her natural appearance or character."[52] For example, a dark-haired girl must never consider dressing as a Scandinavian peasant,[53] while Dorothy Lane writes, "The Egyptian Priestess is an extremely imposing dress and would prove most attractive if worn by a handsome dark girl."[54] If a ball guest chose badly, she risked being ridiculed by journalists, and, perhaps, other guests. Here again, the emphasis on "correct," flattering costumes takes precedence over the accuracy of an item of clothing.

The reference to Egyptian princesses and "dark girls" in Lane's account nods toward a larger shift in the kinds of historical subjects that populated the late-Victorian stage.[55] By the end of the nineteenth century, as fascination with Indigenous, Asian, and Middle Eastern cultures intensified, due in part to growing anxieties about the imperial project, Anglo-American audiences found new pleasure observing "authentic" ethnographic displays of Indigenous peoples and other racialized groups at World's Fairs. Playing to this desire for exotic entertainment, white North American women turned heads in music halls, spas, amusement parks, and other sites of popular entertainment throughout Europe with their interpretations of dances that supposedly originated in Asia, Africa, or the Middle East. Playing out Orientalist fantasies of the sexually available yet mysterious colonized woman, such dancers offered their predominantly (though not exclusively) white male audiences a temporary reprieve from larger concerns about the "threat of the racial Other."[56] The media circus that surrounded the dancer Maud Allan and her dance interpretation of the biblical character of Salome, as presented at London's Palace Theatre in 1908, offers but one example of this Orientalist obsession and its influence on practices of historical reenactment.[57] What made Allan's performance so shocking was not simply her ecstatic interpretation of the young girl's response to receiving the head of John the Baptist but the fact that she danced barefoot and uncorseted, dressed only in a jewel-encrusted bra and gauze skirt that left little to the imagination (Figure 10.4). Indeed, it was the "no-thing-ness" of Allan's costume – to invoke one critic's description[58] – that offended (and titillated) audiences. When called upon to defend herself from accusations of indecency, the dancer stressed that she had drawn inspiration from "Etruscan vases and Assyrian tablets" she had observed in European art galleries.[59] Her performance was therefore authentic ... or so she claimed.

Reenactments in the Twenty-First Century

Today historical reenactment is an extremely popular hobby in North America and in England. As in the nineteenth century, medieval reenactment remains attractive, but there are enthusiasts for nearly every historical moment imaginable: for example, there are Vikings encamped at L'Anse aux Meadows, Newfoundland,[60] there are Jane Austen Societies throwing Regency Balls throughout North America and the UK;[61] there are annual American Civil War reenactments at various key sites,[62] and

Figure 10.4 Maud Allan as Salome, c. 1907. Courtesy of Dance Collection Danse.

the Society for Creative Anachronism, which is dedicated to pre-seventeenth-century skills, arts, combat, and culture, has chapters throughout the world.[63] While sometimes the engagement with costume is as casual as finding the old clothes we wore ourselves when we were in our teens or twenties, wearing them to a decade party at a nightclub in celebration of our own youth and the memories those clothes offer, more frequently costume for historical reenactment refers to a time that the wearer did not personally experience. Today, as in the nineteenth century, the body striving to "get it right" and wearing the clothing is *necessarily* inaccurate, being always too tall, often too old, and almost certainly too healthy to precisely represent the bodies of the past.[64]

Reenactors are concerned about the actual bodies wearing the costumes. One focus is on the moving (seemingly living) costumes, because, when these are animated by living bodies, the costumes create an experience environment. In fact, a new materialist approach to costuming understands the relationship between costume and human body as more dynamic, even symbiotic. Following Bernstein, we might go so far as to suggest that it is not simply living bodies that animate costumes but costumes that script or give shape to the actions of those bodies: one animates the other and vice versa.[65] Or, to return to Hann's "theory of hugging," it is the meeting of flesh and costume that guides human movement and perception. In many reenactment spaces and at major reenactment events, there are often participants and spectators, and therefore, the costume choices influence the wearer's experience as well as the experience of other participants, and potentially, of spectators. However, prior to discussing costume and the experience of spectators or spectator-participants, the other body-based focus related to dress and historical reenactment is on the material experience of the person wearing the costume. Stephen Gapps, a historian and reenactor, writes, "I find dressing and performing historical clothing, often from a culture or past that is not 'my own', to be highly risky work. It is more visceral, insistent, perhaps more creative – but definitely more audacious – than formal historical writing. For these reasons, re-enactment has gotten under my skin."[66]

It is telling that although Gapps's article is about many aspects of participating in reenactments, including the choice of venues and spaces, audience, and the activities reenactors present, his exploration begins with "dressing and performing in historical clothing" and that because dressing and performing in costume is visceral, "re-enactment has gotten under [his] skin." The intimacy of wearing another's time and place seems to do more than create an impression on the skin – it is more than texture, weight, cut, draping, the feel of fasteners, of exposed and covered skin – Gapps suggests clothing does not necessarily sit lightly on the reenactor, implying, perhaps, that the act of wearing and performing in specific clothing can make an impression beyond the surface of the skin and press beneath the surface into the participant's bones – an extreme version of a hug if ever there was one. Exploring costume on the body becomes an opportunity to establish empathy. The significance of clothing's relationship to empathy has been established for a long time. Bruce McConachie is not the first to declare that empathy is "to put it simply, to walk in someone else's shoes," and many argue that clothing is the closest thing to getting inside someone else's skin.[67] In fact, this section examines the conditions participants crave to achieve that kind of empathy. We also consider some complex ethical barriers and identity concerns that arguably render the costume portal leading to empathy with the past completely inaccessible and impassable under some circumstances that harken back to nineteenth-century fancy dress etiquette, but with significantly different implications.

Scholars who have written about reenactors often relate that participants crave connecting with the way the past might "feel," and, as mentioned, if the material conditions of a reenactment moment align for the reenactor, they might experience "period rush" when time seems to fold over the past into the present, setting up the impression of time travel. Gapps, Magelssen, and Shukla all delve into the differences in commitment between what they call "hard-core" reenactors, and "farbs" who are prone to performing anachronisms, and lacking commitment to the historical veracity of a period. Gapps writes, "Reenactors can generally describe their clothing and equipment in great detail, for the authentic object is deeply bound up with the way history might feel. As one reenactor suggests, her 'impression' must be complete in detail or the 'experience' is less convincing."[68] This emphasis on *impression* recalls Sara Ahmed's use of the word to highlight the interrelationship of "bodily sensation, emotion and thought." "We need to remember the 'press' in impression," she writes. "It allows us to associate the experience of having an emotion with the very affect of one surface upon another, an affect that leaves its mark or trace. So not only do I have an impression of others, but they also leave me with an impression; they impress me, and impress upon me."[69]

Many reenactors speak of the power of heavy, itchy fabrics against the skin in helping to transport the wearer out of the present day and into an imagined (understood?) past. As garments of clothing shield the wearers from the air of the present, they seem to be able to transport the wearer into another time, that is both present and past. Wearing a costume as a way to facilitate time travel is not new: in the Victorian era, Cooper argues that fancy dress balls "provided an outlet which one could project oneself into a different time and place."[70] Schneider describes the "queasiness" of this collision of time-spaces, emphasizing the discomfort of being unsettled and uncertain about the presence of the past, while many reenactors seeking the "rush" must find the same feelings thrilling.

While the feel of the past and the connection with the past through the costumes they wear themselves is paramount to the performer, the incorrect costuming of others can also influence the performer's experience of history. The opportunity to "time travel" requires others to travel on the same journey together, which makes these kinds of performative costume displays different from Halloween or even a cosplay convention where performers represent characters from multiple different worlds. The responsibility to perform correctly lies across a spectrum, and many "hard core" reenactors argue that getting the dress right is a historical responsibility. Gapps claims that through costume, reenactors "cite evidence: the footnote to the historian is the authentic (recreated) costume to the reenactor."[71] Shukla, meanwhile, cites multiple rules and requirements for dress at certain reenactment sites, including the importance of historically appropriate footwear, and style of eyeglasses. The intention is to create a whole experience and world that Schneider describes as establishing the conditions of time travel. The relationship to costume anachronism falls across a spectrum, however, in that some reenactors are not troubled by the inevitable lapses in accuracy, considering the effort made to be essential, whereas others regard anachronism as unconscionable, misleading spectators, and ruining the potential experience of participants. The more knowledgeable the participants, the more significant these issues become. Regardless of the importance of space and place in reenactment events, it seems that costume, itself, is an essential element of the time travel. Danielle Robinson details attending a Regency reenactment event for the first or second time, by describing her tentative gestures toward era-specific, but upper-class dress, and being drawn aside by regulars – one who smiled and pulled a more "appropriate" dress out of her bag for Robinson to wear, and another who seemed quite scandalized when she whispered that Robinson should put away her wristwatch. These same reenactors were unperturbed by dinner conversations about (now former) United States President Donald Trump – the performance of Regency gentility required good manners and great costumes, but did not censor the issues that matter in life. As Robinson's experience suggests, putting on a costume is akin to getting into a time machine, and that machine's ability to transport the wearer effectively depends on the quality of their costumes – and the costumes (or time machines) of others around them.[72]

In the twenty-first century, angst about historical accuracy in costumed reenactment events may focus on details like boots and eyeglasses, but it is not unique to the reenactment genre, nor is it unique to the twenty-first century: however, the drive for accuracy and correctness has different implications today than it did in the nineteenth century. In the nineteenth century, the *tableaux vivants* craze encouraged unified expressions of a single (often historical) moment; meanwhile, fancy dress balls were occasionally themed, but more frequently encouraged an eclectic variety of costume choices, not unlike a Halloween party or a cosplay convention today. The onus was on party guests to present an appropriate outfit (and as we mentioned, the idea of "correct" in the nineteenth century had as much to do with the participant's own body, coloring, and personality as it did historical accuracy), and while their costume choice may put their own reputation at stake, the success of the event as a whole was not. At a twenty-first century cosplay event, it is also likely that participants will represent a vast range of characters from a range of fictional (often anime or manga) worlds. When they interviewed cosplay participants, Rahman and colleagues learned that participants shared similar concerns about the significance of costume accuracy as historical reenactors do. Furthermore, they also point out the importance of following the "script" (as Bernstein calls it) embedded in the costume. For example, they quote cosplayer Chelsea as saying "It's not difficult to tell who is a real cosplayer and who is not. The most obvious indicator is that their costumes do not match the original character in terms of style and color. I saw a cosplayer even wearing sneakers with an ancient outfit … some cosplayers just sit there or walk back and forth across the venue without role-playing or performing like their chosen character … To me, authentic cosplayers should at least wear the right clothes … and engage and immerse themselves completely in the performance."[73] Just like historical reenactors, this cosplayer is concerned with getting the costume "right" and allowing the costume to dictate appropriate behaviors.

As we mentioned at the beginning, one of the challenges with historical reenactments today hinges uncomfortably on the bodies that wear the costumes: which bodies are "allowed" to reenact which pasts? Rebecca Schneider notes that when reenactors are attempting to "*touch* the Civil War" or are "fight[ing] to get the times right," what they are actually aiming for is an "idealized time, and the drive to authenticity was a drive to an authenticity that *should have been* according to reenactors' interpretations, not necessarily an authenticity that was."[74] Indeed, as our earlier discussion of Victorian obsession with the medieval period suggests, historical reenactment and the drive to authenticity is almost always fueled by a desire to capture the *should have been*.

This quest becomes complicated when addressing cross-dressing practices, for example. Cross-dressing female fighters are well-documented in the Civil War, and it is believed that many women fought as men, undetected. But supposedly, in their time, they were understood to be men. If a woman is performing as a man in a Civil War reenactment, and, despite her costume, other participants know she is "really" a woman, how does this disrupt their efforts to touch time? Is the message her costume is sending inadequate under the circumstances? In fact, Schneider refers to a lawsuit against Lauren Cook Burgess (1989) who was discovered crossdressing in a reenactment. Burgess won her suit, but the issue remains that for reenactors, the costume is only part of the message – the body is also a communicator. While it is already clear that most reenactors make allowances for height, weight, and good health, other body features seem to clash more awkwardly with the past, and in fact, some clash in similar ways in the cosplay community. Jordan Kass Lome points to the "policing" of the cosplay community, while Schneider and Gapps recount the ways hard-core reenactors try to maintain what they perceive as "standards" of costume (and bodies in costumes) in their chosen era. But a costume is something a player or a reenactor can choose; choosing biological gender, hair color, and skin color is not (or at least not as easy). Lome suggests that despite increasing emphasis on body positivity, "cosplayers still encounter misconceptions as to whether people can cosplay characters of different genders, races, heights, weights, and so on."[75] Schneider also notes that in the Civil War reenactment community that the presence of African American reenactors can cause tensions because their bodies point out difficult social and moral dilemmas that reenactors have tried to expunge from the discourse around their events.[76] More recently, African American reenactors like Cheney McKnight have developed educational programs that use objects, costumes, and performance to directly engage with the history of slavery in the United States.[77]

Yet the question of the body performing in the costume becomes an ethical question when we consider two of Shukla's assertions. First, she writes "Costume provides an outlet for expression of certain identity markers that do not have an outlet in ordinary life."[78] Shukla cites common examples of Halloween costumes – humorous for men, sexy for women, "Princess-y" for little girls, and superheroes for little boys. Cooper argues that these conditions of expression were also present in nineteenth-century fancy dress balls, and Rahmen and colleagues demonstrate that costume is equally important in offering cosplay participants a vehicle to express aspects of themselves that they cannot explore in quotidian life. In Shukla's description, costume – used to communicate something meaningful to others – seems to necessarily communicate something about the living body and the living person wearing the costume. In other words, even if the reenactor is trying to connect, through costume, with the past, the clothing itself is always also communicating something to spectators about the wearer.

If, in the nineteenth century, this meant that certain costumes were off-limits for people with certain "complexions" because of concerns about "correctness" and "accuracy," today those concerns are much more deeply connected to questions around appropriation and even more significantly, ethical practice. Gapps writes, "the body, clothed in history, forces ethics into being: the practice of re-enacting the past is close to an ethics of what can be redone, what should be redone or what cannot be redone."[79] Megan Norcia's descriptions of costumed performances suggested by nineteenth-century geography primers (or textbooks) point out how deeply connected costumed performance is to the dominant discourses of the day. Norcia explores ways that white, English, middle-class girls (themselves marginalized citizens) could use performing otherwise as racialized, non-English people as opportunities to experiment with having power, even as their actions joined the imperialist discourses that subjugated the people whose countries they portrayed.[80] Today, those racist, imperialist discourses that shape our lives in North America still exist, but unlike the nineteenth-century girls who rarely, if ever, had the power to critique those discourses, criticism of racialization, the legacies of settler colonialism, and the imperial project are readily available today – even if meaningful responses are not.

While in today's intellectual climate it seems logical that any person should be able to perform supposedly white, male (normalized and idealized) characters in historical reenactments, regardless of their physical appearance, the idea of saying the same thing about white bodies who want to perform non-white roles is complicated by legacies of oppression, imperialism, and colonialism, current power dynamics supported by systemic injustices that favor white people and white bodies. Despite nineteenth-century ideas about "correctness," as a white woman, Maud Allan danced in the glow of what Bernstein describes as innocence that was "raced white."[81] While Bernstein is specifically examining the construction of childhood innocence, she convincingly demonstrates how whiteness became equated with moral "goodness" over the course of the nineteenth century. At the same time, whiteness carried the privilege of being at the civilized pinnacle of the normative hierarchy (very popular in the nineteenth century, and commonly accepted), known as "The Great Chain of Being," which "offered an irresistible way to rank people from every social class, race, and gender."[82] Through the Great Chain, white people positioned themselves as the morally righteous, intellectually superior, and powerful top of the chain. The result was that white audiences could watch Allan dance without discomfort, because as a superior person within that discourse, it made sense that she could interpret and perform an "Oriental" character like Salome. Simultaneously, her whiteness supposedly shielded her with innocence and protected her from any kind of salacious concerns associated with the stereotypes of the Orient.

But in the twenty-first century, whiteness does not and should not slip easily into any costume nor does it unproblematically permit cross-cultural costumed role play or reenactment. Increasingly, as some North Americans understand the pervasiveness of racist, imperialist discourses in the shaping of North American institutions and systems, they see that wearing a cultural costume can be offensive because it suggests that the wearer is oblivious to the weight of the past that should be felt in the hug of the fabric. In October 2011, Students Teaching Against Racism in Society (STARS) at Ohio University launched a poster campaign to raise awareness about insensitive Halloween costumes, and subsequent campaigns followed, such as Teen Vogue's "My Culture is Not a Costume." In terms of viewership, the campaigns have been radically successful,[83] and while it was still easy to order a range of racialized costume-types on eBay in 2018, the campaigns have ensured that it is much more difficult to ignorantly wear culturally specific costumes that do not connect to the wearer's own heritage.[84] In her discussion of the Boston MFA kimono protests, Michelle Liu Carriger draws attention to the message wearing a costume communicates. Carriger argues that at the exhibit when a white person put on a kimono, the action demands that viewers interrogate (for example) what a kimono has come to symbolize in North America and what Orientalist fantasies do to Asian American women.[85] The hug of the culturally specific costume does more than transport the wearer into another space or time, it simultaneously drags with it concerns about the present. If costume sends a message and communicates something meaningful to the world about the wearer, one of the messages the costume can communicate is a willful obliviousness to the implications of history and human interrelations in today's world. Certain events cannot and should not be represented, and because of historical power relations, white bodies should avoid performing non-white roles.

The nuanced questions about crossing (gender, age, race, and most obviously, time) when participating in historical reenactment demonstrate that the spaces created when a participant decides to put on a costume may be extremely productive sites for learning. Gapps writes that through the embodied reenactment practices, "crossing social, cultural, gender or ethnic boundaries creates tension and unease, but it also generates possibility – much more so I believe, than speaking or writing across those borders."[86] Behaving in offensive and culturally insensitive ways cannot be condoned, but it is possible that through thoughtful decisions concerning historical dress and participating in costumed reenactment, the power of costume to not only transform but to transport the wearer, creates conditions for critical knowledge creation.

Historical reenactment complicates a second assertion of Shukla's about the function of costume: "In wearing costume we do not become someone else: rather we become in some context a deeper or heightened version of ourselves."[87] Gapps also argues that "the reenactor's clothing and equipment are particularly vivid sites of cultural meaning and expressions of social self."[88] Yet, while many reenactors want to *feel* as if they are in the past and part of a past event, portraying a version of the self is not necessarily the goal of the reenactor. While the reenactor *may* want to explore their own potential in the form of an enhanced identity, often they want to touch time and connect with the ghosts of their own or someone else's past, and many are hoping that if they speak to and for the past, the past will speak to and through them – that through their costumed body, they will touch time in whispers and wrinkles that suggest that time repeats, bends, folds, and moves sideways. As the fabric hugs the wearer, the weight and pressure of the fabric may bring the person *beyond* themselves. In these instances, costumes are the primary vehicle for connecting to this otherness. Gapps relates the experience of one reenactor who calls herself a "mobile monument" to the memory of her great-grandmother.[89] She does not perceive her performance as a deeper version of herself, but rather, as a testament to her great-grandmother's life, an act of public commemoration, and a memorial to a person she cannot actually remember but can connect with through the performance of the past. The reenactor goes on to explain that she promotes the idea that reenactors might benefit from choosing a person to represent because, not only is that a meaningful exercise, it can improve the possibility of accuracy.

Yet accuracy, historical reenactment, and costume are uneasily linked together. Today, as in the nineteenth century, costume has the power to send a message *about the past* to spectators, *about the past* to the wearer, and simultaneously, complicates our understanding about the body wearing the costume *in the present* and the *possibility of that body in the past*. The body, itself, has the potential to challenge any message the costume might communicate.

A third question arises when a racialized performer is historically costumed and performs what (in Gapps's terms) might be considered a "heightened version" of the self. Laura Peers analyzes the work of Indigenous interpreters reenacting the past in living history museums at five different Canadian and US living history sites. Her research participants suggest that Indigenous interpreters identify with their work more closely than non-Indigenous interpreters do, and "experience a thinner and more porous boundary between self and representation" because unlike their non-Indigenous counterparts, they told her, "we are playing ourselves,"[90] and in fact a great deal of their work is teaching visitors that Indigeneity is not exclusively a part of history (although it is that too), but that it is a part of contemporary life. Heather's research with volunteers at Fort Edmonton Park interpreting nehiyawak (Cree) and Métis people's experiences in 1846 and 1885 has led to similar conclusions. Lynne, one of the volunteers representing a Métis mother, observed that the nehiyaw women at the fort were often sharing aspects of their culture as it exists today (Figure 10.5).[91]

The racialized bodies of Indigenous interpreters means that their cultural identity is foregrounded before and after they take off the historical clothes.[92] The hug of the clothing intensifies racialization of the body, but unless an interpreter regularly "passes" as white in their quotidian life, interpreters may not be able to choose to leave aspects of their performance identity behind at the end of the day. The young volunteers Heather interviewed spoke about ignorant, racist remarks visitors have made toward them that historically located dress seems to make permissible. Somehow, for some visitors, the clothing objectifies the racialized wearer, and some visitors make rude comments reflecting a racist, imperialist, ignorant legacy of Indigenous-settler relations. While some young Indigenous Edmontonians are certainly subjected to racist remarks in their daily lives, these volunteers told Heather that they did not experience that, except for occasionally at the fort. Volunteers told Heather they received training in how to deal with inappropriate racist and sexist comments directed toward them, and often chose to use second person or third person language to emphasize their knowledge of the era and the people occupying the fort and the Métis camp. Lynne explains that she tells visitors, "I *would be* a Métis woman" when she is in the fort (rather than "I *am* a Métis woman"), while teenaged interpreters Evelyn and her brother Mclovin both explain how they address racist remarks by helping visitors understand why they were inappropriate. While Evelyn handles the racism entirely outside of character, Mclovin rejects the comment with a joke, and then moves out of character to directly address the ignorance, using the opportunity to educate the visitor in what he calls a "proper" way.[93] Indigenous, racialized costumed interpreters are reenacting a past,

Figure 10.5 Image of two young Métis volunteers at winter camp. Courtesy of Fort Edmonton Park.

while simultaneously taking on the responsibility to educate visitors about how that past needs to be understood in the present.

If we return now to the girls in Heather's nineteenth-century theater and dance workshop as they "bodied forth" girls of the past, we can see that their experiments with corsets vividly draw attention to ways a garment of clothing communicates through reenactment. A corset is an undergarment regardless of whether someone is wearing it. And for most middle- and upper-class nineteenth-century girls in England and North America, a corset was daily *dress*. But for the workshop participants, donning the corset was, as Hann puts it, "a performative act." The hug of the corset itself invited participants to think differently about nineteenth-century girls, and the ways they moved, danced, and played. The touch of the corsets drew girls into nineteenth-century spaces, and through the performative act of costuming, encouraged them to ask questions about daily life and daily practices. But putting on the corsets did more than invite girls to think about the material conditions of past lives, and they did even more than think about how those material conditions shaped the action and movement of the past because the corsets – as costumes – made an impression. The pressure and support of the garment, and the necessity of getting help to put it on and take it off brought participants into the realm of acquiring affective knowledge about the past. Experimenting with costumes invites us to think critically about the past and the relationship of that past to our present lives. Costumes allow us to time travel, to feel differently, to reach out (and back) into another time and place. To move and be moved.

Notes

1. Florence Bell, *Fairy Tales and How to Act Them* (London, New York, and Bombay: Longmans, Green, 1896).
2. Rebecca Schneider, *Performing Remains: Art and War in Times of Theatrical Reenactment* (New York: Routledge, 2011), 35.
3. Rachel Hann, "Debating Critical Costume: Negotiating Ideologies of Appearance, Performance and Disciplinarity," *Studies in Theatre and Performance* 39, no. 1 (2019), 2, 12–15.
4. Thomas F. DeFrantz and Gustavo Furtado, "Call for Papers" via email, October 10, 2016, for "The Future of Reenactment" conference at Duke University (April 20–21, 2017) (emphasis added). Cited in Rebecca Schneider, "That the Past May Have Yet Another Future: Gesture in the Times of Hands Up," *Theatre Journal* 70, no. 3 (Sept. 2018), 288.
5. See, for example, Rebecca Schneider, "New Materialisms and Performance Studies," *The Drama Review* 59, no. 4 (Winter 2015), 7–17; Leo Cabranes Grant, *From Scenarios to Networks: Performing the Intercultural in Colonial Mexico* (Chicago: Northwestern University Press, 2016); Robin Bernstein, "Dances with Things: Material Culture and the Performance of Race," *Social Text* 27, no. 4 (2009), 67–94; Robin Bernstein, *Racial Innocence: Performing American Childhood from Slavery to Civil Rights* (New York: New York University Press, 2011); Marlis Schweitzer and Joanne Zerdy, eds., *Performing Objects and Theatrical Things* (Basingstoke: Palgrave Macmillan, 2014).
6. Jane Bennett, *Vibrant Matter: A Political Ecology of Things* (Durham: Duke University Press, 2010).
7. Diana Coole and Samantha Frost, *New Materialism: Ontology, Agency, and Politics* (Durham: Duke University Press, 2010).

8. See, for example, Kim Tallbear, "An Indigenous Reflection on Working Beyond the Human/Non Human," *GLQ: A Journal of Lesbian and Gay Studies* 21, no. 2-3 (June 2015), 230-35; Tim Hutching and Joanne McKenzie, eds., *Materiality and the Study of Religion: The Stuff of the Sacred* (London: Routledge, 2016).
9. Bill Brown, "Thing Theory," *Critical Inquiry* 28, no. 1 (Autumn 2001), 1-22.
10. Bernstein, "Dances," 12.
11. Ibid.
12. Hann, "Debating," 1-2.
13. Hann, "Debating," 2. See also Ali MacLaurin and Aoife Monks, *Costume: Readings in Theatre Practice* (Palgrave Macmillan, 2015); Donatella Barbieri, *Costume in Performance: Materiality, Costume, and the Body* (London: Bloomsbury, 2017).
14. Hann, "Debating," 9.
15. Thomas Carlyle, *Sartor Resartus,* serialized in *Fraser's Magazine* (1833-34) quoted in Inga Bryden, "All Dressed Up: Revivalism and the Fashion for Arthur in Victorian Culture," *Arthuriana* 12, no. 2 Special Issue, *Arthurian Revival in the Nineteenth Century* (Summer 2011), 29.
16. Hann, "Debating," 12.
17. Katherine Newey, "Embodied History: Reflections on the Jane Scott Project," *Nineteenth Century Theatre and Film* 29, no. 2 (2002), 66-70.
18. Kathleen Gallagher, "Theatre Pedagogy and Performed Research: Respectful Forgeries and Faithful Betrayals," *Theatre Research in Canada* 28, no. 2 (2007), 105.
19. Charlotte Canning, "Feminist Performance as Feminist Historiography," *Theatre Survey* 45, no. 2 (2004), 228.
20. Hann, "Debating," 14.
21. Pravina Shukla, *Costume: Performing Identities through Dress* (Bloomington: Indiana University Press, 2015), 1.
22. Shukla, *Costume*, 1.
23. See, for example, Felicity Nussbaum, *Rival Queens: Actresses, Performance, and the Eighteenth-Century British Theatre* (Philadelphia: University of Pennsylvania Press, 2010); Gill Perry, *Spectacular Flirtations: Viewing the Actress in British Art and Theater, 1768-1820* (New Haven: Yale University Press, 2008).
24. Andrew Gibb, "'On the [Historical] Sublime': J. R. Planché's *King John* and the Romantic Ideal of the Past," *Theatre Symposium* 26 (2018), 127-40. See also Alicia Finkel, *Romantic Stages: Set and Costume Design in Victorian England* (Jefferson and London: McFarland, 1996).
25. J. R. Planché, quoted in Richard W. Schoch, *Shakespeare's Victorian Stage: Performing History in the Theatre of Charles Kean* (Cambridge: Cambridge University Press, 1998), 75.
26. Gibb, "'On the [Historical] Sublime'," 129.
27. Ibid.

28. Schneider, *Performing Remains*, 10.
29. Schoch, *Shakespeare's Victorian Stage*, 6.
30. Ibid, 76.
31. Gibb, "'On the [Historical] Sublime'," 137.
32. Schoch, *Shakespeare's Victorian Stage*, 122.
33. Ibid, 123.
34. Ibid, 86–87.
35. Ibid, 87.
36. Louise D'Arcens, "'The Last Thing One Might Expect': The Medieval Court at the 1866 Melbourne Intercolonial Exhibition," *The La Trobe Journal* 81 (2008), 27.
37. Ibid, 26–27.
38. On living history museums, see Scott Magelssen, *Simming: Participatory Performance and the Making of Meaning* (Ann Arbor: University of Michigan Press, 2014); Anthony Jackson and Jenny Kidd, *Performing Heritage: Research, Practice, and Innovation in Museum Theatre and Live Interpretation* (Manchester: Manchester University Press, 2010).
39. On shopping environments, see Maurya Wickstrom, *Performing Consumers: Global Capital and Its Theatrical Seductions* (London: Routledge, 2006).
40. Bryden, "All Dressed Up," 29.
41. Ibid, 32.
42. Charlotte Yonge, "The Mice at Play," *Historical Dramas* (London: Groomsbridge and Sons, 1864).
43. For more on at-home theatricals, see Heather Marie Fitzsimmons Frey, "Victorian Girls and At-Home Theatricals: Performing and Playing with Possible Futures" (Ph.D. dissertation, University of Toronto, 2015).
44. Royal Trust Collection. Excerpt adapted from Jonathan Marsden, *Victoria & Albert: Art and Love* (London: Royal Collection Trust, 2010). See also Caroline Goldthorpe, *From Queen to Empress: Victorian Dress 1837–1877* (New York: The Metropolitan Museum of Art, 1989).
45. Marsden, *Victoria & Albert*.
46. Ibid.
47. Cynthia Cooper, *Magnificent Entertainments: Fancy Dress Balls of Canada's Governors General, 1876–1898* (Fredericton: Goose Lane Editions, 1997); Vicky Ann Cremona *Carnival and Power: Play and Politics in a Crown Colony* (Basingstoke: Palgrave Macmillan, 2018). Alexandra (Sasha) Kovacs, "Beyond Shame and Blame in Pauline Johnson's Performance Histories," in Heather Davis-Fisch, ed., *Canadian Performance Histories and Historiographies* (Toronto: Playwrights Canada Press, 2017), 33–51. Kovacs also discusses costume and questions of authenticity and performance in her analysis of the Indigenous poet/actress E. Pauline Johnson/Tekahionwake.

48. Elizabeth Maddock Dillon, *New World Drama, The Performative Commons in the Atlantic World 1649-1849* (Durham: Duke University Press, 2014), 56.
49. Ardern Holt, *Fancy Dresses Described: or, What to Wear at Fancy Balls* (London: Debenham and Freebody, Wyman and Sons, 1887), 6.
50. Mrs. Eliza Davis Aria, *Costume: Fanciful, Historical and Theatric* (London and New York: Macmillan, 1906), 188. Books such as Cyril Bowen, *Practical Hints on Stage Costume* (London and New York: Samuel French, 1881) also gave nonprofessional performers helpful tips for recreating costumes from earlier historical periods.
51. Cooper, "Dressing Up: A Victorian Passion," in *Magnificent Entertainments*, 37.
52. "Current Modes for Children: Novelties in Fancy Dresses," *Myra's Journal* 4 (1 April 1889), 200.
53. Cooper, "Dressing Up," 30.
54. Dorothy Lane, "Effective Fancy Dresses," *Hearth and Home* 138 (1896), 274.
55. See Edward Ziter, *The Orient on the Victorian Stage* (Cambridge: Cambridge University Press, 2003).
56. Amy Koritz, "Dancing the Orient for England: Maud Allan's 'The Vision of Salome'," *Theatre Journal* 46, no. 1 (March 1994), 7 6. See also Michelle Clayton, "Touring History: Tortola Valencia between Europe and the Americas," *Dance Research Journal* 44, no. 1 (Summer 2012), 30.
57. For more on the Salome craze, see Koritz, "Dancing the Orient for England"; Mary Simonson, "'The Call of Salome': American Adaptations and Re-creations of the Female Body in the Early Twentieth Century," *Women and Music* 11 (2007), 1-16; Judith R. Walkowitz, "The 'Vision of Salome': Cosmopolitanism and Erotic Dancing in Central London, 1908-1918," *American Historical Review* 108, no. 2 (April 2003), 337-76.
58. Quoted in Felix Cherniavsky, *Maud Allan and Her Art* (Toronto: Dance Collection Danse, 1998), 39. For more on Allan's costume as a no-thing, see Marlis Schweitzer, "'Nothing but a String of Beads': Maud Allan's Salomé costume as a "choreographic thing'," in Marlis Schweitzer and Joanne Zerdy, eds., *Performing Objects and Theatrical Things* (Basingstoke: Palgrave Macmillan, 2015), 36-48.
59. Quoted in Walkowitz, "'Vision of Salome'," 356.
60. Ashley Williamson, "How to Act Like a Viking: The New Role of Performance in Experimental Archaeology," *Playing with History: A Performance-Based Historiography Symposium*, Toronto, October 12-13, 2018.
61. Danielle Robinson, "Simpler Times? Exploring Heritage Weekends in Ontario," *Playing with History: A Performance-Based Historiography Symposium*, Toronto October 12-13, 2018.

62. For more on Civil War reenactors, see Tony Horowitz, *Confederates in the Attic: Dispatches from the Unfinished Civil War* (New York: Vintage Books, 1998); Schneider, *Performing*. The politics surrounding such reenactments have intensified in recent years. See Denise Crosby, "Civil War Reenactments: Cultural Insensitivity of Living History Lessons?" *Chicago Tribune* June 27, 2019, https://bit.ly/3n3Z7YR and Mark Guarino, "Time for Civil War Reenactments to Die Out?" *Washington Post* August 25, 2017, https://wapo.st/3om0kKM, accessed August 20, 2019.
63. Society for Creative Anachronism, Inc.
64. Schneider, *Performing*, 45.
65. This view pushes against more traditional understandings of costumes as needing the human body to achieve any kind of agency. See Schweitzer, "'Nothing but a String of Beads'" for a more extended discussion of this idea.
66. Stephen Gapps, "Mobile Monuments: A View of Historical Re-enactment and Authenticity from the Costume Cupboard of History," *Rethinking History: The Journal of Theory and Practice* 13, no. 3 (2009), 396.
67. Bruce McConachie, *Engaging the Audience: A Cognitive Approach to Spectating in the Theatre* (Basingstoke: Palgrave Macmillan, 2008), 99.
68. Gapps, "Mobile Monuments," 398.
69. Sara Ahmed, *The Cultural Politics of Emotion* (London: Routledge, 2004), 6.
70. Cooper, "Dressing Up," 21.
71. Gapps, "Mobile Monuments," 398.
72. Robinson, "Simpler Times."
73. Osmond Rahman, Liu Wing Sun, and Brittany Heim-man Cheung, "Cosplay: Imaginative Self and Performing Identity," *Fashion Theory: Journal of Dress, Body and Culture* 16, no. 33 (2012), 326.
74. Schneider, *Performing Remains*, 55.
75. Jordan Kass Lome, "The Creative Empowerment of Body Positivity in the Cosplay Community," *Transformative Works and Cultures*, no. 22, 2016.
76. Schneider, Performing Remains, 55–56.
77. "Not Your Momma's History." www.notyourmommashistory.com/historical-interpretation.html, accessed September 2, 2019.
78. Shukla, *Costume*, 15.
79. Gapps, "Mobile Monuments," 404.
80. Megan Norcia, *X Marks the Spot: Women Writers Map the Empire for British Children, 1790–1895* (Athens: Ohio University Press, 2010).
81. Bernstein, *Racial Innocence*, 8.
82. Nancy Lesko, *Act Your Age! A Cultural Construction of Adolescence*, 2nd ed. (London: Routledge, 2012), 32.
83. HuffPost, "STARS Student Group Takes a Stand Against Racist Costumes," 24 October 2011; See: https://www.teenvogue.com/story/cultural-appropriation-halloween-costume-video 25 October 2017.
84. Auli'i Cravalho, the actress who voiced Moana for the Disney film, entered this debate by supporting children who want to dress up as

Moana for Halloween, regardless of their ethnicity. Moana's relationship to costume is particularly complicated because she is an Indigenous character, and because the character resonates with practices around cosplay, Disney princesses, and "fangirl" culture. Jennifer McClellan, "Moana Actress Says it's OK for Kids to Dress up as her Disney Character for Halloween," *USA Today*, October 25, 2018.

85. Michelle Liu Carriger, "No 'Thing to Wear': A Brief History of Kimono and Inappropriation from Japonisme to Kimono Protests," *Theatre Research International* 43, no. 2 (July 2018), 165–84.
86. Gapps, "Mobile Monuments," 403.
87. Shukla, *Costume*, 15.
88. Gapps, "Mobile Monuments," 403.
89. Ibid, 395.
90. Laura Peers, *Playing Ourselves: Interpreting Native Histories at Historic Reconstructions* (Lanham: AltaMira Press, 2007), 60.
91. Fitzsimmons Frey. Interview with Lynne, 22 August 2019.
92. Peers, *Playing Ourselves*, 66.
93. Fitzsimmons Frey. Interview with Evelyn and McLovin, August 23, 2019.

11

Indigenous Heritage

Emily L. Moore

In the context of Indigenous studies, "material culture" has a deeply troubled history. The discourse of the field itself is alien to many Indigenous understandings of their heritage: "material" fails to capture the songs, names, and other immaterial prerogatives that are so often bound up with physical objects, and "object" fails to recognize the animacy that Indigenous people frequently accord to their heritage. Western collections that framed Indigenous heritage as "material culture" often did so at enormous cost to Indigenous communities, amassing collections through campaigns of outright and cultural genocide, and displaying heritage in ways that reproduced colonial discourse about Indigenous peoples. Especially, offensive to many Indigenous communities is the fact that anthropologists and lawyers have historically classified their ancestors' human remains as forms of material culture, digging up bones as well as potsherds as "archeological resources," often with no acknowledgment of the sanctity of Native beliefs about their dead.[1]

Since the 1970s, Indigenous peoples have begun to reclaim their heritage, repatriating ancestral remains as well as material treasures to their communities. They have intervened in colonial representations of their culture and demanded the right to self-representation in major museums and their own cultural centers. This chapter offers an overview of some of the milestones in the history of material culture studies and Indigenous peoples, who are defined here as those peoples descended from populations inhabiting lands prior to and continuing through the establishment of modern nation states.[2] Although Indigenous peoples all over the world are engaged in the work of reclaiming their heritage and decolonizing their representation, this chapter will focus primarily on the actions of Indigenous peoples within the settler nations of the United States, Canada, Australia, and New Zealand.

Framing Indigenous Material Culture in Ethnographic Museums

Western ethnographic museums were the first to frame Indigenous heritage as "material culture" in the nineteenth century. Earlier collections of Indigenous objects had been assembled in the "curiosity cabinets" of European elites, but as their name suggests, they were usually jumbled collections of "curiosities" that elicited the wonder or disgust of Western viewers; it was not until the rise of anthropology as a nineteenth-century discipline that Indigenous objects were systematically arranged and studied.[3] Not coincidentally, the rise of material culture displays in ethnography museums, which first developed in the 1840s and blossomed in the "Museum Age of Anthropology" from 1880–1920, overlapped with some of the harshest periods of colonization for Indigenous peoples.[4] Ethnographic museums benefited from military conquest and assimilation pressures that dispossessed Indigenous people of their heritage – and their very lives.

Traffic in Indigenous human remains burgeoned during the nineteenth century as settler nation-states sought to consolidate control over Indigenous lands. In the United States, for example, physical anthropology collections profited from the mid-nineteenth century Indian Wars in the American West. The US Army Medical Museum specifically asked the US military "to aid in the progress of anthropological science by obtaining measurements of a large number of skulls of the aboriginal races of North America."[5] Skulls and scalps – many of them collected during the most infamous massacres of Native peoples in US history – entered museum collections during this period, only to be put to use by the pseudoscience of phrenology to "prove" the racial inferiority of Native people.[6] As George Otis, curator of the Army Medical Museum, stated in 1870: "Judging from the capacity of the cranium, the American Indians must be assigned a lower position in the human scale than has been believed heretofore."[7] Meanwhile, in Aotearoa (New Zealand), a huge traffic in *toi moko* (tattooed preserved heads of Māori elites) arose after the British introduced muskets to the islands in the early nineteenth century, fueling the "Musket Wars" between Māori groups. The sale of *toi moko* to Westerners, who had a lurid fascination with this means of commemorating Indigenous ancestors, became one of the most effective ways that Māori groups could acquire the ammunition and arms that they needed for protection.[8] Hundreds of *toi moko* ended up in English and American museums, where they were reframed as barbaric curiosities rather than honored Māori ancestors.

Museums collecting Indigenous material culture also benefited from colonial assimilation measures that pressured Native people to abandon their ancestral practices. In Canada, for example, the 1884 Indian Act banned the great ceremonial complex of the potlatch on the Northwest Coast and gave the government the right to prosecute any person caught potlatching. In 1921, Indian agent William Halliday learned of a clandestine potlatch at Village Island hosted by Kwakwaka'wakw leader Dan Cranmer. Halliday arrested dozens of people and demanded that they forfeit their masks, rattles, coppers, blankets, and other cultural treasures to avoid jail sentences for themselves or for other family members. In total, Halliday seized more than 600 pieces of Kwakwaka'wakw lineage property from the Cranmer potlatch, taking these treasures to an Anglican church in the nearby community of Alert Bay, where he charged the non-Native public admission to view the "contraband" (Figure 11.1). Halliday later sold most of this "Potlatch Collection" to museums, including George Gustav Heye's Museum of the American Indian (now the Smithsonian National Museum of the American Indian) and the Victorian Memorial Museum in Ottawa (later the Canadian Museum of Man, now the Canadian Museum of History). The Kwakwaka'wakw were left bereft of hundreds of treasures that had animated their connections to ancestors and to each other; as one Kwakwaka'wakw man stated when he had visited Halliday's display at the Anglican church, he had gone to "say goodbye to our life."[9]

Like human remains, the objects sent to ethnographic museums during the colonial period were often used to "demonstrate" the racial inferiority of Indigenous people. As Victor Buchli notes, material culture in the nineteenth century was "the supreme signifier of universal progress and

Figure 11.1 Kwakwaka'wakw masks confiscated by the Canadian government from Dan Cranmer's potlatch, 1921. Image PN 12191. Courtesy of the Royal BC Museum and Archives.

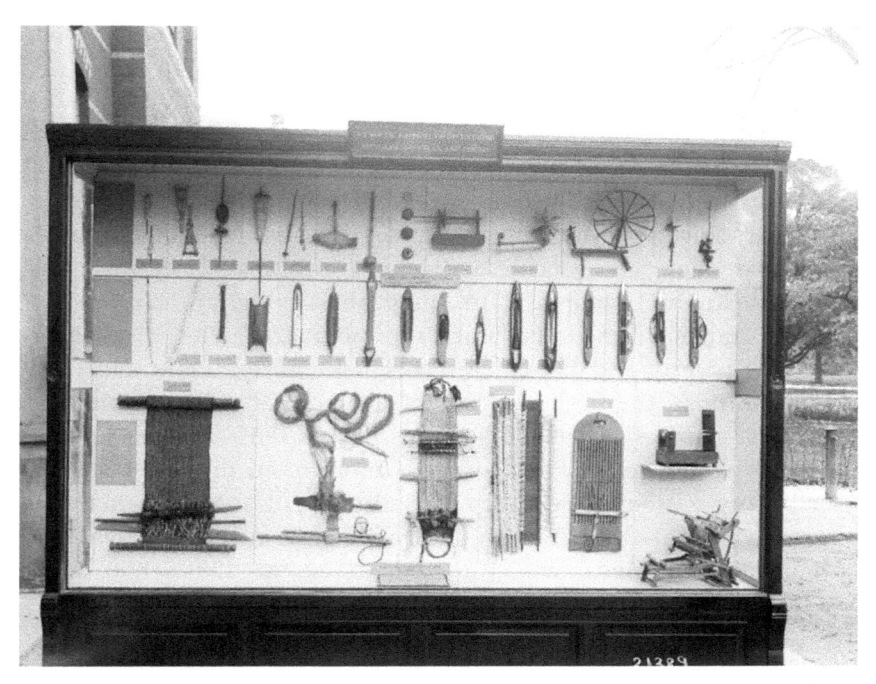

Figure 11.2 Typological display of weaving tools from various Indigenous peoples in the US National Museum, 1890. Smithsonian Institution Archives. Image # MAH-21389.

modernity" and became intimately tied up with the ideology of social evolutionism.[10] Indigenous material culture was used to chart the supposed evolution of technological types: Otis Mason, curator in the 1880s of the US National Museum (the forerunner of the Smithsonian National Museum of Natural History), grouped spindles and other weaving tools from disparate tribes in North America to demonstrate the supposed development of this technology, despite the fact that many of these tribes would never have had contact with each other (Figure 11.2).[11]

The relative sophistication of a people's material culture (as judged by the West) was also used to chart the supposed evolution of humankind, with Indigenous material culture ranking Indigenous peoples as "savages" while Western peoples claimed the highest ranks of "civilization." Such evolutionist displays were especially visible in World's Fairs, where non-Western peoples appeared with "traditional" clothing and tools in staged environments that contrasted with the technological advancements displayed in Western pavilions. At the 1904 Louisiana Purchase Exposition in Saint Louis, for example, W. J. McGee, head of the anthropology exhibits for the fair, arranged African pygmies and Phillipine Igorots on the eastern end of the fair to represent the most "primitive" stages of humanity, opposite of the US pavilions where the "white race represented the endpoint of evolution."[12] Ethnography museums and World's Fairs thus served as exhibitionary agents of colonization, assuring Western cultures of their advanced material culture and civilization, and justifying their domination over non-Western peoples.

Evolutionary displays of Indigenous material culture began to change in the 1890s with curators like Franz Boas, who emphasized cultural relativism rather than social evolution.[13] Boas popularized the diorama at the American Museum of Natural History, displaying Indigenous objects with manikins and reconstructed "life groups" intended to represent specific Indigenous cultures. However, even this "contextualist" approach to Indigenous material culture had damaging impacts on Indigenous representation. The display of Indigenous objects and human remains next to dinosaurs and taxidermied animals continued a kind of evolutionary classification of Indigenous peoples as belonging to uncivilized "nature," while Europeans (whose material culture was more often displayed in fine art or history museums) belonged to civilized "culture." Dioramas are also widely criticized for freezing Indigenous life in the past, portraying Indigenous peoples in an "ethnographic present" that denies them coevality with other peoples.[14] Boas furthered this trope of unchanging Indigenous life by refusing to collect material culture that showed signs of acculturation – part of a wider movement of "salvage anthropology" to find and record the last vestiges of "traditional" Native cultures before they were consumed by modernity.[15] Such displays supported the pernicious nineteenth-century trope of the "vanishing Indian" doomed to perish because they could not adapt to the modern age, rather than recognizing the fact that Native peoples were struggling to survive systems of material and immaterial dispossession deliberately imposed by their colonizers (see also Smith, Ralph, de Leiuen, and Pollard in Chapter 5).

Indigenous Material Culture as Fine Art

With a few exceptions, Indigenous material culture did not enter fine art museums until the first half of the twentieth century. Cultural anthropology had turned away from material culture studies in the early twentieth century in favor of fieldwork and participant observation; kinship and social structures, not material objects, were now seen as the locus of culture.[16] Meanwhile, Western modern artists seeking alternative pictorial traditions to the Greco-Roman lineage of realism had turned to so-called primitive art, studying the displays of African, Oceanic, and Native American objects in ethnographic museums for inspiration. Art institutions also began to validate aspects of Indigenous material culture as "fine art," seeking out the "works of art [that] lurked among the ethnographic specimens" in natural history museums and building their own collections.[17]

The inclusion of Indigenous objects in fine art museums is often hailed as a progressive move for the West, a democratic embrace of difference that rejected racial hierarchies of the nineteenth century.[18] But for much of the twentieth century, fine art museums continued to alienate Indigenous heritage from Indigenous worldviews and to perpetuate colonial representations of the Other. The white walls and glass boxes of fine art museums stripped Indigenous objects of cultural context and reframed them as aesthetic objects available for (the West's) visual pleasure (Figure 11.3). Although a few museums, like the Brooklyn Museum and the Denver Art Museum, strove to highlight the cultural *and* aesthetic significance of Native heritage, many art museums elided ethnographic information about social and ritual contexts to focus instead on the formal interests of the work, emphasizing the modernist credo that a "masterpiece" can "speak for itself" and that viewers should engage with the work through a "perceptual-emotional" experience rather than an intellectual one.[19]

This draining of Indigenous context in the fine art museum made Indigenous material culture particularly vulnerable to appropriation by the West. Surrealists, for example, overwrote the function of crests on the Northwest Coast as intangible property earned by ancestors and passed down through physical objects like totem poles, interpreting them instead according to their own interests as symbols of the unconscious mind.[20] Dozens of modern art exhibitions in the twentieth century appropriated Indigenous material culture to serve nationalist narratives of a distinctive "native" modernism. The 1927 exhibit at the National Gallery of Canada in Ottawa, *Exhibition of Canadian West Coast Art – Native and Modern*, argued that abstraction and expressionism had long been part of Canadian Aboriginal arts, offering Canadian modern art history Indigenous roots distinct from Europe's.[21] The 1941 exhibit *Indian Art of the United States* at the Museum of Modern Art in New York City had a similar premise, positioning Indigenous arts as "the most American" of heritage for American modern design (Figure 11.3).[22] Even near the end of the twentieth century, Indigenous heritage continued to be refracted through a Western lens in fine art museums, as in the 1984 exhibit at the Museum of Modern Art, "*Primitivism" in 20th Century Art: Affinity of the Tribal and the Modern*. Although the exhibit claimed to study the West's fascination with "primitive" art, the displays themselves did little to probe modernism's misrepresentation of Indigenous heritage; indeed, the exhibit continued to emphasize the validity of aesthetic experience alone.[23] Pairing Indigenous objects with Western paintings and sculptures to focus on their visual "affinity," the exhibit sought to defend modernist credos of universality from postmodern critiques mounting in the 1980s.[24]

But the "affinity" between Indigenous and Western art was not a two-way street: like ethnography museums, fine art museums also refused to exhibit contemporary Indigenous art that showed signs of "acculturation." Native

Figure 11.3 Installation view of the exhibition "Indian Art of the United States," January 22, 1941 through April 27, 1941. The Museum of Modern Art, New York. Photographic Archive. The Museum of Modern Art Archives, ART470221.

artists who departed from "traditional" Indigenous art forms to engage in modernist pictorial aesthetics were frequently rejected from art shows and museum collections; the "authenticity" of their art, in the view of white juries, was predicated on their adherence to ancestral forms.[25] The message was that Western modernists could draw on the abstract motifs of Indigenous arts, but Indigenous artists could not trespass on Western modern art; they were expected to remain "traditional" in order to be recognized as "Indigenous." Similarly, many museums refused to show Indigenous-made "tourist arts" that had long translated Indigenous material culture into forms that were marketable to non-Natives, as this, too, undermined the West's ideas of authenticity (see also Gnecco, Chapter 6).[26] With few art forms that represented contemporary Indigenous artists or contemporary Indigenous life, many fine art museums continued colonial practices of portraying Indigenous cultures as vanished.

Indigenous Protests and Postcolonial Critiques

Indigenous people have long protested the misrepresentation of their heritage in ethnographic and fine art museums, but it was not until the late twentieth century that their claims gained much traction. A century earlier, both the Apache and Hopi of Arizona asked museums to return sacred objects that had been looted from shrines, but their requests went unheeded.[27] The first successful repatriation case in the United States came in 1938, when George Gustav Heye (whose collection would later become the core of the Smithsonian's National Museum of the American

Indian) agreed to return a sacred bundle to the Hidatsa of North Dakota.[28] But Heye refused to return wampum belts that the Onandaga had sought since they were alienated from the Iroquois Confederacy in 1893, maintaining that he had purchased the belts legally. It was not until 1971 that the New York State Legislature passed a bill promising to return wampum belts in state museums to the Onandaga, and not until the 1980s that the belts were returned.[29]

Indigenous peoples had also protested the collection and display of their ancestors' human remains, defending the sanctity of their funerary practices against the scientific community's desire to study remains and pointing to the blatant racism of unearthing Indigenous burial sites while leaving white burials intact.[30] One of the most infamous examples of the dispute over Indigenous remains came in 1897, when Arctic explorer Robert Peary brought a group of Inuit men – including a young boy named Minik – from Greenland to the American Museum of Natural History in New York City. Peary hoped that the Inuit would be "useful" for Franz Boas's continued studies of Inuit culture, but the Inuit men died of tuberculosis before much work could be done.[31] The only Inuk to survive was the young Minik, who was adopted and raised by a museum employee. To placate Minik's desire for a proper burial for his father, museum staff staged a burial supposed to contain the father's remains; in fact, his body had been processed to remove flesh and organs for further study. Aleš Hrdlička, the museum's physical anthropologist, commandeered all the Inuit men's bodies for his physical anthropology collection and displayed Minik's father's skeleton to the public for many years.[32] When Minik learned about the deception, he pled for his father's remains to be returned to him, but the museum refused. Minik eventually died in the 1918 influenza epidemic, never having the legal recourse to rebury his father's body. It was not until the 1990s, in the middle of international repatriation movements and a blockbuster book telling Minik's story, that the remains of all five Inuit men were returned to Greenland for reburial.[33]

The shift in control over Indigenous remains and material culture from Western collections to Indigenous peoples in the 1970s and 1980s is often credited to a larger postmodern turn in academic disciplines that questioned the authority of master narratives and sought to center previously marginalized voices in narrating their own histories and experience.[34] But as scholars of Indigenous studies point out, it is also important to credit the activism of an international "pan-Indian" movement that developed during this period, wherein Indigenous actors banded together to draw attention to ongoing historical injustices of colonization and to demand the right to self-determination. In the United States, Native American protestors who called themselves Indians of All Tribes (IAT) occupied Alcatraz Island in San Francisco Bay from 1969–71, drawing attention to broken treaties by seizing property that the US government had recently marked as "surplus." In 1972, activists in the American Indian Movement (AIM) occupied the Bureau of Indian Affairs (BIA) headquarters in Washington DC and later BIA offices at Wounded Knee, South Dakota, protesting corruption in agencies dealing with Indigenous affairs. In Canada, the National Indian Brotherhood of the 1970s gave way to the Assembly of First Nations in the 1980s, which advocated (and continues to advocate) for Aboriginal sovereignty in Canada. And in New Zealand in the 1980s, Māori peoples battled the New Zealand government to honor the 1840 Treaty of Waitangi and won important new measures for sovereignty.

Native scholars contributed to the burgeoning literature in postcolonial theory, "writing back" to the imperialist discourses of settler colonialism and making space for their own perspectives on their history and heritage. Dakota scholar Vine Deloria, Jr.'s 1969 book, *Custer Died for Your Sins: An Indian Manifesto* was a landmark for Indigenous studies in the United States, as it satirized hallowed narratives of the American West and the academic disciplines (especially anthropology) that had claimed authority over the representation of American Indians. A decade later, Palestinian expatriate scholar Edward Saïd published another landmark in postcolonial studies, *Orientalism* (1978), which unraveled "the paternalistic privileges unhesitatingly assumed by Western writers who 'speak for' a mute Orient or reconstitute it as decayed or dismembered 'truth,' who lament the passing of its authenticity, and who know more than its mere natives ever can."[35] Although *Orientalism* has been criticized for its own monolithic representation of "The West," Saïd's book highlighted the link between cultural representation and imperialist domination, a critique that was usefully extended to museum representations of Indigenous peoples.

In the wake of this criticism, museums and the academic disciplines that informed them (especially anthropology and art history) engaged in a "far-reaching critique of their representational practices."[36] The "new museology" that began in the 1980s redefined the role of the museum not as a "temple" for the display of expert knowledge, but as a "forum" for discussion, education, and outreach that engaged multiple stakeholders in the representation of culture and history.[37] In 1997, James Clifford famously applied the postcolonial concept of the "contact zone" to the museum, arguing that museums were not just neutral spaces for the one-way transmission of knowledge but sites of contested power relationships where Indigenous peoples and museum officials could meet to hash out differing understandings of heritage, history, and responsibility. "When museums are seen as contact zones, their organizing structure as a collection becomes an ongoing historical, political, moral relationship – a power-charged set of exchanges, of push and pull," Clifford wrote.[38] More museums turned to consultation with Indigenous peoples about their collections, embracing difficult dialogues that slowly established relationships and better understandings about the contested nature of Indigenous heritage within museum walls.

In this context, Indigenous people began to gain ground in their right to self-representation. In the 1980s, Haudenosaunee (members of the Iroquois Confederacy) protested museum displays of their *ga:goh:sah*, often called "False Face" masks in English, which had been staple objects in both ethnographic and fine art museums in the twentieth century. The Haudenosaunee objected that these sacred masks should only be seen by the initiated during appropriate ceremonies, and further condemned Western museums for believing that the masks served to "enlighten" non-Natives about the Iroquois: "The non-Indian public does not have the right to examine, interpret, or present the beliefs, functions, duties of the secret medicine societies of the Haudenosaunee," the Grand Council of the Haudenosaunee wrote in an official statement. "The sovereign responsibility of the Haudenosaunee over their spiritual duties must be respected by the removal of all medicine masks from exhibition and from access to non-Indians."[39] In another famous protest in 1987, Payómkawichum/Ipi/Mexican-American artist James Luna lay for hours in a glass case in the San Diego Museum of Man near dioramas depicting California tribes. Stripped down to a loin cloth to approximate the "traditional" clothing staged in the ethnographic displays, Luna's living, breathing body nevertheless disrupted the static past of the dioramas. The material culture that he displayed near his body – college diplomas, divorce papers, and his personal music collection of Rolling Stones and Beatles albums – further asserted his participation in contemporary American life. The performance enacted an Indigenous intervention in the longstanding representations of Indigenous people as vanished or dead.

One of the most publicized protests of Indigenous material culture displays in Canada was the boycott of the 1988 exhibition *The Spirit Sings* at the Glenbow Museum, which had timed the exhibit of historical Aboriginal arts to coincide with the Olympic Winter Games in Calgary. A curatorial team of mostly non-Aboriginal scholars had worked for three years to assemble more than 650 objects of Aboriginal arts from museums across the world; many of the objects had been collected during the early years of European contact and had not been seen in Canada for a century or more. Curators stated that their intention was to emphasize "the richness and depth of Canada's Native culture" to the international public at the Olympic Games; however, Aboriginal people protested the lack of Indigenous involvement in the exhibit, as well as the display of some sensitive sacred objects and the emphasis on historical (rather than contemporary) Aboriginal arts.[40] The final straw was the museum's announcement that Shell Oil would be the major corporate sponsor of the exhibit. The Lubicon Lake Cree First Nation protested that Shell Oil had profited from drilling on their traditional lands – lands that the Lubicon Lake Nation had been fighting to secure from the Canadian government for decades – and called for a boycott of the exhibition.[41] Soon Aboriginal nations and communities across Canada joined the boycott, and several international museums refused to lend objects to the exhibit. In 1986, the UNESCO-sponsored International Committee for Museums of Ethnography passed a resolution stating that museums should consult with members of living ethnic groups on any exhibit involving the heritage of those groups. When the exhibition moved to its next venue at the Canadian Museum of Civilization in Ottawa, National Chief George Erasmus invited CMC director George McDonald to meet with Indigenous leaders during a symposium on Canadian museums. This symposium led to the creation of a national Task Force on Museums and First Peoples, which in 1992 issued a report with recommendations for how Canadian museums could strengthen relationships with Aboriginal communities.

Repatriation was another key aspect of reclaiming Indigenous heritage. In 1977, before a legal framework existed for repatriation in the United States, the Zuni appealed to the Denver Art Museum (DAM) to voluntarily return sacred figures known as Ayahu:dah (often called "War Gods" in English). Their claims were based on "humanitarian and moral grounds," since the Zuni believe the Ayahu:dah should decay naturally within their shrines at Zuni, yet many figures had been removed illegally by non-Natives.[42] Initially, the DAM administration resisted the Zuni's arguments, countering that "the object has in reality entered the public realm of world art" and that the museum "could not deprive the world public of further access to it."[43] Other museums defended DAM, stating that the return of the Ahayu:dah would be a "devastating precedent" that could "kill the museum" by draining it of its collections.[44] But the Zuni persisted, and public opinion soon turned in their favor, with more people pressuring museum officials to honor Native beliefs about their heritage. In March 1979, more than a decade *before* the passage of federal repatriation legislation in the United States, the Denver Art Museum returned the Ahayu:dah to the Zuni.

Indigenous people also made progress in repatriating human remains. In 1971, Maria Pearson, a Yankton Sioux woman living in Iowa in the United States, learned that state archaeologists had reburied the remains of twenty-six white people disinterred because of a highway project, yet had sent the remains of a Native woman and her baby to the Office of the State Archeologist for study. Pearson demanded a meeting with Iowa's governor to discuss the blatant disregard for the sanctity of Native burials; a few years later, the state of Iowa extended the "violation of sepulcher" rights to ancient cemetery sites, according equal sanctity of burial to Native and non-Native peoples.[45] The state of Kansas passed similar legislation in 1985 after a Native woman protested a tourist site that charged visitors to see the unearthed and shellacked graves of 146 Caddo Indians.[46] In 1988, Māori activists succeeded in stopping an auction house in London from selling a *toi moko* (tattooed head) of an ancestor, and began the process of repatriating *toi moko* to Aotearoa. Despite continued protests by some members of the scientific and museum communities, the tides were turning to favor Indigenous control of human remains and material culture.

Repatriation Legislation and Agreements

Formal repatriation measures for Indigenous material culture and human remains began in the 1990s in the United States, Canada, and Australia. In 1990, after decades of Indigenous activism and heated debates with museum and scholarly communities, the United States passed the Native American Graves Protection and Repatriation Act (NAGPRA), which established a legal framework for federally recognized tribes and Native Hawaiian organizations to repatriate cultural property and human remains from museums in the United States that receive any form of federal funding. The legislation protects four categories of Indigenous heritage: human remains, funerary objects, sacred objects, and objects of cultural patrimony. Funerary objects are defined as objects that were likely associated with human remains in a burial, regardless of whether they are still associated with those human remains in museum collections. Sacred objects are objects that were used in "traditional Native American religious practices" (a definition that has proven difficult to gauge given centuries of colonial assaults on Native religions).[47] Objects of cultural patrimony are those that have "ongoing historical, traditional, or cultural importance central to the Native American group or culture itself, rather than property owned by an individual Native American" – a category that protects an individual from selling collectively owned heritage, even if that sale was conducted "legally" in Western terms.[48] The law requires that all federal agencies and public museums identify the objects and human remains in their collections that are subject to NAGPRA, consult with tribes about the cultural affiliation of those objects and remains, and publish lists of those items in federal registers. Tribes can then study the lists and, if they can prove cultural affiliation to an item, they can initiate a repatriation claim addressed to the museum that houses it. The law enforces penalties on museums that do not comply with NAGPRA and established a NAGPRA Advisory Board to decide on cases that cannot be resolved between museums and tribes.[49]

In Canada, following the boycott of *The Spirit Sings* exhibition discussed above, the Task Force on Museums and First Peoples in 1992 issued *Turning the Page: Forging New Partnerships between Museums and First Peoples*. The report recommended that "appropriate representatives of First Peoples ... be involved as equal partners in any museum exhibition, program, or project dealing with Aboriginal heritage, history or culture."[50] The report also urged museums to repatriate Aboriginal heritage to Aboriginal communities, although it did not establish a legal framework for doing so, favoring "a case-by-case collaborative approach to resolving repatriation based on moral and ethical criteria ... rather than a strictly legalistic approach."[51] Similar to NAGPRA in the United States, the Canadian report recognizes four areas of Aboriginal cultural heritage: human remains, burial objects, sacred and ceremonial objects, and other "cultural objects that have ongoing historical, traditional or cultural import to an Aboriginal community of culture."[52] It recommends that museums holding the human remains of any Aboriginal individual known by name offer those remains to the deceased's relations; the remains of an individual not known by name, but believed to be affiliated with First People, must be reported to a relevant Nation or community in order to start a dialogue about possible repatriation. Objects of cultural patrimony that were illegally acquired should be returned to source communities; objects that were legally obtained should also be considered for repatriation based on "moral and ethical factors above and beyond legal considerations."[53] The report urges museums to loan objects to First Peoples for ceremonial needs, and it encourages a dialogue between First Peoples and museums about the replication of objects – either replicas that could be returned to First Peoples or replicas that museums could keep as replacements for repatriated objects.

In 1992, the New Zealand government passed The Museum of New Zealand Te Papa Tongarewa Act, uniting the ethnographic collections of the former National Museum and the fine art collections of the National Art Gallery into one museum that could better tell "New Zealand's stories in an interdisciplinary way."[54] The new museum opened in 1998, where exhibits emphasized a new partnership between Tangata Whenua (Māori, the indigenous people of New Zealand) and Tangata Tiriti (people in New Zealand by right of the Treaty of Waitangi). In 2003, the New Zealand government mandated Te Papa Tongarewa to develop a repatriation program to help Māori and Moriori peoples repatriate human remains from international institutions to the *iwi* (tribes). Karanga Aotearoa is the authority that negotiates the repatriation on behalf of the Māori and Moriori; it works with the advice of the Repatriation Advisory Panel, whose members are all Indigenous. The museum has successfully repatriated hundreds of *toi moko* (tattooed preserved heads) and *koiwi tangata* (ancestral remains) from international museums.[55] For remains that cannot be returned to *iwi*, often because of poor provenance, the Te Papa and Auckland museums now house ancestral remains in a *wahi tapu* (sacred area), where they are subject to different ritual and restricted uses than the areas housing objects.[56] Only members of the *iwi* can authorize visits to or research in the *wahi tapu*.

In 1993, Australia issued *Previous Possessions, New Obligations: Policies for Museums in Australia and Aboriginal and Torres Strait Islander Peoples*; the report was revised in 2005. The report called for the "unconditional return" of "ancestral remains and secret sacred objects to their communities of origin to help promote healing and reconciliation."[57] Since

2012, the Australian government has provided funding to eight national museums to involve Indigenous people directly in repatriation. The department works with individual Aboriginal communities to understand how best to handle the repatriation or protection of human remains and secret sacred objects originating from those communities; for wider repatriation issues, it relies upon a rotating board known as the Advisory Committee for Indigenous Repatriation, whose members are all Indigenous. In 2014, this advisory committee issued a report recommending that the Australian government establish a National Resting Place for repatriated Aboriginal remains with unclear provenance. Since 1993, repatriated Indigenous Australian remains not traceable to a specific community have been held "in trust" by the National Museum of Australia. But many Indigenous people objected to the museum as a culturally inappropriate site for holding human remains; international museums also expressed reluctance to return Aboriginal remains to Australia if they were only going to be transferred to another museum, not restored to Aboriginal or Torres Strait Islander control.[58] After many meetings with Aboriginal communities, the advisory committee recommended that a National Resting Place be established in the capital of Canberra within the Parliamentary Triangle. Here the National Resting Place could serve not only as a culturally appropriate place for showing respect to the ancestors, but also as a "beacon of conscience" for lawmakers and visitors in the Australian capital.[59]

Problems with Repatriation Measures

Although the repatriation measures of the past few decades represented a welcome change from colonial collecting practices, numerous problems remain. A common complaint in the United States is that NAGPRA places the burden of repatriation claims on tribes, which often do not have resources or personnel to devote to pursuing a lengthy repatriation process. Tribes must initiate a repatriation claim for each item they wish returned, and they must produce extensive documentation to prove their "cultural affiliation." Many tribes simply do not have the personnel who can conduct this research on top of their regular duties in tribal government.[60] The legal terminology of NAGPRA has also clashed with Indigenous understandings of their cultural patrimony. For example, the collective ownership required to claim heritage as "cultural patrimony" under NAGPRA does not recognize individual ownership of communally significant objects.[61] Claiming a sacred object that is necessary for "traditional Indian religions" can expose religious practices that some Native people do not believe should be shared publicly. The law's persistent use of "tribe" also undermines Indigenous movements to recognize Native polities as nations, "an insidious effect on intertribal discourse regarding sovereignty."[62]

Reincorporating repatriated objects and human remains into Indigenous communities has also been difficult. Following standard conservation practices at the time, many museums treated objects with poisonous chemicals to ward off pests and other threats to the materials: arsenic has been found on several Tlingit tunics, for example, and high levels of mercury, napthalene, and DDT have been detected in Hupa baskets.[63] Although some museums are now offering assistance in trying to remove these chemicals, it can be difficult for communities to trust that they can reincorporate contaminated objects into ritual practice.[64] Another issue is that so many objects are dispersed in different museums and lack the data that would help reunite them. Elders in the Caddo Nation of Oklahoma, for example, do not want to rebury human remains without all of the associated funerary objects that were intended for the body.[65] Yet, funerary objects were frequently dispersed to multiple museums, requiring extensive research and multiple repatriation claims to reunite them; even human remains, following the disarticulation practices common in nineteenth-century physical anthropology, must be reassembled from different collections.[66]

Repatriating human remains has proven especially onerous given poor documentation of provenance. In the United States alone, even twenty years after the passage of NAGPRA, only 27 percent of Native American human remains in 650 museums had been affiliated with a particular tribe.[67] Whether to keep unaffiliated remains in museums or return them to tribes that *might* be related is still controversial: in the 1990s, many archaeologists maintained that returning unidentifiable remains for reburial equaled the "unwarranted destruction of our human heritage," while many Native people held that there was no such thing as an "unaffiliated" Native ancestor.[68] The issue was so difficult to resolve that Congress passed NAGPRA in 1990 without specifying action for culturally unidentifiable human remains, placing that section of the bill "in reserve" and asking the newly formed NAGPRA Review Committee to determine its fate. It took another twenty years – until May 14, 2010 – for the committee to issue language for Section 10.11, which holds that museums must consult with tribes on culturally unidentifiable remains (first with those tribes whose reservations or trust lands the remains came from, then those tribes whose traditional territory encompassed the site of the remains, and then any federally recognized tribe who wants to claim them). If a tribe claims the remains, the museum must return them, regardless of whether affiliation can be proven.

There is also a debate over whether some human remains are so old that they cannot be connected to a living people. Such was the case for "Kennewick Man," a 9,000-year-old skeleton found on the banks of the Columbia River in the Northwest United States in 1996. When archaeologists tried to stop local tribes from claiming the skeleton for reburial under

NAGPRA, a federal court ruled that the skeleton was not subject to NAGPRA because its age disassociated it from NAGPRA's definition of a Native American as "of, or relating to a tribe, people or culture that is indigenous to the United States."[69] Archaeologists proceeded to study Kennewick Man until 2015, when another group of scientists succeeded in sequencing DNA from the remains and showing that Kennewick Man was more closely related to Native Americans – including the local Colville tribe that had wished to rebury him – than any other people. Kennewick Man was repatriated to an association of Columbia River basin tribes in February 2017 and given a Native American burial.[70]

Finally, a problem for many Indigenous peoples locked within settler nation-states is the lack of international agreements on repatriation. The United Nations Educational, Scientific and Cultural Organization (UNESCO)'s Convention on the Means of Prohibiting and Preventing the Illicit Import, Export, and Transfer of Ownership of Cultural Property works to pressure member states to return cultural property removed from other member states; however, the convention cannot be applied retroactively to cultural property removed before ratification of the convention in 1970 (and some member nations, like the United States, did not sign on until 1983).[71] The United Nation's 2007 Declaration on the Rights of Indigenous Peoples includes a statement on the right of Indigenous peoples "to practice and revitalize their cultural traditions and customs," which includes "the right to maintain, protect and develop the past, present and future manifestations of their cultures"; however, the declaration is not legally binding. Moreover, the United States, Canada, New Zealand, and Australia initially refused to ratify this declaration, although all four nations have since supported it.[72]

Despite the lack of international law on repatriation, some museums have voluntarily repatriated cultural treasures across national boundaries. The Museum of Ethnography in Stockholm was one of the first to do so, repatriating a Haisla totem pole to British Columbia in 2006.[73] Other museums have agreed to lend objects back to originating communities for a short period of time to allow community members to renew contact with their heritage. In 2008, the Château Musée in Boulogne-sur-Mer, France sent thirty-four Alutiiq masks collected in 1871 from Kodiak Island back to Alaska for an exhibition in both Kodiak and Anchorage. The museum also invited Alutiiq artists to come to France to study the larger collection of masks so that these artists could bring photographs and knowledge of the masks back to their communities. However, the museum has so far refused to repatriate the masks permanently to the Alutiiq people.[74]

Museums in the Age of Repatriation

Despite the initial resistance to repatriation, many scholars now champion repatriation for generating stronger relationships between

Indigenous communities and museum staff, which has resulted in better understandings of Indigenous heritage in museum collections. Chip Colwell, senior curator of anthropology at the Denver Museum of Nature and Science, writes: "Repatriation did kill the museum. More exactly, repatriation extinguished the old idea that museums could preserve and present Native American culture without any input from Native Americans themselves ... Repatriation has given museums a second life."[75] Ruth Phillips argues that the repatriation era initiated a model of "shared authority" between Indigenous communities and museum curators, catalyzing a "second museum age" that revitalized the display of Indigenous material culture in both Western and Indigenous-managed museums.[76] The colonial museum of the "first museum age" that benefited from genocide and assimilation now has the opportunity – and the responsibility – to partner with Indigenous communities in the work of decolonization, to "assist in tribal nation building, empowerment, and healing," as Ho-Chunk scholar Amy Lonetree has argued.[77]

The commitment to shared authority between Indigenous communities and museum curators (an increasing number of whom are Indigenous themselves) has replaced the colonial museum model of a single authoritative voice with a "multivocal model" that privileges Indigenous worldviews of their heritage.[78] It is now almost unthinkable for a major museum to exhibit Indigenous material culture without consulting Indigenous people, and many more have committed to positioning Indigenous people as the primary authorities in exhibitions and research. In 2004, for example, the National Museum of the American Indian (NMAI) opened on the National Mall in Washington, DC with a promise that every exhibit would operate on a model of shared authority. The NMAI works closely with "community curators" from any culture represented in an NMAI exhibit and trains a growing number of Indigenous interns to be curators and scholars in the field.[79]

Other museums have worked with Indigenous knowledge bearers to honor Indigenous approaches to caring for their heritage even in museum collection spaces. This includes labeling heritage with Indigenous terms in Indigenous languages, smudging shelves to sanctify them, feeding other-than-human-beings with corn meal or appropriate nourishment, and restricting access to people who are trained to respect protocols. Conservators trained to preserve "the integrity of the object" are now working to preserve "the integrity of culture" – by loaning a mask to an Indigenous dance group, for example, even if it risks damaging the mask, and thus recognizing that the mask's well-being is better served by being danced than by being "preserved" as a pristine object.[80]

Even colonial-era museums have become newly relevant to Indigenous peoples as they honor Indigenous worldviews and involve more Indigenous people in their decision-making processes. For example, the Auckland Museum in Aeotearoa (New Zealand) created the position of

Tamuaki (Director of Māori) out of Māori pressure to have more Māori people in the museum's leadership. In 2005, Dr. Paul Tapsell, then the Tamuaki of the Auckland Museum, curated the exhibition *Ko Tawa – Taoanga from Our Ancestral Landscapes*, basing it on the Māori philosophy of *whakapapa* – the genealogical relationship between all things, thoughts, and beings in the universe.[81] The exhibition worked to reconnect Māori *taonga* (tangible and intangible cultural treasures) with their "ancestral trajectories," recognizing the *taonga* as ancestors and making clear their relationships as gifts between *iwi*. In contrast to colonial displays of this same heritage, the new curatorial team decided it would be "rude to push their grandparents up against the wall and objectify them as static beings suffocated within glass cabinets."[82] Instead, they built a plinth resembling a traditional elevated box in which *taonga* were often kept in the rafters of Māori houses, so that "our ancestors could look down on us" in the museum's halls, and so that they "could share each other's breath."[83] Dr. Tapsell wrote that although he was initially concerned that Māori elders would not support the exhibition, given the colonial history that many saw the Auckland Museum as encapsulating, he was deeply moved when elders in the *marae* (traditional community centered on a ceremonial plaza) welcomed him as *mokopuna* (grandchild, descendant) and seized the opportunity to use the exhibition as a "vehicle by which they could meaningfully transfer knowledge to their unknown *mokopu* growing up away in cities."[84] A colonial museum was thus transformed into a vehicle for the intergenerational transmission of Māori values, with Māori curators at the helm.

The repatriation era has also catalyzed new solutions for providing museums with Indigenous heritage that is *intended* for collection and public display. Contrary to the fears that repatriation would drain museums of their collections, repatriation has built stronger relationships between museums and Indigenous communities and innovative new ways to share Indigenous heritage. Several museums in the United States, for example, have commissioned contemporary Indigenous artists to replace objects that were repatriated under NAGPRA – an exchange I have labeled "propatriation."[85] The Harvard Peabody Museum, for example, commissioned a new Tlingit totem pole to replace a nineteenth-century totem pole repatriated to Alaska to fill the space left behind in their Northwest Coast Native art gallery after repatriation. Tlingit people initiated the exchange; however, the village corporation for the Saanya ḵwáan Tlingit, acting on Tlingit protocols of "balance" and reciprocity, gifted the museum a cedar log to acknowledge the return of their clan pole. The museum then decided to commission Tlingit carver Nathan Jackson to carve the gifted log, acknowledging the "new relationship" between the Peabody and Tlingit people. In addition to providing the museum with a new totem pole that was created for public display, the museum worked with the Tlingit community to produce a video documenting the history of the pole, including its wrongful removal from the Tlingit community in 1899, the work of the Saanya ḵwáan to repatriate their pole under NAGPRA, and the subsequent commission of the new pole by Nathan Jackson. The museum has now become a space that exhibits its own colonial history and as well as Indigenous heritage made with the approval and involvement of Indigenous people.

Other museums have turned to digital printing technologies to create replicas of repatriated objects, with permission from Indigenous leaders. The Smithsonian Natural History Museum, for example, gained permission to replicate a Tlingit clan hat repatriated to the Daḵl'weidi clan in Alaska. The clan leader reasoned that a 3D copy of the original clan hat would allow the museum to educate the public about Tlingit clan property and the repatriation process, and safeguard for the clan the exact design of the original in case fire or other accident destroyed it. The museum scanned the original clan hat using 3D scanning software and then milled the hat out of a piece of alder wood, the original wood used to carve the hat. The 3D replica of the *Ḵéet S'aaḵw* now stands on display at NMNH with wall text that tells the story of the original hat and its repatriation, again teaching the museum public the history of colonial collections and new postcolonial relationships made possible with Indigenous involvement.[86]

Virtual Repatriation

In addition to repatriating physical objects to Indigenous communities, many museums have worked to "virtually repatriate" their collections to Indigenous people by making their collection databases available online. The Great Lakes Research Alliance for the Study of Aboriginal Cultures (GRASAC), founded in 2004 by researchers at Carleton University and funded by a grant from the Canadian government, uses "information technology to digitally reunite Great Lakes heritage that is currently scattered across museums and archives in North America and Europe with Aboriginal community knowledge, memory and perspectives."[87] Another example is the Reciprocal Research Network (RRN), based at the Museum of Anthropology at the University of British Columbia. The RRN taps into databases from multiple museums and Aboriginal cultural centers in Canada and abroad to "facilitate reciprocal and collaborative research about cultural heritage from the Northwest Coast of British Columbia."[88] For both databases, users must request approval to create an online account; they can then access images of Indigenous heritage from numerous museums and share their knowledge about this heritage by adding entries to the databases.

Other museums have worked to create new types of databases that honor "Indigenous provenance" – such as the kinship rights associated with objects, the history of their ceremonial transfer and their new meanings with new owners – rather than the usual taxonomies of "culture," "object type," "date," etc.[89] The Burke Museum at the University of Washington, for example, is building a database that houses photographs of objects, song recordings, and videos of dance in the same entry, uniting tangible with intangible heritage scattered in multiple museums and archives. Thus, a Kwakwa̱ka'wakw dance frontlet removed from its ermine headdress when it was sold to a collector can be reunited on the database with images of the complete headdress, a 1930 film showing Lucy Martin Nelson dancing in the headdress, and a 1955 sound recording of the song sung during this dance. The reunification of the tangible frontlet in the Burke's collection with the intangible performance of music and dance recognizes the more holistic context in which Kwakwa̱ka'wakw crests and privileges were displayed, danced, and validated in public ceremonies.[90] The database can compile Indigenous understandings of heritage in ways that a single museum and its physical collections cannot.

Some Indigenous communities and Indigenous scholars, however, have criticized virtual repatriation for celebrating the museum's "outreach" to Indigenous communities without restoring heritage to Indigenous people. Virtual repatriation can be seen as a "capacity building exercise" for museums to benefit from Indigenous knowledge about their collections, without as much benefit to Indigenous communities.[91] Others have called for replacing virtual or "digital repatriation" with terms like "e-patriation" to acknowledge that "what is being returned is very different from what left."[92] Virtual repatriation must also be carefully orchestrated, as Indigenous knowledge and heritage is not always meant to circulate in ways allowed by the Internet. Some databases, like "Mukurtu" ("dilly bag" or safe keeping place for sacred materials in the Warumungu language of northern Australia), have built in careful protocols for ensuring appropriate access to its contents. Every user must create a profile that includes his/her name, gender, country, traditional territory, mother's country and father's country, mother's dreaming and father's dreaming, etc.[93] As Kimberly Christen writes, "The digital archive allows cultural material – and their attendant knowledge and narratives – to circulate through established Warumungu cultural protocols without the threat of permanent loss of a physical object."[94] But for some Indigenous communities the fact that these objects remain in museums at all is itself a "permanent loss" for their communities.

Tribal Museums and Indigenous-Managed Cultural Centers

One especially interesting recent development in Indigenous heritage is the proliferation of Indigenous-managed museums and cultural centers. In North America alone, there are now upwards of 150 tribal museums; other estimates place the number closer to 200.[95] Australia has a growing number of Aboriginal-owned cultural centers, as do the Māori in Aoetearoa.[96] These centers have become important sites where Indigenous people can intervene in centuries of misrepresentation of their heritage and house repatriated heritage that benefits their own community's research, nation building, and ceremonial use.[97]

One of the first Indigenous-controlled cultural centers in Canada was the U'Mista Cultural Centre, which opened in 1980 in Alert Bay to house the "Potlatch Collection" of Kwakwaka'wakw lineage treasures that had been confiscated from the Cranmer Potlatch in 1921 (see earlier). Following amendments to the Indian Act in 1951, when Canada dropped the ban against potlatching, the Kwakwaka'wakw began to seek the return of the treasures that their parents and grandparents had never forgotten. In 1975, the Canadian Museum of Man agreed to return its portion of the collection – on the condition that the Kwakwaka'wakw build a museum to "properly care" for the objects.[98] This requirement struck many Kwakwaka'wakw as paternalistic – assuming that the "proper" care for these objects was not with their own people but in a Western-style institution; it also delayed the return of the treasures for years as the Kwakwaka'wakw sought funding to construct not one but two museums, one in Cape Mudge to house the objects from families in that area, and the other in Alert Bay.[99] In 1979, the Kwakiutl Museum opened in Cape Mudge; the following year, U'mista Cultural Centre opened in Alert Bay.[100] Significantly, while both centers conformed to the climate-controlled display requirements of the Canadian Museum of Man, they represented their collections in ways that honored Indigenous protocols. The U'mista Cultural Centre, for example, displays the Potlatch Collection in the order in which these treasures would be "brought out" for a potlatch, and visitors are encouraged to circulate the room from the right "as a dancer does at potlatch ceremonies" to further inscribe this display in the logic of a Kwakwaka'wakw ceremony (Figure 11.4).[101] None of the masks are ensconced in glass cases, ensuring they can breathe, and certain sacred items are not displayed.

In the United States, the Makah Cultural and Research Center (MCRC) opened in 1979 on the Makah Indian Reservation in Washington State with hundreds of objects recovered from a sixteenth-century ancestral village site on the reservation. The Makah Tribal Council had worked with archaeologists from Washington State University and the federal government to study the Ozette site, with the condition that all artifacts uncovered remain in the new cultural center.[102] The Makah Cultural and Research Center honored the traditional system of Makah property ownership by arranging artifacts according to the house group to which they belonged (identified based on the distinctive crests that four house groups at Ozette had used to mark their belongings). Staff at MCRC also categorized objects according to the Makah language, reawakening Indigenous knowledge systems for the entire community. For example, after twenty

Figure 11.4 U'Mista Cultural Centre exhibition, Alert Bay, British Columbia, 2003. Photo: Aaron Glass.

years of storing canoe paddles with boat gear and wedges with woodworking tools, MCRC staff noticed that the Makah words for these objects all began with a prefix (a barred lambda a). When they arranged canoe paddles, wedges, adzes, and chisels together, based on their Makah names, they realized that these objects shared "a working surface that was perpendicular to the plane of action," uncovering a dormant classification system embedded in the Makah language.[103] This is just one example of how the MCRC has become an "authoritative center" for the production of knowledge of Makah culture based on Makah epistemology.

Given the colonial histories of collection and research embedded in many museums, it may seem surprising that Indigenous communities would adopt these institutions at all. Certainly some communities have resisted naming their heritage-houses "museums" because of the negative connotations the term has for many Indigenous people ("It shall not be called a museum, for we are not a dead people," stated one Kitwancool leader about a new building project in the 1960s).[104] But as Patricia Pierce Erikson argues, Indigenous communities are highly aware of the "dangers inherent in being defined by others" and have turned to the museum as a "globally respected knowledge-making institution" where they can control the representation of their heritage.[105] Tribal museums build on "the authority of museums in Western societies to establish truth, beauty and history" and to build a critical consciousness – not just for non-Indigenous visitors, but for

Indigenous communities as well.[106] In this way, Indigenous-owned cultural centers have turned museums from being "handmaidens of colonialism and assimilation" to sites that strengthen Indigenous nationhood and vital centers for the ongoing work of decolonizing Indigenous heritage.[107]

Future Paths for Indigenous Heritage Studies

In her description of Indigenous futurisms, Anishinaabe scholar Grace Dillon highlights the fluidity of narratives that unite past, present, and future in order to reimagine the possibilities for Indigenous experience. In the circular notion of space-time that Dillon calls the "Native slipstream," where the past and future inform each other and alternative realities are always at hand, histories of colonization become but one part of a larger narrative of Indigenous heritage, while the strength of that heritage becomes the source for robust futures.[108] "It might go without saying that all forms of Indigenous futurisms are narratives of *biskaabiiyang*, an Anishinaabemowin word connoting the process of 'returning to ourselves,'" Dillon writes. "[This] involves discovering how personally one is affected by colonization, discarding the emotional and psychological baggages carried from its impact, and recovering ancestral traditions in order to adapt in our post-Native Apocalypse world."[109] Dillon notes that "decolonization" is another term often used for this work of "returning to ourselves," and highlights the importance of narrative and a strong understanding of one's heritage to undergo the physical, mental, and emotional labor of this process.

In this sense of strengthening understandings of Indigenous heritage, scholars of material culture studies can be allies to Indigenous communities in the work of decolonization – but only if they make space for profoundly different approaches to their study than those derived from Eurowestern worldviews. Increasing numbers of scholars and curators are Indigenous themselves, bringing their perspectives and relationships with Indigenous communities into museums and university departments. Non-Native scholars are also more aware of the biases of their disciplines and the need to "pass the mic" to Indigenous knowledge bearers who can speak for themselves when it comes to exhibit planning and research design. Interdisciplinary and especially post-disciplinary approaches will be critical to the future of Indigenous heritage studies, since so many academic disciplines are rooted in Eurowestern worldviews. By basing research methodologies in Indigenous values of relationality, respect, relevance, and reciprocity, those involved in the study of Indigenous heritage can contribute to narratives of healing and strength told by Indigenous peoples themselves.[110]

Notes

1. Jack F. Trope and Walter R. Echo-Hawk note that the American Antiquities Act of 1906, which was intended to protect archaeological resources on federal lands from looters, included human remains among its definition of "archeological resources" and effectively "converted dead persons into federal property." See Jack F. Trope and Walter R. Echo-Hawk, "NAGPRA: Background and Legislative History," in Devon A. Mihesuah, ed., *Repatriation Reader: Who Owns American Indian Remains?* (Lincoln: University of Nebraska Press, 2000), 127.
2. Compare to the definition of Indigenous peoples by the International Labour Organization, C169 "Indigenous and Tribal Peoples Convention," No. 169 (1989).
3. Janet C. Berlo and Ruth B. Phillips, *Native North American Art*, 2nd ed. (Oxford: Oxford University Press, 2015), 7.
4. William C. Sturtevant, "Does Anthropology Need Museums?" *Proceedings of the Biology Society of Washington* 82 (1969), 22.
5. US Surgeon General, 1868, quoted in Chip Colwell, *Plundered Skulls and Stolen Spirits: Inside the Fight to Reclaim Native America's Culture* (Chicago: University of Chicago Press, 2017), 85.
6. For example, at least six skulls of Cheyenne and Arapaho victims of the 1864 Sand Creek Massacre in eastern Colorado were sent to the US Medical Museum, and later transferred to the Smithsonian. See Colwell, *Plundered Skulls*, 87.
7. Otis quoted in Daniel S. Lamb, *A History of the United States Army Medical Museum* (Washington, DC, 1917), 56. https://bit.ly/3nir8fr.
8. Christian Palmer and Mervyn Tano, "Mokomokai: Commercialization and Desacralization," Report for the International Institute of Indigenous Resource Management (2004), 4–5. https://bit.ly/3ovstyZ.
9. James Charles King, interview at Alert Bay in 1977, quoted in the *Living Tradition Virtual Exhibit*, U'mista Cultural Centre, https://bit.ly/3cckCjZ. See also Gloria Cranmer Webster, "The Potlatch Collection Repatriation," *UBC Law Review* 137 (1995), 137–41.
10. See for example Victor Buchli, "Introduction," Victor Buchli, ed., *The Material Culture Reader* (Oxford: Berg, 2002), 3.
11. Ira Jacknis "Franz Boas and Exhibits," in George W. Stocking, Jr., ed., *Objects and Others: Essays on Museum and Material Culture* (Madison: University of Wisconsin Press, 1985), 77.
12. Robert Rydell, *All the World's a Fair: Visions of Empire at American International Expositions, 1876–1916* (Chicago: University of Chicago Press, 1984), 162.
13. On Boas's curatorial philosophy, see Jacknis "Franz Boas and Exhibits," 75–101.

14. See Johannes Fabian, *Time and the Other: How Anthropology Makes Its Object* (New York: Columbia University Press, 1983).
15. On salvage anthropology, see Douglas Cole, *Captured Heritage: The Scramble for Northwest Coast Artifacts* (Seattle: University of Washington Press, 1985), 49. On twentieth-century discourses of authenticity, see Karen Lusek and Bruce Bernstein, "In Pursuit of the Ceremonial: The Laboratory of Anthropology's 'Master Collection' of Zuni Pottery," *Journal of the Southwest* 50, no.1 (2008), 1–102.
16. Buchli, "Introduction," 7.
17. Susan Vogel and Francine N'Diaye, *African Masterpieces from the Musée de l'Homme* (New York: Center for African Art and Harry N. Abrams, 1985), 11.
18. See for example, Sally Price, *Primitive Art in Civilized Places* (Chicago: University of Chicago Press, 1989).
19. Price, *Primitive Art in Civilized Places*, 83.
20. Artist Max Weber told MOMA director Alfred Barr that totem poles were evidence that "we have the real Surrealists right here in America." W. Jackson Rushing, *Native American Art and the New York Avant-Garde: A History of Cultural Primitivism* (Austin: University of Texas, 1995). For the Surrealist movement's turn to and construction of "primitive" arts as its aesthetic and intellectual "soul mate," see Louise Tythacott, *Surrealism and the Exotic* (London: Routledge, 2003).
21. Ann Katherine Morrison, Canadian Art and Cultural Appropriation: Emily Carr and the 1927 Exhibition of Canadian West Coast Art, MA Thesis (Vancouver: University of British Columbia, 1991), iii. See also Leslie Dawn, *National Visions, National Blindness: Canadian National Art and Identities in the 1920s* (Vancouver: University of British Columbia Press, 2006).
22. René d'Harnoncourt and Frederic Douglas, "Indian Art for Modern Living," in *Indian Art of the United States*, repr. (New York: Arno Press for the Museum of Modern Art, 1969 [1941]), 181.
23. Kirk Varnedoe wrote that "modernist primitivism depends on the autonomous force of objects – and especially on the capacity of tribal art to transcend the intentions and conditions that first shaped it." Kirk Varnede, "Preface," in William Rubin, ed., *"Primitivism" in 20th Century Art: Affinity of the Tribal and the Modern*, Vol. 1 (New York: Museum of Modern Art, New York Graphic Society Books, distributors, 1984), 3.
24. Thomas McEvilley, "Doctor Lawyer Indian Chief: 'Primitivism' in Twentieth-Century Art at the Museum of Modern Art in 1984," *ArtForum* 23 (November 1984), 54–61.
25. For example, when Oscar Howe, a Yankton Sioux painter, submitted an abstract painting to the 1958 Contemporary American Indian Painting Exhibition in Tulsa, Oklahoma, the jury rejected it as a "fine painting ... but not Indian." See Bill Anthes, *Native Moderns: American Indian Painting, 1940–1960* (Durham: Duke University Press, 2006).

26. Ruth Phillips, *Trading Identities: The Souvenir in Native North American Art from the Northeast, 1700–1900* (Montreal: McGill-Queen's University Press, 1998), 24.
27. John R. Welch, "The White Mountain Apache Tribe Heritage Program: Origins, Operations, and Challenges," in Kurt E. Dongoske et al., eds., *Working Together: Native Americans and Archaeologists* (Washington, DC: Society for American Archeology, 2000), 67–83.
28. Colwell, *Plundered Skulls and Stolen Spirits*, 35.
29. Karen Coody Cooper, *Spirited Encounters: American Indians Protest Museums Policies and Practices* (Lanham: AltaMira Press, 2008), 71–73. The delay in returning the wampum belts was caused, in part, by the State Legislature's requirement that the Onandaga build a storage facility to "properly care" for the wampum.
30. See, for example, Maria D. Pearson, "Give Me Back My People's Bones: Repatriation and Reburial of American Indian Skeletal Remains in Iowa," *Journal of the Iowa Archeological Society* 52, no. 1 (2005), 7–12.
31. Cooper, *Spirited Encounters*, 89.
32. Ibid, 90.
33. The book that publicized Minik's story was Ken Harper's *Give Me My Father's Body: The Life of Minik, The New York Eskimo* (Iqaluit: Blacklead Books, 1986).
34. Amy Lonetree, *Decolonizing Museums: Representing Native America in National and Tribal Museums* (Durham: University of North Carolina Press, 2012), 17.
35. This description of Saïd's project is from James Clifford, *The Predicament of Culture: Twentieth-Century Ethnography, Literature, and Art* (Harvard University Press, 1988), 258. Clifford's book, influenced by postcolonial critics like Saïd, stands as a landmark in the revisionary texts of Western ethnography and the authority of Western anthropologists and art institutions to control the description of Indigenous cultures.
36. Ruth Phillips, "Fielding Culture: Dialogues between Art History and Anthropology," in *Museum Pieces*, 103.
37. See Ivan Karp and Steven D. Lavine, eds., *Exhibiting Cultures: The Poetics and Politics of Museum Display* (Washington, DC: Smithsonian Institution Press, 1991). It is published proceedings stemming from a 1988 symposium at the Smithsonian Institution that presented a critical self-assessment of museum exhibition techniques.
38. James Clifford, "The Museum as Contact Zone," in *Routes: Travel and Translation in the Twentieth Century* (Cambridge: Harvard University Press, 1997), 192–93.
39. The Grand Council of the Haudenosaunee, The Six Nations Iroquois Confederacy, "Haudenosaunee Confederacy Announces Policy on False Face Masks," *Akwesasne Notes* 1 (Spring 1995); www.nativetech.org/cornhusk/maskpoli.html.

40. Duncan Cameron, director of the Glenbow Museum, 1986, quoted in Phillips, *Museum Pieces*, 48.
41. As Ruth Phillips writes, "The announcement that one of the companies exploiting the oil on their traditional lands was to fund an exhibition celebrating the glories of early contact-period Aboriginal cultures struck Lubicon strategists as the ultimate hypocrisy." Phillips, *Museum Pieces*, 49.
42. Colwell, *Plundered Skulls*, 41.
43. Ibid, 37.
44. Ibid, 37–38.
45. Pearson, "Give Me Back My People's Bones," 7–12.
46. Devon A. Mihesuah, *Repatriation Reader: Who Owns American Indian Remains?* (Lincoln: University of Nebraska Press, 2000), 5.
47. Michael F. Brown and Margaret M. Bruchac, "NAGPRA from the Middle Distance," in John Henry Merryman, ed., *Imperialism, Art and Restitution* (Cambridge University Press, 2006), 196.
48. NAGPRA Glossary, National Parks Service. www.nps.gov/nagpra/TRAINING/GLOSSARY.HTM.
49. For the complete text of the law, see the National Park Service "National NAGPRA" site: www.nps.gov/nagpra/.
50. Assembly of First Nations and Canadian Museums Association, "Turning the Page: Forging New Partnerships between Museums and First Peoples," 3rd ed. (1994), 7. https://bit.ly/3FhT8WH.
51. Ibid, 5. Although some Aboriginal people in Canada yearn for the teeth of legislation like NAGPRA, Ruth Phillips argues that "the Canadian process of negotiation has shown to be more capable of arriving at a harmonious compromise that satisfied the largest number of goals of both the Indigenous claimants and the archaeological researchers." Phillips, *Museum Pieces*, 137.
52. "Turning the Page," 8.
53. Ibid.
54. Te Papa museum, "Our History/Te whakapapa o Te Papa," www.tepapa.govt.nz/about/what-we-do/our-history.
55. Piripi Taylor, "Largest Collection of Ancestral Remains in NZ History to be Repatriated," Maori Television, December 2, 2014, https://bit.ly/3nia3T9.
56. Lynn Heidi Stumpe, "Restitution or Repatriation? The Story of Some New Zealand Māori Human Remains," *Journal of Museum Ethnography* 17, Pacific Ethnography, Politics and Museums (2005), 136.
57. "Indigenous Repatriation," Australian Government, Department of Communications and the Arts. https://bit.ly/3kZ6WxV.
58. Advisory Committee for Indigenous Repatriation, "National Resting Place Consultation Report" (Canberra: Commonwealth of Australia, 2014), 9.
59. Ibid, 15.
60. Brown and Bruchac, "NAGPRA from the Middle Distance," 196.

61. The Makah, for example, must twist their traditions of individual ownership of cultural patrimony into language that conforms with NAGPRA even though it does represent their own practices. Ann Tweedie, *Drawing Back Culture: The Makah Struggle for Repatriation* (Seattle: University of Washington Press, 2002), 119.
62. Brown and Bruchac, "NAGPRA from the Middle Distance," 203.
63. Ibid, 199.
64. The Burke Museum, University of Washington is one institution that has worked with tribes to remove contaminants from Indigenous heritage before repatriating those objects. See, for example, the Burke's help in cleaning a Kaagwaantaan Brown Bear Tunic in "Prized Tunic on its Way Home to Chilkat Valley," *Chilkat Valley News*, October 6, 2005.
65. Bobby Gonzalez, quoted in Martha Graham and Nell Murphy, "NAGPRA at 20: Museum Collections and Reconnections," *Museum Anthropology* 33, no. 2 (2010), 120.
66. On the historic practices of disarticulation in physical anthropology and its impacts on NAGPRA, see Margaret Bruchac, "Lost and Found: NAGPRA, Scattered Relics, and Restorative Methodologies," *Museum Anthropology* 33, no. 2 (2010), 137–56.
67. Colwell, *Plundered Skulls*, 200.
68. Ibid, 221, 225.
69. Ibid, 224.
70. "Tribes Lay Remains of Kennewick Man to Rest," *The Spokesman-Review* (Spokane, Washington), February 20, 2017. https://bit.ly/3DviDmQ.
71. "International Repatriation," National NAGPRA, National Parks Service, https://home.nps.gov/nagpra/SPECIAL/International.htm.
72. Article 11.1 and 11.2, United Nations Declaration on the Rights of Indigenous Peoples, March 2008. www.un.org/esa/socdev/unpfii/documents/DRIPS_en.pdf.
73. Stacey R. Jessiman, "The Repatriation of the G'psgolox Totem Pole: A Study of Its Context, Process and Outcome," *International Journal of Cultural Property* 18, no. 3 (August 2011), 365–91.
74. Sven D. Haakanson and Amy F. Steffian, eds., *Giinaquq: Like a Face: Sugpiaq Masks of the Kodiak Archipelago* (Fairbanks: University of Alaska Press, 2009).
75. Colwell, *Plundered Skulls*, 264.
76. Ruth Phillips, "Re-placing Objects: Historical Practices for the Second Museum Age," *Canadian Historical Review* 86, no. 1 (2005), 83–110.
77. Amy Lonetree, *Decolonizing Museums: Representing Native America in National and Tribal Museums* (Durham: University of North Carolina Press, 2012), 4.
78. Ruth B. Phillips, *Museum Pieces*, 194.
79. Cynthia Chavez Lamar, "Collaborative Exhibit Development at the Smithsonian's National Museum of the American Indian," in

Amy Lonetree and Amanda J. Cobb, eds., *National Museum of the American Indian: Critical Conversations* (Lincoln: University of Nebraska Press, 2008), 144–64.

80. On the changing attitudes of conservators for First Nations material culture, see especially Miriam Clavir, *Preserving What Is Valued: Museums, Conservation, and First Nations* (Vancouver: University of British Columbia Press, 2002).
81. Paul Tapsell, "*Ko Tawa*: Where Are the Glass Cabinets?" in Raymond A. Silverman, ed., *Museum as Process: Translating Local and Global Knowledges* (London and New York: Routledge, 2015), 263.
82. Ibid, 268.
83. Ibid, 269.
84. Ibid.
85. Emily Moore, "Propatriation: Possibilities for Art After NAGPRA," *Museum Anthropology* 33, no. 2 (Fall 2010), 125–36.
86. Eric Hollinger, Edwell John, Jr., Harold Jacobs, Lora Moran-Collins, Carolyn Thome, Jonathan Zastrow, Adam Metallo, Gunter Waibel, and Vince Rossi, "Tlingit-Smithsonian Collaborations with 3D Digitization of Cultural Objects," *Museum Anthropology Review* 7 no.1–2 (Spring–Fall 2013), 206.
87. Great Lakes Research Alliance for the Study of Aboriginal Arts and Cultures "About GRASAC," https://grasac.org/gks/gks_about.php.
88. Reciprocal Research Network, "Who's Involved," www.rrncommunity.org/pages/about#whos_involved.
89. Aaron Glass, "Indigenous Ontologies, Digital Futures: Plural Provenances and the KwakwaKa'Wakw Collection in Berlin and Beyond," in Silverman, *Museum as Process*, 24.
90. Kathryn Bunn-Marcuse, "Textualizing Intangible Cultural Heritage: Querying the Methods of Art History," *Panorama: The Online Journal of American Art* 4, no. 2 (Fall 2018), https://bit.ly/3Cjotq7.
91. See, for example, David Houghton, "What Is Virtual Repatriation?" 30 April 2010. www.museumsandtheweb.com/forum/what_virtual_repatriation.html.
92. Glass, "Indigenous Ontologies," 23.
93. Kimberly Christen, "Archival Challenges and Digital Solutions in Aboriginal Australia," *The SAA Archeological Record* 9, no. 2 (March 2008), 24.
94. Christen, "Archival Challenges and Digital Solutions in Aboriginal Australia," 24.
95. Lonetree, *Decolonizing Museums*, 19.
96. See, for example, the Aboriginal Cultural Center called Muru Mittigar "Pathway to Friends," which represents the Darug people as the Traditional Custodians of the land in New South Wales. www.murumittigar.com.au/. Te Puia has become a Māori cultural center,

absorbing the New Zealand Māori Arts and Crafts Institute established in the 1920s. See https://tepuia.com/about-us/.
97. Patricia Erikson, *Voices of a Thousand People: The Makah Cultural and Research Center* (Lincoln: University of Nebraska Press, 2002), 17.
98. Webster, "The Potlatch Collection Repatriation," 138.
99. Karen Coody Cooper writes:

> In the minds of many Native people, it is inappropriate for museums and governments to impose standards of care on objects owned by Native entities (and we have found it especially galling to visit non-Native museum facilities that do not meet, or have not met, basic standards of protective, care, and are not, nor have been, required to meet such standards themselves).

Cooper, *Spirited Encounters*, 72.
100. Webster, "The Potlatch Collection Repatriation," 140.
101. Ira Jacknis, *The Storage Box of Tradition: Kwakiutl Art, Anthropologists, and Museums* (Washington, DC: Smithsonian Institution Press, 2002), 366.
102. Erikson, *Voices of a Thousand People*, 21.
103. Janine Bowechop and Patricia Pierce Erikson, "Forging Indigenous Methodologies on Cape Flattery: The Makah Museum as a Center of Collaborative Research," *The American Indian Quarterly* 29, nos. 1/2 (Winter/Spring 2005), 268.
104. Quoted in Jacknis, *The Storage Box of Tradition*, 354.
105. Erikson, *Voices of a Thousand People*, 17.
106. Ibid, 27.
107. Christopher McCormick, spokesperson for the Native Council of Canada, quoted in Michael Ames, *Cannibal Tours and Glass Boxes: The Anthropology of Museums* (Vancouver: University of British Columbia Press, 1992), 146.
108. Grace Dillon, "Introduction," in Grace Dillon, ed., *Walking the Clouds: An Anthology of Indigenous Science Fiction* (Tucson: University of Arizona Press, 2012), 3.
109. Dillon, "Introduction," 10.
110. Lewis Cardinal, "What Is an Indigenous Perspective?" *Canadian Journal of Native Education* 25, no. 2 (2001), 180–82.

Part III

Engaging Across Cultures and Around the Globe

Perhaps home is not a place but simply an irrevocable condition.

James Baldwin, *Giovanni's Room*

12

The Matter of Cultural Exchange

China, Europe, and Early Modern Material Connections

Anna Grasskamp

Through the study of material exchanges between China and Europe during the early modern period, this chapter examines not only the movement of artifacts between continents but ways in which the transported matter moved humans, causing physical and emotional responses, transferring aesthetic and cultural knowledge, and influencing systems of taste and technology. Aesthetic, economic, social, political, environmental, technological, terminological, cultural, and ideological ways of understanding the role of these artifacts are addressed and the diverse methods and models scholars have developed to analyze cultural exchange in early modern material culture are considered. The chapter consists of three sections: in the first, a blue-and-white porcelain jug made in China and received in Europe is used as an exemplar of transcultural material exchange and briefly examined from a number of disciplinary angles; the second section discusses prevailing terminologies and related ideological issues in scholarship on transcultural material culture, and the third part situates the blue-and-white jug, or *kendi*, in its wider material, cultural, and historical contexts and serves as a guide to scholarly literature in the field. The third section also discusses interpretative approaches and concepts that transcend interactions between Europe and Asia, particularly the social and global lives of artifacts, the idea of object agency, and the notion of vital materiality in transcultural contexts.

Scholars from the fields of economic history, the history of science, and art history have approached the narrow field of specialization that studies material connections between East Asia and Europe from 1500 to 1800 in a variety of ways.[1] Recently, two books have gone beyond an overarching history of exchanges and nuanced grand narratives of century-long interactions by treating selected objects not as mere examples of commodities and footnotes to stories of sociopolitical, economic, and epistemic connectivity, but by carefully analyzing them in their own right: the edited volume *EurAsian Matters: China, Europe, and the Transcultural Object, 1600–1800* focuses on the entanglement of transcultural matter and aesthetics while also addressing aspects of economic value creation, technological transfer, epistemic connectivity, and object-body relationships; the edited volume *Entangled Itineraries: Materials, Practices, and Knowledge across Eurasia*, on the other hand, concentrates on the relationships between matter and knowledge (including knowledge on aesthetic practices) in the framework of the history of science and technology.[2] Although the volumes differ, for example, in the use of the term "Eurasian" to indicate the interconnectedness of Asian and Europe geographic space and "EurAsian" to label the merging of two distinct cultural traditions in one artifact, they both aim to nuance and complicate grand monocultural narratives through selected transcultural case studies. In a similar vein, this chapter uses a small number of key EurAsian objects to unravel and showcase the wider conceptual implications of matters in exchange and the matter of material exchange.

A prime example of early modern material exchange is provided by a sixteenth-century blue-and-white Chinese porcelain vessel furnished with a European mount of silver gilt, kept today at the Museum of Applied Arts in Berlin (Figure 12.1). The porcelain jug was made by unidentified artisans during the reign of Emperor Wanli (r. 1572–1620) in Jingdezhen, China. The shape is that of a *kendi*, a container for liquids with

Figure 12.1 Unidentified maker, *Ewer*, China, Ming dynasty, Wanli reign (1572–1620). Porcelain, painted in underglaze blue, h. 19 cm. Gilded silver mounts by Georg Berger (active c. 1547–77), Erfurt. Berlin, Staatliche Museen Preussischer Kulturbesitz, inv. no. 1889,305. Photo: bpk/Kunstgewerbemuseum, smb/Funke.

a spout but no handle. This type of vessel was made for markets throughout Southeast Asia, where *kendi* were used for a variety of purposes, for example, the ritual pouring of holy water. The jug is decorated with six framed segments of floral motifs on its body and several bands around the shoulder. Two birds perched on branches decorate the *kendi*'s neck and leaf-like ornaments encircle its star-shaped lip. The vessel's spout is sculpted in imitation of a tree trunk with roots, with a painted knothole adding to the effect.

Within a few years of its production, the Chinese vessel in the Southeast Asian shape was set in metal mounts by Georg Berger, a goldsmith active between 1560 and 1577 in Erfurt, Germany, which then formed part of the Holy Roman Empire ruled by Ferdinand I (r. 1556–64) and then by Maximilian II (r. 1564–76). The mounts add a metal frame to the *kendi*, including a handle, a star-shaped lid covering the vessel's mouth, a stoppered chain for the spout, and a base. Some of the mounts incorporate figurative elements: a lion's head appears among the volutes that connect handle and base, a female head and a flower-shaped ornament decorate the lid hinge, and underneath the vessel's spout appears a hybrid creature with a human head and a fish-tailed lower body.

We can conceptualize and understand this artifact in the framework of transcultural material exchange in several ways. We might, for instance, approach it according to aesthetic criteria, considering the relationship between the *kendi* as a centerpiece and its metallic mounts. These mounts reframe the *kendi*'s blue underglaze decoration by reinforcing some of the linear divisions that the Chinese craftsman employed to separate the pictorial spaces of the object's surface. Furthermore, the shiny metal mounts delineate and contain the ceramic object much as a golden picture frame embellishes the margins of an oil painting. They form an extension to, and arguably also an enhancement of, the central work of porcelain. The framed *kendi* exemplifies an aesthetic relationship between work and by-work – in Greek, *ergon* and *parergon* – that is pivotal to many European sculptural and architectural forms. For ancient rhetoricians such as Quintilian, these concepts were key to crafting an efficient speech: central arguments should be combined with supplementary by-works (*parerga*) to make them more powerful and convincing. Taking into consideration that the European frame (*parergon*) contains a centerpiece (*ergon*) made in Asia, the object's materiality and its aesthetics can be described as transcultural. An aesthetic approach toward the mounted *kendi* helps to situate it within the European history of thought from the early modern period until today in which ways of material framing constituted a type of appropriation. In the instance of a Chinese vessel provided with a European-made handle, lid, and base, this act of appropriation amounts to a Europeanization of a foreign object's shape, surface qualities, and materiality; whoever touched or utilized this object would do so by engaging primarily with

European material surfaces, by grasping the golden silver handle and lifting the gilded lid.

Another way of understanding the *kendi* is through the lens of economics: in early modern Germany, it would have been a luxury item, a rare and foreign porcelain artifact from Asia framed in precious materials, enhanced by the expensive craftsmanship of a goldsmith working on behalf of collectors with refined taste. Porcelain had for centuries entered Europe through Silk Road trade connections, as when a German traveler purchased a ceramic item from Asia during a pilgrimage to the Levant, an area well-supplied with East Asian goods. By the sixteenth century, Chinese porcelain reached Europe through more direct maritime connections via Portuguese and Spanish trade and gift-giving relationships with Asia. In Germany, however, porcelain remained rare and expensive until the seventeenth century when Dutch trade made Asian ceramics cheaper and more widely available.

A piece of Chinese porcelain like the Berlin *kendi* would have been one Asian commodity among many travelling along the early modern trade routes. Mass-produced artifacts made in the imperial or the unofficial kilns and workshops of Jingdezhen would have been intended for use and display at court or sold at local markets, many ending up on the back of a Silk Road camel or a westbound ship, travelling onboard a Portuguese vessel or Spanish carrack, as part of the load of a small unregistered junk operated by a private merchant, or on one of the official "treasure boats" employed by the Chinese during their military and economic explorations throughout Asia. While being transported and transferred from one carrier to another for months or years on end, porcelain was vulnerable to any number of external threats, such as desert winds, ocean waves, Silk Road bandits, and sea pirates. If the transported item survived the trip intact, a new stage in its life began: removed from the local context of its making, detached from previous modes and means of transportation, the object became a rarity that had withstood the test of time and the hazards of transportation, a highly prized luxury item that only members of an exclusive social elite were able to acquire (often via agents specializing in the trade in artifacts).

In addition to their economic value, porcelain objects in Europe could also accrue a high social value through gifting. Their mounts, like those on the Berlin *kendi*, often bear indicators of social meanings, such as goldsmiths' marks identifying the maker and the quality of the materials, or engraved dedications to gift recipients on behalf of their patrons. Exchanged between members of Europe's social and political elites, the gifted objects carried diplomatic as well as personal significance. Whether porcelain was stored away, put on display in cabinets of curiosity, used during exclusive dinners, or depicted in still life paintings, during the sixteenth century it was an object of conspicuous consumption that functioned within socially defined European systems of taste.

This changed during the seventeenth century when trade conducted by the Dutch East India Company and the British East India Company significantly increased the availability of Chinese ceramics in northern Europe. A variety of different types of Chinese ceramics entered Europe in bulk; the more expensive and rare pieces were transported with great care, while the cheaper ones served as ballast for vessels filled with the comparatively lightweight but more expensive commodities of tea, silk, and spices. Select pieces continued to have high monetary and social value throughout the eighteenth century, among them the 151 vases exchanged for 600 elite soldiers in 1717 by August the Strong (Elector of Saxony 1694–1733; King of Poland and Grand Duke of Lithuania 1697–1706). Yet, from the seventeenth century onward some types of Chinese ceramics increasingly appeared in the households of Europeans of lower social strata. As porcelain became more widely available it was differentiated into various types – some pieces were precious and hence gifted among members of the elite, others sold at low prices in Amsterdam and elsewhere – its economic and social values changed across time and space.

During the sixteenth century the social framing of objects of non-European origin was closely tied to European politics. If an item of Chinese porcelain was given, for instance, by a Portuguese member of the Habsburg family to Archduke Ferdinand II (r.1564–195), it was not just an exclusive, high-quality gift, but effectively connected Innsbruck to Lisbon, which was then the most important European harbor for Asian trade. The gifted object thus became a symbolic representation of the Habsburg empire's worldwide networks of trade and political influence. While diplomatic gifts between rulers carried political messages, strong symbolic meanings were also evoked by looted porcelain. The Dutch term *kraak* denotes a certain type of Chinese porcelain made during the same period as the Berlin *kendi*. It allegedly derives from the Portuguese term *carraca*, meaning carrack, and was coined after the Dutch fleet captured a Portuguese vessel (*carraca*) and looted its cargo of porcelain. Although this etymology might be fabricated, it remains a powerful tale, cited by scholars throughout the centuries and illustrating the symbolic role that looted Chinese porcelain played among European power-holders. It represented the intra-European fight for maritime access to Asia, where increasing quantities of valuable spices and tea leaves, expensive silk fabrics and dyes, and precious pieces of lacquerware and ceramics were exported to Europe, facilitating the rapid and unprecedented economic rise of Amsterdam and the Dutch "Golden Age."

While China could steadily supply European markets with porcelain (except during the so-called transitional period, a time of political turmoil from 1620 to 1683), the European exploitation of many other Asian goods was subject to environmental circumstances such as harvest seasons, the quality of the available crops, and weather conditions during transportation. The first successful recreation of Chinese porcelain in Europe was also partly related to environmental resources. The alchemist Johann Friedrich Böttger (1682–1719) was the first to use a German equivalent to kaolin, the rare clay that was an essential constituent of all Jingdezhen porcelain. Other natural resources crucial to the production of Asian artifacts that were in high demand included the sap of Asian lacquer trees (*Toxicodendron vernicifluum*), which could be used as varnish on lacquerware objects, and the mulberry leaves that fed worms needed for silk.

While certain ecological conditions related to the availability of natural resources and the environment were necessary for making artifacts such as the Berlin *kendi*, we cannot fully understand them without understanding the ecologies of making, craftsmanship, and technology. Jingdezhen, where the *kendi* was made, was situated near a rich supply of kaolin and had for decades been a center of refined artistic activity. Generations of well-trained craftsmen were active there, highly skilled at molding, spinning, carving, and painting porcelain. Some kilns at Jingdezhen fired wares commissioned by the imperial court, which imposed strict systems of supervision overseen by workshop superintendents. The best known was the scholar Tang Ying (1682–1756) who, during his twenty years in office, made a lasting impact on porcelain design and technology and wrote extensively about it in illustrated treatises. Technological knowledge was hence not limited to masters who passed it down orally and by example to their apprentices through tacit processes of knowledge transfer; it was also communicated in writing and documented by imagery.

European alchemists and artisans who experimented with ceramics, such as Böttger who reinvented porcelain in eighteenth-century Dresden, and his sixteenth- and seventeenth-century predecessors who worked on imitations of Chinese porcelain at the Medici court in Florence and the ceramic workshops at Delft, tried to learn the Chinese "secrets" of porcelain production by visually and materially studying objects rather than by reading texts. Some Renaissance descriptions of porcelain production in European languages were misleading, as they erroneously described it as made of such materials as seashells or eggshells. This changed when the Jesuit missionary François Xavier d'Entrecolles (1664–1741) shared eyewitness accounts of his visit to Jingdezhen and his knowledge of various important Chinese texts related to artisanal production. In sixteenth-century China, porcelain was a century-old material, omnipresent in the households of ordinary people and imperial palaces, well researched and recorded in writing. In sixteenth-century Europe, by contrast, it was relatively novel, misunderstood in terms of its chemical composition, and feverishly experimented with by craftsmen who sought to reinvent it.

Among all goods of Chinese origin that were traded with or gifted to European recipients between 1500 and 1800, porcelain objects are by far the most researched and best recorded. The approaches and observations outlined above are informed by a body of scholarship published in English and other languages from different disciplines using their respective terminologies. These terminologies warrant clarification: words such as "East" and "West," "transcultural" and "global," artistic "influence" and "mimesis," cultural "appropriation" and "domestication" are not neutral labels attached to spaces, phenomena, material processes, and social interactions; they have conflictual histories of their own, are loaded in their cultural and historical implications, and relate to ideologies that not all scholars share.

While the geographic division of the world into east, west, north, and south is a legitimate one, many contemporary scholars refrain from referring to "Eastern" and "Western" cultures. This division is a Eurocentric one according to which anything east of Europe is considered "Eastern," while to people in Asia the same regions would be Western. The division of the world into Eastern and Western hemispheres establishes a dichotomy that neglects other geographically and sociopolitically defined cultural entities such as the "global South." The East-West dichotomy also implies the hegemony of Western concepts, terminologies, and disciplinary frameworks, which are imposed on Eastern cultures in academic literature, a colonialist attitude commonly understood as Orientalism.[3] In an effort to challenge the orient/occident dichotomy, recently scholars have highlighted global connectivity and brought to the fore the existence of early modern networks of material transfer and knowledge exchange.[4] While the geographic labels "Asia" and "Europe" figure prominently in the titles of exhibitions and institutions,[5] recent research often narrows its field of investigation to specific parts of "Asia" or "Europe," as illustrated by such book titles as *Mediating Netherlandish Art and Material Culture in Asia* and *Qing Encounters: Artistic Exchanges between China and the West.*[6]

Speaking of "encounters" or "meetings" in art stresses aspects of reciprocity and highlights sociocultural rather than material aspects; the usage of the term "transcultural," on the other hand, marks an artifact's state of belonging to more than one culture, as manifested in matter *or* man-made design (or both). In contrast to terms such as cross-cultural or intercultural, which imply a duality between two entities across which or between which they are situated, "transcultural" marks the presence of two or more cultures in a given object of study; in contrast to the term "multicultural," it highlights the possibility that the dominant identity of an object vis-à-vis its culture of origin can be overwritten by new attributions. The Berlin *kendi*, for example, is a transcultural object as it was made in China for a Southeast Asian market and later materially transformed in Europe, its Chinese origin and "Asian" identity supplanted by a massive frame of European mounts that mask the artifact and render it "German."

Transculturation, a term used to describe cultural processes in which transcultural objects play a crucial role, derives from anthropological research on the converging of cultures in an American context,[7] but has also been used widely in historical studies of regions outside of the

Americas.[8] Anthropologists also use "hybridization" and "creolization" to describe the "presence of exotic objects," among them Chinese porcelain, within a "materially creolized Europe."[9] Both concepts carry distinct connotations. The term hybrid derives from biology, where it describes the breeding of two different entities to produce a "hybrid," as, for example, in the creation of a mule from a horse and a donkey. Its usage has been criticized as the term presupposes the existence of two cultures that are essentially different and unrelated, while all cultures in fact share histories of entanglement and are by definition transcultural; "hybridity" furthermore connotes infertility (e.g., the infertility of the mule), an undesirable attribute in relation to transcultural phenomena or objects.[10] The concept of creolization, on the other hand, derives from contexts in which new forms of linguistic and artistic expression emerged from the blending of colonizing and colonized cultures; it implies processes of acculturation under unequal or even forced circumstances.

Anthropologists have conceptualized the relations between material and culture as dynamic, "fluid," or "wavy,"[11] and have described objects as being "entangled"[12] or exhibiting "creole" designs. Furthermore, certain early modern artifacts have been understood as "in motion,"[13] migrant, or "nomadic."[14] Scholars often label objects new to another culture as "foreign" or "alien" despite their local integration, which makes them transcultural rather than foreign.

"Exotic" also appears frequently in scholarly literature, a term with a long European etymology applied to things coming from "outside" a certain place or space. In premodern Chinese, the period term *xiyang* (literally "Western ocean") carried connotations similar to "exotic." *Xiyang* designated objects exported from the Indian Ocean region to today's China, which Ming dynasty sources commonly referred to as "Great Ming" and Qing dynasty texts as Middle Kingdom (*Zhongguo* in Mandarin and *Dulimbai gurun* in Manchu).[15] A Chinese period term equally, but not exclusively, applied to foreign artifacts is *qi* (rare, strange, or exceptional),[16] its European equivalent in expressions such as the early modern German *Rariteyt* (rarity) or the Dutch *curiositeit* (curiosity) frequently indicate collectibles of extra-European origin in European cabinets of curiosity. While it would therefore, according to period terminology, be appropriate to speak of "rare" rather than "foreign" or "transcultural" objects, it would also be more accurate to speak of the Holy Roman Empire when referring to Germany and other parts of Western Europe, and to the "Chinese Empire" rather than "China," a denomination we associate with the modern nation-state. For the sake of comprehensibility, and to avoid repeating the same terms again and again, many authors draw on period expressions as well as contemporary jargon.

The gap between modern language and early etymologies is also apparent in the case of porcelain. The term *porcellana* had first been given in Italy to the cowry shell due to its formal resemblance to a vulva (colloquially *porcello*).[17] Starting with its late thirteenth-century use by the scribe of *The Travels of Marco Polo*, the term took on another meaning: *porcellana* still denoted shells, but increasingly also Chinese ceramics.[18] This second meaning spread throughout Europe; sixteenth-century variations include the German *Porzelana* and the English *Purselyne*. This terminological conflation illustrates the likeness perceived between *porcellana* shells and Chinese *porcellana* ceramics based on their equally smooth and reflective surfaces and comparable semitransparence and brittleness, an etymological aspect which commonly escapes contemporary users of the term porcelain.

Our contemporary divisions between human and natural aesthetics did not apply in the early modern period. The distinction between the creations of nature (e.g., an Asian sea shell as translucent and shiny as chinaware) and the products of human hands (such as a porcelain *kendi*) was not clearly established: to sixteenth-century beholders in Europe, God's creative powers expressed themselves both through the products of nature *and* human craftsmanship. It is therefore not surprising to see shells equipped with German metal mounts like those on the Berlin *kendi*, such as the nautilus shell framed by Nuremberg goldsmith Bartel Jamnitzer (ca. 1548–96) around 1590 (Figure 12.2). While the Southeast Asian shell had been polished and incised with Chinese-style decorations in Asia,[19] its substance is organic, in contrast to the ceramic matter of the

Figure 12.2 Unidentified maker, *Carved Shell*, probably South China, before 1590. Gilded silver mounts by Bartel Jamnitzer (c. 1548–96), Nuremberg, c. 1590. Stuttgart, Landesmuseum Württemberg, inv. no. KK hellblau 10. Photo: Hendrik Zwietasch.

kendi, which is entirely manufactured. Like the mounts on the Berlin vessel, those attached to the shell show the motif of the mermaid.[20] While further iconographic interpretation of the mounts and carvings lies beyond the scope of this chapter, the mere fact that both shell and porcelain received framing by-works of a similar type illustrates the period understanding of "art" and "nature," man-made matter and organic substances, as entangled rather than divided. Accordingly, both objects are transcultural in more than one sense. First, they are not merely examples of Sino-European relations in art, but form complex and multilayered "EurAsian matters":[21] the *kendi* had been made in Jingdezhen for a South Asian market but ended up in Germany, while the nautilus shell derived from Southeast Asian waters, was likely polished and carved in southern China and eventually reframed by a Nuremberg goldsmith. Second, the *kendi*-jug and shell-cup would have been transcultural in the eyes of a period beholder, as both mediated the "cultures" of human craftsmanship and natural production and thereby transcended the divisions between human and environmental ecologies that characterize our own day.

Scholarship on the material and visual integration of artificial or natural objects new to a particular culture frequently refers to the concept of "appropriation" employed by those anthropologists who define "cultures as open systems, where individual actors negotiate access to, and traffic in, symbolic elements which have no fixed meaning."[22] More recently, historians dealing with matter (rather than "symbolic elements") have considered the case of Chinese porcelain in European culture more specifically as "domestication"[23] of materiality and of symbolic meanings. Similarly, the remaking of a material in a new local context, for example, the reinvention of Chinese porcelain by Johann Friedrich Böttger, can be an act of (symbolic) appropriation and (material) domestication. To overcome dichotomies between original and copy, active invention and passive reproduction, historians of art have discussed the "transformative power"[24] of the creative copy and the use of foreign models in terms of "material mimesis"[25] rather than artistic influence or stylistic impact. Originating from experiments inspired by the arrival of Chinese ceramics in Europe, Western porcelain travelled eastwards during later centuries. A lidded cup made in the French porcelain workshops at Sèvres was received at the court of Emperor Qianlong, after which it received a new material frame in the form of a wooden box inscribed with a Chinese description of the foreign object (Figure 12.3). This container is one among many that reframed artful collectibles of Chinese and non-Chinese origin in the collections of Emperor Qianlong, an aesthetic practice recently labeled an act of "branding."[26]

The aesthetic approach to chinaware engages with theories of what constitutes porcelain vessels as objects of material and visual "beauty." Scholarship on the "appropriation" of porcelain in global history has addressed sixteenth-century mounts on Chinese ceramics, recognizing

Figure 12.3 Unidentified maker, *Lidded jar with gold-painted flowers on white glaze ground*, Sèvres ware, Sèvres, France, eighteenth century, h. 9.7 cm, d. 5.7, h. (lid) 3.6 cm. With inscribed wooden container by Qing imperial workshop, 1736–96. Taipei, National Palace Museum, inv. no. 015560–392–1.

European mounting as "an important part of the exceptionalizing process" by which vessels that were essentially ordinary in their original context became elite objects abroad. The act of mounting arguably "represented a very localized form of appropriation" performed through the "physical transformation" of a given object.[27] Furthermore, the mounts frame and materialize a European system of aesthetic appreciation for porcelain.[28] Eighteenth-century French rococo mounts on Chinese ceramics have been interpreted as "an ornamental mode to enhance" Asian wares, signaling "more dynamic engagements with imports from distant lands" and indicating "how objects mediated in the imagining of eighteenth-century selves in relation to, rather than in opposition to, an other."[29]

While the imported wares set in precious-metal mounts were highly esteemed by early modern European collectors, they did not necessarily meet the standards of taste arbiters within Chinese aesthetic systems. A particularly interesting example that illustrates the disparity between European and Asian aesthetic criteria is provided by porcelain made in China to cater to Western tastes, such as vessels decorated with the heraldic signs of seafarers and noblemen,[30] and other motifs derived from European prints.[31] The previously mentioned *kraak* is often categorized as "export porcelain" due to Europe's high demand for it, which not only resulted in increased production but also the use of certain European decorative elements and the creation of Europeanized shapes.

The *klapmuts*, for instance, received its name from a Dutch term for "hat," as it looks like an upside-down cap; it was more suitable for the consumption of European stews than Chinese bouillon bowls as it was flat and had a shoulder where a spoon could conveniently be rested during the meal. Yet *kraak* ware has also been found in the tombs of Chinese social elites and was hence not limited to consumption by people foreign to the Middle Kingdom. The eighteenth-century expression *Chine de commande*, the terms "export porcelain" and "company art" used in twentieth-century scholarship, and the expression "*kraak* ware" all highlight the imposition of non-Chinese aesthetic criteria on the making of Chinese artifacts. The resulting terminological framework privileges European target audiences. Labels "such as chinoiserie, export or company art and categories like 'Euroiserie', 'Européenerie' or 'Chinese Occidenterie' flag oppositions between 'Chinese' and 'European' market demands and highlight differences in ways of looking and systems of collecting and consumption," yet artifacts like the Berlin *kendi* also exemplify connected rather than opposed (or dichotomous) materiality – objects in which the authorships of European and Chinese craftsmen mix and merge rather than hierarchically dominate each other. Artifacts such as the *kendi* are "communicative in their own right and have the potential to create unpredictable actions in unforeseen spaces, for example as material stimuli to artists and artisans"[32] in Europe. The potential for change brought about by the introduction of foreign artworks was not limited to aesthetics, although changes in aesthetic taste and iconography appear most conspicuous if we think, for example, of the impact that the transfer of European prints rendered with one-point perspective had on Chinese and Japanese visual and material culture.[33]

The mobility of objects also triggered economic change. Geoffrey Gunn has argued that the exchange of knowledge and material culture between Europe and Asia produced a "first globalization" between 1500 and 1800.[34] While the term "globalization" evokes interaction and integration, postcolonial scholars have focused on the unequal and non-integrative aspects of trade exchanges between Europe and Asia and especially the exploitation of resources and people for the benefit of Western colonizing powers. Similarly, economic historians highlight the differences that explain the "great divergence"[35] between Europe's and China's economic developments in relation to European colonial trade. In the past decade, historians have examined a wide variety of materials and artifacts that were transported from the East to the West and vice versa.[36]

During the sixteenth and seventeenth centuries foodstuffs sent from China to Europe included tea leaves,[37] citrus fruits,[38] ginger root and other spices, rhubarb,[39] and soy sauce.[40] Chinese foodstuffs and medical substances reached Europe preserved in containers such as earthenware bottles and ceramic jars. European craftsmen later imitated soy sauce bottles as they provided attractive packaging for foreign merchandise.[41] A particular type of blue-and-white decorated Chinese porcelain vessel became widely known as a "ginger jar" based on the assumption that it originally preserved pickled goods.[42] In the opposite direction, the most notorious substance that Europeans exported to China on a large scale was opium, made in India but distributed by the British from the eighteenth century onward. The so-called Opium Wars received their name from the drug and the economic dependency it allegedly created, although the reasons for China's nineteenth-century economic decline, which included the dissemination of silver in exchange for opium, have recently been reevaluated in a more critical and nuanced light.[43]

Glass items made in Europe and Africa traveled eastward to satisfy a Chinese demand for objects that could not yet be produced by local Asian craftsmen in comparable quantities and with the same levels of translucency and other material qualities. This changed during the Qing dynasty when European missionaries helped establish an imperial glass-making workshop.[44] Elite collections, such as those held at the imperial court, included foreign glass items, but glass objects also played an important role in temple collections and Buddhist material culture: a transparent glass container became an iconographic attribute of the Bodhisattva Guanyin who employed it to contain the sacred water and willow branch that she used to issue blessings upon worshippers.[45] A considerable number of glass beads also entered China through Dutch settlements in Taiwan, alongside other examples of everyday material culture, such as tobacco pipes and German *Bartmann* jugs.[46]

Chinese furniture also began to reach Europe in increasing quantities, a very early example of which is an extant folding chair of circa 1570 from the possessions of Philip II of Spain (r. 1556–198), who allegedly used another armchair of Asian provenance as his main seat during the last years of his life.[47] Another outstanding example of a Chinese chair that received a second life as "a throne" in a European collection is a refined red-lacquerware seat made for use by the emperor, which was among the items looted in 1860 by Anglo-French forces at the Yuanming Yuan close to Beijing (the Old Summer Palace). The lacquer piece ended up at the Victoria and Albert Museum in London where its display at some point suggested that it was *the* imperial "throne" of the Emperor of China.[48] Examples of early modern European furniture designs influenced by Chinese pieces are countless and commonly interpreted in the framework of scholarship on chinoiserie, a term for the use of Chinese motifs and techniques in European art and material culture, especially during the eighteenth century.[49] In China, European furniture imports had an impact on interior design at the imperial court during the Qing dynasty (1644–1911), as evidenced by a European-style table in the collections of the Palace Museum, Beijing, possibly the one that Emperor Yongzheng commissioned in 1730.[50] European and European-style furniture also entered the daily life of ordinary people outside of the courtly context. In the area of Guangzhou (Canton) imported tables were "uniquely compatible with a new trend then emerging within domestic material culture: the use of round dining tables derived from earlier forms of Chinese furniture." Such tables "partook in the formation of a new social dining practice that emphasized casualness and intimacy," substituting previous seating arrangements that highlighted social hierarchy and gender division.[51]

Early eastbound exchanges in material culture can also be seen in architecture such as the importation of Dutch bricks for architectural projects in Taiwan.[52] Foreign merchants also notably impacted harbor cityscapes, especially in Guangzhou where local houses in the trade district were clad with Western facades.[53] Portuguese building activities in Macao are still visible; perhaps the most widely known example is the church of Saint Paul facade.[54] European Jesuits established churches in China and contributed to the design of Qing imperial palaces and gardens.[55] The Old Summer Palace (Yuanming Yuan, meaning "Garden of Perfect Clarity") included European-style buildings depicted in copperplate engravings by the Chinese court artist Yi Lantai (active 1738–86), and surviving in fragments at the original site and in collections worldwide.[56]

An architectural ornament from one European-style building at the Old Summer Palace represents a case of transcultural matter in two ways: first through its design, in which an asymmetrical European rococo shape meets the proportionality, materiality, and color schemes associated with Chinese ceramic tiles, and second through its collection history (Figure 12.4). Like the previously mentioned lacquerware seat, the fragment reached Europe as a result of the palace looting by Anglo-French forces in 1860 and is today at the Victoria and Albert Museum. In 2009, two sculptural fragments of a European-style fountain in the Old Summer Palace were offered at auction, causing an international public debate on questions of belonging and cultural heritage (before being removed from the art market and repatriated in 2013). This case inspired contemporary artist Ai Weiwei (b. 1957) to produce gigantic copies of the sculptures.[57] He claims the original objects from the Old Summer Palace do not qualify as national treasures as they belonged to more than one culture from the start. That is, they are transcultural objects, designed and produced by European Jesuits on behalf of Emperor Qianlong, who, according to Ai, is among those who historically "invented China"[58] before the nation-state and therefore before the formation of modern understandings of national heritage. Ai's work provokes us to rethink the place of early modern transcultural objects in Communist systems, in relation to the global history of national heritage as well as the commodification processes of the art market.[59] Having been neglected and almost forgotten for most of the twentieth century, in recent years the Old Summer Palace's architectural and sculptural fragments have been invested with extraordinary

Figure 12.4 Unidentified maker, *Architectural fitting*, stoneware with turquoise-blue glaze, Yuanmingyuan, China, 1747–70, h. 34.5 cm, w. 38.0 cm, d. 23.0 cm. London, Victoria and Albert Museum, inv. no. C.382–1912.

symbolic value and stand *pars pro toto* for other cases of transcultural material heritage and Elginism in China.

In Europe, Chinese pavilions were constructed in royal gardens from Versailles to Brighton,[60] Potsdam to Drottningholm. These sites employed architectural shapes of Chinese style, or of an imagined "Chinese" style, as well as Chinese materials. The interior of the pavilion at Sanssouci, the summer palace of Frederick the Great (r. 1712–86), was furnished with porcelain vessels with blue-and-white, *famille rose*, *famille verte*, and other Chinese decorative types, placed on golden consoles along the walls. The ceiling of the former Santos Palace in Lisbon is completely covered by plates, bowls, and vases, which have a decorative rather than supportive function. Seventeenth- and eighteenth-century porcelain rooms established at many residences throughout Europe combine walls, consoles, and porcelain objects in ways that blur the distinction between architecture and artifact.

Comparable to porcelain, lacquer was a material that could not be reproduced in Europe before the eighteenth century: early experiments with materials that had properties comparable to the sap of Asian lacquer trees remained unsuccessful.[61] As a result, Asian lacquerware objects were highly desirable.[62] Lacquerware boxes and bowls were avidly collected, and lacquered pieces of furniture, among them screens (and panels that originally belonged to screens), became integrated into the interior designs of European palaces. Furthermore, Chinese textiles, paintings, and wallpapers were employed as wall decoration in European residences.[63] In 1766, tapestries made in Beauvais were offered to Emperor Qianlong, who displayed them in special buildings.[64] In Sino-European exchanges, consumable plants, such as tea leaves and rhubarb stalks played an especially crucial role. In addition, trees, flowers, and other garden plants could also be transcultural, as they were exchanged between Europe and China to serve as ornaments in private and public spaces.[65]

Textiles and clothing were likewise traded in both directions. Chinese silk was imported into Europe in large quantities,[66] and some European textiles were introduced into China where they played an important role in the self-fashioning of Qing dynasty Emperor Qianlong.[67] From the sixteenth century on, individual pieces of exotic fashion, such as a cap from "the kingdom of China"[68] kept at a late sixteenth-century private collection in London, were collected in cabinets of curiosity and, on occasion, worn during European court festivals. The Asian-style *banyan*, a male's gown to be worn at home, became increasingly fashionable in Europe throughout the eighteenth century. In Qing dynasty China, a painting of Emperor Yongzheng shows him dressed in a European-style gown and wig.[69] We also have pictorial evidence of women's use of Western attire at the court of Emperor Qianlong.[70] Personal care items were also exchanged, as evidenced by a "China cabinet" filled with Chinese ear-cleaning devices that reached seventeenth-century England.[71]

Among those foreign artifacts collected and used at the Chinese imperial court, European-made mechanical clocks and automata played an important role.[72] Clocks were commonly exchanged as diplomatic gifts by European rulers, and were also presented to Ottoman sultans, Mughal emperors, and other rulers of extra-European territories.[73] In China, the earliest known example is the clock gifted to Emperor Wanli of the Ming dynasty, after which point clocks quickly became standard items brought by foreign "tribute-bearers" to the Chinese court. Hundreds of automata made by goldsmiths and clockmakers of different European nationalities reached the Middle Kingdom until the eighteenth and nineteenth centuries when local clockwork and automaton factories were established in Jiangsu and Guangdong for the Beijing court. The clock given to Emperor Wanli was accompanied by a clavichord, the first European musical instrument that contributed to courtly musical life in early modern China.[74]

In addition to musical automata, clocks, and watches, other enameled metal objects traveled from Europe to China and vice versa. European enamel wares made in the workshop at Limoges, France were well-received at the Chinese imperial court, where European Jesuits assisted in developing new enamel techniques.[75] In return, eighteenth-century French connoisseurs avidly collected Chinese cloisonné and other enamel wares. Bronze objects, which played a central role in Chinese cultural practices including ancestor worship, entered Europe in small numbers in the early modern period, but had impact and even triggered intellectual debates. In the seventeenth century, for instance, a Chinese bronze mirror in Amsterdam formed part of a Eurasian network of knowledge exchange as scholars tried to decipher its inscription.[76] During the late nineteenth century, other metal objects manufactured in Guangzhou, most prominently Chinese "export" silver wares, were used and collected in China and abroad.[77]

A small number of artifacts carved in the organic materials of ivory, wood, and bone traveled from Europe to China where they inspired changes in local craft practices. Glass-covered bone and wood sculptures manufactured in the South German town of Berchtesgaden were in high demand and prompted the creation of local glass-encased artifacts and "vitreous views"[78] at the Qing court, but were gifted in small numbers rather than traded.[79] A set of 100 wooden cups carved to neatly fit inside each other, a type associated with Nuremberg craftsmanship, was held in high esteem and received a special place in Beijing's imperial collections[80] where a European machine for turning ivory was also used.[81] Although they transformed Chinese craftsmanship at the court workshops, the nesting cups and ingenious ivory-carving machine were highly exceptional pieces whose direct impact was limited to imperial circuits. Objects carved in ivory by European hands did become widespread in China outside of the courtly context – appearing in local churches and among Guangzhou craftsmen and merchants – but they remained exclusive and pricey commodities.[82] Chinese carved ivory items in European collections were equally rare and costly, as were eighteenth-century Guangzhou sculptures made of wood or clay, which formed stereotypical as well as individual portraits of European merchants.[83] While some of the wood or clay sculptures reached life-size dimensions, the illustrated ivory carving which shows three men on a sloop painted in Dutch colors, is rather small (Figure 12.5). The plaque may have once belonged to a screen with a painted, appliqued representation of the Canton harbor.[84] While rhinoceros horn pieces transformed into artful cups by Chinese craftsmen appear in the sixteenth- and seventeenth-century courtly collections of Dresden and Prague, they, too, were restricted to elite collecting.

European religious sculptures reached China through foreign missionaries and Chinese craftsmen in China and the Philippines carved local versions of motifs such as the Madonna and Child in ivory and other materials.[85] Archduke Ferdinand II of Austria kept an "Indian idol" in his bedchamber at Ambras Castle in Innsbruck and a single "broken Indian idol" appears in an early seventeenth-century cabinet inventoried by the Augsburg art agent Philipp Hainhofer, both possibly of Chinese origin.[86] A 1598 inventory of the Wittelsbach dukes' collections at Munich features an item convincingly identified as a Chinese soapstone sculpture of a Buddhist figure.[87] Soapstone sculptures with religious and secular motifs entered collections (such as that of August the Strong) in remarkable numbers, and in Dresden influenced the iconography of Meissen

Figure 12.5 Unidentified maker, *A Sloop with Dutchmen and their Goods*, Guangzhou, China, 1700–50, ivory and paint, l. 16 cm. Amsterdam, Rijksmuseum, inv. no. NG-1994-12.

porcelain.[88] For the early modern trade in gemstones such as rubies and diamonds, India and Sri Lanka were the most important sources for Europe and China.[89] Small amounts of amber and relatively large quantities of coral were transported from the Mediterranean to the Middle Kingdom directly or via merchants in South Asia.[90] Jade items, which Chinese collectors and connoisseurs held in high esteem, reached Europe in small numbers, but did not create a significant market interest.

Among European scientific objects available in China, optical lenses and metal mirrors became widespread commodities.[91] During the reign of Emperor Kangxi, astronomical instruments were designed and made with the support of Jesuit missionaries at the imperial observatory.[92] Commissioned by the emperor, European Jesuits also worked on the design and installation of mechanical devices for fountains and other hydraulic constructions,[93] which remained as limited to court circles as astronomical instruments. Chinese gunpowder was crucial to the emergence of the European elite spectacle of fireworks,[94] while weapons and other military equipment moved in both directions.[95]

Countless items could be added to this survey; I have highlighted items traded in large quantities and those which traveled in small numbers but made an important contribution to local material cultures and craftsmanship in their destinations. Paper-based exchanges were also significant in this context. Blank sheets of Chinese paper were traded to Europe,[96] and books, prints (including maps), and paintings traveled both ways. Some are "EurAsian"[97] objects, such as a Chinese book rebound in a European library and endowed with its new owner's inscriptions and stamps,[98] and a Latin treatise translated into Chinese through collaboration between European Jesuits and local scholars. Full-page printed imagery and pictorial details of images were "re-layered" and "re-framed"[99] in the context of newly created pictures and in illustrated books, while motifs were transferred from paper to other surfaces. Paintings received new textile mounts or wooden frames upon reception in a different cultural context, or were newly categorized according to their material properties: in the inventories of German and Austrian cabinets of curiosities we find references to a Chinese painting on translucent paper and others on silk scrolls described as "windows"[100] and "cloth,"[101] listed in a section separate from European paintings on wooden panels. These examples illustrate important aspects of sources that many historians have tended to research as if they merely consisted of two-dimensional surfaces, ignoring aspects of their materiality. The briefly sketched material culture approach toward objects is necessarily limited, as every single approach to an object is. To truly understand the complexity of objects such as transcultural texts, printed book illustrations, maps, drawings, and paintings, we need to add other analytical tools and methodological perspectives that lie outside of the goal of this chapter.

Reconstructing the trade flow between Europe and Asia provides a glimpse of porcelain, lacquerware, and silk objects as well as the commodities of silver, coral, and opium during one moment in their "social" lives. Before a porcelain item entered the circles of commodity exchange and became part of a European ship's load of Asian goods, it was an artifact made from local natural resources by technologically advanced and artistically sophisticated craftsmen. After its maritime journey the object was sold or gifted and thereby reached another stage in its "social" life. It might have then entered a European kitchen and been used as tableware, or a cabinet of curiosity displayed alongside other precious collectibles and rarities. The notions of an object's "biography" or "social life" have allowed scholars to theorize the cultural meanings of commodities in a way that has built on, but also deviated from, Karl Marx's understandings of material culture.[102] In addition to having social lives, objects involved in Sino-European exchange led "global lives":[103] their biographies are defined by social circumstances but also by conditions that vary between cultures and places across a global network. Among things with "global lives," cross-cultural gifts have attracted special scholarly attention at the intersection of diplomatic history and material culture studies.[104] They include politically motivated presents, religious donations, material exchanges among members of the elite, and what the Chinese called "tributes." Objects in the latter category were, for example, documented in the *Records of Tributes from the Western Ocean Countries*, a printed account from 1520 listing places throughout the Indian Ocean region where certain European and South Asian goods could be acquired.[105]

From the seventh to the early tenth century, Buddhist monks from the Indian Ocean region brought foreign objects to China through networks of "reciprocity, redistribution, and exchange." They supplied China with religious items as well as pearls and Mediterranean coral, which changed the material world of the Chinese in secular and religious contexts.[106] Later, from the mid-tenth to the fifteenth century, a "new pattern of Sino-Indian commercial and cultural interactions" emerged, "dominated by mercantile concerns instead of Buddhist doctrines and pilgrims,"[107] and indicating a shift from gift to commodity exchange. In China, Jesuit "gifts" played an important role from the sixteenth century onward. Some were conspicuously religious (such as sculptures of the Virgin Mary), while others were secular, but nevertheless designed to aid the Jesuits to spread their mission by showing the achievements of Western civilization, which, they believed, God had bestowed upon humanity. In Europe, religious objects of non-European origin appeared in cabinets of curiosity.[108] While in their original Asian contexts many religious icons had been consecrated through eye-opening ceremonies and were considered "living presences,"[109] in their new European surroundings they often lived the social life of a dusty collectible occasionally incorporated into temporary displays but excluded from ritual practices and worship.

The potential of Asian sculptures to function as "agents" has received attention from historians of European art and is treated in depth by area specialists.[110] Over the past twenty years, major scholarly debates have revolved around the question of whether objects in general have "agency." As argued elsewhere,[111] it is possible to define EurAsian artifacts "in performative terms as systems of actions, intended to change the world rather than encode symbolic propositions about it."[112] A porcelain artifact manufactured in Jingdezhen that reached sixteenth-century Florence, where an Italian potter imitated it,[113] has an agency that changes the world of European craftsmanship. The piece of chinaware made the Florentine potter's body (especially his fingers) move in imitation of the performance of Chinese craftsmen, and thereby it possesses agency that prompts an active visual and material communication between artisans from two different cultures.

In contrast to understanding things as "actors," Tim Ingold argues that

> the forms of things are ... continually generated and dissolved within the fluxes of materials across the interface between substances and the medium that surrounds them. Thus, things are active not because they are imbued with agency but because of ways in which they are caught up in these currents of the lifeworld. The properties of materials, then, are not fixed attributes of matter but are processual and relational.[114]

Similarly, for Marta Ajmar, design develops "within a physical environment from the interconnection of human action and materials";[115] she suggests looking *into* objects in addition to looking *at* them. Ajmar sees "fifteenth- and sixteenth-century Italian lacquer and color-glazed pottery" including objects made in imitation of Chinese wares, as "significant actors within global processes of material, technological, and epistemological interconnectedness."[116] They are globally connected to other artifacts "not just as commodities in motion but as technological compounds relying on material mimesis"[117] that is, the cognitive imitation of ancient and foreign artworks by sixteenth- and seventeenth-century Italian craftsmen through material and technological means. In terms of further technological change that porcelain inspired in Europe, Chinese models of modular production at Jingdezhen may have inspired the establishment of similar production systems in the West.[118]

Furthermore, EurAsian artifacts that conspicuously embody the meeting and merging of elements from different cultures have been mapped using social terminology, a rhetoric that goes beyond the attribution of a "life" to an object. Sabine du Crest understands them as "border" or "boundary objects" (*objets frontières*), attributing to some a "double life" (*double vie*), interpreting others as representing a "marriage" (*mariage*) of different parts or belonging to a "patchwork family" (*famille recomposée*).[119] Among such "border" or "boundary objects," mounted Chinese ceramics like the Berlin *kendi* had social and global lives and other characteristics that make them comparable to human agents.

Understanding EurAsian material culture in terms of its sociopolitical implications also requires considering colonial relations. Kristel Smentek sees "imports" to eighteenth-century France, for example, Chinese porcelain vessels, as "primary sites of cultural contact" and claims that "the new items created in response to them are thus productive areas for examining the processes by which otherness was engaged in noncolonialist, intercultural relations."[120] This contrasts with the conclusions of other scholars who see European materiality as inevitably entangled with and informed by the experience of colonialism. Christopher Pinney, for example, condemns the existence of "an originary Europe" as fictional and sees it instead as "hybridized" and "materially creolized," arguing that "Europe was always a reflection of other times and places" due to the "parallel, uncanny, presence of exotic objects."[121] Pinney's view that we do not entangle objects, but that "objects entangle us" is consistent with recent attempts to shift our focus from the human experience of things to a "vital materiality" in things. According to Jane Bennett, "vital materiality" runs through and across bodies, the bodies of people and animals as well as the "bodies" of things; its acknowledgment helps us to fully recognize the active participation of nonhuman forces in events.[122] Such events naturally include transcultural encounters, whether on the battlefield or in the artisan's workshop, involving human agency and "vibrant" matter.

Contemporary museums are not likely to incorporate departments dedicated to "EurAsian Matters" or "Sino-European Artifacts"; instead, galleries filled with Chinese art exist apart from Renaissance hallways and Baroque period rooms. Many museums worldwide have, however, featured temporary exhibitions and small permanent displays highlighting the matter of cultural exchange between China and Europe.[123]

In parts of the museum with a monocultural emphasis, gallery statements refer to a multiplicity of artifacts and usually highlight an object's cultural belonging to the place and the period at the heart of the display, while object labels often dedicate some space to transcultural aspects. In these settings, the museum label functions as an "object passport": it states the object's place of origin and refers to visible or invisible "visa stamps" that reveal its path through the world, perhaps pointing to later additions to the piece or damage caused by transportation. The label also states the artifact's present residence, indicating whether it is "on loan" or in the permanent possession of the exhibiting museum. Usually, the dominant narrative of the gallery (or the special exhibition) presents objects as either "European" or "Chinese," while object labels, which increasingly are bilingual or trilingual, offer the possibility of "dual citizenships." Similarly, the artifacts and objects presented in this chapter inhabit different spaces, those of their makers as well as those of their collectors, those of their transporters and traders as well as those of their gift givers and recipients. The works belong to the period between 1500 and 1800 as well as to our times. They can be understood through aesthetic, economic, social, political, ecological, technological, etymological, cultural, and ideological narratives which are not mutually exclusive, but, like an ideal museum exhibition, offer themselves as frames or lenses through which we better understand an artifact from as many mutually enriching angles as possible.

Notes

1. Monographs include: Harold Cook, *Matters of Exchange: Commerce, Medicine, and Science in the Dutch Golden Age* (New Haven: Yale University Press, 2007); Geoffrey Gunn, *First Globalization: The Eurasian Exchange, 1500–1800* (Lanham: Rowman & Littlefield, 2003).
2. Anna Grasskamp and Monica Juneja, eds., *EurAsian Matters: China, Europe and the Transcultural Object, 1600–1800*, Transcultural Research – Heidelberg Studies on Asia and Europe in a Global Context (Cham: Springer, 2018); Pamela Smith, ed., *Entangled Itineraries: Materials, Practices, and Knowledge across Eurasia* (Pittsburgh: University of Pittsburgh Press, 2019).
3. Edward Said, *Orientalism* (London and Henley: Routledge, 1978).
4. Anne Gerritsen and Giorgio Riello, eds., *The Global Lives of Things: The Material Culture of Connections in the Early Modern World* (Basingstoke: Routledge, 2016).
5. For example: *Encounters: The Meeting of Asia and and Europe, 1500–1800*, exhibition, Victoria and Albert Museum, September 23–December 5, 2004; "Cluster of Excellence," *Asia and Europe in a Global Context*, exhibition, Heidelberg University.

6. Michael North and Thomas DaCosta Kaufmann, eds., *Mediating Netherlandish Art and Material Culture in Asia* (Amsterdam: Amsterdam University Press, 2014); Petra ten-Doesschate Chu and Ning Ding, eds., *Qing Encounters: Artistic Exchanges between China and the West, Issues & Debates* (Los Angeles: Getty Publications, 2015).
7. On Fernando Ortiz's coinage of the term in 1940 see Jossianna Arroyo, "Transculturation, Syncretism, and Hybridity," in Y. Martínez-San Miguel, B. Sifuentes-Jáuregui, and M. Belausteguigoitia, eds., *Critical Terms in Caribbean and Latin American Thought: New Directions in Latino American Cultures* (New York: Palgrave Macmillan, 2016), 133–44.
8. Hans-Georg Sandkühler, *Transculturality: Epistemology, Ethics, and Politics* (Frankfurt a. M.: Lang, 2004); Madeleine Herren, Martin Rüesch, and Chrisiane Sibille, eds., *Transcultural History: Theories, Methods, Sources* (Berlin: Springer, 2012).
9. Christoper Pinney, "Creole Europe: The Reflection of a Reflection," *Journal of New Zealand Literature* 20 (2002), 125–60.
10. See, for example, Amar Acheraiou, *Questioning Hybridity, Postcolonialism and Globalization* (Basingstoke: Palgrave Macmillan, 2011).
11. Ibid.
12. Nicholas Thomas, *Entangled Objects: Exchange, Material Culture, and Colonialism in the Pacific* (Cambridge: Harvard University Press, 1991).
13. *Objects in Motion in the Early Modern World*, special issue, Daniela Bleichmar and Meredith Martin, eds., *Art History* 38, no. 4 (2015).
14. Christine Göttler and Mia Mochizuki, eds., *The Nomadic Object: The Challenge of World for Early Modern Religious Art* (Leiden: Brill, 2017).
15. Craig Clunas, "Connected Material Histories: A Response," *Modern Asian Studies*, 50 (2016), 61–74.
16. Anna Grasskamp, "EurAsian Layers: Netherlandish Surfaces and Early Modern Chinese Artifacts," *The Rijksmuseum Bulletin* 63, no.4 (2015), 363–98, 382, note 58.
17. *The Merriam-Webster New Book of Word Histories* (Springfield: Merriam-Webster, 1991), 371.
18. Robert Finlay, *The Pilgrim Art: Cultures of Porcelain in World History* (Berkeley and Los Angeles: University of California Press, 2010), 70.
19. Anna Grasskamp, "The Frames of Reflection: 'Indian' Shell Surfaces and European Collecting, 1550–1650," in Sabine Du Crest, ed., *Exogenèses: Objets frontière dans l'art européen* (Paris: Boccard, 2018), 69–83.
20. Many other period examples also show mermaids or other female hybrids with half-human, half-animal bodies. See Anna Grasskamp, "Spirals and Shells: Breasted Vessels in Sixteenth-Century Nuremberg," *Res: Anthropology and Aesthetics* 67/68 (2016/17), 146–63.
21. Grasskamp and Juneja, *EurAsian Matters*.
22. Arnd Schneider, "On 'Appropriation': A Critical Reappraisal of the Concept and Its Application in Global Art Practices," *Social Anthropology* 11, no. 2 (2003), 215.

23. Dawn Odell, "Delftware and the Domestication of Chinese Porcelain," in Grasskamp and Juneja, *EurAsian Matters*, 175–202. Anne Gerritsen, "Domesticating Goods from Overseas: Global Material Culture in the Early Modern Netherlands," *Journal of Design History* 29, no. 3 (2016), 232.
24. Corinna Forberg and Philipp W. Stockhammer, eds., *The Transformative Power of the Copy: A Transcultural and Interdisciplinary Approach* (Heidelberg: Heidelberg University Press, 2017).
25. Marta Ajmar, "The Renaissance in Material Culture: Material Mimesis as Force and Evidence of Globalization," in Tamar Hodos, ed., *The Routledge Handbook of Globalization and Archaeology* (London and New York: Routledge, 2016), 684.
26. National Palace Museum, ed., *Story of a Brand Name: The Collection and Packaging Aesthetics of Emperor Qianlong in the Eighteenth Century* (Taipei: National Palace Museum, 2018).
27. Stacey Pierson, "The Movement of Chinese Ceramics: Appropriation in Global History," *Journal of World History* 23, no. 1 (2012), 36.
28. Anna Grasskamp, "Frames of Appropriation: Foreign Artifacts on Display in Early Modern Europe and China," in ten-Doesschate Chu and Ding, *Qing Encounters*, 29–42; Anna Grasskamp, "Porcelain in Frames: The Europeanization of Chinese Ceramics through Sixteenth-Century Metal Mounts," in *Objects in Frames: Displaying Foreign Collectibles in Early Modern China and Europe* (Berlin: Reimer, 2019), 25–52.
29. Kristel Smentek, "Global Circulations, Local Transformations: Objects and Cultural Encounter in the Eighteenth Century," in ten-Doesschate Chu and Ding, *Qing Encounters*, 54; see also Kristel Smentek, *Rococo Exotic: French Mounted Porcelains and the Allure of the East* (New York: Frick Collection, 2007).
30. See David S. Howard, *Chinese Armorial Porcelain* (London: Heirloom & Howard, 2003).
31. For examples, see D. F. Lunsingh Scheurleer, *Chinese Export Porcelain: Chine de Commande* (London: Faber and Faber, 1974).
32. Grasskamp, "EurAsian Layers," 393.
33. Research on this subject has been widely published in English. Literature on China includes Kristina Kleutghen, *Imperial Illusions: Crossing Pictorial Boundaries in the Qing Palaces* (Seattle and London: University of Washington Press, 2015). Literature on Japan includes Timon Screech, *The Lens within the Heart: The Western Scientific Gaze and Popular Imagery in Later Edo Japan* (Richmond: Curzon, 2002); Mia Mochizuki, "The Movable Center: The Netherlandish Map in Japan," in Michael North, ed., *Artistic and Cultural Exchanges between Europe and Asia, 1400–1900: Rethinking Markets, Workshops and Collections* (Aldershot: Ashgate, 2010), 109–33; Mia Mochizuki and Yoriko Kobayashi-Sato, "Perspective and Its Discontents or St. Lucy's Eyes," in Dana Leibsohn and Jeanette Favrot Peterson, eds., *Seeing Across Cultures in the Early Modern Period* (Farnham:

Ashgate, 2012), 21–48. Matthi Forrer, "From Optical Prints to *Ukie* and *Ukiyoe*: The Adoption and Adaptation of Western Linear Perspective in Japan," in North and DaCosta Kaufmann, *Mediating Netherlandish Art*, 245–66.
34. Gunn, *First Globalization*.
35. Kenneth Pommeranz, *The Great Divergence: China, Europe, and the Making of the Modern World Economy* (Princeton: Princeton University Press, 2000).
36. See, for example, Maxine Berg, ed., *Goods from the East, 1600–1800: Trading Eurasia, Europe's Asian Centuries* (Basingstoke: Palgrave Macmillan, 2015) and other outcomes of the project *Europe's Asian Centuries: Trading Eurasia 1600–1830*, University of Warwick.
37. Annette Kanzenbach and Daniel Suebsman, eds., *Made in China: Porzellan und Teekultur im Nordwesten im 18. Jahrhundert. Ein Kapitel Handelsgeschichte* (Emden: Isensee, 2015).
38. Ulrich G. Grossmann, ed., *Die Frucht der Verheißung: Zitrusfrüchte in Kunst und Kultur* (Nuremberg: Germanisches National Museum, 2011).
39. See Anne Gerritsen and Giorgio Riello, "Introduction. The Global Lives of Things: Material Culture in the First Global Age," in Gerritsen and Riello, *The Global Lives of Things*, 1–28.
40. Anne Gerritsen, "'Soja, Zoals Die Uit Oost-Indien Komt'; De Vroege Geschiedenis Van Sojasaus in Nederland," *Aziatische Kunst* 45, no. 3 (2015), 24–33.
41. Anne Gerritsen, "The Global Life of a Soya Bottle," inaugural lecture, Leiden University, December 12, 2014. https://bit.ly/3HGBf6f.
42. Anna Grasskamp and Wen-ting Wu, "We Call Them 'Ginger Jars': European Re-framings of Chinese Ceramic Containers," *Vormen uit Vuur* 232, no. 3 (2016), 64–71.
43. Richard von Glahn, "Economic Depression and the Silver Question in Nineteenth-Century China," in Manuel Perez Garcia and Lucio De Sousa, eds., *Global History and New Polycentric Approaches. Palgrave Studies in Comparative Global History* (Singapore: Palgrave Macmillan, 2018), 81–118.
44. Emily Byrne Curtis, *Glass Exchange between Europe and China, 1550–1800: Diplomatic, Mercantile and Technological Interactions* (Farnham and Burlington: Ashgate, 2009). Emily Byrne Curtis, "A Plan of the Emperor's Glassworks," *Arts Asiatiques* 56 (2001), 81–90.
45. Emily Byrne Curtis, "Poem of the Glass Bowl," in Emily Byrne Curtis, ed., *Pure Brightness Shines Everywhere* (Burlington: Ashgate, 2004), 49–58.
46. Wang Su-chin and Liu Yi-chang, "Shiqi Shijie Qianhou Taiwan Boli Zhushi Yu Yancao, Yan Dou De Shuru Wanglu: Yi Ge Xin De Jiaohuan Jieduan (The Import Networks of Tobacco, Tobacco Pipes, and Glass Bead Ornaments into Taiwan Circa the Seventeenth Century: A New Phase of Exchange)," *Guoli Taiwan Daxue Meishushi Yanjiu Jikan* 22 (2007), 51–90. Hsieh Ming-Liang, *Taoci Shouji* (Handbook of Ceramics) (Taipei: Shitou, 2008).

47. Karl Rudolf, "Exotica bei Karl V., Philipp II. und in der Kunstkammer Rudolfs II," in Helmut Trnek and Sabine Haag, eds., *Exotica: Portugals Entdeckungen im Spiegel fürstlicher Kunst- und Wunderkammern der Renaissance, Jahrbuch des Kunsthistorischen Museums Wien* 3 (Mainz a. R.: Philipp von Zabern, 2001), 181.
48. Craig Clunas, "Oriental Antiquities/Far Eastern Art," *positions* 2, no. 2 (1994), 318–55.
49. Oliver Impey, *Chinoiserie: The Impact of Oriental Styles on Western Art and Decoration* (New York: Scribner, 1977); Hugh Honour, *Chinoiserie: The Vision of Cathay* (London: J. Murray, 1961); Stacey Sloboda, *Chinoiserie: Commerce and Critical Ornament in Eighteenth-Century Britain* (Manchester: Manchester University Press, 2014).
50. Kyoungjin Bae, "Along the Round Globe: The Material Culture of European Round Tables in Mid-Qing China," in "Joints of Utility, Crafts of Knowledge: The Material Culture of the Sino-British Furniture Trade during the Long Eighteenth Century." Ph.D. dissertation (New York: Columbia University, 2016), 180–81.
51. Kyoungjin Bae, "Around the Globe," in Grasskamp and Juneja, *EurAsian Matters*, 37–55.
52. Thomas DaCosta Kaufmann "Scratching the Surface: On the Impact of the Dutch on Artistic and Material Culture in Taiwan and China," in North and Kaufmann, *Mediating Netherlandish Art and Material Culture in Asia*, 205–38.
53. Johnathan A. Farris, *Enclave to Urbanity: Canton, Foreigners, and Architecture from the Late Eighteenth to the Early Twentieth Centuries* (Hong Kong: Hong Kong University Press, 2016). Johnathan A. Farris, "Thirteen Factories of Canton: An Architecture of Sino-Western Collaboration and Confrontation," *Buildings and Landscapes: Journal of the Vernacular Architecture Forum*, 14 (2007), 66–83.
54. Cesar Nuñez, *Macao's Church of Saint Paul, A Glimmer of the Baroque in China* (Hong Kong: Hong Kong University Press, 2009).
55. On imperial architecture, see, for example, Ellen Uitzinger, "For the Man Who Has Everything: Western-Style Exotica in Birthday Celebrations at the Court of Ch'ien-lung," in Leonard Blussé and Erik Zürcher, eds., *Conflict and Accommodation in Early Modern East Asia* (Leiden: Brill, 1993), 216–39. On Jesuit churches see: Cesar Nuñez, "Matteo Ricci, the Nantang, and the Introduction of Roman Catholic Church Architecture to Beijing," in *Portrait of a Jesuit: Matteo Ricci* (Macau: Macau Ricci Institute, 2010). On gardens see: Zou Hui, *A Jesuit Garden in Beijing and Early Modern Chinese Culture* (West Lafayette: Purdue University Press, 2011); Wang Ling, "From La Flèche to Beijing: The Transcultural Moment of Jesuit Garden Spaces," in Grasskamp and Juneja, *EurAsian Matters*, 101–23.
56. Greg Thomas, "Yuanming Yuan/Versailles: Intercultural Interactions between Chinese and European Palace Cultures," *Art History* 32 (2009), 115–43; Michelle Pirazzoli-t'Serstevens, *Le Yuanmingyuan: Jeux d'eau et*

Palais Européens du Xviiie Siecle a la Cour de Chine (Paris: Editions Recherche sur les Civilisations, 1987); Chiu Che-Bing, *Yuanming Yuan: Le Jardin de la Clarté Parfaite* (Besancon: Les Editions de l' Imprimeur, 2000).

57. Susan Delson, ed., *Ai Weiwei: Circle of Animals* (New York: Prestel, 2011).
58. A. Klayman, *Ai Weiwei Circle of Animals/Zodiac Heads*. Documentary trailer, 2010, 2:30. www.zodiacheads.com/about_exhibit_bronze.html.
59. James Hevia, "Plunder, Markets, and Museums: The Biographies of Chinese Imperial Objects in Europe and North America," in Jan Mrazek and Morgan Pitelka, eds., *What's the Use of Art? Asian Visual and Material Culture in Context* (Honolulu: University of Hawai'i Press, 2008), 129–41.
60. Thomas, "Yuanming Yuan/Versailles;" Greg Thomas, "Chinoiserie and Intercultural Dialogue at Brighton Pavilion," in ten-Doeschatte and Ding, *Qing Encounters*, 232–47.
61. On experiments with lacquerware at the court of Dresden see Monika Kopplin and Gisela Haase, eds., *"Sächßisch Lacquirte Sachen": Lackkunst in Dresden unter August dem Starken* (Münster: Museum of Lacquer Art, 1998); Monika Kopplin, "Chrysanthemen am Ostzaun und andere ostasiatische Motive in der Dresdner Lackmalerei," in *Jahrbuch der Staatlichen Kunstsammlungen Dresden* 28 (2000),47–55; Monika Kopplin, *Schwartz Porcelain: Die Leidenschaft für Lack und ihre Wirkung auf das europäische Porzellan* (Münster: Museum of Lacquer Art, 2003); and Monika Kopplin, "Sakesen Gongting Qijiang: Madung Shunier Yu Dongya de Genyuan (Laquer Production at the Court of Saxony: Martins Schnell and his East Asian Sources)," *Gugong Wenwu Yuekan* 320 (2009), 90–105.
62. Patricia Frick, "Die Lackkunst und ihr Weg nach Europa," in Kanzenbach and Suebsman, *Made in China*, 64–73.
63. Friekerike Wappenschmidt, *Chinesische Tapeten für Europa: Vom Rollbild zur Bildtapete* (Berlin: Deutscher Verlag für Kunstwissenschaft, 1989).
64. Kristel Smentek, "Chinoiseries for the Qing: A French Gift of Tapestries to the Qianlong Emperor," *Journal of Early Modern History* 20, no. 1 (2016), 87–109.
65. Chiu Che-Bing, "Vegetal Travel: Western European Plants in the Garden of the Emperor of China," in ten-Doeschatte and Ding, *Qing Encounters*, 95–110; Wang, "From La Flèche to Beijing;" Chang Sheng-Ching, *Dongfang qimeng Xifang: Shiba Shiji Deguo Wolizi (Wörlitz) Ziran Fengjing Yuanlin Zhi Zhongguo Yuansu* (The East Enlightening the West: Chinese Elements in the Eighteenth-Century Landscape Gardens of Wörlitz in Germany) (Taipei: Furendaxue chubanshe, 2015).
66. Andrea Schneider, *Die Handelsgeschichte der Seide: Historische und kulturgeschichtliche Aspekte* (Munich: GRIN Verlag, 2007); Maria João Ferreira, "Chinese Textiles in Portuguese Sacred Interiors During Early Modern Age," in Sabine du Crest, ed., *Exogenèses: Objets frontière dans l'art européen* (Paris: Boccard, 2018), 72–87. Amelia Peck, ed., *Interwoven Globe: The World-Wide Textile Trade, 1500–1800* (New York: Metropolitan Museum of Art, 2013).

67. Mei Mei Rado, "Encountering Magnificence: European Silks at the Qing Court during the Eighteenth Century," in ten-Doeschatte and Ding, *Qing Encounters*, 58–78.
68. Listed in Thomas Platter, *Beschreibung der Reisen durch Frankreich, Spanien, England und die Niederlande, 1595–1600*, ed. Rut Keiser (Basel/Stuttgart: Schwabe, 1968), vol. II, 796f. Translated into English in Clare Williams, *Thomas Platter's Travels in England 1599* (London: Jonathan Cape, 1937), 171–73.
69. For a discussion of the painting see Wu Hung, "Emperor's Masquerade: Costume Portraits of Yongzheng and Qianlong," *Orientations* 26, no. 7 (1995), 25–41.
70. See Grasskamp, "EurAsian Layers," 392, notes 90, 91.
71. "Hans Sloane Describes a 'China Cabinet'," in Susan Pearce and Ken Arnold, eds., *The Collector's Voice: Critical readings in the History of Collecting, Volume II: The Early Voices* (Farnham: Ashgate, 2001), 106–09.
72. Wilt Idema, "Cannon, Clocks and Clever Monkeys: Europeana, Europeans and Europe in some Eighteenth-Century Chinese Novels," in W. J. J. Schipper et al., eds., *White and Black Imagination and Cultural Confrontations, Bulletin of the Royal Tropical Institute* 320 (Amsterdam: Koninklijk Instituut voor de Tropen, 1990), 54–82; Brigitte Kremer, "Kunstfertigkeit und Glockenklang: Mechanische Uhren und Automaten für die Kaiser von China," in Renate Eikelmann, ed., *Die Wittelsbacher und das Reich der Mitte: 400 Jahre China und Bayern* (Munich: Hirmer, 2009), 130–39; Joseph Needham, Wang Ling, and Derek J. De Solla Price, *Heavenly Clockwork: The Great Astronomical Clocks of Medieval China* (Cambridge: Cambridge University Press, 1960); Joanna Waley-Cohen, "Diplomats, Jesuits, and Foreign Curiosities," in Evelyn Rawski and Jessica Rawson, eds., *The Three Emperors: Art and Power in Qing Dynasty China* (London: Royal Academy of Arts, 2005), 178–207; Zhang Baichun, "The Importation of European Clock and Watch Technology into China and the Questions Related during the late Ming and Qing Dynasties (1580–1911)," *Journal of Dialectics of Nature* 17, no. 2 (1995), 38–46; Zhang Pu and Guo Fuxiang, *L'art de L'horlogerie Occidental et la Chine* (Beijing: China Intercontinental Press, 2005); Zheng Yangwen, *China on the Sea: How the Maritime World Shaped Modern China* (Leiden: Brill, 2012), 135–68.
73. Jessica Keating, *Animating Empire: Automata, the Holy Roman Empire, and the Early Modern World* (University Park: Penn State University Press, 2018).
74. Joyce Lindorff, "Missionaries, Keyboards and Musical Exchange in the Ming and Qing Courts," *Early Music* 32, no. 3 (2004), 405–14.
75. Shih Ching-fe, *Riyue guanghua: Qinggong huafalang* (Radiant Luminance: The Painted Enamelware of the Qing Imperial Court) (Taipei: National Palace Museum, 2012); Shih Ching-fei, "Shiba Shiji Dongxi Jiaoliu De Jianzheng: Qinggong Huafalang Zhizuo Zai Kangxi Chao De Jianli

(Evidence of East-West Exchange in the Eighteenth Century: The Establishment of Painted Enamel Art at the Qing Court in the Reign of Emperor Kangxi)," *Gugong Xueshu Jikan* 24, no. 3 (2007), 45–95.
76. Willemijn van Noord and Thijs Weststeijn, "The Global Trajectory of Nicolaas Witsen's Chinese Mirror," *The Rijksmuseum Bulletin* 4 (2015), 325–61.
77. Libby Lai-Pik Chan and Nina Lai-Na Wan, eds., *The Silver Age: Origins and Trade of Chinese Export Silver* (Hong Kong: Hong Kong Maritime Museum, 2017).
78. Liu Lihong, "Vitreous Views: Materiality and Mediality of Glass in Qing China through a Transcultural Prism," *Getty Research Journal* 8 (2016), 17–38.
79. Juneja and Grasskamp, "EurAsian Matters," in *EurAsian Matters*.
80. Shih Ching-fei, "The Wooden Hundred-layered Goblet from the Western Ocean," *Orientations* 48, no. 4 (2015), 60–64; Shih Ching-fei, "'Xuanzi' ji 'Zhuanyi': Quanqiushi Shiye Xia De 'Xiyang' Duo Ceng Mu Tao Bei (Global Visual Studies Perspectives on Multi-Layered Wooden Cups from the 'Western Ocean')," *Yishuxue Yanjiu* 21 (2017), 1–76.
81. Shih Ching-fei, "Unknown Transcultural Objects: Turned Ivory Works by the European Rose Engine Lathe in the Eighteenth-Century Qing Court," in Juneja and Grasskamp, *EurAsian Matters*, 57–76.
82. Craig Clunas, *Chinese Carving* (Singapore: Sun Tree, 1996); Shih Ching-fei, "Xiangya qiu Suojian Zhi Gongyi Jishu Jiaoliu-Guangdong, Qinggong Yu Shensheng Luoma Diguo (Concentric Ivory Spheres and the Exchange of Craft Techniques: Canton, the Q'ing Court and the Holy Roman Empire)," *Gugong xueshu jikan* 25, no. 2 (2007), 87–138.
83. For example: Chitqua (attributed to), *A Dutch Merchant, Possibly Andreas Everardus van Braam Houckgeest*, c. 1770, Canton (Guangzhou), unfired clay and polychrome glaze, h 6.5cm × w 31.5cm × d 20.0cm, Rijksmuseum, Amsterdam.
84. Jan van Campen and Ebltje Hartkamp-Jonxis, *Asian Splendour: Company Art in the Rijksmuseum* (Zutphen: Walburg, 2011), 73.
85. Clunas, *Chinese Carving*; Beatriz Sanchez Navarro de Pintado, *Marfiles cristianos del oriente en México* (Mexico: Fomento Cultural Banamex, 1986).
86. On uses of the term "Indian" in German inventories and other written sources around 1600 see Anna Grasskamp, "Unpacking Foreign Ingenuity: The German Conquest of 'Artful' Objects with 'Indian' Provenance," in Richard Oosterhoff, José R. Marcaida, and Alexander Marr, eds., *Ingenuity in the Making: Matter and Technique in Early Modern Art and Science* (Pittsburgh: Pittsburgh University Press, 2021), 213–28..
87. Frederike Wappenschmidt, "Object Commentary 1725 (1617)," in Willibald Sauerländer, Peter Diemer et al., eds., *Die Münchner Kunstkammer* (Munich: C. H. Beck, 2008), 538.

88. Maureen Cassidy-Geiger, "Changing Attitudes towards Ethnographic Material: Rediscovering the Soapstone Collection of Augustus the Strong," *Abhandlungen und Berichte des Staatlichen Museums für Völkernkunde Dresden* 48 (1994), 26–31; Maureen Cassidy-Geiger, "Forgotten Sources for Early Meissen Figures: Rediscovering the Chinese Carved Soapstone and Dutch Red Earthenware Figures from the Japanese Palace of Augustus Strong," *American Ceramic Circle* 10 (1997): 55–72.

89. On Europe: Kim Siebenhüner, *Die Spur der Juwelen: Materielle Kultur und transnationale Verbindungen* (Vienna, Cologne, and Weimar: Böhlau, 2018); On China: Craig Clunas, "Precious Stones and Ming Culture, 1400–1450," in Craig Clunas et al., eds., *Ming: Courts and Contacts* (London: The British Museum, 2016), 236–44.

90. Anna Grasskamp, "Branches and Bones: The Transformative Matter of Coral in Ming Dynasty China," in Michael Bycroft and Sven Dupré, eds., *Gems in the Early Modern World: Materials, Knowledge, and Global Trade, 1450–1800, Europe's Asian Centuries* (Basingstoke: Palgrave MacMillan, 2018), 118–47; Pippa Lacey, "The Coral Network: The Trade of Red Coral to the Qing Imperial Court in the Eighteenth Century," in Gerritsen and Riello, *The Global Lives of Things*, 81–102; Olivier Raveux, "Du Corail de Méditerranée pour l'Asie: Les Ventes du Marchand Marseillais François Garnier à Smyrne vers 1680," in Xavier Daumalin, Daniel Faget, and Olivier Raveux, eds., *La Mer en Partage: Sociétés Littorales et Économies Maritimes (XVIe–XIXe siècle)* (Aix-en-Provence: University Press of Provence, 2016),343–59; Gedalia Yogev, *Diamonds and Coral: Anglo-Dutch Jews and Eighteenth-Century Trade* (London: Leicester University Press, 1978).

91. Chen Kaijun, "Transcultural Lenses: Wrapping the Foreignness for Sale in the History of Lenses," in Grasskamp and Juneja, *EurAsian Matters*, 77–98.

92. Nicole Halsberghe, "The Resemblances and Differences of the Construction of Ferdinand Verbiest's Astronomical Instruments, as Compared with Those of Tycho Brahe," in John Witek, ed., *Ferdinand Verbiest, S.J. (1623–1688), Jesuit Missionary, Scientist, Engineer and Diplomat*, (Nettetal: Steyler, 1994), 85–92; Catherine Jami, "Western Devices for Time and Space Measurement: Clocks and Euclidian Geometry in Late Ming and Ch'ing China," in Huang C Chün-chieh and Erik Zürcher, eds., *Time and Space in Chinese Culture* (Leiden: Brill, 1995), 169–200.

93. Wang, "From La Flèche to Beijing."

94. Lihong Liu, "Pyrotechnic Profusion: Fireworks, Spectacles, and Automata in Time," *Journal 18: A Journal of Eighteenth-Century Art and Culture* 3 (2017), www.journal18.org/1550; Brenda Buchanan, "Making Fireworks," in Brenda Buchanan, ed., *Gunpowder Plots: A Celebration of 400 Years of Bonfire Night* (London: Penguin Books, 2005), 145–88.

95. Tonio Andrade, "Cannibals with Cannons: The Sino-Portuguese Clashes of 1521–22 and the Early Chinese Adoption of Western Guns," *Journal of Early Modern History* 19, no. 4 (2015), 311–36.
96. As mentioned in an early seventeenth-century letter, see Philipp Hainhofer, "Letter to Duke August of Braunschweig-Lüneburg, 1613–47," R. Gobiet, transcriber, in Philipp Hainhofer, *Der Briefwechsel zwischen Philipp Hainhofer und Herzog August d. J. von Braunschweig-Lüneburg* (Berlin: Deutscher Kunstverlag, 1983), 846f.
97. Grasskamp, "EurAsian Layers"; Grasskamp and Juneja, *EurAsian Matters*.
98. Ulrike Gleixner, "Unlesbare Schriften: Bestände von Weltensammlern des 18. Jahrhunderts in der Herzog August Bibliothek," in Birgitte Neumann, ed., *Präsenz und Evidenz fremder Dinge im Europa des 18. Jahrhunderts* (Göttingen: Wallstein Verlag, 2015), 203–17.
99. Grasskamp, "EurAsian Layers."
100. *fenster*. Frederike Wappenschmidt, "Object Commentary 1955 (1854)," in *Die Münchner Kunstkammer*, vol. 2, 600.
101. "*tuech*. Regest 5556," in Heinrich Zimerman, "Urkunden, Acten und Regesten aus dem Archiv des Ministeriums des Innern Herausgegeben," *Jahrbuch der Kunsthistorischen Sammlungen des Allerhöchsten Kaiserhauses* 7 (1888), II, 307.
102. Igor Kopytoff, "The Cultural Biography of Things: Commoditization as a Process," in Arjun Appadurai, ed., *The Social Life of Things: Commodities in Cultural Perspective* (Cambridge: Cambridge University Press, 1986), 64–91.
103. Gerritsen and Riello, *The Global Lives of Things*.
104. Zoltan Biedermann, Anne Gerritsen, and Giorgio Riello, eds., *Global Gifts: The Material Culture of Diplomacy in Early Modern Eurasia* (Cambridge and New York: Cambridge University Press, 2017).
105. Huang Xingzeng, *Xiyang Chaogong Dianlu* (Records of Tributes from the Western Ocean Countries), 1520.
106. Tansen Sen, *Buddhism, Diplomacy and Trade: The Realignment of Sino-Indian Relations, 600–1400* (Honolulu: University of Hawai'i Press, 2003), 210, referencing Liu Xinru, Ancient India and *Ancient China: Trade and Religious Exchanges, AD 1–600* (Delhi: Oxford University Press, 1988); John Kieschnick, *The Impact of Buddhism on Chinese Material Culture* (Princeton: Princeton University Press, 2003).
107. Sen, *Buddhism, Diplomacy and Trade*, 198.
108. Christine Göttler, "Extraordinary Things: 'Idols from India' and the Visual Discernment of Space," in Göttler and Mochizuki, *The Nomadic Object*, 37–73.
109. Robert S. Sharf, "Introduction: Prolegomenon to the Study of Japanese Buddhist Icons," in Robert Sharf and Elizabeth Horton Sharf, eds., *Living Images: Japanese Buddhist Icons in Context* (Stanford: Stanford University Press, 2001), 8. The case of Chinese sculpture is treated in

Bernard Faure, "Metamorphoses of the Double (II): 'Sublime Corpses' and Icons," in *The Rhethoric of Immediacy: A Cultural Critique of Chan/Zen Buddhism* (Princeton: Princeton University Press, 1991), 148–79.

110. David Freedberg, *The Power of Images: Studies in the History and Theory of Response* (Chicago: University of Chicago Press, 1989), 84ff. For a critique of Freedberg's interpretation of the consecration of a Buddha statue see Ernst Gombrich, "Review of David Freedberg, *The Power of Images: Studies in the History and Theory of Response*," *New York Review of Books* 15 (1990), 7. Gell's anthropology of art and his concept of agency is discussed in relation to religious representations, including a thirteenth-century Japanese statue, in Jeremy Tanner, "Portraits and Agency: A Comparative View," in Robin Osborne and Jeremy Tanner, eds., *Art's Agency and Art History* (Malden and Oxford: Blackwell, 2007), 70–94.
111. Grasskamp, "EurAsian Layers," 374.
112. Caroline van Eck, "Living Statues: Alfred Gell's Art and Agency, Living Presence Response and the Sublime," *Art History* 33, no. 4 (2010), 644, which refers to Alfred Gell's posthumously published *Art and Agency: An Anthropological Theory*, 1998.
113. Marco Spallanzani, *Ceramiche Orientali a Firenze nel Rinascinto* (Florence: Chiari, 1978); Marco Spallanzani, *Ceramiche alla Corte der Medici nel Cinquecento* (Modena: Franco Cosimo Panim, 1994).
114. Tim Ingold, "Materials against Materiality," *Archaeological Dialogues* 14, no. 1 (2007), 1–16.
115. Marta Ajmar, "Mechanical Disegno," *RIHA Journal* 84 (2014), 27.
116. Ajmar, "The Renaissance in Material Culture," 684.
117. Ibid.
118. Lothar Ledderose, *Ten Thousand Things: Module and Mass Production in Chinese Art* (Princeton: Princeton University Press, 2000).
119. Susan Du Crest, *L'Art de Vivre Ensemble: Objets Frontière de la Renaissance au XXIe siècle* (Rome: Gangemi, 2017).
120. Smentek, "Global Circulations, Local Transformations," 41.
121. Pinney, "Creole Europe," 126.
122. Jane Bennett, *Vibrant Matter: A Political Ecology of Things* (Durham: Duke University Press, 2010).
123. Exhibition examples include *Imperial China: The Forbidden City and the Royal Danish Court* at Christiansborg Slot (Copenhagen, October 5–December 10, 2006), *Goldener Drache–Weißer Adler: Kunst im Dienste der Macht am Kaiserhof von China und am sächsisch-polnischen Hof (1644–1795)* at Staatliche Kunstsammlungen Dresden, Residenzschloss (Dresden, October 11, 2008–January 11, 2009), *Die Wittelsbacher und das Reich der Mitte. 400 Jahre China und Bayern*, Bayerisches Nationalmuseum (Munich, March 27, 2009–July 26, 2009), and *China: Through the Looking Glass* at the Metropolitan Museum of Art (New York, May 7–September 7, 2015).

13

Migration and Material Culture

Magdalena Naum

Introduction

When people migrate, so do their material possessions. Carefully packed or grabbed in a hurry, material objects shape the experiences of migration, processes of home making, and a sense of belonging. Attention to the material dimensions of migration is a prominent aspect of the recent anthropological and sociological research focusing on mobility and cultural practices of migrants and diaspora communities. This interest is reflected in the exemplary questions asked by this scholarship: what are the migrants' relationships with material objects in a moment of packing, unpacking, and furnishing their new homes? What is the impact of displacement on the real and imaginary engagements with material objects? What is the role of objects in shaping identity and structuring the experience of migration?

The attention to material culture was not always explicit or at the forefront of migration studies in the humanities and social sciences.[1] For a long time the scholarship was preoccupied with understanding the reasons and patterns of migration, modeling the mechanisms of human movements, and mapping integration strategies. This was the focus of the pioneering research of the nineteenth-century geographer Ernst G. Ravenstein who viewed migration as arising "from the desire inherent in most men to 'better' themselves in material respects"[2] and who formulated general, apolitical, and ahistorical laws governing migration.[3] These basic laws were refined and developed by subsequent scholarship of, for example, William Petersen and Everett Lee who proposed the so-called push and pull model or equilibrium model.[4] Lee explained migration as the interplay of push causes (negative conditions in home region) and pull factors (positive conditions in destination region) mediated through the availability of transport and channeling of the flow of information about the destination. He also stressed a transitional and ambivalent relationship of migrants with their place of origin and destination, pointing out that immigrants take on characteristics of the population at the destination to eventually assimilate but they may hold on to the practices they share with the population at the point of origin for a long time.

In the 1960s and 1970s, in the wake of large-scale labor migration from the global South to the global North, this way of framing migration was challenged by structuralist approaches drawing on Marxist thought and world-system theories. These approaches shifted attention to the macro-level processes that shaped and sustained population movements.[5] Migration was regarded as an aspect of the world capitalist system founded on social disparity and domination (human movement was seen as a means of providing cheap labor for the capitalists in the developed countries), where the role of migration was "to maintain inequality, not to reduce it."[6] It was assumed and observed that these conditions would lead to segregation (imposed by the host society) and creation of ethnic enclaves (by the migrants) with transplanted material practices decreasing the chances of immigrant assimilation with the host communities.

The current way of conceptualizing migration, and cultural processes it fosters, stems from another historical, theoretical, and methodological shift that happened in the late 1980s and 1990s. The observed diversity of migration and migrant experiences, complex cultural negotiations that were happening within and between migrant communities and the host groups, made the previous model-thinking too rigid and inadequate. Selecting individuals and migrant households as the units of analysis, this new paradigm brought the "migrant-as-decision-maker" into major focus reintroducing, at the same time, social and cultural factors as crucial for understanding migrant and diaspora experiences and practices. The standard sets of questions started to include processes of belonging and exclusion, transnational practices, use of memory in construction of diaspora and migrant identities, interactions within migrant/diaspora communities, and between these communities and the majority of the society, as well as the role of institutions in mediating identities and as forums for socializing and status seeking.[7] Simultaneously, the ongoing material and affective turns that emerged in the 1990s drew attention to the importance of material objects as emotional and biographical devices framing and shaping experiences of dislocation. Case studies of historical and contemporary migrations attuned to this materiality perspective show how movements of people and things are interrelated and how this interrelatedness may be influenced by the gender and socioeconomics of migrants as well as the circumstances of migration.[8] They draw attention to how material possessions of the migrants become incorporated into routines and rituals in their new homes, as practical and symbolic semblances of old life, comforting tokens of the home country, or enshrined mementoes of the past.[9] They illustrate the emotional resonance of specific objects around which migrants build narratives of belonging, identity, and continuity with a time and place.[10] However, they also draw attention to the complexities, even contradictions the experiences and encounters with objects engender. While physical presence of material possessions and the memory and imagination surrounding them may help the migrants to experience existential continuity, the same concreteness of objects and their association with past life proves to be a painful reminder of loss, dissolution, and unhomeliness for some.[11] Another thread that is explored in recent studies of migration is the central role material objects play in maintaining transnational connections as a way of compensating for physical absence and retaining social relations.[12]

These concerns and interests are also guiding my diachronic exploration of the subject of migration and material culture in this chapter. Reviewing case studies spanning from early modern colonial transatlantic migration to modern economic and political displacement, I focus on how the historically, economically, and socially diverse individuals and groups used and continue to use material objects in dealing with dislocation and how material objects are structuring their experience of migration and belonging.

Packing and Unpacking the Suitcase

A material object that is intrinsically connected with mobility is a suitcase (or its pre- and early modern version of sea chest, trunk, or knapsack).[13] Besides its obvious practical character, as a container of selected belongings packed together and carried from the point of departure to the destination, a suitcase is also a highly symbolic and emotional object. Örvar Löfgren theorizes it as a physical and cultural container "of not only stuff but also emotions, longings and memories,"[14] a material concentration of a person. A suitcase is "a condensation of future, an icon of mobility, a nostalgic museum, a threatening or comforting object, a defense against a hostile world."[15] He observes that the objects that are put together in the migrant suitcases, as well as the act of packing, respond to different temporalities and realities. The packing is done in a present, yet a suitcase simultaneously looks to the future and harks back to the past. It contains things that are available at hand but already in the moment of packing they acquire an aura of the past, encapsulating life that is soon to be ruptured, changed, and relocated to memories. But packing is also about the future, anticipation and planning for the journey and new life, evaluation of what objects are essential, useful, and meaningful. A suitcase thus is a continuity, an invocation, "an attempt at controlling the future and materializing the past."[16] In that sense packing is also about engaging with different realities and projections. On the one hand, it is a multisensory engagement with objects at hand, encounters with their materiality connected with one's physicality and history. On the other hand, it is about imagining, placing oneself and the contents of the suitcase in the future, making abstractions, envisioning the destination and the new home.

The content of migrant suitcases varies. Those who have time to plan their relocation in advance pack carefully most of their possessions. (One of the post-World War II migrants to Australia reminisced: "We brought all the furniture over from Holland, all our beds and lounge suite, you name it. The whole house was empty and put in the big crate."[17] Another: "The farm was sold to family members; men came and packed up everything we thought we would need in Australia into two big packing cases. ... We brought our fridge, washing machine, pushbikes, stoves, clogs, household items and kitchenware.")[18] The exilees and refugees leaving in panic pack hastily, throwing together only a few essential things. (Bosnian refugees recall: "We decided to leave everything. I came to Vienna with a paper bag for a suitcase ... my father and my mother came here as refugees with a plastic bag, leaving everything behind like me."[19] "I only brought my name with me.")[20] What is taken by the migrants is also historically and culturally specific and depends on the socioeconomic background of those who move.

In the seventeenth century, a period that brought about huge global dislocations of free, indentured, and enslaved populations, the art and skill of packing for the colonies was supported by manuals and instructions. Learning from the problems and mistakes of the earliest groups of European settlers and the observations of the explorers, broadsheets and provision lists were put together and published for those considering transatlantic migration. Francis Higginson, an early Puritan minister in colonial New England, advised prospective migrants: "Before you come ... be careful to be strongly instructed what things are fittest to bring with you for your more comfortable passage at sea, as also for your husbandry occasions when you come to land. For when you are once parted with England you shall meet neither with taverns nor alehouses, nor butchers, nor grocers, nor apothecaries' shops to help with things you need, in the midst of the great ocean nor when you come to land."[21] Higginson also authored a general provision list, one of several targeting Englishmen relocating to America in the 1630s. This and other lists published in England and the Netherlands included food and drink, apparel for different seasons, sewing implements, bedding, arms, and a variety of household utensils and tools that were supposed to sustain a migrant for a period of one year to eighteen months.[22] These colonial packing lists reflected expectations as to the establishment of one's own bearings in the colonies and were meant to assure survival and minimal liability of the newcomers for the already established settlers. They were also comforting documents for the prospective settlers: enumeration of familiar objects "domesticated" the image of America making it a little less strange and a little more tangible.

What was actually packed by individual families varied considerably according to their means. Some individuals packed well beyond what was suggested by the lists; others could only afford minimal amounts of victuals, basic tools, and apparel. Among the belongings were also sentimental objects, like a "parcel of very fine linen of great value, which she set her heart too much upon."[23] Provision lists read along with the probate inventories of the first generations of settlers and reviewed against archaeological material give an impression of migrants, at least those better off, carrying all or most of their possessions to America allowing them to reconstruct the exteriors and interiors of their lost homes and continue with familiar domestic practices.

Complex relationships with material culture and difficult processes of packing were experienced by the community of Mormons who in the 1840s–60s were forced out of Illinois, Iowa, and Missouri and tracked westward to Utah and California. Russell Belk studied diaries and letters of this displaced group to understand their material world – the contents of their chests and trunks and the utilitarian and sentimental value the packed objects had for the individuals.[24] The migration was styled in strong religious and mythological terms as a march toward the Promised Land. This metanarrative partially conditioned attitudes toward possessions as related to three stages of the journey: sacrifice, trial, and rebirth in paradise. Many prized possessions that could not fit into the limited space of chests had to be left behind, sacrificed for the sake of the journey. What was taken were often practical things: "Just our commonest clothing, which would stand the hard wear of traveling as we did. The tent was our covering, and the overcoat spread on the bare ground with the shawl over us was our bed. My feather bed and bedding, pillows, all our good clothing ... all had to be left."[25] This act of packing had to be repeated several times along the route, each time reducing the number of possessions allowed to be taken along. This selectiveness was considered a necessary sacrifice and trial, a physical and religious purge of material things, attachment to which was discouraged by Mormonism. Still, parting with familiar objects was met with anxiety and strong emotional reactions, especially by women who were more likely to anguish over the move and unwilling to leave without treasured household possessions. Belk observed also gendered differences in the objects prioritized to be packed: men valued tools, guns, and watches, while women were more likely to keep domestic objects, sewing machines, spinning wheels, clothing, heirlooms, and furniture.[26] Heirlooms provided emotional comfort and security, awaking memories of home and family, countering the sense of loss, confusion, and "stripped" identity. Belk found that the possessions that were kept and unpacked at the new location helped in creating or reestablishing feelings of competence and domesticity. The process of unpacking, appropriating salvaged objects to decorate new homes was an especially common thread in the diaries of women who, in the era of the Victorian cult of domesticity and after suffering the ordeal of a cross-country journey, regarded homemaking as an integral aspect of their gendered identity and a reassuring act of creating permanence.[27]

The gendered differences in what was packed and how objects feature in the narratives of migration and relocation are also present in the oral stories of post–World War II migrants moving to Australia recorded in the project Belongings: Post-WW2 Migration Memories and Journeys (Case Study 13.1). Reviewing these first-person narratives, Ilaria Vanni argued that the objects migrants brought with them and continued to engage with are central to their identities grounded in the experience of migration:

Case Study 13.1

Belongings: post-World War II migration memories and journeys

"Belongings" was an online project initiated by John Petersen and curated by Andrea Fernandes at the North South Wales Migration Heritage Centre. It documented oral histories of about 90 immigrants from 44 different countries/ cultural backgrounds who arrived in Australia between 1947 and 1974. The interviewed persons were encouraged to incorporate their material belongings in their stories by answering the questions: "What did you bring with you and why? How much could you bring with you? Were there items you regretted leaving behind? Why?"

The full project is archived at www.migrationheritage.nsw.gov.au/belongings/index.html. Below are a few selected narratives:

> Rosina Rombola (from San Ferdinando, Italy; arrived in 1952):
>
> The ladies from the neighborhood came to help me pack. The old ones would say, "They don't have this in Australia so take this with you." I packed three trunks plus suitcases to bring with us. I had walnut veneer trunks: two I still keep in my bedroom and use to store my extra blankets and the other I keep in the shed. My mother and father had them made for me when I married. The trunks have cracked with the heat over the years but I still use them. I tried to get as much in them as possible when I came to Australia. I packed our clothes, saucepans, glasses, cups, the *sculla pasta* (colander). The *zuppa* (soup) bowls [once] were a set of six. I have only two left now but I used them at breakfast time every morning. … I have used these enamel mixing bowls for everything: making dough for pasta and breads, cakes. As you can see they are well used and I always said when they get a hole in them I will throw them away but they still haven't. … I probably would not have brought so much but the older relatives would say 'take this' and 'take that, so I brought anything that would fit.
>
> Anna Grenadier (from Biecz, Poland; arrived in 1973):
>
> I brought things out with me from Poland that are very special and could not be left behind. These are things that are meaningful to me. They remind you of your people and friends whom you love. …

> Case Study 13.1 (cont.)
>
> This beautiful crystal plate is from my godmother and it was one of her wedding presents. My mother, Emilia, gave me this very small one-flower crystal vase and pressed dried flower; it is the only thing that I have from her. When my father retired, he bought me a sewing machine and a huge dinner set. I couldn't bring the sewing machine and I was trying to bring the dinner set but the Polish authority would not let me. They considered it to be a Polish antique and would not allow it out of the country. My sister now has it in her house, although I pinched one plate and two smaller salt and pepper plates. Every time we have family get-togethers or Christmas, these are on the table.
>
> Antonio Cunial (from Possagno, Italy; arrived in 1948):
>
> I only had one change of clothes and brought the wooden case with barbers' tools with me. I never paid for the case because a man made it in return for cutting his hair. I had been conscripted into the Italian Army and one of my jobs was to cut my company's hair [1st Infantry Regt, in 5th Company at Cividale, Udine]. There were about 60 men and I cut their hair for 18 months.
>
> Walter Schmied (from St Polten, Austria; arrived in 1959):
>
> We brought a few belongings out with us to Australia, including a gold coffee set from Austria. It was a wedding present from my friend who was best man at my wedding and I treasure it as a memory of my migration and also of my friend. The decanter set which is of china and in the shape of a barrel was also a wedding present from another of the best men. I value it for the memory of him and of Austria. The glass wine dispenser also came out from Austria with us. We purchased it ourselves as we liked to entertain and it is used by us often in dispensing the wine at parties. It is very attractive and unusual and a fond memory of my homeland.

"they emplace and enact multiple geographies of 'home', including its opposite, 'the unhomely'" or being out of place.[28] As building blocks of migrant biographies, the salvaged, often everyday objects help in reestablishing familiar domestic interiors, habits, and routines, and by doing so combat the overwhelming sense of homesickness and estrangement. The interviewed immigrant women especially, articulate how continuous handling of brought objects in mundane and ritualized situations creates a sense of home as remembered from their childhood and youth prior to migration.

This ability of objects to lessen feelings of loneliness, estrangement, and isolation and to anchor identity and create a sense of homeliness is documented in many studies of postwar and more recent migration (Case Study 13.2 and 13.3).[29] In John Berger's study of migrant guest workers moving to

Case Study 13.2

What reminds me of home in Syria

What reminds me of home in Syria by Michel Youssef (Figure 13.1)

> I am from Syria and came to the Netherlands as a refugee. These two objects remind me of home a lot.
>
> I left Syria in 2014. I had a great life there. I worked at the Indonesian embassy, had my own apartment and a car. I was happy.
>
> When the war started everything changed, life became worse and worse in my area. We moved to another city, and then to another city. It affected my work and my life. As a man, I was being forced to fight – I could not, it's not me, it's not my war.
>
> I had to run away with my mother and sister. I had to protect them. Still the war was getting worse and worse, so I moved to Istanbul in Turkey. I found a job there but after 6 months the job ended. I had nothing, I couldn't go back to Syria, or stay in Istanbul. Moving to Europe was not a choice from beginning. I had skills and didn't think of myself as a refugee.
>
> Eventually, I came to the Netherlands after having travelled through Greece and Italy. It was very expensive to come to Europe, I had saved money and spent €12,000 to get a boat from Turkey to Greece. The boat was very small, with 60 people. I was afraid for others, for the children and the woman. It was super dangerous.
>
> As soon as I arrived in Italy, I became a refugee. It wasn't easy to accept myself as a refugee. I had two cousins in Netherlands, who suggested to come there.
>
> In Syria, I had my own house and car and suddenly I have nothing. I was living in a refugee camp in Netherlands. I was sharing a room with 15 people. It was really traumatizing. I had to start again from zero. I didn't have a network, didn't speak the language.
>
> Over time, I eventually got a job and found an apartment in Amsterdam. When I was more settled in Netherlands, I asked my mother, who still lives in Damascus, to send these things to me as I missed having them around me.
>
> The first is an award I got when I was in the scouts. I got this in 2005. There was an event where around 250 people were camping. As part of the event, there was a competition and award for the best leader. I won this award. It really opened my eyes about who I could be. Before, I was a bit insecure about myself but this showed me who I could be. I promised myself that I would keep it until I died, it is very important to me.
>
> The second is my shisha. Shisha for us is about time spent with family and friends. We invite them, the shisha brings us all together. We connect shisha with talking, fun, love, being *gezellig*, as the Dutch say. If there is no shisha, we feel bored. This shisha is very old, I've had it for around 15 years. Part of the shisha is broken. I remember when it broke, the accident was funny. We laughed a lot and I remember that when I see the broken part.

Case Study 13.2 (cont.)

I still miss a lot from Syria. I once thought that I missed the community, the way we live there – big things. But sometimes it's very small things I miss: the steps I used to sit on with friends, shisha, cafes I used to visit, the jasmine trees in the garden that I sat under every morning.

I now don't really feel I belong to one country, but more in places which have meaning for me or good memories. In a while, I wonder there will be places here that have that same meaning for me.

Courtesy of Europeana Foundation,
2084002_Ag_EU_Migration_ugc

Figure 13.1 What reminds me of home in Syria. Courtesy of Europeana Foundation.

> **Case Study 13.3**
>
> **Feeling at home in a new home**
>
> Feeling at home in a new home/Macrameul de acasa by Simina Badica (Figure 13.2)
>
>> I never appreciated very much these decorations when I was back home. They were everywhere in my grandmother's apartment in Bucharest and more or less in everybody else's grandmothers' homes, on cupboards, beneath flower vases, on the TV sets.
>>
>> I actually found them quite ridiculous – until I moved from Bucharest to Brussels to work as a curator in the House of European History.
>>
>> I took one of these macrame aprons with me by chance as I had borrowed one from my grandmother for an exhibition I had curated that year.
>>
>> I remember walking around my new big, already furnished house in Brussels, trying to make it feel like home. I was failing. And then I put the macrame on a cupboard and there it was: HOME!
>>
>> Courtesy of Europeana Foundation, Europeana Migration Collection Day: Brussels, House of European History, Brussels, 2018–03–15–2018–03–17; 2084002_Ag_EU_Migration_ugc

Figure 13.2 Feeling at home in a new home/Macrameul de acasa. Courtesy of Europeana Foundation.

northern Europe from the southern and eastern part of the continent in the 1960s and 1970s, the sense of dwelling and overcoming alienation was achieved by "remembering through physical things of personal importance."[30] The lives of Turkish migrants, one of the largest groups among guest workers, were generally marked by rupture and loss of familial and social relations. Their suitcases filled with everyday objects, such as clothing, household objects, and food, also enclosed photographs and other personal objects. Berger observes the deeply emotional value of the objects and suitcases as protective containers:

> In certain barracks the authorities have tried to forbid migrant workers keeping their suitcases in their sleeping rooms on the grounds that they make the room untidy. The workers have strongly resisted this, sometimes to the point of going on strike. In these suitcases they keep personal possessions, not the clothes put in the wardrobes, not the photographs they pin to the wall, but articles which, for one reason or another, are their talismans. Each suitcase, locked or tied around with cord, is like a man's memory. They defend their right to keep the suitcases.[31]

The limited spaces of suitcases meant that not all objects involved in the material habits and visual grammar of everyday life were transported from Turkey. Sometimes their absence produced a deep discomfort reaffirming or deepening the sense of being out of place. This feeling of out-of-placeness caused by the lack of specific objects and the contrasting sense of homeliness when these objects were retrieved is poignantly recalled by guest workers who migrated from Turkey to Vienna interviewed by Özlem Savaş:

> I had a very hard time my first two years in Vienna. Everything, even the lack of tea glasses was a big problem. I am addicted to tea, like many Turkish people. But I could not drink proper tea in Vienna in those years. I was told that I could not find a teapot and tea glasses in Vienna. I brought a teapot with me, but forgot the glasses. Cups or big ordinary glasses do not make me feel like drinking tea. It does not taste like tea. Anyway, after two years, I could finally go back to Turkey and of course bought tea glasses. I brought back a set of six tea glasses with their plates, spoons, everything. Believe me, my life became easier. I remember. On the evening of the day I arrived back in Vienna, I made tea and drank it with my glasses. That was the first time that I delightfully drank tea in Vienna. I felt that I was drinking tea. But also, it is strange; I felt as if I was drinking tea *at home*.[32]

Savaş's research draws attention not only to the importance of specific objects brought from home in recreating a sense of belonging and emplacement. He also signals that the Turkish community in Austria developed its own understanding of materialized Turkishness or "Turkish taste," the meaning of which is negotiated between the first and the second generation of migrants. For many Turks, what was originally planned as a temporal economic sojourn in northern European countries, turned into permanent stays followed by family reunification programs.[33] This development resulted in a mass migration of objects from Turkey and a proliferation of specialized shops shaping and answering to a particular "Turkish taste." Savaş concluded that this taste is not a self-evident inherited cultural form existing prior to migration. It is neither a simple blending of material elements stemming from the mainstream Turkish and Austrian cultures. Rather it is a taste shaped within specific processes and paths of displacement and dwelling of both people and objects: by biographies of migration and resettlement, particular experiences of Western Europe and Turkey, and locally articulated relations of production, retail, and consumption.[34] A parallel process of defining Turkishness was observed in case studies conducted in Germany and the Netherlands. There too it is about creating a specific feel or ambiance with the use of traditional, sometimes region-specific objects brought from Turkey arranged in a way that resonates with a particular sense of homeliness.[35]

Packing and unpacking done by the refugees entails yet other negotiations and logic. Those that flee because of violence, war, and the denial of human rights do not always have time to pack. Critically, what is often lacking among their belongings are specific pieces of paper – the appropriate passports and visas. This material absence marks them as "the undocumented" and "the illegal" and more than anything else inhibits their journey.[36]

Bosnian refugees that fled the genocide of the Bosnian War recall the stories of crossing multiple borders, being variously identified as unwanted and protected, and the hurried packing preceding their flight. With no time to search for and fill suitcases, they stuffed only a few belongings into shopping bags.[37] These belongings, as well as souvenirs brought on the subsequent visits to Bosnia and Herzegovina, tend to become physically and emotionally enshrined. They emanate strong affective auras. An extreme example, quoted by Eleanor Ryan-Saha, is that of an older couple of refugees living in the UK, called Baba and Deda (grandma and grandpa) by the Bosnian community, who turned their living room into a kind of museum to their personal ordeal as well as a memory-inducing gathering place for the diaspora. This is "a repository of Bosnian culture," containing photographs, home videos, handmade objects – a testament to traditional cultural expressions.[38] Similar "museumization" of material artifacts blurring private-public/personal-collective boundaries takes place in Palestinian refugee camps in Jordan studied by Beverly Butler and Fatima al-Nammari.[39] In Talbiyeh Camp, established in 1968, some people keep and continue to collect objects closely connected with Palestine – pots, headdresses, traditional camel-hair carpets, embroidered cross-stitched dresses, maps, and photographs. In the "permanent impermanence," which the camp effectively is, the memory of the lost country and a sense of belonging is maintained by the elders – the first generation of the displaced, and through creative engagements with traditional crafts. On a more personal level, it is captured in heirlooms, photographs, and title deeds to the lost land. In these objects, presence and absence are enmeshed with each other.

For the Central American refugees studied in The Undocumented Migration Project led by Jason De León, packing evolves into a strategic negotiation of the absolute necessities, balancing between minimum weight and maximum chances for survival.[40] The violent process of Mexico–US border crossing is associated with routinized techniques and tools that follow specific migrant logic. These include the use of earth tone or dark backpacks, packing cans of food, water, and first-aid supplies that increase the chances of enduring the long trek across the desert and dark color or camouflage t-shirts supposedly decreasing risks of being spotted by the border patrol at night. All these commodities are supplied by what De León calls a "Border Crossing Industry," "smugglers, criminals, vendors, and manufacturers who profit by robbing and selling products and services to migrants."[41] The industry capitalizes on a specific migrant folk logic designing, advertising, and branding commodities as necessary or advantageous to the prospective migrants. In reality these objects may not increase the chances of successful crossing, some (e.g., black water bottles) cause additional stress and they mark their users as "illegals" putting them in further danger.[42] Few things survive this arduous journey, many are left behind at the so-called migration stations building archaeological strata, a material archive of migrant dispensable materialities too heavy to carry, no longer necessary, abandoned by captured migrants or left behind for some other reasons.[43] Cemeteries of toothbrushes, water bottles, emptied cans, broken shoes, soiled clothes, lost family photographs, and backpacks are materializing human desperation and tragedy, hope, and resilience. Similar scenes dot the coast of the Mediterranean and other European Union border crossings, which are sites of landing and encampment of refugees from Africa, the Middle East, and South Asia.[44]

The object that is an essential component in the migrants' and refugees' packs is a mobile phone, often identified as a lifeline and a critical tool for navigating the journeys, self-empowerment, and connection.[45] This is a hyper-object compressing time and space, fusing "communication, sociability, entertainment, storage, and archival functions (including the storage of digital photos of loved ones and of favorite places and home locales), emotion, and affect."[46] Mobile phones are used for capturing and documenting the ordeal of border crossings, and storing autobiographical registers of the experiences.[47] Studying the use of smartphones and the meaning of connectivity among migrants in Naples, Italy, and across France respectively, Nicholas Harney and Marie Gillespie, and Souad

Osseiran and Margie Cheesman show the enormously varied roles the smartphones play in managing the insecurity of migrants' lives and in achieving a form of safety, even if highly symbolic (e.g., a Syrian refugee: "Without my phone, I feel completely lost, stripped, naked, like missing a limb").[48] Phones are used as a basic tool of communication and networking between migrants to warn against custom police, for example, or to check on each other's well-being. In that sense, they help to navigate the precariousness of everyday life. The powerful, affective dimensions of smartphone affordances also reside in them being a medium of contact with family back home, collapsing the distance and isolation and momentarily erasing a sense of absence. They also offer instant access to familiar cultural forms, alleviating some of the homesickness and alienation of displacement: "the other day I went on YouTube and I listened to some music from my Mali. I felt like I was at home, with my sounds, with my rhythms. It made me happy."[49]

Material Translocality and Remittance

The most recent shift in migration studies that brought greater attention to cultural practices and material engagements of migrants also illuminated the dynamism, complexities, and contradictions shaping the lives of these communities. Numerous case studies showed that the lives of migrants are often predicated on multiple social and cultural relations stretching across borders. They rest upon real, virtual, or imaginary travel between places of residence and places of origin and attachments to these places. This dual existence is captured in the concepts of translocality and transnationalism that describe the nature and mechanisms of multiple ties and interactions linking people across borders, allowing migrants to sustain various identities and allegiances and to participate in communal life in their places of residence and places of origin.[50] Translocality is an ability not just to experience the social relations that are located in a place in which one is corporeally standing, but also to experience social relations that are "located" elsewhere.[51] Material objects – gifts, everyday objects sent as parcels and carried in suitcases by visiting expatriates on the ritualized visits back home – are important elements in sustaining these synchronic lives (Case Study 13.4). They are a very tangible extension and materialization of social relations, a way of reaching out, symbolically and emotionally being involved with people who are physically distant.

Practices of remittance and material exchanges as a way of maintaining social relations in premodern cases of migration are understudied and consequently poorly known. David Cressy, who studied seventeenth-century English migration to New England observed, however, how letters, of which several hundred are still preserved, "provided an emotional lifeline, a cord of communication" to inform, comfort, advise, and stay

Case Study 13.4

The taste of my whole life

The taste of my whole life by Luisito (Figure 13.3)

> I'm Peruvian, and I live in Amsterdam. I've first moved here in 2011, and then moved to Argentina between 2012 and 2014. I moved here when I was 20, very young.
>
> I've just come back from a trip to Peru, and brought all this food back with me. My two luggage of 23 kilos were full!
>
> I brought lots of traditional food from my country, like spices for cooking, and the Turron de Doña Pepa, a cake/nougat which is eaten in August but it sold the whole year nowadays. There is also Mazamorra negrita, the taste of my childhood. Mostly there is a lot of candies, cookies – all kind of delicious things I used to have when I was a child.
>
> There are also some medicine, antibiotics that can be bought without prescription, and some natural stuff that help your body get the nutrients it needs.
>
> Some of this Peruvian food cannot be bought here, or they are really expensive.
>
> These are the little things that I miss so much. This trip was very sensitive for me, it was my first trip home for 5 years. I wasn't able to afford a trip before this.
>
> Courtesy Europeana Foundation,
2084002_Ag_EU_Migration_ugc

Figure 13.3 The taste of my whole life. Courtesy of Europeana Foundation.

connected with family and friends.[52] "The letter I received from you lay by me as a cordial which I often refresh myself with," wrote a mother to her daughter across the ocean, indicating the deep affective value of the correspondence and the fact that letters were reread for comfort and a sense of closeness to those that were physically absent. Some of these letters contained requests for objects, exchange of which provided further means of staying connected.

Exchange of letters and news played an important role in creating a sense of continuity in the colony of New Sweden. A few individuals had the necessary skills and means to correspond with family and friends back in Sweden. The most avid writer was Governor Johan Printz, whose correspondence, besides reporting successes and struggles of the colony, revealed emotional difficulties in dealing with dislocation as well as his continuous insistence on regarding Sweden as his only home.[53] Replies to the governor's letters containing assurances, instructions, and bits of news were probably read aloud and spread among the colonists. The few known private letters of the colonists, written toward the end of the seventeenth century, contained descriptions of the conditions in America and calming assurances of well-being. They were not, however, free from anxieties over irregular contact and worries about their family's situation in Sweden. These letters indicate that money and goods were sent from the colony to those who were left behind.[54] In the eighteenth century, when the colony no longer existed as a political entity, but the Swedish-speaking population continued to insist on maintaining transatlantic contacts, the regularly arriving pastors proved to play a crucial connecting role. Besides helping in letter exchanges, they were also directly involved in the circulation of objects, bringing with them and importing books, both religious and secular, and occasionally articles impossible to obtain in the colony, and sending back to Sweden colonial commodities such as pelts, skins, and *curiosa*.[55]

In modern cases of migration, remittance practices and insistence on maintaining material connections are ubiquitous and once again revolve in some sense around suitcases.[56] Kathy Burrell, who conducted a series of interviews with Polish migrants living in the UK, observed that the acts of shopping, packing, and unpacking the suitcases before reoccurring trips home "bridges the gap between the migrants' two lives, and creates a time and space when both lives are effortlessly intermingled."[57] This packing and unpacking requires engagement with personal needs and tastes. The physical reality and imagination/daydreaming that coalesce during this process illustrate the emotional work of migration and transnationalism. On the journey to Poland the suitcases are filled with objects that fulfill the role of remittance (practical things that are cheaper and of better quality in the UK) and carefully chosen personalized gifts that speak more about emotional entanglements than economic relationships between separated families. The choices of English brands (made by the migrants and requested by families back in Poland) are, according to Burrell, closely intertwined with personal biographies of the migrants; they "mark themselves out as the carrier of different goods, exposed to a different material life abroad, and, in return, are marked out at home as the person who is 'away.'"[58] Suitcases on the return journey to the UK are stuffed with things from home: recordings of Polish TV programs and films, magazines, presents from friends and family, souvenirs, and home cooked or Polish food hard to obtain in the UK. Discussing the rationale of bringing "Polish" things back, Burrell repeatedly heard from her respondents that these material things carry emotional symbolism allowing the embodiment and display of Polishness abroad.

Another way of maintaining transnational connections is through maintenance of multiple places of residence and building houses "back home." On one level, the meaning of such dual home ownership is perceived as a symbol of success and economic stability. On another level, it is about continuity and the simultaneity of migrants' lives stretched across several state borders, reflections of their wish to be "here" and "there," possibilities of return and complicated meanings of "belonging";[59] The dream of building a house back home frequently propelled decisions to join the migrant labor pool in Western Europe. A completed house was an emblem of an accomplished sojourn, marking the final return home. Except that for many migrants – for example, Turkish in Germany, Austria and the Netherlands, Albanian in Greece and Italy, and Caribbean in the UK – the final return is difficult or even impossible. Many interviewed migrants admit that life in what was supposed to be a temporary place of residence exercises strong pulls and, with the passing of time, "home" feels increasingly alien.[60] But to give up the idea of having a concrete place made of concrete materials in the place of origin feels like a betrayal or even erasure of oneself from the physical landscape and network of social relations. Consequently, many migrants invest their savings in building and furnishing, often elaborately, their homes back in Turkey, Albania, or Jamaica. However, as this project often results in a series of contradictions and ambivalences, the "continuity of commitment to the house itself" becomes separated from "any personal commitment to actually living there."[61] These houses are often "unlived." Some become seasonal residences that are continuously in the process of being fixed, redecorated, expanded, or altered; others turn into more or less permanent residences for the members of the family who never moved. Some remain indefinitely vacant, and, for those that stay behind, become museum-like structures. In Albania there is a whole vocabulary to describe these houses in terms of temporality ("houses for the future"), social relations (e.g., "houses for children," "houses for parents") and connotation to migrant lives ("houses built with blood and sweat").[62] Their emptied presence causes anxiety and feelings of loss among family members that stayed, which is countered by constant care and attention given to their interiors. As observed by Eckehard Pistrick and Florian Bachmeier,

> The obsessive ritual care given to these rooms was the care which was destined to the bodies of the absent; a care which made us understand that these places are material but at the same time material substitutes for physical bodies of flesh and blood, and "memory boxes" of the immaterial. ... Empty migrant rooms are real, hyper-real. They seem to be livable, but they are not. They seem to wait for being inhabited but at the same time resemble a museum, filled with requisites which do not serve everyday life and whose almost ritualistic order resists any change or adaption.[63]

When Objects Are Burdens

Sometimes moving away is seen a possibility to shake off the weight of social relations, entrapment of physical space and all associated materiality. This type of relocation as a way of escaping the burdens of things, conventions, and people is a less commonly explored subject in migration studies but one that offers yet another view of the evocative nature of human-object interactions in the context of mobility. It also draws critical attention to the idea of home as a space of comfort, familiarity, and refuge showing that sometimes home is a site of oppression, estrangement, or even violence.[64] Migration as an escape from the material and psychological confines of life featured in the interviews with migrant residents in South London conducted by Fiona Parrott and Daniel Miller.[65] One man, for example, framed the move to London from New Zealand as an escape from nonexistence. "This is where my life began as far as I'm concerned, in England not New Zealand."[66] Bringing no belongings of meaning to the UK, after migration he amassed personal objects relating to his self-discovery, independent life, and early adulthood, objects he was planning to take with him back to New Zealand. Another person, an Australian Aboriginal, spoke about the heaviness of material things, their physical size and permanence as hindering his preferred mobile lifestyle, freedom, self-invention, and the search for authenticity and aboriginal heritage. Continuously moving between places, he divested himself of bulky possessions. He digitized photographs, letters, family archives, and music that mattered and linked the different facets of his personal and family history.[67] His laptop was the only object that mattered, a hyper-object of condensed materiality and a solution to his "cosmological tussle with materiality."[68]

The theme of disassociation with objects as a way of starting a new life runs through Jean-Sébastian Marcoux's study of mobility in Montreal.[69] A woman that suffered domestic abuse ran away from her home with nothing, the burden of things and their association with violence being too much to bear. Instead, after the move, or rather a series of almost ritualized and continuous relocations in the city, she accumulated collections of objects that are about herself and have no relation to other people; "she wanted to show that she owed nothing to anybody, as if she wanted to be the sole tributary to her past."[70] The haunting burden of things, albeit of a different nature, motivated the relocation of a widowed man. He moved out of the house he built and spent all his married life leaving all material possessions behind. The house and everything in it reminded him of his departed wife, nothing "was not hers, nothing was not her."[71] The sense that it was his wife and their former joint life that "belonged" to the house made him believe that taking the possessions would constitute an act of uprooting her, a transgression he did not want to commit. His coping strategy to come to terms with loss involved cutting himself from the place and leaving behind all those things he was attached to.

Conclusions

The numerous case studies of migration document complex intersections between mobility and material culture. They illustrate the centrality of material objects in the experience of migration, establishing new bearings and staying connected; they also expose the highly personal, contextual, and diverse way in which the present and absent things act and induce emotional reactions. They point to the fact that when objects move, when they are selected, packed, unpacked, and placed in the new home, their ontological meanings are transformed. Migration leads to material separation from the familiar, domesticated background; taken possessions "escape their frame" too, becoming separated from their homely context.[72] These salvaged belongings (as well as those that were not packed and are missed) are "translated," charged with specific meanings; they are often singularized and acquire certain affective stickiness.[73]

In the migrants' narratives, objects frequently emerge as a stabilizing and comforting force, a material extension of oneself. Their physical constancy has a capability of counteracting the feeling of transiency and insecurity that migration brings about. David Parkin, studying African refugees, noticed how the few personal, sentimental objects taken by people escaping violence can form the bases of future resettlement, "the 'transitional objects' carried by people in crisis inscribe their personhood in flight but offer the possibility of their own de-objectification and re-personalization afterwards."[74] Through multisensory interactions, these objects shape migrants' biographies. As "life-story objects" they give meaning, texture, and shape to self-narratives.[75] This is the way the objects act in the quoted studies of Mormon migrants, Turkish guest workers, or Palestinian refugees.

Yet the process of unpacking suitcases and furnishing new homes with familiar objects is more complex. Objects that move with migrants are not always comforting and reassuring. They can emerge as disrupters reminding of other places and times, magnifying the sense of strangeness and nonbelonging. The migrants sometimes speak about disquieting feelings stirred up by handling objects brought from the home country, homesickness, out-of-placeness, and disjuncture. Rather than simply assisting them to "re-establish or re-define personal and collective origins," as suggested by Parkin,[76] these belongings may simultaneously unsettle, re-entrench a sense of separation by materializing loss. Objects that are often singled out as particularly ambiguous and emotionally laden are photographs. They are potent expressions of absence and loss.[77] "Every now and again I'll go into the hall and I've got a box of photos sitting there. I just look at them and in one way I'm sad because you sort of have lost touch with the people,"[78] reflected Julie Mesic, who migrated to Australia from Croatia in 1967. A sense of loss and "negative energy" also emanates from objects relating to the displacement and dispossession of Bosnian refugees. Eleanor Ryan-Saha's conversations with the Bosnians in Britain about the materiality of diaspora often centered around photographs and ultimately stirred feelings of irreversible loss: of home, family, and friends. On a larger, more abstract, scale they were provoking realization about not belonging anywhere, discomfort, and in-betweenness.[79] In this case, the little that is salvaged only adds potency to what is absent, everyday objects and personal mementoes that were not taken, signaling incompleteness and out-of-placeness.

The ubiquitous migrant hyper-object such as the mobile phone is experienced as a medium of connecting as much as a constant reminder of loss. Calls to family can be full of unease and expectations ("I can't call Bangladesh. My wife just cries and asks when I will come home"),[80] participating in family life through Skype video calls, observing how it happens through Facebook posts magnify anxieties of absence. Phones and connectivity are also perceived as tools of surveillance and exploitation injecting an additional sense of insecurity, vulnerability, and nonbelonging into the undocumented migrants' lives.[81]

Migration is an extremely complex phenomenon, not only in its geographical scope (short distance, internal, transoceanic, long distance), motivations (economic, political, threat to life), and temporality (short-term, permanent), or the difficulties of untangling one reason of migrating from another. Its complexity also rests in a powerful and varied intertwinement of material culture in these movements: from the materials containing practical and personal belongings for the future and of the past (suitcases, backpacks, chests), shaping the journey and border crossing (passports, smart phones, water bottles) to the objects unpacked and missed, allowing or forbidding to settle and shaping ideas of the self and belonging. Regardless of the circumstances, motivations, and experiences of the migrants themselves, material culture is always involved in these crossings: physically moving with people and moving people emotionally.

Notes

1. Paul Basu and Simon Coleman, "Introduction: Migrant Worlds, Material Cultures," *Mobilities* 3, no. 3 (2008), 313–30.
2. Ernst Ravenstein, "The Laws of Migration," *Journal of the Royal Statistical Society* 52, no. 2 (1889), 286.
3. Ravenstein formulated six "laws" governing migration: (1) the migrants move no further than they have to and their movement is a gradual one; (2) majority of migrations are short-distance; (3) each migration stream produces a counter stream of returning immigrants; (4) in most cases there is a strong tendency toward movement from rural landscapes to urban areas; (5) women appear to comprise the majority of short-distance immigrants; and (6) migration tends to increase with the development of commerce and production. Ernst Ravenstein, "The Laws of Migration," *Journal of the Royal Statistical Society* 48 (1885), 167–235; Ravenstein, "The Laws," (1889), 241–301.
4. William Petersen, "A General Typology of Migration," *American Sociological Review* 23, no. 3 (1958), 256–66; Everett Lee, "A Theory of Migration," *Demography* 3, no. 1 (1966), 47–57.
5. Charles H. Wood, "Equilibrium and Historical-Structural Perspectives on Migration," *International Migration Review* 16, no. 2 (1982), 298–319; Kingsley Davis, "Social Science Approaches to International Migration," *Population and Development Review* 14 (1988), 245–61; Barbara Schmitter Heisler, "The Future of Immigrant Incorporation: Which Models? Which Concepts?" *International Migration Review* 26, no. 2 (1992), 623–45; Barbara Schmitter Heisler, "The Sociology of Immigration: From Assimilation to Segmented Integration, from the American Experience to the Global Arena" in Caroline Brettell and James Hollifield, eds., *Migration Theory: Talking across Disciplines*. (New York and London: Routledge, 2000), 77–96; Caroline Brettell, "Theorizing Migration in Anthropology: The Social Construction of Networks, Identities, Communities and Globalscapes," in Caroline Brettell and James Hollifield, eds., *Migration Theory*, 97–136.
6. Schmitter Heisler, "The Future of Immigrant," 628; see also John Berger and Jean Mohr, *A Seventh Man* (London: Verso, 1975); Aristide R. Zolberg, "The Next Wave: Migration Theory for a Changing World," *International Migration Review* 23, no. 3 (1989), 403–30.
7. For example, Nadje Al-Ali and Khalid Koser, eds., *New Approaches to Migration? Transnational Communities and the Transformation of Home* (London: Routledge, 2002); Katherine Brickell and Ayona Datta, eds., *Translocal Geographies: Spaces, Places, Connections* (Aldershot: Ashgate, 2011).
8. Russell Belk, "Moving Possessions: An Analysis Based on Personal Documents from the 1847–1869 Mormon Migration," *Journal of Consumer Research* 19 (1992), 339–61; Divya Tolia-Kelly, "Locating

Processes of Identification: Studying the Precipitates of Re-memory through Artefacts in the British Asian Home," *Transactions of the Institute of British Geographers* 29 (2004), 314–29; Basu and Coleman, "Introduction"; Maruška Svašek, ed., *Moving Subjects, Moving Objects: Transnationalism, Cultural Production and Emotions* (New York: Berghahn, 2012); Special Issue, "'The Material Turn' in Migration Studies," Cangbai Wang, ed., *Modern Languages Open*, September 26 (2016).

9. Jean-Sébastian Marcoux, "The Refurbishment of Memory," in Daniel Miller, ed., *Home Possessions: Material Culture behind Closed Doors* (Oxford: Berg, 2001), 69–86; Patricia Ehrkamp, "Placing Identities: Transnational Practices and Local Attachments of Turkish Immigrants in Germany," *Journal of Ethnic and Migration Studies* 31 (2005), 345–64; Anna Pechurina, *Material Cultures, Migrations, and Identities: What the Eye Cannot See* (London: Palgrave Macmillan, 2015).

10. Raj Mehta and Russell W. Belk. "Artifacts, Identity, and Transition: Favorite Possessions of Indians and Indian Immigrants to the United States," *Journal of Consumer Research* 17, no. 4 (1991), 398–411; David Parkin, "Mementoes as Transitional Objects in Human Displacement," *Journal of Material Culture* 4 (1999), 303–20; Tolya Kelly, "Locating Processes"; Kathy Burrell, "The Objects of Christmas: The Politics of Festive Materiality in the Lives of Polish Immigrants," in Svašek, *Moving Subjects*, 55–74.

11. Magdalena Naum, "The Malady of Emigrants: Homesickness and Longing in the Colony of New Sweden," in Mary Beaudry and Travis Parno, eds., *Archaeologies of Movement* (New York: Springer, 2013), 165–77; Fiona Parrott, "Materiality, Memories and Emotions: A View on Migration from a Street in South London" in Svašek, *Moving Subjects*, 41–54; Eleanor Ryan-Saha, "Repossessions, Material Absences, Affective Presences, and the Life-Resumption Labors of Bosnians in Britain," *Social Analysis* 59, no. 1 (2015), 96–112.

12. Ruben Gielis "A Global Sense of Migrant Places: Towards a Place Perspective in the Study of Migrant Transnationalism," *Global Networks* 9 (2009), 271–87; Steven Vertovec, "Transnationalism and Identity," *Journal of Ethnic and Migration Studies* 27 (2001), 573–82; Kathy Burrell, "Materializing the Border: Spaces of Mobility and Material Culture in Migration from Post-Socialist Poland," *Mobilities* 3, no. 3 (2008), 353–73; Magdalena Naum, "Premodern Translocals: Hanseatic Merchant Diaspora between Kalmar and Northern German Towns (ca 1250–1500)," *International Journal for Historical Archaeology* 17, no. 2 (2013), 376–400; Magdalena Naum, "Migration, Identity and Material Culture: Hanseatic Translocality in Medieval Baltic Sea" in Hakon Glørstad, Lene Melheim, and Zanette Glørstad, eds., *Comparative Perspectives on Past Colonisation, Maritime Interaction and Cultural Integration* (London: Equinox, 2016), 129–48.

13. Divya Tolia-Kelly, "A Journey through the Material Geographies of Diaspora Cultures: Four Modes of Environmental Memory," in Kathy Burrell and Panakos Panayi, eds., *Histories and Memories: Migrants and their History in Britain* (London: I. B. Tauris, 2006), 149–70; Burrell, "Materializing the Border," 353–73, 362–67; Orvar Löfgren, "Containing the Past, the Present and the Future: Packing a Suitcase," *NU* 53, no. 1 (2016), 59–74.
14. Löfgren, "Containing," 60, 69.
15. Ibid, 60.
16. Ibid, 72.
17. Marius (Rien) de Vos, Migration Memories, https://bit.ly/3qLvcad.
18. Maria Goulding, "Migration Memories," https://bit.ly/3FFmmPN.
19. Nizima, "I am not a Balija," in Julie Mertus, Jasmina Tesanovic, Habiba Metikos, and Rada Boric, eds., *The Suitcase: Refugee Voices from Bosnia and Croatia* (Berkeley: University of California Press, 1997), 32, 34.
20. Ryan-Saha, "Repossessions," 99.
21. Higginson quoted in David Cressy, *Coming Over: Migration and Communication between England and New England in the Seventeenth Century* (Cambridge: Cambridge University Press, 1987), 111.
22. Cressy, *Coming Over*, 110–19; John B. Linn and William H. Eagle, eds., *Pennsylvania Archives* 2 series, vol. 5 (Harrisburg: Clarence M. Busch, 1896), 839–42.
23. John Winthrop, *History of New England, 1630–1649*, ed. James K. Hosmer (New York: Charles Scribner's Sons, 1908), 30.
24. Belk, "Moving Possessions."
25. Ibid, 343; see also Gretchen Buggeln, this volume, on materiality of religion.
26. Ibid, 350.
27. Ibid, 355.
28. Ilaria Vanni, "Oggetti Spaesati, Unhomely Belongings: Objects, Migrations and Cultural Apocalypses," *Cultural Studies Review* 19, no. 2 (2013), 151.
29. Berger and Mohr, *A Seventh Man*; Mehta and Belk, "Artifacts"; Parkin, "Mementoes"; Tolia-Kelly, "Locating Processes."
30. Berger and Mohr, *A Seventh Man*; Özlem Savaş, "Taste Diaspora: The Aesthetic and Material Practice of Belonging," *Journal of Material Culture* 19, no. 2 (2014), 189.
31. Berger and Mohr, *A Seventh Man*, 179.
32. Savaş, "Taste Diaspora," 188.
33. Ibid, 190–91.
34. Ibid, 193–204.
35. Başak Bilecen, "Home-Making Practices and Social Protection across Borders: An Example of Turkish Migrants Living in Germany," *Journal of Housing and the Built Environment* 32 (2017), 84; see also Ehrkamp, "Placing identities" and Hilje van der Horst, "Dwellings in

Transnational Lives: A Biographical Perspective on 'Turkish-Dutch' Houses in Turkey," *Journal of Ethnic and Migration Studies* 36, no. 7 (2010), 1175–92.

36. Heath Cabot, "The Governance of Things: Documenting Limbo in the Greek Asylum Procedures," *Political and Legal Anthropology Review* 35, no. 1 (2012), 11–29; Yannis Hamilakis, "Archaeologies of Forced and Undocumented Migration," *Journal of Contemporary Archaeology* 3, no. 2 (2016), 129.
37. Mertus et al., *The Suitcase*; Ryan-Saha, "Repossessions."
38. Ryan-Saha, "Repossessions," 101.
39. Beverly Butler and Fatima al-Nammari, "'We Palestinian Refugees' – Heritage Rites and/as the Clothing of Bare Life: Reconfiguring Paradox, Obligation, and Imperative in Palestinian Refugee Camps in Jordan," *Journal of Contemporary Archaeology* 3, no. 2 (2016), 147–59.
40. Jason De León, "'Better to Be Hot Than Caught': Excavating the Conflicting Roles of Migrant Material Culture," *American Anthropologist* 114, no. 3 (2012), 477–95; Jason De León, "Undocumented Migration, Use Wear, and the Materiality of Habitual Suffering in the Sonoran Desert," *Journal of Material Culture* 18, no. 4, (2013), 321–45; Jason De León, *The Land of Open Graves: Living and Dying on the Migrant Trail* (Oakland: University of California Press, 2015).
41. De León, "Better Be Hot," 482.
42. Ibid, 484–92.
43. De León, "Undocumented Migration."
44. Hamilakis, "Archaeologies"; Oula Ilari Seitsonen, Vesa-Pekka Herva, and Mika Kunnari, "'Abandoned Refugee Vehicles in the Middle of Nowhere': Reflections on the Global Refugee Crisis from the Northern Margins of Europe," *Journal of Contemporary Archaeology* 3, no. 2 (2016), 244–60; George Tyrikos-Ergas, "*Orange Life Jackets*: Materiality and Narration in Lesvos, One Year after the Eruption of the 'Refugee Crisis,'" *Journal of Contemporary Archaeology* 3, no. 2 (2016), 227–32.
45. Nicholas Harney, "Precarity, Affect and Problem Solving with Mobile Phones by Asylum Seekers, Refugees and Migrants in Naples, Italy," *Journal of Refugee Studies* 26, no. 4 (2013), 541–57; Marie Gillespie, Souad Osseiran, and Margie Cheesman, "Syrian Refugees and the Digital Passage to Europe: Smartphone Infrastructures and Affordance," *Social Media + Society* (2018), 1–12.
46. Hamilakis, "Archaeologies," 135.
47. Koen Leurs, "Communication Rights from the Margins: Politicizing Young Refugees' Smartphone Pocket Archives," *The International Communication Gazette* 79 (2017), 674–98; Gillespie et al., "Syrian Refugees," 4.
48. Gillespie et al., "Syrian Refugees," 6; Harney, "Precarity."
49. Harney, "Precarity," 553.

50. Gielis, "A Global Sense"; Nina Glick Schiller, Linda Basch, and Cristina Blanc-Szanton, eds., *Towards a Transnational Perspective on Migration: Race, Class, Ethnicity, and Nationalism Reconsidered* (New York: New York Academy of Sciences, 1992); Alejandro Portes, Luis E. Guarnizo, and Patricia Landolt, "The Study of Transnationalism: Pitfalls and Promise of an Emergent Research Field," *Ethnic and Racial Studies* 22 (1999), 217–37; Vertovec, "Transnationalism and Identity"; Steven Vertovec, "Migrants, Transnationalism, and Modes of Transformation," *International Migration Review* 38 (2004), 970–1001; Steven Vertovec, *Transnationalism* (London: Routledge, 2009); Al-Ali and Koser, *New Approaches*; Brickell and Datta, *Translocal Geographies*; Elliott Robert Barkan, ed., *Immigration, Incorporation and Transnationalism* (New York: Routledge, 2017); Richard K. Brail, ed., *Transnational Ties: Cities, Migrations, and Identities* (New York: Routledge, 2017).
51. Gielis, "A Global Sense," 275.
52. Cressy, *Coming Over*, 213–34; see also Sarah Pearsall, *Atlantic Families: Lives and Letters in the Later Eighteenth Century* (Oxford: Oxford University Press, 2008).
53. Printz's letters to Per Brahe and Axel Oxenstierna in *The Instruction for Johan Printz, Governor of New Sweden*, ed. Amandus Johnnson (Philadelphia: The Swedish Colonial Society, 1930); Naum, "The Malady," 165–77.
54. Gunlög Fur, Magdalena Naum, and Jonas M. Nordin, "Intersecting Worlds: New Sweden's Transatlantic Entanglements," *The Journal of American Transnational Studies* 7, no. 1 (2016), 4–5; Peter Stebbins Craig and Kim-Eric Williams, eds., *Colonial Records of the Swedish Churches in Pennsylvania I* (Philadelphia: Swedish Colonial Society, 2006), 195–201.
55. Fur et al., "Intersecting Worlds," 8.
56. Mariano Sana and Douglas S. Massey, "Household Composition, Family Migration, and Community Context: Migrant Remittances in Four Countries," *Social Science Quarterly* 86, no. 2 (2005), 509–28; Kankonde Bukasa Peter, "Transnational Family Ties, Remittance Motives, and Social Death among Congolese Migrants: A Socio-Anthropological Analysis," *Journal of Comparative Family Studies* 41, no. 2 (2010): 225–43.
57. Burrell, "Materializing the Border," 267.
58. Ibid, 265.
59. Peggy Levitt and Nina Glick Schiller, "Conceptualizing Simultaneity: A Transnational Social Field Perspective on Society," *International Migration Review* 38, no. 3 (2004), 1002–39; Mirjana Lozanovska, "Diaspora, Return and Migrant Architectures," *International Journal of Diversity in Organizations, Communities and Nations* 7, no. 2 (2007), 239–50; Daniel Miller, "Migration, Material Culture and Tragedy: Four

Moments in Caribbean Migration," *Mobilities* 3, no. 3 (2008), 397–413; Dimitris Dalakoglou, "Migrating-Remitting-'Building'-Dwelling: House-Making as 'Proxy' Presence in Postsocialist Albania," *Journal of the Royal Anthropological Institute* 16, no. 4 (2010), 761–77; Gerda Dalipaj, "Migration, Residential Investment and the Experience of 'Transition': Tracing Transnational Practices of Albanian Migrants in Athens," *Focaal* 76 (2007), 85–98; Eckehard Pistrick and Florian Bachmeier, "Empty Migrant Rooms: An Anthropology of Absence through the Camera Lens," *Journal of Contemporary Archaeology* 3, no. 2 (2016), 205–15.
60. Van der Horst, "Dwelling"; Bilecen, "Home-Making"; Miller, "Migration."
61. Miller, "Migration," 405.
62. Pistrick and Bachmeier, "Empty Migrant Rooms," 205.
63. Ibid, 207.
64. Bilecen, "Home-Making."
65. Daniel Miller, *The Comfort of Things* (Cambridge: Polity Press, 2008), 67–72; Parrot, "Materiality."
66. Parrott, "Materiality," 44.
67. Ibid, 45.
68. Miller, *The Comfort*, 72.
69. Marcoux, "The Refurbishment."
70. Ibid, 73.
71. Ibid, 81.
72. Vanni, "Oggetti Spaesati," 163.
73. Basu and Coleman, "Introduction," 327–28; see also Julian Yates's Chapter 2 in this volume.
74. Parkin, "Mementoes," 303, 313.
75. Basu and Coleman, "Introduction"; van der Horst, "Dwelling," 1178.
76. Parkin, "Mementoes," 303.
77. Berger and Mohr, *A Seventh Man*, 13–17; see also Roland Barthes, *Camera Lucida: Reflections on Photography* (London: Vintage, 1993).
78. Julie Mesic, Migration Memories, https://bit.ly/30vv58h.
79. Ryan-Saha, "Repossessions," 101–02.
80. Harney, "Precarity," 549.
81. Gillespie, Osseiran, and Cheesman, "Syrian Refugees."

14
Identity and Agency

Veronica Strang

Identity and Materiality

Identity is a fundamental issue about who we are, which group(s) we belong to, and where we belong. Identity is ineluctably material, located in bodies, and embedded in places and environments. In highly mobile societies, people often move from place to place, but they nevertheless strive to engage with each locale. The connections between identity and place are more visible in place-based societies, where relationships between people and their homelands are permanent and inalienable. This chapter therefore focuses primarily on a place-based community to illustrate the centrality of place in identity. By elucidating the simultaneous process of place and identity-making, the ethnographic account makes it easy to see how, even in societies where geographic mobility is the norm, identity is composed via engagement with local places, environments, and communities.

Identity has long been a focus of interest in anthropological research, raising research questions across all areas of the discipline. As this implies, identity is both social and material, having as much meaning for paleoanthropology, biological anthropology, and archaeology as it does for anthropologists examining contemporary human societies. Thus, when human remains thousands of years old are found in a peat bog, the first questions are concerned with identification: "who was this person? where did they come from? how did they live? how do we know who they were?" Answers to such questions rely on physical "identifiers": bones that indicate gender and age; material traces that suggest temporal and spatial origins; dental configurations and other physical clues to diet and lifestyle.[1] With luck such discoveries also include material objects that reveal technologies, methods of production, and conventions of design, and which provide hints about beliefs, ideas, and practices.[2] Both human remains and objects will carry material traces of particular ways of engaging with environments.

Historically, ideas about the material aspects of identity have some painful baggage, reifying ideas about race in ways that were often pejorative and Eurocentric.[3] Although contemporary scholars recognize that race is a social construct, this is not a legacy that should be forgotten, and it serves as a useful caution about the dangers of essentializing identity.[4] However, it also reminds us that some dimensions of identity are ineluctably material, and that this is imagined cross-culturally in a variety of ways, whether through the scientific language of DNA and genealogy or through persons being seen as composed of the matter and spiritual essence of a particular place.

An example of the latter is provided by the ways in which identity is constructed according to the cultural beliefs and practices of the Indigenous Australian communities inhabiting the Cape York Peninsula, with whom I have worked for many years. Located in Far North Queensland, this is a tropical region with extreme wet and dry seasons, resource-rich savannahs, wetland areas, and rainforest. Prior to colonial settlement the area was densely populated by a number of different language groups. Located in Kowanyama, near the Gulf of Carpentaria coast, the Kunjen, Kokobera, and Yir Yoront language-speakers share ideas about identity that are similar, in their core principles, to those of other Australian Aboriginal communities.[5]

There are hundreds of indigenous language groups across the continent and some, for example those in Arnhem Land, are subdivided into moieties: social "halves" that facilitate exchange relationships within the group.[6] In Cape York there are some broad divisions, for example between saltwater and freshwater people, coastal or inland groups, but, for the most part, language groups are directly subdivided into small clans, each identified by an estate centered upon particular sacred sites and ancestral beings.

Aboriginal Australians lived successfully as hunter-gatherers for many millennia prior to the European colonization and settlement of Australia. As in many other hunter-gatherer societies, their ancestral beings are believed to be totemic, usually taking the form of animals or birds, aspects of the environment, or local material culture. These beings are said to have emerged from the landscape in the Dreamtime[7] and more particularly to have "come from" the major ancestral being: the Rainbow Serpent, a central ancestral figure manifesting the life-creating powers of water.

In this period of cosmogenesis, the ancestors formed the land and waterscape and its features and inhabitants, and demonstrated the "right way" to live as hunter-gatherers, defining, for example, marriage laws, social responsibilities, and how to harvest and use resources sustainably. Having established what Aboriginal people call "The Law," which is transmitted intergenerationally through songs, stories, dance, and artworks, the ancestors "sat down": that is returned into the land, like water, where they remained as a potent creative and potentially punitive force, sentient,

Figure 14.1 Kunjen elders at sacred site. Photo: Veronica Strang.

observant, and linked to their human descendants. Communication with this nonmaterial domain includes "increase rituals" at specific sacred sites where, through the scattering of leaves or dirt, or through rubbing bark or rock, the environment is stimulated and the ancestral beings are encouraged to provide resources (Figure 14.1).[8]

Each Aboriginal clan's estate therefore centers upon the sacred sites of specific totemic ancestors, creating a cultural landscape based upon ancestral connection.[9] In Cape York, the majority of sacred sites are water sources, and, even in drier areas, water places are typically among the most important sites. This is because water both embodies and provides a way of thinking about ancestral forces, and how they support hydro-theological movements of life out of the land and back into it.

Water is central to identity: concentrating ancestral power at sacred sites, it generates the spirits of the individuals who will thus be "born into" a local clan, with commensurate rights and responsibilities. The human spirit "jumps up" from the water, to enliven the fetus in a woman's womb, and a sign, perhaps a peculiar bird call, or an unusual event, is given by the ancestors to inform the parents that it has arrived. That site will therefore be regarded as the individual's "home place": in Kunjen, *errk elampungk*, which translates as "place-eye-home" or "the home place of your image."

An individual matures, drinking the waters and eating the foods from the clan estate, and is therefore seen as having been "grown up" by it. Underlying this term is a belief that a person is substantially, both materially and spiritually, composed of the place in which they live. This co-substantiality is further illustrated by ideas about blood that link people within and across totemic clans, and to the land itself. In the ancestral stories, the blood of the ancestral beings is often conflated with or interchangeable with, the waters of the landscape. Thus Morphy describes a Yolngu creation story in Arnhem Land, in which the blood of a female ancestral being, Nyapililngu, "flowed into the lake and became the spiritual generator of subsequent generations of Manggalili clan members."[10]

This is, therefore, a belief system in which places themselves, and locally generated spirit and matter, are seen to compose the substance and identity of the individual and the group to which they belong. On a larger scale, it unites the multiple and interconnected Aboriginal clans and language groups across the continent. This concept of material being is further illustrated by an Aboriginal ritual of baptism involving rubbing sweat from the bodies of local people, or splashing water from local sources onto strangers, so that the related ancestral beings will "recognize" them. When an individual dies, their spirit will be ritually sung back, by their relatives, to its original "home place," to be reabsorbed into the generative pool of ancestral force from which it arose.

There is obvious resonance with Christian practices of splashing "holy water" onto the heads of babies, to christen them and, to use a suitably pastoral term, to bring them into the fold as members of a local "congregation." Such ties between blood, water, and the spirit are readily evident in many belief systems. In English foxhunting, to be "blooded" with the gore of a slaughtered fox traditionally brought newcomers, especially children, into the social group of the hunt.[11] There are similarly connective material notions about soil that "grounds" people in place. For example, Gomez-Temesio describes how, in Senegal, the term "son of the soil" defines an identity as a local citizen, and a responsibility to promote the interests of local communities by acting as a "spiritual godfather" to local water sources.[12]

Ideas about the material substantiality of identity, and of course most kinship systems, rest on concepts of blood and other identifying matter flowing down generations. As well as linking people and places across space and time, this connectivity traverses scale: individual identity nests within family and kin, but it is also part of the larger "imagined communities" of local neighborhoods, cities, regions, or catchment areas; ethnic or religious communities, and nations.[13] The nation is conceptually linked by shared cultural beliefs, knowledge, and values, and by extended notions of substantial connection, most poignantly expressed by Rupert Brooke's poem, "The Soldier," valorizing the blood spilled by young men in World War I:

> If I should die, think only this of me:
> That there's some corner of a foreign field
> That is for ever England. There shall be
> In that rich earth a richer dust concealed;

A dust whom England bore, shaped, made aware,
Gave, once, her flowers to love, her ways to roam,
A body of England's, breathing English air,
Washed by the rivers, blest by suns of home.[14]

Identity and Gender

The materiality of identity is most obvious in the anatomical form of the physical self. Just as categories of race and color have been critiqued over the last few decades, though persist in popular discourses, those pertaining to gender have increasingly been brought into question. Writers such as Butler and Strathern sparked a debate by emphasizing that gender is a matter of signification and learned practice, rather than embodiment, and Moore observed that "gender is a construct, a performance, a masquerade."[15] Debates broadened further with the emergence of gender studies, transgender studies, and queer theory in the 1990s, and these areas of scholarship continue to explore new ways to think about gender and identity.[16]

The anthropological literature in this area usefully describes diverse cultural views on gender categories. Although binary categories may be the most common model, there are various societies traditionally containing "in-between" gender categories,[17] and some in which gradations are finer still, such as the Bugi groups in Indonesia, in which gender identity is located in five categories.[18] However, Astuti argues that there is a need to retain a dichotomy between sex and gender to distinguish between what is "biologically intractable ... and what is culturally constructed," while Braidotti suggests that gender is "bioculturally located."[19]

Although sexual anatomy is most often regarded as the basis for defining gender, this is also challenged by alternative cultural views: for example in Nepal, where the material characteristics of flesh and bone are regarded as more telling.[20] Nevertheless, in material terms, the biological sex of the body and how this affects people's experiences, continue to exert an intense influence on thinking about gender and identity. Gender is perhaps most realistically considered in fluid terms, as a continuum along which identity can shift. But it remains common for those hoping to move away from assigned categories to try to match such moves with adjustments to their physical selves, suggesting that gender identity retains an important material, bodily dimension.

The social obstacles faced by those making gender transitions highlights a recurrent reality about identity: that while some people are appreciative of fluidity, others prefer certainty about identity categories. Anxieties about, and thus hostility to, "transgressive" behaviors may be seen, to some extent, as a reflection of cognitive processes in which categorical uncertainties create dissonance and discomfort. Ideas about social order are intrinsically visions of stability, and this implies some control over categories, including those that define identity. Because categories are composed in part by materialities, transitions that seek to contradict perceived alignments between gender and physical anatomy are inevitably the most controversial.

Socially constructed definitions of gender identity are also materialized through the gendering of material culture. Everyday objects carry gendered associations, and are often influenced by homologous ideas about gender. Returning to Cape York, for example, ethnographic research demonstrates that traditional material culture objects, such as string bags and boomerangs, are highly gendered. They are not only produced by women and men respectively, they embody specific gender roles, and express ideas about specific gender characteristics. Thus the dilly bag, a soft string container, is associated with the womb, for which the Kunjen term is *idn afum*, "breeding bag," with *afum* also referring to "breast" and employed as a kin term to describe mother and child relationships (Figure 14.2).[21]

The materiality of identity is therefore composed of a number of elements: bodily anatomy and appearance, blood, organic matter, genes, water, and perceived spiritual substance. It is further materialized by the encoding of identity in everyday objects. And it requires location in place.

Figure 14.2 String ("dilly") bag containing goose eggs, Kowanyama. Photo: Veronica Strang.

Identity and Place

Constructing places is, as Kaul points out,

> a deeply political process: one that embeds and inscribes power structures and conflicts into the material production of places. In other words, political conflicts do not simply exist during the act of place-making; they also exist in the physical developments that result from that process…Places can therefore be seen as sites in which the built environment reveals and also creates the social environment. Knowledge, narratives, and power articulate and interact with buildings, land, and boundaries.[22]

For Aboriginal Australians place is central to identity: there is a permanent, inalienable relationship between people and their "country."[23] The land and its waters are not commodities that can be bought or sold, and it is this intimate relationship to place, and the related trauma of dispossession, that lies at the heart of the land rights movement and challenges to Western notions of "property" and ownership.

While European settlers in Australia have often put down strong roots into places through farming the land over several generations, a concept of land as alienable property necessarily creates more transitory kinds of engagements.[24] For people living in urban environments[25] it is even more difficult to maintain permanent ties to place. In Australia as a whole, about 15 percent of the population now moves each year. In the UK people move, on average, eight times during their lives, and in the United States the average is over eleven times.[26] Yet identity remains place-based in a variety of ways. A first question for new acquaintances is often about origins: "where are you from?" and, particularly in the UK, accent continues to provide a key identifier of both location and class. Job seeking in a global economy dominated by neoliberalism continues to demand increasing levels of population mobility, and yet, even as they shift nomadically from place to place, people seek ways to connect with local environments and to compose their identities accordingly.

It is perhaps more useful to think about place and identity as an intricate coproduction, dependent on complex daily processes of engagement (see Gaddis, Chapter 19). At an individual level, the making of place and self is expressed in multiple material expressions: in home furnishing and decoration; in gardening small patches of land; in the tiny colonization of workspaces with personal items. Even on brief visits to the beach, families "make a place" for themselves with careful arrangements of windbreaks, deckchairs, towels, and, with inescapable symbolism, sandcastles. As this implies, place-making has a vital territorial dimension. Domestic households establish core individual and familial space, and few social interactions are as fraught with tension as boundary disputes with neighbors.[27]

Colonization and the making of nations represent the territorial dimensions of place-making processes on a grand scale. An inevitable first step is the renaming of rivers, mountains, and regions, often with names celebrating the "home" country.[28] Thus the Mitchell River, which runs through the country of the indigenous groups in Kowanyama, was named in 1845 by overland explorer Ludwig Leichhardt to commemorate Sir Thomas Mitchell, an earlier surveyor and explorer in south-east Australia. A second colonizing step, along with the imposition of new forms of governance and the parceling out of land to settlers, is the casting of a net of roads, fences, and other appropriating infrastructure, and the drawing of maps in which these feature centrally.[29] National boundaries are marked not only in representational media, but also with physical markers: border posts, sentry posts, watchtowers, and fortifications and, on the coast, the surveying beam of lighthouses.[30]

Places and identities vary in the extent to which they are boundaried. As noted above, Aboriginal clan country in Australia is defined not by perimeters but by the concentrations of ancestral power emanating from key sacred sites. Prior to the colonial era, in a society where relations between people and places were intimately known and understood, such diffuse notions of territory were very workable, although that is not to say that they invariably prevented disputes over land and resources. With networks of contiguous clans maintaining exchange relationships, and a variety of kinship systems facilitating the systematic movement of people between them, identity remained similarly permeable. People in Cape York still typically describe connection with their father's and their mother's country, and adoptive connections with the clan estates of other kin; and archaeological records reveal major networks of trade across the continent.

But it is a truism, even in small-scale, egalitarian, and relatively cohesive societies, that articulations of identity require some degree of "us" and "other." Moieties and clans provided this within indigenous societies. Aboriginal Australians, particularly in the Far North, also had centuries of contact with outsiders: Macassans seeking trade preceded Chinese, Portuguese, Dutch, and English seafarers, and overland European explorers. Being remote from the early centers of European government in Australia, Cape York has a relatively recent colonial history, but the Palmer River gold rush of the late 1800s was a violent incursion. As the land was given to settlers for mines and cattle stations, there was genocide, dispossession, slavery, and the enforced concubinage of women, which persisted into the early decades of the twentieth century.[31]

As a tiny minority within a much larger colonial society, Aboriginal people across Australia found that a new identity was imposed upon them, based on eighteenth-century European ideas about race and "civilization." Their subsequent efforts to redefine Aboriginal identity in their own terms are illustrative of the kinds of efforts made by many indigenous, ethnic, or religious minority groups in the postcolonial era. A civil rights movement in the 1960s achieved several important things: in 1967, it led to Aboriginal citizenship and enfranchisement as part of the Australian nation. It also initiated the land rights movement, beginning a long struggle by indigenous communities to reclaim their traditional land, in part by carrying into Australian law an understanding of the cultural centrality of co-identification between people and place.

It took some time for the Australian judiciary to recognize the collective forms of land ownership that this entailed: in the 1970s, Justice Blackburn famously described Aboriginal people as "belonging to" the land, rather than *vice versa*.[32] However, in 1993, the Mabo case established that, prior to European settlement, Aboriginal people had a form of collective land ownership. This opened the door to Native title claims, which continue to rumble through the courts, not only seeking social justice and equality (see Smith, Ralph, de Leiuen, and Pollard, Chapter 5), but also providing a detailed elucidation of Aboriginal relationships between place and identity.

The land rights movement has had a range of implications for the ways in which Indigenous Australian identity is represented by Aboriginal people and by others. In foregrounding the abuses of the colonial era, land tribunals and revelations about the Stolen Generations have highlighted the victimhood of Aboriginal Australians, creating some knotty questions about the recursive social effects of this kind of identification.[33] Such questions are equally relevant for other groups who have experienced genocide, slavery, dispossession, or dislocation, such as Holocaust survivors; groups fleeing territorial aggression; and villagers dispossessed by governments to enable the building of dams and other infrastructures. Seeking justice, and restoration or compensation, often requires the inhabitance and performance of a victim identity over long periods of time. As well as carrying a significant psychological cost, this can generate hostility from those directly or implicitly held responsible, as illustrated by the right-wing Australian prime minister John Howard's dismissal of such narratives as "black armband history."[34]

It has therefore been a long journey for Aboriginal people in Australia, with an important supporting role from anthropology, to reject colonial perceptions, to establish respect for Indigenous lifeways, and to promote their rights and interests. In composing more positive representations of identity, like many indigenous groups internationally, Aboriginal Australians have been astute in highlighting the importance of their close spiritual relations to place, their deep ecological knowledge, and the long-term sustainability of their lifeways. Providing both an exemplar and a critique of non-Aboriginal failures to achieve sustainable environmental practices, this has been inspirational to conservationist groups concerned about environmental degradation, as well as to people, particularly those living in urban areas, who feel that they lack sufficient social and spiritual connection to place. A more positive view of Aboriginal identity is therefore co-represented by indigenous communities themselves, and by groups sympathetic to their cultural beliefs and values.

Discourses about Indigenous connections to place have also helped to articulate ideas about cultural heritage, a concept recognizing that embedding of identity in places creates a legacy that is both tangible and intangible. Material heritage may be expressed through the shaping of cultural landscapes: the scars on ironwood trees where shields have been cut with stone axes; the roads and fences imposed by settlers. It may rest on visual and written records. But for "heritage" and cultural identity to be maintained it must also be accompanied by intangible legacies: social histories and memories, and specifically cultural beliefs and practices.

While the concept of cultural heritage has helped to widen understandings about Indigenous lifeways, it has also enlivened thinking about place and identity in more recently established communities. In Australia, Aboriginal narratives about long-term prior belonging are countered by the valorization of European "lone pioneers" and "outback battlers," as celebrated for example, by the Stockman's Hall of Fame in Longreach (Figure 14.3). As Gnecco points out in Chapter 6, agency and authority are acquired through the "specific materialities" of heritage. In rural areas, cattle farming dynasties collate family histories and celebrate the sites of historical action undertaken by their "pioneering" ancestors. In urban

Figure 14.3 Stockman's Hall of Fame, Longreach, North Queensland. Photo: Veronica Strang.

areas, community groups produce books about local history, recognizing that possessing historical and locally cultural knowledge is intrinsic to belonging. This raises another material aspect of identity: the capacity to connect or "cathect" to place.

For Indigenous Australians, every dimension of traditional life is mediated by the landscape, and place-based identity is therefore assured. Members of more mobile societies, however, see such deep local connection as aspirational. Homemaking efforts and community engagement provide a partial response but, for urban dwellers in particular, recreational engagement with places has become an important way of reconnecting with "nature" and with lifeways that they see as containing the kinds of sociality less easily achieved in larger-scale urban environments.

As I have noted elsewhere, the term "recreation" is revealing. It contains elements of play, and the relaxing of normal adult social boundaries. It often entails intimate sensory engagement with place: literal immersion in water; the close attention required for fishing or bird watching; slow and observant traversal of landscapes; and the phenomenological experience of visual and audial stimuli, scents, textures, wind, and weather. Its aim is the "re-creation" of the self, suggesting a renewal or rediscovery of individual or group identity, and it enables a sense of connection that, as Milton and others have observed, engenders concern for the well-being of places and their human and/or non-human inhabitants.[35] Much could be said about how this intersects with countermovements seeking social and ecological justice. But the key point here is that the composition of identity, and the values through which it is defined, is in part an emergent outcome of sensory and phenomenological experience and engagement with places and environments.

Knowledge and Identity

Acquisition of intimate knowledge about place also enable connections to them. To have deep memories about a place; to know every detail about what is where; to know the things of which places are composed; and to understand the complex relationships between them, is essential to the processes through which people co-constitute place and identity. The ecological expertise essential to successful hunting and gathering requires a vast lexicon of local knowledge and shared memories, as does understanding the complexities of a cultural landscape deeply imbued with spiritual meanings.[36]

Although more temporarily, and without the support of inalienable connections to place, recreational activities such as fishing similarly encourage close material observation and knowledge acquisition. In more specialized ways, so too do scientific investigations, farming and raising livestock, mining, and so forth. In other words, all engagements with place involve a process of knowledge acquisition, with varying degrees of depth and breadth. Conversely, identities are composed of many kinds of knowledge and memory, in which place is always present. Family histories may focus on accounts of ancestors, relationships, marriages, progeny, and events, but all will "take place" implicitly, in particular locations, amid particular objects. Professional expertise and the identity it confers require imaginative location in particular bodies, communities, institutions, and wider social and material environments.

Like places, knowledges can be highly boundaried, supporting belonging and co-identification, and giving exclusive access to status, resources, and political power. Knowledge boundaries can also be transgressed, and this raises the point that there are multiple social and material levels at which identity is perceived as being vulnerable to pollution: in bodily terms, influxes of foreign blood and "other" genetic inheritances; at a collective group or societal level, the immigration of "foreign" bodies into society; and, in less tangible terms, the inflow of "corrupting" ideas that challenge accepted beliefs and knowledges.

As Douglas established, concepts of pollution are comprehensively cross-cultural, reflecting a shared human need to envisage order. She highlights the spatiality of the concept by defining "dirt," in whatever form, as disorderly "matter *out of place*."[37] This suggests some internal tension in the composition of identity: on the one hand, it is a creative and dynamic process, an active engagement with the world aimed at self-making; but it also entails some striving for stability, for an ordered and boundaried self that has wholeness and integrity. A useful analogy is that of health, which similarly rests on ideas about wholeness.[38] Just as ecosystems require water flows of the right volume, at the right time, physical health relies upon systemic order and integrity, with properly regulated incoming and outgoing flows of matter. Similar principles of balance might also be applied to emotional and mental well-being.

Thus, identity-making entails some regulation of flows, in particular those constituting "otherness." Both individual and collective processes of composing identity depend on conceptual and material boundaries. Increasingly fierce contemporary conflicts about immigration demonstrate all too clearly that there are wide variations in the degree to which permeability is seen as desirable, and in the extent to which people valorize inclusion and exclusion, diversity and homogeneity.

Identity and Agency

The preceding section illustrates that identity is creative and dynamic. It is not something that people merely "have," or "become," but something that they compose in relation to others. This draws attention to the reality that identity is expressed and recursively constructed through representation, performance, and action, and that this "doing" is the basis of social agency.

Visual anthropology has made a vital contribution to understandings of how "self" and "other" identities are represented and communicated through art and material culture. Edwards's analyses of colonial photographs illuminates the role played by visual images in presenting the identities of both colonial settlers and colonized communities, and in shaping the relationships between them.[39] This work also underlines the materiality of images: "photographs are both images and physical objects that exist in time and space and thus in social and cultural experience."[40] As Moore observes in Chapter 11, political relations are sharply revealed in decisions about who controls the production, representation, and interpretation of images and objects.

Indigenous communities are fully cognizant of the importance of reclaiming control over representational processes, and appreciative of the power of objects to produce political and affective responses. Gell, writing about art and agency, explored how artworks such as Gawan canoe carvings, are designed to act upon the viewer and elicit particular ideas and emotions. Morphy considers how Indigenous communities represent their own identity and agency by employing artworks, objects, and performance to explicate their worldviews and promote their rights and interests in the political arena. He describes the production of Yolngu art as a form of action in the world, which centers on ideas about personhood and agency. "Yolngu art is a form of representational and expressive practice that can be used to achieve or at least attempt to achieve certain objectives; these can vary from transporting a person's soul, to affirming group identity, to demonstrating rights in land or the ownership of a motor vehicle."[41]

There is an abundance of seminal anthropological literature on identity and performance and this has often highlighted the importance of ritual and what Turner classically described as "theatre."[42] Religious rituals have an obvious focus on the inculcation of identity, as their core aim is to restate and reaffirm cultural visions of order and concomitant beliefs and values. In Aboriginal ceremonies, such as initiation or mortuary rituals, bodies are painted with totemic clan designs, and songs and dances relate ancestral stories, simultaneously transmitting religious knowledge intergenerationally and reaffirming the shared identity of the participants (Figure 14.4).

Rites of passage are directed specifically toward effecting transformations in identity.[43] Indigenous Australian ritual practices not only include key initiation ceremonies, but also conceptualize the development of identity over time as a series of stages at which, through participation in rituals, people acquire the secret, sacred knowledge that confers gerontocratic authority. In Cape York, a particularly important ritual, undertaken by only a few, is known as "passing through the Rainbow." Via immersion in

Figure 14.4 Children painted with clan designs for ceremony, Kowanyama. Photo: Veronica Strang.

water (the Rainbow Serpent) at a particular sacred site, the acolyte acquires deep sacred knowledge, thus becoming a "clever doctor" or shaman.

There are many everyday ritual behaviors composing identity too. For the European settlers in Cape York, the stages through which young stockmen become experienced "ringers" involve various baptisms of fire, such as breaking a first horse, riding a wild rodeo bull, or killing the livestock sacrificed weekly to feed the station.[44] All societies contain such everyday rituals, though generally requiring a little less fortitude. Small rites of passage, such as giving professional presentations, are meshed with more formal occasions of graduation, or acceptance into professional associations. Across cultures, religious initiations into adulthood are ubiquitous, though are more often directed at men, or regarded as more critical for them.

In most societies, the most transformative rite of passage for many women is that of marriage, which often entails moving to a locale inhabited by the husband's kin, and adopting the husband's family name, which will then also apply to any children issuing from the marriage. Just as the renaming of rivers, mountains, and whole continents, and the renaming of conquered and sometimes enslaved peoples, asserts colonial authority, the adoption of a husband's family name is a useful illustration of the relationship between identity and power. Names are central to identity: the subsuming of one by another is intrinsically unequal, and supports related structural inequalities. Place comes into the equation here too, illustrating the way that that identity is often imagined spatially, in terms of closeness and distance, or relative elevation. Women, people of color, and the "lower" classes, are expected to "know their place."

In understanding links between identity, power, and agency, much depends on who gets to decide what the categories of identity should be, what these will mean, and how categorical boundaries will be maintained. All groups make self-representations and those of "the other," and these can both act upon and counter each other. Stereotypes provide a shorthand way of boxing people into identity categories, and these can range from affectionately humorous to cruelly demeaning. The latter extreme serves to excuse a spectrum of aggressive behaviors: bullying; exclusion; lack of access to opportunities; appropriation of land and resources; subjugation and enslavement; and even genocide.

Identity-making can therefore be seen as a highly competitive process. The representation and performance of identity flows through all aspects of everyday life, and all social interactions. Families continually perform and negotiate familial roles, and relative power; social mobility is concerned with "climbing up"; and professional domains are often extreme in the extent to which they involve jockeying for superior positions. All such efforts are concerned with the enactment of power and agency.

Identity and Agency along the River

Identity, agency, and power are negotiated in multiple ways, and it is useful to consider an example in which highly diverse groups, carrying considerable historical baggage, try to work together. An example is provided by the Mitchell River Watershed Management Group (MRWMG) in North Queensland. The river catchment has an area of 72,000 km^2, which is larger than Tasmania, and it extends from the Coral Sea across the Cape York Peninsula to the Gulf of Carpentaria.

There are many local and regional catchment management groups in Australia, but the MRWMG is unusual in that the Kowanyama Land and Natural Resources Office initiated it in 1990, with a view to increasing indigenous involvement in the management of the river (Figure 14.5). Located near its estuary, the community inherits the effects of many

Figure 14.5 Nelson Brumby (deceased), one of the first Aboriginal rangers in Kowanyama. Photo: Veronica Strang.

economic activities upstream, which include pastoralism, arable farming of fruit and coffee, intensive irrigation farming of sugar cane, and gold mining. Since its inception, as the MRWMG's website says:

> It has grown into an independent, not-for-profit organization working in partnership with local communities and stakeholders toward:

- A balanced approach to the use of the catchment resources; and
- sustainable and integrated management of the Mitchell River catchment area.[45]

The MRWMG has an office donated by the Northern Gulf Natural Resources Management organization, and a coordinator funded via membership and donations. It hosts a number of research projects supported by various funding bodies: for example, recent projects have included one investigating links between ecology and water flows, and another on soil and water quality, focusing on groundwater and salinity. In accord with a politically dominant model describing the river and local ecosystems as economic "assets," the participants are described as "stakeholders." Each group acts as hosts and provides meeting locations, though given their spatial distribution these are more often upriver, or on the eastern coast of the Peninsula.

Typically, MRWMG meetings include cattle farmers from the area and the related Gulf Cattleman's Association; elders from local indigenous communities, and staff, including Aboriginal rangers, from Kowanyama's Aboriginal Land and Natural Resources Management Office; and representatives of relevant government departments: the Queensland National Parks and Wildlife Service (QPWS); the Department of Natural Resources and Mines; and the Environment Agency.

The small alluvial miners, represented by the North Queensland Mining Association, attend more sporadically. The larger mines, active in the area until the late 1990s generally sent their own "environmental officers" to MRWMG meetings. Since the 1980s, tourism has grown rapidly in Cape York, bringing more representation from recreational industry operators. There are people representing recreational and commercial fishers. There are biologists, botanists, ecologists, or hydrologists, either employed by government agencies or conducting university-based research, and the occasional anthropologist, sometimes employed by indigenous organisations. Formerly strong representation by local environmental and conservation groups has declined, as funding to this area has dried up, but the MRWMG counts itself as a survivor in this regard.

In a catchment group primarily composed of professional land and water managers and users, and elders from indigenous communities, women can and do speak up, particularly in relation to health and social issues, but the major conversations about how to manage the river tend to be dominated by men. Government agencies might be represented by women, but the major stakeholder groups concerned with economic matters[46] are largely represented by men. There is a similar gendered pattern in representation from the social and material sciences. "Management," as in other areas, is seen as a primarily male enterprise.

The group has a range of long-term concerns. These include the challenges of controlling invasive weeds and feral animals, in particular pigs and cats. There are debates about fire management, and the use of pesticides and herbicides. There are major water and soil quality issues: erosion from cattle intensification; turbidity from alluvial mining; mine leachate, particularly from older abandoned mines; and, more recently, salinity caused by the irrigation scheme in the upper reaches of the river. There are concerns about tourists, and especially the "bush bashers" who drive through cattle fences and camp illegally. Coastal and estuarine concerns include falling populations of aquatic species, illegal fishing, which is a particular issue for indigenous communities for whom fishing is a major source of food, and the ghost nets that have had a major impact on marine life.

The focus is determinedly on these practical problems, with thornier issues, such as local colonial history, tacitly left outside the door. However, history seeps into discussions about local Native title claims; tensions around traditional access, facilitated by Indigenous Land Use Agreements (ILUAs); and hunting, both on cattle stations and in the national parks. It comes through in debates as to whether populations of local fauna, for example agile wallabies, are plummeting because of increased competition for grass from an intensifying cattle industry; overhunting by indigenous people or visitors; or because of climate change and its effects on seasonal rains.

As elsewhere in Australia, with intensification in all areas of farming, recent conflicts have arisen over water allocations. Some of the rivers in north Queensland were designated as "wild rivers" and protected against riparian developments, but this legislation, established in 2005, was repealed in 2014, restoring planning control to local and state governments. The Mitchell Water Plan from 2007 expired in August 2018, and there are proposals to divert water from the Palmer River, a Mitchell tributary, to a major irrigation property at Lakeland.

Underlying all discussions is the group's core concern: *who* is managing the river? In theory, the common aim is co-management that balances the needs and interests of the diverse stakeholders and the catchment ecosystems. But there are often more self-interested motivations for participation. As noted above, the community in Kowanyama established the group to try to ensure that indigenous voices were heard in debates about the river. And farmers in Queensland readily admit that they deliberately distribute family members across such organizations "to keep an eye on things" and make sure that "sensible" priorities are maintained.[47]

In this way, the regular meetings of the group provide a forum in which identity, agency, and power are negotiated. Hosting meetings is an important way for participants to take center stage and promote their interests, and some can afford to do this more readily than others.

The ritualized format of the meetings depends upon which group hosts the event, and the materialities of the context. Upriver, in the small towns such as Mareeba or Chilligoe, or in Cairns, meetings are shaped by the arrangement of conventional meeting rooms, with seats in neat rows, lecterns for speakers, and in general some formal data presentation. This is a format that imbues speakers with particular authority. The group does strive for less formality in general, but even roundtable arrangements have a hierarchy, with key players literally claiming a seat at the table, and more peripheral participants in an outer perimeter, with their backs to the wall.

There is a performative pattern: a representational dance between groups recurs with some consistency. Representatives from government departments have a strongly mediatory role, and their aims cohere with the respective remits of the departments involved: economic development, environmental protection, and so forth. Their input is often a "carrot and stick" combination, in which they hope to persuade landowners to undertake positive catchment management activities, such as protecting important biodiversity areas, or undertaking weed control; and to dissuade them from activities that have negative impacts, such as overgrazing, building too many dams, or discharging pollutants into watercourses. However, their relative access to funding is naturally reflective of dominant political realities, and material activities promoting economic growth and expansion generally receive more support than those directed toward ecological or social well-being.

Government agencies' ability to provide funding or other resources, or to enforce regulations, for example by prosecuting polluters, are very real forms of agency and power. But the major avenue to having power to affect the material landscape comes through ownership of land and water. In Australia, the states claim ownership of water, and they issue water allocations to different groups of users. However, as these are then tradeable in a water market, and can be traded away from the land from which they arise, water ownership has, de facto, been privatized. Farmers and cattle station owners can dig boreholes and build dams up to a certain height without a license, and thus the road from Cairns to Kowanyama is dotted with small farm dams aiming to retain annual floodwaters. Upriver, around Mareeba, there is considerable irrigated farming, and, as in many Australian river catchment areas, there is pressure to expand existing irrigation schemes.

Land tenure in Far North Queensland falls into several categories that deliver varying degrees of agency and control. There is collective ownership by indigenous groups, arising from former Deeds of Grant in Trust and more recent Native title claims. However, such tenure does not cover mineral rights, water rights, or rights to use local resources other than via traditional methods. There are long-term leases to farmers and mining companies: these are time limited and demand economically productive activities, although the Australian Wildlife Conservancy has purchased one station to preserve local biodiversity. Freehold property includes the small blocks of land owned by recreation industry operators and "blockies" aiming at alternative lifestyles. The Kunjen people have reclaimed the former Alice-Mitchell National Park near Kowanyama under the Native Title Act, and it is now co-managed with the Queensland Parks and Wildlife Service. When the claim succeeded, the colonial nomenclature was reversed, and it was renamed Errk Oykangand National Park, which means "the place of the Kunjen/Oykangand speaking people."[48]

Cattle station leaseholders control most of the land in the catchment, as stations are typically several thousand square miles in size (Figure 14.6). The stations were established in the late 1800s and early 1900s to provide meat to the mining industry, but now sell their cattle to global markets. Their homesteads are often architectural exemplars of the colonial period, and, because they are built at the most reliable waterholes/lagoons, are generally located in places that, for the same reason, were important sacred sites to local indigenous groups.

The cattle farmers express their agency through highly instrumental engagement with the land and waterscape. Their lives are focused on building and maintaining fences, and directing the movements of cattle

Figure 14.6 Dunbar cattle station homestead. Photo: Veronica Strang.

around grazing areas, ensuring they are on higher ground in the Wet, and bringing them in for drafting and transfer to the market in the Dry. Ongoing efforts to increase the "carrying capacity" of the land, and thus its profitability, has led to much dam building and borehole drilling. One result is increased soil degradation and turbidity in the river; another is pressure on local wildlife.

There have been critiques of this intensification by indigenous communities and local conservation groups, but dominant political ideologues insist that growth is necessary for economic viability. Equally important are the identity politics involved. The cattle farmers are members of a powerful, long-established "squattocracy," which "settled" the land and displaced indigenous communities in the first place, and can now draw on several generations of "pioneering" cultural heritage. The industry is represented in both state and federal governments. Thus, at MRWMG meetings, the cattle farmers generally highlight the importance of their activities to the local economy, their expertise and practical experience, and their long-term emplacement and investment in the area.

Though the small alluvial miners in the catchment rarely attend MRWMG meetings, they insist in the political arena that the ecological impact of their activities is minimal. Their representational efforts highlight the historical importance of mining in the area, and this has led to transformation of a number of old mines into sites for historically oriented tourism (Figure 14.7).

Figure 14.7 Maytown historic mine site, Palmer River. Photo: Veronica Strang.

The large-scale gold miners, led in the Mitchell River area by Red Dome, have been regular attendees at MRWMG meetings whenever the mine has been active. Their "environmental officers" have invariably underlined the centrality of mining in the regional and national economy, and foregrounded the technical changes and infrastructure that they say improved the control of poisonous chemicals, such as cyanide, used in production. Their visual representations of identity feature tree-planting on site and colorful birds and flowering plants, juxtaposed with images of showers of gold and robust machinery signifying the "hard yakka"[49] and large profits involved. But the fortunes of large mines are volatile: taken over by Nuigini Mining in 1991, Red Dome was highly profitable for a number of years, but closed in 1997, having spent AUD 5.2 on environmental remediation. Interest in its minerals revived in 2009, but the most constant concern for the MRWMG, as with the other local mine sites no longer owned by the original companies, is the legacy of the poisonous chemicals remaining in tailings dams and ponds, and the ongoing need to prevent such chemicals from leaking into neighboring watercourses.

The commercial fishing industry similarly foregrounds its contribution to the regional economy and the employment opportunities it provides, as do the tourist industry operators, who seek to represent the interests of recreational land and water users. In both cases, there is some incentive to protect the material and ecological well-being of the catchment area, but also to exploit its land and waterscapes.

The scientists' performance of identity rests upon demonstrating specialized knowledge, and presenting problems, analysis, and solutions, much as they would in any professional context. Their representational efforts focus on mostly quantitative data, in the form of graphs and charts. This transferable and purportedly objective expertise supports their agency and authority in decisions about the river. In many instances, their work overlaps with that of conservation groups and the Queensland Parks and Wildlife Service, so their particular "moral high ground" is that scientific research and application supports biodiversity in the catchment, and promotes "sustainable" use of its resources (Figure 14.8).

Aboriginal rhetoric is of a different style. In an indigenous cultural landscape, all places are unique, broad generalizations are rare, and problems are illustrated by specific examples: contiguous engineering work has drained a sacred waterhole at Red Lily, with concomitant impact upon the ancestral landscape. Too many tourists are going to White Water Place, and the "boss" feels the effects of strangers' footprints on his health. Illegal fishing in the estuary is depriving the community of traditionally vital "bush foods."

Achieving agency through "showing rather than telling" is also evident when the indigenous community hosts catchment group meetings. These take place out of doors, often at key sacred sites or those where management issues such as weed invasions or feral pig damage are very evident. Communication with the ancestors is demonstrated performatively, sometimes with increase rituals, but more often with newcomers undergoing the baptismal ritual noted earlier. Thus the indigenous elders demonstrate

Figure 14.8 MRWMG meeting in Kowanyama. Photo: Veronica Strang.

the depth of indigenous traditional knowledge, and the close intimacy of their social, spiritual, affective, and above all *prior* connections to place.

Cultural heritages of various kinds therefore run underneath and sometimes surface in discussions: not only in the deep heritage represented by millennia of indigenous lifeways, but also in the cattle station families' "pioneering" histories; in the reformation of old mine sites as historical places of interest; and in the proudly displayed technical advances within the mining industry.

Maps of the different cultural landscapes of the participant groups are also important in understanding the relationships between identity, agency, and place. They foreground what each group values the most. Thus conservation maps of wildlife distribution present a wilderness to be experienced. Scientific maps focus on elucidating the state of species distributions, geology, soils, and hydrology. Mining maps seek to look under the surface of the land for treasure. Cattle station maps of roads and fence lines assert the net of settlement cast over the land, and its forms of productivity. Aboriginal maps highlight indigenous place names and, though careful about sharing secret sacred knowledge, hint at the depth of indigenous relations with place.

Conclusion

It will be plain that, although there is a broadly shared goal of ecological and social well-being throughout the catchment area, the stakeholders have diverse and sometimes incompatible interests. One of the key aims of the MRWMG is to try to prevent or resolve conflicts in the catchment area, and it has been quite successful in this regard, albeit to some degree by working carefully within a well-established set of social and political relations. These are framed, of course, by dominant ideologies, in which the environment is merely a series of assets to be exploited, as Hutchings describes in Chapter 4. While some groups clearly retain a lot more agency and power than others, the MRWMG has some capacity to subvert the status quo. It has been effective in establishing a strong co-management position for the Indigenous groups in the area. And although it has required them "to talk the talk, and walk the walk" of more powerful groups,[50] it has opened up a space in which they have been able to critique exploitative ideologies and press for more sustainable practices.

With this thumbnail ethnographic sketch of the interactions within the MRWMG, it is possible to gain a glimpse of the different ways in which identity, agency, and power are performed by the participants and the various forms of representation that they employ. A similar analytic approach is applicable within any ethnographic context, tracing the conceptual and material aspects of identity and agency, and the processes through which these are negotiated.

Notes

1. Miriam Nafte, *Flesh and Bone: An Introduction to Forensic Anthropology* (Durham: Carolina Academic Press, 2016).
2. Peter Glob, *The Bog People: Iron-Age Man Preserved* (New York: New York Review of Books, 2004).
3. Charles Loring Brace, *Race is a Four-Letter Word* (Oxford and New York: Oxford University Press, 2005).
4. Linda Alcoff and Eduardo Mendieta, *Identities: Race, Class, Gender, and Nationality* (Oxford: Blackwell, 2003); Richard Schaefer, ed., *Encyclopedia of Race, Ethnicity, and Society* (London: Sage Publications, 2008); Paul Taylor, Linda Alcoff, and Luvell Anderson, eds., *The Routledge Companion to Philosophy of Race* (London: Routledge, 2017).
5. Francesca Merlan, "Land, Language and Social Identity in Aboriginal Australia," *The Australian Journal of Anthropology* 13 no. 2 (1981), 133–48; Laurent Dousset, *Australian Aboriginal Kinship: An Introductory Handbook with Particular Emphasis on the Western Desert* (Marseille: Pacific-credo Publications, 2011).
6. Frances Morphy, *The Macquarie Atlas of Aboriginal Australia* (Canberra: Australian National University, 2017).
7. The Dreamtime or, as it is now more often called, the Dreaming, is also known in Cape York as the Story Time.
8. John Morton, "The Effectiveness of Totemism: Increase Rituals and Resource Control in Central Australia," *Man* 22 (1987), 453–74.
9. Edward Morphy, *Ancestral Connections: Art and an Aboriginal System of Knowledge* (Chicago: University of Chicago Press, 1991).
10. Ibid, 283. See also Howard Morphy and Frances Morphy, "Tasting the Waters: Discriminating Identities in the Waters of Blue Mud Bay," *Journal of Material Culture* 11, nos. 1/2 (2006), 67–85.
11. Matt Cartmill, *A View to a Death in the Morning: Hunting and Nature through History* (Cambridge: Harvard University Press, 1993); Garry Marvin, "Research, Representations and Responsibilities: An Anthropologist in the Contested World of Foxhunting," in Sarah Pink, ed., *Applications of Anthropology* (London and New York: Berghahn, 2006), 191–208.
12. Veronica Gomez-Temesio, "Home is Claiming for Rights: The Moral Economy of Water Provision in Rural Senegal," in Franz Krause and Veronica Strang, eds., *Thinking Relationships through Water*, Special Issue, *Society and Natural Resources* 29, no. 6 (2016), 654–67.
13. Benedict Anderson, *Imagined Communities* (London: Verso, 2003).

14. Robert Brooke, "The Soldier," *1914 and Other Poems*, 1915. Chosen by Philip Larkin in *The Oxford Book of Twentieth Century Verse* (Oxford: Oxford University Press, 1973), 213.
15. Judith Butler, *Gender Trouble: Feminism and the Subversion of Identity* (London: Routledge, 1990); Marilyn Strathern, *The Gender of the Gift: Problems with Women and Problems with Society in Melanesia* (Berkeley: University of California Press, 1988); Henrietta Moore, A *Passion for Difference: Essays in Anthropology and Gender* (Cambridge: Polity Press, 1994), 143.
16. Talia Betcher and Ann Garry, "Transgender Studies and Feminism: Theory, Politics, and Gendered Realities," *Hypatia* 24 no. 3 (2009), 1–10; Jodi O'Brien, *Encyclopedia of Gender and Society* (London: Sage, 2009); Susan Stryker and Stephen Whittle, eds., *The Transgender Studies Reader* (New York: Routledge, 2006).
17. Harriet Whitehead, "The Bow and the Burden Strap: A New Look at Institutionalized Homosexuality in Native North America," in Sherry Ortner and Harriet Whitehead, eds., *Sexual Meanings: The Cultural Construction of Gender and Sexuality* (Cambridge: Cambridge University Press, 1981), 80–115; see also Lynn Morgan and Evan Towle, "Romancing the Transgender Native: Rethinking the Use of the 'Third Gender' Concept," *GLQ: A Journal of Lesbian and Gay Studies* 8, no. 4 (2002), 469–97.
18. Sharon Graham-Davies, *Challenging Gender Norms: Five Genders Among Bugis in Indonesia* (Belmont: Thomson Wadsworth, 2007).
19. Rita Astuti, "'It's a boy!', 'It's a girl!', Reflections on Sex and Gender in Madagascar and beyond," in Michael Lambek and Andrew Strathern, eds., *Bodies and Persons: Comparative Perspectives from Africa and Melanesia* (Cambridge: Cambridge University Press, 1998), 29–52; Rosi Braidotti, *Patterns of Dissonance: A Study of Women in Contemporary Philosophy* (New York: Routledge, 1991), 139.
20. Moore, *A Passion for Difference*, 1994.
21. Veronica Strang, "Familiar Forms: Homologues, Culture, and Gender in Northern Australia," *Journal of the Royal Anthropological Society* 5, no. 1 (1999), 75–95.
22. Adam Kaul, "The Village That Wasn't There: Appropriation, Domination and Resistance," in Veronica Strang and Mark Busse, eds., *Ownership and Appropriation*, ASA Monograph (Oxford and New York: Berg, 2010), 255.
23. Fred Myers, *Pintupi Country, Pintupi Self: Sentiment, Place and Politics among Western Desert Aborigines* (Canberra, Washington, and London: Smithsonian Institute and Australian Institute of Aboriginal Studies, 1986).
24. Veronica Strang, *Uncommon Ground: Cultural Landscapes and Environmental Values* (Oxford and New York: Berg, 1997); David Trigger and Gareth Griffiths, eds., *Disputed Territories: Land,*

Culture and Identity in Settler Societies (Hong Kong: Hong Kong University Press, 2003).

25. More than half of the world's population, and three-quarters of it in Europe, live in urban areas.
26. Australian Bureau of Statistics 2017; UK Office for National Statistics 2018; United States Census Bureau 2018.
27. Tony Cassidy, *Environmental Psychology: Behavior and Experience in Context* (Hove: Psychology Press, 1997); Elizabeth Stokoe, "Public Intimacy in Neighbour Relationships and Complaints," *Sociology Online*, 11, no. 3 (2006). www.socresonline.org.uk/11/3/stokoe.html.
28. Barbara Bender and Margot Winer, eds., *Contested Landscapes: Movement, Exile and Place* (Oxford and New York: Berg, 2001); Paul Carter, *The Road to Botany Bay: An Essay in Spatial History* (London and Boston: Faber and Faber, 1987).
29. Roberts Les, ed., *Mapping Cultures: Place, Practice, Performance* (London: Palgrave Macmillan, 2015).
30. Thomas Wilson and Hastings Donnan, *A Companion to Border Studies* (Chichester: Wiley, 2012); Veronica Strang, Tim Edensor, and Joanna Puckering, eds., *From the Lighthouse: Interdisciplinary Reflections on Light* (London: Routledge, 2018).
31. Raymond Evans and Robert Ørsted-Jensen, "'I Cannot Say the Numbers that Were Killed': Assessing Violent Mortality on the Queensland Frontier" 2014. https://ssrn.com/abstract=2467836.
32. Australian Supreme Court (NT) 1971. See also Henry Reynolds, *The Law of the Land* (London and New York: Penguin, 1987).
33. Veronica Strang, "Raising the Dead: Reflecting on Native Title Process," in S. Toussaint, ed., *Crossing Boundaries: Cultural, Legal, Historical and Practice Issues in Native Title* (Melbourne: Melbourne University Press, 2004), 9–23.
34. Stuart Macintyre and Anna Clark, *The History Wars* (Carlton: Melbourne University Publishing, 2003).
35. Veronica Strang, *Gardening the World: Agency, Identity, and the Ownership of Water* (Oxford and New York: Berghahn, 2009); Tim Ingold, "Footprints through the Weather-World: Walking, Breathing, Knowing," *Journal of the Royal Anthropological Institute*, Special Issue (2010), S121–39; Kay Milton, *Loving Nature: Towards an Ecology of Emotion* (London and New York: Routledge, 2002).
36. Krim Benterrak, Stephen Muecke, and Paddy Roe, *Reading the Country: An Introduction to Nomadology* (Liverpool: Liverpool University Press, 1996).
37. Mary Douglas, *Purity and Danger: An Analysis of Concepts of Pollution and Taboo* (London: Routledge, 2002 [1996]).
38. The terms "health" and "wholeness" are related etymologically through "haleness."

39. Elizabeth Edwards and Matt Mead, "Absent Histories and Absent Images: Photographs, Museums and the Colonial Past," *Museums and Society* 11, no. 1 (2013), 19–38.
40. Elizabeth Edwards and Janice Hart, eds., *Photographs, Objects, Histories: On the Materiality of Images* (London and New York: Routledge, Taylor and Francis, 2004).
41. Alfred Gell, *Art and Agency: An Anthropological Theory* (Oxford and New York: Berg, 1998); Howard Morphy, "'Not Just Pretty Pictures': Relative Autonomy and the Articulations of Yolngu Art in its Context," in Strang and Busse, *Ownership and Appropriation*, 264.
42. Richard Schechner and Willa Appel, eds., *By Means of Performance: Intercultural Studies of Theatre and Ritual* (New York: Cambridge University Press, 1991); David Parkin and Lionel Caplan, eds., *The Politics of Cultural Performance* (Providence: Berghahn Books, 1996); Victor Turner, *From Ritual to Theatre: The Human Seriousness of Play* (New York: Performing Arts Journal Publications, 1982).
43. Van Gennep, *Rites of Passage*, 1960.
44. Strang and Busse, *Ownership and Appropriation*, 2011.
45. Mitchell River Watershed Management Group. www.mitchell-river.com.au.
46. The major economic players are the mining and cattle industries, tourist operators, and various development agencies.
47. Strang, *Gardening the World*, 2009.
48. Oykangand is another way to describe the Kunjen language.
49. Yakka is a colloquial term for "work."
50. Veronica Strang, "The Strong Arm of the Law: Aboriginal Rangers and Anthropology," *Australian Archaeology* 47 (1998), 20–29.

Part IV

Cultural Production and Reproduction

Objects are made to be completed by the human mind.

Alvar Aalto

15

Modes of Representation

Sebnem Timur

In this chapter, I explore the representative power of things, objects, images, products, the built environment, design, and material culture in general. The argument has two components: how objects can convey messages and how messages can be inscribed on objects so that they become carriers of meaning, action, and transgression. I explain representation principally within the theoretical framework of semiotics and sign-based signification. A wide spectrum of objects exemplifies the representative capacity of things, including diamond rings, Vespa scooters, coffee tables, numbers, and maps. Lastly, I demonstrate the changing relationship of material things and people through different disciplinary conceptions, yielding to a discussion of the concept of representation itself.

Objects/Things as Carriers of Meaning

> A garment, an automobile, a dish of cooked food, a gesture, a film, a piece of music, an advertising image, a piece of furniture, a newspaper headline – these indeed appear to be heterogeneous objects.
> What might they have common? This at least: All are signs. When I walk through the street – or through life – and encounter these objects, I apply to all of them, if need be without realizing it, one and the same activity, which is that of a certain *reading*; modern man, urban man, spends his time reading. He reads, first of all and above all, images, gestures, behaviors: this car tells me the social status of its owner, this garment tells me quite precisely the degree of its wearer's conformism or eccentricity, this *apéritif* (whiskey, Pernod, or white wine and cassis) reveals my host's lifestyle.[1]

Roland Barthes[2] opens his "Kitchen of Meaning" with these paragraphs and points to the signification capacity of things, objects, the built environment, and different outcomes of human production and appropriation of nonhuman production. This notion refers to the Marxian conception of the object and commodity's representational character in which objects become the mirror of their production. The mirroring implies that the social relations among human beings are transferred to objects and now they can represent these values.

In order to explain modes of representation, I start with the concept of representation. The semiotic conception of representation refers to the notion of the "sign." Umberto Eco[3] defines a sign as "everything which can be taken as significantly substituting for something else." Anything that has a representational capacity has the ability to act as a substitute for that to which it refers. The representational capacity is determined by the person who uses, beholds, or simply faces the sign. This sign can be anything from a garment to a piece of music, a photograph, and so on.

Let us start with modes of signs to explain modes of representation. Charles Sanders Peirce described three modes of signs: icon, index, and symbol (Table 15.1).[4] They are called modes instead of types because the categories are permeable.

These three modes of signs are useful in providing an analysis consisting of different layers of interaction. The iconic mode refers to the visual or sensory layer of our interaction with things. It functions through "resemblance," providing a basic perceptive base of interaction, and works on the level of survival and identification. The indexical mode of sign refers to a functional relationship, and is about the cues that the object carries related to how it can be operated or used. The symbolic mode of the sign is related to the qualities of the object comprised by the members of the society. The meaning is social, cultural, contextual, and reflexive. If we are to deconstruct the three sign

Table 15.1 *David Chandler's (2002) explanation of C. S. Pierce's three modes of signs*

1. Symbol/symbolic: a mode in which the signifier does not resemble the signified but which is fundamentally arbitrary or purely conventional – so that this relationship must be agreed upon and learned: e.g., language in general (plus specific languages, alphabetical letters, punctuation marks, words, phrases, and sentences), numbers, morse code, traffic lights, national flags.
2. Icon/iconic: a mode in which the signifier is perceived as resembling or imitating the signified (recognizably looking, sounding, feeling, tasting, or smelling like it) – being similar in possessing some of its qualities: e.g., a portrait, a cartoon, a scale-model, onomatopoeia, metaphors, realistic sounds in "program music," sound effects in radio drama, a dubbed film soundtrack, imitative gestures.
3. Index/indexical: a mode in which the signifier is not arbitrary but is directly connected in some way (physically or causally) to the signified (regardless of intention) – this link can be observed or inferred: e.g., "natural signs" (smoke, thunder, footprints, echoes, non-synthetic odors and flavors), medical symptoms (pain, a rash, pulse-rate), measuring instruments (weathercock, thermometer, clock, spirit-level), "signals" (a knock on a door, a phone ringing), pointers (a pointing "index" finger, a directional signpost), recordings (a photograph, a film, video or television shot, an audio-recorded voice), personal "trademarks" (handwriting, catch-phrases).

modes of a plastic water bottle, an industrial product that is consumed on a daily basis, we can say that on an iconic level, the bottle is quickly discernable typologically as a bottle by its neck, cap, and body. The transparent plastic shows the water, so visually the product reflects what it carries as a packaging. On an indexical level, the different material, color, and the texture on the cap implies and directs us to a motion of turning, whereas the waves on the body of the bottle gives clues that after the bottle is emptied, the plastic body can be compressed from those ribs, so that it will occupy less space. The size of the bottle neck clues about the way it is produced, being the only remaining part after the blow molding. Symbolically, the PET (polyethylene terephthalate) bottle conjures many messages related to problems about sustainability, excessive use of the world's resources, throw-away culture, and shrinking of drinkable water. The whole category of PET bottles have become the symbol of industrial production and consumption that challenge a sustainable future. These three modes of signs are the keys of our interaction with the built environment. They depend on our cognitive abilities and how we make sense of the world to survive.

Although not making an explicit connection, Donald Norman, first in his book *Emotional Design*[5] and then in the revised edition of *The Design of Everyday Things*,[6] describes a similar triad of human emotion and cognition that he defines as the visceral, behavioral, and reflective levels. The visceral level resembles the iconic mode of the sign because it works with senses. The behavioral level parallels the indexical mode of the sign, because it relates to operational cues, for example, combining and separating two parts of the object, opening and closing things that have hinges, using certain things for their physical properties, such as using a heavy object as a paperweight (Table 15.2).

Table 15.2 *Comparisons, modes of representation*

Modes of sign[7]	Three levels of processing[8]	Explanation	Relation	Dimension
ICONIC	VISCERAL	Visceral, for the elementary levels of motor action performance and perception	SENSES	INSTINCTS
INDEXICAL	BEHAVIORAL	Behavioral, for the levels of action specification and initial interpretation of the outcome	USABILITY, ACTION, and AFFORDANCES	BODY (FUNCTION)

Table 15.2 Continued

Modes of sign	Three levels of processing	Explanation	Relation	Dimension
SYMBOLIC	REFLECTIVE	Reflective, for the development of goals, plans, and the final stage of evaluation of the outcome	THINKING, EVALUATION, ANALYSIS, RESPONSIBILITY, MEMORY, etc.	MIND (MEANING)

What does this argument about modes of signs and cognitive level of processing have to do with modes of representation and material culture respectively? The reason to start with this background and basic information is that the materiality of objects and our interactions with them determine both our intuitive way of using them and political manipulations of them. The manipulation of objects to signify certain things and the representative capacity of material culture as a whole is critical at this point. The three modes of signs and the three levels of processing relate to the functioning of the triune model of the human brain: the reptilian brain, the paleomammalian brain (limbic system), and the neomammalian brain (neocortex).[9] The neocortex is what makes us human and separates us from other mammals. Reflective and abstract cognitive abilities make reasoning possible: thinking, reflecting, reasoning, questioning, criticizing, and then taking action accordingly. Although the neocortex acts on an abstract level, cues are fed to it through physical, concrete, and material objects. The representative qualities of material culture derive from the concrete and are processed on an abstract level. They can be changed, manipulated, or analyzed through these modes of signs and levels of human processing.

Imposed or Emanated Meanings of Objects/Things

While objects have values and meanings attached to them, a new meaning can be created through strategies of marketing. Objects can also gain new meanings and be manipulated to function in different contexts. An example is the story of diamonds and how they became defined as the symbol of love, attachment, and eternity.

> before World War II, only 10 percent of engagement rings contained diamonds. With a carefully executed marketing strategy, N. W. Ayer could strengthen the tradition of engagement rings and transform public opinion about diamonds – from precious stones to essential parts of courtship and marriage. Eventually, Ayer would convince young men that diamonds are the ultimate gift

of love, and young women that they're an essential part of romantic relationships.[10]

As a result of this marketing campaign, diamonds became the symbol of weddings. De Beers's marketing success was to create a new category of products by manipulating the meaning of an object. This functioned as a "strategy" as opposed to a "tactic" as De Certeau[11] suggests. Strategies work as top-down pressures imposed by the possessors of power, the institutional; against these strategies people use tactics to resist. They find and define their own positions. Deploying the everlasting motto, "A diamond is forever," De Beers created a message that appealed to a collective unconscious such that everyone who is about to make a commitment felt obliged to exchange this piece of stone.

"A diamond is forever" is what Barthes describes as a "Myth Today,"[12] a naturalized type of speech that hides the political, manipulated, the constructed. "A diamond is forever" because the diamond cartel wanted to monopolize and expand the diamond market. The metonymic overlapping of love and diamond is so strong and the story is constructed over a tradition of ring-wearing as the symbol of attachment. There was the ring and what they did was to add the diamond to the engagement ring.

In another example, Dick Hebdige[13] explains in detail the story of the Vespa scooter. In "Object as Image: The Italian Scooter Cycle," he defines the three moments of an industrial product: production, mediation, and consumption. The Vespa scooter was an innovative, new type of product, but the way it was mediated did not match how it was consumed. The marketing campaign was directed at women, yet they are not the sole users of the scooter. Instead, thanks to its light motor and new chassis design, middle-class urban men adopted it to travel to work without their pants getting dirty. Whereas motorcycles were seen as more masculine, Vespa was marketed to be the feminine response to a motorcycle, but in the end it is widely used by men and women in different parts of the world. Even a British subcultural group called "mods" embraced the Vespa because it so precisely aligned with their way of dressing, outfits, and style.

While the industrial product is produced, mediated, and consumed in different ways, Judy Attfield, a foundational theorist of design and material culture, pioneered the detailed explanation of the object's significance opposed to the product. Among other household objects she beautifully defines the phenomena of the coffee table[14] and the empty cocktail cabinet[15] as the symbols of modernity by explaining they and other objects can carry and reflect cultural norms, attitudes, and transformations of meaning.

Simsek Caglar also examines the meaning of tables in "A Table in Two Hands," which focuses on the difference between tables and the arrangements of Turkish immigrants' homes in Germany and Turkey.[16] An ethnographic study of both homes revealed that while the table that the Turkish immigrants living in Germany chose is affordable, modest, and utilitarian, their tables and the furnishing of their homes in Turkey are shaped differently, according to a logic of symbolic qualities, rather than indexical or functional properties. She explains that Turks identify their German homes to be their "real" homes, whereas their homes in Turkey represent their "ideal" homes that carry the idea of what an "ideal household" should be, furnished with all the necessary objects, details, arrangement of things, and use of space.

The representational potential of material culture opens up a space against the theory of consumer culture and the culture industry. The material properties of things around us enable users to speak through the language of matter. The way they are incorporated, appropriated, customized, brought together, organized, and manipulated carries the user from a mere consumer state to a more proactive producer of meanings. Especially, Daniel Miller's wide variety of work, from material things[17] and homes[18] to the practice of shopping[19] and the use of the Internet,[20] has taught us that consumption is a form of production where people have the chance to represent themselves, and how these different relationships, values, and subjectivities become visible or enacted. The theory of material culture of the everyday can act as the arena toward and against the mechanisms of consumer culture and its homogenizing effects.

When the Signified "Seizes" to Be the Signifier

"*Gegenstand*" means "object" in German and translates in English as "that which stands against the body." The object is defined in relation to the body; in return the representation of self is conveyed through objects, garments, accessories, gestures, and music. It is not surprising to see Erving Goffman's early work on the presentation of the self in everyday life[21] remains useful today. Understanding the human face to be a mask or the human body to be an actor/actress playing different roles in everyday life captures their power as representational media on which we reflect our identities. The body, simultaneously a cover and a canvas, makes it the signifying medium, a signifier, whereas the signified is how we want ourselves to be perceived (Figure 15.1). The signifier is the visible and perceivable part of the sign. The signifier stands for the invisible and immaterial part of the sign, the concept to which the signified refers. In this section I will present two examples in which the signified leaks into the "visible" and shapes the perceivable part of the sign (the signifier).

I begin with a homunculus statue that I experienced and remember (Figure 15.2). It was rather startling to see the homunculus statue in the entrance of a science center when I was young. I could not understand why someone put such a strange human figure in front of a place wherein knowledge and the truth about nature is taught. A guide explained the reason for the distortion of certain parts of the human body. The larger the

Figure 15.1 A tattoo designed by the wearer to represent her identity. Photo: Sebnem Timur.

Figure 15.2 Statue of a homunculus in front of Feza Gürsey Science Center in Ankara, Turkey. https://bit.ly/3GbOGc7.

body part in the statue, the larger the area that it occupies in the human cortex based on Wilder Penfield and Edwin Boldrey's analysis.[22]

This homunculus statue was the first type of infographic that I came across and it was truly more inspiring and interesting than anything I had seen before. One reason for my curiosity and wonder was my realization that it is possible to explain an abstract concept by means of a physical entity that was such a powerful explanatory tool. If the representation depended on a correct mathematical relation, then it was possible to convey the relative impact of things both physically and visually.

Using representation as a means to explain facts, phenomena, how things work, or how they are related fits well within the context of education. While representation can demonstrate how things are, Eco[23] reminds us that "a sign is something you can use to tell a lie"; similarly nearly all kinds of representation can easily be used to distort, manipulate, and construct new realities and spaces of discourse.

In response to the homunculus, Paula Di Noto and her co-authors[24] ask in "The Hermunculus" why only the brain cortex of male body parts is represented, even though Penfield also worked with women to map the human cortex. They ask why there is not a hermunculus opposed to or besides a male homunculus representing the female body within the brain. The answer to this question, while providing valuable insight into female physiology and cures for certain illnesses, also illustrates the representational bias in the history of science in terms of dealing with female sexuality. A scientific body is most of the time a male body, like the skeleton in most doctor's offices is perceived to be a skeleton of a male. So, what is visible is also political.

To exemplify the display of both power and resistance in self-expression and identification, we turn to the work of the Afro-Cuban American artist Harmonia Rosales. Her work critiques the white-male dominant history of oil painting through the power of representation in her paintings. She redraws well-known oil paintings, replacing the white-male characters with Black women. This shift opens up a large gap in our perception of both the subject of paintings and the context in which they are created and consumed. She explains her work thus: "The visual narratives of the 'masters' depicting a White heaven and the idealized subordinated woman lay at the foundation of our mediated reality of social order and a power hierarchy. They block our path to the truth. My exhibits intend to begin to clear that blockage by deconstructing the dominant social narrative through the same medium that helped create it."[25]

In her paintings, Rosales turns the invisible, unrepresented, absent, and omitted subject into the signifier itself, and the signified is presented openly and visually, with all its unexpectedness. In the *Introduction to Communication Studies*, John Fiske estimates that about 50 percent of daily communication in English relies on the concept of redundancy, implying that if we remove 50 percent of the words we use, we would still be communicating properly. This means that most subsequent literary and social acts can be predicted. Owing to the literary and grammatical rules, sentence types and the way the information is structured can be anticipated even before their utterance. The power of Rosales's paintings reside in this reciprocal displacement of the redundant signifier with the entropic one through visuality. What is truly redundant within the context of oil painting is exchanged with the most unexpected. Placing the Black woman as the primary subject of the oil painting enables the viewer to question and rethink the story in which it is embedded. The canonical is not as unquestioned, given, taken for granted, or accepted as it was. The canonical is now ordinary, mundane, and human made. This is the power of representation itself: to shake the throne of the invisible signifiers through playing with the visible signifieds.

All modes of representation are by nature political in that they depend on the absence of what the representation stands for. Representation can be considered the shape of absence, as in the case of the number zero. Representation is a kind of social and cultural construction. It reflects beliefs, cosmologies, the way the society works, the way the economic and political system works. It is not only a reflection; for example, democracy itself functions on absence. The whole parliamentary system depends on the absence of the voters.[26]

Case Study 15.1

The story of zero

Representation in mathematics depends on abstraction of information, knowledge, or physical phenomena.[27] Mathematics as representation refers to a specific type of language that enables observation, calculation, and therefore manipulation. One of the most interesting elements of mathematical language is the invention of zero. Hannah Fry explains in a beautiful animation called "The Story of Zero: Getting Something from Nothing," that zero is the absence of value.[28] At first, it was just a placeholder, but Indians used zero as a number in its own right, revolutionizing mathematics."[29]

> Why did the Indians make this imaginative leap? Well we will never know for sure, but it is possible that the idea and the symbol that the Indians used for Zero came from calculations they did with stones in the sand. When stones were moved from the calculation, a small, round hole was left in its place representing the movement from something to nothing.
>
> Perhaps, there is also a cultural reason for the invention of Zero. For the ancient Indians the concepts of Nothingness and Eternity, they are at the heart of their belief system. In the religions of India, the religions were born out of Nothingness and Nothingness is the ultimate goal of humanity. So it is perhaps not surprising that a culture that so enthusiastically embraced the void should be happy with a notion of Zero.[30]

With the invention of zero comes the shockingly simple idea of the void becoming a number in its own right. This signifier of emptiness marks the representational quality of numbers as signifying systems. John Barrow, writing in *The Book of Nothing*, explains the different historical conceptions of Zero and, quite amusingly, its different uses:

> Some zeros seem positively obscure, almost circumlocutory. Tennis can't bring itself to use so blunt a thing as the word "nil" or "nothing"

> **Case Study 15.1 (cont.)**
>
> or "zero" to record no score. Instead, it retains the antique term "love," which has reached us rather unromantically from l'oeuf, the French for an egg which represented the round 0 shape of the zero symbol. Likewise, we still find the use of the term "love" meaning "nothing" as when saying you are playing for love (rather than money).
>
> Barrow explains in detail Western cultures' intolerance toward the concept of emptiness and the void, whereas non-Western cosmologies imagine a habitat in which it is possible to envisage and dwell with the notion of the nonexistent.

Representation of Reality

Documentary films are useful in demonstrating the ways in which reality can be represented. In 1969 Kenneth Clark launched the television series *Civilization*, a thirteen-episode BBC series later published as a book. The project focused on Western art and philosophy, based on research that spanned an "80,000 mile journey visiting 13 countries, 117 locations, 18 libraries, and 118 museums."[31] It is criticized for being a white-male oriented depiction of Western civilization. John Berger responded in 1972 with a sort of counter-series, entitled *Ways of Seeing*. Berger's series critiqued the Western representational tradition and art, following the narrative from oil painting to contemporary visual mechanisms of advertising.

Berger begins his depiction of Western art by introducing the concept of perspective. In Western art, the perspective represented was generally the single-pointed Cartesian world view, situating the human subject at the center of the gaze. Different world views are suggested through different modes of representation, such as miniatures. Unlike perspective drawings, in miniatures, the subject, who is the beholder of the gaze, floats above the picture plane. In perspective drawings, the painter depicts the world from the viewpoint of the viewer, which is the most accurate optical representation of reality. On the other hand, in miniatures, the miniaturist's viewpoint is not a fixed and steady one. For example, if a castle is to be represented, the walls on the left side would be drawn as if viewed from the left side; the right side of the castle walls would be drawn as if observed from the right side. It is like introducing different viewpoints into the field of vision. This provides a three-dimensional conception of the world being depicted, one which works quite differently than the fixed single point gaze of the perspective. While the Western perspective suggests a steady but true representation of reality, miniatures provide a more flexible and mobile representation of reality. Perspective aims to reflect what the eye sees, whereas the latter acts like human thought itself, acentered and moving. If we are to equate the painter to our avatar in a board game, the Western perspective presents us a single avatar to view the world from a single point of view; miniatures allocate different avatars, in different parts of the board in a single image. This comparison does not aim to imply one conception is superior to the other, but rather to point to the differences in modes of representation.

There are similar cosmological practices that demand new orders of signification and representation that are like extensions of different world views, thoughts, or cosmologies, like the one in miniatures. The most well-known are iconoclastic traditions of representation. The underlying motif of most iconoclasm is that what is represented is so transcendent that it cannot have a visible, perceivable signifier. An example is most Islamic patterns, in which the idea of eternity is represented through geometric patterns that allude to unity in the endless fractal combinations of a single source. Most Islamic patterns are the abstractions of the "divine creator," which is beyond human perception and cannot be represented with figurative images that we know or recognize. Instead, the recurring and repeating endless geometric forms are used to imply the idea of being endless, something that has no beginning and no end. The meaning itself becomes the signifier relying on the fact that just like the conception of God that is eternal, the patterns have no end and beginning.

Case Study 15.2

Act of mapping and politics

Maps are the representations of the world we live in. There are different ways to make a map depending on the technique and the intention of the mapmaker. Aslıhan Şenel[32] defines this intentionality in mapmaking and also the deliberate act of map-using as the "performance of place." The political is marked and reproduced through this act of mapping. Mapping can become an object of resistance, a way to make visible and become visible. Consider, for example, Mercator's projection:

> Mercator's projection of the world continues to be beneficial for navigation for sailors and pilots, who rely on the straight lines depicted on the map and which match up with the four cardinal directions on a compass. The downside to Mercator's projection is that it is nearly impossible to show both the shape and size of landmasses on a map – one must be sacrificed, and this tends to be size (as shape is very important on a map!). Cartographers call this size/shape discrepancy "the Greenland Problem" as the Mercator projection shows the small island of Greenland (0.8 million square miles in size) to be roughly the same size as the continent of Africa (1.6 million square miles). Mercator's projection most compromises

Case Study 15.2 (cont.)

the true size and shape of the continents on Earth closer to the Equator, and the farther you get away from the equator the less accurate size is able to be depicted.[33]

Şenel describes Guy Debord and Ager John's[34] illustration called the "Naked City," which presents a visual and spatial experience of Paris, rather than a formal and geographic representation of the city. Şenel defines mapping as a performative act rather than a representational tool.[35] "The shift from theories of map-making to mapping represents a desire to transform the worldview that seeks a single objective and quantitative knowledge of place to one that embraces subjective and qualitative multiple knowledges of place. The shift refers to a change from representative theories to performative ones."[36]

The map as an object is and can be designed according to different purposes. One of the most famous maps that enabled simplicity and comprehension in reading the paths, lines, and relations is the London tube map. Designed by Harry Beck in 1931, the map provides a schematic and geometric representation of the intersecting lines, while disregarding the geographical distances. Although two stops may seem close and adjacent to each other, they may be geographically distant from each other. Sacrificing geographic relations contributed to the clarity and power of the map.

Contrary to the London tube map, a map designed by Hajime Narukawa called the AuthaGraph World Map, aims at representing the true geographical relations and proportions (Figure 15.3a and b). It received a Good Design Award of Japan in 2016. On this map there is no direction, no hierarchy, no East, no West, no North, no South, no center. Thinking of the globe as a seamless structure, without borders, it is quite stunning to see the real size of Africa as opposed to Europe and to envision the places and proximities of continents, oceans, and lands anew. The materiality of representation creates and rearranges our perceptions through new designs like this map. Prejudices, ideas, and opinions can be altered by changing the way we see and perceive the world. This map is one of the best examples of representing a vast array of different kinds of information: political, geographical, atmospheric, seismic, social, cultural, dimensional, directional, and so on. All this information is materialized as signifiers that are visible, defining the politics of representation. It shows there are no "four corners of the earth" by arranging several world maps without visible seams around a world map with color. You can see Antarctica at the right bottom is close to not only South America but also Africa and Australia.[37]

> This rectangular world map called AuthaGraph World Map is made by equally dividing a spherical surface into 96 triangles, transferring it to a tetrahedron while maintaining areas proportions and unfolding it to be a rectangle. The world map can be tiled in any directions without visible seams. From this map-tiling, a new world map with

Case Study 15.2 (cont.)

triangular, rectangular or parallelogram's outline can be framed out with various regions at its center. The name, AuthaGraph is from authalic and -graph.[38]

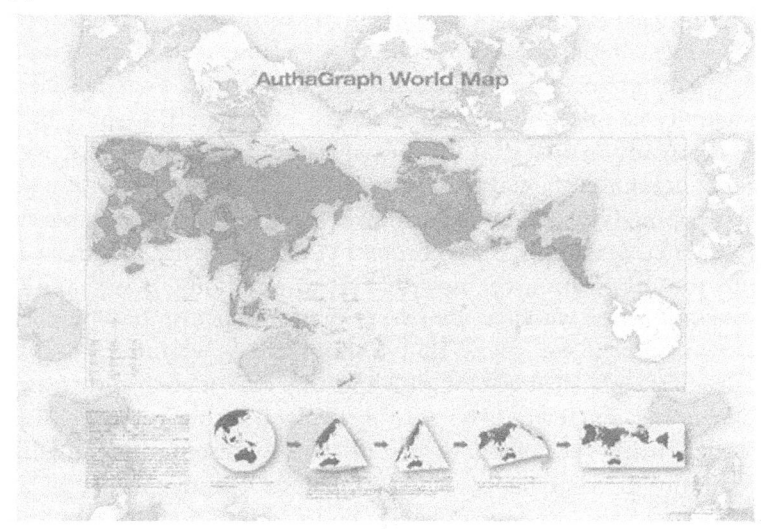

(a)

(b)

Figure 15.3a and b The AuthaGraph World Map created by Hajime Narukawa, www.authagraph.com.

Objects, Representation, Design, and Material Culture

Elizabeth Shove, Matthew Watson, Martin Hand, and Jack Ingram,[39] in *The Design of Everyday Life*, chart the transformation from product-centered design to user-centered design, and finally to practice-centered design (Figure 15.4). Their argument relies heavily on Bruno Latour's[40] actor network theory (ANT), but the notion of practice-oriented design also correlates to nonrepresentational theory, in which the object or representation of it is no longer important; rather the way it is engaged in any kind of practice, use or motion gains significance. In this kind of negative theory of representation, one does not look at the object or the spot that it occupies positively in space, but rather at its negative space, as it were, the larger context and the field of action the object belongs to or is a part of. Since mapping is described as performing space,[41] can we assume that practice-oriented design performs context? Performing context can be one answer to the proposition of "negative representation." If we take the Latourian stand, then we have to assume that objects also have agencies in their own right. If we follow Hans Gumbrecht,[42] we understand the importance of the physical and tangible together over mere interpretation and sole meaning, and it would be possible to dwell in the "presence." If we rely on Nigel Thrift,[43] we read it as part of "non-representational theory," the "geography of what happens" that suggests embracing action and movement together among objects, bodies, buildings, mountains, cities, etc.

Jane Fulton Suri has tried to bring a social science perspective to the field of design. While working in one of the most influential design consultancy

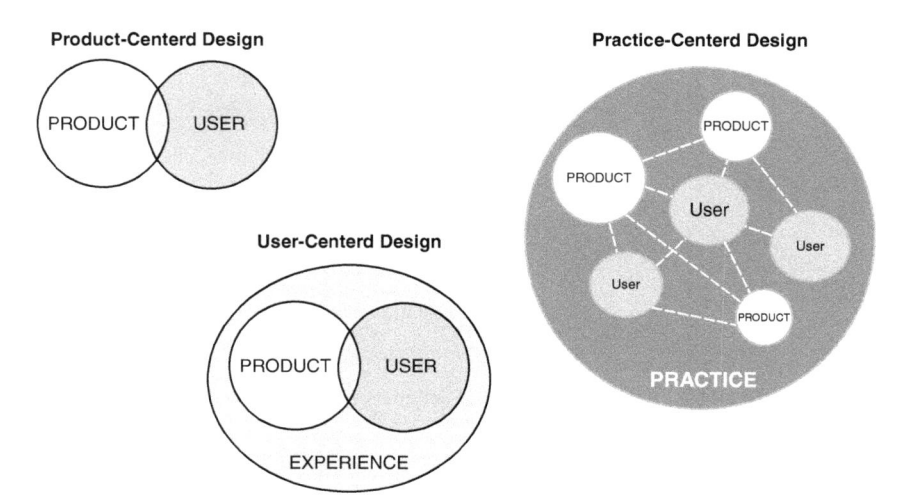

Figure 15.4 Diagrams showing the three phases of design (illustrated by the author from Shove et al. (2007)).

firms IDEO, she wrote *Thoughtless Acts?*, which describes and illustrates different uses of things, objects, spaces, and products. She developed a categorization based on the ways we interact with the world through reacting, responding, co-opting, exploiting, adapting, conforming, and signaling. Different appropriations of objects around us can no longer be static with predefined relations, rather they are dynamic reconstructions performed through the course of the everyday. The streets of Istanbul provide an example. Furniture upholstery makers demonstrate their work on the pavements that function to mark the existence of the shop and attract attention; at the same time, taking the spacious furniture out of the shop saves interior space for work (Figures 15.5 and 15.6). The furniture has a bodily existence in the street, marking a presence, marking the public space with individual objects. Sometimes these objects, mostly different types of old, worn furniture, are used to mark this presence in the public space, implying they have an owner. This continuous movement of objects that belong to the private domain within the public sphere is exemplary of

(1) The agency of objects: chairs can stand on their own, thus chairs can stand on the streets by themselves. By their weight, they can withstand wind and other forces. By their volumes they can occupy space, so that they do not let other cars park in empty slots. Unlike the trees or concrete elements used to block

Figures 15.5 and 15.6 Furniture demonstrated on the pavements by upholstery makers in Istanbul. Photos: Sebnem Timur.

Figures 15.5 and 15.6 (cont.)

parking, they are mobile and have a temporary status, so that they gain the right to exist in the temporality of the flow of the street.
(2) Human/user-centered and practice-centered design. The furniture is reminiscent of its producers, designers, users, or any other stakeholder in the practice of upholstery making which still exists as part of a repair-craft tradition against the mechanisms of a capitalist mode of production and consumption patterns.
(3) Signifying practices that describe current trends in colors, patterns, styles, accepted and valued types of furniture that represent certain lifestyles. The newness of the upholstery, the way the objects have been refurbished in terms of craftsmanship implies that the shop is working well and reliably. As the new or newly refurbished furniture is demonstrated on the street, it also gives the impression that there is significant workflow within the shop.

Anthony Dunne and Fiona Raby's work renders a quite different image. By being both speculative and bold, they demonstrate possible futures with a critical tone. Their work consists of projects that look quite realistic. Etymologically the word "project" means throwing something further away. The strength of a project is that it is not produced, it is not material yet. A project is a representation of how an object or a product would look and work, for example within an imagined scenario. Making things look like they are part of a material setting, Dunne and Raby find a convenient zone in this immaterial aspect of the "project"ness of things and use the representative character of objects as their form of expression. The publisher introduces their book *Speculative Everything* this way:

> *Speculative Everything* offers a tour through an emerging cultural landscape of design ideas, ideals, and approaches. Dunne and Raby cite

examples from their own design and teaching and from other projects from fine art, design, architecture, cinema, and photography. They also draw on futurology, political theory, the philosophy of technology, and literary fiction. They show us, for example, ideas for a solar kitchen restaurant; a flypaper robotic clock; a menstruation machine; a cloud-seeding truck; a phantom-limb sensation recorder; and devices for food foraging that use the tools of synthetic biology. Dunne and Raby contend that if we speculate more "about everything" reality will become more malleable. The ideas freed by speculative design increase the odds of achieving desirable futures.[44]

While it is possible to speculate through objects for the future, it is also possible to design objects accordingly to make them socially responsive,[45] to prevent crime,[46] to promote social innovation,[47] or contribute to a critical discourse.[48] This is the role of designers. Users similarly share in appropriating things accordingly to fight against forces, and to create nodes of resistance and fields of expression for themselves. Catherine Flood and Gavin Grindon provide an instructive compilation of such objects in real life settings in their book *Disobedient Objects*. Unlike Fulton Suri's everyday appropriations, disobedient objects are part of outbreaks or civil commotions against antidemocratic acts. These objects, while widespread and affordable enough to be dispensable, are utilized for tasks that are otherwise unthinkable; for example, the plastic water bottle transformed into a gas mask in the 2013 Gezi Park protests in Istanbul, or the use of pans, pots, and scoops for noise making in the 2008 protests in Buenos Aires.[49]

Representation of Relations of Objects and Subjects

All scientific inquiry depends on the separation between subject and object. Placing the object on one side of the spectrum and placing the subject on the other end gives us the whole scale of differences in scientific thought. While object-based scientific inquiry supposes that the truth resides in the object itself, subject-based inquiry supposes that the truth resides in the subject. Constructionism is in the middle and looks at the interaction between the object and subject. On the other hand, contemporary theoretical approaches like ANT and non-representational theory tend to dissolve these boundaries of object and subject. Actor Network Theory includes objects within the scope of sociology, which had only considered subjects, and proposes to build the broken bridge over this fissure opened by modern thought. Nonrepresentational theory targets actions, movements, or happenings, rather than objects and subjects. These two lines of thought redefine new modes of representation that build the link between

Table 15.3 Subject–object spectrum in representation

OBJECT	SUBJECT	
PRODUCT	USER	DESIGN
COMMODITY	CONSUMER	ECONOMY
ARTIFACT	SOCIETY	SOCIOLOGY-ANTHROPOLOGY
SIGNIFIER/SIGN	READER	SEMIOTICS
THINGS	PEOPLE	MATERIAL CULTURE
ACTORS, HUMANS, NONHUMANS, HYBRIDS		ACTOR-NETWORK THEORY
MOVEMENT, HAPPENINGS, ACTION, FLOWS		NONREPRESENTATIONAL THEORY

and among objects and subjects. The significance of this new way of thinking about objects, subjects, and how they are related is that the relationship itself has become an entity to be embodied, studied, constructed, represented, and/or designed (Table 15.3).

New media, for example, relies on this link or relationship between and among objects and subjects. Information technologies, the Internet, and social media are making these kinds of relations more visible in ways that are elaborated by Cordell in Chapter 23 and Chuk in Chapter 24. Artificial intelligence is learning existing links and offering new ones for different kinds of user purposes. Information and representation of information have never been so traceable and trackable, both in terms of quantity and visuality. For example, the rise of the tag or word clouds work on the principle of representing the most frequent words within a site or a text with larger font sizes.[50] This statistical analysis provides an opportunity for the viewers to get an idea of which words and concepts stand out in the text just at a glance. Visualization of information according to reliable and accurate data has changed the relationship between both graphic production and perception. The information that we face today has become more relational. For example, social network sites not only combine friends, but also help to create and sustain a network that works over a collective visibility. Our perception or value propositions of things have become highly attached to the number of other people that "look," "click," or "like" them. They are gaining value from another layer of information beside their content: number of likes, or number of good comments, number of recommendations, etc. While Jean Baudrillard[51] added the "sign value" proposition to objects beside the Marxian "exchange" and "use values," now we are facing another type of value that I call "relational value." Relational value relies on the abstract layers of different informational representations over objects, products, films, articles, games, experiences, places, etc. Designers in the future may be responsible for implementing this new mode of representation while still dealing with the materiality of things.

Conclusion

There were three basic axes of the argument in this chapter: (1) objects/things are carriers of meaning (either imposed or emanated); (2) objects/things are representations themselves (of their functional properties); and (3) meaning occurs between and/or among networks of things/objects and/or people. In concluding, I am reminded of Attfield's statement on the tension between material culture and signification. She argues that a material culture perspective puts matter over meaning; she does not propose completely denying meaning, but rather suggests we examine them both and relatively. "A material culture perspective de-emphasizes the importance given by the theory of representation that prioritizes meaning over matter through the interpretation and explanation of ideological cultural codes that are seen to reside behind the false front of appearance conceived as a 'system of signs.'"[52]

This chapter, while relying on the theory of a system of signs and signification, also "projects" the object/thing itself with all its materiality as a representational medium. The object/thing as a representational medium means that meaning moves both toward the object/thing and from the object/thing, and that despite all these representative movements occurring through and over the object, the object/thing remains to represent itself.

Crome and Williams[53] explain in their *Lyotard Reader*:

> as Mallarme himself stressed, in its communicative function language negates the reality of its referent. For example, the word "table" stands in for the actual object that it refers, taking its place; but it does not just stand in for the particular object, since in so doing it destroys its particularity. The word "table" can be used not just of this table that I am sitting at now, but of all tables. In this sense, the word has a universal and ideal significance; it negates the actual, particular thing and replaces it with the concept. It is because the word works in this way, we are able to communicate by its means. To put this

another way, language imposes truth on experience, because it imposes the unchanging and non-contingent identity of the concept upon it. In drawing attention to this capacity of language to negate the reality of things.

The power of material culture is that while embracing all the representative load of the thing/object, it can remain still and silent with the singular, one and only thing itself, with its iconic, indexical and symbolic qualities; with its visceral, behavioral and reflective characteristics; with all its mundane, material, everyday existence, even as the object/thing is being re-produced, re-experienced, re-contextualized or re-enacted in different settings, contexts, scenarios, and agents of any kind.

Case Study 15.3

"This is Not a Pipe" versus "Banana with Duct Tape"

Judy Attfield argues that "whereas art enchants the ordinary object and makes it special, design disenchants it." The threshold between an ordinary object and art has never been this close, as we have witnessed by the incident of the "banana duct-taped to the wall of a gallery." Talking with and representing with objects have long been tools of art and design. When Magritte was painting the pipe, with the subtext "This is not a Pipe," he was questioning the notion of representation itself, whereas taping the banana to the gallery wall is like writing "This is a Banana" on the wall with the thing/object itself. Representation has overlapped itself, losing all meaning and capacity of signifying anything other than itself. This can be considered the end of representation itself.

Notes

1. Roland Barthes, "The Kitchen of Meaning," in *The Semiotic Challenge* (Berkeley: University of California Press, 1994), 157–59.
2. Ibid.
3. Umberto Eco, *A Theory of Semiotics* (Bloomington: Indiana University Press, 1976).
4. David Chandler, *Semiotics: The Basics* (New York: Routledge, 2002).
5. Donald Norman, *Emotional Design: Why We Love (Or Hate) Everyday Things* (New York: Basic Books, 2004).
6. Donald Norman, *The Design of Everyday Things: Revised and Expanded Edition* (New York: Basic Books, 2013).

7. Charles Sanders Peirce, "Collected Papers of Charles Sanders Peirce," in Charles Hartshorne and Paul Weiss, eds., *Collected Papers* (8 vols., vol. 1) (Cambridge: Harvard University Press, 1931).
8. Norman, *Emotional Design*.
9. Paul D. MacLean, "Triune Brain," in Louis N. Irwin, ed., *Comparative Neuroscience and Neurobiology* (1998), 126–28.
10. Lindsay Kolowich Cox, "The Engagement Ring Story: How De Beers Created a Multi-Billion Dollar Industry from the Ground Up," June 13, 2014. https://bit.ly/3nEz7Dy.
11. Michel De Certeau, *The Practice of Everyday Life* (Berkeley: University of California Press, 1988).
12. Roland Barthes, "Myth Today," *Mythologies* (New York: Hill and Wang, 1972), 109–59.
13. Dick Hebdige, "Object as Image: The Italian Scooter Cycle," in Dick Hebdige, *Hiding in the Light: On Images and Things* (London and New York: Routledge, 2001), 77–115.
14. Judy Attfield, "Design as a Practice of Modernity: A Case for the Study of the Coffee Table in the Mid-Century Domestic Interior," *Journal of Material Culture* 2, no. 3 (1997), 267–89.
15. Judy Attfield, "The Empty Cocktail Cabinet: Display in the Mid-Century British Domestic Interior," in Tim Putnam and Charles Newton, eds., *Household Choices* (London: Futures Publication, 1990), 84–88.
16. Ayse Simsek Caglar, "A Table in Two Hands," in Deniz Kandiyoti, ed., *Fragments of Culture: The Everyday of Modern Turkey* (London: Tauris, 2002), 294–307.
17. Daniel Miller, *Stuff* (Cambridge and Oxford: Polity Press, 2009).
18. Daniel Miller, ed., *Home Possessions* (Oxford: Berg, 2001); Daniel Miller, "Designing Ourselves," in Alison Clarke, ed., *Design Anthropology* (New York: Springer, 2010), 88–99.
19. Daniel Miller, *A Theory of Shopping* (Cambridge and Oxford: Polity Press, 1998).
20. Daniel Miller, "Social Networking Sites," in Hans Horst and Daniel Miller, eds., *Digital Anthropology* (Oxford: Berg, 2012), 156–61.
21. Erving Goffman, *The Presentation of Self in Everyday Life* (Garden City: Doubleday, 1959).
22. Wilder Penfield and Edwin Boldrey, "Somatic Motor and Sensory Representation in the Cerebral Cortex of Man as Studied by Electrical Stimulation," *Brain* 60, no. 4 (December 1, 1937), 389–443. https://doi.org/10.1093/brain/60.4.389.
23. Eco, *A Theory of Semiotics*.
24. Paula M. Di Noto, Leorra Newman, Shelley Wall, and Gillian Einstein, "The *Hermunculus*: What Is Known about the Representation of the Female Body in the Brain?" *Cerebral Cortex* 23, no. 5 (2013), 1005–13. https://bit.ly/3ueHZnk.

25. Harmonia Rosales, *The Creation of God*. Oil on Linen. 48˝ h x 60˝ w. B.I.T. C. H. Black Imaginary to Counter Hegemony: Art Series, 2017, https://bit.ly/32hk37o.
26. Bernhard Weßels, "Political Representation and Democracy," in Russell J. Dalton and Hans-Dieter Klingemann, eds., *The Oxford Handbook of Political Behavior* (Oxford: Oxford University Press, 2007), 833–49.
27. Christopher Pincock, *Mathematics and Scientific Representation* (Oxford: Oxford University Press, 2012).
28. www.youtube.com/watch?v=9Y7gAzTMdMA.
29. See the documentary "The History of Zero: Discovery of the Number 0 by Ancient India." BBC's Story of Maths. www.youtube.com/watch?v=LQEuywkWa2U, 3.20–4.30 sec.
30. Ibid.
31. Amazon review of Kenneth Clark, *Civilization*. https://amzn.to/3GJCSz7.
32. Senel, "Mapping as Performing Place."
33. Elizabeth Borneman, "Cartographic Anomalies: How Map Projections Have Shaped Perceptions of the World" (February 2014). https://bit.ly/34VcN1O.
34. Guy Debord and Asger Jorn, *The Naked City* (New Haven: Beinecke Rare Book and Manuscript Library, 1957).
35. Senel, "Mapping as Performing Place."
36. Ibid, 95.
37. www.authagraph.com/category/products/?lang=en.
38. https://bit.ly/35ANjr1.
39. Elizabeth Shove, Matthew Watson, Martin Hand, and Jack Ingram, *The Design of Everyday Life: Cultures of Consumption Series* (London: Berg, 2007).
40. Bruno Latour, *Reassembling the Social: An Introduction to Actor-Network-Theory* (Oxford and New York: Oxford University Press, 2005).
41. Aslihan Senel, "Mapping as Performing Place," *disClosure: A Journal of Social Theory* 23, no. 8 (2014). https://doi.org/10.13023/disclosure.23.08.
42. Hans Ulrich Gumbrecht, *Production of Presence: What Meaning Cannot Convey* (Stanford: Stanford University Press, 2004).
43. Nigel Thrift, *Non-representational Theory: Space, Politics, Affect* (London and New York: Routledge, 2007).
44. Anthony Dunne and Fiona Raby, *Speculative Everything: Design, Fiction, and Social Dreaming* (Cambridge: The MIT Press, 2013).
45. Loraine Gamman and Adam Thorpe, "What is 'Socially Responsive Design and Innovation'?" in Fiona Fisher and Penny Sparke, eds., *Routledge Companion to Design Studies* (London: Routledge, 2016), 317–29.
46. Paul Ekblom, ed., *Design Against Crime: Crime Proofing Everyday Objects* (Boulder: Lynne Rienner Publishers, 2012).
47. Ezio Manzini, *Design, When Everybody Designs: An Introduction to Design for Social Innovation* (Cambridge: The MIT Press, 2015).

48. Matt Malpass, *Critical Design in Context: History, Theory, and Practice* (London: Bloomsbury, 2017).
49. Catherine Flood and Gavin Grindon, eds., *Disobedient Objects* (London: Victoria and Albert Museum, 2014).
50. Florian Heimerl, Steffen Lohmann, Simon Lange, and Thomas Ertl, "Word Cloud Explorer: Text Analytics Based on Word Clouds," *47th Hawaii International Conference on System Sciences*, 1833–42, January 2014.
51. Jean Baudrillard, *For a Critique of the Political Economy of the Sign* (St. Louis: Telos Press, 1981).
52. Judy Attfield, *Wild Things: The Material Culture of Everyday Life* (Oxford: Berg, 2000).
53. Jean François Lyotard, Keith Crome, and James Williams, *The Lyotard Reader and Guide* (Edinburgh: Edinburgh University Press, 2006).

16

Aesthetics

Timothy Carroll[1]

Within social theory, scholars have used aesthetics to discuss four main theoretical concerns. The first follows closely upon the philosophical tradition of Immanuel Kant and takes aesthetics as an ancillary to rational cognition, or as the mediating interchange between internal cognition and the external world. The second puts a more phenomenological emphasis on this and takes aesthetics as relating to the somatic experience of sensual forms in the world. The third takes aesthetics as the domain of the formal constituting elements of these external sensual forms, the style and harmony of relations within art-like, or quotidian, artifacts, and social practice. The fourth takes aesthetics as akin to beauty or ornamentation, often using it as an adjective used to mark the main noun as somehow analytically complex, a mix of beauty, elaborate, and ethically or cosmologically weighted.

In many cases, the use of "aesthetics" reads as an almost intentionally indeterminate term, as if the author wishes to sidestep the hazy quagmire that is "aesthetics" with its many meanings and complex array of implications. Even in contexts where an author provides a clear analytical frame for the term's use, there is often slippage in its specific meanings. This complexity is no doubt our inheritance passed down through the generations of philosophical, art critical, and social theoretical developments, critiques, and adaptation of "aesthetics". There is also the clear problem – at least from the perspective of intellectual coherence – of the collapse of the clarity and coherence offered by the grand narrative of European scholasticism. The deeply Eurocentric elitism that was indistinguishable from the development of aesthetics as a philosophical concept has left a bad taste in the mouth of subsequent generations. Moreover, the inherently subjective nature of the subject of study (in at least the second, third, and fourth senses of aesthetics) also makes difficult any attempt at maintaining aesthetics as a coherent overarching theoretical project.

In this chapter, I advance an argument in favor of Aesthetics (in the capital) as an area of comparative study, which examines the role of aesthetics (in the lower case) as means to access the internal, intuitive geometries of logic and society. This is an attempt to bring the first three definitions offered above into a mutually informed model. If we accept, as I argue below, that there is necessarily correlation between the interior mind and the exterior forms in the world, and that the rational capacity of mind relies on the somatic perception of being-in-world, and that the formal elements of artifacts and performance trigger intuitive cognitive function, then we can take aesthetics as a phenomenon linking the interior mind and the exterior concretizations of society. Aesthetics, then, is a comparative anthropological science of understanding how these internal, intuitive geometries of logic are concretized in the exterior forms of human experience.

I do not review the breadth and variety of uses, but rather sculpt a specific trajectory in order to offer a way forward.[2] There are very well articulated reasons to abandon the term entirely, and scholars who have sought to do so. However, the term remains, and it is almost seductively profitable. It is therefore my proposal that the project be harnessed for specific aims needed most by those – namely scholars in material culture and the social sciences of sensible forms – tempted to reach for this specific analytical tool. I start with a brief history – highlighting key aspects of aesthetics in philosophical and cross-cultural studies – and then move to examine Gregory Bateson's ecological understanding of mind and nature, and specifically the role of abduction, or intuitive inferential thinking, in the relationship between the interior mind and the exterior artifactual domain.

From Baumgarten

In 1750, Alexander Gottlieb Baumgarten proposed aesthetics as a way to address the role that the senses play in judgment – that is, the perception and valuation – of sensation. In this sense, "aesthetics" was opposed to rational cognition. Baumgarten was interested in the perception of beauty itself, and argued that whereas objects of thought, like mathematics and the physical sciences, were the rightful subjects of the discipline of Logic. Objects of the senses, which cannot be understood by reason alone, should be studied by the discipline of Aesthetics. Aesthetics, he defined as "the science of sensible cognition." Baumgarten took the term from the Greek for "sensitive" or "relating to sense perception." However, up to that point, the word *aisthetikos* was used to discuss the bodily response to stimulation. In the new coinage, Baumgarten gave the term important new analytical weight.

As a science, it is methodological, and invites systematic study. He argues that "the purpose of aesthetics is the perfection of sensible cognition, that is beauty; the imperfect is avoided, however, as it is deformity."[3] In framing "aesthetics" as being purposive toward the perfection of beauty, and to the resistance of deformity, he gives aesthetics a moral valence within a context where the classical virtues of Goodness, Truth, and Beauty were indelibly united. Being beautiful, and being able to correctly identify beauty, was indicative of moral superiority and veracity.

For generations of philosophers following Baumgarten, the debate was therefore *how*, not *if*, exposure to beauty helped in people's moral formation. Immanuel Kant, in his late-eighteenth-century treatise *The Critique of Judgement*,[4] addressed the nature of objects of the senses, arguing that aesthetics is the cognitive capacity for judging or evaluating things, in order to determine if that thing is truly Beautiful.[5] If Beautiful, then it is consequently also True and Good. This aesthetic judgment, however, is – in Kant's understanding – only possible when the viewer is neutral, unbiased, and therefore able to offer a disinterested and objective evaluation. If one can evaluate the thing in question with such a passionless gaze, then recognition of Beauty can bring about the sensation of pleasure because of the beautiful or sublime aspect. This assessment, done from a "disinterested" position, worked, it was reasoned, because Beauty was an essential – that is true and inherent – quality of the object,[6] not a subjective assessment of preference.

Aesthetics, then, as a faculty of cognition, is a process of assessing the qualities of an object without assigning it into any logical categorization. So, instead of seeing light in the sky and saying, "that is a sunset" (which would be an act of rational cognition), the act of aesthetic judgment is to appraise without assumption, and thereby the viewer is able to appreciate the beauty of the luminescent drama, which far surpasses the typological marker of "sunset." There is an excess, a true beauty that can be appreciated only via the disinterested act of just, simply, looking. This is what Kant meant by his famous suggestion that aesthetics is "purposive without purpose"[7]; aesthetics pursues cognitive exploration without finding a rational explanation. In its ancillary role, aesthetics acts like reason (it is purposive), but instead of facilitating cognitive comprehension (purpose), it brings pleasure via the appreciation of Beauty.

The possibility of seeing and appreciating Beauty, and the moral (and moralizing) implications it shares via its connection to Goodness and Truth, meant that scholars instrumentalized aesthetics in the subsequent centuries. Projects throughout the nineteenth and twentieth centuries, aimed at educating the masses through public collections, rested on the understanding that moral betterment – the formation of good citizens and good souls – could be facilitated via exposure to beautiful things. In debating "how" to best achieve this end, philosophical and art critical discussions revolved around articulating how to form beautiful works of art and how to appreciate that art.[8]

The Kantian notion, or various derivations of his principal ideas, has become the basic presupposition (both academic and popular) in Euro-America,[9] with emphasis on the ancillary (*ancilla*, handmaid) nature of aesthetics as subordinate to rational cognition. Particularly when coupled with a Cartesian preference to the purity of the conceptual realm, this ancillary role means that as a sort of handmaid to reason, aesthetics fills an intermediate role between the purity of the higher intellect and the messy quagmire of the world out there. Kant's philosophy is, better or worse, fundamental to the anthropological and wider social scientific enquiry, and the modern coinage of "anthropology" is, in fact, also part of the Kantian legacy. He framed anthropology – "the philosophical study of society" – with reference to the cognitive, ethical, and aesthetic.[10] "For Kant," writes Keith Hart, "community and common sense were generated through social interaction; the aesthetic was primarily social, having its roots in good food, good talk and good company."[11] In the popular derivations of this Kantian norm, beauty is rendered nice and pleasing, but without function – a related, but distinctly different, notion of "purposive without purpose."

Power and Contest

As the grand narrative of European ideals began to slip, the debates about "how" aesthetics was formative of persons also became "what," in terms of what notions of beauty were legitimate. The ability (and power) to establish which aesthetic regime would prevail became increasingly important. As Terry Eagleton highlights in the use of aesthetics within European political history,[12] and Susan Buck-Morss elaborates in her discussion of Nazi aesthetics, the capacity to capture the imagination and drive forward a group of people via the actions to "create art – destroy the world" instrumentalizes, and weaponizes, aesthetics.[13]

Even outside the explicitly political world of governance, the politics of art production and aesthetic appreciation is, as many authors have noted, deeply entrenched and causes far-reaching effect in various social spheres.[14] Rather than being inherent in objects, the specific aesthetic qualities – and particularly the evaluative schema for valuing certain aesthetic forms – is, as Pierre Bourdieu demonstrates in his study of taste in France, the product of socioeconomic elite privilege.[15] In each society, and within the variety of subgroups and economic brackets, taste and valuation are part of the habituation of society.

Complementary to Bourdieu's argument concerning variation and the socioeconomic stratification seen in aesthetic valuation in a European society, the evaluative framework of aesthetics as deployed in non-European society proved deeply fraught and problematic. Work by those like Eric Michaels, in an Aboriginal Australian context, highlighted the problem of using aesthetic valuation as a schema for appreciating and interpreting indigenous "art."[16] Others also called for moving away from using indigenous notions of beauty as the basis for a comparative anthropology of, or critical evaluation of, art.[17] The intellectual burden that "aesthetics" as a concept owes to Kantian notions of cognition was, as the anthropologist Fred Myers points out in his work on Australian Aboriginal art production, overly ethnocentric in its valuation of the judgment of beauty alongside logic and utility.[18]

Myers's argument, however, raises the point that there is no need to hold strictly to a rigid definition and that in discursive traditions – such as art and anthropology and we might add material culture studies – there is good reason to shift the analytical framing of key terms. His specific concern is with elaborating the notion of criticism, a project he articulates thoroughly in his later work *Painting Culture*, outlining in detail the move between the source communities and the gallery settings in terms of what the art object is and why it generates the attention it does.[19] In examining why acrylic paintings sell in the gallery, Myers quotes the gallerist and critic Christopher Hodges, saying: "The best pictures, they hit you. That ability to hit, even though there's no cultural records. It really makes the difference."[20] This demand for "stronger" art echoes earlier art critical re-evaluation of aesthetics along the lines of impact, rather than strictly beauty (Case Study 16.1).

> ## Case Study 16.1
>
> ### Aesthetics across genres
>
> In her work on Oaxacan woodcarvers in San Martín Tilcajete, Alanna Cant highlights how one pair of artisans – Miguel and Catalina García – are able to position their work not as Mexican craft, but as indigenous art.[21] Even though the Garcías are using the same materials, working in the same village, and within the same established style, they are considerably more successful at attracting international attention from the art market, rather than solely the tourist trade. Some of this is marketing, and the neighbors admit that Miguel is a very good salesman. His shop is open for demonstrations, and in talking to his guests he highlights the importance of indigenous animals within the ancient Zapotec calendar, and the use of wood from specific trees that likewise are situated in the long history of regional myth and religion. However, the specific histories, and especially the discontinuities, between the recently invented practice of Oaxacan carving and the increasingly tangential connections to Zapotec language and cultural heritage are quietly passed over.
>
> However, while some of the Garcías's success can be credited to good salesmanship and an entrepreneurial spirit, it does not account for everything. Cant offers a contrasting example of Lázaro Ramos who, in

Case Study 16.1 (cont.)

a spirit of enterprise and creativity, uses fluorescent paint on some carvings, in order for them to glow under a black light. "Like the conquistadors and Cortez, who were enchanted by the gold of the Aztecs, these will enchant the tourists," Ramos explained.[22] Tourists, however, were not enchanted by the glow, and the fluorescent paints were eventually discarded. By contrast, Cant explains, the Garcías were "able to satisfy the desires of consumers of ethnic art for objects that are locally produced by authentic indigenous people" by "connecting their aesthetics of indigeneity to ... local indications of Zapotecness."[23]

To claim that one kind of indigenous art is more authentic than another is deeply fraught. On one level, there is nothing more indigenous than the Tilcajete woodcarver Ramos using fluorescent paint to make his carvings more enchanting. As a local artist his work is, by definition, indigenous. However, his innovation strikes outside the anticipated registers of what a global market (of tourists and art collectors) expect of indigeneity. As Charlotte Townsend-Gault observes in the context of the art of the First Nations Peoples in British Columbia, the non-native is drawn to the object because it contains "some coveted fragment of sacro-animist imagery that they do not understand, something aboriginal."[24] This quality works as "evidence" of the "aesthetic credentials" of what is indigenous.[25] In this way, while the work of the Garcías is clearly within the same aesthetic register shared by their neighbors in San Martín Tilcajete, their unique success is due in large part to their ability to match two aesthetic registers. Not only are they beautiful and aesthetically masterful artifacts in terms of Oaxacan sensibilities, they also "evidence" the credentials of indigeneity in a way that is intuitively recognizable by those in the global art market.

Significant Form and Affect

Clive Bell, in his 1914 work *Art*, advanced the idea of "significant form" as key to the value and purpose of art, over and against any value attributed to the representational subject present in the piece.[26] He says, "lines and colors combined in a particular way, certain forms and relations of forms, stir our aesthetic emotions. These relations and combinations of lines and colors, these aesthetically moving forms, I call 'Significant Form'; and 'Significant Form' is the one quality common to all works of visual art."[27] Significant form, present in all art (Bell was interested in visual, but for our argument let us expand it), stirs "aesthetic emotion." This emotion, for Bell, was not felt by everyone, but was felt by everyone in their appreciation of the significant form of art. Speaking of a friend who, though interested in aesthetics and art, had "no faculty for distinguishing a work of art from a handsaw," Bell suggested that he had "never during a life of almost forty years been guilty of an aesthetic emotion."[28] This emotion, which artists may experience in response to significant forms in the world, is communicated via the art to others.[29] The critic helps the audience appreciate significant form, and thereby experience the aesthetic emotion in response to the art.[30] While admitting the role of taste – such that some people will feel emotion in response to an art object while others may not – Bell paints a picture of art appreciation similar to William James's views on "religious experience." James argued that some are more naturally skilled, and the views of those most skilled in the experience give shape to the genre for others – including those who appear to have natural capacity for it, and struggle to acquire it.

One of the interesting aspects of Bell's discussion of aesthetic emotion is that he admits that while most experience it only for crafted objects (cathedrals, pictures, etc.) a few people appear to have it sometimes for "natural" phenomena (such as butterflies, birds, flowers). I would venture that the distinction between the two classes is what Gell would subsequently call the "abduction of agency,"[31] in marking a class of objects as intentionally significant in form, versus those simply existing in the "causal milieu." In placing the distinction along lines of intentional craft, and not in the presence of beauty, Bell also dislodges the discussion of aesthetics as the judgment of beauty, and instead positions it as an affective realm of social relation. It is recognition of intelligent production of significant form that arouses aesthetic emotion.

Bell's separation of aesthetics from beauty, moving in favor of "significant form" and "aesthetic emotion" – particularly in the indefinite ambiguity of what, exactly, defines that emotion, poses a question best answered by a psychological approach to affect. This approach, taken by the art historian Susan Best, applies the theory of affect, as advanced by Silvan Tomkins, to illuminate the variability of aesthetic response. As she explains, "while the affective system is relatively fixed – there are nine and only nine affects, and these are clearly anchored in the subject … the range of objects that elicit or provoke affect is not fixed or prescribed."[32] Best focuses most on the effect of "interest-excitement" in relation to art appreciation; however, if we move away from the strict canonical context of "art," and move to a wider distinction between, as suggested above, abducted agency and the causal milieu, any of the nine affective states[33] could – I venture – give rise to an aesthetic emotion. This would, however, place us in danger of collapsing aesthetics and affect, were in not for another aspect that Bell emphasizes, namely rhythm.

In an important limiting manner, Bell marries the idea of aesthetics to rhythm. In a rhetorical move, he admits that "significant form" could also be "significant relations of form," and the aesthetic and the metaphysical worlds can be united "by calling these relations 'rhythm.'"[34] This notion of rhythm, also called "harmony," within an object is important in shaping the kind of significant form and the subsequent aesthetic emotions. As such, the role of aesthetic appreciation (more than strictly judgement) is one that maps the distance between the interiority of the person and the material qualities of the exterior object. However, rather than being articulated in the cognitive faculties of rational categorization (*a la* Kant), here it is a passion play of the emotional arousal in recognizing the intention of design in the work. In a move paralleling Franz Boas's arguments on virtuosity in the indigenous artisan's manipulation of materials,[35] Bell links the importance of intention to the presence of precision,[36] which as Boas argues, manifests in the rhythmic regularity of the object's physical form.

This more affective, emotional response to the crafted world has found resonance more recently, as some scholars have sought to avoid the problematic legacy of Kant by working with a phenomenological approach, most notably shaped by the work of Maurice Merleau-Ponty.[37] While still rooted in the European philosophical tradition, Merleau-Ponty's collapse of interiority and exteriority blends the lines between the self and the world. He writes, "Inside and outside are inseparable. The world is wholly inside and I am wholly outside myself,"[38] offering a radical reframing of the role of aesthetics as the ancillary handmaiden to reason, which mediates the distance between pure, clean cognition and the mess of the outside world.

At one level, Merleau-Ponty's phenomenology returned to Baumgarten's interest in the senses as a way to escape the dominant European discourse concerning beauty as an ideal type, and sense as ancillary to rationality. In taking aesthetics as embodied knowledge, the phenomenological approach offered social scientists of material a way to sidestep some of the more problematic aspects of the ethnocentric and highly normative notions held in a Kantian sense of aesthetics.

Thought, Comparison, and Modeling

In the latter half of the twentieth century, and into the turn of the present one, as aesthetics became increasingly loosed from its role in the European project of judgment and beauty, a plethora of new approaches sprang up. Significant contributions on indigenous notions of aesthetics – such as by Shirley Campbell,[39] Jennifer Deger,[40] Diane Losche,[41] Nancy Munn,[42] and Marilyn Strathern,[43] among others – pushed the analytical framework forward. Together, they demonstrated the importance of aesthetics (maybe in this period best defined as the perceivable and intelligible form of objects and practices) as part of the negotiation of social relations, and, thereby, a means for anthropological study of social relations.[44] They drew on the intellectual capital and affective certainty of "the aesthetic," but wrestled with the problem of its utility as an analytical concept and with its acceptability in a postmodern global context. The possibility of aesthetics as a cross-cultural category forced many scholars to work toward an articulation of aesthetics removed from the Eurocentric and colonial heritage of art evaluation.⁴⁵ In our present concern, interested in what aesthetics is – or better might be – for the study of material culture, a few of these are worthy of extended meditation.

The art historian Robert Farris Thompson, with a long and productive career working across multiple culture groups in Africa and in the diaspora in the New World, argued in favor of the legitimacy of a local practice of critical judgment and evaluation of art in the Yoruba context. He used "the aesthetic" to indicate the "deeply and complexly motivated, consciously artistic interweaving of elements serious and pleasurable, of responsibility and of play."⁴⁶ In Yorubaland, Farris Thompson sought the insight of eighty-eight "critics" – people who either self-acknowledged expertise, or were socially recognized as experts in their ability to identify good pieces of Yoruba art.⁴⁷ He gathered from these critics a list of eighteen contributing factors shared across the collections he studied. While not universally acknowledged (i.e., all critics did not identify the same qualities, nor did every object demonstrate all factors), these contributing factors were recurrent across the sample set.

His set of eighteen qualities included: midpoint mimesis; hypermimesis; excessive abstraction; visibility; shining smoothness; emotional proportions; positioning; composition; delicacy; roundness; protrusions; non-pleasing protrusions; sinister bulges; pleasing angularity; straightness; symmetry; skill; and ephebism.⁴⁸ Apart from ephebism – having the quality of youthfulness – the qualities are all about ratio, harmony, and proportion of form. It is strength or significance of form that appears to be the general guiding principle across the catalogue. This strength of form allows, in Farris Thompson's understanding, the object to facilitate "aesthetic activation, turning ancient objects of thought into fresh sources of guidance and illumination."⁴⁹ The artifact is capable of provoking new understanding and insight through its contemplation. It, as a static object, is generative of new thought.

As an advocate for studying indigenous notions of aesthetics, Farris Thompson also saw the need to refute the functionalist interpretations of "ethnographic" art. Social scientific study of material culture has had a long tradition of giving artifacts a functionalist role in their interpretation of sociocultural practice. In recognizing the importance of aesthetic objects as "fresh sources" for ongoing guidance and insight, Farris Thompson argues for something more abstract, almost philosophical, for the object, rather than its "use" as a tool or ritual representation. He argues that the functionalist predisposition to labelling an ethnographic object to be "for" some specific purpose was born out of the mutual distrust between the local expert and the foreigner. It is, he suggests, a mutual distrust born of each's inability to believe in the other's capacity to truly appreciate art. The beauty of functionalism, then, is that it offers an easy common denominator – a reliable discourse that each side can use, and thereby avoid what is actually happening in and around the object.

In anthropology, Alfred Gell, in his *Art and Agency*, focused on exactly this issue of what happens in and around the object.[50] While Gell overtly rejects aesthetics, he does so because of the intellectual baggage the term carries, belonging as it does to the project of European philosophy. However, rather than completely doing away with the project of aesthetics (broadly conceived), he articulates an approach to art that, ultimately, recreates aesthetics from the ground up, composing a study of art in terms of style, abduction, and enchantment.

The project of aestheticizing ethnographic objects – exemplified most famously in Jacques Chirac's establishment of the Musée du Quai Branly and the Pavillon des Sessions in the Louvre[51] – went against Gell's core methodological ideal of philistinism. Rejecting the idea that aesthetic criticism should be reserved for "art" objects, separate from a wider genre of mundane objects, Gell argued that a theory of objects must be coherently applicable to both canonical high art and any other kind of artifact.

In response to the 1984 exhibition on "primitive art" and its influence on modernism in the Museum of Modern Art,[52] Gell wrote his essay on the technology of enchantment[53] (written in 1985, published 1992). At the same time, he also wrote his first extended discussion of the *oeuvre* of Marcel Duchamp[54] (published only later, in 2013). In these two works, Gell makes two very different, but complementary, arguments.

The first is similar to Bell's in that the work of art, because of the intentional and skilled precision of its making, is able to enchant, or captivate, the viewer, and thereby render the viewer subject to its power. Also like Bell, Gell's emphasis is not on the representational aspects of the work, however, he does not dismiss them outright as Bell does in his arguments on significant form. Like with magic, the content is important, but is only fecund because of the incantational quality of the spell. Gell argues for art to be seen as a technical system, and in doing so blurs a boundary between what in a Kantian system would have been the realm of pure reason (and with "purpose") and the realm of aesthetic judgment ("purposive without purpose"). As a technical system, it is an apparatus for moving thought along logical paths that can – at least by the skilled craftsperson, artist, magician, and technician – be anticipated and molded. This purposeful movement of thought – designed by the artist, and achieved in the mind of the viewer – also carries forward Farris Thompson's suggestion that objects initiate "aesthetic activation," and bring new insight and understanding. In this light, we see that the excess identified by Kant is not a lack of purpose, but a surplus of purpose; objects with significant form are fertile, able to drive forward thought and society.

In the second paper that Gell was working on in 1985, he examined the work of Marcel Duchamp, focusing on the sequence of art works from 1911 to 1914 that mark the significant shift in Duchamp's *oeuvre*.[55] Duchamp painted *Dulcinea* (1911) and *Nude Descending the Stairs* (1912) in a brief period during which he was moving in cubist circles. Unlike the cubist interest in portraying a single object from multiple vantage points, Duchamp's cubist work showed a single perspective of a moving object. *Dulcinea* is composed of five stages of a dancer moving in a circle, superimposed upon each other, and *Nude* is a highly stylized side view of a figure moving down stairs. These works offended the cubists, and Duchamp stopped painting; his subsequent two works, *The Three Standard Stoppages* (1913) and *Network of Stoppages* (1914), marked his move toward conceptual art and an earnest drive toward understanding what Gell later calls "the unrepresentable but very *conceptualizable* and by no means 'mystic' fourth dimension."[56] In discussing Duchamp's works, Gell demonstrates how works of art function as objects of thought and the virtuosity of an artist's style make concrete and external the mind so viewers can apprehend and contemplate it.

In framing art as objects of thought, Gell is echoing the truly illuminating work of Nancy Munn. As she notes in her work on Walbiri iconography, the material form – and specifically the use of repetition within the visual motif – is an element of the "logico-aesthetic function" of art. "Such [simple elemental] shapes are flexible," she argues, such that "their generality makes possible indefinite specific variation within a framework of standardized forms, and the inclusion of 'new' meanings or content without destroying continuity and order. The experience of sameness and tradition can be maintained while at the same time the system is not fixed to a limited range of particulars in its expression of the phenomenal world." She continues, "Metaphoric meanings can be easily manipulated within this framework since it allows for a density of meanings in conjunction with a simplicity of form. This inverse relationship between semantic density and formal complexity is a general characteristic of visual symbol systems."[57] The logico-aesthetic function of art (or indeed wider artifact) objects here is the concretization of the mind in material form.

Read with this insight, Gell's two papers frame the two sides of the object's relations. The first outlined the relation between the work of art and the recipient, the second focused on the relation between the work of art and the artist. This basic framework, brought together in more detail in his paper on "Vogel's Net"[58] and then culminating in *Art and Agency*, was the basis for his "art nexus." The nexus, holding together in relation the art object, the artist, the recipient, and the prototype – that is the likeness or intention after which it was modeled – were held together in Gell's theory by abduction.

The Logico-aesthetic Labor of Abduction

Abduction is a type of thought process introduced into formal logic by the philosopher Charles Sanders Peirce. Like inductive and deductive reasoning, abductive reasoning designates a kind of logical step, specifically one based on lateral or associative reasoning. In some contexts, Peirce also called abduction "hypothesis." Gell takes his definition of abduction from Umberto Eco, quoting Eco to say: "Abduction ... is a tentative and hazardous tracing of a system of signification rules which allow the sign to acquire its meaning ... [It] occurs with those natural signs which the Stoics called indicative and which are thought to be signs, yet without knowing what they signify."[59] Gell's interest in the work of art as action means he focuses on abduction as an intuitive inference of relation. As an act of cognitive processing, it is the way in which a person, when seeing a work of art (or broadly an object or even act of nature), is able to understand intuitively that the object in question was achieved with some intention behind it.

While Gell does not cite him in framing abduction, it is evident that he was influenced by the work of Gregory Bateson, for whom abduction holds a central role in art appreciation, and indeed in all manners of thought. Bateson, in *Steps to an Ecology of Mind* and *Mind and Nature*, outlined the way that the mind probes the world for "patterns of relation."[60] For Bateson, abduction moves the mind from the seen and observable to what might otherwise be. Paired with deduction, it forms what Bateson calls "double description" or "binocular vision," where the two – in an intuitive fashion – map out the possibilities of similarity and difference. This partnership, between the modes of logical thought, are the basis for abstract modelling as well as predictive reasoning. It is pattern recognition and extension. This extension has its root in the interplay of sameness and difference. It is also how a system is able to make infinitely variable permutations of itself, wholly within a coherent style.

The possibility of coming to know an object, then, is based on the process of description, which Bateson identifies as an antecedent to explanation. In explanation, there is meaning making, which is inherently an interpretive process of limitation. In deciding what is meaning and what is noise, the act of explanation limits the object (or, more broadly, the phenomenon). Description, however, can be complete and expansive. For Bateson, when the mind makes choices about what parts of the observational field to ignore, it limits the range of possibilities that rest in the relation between the mind, the thing, and the range of lateral inferences available via abduction. Similar to Bourdieu's later work on taste,[61] Bateson sees this interpretive process as linked to inculcation via learning, whereby one's predispositions – and the pathways of possible abductive inferences – are shaped. For Bateson, abduction undergirds rational thinking. This form of lateral and intuitive thought interprets the data not on a one-to-one correlation, but allows a single stimulus to call to mind a range of possible implications at any given moment. The same stimuli will evoke different lateral connections in different persons, and the same stimuli may evoke multiple responses in a single person. In contexts like art or ritual, any specific aspect of the object or behavior may stimulate the person toward abductive inferences linked with any number of multiple possible *relata*. When perceiving the same phenomenon, some people will know intuitively how to interpret the data, making careful selection from within the noise, and some will be lost in the overwhelming availability of sensory input. Some may be abducted to wrong – say, socially improper or ill-informed – interpretations.

The phenomenon, being a thing in relation, is demarcated as a distinct entity based on the recognition of difference. As such, it also articulates a distinction between those who have a specific kind of understanding and those whose knowledge is different or partial. Aesthetic perception is, then, for Bateson, a matter of epistemology, and "any change in our epistemology will involve shifting our whole system of abductions."[62] However, even while being a matter of epistemology, it is important to note that "aesthetic comprehension" is nonetheless non-discursive,[63] or maybe better pre-discursive[64] or pre-hermeneutic,[65] in that it shapes the very foundation of discourse itself.[66] Aesthetics is, for Bateson, ultimately about "recognition and empathy," being defined as a "responsive[ness] to the pattern which connects."[67]

Like for Farris Thompson, the art object is able to catalyze novel thought via the recognition of the patterns within the form. For Bateson, the project of art is primarily a quest for "grace"; in this, he follows Aldous Huxley in defining a naiveté, shared by God and the animals, but lost to humankind.[68] For Gell the cognitive response to art objects is also true of any sort of object that elicits abductive inferences – ultimately it does not matter if the object was actually "caused" by an intentional artist, but only if the viewer *thinks* it was. This opening up of the framework is largely because Gell is consciously moving away from the strictures of the philosophical debate of "aesthetics" *qua* judgment of beauty. Being more interested in social sequencing than aesthetic emotion, the frame is shifted from great works of "significant form," or even the human attempt toward "grace." However, the conceptual framework that guides the perception of external form is still at the heart of the matter.

The Quotidian Reality of Aesthetics

One of the critical moves in wider aesthetic theory that guides this move away from a reified stricture of aesthetic objects is the movement, exemplified in the work of Jeremy Coote, toward everyday aesthetics.[69] Coote's argument, based on Nilotic cattle-keeping peoples of East Africa, draws out similarity between the valued qualities of cattle and the wider artistic and ethical framework of the societies. Even in disagreeing with Coote, Gell acknowledges that he is "indebted to him for his basic methodological insight, which is, that if one wants to get to grips with art as an anthropological problem, it is precisely to societies which ostensibly 'don't have any art' that one should turn one's attention."[70] Where Gell differs is that while Coote argues the Dinka have aesthetics without having art, Gell argues that they have art,[71] much like the Trobriand garden is a collective work of art.[72] This argument about "what is art" is, I think, futile, and no doubt part of the reason Gell moves to "index" in his later work.

The possibility of demarcating aesthetic objects from non-aesthetic objects is, however, productive. While the distinction made by Bell between the handsaw and the painting may not be useful,[73] and Arthur Danto's argument about the hypothetical pot-people and the basket-people problematic,[74] even Gell admits that some indexes are more suitable to contemplation than are others. They served as better "perches,"[75] being more centrally situated within the coherence of a style (and logic), than others.

One way to distinguish between the aesthetics of an object and an aesthetic object is to consider Eduardo de la Fuente's reading of Georg Simmel and the notion of the "aesthetic threshold." He says:

> A consistent theme in Simmel's [1896] writings on the aesthetics of social life is that "aesthetic feelings" and "aesthetic value" don't develop until "immediate utility has been cleared away in the course of historical development ... [and] the materialistic motives on which our aesthetic sensibilities are based have been effaced in time". This model of aesthetics is based on a theory of form that holds that aesthetic sensation requires the transformation of content into something that transcends utility. There are strong echoes here of the Kantian maxim: "Beauty is the form of finality in an object so far as perceived in it apart from the representation of an end."[76]

The "aesthetic threshold" marks the stage when the form becomes more than simply operational, and this extra flourish of sociability is aesthetically pleasing because it holds within it a condensed form of reality.[77]

This is a very helpful point, and brings into view a line of thought traced through Farris Thompson's resistance to functionalist interpretations and the elaboration of novel thought possible via the object – seen in various ways in Farris Thompson, Munn, Bateson, and Gell. The "condensed and sublimated form" of reality held within the aesthetic form (object or behavior) acts as a model for that reality it holds. The consideration of the form – either in the brief intuitive abductive inferences of double description, or the more elaborated contemplation of masterpieces, allows the experiencing subject to be situated within the spatial, patterned, model of reality. In its condensed form, however, it – as a miniaturization of that reality, which "manages to synthesize these intrinsic properties [of a diagram] with properties which depend on a spatial and temporal context"[78] – allows it to be grasped (either physically or conceptually), and manipulated in a way that is pleasing (Case Study 16.2).[79]

Case Study 16.2

Antiphonal relations

Nadia Seremetakis, in examining how mourning songs work among Greeks living on the Mani Peninsula, explains the importance of antiphonal singing. Antiphony, she says, "possesses a social and juridical sense in addition to its aesthetic, musical, and dramaturgical uses."[80] While in English, "anti" generally has the connotation of oppositional antagonism, in Greek "anti" can also connote reciprocity or equivalence. In mourning, Seremetakis explains, the reciprocal arrangement is such that the singer may position themselves within the song (or physically)[81] as if facing the dead so as to come and represent the dead. The word *antiprósopos*, meaning "representative," uses the root *prósopo* (face or person) in such a way to position the singer face-to-face with the dead, giving voice to the silence of the unspeaking departed.

In the highly choreographed ritual setting of the Greek Orthodox Liturgy, the hymnography of the service is sung in alternating antiphons between two sets of cantors, positioned at either end (north and south) of the church's transept. In large churches, such as the main church in a monastery like Vatopedi in Mount Athos, Greece, a pilgrim will stand facing east, toward a large icon screen (the iconostasis), behind which clergy are leading the service. In front of the iconostasis is an open space with a group of cantors to the left and right. During extended periods of song, each set of cantors will take a stanza in turn, such that the sound shifts from north to south, back and forth, as each group fills the church with their chanting voices and the *ison* (or drone) that sets the tone for the hymnody. In addition to these, an *archon* (leader) goes back and forth across the open space in front the iconostasis, calling out the first line of the next stanza to each group in turn. This choir of antiphonic chanting and the archon guiding the hymnography are layered atop each other, as the antiphon is begun before the voices of the previous stanza die out. In addition, the chamber of the stone church also is filled with the voices of the clergy behind the iconostasis. In this way, the antiphony is part of a larger polyphony, with multiple relations between those living and the saints, and the dead have a voice within the liturgical cycle of Orthodox Christianity.[82]

Polyphony is, according to Seremetakis, the "raw material" for antiphonic practice. This is most evident in the *kláma* (wake), which is characterized by a multiplicity of vocalized utterances of different kinds: spoken, sung, unintelligible, improvised, or planned. As she explained, "The antiphonic relation emerges as an articulation between these linguistic and extralinguistic media, between poetry and prose, music and screaming, and it is distributed and redistributed through this multidimensional polyphony."[83] The capacity of the mourning to "scream the dead" rests in this antiphonal positionality, whereby the singer, mimicking the local customary legal system, structures their witnessing of the event as a dramatization of the event, through ritualized gestures and discourse, to show themselves as a witness and guarantor.[84]

In the two contexts – that of the *kláma* and the liturgy – the performance of antiphony and polyphony are markedly distinct, such that Seremetakis argued that the "Byzantine chant sung by the priest and

> **Case Study 16.2 (cont.)**
>
> his choir is aesthetically, stylistically, and ideologically antithetical to the *moirolôi* (lament)."[85] However, it is worth considering this "anti" of antithetical as having the connotation of reciprocity and equivalence, not opposition. While the texture of polyphony is different in the two settings, both afford the rich arrangement of sound, meaning, and performance for the antiphonal representationalism whereby the voice of the witness and the voice of the witnessed are heard in conversation. In both settings, the aesthetics of song and performance materialize the internal logics of relation.

Following Bateson, it is metacognition, working with metapattern, which allows for thinking with models. The pattern connects the sameness and difference with and around the object, and across genre, and is recognized by abduction. As he says, "The *pattern which connects is a metapattern*. It is a pattern of patterns. It is that metapattern which defines the vast generalization that, indeed, *it is patterns which connect*."[86] Bateson elaborates saying that, "Mind is empty; it is no-thing. It exists only in its ideas, and these again are no-things. Only the ideas are immanent, embodied in their examples. And the examples are, again, no-things";[87] this erasure of distinct categories, like Merleau-Ponty's erasure of the self as separate from the world, is part of Bateson's argument that mind and nature are a "necessary unity,"[88] and based on an ecological relation, drawing all *relata* into the same metapatterning of the world.[89] There is, for Bateson, contra Heidegger, no thing in itself, there is only thing as relation.

In this view, aesthetics is an essential aspect to the abductive work that facilitates the individual's movement within and understanding of the metapattern. Aesthetics allows the person to be able to contemplate the nature of relation itself, as it is condensed within the object's aesthetic excess.

Aesthetics as a Methodological Imperative

In this light, the question of what art "does" re-emerges and allows us to frame aesthetics as the point of access into the abstract, but intuitive and logical geometries of society. It is the means by which reality becomes sensibly apprehended. Having moved away from the Kantian notion of aesthetics as the perceptual judgment of beauty, we can now frame the concept in terms of what perception of the purposive capacity of an object does for the recipient – both the indigenous viewer and the social scientist.

Following Bateson, I argue that the process of abduction helps explain the mechanism by which aesthetics can provide access to the internal, intuitive geometries of the artifactual form. The object, as an agentive and polyvalent thing, emerges through design and the interartifactual sequentiality of each artifact as a condensation of reality within the ongoing metapattern of the world.[90] This invites a renewed engagement with aesthetics as a methodological imperative for the study of human practices of association and distinction.

I am calling for ethnographically grounded research into what aesthetics does. If we accept the concept of aesthetics as somatic apprehension, and with Bateson we see aesthetics as the intuitive and empathetic responsiveness to patterns that connect an entire ecology of *relata*, then we can frame aesthetics as a concrete thing coming out of the architectonics of the mind and brain within social and artifactual contexts. Consequently, we need (1) a new dedication to aesthetics as part of the social scientific project; and (2) a recognition of aesthetics as an empirical, ethnographically grounded analytical sphere that must be articulated in the artifactual form and the phenomenological body. It is, in Baumgarten's sense, a science of sensible cognition, but one that must be grounded in the "material ecology"[91] which connects various *relata* – person and thing, mind, and concept.

Notes

1. This chapter has been written the same time as two other collaborative projects that have shaped my position significantly. The first, working with Alanna Cant, has been a panel at the Royal Anthropological Institute (RAI) and a subsequent co-authored paper on aesthetics and religious collectivities. The second, with Susanne Küchler, is the co-authored book, titled *A Return to the Object: Alfred Gell, Art and Social Theory* (London: Routledge, 2021). I am deeply indebted to both Alanna and Susanne, whose genius and critical insight has heavily shaped my own understanding of this topic. Many key ideas, and no doubt some specific phrases, are credit to them. The errors, however, are all my own.
2. Janet Wolff very convincingly shows that aesthetics has a distinct social history, fraught with "terms, assumptions, and judgements" that are "socially located and, in an important sense, ideological" (Janet Wolff, *Aesthetics and the Sociology of Art: Second Edition* (London: Macmillan Press, 1993), 105). While mindful of this larger interdisciplinary and historically contextual movement, in this chapter I make a specific ideological choice to cut a line of argument that moves somewhat freely between disciplines and periods – a method very much born of Material Culture Studies (see Peter Ucko, "Penis Sheaths: A Comparative Study," *Proceedings of the RAI* (1969), 24–67; Timothy Carroll, Antonia Walford, and Shireen Walton, "Introduction," in Timothy Carroll, Antonia Walford, and Shireen Walton, eds., *Lineages and Advancements in Material Culture Studies: Perspectives from UCL Anthropology* (London: Routledge, 2021) and its own historical context.

3. Alexander Gottlieb Baumgarten, *Theoretische Ästhetik: die grundlegenden Abschnitte aus der "Aesthetica" (1750/58): Lateinisch-Deutsch*. trans. Hans Rudolf Schweizer (Hamburg: Meiner, 1983[1750]), 10, author's translation.
4. Immanuel Kant, *The Critique of Judgement*, Nicholas Walker, ed. and James Creed Meredith, trans., rev. ed. (Oxford: Oxford University Press, 2007 [1790]).
5. For a good overview of Kant, see Elisabeth Schellekens, "Immanuel Kant (1724–1804)," in Alessandro Giovannelli, ed., *Aesthetics: The Key Thinkers* (New York: Continuum, 2012), 61–74.
6. Kant, *The Critique of Judgement*, 51ff.
7. Ibid, 52.
8. Owen Jones, *The Grammar of Ornament: Illustrated by Examples from Various Styles of Ornament* (London: Day and Son, 1856); Georg Simmel, *Rembrandt: An Essay in the Philosophy of Art*, Alan Scott and Helmut Staubmann, trans. (London: Routledge, 2005 [1916]).
9. Roger Sansi, *Art, Anthropology and the Gift* (London: Bloomsbury, 2014).
10. Immanuel Kant, *Anthropology from a Pragmatic Point of View*, Robert B. Louden, ed. (Cambridge: Cambridge University Press, 2006 [1798]).
11. Keith Hart, "Forward," in Roy Rappaport, *Rituals and Religion in the Making of Humanity* (Cambridge: Cambridge University Press, 1999), xix.
12. Terry Eagleton, *The Ideology of an Aesthetic* (London: Wiley-Blackwell, 1990).
13. Susan Buck-Morss, "Aesthetics and Anaesthetics: Walter Benjamin's Artwork Essay Reconsidered," *October* 62 (1992), 4, quoting Walter Benjamin.
14. Howard Becker, *Art Worlds* (Berkeley: University of California Press, 1982); Pierre Bourdieu, *Distinction: A Social Critique of the Judgement of Taste* (Cambridge: Harvard University Press, 1984); Alanna Cant, *The Art of Indigeneity: Aesthetics and Competition in Mexican Economies of Culture* (Austin: University of Texas Press, 2019); Arthur Danto, "The Artworld," *Journal of Philosophy* 61 (1964), 571–84; George Dickie, *Art and Aesthetic: An Institutional Analysis* (Ithaca: Cornell University Press, 1975); Ruth Phillips, *Museum Pieces: Toward the Indigenization of Canadian Museums* (McGill-Queen's University Press, 2011); Charlotte Townsend-Gault, "Northwest Coast Art: The Culture of the Land Claims," *American Indian Quarterly* 18, no. 4 (1994), 445–67 and "Circulating Aboriginality," *Journal of Material Culture* 9, no. 2 (2004), 183–202; Suzanne Vogel, ed., *Art/Artifact: African Art in Anthropology Collections* (New York: Center for African Art and Preston Verlog, 1988); Janet Wolff, *Aesthetics and the Sociology of Art*, 2nd ed. (London: Macmillan Press, 1993).
15. Bourdieu, *Distinction*.
16. Eric Michaels, *Bad Aboriginal Art: Tradition, Media, and Technological Horizons* (Minneapolis: University of Minnesota Press, 1993); Vivian Johnson, "Especially Good Aboriginal Art," *Third Text* 56 (2001),

33–50. See also Jennifer Deger's review and critique concerning the traditionalism in Michaels' approach, and her arguments demonstrating the ways "indigenous Australians negotiate their Aboriginality across a mediascape where local meanings intersect with regional, nation (and international) discourses." Jennifer Deger, "Review: *Bad Aboriginal Art*," *Oceania* 66, no. 4 (1996), 333; and "Thick Photography," *Journal of Material Culture* 21, no. 1 (1996), 111–32.

17. James Clifford, *The Predicament of Culture: Twentieth-Century Ethnography, Literature and Art* (Cambridge: Harvard University Press, 1988); Alfred Gell, "The Technology of Enchantment and the Enchantment of Technology," in Jeremy Coote and Anthony Shelton, eds., *Anthropology, Art and Aesthetics* (Oxford: Clarendon, 1992), 40–63; Hal Foster, ed., *The Anti-Aesthetic: Essays on Postmodern Culture* (Port Townsend: Bay Press, 1983); Thomas McEvilley, "Doctor, Lawyer, Indian Chief," *Artforum* 23, no. 3 (1984), 54–60.
18. Fred Myers, "Beyond the Intentional Fallacy: Art Criticism and the Ethnography of Aboriginal Acrylic Painting," *Visual Anthropology Review* 10, no. 1 (1994), 12.
19. Fred Myers, *Painting Culture: The Making of an Aboriginal High Art* (Durham: Duke University Press, 2002).
20. Myers, *Painting Culture*, 223.
21. Alanna Cant, *Value of Aesthetics: Oaxacan Woodcarvers in Global Economies of Culture* (Austin: University of Texas Press, 2019), 85ff.
22. Cant, *Value of Aesthetics*, 30.
23. Ibid, 97.
24. Townsend-Gault, "Circulating Aboriginality," 197.
25. Ibid, 188, 197.
26. Clive Bell, *Art* (New York, Frederick A. Stokes, 1914).
27. Bell, *Art*, 8.
28. Ibid, 4.
29. Ibid, 46; see also Susan Feagin, "Roger Fry (1866–1934) and Clive Bell (1881–1964)," in Alessandro Giovannelli, ed., *Aesthetics: The Key Thinkers* (Continuum, 2012), 113–25.
30. Feagin, "Roger Fry," 119.
31. Alfred Gell, *Art and Agency: An Anthropological Theory* (Oxford: Clarendon Press, 1998).
32. Susan Best, "Rethinking Visual Pleasure: Aesthetics and Affect," *Theory & Psychology* 17, no. 4 (2007), 506.
33. The nine states are: enjoyment-joy, interest-excitement, surprise, anger-rage, disgust, dissmell, distress-anguish, fear-terror, shame-humiliation. Silvan Tomkins, *Affect Imagery Consciousness: Vol. 1. The Positive Affects* (New York: Springer, 1962); *Affect Imagery Consciousness: Vol. 2. The Negative Affects* (New York: Springer, 1963); *Affect Imagery Consciousness: Vol. 3. The Negative Affects: Anger and Fear* (New York: Springer, 1991).
34. Bell, *Art*, 16.

35. Franz Boas, *Primitive Art* (Toronto: Dover, 1955 [1927]).
36. Bell, *Art*, 64.
37. For example see: Frances Mascia-Lees, "Aesthetics: Aesthetic Embodiment and Commodity Capitalism," in *A Companion to the Anthropology of the Body and Embodiment*, Frances Mascia-Lees, ed. (London: Wiley Blackwell, 2011), 3–23; Christopher Pinney, *Photos of the Gods: The Printed Image and Political Struggle in India* (London: Reaktion Books, 2003); Alanna Cant, *The Value of Aesthetics: Oaxacan Woodcarvers in Global Economies of Culture* (Austin: University of Texas Press, 2019); Susan Best, "The Trace and the Body," *First Liverpool Biennial of International Contemporary Art: Trace* (Liverpool: Tate Gallery, 1999), 172–77.
38. Maurice Merleau-Ponty, *The Phenomenology of Perception* (London: Routledge, 2007 [1962]), 407.
39. Shirley Campbell, *The Art of Kula* (Oxford: Berg, 2002).
40. Jennifer Deger, *Shimmering Screens: Making Media in an Aboriginal Community* (Minneapolis: University of Minnesota Press, 2006).
41. Diane Losche, "The Sepik Gaze: Iconographic Interpretation of Abelam Form," *Social Analysis* 38 (1995), 47–60.
42. Nancy Munn, *Walbiri Iconography: Graphic Representation and Cultural Symbolism in Central Australian Society* (Ithaca: Cornell University Press, 1973).
43. Marilyn Strathern, "The Aesthetics of Substance," in *Property, Substance and Effect: Anthropological Essays on Persons and Things* (London: Athlone Press, 1999) and *The Gender of the Gift* (Berkeley: University of California Press, 1988).
44. As Strathern notes, aesthetics is thus, in two distinct ways, "purposive" in this genre of work. Marilyn Strathern, "Reflections," in Raminder Kaur and Parul Dave-Mukherji, eds., *Arts and Aesthetics in a Globalizing World* (London: Bloomsbury, 2014), 261.
45. Charlotte Otten, ed., *Art and Aesthetics: Readings in Cross-Cultural Aesthetics* (New York: Doubleday, 1971); James Weiner, ed., "Aesthetics is a Cross-Cultural Category," *Group for Debate in Anthropological Theory no. 6*, Department of Social Anthropology (University of Manchester, 1996); Russell Sharman, "The Anthropology of Aesthetics: A Cross-Cultural Approach," *JASO* 28, no. 2 (1997), 177–92.
46. Robert Farris Thomson, "The Aesthetics of the Cool," *African Arts* 7, no. 1 (1973), 41.
47. Robert Farris Thomson, "Yoruba Artistic Criticism," in Howard Morphy and Morgan Perkins, eds., *The Anthropology of Art: A Reader* (Oxford: Blackwell Publishing, 2006 [1973]), 242–69.
48. Farris Thomson, "Yoruba Artistic Criticism."
49. Farris Thomson, "Aesthetics of the Cool," 67.
50. Alfred Gell, *Art and Agency*.
51. See James Clifford, "Quai Branly in Process," *October* 120 (2007), 3–23; Michael Kimmelman, "A Heart of Darkness in the City of Light,"

New York Times (2 July 2006); Sally Price, *Paris Primitive: Jacques Chirac's Museum on the Quai Branly* (Chicago: University of Chicago Press, 2007).
52. William Rubin, *Primitivism in Twentieth Century Art* (New York: Museum of Modern Art, 1984).
53. Gell, "Technology of Enchantment." I am indebted to Susanne Küchler for filling in some of the backstory on the timing and intention behind Gell's articles.
54. Alfred Gell, "The Network of Standard Stoppages (c. 1985)," in Liana Chua and Mark Elliot, eds., *Distributed Objects: Meaning and Mattering after Alfred Gell* (Oxford: Berghahn, 2013), 88–113.
55. Gell, "Network of Standard Stoppages."
56. Gell, *Art and Agency*, 250, emphasis original.
57. Munn, *Walbiri Iconography*, 173.
58. Alfred Gell, "Vogel's Net: Traps as Artworks and Artworks as Traps," *Journal of Material Culture* 1, no. 1 (1996), 15–38.
59. Umberto Eco, *Semiotics and the Philosophy of Language* (London: Macmillan, 1984), in Gell, *Art and Agency*, 14.
60. Gregory Bateson, *Steps to an Ecology of Mind: Collected Essays in Anthropology, Psychiatry, Evolution, and Epistemology* (Chicago: University of Chicago Press, 1972) and *Mind and Nature: A Necessary Unity* (New York: E. P. Dutton, 1979).
61. Bourdieu, *Distinction*.
62. Bateson, *Mind and Nature*, 143.
63. Roy Rappaport, *Ritual and Religion in the Making of Humanity* (Cambridge: Cambridge University Press, 1999), 386.
64. Julia Kristeva, *Power of Horror: An Essay on Abjection* (New York: Columbia University Press, 1982).
65. Susanne Küchler, "Threads of Thought: Reflections on Art and Agency," in Liana Chua and Mark Elliot, eds., *Distributed Objects: Meaning and Mattering after Alfred Gell* (Oxford: Berghahn, 2013), 25–38 and "Materials: The Story of Use," in Adam Drazin and Susanne Küchler, eds., *The Social Life of Materials* (London, Bloomsbury, 2015), 267–82.
66. Don Ihde, *Expanding Hermeneutics: Visualism in Science* (Evanston: Northwestern University Press, 1998).
67. Bateson, *Mind and Nature*, 8.
68. Bateson, *Steps to an Ecology of Mind*, 128–29.
69. Jeremy Coote, "Marvels of Everyday Vision: The Anthropology of Aesthetics and the Cattle Keeping Nilotes," in Jeremy Coote and Anthony Shelton, eds., *Anthropology, Art & Aesthetics* (Oxford: Oxford University Press, 1992).
70. Alfred Gell, "On Coote's 'Marvels of Everyday Vision,'" *Social Analysis* 38 (1995), 18.
71. Gell, "On Coote's," 25.
72. Gell, "Technology of Enchantment," 60.
73. Bell, *Art*, 4.

74. Arthur Danto, "Artifact and Art," in Suzanne Vogel, ed., *Art/Artifact: African Art in Anthropology Collections* (New York: Center for African Art and Preston Verlog, 1988), 18–32; Gell, "Vogel's Net."
75. Gell, *Art and Agency*, 250.
76. Eduardo de la Fuente, "On the Promise of a Sociological Aesthetics: From Georg Simmel to Michel Maffesoli," *Distinktion: Journal of Social Theory* 8, no. 2 (2007), 96–97, quoting Simmel, "Sociological Aesthetics" and Kant, *Critique of Judgement*.
77. de la Fuente, "On the Promise of Sociological Aesthetics," 95.
78. Claude Lévi-Strauss, *The Savage Mind* (Chicago: University of Chicago Press, 1966), 25.
79. See Jack Davy on miniaturization in this regard, notably: John (Jack) Davy, "Miniaturization: A Study of a Material Culture Practice among the Indigenous Peoples of the Pacific Northwest." Ph.D. dissertation (University College London, 2016); "The 'Idiot Sticks': Kwakwaka'wakw Carving and Cultural Resistance in Commercial Art Production on the Northwest Coast," *American Indian Culture and Research Journal* 42, no. 3 (2018), 27–46; Jack Davy and Charlotte Dixon, eds., *Worlds in Miniature: Contemplating Miniaturisation in Global Material Culture* (London: University College London Press, 2019).
80. Nadia Seremetakis, *The Last Word: Women, Death, and Divination in Inner Mani* (Chicago: University of Chicago Press, 1991), 102.
81. See also Loring Danforth and Alexander Tsiaras, *The Death Rituals of Rural Greece* (Princeton: Princeton University Press, 1982).
82. For more on this, see Timothy Carroll, *Orthodox Christian Material Culture: Of People and Things in the Making of Heaven* (Routledge, 2018), especially chapter 9.
83. Seremetakis, *The Last Word*, 106.
84. Ibid, 102.
85. Ibid, 165.
86. Bateson, *Mind and Nature*, 11, emphasis original.
87. Ibid.
88. Bateson, *Mind and Nature*.
89. Bateson, *Ecology of Mind*.
90. Küchler and Carroll, *A Return to the Object*; Gell, *Art and Agency*.
91. Carroll, *Orthodox Christian Material Culture* and "Axis of Incoherence: Engagement and Failure between Two Material Regimes of Christianity," in Timothy Carroll, David Jeevendrampillai, Aaron Parkhurst, and Julie Shackelford, eds., *Material Culture of Failure: When Things Do Wrong* (Bloomsbury Press, 2018), 157–78.

17

Objects Are Alive

Producing Animacy in the Inanimate

Peter Roe

> Although we wish for better worlds, and dream of perfect ones, we end by leaving behind things *made* more often than things wished for.
>
> Adam Gopnik

Preface: Peoples and Cultures Selected

This chapter seeks to demonstrate that objects are alive in the belief systems of Native Americans in the sense that everything from the raw materials and fabrication processes to the artifacts themselves emulated the morphology and ethology of nature's species, from plants and animals to entire sacred landscapes and their "living" hydrological, geological, and climatological aspects. This sharing of vital energy starts with corporeal art and quotidian objects, extends to the hut lived in, the village, and ultimately the civic-ceremonial centers and urban spaces that emerged as these cultures developed. Rooted in animism and shamanism, ideological aspects maintained as these societies evolved; unlike the Old World, this perspective presents a profoundly alien perspective on material culture that Western students should understand and respect. Amerindian consciousness is not unlike similar rootedness in land and life that continues to shape awareness and behavior among other traditional populations adapting to the modern world, such as Australian aborigines (see Smith and colleagues, Chapter 5 and Strang, Chapter 14 in this volume).

The cultures referenced here derive from my ethnographic and prehistoric archaeological fieldwork in South America and the Caribbean, and conducted archaeological tours in Mexico.[1] Comparative work among the Shipibo of the eastern Andes,[2] the ancient Chavín of northeastern Peru,[3] the pre-Taino Saladoid horticultural migrants to the Antilles,[4] and the Waiwai of the Upper Essequibo River of Guyana,[5] focused on art and technology, and the ideologies they encapsulate. Using examples from Mesoamerican (Mexico to Honduras) and Caribbean-South America, this diverse culture-geographic area becomes "Amerindia" after the regional name for Native Americans. My "informants," both living and dead, span the *longue durée* of deep time, across a broad, but by no means comprehensive, swath of the New World.

Material Culture Begins with Attitudes Toward Nature

Before one can have technology or art, one must first have a set of "attitudes toward nature" from which culturally recognized resources are selected, and the "inherent perfectibility of form"[6] of their raw materials. The affect intrinsic in human/nature interactions means these attitudes reside in magico-religious realms. Heuristically, I propose a fundamental dichotomy in the sacred between two grand cultic systems and their contrasting attitudes toward nature, perhaps derived from their origin biomes: the "Desert Religious Tradition" (DRT), and the "Jungle Religious Tradition" (JRT). These two systems of the numinous can be mapped onto the "West" and "the Rest" (African-Asian-Amerindian-Melanesian-Oceanic). Eglee Zent's review of Western/Non-Western attitudes toward nature elaborates an isomorphic dyadic set:

> Religions such as Buddhism, Hinduism and Jainism [all JRT] tend to emphasize the intrinsic value inherent in biota, and by extension, nature. These religions conceive people's relationship with their surrounding as more biocentric and even ecocentric, just as those of Amerindians' traditions. On the contrary, religions such as Baha'i, Christianity, Judaism and Islam [all DRT] are more inclined to weigh the instrumental value of the environment, thus being closer to theocentric and anthropocentric environmental ethics.[7]

The DRT originated in ancient Mesopotamia with the birth of settled civilization in Sumer (and thence to succeeding Akkadian, Babylonian, Phoenician, Canaanite, and Hebraic cultures; cf. the Old Testament).[8] That tradition continued through Christianity to Islam and, ultimately, Mormonism, a New World DRT variant, and the most recent in "redeeming Zion" by turning the desert of Utah into a simulacrum of the Garden of Eden via irrigation and collapsing earthen dams.[9]

Because the ancient Middle East was desertified (although not as arid as currently), the idea of the "Wilderness" (untamed nature) arose as early as the Sumerian *The Epic of Gilgamesh* (2094–2047 BCE).[10] The Wilderness, a sterile, or foreboding domain filled with monsters like hairy *Humbaba*, needed redemption via human-engineered irrigation technology. Based on ancient Dilmun, the aim was to create a well-watered "Garden of

Eden." This "artifactual" view of nature became the West's key ideological leitmotif.

From thence comes the "Conquest of Nature," as in Genesis 1:28 (King James Version), where humans are given "dominion" over all life and enjoined to go forth and "subdue" it (multiplying at its expense). The insidious consequences of this "dominionist" view of nature[11] was recognized by the historian of technology, Lynn White, in his 1967 "The Historical Roots of Our Ecological Crisis."[12] This precocious "cultural critique"[13] remains fundamental to understanding our current fossil fuel dependency despite its catastrophic externality of global warming, as well as our depletion of the world's fisheries, and the human-induced greatest extinction event since the Permian/Triassic.

This dominionist perspective treats nature as a bank or storehouse from which resources are extracted until they run out.[14] Perhaps this attitude originated in the experience of death in the deserts of the ancient Middle East. As an animal dies in such an environment its body desiccates, becoming a dry and inert husk, iconic of the bleakness of the arid wasteland. This becomes a metaphor for life's fate without the intervention of an interfering, anthropomorphic, and warlike Storm God bringing the heavenly waters from the mountains, yielding verdant life in the desert wastes. This is what the Sumerian deities did, chief among them Enlil, the "Bull of Heaven," "Lord Wind,"[15] and his successor deities like the Canaanite El ("Bull-El") and Baal, as well as the last of the Middle Eastern Warrior Storm Gods, the Hebraic bull-like Yahweh[16] (Isaiah 19:1), depicted, along with his wife-Asherah (Athirat) – soon "edited out" in such a patriarchal ethos – as bull-headed anthropomorphic graffiti on a sherd (*pithos*) from Kuntillet Ajrud.

As DRT Christianity penetrated animistic Europe (or, later, the New World with its Extirpation of Idolatry) its first duty was to kill the spirit guardians of the springs, the rivers, the groves (sacred to both Germanic and Celtic tribes), and the mountains, replacing them with a single set of interfering, anthropomorphic masculine deities (God-the-Father, and his patriarchate-modeled son-Jesus, as well as the Father's seminal emanation, the Holy Ghost). It is a short step from killing the Sacred Grove's spirit to cutting the forest down as so much lumber, like we continue cutting and burning the world's rainforests, from Southeast Asia to the Amazon.

While the ancient animal gods of the West anthropomorphized as society stratified, these mighty theriomorphs kept their allure in transcultural Amerindia. Witness the Quechua image of the clash between the DRT and the JRT in Hispanic hegemony over their indigenous culture. In their melancholic *Yawar* Fiesta, a giant Andean condor is tied to the back of a raging Spanish fighting bull, bloodying its back with its tearing beak but unable to free itself.[17] This is a fit metaphor for the economically impoverished, but spiritually resilient, Amerindian underclasses oppressed within such Iberian-descendant élite and mestizo societies!

Like most cultural values, this Western tendency to treat nature as inert, and its denizens as mere furniture designed for human consumption, is a two-edged sword. It is the key to our technological dominance (think Pavlov and his horrific treatment of dogs to discover operant conditioning, or our recent medical experiments on our closest-and endangered-primate relatives, the self-conscious and proto-cultural chimpanzees). One could hardly have a techno-physics if the subjects of inquiry could respond interactively with the investigator, and whose integrity must be respected and negotiated. Hence the taboo against "anthropomorphization" in animal behaviorist studies lest the "non-animal," semidivine nature of humans be questioned. Yet it also leads to the present ecological nightmare of unbridled consumption and unconstrained pollution (Hutchings elaborates on material culture studies' complicity in Chapter 4).

Our only forlorn hope is for the "greening" of the DRT's edges via incrementally borrowing portions of the JRT's worldview.[18] Yet these hesitant beginnings may not be enough to forestall worldwide ecological Armageddon. But even then, DRT believers will have moved on, either in the "Rapture" of Christianist Evangelicals as they imagine themselves instantaneously transported to the Divine from a ravaged earth, or in science fiction, the ultimate dream of Western technological infatuation. Our new "myths," transported by "progress" from the Golden Age past to the utopian/dystopian future, these fantasy worlds invariably envision a few intrepid survivors abandoning a wasteland earth to colonize the universe (the ultimate lifeless wasteland turned paradisiacal by gigantic "terra-forming" machines) in completely mechanized space ships, aided by artificial humans-HAL, robots, or cyborgs. These envisioned heavenly chariots become the ultimate creations of humans-as-gods, gigantic in scale, self-replicating in number, and totally unnatural in character.

In contrast, the second grand cultic system, the JRT, can be traced to the etymological origin of the Sanskrit word "jungle" describing the subtropical, tangled, and impenetrable vegetation of the northern Indian subcontinent. At a deeper cultural horizon, it derives from humankind's oldest "default" religion, animism. That 32,000-plus-years-old spiritual awakening is depicted in the avi- and theri-anthropic rock art and sculpture of the European Upper Paleolithic.[19] As Edward Tylor noted in 1871, this ancient and remarkably uniform religious system is "nature worship," all of the environment being "alive," invested with movement and "souls."[20] This analogical viewpoint decenters people, unlike the DRT, which grants pride-of-place to humans ("human-centric") as the only beings with souls. Animism seeks to maintain equilibrium in nature by treating it as a sentient being worthy of a "dialogue" of negotiation and adulation, rather than the DRT's "monologue" of domination and extraction.

Animism's agents are shamans and shamaneses, the curing/bewitching specialists of band and tribal societies (persisting, subordinate to priests, into chiefdoms and states). They have direct contact with the spirits via altered states of consciousness. Shamanism is associated with power animals ("familiars"), frequently impressive carnivores or raptors.[21] They are humans' guides to nature's embedded knowledge, hence the shaman's magical ability to transform into such animals/birds ("were-creatures"). Hence also "shamanic flight" through the levels of the universe to recapture the souls of patients from afflicting spirits (from the talons of giant harpy eagles in the Amazonian Sky World, or the maws of enormous ophidian-caimanic dragons in its Subaquatic Underworld). Shamanistic curing rituals also utilize convincing sleight-of-hand magic and spectral voice-projection (ventriloquism).

Shamanic interconnectedness with nature parallels the laity's multiple "animal double" souls in need of curing. Wild creatures share a person's soul and fate, from the *noreshi* of the Yanomamö in the Venezuelan-Brazilian jungle[22] to the alter-egos of modern Zinacanteco Mayans "clearly cognate with the *wahy* of the Classic Maya."[23] Even raw materials like reeds, and their resultant woven artifacts, have their own invisible and perfect double (*akato*), à la "Primitive Platonism," among the Ye'cuana,[24] Caribs of the Upper Orinoco in Venezuela. Elements like water are also "alive," from the fish-like rigid Moche "Wave Creature,"[25] to the plunging, be-plumed ocean waves of Lambayeque (Sicán), 750–1375 CE.[26]

"Sacred devolution" from primordial beings, both human and animal, also marks the *no badabö* of the Yanomamö, like *Iwariwä* ("caiman ancestor"), the stingy owner of fire.[27] All cultural skills came from nature, from such animal and plant "Proto-Cultural Custodians."[28] They possess culture naturally, as part of their anatomy, but refuse to share it with questing proto-humans. In contrast to DRT human heroes, who actively invent cultural traits via "social agency," JRT culture heroes tend to steal these skills/traits from such were-creatures via "mythic agency," tricking them through helpful bird intermediaries. Cultural characteristics were obtained by killing and skinning the mythic custodians, as with *Urufiri*, the Waiwai ophidian flying dragon, owner of designs, so that humans could decorate their bodies and objects.[29] Dragons, composite caimanic monsters, first appear in Amerindia in Formative Period Olmec[30] and Chavín.[31] They slither through successor cultures like the Maya in Mesoamerica (the "Cosmic Monster"),[32] and the South American Moche,[33] eventually yielding preeminence to were-jaguar chieftains in increasingly stratified successor societies.

Perhaps this tropical worldview is also motivated by the observation of death and decay in the jungle. Where the carcass in the desert is inert, merely shriveling and desiccating, a similar body in the jungle soon teems with life, maggots "animating" its rapidly disappearing skin in the same manner that microbial and insect detritivores recycle the nutrients of fallen leaves into the tree's rootlets. Amerindians encode this continuous transformation in mythology. Consider Huxley's recounting of *Mair*, the Solar Culture Hero of the Urubu Brazilian Indians.[34] As he flies over the forest's canopy, in his guise as the *yapu* bird, *Mair* sees a rotten tree fruit lying on the ground, teeming with worms. He thinks to himself, "that would make a nice woman" (menstruation, or metonymic rot, being the bridging metaphor). After her human metamorphosis she becomes his wife. All of these jungle "Eves" – and derivative Antillean females – come in round, hollow "natural" forms as Gourd Mothers and Fruit Women: the Yanomamö *wabu* fruit First Woman,[35] and water-related forms: as fish – The "Mermaid," the "Turtle Progenitrix," the "Mud Maid," as well as hollow trees such as "The Wooden Bride."[36]

These mythic transformations annotate their material culture correlates. Appropriately, the first serving twill-weave basket a Ye'cuana man makes for his new wife is the *Kutto shidiyu*, the "Frog's Bottom" design.[37] The culturally related Cariban Waiwai concur, a man addressing his wife as "my *wayamnu*" ("my little turtle"). The message resonates, out of death comes life; childbirth in natural populations often is lethal, in reality and in mythology – the Shipibo "First Woman," a gourd, is broken open, "killed," in a forced caesarian section to yield the Magical Twins and six gourd siblings. Similarly, in the distant Greater Antilles, the proto-historical Taíno's *Itiba Cahubaba* ("Bloodied Aged Mother") dies in childbirth, her four sons extracted postmortem.[38]

Mythology, "rooted" in jungle ecology, supports an unparalleled diversity of life maintained by death and decay. One's first entry into a tropical forest yields an impression of the extreme profusion of life, a green riot of vegetation accompanied by the incessant cacophony of bird and monkey calls from high above in the forest canopy. Yet this paradisiacal sensation is immediately coupled with the overwhelming stench of humid decay. Amerindians, while modifying this biome,[39] go with nature's flow, achieving cultural homeostasis in a "socialization of nature."

Where members of the DRT are puzzled by the mysterious disappearance of animals like the North American bison, the extinction of birds like the once myriad passenger pigeons, or the radical decline of the Eastern shad, all due to over-extraction and environmental disruption, members of the JRT, like the Tukano Indians of the Northwest Amazon, forestall such collapse. In the "Master of Animals,"[40] they conceive of large species paragons who animate the game animals, provided that hunters ask forgiveness of the animals they kill and cull no more than they need. Indiscriminately slaughtering all the available game angers these *Humbaba*-like guardians, who cease animating and sending game out into the world, hence their disappearance. Ecological equilibrium results from treating non-humans, natural and supernatural, like fellow humans.

Such "anthropomorphization" of nature is a JRT universal. Humans project their image, and social relations, outward to the spiritualized environment as a way of understanding it, labeling its bounty in endlessly variable ethno-taxonomies, making interaction with it like the politics of social life. Andean highlanders view the surrounding craggy massifs as large humans, fit for worship and emulation; so too do they and others invest human agency in plants, animals, and birds.[41]

The first step in material production being to procure the necessary raw materials, I begin with these resources' animacy, and the processes that manipulate them. Next, in the "operational chain"[42] of decisions creating material culture, sacred or profane, I examine the selection of fabrication processes, there being "styles in technology" as in art.[43]

Living Fire and "Color Energies"

In the JRT the procurement of resources from nature is social interaction, a dialog, with living beings. Zent, citing the Jodï of the Venezuelan *Amazonas*, explains that "the Amerindian life sphere conceives nature as inter-subjective, it establishes permanent negotiations and dialogic relations between the different entities."[44] This attitude extends from the raw materials to their modification (fire) and properties (color).

Fire must be "gestated," "birthed," and "grown." The Yanomamö ("Waika") make fire using friction in a simulacrum of intercourse, rotating the hard, vertical "Father" stick on the soft, horizontal "Mother" stick while "feeding it" tinder and fanning it with the "breath" of oxygen. Only men aid in this "birth," doing so in the forest, a realm prohibited to unescorted women. Life-force fire produces their *curare* hunting poison, which cannot be abandoned in cold coals but must be ritually "killed," returning fire's essence to the natural world.[45]

Just as technological processes, like fire, are "alive," possessing a "life trajectory," so too do other raw materials and properties have their own "hyper-animacy."[46] Colors are one fertile field for comparison between the DRT's static, dyadic dualism and the "dual-triadic dualism"[47] continuum logic of the Amerindian JRT. In old westerns, the good guys wore white hats and rode white horses while the bad guys wore black hats and rode black horses, replaying the DRT binary opposition of good/evil "bedeviling" Western thought.

Contrasting Amerindian conceptions of living "color energies"[48] derive from their most highly valued raw material: shiny, iridescent bird feathers. Elaborated by jungle groups like the Waiwai[49] and Cashinahua,[50] these feather accoutrements give the lie to "naked Indians" (the frontiersmen's justification for killing them because they are "naked like animals, like cattle")[51]; they transform men into birds, often fierce ones. Birds being venerated as benevolent spirit intermediaries between the masculine celestial world and the feminine earth plane, what better goal than to dress like them? Avian transformation starts at the crown of a Cashinahua warrior's head, the somatic portion nearest Sky World. Hence his most highly prized accoutrement, a white Harpy Eagle headdress emulates the erectile crest of that largest of raptors. Below, on the chest, comes feathered breastplates, copying the enlarged breasts of birds, as well as feathered back-racks, simulating their tails. (Figure 17.1.)

This "feather code" also embraces the type (species, color) of plumes as sartorial microcosm, recapitulating the vertical order of the rainforest macro-cosmos. Beginning again at the somatic apex, now with a Waiwai headman,[52] the same vertically plummeting, masculine-personifying (white) solar Harpy Eagle, nesting 200 feet above the forest floor in the branches of the sacred World Tree, the towering silk cotton kapok (*Ceiba pentandra*), constitutes the primary upper element in his headdress.[53] The next level down in his "terrain" are broad, sweeping scarlet macaw tail feathers projecting from his perforated nasal septum,[54] or red and yellow toucan breast feathers dangling from his perforated cheeks. On the upper arms, from tight ligatures cinched above his biceps, project the long tail feathers of the scarlet macaw, his "wings." The scarlet macaw and toucan

Figure 17.1 A Cashinahua warrior, Peruvian jungle, as a Bird Man in feather art. The Chonta palm lance is in the author's collection. Drawing: Author, 2018.

are mid-level fliers visiting the fruiting trees of the eighty-foot medium canopy. Descending from those same ligatures, but from behind, dangles a giant bulb of black curassow tail feathers,[55] hanging close to the ground, below his calves. The somber-colored curassow is a feminine-associated forest floor-dwelling fowl, a reluctant flier and favored game bird, the "turkey" of the jungle.[56]

À la Leach's "magical hair,"[57] a "cultured" Waiwai man's coiffure is controlled, while a Waiwai woman's hair hangs loose and longer in back, befitting her "natural" status.[58] He wears a beaded and feathered hair tube enclosing the tip of his long, tightly wrapped pigtail, dangling to his buttocks. This unique artifact recapitulates the same color and species code of terminal feather adornments (white, yellow, black). The tufts of white, filmy down from captured harpy eagle nestlings plaster the front of his palm-oil slicked and gleaming black hair, carefully cut bangs in front.[59] They turn his dull black coiffure shiny and white (like the Yanomamö ceremonial coiffure);[60] the downy feathers fall like snow as he dances,[61] fulfilling the "kinetic necessity" of living Amerindian art. A man's avian "cosmological body" reflects, in its color and species symbolism, a moving microcosm of the forest macrocosm, turning men into "flying" avi-anthropic beings, a wish, instantiated in art, as old as the Upper Paleolithic.

Amazonian male dance patterns also parallel the mating system of colorful jungle birds like cock of the rock. These spectacularly orange-plumaged males strut and pirouette in a "dance ground" clearing for apprising drab females in the surrounding bushes.[62] In like fashion masculine dancers, splendidly be-feathered, "fly" across the cleared plaza under the evaluating eyes of the surrounding, less-elaborately costumed, feminine observers, a similar pantomime of sexual selection.

The shining hyper-animacy of color energies also adorned the "bodies" of living Maya temples as shiny, black obsidian insert disks.[63] These incrustations of dark, but high chroma reflective elements made the structures glint in the sun, reinforcing the liveliness of the building and its adorning sculpture. Chroma thus trumps hue; a shiny black or blue carries more semantic weight, and life energy, than a dull light brown. To live, an object must shine, as when Moche royals, dressed in armored tunics composed of myriad flashing golden plates, flashed like walking mirrors.[64]

"Color energies" characterized South Amerindian metallurgy.[65] Thin gold and silver "feathers" embodied a unique "depletion gilding" technology. *Tumbaga*, an 80 percent copper/20 percent gold alloy, its surfaces enriched with gold ions and depleted of copper ions by repeated bathing in oxidizing plant acids, appeared as pure gold. This technological style "revealed the essence" of the gold hidden within the base object. In contrast, Western Sheffield plating "occludes essence" by coating a copper object with a thin layer of gold or silver, thus "dominating" the metal.

Colombian-Ecuadorian and Peruvian Indians employed *tumbaga* for sacred and aesthetic reasons, realizing a range of color energies from pink to red, to gold, the "Sweat of the Sun," and silver, the "Tears of the Moon."[66]

This parameter derives from the light in living eyes, the eerie white "mirrors" of the feared, but admired, jaguar's eyes at night.[67] Death is signaled when the light goes out of the eyes. South Amerindians, like the Ye'cuana, often have multiple souls with different "half-lives": ephemeral "water souls," one's reflection in still water, "sun souls," one's diurnal shadow, and "moon souls," one's nocturnal full-moon shadow, etc.[68] But the eternal form of these multiple souls, at least for the Shipibo, is the *caya*, the "eye soul." The *caya* leaves the body upon death, flying on a scarlet hummingbird's back to the sun, to enjoy eternal life in Sky World.

In Shipibo, the semantic range of "brightness" ranges from "reflective," as in sunlight glinting off water at noon, on the sensual pole, to their defining ethno-aesthetic criterion, *shina*, on the normative pole. *Shina* implies skill and creative "insight." Hence the famous Shipibo polychrome pottery is covered with a brilliant white pre-fire slip. Then their elaborate geometric designs are painted in yellow limonite and cordovan-brown manganese paints, the pot fired (when the hydrous ferric oxide limonite transforms into anhydrous ferric oxide, red hematite). Still hot from the teepee firing, its exterior is rapidly covered with a fine resin, protecting its paints like a car's clear coat, shining like a reflective glaze. The Shipibo, having an aesthetic of the "pristine" (unlike our own aesthetic, as a historical civilization, of the distressed "antique"), produce shiny, never-used pottery for honored guests at feasts. Old, worn pottery, especially if it has lost its post-fire resin crusting, is relegated to chicken coops. No wonder Shipibo women are bemused by Western tourists who insist on buying their older, worn pottery over their brand-new gleaming production (which to tourist eyes looks like it was made in China, too perfect for such "savages").

This preoccupation with *shina* is not restricted to pottery. The women's wrap-around skirts, *jośho chitonte* ("white skirt"), are woven on backstrap looms from native tree cotton. They are decorated with warp-patterned colorful designs, or, recently, with bright aniline-dyed wool embroidery. Likewise, men's ponchos, *jośho tari* ("white poncho"), similarly decorated, are valued as ethnic badges of emblematic style.[69] However, before being worn, the newly painted textiles are buried under a layer of mud rich in iron oxide, gathered by women from nearby swamps. A classic phenolic reaction follows whereby the design's plant dyes react with the mud's iron oxide, oxidizing, darkening, and becoming fixed. Not all chemistry takes place in Western laboratories.

When old and soiled, the *chitonte* and *tari*, as well as a woman's shawl (*racote*), will once again go under the mud, but for a longer time. The result is a warm brown color, the black designs muted, almost fugitive, the stains hidden. Such textiles are suitable for daily wear, but *verboten* for ceremonial attire. Again, the Shipibo women are surprised when tourists prefer the old, dyed fabrics to their new white, bright ones. To answer this demand, they have taken to dying new textiles, proof that the *nahuan joshinbo* ("white savages") are truly infrahuman!

There was even a fashion in the mid-seventies for Shipibo white dresses to be embroidered with bright pink and red imported aniline-dyed wool yarn, creating contour ambiguity like "dazzler" Navajo rugs. Once the fashion shifted to black dresses in the 1980s, better to showcase the yarn's brilliant colors, Shipibo maidens, as ardent followers of fashion as modern Westerners, added reflective sequins to the design's form-lines, the dresses sparkling more ardently. Shipibo women wear their wealth on their bodies, as in all traditional societies, displaying a massive belt of white glass beads, the *morochënëšëti*. This adds the appropriate light hue and chroma to the "equator" of her somatic geography. These fashions continue women's concern with *shina*, confirming their sobriquet as "painted doves."

A culture's central metaphors manifest themselves on ever-encompassing levels, from micro to macro. If Clifford Geertz's apocryphal informant's response, "Ah Sahib, its turtles all the way down," to his questions concerning Hindu cosmology is accurate for the macro-to-micro intellectual journey, it is also "turtles all the way up."[70] Thus *shina* manifests itself from the object (the pot) to the person (clothing), and thence to the settlement. Shipibo village matrilocal compounds are like strings of pearls, strung along the high bluffs fronting the rivers and lakes of the Upper Amazon, high above the flood waters of the torrential rainy season.[71]

During the dry season Shipibo descend to the floodplain's sandbars to collect brilliant white sand. They haul it back up the steps cut into the clay walls of the bluff to the village plaza and spread it over the hard-packed clay substrate to yield a blindingly white plaza. The whole village, now "enlightened," cleansed, made beautiful, manifests purified *shina* before invited guests arrive for fiestas, an advertisement of civic pride (and the host's political strength). A dirty, dull-clayey, weed-infested plaza would constitute a sad commentary about the corporate weakness and moral lassitude of the irresponsible denizens of an unkempt village.

Objects Move, Therefore They Are Alive

Another defining characteristic of life is mobility, stasis implying death. For the animist, the infusion of life into what for Westerners is inert (dead) nature, derives from its unceasing movement. Do not rivers flow, rise, and recede in flood, their waters circling in whirlpools, or cascading in waterfalls? Do not mountains erode, suffer mass movement, or explode in volcanism? Does not the very ground move in earthquakes (all these perturbations characterizing the Andes)? The same kinetic processes occur in the biosphere; do not trees grow, move (a species of palm even "walks" in the Amazon), bend and shake, crashing in heavy wind, even the mightiest among them? All this activity surrounds humans with animated, moving beings, larger and stronger than they are, requiring both obeisance and negotiation.

A "living" material culture, made from such animated raw materials, must also be infused with movement, a kinetic function, with the same appearance (effigies) and "somatic geography" as their human creators. Those Waiwai headdress elements have their feather ends weighted with tree resin, attaching contrast-colored smaller feathers, so that the plumes bob and weave in dance. The ancient Moche "embodied" the same idea in an owl headdress with multiple huge, metal "feathered" wings with danglers[72] glistening and bending in movement. A metal fox-head mask with movable tongue[73] clattered and barked as its bearer moved. Moche nobles also wore delicate sheet-gold hummingbird earrings with inlaid turquoise eyes, whose dangling wings and feathers were suspended from golden wires, quivering and jingling with their owner's slightest movements.[74] More broadly, Inuit-to-Northwest Coast transformation masks, and the latter's masks with moveable and interchangeable mouth parts and theatrical animated puppets, demonstrate that living material culture pervaded indigenous thinking from the Arctic to Peru.

Life Does Not Last, or Does It?

The ephemerality/eternity of JRT artifacts made from perishable materials also applies to the human body and its artifactual embodiment in the hereafter. Lowland cultures modeled anthropomorphic funeral urns for secondary burials. Others employed large burial urns containing the dead in fetal positions.[75] Both strategies entombed the deceased within hollow "wombs" in the feminine earth for rebirth. Nor did the descendants' attentions end with burial. In the Marajoara culture's mounds at the mouth of the Amazon, in situ large, decorated anthropomorphic burial urns were only partially interred. Their capped orifices, left above ground and protected by a roofed enclosure, allowed the descendants to revisit the urns, uncap them, and provide ritual libations and food offerings for their ancestors.[76] These effigy urns, the reconstituted bodies of the skeletons within them, still needed sustenance, as alive as the famous Incan mummies.

The living hoped to carry with them helpers into the other world, first by sacrificing real attendants and animals and, as cultural attitudes softened, modeled attendants, who would revivify in the afterlife and serve their owners. Hundreds of small human effigy press-molded, face-neck jars were interred with Moche rulers (along with "real" concubines, warriors, servants, and pet dogs), to reanimate as complete human servants and guardians in the next life.[77] Being intended for sacrifice, sometimes their workmanship is crude or unfinished. The small golden lost-wax caste figurines of the Colombian Chibcha still sport rough edges, fresh from the casting.[78]

Another example of subprime manufacture and the killing of funerary pottery "people" comes from the Huaca de la Luna pyramid in the Moche Valley. In addition to sacrificed young males, large and unfired effigy jars of seated, naked warrior prisoners with ropes around their necks and hands tied behind their backs[79] were ceremoniously "killed," smashed to pieces in situ. More than just standing in for people, these pots *were* people, augmenting the number of propitious victims.

"Killing pots" was not unique to the Moche. In the American Southwest, numerous, otherwise intact Mimbres (1,000–1,200 CE) open bowls with stylized animals painted on their interiors[80] were also mortuary goods, "cancelled" for mortal use by punching holes in their bottoms. I encountered a similar context, but with pot sherds, in excavations of ancient Puerto Rican Amerindian sites. From the excavation of one secondary burial dating to the initial phase of the Saladoid occupation at the large residential Maisabel site, excavators recovered a set of large white-on-red rim sherds of complex-silhouette bowls (Figure 17.2). Why were whole vessels not left as grave goods? Of what use would sherds, even large and pretty ones, be to the dead?

Years later another puzzling situation resurfaced at Punta de Mameyes. In the Monserrate vessels (the Epi-Saladoid phase, 600–800 CE) of this

Figure 17.2 The author excavating a secondary burial with partial vessels as a funerary offering at the Maisabel site, north coast Puerto Rico. Photo: unknown student from author's field school, 1985.

multicomponent site, otherwise whole cook pots had their bottoms knocked out. The missing sherds were never found, indicating that breakage occurred before deposition. Orifice-up, seated on the ground, with other large sherds inside, they once contained burial food offerings. Since the dead were "broken" so did their pots need to be "killed," accompanying them to *Coaybay* (the western land of the dead). There they would reassemble, to continue their culinary function.

More than treating a pot like a living entity, the nature of the sherds found inside these "killed" vessels represented the same pattern as the earlier burial offerings at Maisabel. In one feature a whole cooking "kit" appeared as broken sherds including a large fragment of a *burén*, the clay griddle on which unleavened cassava bread prepared from bitter manioc flour was toasted. As with the Waiwai, the "killed" vessel itself was the cookpot in which a fish and sweet potato soup, the original "gumbo," was cooked, the protein source complementing the bread carbohydrate. Lastly, a large, decorated dish sherd was the fineware plate on which prepared solid food like fruit was served, a complete "tableware" set. Another Monserrate example of multiple bottom-knocked-out cook pots appeared at the later inland site of San Lorenzo as these coastal peoples penetrated the island's interior. One such bottomless cook pot even had an earlier Cuevas-style plate fragment, an ancient "curio," placed over the perforated bottom, better to contain the food offering![81]

Pots as Living Portable, Utilitarian Sculpture

To "kill" a pot it must first have been "alive." In the West, a ceramic vessel is usually just an inert container, like the ubiquitous red (*terra cotta*) earthenware flowerpot (or its plastic skeuomorph). But in the Amerindian JRT, earthenware vessels are "living" portable, utilitarian sculpture.[82] Moche-painted stirrup spout bottles, 100–800 CE, revealed this sculptural intent, sometimes treating human effigy vessels to decorative semi-precious stone inclusions, imitating face paint,[83] and creating their famous portrait jars,[84] or their "infamous" pornographic pots.[85] Moche effigy pots included everything from fruits,[86] cultigens,[87] and insects,[88] to fish,[89] animals (a llama effigy),[90] and birds.[91] This incredible corpus enables a veritable "ceramic ethnography," despite Moche's lack of writing.

This effigy tradition also appears throughout Amazonia-Guiana (Cumancaya),[92] and the ancient Caribbean (Elenoid)[93] in ceramic *adornos*, or figural lugs of human or animal heads, facing inward on vessel rims. When provided with raised arms or extended legs, the whole pot becomes a bodily effigy, forcing one to eat out of the being's open belly,[94] or snorting, via the nose, psychotropic liquid tobacco juice through the effigy vessel's hollow legs (Huecan Saladoid)![95] In one standing Moche skeletal, anthropomorphic effigy jar with an enormous erection,[96] holes round the hollow figure's headband made it impossible to drink from the macabre figure's main head orifice, forcing the drinker to imbibe the liquid from the tip of the hollow penis-spout in an act of simulated fellatio!

These sculptural figures, usually destined for the dead, were "animated objects" demonstrating life's *stigmata*, movement. Not merely utilitarian sculpture, they were "kinetic sculptures" allowing liquids like the vessel's "blood," "urine," and "semen" to move in peculiar and elaborate ways. Instead of the Western pitcher's single, practical orifice, the stirrup-spout of a northern coastal Peruvian bottle[97] channeled liquid from either direction in the stirrup, flowing into the central spout. In similar dualistic fashion, the double-spout-and-bridge bottles[98] allowed the liquid to pour from either spout,[99] the forward one often an effigy head, or whole figure.[100] A Moche specimen exhibits greater complexity, with a modeled, hollow rim and a double (hollow) base, allowing water to be channeled first to an orifice in the rim, and from thence to a hollow standing male figure in the base urinating to fill the bowl; or in another case, submerging a group of metal smiths with blow-tubes![101] In a modern Canelos Quichua effigy bowl from the Ecuadorian jungle, a hollow basal monster's (*supai*'s) head "vomits" beer as the bowl is emptied.[102]

To this index of kinetic vivacity, Amerindians added another life indicator, sound. Peruvian double-spout-and-bridge bottles have a built-in whistle modeled into the forward effigy head. When the vessel is tipped, the displacement of liquid and air causes the pot to whistle.[103] Shipibo *quënpo* ("manioc beer mugs") also couple kinetic features with sound. Inside their hollow base ceramic beads rattle as the beer is quaffed. South Amerindian pottery, ancient and modern, "talks" and "moves," announcing the life it embodies.

Not just human effigies, these pots exhibit the "micro-macrocosmic recapitulation" of human body art. A large Shipibo anthropomorphic beer fermentation and storage jar (Figure 17.3a) is a female; these vessels come in consort pairs. It is a *joni chomo ani* ("human" "liquid storage-transport jar," "large size mode") exhibiting dual design fields that reflect the vertical order of the cosmos: (1) sub-rim, above the keel, and (2) body=*poro*, the lower band, near the base, the vessel's *poinqui*, or "ass"). The lower field pictures a *ronin quënëya* ("boa," "design," "with") angular fret design layout representing the constrictor's body (Figure 17.3b) and has the stylized boa turning into that geometric figure in a nineteenth-century tunic. This ophidian icon represents the Earth World platter the pot sits on, and below it, the aqueous Underworld. The vessel's upper segment depicts a *caros quënëya* ("cross" "design," "with") layout, derived from the celestial "World Cross," the Southern Cross asterism representing Sky World[104] and the universe's quadrants. Such anthropomorphic pots bear the same cosmic recapitulation designs, in the correct order, of Shipibo body painting, costume, and feather art: Sky World above, Earth World in the middle, and Subaquatic Underworld below.[105]

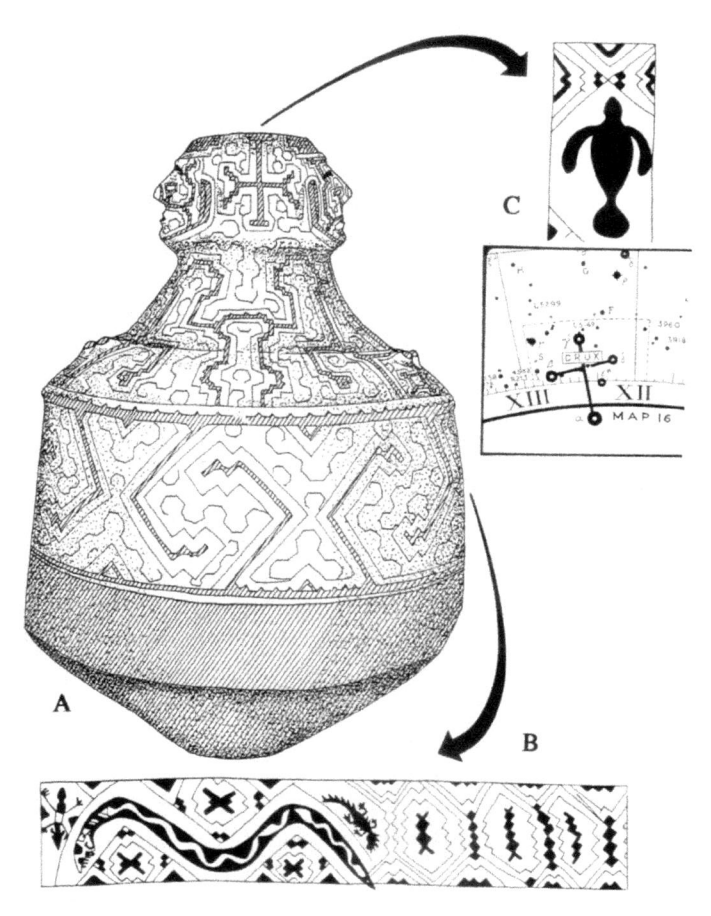

Figure 17.3a A Shipibo effigy pot whose upper design mirrors Sky World.
Figure 17.3b The lower designs represent Earth World and the Sub-Aquatic Underworld. Drawings: author, 1981.

From Living Effigy Pots to Ensouled Textiles

Transitioning from the artifact handled to the artifact worn, for Central and South Amerindians clothing is a backstrap loom-woven cotton or wool textile. The tree cotton's bolls originally grew from the body of the were-jaguar Chavín female Cotton Goddess. The Andean form of the lowland "Mermaid," she sports her fearsome *vagina dentata*, as well as a main mouth of snarling interlocking felinic canines, and a projecting crown of an anatropic mouth sporting caiman's teeth.[106] As with the caimanic Dragon from Shipibo mythology, this figure is recapitulated in Waiwai myth.[107] Soft cotton, the prototypical feminine raw material, grows in every woman's house garden.

The act of weaving warp and weft, a feminine "gestational" technique, constitutes a form of worship. Schaefer's description of Huichol women in Mexico[108] equally applies to a Shipibo woman at her loom. She similarly "gives birth" to her textiles, which retain her *caya* (eye-soul), as well as the soul-stuff of the person, male or female, who will wear it. Using contagious magic, a person's garment or accoutrement, once worn, continues to be suffused with their wearer's oils and odor, partaking of his/her soul as I learned when I had to hastily return a Shipibo poncho I was drawing the designs from when its owner, a shaman (Figure 17.4), complained that, bereft of it, he had become sick as a portion of his soul was missing![109]

Another woven domain, basketry, has the same "animated" nature as textiles and their twill-weave designs from the Ye'cuana,[110] or the Waiwai of neighboring Guyana,[111] are derived from nature. They originate in, and are patterned after, animal "Masters": capuchin and spider monkeys, stingrays, caiman, and anacondas, taking both the shape and decoration of these donors. They all wear "art," a defining characteristic of culture, *naturally* on their skins, hides, and feathers. Hence the twill-weave designs on Waiwai baskets came from the scaly skin of *Urufiri*, the gigantic mythological flying Dragon. Malignant and unwilling to share, he must be killed and skinned, and the skin's intricate pattern studied by a culture hero who learns the designs and transmits them to succeeding generations, now as culturally learned skills, not natural attributes.

Not just the designs, but these artifacts' shape and function, come from these once-living things, continuing their lives. As the Ye'cuana observe, their drums were originally vivified and ferocious: "The drum was a

Figure 17.4 A Shipibo shaman, *Bahuan mëtsa* ("Like a Green Amazonian Parrot"), with his painted *tari* (cotton poncho). Photo: author, 2010.

different shape. It was pointed and could run right through a person like a sword."[112] Or like their unique telescoping baskets, the *Kungwa*, or the Waiwai man's vanity basket, the *fakara*, once ferocious caimans who went along the shore snapping their jaws (the upper and lower parts of the elongated baskets), devouring hapless creatures.[113] Ethology following morphology, their basketry descendants "eat," and thereby store in their woven bellies a man's feathers, face, and body paint, and a shaman's quartz crystals, maraca, and tobacco. Another basketry artifact, the triangular fire fan, the simplest, and therefore the first basket made by young men, reveals, in its triangular shape, its origin in the freshwater stingray. Such analogies pervade their woven repertory.

The designs, like *Mado*, the Jaguar's intricate quatrefoil spots, turn into mirrored rectangular frets, *Mado fidi*. They decorate and energize Ye'cuana baskets.[114] Yet they are "toxic" for women because of their dangerous wild creature origin. Because women are regarded as more "natural" than men, and easily seduced, they could be drawn back into nature by Jaguar therianthropic lovers, or by "phallic" Were-caiman and Were-anaconda paramours, lost to culture forever. After all, women originated as Mermaids, the daughters/lovers of the *Okoimyo yenna*, the Anaconda Folk in Waiwai mythology. They could easily be pulled back into that aquatic domain, abandoning their human husbands and sons, ending human society. Analogous Ye'cuana women are forbidden to use twill-weave-decorated flat serving baskets (*waja tomenato*, the "painted" ones with stylized animal designs) woven by their men until "domesticated" by their first year of marriage. Until then, women must employ the appropriately aquatic, and non-pictorial, "Frog Bottom" serving baskets, especially when they are in their most "watery" and "natural" menstrual state.

Predictably, the only basket women make is an undecorated wickerweave *wuwa* burden basket. With its sturdy, round, and waisted form, it mimics their body image and garden tuber and firewood gathering duties. In contrast, Waiwai men's baskets, like the Ye'cuana *tudi*, are twill-weave decorated, with a linear form that recalls men's own bodily image and an open U-shaped back to accommodate unusually shaped things like a deer's carcass; both types "embodying" a "sexist technology."

The Next Level, Animated Structures: Huts, Temples, and Cities

From the gendered human body, its effigies, and accoutrements, we arrive at larger contexts: the hut lived in, the temple worshipped in, and the city dwelt within. The most inclusive level, that of the entire "sacred landscape," anchored these civic-ceremonial centers.[115] The Nazca Valley, on the south coast of Peru, with its gigantic geoglyphs of monkeys and spiders[116] each a sacred trackway, "form[ing] a continuous line that never crosses itself ... a ritual pathway," is a famous example of such a setting.[117] Many of its trackways led to hidden sources of water, crucial for such moisture-challenged environments.

For the elementary level, the individual hut, I return to the Cariban Ye'cuana and Waiwai where the settlement pattern is a circular village. Like the ancient Saladoid villages of their Antillean precursors, these sites consist of large round communal huts clustered around a cleared plaza. These *malocas* exhibit "sexed space" (men : upper :: women : lower, men : center :: women : periphery). Around the feminine periphery, the occupants string their hammocks (men's above, women's below). Men's ceremonial activities control the center, under the towering roof apex.

These huts are "living" beings built by complementarily gendered labor, the soft round structure and the finer lower thatch, feminine (gathered by women from the lowest palms), while the rougher upper thatch, and the central projecting hut pole, masculine, obtained by men from the tallest palms. The central pole is nonstructural, but symbolically necessary, being brought in after the hut is built. It is carried on the shoulders of the men from a neighboring village, the prospective exogamic marriage mates of the village's women. Like a long and hard phallus, it enters the single vaginal doorway in an act of symbolic intercourse. The men then "erect" (the *double entendre* applies) the post in the structure's center, penetrating it (the pole extends several meters beyond the apex). Finally, a round gourd, a uterine symbol, is placed over the phallic tip of the projecting post in yet another mime of intercourse, the communal hut becoming a self-copulating "being," the social totality of the village.[118]

These Guianan peoples' Arawakan precursors took the "living hut" one step further. Just as their Taíno descendants envisioned a Turtle Woman progenitrix for whom primordial men constructed the first *maloca*, the Saladoid village of Golden Rock in St. Eustatius, Lesser Antilles (248–610 CE), consisted of structures shaped as massive sea turtle effigies. They even ceremonially buried an intact (though decapitated) sea turtle in the midden. The ground plans of these circular communal huts, ancestral to the Taíno *bohio*, included wind screens that arched from their sides, mimicking the turtle's paddles.[119] Instantiating their round and "hollow" feminine symbolism, "[b]y far the most common zoomorphs appearing in Saladoid *adornos*, painted motifs, and effigy pots were turtles."[120] Lastly, the term "*maloca*" has its etymology in "*morocoy*," "commonly used to denote tortoises."[121] Humans thus grew up "children of the turtle."

As living beings, these stationary structures also "move." The Ye'cuana hut is not located at random. Rather, it is situated so that the doorway faces east to the rising sun. Then, to mark the seasons, a roof door (the *mentana*)[122] is opened so that the sunlight at the equinoxes and solstices illuminates the central and nearby posts, the former decorated with a solar snake. The entire structure becomes a functioning celestial being, changing with the seasons of the horticultural year. In late-prehistoric times, the massive wheel-like villages of the Xingú in central Brazil, composed of multiple huge, encircling oblong communal huts surrounding a cleared central plaza, elaborated that symbolism. The villages projected cardinal-point avenues radiating toward other hub-like villages in "distributed urbanism."[123]

Huts "moving" to the seasons also characterizes the next level of "micro-macro cosmic recapitulation," the temple (the god's hut writ large). From the earliest times (Initial Period, 2,200–1,750 BCE) Peruvian coastal pyramids had an astronomical function.[124] The Chavín inherited both a U-shaped pyramid and circular sunken plaza embraced by twin wings from earlier coastal centers, yet unlike them its associated polities possessed clear social stratification with theocratic/military élites. Chavín innovated a highly developed multimedia technology, including monumental stone sculpture and unusually complex stone architecture. Like analogous Balinese temples and palaces of the Negara, the "Theatre State," the objective behind the monuments was "to make inequality enchant."[125]

To accomplish this the priesthood's knowledge (their calendrical and astronomical mastery) became essential to the peasantry by "ritually regulating" their subsistence cycle. In the eastern Andes, fronting the *montaña*, this centers on the prediction of the rainy season. On the western desert coast it anticipated the summer runoff from the glaciers on the deified mountains (*Apus*). These torrents swell the fifty-odd, intermittently dry, coastal rivers that feed the irrigation systems, nurturing the crops that nourish the commoners. Just as the mountains were "alive" as gods (Masters/Mistresses of Water), so too were the pyramids, as living beings, artificial mountains oriented to the real ones, and charged with the same responsibilities.

Lumbreras in his excavations of the "Old Temple" portion of the Chavín de Huántar pyramid, discovered a set of interior stone galleries ("intestines of the Dragon's belly").[126] One descended under the seven-riser monumental stairway ("Pleiades Staircase," from the asterism's seven stars) to a circular semi-subterranean ("sunken") plaza in the center of the temple's extending "wings." Lumbreras hypothesized that the seven-foot Tello Obelisk had originally stood in the center of that circle. Vertically mounted stone slabs inside the descending gallery caused rainwater runoff from the pyramid's upper structure to form turbulent vortexes within its resonating chamber; as the rains arrived the gallery, the temple "roared" (bull caimans, in mating displays, utter infrasonic roars that cause the water to "dance" around them). During the rainy season, the pyramid, shaped like a caiman's jaws,[127] bellowed at the same time that black caimans surfaced to hunt fish in the flooded forests of the Amazon. The temple was "a living being" designed to impress pilgrims that came from afar to consult the center's oracle and leave offerings in its hidden galleries.

In transit and sextant-aided fieldwork, coupled with computer ("Starry Night") astral simulation, my colleague and I discovered that the Old

Temple was oriented to the heliacal setting of the Pleaides at 1,000 BCE, heralding the arrival of the rains from the Dragon's jungle home to the east, as necessary for highland potato gardeners as for lowland manioc cultivators.[128] The Tello Obelisk was decorated with two monstrous black caimanic Dragons (with piranha and ophidian attributes). Incised in bas-relief, vertically ascendant, cultigens sprouting from their bodies, these consort Dragons precisely reflected a Shipibo myth.[129] It recorded the origin of the Pleiades, Orion, and the Hyades and multi-cropped horticulture, demonstrating over 3,000 years of mythic continuity. The ability to predict the rains for these cultigens gave the site's priests an aura of sacred authority for visiting worshippers utterly dependent upon those rains in the semi-arid highlands.

We were also the first identify the L-shaped terminus of the obelisk, like the "V" of rifle sights, as a sighting gnomon to establish the midline of the structure and its central entombed, cross-based gallery. In line with the Pleiades Stairway, the latter housed an earlier L-shaped sighting gnomon, circa 1,200 BCE, the monstrous Lanzón. Originally erected on ground level, the pyramid and its galleries built around it, the sunken plaza Tello sightline followed the long axis of the Lanzón's gallery, continuing beyond the structure to bifurcate a V-shaped valley, the lowest break in the surrounding mountain wall, as well as an ancient mountainside path descending from that pass to the site. The temple's valley location was selected because of its sacred confluence of two rivers,[130] both joining the Marañon, a major tributary of the Upper Amazon, the caimans' home.

The fearsome Lanzón ("Lance" from its adventitious shape), is a Medusa-coiffured theri-anthrope with a caiman's agnathic-fanged mouth housed in the center of the Old Temple's St. Andrew's Cross-shaped subterranean gallery, an *axis mundi* shrouded in darkness. The consort Dragon's son, he is climbing a Sky Rope to escape to the heavens from the belly of the pursuing cannibalistic, dragonic temple (real caimans sometimes feast on their own juveniles). Above the Lanzón, tenoned into the ceiling, is another gallery from which hidden priests issued oracular prognostications to visiting pilgrims, their booming voices echoing among the stones.[131]

The Lanzón, a "living and speaking idol," had to be fed with libations of human blood to energize him for his arduous climb out of the Underworld dragon's bowels. In the Sky World he realized his astral destiny, becoming Alcyone, the brightest star (first magnitude) in the Pleiades, the herald of the rains and subsequent horticultural fertility.

Feeding the Lanzón was via a pour channel carved into the idol's "L" extension. It ends in a cosmogram (the "Andean Cross," the *chakana*, another St. Andrew's Cross) with a central circular "pool" on the Lanzón's forehead. The same priest that made the idol talk from the hidden gallery above poured the blood offering using that channel.[132] The Tello Obelisk's consort Dragons actively pursue him, both on the Tello's sculptural friezes, and from their architectural position in the sunken circular plaza outside the temple. Unlike DRT's temples, passive stages for human movement, JRT temples self-animate.

There was no exit drain for the descending waters from the acoustic gallery as they debouched into the sunken circular plaza where the Tello caimans stood. As the rains fell and the temple roared, the water flowed into the plaza, the lithic reptilian Dragons "breaching" out of the resultant standing pond, emulating the caiman's lake in the Shipibo myth. Then, as the dry season approached, the lake evaporated, permitting the peasants to harvest. The Dragons would then (metaphorically) dive in a six-month cycle to await the next year's rainy season of planting. This cycle adds the same "kinetic" function to a temple (the macrocosm) as in pot effigies and communal huts (the microcosms); truly it is "caimans all the way down."

Such "living temples" are replicated in Mesoamerica's "animated buildings."[133] An uncanny parallel to the "watery" and astronomical functions of Chavín's Old Temple comes from the contemporary Olmec center of Teopantecuanitlán in Guerrero, Mexico. In Phase 3 (1,000–800 BCE), a series of stone masonry platforms were placed above and below a sunken rectangular court with double stairways descending into it, their balustrades decorated with stone Olmec feline heads. "Four large sculptures resembling an inverted T crowned the east and west walls of the courtyard."[134] These inverted T-shaped monoliths were decorated with split-representation, were-jaguar Maize God heads. With their rectangular topknots, they approximate the L-shaped sighting gnomons of Chavín, serving a similar archaeo-astronomical function by marking the solstices and equinoxes (also accomplished at Chavín). To continue the parallels, the sunken court received rainwater runoff from the slopes above, and was constructed complete with two stone outlets and drains identical to those employed for water drainage at other Olmec centers like San Lorenzo and La Venta.

> Some archaeologists believe the drains were just part of a larger hydraulic system that emptied water *into* the Sunken Court from the east to create an artificial pond before it exited through the west drain. Karl Taube [the deity's identifier] believes local leaders deliberately flooded the court during rituals devoted to agricultural fertility. If so, the Maize God sculptures seeming to emerge from the water at the edge of an artificial pond set in the arid Guerrero countryside must have been a spectacular sight.[135]

Those leaders also constructed mundane irrigation systems at the site.

Such architectural "theatrical trickery" is rooted in the sleight-of-hand magic and ventriloquism of the ancient, and still-enduring, shamanic tradition. Therefore the Old Temple's acoustic deception is not unique to the high civilizations of Mesoamerica and Peru. In the Caribbean, Columbus's testimony (circa 1496) records entry into a Taíno chief's (*cacique*'s) hut (*caney*) in Hispañola. That large, thatched hut, complete with multiple gourd apex finials, functioned like a temple. Inside he discovered a carved wooden *zemi* idol (*cemí* – originally animistic spirits, later morphing into "departmental gods" as Taíno chiefdoms emerged), connected by an acoustic tube to a hidden outside speaker, thus overawing supplicants with the image's apparent pronouncements. The *cacique* subsequently pleaded with the Spaniards not to reveal the ruse to his subjects "because he held them all in obedience with that trick ... for they believe the *zemi* is the one who speaks, and all of them generally are deceived, and only the *cacique* knows and conceals the false credulity he uses to extract from his people all the tributes he wants."[136]

Back in Mesoamerica, animated sculpture and associated temples persisted from the Olmec into the later Maya civilization. "Foundation offerings" including infant or adult sacrifices, marked the "birth" of a construction level, as well as "temple internment," or "burial," when it was ritually "killed" to be capped by a "reborn" structure. These new levels grew ever grander in scale, "gestating" temples, like 10L-16 pyramid's construction sequence at Copán. It "entombed" the earlier "Rosalila" temple built over the founder's tomb, together with its "termination" (death) offerings.[137] Other site structures repeat this "life cycle," renewed every fifty-two years as part of the calendrical round.[138]

The Rosalila's façade still boasts its painted red color, symbolic of blood, hence life; the whole façade, below a bicephalic, arched sky-serpent, writhes with animacy. Such temples, as human-made stone mountains, emulate the mythic mountain itself, its upper story emblazoned with the face of a mountain deity, from whose forehead sprouts scrolls of yellow corn kernels. The image invokes the myth of the sacred mountain where maize originated. Above the mountain deity is a skeletal head representing death and rebirth. In Maya religion, death was followed naturally by rebirth, just as the sun is reborn each day, maize regenerates every year, and Maya children are believed to be the regeneration, or *k'exal* (replacements), of their grandparents and ancestors. Elaborate termination rituals for one building were precursors for the dedication rituals of the next continuing the cycle of architectural life.[139]

Killing Stone Bodies via Beheading

If the temple and its associated stone sculptures were "alive," they could also be "killed." Unlike the DRT Old World, the JRT New World never left animism behind. As in South America, the "trophy head cult" was an integral part of Central Mexican[140] and Mayan culture. When the king of a Mayan city was defeated, he was beheaded as was his temple sculpture.[141] Upon temple internment, all its "sculptures were then partially broken or demolished, perhaps as part of a termination ritual." "The Maya saw decapitating a statue as a means of destroying its spirit, or *ch'ulel*.

This is why we find many figures without their heads."[142] Hence stone skulls decorated pyramid façades not just as icons of mortality, but also harbingers of rebirth.[143] The Maya concept of a spitting skull impregnating a mythic goddess in the *Popol Vuh* illustrates this, since the soul as *sak nik*, "white flower," links "the regeneration of plants, especially maize and fruits, [which] parallel[s] the cycle of human life."[144] After all, the youthful Maize God was decapitated just as the maize plant lost its "head" (the cob) when harvested, reborn as its kernels were planted and germinated.

These conceptions derive from an "androcentric theory of conception," the skull being a round, hollow, bony, portable "womb" that men use, via the *foramen magnum* "birth canal," to magically propagate game (in the jungle, as in the *Bi Yoshin* myth), or cultivated plants (in the Andes and coast, as when peanuts emerge from the trophy head hauled by the hind foot of the Dragons on the Tello Obelisk, or a pineapple sprouts from another trophy head).[145]

Cities "Live" as Animal/Bird Masters of the Universe

The animation of architecture and its adorning sculpture does not end with the individual pyramid or pyramid group. It extended to the city that enclosed the temples, the urban space writ large. The nineteenth-century explorer, Ephraim Squier, produced an accurate map of the Inca Empire's capital, Cusco (Cuzco) showing it as a gigantic profile mountain lion,[146] the Emperor's and the empire's icon.[147] In the jungle to the east, as with Chavín, the jaguar is the icon of warriors and chiefs,[148] but it does not roam into the Andes; the cougar does, becoming the jaguar's highland "mythic substitute."

The contemporary "Pristine Civilization" to Chavín in Mexico, the Olmec (1,500–200 BCE) also constructed their centers as living effigies of the same "savage trinity" of natural icons: Jaguar (along with similar were-jaguar human transformation),[149] Harpy Eagle,[150] and Snake, each "Masters" of their respective realms. The Olmec substituted the Rattlesnake,[151] the prototype for the "Feathered Serpent," is the Amazonian Anaconda, there is also a Feathered Serpent in the Guianas, the Waiwai *Urufiri*.[152] Michael Coe argued that the multiple, artificial platforms constructed at the Olmec San Lorenzo site were an attempt to transform it into a gigantic flying bird,[153] that king of neotropical raptors, the harpy eagle.

Effigy cities, incomprehensible for the DRT, also reappeared among the Maya with another cosmic "Master," the caiman. This "living city," Nixtun-Ch'ich', located on a peninsula jutting into Lake Petén Itzá, northern Guatemala, is "the only Maya city with an urban grid [that] may [also] embody an ancient creation myth"[154] as the early Mayans were "trying to embed their worldview, their cosmology, into their city."[155] Built before 500 BCE, the presence of a *cenote*, a natural sink-hole and earth portal, suitable for sacrifices of humans and their artifacts[156] because it was the

Sun's entry point into the dark Underworld at dusk, was a cosmological inducement for the Maya settlement.

Nixtun-Ch'ich's peninsular location suggested a creature that could move between land and water, straddling two of the three cosmic platter worlds. An origin myth identifies that creature as our Formative icon, the caiman. Floating in a primordial sea, glyphs at Palenque describe it as having a hole in its back (the *cenote*), the gods slitting its throat. The ensuing torrent of blood formed the waters, its body the earth. Hence Nixtun-Ch'ich' emulated a crocodilian sliding into the lake, the regularly spaced city blocks of its urban grid forming its scales, the lake its blood. "A defensive wall, lined with a ditch ... represented the gash the gods made in the crocodile's neck."[157] Nixtun-Ch'ich' as a giant caiman slithering into the lake to the timing of the seasons parallels the giant black caimanic Dragons of the earlier ceremonial center of Chavín de Huántar far to the south, as well as sharing its bloody fate.

Conclusions: The Vestigial Animism of Objects

The investment of life in artifacts is not limited to tribal people, or the inhabitants of traditional chiefdoms or states, but includes us all. There persists a Western tendency to invest inanimate objects with animacy, often by giving transportation and war machines the attributes of formidable carnivores like sharks (Figure 17.5), or, conversely, endowing them endearing names. In our technology of the "foreseeable" we work hard to realize the "technological dream" of the ultimate "living machines," AI-enabled autonomous robots.[158] In Japan, with its reluctance to import caregivers from the Philippines or elsewhere to serve an increasingly geriatric population, great emphasis has been placed on robot design to fulfill that function. Such Japanese robots are often regarded by the elderly as "persons," and interacted with accordingly, particularly if they are given "cute" or "adorable" visages (exemplifying *Kawaii*, a key Japanese value), for example, the "Hello Kitty" phenomenon with big endearing eyes like *Paro*, a baby electro-mechanical harp seal.[159] The same findings have been recorded for Western anthropomorphic robots, such as the early Kismet emotive robot (Figure 17.5).[160]

More fascinating is the tendency for even humble technological devices, such as electronic personal assistants, like Siri, to be given personhood by their users: "dozens of experiments over the years have shown that people readily build strong bonds with computerized helpers which are endowed with anthropomorphic features, whether visual or vocal." These responses can even include embarrassment to admit ignorance, preventing some users from asking for help from these electronic aids.[161] As DRT denizens of the Information Age, from the dystopia of HAL to the utopia of Alexa™, we rediscover the animacy of objects, but from biomimetic machines, not nature.

Figure 17.5 A tour boat in the Boston harbor with shark-mouth decoration. Photo: author, 2017.

Notes

1. Prehistoric fieldwork began with the ninth-century CE Alto Ucayali River Cumancaya culture, Upper Amazon, utilizing Shipibo field assistants. See Raymond J. Scott, Warren R. DeBoer, and Peter G. Roe *Cumancaya: A Peruvian Ceramic Tradition* (Calgary: University of Calgary, 1975).
2. The Shipibo, famous for their elaborate polychrome pottery and textile arts, are Middle Ucayali "Canoe Indians" (Amazonia's most productive adaptation, utilizing its abundant aquatic fauna, and the rich alluvial soils deposited by annual inundations from the Andes's Eastern slopes, ideal for intercropped sweet manioc horticulture). Archaeological and ethnographic research focused on Shipibo mythology, ethno-astronomy, and ceremonies, as well as the structure and iconography of their complex geometric art in multimedia: ceramics, body art, textiles, beadwork, and wood-carving. See Peter G. Roe, "Paragon or Peril? The Jaguar in Amazonian Indian Society," in Nicholas J. Saunders, ed., *Icons of Power: Feline Symbolism in the Americas* (London and New York: Routledge, 1998), 171–202; Roe, "Mythic Substitution and the Stars: Aspects of Shipibo and Quechua Ethnoastronomy Compared," in Von del Chamberlain, John B. Carlson, and M. Jane Young, eds., *Songs from the Sky: Indigenous Astronomical and Cosmological Traditions of the World* (Washington, DC: Smithsonian Institution, 2005), 193–227; Roe, "Art and Residence among the Shipibo Indians of Peru: A Study in

Microacculturation," *American Anthropologist* 82 (1980), 42-71; Roe, *The Cosmic Zygote: Cosmology in the Amazon Basin* (New Brunswick: Rutgers University Press, 1982); Roe, "At Play in the Fields of Symmetry: Design Structure and Shamanic Therapy in the Upper Amazon," in Dorothy Washburn and Donald W. Crowe, eds., *Symmetry Comes of Age* (Seattle: University of Washington Press, 2004), 215-303.

3. Comparative research in the northeastern Peruvian Andes centered on the textiles, monumental stone sculpture, and architecture of ancient Chavín. Anomalously for a "highland" culture, Chavín's iconography was filled with powerful *montaña* megafauna. South America's first "civilization," Chavín spanned all three biomes of Peru: the jungle, the highlands, and the coast. Emerging out of coastal Cupisnique roots, (also a predecessor of the later Moche style) at 1200 BCE, it endured as a "regional cult" until 200 BCE. Shipibo astral and horticultural origin myths helped to decode the archaeo-astronomical functions of the eponymous civic-ceremonial center of Chavín de Huántar. Those myths also provided a detailed iconographic reading of the site's central monumental sculptures: the gigantic entombed Lanzón monolith and the freestanding Tello Obelisk, both Pleiades sighting gnomons. Hitherto unread, their bas-relief figures embodied lithic versions of this long-enduring (over 3,200 years), multi-tribal, jungle narrative. See Peter G. Roe, "How to Build a Raptor: Why the Dumbarton Oaks 'Scaled Cayman' Callango Textile is Really a Jaguaroid Harpy Eagle," in William J. Conklin and Jeffrey Quilter, eds., *Chavín: Art, Architecture and Culture* (Los Angeles: University of California, 2008), 181-216; Jeffrey Quilter, *The Moche of Ancient Peru: Media and Messages* (Cambridge: Peabody Museum Press, 2010), 20. Richard L. Burger, *Chavin and the Origins of Andean Civilization* (London: Thames and Hudson, 1992); Roe, "Mythic Substitution."

4. In the lowlands, archaeological studies focused on the initial Saladoid horticultural migrants to the Antilles (pre-500 BCE), their elaborate polychrome pottery, and innovative rock art adorning ball parks, human bone artifacts, and shell art. This transitional culture led to the ceramics and rock art of the protohistoric Taíno, 1200-1550 CE, the complex chiefdoms encountered by Columbus. See Peter G. Roe, "A Grammatical Analysis of Cedrosan Saladoid Vessel Form Categories and Surface Decoration: Aesthetic and Technical Styles in Early Antillean Ceramics," in Peter E. Siegel, ed., *Early Ceramic Population Lifeways and Adaptive Strategies in the Caribbean* (Oxford: British Archaeological Reports International Series, 1989), 267-382; Roe, "Rivers of Stone, Rivers Within Stone: Rock Art in Ancient Puerto Rico," in Peter E. Siegel, ed., *Ancient Borinquen: Archaeology and Ethnohistory of Native Puerto Rico* (Tuscaloosa: The University of Alabama Press, 2005), 285-336; Roe, "Walking Upside-Down and Backwards: Art and Religion in the Ancient Caribbean," in Timothy Insoll, ed.,

Oxford Handbook of the Archaeology of Ritual and Religion (Oxford: Oxford University Press, 2011), 518-39.

5. To flesh out the extinct cultures of the lowlands, a multidisciplinary team headed to the remote interior of the Upper Essequibo River of Guyana, the region of the Saladoid departure. There the Carib-speaking Waiwai are classic "Foot Indians" (the other adaption to the Amazon-Guianas, where hunting arboreal game is coupled with extensive slash-and-burn bitter manioc horticulture). In addition to their vibrant oral tradition, the Waiwai possess uniquely developed corporeal, feather, and basketry arts. See Peter G. Roe, "Of Rainbow Dragons and the Origins of Designs: The Waiwai *Urufiri* and the Shipibo *Ronin ëhua*," *Latin American Indian Literatures Journal* 5, no. 1 (1989), 1-67; Roe, "The Language of the Plumes: 'Implicit Mythology' in Shipibo, Cashinahua and Waiwai Feather Adornments," in Mary H. Preuss, ed., *L.A.I.L. Speaks! Selected Papers from the Seventh International Symposium, Albuquerque, 1989* (Culver City: Labyrinthos Press, 1990), 105-36; and Roe, *Arts of the Amazon*, Barbara Braun, ed. (London and New York: Thames & Hudson, 1995).
6. Carol Link, "Japanese Cabinetmaking: A Dynamic System of Decisions and Interactions in a Technical Context." Ph.D. dissertation (Urbana-Champaign: University of Illinois, 1975).
7. Egleé L. Zent, "Unfurling Western Notions of Nature and Amerindian Alternatives," *Ethics in Science and Environmental Politics* 15 (2015), 1-19.
8. Robert Wright, *The Evolution of God* (New York: Little, Brown, 2009).
9. Mark P. Leone, "The Role of Primitive Technology in Nineteenth-Century American Utopias," in Heather Lechtman and Robert Merrill, eds., *Material Culture: Styles, Organization, and Dynamics of Technology* (St. Paul: West Publishing Company, 1977), 87-107.
10. Andrew George, *The Epic of Gilgamesh: The Babylonian Epic Poem and Other Texts in Akkadian and Sumerian* (London: The Folio Society, 2010).
11. Ronald B. Tobias, "Theodore Roosevelt's Last Hunt: How to Reconcile the President's Protection of Nature with His Seeming Desire to Destroy It?" *Natural History* 127, no. 3 (2019), 37.
12. Lynn White, Jr., "The Historical Roots of Our Ecological Crisis," *Science* 155, no. 3767 (1967), 1203-07.
13. George E. Marcus and Michael M. J. Fischer, *Anthropology as Cultural Critique: An Experimental Moment in the Human Sciences*, 2nd ed. (Chicago and London: The University of Chicago Press, 1999).
14. J. Stephen Lansing, *Priests and Programmers: Technologies of Power in the Engineered Landscape of Bali* (Princeton: Princeton University Press, 1991), 10-12.
15. H. W. F. Saggs, *The Babylonians: A Survey of the Ancient Civilization of the Tigris-Euphrates Valley* (London: The Folio Society, 1988), 257.
16. Saggs, *The Babylonians*, 257, 262.

17. José María Arguedas, *Señores e indios: Acerca de la cultura Quechua*, Angel Rama, ed. (Buenos Aires: Arca Editorial, 1976).
18. Zent, "Unfurling Western Notions."
19. John Boardman, *The World of Ancient Art* (London: Thames & Hudson, 2006), figures 1-2, a pictographic deer-man, a bison-man, a bird-man, and, elsewhere, a sculptural lion-man.
20. Sir Edward Burnett Tylor, "Religion in Primitive Culture," *Primitive Culture* Part II, chs XI-XIX (New York: Harper & Row Publishers, 1958).
21. Mircea Eliade, *Shamanism, or Archaic Techniques of Ecstasy* (Princeton: Princeton University Press, 1974).
22. Napoleon A. Chagnon, *Yanomamo*, 6th ed. (New York: Harcourt Brace College Publishers, 2013), 116.
23. Michael D. Coe and Stephen Houston, *The Maya*, 9th ed. (New York: Thames & Hudson, 2015), 294.
24. David M. Guss, *To Weave and To Sing: Art, Symbol, and Narrative in the South American Rain Forest* (Berkeley and Los Angeles: The University of California Press, 1989), 31.
25. Elizabeth P. Benson, *The Worlds of the Moche on the North Coast of Peru* (Austin: University of Texas Press, 2012), figure 13.6, Phase V.
26. Carlos G. Elera, "The Face behind the Mask," in Victor Pimentel, ed., *Peru: Kingdoms of the Sun and the Moon* (Montreal: Montreal Museum of Fine Arts, 2013), figure 1.
27. Chagnon, *Yanomamo*, 104.
28. Roe, "Of Rainbow Dragons."
29. Ibid.
30. Richard A. Diehl, *The Olmecs: America's First Civilization* (London: Thames & Hudson, 2004), figure 64d.
31. Roe, "How to Build a Raptor," figure 7.1e.
32. Linda Schele and David Freidel, *A Forest of Kings* (New York: Quill William Morrow, 1990), 408.
33. Benson, *The Worlds of the Moche*, figure 7.2.
34. Francis Huxley, *Affable Savages: An Anthropologist among the Urubu Indians of Brazil* (New York: Capricorn Books, 1956), 273.
35. Chagnon, *Yanomamo*, 107.
36. Roe, "Art and Residence"; Roe, *The Cosmic Zygote*, figure 4.
37. Guss, *To Weave and To Sing*, 81.
38. José Juan Arrom. "The Creation Myths of the Taíno," in Fatima Bercht et al. eds., *Taíno: Precolumbian Art and Culture from the Caribbean* (New York: Monacelli Press, 1997), 68.
39. Zent, "Unfurling Western Notions."
40. Gerardo Reichel-Dolmatoff, "Cosmology as Ecological Analysis: A View from the Rain Forest," *Man* 11 (1976), 307-18.
41. Andrea M. Heckman, *Woven Stories: Andean Textiles and Rituals* (Albuquerque: University of New Mexico Press, 2003), 5.

42. Pierre Lemonnier, *Elements for an Anthropology of Technology* (Ann Arbor: University of Michigan Press, 1992).
43. Heather Lechtman, "Pre-Columbian Surface Metallurgy," *Scientific American* 250, no. 6 (1984), 56–63.
44. Zent, "Unfurling Western Notions," 15.
45. Barbara Brändli, *Curare*. Documentary film, 1970.
46. Roe, *Arts of the Amazon*.
47. Peter G. Roe, "Style, Society, Myth and Structure," in Christopher Carr and Jill E. Neitzel, eds., *Style, Society, and Person* (New York: Plenum Publishing Corporation, 1995), 27–76.
48. Gerardo Reichel-Dolmatoff, "Desana Animal Categories, Food Restrictions, and the Concept of Color Energies," *Journal of Latin American Lore* 4 (1978), 243–91.
49. Roe, "The Language of the Plumes."
50. Kenneth M. Kensinger, "Feathers Make Us Beautiful: The Meaning of Cashinahua Feather Headdresses," in Ruben E. Reina and Kenneth M. Kensinger, eds., *The Gift of Birds: Featherwork of Native South American Peoples* (Philadelphia: The University Museum of Archaeology and Anthropology, 1991), 40–49.
51. Bernard Arcand, *The Last of the Cuiva*. Documentary film, 1991.
52. Roe, "The Language of the Plumes."
53. Nicholas Guppy, *Wai Wai: Through the Forests North of the Amazon* (London: John Murray, 1958).
54. Ibid, first black and white plate.
55. Ibid.
56. Roe, "How to Build a Raptor," figure 7.7.
57. Sir Edmund Leach, "Magical Hair," *Man* 88 (1958), 147–64.
58. Guppy, *Wai Wai*, fourth black and white plate group, plate 1.
59. Ibid, second black and white plate group, plate 1.
60. Chagnon, *Yanomamo*.
61. Timothy Asch and Napoleon A. Chagnon, *The Feast*. Documentary film (Watertown: Center for Documentary Anthropology, 1970).
62. Guppy, *Wai Wai*, 79–80, 90–92.
63. Barbara W. Fash, *The Copan Sculpture Museum: Ancient Maya Artistry in Stucco & Stone* (Cambridge: Peabody Museum Press, 2011), 77.
64. Walter Alva and Christopher B. Donnan, *Royal Tombs of Sipán* (Los Angeles: Fowler Museum of Cultural History, 1993), figure 245.
65. Lechtman, "Pre-Columbian Surface Metallurgy."
66. Carole Fraresso, "The Sweat of the Sun and the Tears of the Moon: Gold and Silver in Ancient Peru," in Victor Pimentel, ed., *Peru: Kingdoms of the Sun and the Moon* (Montreal: Montreal Museum of Fine Arts, 2013), 142–55.
67. Roe, "Paragon or Peril?"
68. Guss, *To Weave and To Sing*, 50–51.

69. Polly Wiessner, "Style and Social Information in Kalahari San Projectile Points," *American Antiquity* 48, no. 2 (April 1983), 253–76.
70. Clifford Geertz, *The Interpretation of Culture* (New York: Basic Books, 1973).
71. Roe, "Art and Residence."
72. Alva and Donnan, *Royal Tombs of Sipán*, figure 169.
73. Ibid, figure 199.
74. David M. Jones, *The Everyday Life of the Ancient Incas: Art, Architecture, Religion, Everyday Life, Culture* (London: Hermes House, 2010) figure 237 upper.
75. Warren R. DeBoer, "Report of Archaeological Excavations on the Río Shahuaya: A Western Tributary of the Upper Ucayali, Peru," MA thesis (Berkeley: University of California, 1970).
76. Margaret Young-Sánchez and Denise P. Schaan, *Marajó: Ancient Ceramics from the Mouth of the Amazon* (Denver: Denver Art Museum, 2011), 74.
77. Alva and Donnan, *Royal Tombs of Sipán*, figures 42, 51, 127–28, 131, 174–76, 181, 191.
78. Geoffrey H. S. Bushnell, *Ancient Arts of the Americas* (New York: Frederick A. Praeger, 1965), figure 230.
79. John W. Verano, "Communality and Diversity in Moche Human Sacrifice," in Steve Brändli and Kimberly L. Jones, eds., *The Art and Archaeology of the Moche: An Ancient Society of the Peruvian North Coast* (Austin: University of Texas Press, 2008), figures 11.18–19.
80. Boardman, *The World of Ancient Art*, plate 619; Bushnell, *Ancient Arts of the Americas*, figure 131.
81. Peter G. Roe, Juan González Colón, and Amy W. Roe, "To Feed the Dead: The Fine Ware from the Monserrate Site of San Lorenzo, Puerto Rico," *Proceedings of the 27th Congress of the International Association for Caribbean Archaeology* (St. Croix, USVI, 2019).
82. Peter G. Roe, "The Ghost in the Machine: Symmetry and Representation in Ancient Antillean Art," in Dorothy Washburn, ed., *Embedded Symmetries: Natural and Cultural* (Albuquerque: University of New Mexico Press, 2004), 95–143.
83. Benson, *The Worlds of the Moche*, figure I.5.
84. Michael E. Moseley, *The Incas and their Ancestors* (London and New York: Thames and Hudson, 2001), plates 57–58.
85. Benson, *The Worlds of the Moche*, figure 12.7.
86. Steve Bourget and Kimberly L. Jones, *The Art and Archaeology of the Moche: An Ancient Society of the Peruvian North Coast* (Austin: University of Texas Press, 2008), color plate insert, "*ulluchu* bowl."
87. Benson, *The Worlds of the Moche*, figure 3.1, maize with god image; figure 3.2, manioc; and figure 3.3, a peanut man with a spout erection.
88. Bourget and Jones, *The Art and Archaeology of the Moche*, spider.
89. Benson, *The Worlds of the Moche*, figure 11.2, a bonito.
90. Benson, *The Worlds of the Moche*, figure 3.4.

91. Bourget and Jones, *The Art and Archaeology of the Moche*, figure 9.16, a duck "warrior."
92. Scott, DeBoer, and Roe, *Cumancaya*, figures 8, 21.
93. Roe, "The Ghost in the Machine," figures 7, 8.
94. Ibid, figure 7.17.
95. Ibid, figure 7.3.
96. Quilter, *The Moche of Ancient Peru*, 55.
97. Ibid, plate 2.
98. Cecilia Bákula, "The Art of the Incas," in Laura Laurencich-Minelli, ed., *The Inca World: The Development of Pre-Columbian Peru, A.D. 1000–1534* (Norman: University of Oklahoma Press, 2000), figure 76.
99. Moseley, *The Incas and their Ancestors*, plate 68.
100. Ibid, plate 71.
101. Ibid, plate 66.
102. The vessel is in the collection of the author.
103. Bákula, "Art of the Incas," figure 76.
104. Roe, "Mythic Substitution and the Stars."
105. Roe, "Art and Residence;" Roe, *The Cosmic Zygote*, figure 2.
106. Roe, "How to Build a Raptor," figure 7.6.
107. Roe, "Art and Residence;" Roe, *The Cosmic Zygote*, 167.
108. Stacy B. Schaefer, "The Loom as a Sacred Power Object in Huichol Culture," in Richard L. Anderson and Karen L. Field, eds., *Art in Small-Scale Societies: A Contemporary Reader* (Englewood Cliffs: Prentice-Hall, 1993), 118–30.
109. Sir James George Frazer, *The Golden Bough*, abridged (New York and London: Penguin Books, 1922).
110. Guss, *To Weave and To Sing*.
111. Roe, "Of Rainbow Dragons."
112. Guss, *To Weave and To Sing*, 94.
113. Ibid, 103.
114. Ibid.
115. Richard F. Townsend, ed., *The Ancient Americas: Art from Sacred Landscapes* (Chicago and Munich: The Art Institute and Prestel-Verlag, 1992); and Lizzie Wade, "The City at the Beginning of the World: The Only Maya City with an Urban Grid May Embody an Ancient Creation Myth," *Archaeology* 71, no. 4 (2018), 26–31.
116. Moseley, *The Incas and their Ancestors*, plate 67.
117. Jones, *The Everyday Life of the Ancient Incas*, 126.
118. Roe, "Of Rainbow Dragons."
119. Roe, "How to Build a Raptor"; Roe, "Walking Upside-Down and Backwards," figure 33.2i.
120. Lawrence Waldron, "Whiskers, Claws and Prehensile Tails: Land Mammal Imagery in Saladoid Ceramics," in Samantha A. Rebovich, ed., *Proceedings of the XXIII Congress of the International Association for*

Caribbean Archaeology (IACA) (English Harbour, Antigua: Dockyard Museum, 2011), 4.
121. Ibid, 5.
122. Guss, *To Weave and To Sing*, 23–24.
123. Michael J. Heckenberger, "Amazonian Mosaics: Identity, Interaction, and Integration in the Tropical Forest," in Helaine Silverman and William H. Isbell, eds., *Handbook of South American Archaeology* (New York: Springer, 2008), 941–61.
124. Robert A. Benfer Jr., "Monumental Architecture Arising from an Early Astronomical-Religious Complex in Perú, 2200–1750 BC," in Richard L. Burger and Robert M. Rosenswig, eds., *Early New World Monumentality* (Gainesville: University Press of Florida, 2012), 313–63.
125. Clifford Geertz, *Negara: The Theatre State in Nineteenth-Century Bali* (Princeton: Princeton University Press, 1980).
126. Luís G. Lumbreras, C. González, and B. Lietaer, "Acerca de la Función del Sistema Hidráulico de Chavín," *Investigaciones de Campo No. 2* (Lima: Museo Nacional de Antropología y Arqueología, 1976).
127. Donald W. Lathrap, "Jaws: The Control of Power in the Early Nuclear American Ceremonial Center," in Christopher B. Donnan, ed., *Early Ceremonial Architecture in the Andes* (Washington, DC: Dumbarton Oaks, 1985), 241–67.
128. Roe and Roe, "Jungle Religion."
129. Roe, "Art and Residence;" Roe, *The Cosmic Zygote*, 63–66.
130. Tom Cummins, "The Felicitous Legacy of the Lanzón," in William J. Conklin and Jeffrey Quilter, eds., *Chavín: Art, Architecture, and Culture* (Los Angeles: Cotsen Institute of Archaeology, 2008), 239–59.
131. Jones, *The Everyday Life of the Ancient Incas*, 67.
132. Ibid, 142.
133. Fash, *The Copan Sculpture Museum*, 3.
134. Diehl, *The Olmecs*, figure 168.
135. Ibid, figure 169. (Emendation mine.)
136. Susan C. Griswold, "Appendices," in Fatima Bercht, Estrellita Brodsky, John Alan Farmer, and Dicey Taylor, eds., *Taíno: Precolumbian Art and Culture from the Caribbean* (New York: Monacelli Press, 1997), 170–71.
137. Fash, *The Copan Sculpture Museum*, figure 41, 38.
138. Ibid, figure 124.
139. Ibid, 43.
140. Gabriel Wrobel, Christophe Helmke, Sherry Gibbs, George Micheletti, Norbert Stanchly, and Terry Powis, "Two Trophy Skulls from Pacbitun, Belize," *Latin American Antiquity* 30, no. 1 (2019), figure 3.
141. Fash, *The Copan Sculpture Museum*, 98.
142. Ibid, 88, 97.
143. Ibid, 71.

144. Ibid, 84–85.
145. Roe and Roe, "Jungle Religion," figure 3, 2a.
146. Moseley, *The Incas and their Ancestors*, figure 35.
147. R. Tom Zuidema, "The Lion in the City: Royal Symbols of Transition in Cuzco," in Gary Urton, ed., *Animal Myths and Metaphors* (Salt Lake City: University of Utah Press, 1985), 183–250.
148. Roe, "Paragon or Peril?"
149. Diehl, *The Olmecs*, figures 69, 80.
150. Ibid, figure 64.2, 102.
151. Ibid, figure 39.
152. Roe, "Of Rainbow Dragons."
153. Coe and Houston, *The Maya*, 35.
154. Wade, "The City at the Beginning of the World," 27.
155. Ibid, 30.
156. Kristin M. Romey, "Diving the Maya Underworld: An Adventure in the Sacrificial Sinkholes of the Yucatán Jungle," *Archaeology* 57, no. 3 (2004), 16–23.
157. Wade, "The City at the Beginning of the World."
158. David Hakken, *Cyborgs@Cyberspace: An Anthropologist Looks to the Future* (Routledge: New York, 1999); and Steve Mann, "Cyborg Seeks Community," *Technology Review* (May–June 1999), 36–42.
159. Adam Piore, "Friend for Life: Robots Can Already Vacuum Your House and Drive your Car, Soon, They Will Be Your Companion," *Popular Science* 235, no. 5 (2014), 44.
160. Anonymous, "Babybot," *Discover* 19, no. 12 (1998), 18.
161. Anonymous, "Digital Assistants: Losing Face," *The Economist* 426, no. 9073 (2018), 57–58.

18

Technology

Ludovic Coupaye

Technology itself has no agency: it is the choices people make about it that shape the world.

"Pessimism v Progress," *The Economist*, December 21, 2019

Whether your greatest concern is climate change, air pollution, plastics, food security or one of the many existential threats the world is facing today, it seems that there are technological solutions that may actually help us meet the goals of the 2015 Paris climate agreement or achieve the Sustainable Development Goals by 2030.

Felicia Jackson, *Forbes*, January 17, 2019

Both viewpoints [techno-utopia and techno-dystopia] treat technology as if it had a life of its own, as if it possessed agency. This makes it more difficult to answer the vital question: not "Is technology good or bad?"; but "How should we organize ourselves as citizens to make the best use of technology?"

Kenan Malik, *Guardian*, October 20, 2019[1]

An anthropology of technology might as well use these epigraphs as ethnographic vignettes or, perhaps even, as transcripts of field interviews. They indeed summarize the place "technology" occupies in contemporary imagination: they seem to refer to a set of means designed to serve specific ends, after all, not unlike a simple hammer. As such, then, it appears logical that it can be used to solve some of the most pressing issues, such as climate change, democracy, social and economic development, or that, in a more pessimistic or even dystopian view, it can invoke the spectre of global surveillance, environmental degradation, or unemployment. Implicit in these debates is the issue of responsibility for either positive or negative effects. The answer is easy: if "technology" is neutral, then indeed anthropology should investigate mainly humans and their (good or bad) choices. Maybe when we deal with a hammer, this is a valid argument (this remains to be demonstrated). But then, if the neutrality of "technology" is itself under scrutiny, we might want to think about whether indeed the powerful machines and organizations that have emerged over the last 150 years, and the transformations these have brought to society, environment, health, warfare, or indeed politics, are just about choices.

I would add that we could also wonder about the actual ground on which one can really put together a hammer, social media, a driverless car, and an automated border control system. Indeed, the authors of the above epigraphs are not talking about hammers. We implicitly know that they are referring to "digital technologies." The shortcut "technology" covers such a wide array of things, people, and organizations and at such a wide scale (far beyond the one of a hammer), that it cannot but appear ubiquitous. In this perspective, "technology" is everywhere and everything.

Despite both its ubiquity and these recurrent moral and ethical dimensions, "technology," as a phenomenon deeply associated with colonial, industrial, and modern capitalism, does not constitute an anthropological subfield, such as art, religion, politics, or gender. While there have been attempts from both anthropologists and archaeologists,[2] material culture studies seem to have a hard time in making it a proper focus of inquiry, and what pertains to "technology" seems to be distributed between several subjects: digital anthropology, anthropology of infrastructures, design, art, the body, etc. This is even more surprising given that, as a topic, it has been explicitly examined by many twentieth-century influential thinkers working at the intersection between philosophy[3] and sociology.[4]

There are several reasons for this paradoxical situation, some pertaining to the actual phenomenon and the possibility of ethnography – technology being so ubiquitous that it would be hard to locate the field site – others being epistemological or emerging from the particular histories of anthropological traditions. But all stem from the complexity of "technology" as a domain of inquiry and the type of knowledge required to anthropologically investigate it. Indeed, the exponential increase in technical innovation since the end of World War II presents the ethnographer with such a diversity of phenomena, devices, and organizations, that it can be seen as thwarting any attempt to elaborate an interpretive frame able to unpack the trope "technology" presents.

Yet, in this chapter, my aim is both to present a range of analytical and methodological approaches which have tackled and tackle today what is encompassed in the category of "technology," and to propose a wider analytical frame which might help us to investigate it. To do so, I start by a brief summary of the epistemology of Euro-American perceptions of technical phenomena and examine "technology" as a problematic analytical category of the same order as "Nature" or "Society," before suggesting resorting to the category of "technique"/"technical" to qualify the ethnographic content of what constitutes "technology."

"Technology" as an Epistemic Category

"Technology" finds its etymological source in the combination of the Greek words, *techné* (τέχνη, in latin *ars*), that is "skills," "arts," or "crafts" and *logos*, "discourse," "knowledge," or "science." "Technology" was thus supposed to be to techniques and material culture, what *meteorology* was to the *weather*, or *biology* to *living processes*: the science/discipline which study arts, crafts, or material culture.[5]

Originally meant to refer to a reflexive attitude toward the performance of techniques and practices, the "study of the thing" has become replaced with "the thing itself," in a classical Magritte manner. "Technology" today encapsulates a diversity of empirical phenomena under a single universalizing category which is used to refer to such a broad range of actions, material things, and contemporary phenomena that it can literally encompass anything. This is particularly relevant when examining how, like with many categories, attempting to define "technology" does not always help identifying the anthropological or even sociological domains it is supposed to cover.[6] As Tim Ingold suggested some time ago,[7] instead it is more fruitful to examine the types of implicit claims made when using the term "technology."

The main clue for a critical analysis can be found in how "technology," as a category, is intimately linked to the emergence of a white, middle-class male form of capitalist modernity.[8] Following Leo Marx,[9] Eric Schatzberg, in his recent book on the critical history of the concept of technology,[10] details how, since the end of the eighteenth century, translations into English of French and German classical texts,[11] combined with both spectacular changes in the material culture of the era and the conceptual divide between, on the one hand, fine arts and, on the other hand, useful or mechanical arts, progressively led to the use of "technology" to refer to modern industrial material processes. Wedged between deterministic discourses of progress and what Schatzberg called a "continued confusion between technology as industrial arts and technology as technique,"[12] both public and academic discourses ended up confusing the means and methods for transforming the material world with the skills, devices, and procedures for achieving a specific end (material or not), erasing its original meaning of a discipline dedicated to analyzing them. Such a conflation not only led to "consigning technologies to the realm of things" thus distracting "attention from the human – socioeconomic and political – relations which largely determine who uses them,"[13] but the confusion also helped sustain "a mystifying, deterministic discourse that portrays technological change as the inevitable fruit of scientific discovery," as Schatzberg concludes.[14]

As seen in the epigraphs at the start of the chapter, the use of "technology" in public discourse and the media refers directly to a neutral force of progress, inherently rational, whose positive or negative effects only lie in social choices made about its use. More critically, as both Ruth Oldenziel and Judy Wajcman[15] have demonstrated, the category is not only associated with Euro-American vernacular ideas of rationalist, deterministic, and efficiency-driven conceptions, it is also profoundly gendered and politically loaded. While this appears to be an issue of semantics, the black boxing of several phenomena (objects, skills, scientific and applied knowledge, infrastructures, etc.) within the single term of "technology" contributed to making it a hegemonic category. It is not only ubiquitously used in daily public life and the media as shown in the epigraphs, but it has also colonized other languages.[16] While the term "technology" might convey the importance of particular modalities of action which intertwine devices, ideas, and standardized forms of behaviors,[17] its semantic void also folds these modalities within a universalizing neutral and utilitarian category.

"Technology" has become a category vernacular to Euro-American-led modernity, infused with forms of essentializing determinisms, placing it implicitly outside of the scope of most social sciences. The question, then, is to find which analytical category might be less intrusive and still able to take account of the phenomena encompassing such a diverse range of operations involving material culture, which anthropologists are able to recognize in their many guises, from fertility rituals to political actions, from New Guinea gardens to London design studios and the emergence of "machine-learning."

The issue lies in the sheer diversity of phenomena that the category itself can be (and has been) applied to, and it is perhaps this very pervasiveness that creates an obstacle to its coalescence into a specific subfield. Investigating the ways in which "technology" is mobilized in anthropology shows that, at its most basic scale, it refers implicitly to modes of action and processes of creation or transformation (including destruction), which themselves can be observed in the field and commented upon by actors. At a minimal empirical level, what "technology" seems to be dealing with is ways of doing and making,[18] weaving together living beings (humans and/or nonhumans) and things or artifacts, enrolled in a process, within specific historical and socio-historical settings. At a more general level, including in its vernacular use, "technology"[19] includes three orders of phenomena: (1) technical processes and knowledge, usually referred to in English as "technique"; (2) devices and objects (virtual or actual) such as tools, instruments, machines, apparatus, weapons, often implicitly "High-Tech" – to which one can add digital objects such as software and algorithms; and (3) modern infrastructures, modes of organization, sociotechnical systems and/or networks. These three orders of phenomena, though not happening at the same scale, are nevertheless deeply – one can say *structurally* – interrelated. In addition to revealing the vernacularity of the category of "technology," the task of an anthropological investigation of "technology" should be to examine and specify the modalities of these relations. In what follows, I shall examine all three orders. However, as with every anthropological enquiry, one should be aware of the issue of scales: of the phenomenon to be studied; of (ethnographic) observation; and of analysis itself. In this particular topic, and because of its conceptual payload, I take my starting point on a premise: whatever "technology" refers to, our first ethnographic point of entry should be at the level where humans actually experience it: it arguably starts with the body and its modalities of actions.

From Bodies to Subjects, Skills, Materials, and Magic: Technical Activities and Techniques

Over the course of the past three decades, a renewed interest in the body has brought "practice," "performance," or "embodiment" to the center of many ethnographies of material culture. These analyses weave together – though not all with the same weight and at times in debates with one another – several theoretical strands: phenomenology, cognition, praxeology, identity, and politics constitute some of the major theories investigating the body. However, actual practices do not occupy the same analytical position in all.[20]

Shifting from "technology" to "techniques," the adjective "technical" might prove analytically fruitful particularly because of its empirical and descriptive dimension. The idea of techniques as analytically paramount was first formulated by Marcel Mauss, in his foundational text on *Body Techniques*,[21] where he pointed out the fundamental relational performativity of techniques in a simple definition: "I call technique an action which is *effective* and *traditional* (and you will see that in this it is no different from a magical, religious or symbolic action). It has to be effective and traditional. There is no technique and no transmission in the absence of tradition."[22]

Despite a deceptively anodyne quality, Mauss provides us here with a formula[23] powerful enough to deal with "technology" in its different guises. Its analytical power lies in the combination of the two conditions, "effective" – or "efficacious" – and "traditional." By "efficacy" (not to be confused with "efficiency"), Mauss brackets the Western concern for an actual result, turning our attention instead toward the efficacy *according to the actor*, to vernacular conceptions of effectiveness, that is intentionalities (realized or not) and reasons for actions,[24] a focus which is indeed ethnographically essential to dislodge Eurocentric definitions of rationality. With the second condition, "tradition," Mauss points out the fundamental sociohistorical dimension of practices as being inscribed within a longer history of transmission and change.

Mauss's methodological stance is that the study of techniques begins at the scale of the body itself and in the ways in which people do things, be it walking, sleeping, or weaving – even having sex.[25] This claim was based on three central premises: first, a holistic conception of the body, not only biological but also both psychologically and socially molded, the three aspects being "indissolubly mixed together";[26] second, the central role of the set of acquired bodily abilities, or *habitus*,[27] embedded within a sociohistorical frame; third, the recognition that body techniques were also central to magical and ritual actions, something already adumbrated in his work *On Prayer*.[28] Through a focus on bodily practices themselves, Mauss offered a crucial analytical shift toward *the modalities of actions*, rather than on their actual (material) results. These three premises broaden the analysis of technical activities in three directions, often intersecting one another.

The first direction deals with the way a holistic understanding of the performing body allows for an empirical and pragmatic approach to processes of subjectification, be it political, sexual, or racial. This is particularly exemplified in the works of Jean-Pierre Warnier and his group Matière à Penser ("Matter to Think"), which combines Foucauldian, praxeological, and phenomenological frames to extend Mauss's conception of efficacy onto other modes of action to include the self and others.[29] Categories such as "identity" or the "subject" appear then as immersed in and emerging from sets of efficacious and traditional actions – be they on and with materials (tangible and intangible, or even invisible, such as spirits or substances such as the Polynesian *mana*), on and with the subject/self (e.g., sport or ritual), or on and with others (e.g., military training or sports.)[30] The crucial point here is that this subject/self construction happens everywhere and every time *with* material culture: built environments direct, encourage, or hinder mobility and possibilities of action; chefs master their knives to the point of sensorial perfection; drills turn weapons into a soldier's bodily extension. Workshops become not only places of production, but also of socialization as masters and apprentices perform, transmit, and learn their technical skills, in a web of social relations with the space, the materials, and with each other, and where the learning of a craft implies also the transforming of the self.

The second direction prolongs the previous one and deals with how, while bodily practices are evidently highly social, their performance does not necessarily require actors' consciousness. The *habitus*, as a set of norms and discipline,[31] by becoming embodied through the learning of skills, including through the complex cognitive processes at play in the performance of activities, becomes a constitutive part of the body itself. It encompasses both a "tradition" – a sociohistorically inscribed modality of action transmitted and sanctioned by a community as being appropriate – and a vernacular conception of efficacy – social values striate everyday gestures and actions lending it a capacity to bring results, in a way that can impose political domination without direct violence, as Warnier brilliantly demonstrated.[32]

Ethnographically speaking, the crucial point is that, at this level, an analysis of technical activities opens a window into both conscious and unconscious norms, some verbalized and others only embodied. The verbal dimension – particularly the modalities of evaluation of actions, of actors or of what is acted upon – thus gives an insight into vernacular conceptions of efficacy (in its pragmatic sense) and appropriateness (aesthetics, reference to a "tradition") as a background against which all actions are judged. As for the embodied nonverbal dimension, techniques imply the acquisition of skills, imparting the actor with a procedural knowledge or memory, shaping together the body and the mind of the actor through the acquisition of *habitus*, and actively partaking in the construction of the socialized, sexual, and political self. Simultaneously, skills appear as performances that actualize and reaffirm both technical ("efficacy" and "tradition") and social values, through the ways in which actions and their results are evaluated.

The nonverbal dimension of skills also brings in two other scales of analysis. The closer scale deals with cognition and how actions, bodies, and material things can be experienced as both a material flow and a flow of consciousness by the actor,[33] as well as extending beyond his/her actual body. Cognition and operational memory[34] appear then as situated, extended, and distributed over the human and nonhuman (materials, technical objects, spaces, texts) participants of the technical activities.[35] From an ethnographic perspective, this means paying attention to the ways humans perceive, engage with, and imagine materials.[36] At the wider scale – which leads to my discussion of technical systems – it deals with the socializing effect of technical activities, particularly relevant in terms of gender,[37] social hierarchy,[38] as well as community[39] and politics.[40]

At both levels, though, nothing is static or homogenous. Some technical activities are subject to dynamics of change and improvisation, even resistance or rebellion. Depending on the scale of analysis, they can, more rarely, be smooth and continuous or, instead, have different rhythms and velocities, and include breaks, both intended and unintended. The introduction of new technical objects might require a change in the activity to follow the operational mode of the new tool/instrument, or, on the contrary, a tinkering of the introduced object to adapt it to the local practice – and even at times, reject it.[41]

The third direction pushes further the very notion of technical activities themselves and challenges the category's restriction to material activities of production and/or consumption, and the suspension of Euro-American conceptions of rationality.[42] This is where Indigenous (vernacular) conceptions come back into the fore, through Mauss's simple yet powerful realization that technical action, physical action, and magico-religious action were often undifferentiated by actors themselves.[43] Mauss's original formula thus extends our analytical frame to activities usually excluded from the classical field of "technology," such as religious or magical rituals,[44] often contrasted in anthropology.[45]

It concretely means paying attention to vernacular conceptions of actions, of their efficacy, as well as of the things acted upon, be it persons, materials, or substances. Hence, whether associated with metallurgy,[46] gardening,[47] tattooing,[48] art[49] or interactions with animals,[50] magical or ritual practices are not only undifferentiated from "purely material" ones,[51] but because of their vernacular efficacy, they also qualify as "technical activities." This third direction is also analytically crucial for exploring how the logic of actions, in rituals and in other production processes, allows for an investigation of Indigenous ontological regimes.[52] Indeed, the logic of actions is necessarily related to the underlying assumptions about the actor, the thing acted upon and the action itself. Yam growers of the Nyamikum village in Papua New Guinea sing to the yam vines to make them grow;[53] such an action mobilizes vernacular conceptions of singing, of songs, of breath, of the singer's body, as well as of the plant and the processes which make it grow,[54] in turn delineating Indigenous conceptions of vital processes.[55]

Moving to a wider scale, the analysis of technical activities thus requires making visible the complexity, the heterogeneity, the temporality and spatiality of processes, as well as the logics, including vernacular ones, as performed by actor(s). Body techniques are indeed performed in relation with technical objects and their functioning, as well as spaces and places where the activity takes place – be it a workshop or a hunting territory. In order to empirically examine the interactions between the different elements, human and nonhuman, at play in a single technical process, the ethnographic method of the *chaîne opératoire* (operational sequence)[56] appears as one of the most fruitful, though demanding, ways to document and visualize the unfolding and the interweaving of logics, the role of materials, tools, instruments, or machines, the cooperation of human and nonhuman actors, the contingencies, incidents, and accidents that populate the technical process.

There is, however, a risk of confusion – like that plaguing the category of technology – between the technical process, the experience of the actor(s), and the analytical model built by the anthropologist. Far from referring to the ways in which processes are experienced by actors or to a strict protocol that they would follow,[57] the *chaîne opératoire* is nothing but both a guideline for documenting and a graphic rendering[58] of a real occurrence, observed in the field – in contrast with the ways in which archaeologists use the concept to describe a generalized model of artifact production to reconstitute past processes.[59]

From an anthropological perspective, the *Chaîne Opératoire* has thus been used to document variations and technical choices,[60] as well as the interactions between its different elements, such as materials, tools, knowledge, energy, and actions.[61] It is a method that can be used to reveal the profound ontological heterogeneity of the logics at play[62] as well as the cognitive aspects of technical processes,[63] or their socialized and socializing dimensions.[64]

The adjective "technical," in its pragmatic Maussian perspective, thus offers an opportunity to account for what would be usually coined as the "materiality" of technology. As Bruno Latour recently pointed out, "technical" skirts around the Eurocentric inflexions of concepts such as "matter" or "materiality,"[65] allowing instead for the identification, not of the essence of "technological" phenomena, but of the specific and empirical manifestations of these phenomena in a given setting. The examination of technical activities, and their temporal and spatial unfolding, reveals the places, roles, and agencies of what surrounds the human actor's body, whether other human or livings beings, or spirits, tools, instruments, machines, algorithms, materials, buildings, or landscapes. As we enlarge the scale and ethnographically follow these "actors," we indeed trace associations and assemblages, of practices, objects, and institutions. I call these associations "technics," firstly, to avoid the confusing and black boxing effect of "technology," but also to refer to both the implicit logic of "efficacy" they manifest (according to the actors) and to their historical and "oecological" ("traditional") groundings. We can then recognize that technics can form networks, either informal and implicit or, on the contrary, taking the shape of planned and purposive infrastructures. But in all cases, at every point of the "network" or "sociotechnical system," technics manifest themselves as the unfolding relations between activities (actions) and assemblages of objects, in more or less structured forms. The next section will focus on the latter, to examine "technical objects" as artifacts or things (including digital objects) that are made for and/or enrolled in technical activities. The last section will explore the wider scale of "technical systems," in particular the ways in which both activities and objects can never be isolated, not only from each other but also from other social phenomena such as religion, environments, or politics.

Technical Objects: Evolution, Design, Agency

Open up the black box of "technology" and a plethora of things spring out: spears, pots, traps, pebbles, bricks, painted masks, religious figures, door closers, speed bumps, mobile phones, algorithms ... all result from and/or are actors in technical (ritual, aesthetic, political, etc.) activities. However, "technical objects" do not necessarily designate solely tools or machines; instead, I use the term mainly to refer to the specific "traditional" and "efficacious" properties any artifact adopts when examined from the angle of technical activities.[66]

This type of analysis of artifacts also has its place in anthropology. First, in its origin with the works of A. H. L. F. Pitt-Rivers,[67] but also in the elaboration of material culture itself.[68] In almost every early ethnographic collection, categories such as "weapons," "tools," "fishing implements," "ritual," etc. were indeed referring to the relations between a "specimen" and a specific technical process. However, such classifications referred mostly to the context of utilization of objects.

Yet, use and function might prove insufficient to analyze their technical dimension; every object can be used for different purposes: the same knife can be a tool, a weapon, an ornament, paraphernalia for an office, or a museum object; similarly, a bow and a crossbow can both be used for hunting, war, or sport competition. However, their *functioning*, or modes of operation, present some important *technical* differences. In the case of the knife, its sharpness might condition its use for cutting or piercing, but a dull knife, or even the blade or the handle (but not both, evidently!) of which might be missing, does not prevent its other usages. The importance of functioning is even clearer in the case of the bow, the mode of functioning of which is based on the combination of the traction of the string and the aiming of the actor, while the crossbow removes the traction from the release and delegates it to either a crank or a lever, which can be done before and independently of the aiming itself, the string being maintained by a notch. What distinguishes an eighteenth-century carriage from one in 2020 is not necessarily their use (transporting people, living beings and/or things). Instead the motor of a carriage is an animal, a horse for instance, attached to the transporting frame; it can be replaced by another horse or perhaps another animal, such as mule or an ox, whilst the 2020 car's motor is *integrated within* the structure of the whole artifact.[69] These differences generate different relations in the technical activity in which the object is involved, as Carlos Sautchuk demonstrated: using a spear to catch a *piracuru* fish in the Amazon materializes an egalitarian relation between the fisherman and the fish, whereby both are treated as persons; using a net instead is considered as cowardly and abusive of the fish's trust; in other words, the two technical objects, net and spear, manifest two very different relational regimes.[70]

As with activities, the adjective "technical" here refers to the relationality encapsulated and generated by objects, as the functioning structure of an object both condenses past relational regimes and can generate new ones in its vicinity. But the very idea of a relational regime generated by the functioning of a technical object, an actual form of agency, also hints at the profound ecological dimension of technical objects.

This historical and ecological aspect of the design of artifacts (tools, objects, things) was arguably highlighted first by André Leroi-Gourhan, anthropologist and prehistorian student of Mauss, who conducted an extensive survey of the Musée de l'Homme collections. This survey produced two books on *Evolutions et Techniques*,[71] which laid out methods and concepts for an analysis of artifacts that would deal once and for all with old deterministic and ethnocentric evolutionist and diffusionist models. Instead, he proposed what could be called an ecological analytical framework for the study of technics. Be they tools, instruments, or machines, all technical artifacts were to be understood as the historical convergence of a gesture (or several operations) and a material, both engaged in a technical activity, coalescing into an object. The materializations of these convergences in the shape of artifacts was the product of both a specific environment (which included climate) and history – in fact the history of the human species itself saw the correlation of the emergence of hominids, their physiology, their cognitive, technical, and symbolic abilities.[72] For Leroi-Gourhan, the material structure of tools and instruments had thus to be thought of as localized and situated instances of complex sociohistorical and ecological dynamics of innovation, change, and borrowing, as well as applications of empirical knowledge of the world, its materials and their physical qualities. Combined with the specific sociocultural context, all formed what he summarized as "milieus" – a resolutely ecological term.[73]

What Leroi-Gourhan did with Indigenous and archaeological artifacts, was done with industrial machines and tools by his contemporary Gilbert Simondon – to whom we owe the term of "technical objects"[74] – more known in anglophone academia for his contributions to philosophy[75] than for his teaching and methods for analyzing technical objects. In a philosophical move that precedes the more recent analytical "posthuman" turn to objects, their agencies, biographies, and social lives, Simondon proposed an enquiry into technical objects which, refusing anthropocentrism, sets aside use, consumption, and other forms of social metaphors, to examine instead their "mode of existence."[76] Like Leroi-Gourhan, Simondon started by considering that the mode of existence of a given technical object could not be investigated without considering it as a singular instance of a longer evolutionary – though not evolutionist – temporal process of re-production. Technical objects are thus historical beings emerging at the point of concurrence of ecological, cultural, and social settings, each as a form of potential realized in a unique, though reproductive, form.

The philosophical centrality of the mode of existence of technical objects was more than an intellectual inquiry only, and Simondon also practically experimented on methods for analyzing artifacts. In a similar way to Leroi-Gourhan, he saw technical objects as emerging/becoming at the point of concurrence between an organism (a body, then, but not solely human) and an environment. This point was the moment/place where mediation occurred and coalesced into the particular form, or structure, of the technical object: a hammer emerges at the junction between an efficacious (bodily) action of percussion and the type of materials (hardness, density, etc.) it is supposed to have an effect on. Hence, the different shapes and sizes of hammers.

This idea of coalescence of mediations allowed Simondon to approach the emergence of complex technical objects as a form of ontogenesis, always in becoming, encapsulating changes and dynamics according to the contexts and domains in which they were used. Their functioning structure changes with time, developing synergies between heterogeneous and at times incompatible effects (heat, vibration, noise in an engine, for instance). Technical objects thus become more "concrete," that is encapsulating, in a tighter way, modalities of self-regulation and autocorrelation, as they move toward autonomization and automation.[77]

The latter form opens up the possibility of expanding Simondon's method to digital objects such as software and algorithms, the mode of behavior and roles of which, in combination with other types of technical objects, such as cars, mobile phones, and computers, indeed seem to fit Simondon's ideas of technical objects, while at the same time being more analytically demanding.[78]

The second main strand in the study of technical objects is more familiar to anthropologists and emerges out of the sociology of knowledge and science and technology studies (STS, hereafter). This strand both enlarges our analytical frame of artifacts and challenges the Euro-American society/technics dichotomy by revealing the inherent heterogeneity of social and technical relations. It promotes a fundamentally sociological approach to the technicity of artifacts, how their design and functioning can itself be subject to sociological analyses, and the effects on their (mis)use. Beyond this common ground, methods and positions diverge into two further directions, intersecting one another: whether technical objects are analyzed within wider sets of relations – and this brings us closer to the scale that corresponds to "technical systems" – or whether technical objects encapsulate within themselves modalities of actions that translate and transduct moral, ethical, and political values, which in turn shape their behaviors and the interactions that humans have with them. In terms of themes, these approaches often look at processes of design, innovation, or "technology transfer" and their explanatory models often spill over into the larger scale of socio-technical systems.

In the first direction, the SCOT approach (social construction of technology) proposes a range of works on innovation, technical change, design of artifacts, and materials.[79] Based on empirical and precise descriptive methods, these authors consider technical objects as fundamentally socially constructed. In the deeply constructivist vein, technical designs and changes are seen to result from heterogeneous social negotiations of positions, framing the analysis of objects within wider political and gendered approaches to technics – and to technology as a discourse or conception of technics.[80]

The second trend questions in more depth the ontological premise that separates human and nonhuman entities and investigates ways in which political and moral dimensions are delegated to *and* translated *into* the functioning of technical objects.[81] Translations of moral and political statements and agendas are seen as "programmed" into the functioning of technical objects that then become agents through the affordances and behaviors they present to their human counterparts. By doing so, door closers, seatbelts, hotel keys, generators, casino machines, or speedbumps become actors, in wider socio-technical networks, both materializing and stabilizing social relations.

"Technical object" as an analytical frame synthesizes these different approaches, while keeping actual artefacts and their material properties at the center of inquiry. They appear then as historical entities designed to be "efficacious" (their functioning structure, which is a condition for their actualization, is operational) and "traditional": along with humans, they are part of wider networks, from which they both emerge (history, geography, social relations) and depend on for their efficacious functioning. A mobile phone requires radio wave infrastructure (towers, roads to access these and allow their maintenance) to receive and transmit information, be it messages or upgrades, as well as a power supply for its battery; a car implies fuel – or electricity – supply, as well as mechanics, roads suitable for vehicles and increasingly, due to the inclusion of chips, computers. While all implicate human negotiators, these necessary requirements fall within what Winner aptly defines as "technological imperatives,"[82] which structure the conditions of successful functioning of technical objects and reframe the crude conceptualization of "technological determinism" in a less rigid way.

This analysis of the functioning of technical objects[83] opens into the larger scale of socio-technical systems, where control – or "power" – circulates through larger networks and infuses the relations between technical activities and technical objects.

Technical Systems: Scale, Relatedness, Behavior

No activity or object exists in isolation. Consider the simple operation of hammering a nail: it can be part of putting a picture on a wall or of the building of a mosque (or worse, crucifying someone!). The hammer, the nail, and the thing to be nailed are themselves the products of sequences of action that have gathered and transformed materials and brought them together at the moment and place of the actual nailing. Simultaneously, each sequence of operations is also molded by vernacular modalities of actions and logics, infused with conscious or unconscious intentionalities, values, and meanings such as "efficiency," "appropriateness," or even "rationality." These values can also operate in other domains, technical or not – a point I can easily *hammer home*. Even the carving of the visible parts of a wooden beam into figures or geometric patterns is part of a longer iconographic "tradition," learned and transmitted from one generation of carvers to the next, perhaps following kinship patterns or specific workshop practices.

Technical objects, themselves, while deceptively discrete entities, are instantiations of longer and wider chains of (re)production, change, and design (the Maussian "tradition"), themselves materializations of wider conceptions of "efficacy" and intentionality. Crucially, they also emerge from and are embedded in (increasingly so in contemporary contexts) wider material (such as "resources") and technical organizations, which are required for their functioning (from watermills requiring rivers, to mobile phones requiring radio waves) and relate their purpose to their wider environmental, sociological, political, and cosmological settings.

Investigating such relations implies widening the scale of analysis of the modes of relations between technical activities and technical objects. As we do so, we can see the nailing of a roof beam of a cathedral or synagogue as being part of a religious but also economic and political endeavor, mobilizing many materials and people as well as several institutions (the Church, the State) and organizations (guilds of carpenters, miners, transport workers, etc.). Even a simple gesture which handles a tool – prepared or improvised, such as a stick picked up in a forest – is always part of a longer and larger process that connects making, doing, using, and thinking, both here and then, or further away in time and space.

This web of relations takes the form of networks, dynamically relating energies, materials, information, things, ideas, and concepts at a larger scale than the one usually directly observed in the field. This implies that, arguably, *one cannot really see networks – or systems*: one can only encounter some features taking the form of emerging effects, or manifestations as the process unfolds (as I try to make a call, then I realize that the absence of a "signal network" stops me from using my phone). These features and events, which can be seen as indexes of distant phenomena (in time and space), are, *mutatis mutandis*, like a journey through a landscape, when one encounters on one's path other roads, skirts around emerging rocks, crosses rivers, climbs mountains, or follows ridges. Actors of a technical process are thus navigating within a wider spatial and temporal reticulated frame, the whole extent of which remains beyond their direct experience, but the effects of which can be felt and encountered along the path itself.

The ways in which technical processes are always embedded within wider phenomena is also one domain in which anthropology and material culture studies have a long research tradition, though often developed in different ways. These can be traced back at least to the ways Lewis H. Morgan identified the different components of society, such as subsistence, government, language, or family, and interpreted their relations as indexes of different "ethnic stages."[84] In the course of the twentieth century, this static model was pushed further by authors such as Mauss and Leroi-Gourhan, but also by Bronislaw Malinowski, C. Daryll Forde, and researchers from the American school of cultural ecology, such as Julian Stewart and Roy Rappaport.[85] To various degrees, all examined, documented, and analyzed how technical activities, often under the terms of "modes of subsistence," "crafts," or "arts," were related to other domains such as magic, religion, kinship, economics, or politics. Together, these works demonstrated, sometimes indirectly, how the production and use of artifacts were always in interdependence, material or conceptual, with their environmental, geographical, historical, cultural, and social settings – in other words, the tradition part of Mauss's formula.

From a theoretical point of view, Karl Marx was one of the first to use anthropological and historical examples to demonstrate the link between modes of production and social relations.[86] His analysis of the interdependency of technics, political economy, and general social organization aimed at demonstrating the deeply transformative potential brought by technical changes. It pointed out how time is crucial to analyze the ways in which technical change could have social and material repercussions, both intended and, more dramatically, unintended – as contemporary climate change and environmental pollution keep reminding us. However, such interactions, notably with social and political organization, were at the heart of 1970s' Marxist anthropology, which investigated the relations between kinship systems, religious belief, and social relations such as gender and inequality with modes of subsistence and Indigenous economy.[87] But arguably the main aim of these anthropological analyses was definitely the study of social relations and/or political economy; technical activities such as gardening or cattle herding[88] were rarely analyzed in and of themselves and were instead mobilized just as evidence for broader social analyses.[89]

By contrast, historians, because of their interest in dynamics of technical invention and innovation, had an earlier concern for how technical and social change were correlated. Lewis Mumford, one of the founders of the journal *Technology & Culture*, examined after World War II the ways in which the introduction of new artefacts transformed technical activities and were linked to profound historical and cultural changes.[90] While some reconstitutions were far too linear (such as in Lynn White Jr.'s hypothesis about how the introduction of the stirrup was almost directly related to the emergence of medieval social organization)[91] the fundamental idea was to examine the systemic relation between technical changes and historical and social dynamics.

Mauss was, again, one of the first anthropologists to explicitly point out that "techniques, industries and crafts, taken together, constitute the [technical] *system*[92] of a society which is essential to it."[93] However, inspired by the theory elaborated by the Austrian biologist Ludwig von

Bertalanffy,[94] the term "system" was first consistently applied to technics by two main authors. One is the French historian Bertrand Gille, less known in the anglophone than in the francophone tradition, and the other is the American Thomas P. Hughes.

Gille edited – and was the main contributor to – a *magnum opus* on the history of techniques,[95] which had a huge influence on the development of the French research group around *Techniques & Culture*.[96] His main contributions were threefold. Firstly, like Simondon, technics could not be understood without paying attention to the specificities of historical dynamics of change and innovation. Secondly, he showed how technics – constituted by devices, their mode of functioning and technical activities – were interrelated in ensembles and structures, aiming at producing specific types of results, such as textiles, aviation, or agriculture, which formed technical systems. Thirdly, these technical systems could not be isolated from other phenomena and activities, such as the economy or social organization, but were ensconced within their context – and a crucial part of it.

Inspired by Gille, Pierre Lemonnier spelled out for ethnographers the three main levels of these systemic relations,[97] to which I have alluded at the beginning of this section: (1) at the closer scale, the five elements (materials, tools, gestures, knowledge, energy) of a given technical process are related in a systemic way; they must all be in interaction to produce the desired effect ("efficacy"): a change in one of them, such as in a material, can have repercussions on the tools used, on the actions performed, or on the knowledge required, and a change in the energy necessary to animate the action will affect either the technical objects or the gestures, and so on; (2) every element of a technical activity is itself part of a wider trajectory involving other technical activities and objects (a hammer has been made, a wooden frame has been grown as a tree, nails are factory made); similarly, every process is part of longer process (the building of a Catholic cathedral, which might also require sawing planks, building stone walls, quarries, transport infrastructure etc.); (3) every technical process is thus in relation with other social phenomena and all technics are necessarily enmeshed in economic and social (gender, class, etc.) relations, as well as political and legal institutions.[98]

When used as an analytical tool in Indigenous and historical contexts, this systemic approach examines how activities, such as gardening, fence building, mining or metallurgy, and even rituals, mobilize objects, actions, and representations[99] – where, in particular, vernacular conceptions of efficacy, the other element of Mauss's formula, play a central role. As a result, anthropological studies of technical systems necessarily mobilize topics, often seen as distinct, such as kinship, religion, economics, politics, art, or even ontology and/or environment.[100] One of the best examples is Michael Rowlands and Warnier's description of the ways in which Cameroon Grassland iron-smelting is equated with human reproduction;

what is made visible here, on the ritual and female features of the furnace, is not a metaphorical relation, but instead a vernacular ontological parity between object and subject production.[101]

Hughes's work on the electrification of the United States focused more directly on the political economic conditions that fostered the development and the materialization of large-scale infrastructures.[102] For Hughes, the analytical dichotomies between technics and science, and technics and society ("technology" in his writings) – an analytical distinction based on categories profoundly vernacular to modernity – rely on mechanistic explanatory models which foreclose any analysis, other than deterministic ones, which would give historical change its proper place. Instead, Hughes claims, we are in the presence of a "seamless web,"[103] where dichotomies evaporate as the description of the development of an infrastructure reveals how they are inherently embedded within, and inseparable from, a political, social, and economic setting.

Both Gille's and Hughes's approaches were originally dedicated to the analyses of wider, large-scale technical systems but are also analytically valid for both Euro-American and Indigenous settings. They use a theory of interconnections and interactions of practices, apparatus, and organizations which leads the way to think about questions of control and agency, by tackling more or less directly the issue of determinisms, be they technical ("technology shapes society") or social ("society shapes technology"), to which we could add environmental determinism. These issues, however, emerged from Eurocentric conceptions of technical systems. Bertalanffy's general system theory had a huge influence on contemporary modernist thought, spilling out of academia and often leading to rigid, deterministic, and teleological models, particularly within corporate, financial, economic, social, and political discourse, as Langdon Winner rightly summarized.[104] As a result, the very idea of "technical systems," even in sociology and anthropology, is mostly equated with industrial ones, and seen as a rigid deterministic and instrumental analytical frame.

This modern, industrial, vernacular interpretive frame led to the development of technical systems as mainly "purposive,"[105] that is identified by actors according to their purpose, or the domains they are directed to, sometimes identified as "industries": food supply, health (both physical and mental), energy, mobility, communication as well as security and culture.[106] Though they manifest themselves at the level of technical objects and activities (including knowledge) associated with them, they are fundamentally different, appearing as infrastructures that "create the grounds on which other objects operate, and when they do so they operate as systems."[107] Analyses of these industrial technical systems are thus often implicitly framed within the old philosophical question of the moral dimension of "technology" as either neutral, evil, or, on the contrary, making human lives fundamentally better by solving (social and/or material) problems, and fulfilling their "needs," as this chapter's epigraphs illustrate. Themes emerging from these analyses deal with issues of connectedness, determinism, and control – or "power" – and have a long-lasting influence in anthropological and sociological studies of contemporary societies.

From an ethnographic perspective, however, and summarizing what authors such as Gille, Mumford, Hughes, or Lemonnier have described, I venture that it is possible to characterize further the systemic modalities of technics through three provisional analytical categories, perhaps able to specify their local ontological dimensions: their *scale*, their *relatedness*, and their *behavior*.[108] All three analytical characteristics apply both to Indigenous and non-Indigenous cases. Although the themes that emerge from the literature are not necessarily the same, small-scale communities became and keep becoming increasingly enrolled in globalized networks, infrastructures, and systems (pertaining to, among other things, resource extraction such as logging and mining).

The *scale* deals with what lies within and beyond the level of an ethnographically observed phenomenon – such as the use and discarding of a mobile phone, what happens in a local workshop, a group meeting within a design studio, the building of a canoe or a mortuary ceremony. While networks and systems are too broad a frame to be experienced fully (one cannot *see* them, but mostly their effects), following Lemonnier's three levels of systemic properties, it is at the level of processual relations – which involve activities and objects – that one can reveal structural relations with a larger world of materials, energy, knowledge, and social relations, and which merges together heterogeneous domains such as material, ritual, legal, economic conditions or relations of expertise and authority. It is possible to extend the scale temporally, to show how systems emerge slowly through time and change with "innovations" and "improvements" (and are thus "traditional" in the Maussian sense), and spatially, as the "resources" and "supply chains" (energy, information, humans, and materials) that are mobilized transcend the local to extend into – and can end up mobilizing – the global.[109] The spatial and temporal extension of the scale also helps in expanding and confirming specific conceptions of efficacy and logics that lead to and sustain their emergence: rational efficiency[110] and effective management[111] are contemporary examples of global logics made real and self-justified.

Relatedness refers to the properties of interconnection of heterogeneous assemblages of humans' technical objects and activities, whether in Indigenous settings[112] or elsewhere. While often simplified in terms of determinisms, this characteristic refers to two broad types of phenomena. On the one hand, it refers to the ways in which any event – be it exercise of control or resistance, accidents, shortages, etc. – in a specific place and time, has potential ripple effects on others, through the organic chain of people, things, and/or institutions, wherever the starting point may be, at whatever the scale the ethnographer is locating her/himself. The larger the system (or "infrastructure") may be, the larger the number of elements affected and the further away they are. On the other hand, relatedness also refers to the circulation of "resources" in order to maintain the network itself, especially through the making, functioning, and maintenance of technical objects, and whether these can be decided and done locally or not.

Qualifying the actual modes of relation becomes a crucial analytical objective. For instance, relatedness is central to the ANT concept of "network." As a category which has come to replace "system,"[113] "network" has helped circumvent the compartmentalization created by analytical categories that separate technical systems from social ones, as well as human actors from nonhuman ones (materials, plants, animals, technical objects). Relatedness, whether in networks or system, refers thus to the ways in which "nodes" of humans and nonhumans are linked together in what appear then as multidirectional and heterogeneous reticulated relations of causalities.[114] For ANT, these relations are material-semiotic and can be expressed in terms of delegation, translation (or transduction), and stabilization of programs[115] which link designers/engineers, artefacts, and their users, as well as all the intermediaries. Events – decisions, incidents, accidents, hopes, and regulations – do not travel neutrally through the network, but are translated to other nodes in the network, through processes of socio-material delegations (and at times through the very functioning of technical objects) and, like ripples in a pond, actualize, make present and visible the types of relations (including power relations) that connect the "nodes." In a manner familiar to anthropologists, nodes are thus less defined by their own ontic existence, than by the relations they are enmeshed in, which can be smooth, fluid, cut, or even inherently hierarchical.[116] One contemporary example of this might be found in the velocity and the extension of contemporary digital connectivity (of people and of things), which means that decisions about updates, upgrades, and auditing ("data") can have a faster, further, and bigger reach – whether actors want or know them or do not – through a whole chain of human and nonhuman intermediaries.

Finally, I use *behavior* to refer to the dynamics, temporal and spatial, of interactions and interdependencies that animate technical systems/networks and to how different agencies, while circulating and encountering each other, manifest themselves at a more empirical level. This is arguably the main way in which an ethnographer can witness, if not the network (or the system) itself, but some of its *effects*, as indexes of wider (longer, larger, older) reticulated entities (organizations, systems, institutions). What I call their behavior concerns the modalities of concretization, thus of actualization of intended (and unintended) effects and the ways in which these relate to, at the closer scale, both human and nonhuman agencies, activities, functioning, hopes, or desires.

This is particularly relevant for modern settings (including in developing countries), as the inherent Euro-American *vernacularity* of the purposive dimensions of technical systems[117] orients them toward general *ends*,[118] not only "material" ones, such as food supply, mobility, communication, or health but also more abstract ones, such as entertainment, safety, justice, or democracy. To reach these ends, they require setting up, at a very large scale, an organized control ("management" and "audit") of the functioning and activities ("training," "maintenance," "repair") of both human and nonhuman participants, so that they can then act as indeed efficacious, but mostly *efficient* delegates: as the input/output ratio becomes paramount, it implies, as Winner remarks, that the *means* of organization become, *at the very least*, as important as the results.[119]

This is where the idea of technical "imperative" appears politically crucial, sometimes taking the appearance of technical "determinism," when technical objects impose upon human activities, or of "technocracy," when the organization imposes its (vernacular) values of "rationality" and "efficiency" upon people's activities and behaviors.[120] On the one hand, technical systems – or networks – indeed *tend to* stabilize social relations,[121] while also creating effects of black boxing and invisibility. On the other hand, because of their temporal and spatial nature, they also are, like all nonlinear systems, *simultaneously* determined and unpredictable, shifting with time and space.[122] Thus, for technical systems, modern ones in particular, to achieve their assigned role in an efficient way they require constant control, maintenance, and readjustments, the effects of which give protocols and regulations an increasingly central role, at the expense of contingencies and idiosyncrasies, folding together technical imperatives with technocracy in an obviated form of socio-technical determinism. This is what concepts such as Ellul's "technical order"[123] or Feenberg's "technical code" refer to: a "'regime of truth' that brings the construction and interpretation of technical systems into conformity with the requirements of a system of domination."[124]

Such domination is not smooth, however. Technical systems constitute, at the ethnographic level, the theater where "technological dramas" of regularizations, adjustments, and reconstitutions[125] are played out, and where every counter-signification and counter-appropriation of technical processes or technical objects ends up being reintegrated within the system – such as personal computers that emerged out of wresting power away from corporations before becoming their main products,[126] or hackers recruited to design security systems or new Apps in a start-up. As Feenberg noted (and note the use of the category of "technology" here):

> [t]echnology is power in modern societies, a greater power in many domains than the political system itself. The masters of technical systems, corporate and military leaders, physicians and engineers, have far more control over patterns of urban growth, the design of

dwelling and transportation systems, the selection of innovations, our experience as employees, patients, and consumers, than all the electoral institutions of our society put together.[127]

At the same time, unpredictability and the effect of time and expansion of scale means that breaks and bugs, such as bridges collapsing, nuclear reactor meltdowns, high-speed train collisions, or even local wars and financial crises are bound to occur. These unpredictable events make the network and its dys/functioning visible, as the anthropology of infrastructure demonstrates.[128] However, responses to such events rarely imply the scrapping of the whole technical system, but instead prompt the setting up of a heterogeneous combination of technical objects and practices, updates, and new regulations, which, however, because of the technical imperatives that emanate from the objects involved, stop any in-depth challenge to the original "technological code."

These three characteristics, scale, relatedness, and behavior, hint at the inherent political dimensions of artefacts, activities, and systems, and at how they are locally manifested. This is also a venerable theme, whether in philosophy or sociology,[129] and the issue of power, control, and resistance has been examined in many instances.[130] Collectively, these works all think through the actual unfolding of technical (efficacious and traditional) relations between activities, objects, and systems. They give the means to investigate how the manifestations of these systemic relations in technical objects and performance of technical activities are the crucial loci of power struggles of agency and autonomy, as well as inviting imaginations and desires for equality, change, or democracy.

Conclusion

The anthropology of technology exists, then, though parsed through different domains and dealing with different scales. With the emergence of contemporary concerns and phenomena such as post- and transhumanism, the Internet of Things,[131] or artificial intelligence within a context of climate change and global tensions between populism and technocracy, the politics of technics as a general topic is far from anthropologically irrelevant. Technology as a theme is still at the forefront of public debates in the media, often mobilized as a solution to specific issues such as immigration and border control, aging and well-being, social justice and democracy, or indeed security. As a trope, it often acts as the ultimate black box, which can only appear then either as a Pandora's box, or as a treasure chest.

In this chapter I have suggested that an anthropology of technology today can be crafted by fully acknowledging the fundamental relational dimension of what the epigraphs I started with call technology. From there we can adopt a fully dynamic approach to the ways in which technical processes are situated in (i.e., emerging from and generating) specific milieus. It implies weaving together several theoretical trends on body techniques and performances (technical activities), on things and their mode of existence (technical objects), and on how the relation between both manifest what we call networks or (technical) systems. An anthropology of technology would thus be constituted by the study of technical activities, technical objects, technical systems, and their relations, where the adjective "technical" occupies a heuristic position previously dominated by Eurocentric conceptions of technology.

From this anthropological perspective, the question is neither whether "technology [is] good or bad," nor if "we [should] organize ourselves as citizens to make the best use of technology," but to unveil how contemporary technical configurations might foster specific social, political, and moral preconceptions to the exclusion of others.

Acknowledgments

This chapter owes much to both the undergraduate and postgraduate students in the course "Transforming Worlds: Anthropological Perspectives on Techniques and Technology," as well as the innumerable discussions (and debates) with colleagues, especially Timothy Carroll, Kimberley Chong, Adam Drazin, Hannah Knox, and Aaron Parkhurst. Very crucial were discussions and seminars with Ph.D. students, with special thanks to Chloe Dominique, Raffaele Buono, and in particular to Rosalie Allain, for her rigorous and acute reading and her suggestions.

Notes

1. https://bit.ly/3CTDcs2.
2. Such as Pierre Lemonnier, *Elements for an Anthropology of Technology* (Ann Arbor: University of Michigan Press, 1992); Bryan Pfaffenberger, "Social Anthropology of Technology," *Annual Review of Anthropology* 21 (1992), 491–516; François Sigaut, "Technology," in Tim Ingold, ed., *Companion Encyclopedia of Anthropology* (London: Routledge, 2002[1994]), 420–59); Tim Ingold, "Eight Themes in the Anthropology of Technology," *Social Analysis* 41, no. 1 (1997), 106–38; Michael B. Schiffer, ed., *Anthropological Perspectives on Technology* (Albuquerque: University of New Mexico Press, 2001); and Ron Eglash, "Technology as Material Culture," in Chris Tilley et al., eds., *Handbook of Material Culture* (London: SAGE, 2006), 327–40.
3. See, for instance, Carl Mitcham and Robert Mackey, eds., *Philosophy and Technology: Readings in the Philosophical Problems of Technology* (New York: Free Press, 1972).

4. The list is long and venerable: from the critical works of Thorstein Veblen, *The Engineers and the Price System* (New York: B. W. Huebsch, 1921); Martin Heidegger, "The Question Concerning Technology," in *The Question Concerning Technology and Other Essays* (New York: Harper and Row, 1977[1954]); Jacques Ellul, *The Technological Society* (New York: Vintage Books, 1964[1954]); Herbert Marcuse, *One-Dimensional Man* (Boston: Beacon Press, 1964), we move to more contemporary analyses by Jürgen Habermas, "Technology and Science as 'Ideology,'" in *Toward a Rational Society* (Boston: Beacon Press, 1970[1968]), 81–122; Langdon Winner, *Autonomous Technology: Technics-Out-of-Control as a Theme in Political Thought* (Cambridge: MIT Press, 1985[1977]); David F. Noble, *America by Design: Science, Technology, and the Rise of Corporate Capitalism* (New York: Knopf, 1977); Thomas P. Hughes, *Networks of Power: Electrification in Western Society, 1880–1930* (Baltimore: The John Hopkins University Press, 1983); Carl Mitcham, *Thinking through Technology: The Path between Engineering and Philosophy* (Chicago: The University of Chicago Press, 1994); and more recently Bruno Latour, *Aramis, or the Love of Technology* (Cambridge: Harvard University Press, 1996[1992]); Ruth Oldenziel, *Making Technology Masculine: Men, Women, and Modern Machines in America, 1870–1945* (Amsterdam: Amsterdam University Press, 1999); and Andrew Feenberg, *Transforming Technology: A Critical Theory Revisited* (Oxford: Oxford University Press, 2002). Other, perhaps less direct, scholarship includes a long tradition of the critique of modernity which aligns authors such as Karl Marx, *Capital: A Critique of Political Economy*, Vol. I, Part I (New York: Cosimo Classics, 2007[1867]); Max Horkheimer and Theodor W. Adorno, *Dialectic of Enlightenment* (London: Verso, 1976[1944]); or Hannah Arendt, *The Human Condition* (Chicago: The University of Chicago Press, 1998[1958]). Syntheses of these works include Andrew Feenberg, *Critical Theory of Technology* (Oxford: Oxford University Press: 1991) and Steve Matthewman, *Technology and Social Theory* (New York: Palgrave Macmillan 2011).
5. See Mitcham, *Thinking through Technology*, 116–34 for a full discussion.
6. See François Sigaut, "More (and Enough) on Technology!" *History and Technology* 2 (1985), 115–32; Eglash, "Technology as Material Culture," 329; Matthewman, *Technology and Social Theory*, 8–20.
7. Tim Ingold, "Foreword," in Marcia-Anne Dobrès and Christopher R. Hoffman, eds., *The Social Dynamics of Technology* (Washington, DC: Smithsonian Institution Press, 1999), viii.
8. Oldenziel, *Making Technology Masculine*.
9. Leo Marx, "'Technology': The Emergence of a Hazardous Concept," *Technology and Culture*, 51, no. 3 (2010[1997]), 561–677.
10. Eric Schatzberg, *Technology: Critical History of a Concept* (Chicago: The University of Chicago Press, 2018).

11. One of the most obvious examples comes from the translation of non-English works, for instance French: Michel Foucault's famous text, "Les Techniques de Soi" in French, was translated as "Technologies of the Self," in Luther H. Martin, Huck Gutman, and Pattrick H. Hutton, eds., *Technologies of the Self* (Amherst: University of Massachusetts Press, 1988[1977]), 16–49. Foucault was similarly discussing techniques of production, techniques of power, and techniques of signs. The same translation issue appears in the works of authors such as Jacques Ellul, *La technique ou l'enjeu du siècle* into *The Technological Society* (New York: Vintage Books, 1964[1954]), or Bruno Latour, *Aramis ou l'Amour des Techniques* into *Aramis, or the Love of Technology* (Cambridge: Harvard University Press, 1996[1991]). See also the footnote at the beginning of the recent translation of Gilbert Simondon, *On the Mode of Existence of Technical Objects* (Minneapolis: Univocal Publishing, 2017[1958]), 1, as well as Karl Marx's *Das Kapital*, where *Technologie* had retained its original meaning. Marx's famous footnote 2, chapter XV used the German term *Technologie* which "discloses man's mode of dealing with Nature, the process of production by which he sustains his life, and thereby also lays bare the mode of formation of his social relations, and of the mental conceptions that flow from them" (Marx, *Das Kapital*), 406. The mistranslation was one the sources of critiques of Marx's supposed technological determinism. As Schatzberg finally unveiled, it was *the analysis of technics* ("technology" in its original meaning), which was supposed to provide the ways to reveal these relations, not technics themselves, see Schatzberg, *Technology*, 100.
12. Schatzberg, *Technology*, 232.
13. Leo Marx, "Technology," 576.
14. Eric Schatzberg, "*Technik* Comes to America: Changing Meanings of Technology before 1930," *Technology and Culture* 47, no. 3 (2006), 512.
15. Oldenziel, *Making Technology Masculine*; Judy Wajcman, *Feminism Confronts Technology* (Cambridge: Polity Press, 1991).
16. *Teknologi* in Indonesia, *tecnología* in Spanish, *tecnologia* in Brasilian Portuguese, *teknujori* in Japanese.
17. Andrew Feenberg, *Critical Theory of Technology* (Oxford: Oxford University Press, 1991), 71.
18. Laurence Douny and Myriem Naji, "Editorial," *Journal of Material Culture* 14, no. 4 (2010), 411–32.
19. Winner, *Autonomous Technology*, 10–11; Matthewman, *Technology and Social Theory*, 12.
20. See Jean-Pierre Warnier, *The Pot-King: The Body and Technologies of Power* (Leiden: Brill, 2007), 6 ff; and Wasserman, Chapter 3, this volume.
21. Marcel Mauss, "Techniques of the Body," *Economy and Society* 2, no. 1 (1975[1935]), 70–88.
22. Ibid, 5, original emphasis.

23. François Sigaut, "La formule de Mauss," *Techniques & Culture* 40 (2003), 153–68.
24. There is a common confusion in thinking about techniques regarding the importance given to *causes* at the expense of *reasons*, a confusion which has been analyzed in the philosophy of action, particularly around the work of Ludwig Wittgenstein, *Wittgenstein's Lectures: Cambridge 1932–35* (Oxford: Blackwell, 1979), 4.
25. Mauss, "Techniques of the Body," 84–85.
26. Ibid, 74.
27. Reframed by Pierre Bourdieu, *Outline of a Theory of Practice* (Cambridge: Cambridge University Press, 1977[1972]), 72–95.
28. Marcel Mauss, *On Prayer* (New York: Durkheim Press/Berghahn Books, 2003[1909]).
29. Jean-Pierre Warnier, "A Praxeological Approach to Subjectivation in a Material World," *Journal of Material Culture* 6, no. 1 (2001), 5–24; Urmilla Mohan and Laurence Douny, eds., *The Material Subject: Rethinking Bodies and Objects in Motion* (London: Bloomsbury, 2020).
30. See Warnier, *The Pot-King*, 143–45.
31. See also Foucault, "Technologies of the Self," and Warnier, *The Pot-King*.
32. Warnier, *The Pot-King*.
33. Tim Ingold, *Making: Anthropology, Archaeology, Art and Architecture* (London: Routledge, 2012), 14–31.
34. André Leroi-Gourhan, *Gesture and Speech* (Cambridge: The MIT Press, 1993[1964]), 230–34.
35. Edwin Hutchins, *Cognition in the Wild* (Cambridge: The MIT Press, 1995); Charles M. Keller and Janet Dixon Keller, *Cognition and Tool Use: The Blacksmith at Work* (Cambridge: Cambridge University Press, 1996).
36. James J. Gibson, *The Ecological Approach to Perception* (Hillsdale: Lawrence Erlbaum Associates, 1986); Tim Ingold, "Materials against Materiality," *Archaeological Dialogues* 14, no. 1 (2007), 1–16; Lambros Malafouris, *How Things Shape the Mind: A Theory of Material Engagement* (Cambridge: The MIT Press, 2013); Carl Knappett, "The Affordances of Things: A Post Gibsonian Perspective on the Relationality of Mind and Matter," in Elizabeth DeMarrais, Chris Gosden, and Colin Renfrew, eds., *Rethinking Materiality: The Engagement of Mind with the Material World* (Cambridge: McDonald Institute for Archaeological Research, 2004), 43–51.
37. Francesca Bray, *Technology and Gender: Fabrics of Power in Late Imperial China* (Berkeley: University of California Press, 1997); Oldenziel, *Making Technology Masculine*.
38. Trevor H. J. Marchand, "Muscles, Morals and Mind: Craft Apprenticeship and the Formation of Person," *British Journal of Educational Studies* 56, no. 3 (2008), 245–71.

39. Jean Lave and Etienne Wenger, *Situated Learning: Legitimate Peripheral Participation* (Cambridge: Cambridge University Press, 1991).
40. Warnier, *The Pot-King*; Foucault, "Technologies of the Self;" Margot L. Lyon, "The Material Body, Social Process and Emotion: 'Techniques of the Body' Revisited," *Body & Society* 3, no. 1 (1997), 83–101.
41. See the example of the rejection of the use of iron tools by Māori agriculturalists in William C. Schaniel, "New Technology and Cultural Change in Traditional Societies," *Journal of Economic Issues* 22 (1988), 493–98.
42. Arthur M. Hocart, "The Purpose of Ritual," *Folklore* 46, no. 4 (1935), 343–49; Stanley J. Tambiah, *Magic, Science, Religion, and the Scope of Rationality* (Cambridge: Cambridge University Press, 1990).
43. Mauss, "Body Techniques," 75. Unfortunately, the English translation used the term "confused" for the French *confondus*, a word which I believe is a false friend.
44. Mauss, *On Prayer*.
45. Edward E. Evans Pritchard and Eva Gillies, *Witchcraft, Oracles, and Magic among the Azande* (abridged ed., Oxford: Clarendon Press, 1976); Bronisław Malinowski, *Magic, Science and Religion* (New York: Doubleday, 1954); Alfred Gell, "Technology and Magic," *Anthropology Today* 4, no. 2 (1988), 6–9; Claude Lévi-Strauss, *Structural Anthropology I* (New York: Basic Books, 1963[1958]), 167–231.
46. Michael Rowlands and Jean-Pierre Warnier, "The Magical Production of Iron in the Cameroon Grassfield," in Thurstan Shaw, Paul Sinclair, Bassey Andah, and Alex Okpoko, *The Archaeology of Africa: Food, Metals and Towns*, One World Archaeology, 20 (London: Routledge, 1995), 512–50.
47. Bronisław Malinowski, *Coral Gardens and Their Magic: A Study of the Methods of Tilling the Soil and of Agricultural Rites in the Trobriand Islands* (New York: Dover Publication, 1978[1935]); Ludovic Coupaye, *Growing Artefacts, Displaying Relationships: Yams, Art and Technology amongst the Nyamikum Abelam of Papua New Guinea* (Oxford: Berghahn Books, 2013); "'Yams Have No Ears!': Tekhne, Life and Images in Oceania," *Oceania* 88, no. 1 (2018), 13–30.
48. Sébastien Galliot, "Ritual Efficacy in the Making," *Journal of Material Culture* 20, no. 2 (2015), 101–25.
49. Alfred Gell, *Art and Agency* (Oxford: Clarendon Press, 1998); Sandra Revolon, "Iridescence as Affordance: On Artifacts and Light Interference in the Renewal of Life among the Owa (Eastern Solomon Islands)," *Oceania* 88, no.1 (2018), 31–40.
50. Carole Ferret, "Towards an Anthropology of Action: From Pastoral Techniques to Modes of Action," *Journal of Material Culture* 19, no. 3 (2014), 279–302.
51. Mauss, "Body Techniques," 75.

52. Rowlands and Warnier, "The Magical Production of Iron"; Philippe Descola, *Beyond Nature and Culture* (Chicago: Chicago University Press, 2013[2005]).
53. Coupaye, *Growing Artefacts*, 133 ff.
54. Coupaye, "'Yams Have No Ears.'"
55. Perig Pitrou, "Life as a Process of Making in the Mixe Highlands (Oaxaca, Mexico): Towards a 'General Pragmatics' of Life," *Journal of the Royal Anthropological Institute* 21, no. 1 (2015), 86–105; Ludovic Coupaye and Perig Pitrou, "Introduction: The Interweaving of Vital and Technical Processes in Oceania," *Oceania* 88, no. 1 (2018), 2–12.
56. See Lemonnier, *Elements*; Coupaye, *Growing Artefacts*; "Chaîne Opératoire, Transects et Théories: Quelques Réflexions et Suggestions sur le Parcours d'une Méthode Classique," in Philippe Soulier, ed., *André Leroi-Gourhan "L'homme Tout Simplement"* (Paris: Éditions de Boccard – Travaux de la MAE – Maison de l'Archéologie et de l'Ethnologie, René-Ginouvès, 2015), 69–84; "Making 'Technology' Visible: Technical Activities and the *Chaîne Opératoire*," in Maja Hojer Bruun and Ayo Wahlberg, eds., *The Anthropology of Technology: A Handbook* (New York: Palgrave Handbooks, in press).
57. Ingold, *Making*, 26.
58. See Lemonnier *Elements*, 37–44; Coupaye, "Making Technology Visible."
59. Hélène Balfet, ed., *Observer l'action Technique: Des Chaînes Opératoires, Pour Quoi Faire?* Paris (Editions du CNRS, 1991); Nathan Schlanger, "The *Chaîne Opératoire*," in Colin Renfrew and Paul Bahn, eds., *Archaeology: The Key Concepts* (London: Routledge, 2005), 25–31; Marcos Martinón-Torres, "*Chaîne Opératoire*: The Concept and its Application Within the Study of Technology," *Gallaecia* 21 (2002), 29–43; Marie Soressi and Jean-Michel Geneste, "The History and Efficacy of the *Chaîne Opératoire* Approach to Lithic Analysis: Studying Techniques to Reveal Past Societies in an Evolutionary Perspective," *PaleoAnthropology* 63 (2011), 334–50.
60. Pierre Lemonnier, "Introduction," in Pierre Lemonnier, ed., *Technological Choices: Transformation in Material Culture since the Neolithic* (London: Routledge, 1993), 1–35; Sander E. Van der Leeuw, "Giving the Potter a Choice: Conceptual Aspects of Pottery Techniques," in Lemonnier, *Technological Choices*, 238–88; Olivier Gosselain, "Mother Bella was not a Bella: Inherited and Transformed Traditions in Southwestern Niger," in Miriam T. Stark, Brenda J. Bowser, and Lee Horne, eds., *Cultural Transmission and Material Culture: Breaking Down Boundaries* (Tucson: University of Arizona Press, 2008), 150–77.
61. Lemonnier, *Elements*, 5–7; see discussion in Coupaye, *Growing*, 98–100, 159–63, and Coupaye, "Making Technology Visible."
62. Coupaye, "Chaîne Opératoire, Transects et Théories."

63. Nicole Boivin, "Mind over Matter? Collapsing the Mind-Matter Dichotomy in Material Culture Studies," in Elizabeth DeMarrais, Chris Gosden, and Colin Renfrew, eds., *Rethinking Materiality: The Engagement of Mind with the Material World* (Cambridge: McDonald Institute for Archaeological Research, 2004), 63–71; Matthew Walls, "Making as a Didactic Process: Situated Cognition and the *Chaîne Opératoire*," *Quaternary International* 405 (2015), 21–30.
64. For example Marcia-Anne Dobrès, "Technology's Links and *Chaînes*: The Processual Unfolding of Techniques and Technician," in Marcia-Anne Dobrès and Christopher R. Hoffman, eds., *The Social Dynamics of Technology* (Washington: Smithsonian Institution Press, 1999), 124–46.
65. "'Technical' is an adjective that is able to resonate with any layer of what I hesitate to call materiality: songs as well as wood, noise as well as steel, narratives as well as fences. In effect, whatever is woven together by the highly specific trajectory of 'technical' moves becomes 'material' as a consequence," Bruno Latour, "Technical Does not Mean Material," *HAU: Journal of Ethnographic Theory* 4, no. 1 (2014), 508.
66. While I do not discuss these in this chapter, this category could also potentially include large "objects" such as factories or even large buildings and structures.
67. A. Henry Lane and F. Pitt-Rivers, *The Evolution of Culture and Other Essays* (Oxford: Clarendon Press, 1906).
68. The literature is obviously so vast that there is no space here to recapitulate it. But for the specific topic of technical objects in the anthropology – and archaeology – of material culture, one can quote examples such as Ralph Linton, *The Material Culture of the Marquesas Islands* (Honolulu: Memoirs of the Bishop Museum VIII, no. 5, 1923); Beatrice Blackwood, *The Technology of a Modern Stone Age People in New Guinea*, Occasional Papers on Technology 3 (Oxford: Pitt Rivers Museum of Oxford, 1950); Robert Cresswell, "Of Mills and Waterwheels," in Lemonnier, *Technological Choices*, 181–213; Alfred Gell, "Vogel's Net: Trap as Artworks and Artworks as Traps," *Journal of Material Culture* 1, no. 1 (1996), 15–38; Margaret Conkey, "Style, Design and Function," in Tilley et al., *Handbook of Material Culture*, 355–72; Warnier, *Pot-King*.
69. There are many other differences, and one suspects that today's cars already present some important functioning differences with 1960s' cars, with the increasing role given to processors and algorithms.
70. Carlos Emmanuel Sautchuk, "The Pirarucu Net: Artifact, Animism and the Technical Object," *Journal of Material Culture* 24, no. 2 (2019), 176–93.
71. André Leroi-Gourhan, *Évolution et Techniques I: L'Homme et La Matière* (Paris: Albin Michel, 1971[1943]); *Évolution et Techniques II: Milieu et techniques* (Paris: Albin Michel, 1973[1945]).

72. Leroi-Gourhan, *Gesture*.
73. See François Audouze, "Leroi-Gourhan, a Philosopher of Technique and Evolution," *Journal of Archaeological Research* 10, no. 4 (2002), 227–306, for a summary, and Bernard Stiegler *Technics and Time, 1: The Fault of Epimetheus* (Stanford: Stanford University Press, 1998) for a philosophical discussion.
74. Gilbert Simondon, *On the Mode of Existence of Technical Objects* (Minneapolis: Univocal Publishing, 2017[1958]).
75. Both Leroi-Gourhan and Simondon, because of their profoundly Bergsonian processual approach and interests in processes of *becoming*, were foundational to the works of Gilles Deleuze and Felix Guattari, most known for *A Thousand Plateaus* (Minneapolis: University of Minnesota Press, 1987[1980]). Tim Ingold's recent philosophical discussion of processes in *Making* synthesizes these influences. Technical objects were to be thought of as instances and changing iterations of earlier ones, giving a shape to time, as George Kubler suggested in *The Shape of Time* (New Haven: Yale University Press, 1962). Technical objects were thus to be examined in terms of their *becoming* or, as Simondon puts it, their ontogenesis.
76. Simondon, *Mode of Existence*.
77. Ibid, 25–28.
78. Simon Mills, "FCJ-127 Concrete Software: Simondon's Mechanology and the Techno-social," *The Fiberculture Journal* (2011), Open access: https://bit.ly/3ra4NTY; Yuk Hui, "What is a Digital Object?" *Metaphilosophy* 43, no. 2 (2012), 379–95; *On the Existence of Digital Objects* (Minneapolis: The University of Minnesota Press, 2016); Bernard Stielger "Teleologics of the Snail: The Errant Self Wired to a WiMax Network," *Theory, Culture & Society* 26, nos. 2–3 (2009), 23–45.
79. For instance, Bakelite in Wiebe J. Bijker, "The Social Construction of Bakelite: Towards a Theory of Invention," in Wiebe E. Bijker et al., eds., *The Social Construction of Technological Systems* (Cambridge: The MIT Press, 1989), 159–87; bicycles in Trevor J. Pinch and Wiebe E. Bijker, "The Social Construction of Facts and Artifacts: Or How the Sociology of Science and the Sociology of Technology Might Benefit Each Other," in Bijker et al., eds., *The Social Construction*, 17–50; or missiles in Donald MacKenzie, *Inventing Accuracy: A Historical Sociology of Ballistic Missile Guidance* (Cambridge: The MIT Press, 1990).
80. See Bijker et al., *The Social Construction*; Wiebe E. Bijker and John Law, eds., *Shaping Technology/Building Society: Studies in Sociotechnical Change* (Cambridge: The MIT Press, 1992); Wieber E. Bijker "How is Technology Made? That is the Question!" *Cambridge Journal of Economics* 34 (2010), 63–76; Oldenziel, *Making Technology Masculine*; Judy Wajcman, *TechnoFeminism* (Cambridge: Polity Press, 2004).
81. John Law, "Technology and Heterogeneous Engineering: The Case of Portuguese Expansion," in Bijker et al., *The Social Construction*, 111–34;

Michel Callon, "The Role of Hybrid Communities and the Socio-Technical Arrangements in the Participatory Design," *Journal of the Center for Information Studies* 5, no. 3 (2004), 3–10; Madeleine Akrich, "The De-Scription of Technical Objects," in Bijker and Law, *Shaping Technology*, 205–24; Latour, *Aramis*; Latour, "The Berlin Key or How to Do Words with Things," in Paul Graves-Brown, ed., *Matter, Materiality and Modern Culture* (London: Routledge, 2000), 10–21; Natasha Dow Schüll, *Addiction by Design: Machine Gambling in Las Vegas* (Princeton: Princeton University Press, 2012).
82. Winner, *Autonomous Technology*, 100–06, 251–62.
83. See Ludovic Coupaye, "'Things Ain't the Same Anymore': Towards an Anthropology of Technical Objects (or 'When Simondon meets MVC')," in Timothy Carroll, Antonia Walford, and Shireen Walton, eds., *Lineages and Advancements in the Anthropology of Material Culture* (London: Routledge, 2020), 46–60.
84. Lewis H. Morgan, *Ancient Society* (Tucson: University of Arizona Press 1985[1877]).
85. Bronislaw Malinowski, *Coral Gardens and their Magic: A Study of the Methods of Tilling the Soil and of Agricultural Rites in the Trobriand Islands* (New York: Dover Publication, 1978[1935]); C. Daryll Forde, *Habitat, Economy and Society* (London: Methuen, 1934); Julian Stewart, *Theory of Culture Change: The Methodology of Multilinear Evolution* (Urbana: University of Illinois Press, 1955); Roy Rappaport, *Pigs for the Ancestors: Ritual in the Ecology of a New Guinea People* (New Haven: Yale University Press, 1968).
86. Marx, *Das Kapital*.
87. For example Maurice Bloch, ed., *Marxist Analyses and Social Anthropology* (London: Malaby Press, 1975); Maurice Godelier *The Making of Great Men: Male Domination and Power among the New Guinea Baruya* (Cambridge: Cambridge University Press, 1986[1982]).
88. Godelier, *The Making of Great Men*; Claude Meillassoux, *Anthropologie Economique des Gouro de Côte d'Ivoire: De l'Economie de Subsistance à l'Agriculture Commerciale* (The Hague: Mouton, 1964).
89. See Lemonnier, *Mundane Objects*, 16.
90. Lewis Mumford, *Technics and Civilization* (Chicago: University of Chicago Press, 2004[1934]).
91. Lynn White Jr., *Medieval Technology and Social Change* (Oxford: Oxford University Press, 1962), 1–38.
92. The original French – unsurprisingly – uses *système technique*.
93. Marcel Mauss, *Manual of Ethnography* (New York: Berghahn Books, 2007[1967]), 24, my emphasis.
94. Ludwig von Bertalanffy, *General System Theory: Foundations, Developments, Applications* (New York: George Braziller, 1968).
95. Bertrand Gille, *The History of Techniques* (New York: Gordon and Breach Science Publishers, 2 vols., 1986[1978]).

96. Bertrand Gille, "La Notion de Système Technique (Essai D'épistémologie Technique)," *Technique & Cultures* 1, 8–18; Pierre Lemonnier, "A Propos de Bertrand Gille: La Notion de 'Système Technique,'" *L'Homme* 23, no. 2 (1983), 109–15.
97. Lemonnier, "The Study of Material Culture Today: Toward an Anthropology of Technical Systems," *Journal of Anthropological Archaeology* 5, no. 2 (1986), 154–56; *Elements*, 8–11.
98. Lemonnier, *Elements*; Francesca Bray, *Technology and Gender: Fabrics of Power in Late Imperial China* (Berkeley: University of California Press, 1997); Oldenziel, *Making Technology Masculine*.
99. See Lemonnier, *Elements*; "L'étude des Systèmes Techniques : Une Urgence en Technologie Culturelle," *Techniques & Culture* 54–55 (2010[1976]), 46–67; and *Mundane Objects: Materiality and Non-Verbal Communication* (Walnut Creek: Left Coast Press, 2012).
100. For example Malinowski, *Coral Gardens*; André-George Haudricourt, "Domestication of Animals, Cultivation of Plants and Human Relations," *Social Science Information* 8, no. 3 (1969[1962]), 163–72; Philippe Descola, *In the Society of Nature: A Native Ecology in Amazonia* (Cambridge: Cambridge University Press, 1994); Coupaye, *Growing*; Laurence Douny, *Living in a Landscape of Scarcity: Materiality and Cosmology in West Africa* (London: Left Coast Press, 2014).
101. Rowlands and Warnier, "The Magical Production of Iron." Philippe Descola also developed this fundamental idea of resonances of logic through his discussion of the schemas of practices, in *Beyond Nature and Culture*, 91–111.
102. Thomas Hughes, *Networks of Power: Electrification in Western Society, 1880–1930* (Baltimore: The John Hopkins University Press, 1983).
103. Thomas Hughes, "The Seamless Web: Technology, Science, Etcetera, Etcetera," *Social Studies of Science* 16, no. 2 (1986), 281–92.
104. Winner, *Autonomous*, 223 ff.
105. Ibid, 241.
106. Ibid, 234.
107. Brian Larkin, "The Politics and Poetics of Infrastructure," *Annual Review of Anthropology* 42 (2013), 329.
108. These three analytical categories are exactly what I indicated they were: provisional. While they might be operational, they might not be as "effective" with every case study.
109. For example Joshua A. Bell, Briel Kobak, Joel Kuipers, and Amanda Kemble, "Unseen Connections: The Materiality of Cell Phones," *Anthropological Quarterly* 91, no. 2 (2018), 465–84.
110. For example Lewis Mumford, *The Myth of the Machine*, 2 vols. (San Diego: Harcourt, Brace, Jovanovich, 1967 and 1970).
111. Kimberley Chong, *Best Practice: Management Consulting and the Ethics of Financialization in China* (Durham: Duke University Press, 2018).

112. See Ludovic Coupaye, "At the Power Plant's Switchboard: Controlling (Fertile) Energy amongst the Abulës-Speakers of Papua New Guinea," in Thomas Galoppin and Cécile Guillaume-Pey, eds., *Ce que peuvent les pierres: Vie et puissance des Matièries lithiques entre rites et savoirs* (Liège: Presses universitaires de Liège, 2021), 87–107.
113. Hughes, "The Seamless Web"; Callon, "The Role of Hybrid Communities"; Bruno Latour, *Reassembling the Social: An Introduction to Actor-Network-Theory* (Oxford: Oxford University Press, 2005).
114. See Akrich, "The De-Scription of Technical Objects."
115. For example Bruno Latour, Philippe Mauguin, and Genevieve Teil, "A Note on Socio-technical Graphs," *Social Studies of Science* 22 (1992), 33–58, 91–94.
116. See critiques and discussions in Marilyn Strathern, "Cutting the Network," *The Journal of the Royal Anthropological Institute* 2, no. 3 (1996), 517–35, and in Anna Tsing, "Worlding the Matsutake Diaspora: Or, Can Actor-Network Theory Experiment With Holism?" in Ton Otto and Nils Bubandt, eds., *Experiments in Holism: Theory and Practice in Contemporary Anthropology* (Oxford: Wiley-Blackwell, 2010), 47–66.
117. Winner, *Autonomous Technology*, 241.
118. Ibid, 234.
119. Ibid, 220ff.
120. Chong, *Best Practice*, chapter 3, especially 108–09.
121. Akrich, "The De-Scription of Technical Objects"; Bruno Latour, "Technology is Society Made Durable," in John Law, ed., *A Sociology of Monsters? Essays on Power, Technology and Domination* (London: Routledge, 1991), 103–31.
122. Thinking with nonlinear theory at this level allows the investigation of phenomena of sensitivity to initial conditions, unpredictability and irreversibility, and their role in wider social and environmental change; see Mark S. Mosko and Fred H. Damon, eds., *On the Order of Chaos: Social Anthropology and the Science of Chaos* (New York and Oxford: Berghahn Books, 2005).
123. Ellul, *The Technological Society*.
124. Feenberg, *Transforming Technology*, 76–77. This concept of "code" strongly echoes with works of thinkers such as Gregory Bateson, "Style, Grace, and Information in Primitive Art," in Anthony Forge, ed., *Primitive Art and Society* (London: Ely House, Oxford University Press, 1973), 235–55, or, indeed, Marshall McLuhan, *Understanding Media: The Extension of Man* (Cambridge: The MIT Press, 1995[1964]), in showing how the materialization of values into functioning objects and systems can indeed become more important than the function or purpose.
125. Bryan Pfaffenberger, "Technological Drama," *Science, Technology and Human Values* 17, no. 3 (1992), 282–312.

126. Bryan Pfaffenberger, "The Social Meaning of the Personal Computer: Or, Why the Personal Computer Revolution Was No Revolution," *Anthropological Quarterly* 6, no. 1 (1992), 39–47.
127. Andrew Feenberg, *Questioning Technology* (London & New York: Routledge, 1999), 131.
128. For example Larkin, "The Politics and Poetics of Infrastructure"; Penny Harvey and Hannah Knox, "The Enchantments of Infrastructure," *Mobilities* 7, no. 4 (2015), 521–36.
129. See Winner, *Autonomous Technology*; Feenberg, *Critical Theory of Technology*; Sarah Grimes and Andrew Feenberg, "Critical Theory of Technology," in Sara Price, Carey Jewitt, and Barry Brown, eds., *The SAGE Handbook of Digital Technology Research* (Los Angeles: SAGE, 2013), 121–29.
130. Langdon Winner, "Do Artifacts Have Politics?" in *The Whale and the Reactor* (Chicago: University of Chicago Press, 1986), 19–39; Pfaffenberger, "Technological Dramas."
131. "Technology Quarterly," *The Economist*, September 14, 2019.

Part V

Experience

To dwell means to leave traces.

Walter Benjamin

19

Place and Materiality

Elijah Gaddis

Place coheres around abstraction. Itself conceptual, and indeed, immaterial, place is nonetheless a process deeply imbricated in the material of the world and the actors who make it. As a concept, it forces us to pay attention to the materiality of physical locality and the processes and experiences that *take* place within and around it. The paradox of place is its relationship to materiality and to material culture as at once an abstraction and an enduring material presence.

In this chapter, I focus on the distinction between landscape and place as a way of reflecting the multitudinous ancestors of place as a field of inquiry within interdisciplinary material culture studies. This academic genealogy reveals the central problem of this essay and indeed, of this field of study: the ways by which we might go about materializing the immaterial and considering abstract place as material cultural reality. We have long used landscape as both a default term and a structuring understanding of the material and conceptual dimensions of dwelling.[1] But landscape carries with it linguistic, material, and conceptual weight that replicates its originary, colonialist impulses. To these problems I add the difficulty of researching, writing, and conceptualizing place from a perspective focused on the everyday. Though the spectacular, the planned, the exceptional, and the photogenic are our most ready entries to understanding place, they also tend to flatten our comprehension of the complexity of the daily processes that go into its making. Accordingly, I propose here an interdisciplinary method designed to recall place to its material origins, and to have a material culture practice more conversant with place. Just as we have seen geography move increasingly away from an understanding rooted in maps, I suggest that we might better understand place through its material traces, objects that recall significance but are not themselves representations of the fractured and always incomplete individual and collective understandings of a single place.[2] In what follows, then, I both explore literature on the ways in which we can consider the (im) materiality of place, and through a case study of memorializations of slavery, the Civil War, and the Confederacy, propose a material culture approach to place as a way of better understanding the lived, material complexities of people in the world.

Materializing the Spatial Turn

Place has emerged as a robust and full-fledged theoretical concept in the past several decades. Though debates about meaning and precise definitions are central to the field of study, a collective definition would define space as a physical embodiment of potentiality, an "undifferentiated" and unknown locality.[3] Place is space enriched, made useful or at least meaningful. Never merely derivative of space, it is both the process and the result of meaning making in physical surroundings. Though place as a theoretical concept has a fairly clear lineage (some of which will be detailed below) its embrace in the recent past has been part of a so-called spatial turn in the humanistic and social scientific disciplines. This turn saw both space and place redefined and reduced, often to "somewhat arbitrary or constructed notions," for the various uses of individual disciplines.[4] The irony here is that, though place is embedded in a materialist reading of the world, the multidisciplinary borrowing of space and place as concepts has largely left material culture and materiality aside. Material culture studies can make a useful intervention by recalling the materiality of places. The spatial turn is an opportunity for material culture studies to both engage with this recent spatial scholarship and look to its own interdisciplinary past and methodologies as a way of materializing the spatial turn. In other words, the spatial turn might push the leading edge of material culture studies toward a fuller engagement with the broad strokes of multi- and interdisciplinary scholarship and help restore material culture studies to their one-time centrality within that broader discourse.[5]

As Jo Guldi's brief but comprehensive overview of the spatial turn suggests, it is a movement both rooted in long disciplinary histories and one that shows up well before the recent advent of the spatial mapping technologies that constitute this turn in the scholarly imaginary.[6] Starting in the late 1970s, humanistic disciplines embraced an emerging body of philosophical work on place as a solution to a lack of groundedness. Building on then recent translations of French theory, the expanded temporal and geographic focus of the Annales school, and on emerging fields of human and cultural geography, place became a way to understand embeddedness and human interaction with the world. This "turn" was particularly influenced by the work of geographers like Yi Fu Tuan, and the translation of scholarship by Michel Foucault, Pierre Bourdieu, Gaston Bachelard, and particularly Henri Lefebvre. While certainly engaging with one another's ideas in their original French, it was the translation of these ideas into English that brought them together as a new school of philosophy centered on the spatial. And it has been English language scholarship that has most embraced and tried to work with these ideas as a coherent school of philosophical thought and scholarly practice. Lefebvrian acolytes like David Harvey and Edward Soja continued the project of conceptualizing abstract space and equally philosophized place and themselves gained many imitators and would-be spatial theorists. By the late 2000s when GIS and accessible digital technologies were on the rise, there was already a body of theory in place to help contextualize and interpret even the earliest, fumbling efforts at a new mode of scholarship.[7] In some ways of course, none of this was new, but rather refinements and corrections to older ideas which had not become a central part of disciplinary methodologies. The "turn" then, as Guldi notes, was both about facing backward and about integrating new ideas in search of lost or ignored disciplinary pasts.

By the time that other disciplines were embracing spatial (or in Edward Casey's awkward neologism "placial") thinking and theory, geographers like Peter Jackson were already reacting to the theoretical, semiotic research in their own discipline.[8] Jackson's collaborations with Daniel Miller sought to "rematerialize" human geography and served as a mission statement for the social and cultural wings of the field and its new journal.[9] Other disciplines were slower to follow. But in the decade and a half since Jackson's article, history, anthropology, art history, and literary studies have followed suit and material culture and materiality has emerged (or reemerged) as a concern. Frustrations with the ephemerality of scholarly fashion aside, I think that we might now view the spatial turn and its adjustments and reactions as useful fodder for reformulating a wing of material culture centered on concerns with place and space. Though certainly that was not the intention, the formulations and reactions of it clearly suggest the necessity of an interdisciplinary approach that can deal with both the abstractions of place and space and their real, material consequences. Material culture can serve those purposes, both because of its ability to encompass each of these branches of thought and because of its long history of doing just that. Far from being a recuperative effort, I argue that place has been a central concern of material culture studies since its inception. This requires that we view material culture studies as a field (if not a discipline) in its own right. Indeed, we might think of the overlaps between would-be material and spatial turns, a broad expanse of object-centered study that builds on many disciplinary homes (art history, history, anthropology, geography) but exists in the interstitial spaces between them. Though the approaches and methods of material culture have certainly been used by other disciplines, at least in an Anglo-American context there is ample evidence to both claim material culture studies as a field distinct from its many antecedents and contributing disciplines and to find its long-standing concern with what we would now call place as a central organizing principle of that field. This volume is, I think, evidence that material culture studies has already emerged in the twenty-first century as its own field of study worthy of attention as a scholarly practice rooted in and informed by a wide range of disciplinary perspectives and methodologies. Reflecting the multiple origins of material culture, this is not about claiming scholarly territory but rather about acknowledging the utility that comes with emphasizing interdisciplinarity and the energy that can come from a range of scholars working toward a project with similar ends, if not necessarily similar tools, methods, or approaches.

All of this adds up to an understanding of place that is incomplete, tenuous, even confused. But it also points to a range of possibilities for the study of place and material culture. This recent attention to place has made its usage increasingly commonplace in the vernacular of scholars, practitioners of city planning and development, and ordinary people. This has made the concept both more exploitable and more readily usable for scholars seeking to link it to everyday experience. The other is the immateriality of place as it is presently conceived. Material culture scholars can reckon with this not just as scholarly omission, but rather as a critical stance. To conceive of place in this way is, perhaps, to pay closer attention to material objects and material landscapes, but also to the relationships and attachments that cohere in and around them. As an organizing principle, place allows us to leave behind the restrictions of landscape or indeed of presence in the material sense altogether. Material culture studies, particularly in the context of the everyday, have been object-centered sometimes to the detriment of our field.[10]

As Sarah Wasserman also suggests in Chapter 3 on representation, place calls us to think about absence and immateriality, with the paradoxes of a material culture that is at once everywhere and nowhere, surrounding us and largely invisible to our visual scrutiny. This also allows for a reordering based on spatiality rather than temporality and to see the world of people and their localities as linked as much by space as by time (and perhaps more so). Though not without its own problems, place nonetheless speaks to the complexity of the visual, the material, and the lived. Indeed, part of its appeal comes from its ambiguity and fragmentation. Whereas landscape is about making order of the material world, the range and proliferation of ideas around place can reflect the messiness of those same interactions without trying to bring it into an overarching organizational conceptualization. As Michel de Certeau suggests in one of the pioneering works on the understanding and navigation of everyday life "places are fragmentary and inward-turning histories, pasts that others are not allowed to read, accumulated times that can be unfolded but like stories held in reserve, remaining in an enigmatic state, symbolizations encysted in the pain or pleasure of the body."[11] Place opens up the possibilities and the necessity of thinking about the personal, the collective, and the bodily making meaning amid locality. Material culture scholars then might prefer the use of place rather than the totalizing visual array of landscape which too often gets read as the sum of all interactions between human and environment. The concept of landscape, even in its most expansive cultural formations, is one descended from and still beholden to a fundamentally visual range of understanding. Accordingly, material culture studies as a field has dealt with the tensions between landscape and place, between representation and experience, between evident materiality and symbolic abstraction.

This adoption of place better reflects the evolution of work in material culture studies. So too does the concept of materiality. As Daniel Miller suggests, objects are "appearances ... emerging in the wake of the process of objectification as it proceeds as a historical process."[12] In other words, he reframes the point of material culture studies to center more fully on the process of creation, rather than the outcome of that process as it has been traditionally studied in the object itself. Materiality is more appropriately seen as process or performance, and in this formulation, material culture studies might focus alike on the ephemeral traces of interaction and creation embedded in objects. This understanding of materiality necessarily means a co-constituting relationship between objects and places, rather than the long Western tradition of seeing space as a "pre-existing container" for objects.[13] Materiality and place then function as interlocking concepts that allow scholars to both better understand place and contradict assumptions of the fixity of an object's meaning and material presence. In other words, place and materiality suggest a material culture studies focused on the processual and performed, on the evolution of objects and experience.

The Problem with Landscape

This chapter, and indeed this volume, are reflective of both the long development of material culture studies, and more recent theoretical and methodological transformations within the field. Accordingly, this chapter tends to the materiality of place, rather than exploring landscape as similar, earlier collections might have done. But it is also in recognition of the work that the spatial turn has done in causing humanistic and social scientific scholars to reformulate the frameworks by which we understand the interactions between the world and the beings that live within it. My concern with landscape then lies with its flattening of the complexity of the material world. It reifies the historical construction of landscape as a subject. We end up as spectators looking out over a vista removed of people, rather than placing ourselves amid the muck and mire of human intention and action. Perhaps we cannot escape our impulse toward visual accumulation, but we can counter it by conceptualizing the impacts this narrowed range of vision has, and the way it proceeds to forms of dominance in the material world.

The genealogy of landscape as a scholarly subject is well known. Its linguistic origins, as John Brinckerhoff Jackson noted in an early essay, "hark back to that ancient Indo-European idiom" that served as the basis for most contemporary European languages.[14] Of course, Jackson's concern was not principally linguistic. Instead, he was interested in the uses of the word as an organizing principle and mode of aesthetic understanding. He finds the earliest uses of landscape corresponding to artists' interpretations, to a definition that "did not mean the view itself" but rather "a picture of it, an artist's interpretation."[15] Landscape emerged first as a genre of aesthetic expression, taking as its initial subject a visual pastoralism that was a modification of a long-standing and multi-format artistic interest in the expressive material world in which and from which the artist created.[16] This same totalizing impulse extended to literature, where pastoralism created visions of landscape untrammeled by all but the most gentle of human interventions.[17] The inheritances of this early aesthetic persist well beyond the temporal contours of its initial creation.

As an idiom in the English language then, landscape represented not just a visual array but an aestheticization that hewed toward the romantic and the reductive. It spoke to an increasingly familiar impression of the material world and its symbolic meaning as one deeply divided by the reductive dichotomies of nature and civilization, rural and urban. As W. J. T. Mitchell suggests, "landscape aesthetics" arose as a production of European modernity intended to constitute a "new way of seeing."[18] This was a practice designed to turn representation into reality and into knowledge and by extension, domination. Landscape's own definitions – linguistic, artistic, and imperial – were formulated out of its own representational inadequacies.

Jill Casid notes that it was the landscape ideal and the practice of landscaping that served as a tool of empire in conquering the colonies and literally spreading colonization. The act of planting – metaphorically, the scattered seed of heterosexual reproduction – was, in Casid's words, "both to produce colonies and to generate imperial subjects to sustain them."[19] As in Mitchell, landscaping for Casid is a larger aesthetic form that "should be understood as united discursive and material practices that came to the fore in the eighteenth century as techniques of empire."[20] Casid's work tracks the expansion of landscape to the material practice of *landscaping*, still perhaps the most prominent vernacular usage of the term. These linguistic expansions, paradoxically, led to a conceptual retraction, making landscape an ever more focused project of insidious, imperial control over the appearance, if not the experience, of everyday life. As a practice of imperial domination, landscape practice often failed in the face of native resistance both human and nonhuman. The careful attempts at ordering and cataloging that Casid chronicles were betrayed by a fecundity that surpassed the colonial imagination, a human resistance that undermined assumptions about Western superiority, and an inability to translate ideas of theoretical order into actual practice. But landscape's material and conceptual shortcomings are also ones that extend to scholarly practice.

Material culture studies largely inherited that struggle over representation and meaning. Even as the field emerged as a more full-fledged approach rather than a corollary to art historical discourses, it has not abandoned the notion of landscape as visual, or more accurately, fully *comprehensible*. The many scholars critiquing the visual supremacy of landscape as term and field of study hint at this totalizing epistemological framework.[21] In his critique of the visual culture of landscape, Anthony D. King points to further problems with visuality itself as part of an academic-imperial project. For King, "the notion that until things are seen they cannot be known" has formed the basis of multiple scholarly disciplines and "privileged the unknown Other as an object of knowledge."[22] The deeper, unarticulated critique of this form of visuality is not about particular sensorial dominance, but about the substitution of observation for knowledge. Landscape's definitions are entangled with early forms of modernity, which sought (and seek) a full comprehension of the world through human documentation and knowledge. Even our constructions of the wild and the natural presuppose a form of understanding that is limited in actuality.[23] The inheritance of the visual is not just that we still tend to "see" the landscape but that we substitute any kind of documentation for a deeper form of understanding. An alternate genealogy of landscape studies in material culture reveals nascent frameworks for a more complex understanding. This materialist reading can help recast the proliferation of spatial theory in recent decades toward its lived, material realities.

Places, and the people making and using them, resist the order of the visible and definable. More than thirty years ago, Jackson was already looking for a new definition of landscape that served the purposes of the emergent academic field of cultural landscape studies and to reflect the realities of human usage. These emergent materialist discourses on landscape and habitation have continued to run largely parallel to art historical ones. A variety of scholars, most notably the geographer and anthropologist Fred Kniffen and his mentor Carl Sauer, were likewise trying to forge a new field of materially inclined studies of landscape. Kniffen, and his student Henry Glassie, focused on the vernacular built environment, seeing in ordinary buildings and their surroundings an important measure of cultural production and social understanding.[24] The careers of each of these scholars was in large part devoted to the project of documenting, interpreting, and theorizing material environments.[25] Their legacy is measured in the persistence of material cultural study in fields as diverse as folklore, vernacular architecture studies, and cultural geography.

For scholars, landscape as practice fails on an epistemological level. In and of itself, that may not be reason enough to abandon or otherwise neglect the use of landscape as an organizing principle of spatial and geographic understanding. Indeed, the world around us bears the evident marks of settler colonial expansion, particularly in the United States. In Alabama, where I currently reside, place names of imperial conquest abound. Take for instance Opelika, the rapidly gentrifying small town one over from the university where I teach. The name is, of course, native – an appellation borrowed from the Muskoghean language of the Creeks who inhabited the land before it was claimed, sold, or otherwise stolen. This matters in a conceptual sense for anyone concerned with the ethics of habitation and dwelling, but it also has daily repercussions. The barista in the coffee shop where I am writing this paragraph is wearing a shirt proclaiming that things are "cooler in Opelika." Besides the unconscious resonance with forms of materiality, I wonder what this phrase includes and excludes? Are the tribes subjected to removal of a part of the indexing of cool in this commoditizing form of ownership? Does the history embedded here matter in this definition as anything more than the material repositories for the desires of new residents? This hints at the kind of omissions that the geographer Tim Cresswell has criticized for decades as he has tried to bring first practice and more recently mobility into the study of what most in his discipline continue to call landscape. More recently he has identified (somewhat tongue in cheek) the scholarly practice of *landscaping*, whereby scholars are complicit if not active in the creation of "a particular aesthetic that hides all kinds of other processes that are going on in it."[26] Its imperial mission, if not intention, remain. Earlier in Cresswell's campaign for an alternative to landscape, he remarked that landscape has little room for the living, the processual, and the in-progress. Its inert sense of captivity "does not have much space for temporality, for movement and flux and mundane practice. It is too much about the already accomplished and not enough about the processes of everyday life."[27] Despite the ahistoricism seemingly implied here, Creswell's point is that landscape is so laden with its long history of usage as to be virtually unmodifiable. Landscape has run its course.

Nowhere is this more evident than in the monumental and memorial landscapes of the American South. As I write this, the region and the country have been embroiled in debates over the preservation, alteration, and removal of Confederate monuments. While the terms of debate have centered on history and pastness, both the critique and defense are rooted in an understanding where history, heritage, and memory are central to the claiming of public, civic, and other shared places.[28] This debate highlights the centrality of the interplay between material objects and symbolic structures of feeling in determining how people live, experience, and interact with and in the places they are from. In the remainder of this chapter, then, I will reflect on what it would mean to rethink the grounds of this debate as primarily spatial, and to see the long histories of contestation and conflict as ones that are centrally about the creation and navigation of the material and symbolic manifestations of place.

Monument Building and White Supremacist Spatial Formation

By the 1890s, the states of the former Confederacy were at war again over territory. The much-documented memorial impulse of the United Daughters of the Confederacy (UDC) and other women's organizations was only the most prominent movement of a society obsessed with claiming places around competing visions of the past.[29] As Black migrants helped remake the material and demographic environments of New Southern cities, both local law, emergent customs, and dedicated organizations sought to reverse any claim they made to civic or public space and to reify a white supremacist imaginary in the material world.

Between the 1890s and the 1920s, thousands of monuments to the Confederate dead, individual leaders and soldiers, and the cause of slavery were erected, mostly but not exclusively in the former Confederate states (Figure 19.1). These statues, columns, buildings, and roads dominated the urbanizing landscape and established a permanent physical presence that reinforced the increasing restrictions and revocations on rights as basic as mobility for African Americans, Native Americans, and other marginalized people of color. In effect, they created a southern sense of place that was synonymous with whiteness and exclusion. Less permanent though equally important were the parades, protests, and programs put on by Black fraternal lodges and community organizations. These countermemorials laid claim to many of the same spaces in ways more fleeting and performative. Their vision of southern sense of place was one rooted in an acknowledgment of the struggles of the past as a clarifying point of remembrance for moving forward in the future. These two competing visions of placemaking represent the complexity of the materiality of place. The physical, often imposing monuments that litter the landscape are the most tangible markings of these geographic claims. But they represent omissions not just of historical narratives, but of the actualities of place and the way in which it was conceived and used. These monuments were erected as the cultural and material arms of a campaign of white supremacy. We can, and should, fault their continued existence on the landscape for instantiating a particular version of history and memory. But that continued material presence also occludes both their original intent and the ways in which they have influenced their environments in the generations since.

Though these monuments have, in the past two decades, become objects of scholarly scrutiny, rarely have the historians and geographers writing

Figure 19.1 Confederate monuments achieved central placement in civic spaces and in cultural expression of place, as in this dedication ceremony in Tennessee, c. 1910. Dedication ceremony for Confederate Monument in Mulberry, Tennessee, Prints and Photographs Division, Library of Congress.

about them conducted a focused longitudinal study that documents the experience of, with, and around these monuments. We know, often implicitly and sometimes through written records, that African American people in cities and towns walked past (or around) these markers of revanchist white supremacy from their inception in the 1880s and 1890s. Once places of provisional promise for African American rural migrants, these growing southern cities were increasingly dominated by the culture of whiteness materialized in the form of monument building and expressed otherwise in the violence of racial terror lynching, intimidation, and the practices of spatial segregation. This caused many African Americans to leave, becoming political and economic refugees as part of the Great Migration. Others continued to navigate cities whose civic spaces and then, increasingly, public streets were marked as commemorations of an exclusionary past and contemporary memory driven by that misapprehension. These broader changes came amid the destruction of Black places in cities across the South and nation, a process linked to this memorialization and the devaluation of Black life and landscapes that it represented. But amid these macro changes, we can also see traces of the responses to these monuments, their erection, their contestation, and their persistence. Documenting that response means being attentive to written, material, and experiential archives of memory such as the one that exists around the Confederate memorial in Oxford, North Carolina.

Memorializing and Contesting Place

Oxford's "Granville Grays" chapter of the UDC raised the funds for a prominent granite memorial in 1909. News of the $3,000 contract for the statue made it the 200 miles to Charlotte in early March of 1909.[30] Two months later the laying of its cornerstone was sufficient occasion for "imposing ceremonies" amply documented by both reporters on site and a booklet published by the Granville Grays. The day's grand events featured a massive procession through the streets, speeches, hymn singing, and the participation of groups ranging from schoolchildren and orphans to the local guard.[31] When the monument itself was completed and dedicated seven months later in October, news of the ceremonies and celebrations was again detailed on newspaper front pages to apparently universal adoration (Figure 19.2). The statue itself was (and is) both starkly simple and utterly imposing. Thirty-four feet high, formed from local granite into a variation on the cross-vault obelisk, it is topped with a seven-foot tall bronze soldier manufactured in Chicago. On the east and west sides there are large Confederate States of America emblems wreathed in laurels carved into the statue. At nine feet above the ground, they were almost exactly at eye level for Oxford inhabitants walking by the statue from several paces away, as its position in the street's center necessitated. Its boy soldier was faced northward "gun in hand, standing at the position of 'Ready!'"[32] One commenter called it "an adornment to the city" occupying as it did "the elevation in the center of the city, an everlasting sentinel addressing in soul-words all who view it."[33] And if its north-facing, gun-toting posture left any ambiguity about its meaning, the dedication speeches were even more explicit in their purpose. Local dignitary D. G. Brummitt invoked the Lost Cause of the Confederacy by name[34] while then governor William Walton Kitchin defended the Ku Klux Klan, praised the steadfast virtue of white womanhood during the "dark days of Reconstruction," and spent much of his time speaking in "tribute to the white race."[35] The dedication of the speech was similar to others in the period, each of which had the impact of setting aside a would-be sacral space of whiteness around the monument and all it surveyed. The

Figure 19.2 "Confederate Monument, Oxford, NC." Durwood Barbour Collection of North Carolina postcards (P077), North Carolina Collection. Photographic Archives, Wilson Library, UNC-Chapel Hill.

monument recognized Oxford's growing importance as a center of trade and production with a population both sufficiently proud and wealthy enough to provide the grand monument that spoke to their own civic ambitions and pride in their collective memory of the past.

Black residents of Oxford, Granville, and surrounding counties were less enthusiastic about the monument and its stated purposes. Unsurprisingly, no mention of any African American organizations or individuals appears among the accountings of either dedication ceremony. The context in which African American residents of Oxford reacted to the monument originally and in a formal public context was through their annual Emancipation Day procession through the town center. Themselves the performative, ephemeral counterpoint to the civic permanence of Confederate memorials, these parades occurred in numbers and on a scale virtually unrivaled in American history to that point. In the years after formal emancipation, these celebrations were organized in virtually every town and county geographically southern, and many beyond it. Emancipation Day celebrations, and particularly processions, were the most prominent and visible form of Black commemoration and place-claiming in the postbellum United States.[36]

In 1910 then, the African American residents of Oxford had to contend with the new statue squarely in the path of their daily movements around town and amid their annual processional route. Whether intentional or not, this new landscape feature impacted the day's commemorations. Doubtless individual members of the crowd had their own reactions to the thirty-foot-high obelisk. Since the parade happened at the first of the year and only a little over two months since its building, it may have been the first time that some of the rural residents who flocked to the tri-county metropolitan Oxford had experienced it in person. The official reaction of the local organizing committee for the event was complicated and clearly designed toward a spirit of compromise. How much that position was compelled by either spatial or social coercion is impossible to tell. But the position concretized in the resolutions voted on at the Emancipation Day meeting show a rhetorical position born out of necessary restraint even amid the realities of celebrating in this place. The resolution opens with a paean to Oxford as "a community where peace and harmony reign between the races."[37] Much of their basis for this judgment of the town was based on its aesthetic, rather than social characteristics. Their resolutions describe Oxford as a "beautiful town," and the monument as a "beautiful monument." Redundancies aside, the town they invoked was one spatially and socially harmonious.

Continuing their recitation of the day's events, the Resolutions and Statistics Committee of the local Emancipation Day organization talked about the morning's procession. "We have marched through the streets and under the shadow of a beautiful monument erected to the memory of the Confederate dead, who, fought heroically for what they conceived to be the right."[38] This is subtly crafted critique disguised as praise. The repetition of "beautiful" seems to suggest not a paucity of vocabulary (the resolutions are otherwise verging on the verbose,) but rather the facile nature of appearance as a judgment of worthiness. The monument is beautiful but perhaps not otherwise praiseworthy. Indeed, the second usage of the word turns the description of the town into another subtle criticism; a place that has aesthetic appeal, but perhaps little else. More overt is the Lost Cause reference "for what they conceived to be the right." Probable mistype and all, it clearly portrays the monument as a one-sided and exclusionary tribute. More importantly, it also provides a segue for the resolutions to insist on support for their similarly proud, though not divisive or supremacist, celebration. Their official, complicated acknowledgment of the monument hints at approval of its content for all but the most careful reader. They use that faint praise to ask that "the white people in turn unite with us in the celebration of this day." This "harmonious blending of what was once diverse and antagonistic feeling," suggests the realities of the recently calcified spatial segregation and its possibilities for community building.[39] This monument represented a revision of the New South credo, a tenuous truce that saw cities and towns no longer violently expelling Black residents but now passively, reluctantly allowing their physical presence while symbolically creating places inhospitable to them. The slight hint at a rejection of this culture that we get in this official statement of approval can doubtless be taken as evidence of both the statue's clear meaning and a much wider rejection of the spatial order that it represented.

That new spatial order lasted for the next several decades, in part because of the massive outmigration of Black southerners to industrial opportunity and the promise, if not reality, of a more welcoming place outside the confines of the former Confederacy. Some older residents of Oxford even linked the monument and the potential for those migrations explicitly. During his childhood in the years just after the monument was erected, William Henry Daniel recalled that he been told it was there to "keep the black man down ... some said he had the gun pointed ... to keep the nigger down south."[40] Others who grew up in early twentieth-century Oxford and were later interviewed by the local historian Eddie McCoy agreed. The monument was a part of their daily lives, sometimes unregarded but possessing a symbolic significance whose meaning was never lost on them. These repeated comments also suggest a kind of spatial knowledge of the monument rather than one rooted solely in actual encounter. Indeed, part of its significance was in the comprehension that it made Black residents carry with them as they navigated the town. Jerome Anderson, among the oldest of McCoy's interviewees in the early 1980s, even recalled a time before the monument was erected when there "use to be a well sitting right there where the city use water out of. And they had a watering trough there on the corner."[56] Less utilitarian in this new commemorative formulation, the intersection of Main and Williamsboro streets became both less necessary to visit as part of the functioning of life in the town and more forbidding as a symbol of the town's white supremacist governing structure. That kind of roving geographic knowledge was deeply ingrained in McCoy's interviewees as they mentioned the monument even in passing. Clearly, African American residents of Oxford understood their literal and conceptual navigation of the city through the lens of the statue dominating its de facto public square.[41]

Over time, the implicit critiques of 1910 turned far more open. In 1970 the conflict between a white shopkeeper and his mostly Black customers turned first into a boycott and eventually multiple episodes of violence. The violence of the white merchant and his family eventually resulted in their store being burned, the protestors' actions being labeled a riot, and the town briefly enacting a curfew and other restrictive measures.[42] The monument unsurprisingly became a target of the protestors and their open expression of decades of sublimated anger at the city's racist spatial order. As the historian Tim Tyson recounts in his memoir of the riots, at least one group of activists attached a rope to the monument in its prominent Main Street location and attempted to pull it down. So central was the symbolic destruction of this hated symbol that one of the protestors reflected years later "the only thing I really hate is that we couldn't pull down that damn Confederate monument."[43]

Though this attempt got fairly little press coverage at the time, the monument became a central part of the plan for reconciliation on the part of the politicians and other leaders of Oxford. In 1971 the monument was relocated to the newly built library as part of a compromise in the wake of the riots.[44] That the monument would play such a central role here is illustrative less of its central importance to town leaders and others and more of the fungibility of its purpose. The monument was always a stand in for a broader symbolic spatial and social order and its relocation was at once a way of offering a real, material response without engaging with the underlying issues. In other words, the movement saw the material presence of the statue change but not its underlying functionality or purpose. It still broadcast a particular, exclusionary sense of place to townspeople walking or driving past it, and it still dominated the small downtown of Oxford even in the absence of its formerly central place in the town's spatial order.

Its new place is one filled with the contradictions of a town looking to at once embrace the original message of the monument and formally mitigate its impact. It still sits at a prominent address – 210 Main Street – and across the street from the First Baptist Church and other central downtown institutions. Indeed, the land on which it sits is that of the town's mid-twentieth century library. But that prominent address is somewhat illusory. The monument is actually sited on Spring Street along the southeast facade of the library. It is obscured now, to the extent that a thirty-foot-tall granite statue can be blocked, by ten to fifteen years of growth of a willow oak. From Main Street, the monument is barely visible to those passing by, a fact made less meaningful by the automobile age which makes even small towns like Oxford virtually unnavigated on foot. But that modified navigability of the town center is certainly a part of the monument's current placement as well. It sits at what has become the main entrance of the town's public library through the custom of use. In my observation, virtually everyone entering the library used this newer entrance rather than the front one. Its seemingly innocuous placement is belied by the fact of that interaction. Were it at the courthouse or county offices, it might have more official status cast on it by the proximity of governmental power. But by the same token, it would hardly be a part of daily experience for most people in town who would rarely enter the doors of or even approach buildings whose innerworkings are still somewhat mysterious and foreboding to anyone who does not have to enter them on a daily basis. This new location, directly to the left of those entering the library, is one better suited to the uses of the contemporary town. Its redirected monumentality is one that that accompanies not the judicial, official, arms of the government but rather its friendly front door. It is a monumentality suited to a town and to a governmental institution which is perhaps one of the very few that people will regularly enter on foot, even if it is from a car parked nearby. Given semi-official status by its placement on town property, the monument was also brought more forcefully into a spatial modernity by its association with the modernist, architect designed library. The statue is still a relic of the past, but one that has been recontextualized for the modern town dweller.

Indeed, its contradictions extend beyond its strictly spatial orientation. Its place seems willfully calculated to reflect the ambiguities of its kind of tenuous spatial modernity and to contain most of its symbolic memorial purposes. This begins with its geographic orientation. It is directed northward in the long tradition of monuments of its type. It is surely not coincidental either, that the re-sited monument was faced toward the edges of the elite, tony houses of downtown. The forward-facing soldier when relocated in the 1970s must have seemed a kind of protective, calming presence for the residents of this district still shaken by the eruption of a destructive anger in their town. If his almost-conversational orientation toward their houses, schools, and institutions seemed more benevolent than protective, they had the resolution of the previous year's riots and its few accommodations to legitimate grievances to reassure them of their continued centrality in the town.

But just as surely as this new placement was seemingly directed toward the comfort and pride of many of the town's prominent white citizens, it was clearly likewise intended as a message for African American citizens living on the other side of the town's racial-geographic dividing line. To the south of the statue – segmented by one block filled with parking lots and two unremarkable office buildings – is Martin Luther King Jr. Avenue. As in other towns and cities across the South, this street represents a very real demarcation between white and Black neighborhoods.[45] Clearly intended to have symbolic purpose, these streets practically helped materialize already existing social divisions with a concrete practice of placemaking. Part of the purpose of this street naming then, is the widening and deepening of that division and exacerbating the existing material inequalities of cities and towns like Oxford and others in the south.

Those material differences were stark when I last visited Oxford. Partially this is an issue of scale. Martin Luther King Jr. Avenue is a busy street that widens to four lanes heading out of town, just south and east of the monument. In that sense, its role as a dividing line is all the more prominent since it is virtually unnavigable for those on foot or bicycle. It is a material border between the two sides of the town that makes the stone soldier's backward-facing orientation seem even more insulting. The statue is hardly on guard because the landscape has been transformed to make it unnecessary. It is as if he will not even deign to turn his defenses toward the poorer district. And while the monument can be selectively ignored from the north side of town, it is omnipresent here, even over the buildings, because of a shift downward in grade. More than when it was on the level ground of the more central district, the material landscape has been formed in such a way as to ensure its looming presence.

Naturally, this has not gone unnoticed for African American residents in the town. A decade ago, as expansions to the library were planned, some local leaders tried to advocate that the monument be moved again to a final resting place in the town's cemetery just a few hundred feet away. They objected to its placement and argued, correctly, that the library's renovations would allow "more people [to] see the statue."[46] Predictably, the local chapter of the Sons of Confederate Veterans opposed the move and city leaders demurred, promising only to relocate the statue if opposing groups found the money to do so. Instead the statue remained where it was and as a marker not only of the town's memories of itself, but as the very real dividing line between the experience of the town for people living there.

This symbol of the statue becomes all encompassing, a material representation whose presence stands in for the material realities expressed in the geography of the town. In some sense this reveals the preference for place over landscape as purely academic in both the literal and figurative senses. But the smaller houses, bigger roads, and low-lying topography are both actual conditions and ones that find their origin in these symbolic realities. And the material and social organization of these places clearly plays out in ways that have a real impact on the lives of their inhabitants, from lower home values and therefore less accumulated family wealth to the linkages between poor health outcomes and environment. As material culturalists, we might pay more attention to those macro factors that result in and from interaction with the material world. Place is both symbolic and material, and acts as a call to balance the two and to seek fields of study less concerned with disciplinary endeavors than with empathy and human response.

Conclusion

As of this writing, the Oxford monument still stands. There is seemingly little threat to its removal. Indeed, despite prominent cases in New Orleans, Birmingham, Charlottesville, Durham, Chapel Hill, and a few other southern cities and towns, the vast majority of Confederate monuments remain both up and in their original locations.[47] In 2017 there was even the dedication of at least one new monument to "Unknown Alabama Confederate Soldiers." Its location (at a private Confederate memorial next to an RV park in rural Alabama) and scale (a roughly two by four foot piece of granite, the size of a contemporary gravestone) suggest the reduced audience and purpose for such a memorial.[48] It both preempts the criticism of placement in a city center and plays on the appeal of the flag and the Confederacy as symbols of rural resistance. The monuments, once the height of memorial splendor in their day, are now seen as objects of veneration themselves rather than the symbols of modernity and progress that they were once posed as. Placing this new memorial in the rural countryside allows it to carry the symbolic valences that have accumulated around Confederate memory in the century or so since most of the monuments were erected.

But still, these retrograde material remainders sit in city and town centers across the South. The likelihood of their being removed in Oxford, North Carolina, Charleston, South Carolina, or Montgomery, Alabama seems slim. So too does the kind of contextualization favored by moderate voices. Plaques and other historicizing materials are fine from a public historical context, but do not override the overwhelming, literally monumental scale of the statues or the long accretion of experience. Often lost in this debate are the voices of material cultural scholars who could point out not only the material histories of these statues as objects, but likewise their meaning across space and time. These memorials are obliterative, dominating landscapes through sheer scale and projecting a sense of exclusion that can hardly be counteracted – visually or otherwise – with contextualizing material of anything other than an equally monumental scale. Standing in their shadow for any amount of time suggests the inadequacy of scholarly representation, the limits of landscape, and the powerful phenomenological impact of an object designed to project its meaning out into and beyond its surroundings. Refiguring our material readings of what we have long called landscape can help us form a material culture practice that works at the intersections of the immaterial and material, the past and the present, the symbolic and the actual.

Place helps make the material world. As the old maxim has it, events (and things) *take place*. But this all-encompassing theorization of place and the material world threatens to obliterate much of its lived realities. The outgrowth of the spatial turn has seen a multidisciplinary move toward theories of place divorced from the quotidian, the practiced, the minute and overlooked. An embrace of the materiality of place in the world can move us back toward a subtler and smaller-scale place that embraces at once the world-spanning and the microscopic. This is deeply tied to the long project of understanding what we have most often called landscape in material culture studies. Our attempts to complicate the physical environment through its entangled social, cultural, and political implications has been a process of unlearning the totalizing knowledges that is our inheritance from epistemologies of modernity. Place calls our attention to the performed and experienced, essential components both of making the material world and the subjects that live in it. As Dell Upton notes, "the self is always a self in space."[49] The act of place becoming is an act of transformation into a new selfhood located amid the material processes of the world. The material culture of place reminds us of these deep networks of mutuality, and the ways in which even the smallest things can make a world. This is paradoxically a way of widening the scope of material culture studies, and of returning us to our long-standing practices of observation, iteration, and repeated attempts to begin to understand the object worlds we inhabit.

Notes

1. Christian Norberg-Schulz, *Genius Loci: Towards a Phenomenology of Architecture* (New York: Rizzoli, 1980).
2. See J. B. Harley, "Deconstructing the Map," *Cartographica* 26, no. 2 (Spring 1989), 1–20. Harley's argument has been widely adopted in geography as well as its narrower subdisciplines and related fields like cartographic history. This article and its antecedents are often, if not widely, cited in other fields like history as well. But, as I suggest in this chapter, representation of geographic space continues to matter and indeed, even geographers themselves have been calling for a rematerialization of the field for the better part of two decades: Peter Jackson, "Rematerializing Social and Cultural Geography," *Social and Cultural Geography* 1, no. 1 (2000), 9–14.
3. Yi Fu Tuan, *Place and Space: The Perspective of Experience* (Minneapolis: University of Minnesota Press, 1977).
4. Jeff Malpas, "New Media, Cultural Heritage, and the Sense of Place: Mapping the Conceptual Ground," *International Journal of Heritage Studies* 14, no. 3 (May 2008), 201.
5. This of course means engaging with new theories of materiality as well, particularly those in science and technology studies and actor network theory as well as the literary and cultural studies inflected new materialists.
6. Jo Guldi, *What is the Spatial Turn?* (Charlottesville: Scholars Lab, University of Virginia Library, 2012). https://bit.ly/3r7Ak8K.
7. See David J. Bodenhamer, John Corrigan, and Trevor M. Harris, eds., *The Spatial Humanities: GIS and the Future of Humanities Scholarship* (Bloomington: Indiana University Press, 2010.) This collection both seeks to historicize the spatial turn and provide a series of case studies on new methods and approaches based on the application of spatial theory to geographic information systems.
8. Edward S. Casey, *The Fate of Place: A Philosophical History* (Berkeley: University of California Press, 1997).
9. Peter Jackson "Rematerializing Social and Cultural Geography," *Social and Cultural Geography* 1, no. 1 (2000), 9–14.
10. Material culture studies, particularly those by archaeologists, have recently engaged the idea of immateriality as part of the larger discourse on the relationship between objects and intangible heritage and culture. See for instance Elizabeth S. Chilton, "The Archaeology of Immateriality," *Archaeologies* 8, no. 3, (December 2012), 225–35 or the more recent theorization of Victor Buchli: Victor Buchli, *An Archaeology of the Immaterial* (New York: Routledge, 2016). Though work on immateriality specifically is more recent, scholars of material culture and particularly the built environment have long focused on the

relationships between presence and absence. See Bernard L. Herman, *The Stolen House* (Charlottesville: University of Virginia Press, 1992). This attention to the vanished, the unmade, the destroyed, or otherwise absent material objects has been more prominent in this field because of the size and scale of these objects which makes their presence, or at least traces of it, more enduring. Clearly this applies alike to archaeology and its focus on traces as an organizing principle. The utility of such an approach is perhaps not as evident in other kinds of material culture studies though equally vital to them.

11. Michel de Certeau, *The Practice of Everyday Life*, Steven F. Rendall, trans. (Berkeley: University of California Press, 1984), 108.
12. Daniel Miller, "Materiality: An Introduction," in Daniel Miller, ed., *Materiality* (Durham: Duke University Press: 2005), 10.
13. John Law "Objects and Spaces," *Theory, Culture, and Society*, 19 nos. 5–6 (2002), 96.
14. John Brinckerhoff Jackson, "The Word Itself," *Discovering the Vernacular Landscape*, (New Haven: Yale University Press, 1986), 5.
15. Jackson, "The Word Itself," 3.
16. W. J. T. Mitchell, "Imperial Landscape," in W. J. T. Mitchell, ed., *Landscape and Power* (Chicago: University of Chicago Press, 1994), 5–34.
17. Leo Marx, *The Machine in the Garden: Technology and the Pastoral Ideal* (Oxford: Oxford University Press, 1964).
18. Mitchell, "Imperial Landscape," 7.
19. Jill H. Casid, *Sowing Empire: Landscape and Colonization* (Minneapolis: University of Minnesota Press, 2005), xiv.
20. Casid, *Sowing Empire*, xxii.
21. See for instance Diane Harris and D. Fairchild Ruggles, *Sites Unseen: Landscape and Vision* (Pittsburgh: University of Pittsburgh Press, 2007).
22. Anthony D. King, "The Politics of Vision," in Paul Groth and Todd Bressi, ed., *Understanding Ordinary Landscapes* (New Haven: Yale University Press, 1997), 135.
23. William Cronon, "The Trouble with Wilderness; or, Getting Back to the Wrong Nature," in William Cronon, ed., *Uncommon Ground: Rethinking the Human Place in Nature* (New York: W. W. Norton, 1995), 69–90.
24. On the importance of Kniffen to vernacular material culture studies see John Michael Vlach, "Fred B. Kniffen's Milestones in American Folklife Study," *The Journal of American Folklore* 108, no. 429 (Summer, 1995), 328–33.
25. Kniffen's early, important work on house types in Louisiana provided the early vocabulary and object of study for vernacular landscape studies. Fred B. Kniffen, "Louisiana House Types," *Annals of the Association of American Geographers* 26, no. 4 (December 1936), 179–93. Kniffen best summarizes his own career with his 1965 presidential address to the Association of American Geographers: Fred B. Kniffen,

"Folk Housing: Key to Diffusion," *Annals of the Association of American Geographers* 55, no. 4 (December 1965), 549–77. Henry Glassie very consciously expanded Kniffen's projects with his first two books, bringing a material culture approach to American folklore and folklife studies and broadening the type and scale of objects that Americanist scholars studied. That he does not get more credit for this work outside the fields of folklore and vernacular architecture speaks to the disciplinary narrowing of the fields in subsequent decades. Henry Glassie, *Pattern in the Material Folk Culture of the Eastern United States* (Philadelphia: University of Pennsylvania Press, 1971); Henry Glassie, *Folk Housing in Middle Virginia: A Structural Analysis of Historic Artifacts* (Knoxville: University of Tennessee Press, 1976.)

26. Peter Merriman, George Revill, Tim Cresswell, Hayden Lorimer, David Matless, Gillian Rose, and John Wylie, "Landscape, Mobility, Practice," *Social & Cultural Geography* 9, no. 2 (2008), 194.

27. Tim Cresswell, "Landscape and the Obliteration of Practice," in Kay Anderson, Mona Domosh, Steve Pile, and Nigel Thrift, eds., *Handbook of Cultural Geography* (London: Sage, 2003), 269.

28. I make the distinction between public and civic space here as that split (between land that served in some official governmental capacity, i.e., a courthouse square, versus land made accessible to the public but not necessarily owned by the people) was heightened during these decades. Indeed, part of the contestation over Confederate memorials revealed these distinctions as well as the complicity of governments in allowing places belonging equally to the entire polis to be permanently occupied by the symbols of a particularly isolating form of material ideology.

29. In particular see W. Fitzhugh Brundage, *The Southern Past: A Clash of Race and Memory* (Cambridge: Belknap Press of Harvard University Press, 2008) and Karen L. Cox, *Dixie's Daughters: The United Daughters of the Confederacy and the Preservation of Confederate Culture* (Gainesville: University Press of Florida, 2003).

30. "Contract for Oxford Confederate Monument Awarded," *Charlotte Observer*, March 13, 1909.

31. "Laying of the Corner Stone of Confederate Monument," *Oxford Public Ledger*, May 7, 1909.

32. Edward L. Conn, "Confederate Monument Dedicated," *Cornerstone of Confederate Monument Laid* (Oxford: Orphanage Press, 1910), 8.

33. Conn, "Confederate Monument Dedicated," 9.

34. D. G. Brummitt, "Address of Acceptance by D. G. Brummitt," *Cornerstone of Confederate Monument Laid* (Oxford: Orphanage Press, 1910), 15. 50. "[Governor Kitchin]," *Cornerstone of Confederate Monument Laid* (Oxford: Orphanage Press, 1910), 21.

35. Ibid.

36. Despite their ubiquity, relatively little has actually been written about Emancipation Day celebrations. Mitch Kachun has the broadest

overview of these and other "festivals of freedom" during the late nineteenth and early twentieth centuries: Mitchell Kachun, *Festivals of Freedom: Memory and Meaning in African American Emancipation Celebrations, 1808–1915* (Amherst: University of Massachusetts Press, 2003). And Kathleen Clark likewise writes about Emancipation Day celebrations, but generally only in relation to an emergent African American political class: Kathleen Clark, *Defining Moments: African American Commemoration & Political Culture in the South, 1863–1913* (Chapel Hill: University of North Carolina Press, 2005). For my purposes here, both accounts largely leave out the spatial and material implications of these celebrations, though large processions through a variety of urban spaces were the centerpiece of virtually every town's commemoration. For a sense of the scale of these memorializations, albeit in a single state, see my "Visualizing Emancipation Day," http://elijahgaddis.com/visualizing-emancipation.

37. "Celebrate Emancipation Day," *Oxford Public Ledger*, January 7, 1910.
38. Ibid.
39. Ibid.
40. Interview with Judge and Ellie Chavis by James Eddie (James Edward) McCoy, May 15, 1981 Q-0121, in the Southern Oral History Program Collection #4007, Southern Historical Collection, Wilson Library, University of North Carolina at Chapel Hill.
41. Interview with William Henry Daniel by James Eddie (James Edward) McCoy, September 4, 1981 Q-0012, in the Southern Oral History Program Collection #4007, Southern Historical Collection, Wilson Library, University of North Carolina at Chapel Hill; Interview with Mary W. Harris by James Eddie (James Edward) McCoy, September 9, 1981 Q-0053, in the Southern Oral History Program Collection #4007, Southern Historical Collection, Wilson Library, University of North Carolina at Chapel Hill.
42. This event is detailed in Tim Tyson's book: Timothy Tyson, *Blood Done Sign My Name: A True Story* (New York: Crown Publishers, 2004).
43. Tyson, *Blood Done Sign My Name*, 6.
44. "Granville County Confederate Monument, Oxford," *Commemorative Landscapes of North Carolina*, https://docsouth.unc.edu/commland/monument/17/.
45. Derek H. Alderman, "Martin Luther King Jr. Streets in the South: A New Landscape of Memory," *Southern Cultures* 14, no. 3 (Fall, 2008), 88–105.
46. Some Oxford Residents Want Confederate Statue Moved," *WRAL.com*, 19 June 2009. www.wral.com/news/local/story/5397408/.
47. *Whose Heritage? Public Symbols of the Confederacy* (Montgomery: Southern Poverty Law Center, June 2018). https://bit.ly/3raPk64.
48. Connor Sheets, "New Confederate Memorial Unveiled in Alabama," *AL.com*, August 27, 2017. https://bit.ly/2ZlUikI.
49. Dell Upton, "Sound as Landscape," *Landscape Journal* 26, no. 1 (2007), 24.

20
Home and Domesticity

Psyche Williams-Forson

In US contexts, home tends to refer to one's residence and where one makes sense of their social and cultural space. The physical space varies and may include anywhere from an enslaved dwelling, tenement house, dugout, barn, or boardinghouse, to an apartment, townhouse, single-family dwelling, and so on. Moreover, it may be located in a rural, suburban, or urban locale. The concept of house and home has always been a contested topic that scholars from a number of disciplines have approached and studied using a range of methodological approaches including, but not limited to, feminism, Marxism, psychoanalysis, structuralism, and literary criticism.

Domesticity is an ideological way of ordering one's space materially as informed by ideas of gender, race, socioeconomic class, labor, culture, family, and more. In short, it was and is a middle-class construct used by white people (especially women) to exert and uphold power structures and ideals of American exceptionalism. Anyone outside the visage of white heterogeneity had to prove their worth and conform to these principles to be considered an American citizen. This was especially the case for women, specifically, and people of color, more generally. For white women, domesticity was a marker of superiority; consequently, "good" and "bad" housekeeping was believed to define one's morality and access to the American ideal. This doctrine of separate spheres essentially held that the public sphere, or the world of the marketplace, was the domain of men who were able to freely move outside the home to participate in public life. In contrast, the private sphere of the home was dominated by women, who not only took care of household matters but also bore the responsibility of transmitting cultural and moral values to the children.

While the trope of the separate spheres may have always been an ideal, the reality was more multidimensional. For one, most African American, Latina, and Asian American women have always worked outside the home. Most African American women, for example, were ensnared by enslavement and thus never had the option of choosing to remain in the home *or* to work in the public sphere. Even free women and urban middle-class activists such as Maria W. Stewart, Nannie Helen Boroughs, Sojourner Truth, Frances Harper, Ida B. Wells-Barnett, and Mary Church Terrell lived precarious lives making it necessary for their public activism to overlap with their private activities as they advocated on behalf of their enslaved and working-class sisters.

The dichotomy of private/public is further troubled by the overlapping realities of reliance. While there was (and often continues to be) a belief and ideal that the accomplishments of men were achieved in isolation and thus non-constitutive, the reality belies a power dynamic wherein the hegemony of the public success exists and thrives most often because women, from the home, provide the support and care that is needed. In truth, the spheres reinforce and overlap with one another.

The Material Culture of Domesticity

The material culture of domesticity in America is multilayered and complex inasmuch as it is tied to historical discourses on gender, race, and class as well as housekeeping and domestic space. Underpinned by a world in which gender and race differentiated what constituted a proper domestic sphere, the ideology of female domesticity has shifted and changed to fit prevailing beliefs about women in society. It has been argued that this ideal is rooted in concepts of subordination. Consequently, women are perceived to be participating in their own subjection when they seek not only to achieve this ideal but also to perfect it.

The desire to achieve domestic perfection through consumer culture has often made many middle and upper-class women willing to support conditions that keep other women – especially women of color – disadvantaged. This is due in no small part to the economic and political advantages that disguise and mostly outweigh the impact of the greater inequities and inequalities. For some women, who are racially and economically privileged, this ideology helps to reinforce women's inferiority especially when socially legitimate household responsibilities are defined. Simultaneously, for those without the same social privileges, achieving the domestic ideal contributes to equitable domestic and public power relations, and demonstrations of personal integrity, commitment, and hard work.

A central pervasive theme in domestic material culture is citizenship. Emphasizing this argument, Stacey Lynn Camp writes, "Throughout the course of American history, what people do and do not purchase and consume has served as a cornerstone of citizenship and marker of American identity."[1] People have always used goods to claim elements of belonging despite the fact that this was not necessarily their original use. Over time, different groups have used material things to create their own definitions of what it means to belong in American society. For Camp, citizenship is much more fluid than we are led to believe; it is "a process rather than a static, legal state of being." By attending to Renato Rosaldo's "vernacular notions of citizenship," Camp maintains that we are able to understand how and why those considered outside of the mainstream "choose or not choose to adopt certain behaviors and goods expected of American citizens." By studying these practices, we are able to understand the flexibility of citizenship and how the material work centrally factors therein. Yet, even within these various groups there is not always consensus or agreement on what objects or practices constitute successful enjoyment of belonging. Rather, all groups are heterogeneous and so are their practices. Thus, adoption of particular material goods and practices does not necessarily indicate group consensus and not all marginalized individuals equate consumption with the successful achievement of belonging. Thus, studying the material furnishings of one's home equally reveals the conditions of labor – paid and unpaid – that lead to the acquisitions, whether through purchasing, gifting, or bartering.

Further, studying the roles of foods in families and the ways they were acquired and prepared over time lets us see the ways that families practiced traditions and behaviors – old and new – that suited their definitions of what it means to be American. Foods became a major target for reform at the turn of the twentieth century. They became a way to demarcate proper practices of good citizenship. African Americans, whose entry into the United States was forced, found themselves modifying, adapting, and creating a host of culinary practices that has left an indelible imprint on American foods. Other groups had challenges as well. Hasia Diner explores this dynamic in *Hungering for America* where she tells the stories of three distinctive groups – Italian, Irish, and East European Jewish immigrants – who modified and adapted their food practices in America to better suit both their communities and their newfound sense of belonging.[2] Elizabeth Englehardt details Appalachian residents who resisted "the timeclock that industrialization introduced" by insisting upon continuing to garden and forage, despite being able to purchase various foods in canned form.[3]

In all, the domestic world is intricately tied to citizenship and belonging. Studying the domestic world through our material engagements not only reveals how we define what it is to be American but also the struggles we encounter in doing so.

Victorian Era Domesticity and Material Culture

In March 1903, Black Women's Club Movement activist Alberta Moore Smith wrote in the *Colored American Magazine*, "The home, which is the citadel of all truths, influences the lives of the better class of these people, and all that love, education, culture, and a comfortable salary can give, abides within their homes." Writing several years earlier in 1897, American minister and sociologist Charles Richmond Henderson wrote, "the dwellings, the walls, the windows, the furniture, the pictures, the ornaments, the dress, the fence or hedge – all act constantly upon the imagination and determination of its contents." Henderson shared what a wide range of white Americans believed while Smith extolled the virtues of Black women's ability to make good citizens with a good home. Both wrote of the moral implications of objects and nowhere was this more apparent than in the late-nineteenth and early twentieth centuries.

At the dawn of the twentieth century, the home in its physical and ideological senses merged as a place of refuge from the rapid changes in American society for many. Considered the vanguard of consumer society, this period of mass consumption was simultaneously a time of rapid social, political, and cultural change and a time of abundance. Shifts such as Asian immigration and African American freedom brought a great sense of nervousness to white Americans. Mass-produced goods and commodities often were used in an effort to alleviate some of the distress caused by these transformations. Objects were particularly useful for helping individuals contemplate the "possession of an emotional condition, a social circumstance, even an entire lifestyle" by making desires concrete.[4] The utmost desire was to differentiate whiteness from Irish immigrants and African Americans, Asians, and Mexican Americans and to express class superiority through a series of genteel performances. At a time when these latter groups were excluded from civil and social participation, objects took on political significance. A robust print and visual culture involving conduct and etiquette books, domestic manuals, newspaper columns, novels, paintings, sermons, and more reinforced the ways in which Victorians were concerned with unifying the material, spiritual, philosophical, and political dimensions of home and private life.

And, contrary to what studies indicate, this period of consumption was not experienced solely by white elites. Rather, the "domestic ideal" was experienced across racial, ethnic, regional, class, and gender lines, albeit differently. As Amy Ritcher notes, "Despite the initial association of the Victorian domestic ideal with the private lives of the white, native-born bourgeoisie, it crossed lines of race, ethnicity, class, and region, reshaping personal, political, and economic landscapes over the course of the century."[5]

For the rising middle classes, numerous factors served as barriers to preventing the masses from entering privileged elite circles. Racially, during this time, the meaning of material symbolism was whiteness just as the middle class served as the standard bearer for tastes and behaviors and served as the audience for most advice manuals and popular magazines. Consequently, social and material meanings of objects should be interpreted against this backdrop. Some scholars, for example, have considered knickknacks or bric-a-brac like figurines, statuary, and other mass-produced objects of modest cost for the complex meanings they conveyed to those who owned them.

And the home was the site of performance and display because women were expected to tether themselves to the space and place. The atmosphere of the home was seen as having "an almost mystical effect on its inhabitants, determining their moral standards, happiness and success in the outside world."[6] Guidebooks and other forms of popular reading material reinforced the ways in which women were supposed to keep beautiful, clean, and orderly homes. Decoration was linked to order, virtue, and morality. Rooms and furnishings were imbued with symbolism to convey a variety of messages about status, comportment, and proper living (Figure 20.1). Urban historian Cindy Lobel maintains, "The rise of the middle-class dining room [for example] coincided with the prescriptive idealization of the domestic sphere as a cloistered haven, a private shelter devoid of the crassness and dangers of the public sphere of politics and business."[7] Consequently, to have an identifiable living room not only indicated performing domesticity in a proper fashion but also signaled class identification.

While most American homes were small, consisting of only two rooms, more monied dwellings had multiple levels with many rooms. But, overall, the sentiment was that proper morality was best transmitted and

Figure 20.1 Kitchen with ornate stove and dishes. Irma and Paul Milstein Division of United States History, Local History and Genealogy, The New York Public Library. The New York Public Library Digital Collections. 1902–14. https://on.nypl.org/3lVXnQz.

Figure 20.2 Front parlor. Courtesy of the Heurich House Museum

embodied in the house design, its furnishings, and women's domestic roles. And while decorating advice changed over time, when Edith Wharton wrote *The Decoration of Houses*, she called for symmetry, balance, and tastefulness represented by fewer "stuffed furnishings and wall hangings." Many early Victorian rugs represented the Middle East and window coverings were inspired by Asian design and made of silk or velvet in deep red or gold. The rooms appeared dark largely due to less lighting. But, by the end of the nineteenth century more residents were using floral wallpaper and window valances. Furniture was made of dark wood like mahogany and the upholstery was brocade, chenille, and damask, usually in mauve, red, and green. Heavy throw pillows are an excellent example of such design in an accessory. By century's end, furniture was more modern and lighter in construction, less bulky and more portable. Parlors and dining rooms are examples of domestic spaces that underwent rapid change. (Figure 20.2 and 20.3.)

The Parlor and Other Rooms

According to historian Katherine Grier, for Victorian Americans, the parlor was one of the most elaborately decorated spaces in the home, but it was equally often one of the most inconsequential. Like the twenty-first century "great room" where some entertaining and family time occurs, in the

Figure 20.3 Dining room. Courtesy of the Heurich House Museum

early twentieth century, the parlor was a space for the display of social performances exemplifying largesse and/or social striving. Grier explains, "Parlor-making families were participants in a rapidly commercializing world in which readily available goods – center tables, window draperies, and sets of matching chairs – could make manifest core cultural ideals that were, supposedly, timeless and beyond the reach of transient consumer tastes ... parlors were settings that allowed Victorian Americans to represent themselves as full participants in their world."[8]

The parlor was a relatively complicated space because it was a social arena of class performance and theater, filled with the latest that technology and industrialization had to offer. Stimulated initially by the increase in commercial parlors, Grier indicates, it was also a space where the tensions between culture (the practice of gentility) and comfort (family-centered values) were fully exhibited. In the upholstered chairs, tapestries, draperies, tables, and ornamentation was the suggestion of civilized behavior. The physical form and style of this decor, along with the design and textiles, helped to balance the tensions between self-aggrandizement and family contentment. But the rules governing how one was to behave in the parlor – refined and practicing good manners – meant that the needed furniture had to reinforce these practices.

In addition to the parlor, other rooms in the home including hallways and dining rooms, as well as objects such as organs, pianos, center tables, cardstands, sideboards, hallstands, needlework, carpeting, drapery, and textiles had a range of meanings in the Victorian era and thus influenced the meanings of home for white Americans. The dining room, for example, became a necessary space in middle-class homes. While the elite seemingly have always had a space dedicated for dining, the concept of "a dining room" was a novelty. Lobel indicates that "the creation of the dining room involved a huge investment in the public sphere. Consumer items like dining furniture, carpets, textiles, decorations, dishes, silver plate, and other dining accoutrements became de rigueur in middle-class homes and middle-class homemakers modeled their dining rooms and kitchens after the commercial kitchens and dining rooms proliferating in the cities of antebellum America."[9] (Figure 20.4.)

By the early twentieth century, however, the popularity of the parlor began to wane even as dining rooms remained as smaller living spaces, changing influences in the domestic realm, and discretionary spending all began to shift how consumers viewed the usefulness of the space. Museum curator Bradley Brooks maintains that stylistically, domestic interiors also began to shift as the century got underway and mass culture became the order of the day. Due to newer trends in architecture and art shifting toward modernity and with the proliferation of decorating and advice manuals the look of many American homes followed suit. There was less clutter and heavy fabrics, and more simplicity, balance, and harmony brought by muted tones, brighter lighting, and furniture placement. All these conversations in style also dictated what was considered good taste. These new rooms were to articulate less stylistic diversity in an effort to achieve unity.[10]

Progressive era reformers were central to conveying these principles of unity and harmony. Under the guise of campaigns promoting American

Figure 20.4 Biertstube. Courtesy of the Heurich House Museum

exceptionalism and uplifting the masses, they implemented social reforms that sought to transform the home into experiments of social and cultural improvement. Within homes and in communities, messages were conveyed through housekeeping manuals, domestic science classes, and settlement houses that middle-class standards and styles were the order of the day.

American homes in the past, like today, served a variety of functions and incorporated many activities, from performing one's status to everyday activities like eating, drinking, and sleeping. And these rooms took on changing meanings and significance. For example, while the dining room becomes an important site for the performance of social class, the rituals and behaviors, the implements and eating utensils used are of equal significance. For example, in *Ambitious Appetites: Dining, Behavior, and Patterns of Consumption in Federal Washington*, Barbara Carson's study on early social life in Washington, DC, emphasizes this point. Writing from the standpoint of the material culture of social ritual, Carson gives a great deal of attention to the use of tableware like forks, spoons, knives, butter pats, gravy bowls, and other tableware to explore social interactions and the ways in which they revealed gender, race, and class disparities. Moreover, her work on families of the Federalist era introduces how these aspirational concepts of the early republic, like respectability and gentility, demarcated the separation of public and private spheres, participation in civilized society, and the differences in the ways race intersects with gender, class, sexuality, religious affiliation, and other similar identifiers. Thus, studying mealtimes and meal structures, including the actual foods that were eaten, when they were eaten, how they were prepared, and by whom provides a great deal of information about household management, commerce and trade, the roles of individual members of a household, as well as the nutritive value of a range of foods. Such an analysis can go far to dispel myths of "typical" kinds of meals eaten.

Working-Class Domesticity

While scholarship in archaeology and American studies has unearthed rich new ground in domestic material culture by exploring ephemera such as photographs, film, and women's writings, as well as reexamining probate records and other documents through new lenses, the data still tends to skew toward the urban middle class and upper echelon of society. That is not to say, however, that those outside monied confines did not decorate their domestic settings. Indeed, they did and future conversations on domestic interiors would benefit immensely by examining the working class, Native American, Latina, Asian, and African Americans homes for what they reveal about their social and cultural identities.

In the essay, "Embellishing a Life of Labor: An Interpretation of the Material Culture of American Working-Class Homes, 1885–1915," historian Lizbeth Cohen discusses the domestic lives of working-class urban white Americans wherein "working-class material culture was distinctive or part of a larger cultural system." Cohen details the social histories of working-class urbanites who sought to make their dwellings a home. In addition to the external pressures from middle-class women's organizations, Cohen explicates how industries and companies participated in communicating what was considered "proper" values. They often did this through the provision of welfare programs, company housing, employee lounges, recreation, and eating spaces. An example includes the factory and mills dormitories for the girls in New England and elsewhere. Cohen explains, "Interiors promoted the specialization of rooms in an effort to discourage the taking in of boarders and to enforce a middle-class pattern of living revolving around parlor, kitchen, dining room, and bedrooms. Some companies offered employees welfare programs which also affirmed middle-class domestic standards."[11] While some embraced the efforts of reformers, who sought to promote these values and styles, many others rejected these edicts and instructions that called for painted instead of wallpapered walls, shelving versus sideboards, and few pictures in particular rooms, in favor of their own definitions of comfort and style.[12]

As more of the working class either bought homes or rented spaces, they manipulated their interior spaces to suit what was necessary for their own enjoyment and practicality. For example, where middle-class denizens might allocate certain rooms for particular uses, many working-class people saw no need for such separations. Kitchens, for example, then like now, often served as communal spaces where not only cooking occurred but family members and friends would also gather to socialize and even to stay warm during cold nights. Those who persisted in having a parlor were perceived by reformers to be giving a nod to middle-class habits and conduct. Yet, though a parlor was present in the home, it was not necessarily used in the same way. For example, for some this room in the working-class home doubled as a sleeping space; the dining room doubled as a space for hanging laundry or sewing; and the kitchen was the primary space where meals were eaten. The home was an insular space, not one used for miscellaneous entertaining. Thus, it was a true reflection of the separation of public and private spheres. Cohen concludes:

> Whereas the middle-class home provided a setting for a wide range of complex interactions related to work, family and community, and therefore required distinctions between private and public space, workers conceived of home as a private realm distinct from the public world. Because workers only invited close friends and family inside, the kitchen provided an appropriate setting for most exchanges. Relationships with more distant acquaintances took place in the

neighborhood – on the street or within shops, saloons or churches. The transference of these traditional patterns of socializing from an intimate pre-industrial community to the city had the impact of increasing the isolation of the working-class home.[13]

It was not only physical spaces that were subject to the "parlorization" or persistent belief in middle-class values. Food was also subject to such influence by reformers of the settlement movement. Cultural historian Elizabeth Engelhardt details how foods like cornbread and wild greens came under scrutiny by reformers as they were considered basic, lacking in civility and nutrients. These foods, which were easy to cook and to obtain, were considered poverty foods in need of improvement, change, and substitution. In 1902, Katherine Pettit and May Stone founded the Hindman Settlement School in eastern Kentucky and began the campaign "to civilize" the locals by emphasizing that wheat-based breads, like beaten biscuits and soda biscuits, instead of cornbread, become the staple in Appalachian households. While Pettit and Stone considered biscuits a domestic achievement, they were considered a more arduous and time-consuming food to make because they had to be leavened by hand through the beating process. Moreover, biscuits required more specialized equipment – a rolling pin, biscuit cutters, an oven, and the like – making it a much more expensive accompaniment. Meanwhile, cornbread required corn meal, water, maybe some flavoring, and a hot skillet. A more tasty and affordable side for people already struggling to make ends meet.

Biscuits not only were considered by reformers to be a "more healthful, appropriate and civilized alternative," but also a conduit to morality because the cooking process was "cleaner."[14] Wild greens suffered the similar fate. Fresh greens, though perhaps healthier because they had not undergone the processing of commercial canning, were considered dirtier than those that had been processed in the factory. Picking greens was an activity that could be done on one's own time, by either men or women, from anywhere that the leaves could be found. Rather than purchasing canned greens, Appalachian citizens expressed their preference for picking greens from overgrown, empty lots and fields as their time allowed.

Interestingly, white women also subjected Native American women to evolutionary progress reforms; white bread is a good example. In *Making Home Work: Domesticity and Native American Assimilation in the American West, 1860–1919*, Jane E. Simonsen provides one example that occurred in the trans-Mississippi West. Like Appalachian women, some Native women refused white domestication in favor of their own strategies for creating a home that affirmed their indigenous identities. Simonsen argues that "domestic imperialism was mediated not only by gender and race hierarchies but by economics, material conditions and class divisions." Simonsen explains how Native women pushed back against progressive reforms to define their homeplace as they liked. In their model homes with their pine floors and cook stoves, they continued to practice traditional customs. And they used such objects as scrub brushes, needle and other artisanal work, as well as white bread to reinforce how they saw themselves participating in American culture. Using the advocacy work of the Women's National Indian Association, Simonsen illustrates the meanings and responses to ideas of home and women's work and how race, class, and cultural meaning were often on display as the debates surrounding domestic life and citizenship were increasingly in conflict. White middle-class domestic ideals were upheld as "civilized" against the "savage" domestic practices of Native women. In Simonsen's study is a convincing argument that making a "home" was directly connected to nation building, the American expansionist endeavor, and racial hierarchies.

These insights into working-class domestic interiors speak to larger social and cultural changes in America. These discussions are multilayered with most studies providing a glimpse into different and varying ways in which homemaking was carried out. The American boardinghouse, for instance, was exemplar of a dwelling in which multiple people shared living arrangements and thus social and cultural changes were frequent. Boardinghouses made it possible for women to travel to urban environments to seek employment and other opportunities. In addition to offering a space for social mixing, boardinghouses served as a welcome source of income for women and men of all races.

For African Americans, boardinghouses provided income-generating opportunities when other economic doors were closed as a result of racial discrimination. Writing at the turn of the twentieth century, African American journalist, playwright, historian, and editor Pauline Hopkins penned the influential novel, *Contending Forces*. The central location of the story is a lodging house owned by African American widow, Mrs. Smith. Smith lives in the home with her young adult children.[15] The novel provides readers with details from the furnishings, to the foods, and activities – social, cultural, political – that take place in the house. On any given Sunday, for example, Ma Smith's boardinghouse is filled with guests and boarders eating all kinds of good foods from sandwiches to sherbet and cake with hot chocolate. While eating, the house residents, boarders, and other guests discuss many of the political issues affecting African Americans at the time. Hopkins takes great pains to focus on how the private house, and especially the African American parlor, was the center not only for social gatherings but also specifically for important public affairs and women's political engagement.

Though Hopkins creates a fictional event, it resonates with real life occurrences. During the Colored Conventions Movement,[16] for instance, boardinghouses provided a safe place to stay when other spaces were not offered. Not only did these lodging spaces provide access to a communal social life, they also enabled many African Americans to function and survive in inhospitable environments. Fugitive slaves, for example, could rely upon these spaces to offer critical information about where and how they could move about freely and/or evade trouble while learning to navigate their new environment.

Delving into the domesticity of African American boardinghouses offers a window into understanding the ways in which domestic spaces enabled Black women to demonstrate forms of social activism. Food played an important role in the Colored Conventions Movement and by studying committee reports, local boardinghouse advertisements, menus, and other ephemera we can learn more about the types of food provided during and after convention meetings. Regardless of the actual housing or lodging setting, the decision to serve guests certain foods and dishes during convention times allowed Black women to express agency because many of these hosts were cognizant of the relationship between commensality and politics. Consequently, food selection offered Black women an indirect means to express their political viewpoints. These boardinghouse spaces became precursors to those African Americans (mostly women) who hosted rent parties and other social activities in their homes during the Civil Rights Movement and under the pretense of such events used the opportunity to register African Americans to vote.

An example is Georgia Gilmore, one of many African American women who used their homes to feed participants and fund the Montgomery bus boycott. Gilmore's group, the Club from Nowhere, was so named in order to protect the identities of those who aided the resistance. They prepared meals such as fried chicken sandwiches, fried fish, pork chops, greens, lima beans as well as a variety of baked goods (peach pie, poundcakes) and sold them out of their homes, in churches and other local businesses and organizations as well as at protest meetings.[17] This organized effort was one of many that helped sustain and maintain the fight for civil rights.

New Directions in Domestic Material Culture

The varying social, cultural, and historical meanings of domesticity remind us that houses and dwellings are by their nature contested spaces that embody social, cultural, and political life. The public and private spheres come together, overlapping in ways that cause conflict, even as they attempt to pacify. The material artifacts, while being used to decorate, also illustrate work, labor, material conditions, and national concerns. Much of the work done to date has contributed to broadening our understanding of these dynamics, but more is needed.

In his landmark study, *No Place Like Home: Relationships and Family Life among Lesbians and Gay Men*, Christopher Carrington probes the domestic lives of "lesbigay" couples to document how they perform what constitutes family activities in American society. Using a range of methodologies including questionnaires, ethnography, and participant observation, Carrington details the hidden work of labor and caring in same-gender loving households as similar to that of heterosexual families. In a thorough examination of the various components of family domesticity – feeding (including paying attention to ingredients present or lacking, shopping for what is needed, planning and executing meals, and cleaning), and other kinds of consumption work (acquiring material goods and services), housework, and kin work, we are reminded of the hidden labors of family maintenance. He concludes that regardless of the family makeup, domestic labor is still gendered, often hidden, and more often devalued. Yes, Carrington explains, "my analysis does not conceive of domesticity as a great unpleasantness that the person with more resources (e.g., income, prestige and education) forces on the person with fewer. Such a view reduces domesticity to its unpleasant aspects and conceals its attractive ones, therein leaving us with no convincing explanation of why some people prefer, and orient themselves toward, domesticity." For example, Carrington found that while many lesbigay professionals keep their public personas separate from their private lives, those who entertain in their homes do so a great deal. And the burden of preparing the house for guests tends to fall on the partner who is perceived to have the "less powerful" or "less important" career outside the home, despite insistence that the division of labor is equitable.[18]

What of the domestic lives of US Latinx peoples, for instance? Marci R. McMahon's *Domestic Negotiations: Gender, Nation, and Self-Fashioning in US Mexicana and Chicana Literature and Art* illustrates, through fiction and art, some of the domestic practices by US women of Mexican descent from the twentieth and twenty-first centuries. Focusing on Mexicana and Chicana writers and artists, McMahon provides a lens through which we see how domestic space is used "to negotiate the domestic/foreign, white/nonwhite, and legal/illegal binaries that have sought to exclude their communities from belonging in the US nation."[19] From a discussion of clothing to food, McMahon resists binaries of resistance and submission in her object analysis and instead works through the nuances and complications of dominant ideologies of domesticity to reveal how Mexicana and Chicana writers and artists both challenge and reify the norms that inform domestic negotiations.

Food and kitchenscapes are also at the center of Meredith Abarca's *Voices in the Kitchen: Views of Food and the World from Working-Class Mexican and Mexican American Women* and Maria Christie's *Kitchenscape: Women, Fiestas and Everyday Life in Central Mexico*. Food is more than satiety and kitchens are for more than eating. Through *charlas culinarias* (culinary chats) with her mother, female relatives, family friends, and a professional chef, Abarca explains the range of domestic negotiations that take place in Latina households. More than drudgery alone, or a space of racial, class, and patriarchal oppression, for Mexican American women cooking serves a variety of functions from affirming one's identity to empowering through creativity, economic opportunity, and binding kinships.

Similarly, in *Kitchenscape*, Christie details the ways in which house-lot gardens, carnitas, tamales, mole, and other foods, many of which form the culinary bedrock for fiestas, are symbols of how the public and private merge. These foods reveal how "changing cultural identities are negotiated, re-created and celebrated as 'tradition' is continually redefined."[20] In the kitchen space, Mexican women demonstrate the control they have in the community. Christie explains, "inside the home, kitchens are not community spaces. It is there that individual women assert control over their world ... men listen to women ... women tell their stories over and over to each other, to their children, perhaps to themselves."[21] In these spaces, corn and beans, along with tortillas and chilies, are central to the menu.

Building from Brett William's 1975 classic essay, "Why Migrant Women Feed their Husbands Tamales: Foodways as a Basis for a Revisionist View of Tejano Family Life," these books further the discussion of the dynamics of class, gender, race, ethnicity, region, and food. In some of these communities where gender roles are not only clearly demarcated but also starkly performed, Williams, Abarca, and Christie (in their respective contexts) dissect the larger physical, emotional, and cultural meanings of food shared between and among real and fictive kin. In these studies, the focus is on women, yet not at the exclusion of men. In Williams's discussion of the cooking process, for example, "buying the pig's head, stripping the meat, cooking the mash, preparing the paste, and stuffing, wrapping, and baking, or boiling the final tamale," we learn more about how working-class Tejano women negotiate labor, intimacy, and family.[22] In many instances, we learn that in culinary preparations the roles of men are integral, though not necessarily equal, to that of the women. Focusing on domestic labor both in and outside the home for migrant Tejano women, Williams encourages us to be more expansive in our thinking about the ways in which various communities perform domesticity and the material conditions that aid and mitigate against it.

Food is ubiquitous, yet useful for revealing performances of gender, race, and class but also citizenship. Because food and food practices serve as symbols of cultural and racial/ethnic identity they are thus used to index morality and respectability. For example, African American women who ran boardinghouses made it a point to emphasize to their clients when they offered the "finest" foods. Finest, in this context, means foods that were difficult to obtain or dishes that were elaborate to prepare (or those requiring a cookbook and measurements) – in short, beyond standard everyday eats. This might include a combination of beef soup, ham omelets, and Indian meal batter cake, all foods featured in the *Delaware County American* advertisement for Ms. Amie Long's boardinghouse. Because food practices have the ability to demarcate status based on affordability and knowledge they, along with other objects, serve as cultural lifestyle measurements for "national inclusion and exclusion as well as social prestige and hierarchy."[23] These objects serve as conveyors of the proper decorum and respectability; and one object that has been used across cultures to emphasize this practice is the piano.

The Material Culture of Domesticity: The Piano

Chrissy Yee Lau advances this and other arguments in her research on Japanese American respectability. Lau explores the affective agenda of Japanese immigrant elites in California to engage in ethnic uplift amid the oppressive and exclusionary immigration bans on Asian Americans (Yellow Peril) of the late nineteenth and early twentieth centuries. Against this racial civilizing agenda, she maintains that Japanese immigrant elite encouraged their own respectability projects – the reproduction of white middle-class standards – including the practice of "proper" gender roles, especially women's domesticity. One object that came to define this standard of respectability, domesticity, virtue, and luxury was the piano.

Like other ethnic and racial groups in America who found themselves being influenced and intruded upon by elite reformers, working-class Japanese Americans were recipients of similar practices of respectability politics. The Japanese Association of America (JAA) took pains to encourage working-class families to adopt middle-class attitudes and behaviors in their work and leisure activities to acquire a higher status and establish a place of respect among white America. In addition to trying to dissuade farm women from working in the fields and instead become housewives, they also hoped these women would adopt modern health standards and "nice furnishings" like the piano.[24] The piano was more than a symbol of leisure, refinement, and class, it was one of power. As Lu explains,

> high culture played an important role in the debates around citizenship and assimilability. Working-class Japanese Americans were accused of being dirty and thus not abiding by social and cultural rules. But middle-class Japanese Americans impressed upon white people the idea that they could assimilate and live together harmoniously ... If one was not physically white and wealthy, one could appear cultured by acting and expressing oneself as though one were white and middle class. Therefore, high culture became a way to bridge racial and economic differences.[25]

As Craig Roell indicates, the piano was a "cultural totem," the ultimate symbol of Western imperialism and Victorian values. As such it represented an investment in the moral fabric of American culture. As Roell suggests, the piano was a symbol of virtue, the moral dignity of productive work, self-expression, home, and family. It was "medicine for the soul" and because women were the cultural transmitters and conveyers of such virtue, they were closely aligned with the instrument.[26] To play the piano required discipline, perseverance, and sacrifice, making one's ability to do so more noble. Though its mass production and distribution enabled its acquisition across races and classes, symbolizing what Roell calls "a musical democracy," owning a piano placed one well above others in status.

Music and its supposed moral suasive powers had a major role in the domestic lives of many Americans – of all races. It was said to be a tool of uplift and transformation and a way to improve upon one's character and well-being. In the hands of women, playing a "premier instrument" like the piano went hand-in-hand with genteel womanhood. It is a symbol of middle-class values partly due to the discipline and perseverance needed to play but also the significance of these virtues to Victorian society. The piano and the chair, which required a straight back and upright posture, was an artifact that represented morality, uplift, prestige, and refinement. The piano was, therefore, symbolic among the general populace and among "the better class of people" in that it reflected "all that love, education, culture, and a comfortable salary can give." For women, the piano provided an occasion to display feminine accomplishment, respectability, and the Christian virtues of ladyhood.

This edict not only applied to immigrants and working-class whites but African Americans as well (Figure 20.5). Pauline Hopkin's novel *Contending Forces* offers an example of the importance of the piano in African American culture and life. Many of the citizens of Ms. Smith's boardinghouse attended the same space of worship where the women were active in the church's civic affairs; most of these at the turn of the twentieth century had an agenda of African American social and cultural liberation. During one church event we see how domesticity merges the public and private spheres when a fair was held to raise money to offset the church's mortgage.

The primary fundraiser of the fair was a raffle with the members selling the greatest number of tickets eligible to win prizes – a silver set, a gold watch and chain, a diamond pin, and of course, a piano. These items were so important to the competitors that one church member put a sideboard on lay-away in anticipation of her win. There were two top sellers. One had an opossum sent up from the south so she could make a stew to assist her in selling even more tickets. Despite her elaborate efforts, however, she did not win the competition. Hopkins's fictional account highlights the importance for some of practicing middle-class standards in an effort to counter many of the common prejudices against African Americans at that time. Hanna Wallinger argues that during Hopkins's time such an impression "served as proof of respectability, achievement and progress, all of which are virtues that needed to be defined and defended rather than taken for granted."[27] She further suggests that such attention "served as a reminder to [Hopkins's] white readers that African Americans could live in as much comfort [and style] as white people."

Paul Mullins contends along similar lines in his article "Race and the Genteel Consumer." Mullins states that African Americans like most Americans "were deeply attracted to the material self-determination and attendant citizen privileges promised by consumer culture." In this space, he goes on, "African Americans [were able] to articulate social aspirations and class struggle" all the while confronting racism and its

A MUSICAL REHEARSAL.

Figure 20.5 A musical rehearsal. Schomburg Center for Research in Black Culture, Jean Blackwell Hutson Research and Reference Division, The New York Public Library. The New York Public Library Digital Collections. 1914. https://on.nypl.org/3lPhYWl

accommodating implications.[28] But what should be at least somewhat apparent is a need for further probing into the ways in which particular material culture artifacts consumed and used by African Americans lend themselves to better understanding of the conflation of race, class, material culture, citizenship, and belonging.

Conclusion

The literature on American domesticity and material culture is continuously evolving. These interdisciplinary cultural analyses are important not only to material culture studies scholarship but also to a host of other disciplines that seek a deeper understanding of how the material world is intertwined with labor, consumer culture, citizenship, and belonging. The studies introduced here provide a starting point but as illustrated there is much more to be uncovered by delving into the lives of working-class, Native Americans, Latina Americans, Asian, and African Americans. Not only will we better understand those cultures, we will also recognize the common thread of seeking citizenship and belonging and the ways in which the material world reveals those struggles.

Notes

1. Stacey L. Camp, *The Archaeology of Citizenship* (Gainesville: University of Florida Press, 2013), 2.
2. Hasia Diner, *Hungering for America: Italian, Irish, and Jewish Foodways in the Age of Migration* (Oxford University Press, 1991).
3. Vive Griffith, "You Are What You Eat." December 1, 1999. https://perma.cc/ZT75-SDA8.
4. Grant McCracken's discussion is a good one on the ways in which consumer goods helped to preserve hopes and ideals during the Victorian era. Grant McCracken, "The Evocative Power of Things," in *Culture and Consumption: New Approaches to the Symbolic Character of Consumer Good and Activities* (Bloomington: Indiana University Press, 1988), 104–10.
5. Amy Richter, *At Home in Nineteenth-Century America: A Documentary History* (New York: New York University Press), 2.
6. Marilyn Motz and Pat Brown, *Middle-Class Women and Domestic Material Culture, 1840–1940* (Bowling Green: Bowling Green State University Popular Press, 1988), 1.
7. Cindy Lobel, "The Institution of the Household: Domesticity and Consumption in Antebellum New York City." Paper presented at the annual meeting of the American Studies Association Annual Meeting, Washington, DC, 2014, 11, 28. http://citation.allacademic.com/meta/p318141_index.html.
8. Katherine Grier, *Culture and Comfort: Parlor Making and Middle-Class Identity, 1850–1930* (Washington, DC: Smithsonian Books, 2010), viii.
9. Lobel, "The Institution of the Household."
10. Brooks, Bradley "Clarity, Contrasts, and Simplicity: Changes in American Interiors, 1880–1930," in Jessica H. Foy and Karal Ann Marling, eds., *The Arts and the American Home, 1890–1930* (Knoxville: University of Tennessee Press, 1994), 29.
11. Ibid, 758.
12. Lizabeth Cohen, "Embellishing a Life of Labor: An Interpretation of the Material Culture of American Working-Class Homes, 1885–1915," *Journal of American Culture* 3, no. 4 (Winter 1980), 756.
13. Ibid, 766.
14. Elizabeth Engelhardt, "Beating the Biscuits in Appalachia," in Sherrie A. Inness, ed., *Cooking Lessons: The Politics of Gender and Food* (Lanham: Rowman & Littlefield, 2001), 153.

15. Throughout her work – novels, short stories, and editorial contributions – Pauline Hopkins deeply engages history and, as an editor for the *Colored American Magazine*, print culture. See Pauline Hopkins, *Contending Forces*, Schomburg ed. (New York: Oxford University Press, 1991), 110 and see also Richard Yarborough, Introduction to this edition; Claudia Tate, *Domestic Allegories of Political Desire* (New York: Oxford University Press, 1992); and, P. Gabrielle Foreman, *Activist Sentiments* (Urbana: University of Illinois Press, 2009), for more on Hopkins' use of contemporaneous historical debates, historical figures, and locations.
16. The Colored Conventions Movement was a series of national, regional, and state meetings held irregularly during the decades preceding and following the American Civil War. https://coloredconventions.org/about-conventions/.
17. Klancy Miller, "Overlooked No More: Georgia Gilmore, Who Fed and Funded the Montgomery Bus Boycott." *New York Times*, July 31, 2019. https://nyti.ms/31OwGpY.
18. Christopher Carrington, *No Place Like Home* (Chicago: University of Chicago Press, 1999), 67–108, 188.
19. Marci R. McMahon, *Domestic Negotiations: Gender, Nation, and Self-Fashioning in United States Mexicana and Chicana Literature and Art* (New Brunswick: Rutgers University Press, 2013), 3–4.
20. Maria Christie, *Kitchenscape: Women, Fiestas and Everyday Life in Central Mexico* (Austin: University of Texas Press, 2008), 2.
21. Ibid, 3.
22. Brett Williams, "Why Migrant Women Feed Their Husbands Tamales: Foodways as a Basis for a Revisionist View of Tejano Family Life," in Linda Brown and Kay Mussell, eds., *Ethnic and Regional Foodways in the United States: The Performance of Group Identity* (Knoxville: University of Tennessee Press, 1984), 113.
23. Chrissy Yee Lau, "Loving Luxury: The Cultural Economy of the Japanese American Home, 1920s," Ph.D. dissertation, University of California, Santa Barbara, 2013, 10. https://bit.ly/31SfGiA.
24. Ibid, 33.
25. Ibid, 36–37.
26. Craig Roell, "The Piano in the American Home," in Jessica H. Foy and Karal Ann Marling, eds., *The Arts and the American Home 1890–1930* (Knoxville: University of Tennessee Press, 1994), 85.
27. Hanna Wallinger, *Pauline E. Hopkins: A Literary Biography* (Athens: University of Georgia Press, 2005), 158.
28. Paul Mullins, "Race and the Genteel Consumer: Class and African-American Consumption, 1850–1930" *Historical Archaeology* 33, no. 1 (1999), 22–38.

21

The Materiality of Institutional Life

Eleanor Conlin Casella and Linnea Kuglitsch

The institution is a modern entity so ubiquitous and historically important that "most (historical) archaeology throughout the Anglophonic world could be described as the archaeology of institutions."[1] Indeed, a rapidly growing body of archaeological scholarship has explored the modern institution in its many forms: prisons, schools, internment, and prisoner-of-war (POW) camps, alms- and workhouses, orphanages, asylums, and hospitals. Public or private, large or small, these various establishments existed for a shared purpose: to contain and reform – and in certain cases punish – those deemed to be criminal or deviant, elderly or young, sick, poor, or simply racially "different" from mainstream society.

From the mid-eighteenth century onward, these "total institutions," as sociologist Erving Goffman called them, offered tangible solutions to social disorder as industrialization, economic and political change, and increasing migration and social mobility disrupted civic traditions of the previous era. Through their physically isolated and intentionally designed landscapes, their stringently enforced rules, their stark differentiation of inmates and staff, and their choreographed daily rituals, modern institutions delivered a concentrated form of psycho-social transformation that differentiated them from other familiar establishments – households, playgrounds, churches, libraries, and other community organizations – that shaped everyday civic life.[2]

Institutions operate on many types of inhabitants. Prisons confine and punish the criminal. Schools and orphanages acculturate and educate students, preparing them for adult socioeconomic life. Hospitals care for and treat patients to either restore them to a state of mental and physical normalcy, or isolate their contagion to prevent its spread into a morally and medically healthy society. Workhouses discipline those who do not (or cannot) labor, exchanging their energy and effort for food and shelter. While the individuals subjected to these systems of institutional reform tend to be selected based on some immaterial aspect of their identity – their class, race, occupation, gender, age, perceived moral or physical well-being – the processes of institutional reform operate on a material dimension. What, therefore, would constitute a materiality of institutional life? How have archaeologists examined and defined these landscapes? Why do daily institutional operations crystallize into a built environment characterized by bodily discipline, deprivation, and regulation? And where do material narratives emerge for the people who lived and worked within these stark landscapes?

While an "institution" can be non-geographic (particularly in terms of social media and digital communities), this chapter ultimately explores material legacies of the modern institution through archaeological case studies drawn from Britain, North America, New Zealand, and Australia. First, we address penitentiaries and prisons. These carceral institutions focused on confining, punishing, and reforming the criminal. We then turn to archaeological investigations of institutions established for the care, education, and training of the young and the impoverished – the almshouses, asylums, schools, and orphanages established for treatment of the "deserving" unfortunate and uneducated. Our chapter ends with an overview of research focused on hospitals. These institutions were dedicated not only to treating injuries, infections, and diseases, but halting their spread throughout society. Approached together, these broad categories not only highlight the diverse archaeological literature on institutional worlds but emphasize the myriad ways in which deviance was understood, punished, and corrected in modern history.

Ultimately, this chapter demonstrates how elements of punishment, reform, cure, and care materially permeate the institutional landscape. These endeavors forged both architectural environments and lived spaces. They emerged through the archaeological remains of everyday activities – objects that ranged from sewing paraphernalia and tableware, to shop tools and uniform buttons. Enacted upon the criminal, the sick, the indigent, the vulnerable, and the unclean, these interventions all operated on an "intimate"[3] level to restore the individual body to a state of productive acceptability and normalcy within society.

Exploring the Institution: Theoretical and Historical Perspectives

The origins, development, mechanisms, effects, and role of institutional life have proven a point of fascination for scholars across a range of fields. While historians and architects have examined how pre-eighteenth century communal forms of social welfare and punishment transformed into the stark penitentiaries and fortified compounds of the twentieth century,[4] criminologists, legal theorists, and philosophers have debated the relative civic effects of institutionalization as a mechanism for punishment, deterrence, and retribution.[5]

Others from sociology, anthropology, and culture studies have considered the lived experience of institutionalization in terms of the psychosocial impact of the environment on inmates,[6] staff,[7] dependent children and families,[8] and even the researchers themselves.[9] Archaeological perspectives have also illuminated the material conditions of the modern institution.[10]

This multidisciplinary body of work has revealed a profound dissonance between ideal designed landscapes of disciplinary intention, and embodied landscapes of insubordination and compromise. Furthermore, the archaeological shift "from unearthing building footprints to posing research questions that focus on class, inequality, gender, race, ethnicity, and ideology,"[11] has encouraged scholars to embrace a rich variety of sources. Floor plans, photographs, maps, standing structures, salvaged architecture, museum collections, and excavated assemblages have all enriched our understandings of institutional materiality. Ultimately, this widened scope of theoretical and material analysis has depicted confinement as a social practice linked to a disparate set of places "all seeking to fulfill different ideal institutional models."[12]

Despite their varied societal functions, the establishments considered by institutional archaeologists have a similar historical pedigree. As Michel Foucault notoriously observed, radical transformations in both European and American forms of social management unfolded from the mid-eighteenth century, with practices of classification, surveillance, and confinement applied to an increasingly broad spectrum of societal misfits.[13] Culminating in the institutionalization of those persons identified as a threat to social order, this modern "Enlightened" regime initiated a new architectural form as an explicit mechanism of social control.[14] Further refined over the nineteenth century, these broad ideologies of societal "improvement" transformed the industrialized Western world.[15] When combined with growing attention toward the surrounding environment as a primary determinant of both personal behavior and moral character, these ideologies of improvement delivered a fresh social purpose to professions ranging from medicine and criminal reform, to social welfare and urban design.[16] The very materiality of modern society not only could, but *should*, be harnessed to exact improvement.

In 1791, the elite British industrialist Jeremy Bentham published his proposal for the *Panopticon; or the Inspection House*, a circular structure explicitly designed to maximize surveillance of both penitentiary inmates and staff.[17] While far too expensive to ever be fully realized, Bentham's iconic designs inspired the widespread adoption of surveillance as a primary institutional mechanism for "grinding rogues honest, and idle men industrious."[18] These newly founded and redeveloped specialized establishments proliferated as a mechanism of social control from the

1820s onward, providing society with the means to manage, reform, treat, and punish those who would or could not contribute to the social economy.[19] Through their architectural and artifactual worlds, these new palaces of confinement enforced systems of isolation, internal classification, routine ritualized practice, and strict discipline across all categories of inhabitants.[20] Their shared goal was improvement of both the individual and wider society by transforming the criminal to the citizen, restoring the sick to health, and instilling virtue and discipline in the "fallen," "vicious," and "ignorant."

In 1961, Erving Goffman introduced the notion of the "total institution," which has become a vastly influential concept for exploring archaeologies of institutional life.[21] The total institution transforms the deviant into the model through an extended process that Goffman refers to as "mortification." In the process of being admitted to a prison, hospital, industrial school or asylum, an individual enters into the "inmate world." They are excised from the fabric of outside society, stripped of their personal effects, and assigned a new institutional identity. This transformational process both establishes and enforces the internal regime. Thereafter, all personal, domestic, labor, and recreational activities are both scheduled and regulated by the institutional authority, undertaken collectively with fellow inmates, and imposed through exaggerated power differentials between inmates and staff.[22]

Disengaging inmates from society is enforced materially through a number of dimensions. These typically include architectural elements such as "locked doors, high walls, [and] barbed wire," or geographic isolation through selection of a site "hemmed in by natural barriers like cliffs, water, forests, or moors."[23] On a more intimate level, mortification is enacted through the body. Incoming inmates exchange their clothing and possessions for a uniform and standard-issue equipment, in the process of "leaving off and taking on [social identities], with the mid-point marked by physical nakedness."[24]

The very fabric of the landscape has also been used to generate institutionalization. Material culture and sensory deprivations apply a coercive force upon the body.[25] Coarse clothing, inaccessible windows, deprivation of everyday comforts, and, in extreme circumstances, deprivation of food and light produce intentional "pains" that drive inmates to accept the regulations and routines of institutional life, and channel them toward moral or physical reform. Together, these mortifications operated to "soften the mind to virtuous suggestion,"[26] transforming the inmate from recalcitrant to receptive.

In spite of their similarities in purpose, there is no one standardized approach to the archaeological analysis of these material worlds. Instead, scholarship has generally clustered around a shared core element: the power relations that infuse all institutional sites.[27] Recognizing this fundamental dynamic, Suzanne Spencer-Wood and Sherene Baugher refer to these places as "powered cultural landscapes."[28] Drawing from a growing body of archaeological case studies, they have argued for an expansion of Michel Foucault's reductive (if compelling) image of the institution as a factory for "docile bodies."[29] Instead, they draw from feminist scholarship to conceptualize power as a "heterarchical" set of social relations characterized by their numerous, varying, and circumstantial moments of opportunity.[30]

This ability to see beyond the institution-versus-inmate dialectic is one of the key strengths of examining these landscapes through the archaeological lens. As we explore in this chapter, institutional authorities relied upon a wide range of material practices to exact their reforms. But this is only part of the picture. To truly appreciate the realities of past institutional lives, it is essential to recognize and reconcile the official material mechanisms of reform with the myriad of individual needs, goals, agencies, and values of both inmates and staff – social dynamics that over time and practice left their own distinctive mark on the archaeological record. The following sections trace this complex dialectic starting at the pinnacle of institutional discipline and reform: the prison.

Punishment and Reform

As Joseph Gurney observed during his visits to British prisons in the company of prominent reformer Elizabeth Fry: "Prisons *ought to be* so conducted as to produce reform; they too often *are* so conducted as to be the very seminaries of crime."[31] Archaeologies of the prison have scrutinized this fundamental dissonance between the ideal model and lived experience of institutional life. For example, research on the Walnut Street Jail demonstrated how closely the materiality of reform and resistance intertwine.[32] Established in 1790, this early penitentiary operated under the Separate or Auburn system, which promoted a silent and solitary regime. Inmates' days were divided into periods of worship, meals, sleep, and manual labor. By the first decade of the nineteenth century, workshops for stone-working, shoemaking, weaving, and carpentry were added to the prison's rear yard. Excavations of the site in 1973 recovered plentiful evidence of these disciplinary activities in both the general artifact scatters and remains of the workshop structures. Investigations of an early construction trench also produced evidence of an alternative material world. Amid the debris of fragmentary cut marble, button blanks, and worked bone, archaeologists discovered five partly finished bone dice. These curious artifacts suggested that an informal, illicit manufacturing trade was occurring alongside the institutionally sanctioned labor regime.[33]

Likewise, evidence of deviations from the ideal carceral regime have been found in excavations at the Undercourt Jail at the Parliament House in Edinburgh (1836).[34] Victorian era penal codes mandated consistent treatment for all prisoners. They were, for example, expected to surrender their personal possessions for an institutional uniform and a penitential cell. Fabric and a button from a prison uniform recovered from the site indicate the Undercourt Jail abided by this system of regulations. And yet, the presence of several artifacts such as pipe stems and glass from an olive glass Guinness bottle suggested a material departure from these codes. Similarly, regulations also appear to have been interpreted loosely in relation to younger prisoners: several toys, including a spinning top, a rubber ball, and a toy tea set indicate efforts to accommodate children – the youngest of whom was incarcerated at just three years old.[35]

Eleanor Conlin Casella's work at the Ross Female Factory also revealed a material culture of deprivation and reformative labor entangled with one of black-market economies. Located in rural Tasmania, the factory received exiled British convict women between 1848 and 1853.[36] Conversion of the quadrangle from a road station (which had accommodated gangs of male felons) into something deemed suitable for the imprisonment of female convicts and children manifested in the recovery of remnant window glass and sandstone support tiers for floorboards. Activities geared toward moral reform were also represented. Fragmentary slate pencils and tablets indicated efforts to encourage literacy, while copper pins, thimbles, and lead bale seals demonstrated the task-work used to transform female convicts into respectable servants, wives, and mothers. As the institution expanded, its landscape of reform expanded. In 1851, a chapel, workroom, and bank of solitary cells were added to the main quadrangle (Figure 21.1).[37] Taking advantage of the natural slope of the site, factory authorities used the visual relationship between these new buildings to create a moral tableau: though near to the solitary cells, the new chapel was seated on slightly higher ground, thereby spatially reinforcing the inmates' choice "between Salvation and Damnation."[38]

Despite these symbolic and sensory messages of reform, women at the factory were determined to pursue their own needs and ends.[39] The illicit exchange of goods and services left a unique material signature across the Ross Factory site. Casella interpreted unexpected concentrations of bone, glass, and shell buttons as trade tokens within the broader sexual economy of this British penal colony.[40] Although explicitly designed to enforce strict isolation upon recalcitrant inmates, the solitary cells also contained a cache of bone and metal food remains, a kaolin clay pipe stem, and an olive bottle glass base – all hidden within a small pit dug into the earthen floor of the western cell.[41] Thus, even the specific location of recovered artifacts suggested a complex web of heterarchical relations structured this carceral landscape.

Subsequent excavations within the nursery ward recovered copper alloy thimbles and sewing pins, bone and ferrous uniform buttons, and stamped

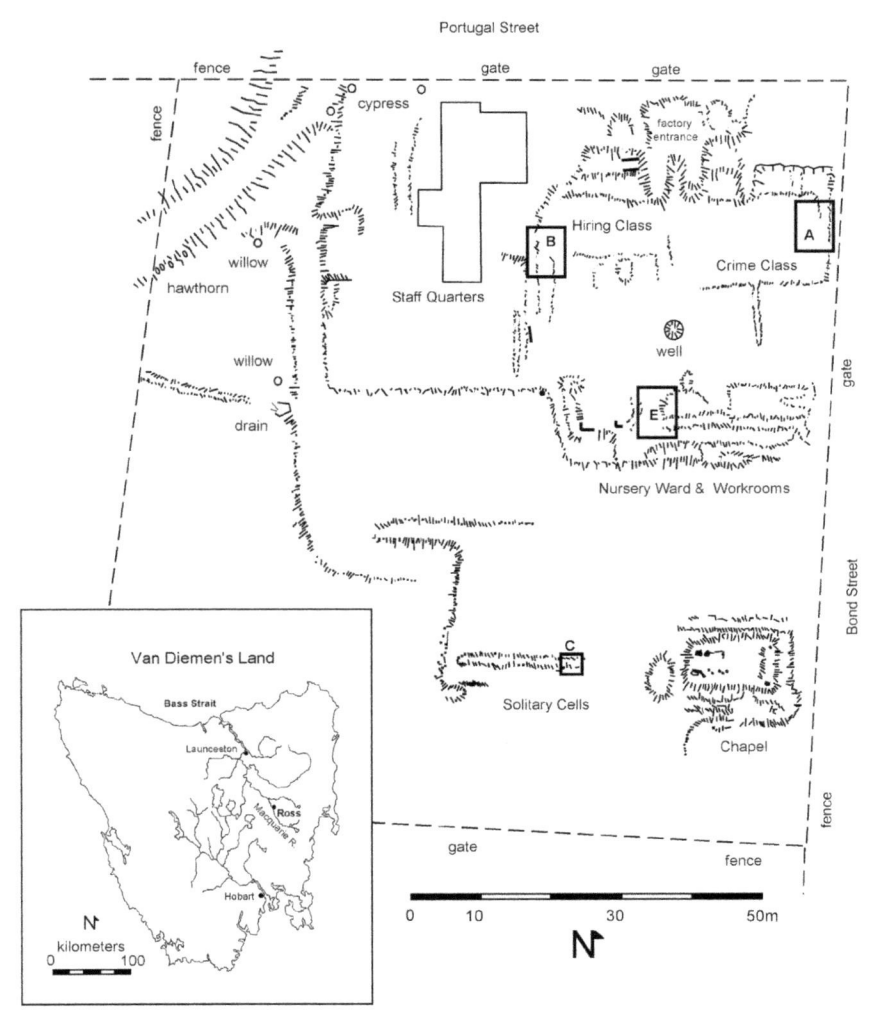

Figure 21.1 Ross Female Factory site plan, with insert location map of Tasmania (Van Diemen's Land). Image courtesy of Eleanor Conlin Casella.

lead seals used to secure bales of woven cloth. Prison regulations issued by the colonial Comptroller-General of Convicts strictly forbade convict mothers from contact with their infants after weaning was enforced at nine months. And yet, the frequent presence of these sewing-related artifacts throughout our excavation trenches suggested that moments of leniency, collusion, and negotiation intercut this stark carceral world.[42]

In the absence of a wealth of excavated material culture, James Garman developed a spatial approach to his work on the Rhode Island State Penitentiary. Founded in 1838, the penitentiary initially adopted the Auburn system of prison management, which sentenced inmates to silent individual labor within their solitary cells. Proving difficult to administer and prohibitively expensive, by 1845 the institution switched to the competing Congregate system – a transformation marked by the addition of a factory-style workshop to the penal compound. By overlaying archival accounts of rule-breaking inside the institution with archaeological remains from the site, Garman created a spatial model of inmates' contempt for their penal labor. Between 1872 and 1877, over half of the prisoner offenses occurred inside the workshops. Despite carefully arranged lines of worktables, acts of resistance ranged from the mundane – breaking the silence, destroying tools and supplies, or willfully slowing down production – to more extreme measures. In 1874, the workshops were destroyed by arson. Prison authorities responded by installing narrow brick paths into the yard to restrict freedom of movement. Inmates were additionally tasked with construction of a fire-proof replacement workshop over the cold winter season.[43]

In some cases, the management of penal labor articulated directly with other racialized forms of unfree labor. Established in the early 1830s, Louisiana's Old Baton Rouge Penitentiary incorporated productive industries such as cloth weaving and tailoring; tanning and production of leather goods; carpentry and cabinet making; and blacksmithing. By 1846, a dedicated cotton factory and engine house had replaced the eastern perimeter wall.[44] However, instead of toiling within the confines of this monumental institution, large battalions of male convicts were leased to private contractors for extensive agricultural and hazardous infrastructure works *outside* the penitentiary walls. With the dramatic increase in African American inmates after the Civil War, this convict leasing system – characteristic of penal corrections throughout the American South – provided a terribly familiar alternative to the unfree labor system of African American enslavement that had previously structured the Southern economy.[45]

Thus, the material world of the nineteenth-century carceral institution reflected its desire to return "undeserving" classes of criminal deviants toward penitence, respectability, and integrity. Penal regimes were equally developed to harness (if not exploit) the unfree labor of their inmates. Punishments and deprivations were a necessary part of exacting moral reformation. To plant seeds of improvement, the carceral institution first had to strip away the corruption of the inveterate criminal. The material culture of these carceral worlds pivoted around the discipline of the inmate body within an intentionally stark and regimented landscape.

Reform, Education, and Care

Not all institutions employed such drastic deprivations to encourage social improvement. Authorities tasked with managing populations less tainted by criminality – vulnerable women, orphans, stolen Indigenous children, and those limited by age or infirmity – instead developed regimes focused on the transformation of more "deserving" individuals. A great deal of this work has been informed by Lu Ann De Cunzo's seminal analysis of ritual, symbolism, and material culture as a holistic system of reform at the Magdalen Asylum in Philadelphia.[46] Opened in 1808, the asylum functioned as a refuge for the "fallen women" of the city – prostitutes, unwed mothers, and others who deviated from the idealized image of the wife and mother.[47]

Reform at the institution mixed ritual and self-discipline, steeped in movement through and engagement with the asylum's distinctive material world. Upon arrival, the Magdalen women shed evidence of their previous lives, exchanging their names and personal clothing for a number and uniform.[48] Once admitted, inmate lives were organized to render them into socially respectable domestic servants, wives, and mothers. Their days were broken into a regime of domestic activities, meals, religious worship, and exercise. The matron and her assistants directed the Magdalens in these activities, training them in tasks such as cleaning, sewing, laundry, and tea service.[49] Social hierarchies and values were inscribed onto the body through symbolic material culture embedded in these rituals of institutional life. For example, tablewares recovered from the site indicated that asylum inhabitants "ate principally from 'refined' white and floral ceramic wares" intended to reinforce ideologies of moral purity.[50] De Cunzo also found that decorated wares were reserved for the matron and her staff, thereby mirroring the material hierarchy between servants and their domestic employers.[51]

Spatial negotiations similarly featured as a prominent element of improvement. For example, the rear garden of the Magdalen Asylum offered a reformative space where inmates could absorb the moral influence of the natural world. In 1842, the Management Board replaced the asylum's eight-foot timber fence with a more substantial stone-topped thirteen-foot brick wall, a fortification intended to deter inmates from escape.[52] Similarly, at the Abbotsford Convent, an Australian Magdalen institution founded in Melbourne during 1863, demarcations of space reflected the disciplinary regime.[53] The site of the convent itself was originally selected for its remoteness, a key mechanism of reform. Social isolation was further reinforced by a series of outbuildings, fences, and barriers that ringed the laundry buildings – themselves serving as centerpiece of this institutional landscape. From the 1870s, as the growing colonial city increasingly encroached upon this rural isolation, the convent explicitly defined its segregated property with a set of robust exterior walls and boundary markers.[54]

A parallel landscape of protective isolation and domesticity was interpreted at St. John's Reformatory for Girls, a Catholic institution established in South Australia during 1897. Founded to correct the behavior of "wayward" and disobedient girls, the reformatory offered material perspectives on an institution uniquely located at the crux of gendered and religious approaches to reform.[55] Cherrie De Leiuen found that Catholic traditions of female confinement informed both the architectural and geographic nature of the institution. Situated out in the countryside and bounded by iron fences and barred windows, the reformatory included solitary apartments reserved for punishment of particularly difficult inmates. Together, these features created a built landscape explicitly designed to prevent escape.[56]

As at the Magdalen Asylum, St. John's Reformatory emphasized the inmates' future roles as wives, mothers, and domestic servants. Girls labored in the sewing rooms and laundries, participated in taught lessons and religious activities, and prepared and served all institutional meals. Recovered assemblages of molded, banded, and transfer-printed teawares, plus a variety of ceramic plates and bowls archaeologically emphasized the importance of food practices, while a diverse range of buttons and sewing equipment highlighted the centrality of domestic training within the daily regime.[57] The importance of religious worship was materially reflected in the discovery of a metal medallion bearing the institution's initials and an image of St. Jude – the patron saint of "difficult" and "desperate" cases.[58] Recovered from the vicinity of the church, and presumably worn by an inmate, it signified efforts to inscribe penitent values onto their bodies through subtle elements of institutional adornment.

Our material studies demonstrate that not all institutions relied on strict deprivation to instill reform. Methods of "soft" control, such as rewarding compliant inmates with privileges and indulgences, helped authorities strengthen their "powers with" inmates and encouraged acceptance of the regulations and routines that structured institutional life.[59] These material rewards took many forms. For example, the matron at Sydney's Hyde Park Barracks (1862–86) was permitted to provide the elderly, invalid, and newly immigrated women under her authority with a weekly ration of tobacco. Numerous pipes and matchbooks recovered from underfloor deposits throughout the barracks indicated a widespread participation in this reward system.[60] Archaeological studies of the Sailors Snug Harbor in New York City (1833) and the Sydney Sailors Home in Australia (1865) also demonstrated the central role of material incentives. These charitable institutions accommodated retired and invalided sailors who promised to follow their rules – including conducting themselves temperately. At Sailors Snug Harbor, rations of tobacco, right to payment for labor, and freedom to visit the nearby community were all contingent upon behavior; any resident caught drunk or disorderly relinquished these privileges.[61]

A further category of establishment was dedicated to improve and educate members of another "helpless" and "deserving" population – children. From residential and day schools to reformatories and orphanages, these institutions employed material culture in novel ways to instill the personal discipline, literacy, and labor skills that their wards would need for later productive success. For example, at both the Infant Orphan Asylum Hall in outer London (1843) and the Schuyler Mansion Orphanage in New York (1886), the sizes of the plates and mugs, and the nature of toys were adjusted to fit the perceived childhood socialization of different ages and genders.[62]

Although a number of voluntary day schools operated across nineteenth-century North America, these civic establishments differed from their strictly institutional counterparts in several ways. They were not residential sites. Focused more explicitly on children's initial socialization, these schools were not typically dedicated to the management of deviant, racially identified, or otherwise vulnerable groups. Furthermore, as Deborah Rotman points out in her analysis of the Wea View School (founded in rural Indiana during the 1860s), day schools frequently doubled as social centers for the wider community. While writing slates and pencils did appear at the site, the recovery of punch cups, tobacco pipes, and sewing needles from the site suggested it was also used to host social activities like sewing circles or May Day celebrations.[63]

Residential industrial schools were characterized by social isolation and compulsory attendance. Operated under the supervision of the United States Bureau of Indian Affairs (BIA), residential schools constituted the main mechanism for assimilating Indigenous North American populations into white American culture from the late nineteenth through mid-twentieth centuries. Following removal from their tribal communities, young Native American children were assigned to a dedicated residential school for basic education and vocational training in mainstream domestic, industrial, and agricultural skills deemed valuable for their future employment.[64]

Owen Lindaeur's examination of the garbage dump site from the Phoenix Indian School (1891) – one of many residential institutions that operated under the BIA's educational program – provided direct insight into the material process of cultural assimilation.[65] Since training schemes focused primarily on skills required for gender-specific employment in mainstream white America, female students were trained in domestic arts (cleaning, sewing, cooking, and childcare), while male students were taught skills related to agricultural or industrial labor (Figure 21.2). All residents were required to write and speak only in English, an aspect of their educational program materially linked to the recovery of numerous ink wells and writing slates during excavations.[66] The large number of toothbrushes recovered – remnants of the thrice-daily "toothbrush drills" introduced in 1916 – highlighted how this acculturative process operated at the intimate level of the individual body.[67]

The Mount Pleasant Indian Industrial Boarding School (1893) in central Michigan pursued a similar institutional regime of cultural assimilation.[68] The division of the grounds at Mount Pleasant reflected

Figure 21.2 Home economics class for women, Carlisle Indian School, Pennsylvania, c. 1900. Photograph by Frances Benjamin Johnston. Library of Congress, Prints and Photographs Division, LC-USZ62-55456.

gender ideologies at the institution. Male students were granted access to the nearly 300 acres of land that constituted Mount Pleasant's campus. These grounds provided ample space for both farming and recreational uses such as fishing and hiking. Conversely, only twenty acres were allotted to the female students since, as at the Phoenix School, their education focused heavily on tasks suited to their presumed futures in domestic service.[69]

Like other institutional types, residential schools enforced complex disciplinary systems of rituals and routines to fuel the cultural transformation of their inhabitants. Nevertheless, archaeological evidence demonstrated that Native American students created and maintained their "home" identities in numerous ways. The Phoenix School dump site, for example, yielded carved fetishes, effigies, and even knapped ceramic whiteware plate edges and fragments – artifacts that suggested students continued to curate their own cultural and spiritual traditions.[70] In her study of Mount Pleasant, Sarah Surface-Evans argued that the contrasting treatment of male and female students led them to challenge the institutional regime through differently gendered activities. The clay marbles and buttons found throughout the archaeological record were exchanged for entrance to pipe-ceremonies and powwows that male students secretly held in the woods around campus. In contrast, with fewer authorized opportunities to roam, female students were more likely to run away from the institution, or set fire to the laundries and dormitories where they lived and worked.[71]

Excavations at Harvard College, a Puritan institution founded in the Massachusetts Bay Colony in 1636, have highlighted the tensions between institutional ideologies and individual needs as they applied to dressing the body.[72] The college provided religious training to young English and Native American men pursuing a career as religious ministers in the growing colony, instructing them in essential "knowledge and godliness."[73] Life for students at Harvard was structured by the college laws, which echoed those of the Massachusetts Bay Colony. Underlying Puritan ideologies considered the body vulnerable to physical and spiritual injury if left undisciplined; Harvard students were therefore expected to adhere to a number of rules governing their dress, deportation, and consumption of food and tobacco.[74]

Excavations undertaken at Harvard College suggest students had more complex relationships with bodily discipline. Diana Loren interpreted the numerous tobacco pipes recovered from excavation of the dormitories as evidence that students' health anxieties were powerful enough to encourage illicit consumption of tobacco – a substance then recommended as a remedy.[75] A pierced coin "touch piece" was also recovered from the site. Worn against the skin as a form of protection against witchcraft and other spiritual malady, these amulets violated the institution's formal dress code, even when placed beneath robes and gowns.[76] Thus, the same ideological framework that governed the rules and regulations of Harvard College simultaneously motivated its residents to defy them.

Care and Cure

The archaeological study of medical care delivered in an institutional setting is a recent development. Termed "hospital archaeology" by Ian Smith and Jessie Garland,[77] its origins can be traced to Roberta Gilchrist's seminal work on English medieval hospitals. Gilchrist interpreted these early medical institutions as liminal spaces that mediated both the physical boundaries between town and parish and divisions between life and death.[78] Subsequent archaeologists have expanded this approach to examine other types of institutions concerned with isolating the sick in order to modify their bodily process, behaviors, and appearances to return them to a state of healthy normality.[79]

Archaeological research has examined both dedicated medical institutions, including hospitals, sanatoriums, and lunatic asylums, and materials derived from specialized medical infirmary wards within other institutions, such as military compounds and prisons.

In the latter cases especially, medical treatment reflected broader efforts to produce uniformity in the inmate body. Or as Fiona Starr observed in her analysis of assemblages excavated from the privies of the Civil Hospital site on Norfolk Island (1826), under ideal circumstances the prevalence of hygiene and medical-related artifacts indicated "an official desire for standardization of behavior."[80] In other contexts, however, these intra-institutional medical facilities fell short of their goals. For example, excavations of the hospital latrines on Johnson's Island (1862–66) – a POW camp that held Confederate army officers captured during the American Civil War – recovered increasing numbers of patent medicine bottles in features dating to the final years of the war. David Bush interpreted this assemblage as evidence that incarcerated officers had supplemented the institutional treatment regime with privately purchased remedies as the war progressed and "official" medical supplies became increasingly scarce.[81]

Hygienic and medical materials have also been interpreted as evidence of bodily improvement and standardization within dedicated healthcare institutions. Excavations at the Radcliffe Infirmary (1770–1900) in Oxford recovered a number of artifacts discarded in an abandoned laundry trough.[82] About a quarter of the materials recovered from this feature were linked to medical and sanitary efforts to control the products and processes of the body. Pharmaceutical bottles, syringes, and toothbrushes, for example, reflected activities that targeted the health of the body.[83] The remaining artifacts recovered spoke to more mundane realities of institutional life at the infirmary. The preparation and serving of food to large numbers of patients is represented in the recovery of broken tableware, utensils, and mugs. Patients also had to be kept clean and dressed, as the presence of buckles, buttons, chamber pot, and washbasin fragments attest.[84]

The prevalence of artifacts relating to caring for patients' daily needs may relate to the size of the institution itself, as Ian Smith and Rebecca Garland discuss in their analysis of materials recovered from a cistern associated with St. Bathan's Cottage Hospital (1891–1918). Founded in a rural mining community in New Zealand, St. Bathans treated conditions ranging from pulmonary complaints to broken bones.[85] By contrast to the Oxford Infirmary, over half of the artifacts recovered from the hospital cistern – including medicine bottles and ampoules, surgical needles, disinfectant – were medical or pharmaceutical in nature. St. Bathans closed frequently and never served more than six patients at once, producing a more marginal material footprint of practices relating to patients' non-medical needs.[86]

While hygiene and medicine are key features of the hospital regime, the spatial arrangement of these institutions also communicates information about the management of sick bodies. The quarantine of contagion offered a fundamental technology for preventing the spread of diseases.[87] Accordingly, lazarets – or institutions for isolating individuals infected with leprosy – were often established in remote locations and landscaped to maximize control over those inflicted. This was the case at the Peel Island Lazaret (1907–59) established off the coast of southeastern Queensland, Australia. Medical authorities on Peel Island divided space into three fenced compounds in accordance with mainstream racial and gendered ideologies. White men and women lived in two separate compounds near the staff quarters; a third enclosure for housing nonwhite patients was built to the south.[88] Individuals were assigned to huts within these enclosures based on the severity of their case, with more advanced cases positioned closer to the center of the island. This spatial differentiation was enforced by fences and policed by lazaret staff, who lived in huts placed between the three compounds.[89]

Spatial control was also a key consideration in planning the lazaret at Kalawao, founded on the isolated Kalaupapa peninsula of Hawaii (1866–1932).[90] Detailed archaeological analysis of the site demonstrated how physical features of this landscape had been intentionally harnessed. The site purchased for the lazaret was no tabula rasa. Stone buildings, enclosures, shines, and agricultural terraces established by the Polynesian communities were already in place. This pre-contact footprint defied efforts to create a settlement based on a grid system, thereby producing a unique palimpsest of culturally and institutionally informed landscape design.[91]

Medical authorities at both Peel Island and Kalawao considered the isolation, categorization, and segregation of patients as imperative to the prevention of leprosy. Nevertheless, patients did not always respond favorably to these regulations. Peel Island residents frequently ignored or damaged the fences that divided the patient compounds. Male patients with recreational boating privileges would often defy their quarantine entirely by taking unauthorized mainland visits.[92] Although fewer opportunities existed to leave the Kalawao settlement, the recovery of a diverse range of decorated tablewares, medicines, and commercial beer bottles suggested that inmates retained connections to their own familial and social worlds through consumer practices.[93]

In hospital contexts, isolation was not envisioned as carceral or punitive; rather, it was deemed necessary to prevent the spread of infectious diseases. By contrast, the isolation and organization of bodies was considered a vital curative mechanism within the lunatic asylum. Rational spaces, experiences, and architecture were believed to re-order and restore the mind. Differently classed wards were arranged, designed, and furnished to reflect the gender of their various residents: male patients were typically provided access to the farm and gardens; their female counterparts were more likely to gain easy access to the sewing rooms and laundries.[94] And yet, as

Susan Piddock observed in her comparative analysis of British and South Australian lunatic asylums, the design of these institutions differed between social and geographical contexts. These divergences reflected the availability of building resources as well as notions of the needs and character of the vulnerable populations they served.[95]

Design of an asylum building therefore reflected the circumstances of its construction. At the Purdysburn Villa Colony (1909) in Ireland, patients lived in detached pavilion-type buildings that resembled everyday homes.[96] Their large windows, skylights, and glass-roofed porches ensured that all ward interiors were brightly lit to deliver a protective and hygienic force of improvement. These discursive qualities, Gillian Allmond argued, were imparted to the rooms of the villas and the bodies that occupied them through this restorative sensory architecture.[97] Similarly, Katherine Fennelly comparatively examined the relationship between soundscapes and the built environment at a diverse range of asylums established across Britain and Ireland from 1808 through the late nineteenth century.[98] As both studies demonstrated, medical authorities believed the general ruckus of institutional life disturbed patients by delaying or preventing recovery. Different building materials and architectural forms muted or amplified institutional sounds, prompting authorities to devise material solutions – encasing noisy metal locks in leather, or insulating the interiors of seclusion rooms.[99]

While asylum architecture was manipulated in order to provide patients with a curative experience, Peta Longhurst has observed that this aspect of the material worlds cannot be treated as "neutral space, or as a direct reflection of the ideology underpinning [them]"; rather, these built environments offer "a potential source of friction."[100] Turning to the artifactual record, the complexity of these sites becomes clearer. For example, while patients' clothing was usually standardized, archaeological evidence indicated that patients actively repurposed these garments. This tension between institutional reform and inmate needs was interpreted through analysis of several aprons retrieved from under the porch of the Ladies Cottage in Tasmania's Royal Derwent Hospital (1826).[101] As part of the institutional uniform, aprons were required apparel for women at the hospital employed in the laundries, kitchens, sewing rooms, and wards.[102] Examples retrieved from the Royal Derwent site also functioned as biographical objects. The choices in material, thread, and pattern, in addition to individual sewing techniques for construction and repair, all reflected the histories, experiences, and skillsets of these patients – as did the words and images embroidered upon them prior to deposition beneath the cottage porch.[103]

Linnea Kuglitsch's analysis of materials excavated from the site of the Eastern Lunatic Asylum (1773–1885) in Williamsburg, Virginia, identified a similar tension between institutional and inmate use of material culture.[104] From the 1840s through the 1860s, the asylum adhered to the moral treatment framework. At the asylum, the "right and religious disciplining of the mind," and "prudent management of the body"[105] championed by the moral treatment model translated into a disciplinary process characterized by a regular schedule, good food, and a regimen of work, worship, and recreation. Together, these choreographed aspects of institutional life were believed to restore patients' self-discipline and health.

This disciplinary regime was materially apparent from the bobbins, chamber pots, utensils, and toothbrushes to the hundreds of pharmaceutical bottles linked to the asylum dispensary.[106] However, not all of the meanings suffusing the archaeological record were institutional. The discovery of fifteen metal buttons, pressed purposefully into mortar joints of a brick-floored privy at the site, indicated that patients adapted their artifactual world to their own ends.[107] Removed from a patient's clothing, this button assemblage was entangled with the discipline of the inmate's body (Figure 21.3). Yet, their presence in the privy floor suggested they had additional meanings. Patients were known for making strange collections. "The trifles that lunatics in asylums are able to acquire may not have much value," advised British asylum writer Charles Mercier, "but are of value to their owners simply because they are their own."[108] It is likely that this "irrational" collection was left in the privy floor to prevent it from being reappropriated by the institution and threaded back into its disciplinary clothing regime. Thus, even the most mundane artifacts offered a wide spectrum of different and sometimes conflicting social meanings within the institutional context.

Figure 21.3 Pair of shanked buttons found pressed into the joints of a brick-floored privy at the Eastern Lunatic Asylum. Photo: Linnea Kuglitsch. Reproduced by permission of the Colonial Williamsburg Foundation, Department of Archaeology, Object ER2284X.

Conclusions

From the late eighteenth century, the institutions of the Western world – prisons, schools, hospitals, workhouses, and asylums – underwent a drastic social and material transformation. Emerging from their origins in the religious cloisters and hospitals of medieval Europe,[109] these modern institutions were expanded and reinvented, embracing an increasingly specialized material repertoire, and applied to an ever-increasing array of populations. Further, the prolific body of work on penitentiaries and prisons has been matched by archaeological research on educational and medical institutions. When considered comparatively, the underlying material dynamics, mechanisms, and processes of the modern institution begin to appear.

As both a social philosophy and architectural form, the modern institution relied upon a cluster of techniques to punish, reform, and rehabilitate its occupants.[110] These mechanisms – customized to suit specific functional, ethnic, geographic, and socioeconomic contexts – left a distinctive material imprint throughout the Western world. Both purpose-built and modified buildings guided inmates through the process of reform, choreographing all internal movement and social interactions. The institutional environment advanced reform by segregating inhabitants, by creating opportunities for surveillance and discipline, by imposing a uniform schedule of daily activities, and (in specific cases) by inspiring trust through a replication of domesticity. The transformative process operated through the regulation of sensory experiences such as sound, textures, light, hunger, temperature, and fatigue. By stripping and reclothing inmates, by applying medical treatments, and by imposing new hygienic regimes, institutional practices had tangible impacts on the bodies, minds, and experiences of all occupants – staff, visitors, consultants, and inmates.

Although united in their efforts to educate, resocialize, improve, and transform, the specific techniques adopted to achieve these shared aims were customized to suit the needs of each type of institution. While the confinement and isolation of the prisoner was enacted as a mode of punishment, the cloistered existence faced by other inmates appeared more protective than punitive. Archaeological work has exposed the enduring dissonance between grand institutional ideals and internal everyday practices. In addition to studying an increased diversity of institutional types, scholarship has also begun to develop a focus upon the materiality of not only inmates, but the range of administrative, correctional, medical, and educational staff that equally inscribed their material signatures upon the modern institution.

Although explicitly designed to enforce a strictly hierarchical power structure, institutional life was shaped by complex systems of overlapping rules, intentions, and actions. These archaeological landscapes embed not only evidence of ritual, labor, discipline, and routine, but also insubordinate actions, desires, and attitudes. Inmates challenged the institution through their own material worlds: they stole and hid objects, defied boundaries, and vandalized property. Even the archaeological presence of small indulgences – a tobacco pipe, a child's toy, a toothbrush – demonstrated moments of resistance and survival within these monuments of discipline and reform.

Ultimately, the archaeology of these complex establishments reveals wider (and frequently dark) moral, socioeconomic, and medical anxieties over the accommodation of those who do not, or cannot, participate in mainstream Western society. By exploring the austere landscapes, buildings, and artifact assemblages of these confronting monuments we open a window into not only the goals and mechanisms of these distinct establishments and their programs of reform, but also the intimacies of human experiences within their walls. In doing so, we can begin to appreciate the enduring social and material legacy of our modern institutional worlds.

Notes

1. James Gibb, "Introduction," in April Beisaw and James Gibb, eds., *The Archaeology of Institutional Life* (Tuscaloosa: University of Alabama Press, 2009), 2.
2. Erving Goffman, *Asylums: Essays on the Social Situation of Mental Patients and other Inmates* (Anchor Books, 1961), 3–4; David J. Rothman, *The Discovery of the Asylum* (Transaction Publishers, 1971).
3. Stacey Camp, "Commentary: Excavating the Intimate," *Historical Archaeology*, 52, no. 3 (2018), 600–07.
4. Robin Evans, *The Fabrication of Virtue: English Prison Architecture, 1750–1840* (Cambridge University Press, 1982); Michael Ignatieff, *A Just Measure of Pain: The Penitentiary in the Industrial Revolution, 1750–1850* (London: Macmillan, 1978).
5. David Garland, *Punishment and Modern Society* (Oxford: Clarendon Press, 1989); Adrian Howe, *Punish and Critique: Towards a Feminist Analysis of Penality* (London: Routledge, 1991).
6. Donald R. Clemmer, *The Prison Community* (Boston: Christopher Publishing House, 1940); Goffman, *Asylums*.
7. David Price and Alison Liebling, *The Prison Officer* (London: Prison Service, 2001).
8. Barbara A. Owen, *In the Mix: Struggle and Survival in a Women's Prison* (Albany: State University of New York Press, 1998).
9. Mark S. Fleisher, *Warehousing Violence* (Newbury Park: Sage, 1989).

10. Lu Ann De Cunzo, "Reform, Respite, Ritual: An Archaeology of Institutions; the Magdalen Society of Philadelphia, 1800–1850," *Historical Archaeology* 29, no. 3 (1995), 1–168; Lu Ann De Cunzo, "On Reforming the 'Fallen' and Beyond: Transforming Continuity at the Magdalen Society of Philadelphia, 1845–1916," *International Journal of Historical Archaeology*, 5, no. 1 (2001), 19–43; Suzanne M. Spencer-Wood and Sherene Baugher, "Introduction and Historical Context for the Archaeology of Institutions of Reform. Part I: Asylums," *International Journal of Historical Archaeology* 5, no. 1 (2001), 3–17; Eleanor Conlin Casella, *The Archaeology of Institutional Confinement* (Tallahassee: University Press of Florida, 2007); April M. Beisaw and James G. Gibb, eds., *The Archaeology of Institutional Life* (Tuscaloosa: University of Alabama Press, 2009).
11. Sherene Baugher, "Historical Overview of the Archaeology of Institutional Life," in Beisaw and Gibb, *The Archaeology of Institutional Life*, 7.
12. Spencer-Wood and Baugher, "Introduction and Historical Context, Part I," 11.
13. Michael Foucault, *Discipline and Punish: The Birth of the Prison* (New York: Pantheon Books, 1977).
14. Foucault, *Discipline and Punish*.
15. Sarah Tarlow, *The Archaeology of Improvement in Britain, 1750–1850* (Cambridge: Cambridge University Press, 2007).
16. Carla Yanni, *The Architecture of Madness: Insane Asylums in the United States* (Minneapolis: University of Minnesota Press, 2007).
17. J. Semple, *Bentham's Prison: A Study of the Panopticon Penitentiary* (Oxford: Clarendon Press, 1993).
18. J. Bentham, *The Works of Jeremy Bentham, Published under the Superintendence of his Executor*, John Bowring (Edinburgh: William Tait, 1838), vol. 4, 342.
19. Casella, *The Archaeology of Institutional Confinement*, 24–32.
20. Evans, *The Fabrication of Virtue*.
21. Goffman, *Asylums*.
22. Ibid, 11–17.
23. Ibid, 4.
24. Ibid, 27.
25. Eleanor Conlin Casella, "Lockdown: On the Materiality of Confinement," in Adrian Myers and Gabriel Moshenska, eds., *Archaeologies of internment* (New York: Springer, 2011), 285–95.
26. Ignatieff, *A Just Measure of Pain*, 74.
27. Casella, *The Archaeology of Institutional Confinement*.
28. Suzanne M. Spencer-Wood and Sherene Baugher, "Introduction to the Historical Archaeology of Powered Cultural Landscapes," *International Journal of Historical Archaeology* 14, no. 4 (2010), 463.
29. Foucault, *Discipline and Punish*, 137.

30. Robert Ehrenreich, Carole Crumley, and Janet Levy, eds., *Heterarchy and the Analysis of Complex Societies*. Archeological Papers of the American Anthropological Association, 1995.
31. Joseph J. Gurney, *Notes on a Visit Made to Some of the Prisons in Scotland and the North of England, in Company with Elizabeth Fry* (London: A. Constable and Company, 1819), 103.
32. John L. Cotter, Roger Moss, Bruce Gill, and Jiyul Kim, *The Walnut Street Prison Workshop: A Test Study in Historical Archaeology Based on Field Investigation in the Garden Area of the Athenaeum of Philadelphia* (Watkins Glen,: Athenaeum of Philadelphia, 1988).
33. Cotter et al, *The Walnut Street Prison Workshop*.
34. Victoria Oleksy, "Conformity and Resistance in the Victorian Penal System: Archaeological Investigations at Parliament House, Edinburgh," *Post-Medieval Archaeology* 42, no. 2 (2008), 276–303, 280.
35. Oleksy, "Conformity and Resistance in the Victorian Penal System."
36. Eleanor Conlin Casella, *Archaeology of the Ross Female Factory: Female Incarceration in Van Diemen's Land, Australia* (Launceston: Queen Victoria Museum and Art Gallery, 2002).
37. Eleanor Conlin Casella, *Archaeology of the Ross Female Factory*, 58–59.
38. Eleanor Conlin Casella, "Little Bastard Felons: Childhood, Affect, and Labor in the Penal Colonies of Nineteenth-Century Australia," in Barbara Voss and Eleanor Conlin Casella, eds., *The Archaeology of Colonialism: Intimate Encounters and Sexual Effects* (Cambridge: Cambridge University Press, 2011), 31–48, 4 1.
39. Casella, *Archaeology of the Ross Female Factory*, 80.
40. Eleanor Conlin Casella, "'Doing Trade': A Sexual Economy of Nineteenth-Century Australian Female Convict Prisons," *World Archaeology* 32, no. 2 (2000), 209–21.
41. Casella, *Archaeology of the Ross Female Factory*.
42. Casella, "Little Bastard Felons."
43. James C. Garman, *Detention Castles of Stone and Steel: Landscape, Labor, and the Urban Penitentiary* (Knoxville: University of Tennessee Press, 2005).
44. Thurston Hahn and Susan Wurzburg, *Hard labor: History and Archaeology at the Old Louisiana State Penitentiary, Baton Rouge, Louisiana* (Fort Worth: General Services Administration, 1992).
45. Casella, *The Archaeology of Institutional Confinement*, 34–35, 90–94; Scott Christianson, *With Liberty for Some: 500 Years of Imprisonment in America* (Boston: Northeastern University Press, 1998); Burk Foster, Wilbert Rideau, and Ron Wikburg, *The Wall is Strong: Corrections in Louisiana*, 3rd ed. (Lafayette: Centre for Louisiana Studies, University of Southwestern Louisiana, 1995).
46. De Cunzo, "Reform, Respite, Ritual."
47. Ibid, 119.
48. Ibid.
49. De Cunzo, "On Reforming the 'Fallen' and Beyond."

50. De Cunzo, "Reform, Respite, Ritual," 107.
51. Ibid, 81–88; De Cunzo, "On Reforming the 'Fallen' and Beyond," 27–29.
52. De Cunzo, "Reform, Respite, Ritual," 113.
53. Edwina Kay, "Containment of 'Wayward' Females: The Buildings of Abbotsford Convent, Victoria," *Archaeology in Oceania* 50, no. 3 (2015), 153–61, 154.
54. Kay, "Containment of 'Wayward' Females."
55. Cherrie De Leiuen, "'Corporal Punishment and the Grace of God': The Archaeology of a Nineteenth Century Girl's Reformatory in South Australia," *Archaeology in Oceania* 50, no. 3 (2015), 145–52.
56. Ibid, 146.
57. Ibid, 150.
58. Ibid.
59. Suzanne M. Spencer-Wood, "Feminist Theoretical Perspectives on the Archaeology of Poverty: Gendering Institutional Lifeways in the Northeastern United States from the Eighteenth Century through the Nineteenth Century," *Historical Archaeology* 44, no. 4 (2010), 130.
60. Peter Davies, Penny Crook, and Tim Murray, *An Archaeology of Institutional Confinement: The Hyde Park Barracks, 1848–1886* (Sydney: Sydney University Press, 2013), vol. 4.
61. Dennis Gojak and Nadio Iacono, "The Archaeology and History of the Sydney Sailors Home, the Rocks, Sydney," *Bulletin of the Australian Institute for Maritime Archaeology* 17, no. 1 (1993), 27; Sherene Baugher, "At the Top of the Hierarchy of Charity: The Life of Retired Seamen at Sailors' Snug Harbor, Staten Island, New York," *Northeast Anthropology* 73 (2009), 59–86; Sherene Baugher, "Landscapes of Power: Middle Class and Lower Class Power Dynamics in a New York Charitable Institution," *International Journal of Historical Archaeology* 14, no. 4 (2010), 475–97.
62. Lois Feister, "The Orphanage at Schuyler Mansion," *Northeast Historical Archaeology* 20, no. 1 (1991), 27–36; Barry Hughes, "Infant Orphan Asylum Hall Crockery from Eagle Pond, Snaresbrook," *London Archaeologist* 6, no. 4 (1992), 382–87.
63. April M. Beisaw, "Constructing Institution-Specific Site Formation Models," in Beisaw and Gibb, *The Archaeology of Institutional Life*, 49–68; Deborah L. Rotman, "Rural Education and Community Social Relations: Historical Archaeology of the Wea View Schoolhouse No. 8, Wabash Township, Tippecanoe County, Indiana," in Beisaw and Gibb, *The Archaeology of Institutional Life*, 80–81.
64. Owen Lindauer, *Historical Archaeology of the United States Industrial Indian School at Phoenix: Investigations of a Turn of the Century Trash Dump* (Tempe: Office of Cultural Resource Management, Department of Anthropology, Arizona State University, 1996), 213–14.
65. Robert Trennart, *The Phoenix Indian School: Forced Assimilation in Arizona, 1891–1935* (Norman: University of Oklahoma Press, 1988),

168; Lindauer, *Historical Archaeology of the United States Industrial Indian School at Phoenix*; Casella, *The Archaeology of Institutional Confinement*, 34–39.
66. Lindauer, *Historical Archaeology of the United States Industrial Indian School*, 156, 163, 133.
67. Owen Lindauer, *Not for School, but for Life: Lessons from the Historical Archaeology of the Phoenix Indian School. Office of Cultural Resource Management Report #95* (Arizona State University, Office of Cultural Resource Management, Dept. of Anthropology, 1997), 135.
68. Sarah L. Surface-Evans, "A Landscape of Assimilation and Resistance: The Mount Pleasant Indian Industrial Boarding School," *International Journal of Historical Archaeology* 20, no. 3 (2016), 574–88.
69. Surface-Evans, "A Landscape of Assimilation and Resistance," 583.
70. Lindauer, *Not for School, but for Life*, 215–20; Owen Lindauer, "Individual Struggles and Institutional Goals: Small Voices from the Phoenix Indian School Track Site," in Beisaw and Gibb, *The Archaeology of Institutional Life*, 95–96.
71. Surface-Evans, "A Landscape of Assimilation and Resistance," 584–86.
72. Diana D. Loren, "Bodily Protection: Dress, Health, and Anxiety in Colonial New England," in James Fleisher and Neil Norman, eds., *The Archaeology of Anxiety: The Materiality of Anxiousness, Worry and Fear* (New York: Springer, 2016), 144.
73. Ibid, 144.
74. Ibid, 144, 151.
75. Ibid, 147, 151.
76. Ibid, 151.
77. Ian Smith and Jessie Garland, "Archaeology of St. Bathans Cottage Hospital, Central Otago, New Zealand," *Australasian Historical Archaeology* 30 (2012), 52.
78. Roberta Gilchrist, "Christian Bodies and Souls: The Archaeology of Life and Death in Later Medieval Hospitals," in Steven Bassett, ed., *Death in Towns: Urban Responses to the Dying and the Dead, 100–1600* (Leicester: Leicester University Press, 1992), 101–18.
79. Julia Epstein, *Altered Conditions: Disease, Medicine, and Storytelling* (London: Routledge, 1995), 7, 14.
80. Fiona Starr, "Convict Artefacts from the Civil Hospital Privy on Norfolk Island," *Australasian Historical Archaeology* 19 (2001), 45.
81. David R. Bush, "Interpreting the Latrines of the Johnson's Island Civil War Military Prison," *Historical Archaeology* 34, no. 1 (2000), 62–78.
82. Nigel Jeffries, Tim Braybrooke, and Jacquai Pearce, "Development of the Former Radcliffe Infirmary, Oxford, 1770–1900," *Post-Medieval Archaeology* 49, no. 2 (2015), 238.
83. Ibid, 238, 250–52.
84. Ibid, 250, 254–55.
85. Smith and Garland, "Archaeology of St. Bathans Cottage Hospital," 53.

86. Ibid, 60.
87. Peta Longhurst, "Quarantine Matters: Colonial Quarantine at North Head, Sydney and its Material and Ideological Ruins," *International Journal of Historical Archaeology* 20, no. 3 (2016), 589–600; April Youngberry and Jonathan Prangnell, "Fences, Boats and Teas: Engendering Patient Lives at Peel Island Lazaret," *International Journal of Historical Archaeology* 17, no. 3 (2013), 445–64; James Flexner, "An Institution That Was a Village: Archaeology and Social Life in the Hansen's Disease Settlement at Kalawao, Moloka 'i, Hawaii," *International Journal of Historical Archaeology* 16, no. 1 (2012), 135–63.
88. Youngberry and Prangnell, "Fences, Boats and Teas," 448.
89. Ibid, 449–51.
90. Flexner, "An Institution That Was a Village," 146.
91. Ibid, 145–46.
92. Youngberry and Prangell, "Fences, Boats and Teas," 451, 453.
93. Flexner, "An Institution That Was a Village," 155–56, 140.
94. Susan Piddock, "To Each a Space: Class, Classification, and Gender in Colonial South Australian Institutions," *Historical Archaeology* 45, no. 3 (2011), 89–105.
95. Susan Piddock, *A Space of Their Own: The Archaeology of Nineteenth Century Lunatic Asylums in Britain, South Australia and Tasmania* (New York: Springer, 2007), 202–09.
96. Gillian Allmond, "Light and Darkness in an Edwardian Institution for the Insane Poor: Illuminating the Material Practices of the Asylum Age," *International Journal of Historical Archaeology* 20, no. 1 (2015), 3–4.
97. Gillian Allmond, "'The Outer Darkness of Madness': The Edwardian Winter Garden at Purdysburn Public Asylum for the Insane," in M. Dowd and R. Hensey, eds., *The Archaeology of Darkness* (Oxford: Oxbow Books, 2016).
98. Katherine Fennelly, *An Archaeology of Lunacy: Managing Madness in Early Nineteenth Century Asylums* (Manchester: Manchester University Press, 2019).
99. Katherine Fennelly, "Out of Sound, Out of Mind: Noise Control in Early Nineteenth-Century Lunatic Asylums in England and Ireland," *World Archaeology* 46, no. 3 (2014), 416–30.
100. Peta Longhurst, "Institutional Non-correspondence: Materiality and Ideology in the Mental Institutions of New South Wales," *Post-Medieval Archaeology* 49, no. 2 (2015), 234.
101. Danica Auld, Tracy Ireland, and Heather Burke, "Affective Aprons: Object Biographies from the Ladies' Cottage, Royal Derwent Hospital New Norfolk, Tasmania," *International Journal of Historical Archaeology* 23, no. 2 (2018), 1–19.
102. Ibid, 6.
103. Ibid, 10.

104. Linnea Kuglitsch, "Materia Medica, Materia Moral: An Archaeology of Asylum Management and Moral Treatment in the United States, 1840–1914," Ph.D. Thesis, The University of Manchester 2019.
105. J. M. Galt, *The Annual Report of the Physician and Superintendent of the Eastern Asylum, in the City of Williamsburg, Virginia, for 1842* (Richmond: Shepherd and Colin, 1843), 9.
106. W. F. Bynum, "The Rise of Science in Medicine, 1850–1913," in Lawrence Conrad, Michael Neve, Vivian Nutton, Roy Porter, and Andrew Wear, eds., *The Western Medical Tradition, 1800 to 2000* (Cambridge: Cambridge University Press, 2006), 111–239.
107. Ivor N. Hume, "Public Hospital ER 2200 & ER 2299 Field Notes" (Colonial Williamsburg Department of Architectural and Archaeological Research, Williamsburg, 1980), 284.
108. Charles A. Mercier, *The Attendant's Companion: A Manual of the Duties of Attendants in Lunatic Asylums* (London: J. & A. Churchill, 1898), 101.
109. Roberta Gilchrist, *Gender and Material Culture: The Archaeology of Religious Women* (Routledge, 1994); Paul Huey, "The Almshouse in Dutch and English Colonial North America and Its Precedent in the Old World: Historical and Archaeological Evidence," *International Journal of Historical Archaeology* 5, no. 2, (2001), 123–54.
110. Casella, *The Archaeology of Institutional Confinement*.

22

Material Religion

Gretchen Buggeln

Material objects that have transcendent importance – skeletal remains, holy books, ritual garments and artifacts, objects of private devotion and intense respect – raise special problems and questions for scholars of material culture. First, there is the problem of definition. What makes an object "religious" or "sacred," and hence require engagement on this plane of inquiry? Since its origin as a field of study, religion has persisted in being notoriously difficult to pin down, and scholars still do not agree on a definition. A second challenge for material culture scholars is that respect for the sacred beliefs and practices of makers, users, and their descendants, means that these objects often require special care in handling and interpretation (see Moore, Chapter 11). Yet the fact that these artifacts carry important meanings and assist human beings in the fundamental ordering of their worlds makes them especially rewarding as objects of study. Questions about agency, identity, embodiment, and practice, in particular, are reshaping the way religion scholars understand the way religion happens in the world, creating endless opportunities for material culture scholars to contribute to the conversation. This chapter will address the history, challenges, and possibilities of this area of scholarship.

The academic study of "religion" per se originated in the nineteenth-century West. Early religion scholars conceptualized their subject as truth claims articulated in doctrine and demonstrated in practices that served that doctrine, all under the umbrella of clearly demarcated, authoritative traditions, such as Christianity or Islam. As Talal Asad and others have argued, these structural assumptions not only shaped the study of Western religions but led Western scholars to invent non-Western "religions" that would have been largely unrecognizable to insiders.[1] However wrongheaded this approach might have been, the desire to establish a stable, shared context of meaning for the study of spiritual beliefs and practices is an understandable and even valuable impulse. Yet there are associated problems with this tendency that have continued to plague the interpretation of religion and its material cultures. Thinking in terms of broad, definable traditions can limit or ignore variability, individuality, and the dynamic character of religious belief and practice. Furthermore, the emphasis on the primacy of belief has often meant that the constitutive agency of religious objects and the practices they assist appears secondary. Even before religion was a field of academic study people thoughtfully considered the material evidence of spiritual beliefs and practices, rich and expressive engagement with the material world in the form of art, architecture, adornment, ritual artifacts, and texts. But scholars who studied these artifacts tended to value them primarily for their aesthetic qualities or as symbolic evidence that proved, elaborated, or contested *belief* – a legitimate approach, to be sure, but one that left untapped other avenues of questioning.

The elusive character of "religion" also stems from the fact that scholars of religion work in widely different fields – anthropology, sociology, history, art history, religious studies, folklore, and philosophy among them – each field operating with its own presuppositions, conventions, and goals. Historians, for instance, have largely focused on telling the stories of religious groups, traditions, and institutions. Sociologists, after Durkheim, have often viewed religion in functional terms and sought to understand the ways it satisfies social needs.[2] Anthropologists have been interested in religion as an expression of culture and a revelation of underlying economic, political, and social structures of power. With the study of the material culture of religion scattered throughout these disciplines, and conflicting claims about what religion actually *is* or *does*, it is not surprising that this field has not developed a widely accepted purpose, logic, or methodological coherence.

Even so, two decades into the twenty-first century, the material culture of religion is one of the most active, interdisciplinary, global, and innovative areas of material culture study. The recent uptick in religion scholarship is in part a response to late-twentieth-century reconsideration of the "secularization theory."[3] This theory had proposed that increasing modernity would inevitably lead to a decline in the presence and power of religion. Yet there is ample global evidence of the variety, mutability, and dogged persistence of religion and spirituality.[4] Responding to this reality, and pushing against the normative claims of modernity that long held sway, scholars have attended to the astonishing diversity of contemporary religious practice. The scholarly initiatives, journals, archives, and published body of work demonstrate wide-ranging vitality and promise. This chapter will focus on a relatively new movement that draws various approaches and methods together into the interdisciplinary terrain of "material religion" studies. Following a brief account of its origins and a bibliographic summary of some important scholarship and approaches, the chapter concludes with thoughts on the future directions of material religion studies. Case studies are included throughout.

Material Religion: Definitions and Explorations

The "material religion" movement emerged out of the expansion and maturation of the field of religious studies in the last three to four decades.[5] Beginning in the 1980s, scholars turned their attention from doctrines and institutions to "lived religion," a term that signified the daily practices of religious people, frequently people on the margins of political and institutional power. Historical works such as Robert Orsi's *Madonna of 115th Street* or Leigh E. Schmidt's *Consumer Rites: The Buying and Selling of American Holidays* opened up ways of studying the popular practice of religion across the socio-economic spectrum and, significantly for scholars of material culture, its multi-faceted engagement with the material world.[6] Colleen McDannell's object-oriented 1995 study *Material Christianity*, for instance, considered Victorian bibles as both sacred texts and "fashion statements" and argued that common figurines sometimes viewed as "kitsch," such as the T-shirts and jewelry marketed by Christian retailers, hold "the power to minister."[7]

Lived religion persists as a theme in religious studies, and material culture studies have much to contribute, because lived religion often happens with ordinary objects in ordinary spaces. Lauren Winner, for instance, in her study of Anglican religious practice in colonial Virginia, structured chapters around needlework, baptismal bowls, and recipes used to mark events in the liturgical year. Winner used objects and rituals to argue for the tangible presence of faith in households assumed by previous scholars to be religiously lukewarm.[8] In addition to reclaiming the religious dimensions of the artifacts of daily life, a lived religion approach has had the added benefit of finding ways to incorporate objects, images, and places into the study of traditions widely viewed as iconoclastic, such as Puritanism or Zen Buddhism. As John Kieschnick argues, "When a Puritan rejects a Catholic rosary, or a Jain refuses to wear clothing, material culture forms the syntax of their arguments."[9] Building on ideas from history of the book studies, scholars of religion are also thinking about texts themselves as material objects.[10] Interest in "lived religion" continues to be evident across many disciplines – art history, anthropology, and sociology among them.

One of the most exciting developments of the new scholarship of religion is the recognition that a sufficiently complex understanding of religion often cannot be grasped within the bounds of a single, traditional, disciplinary approach. Scholars in religious studies and media studies, anthropologists, archaeologists, and historians of art, objects, and the built environment are building a nexus of approaches and questions that encourage the crossing of former disciplinary boundaries.[11] A particularly generative development has been the movement toward conceptualizing religion as something that happens in and through material practices, something experienced and negotiated not just in words but in interactions with objects, places, and bodies. Religion, in other words, is *made* as well as thought. According to this way of understanding religion, beliefs about ultimate truths and the supernatural are still important to religious identity and practice, but these ideas are formed in both ordinary and extraordinary activities, and, significantly, through interactions with material things that have agency of their own. This paradigm shift calls for even more focused study of religion as it happens with material objects, in physical places and in acknowledgment of the broader material conditions, such as economic, social, and political relations that enable or deter religious practice. A material religion approach to pilgrimage, for instance, would be to think of it in multidimensional ways, as a practice that is constitutive of belief rather than something that reflects it only; pilgrimage consists of bodies in motion, landscapes, rituals, and objects, all entangled in a web of meaning in a specific social, economic, political, and material context. Religion *is* pilgrimage as much as it is the ideas that accompany it.[12]

Thinking about religion in this way, as something continuously formed and reformed in daily life, has changed where scholars have looked for religion and religious identity.[13] They are watching what people do with their bodies, taking note of the involvement of sensory processes, habits, and experiences with and around material things. There is no need to privilege public or private worship space over domestic or ordinary spaces and things; kitchens, offices, yards, and sidewalks are equally fair game in the search for religion.[14] As should be clear by now, rather than hold a narrow view of "religion" as structured, systematic human activity, located in belief systems and connected to tradition, institutions, and systems of authority, scholars of material religion define religion very broadly.

Case Study 22.1

The woman of Willandorf: What makes an object "religious"?

In his 2018 Gifford Lectures, "Why We Believe: Evolution, Making Meaning, and the Development of Human Natures," anthropologist Agustín Fuentes noted that it was only about 6,000–8,000 years ago that evidence of something like identifiable, traditional religious belief systems emerged – the origins, scholars think, of the earliest major religions.[15] Yet long before then, Fuentes argued, archaeological evidence demonstrates that humans had the capacity for spiritual belief and practice.

This 11 cm limestone figurine, colored with red ochre, representative of a woman's body with accentuated reproductive organs and possibly a hair design but no discernible face, was discovered at a Paleolithic site in Southern Austria in 1908 and dated 28,000–25,000 BCE[16] (Figure 22.1). By itself, without contextual information, it is difficult to claim it has

> **Case Study 22.1 (cont.)**
>
> any sort of symbolic meaning. But many similar figurines of different sizes and materials have been discovered, dating from 18,000 to 30,000 BCE, across Paleolithic Europe. By introducing American philosopher Charles S. Peirce's idea of the "legisign," a sign vehicle based on conventions which indicate the codification of shared ideas, Fuentes and Mark Kissel argue that this is evidence that a form came to elicit conventional sensations and responses, significant evidence for meaning making.[17] Although from these similar objects alone it is impossible to determine what that meaning was, scholars have speculated that it might be connected to a mother goddess and fertility.

Figure 22.1 Woman (Venus) of Willandorf. Limestone figure, representative of a woman's body. Photo: Mattias Kabel. Wikimedia Commons.

When scholarship in religion took a material turn in the 1990s, studies in religious visual culture, typically by researchers with a background in art history, religious studies, and media studies, often led the way.[18] Art history was the locus of landmark studies that focused on practice, the early influential, theoretical work that restored agency to objects. Art historian David Freedberg's *The Power of Images* (1989) and anthropologist Alfred Gill's *Art and Agency* (1998), for instance, described images as technologies of interaction and placed them in social relationships. Although neither work was about religion only, both turned to religious images as subjects.[19] Particularly through the work of David Morgan, these ideas became more accessible to scholars of material religion. Morgan's introduction to *Visual Piety: A History and Theory of Popular Religious Images*, for example, provides a useful and lucid introduction to the way "popular [religious] images participate in the social construction of reality," and applies equally well to religious objects.[20]

Case Study 22.2

Ukrainian "Icons on Ammo Boxes": strategic transformations

As part of a project, "Icons on Ammo Boxes," Orthodox iconographers Oleksandr Klymenko and Sofia Atlantova painted this Byzantine icon of the Virgin Mary and Child on the wooden lid of a Russian crate used to bring weapons into Ukraine (Figure 22.2). In choosing this medium, the artists are protesting the contemporary war between Russia and Ukraine. But they are also figuring the act of redemption that is at the heart of Christian theology, a reclaiming and sanctification of matter that echoes the belief in incarnation and resurrection.

Klymenko and Atlantova are trained iconographers; their work reflects a long and carefully controlled practice of image making and use within Orthodox worship and devotion. This particular icon symbolizes the transformation of death into life in a sacred image of motherhood, in the same way the Christian cross takes an image of violent death and transforms it into a sign of life and victory. Klymenko claims his icons are examples of antimony, a reconciling of the incompatible: in this case, icon versus weapon, life versus death, and traditional Christian arts versus the material of contemporary war.

Religious objects can challenge and protest. In this age of the image, these iconographers use the materiality of their art to make real for viewers the pain of conflict. Furthermore, the proceeds from the sale of Klymenko and Atlantova's icons support the work of a volunteer mobile hospital in Eastern Ukraine. The religious object is not just a sign, but also an actor, itself part of political, economic, and spiritual exchanges and transformations.

Other important art historical studies demonstrate how far this kind of inquiry can go toward addressing important historical questions. Joseph Koerner's influential *Reformation of the Image* (2004) used religious art in post-Reformation Germany to illuminate the practice of religion as Protestants came to terms with a disenchanted world and invented new

Figure 22.2 Sofia Atlantova (b. 1981) and Oleksandr Klymenko (b. 1975). Our Lady with the Child, 2018. Tempera, gold leaf, and ammunition box fragments, 49 x 53 cm. Collection of the artists. Photo: Yevhen Chorny.

collaborations between art and religion.[21] Mia Mochizuki's study of the remaking of St. Bavo's, Haarlem, where decorative *textborden* replaced pictures in the stripped, formerly Roman Catholic space, was similarly revelatory about the way religious images also figured new social and political relationships.[22] Although these studies can be considered work in visual culture, within the material religion movement distinctions between visual and material culture have faded, visual culture generally being recognized as simply one element of material culture. As Birgit Meyer has argued, "Since images do not only exist in the imagination, but have an objective existence and appeal to the senses, visual culture is obviously a part of material culture."[23] Studying religion as it takes shape in practice incorporates visual culture, material culture, performance studies, history of the book, media studies, somatic (sensory) studies – all the many ways religion is "materialized," including in cyberspace. "Material religion" has come to stand for all these things together.

At the center of material religion studies are many vexing words or terms that are notoriously difficult to define, "religion" and "culture" among them. Fortunately, scholars in this field have done a great deal of definitional work. In 2011, the editors of the influential journal *Material Religion* (established in 2005) published a special issue, "Key Words in

Material Religion." Experts delivered thorough, contemporary yet historically situated definitions for nineteen key words, including belief, body, icon/image, sacred, ritual, and spirit. S. Brent Plate expanded this list to thirty-seven short essays in the 2015 edited collection *Key Terms in Material Religion*, adding terms such as aesthetics, dress, food, prayer, and technology.[24]

In his useful introduction to *Key Terms*, Plate argues that understanding the significance of materiality in human society can help us better understand religion. He writes, "Religious traditions themselves originate and survive through bodily engagements with the material elements of the world." Plate defines "material religion" itself as: "(1) An investigation of the interactions between human bodies and physical objects, both natural and human-made; (2) with much of the interaction taking place through sense perception; (3) in special and specified times and places; (4) in order to orient, and sometimes disorient, communities and individuals; (5) toward the formal strictures and structures of religious traditions."[25] This working definition has the advantage of pointing to growing areas of inquiry in the field of religion: the entanglement of people and things in action; the primacy of bodies and embodiment; identity and community formation; and belief and tradition as something humans do as much as think.

Such a broad and dynamic understanding of material religion is apparent in the scholarship, much of it found in published collections of essays, in academic journals (most notably *Material Religion*), and on websites and blogs. Edited collections of short, focused studies, often the outgrowth of academic conferences, witness the diversity and ever-expanding boundaries of the field. One of the earliest collections, Morgan and Promey, *The Visual Cultures of American Religions* (2001), offered a largely art historical perspective.[26] Scholars from the sociology of religion have made several edited contributions: Arweck and Keenan, *Materializing Religion: Expression, Performance, and Ritual* (2006) and Hutchings and McKenzie, *Materiality and the Study of Religion: The Stuff of the Sacred* (2017).[27] Edited interdisciplinary collections include Morgan, *Religion and Material Culture: The Matter of Belief* (2010) and Houtman and Meyer, *Things: Religion and the Question of Materiality* (2012).[28] The latter volume contains twenty-one essays on topics as various as representations of the Virgin of Urkupina in Bolivia, Muslim prayer beads in North Cameroon, mass-produced Jesus pictures in Ghana, and consumerism and spirituality in Silicon Valley. Other edited volumes display a similar variety of topics with a wide range of disciplinary orientations and approaches. Two new edited collections, Opas and Haapalainen, *Christianity and the Limits of Materiality* (2017), and Meyer and Stordalen, *Figurations and Sensations of the Unseen in Judaism, Christianity, and Islam* (2019) push our understanding of how materiality figures in religions of the book.[29] Some of the contributions to these collections are heavily theoretical, some are historical, and others more ethnographic and based in extensive fieldwork. Although the earliest wave of this new approach to religion came predominantly from North America, as witnessed by these collections, European scholars are equally involved in the material religion movement, and topics circle the globe.

The content of *Material Religion*, the core journal for this approach to religion and material culture, deserves an in-depth account. *Material Religion*'s wide array of articles include studies of everyday objects, sacred objects, fine art, space and place, taste and sound, visual media, and performance – virtually every material channel of human activity and expression. Periodic special issues have pointed to percolating concerns in the field, including: "Global Pentecostalism" (2004), "Gender" (2006), "Media and the Senses" (2007), "Archaeology and Material Religion" (2008), "Muslims and Materiality" (2012); "Heritage and the Sacred" (2013); and "Material Religion in Latin America" (2017). Furthermore, the journal has a regular "In Conversation" feature that brings together a few scholars who exchange ideas on a topic such as "Dress, Religion, and Identity" (2010) or "Cataloging Magic" (2018). Working through a complete run of the journal *Material Religion* will give a reader a thorough understanding of both the field of material religion and the state of international scholarship in the material culture of religion today.

Another important node for scholarship in the material culture of religion is Yale University's Center for the Study of Material and Visual Culture of Religion (MAVCOR), an educational center that facilitates a wide and collaborative network of scholars, practitioners, and institutions, including many affiliated with religious traditions. Launched in 2011, MAVCOR's website states the grounding assumption of this inquiry: "Past and present religious practice, as inherently sensory and material as it is textual, is intimately engaged with 'stuff.'" The website suggests a research field of impressive material variety, worth quoting here at length:

> clothing, costume, jewelry, textiles, tattoos and other body modifications or adornments; landscape and the built environment, architecture and other forms of spatial organization or consolidation; paintings, prints, photographs, postcards, film, television, the internet and digital technologies; toys and games; maps; cartoons; sculpture, statuary, figurines; embroideries and needlework; educational ephemera; coins and currencies and postage stamps; devotional objects and implements; furniture; scrolls and books; bumper stickers, keychains and dashboard decorations; holiday displays; processions and parades; housewares, domesticities, and domestic technologies; certificates and other items commemorating rites of passage and accomplishment; advertisements, broadsides, posters, billboards; as well as images and objects seen and felt with the "interior senses," like the products of visionary experience and sensory imagination.[30]

Indeed, one can no longer consider the material culture of religion to be a category of things as much as one way to consider human interaction with the whole material world.[31]

It should be clear from the foregoing account that material religion is above all an *approach* to studying religion as it happens in the world, and not a category of artifact. Material religion scholarship addresses many types of objects and spaces, in a wide variety of religious contexts, often illuminating questions of political and social power and centering on practice. One benefit of this focus on what people do with objects is that things that are not obviously "religious" are of interest. What is religiously significant about an object may not be inscribed in the object itself and may be relational and temporary. For example, assemblages of nonmanufactured objects, such as those constituting a Vodou altar, have powerful religious presence and significance, but unless the assemblage and context is maintained, the meaning of the things may be lost.[32] The remains of such significant spiritual constructions might not be legible as sacred. Other hidden, sacred meanings can be discovered in the most basic of human activities, such as shopping. In the exercise of consumer choice, religion can inflect the acquisition and use of objects that otherwise appear entirely secular. For instance, in the selection of dress subtle modesty and restraint might be tied to religious practice.

Dress and adornment are a natural fit for material religion's concerns with embodiment and practice, as explored by the contributors to the edited collections *Religion, Dress and the Body* (1999) and *Undressing Religion* (2000).[33] Clothing and personal objects such as jewelry or a headscarf can be especially potent, sometimes controversial expressions of religious identity or even prejudice. Lynn Neal, for instance, studied American T-shirts with offensive anti-Muslim slogans, arguing that the simple T-shirt is, somewhat ironically, "the ideal article of democratic apparel for disseminating religious intolerance."[34]

Case Study 22.3

Muslim head scarves: expressive and contested objects

Religious identity is often deeply connected to what a person wears (or refuses to wear). Possibly no item of religious dress is presently more contested or misunderstood than the Muslim woman's head covering, debated within Muslim communities as well as without. The most limited covering is hijab, or the headscarf, a piece of fabric designed to cover the hair and head of an adult Muslim woman (Figure 22.3). It may be solid colored or patterned, and of many different fabrics.

Wearing the scarf in public company is an outward sign of the practice of hijab, a standard of modesty outlined in the Qur'an. It can thus be a statement of religious conviction, but also a political claim, a fashion statement, or a public declaration of group belonging and allegiance.[35]

> **Case Study 22.3 (cont.)**
>
> Humans read each others' faces for critical information about character and intent, and thus clothing that masks the face, such as the Islamic niqab (face veil, seen in the center of Figure 22.3) or full-body burka, can be perceived as especially threatening. Political bans of the headscarf are met by both outrage and relief. Muslims themselves disagree about the need to wear a head covering and what it means to wear one. What makes clothing such a particularly sensitive category of religious expression?

Figure 22.3 Store selling head scarves in Damascus, Syria, 2010. Photo: Bernard Gagnon. Wikimedia Commons.

Given the current tendency of religious studies to conceptualize religion as something intrinsically practiced and embodied, building bridges to the growing field of sensory studies is a natural development. Sally M. Promey, director of the MAVCOR center, organized an international, multi-year (2008–12) collaborative project on religion and the senses, resulting in a large volume of thirty-five essays, titled *Sensational Religion*.[36] These essays cover a wide variety of global topics, from the ingestion of sacred texts to the perception of angels, to hair embroidery in Chinese Buddhism. The sensory experience of religion is also the driving question behind S. Brent Plate's *A History of Religion in 5½ Objects: Bringing the Spiritual to its Senses*, in which he looks at the religious practices around stones, incense, drums, crosses, and bread. The "1/2" in the title "stands as a symbol of our incomplete natures, the need for a human body to be made whole through relations with something outside itself."[37] This area of scholarship also has the potential to connect in interesting and productive ways with developments in the fields of perception and neuroscience.

This summary of recent work in the field of material religion suggests both the questions scholars are asking and the content they are generating. They are finding religion and religious objects in new places, setting objects back in their multidimensional contexts, pushing for a more global scope of research, and crossing disciplinary boundaries. This amounts to not only new ways of thinking about religious material culture, but about religion itself.

Space, Place, and Religion

One of the most studied types of religious material culture has been architecture. Communal ritual or worship spaces in particular – visible expressions of shared faith, clearly connected to traditions and doctrines, situated in communities of practice, and aesthetically complex and intriguing – are multidimensional artifacts that reward a multidisciplinary approach. What might material religion bring to this enterprise? To begin: a broadening of definitions, an emphasis on practice, questions about how buildings and people work together in the making of religion, and a consideration of the dynamic, ever-evolving lives of buildings.

Case Study 22.4

Dynamic repurposing: Lake View Lutheran Church, Chicago

This choir loft, repurposed as a living room, speaks to the changing nature of a congregation, the flexibility and informality of Protestant architecture, and the practical resourcefulness of a community with limited assets.

Lake View Lutheran Church on Chicago's north side is the fourth building of a congregation founded by Scandinavian immigrants in 1848. By 1961, demographic changes had pushed the congregation to relocate and rebuild. On a small urban lot, the architect Charles Stade designed a simple rectangular sanctuary (seating about 200 in pews) above a full basement that houses classrooms, offices, and social spaces. The upper floor is a nononsense shell of space; the sacristy and choir gallery stand freely within. Flat glue-laminated timbers and wooden decking form the roof.

In the early 1960s, Lake View's congregation numbered in the hundreds. In 2012, a three-quarter time pastor preached in a sanctuary filled with a few dozen chairs. The building was in frank disrepair. Colored windowpanes were broken and patched, floors were peeling, and furnishings worn. Mechanical systems wheezed along. Yet upstairs on the west side of the choir loft, a sunny and comfortable place creatively used

Case Study 22.4 (cont.)

castaway furnishings to shape an intimate place for discussion, relaxation, and prayer. There were two worn upholstered chairs, a discarded couch, and circa 1980s side chairs placed on a plywood riser. Center table and end tables in earlier twentieth-century revival styles added aesthetic variety. A rust-tone carpet remnant with a baroque flourish defined the central space, approximately 12 x 15 feet. Throw pillows, old quilts, and a houseplant softened the edges.

Postwar choir lofts were typically back-of-the-house, minimally detailed spaces with inexpensive furnishings and finishes, that provided functional space for substantial choirs, heard but not seen by the worshippers below. Here, after a congregational space analysis determined that the sanctuary space was underutilized, it was repurposed into a place for council meetings, Alcoholics Anonymous meetings, small group studies, and, during Lent, as a place for quiet meditation.

In the postwar years, with an emphasis on the family and domestic intimacy, multiple casual social spaces were a counterpoint to the sacramental centers in nearly all American churches. Generally those spaces were located at some remove from the sanctuary. Today many Protestants question this division of space. The Lake View Lutheran congregation, however, is motivated not by a countercultural vision as much as a practical necessity. This loft space is an honest expression of the congregation's needs and its unpretentious character (Figure 22.4).

Figure 22.4 Repurposed choir loft, Lake View Lutheran Church, Chicago, Illinois, 1961. Photo: Author, 2012.

Following a late-twentieth-century "spatial turn" in religious studies, scholars of religion are putting more emphasis on how spaces act and are acted on and are turning their attention to a wider range of places. (See explanation of spatial theory in Gaddis, Chapter 19.) With Jonathan Z. Smith, they assume that places are made religious through ritual, and that religion can happen in even apparently secular places such as city streets or coffee houses.[38] David Chidester and Edward Linenthal's 1995 book *American Sacred Space* set the table for much future scholarly conversation about what makes space "sacred," how nonecclesiastical spaces participate in religious experience, and the dynamics of such spaces in community and practice.[39] The work of Thomas A. Tweed has also invited new ways of conceptualizing sacred space and integrating architecture and landscape. His studies of diasporic religion at a Cuban Catholic shrine in Miami, Florida (1997) and the Catholic Shrine of the Immaculate Conception in Washington, DC (2011) connect space and place to nationalism, borders and boundaries, and migration.[40] Tweed theorized further in his influential book *Crossing and Dwelling: A Theory of Religion*, which integrates ideas of materiality and spatiality into major religious studies themes of migration, globalization, and adaptation.[41] Tweed's work is helpful for thinking about the way many human beings – migrants, notably, but also people making sense of conflicting spiritual claims – have navigated multiple religious traditions or practices at the same time in ways not necessarily syncretic. See, for instance, the example of Native American students at the Phoenix Indian School in Arizona (noted by Casella and Kuglitsch, Chapter 21), who kept objects expressive of their inherited religious traditions, such as carved fetishes, while inhabiting a Christian environment.

A great deal of productive interest in religion and civic space is coming from social scientists mapping religious practices. Justin Wilford, in *Sacred Subdivisions*, explored various sacred spaces of the evangelical megachurch in suburban Los Angeles. By looking at how people were operating within a network of places, Wilford was able to argue that the megachurch inverts the expectations of core and periphery, with the heart of the movement not at the central architectural complex, but in the suburban homes of committed members who regularly meet in small groups for prayer and fellowship.[42] Claire Dwyer, leader of the "Making Suburban Faith" project at University College London has studied the material practices of faith in multicultural communities (Muslim, Hindu, Christian) of suburban London, demonstrating how attention to the geographies and material cultures of suburban religion enrich and complicate our understanding of both faith and suburbia.[43] As Kim Knott, Volkhard Krech, and Birgit Meyer note in their introduction to "Iconic Religion in Urban Space," "Visitors to the cities featured in this special issue [of *Material Religion*] – Berlin, London, Amsterdam and Granada – could not walk far without encountering the material traces of religion," such as religious buildings, posters and leaflets, dress, church bells, or an Islamic call to prayer.[44]

Space is clearly a useful concept for the study of religion, but in many cases close attention to the actual bricks and timbers of constructed space becomes secondary. Another vein of scholarship in the material culture of religion and place has closer ties to architectural history, often incorporating vernacular architecture, folklore, or anthropological approaches in which buildings and landscapes remain central and their materiality is explored in depth. An early harbinger of this architectural approach is Dell Upton's *Holy Things and Profane*, a study of Anglican parish churches in colonial Virginia, in which he used a broad social history approach to carefully describe and deeply contextualize buildings and to imagine human actors within them.[45] A more recent book by Gabrielle Berlinger, *Framing Sukkot*, investigates symbolic, ritual Jewish homes in Indiana, Israel, and New York in an interdisciplinary, comparative study that brings a material religion approach to an ancient architectural form in contemporary, cross-cultural settings.[46] Berlinger's work, in particular, points the way for future studies of the built environment that will cross all sorts of disciplinary, interpretive, and material boundaries without losing sight of the objects themselves.

Religion in Museums

An important and distinctive contribution of the material religion movement has been the insistence that academic scholars and museum professionals be in dialogue on the topic of religion. Many types of museums – anthropological, historical, art – contain objects with religious content or history, and scholarship on religious artifacts has long been rooted in museums and their collections. Curators have studied and labeled these objects according to their aesthetic character, iconographic symbolism, and sometimes (particularly in anthropological museums) their role in ritual. For the most part, however, the potential of these artifacts to say something more about religion has remained untapped. In Chapter 11 on Indigenous heritage, Emily Moore notes that, in art museums, Native American artifacts have typically been displayed without attention to ethnographic context. This has been true to a large degree, in fact, for *most* religious objects in art museums, where aesthetic conventions of display have typically outweighed the need for context. In the broader museum universe, exhibitions on the religious practices and material culture of various faith communities have been infrequent at best.

More recently, museums have been alert to the possibility that the exhibition and interpretation of religious artifacts, both historic and contemporary, is ripe for development and experimentation. In 1996, the Ackland Museum at the University of North Carolina hosted a multi-year

"Five Faiths Project" that brought the community together to consider the material expressions of five major faith traditions that had a presence in their community: Christianity, Islam, Buddhism, Judaism, and Hinduism. The project, based in exhibitions, was rich in professional and community conversations and resulted in a publication, *A Place for Meaning*, that tells the story of the project in careful detail.[47] In 2000, Crispin Paine published his path-breaking edited volume, *Godly Things: Museums, Objects and Religion*, which included fourteen essays covering a range of global places and traditions. Paine followed in 2013 with a single-authored volume, *Religious Objects in Museums: Private Lives and Public Duties*, an expansive essay focused on the tremendous variety of religious objects in museums and on the relationships among objects, curators, and visitors activated in the construction of meaning.[48] In 2009, the International Committee for Museums and Collections of the International Council of Museums hosted a conference, *Museums and Faith*, in Luxembourg, of which the proceedings were subsequently published.[49] That conference highlighted the way that museum professionals, in Europe especially, were grappling with an unexpected resurgence in religion that challenged their expectations of secularity. More recently, another edited volume, *Religion in Museums: Global and Interdisciplinary Perspectives*, charts the progress in this field.[50]

Well-attended exhibitions with a focus on religious material culture and practice are evidence of public interest in religion. Just a few examples include: "Hajj: Journey to the Heart of Islam" at the British Museum (2012); "Shalom Chicago" at the Chicago History Museum (2013), "National Geographic Sacred Journeys" at the Children's Museum of Indianapolis (2015–16), and "Encountering the Buddha: Art and Practice across Asia" at the Freer/Sackler museum of Asian Art (2017–20). Some museums have purposefully tackled topics in religion and material culture that challenge their communities, such as the exhibition "My Headscarf" at the Amsterdam Historical Museum in 2006.[51]

The institutions interpreting the material culture of religion for the public are widespread and varied. Some focus primarily on religious material culture and religious history, including St. Mungo Museum (Glasgow, Scotland); the Marburg Museum of Religions (Marburg, Germany); the State Museum of the History of Religion (St. Petersburg, Russia); the Topkapi Palace Museum (Istanbul, Turkey); Glencairn Museum (Bryn Athyn, Pennsylvania, USA); and the new and controversial Museum of the Bible in Washington, DC. There are also, of course, many religiously affiliated sites that serve as places of pilgrimage and group cohesion as well as educational sites. Religious theme parks, such as the Holy Land Experience in Orlando, Florida, or the Hindu Swaminarayan (BAPS) Akshardham theme park and temple in Gandhinagar, Gujarat, India – hybrids of museum, sacred space, and entertainment venue – are less sites of interpretation than themselves revealing subjects of scholarly inquiry.[52]

One of the most intriguing questions about religious artifacts in museums is whether, and in what way, the spiritual significance of certain material things should be affectively present in the secular museum.

Case Study 22.5

Vodou: strategies of interpretation and display

Vodou is a syncretic, decentralized religious practice formed in Haiti and the American South when West African spiritual traditions collided with European Christianity after colonization. The 2014–15 exhibition "Vodou: Sacred Powers of Haiti," an installation of 300 objects at the Field Museum in Chicago, illustrated the opportunities and challenges of presenting highly evocative, magical, and powerful religious objects in a museum setting. In the dimly lit galleries, the lack of barriers between visitors and objects contributed to a rich sensory engagement with the artifacts. Numerous video stations, showing the enactment of rituals and interviews with practitioners, served as context, but the mediation of the curatorial expert faded when the visitor confronted the objects, in particular a low platform with a dense crowd of menacing, life-sized, padded-cloth figures, painted black and red and covered in mirrors. These *lwa* (spirits) represent the "defensive and combative" Vodou practiced by secret societies that emerged during slavery.[53]

One exhibition label read,
SUFFERING, RAGE, POWER

> They are one-eyed, mutilated and maimed. Our *lwa* (spirits) emerged from the battles of the past and present, where no amount of suffering deterred our quest for freedom. They grimace, bare their teeth, carry weapons and seem ready to destroy everything in their path. Our *lwa* were born of our rage in the face of our oppressor's refusal to treat us as equals. As a precautionary measure, we *marre* (tie up) our *lwa*, binding them with ropes and chains. They hold enormous power, proportionate to the ideas that have always sustained us.

To Western eyes, these objects may hold negative associations with magic and the occult. Other parts of the exhibition carefully debunk Hollywood "voodoo" stereotypes. How might a display like this navigate historical truth and stereotype? How might the fact that the encounter between these objects and the viewer takes place in a museum exhibition shape the interaction and response?

Of course, not every visitor will react the same way to a given object or installation, and the received meaning of these things on one level will be impossible for museums to control. In "Sacred to Profane and Back Again," Ivan Gaskell asks, "Should not certain objects be addressed in religious terms, even though they remain in museums? Should certain objects not remain in museums, but be returned to those who would treat them principally in religious terms?"[54] Gaskell offers three examples of compromise responses to these questions: a Tibetan altar installed at the Newark Museum and consecrated by the Dalai Lama in 1990; the spiritually and politically important twelfth-century *Virgin of Vladimir* Orthodox icon, currently exhibited in a historic church building in Moscow connected by tunnel to the State Tretyakov Gallery, an arrangement that preserves both church and state claims to ownership of the icon; and the Peabody Museum at Harvard's return of Hupa dance regalia to its Northern California tribe, who then placed the regalia in the Hoopa Tribal Museum for occasional appearance at dances (not for use). Gaskell's last example reflects ongoing debate about the ownership of Native American/First Nations sacred objects in museum collections in the USA and Canada. Following the Native American Graves Protection and Repatriation Act of 1990 (NAGPRA) in the USA, many museums had to rethink their relationship with these objects and the descendants of the objects' makers, and then negotiate repatriation or collaborative care.[55]

As scholars of religious material culture turn toward the idea that religion is something that exists in experience and practice, as something that is *made* as well as thought, museums have a unique opportunity to convey this dynamic to visitors. Museums can create affective environments that focus attention on objects, encouraging contemplation and questioning that can go beyond dispassionate, didactic instruction to capture some of the sensory and emotional aspects of lived religion.[56] As Crispin Paine notes, the exhibition format can allow learners to get closer to the way religion is actually experienced, to understand that religion does not have to be translated into text.[57]

Future Directions

Shifting the focus to the material aspects of religion has fundamentally changed the way religion is understood by many scholars, particularly regarding the popular experience of "religions of the book" such as Judaism, Islam, and Christianity. Of course, not all scholars of religious visual and material culture would readily identify with this movement. Some, such as those who study Orthodox icons or Native American ceremonial artifacts, may rightly believe they have been attending to presence and practice all along. Yet the vigor and new critical and theoretical approaches of material religion have influenced this corner of material culture studies immeasurably.

In 2015, to mark the tenth anniversary of the journal *Material Religion*, the editors offered a reflection on where the study of material religion has been and where it is going.[58] Taking the journal's content as a measure of activity in the field, they were pleased with its global reach, transdisciplinary nature, and representation of diverse religions, although they noted the need for more work on Asian, South American, and African, ancient and medieval topics, as well as on Oceanic and First Nations religions. They predicted attention to sensory history will continue to grow, as well as the integration of insights from cognitive psychology and neuroscience. They further suggest that more comparative, diachronic, detailed, and descriptive fieldwork in material religion can lead to important insights. Finbarr Barry Flood's 2009 study of material culture at the nexus of interreligious encounter in medieval South Asia indicates what might be learned by recovering the creative interactions around material culture, between peoples of different religious traditions.[59]

Not all those who work in material religion have given concentrated attention to the actual physical qualities of objects and spaces. As Birgit Meyer explained, "Some of us are even more concerned with what people do with things [practices] than the things themselves."[60] This tendency, although not necessarily diminishing the work that has been done, opens opportunities for scholars with particular expertise in object study who can help to ensure that the study of material religion gains the benefits of close attention to tangible materiality.

Case Study 22.6

Ganesha and auspicious beginnings: Does the medium matter?

When religion takes material form, it does so in a particular medium, chosen by its maker and later selected by its user/consumer. Hinduism is a richly visual and material faith, manifest in a wide variety of forms, images, and practices. For instance, Hindus embrace a diversity of colorful material expressions of the deities in a wide range of media, including popular and electronic.

The Hindu elephant god Ganesha, instantly recognizable by his trunk and large ears, is the god of auspicious beginnings, one who welcomes and prospers devotees (Figure 22.5). Ganesha takes form as medieval bronzes now in the collections of major art museums, sculpted stone deities in temples, but also on popular and inexpensive "God posters," or as a cartoon character in a popular children's television show.[61] This example is a small, nine-inch tall, crystal figurine from a household in Bangalore, India, a decorative object that is also revered. Does its particular, fragile medium affect the believer's interaction with the object and experience of religion, or affect the level of care the object receives? What does the *materiality* of material culture convey in the realm of religion? How do differing technologies affect the way a believer experiences the divine?

> Case Study 22.6 (cont.)
>
> **Figure 22.5** Ganesha statue, crystal. Photo: Sundar Ganesh Babu.

Finally, current global conditions will inevitably shape the way religion is conceptualized and studied. As David Morgan noted, "we are in the business of parsing enormous and very intricate assemblages" and attention to both methodology and personal bias is necessary. Just as the late-twentieth-century reinvigoration of religious studies emerged out of the post-secular, transnational experiences of scholars, we may expect the political and ethical concerns of the present age – including identity politics, materialism, consumerism, transhumanism, and nationalism – to inflect future scholarship in material religion in both academia and museums.

Notes

1. See Talal Asad, *Genealogies of Religion: Discipline and Reasons of Power in Christianity and Islam* (Baltimore: Johns Hopkins University Press, 1993).
2. See Emil Durkheim, *The Elementary Forms of Religious Life* (1912; reprint Oxford University Press, 2008).
3. For a survey of the development of the field of religious studies, see Slavica Jakelić and Jessica Starling, "Religious Studies: A Bibliographical

Essay," *Journal of the American Academy of Religion* 74, no. 1 (March 2006), 194–211, 209–10; Peter L. Berger, *The Desecularization of the World: Resurgent Religion and World Politics* (Grand Rapids: Wm. B. Eerdmans, 1999).

4. The use of the term "spirituality" here conveys practices that are, or appear to be, outside the bounds of communal or institutional religion, such as the growing tendency of Americans to label themselves "spiritual but not religious."
5. Jakelić and Starling, "Religious Studies: A Bibliographical Essay."
6. Robert Orsi, *The Madonna of 115th Street: Faith and Community in Italian Harlem* (New Haven: Yale University Press, 1985); Leigh Eric Schmidt, *Consumer Rites: The Buying and Selling of American Holidays* (Princeton: Princeton University Press, 1997).
7. Colleen McDannell, *Material Christianity: Religion and Popular Culture in America* (New Haven: Yale University Press, 1995), 87–98, 267. For early work on popular visual culture and religion, see David Morgan, ed., *Icons of American Protestantism: The Art of Warner Sallman* (New Haven: Yale University Press, 1996) and Morgan, *Protestants and Pictures: Religion, Visual Culture, and the Age of Mass Production* (Oxford: Oxford University Press, 1999).
8. Lauren Winner, *A Cheerful and Comfortable Faith: Anglican Religious Practices in the Elite Households of Eighteenth-Century Virginia* (New Haven: Yale University Press, 2010). See also Louis P. Nelson, *The Beauty of Holiness: Anglicanism and Architecture in Colonial South Carolina* (Chapel Hill: University of North Carolina Press, 2009).
9. John Kieschnick, "Material Culture" in John Corrigan, ed., *The Oxford Handbook of Religion and Emotion*, published online September 2009, 5. https://bit.ly/31Hz01G. See also Pamela D. Winfield and Steven Heine, eds., *Zen and Material Culture* (Oxford: Oxford University Press, 2017).
10. Benjamin J. Fleming and Richard D. Mann's edited collection *Material Culture and Asian Religions* (Routledge, 2014) brings this approach to religions in Asia (including Islam and Christianity). Many of the contributions consider the physical form of texts, objects within texts, and human interaction with them.
11. Interdisciplinary conversations have been helpful, for instance, in furthering the study of religion among archaeologists. See Julian Droogan, *Religion, Material Culture, and Archaeology* (London: Bloomsbury, 2013); Colin Renfrew and Iain Morley, eds., *Becoming Human: Innovation in Prehistoric Material and Spiritual Culture* (Cambridge: Cambridge University Press, 2009); Timothy Insoll, *Archaeology, Ritual, Religion* (London: Routledge, 2004); and Miguel Astor-Aguilera, *The Maya World of Communicating Objects: Quadripartite Crosses, Trees & Stones* (Albuquerque: University of New Mexico Press, 2010).

12. Although not specifically about material culture, two recent collections provide the contemporary contours of pilgrimage studies and illustrate how much material culture study is playing a role within that field. See Dionigi Albera and John Eade, eds., *International Perspectives on Pilgrimage Studies: Itineraries, Gaps, and Obstacles* (London and New York: Routledge, 2015); and Albera and Eade, eds., *New Pathways in Pilgrimage Studies* (London and New York: Routledge, 2017).
13. See Manuel A. Vasquez, *More than Belief: A Materialist Theory of Religion* (Oxford: Oxford University Press, 2010).
14. Elizabeth Perez, *Religion in the Kitchen: Cooking, Talking, and the Making of Black Atlantic Traditions* (New York: New York University Press, 2016); Amy Mills, *Streets of Memory: Landscape, Tolerance, and National Identity in Istanbul* (Athens: University of Georgia Press, 2010); Kathryn Lofton, "The Spirit in the Cubicle: A Religious History of the American Office," in Lofton, *Consuming Religion* (Chicago: University of Chicago Press, 2017); Joseph Sciorra, *Built with Faith: Italian American Imagination and Catholic Material Culture in New York City* (Knoxville: University of Tennessee Press, 2015).
15. Agustín Fuentes, lecture five, "Why Do We Believe?" March 8, 2018, University of Edinburgh. www.youtube.com/watch?v=Im_swwR6hsM.
16. See Colin Renfrew, "Situating the Creative Explosion: Universal or Local?" in Colin Renfrew and Iain Morley, eds., *Becoming Human: Innovation in Prehistoric Material and Spiritual Culture* (Cambridge: Cambridge University Press, 2009), 79–80.
17. Agustín Fuentes and Mark Kissel, "Semiosis in the Pleistocene," *Cambridge Archaeological Journal* 27, no. 3 (2017), 397–412. https://bit.ly/31Bxo9P.
18. See Diana Eck, *Darsan: Seeing the Divine Image in India* (New York: Columbia University Press, 1998); Morgan, *Protestants and Pictures*; Sally M. Promey, *Spiritual Spectacles: Vision and Image in Mid Nineteenth-Century Shakerism* (Bloomington: Indiana University Press, 1993); Hans Belting, *Likeness and Presence: A History of the Image before the Era of Art* (Chicago: University of Chicago Press, 1997); Stewart M. Hoover, *Religion in the Media Age* (London: Routledge, 2006).
19. David Freedberg, *The Power of Images: Studies in the History and Theory of Response* (Chicago: University of Chicago Press, 1989); Alfred Gell, *Art and Agency: An Anthropological Theory* (Oxford: Oxford University Press, 1998).
20. David Morgan, *Visual Piety: A History and Theory of Popular Religious Images* (Berkeley: University of California Press, 1999), 1–20. Quote, 20.
21. Joseph Koerner, *The Reformation of the Image* (London: Reaktion, 2004).
22. Mia M. Mochizuki, *The Netherlandish Image after Iconoclasm, 1576–1672: Material Religion in the Dutch Golden Age* (London: Ashgate, 2008).
23. In Birgit Meyer, David Morgan, Crispin Paine, and S. Brent Plate, "Material Religion's First Decade," *Material Religion* 10, no. 1

(March 2014), 108. See also Hans Belting's use of "iconic presence" in Belting, "Iconic Presence: Images in Religious Tradition," *Material Religion* 12, no. 2 (June 2016), 235–37, in special issue on "Iconic Religion in Urban Space," and David Morgan, *The Embodied Eye: Religious Visual Culture and the Social Life of Seeing* (Berkeley: University of California Press, 2012).

24. *Material Religion* 7, no. 1 (March 2011); S. Brent Plate, *Key Terms in Material Religion*. (London: Bloomsbury, 2015). See also David Chidester's lengthy review of Mark C. Taylor's *Critical Terms in Religious Studies* (Chicago: University of Chicago Press, 1998), in which he notes the rise of embodiment and materiality within religious studies. Chidester, "Material Terms for the Study of Religion," *Journal of the American Academy of Religion* 68, no. 2 (June 2000), 367–80. Chidester suggests that what he calls "new materialism" "implicitly recasts religion as a category for analyzing materiality." For a different and provocative use of the term "new materialism" in religious studies, see Sonia Hazard, "The Material Turn in the Study of Religion," *Religion and Society: Advances in* Research 4 (2013), 58–71. Hazard argues that material religion studies remain too anthropocentric.

25. Plate, *Key Terms*, 4. See also David Morgan, "Religion and Embodiment in the Study of Material Culture," *Oxford Research Encyclopedia of Religion*. March 2015. https://bit.ly/3oygLVn.

26. David Morgan and Sally M. Promey, eds., *The Visual Cultures of American Religions* (Berkeley: University of California Press, 2001).

27. Elisabeth Arweck and William Keenan, eds., *Materializing Religion: Expression, Performance, and Ritual* (London: Routledge, 2006) and Tim Hutchings and Joanne McKenzie, eds., *Materiality and the Study of Religion: The Stuff of the Sacred* (London: Routledge, 2017).

28. David Morgan, ed., *Religion and Material Culture: The Matter of Belief* (London: Routledge, 2010) and Dick Houtman and Birgit Meyer, eds., *Things: Religion and the Question of Materiality* (New York: Fordham University Press, 2012). Other edited collections of note include Ceri Houlbrook and Natalie Armitage, eds., *The Materiality of Magic* (Oxford: Oxford University Press, 2015) and Fleming and Mann, *Material Culture and Asian Religions*.

29. Minna Opas and Anna Haapalainen, eds., *Christianity and the Limits of Materiality* (London: Bloomsbury Academic, 2017), and Birgit Meyer and Terje Stordalen, eds., *Figurations and Sensations of the Unseen in Judaism, Christianity, and Islam* (London: Bloomsbury Academic, 2019). These works are early installments in a promising new book series.

30. Anne Grant, "Adonai/Adidas T-shirt." MAVCOR, Yale University. https://bit.ly/3ozqpax.

31. Websites and blogs in the field of material religion are multiplying. The MAVCOR website presents bibliography, short articles, and object studies. https://mavcor.yale.edu/material-visual-cultures-religions. One of

the first major material religion collaborative projects, the "Material History of Religion" (1995–2001) is still accessible through its website, "Material Religion." See Material Religion, www.materialreligion.org/index.html. David Morgan identified this website as a source for the term "material religion." Email correspondence with author, October 25, 2018. A more recent venture, the "Material Religions" blog, created by anthropologists John J. McGraw and Urmila Mohan, collates news, articles, and bibliography from a predominantly social science perspective. See https://materialreligions.blogspot.com/p/about.html. These are just a few of the online sources that testify to the vitality of the field, its breadth, and its interdisciplinary nature.

32. Natalie Armitage, "Vodou Material Culture in the Museum: Reflections on the Complexities of Demonstrating Material Culture of Assemblage and Accumulation in a Traditional Museum Environment," *Material Religion* 14, no. 2 (2018), 218–34.

33. Linda B. Arthur, ed., *Religion, Dress, and the Body* (Oxford: Berg, 1999); Arthur, ed., *Undressing Religion: Commitment and Conversion from a Cross-Cultural Perspective* (Oxford: Berg, 2000).

34. Lynn S. Neal, "The Ideal Democratic Apparel: T-shirts, Religious Intolerance, and the Clothing of Democracy," *Material Religion* 10, no. 2 (2014), 182–207. Quote, 85. See also Anne Grant, "Adonai/Adidas T-shirt" on MAVCOR website, https://mavcor.yale.edu/conversations/object-narratives/adonaiadidas-t-shirt and Colleen McDannell, "Mormon Garments: Sacred Clothing and the Body," in McDannell, *Material Christianity*, 198–221.

35. See Annelies Moors, "The Affective Power of the Face Veil," in Dick Houtman and Birgit Meyer, eds., *Things: Religion and the Question of Materiality* (New York: Fordham University Press, 2012), 282–95. Joan Wallach Scott, *The Politics of the Veil* (Princeton: Princeton University Press, 2007), though not a material culture study, is a useful source. See also Rafia Zakaria, *Veil (Object Lessons)* (London: Bloomsbury Academic, 2017); Elizabeth Arweck, "Religion Materialized in the Everyday: Young People's Attitudes towards Material Expressions of Religion," in Tim Hutchings and Joanne McKenzie, eds., *Materiality and the Study of Religion: The Stuff of the Sacred* (London: Routledge, 2017), 185–202; "Secular Europe, Headscarves and Identity" with comments by Annelies Moors and Shabana Mir, *Material Religion* 6, no. 1 (2010), 111–16.

36. Sally M. Promey, ed., *Sensational Religion: Sensory Cultures in Material Practice* (New Haven: Yale University Press, 2014). See also Alexandra Grieser and Jay Johnston, *Aesthetics of Religion* (Berlin: De Gruyter, 2017).

37. S. Brent Plate, *A History of Religion in 5½ Objects: Bringing the Spiritual to its Senses* (Boston: Beacon Press, 2014). For sound, see Isaac Weiner, *Religion Out Loud: Religious Sound, Public Space, and American Pluralism* (New York: New York University Press, 2013).

38. Jonathan Z. Smith, *To Take Place: Toward Theory in Ritual* (Chicago: University of Chicago Press, 1987).
39. David Chidester, and Edward T. Linenthal, *American Sacred Space* (Bloomington: Indiana University Press, 1995).
40. Thomas A. Tweed, *Our Lady of the Exile: Diasporic Religion at a Cuban Catholic Shrine in Miami* (Oxford: Oxford University Press, 1997); Tweed, *America's Church: The National Shrine and Catholic Presence in the Nation's Capital, 1917–1997* (Oxford: Oxford University Press, 2011). As Kim Knott argues in a review essay covering new scholarship up to 2010, much of the contemporary way of thinking about religion, space, and place centers either on *poetics* (phenomenological questions of human relationship to the divine), or *politics* (concerns about power, conflict, and identity formation and contestation in human community). Kim Knott, "Religion, Space, and Place: The Spatial Turn in Research and Religion," *Religion and Society: Advances in Research* 1 (2010), 29–43. Some scholars, like Tweed, do both.
41. Thomas A. Tweed, *Crossing and Dwelling: A Theory of Religion* (Cambridge: Harvard University Press, 2008).
42. Justin Wilford, *Sacred Subdivisions: The Posturban Transformation of American Evangelicalism* (New York: New York University Press, 2012).
43. Claire Dwyer, "Spiritualizing the Suburbs: New Religious Architecture in Suburban London and Vancouver," in Victoria Hegner and Peter Jan Margry, eds., *Spiritualizing the City* (London: Routledge, 2017), 115–29; "Making Suburban Faith" website, https://makingsuburbanfaith.wordpress.com/about-2. This project also includes hands-on, collaborative art making, allowing scholars to witness the body-object-idea dynamic in operation. See also Claire Dwyer, "Why Does Religion Matter for Cultural Geographers?" *Social and Cultural Geography* 17, no. 6 (2016), 758–62. www.tandfonline.com/doi/full/10.1080/14649365.2016.1163728.
44. Special issue of *Material Religion* 12, no. 2 (2016). Quote, 125. See also Orsi, *Madonna of 115th Street*; Margaret Olin, "Introduction to the Eruv" on MAVCOR website, https://bit.ly/3lIeZQ0.
45. Dell Upton, *Holy Things and Profane: Anglican Parish Churches in Colonial Virginia* (Cambridge: MIT Press, 1986). Upton's broad interpretive approach influenced much subsequent scholarship. See Louis P. Nelson, *The Beauty of Holiness*; Gretchen Buggeln, *The Suburban Church: Modernism and Community in Postwar America* (Minneapolis: University of Minnesota Press, 2015); Nelson, ed., *American Sanctuary: Understanding Sacred Spaces* (Bloomington: Indiana University Press, 2006); Robert Proctor, *Building the Modern Church: Roman Catholic Church Architecture in Britain, 1955 to 1975* (London: Routledge, 2014); Thomas Carter, *Building Zion: The Material World of Mormon Settlement* (Minneapolis: University of Minnesota Press, 2015).

46. Gabrielle Berlinger, *Framing Sukkot: Tradition and Transformation in Jewish Vernacular Architecture* (Bloomington: Indiana University Press, 2017).
47. Amanda Millay Hughes and Carolyn H. Wood, *A Place for Meaning: Art, Faith, and Museum Culture* (Chapel Hill: University of North Carolina Press, 2009).
48. Crispin Paine, *Godly Things: Museums, Objects, and Religion* (Leicester: Leicester University Press, 2009); Paine, *Religious Objects in Museums: Private Lives and Public Duties* (London: Bloomsbury Academic, 2012).
49. Marie-Paule Jungblut and Rosmarie Beier-DeHaan, eds., *Museums and Faith* (Luxembourg: ICOM and Musee d'Historie de la Ville de Luxembourg, 2010).
50. Gretchen Buggeln, Crispin Paine, and S. Brent Plate, eds., *Religion in Museums: Global and Interdisciplinary Perspectives* (London: Bloomsbury, 2017). See also Gretchen Buggeln and Barbara Franco, eds., *Interpreting Religion at Museums and Historic Sites* (Lanham: Rowman & Littlefield and the American Association of State and Local History, 2018).
51. See Annemarie van den Dekker, review of "My Headscarf" exhibition at Amsterdam Historical Museum, *Material Religion* 2, no. 3 (2006), 399–401. The exhibition included videotaped interviews with, and objects lent by, young Muslim women.
52. Crispin Paine, "Religious Theme Parks," *Material Religion* 12, no. 3 (2016), 402–03. See also Paine, *Gods and Rollercoasters: Religion in Theme Parks Worldwide* (London: Bloomsbury Academic, 2019). See also Annabel Jane Wharton, *Selling Jerusalem: Relics, Replicas, Theme Parks* (Chicago: University of Chicago Press, 2006).
53. See Armitage, "Vodou Material Culture in the Museum," 218–34.
54. Gaskell, Ivan, "Sacred to Profane and Back Again," in Andrew McClellan, *Art and Its Publics: Museum Studies at the Millennium* (Malden: Blackwell, 2003), 149–62. Quote, 150.
55. *Stewards of the Sacred*, proceedings of a conference at Harvard University's Center for the Study of World Religions, is an important collection of responses to these issues. See Lawrence Sullivan and Alison Edwards, eds., *Stewards of the Sacred* (Washington, DC: American Association of Museums, 2004).
56. For an interesting example of affective installations in an art museum, see Gary Vikan, "Bringing the Sacred into Art Museums," in Buggeln, Paine, and Plate, *Religion in Museums*, 205–10.
57. See Meyer et al., "Material Religion's First Decade," 105–11.
58. Meyer et al., "Material Religion's First Decade."
59. Finbarr B. Flood, *Objects of Translation: Material Culture and Medieval "Hindu-Muslim" Encounter* (Princeton: Princeton University Press, 2009).
60. Meyer et al., "Material Religion's First Decade," 105.
61. See Diana Eck, *Darsan*; Christopher Pinney, *Photos of the Gods: The Printed Image and Political Struggle in India* (London: Reakton Books, 2004).

Part VI

Materiality and the Digital World

In the digital world, there are numerous technologies that we are attached to that create infinite interruptions.

Timothy Ferriss

23

Material Cultures of the Digital

Ryan Cordell

Introduction

When Google sought to expand its data center operations in 2009, the company bought an abandoned paper mill in Hamina, Finland. Built in 1953, the Summa Mill had been operated by Finnish pulp and paper manufacturer Stora Enso but was closed in 2008 due to "a drop in newsprint and magazine-paper production" and because "newspapers and magazines are slowly giving way to web services along the lines of, well, Google." According to *Wired* magazine, Google was interested in the mill because it "included an underground tunnel once used to pull water from the Gulf of Finland" to cool "a steam generation plant at the mill." Google needed efficient and ecologically friendly cooling systems, as well – not for a steam plant, but to cool the processors and other components in its massive servers (Figure 23.1). "Google's Hamina data center is," *Wired* declared, "the ideal metaphor for the digital age."[1] We might recognize in *Wired*'s confident emblemizing of this factory a tidy narrative of new media in which the future necessarily subsumes the past, eliding the messier present.

While popular press accounts of Google's paper mill purchase tended to claim the purchase illustrated the digital replacing its preceding media, it might instead remind us of the ways material cultures imbricate across time. Google purchased a space designed to produce one kind of information medium because its design, only slightly modified, would well serve the needs of a new information medium. Through this process the tech giant collapsed "analog" and "digital" material histories into one entwined narrative. As Alan Liu contends, narratives of new media too often hinge on ideas of replacement or conversion, while "the better term is indeed 'encounter,' indicating a thick, unpredictable zone of contact – more borderland than border line – where (mis)understandings of new media are negotiated along twisting, partial, and contradictory vectors." In this

Figure 23.1 A server room at CERN. Creative Commons image via Wikimedia Commons.

encounter, the data center inhabits the paper mill, and the paper mill shapes – at least partially – the data center, a "*déjà vu* haunting of new by old media."[2]

Such encounters are everywhere in the histories of hardware and software. For instance, early Internet companies like Prodigy and America Online relied on the infrastructure of the US Postal Service to distribute CD-ROMS of their software cheaply to potential users, as well as on the infrastructure of telephone lines to connect those users to the World Wide Web. More recently, Nicole Starsielski has traced the global fiber-optic network, a planet-spanning series of "winding cables the size of a garden hose" that run underground and undersea to "transport 99 percent of all transoceanic digital communications, including phone calls, text and e-mail messages, websites, digital images and video, and even some television." Like Google's paper mill-cum-server farm, the extensive infrastructure of the global Internet often "follow[s] ... the contours of earlier networks, layered on top of earlier telegraph and telephone cables, power systems, lines of cultural immigration, and trade routes."[3] We cannot consider the Internet's history or present without also considering the objects and people who have constituted its network, or indeed the previously existing networks the Internet runs along or rides atop.

A popular aphorism in the computing profession reads, "THERE IS NO CLOUD: It's just someone else's computer." This phrase appears on laptop stickers and t-shirts, and on a bevy of coffee mugs found in computer science departments, tech conventions, and the offices of Internet start-ups. This aphorism offers a wry reminder that for all the airy metaphors we use to discuss computation in the Internet age, data does not drift around the atmosphere. A computer is every bit as *material* an artifact as an abacus or printing press, as are the servers, cables, monitors, and other objects that make up the computational ecosystem. According to Tung-Hui Hu's *A Prehistory of the Cloud*, "The cloud is both an idea and a physical and material object, and the more one learns about it, the more one realizes just how fragile it is."[4] It is incumbent on scholars of material culture across disciplines to learn about this constellation of objects we call the cloud if we are to account for this age.

Nevertheless, we often talk of the newly ubiquitous "apparatus" of the digital age – to borrow N. Katherine Hayles's word in *Writing Machines* – as if they were objects made of mist rather than metal, plastic, glass, and wire.[5] In fact, the phrase "It's just someone else's computer" somewhat diminishes the full materiality of the Internet. What we call "the cloud" comprises *a lot* of computers and servers, linked by routers, switches, and overland or undersea cables: the *network* of the World Wide Web. In Chapter 24 of this volume, Natasha Chuk writes, "The World Wide Web is precisely what its name implies: a global network of material and virtual nodes and connections with material impact between them."[6] As of 2017, Google alone operated fifteen data centers around the world, with many other smaller "cloud centers" and "caching sites" supplementing their operations. The largest of these facilities approaches one million square feet, while reports about a new Google data center in the Netherlands claimed, "the company ... contracted for the entire 62 Megawatt output of a nearby windfarm and ran 9,941 miles of computer cable within the facility."[7] The infrastructure for other major tech companies, such as Facebook or Amazon, is just as expansive, while a host of others employ smaller – but still extensive – server farms and data centers. While they exude, perhaps, an aura of corporate sterility off-putting to many scholars of material culture, such data centers comprise the backbone of digital culture and, though often unseen by users, leave enormous economic, environmental, and material footprints in the world.

We are faced with a strange and hazardous irony in the digital age: surrounded by a rapidly proliferating domain of objects, increasingly central to our social, economic, and political lives, we fall back on a strange dichotomy of "digital" versus "analog," eliding the much more complex and interesting ways these two modes entwine and interact. Popular attitudes toward the digital vary widely and are often highly contradictory. Digital content is both unreliably ephemeral and stubbornly eternal; hyperlinks go dead rapidly, and thus cannot suffice as scholarly references, while embarrassing photos posted to social media in high school will surely derail presidential campaigns decades hence. Such contradictions arise in part due to the novel materiality of digital media, which is both widely distributed (i.e., pervasive) and rapidly iterative (i.e., impermanent). For scholars of material culture, the digital represents the fastest-growing domain of material culture in the late twentieth and early twenty-first centuries, both in terms of its literal materials and its broader cultural effects. Understanding and theorizing the material culture of the digital is thus one of the field's most pressing mandates.

"Digital" was never truly a synonym for "virtual," and each year the boundary between digital and analog materiality becomes more difficult to ascertain. Three-dimensional printing technologies manifest computational models in human spaces: everything from pop-culture tchotchkes to artificial human organs. Our digital network now connects a vast, growing, and uniquely vulnerable "Internet of Things" to the Internet and to each other. The Internet of Things comprises the light bulbs, refrigerators, home security systems, thermostats, garage door openers, and other not-obviously computational devices we now can control from other devices, thus scattering the material culture of the digital across a wide swathe of twenty-first century culture writ large. Even more broadly, from our computers, tablets, and phones we summon people into action and spur a host of material objects into circulation. We click a button, for instance, and a worker begins hunting in an enormous factory for the item we have ordered, the first human being in a chain of humans who will close the commercial circuit. As Chuk writes, the digital reconfigures our physical relationship to other people as "our mobile devices encourage habits of remotely socializing with persons who are not physically in present company, instead establishing a space of absent-present company, that is, company that is physically absent but digitally present."[8] For scholars of material culture, the digital is essential to understand both as an assemblage of material objects and as a network that increasingly circumscribes the interactions of people and other material objects.

A Register of Digital Materials

To begin grappling with the materiality of the digital, we might compile a brief and necessarily incomplete inventory of computational artifacts:

- computer cases (desktop, laptop)
- monitors (CRT, LCD, OLED)
- CDs (CD-DA, CD-ROM, CD-R, CD-RW, VCD, SVCD), DVDs (DVD-ROM, DVD-R, DVD-RW, DVD+RW, DVD-RAM)
- CD and DVD drives (internal, external)
- mice (ball, roller, optical, laser, trackpad, 3D, ergonomic)
- server
- network router closets
- circuits
- motherboards

- sound cards
- graphics cards
- RAM chips
- cables (SCSI, PS/2, 3.5 mm, VGA, DVI, USB [many varieties], Firewire, Lightning, Ethernet, HDMI)
- hard disk drives (internal, external)
- flash drives
- solid-state hard drives
- punch cards
- floppy drives
- floppy disks (8", 5¼", 3½")
- Zip and Jazz drives and disks
- keyboards (standard, laptop, flexible, portable, optical, mechanical, illuminated)
- printers (dot matrix, thermal, ink jet, laser, desktop, drum, line)
- laptop or monitor stands
- software packaging
- tablets
- mobile phones
- communications satellites
- chargers (corded, wireless, portable, bicycle dynamos)
- cell phone charging lockers (in airports and public spaces)
- external power supplies, speakers (internal, external, portable, smart)
- headphones
- smart appliances (light bulbs, refrigerators, coffee makers, stoves, garage doors)
- gaming consoles
- controllers (game pads, joysticks, remotes)
- watches (digital, smart)
- fitness trackers
- scales (digital, smart)
- televisions
- virtual reality glasses
- 3D printers
- laser cutters

I expect anyone who reads the list above will think of at least one artifact it misses. It cannot cover the vast array of objects now produced with embedded computer components: everything from automobiles to medical equipment to children's toys to voting machines.

Our material culture is suffused in digital objects and even more, in another stratum of objects designed for carrying, storing, protecting, decorating, or displaying digital-material artifacts: for example, laptop sleeves, mobile phone cases, or computer decal stickers. Moreover, the design of many objects intended primarily for noncomputational purposes has been nonetheless altered for the Internet age. It would be nearly unthinkable to imagine a modern briefcase, for instance, that does not include a separate, padded compartment for a laptop computer or, increasingly, a car without a USB charging port in its front cabin. Fields such as design and fashion have been radically reoriented around the digital – and radically reorganized in practice around digital platforms – so that any account of their material culture must engage the effects of computation. Discussions of twenty-first-century architecture, for example, likely must account for AutoCAD and similar programs, just as discussions of clothing design likely must include accounts of Adobe Illustrator or its kin. Around this amorphous construction of "the digital," then, we find a penumbra of artifacts that exist because of software or hardware, or that manifest the affordances and limitations of software.

Perceiving Digital Materiality

The word "network" has become increasingly metaphorical, describing relationships among devices but also among people, but it was coined because connected systems – whether of wire, rails, roads, or other conveyances for information or people – were thought to resemble the connected ropes of a net, or the "net work." It was, perhaps, easier to remember the material entanglements of computing when users were required to physically connect their computers to hard-wired networks using telephone and then Ethernet cables, establishing a literal and visual link that could pull or even tear, severing one device from the collective. As Chuk notes,

> The web is finite due to its reliance on servers, which are physical components, but it is unfathomably large. It is difficult to gauge just how big it is because its contents are made of bits and bytes, web sites are impossible to count, and it is indexed in different ways across different servers, not to mention exact measures are complicated by its constant fluctuations – new sites emerge and old ones become defunct.[9]

Increasingly, people connect to the Internet's network of servers wirelessly, but still through material devices such as laptops, tablets, and mobile phones that communicate with yet other devices such as wi-fi transmitters or cell phone towers. As our computers have disconnected from wires, the number of computer-centered or computer-driven devices in our daily lives have increased exponentially. The US Environmental Protection Agency reports that "the *average* American household uses about twenty-eight electronic products such as personal computers, mobile phones, televisions and electronic readers (e-readers)"; a good many of these products are, especially if produced in the past decade, in some sense "digital."[10] In becoming more portable, the digital has become for many essential to the minutiae of both public and private life, even to bodily autonomy. Our mobile phones have become extensions of our memory and our digits. We are cyborgs in habit if we are not (yet) corporally entangled with our devices.

Some of the specific sensations facilitated by digital objects are likely novel; how many people in previous generations ran their fingers along perfectly smoothed glass as regularly as a twenty-first-century smartphone user? Nonetheless, our digits manipulate matter when we interact with digital interfaces. Dennis Tenen describes the effects of our fingers on keyboards as initiating a long chain of material changes: "What originates from (1) the keyboard as the mechanical action of a switch becomes (2) an electric signal that (3) leaves electromagnetic marks in computer memory, which (4) morph into phrases of liquid crystal on-screen, leaving behind (5) letters that emanate outward as light."[11] Our interactions with the touch screens on phones or tablets seem to close this loop, encouraging the perception that our fingers interact directly with light-emanated letters. In reality, our fingers brush capacitive touch screens that send small electrical charges into our fingertips, completing circuits and sending signals to our devices about where their screens were contacted.

Paradoxically, the materiality of computation seems to become increasingly difficult to apprehend even as computation increasingly suffuses culture. The room-filling computers of the 1940s and 50s were literally and metaphorically hefty. The cumulative mass of twenty-first-century computation would outweigh these machines by many orders of magnitude, but its ubiquity and even its interfaces serve to mask this reality. The graphical user interfaces (GUIs) through which we typically interact with computers deliberately obscure the machinery that creates and sustains them. Interfaces are largely organized around skeuomorphic representations of older media: we work from a desktop, we delete files through a trash can, we save files by clicking a floppy disk, or we browse the Internet through windows and tabs. These skeuomorphs help communicate functionality to users, to make new and unfamiliar operations tractable, but they also serve to separate the objects we interact with from their own materiality – the simulation on the screen encourages us to look past the screen itself, along with its attendant components, and imagine something like a disembodied cloud of software rather than a warehouse full of servers.

Marlene Manoff outlines some of the dangers that result from scholars misrecognizing the digital space as immaterial. Writing primarily to librarians, she cautions them not to replace the term "collection management" with "content management," because "when one calls collection management 'content management,' librarians are encouraged to think about content in the abstract, as if it existed apart from any particular physical embodiment ... The term 'content management,'" she continues, "suggests that we have somehow moved beyond mundane considerations of physical reality when, in fact, the electronic environment introduces a whole new set of questions about the material aspects of library collections." One danger of making a mental shift from "collections" to "content," Manoff argues, is that such a shift will encourage notions of surrogacy between digitized materials and their archival originals that can flatten the unique properties of either medium. As a result, "some librarians are rushing to identify funds that can be freed by canceling print subscriptions that are duplicated in electronic formats. Others are eager to jettison paper back-files in order to free up shelf space without much consideration of the reliability of the back-files or the digital archive."[12] By failing to fully account for the digital medium's specific materiality, in other words, we place the past and future at greater risk. In my own research I have suggested that the "myth of surrogacy" stunts our historical and contemporary imaginations alike, shrinking the materials of the past to the size of a computer screen and, perhaps paradoxically, encouraging us to use digitized materials as if they had no unique properties to their medium.[13]

Digital Environments

As Jussi Parikka reminds us, we cannot separate the myriad objects of the digital world from the materials and systems underlying their construction, use, and eventual disposal: "Media and information technology are far from zero entropy mathematical dreams, and embedded in physical networks, afforded by hardware and hard*work* – practices of mining, shipping, polishing, constructing, and then the other way round, when disgorging such machines." Parikka insists "the materiality of information technology starts from the soil, and underground" before listing the minerals necessary for the creation of many digital artifacts:

Cobalt Lithium-ion batteries, synthetic fuels
Gallium Thin layer photovoltaics, IC, WLED
Indium Displays, thin layer photovoltaics
Tantalum Micro capacitors, medical technology
Antimony ATO, micro capacitors
Germanium Fiber optic cable, IR optical technologies
Platinum (PGM) Fuel cells, catalysts
Palladium (PGM) Catalysts, seawater desalination
Niobium Micro capacitors, ferroalloys
Neodymium Permanent magnets, laser technology.[14]

While it may seem obvious that computer hardware is material, common metaphors such as "the cloud" obscure the gritty realities of cobalt, tantalum, and niobium, and the human labor required to extract these materials from the ground. Creating, running, and maintaining our digital infrastructure takes a substantial environmental toll. Moreover, the energy costs of our ubiquitous devices are even more substantial, and only growing. Social scientists Richard Maxwell and Toby Miller note in their book *Greening the Media*,

> residential electricity consumption for powering ICT/CE [Information and Consumer Technology/Consumer Electronics] is also growing at unprecedented rates, accounting for about 15 percent of global residential electricity consumption by 2009. By 2011, upwards of ten billion devices needed external power supplies, including two billion TV sets, a billion personal computers, and cell phones, which reached five billion subscriptions in 2010, including 85 percent of the US public. In 2011, nearly three-quarters of the world's population owned one, and three-quarters of these accounts were held in the Global South. By 2009, about 40 percent of US homes had video-gaming consoles, which collectively consumed electricity at the same annual rate as San Diego, the ninth-largest city in the country. If media usage continues to grow at this rate, the IEA estimates that electricity consumption by electronic equipment will rise to 30 percent of global demand by 2022, and 45 percent by 2030.[15]

These predictions have largely proven accurate, save minor improvements made through the development of more energy efficient devices in the years since 2012. However, new environmental wrinkles have also emerged during this same period. For example, the networks of people and machines mining Bitcoin, a "cryptocurrency" that exists entirely in code, are estimated to consume as much electricity as countries such as Ireland or Austria.[16] The process of verifying electronic transactions, which is required to produce new digital currency, is referred to as "mining." These processes are often automated for speed, scale, and efficiency, set running on computers and servers twenty-four hours a day. It might seem a strange skeuomorph to call these operations "mining," but just as mining for natural resources requires large expenditures of human and machine energy and can damage the natural world, technologies for extracting digital resources require substantial investment of time and resources and take an environmental toll.

Our digital devices take a human toll as well. Mined minerals are shaped into computer components and devices in massive factories, many in the developing world, and often with poor records regarding employee health and happiness. Most prominently, in 2010 at least eighteen workers attempted suicide at a complex of Foxconn factories in China, where, among other products, workers assembled Apple's iPhone smartphones and iPad tablet computers. Accounts of conditions in these factories vary widely, but grim images of suicide nets, installed to prevent workers jumping off factory buildings to their deaths, circulated online and in broadcast media, soberly remind consumers of the human costs of building digital devices – though sales of Foxconn-made products have not seemed to slow as a result. Stories juxtaposing the hard labor of device assembly with the conveniences of digital access often deliberately recall the factory literature of the nineteenth century and early twentieth centuries, which challenged readers to recognize the human costs of that age's technical marvels. Frankly, this is not a reckoning well undertaken by either the public or scholars: myself included, as I type this article on a device made by unknown workers under unknown conditions.

Concerns about material and economic exploitation attend the entire digital life cycle. While as a category, digital devices are ubiquitous in the early twenty-first century, *particular* digital devices have very short shelf lives: new software often will not run on models only a few years old, new features convince users to upgrade, or older devices simply become unfashionable. Many companies prioritize "planned obsolescence" in their design and marketing to keep consumers buying. Because older digital devices remain physical objects, however, they must go somewhere when discarded. In the best cases, components or even whole devices can be recycled or "up cycled" toward new uses: an old laptop becomes an interface for a home entertainment system, perhaps, or components from an old phone are reused in a different device. But old electronics all too often become simply waste, and often dangerous waste. Developed countries often ship "e-waste" to developing countries, where it can be stripped for parts and chemical components more cheaply and often under much more hazardous conditions for workers. In early 2018 China refused to take any more imported plastic waste from other countries, citing a desire to clean its air, water, and land, while working toward greener technologies across the country. The move threw countries like the United States into crisis, with nowhere to ship the huge volumes of plastics, including e-waste, that accumulate in waste or recycling bins each day.[17]

In other words, the digital or virtual environments we navigate on our screens are made of terrestrial stuff and make lasting terrestrial changes. A stunning, comprehensive account of "the full stack" – another weighty, materialist phrase – of labor, technology, and economics required for humans to interact with a single digital device, the Amazon Echo, can be found in Kate Crawford and Vladan Joler's essay and map, "Anatomy of an AI System: The Amazon Echo as an Anatomical Map of Human Labor, Data and Planetary Resources."[18] This remarkable piece begins noting,

> A brief command and a response is the most common form of engagement with this consumer voice-enabled AI device. But in this fleeting moment of interaction, a vast matrix of capacities is invoked: interlaced chains of resource extraction, human labor and algorithmic processing across networks of mining, logistics, distribution, prediction, and optimization ... each small moment of convenience – be it

answering a question, turning on a light, or playing a song – requires a vast planetary network, fueled by the extraction of non-renewable materials, labor, and data.

From here, Crawford and Joler outline those extractions, connecting work mining the lithium reserves of the Salar in southwest Bolivia; to Athanasius Kircher's 1673 invention of "the *statua citofonica*, or the 'talking statue'"; to "hardware manufacturing and assembly processes in Chinese factories" and "exploited outsourced cognitive workers in developing countries labelling AI training data sets"; to the Victorian destruction of the trees that produced *gutta percha* for insulating telegraphic and other cables; to the shipping boats full of cargo containers that "produce 3.1 percent of global yearly CO_2 emissions" today.

This summary unfortunately elides most of their essay's points, but hopefully hints at the complexity of the material-social-technical systems they demonstrate as necessary for understanding a single computational device. Scholars of material culture could and should take on the responsibility of producing similar accounts of the many other devices and artifacts of the digital age. Doing so will require both the analytical capacities we typically associate with humanistic inquiry and the technical capacities that will enable scholars to understand interplays between hardware and software, devices and networks, or users and systems.

Soft(ware) Materials

Even less apparent than the materiality of hardware is the materiality of the software running on it. We too often overlook the intimate connections among hardware and software, strangely failing to link – intellectually, at least – our ubiquitous devices to the programs that run on them. But software is also a *thing* with a physical presence in the world or, as Chuk describes it, "a negotiation between abstract and machine systems."[19] In a 2014 lecture, Matthew Kirschenbaum looked at software from fourteen perspectives to outline all the ways in which it is a "thing": "software as asset," "software as shrinkwrap," or "software as epigraphy," to name just a few of the frames he draws around a category that for libraries, archives, and museums "remains a narrow, niche, or lesser priority" for preservation.[20] Software exists in particular material states and on particular media. Software can be transmitted from device to device through wireless signals, but it must ultimately *be* somewhere, and be some*thing*.

The field of digital forensics often relies on the material relationships among software and hardware, the inscriptions (and similar traces) that software makes on its hardware. The field was developed and is typically employed to find digital evidence of crimes – shady bank transactions or incriminating emails – though its methods have been adapted by scholars for other purposes. In his 2008 book, *Mechanisms: New Media and the Forensic Imagination*, for example, Kirschenbaum excavates the material traces left on disks and hard drives to show how techniques adapted from book history and media archeology can locate the physical traces of digital texts. Beginning from the question, "In what ... does the materiality of electronic texts consist?" Kirschenbaum argues that, like the letters inscribed on paper through print,

> electronic textuality is similarly locatable, even though we are not accustomed to thinking of it in physical terms. Bits can be measured in microns when recorded on a magnetic hard disk. They can be visualized with technologies such as magnetic force microscopy (MFM), which is a variation on the scanning tunneling microscope (STM). When a CD-ROM is burned, a laser superheats a layer of dye to create pits and lands, tiny depressions on the grooved surface of the platter. The length of these depressions is measured in microns, their width and depth in nanometers.[21]

Cold metal bites into rag paper to print a hand-press era book; electrons are stored in the cells of a solid-state hard drive to save a Word file. As Kirschenbaum acknowledges, the materiality of something like a Word file is less immediately tangible to human senses, which makes it harder for scholars to apprehend.

Nevertheless, scholars must develop new analytical capacity to close this intellectual distance. As Alan Galey notes in his bibliographic reading of Johanna Skibsrud's *The Sentimentalists* in both print and digital editions, understanding such objects will "require a synthesis between forensic methods and the humanities' interpretive strengths." Such a synthesis is necessary, Galey argues in his conclusion, because,

> e-books, like all digital texts, require us to interpret phenomena not directly observable by the senses. We must rely on layers upon layers of digital tools and interfaces, as we have seen in the examples above. A purely empirical and forensic perspective assumes that objects speak for themselves, and yield up their evidence to the observation of human senses and the inquiry of human reason.[22]

The peculiar materiality of software cannot be entirely understood through direct observation and will require researchers to develop new standards of evidence, as well as new methodologies for gathering it.

Scholars of material culture studies must cultivate such proficiencies, as the future of storage promises to write digital data onto new, even less-apprehensible material substrates. In their ongoing efforts to find more efficient, capacious, and compact media, researchers have succeeded in saving "502 terabits per square inch" in a "flat two-dimensional lattice" of chlorine atoms and vacancies. These researchers tout the potential capacity of atomic memory, noting in conclusion that "translating the two-dimensional storage density presented here to three dimensions, would ... allow the storage of the entire US Library of Congress in a cube 100 μm [micrometers, or millionths of a meter wide]."[23] Another area of current research marries computation and biology, using DNA as a data storage medium. One group of researchers, for example, "encoded computer files totaling 739 kilobytes of hard-disk storage and with an estimated Shannon information of 5.2 3 106 bits into a DNA code, synthesized this DNA, sequenced it and reconstructed the original files with 100 percent accuracy." Currently DNA storage is too time- and resource-intensive for most archives, but researchers believe "if current trends continue," then "DNA-based storage becomes practical for archives with a horizon of less than 50" years within a decade. Researchers are looking to DNA as an archival medium:

> The DNA-based storage medium has different properties from traditional tape-or disk-based storage. As DNA is the basis of life on Earth, methods for manipulating, storing and reading it will remain the subject of continual technological innovation. As with any storage system, a large-scale DNA archive would need stable DNA management and physical indexing of depositions. But whereas current digital schemes for archiving require active and continuing maintenance and regular transferring between storage media, the DNA-based storage medium requires no active maintenance other than a cold, dry and dark environment (such as the Global Crop Diversity Trust's Svalbard Global Seed Vault, which has no permanent on-site staff) yet remains viable for thousands of years even by conservative estimates.[24]

While these media may be almost impossibly microscopic, that we can encode digital data onto atoms or into DNA strangely makes the intrinsic materiality of those data plainly apparent. Data can be digital, chemical, or even biological.

Preserving and Accessing Digital Culture

One of the most potent and sobering reminders of the digital's materiality is its rapid dilapidation. Technologists and archivists both increasingly use the phrase "digital dark age" to refer to the early era of modern computing, which becomes less accessible each year as its hardware degrades and its software grows less compatible with new hardware. These processes are often called "bit rot" or "data rot" – an intriguingly biological metaphor for the decay of digital artifacts. Google Vice President Vint Cerf has been perhaps the highest profile voice worried that "even if we accumulate vast archives of digital content, we may not actually know what it is" very far into the future.[25] Due to material decay and the obsolescence cycles of the computer industry, an entire generation of cultural heritage is in critical danger of being lost to history. These endangered artifacts include software objects themselves – programs, computer games, operating systems – and objects created with them, such as the correspondence or working documents of important social, political, or artistic figures.

As it is written today, computer code operates at several removes from machine language. Programmers do not write in binary, they write in C++, Python, R, or any number of programming languages that are compiled or assembled, translated into machine code that the computer can execute directly. Machine code depends quite literally on hardware parameters; the set of available instructions differs for each processor, though newer processors may include instructions from their predecessors. When hardware evolves too far past the parameters for which a given piece of software was written, however, that program can no longer be translated and run as intended.

Storage formats change even more rapidly, and many storage technologies physically degrade, in some cases at faster rates than pre-digital media, such as paper or vellum. As Roy Rosenzweig writes, "Print books and records decline slowly and unevenly – faded ink or a broken-off corner of a page. But digital records fail completely – a single damaged bit can render an entire document unreadable." Even if data saved to a floppy disk is compatible with a modern program – and the floppy disk has not itself deteriorated – accessing that data would require access to a dwindling number of functional floppy disk drives, and an operating system capable of reading from the drive and disk. Rosenzweig asserts, "Well before most digital media degrade, they are likely to become unreadable because of changes in hardware (the disk or tape drives become obsolete) or software (the data are organized in a format destined for an application program that no longer works). The life expectancy of digital media may be as little as ten years, but very few hardware platforms or software programs last that long."[26] The challenges of preserving born-digital materials, then, comes not from the development of media, hardware, or software in isolation, but instead from simultaneous – but not necessarily *coordinated* – change across all three.

The project *Preserving Virtual Worlds* brought together researchers from the Rochester Institute of Technology, Stanford University, the University of Maryland, the University of Illinois at Urbana-Champaign, and Linden Lab to investigate the challenges of preserving video games and interactive fiction from the 1960s to early 2000s. In the project's final report, team members identify obsolescence as the first obstacle to their work:

> The most obvious problem affecting these materials is the obsolescence of the hardware and software infrastructures necessary to allow software to run. The earliest game in our case set, *Spacewar!*, currently

exists in its original form stored on a punched paper tape intended to be read into the memory of a PDP-1 computer. There is, to the best of our knowledge, only one functioning PDP-1 computer left in the world, at the Computer History Museum in Mountain View, California, and paper tape readers are not exactly common equipment at this time. The fate of the paper tape of *Spacewar!* is the fate awaiting all games without the active intervention of preservationists. A book may pass 50 years on a shelf and still be readily accessible; rapid technological change and the resulting obsolescence of the technology necessary to access software mean that a computer game will not.

Beyond this "most obvious" problem, however, the team noted the difficulty in bounding precisely what object must be preserved, because "while we tend to think of the game as a relatively discrete package of software, the reality is that a *functioning* game involves a web of interconnections between the game's executable, an operating system, the hardware platform used to execute both, and potentially network hardware and software and a multiplicity of other computer systems."[27]

Scholars and archivists alike wrestle with different ideas about how best to preserve and present histories of hardware and software, and it is likely that some combination of these ideas will be required as the urgency and scope of the problem increase. One of the primary methods for born-digital preservation requires the maintenance of original hardware, on which researchers can access pertinent software, while the other relies on the emulation of older software environments on newer hardware. The Emory University Libraries, for instance, rely on emulation to present the digital "papers" of writer Salman Rushdie. Emory Libraries' help sheet for this collection offers insight into the preservation challenges that digital technologies raise for libraries, museums, and other cultural heritage institutions:

> Welcome to the Salman Rushdie digital archive. On this workstation, you will find selected digital files from Rushdie's Macintosh Performa 5400, one of several computers and other related devices that form the born digital component of the Salman Rushdie papers in Emory University's Manuscript, Archives, and Rare Book Library (MARBL).
>
> The majority of the digital files date from 1992–2002, and consists [sic] of notes and drafts of Rushdie's writings and selected correspondence. Of particular interest is a small cache of email correspondence, representing Rushdie's first foray into this emerging form of communication in the late 1990s. Writings include drafts of Rushdie's fiction, such as *East, West* (1994), *The Moor's Last Sigh* (1995), and *The Ground Beneath Her Feet* (1999). Nonfiction writings include notes and drafts for *Step Across this Line*, Rushdie's collection of essays and criticism, published in 2002. Other writings include drafts of the *Midnight's Children* and *The Courter* play scripts, as well as drafts of letters to the editor,

newspaper columns, poems, and speeches. The Performa 5400 contains a backup of an earlier computer, which Rushdie entitled "OLD MAC," and a laptop, the "Powerbook," which Rushdie likely used in tandem with the Performa 5400.

Emory Libraries allows researchers to access these materials through a searchable database, but also through an emulation of Rushdie's Macintosh Performa 5400. "In this environment," the library's help sheet reports, "you will be able to view Rushdie's exact directory structure and open each file in the application in which it was created, such as MacWrite Pro or ClarisWorks."[28] These two projects evidence ideas of emulation that are becoming increasingly important for thinking historically about digital artifacts and culture.

By contrast, other scholars seek to preserve historical computing objects in working order for future study. Founded in 2009, the Media Archeology Lab (MAL) at the University of Colorado at Boulder, describes itself as "a place for cross-disciplinary experimental research and teaching using still functioning media from the past." Contrasting its mission to media labs focused on the latest technologies, the MAL claims to be "propelled equally by the need to both preserve and maintain access to historically important media of all kinds – from magic lanterns, projectors, and typewriters to personal computers from the 1970s through the 1990s, as well as early works of digital literature/art which were created on the hardware/software housed in the lab."[29] In spaces like the MAL, students or scholars can play the 1987 adventure game *King's Quest III: To Heir is Human* on an Amiga computer or experience writing in WordPerfect on an Apple IIe. Such resources are an enormous boon to those concerned with the social and material histories of the digital age, but are also an enormous undertaking to create and, especially, maintain as parts and expertise in older computers alike disappear. Whether through emulation or preservation, it has become increasingly clear that the early history of computing – a phase, I would argue, that continues to this day – will require substantially more engagement from scholars if we hope to preserve its texts and artifacts for future students, scholars, or the public.

Digital-Material Circuits

While the digital realm certainly is material, its materiality is in many ways distinct from those objects we identify as "analog." The objects we encounter on a screen often mimic a physical form quite distinct from the form they inhabit. As Kirschenbaum argues, "a digital environment is an abstract projection supported and sustained by its capacity to propagate the illusion (or call it a working model) of *immaterial* behavior: identification without ambiguity, transmission without loss, repetition without originality."[30] It is the domain of images displayed by computer screens that we mark as "virtual reality"; these are models of the real or fantasy worlds. Increasingly, however, the digital and analog worlds bleed into each other. When the mobile game *Pokémon Go* was released in July 2016, it sent players scrambling around their towns and cities in search of the cartoon creatures, which, though an "augmented reality" application, could be found on real streets, in real buildings, and even, sometimes problematically, at real historical sites and monuments. In 2016, for instance, the Holocaust Museum in Washington, DC requested that *Pokémon Go* players stop catching the cartoon creatures in the memorial space. The game's developers automated the creation of "Pokestops" to coincide with landmarks as identified on digital mapping platforms, but without considering that some landmarks might be inappropriate locations for such play.

While this implementation of augmented reality was rightfully decried – and soon corrected – there are arguments in favor of interfaces that blend digital and analog environments. Even *Pokémon Go* was praised for urging players toward fresh air and exercise, and some scholars and cultural heritage institutions have turned to augmented reality to engage the public. The Museum of London launched the app *Streetmuseum* in 2010 (currently unavailable). The Histories of the National Mall website, developed by the Roy Rosenzweig Center for History and New Media at George Mason University, allows visitors to this Washington, DC spot to explore historical maps, photos, stories, and other materials related to the National Mall as they explore the physical space itself.[31] The Smithsonian's Museum of Natural History's *Skin and Bones* app attempts to breathe new life into one of its oldest exhibit halls, allowing visitors to overlay muscles, skin, and other anatomical features onto the skeletons in the exhibit hall, and even breathe virtual life into the creatures on display.[32] These applications bring virtual reality into explicit dialogue with the "real world," layering the digital and analog.

In the past decade or so, the digital world has manifest in the analog in another significant way, through the growth of technologies such as 3D printing that express computer models in materials such as plastic, resin, ceramic, metal, and even tissue. The practical and theoretical applications of 3D printing are expanding rapidly, and the technology can be found everywhere from engineering firms, to hospitals, to libraries. The broadest application of 3D printing has been for creating physical models relatively quickly and cheaply, allowing engineers (or other researchers) to create a digital schematic of a design and then generate a physical representation of it. These models can be used to test structural properties of designs before production, compare different design options or simply to demonstrate for clients.

As with augmented reality, museums and other cultural heritage institutions experiment with 3D printing to bring students, researchers, and the public into contact with artifacts with which they might not otherwise be able to interact. New York's Metropolitan Museum of Art was one of the first museums to make 3D models of its artifacts available for download and reproduction, as have national museums such as the Smithsonian Institution and British Museum, alongside a host of smaller institutions and individual research projects. The University of North Texas's *3Dhotbed* is "a collaborative project that seeks to enhance book history instruction by providing access to affordable teaching tools and related materials for pedagogical purposes."[33] The project has created 3D models of hard-to-find artifacts from the hand-press era that teachers of book history, bibliography, and related disciplines can use to demonstrate objects' use to students. The project's current models include a two-part type mold and matrix used to demonstrate to students how individual pieces of movable type were created, a facsimile of a Renaissance-era woodcut image, and a facsimile of a Chinese xylographic woodblock. These are materials not likely to be available for most classroom instructors, made accessible through 3D models and printing.

As the possibilities expand for material substrates used in 3D printing, so too have its applications. Practically, 3D printers can be used to create hard-to-find replacement parts for rare or outdated machines. Though there are relatively few replacement parts that justify the time and cost of creating a 3D model and printing it, groups such as NASA are experimenting with ways the technology might assist with repairs on highly customized tools in places such as outer space.[34] Experiments also continue in 3D printing another kind of rare "spare part," as biologists and doctors work toward 3D printing viable human organs for use in transplants. While it might sound like science fiction, this technology has produced near-viable organs. A 2014 review article in *Nature Biotechnology* describes the major approaches to "3D bioprinting," including biomimicry, autonomous self-assembly, and mini-tissues, as well as overviewing the primary technological approaches to this challenge. In this instance, the material culture of the digital becomes the biological culture of the digital, a new corporal entanglement between computers and us.[35]

In addition, the past decade has seen a growing body of research and practice around ideas of "data physicalization" or "haptic data," both movements that seek to challenge the domination of sight in expressions or analysis of data, and both movements that bring computerized data viscerally into the material world. In contrast to data visualization, "a *data physicalization* (or simply physicalization) is a physical artifact whose geometry or material properties encode data." The authors of this research go on to imagine a museum exhibit in which visitors pick up stones of various temperatures to experience changes in Earth's climate over time, as well as describing existing data physicalization, such as "a wooden three-dimensional model of

Mexico City where height encodes population density."[36] Such physicalizations blend data science with the art installation and close the circuit of data collected from physical or built environments, aggregated and analyzed computationally, and then expressed – transformed – in material form.

These kinds of experiments bring information out of screens and into human spaces, often putting people into literal contact with data representations. Haptic data experiments do not simply encode data through material properties but invite people to experience data using senses beyond (though perhaps including) sight. The *Vibrant Lives* project, for instance, describes an approach that "look[s] to somatic and contemporary dance practices for new design strategies that engage users in affective, felt relationships with personal technologies and personal data."[37] In installations sponsored by this project, participants experienced the data streaming from their mobile phones as vibrations felt through devices worn on their clothing, or they both heard and felt the history of forced eugenic sterilization in California. In a blog post about the latter event, Jacqueline Wernimont describes participants "leaning in to feel a history of sterilization." She notes that "the haptics are being shared with a thin, red metal wire that the participants have to touch lightly in order to not dampen the signal for others," which is part of the *Vibrant Lives* team's "effort to bring care for the experiences of others into the performance."[38]

None of the above manifestations of the digital within the material quite touch an even broader set of ideas and practices gathered under the heading of "wearable technology." These include the kinds of commercial trackers (e.g., the Fitbit) critiqued by projects such as *Vibrant Lives*, but also a range of experimental interfaces born from maker culture, most excitingly in dialogue with feminist or other ethical frameworks. Kim Brillante Knight surveys a range of feminist interventions in wearable technology, including this description of Kathleen McDermott's work:

> Kathleen McDermott's Urban Armor collection is a series of wearable garments in which we glimpse the cyborg's radical possibility. Of particular note is the "Personal Space Dress"; its skirt expands when activated by a proximity sensor in order to protect the wearer from unwanted contact... The choice of a feminine garment – a dress – calls attention to the way women in particular are subject to harassment in public spaces.

Knight describes her own research project *Fashioning Circuits*, which works in undergraduate classrooms "to articulate a counterpublic to dominant computing publics by creating a space in which women and underrepresented people of color feel comfortable learning and have the freedom to pursue projects that reflect their priorities and needs."[39] They do this through a range of theoretical readings and discussions alongside making their own wearable technology that works against the dominant models of commercial devices.

The kinds of pedagogical, research, and artistic experiments described in this section certainly create new material artifacts for description and study by scholars. In such work we identify another way in which the abstruse digital realm is brought into meaningful, physical contact with people. For scholars of material culture, physicalizations, haptic data, and wearable technology are doubly resonant, as both objects of potential study and as modeling potential modes of analysis or engagement. As in the catalog of digital devices, this section cannot fully document the many ways in which the digital re-emerges into the analog world. With several decades of digitization past, we are now coming full circuit, and such manifestations of the digital are only due to increase.

Conclusion

In *Writing Machines*, Hayles argues that the need for "media-specific analysis" became more important, rather than less, upon the introduction of the computer:

> As the vibrant new field of electronic textuality flexes its muscle, it is becoming overwhelmingly clear that we can no longer afford to ignore the material basis of literary production. Materiality of the artifact can no longer be positioned as a subspecialty within literary studies; it must be central, for without it we have little hope of forging a robust and nuanced account of how literature is changing under the impact of information technologies.[40]

For Hayles, this moment of transition or remediation makes media apparent where it was once functionally transparent. The digital makes clear the unique material properties of the media that came before, though – as this chapter has discussed – the new medium can be difficult to perceive so clearly. Scholars of material culture must conscientiously address this self-effacing property of new media: to recognize that it mediates no more or less than its predecessors, and to attend deliberately to its affordances and limitations.

There is no cloud. What does exist is a vast plethora of digital devices, and a rapidly growing ecosystem of materials related to the creation, use, and maintenance of those devices. It would be a mistake to conflate digital culture with twenty-first-century culture writ large, but it would be equally misguided to cordon digital studies from other forms of cultural analysis: material culture studies perhaps most of all. Hardware, software, and even data have material properties that warrant investigation and robust theorization.

Notes

1. Cade Metz, "Google Reincarnates Dead Paper Mill as Data Center of Future | WIRED" *Wired* (January 26, 2012). www.wired.com/2012/01/google-finland/.
2. Alan Liu, "Imagining the New Media Encounter," in Ray Siemens and Susan Schriebman, editors, *Companion to Digital Literary Studies*. Blackwell Companions to Literature and Culture (Hoboken, NJ: Blackwell, 2008). https://bit.ly/3EB8khK.
3. Nicole Starosielski, *The Undersea Network: Sign, Storage, Transmission* (Durham: Duke University Press, 2015), 1–3.
4. Tung-Hui Hu, *A Prehistory of the Cloud* (Cambridge: The MIT Press, 2015), 10.
5. N. Katherine Hayles, *Writing Machines* (Cambridge: MIT Press, 2002), 15.
6. Chuk, p. xxx.
7. "Google Data Center FAQ." Data Center Knowledge (March 16, 2017). https://bit.ly/3pHZPvj.
8. Chuk, p. xxx.
9. Ibid, p. xxx.
10. OSWER US EPA, "Basic Information about Electronics Stewardship." Overviews and Factsheets. US EPA (September 3, 2015). www.epa.gov/smm-electronics/basic-information-about-electronics-stewardship (my emphasis).
11. Dennis Tenen, *Plain Text: The Poetics of Computation* (Palo Alto: Stanford University Press, 2017), 24.
12. Marlene Manoff, "The Materiality of Digital Collections: Theoretical and Historical Perspectives," *Portal: Libraries and the Academy* 6, no. 3 (2006), 314, 316. https://doi.org/10.1353/pla.2006.0042.
13. Ryan Cordell, "'Q i-Jtb the Raven': Taking Dirty OCR Seriously," *Book History* 20 (2017), 193.
14. Jussi Parikka, "Turf Instead of Turf Wars," *Machinology* (August 30, 2012). https://jussiparikka.net/2012/08/30/turf-instead-of-turf-wars/.
15. Richard Maxwell and Toby Miller, *Greening the Media* (New York: Oxford University Press), 32.
16. Alex de Vries, "Bitcoin's Growing Energy Problem," *Joule* 2, no. 5 (2018), 801–05. https://doi.org/10.1016/j.joule.2018.04.016.
17. See for instance Yen Nee Lee, "The World Is Scrambling Now That China Is Refusing to Be a Trash Dumping Ground," CNBC (April 16, 2018). https://cnb.cx/3m7t2ij or Laura Parker and Kennedy Elliott, "Plastic Recycling Is Broken: Here's How to Fix It," *National Geographic News* (June 20, 2018). https://on.natgeo.com/3EDUkDU.
18. Kate Crawford and Vladan Joler, "Anatomy of an AI System: The Amazon Echo as an Anatomical Map of Human Labor," AI Now Institute and Share Lab (2018). www.anatomyof.ai.

19. Chuk, p. xxx.
20. Matthew Kirschenbaum, "Software, It's a Thing" *Medium* (July 24, 2014). https://bit.ly/3oyVxqp.
21. Matthew G. Kirschenbaum, *Mechanisms: New Media and the Forensic Imagination* (Cambridge: MIT Press, 2008), 9, 5.
22. Alan Galey, "The Enkindling Reciter: E-Books in the Bibliographical Imagination," *Book History* 15, no. 1 (2012), 211, 240. https://doi.org/10.1353/bh.2012.0008,.
23. F. E. Kalff, M. P. Rebergen, E. Fahrenfort, J. Girovsky, R. Toskovic, J. L. Lado, J. Fernández-Rossier, and A. F. Otte, "A Kilobyte Rewritable Atomic Memory," *Nature Nanotechnology* 11, no. 11 (2016), 926, 929. https://doi.org/10.1038/nnano.2016.131.
24. Nick Goldman, Paul Bertone, Siyuan Chen, Christophe Dessimoz, Emily M. LeProust, Botond Sipos, and Ewan Birney, "Towards Practical, High-Capacity, Low-Maintenance Information Storage in Synthesized DNA," *Nature* 494, no. 7435 (2013), 77, 79. https://doi.org/10.1038/nature11875.
25. Pallab Ghosh, "Net Pioneer Warns of Data Dark Age," *BBC News*, Science & Environment (February 13, 2015). www.bbc.com/news/science-environment-31450389.
26. Roy Rosenzweig, "Scarcity or Abundance? Preserving the Past in a Digital Era," *American Historical Review* 108, no. 3 (2003), 741–42.
27. Jerome P. McDonough, Robert Olendorf, Matthew Kirschenbaum, Kari Kraus, Doug Reside, Rachel Donahue, Andrew Phelps, Christopher Egert, Henry Lowood, and Susan Rojo, "Preserving Virtual Worlds Final Report" (August 2010), 5. www.ideals.illinois.edu/handle/2142/17097.
28. Emory Libraries Manuscript, Archives, and Rare Books Archive, "The Digital Archives of Salman Rushdie Help Sheet." https://bit.ly/304ZHgm.
29. Media Archaeology Lab, "What" (2018). https://mediaarchaeologylab.com/about/what/.
30. Kirschenbaum, *Mechanisms*, 11.
31. Roy Rosenzweig Center for History and New Media, "Histories of the National Mall" (2018). http://mallhistory.org/.
32. Smithsonian National Museum of Natural History, "Skin and Bones: Mobile Augmented Reality App for NMNH's Hall of Bones." https://naturalhistory.si.edu/exhibits/bone-hall/.
33. Courtney Jacobs, Kevin O'Sullivan, and Marcia McIntosh, "3Dhotbed." 3Dhotbed (2018). www.3dhotbed.info/.
34. Loura Hall, "3D Printer Headed to Space Station," Text. NASA (July 12, 2016). www.nasa.gov/content/3d-printer-headed-to-space-station.
35. Sean V. Murphy and Anthony Atala, "3D Bioprinting of Tissues and Organs," *Nature Biotechnology* 32, no. 8 (2014), 773–85. https://doi.org/10.1038/nbt.2958.
36. Yvonne Jansen, Pierre Dragicevic, Petra Isenberg, Jason Alexander, Abhijit Karnik, Johan Kildal, Sriram Subramanian, and

Kasper Hornbæk, "Opportunities and Challenges for Data Physicalization," *Proceedings of the 33rd Annual ACM Conference on Human Factors in Computing Systems – CHI '15* (Seoul: ACM Press, 2015), 3227–36. https://doi.org/10.1145/2702123.2702180.

37. Jessica Rajko, Michael Krzyzaniak, Jacqueline Wernimont, Eileen Standley, and Stjepan Rajko, "Touching Data Through Personal Devices: Engaging Somatic Practice and Haptic Design in Felt Experiences of Personal Data," *Proceedings of the 3rd International Symposium on Movement and Computing*, MOCO '16 (New York: ACM, 2016), 16: 1–16:8. https://doi.org/10.1145/2948910.2948937.
38. Jacqueline Wernimont, "Hearing Eugenics," *Sounding Out!* (July 18, 2016). https://soundstudiesblog.com/2016/07/18/hearing-eugenics/.
39. Kim A. Brillante Knight, "Wearable Interfaces, Networked Bodies, and Feminist Interfaces," in Jentery Sayers, ed., *The Routledge Companion to Media Studies and Digital Humanities* (London: Routledge, 2018), 207–08, 210.
40. Hayles, *Writing Machines*, 19.

24

Curating the Digital

Understanding Flows of Data and Their Relations

Natasha Chuk

We have long understood our world through objects of creation: design, ingenuity, and creativity come together in various physical objects that reflect aspects of our daily life, values, desires, and innovations. The advanced communications technologies of the past several centuries helped usher a significantly new form in the partially or entirely digital object. As a result, the Information Age brings a system of not only information exchange, storage, and retrieval, but also new ways of thinking and being in the world, and in particular new ways of understanding materiality and our relations to objects and systems that are intangible but increasingly ever-present. This marks an affordance of efficiencies and changes in personal habits, interpersonal communication, and individual and collective identities.

In this chapter, I discuss the makeup of digital objects, their curation, or care, organization, and storage, and how they are intertwined with material objects and conditions. I refer to the rich history of digital objects and information flows and the experiments in mass communications that produced systems organized around virtual connections, which led to shifting definitions and applications alongside new technologies, user habits, and behaviors. Medium theory helps to situate their histories and definitions in relation to material objects, encouraging understanding of meaning-making and cultural context for the ways they work together to facilitate information gathering, sharing, and manipulation. I also consider the empowerment users, producers, and consumers feel by their exchanges of and through digital objects; this is a key component to understanding their organization and the social spheres they engender, not least the ways that identities – individual and collective – form around and through them. (Strang, in Chapter 14, elaborates on social and material ties to individual and collective identity and agency.) Economies of sharing and collective action also contribute to our understanding of digital curation and access, as the cultivation of fantasy, play, protest, business, and other organized activities occur in networked digital environments. (Cordell writes about the relations between cultures and digital objects in Chapter 23.) Finally, alternative networks, currencies, and emerging economies are by-products of these digital outputs, including considerations of privacy, data management and collection, and the expansion of the Internet of Things (IoT).

Understanding Digital Objects

An unavoidable and tangled relation links material and intangible objects: today's networked devices are the interfaces through which we interact with physically untouchable information exchanged between different nodes. This condition generally produces a sense of mystery or secrecy around data and digital objects, but they are more physically dependent than we tend to acknowledge. The interrelations between material and virtual components of computing systems are situated within the original meaning of the term digital, which Benjamin Peters reminds us is related to the digit, or index finger and, more importantly, that this relationship is based on their shared capabilities: "how digits do what index fingers do – namely, count, point, and manipulate." This simplification draws attention to the physical components of actions and tactility and to abstract notions of their outcomes. He adds, "[L]ike fingers, digital media carry out at least three fundamental (Lacanian) categories of actions: digits count the symbolic, they index the real, and once combined and coordinated, they manipulate the social imaginary."[1] The process of translating the material to the symbolic is described differently by Marcelo Vitali-Rosati:

> [D]igital is a particular way of representing information, in opposition to analog. *Analog* is a form of representation that has the same shape as the original – and thus is continuous with its reality – while *digital* representation is achieved by translating the continuity of the real into discrete numbers through a sampling process in which a continuous signal is cut into a set of discrete "samples."[2]

One should also consider the relations between the visual and the digital. "The human-computer interface; the operating system (OS)" assists users with navigating data and enacting computer processes, a very modern concept.[3] "[B]efore 1935, a computer was a person who performed arithmetic calculations. Between 1935 and 1945 the definition referred to a machine, rather than a person. The modern machine definition is based on [John] von Neumann's concepts: a device that accepts input, processes data, stores data, and produces output."[4] The machine requires a system that mediates between the user and computation, processes, and functions.

"In semiotic terms, the computer interface acts as a code that carries cultural messages in a variety of media." Such codes are necessary forms of accessible language and interaction to users. "When you use the Internet, everything you access – texts, music, video, navigable spaces – passes through the interface of the browser and then the interface of the OS."[5] Lev Manovich approaches the study of what he refers to as a *new media object* – "a digital still, digitally composited film, virtual 3-D environment, computer game, self-contained hypermedia DVD, hypermedia web site, or the web site as a - whole."[6] Similar to Vitali-Rosati, he notes the analog/digital distinction as well as the capabilities associated with computer "translation of all existing media into numerical data," called *digitization*.[7] This involves "two steps: sampling and quantization. First, data is *sampled*, most often at regular intervals, such as the grid of pixels used to represent a digital image. The frequency of sampling is referred to as *resolution*. Sampling turns continuous data into *discrete* data, that is, data occurring in discrete units." A discrete unit can be modified, as it remains unhindered. Each sample is *quantified*, or "assigned a numerical value drawn from a defined range."[8] Digitization, for Manovich, is summarized in five basic principles: numerical representation, modularity, automation, variability, and transcoding all common behaviors of everyday computer user interactions, well beyond numerical calculations.

Modern computer memory has shifted in form, beginning as electronic memory, then transitioning to magnetic memory, and finally to semiconductor memory chips. Dramatic decreases in size and increases in storage capacity caused these developments, especially improvements in durability and declining costs. In 1970, IBM introduced the System 370 Model 145 mainframe computer, their first all-semiconductor memory computer, which could store twice the amount of data using half the amount of space.[9] As the number of computer users increased, developers found new ways to store information outside of the capacity of a system's core memory, which enabled additional storage as well as sharing possibilities. Different formats allowed for different capabilities: cassette tapes, floppy disks, CD-ROMs, flash disks, cartridges, zip disks, DVDs, and all their variations provided ways to buy, access, share, store, and alter information. The latest and increasingly the first choice for digital data storage is cloud computing, introduced in 2009, which, with the help of the Web, automatically backs up data onto remote servers.[10]

Zero is the basis of all computing, which organizes zeros and ones in forms that information users can easily understand. "Whether they are gathering information, telecommunicating, running washing machines, doing sums, or making videos, all digital computers translate information into the zeros and ones of machine code. These binary digits are known as *bits* and strung together in *bytes* of eight."[11] From a mathematical standpoint, the value of zero has been significant to information organization since the fifth century CE. "Indian mathematicians did more than simply accept zero. They transformed it, changing its role from mere placeholder to number."[12] Its function as both a placeholder and a valued number led to many sophisticated discoveries in philosophy, theology, astronomy, and other areas of life, and eventually digital computing (see Timur's story of zero in Chapter 15).

Manovich is very keen to trace the parallel histories between modern media and computing. "The connection between the Jacquard loom and the Analytical Engine," he writes, "is not something historians of computers make much of, since for them computer image synthesis represents just one application of modern digital computer among thousands of others, but for a historian of new media, it is full of significance." The Jacquard loom was invented early in the nineteenth century and set the stage for modern mechanization with the inclusion of punched paper cards that automatically controlled it. A short time afterward, inventors incorporated the same punch card technology to create the Analytical Engine, which had "most of the key features of the modern digital computer," using the punch cards "to enter both data and instructions" and to store information in its memory.[13]

The symbolism and significance of zero is at the heart of how the Web works, a vast encyclopedia of storage and retrieval. The fundamental attributes of the digital have been in place for centuries, and mainly their translation processes and signals have changed considerably with the addition of digital formats and networked computing.

The Internet and Its Material-Virtual Relations

Vast amounts of information today are digitally processed and visualized. Without human agents directly operating the systems, and with hidden equipment and intangible components, the term "Internet" does little to explain how it works. "The term *Internet* is often used to refer to a host of different technologies, from non-TCP/IP systems of connection like local area networks and mobile phone data networks, to major 'Internet backbone' connections involving core routers, fiber-optic long-distance lines, and undersea cables."[14] However, because a single term can refer to many disparate functions, a closer examination of what the Internet actually *is* underscores its complicated mix of physical and virtual objects. Our devices allow us to easily access and change content to "point, index and reference objects at a distance, as well as combine into new tool suites capable of profound acts of social manipulation, handling, and management."[15]

Remote applications are enabled by data centers around the world that house massive storage information; underground and underwater cables facilitate the transfer of signals and information flows between users. These largely unknown or hidden physical counterparts to the Internet are sizable and crucial to its functioning. They help illustrate a distinction between the Internet and the World Wide Web, or simply web. The former is the global system or network that provides the underlying blueprint for the web. The web is the visible application, zeros and ones converted to text and images, of the system that enables users to navigate between various locations.[16] Together they organize information and establish flows and suspensions. Websites, for example, offer users visual navigation through information, the equivalent to doors and hallways that lead to information that can be accessed (viewed) and potentially transformed (downloaded, shared). Apart from websites, other domains and applications organize information with visualized thresholds that separate them with the help of our computer interfaces, which organize information in recognizable tabs and icons.

While seemingly accessory to the Internet and web, the material conditions of our networked environments are vital to our interactions within them. "It would be problematic to understand networks," Christiane Paul argues, "as a separate kind of territory that has no connection to our physical environment."[17] They are inextricably connected and inform one another, perhaps most notably regarding questions of public and private spaces, interactions, and behaviors. As Manovich notes, "Telepresence allows the subject to control not just the simulation but reality itself ... [providing] the ability to manipulate remotely physical reality in real time through its image." Examples beyond the social sphere of telepresence at work include remote surgery, distance education, the Mars Exploration Rover, and others; because of their remote material effectiveness, Manovich suggests a better term might be *teleaction*, "acting over distance. In real time."[18]

Actions and automatic processing of information are inherent qualities of human behavior and activity. For Yuk Hui, digital "has a specific orientation toward the automation of data processing." Data and metadata "embody the objects with which we are interacting, and which machines are simultaneously operating." As a result, "data directly intervenes throughout our human experiences in a double sense. When we look at the term *data*, we generally do not recognize its Latin origin, as the plural form of *datum*, meaning "[a thing] given." The French word for data, *donnée* ("given," from *donner*, "to give"), retains the Latin sense exactly.[19] This doubled manner of looking at data comes together nicely when describing the interactions between hardware and software of video (or computer) games. As Alexander Galloway writes, "Software is data; the data issue instructions to the hardware to the machine, which in turn executes those instructions on the physical level by moving bits of information from one place to another, performing logical operations on other data, triggering physical devices, and so on." Then, echoing Manovich, he stresses the activity of the medium, "whose very materiality moves and restructures itself – pixels turning on and off, bits shifting in hardware registers, disks spinning up and spinning down."[20] Combined with Hui's reflection on process as a counterpart to digital objects, the materiality of systems is an essential but often overlooked component to digital computing, in part because many of our experiences with data mingle with everyday life and the physical aspects of computing are increasingly hidden by design. Tung-hui Hu writes, "[E]ven as digital networks seem to annihilate or deterritorialize physical space, space seems to continually reappear." Cloud computing, for example, "buries or hides its physical location by design" and turns "geography into the virtual flows of market capital," which distributes virtual geographies in ways that have no noticeable physical impact.[21] In turn, users benefit from being anywhere, geographically speaking, with the ability to access data stored on the cloud, regardless of the server's physical location.

Access and Organization of Digital Objects

Cloud computing and mobile technologies mean a user's physical location no longer impedes access to data and interaction with systems and other users. These data spaces, writes Paul, "constitute an environment with no fixed entry points, consisting of nodes and synapses that can be reconfigured. The ability to create context and meaning in the networked environment largely relies on possibilities of filtering information and creating some form of 'map' and classification that can allow for orientation, even if the map is constantly reconfiguring itself in front of our eyes."[22] The ever-changing constitution of the web is taken in strides, as users navigate it in personal ways, essentially producing individual maps of activity, which are rather organic in their organization. "The growth of the Net has been continuous with the way it works. No central hub or command structure has constructed it, and its emergence has been that of a parasite, rather than an organizing host."[23]

The World Wide Web is precisely what its name implies: a global network of material and virtual nodes and connections with material impact between them. "Digital technologies also allow for recording our itineraries and for the processing of navigation and data transmission – be it in the form of personal bookmarks, server traffic statistics or consumer histories."[24] These tools seamlessly converge on- and off-line activities and provide serve searchable archives and real-time connections to information and other users. However, the size, navigation, and overall experience of the Web prior to Web 2.0 greatly differed.

> While the network was doubling in size every year, screens were gray, the options limited, and the number of users relatively small until the late 1980s. Access was hardly limited to students, hackers, and academics, but certain skills and commitments to computing were prerequisites of any tangible input into the system, and the users of the network occupied a strange frontline between state institutions and anarchic private use.[25]

Spatial designations when referring to the web originally meant being online or off-line. "Cyberspace," coined by the novelist William Gibson, offered a more elusive and perhaps romantic classification, referring to the complex and mysterious online world into which one could willingly enter and leave. Vitali-Rosati provides useful definitions of web space, denoting variations between the virtual and material, allowing us to understand how we navigate each, how they are interdependent, and where authority is situated within them.

> A space is a particular dynamic set of relationships between objects. These relationships can be of different kinds, including distance, visibility, and position. Structuring a relationship between objects also means determining certain values: the fact that something is more visible than something else, for example, implies that the former is more important than the latter. For his reason, a space always carries values. The relationships are always something written, and there is a deep link between inhabiting a space, reading it, and writing it.[26]

He defines digital space as "the set of relationships between a hybridization of connected and non-connected objects ... Digital space is a well-structured material space. We should not consider digital space as immaterial or as something without a given structure." Though digital space is constantly in flux, and therefore resists stasis, this does not devalue its materiality. It is kept in motion through editorialization, the set of dynamic "interactions of individual and collective actions within a particular digital environment."[27] This reinforces Manovich's ideas about teleaction and further argues that digital objects are material constituents, not part of a separate, imagined space in which we enter and exit.

"The most common interpretation of digital space," Vitali-Rosati argues, "does not recognize this element of continuity. In the public discourse, at least, digital space is mostly understood as a parallel space, separated from 'real' space and often interpreted as imaginary." Digital objects are indeed real, and they operate within immaterial systems that enable material actions. Actions are "everything that one can do."[28] Networked (online) banking, shopping, and socializing are inextricably linked to material actions, goods, and people. The web is organized and optimized for the integration of and interaction between immaterial and material objects and actors. Websites are designed with navigational principles in mind, guiding users toward specific material actions and desired outcomes.

Users' behaviors, activities, and outputs are determined by various affordances and limitations of designs on a micro and macro level. Websites and applications (or apps) for mobile devices rely on visual layouts, navigation cues, file support options, and storage possibilities to shape how users will interact with data on their platform. Everything, from restrictions on file sizes through email to whether an app allows you to connect to your contact list, reflects the kind of experience a user might have. Internet service providers (ISPs) manage users' accounts and maintain access to the networked system. Mobile data allow users to regionally connect to the network through available wireless signals on a mobile device. Data roaming looks for a signal, and most ISPs have limitations on how much data roaming is allowed or if an additional charge will incur in a particular region. The restrictions are about the management of data, and not all data are equally valuable from a data roaming charge perspective. Likewise, a server can crash, or become dysfunctional, as a result of a large queue, or too much user traffic.

Users can also be organized into consciously and unconsciously created social groups through these systems. "The convergence of social evolution and information technologies has created a new material basis for the performance of activities throughout the social structure. This material basis, built in networks, earmarks dominant social processes, thus shaping social structure itself."[29] For example, wikis attract users to convene, share, and collaborate around the collective interest or expertise on a subject with "software that enables users to edit the content of Web pages." The largest and most well-known is Wikipedia, a portmanteau combining "wiki" and "encyclopedia," which is "a collaboratively created encyclopedia, owned by no one and authored by tens of thousands of enthusiasts." Wikipedia is modeled on the tenets of collective intelligence and peer production, "a new mode of innovation and value creation" by volunteer experts, amateurs, and interested participants who maintain the wiki, and is enjoyed by millions of non-contributors who regularly use it as a resource.[30]

Wikis promote editing, while other websites are optimized for different activities and behaviors based on their technical offerings and principles of experience design. Instagram is an image-based sharing platform that allows users to edit still images and video and to caption them before sharing them with followers. Image filters and hashtags further customize personal images, and the latter potentially increase organization, access, and viewership. A hashtag is "a type of label or metadata tag primarily used on social networking websites and microblogging services. It makes it easier for users to find content of the same topic. Hashtags are created by inserting the hash character (#) in front of a word or unspaced phrase."[31] Hashtags can also serve as commentary and create meaning through the association between the content and the word or phrase of the hashtag. The frequent and collective use of a hashtag can effectively amplify the message and dominate headlines in networked environments.

Hashtags are only one kind of metadata, which are tied to every communication system and aid the identification and dissemination of information. Users can consciously or unconsciously create metadata; keywords or phrases can be added. "Nearly every device you use relies on metadata or generates it, or both."[32] Information, or metadata, is encoded into the message by the generating system: telephone numbers, timestamps, duration of activities, and other such data are automatically collected in networked environments. This information allows systems developers to track and observe users' activities, inadvertently and intentionally shaping them and the digital objects being disseminated.

Flows of Information and the Bias of Communication

After the transition to Web 2.0 in the early 2000s, which encouraged users to actively participate in the creation and distribution of content, users can collect, share, and store content on social media with increasing ease and frequency. Social media refers to "a group of Internet-based applications that build on the ideological and technological foundations of Web 2.0, and that allow the creation and exchange of User Generated Content."[33] Some of the most popular social media platforms today include Facebook, Twitter, Instagram, TikTok and YouTube. Within social media channels of communication, interaction design plays a significant role in determining in the ways, kinds, and quality of information flowing through the system.

Social media platforms are among the most popular default platforms of corporate entities, commercial actors, and individual users. Tim O'Reilly compares the search engines of the past and present to illustrate the fundamental differences in the way information flows. "Google requires a competency that Netscape never needed: database management. Google isn't just a collection of software tools; it's a specialized database. Without the data, the tools are useless; without the software, the data is unmanageable." Google's core competency is in the management of a vast and growing set of data and number of users. The accommodation of an expanded user base is a key principle of Web 2.0, in which "the service automatically gets better the more people use it."[34] Moreover, Google's search function incrementally improves with every user's search as its algorithm learns from human habits and methods of inquiry. Google is one example of how, by design, the current web is optimized for expansion, which helps it grow while remaining effective despite its size.

Medium theory presents ways of thinking about the character and effects of information flows, particularly the bias of communication. In the 1950s, communication theorist Harold Innis developed the idea of "communication bias":

> A medium of communication has an important influence on the dissemination of knowledge over space and over time and it becomes necessary to study its characteristics in order to appraise its influence in its cultural setting. According to its characteristics it may be better suited to the dissemination of knowledge over time than over space, particularly if the medium is heavy and durable and not suited to transportation, or to the dissemination of knowledge over space

than over time, particularly if the medium is light and easily transported. The relative emphasis on time or space will imply a bias of significance to the culture in which it is embedded.[35]

The Internet and World Wide Web have dominated mass communication for the past couple of decades, and many argue that networked communication is neither fully biased toward space or time. However, Innis's observations of medium characteristics as indicators of cultural significance are deeply relevant to networked communication and how it facilitates information spread and flow. It is biased toward and optimized for communication across both space *and* time: global networks allow for information to travel great distances without much effort, and the organization allows one to search databases, archives, and storage centers to retrieve information across time. Medium theorist Marshall McLuhan, in contrast, famously proposed that "the medium is the message," because it "shapes and controls the scale and form of human association and action," not the message contents.[36] Like Innis, McLuhan emphasizes the character of the medium is essential to fully grasp the meaning of the message.

The design of the web encourages access anytime and anywhere by users who greatly value speed and convenience. Indeed, more recent additions of Wi-Fi signals, mobile devices, and cloud computing allow users to experience the web's features and benefits as an extension of the self on-the-go. This, in a way, personalizes and democratizes the medium. Speed and convenience are also shared by the proliferation of social media websites, SMS (short message service) and other text-based communications via mobile or other devices. The cultural significance is not so much dependent on the content of each message or exchange as the popularity of networked communication over other forms. McLuhan would argue the speed, ease, and scale of these communications are themselves the message of this era.

A New Web and the Proliferation of Digital Objects

Web 2.0 made it easier for everyone to use the web with no computer skills. It embraced its biases toward space and time, accommodating many users in many places with the ability to support a massive amount of data. The primary means of organizing vast archives is through the principle of connection.

> Hyperlinking is the foundation of the web. As users add new content, and new sites, it is bound into the structure of the web by other users discovering the content and linking to it. Much as synapses form in the brain, with associations becoming stronger through repetition or intensity, the web of connections grows organically as an output of the collective activity of all web users.[37]

Google (now part of parent company Alphabet), was one of the most successful pioneers of the Web 2.0 transition. While Google offers numerous technologies, it began as and is best known for its search engine, which dominates because of its breakthrough technology called PageRank, "a method of using the link structure of the web rather than just the characteristics of documents to provide better search results."[38] This method took advantage of users' searches and ranked pages based on relevance, honing the collective patterns of activities. Today, Google relies on multiple algorithms to facilitate its searches, continuously evolving as the web grows into a larger and more complex network.

"A networked-based social structure is a highly dynamic, open system, susceptible to innovating without threatening its balance."[39] The web, a vast network of nodes, continues to grow without many notable hitches. The addition of cloud computing has made it easy to feel a boundlessness of size, spatial dimensions, and continuity of time. However, the web is finite because of its reliance on (physical) servers and limitations on underground and underwater cables. Despite its materiality, the web is unfathomably large in scope, data, and interconnectivity, though precise measurements are difficult to assess. The big four online storage and service companies are Google, Amazon, Microsoft, and Facebook (now Meta). At the time of this writing, one report estimates that they store at least 1200 petabytes, or approximately 1.2 million terabytes of data.[40]

Great expansion requires great organization, particularly as it relates to users' experiences. "As a corporate concept, Web 2.0 provides contextual 'warehouses' that allow for the automated filtering and networking of user-generated content."[41] Social media platforms thrive because they bolster innate social qualities of human nature. "Human brains are social brains," writes Tom Standage, "tuned to analyze the shifting intentions and allegiances of friends and rivals within a group. Our brains were literally made for social networking."[42] The Pew Research Center reported that approximately 69 percent of Americans used some type of social media as of early 2018, compared to 5 percent in 2005.[43] The center also reported that "Facebook is the most-widely used of the major social media platforms, and its user base is most broadly representative of the population as a whole. Smaller shares of Americans use sites such as Twitter, Pinterest, Instagram and LinkedIn."[44]

Each social media platform offers different affordances and limitations, attracting and promoting different activities, communities, and behaviors among users. Jose van Dijck describes this as "a new online layer through which people organize their lives."[45] Facebook focuses on sharing; Twitter on following and trending information; Instagram on imagery and geographic location; Pinterest on vision boards; and LinkedIn on professional profiles. But these are merely broad, superficial summaries of each platform's objective. Facebook frequently uses "sharing" as part of its marketing language, connoting openness and transparency as a company and through its platform. But sharing is not new to Facebook or any other social media platform, rather it is the basis of the web's function and design.

Van Dijck drills down further to unpack what sharing means from a technical standpoint, suggesting it relates to two types of coding qualities. "The first type relates to *connectedness*, directing users to share information with other users through purposefully designed interfaces."[46] Sharing and connection involve numerous activities and types of content encouraged by Facebook's interface design, which van Dijck explains in some detail:

> Facebook's interface allows its members to create profiles with photos, lists of preferred objects ... and contact information; users can also join groups and communicate with friends by means of chat and video functions. Several features channel social interaction, including News Feed, for updates of stories from people and pages, the Wall for (public) announcements, Poke for attracting attention, and Status for informing others about your whereabouts or for announcing changes in your (relational, professional) status.[47]

Facebook's design powerfully persuades users to engage, create, and share content in specific ways. The ability to form a group – with a separate name, page, profile, and stream of activities – encourages users to think in terms of collectives and, secondarily, ushers a sense of community and belonging. When Facebook added video and chat capabilities, users were encouraged to create and share content via moving images, and real-time text messaging became part of the Facebook community's language of digital content sharing. Such available platform options may seem innocuous, but they inform the expectations of users and their behaviors around digital content. Features and file supports that are popular influence the design and development of new and competing technical products. These design choices influence the file type, scale, and aesthetic of digital objects generated online.

The second coding quality van Dijck observes is *connectivity*, which relates to the aggregation and sharing of users' data with third parties. Ted Nelson, who coined the term hypertext, laid out the basis for the web's arrangement in a 1965 paper, describing a system he called the ELF (Evolutionary List File) in which an entry is "a discrete unit of information designated by the user" that can be comprised of "text (long or short), a string of symbols, a picture or a control designation for physical objects or operations." The list orders these entries, while a link (or hyperlink) is "a connector, designated by the user, between two particular entries which are in different lists," thus creating a vast network of connections.[48] As users connect to information, they ultimately reveal their interests (superficial or otherwise). This is evident in the ways that Web 2.0 operates but was also visible in the prototypes and designs of early networked systems of the 1940s and 50s. As Sadie Plant writes, "The user of [Vannevar] Bush's imagined system left 'a trail ... of interest through the maze of materials available,' adding links and connections, inserting passages, and making routes through an immense virtual library whose composition continually shifts" through user activity.[49] This imagined system is a "memex," which Bush described as "a sort of mechanized private file and library."[50] The so-called memex of today is both individual and collective, thanks to hyperlinks that allow shared connections between individual inputs, and to Web 2.0 guidelines, which encourage a vast number of participants to contribute to the "library."

Content Creation and Ownership

Personalization and customization of content is encouraged across social media platforms, which draw scores of users because they encourage and facilitate speedy and convenient communication across geographic locations and time zones. A feeling of individuality is galvanized among users who create and share content, that they believe they own, with others who are part of the platform community. However, web tracking and user data collection are two common practices today that are part of the invisible backbone helping to underwrite online, social media, and website services. Websites and social media platforms want to know more about their visitors, potential customers, and communities: tracking users' behaviors provides a snapshot of popular and unpopular features, and, more controversially, platform owners profit by collecting and analyzing metadata that users do not see or realize is embedded in their digital content to offset technically free membership or registration. Web browsers have a cache of search activity and web history accessible to users and platform owners. However, websites also track the things a user clicks on or hovers over.[51]

An example of this is a cookie, or "a small piece of data that a website loads onto your browser. Every time you visit that site in [the] future, the browser sends that cookie back to the server so that the website can correlate this with your previous activity."[52] This creates a relationship between discrete visits. Cookies are not visible to users, rather programmed into the system so as not to obstruct user activity. They are virus-free, but they are not necessarily owned by the platform, and instead can belong to third-party trackers paid to collect information for marketing purposes. Connections and activities between users and digital content are valuable assets to platform owners who can profit by offering proof of user engagement to potential advertisers, investors, and others, which expanded the possibilities for both first- and third-party web tracking.

Linking user data between platforms follows the web's basic foundation of hyperlinking information for the benefit of greater access. But this kind of link is hidden and thus raises questions about users' privacy.[53] Online privacy is difficult to define. After reviewing many perspectives on defining privacy, Christian Fuchs suggests they have the following in common: "they deal with the moral questions of how information about people should be processed, who shall have access to this data, and how this access shall be regulated."[54] Access to information about users through surveillance can ultimately lead to power over them, often without users' acknowledgment of these activities, or the extent of the intentions behind them. "Social media that are based on targeted advertising sell prosumers as a commodity to advertising clients. There is an exchange of money for the access to user data that allows economic user surveillance."[55] Issues of privacy are complicated by more than web tracking and data collection, especially since the web advances participatory culture and proliferates sharing. The blurred lines between public and private life involve new negotiations of personal and communal behaviors, ways of life and the shaping of identities. "The shift from distribution to circulation signals a movement toward a more participatory model of culture, one which sees the public not as simply consumers of preconstructed messages but as people who are shaping, sharing, reframing, and remixing media context in ways which have not been previously imagined."[56] It is fair to say that social life has migrated to networked environments in truly substantial ways.

Participation, Socializing, and Sharing of Digital Objects

Digital objects in networked environments are in constant flux: they move from node to node and shift in meaning as their context fluctuates. As there are no set rules, "this fluctuation of context," writes Paul, "affects the formation of identity, our social systems, and cultural production at large."[57] One concern is with the quality and character of socialization and changes in interpersonal communication. Sherry Turkle argues that, as mobile devices become ubiquitous, we spend an increasing amount of time being "alone together," choosing when and how we interact with each other through means that offer more social control than person-to-person communication. "Texting offers just the right amount of access, just the right amount of control." For Turkle, this endangers facing the difficult but necessary conditions of social interactions. Opting out of face-to-face or voice interactions means keeping one another at a comfortable distance. Moreover, though we are tangibly present in one another's company, our mobile devices encourage habits of remotely socializing with persons who are not physically present, establishing a space of absent-present company. Turkle argues these conveniences give us "more control over human relationships" at the detriment of getting too close or uncomfortable.[58]

This is merely one example of many of how digital content intersects with material apparatuses to combine and forge new experiences and ways of life. Being "alone together" has become a new, increasingly acceptable way of socializing, with participants shifting between remote, intangible contacts and those who are physically present. Tom Standage argues this effect is not unique. "In modern societies the exchange of social information is not limited to people who are physically present. Just as gossip is grooming at a distance, various forms of media make possible gossip at a distance, by capturing information so that it can be sent across time and space."[59] This includes everything from letter writing to making a phone call to online interaction. Telepresence, being present at a distance, "encompasses two different situations – being 'present' in a synthetic computer-generated environment (what is commonly referred to as 'virtual reality') and being 'present' in a more remote physical location via a live video image."[60] However, to reconnect with Turkle's concerns, the social etiquette around these behaviors has not fully formed and we can expect that it will continue to shift at pace with advancements and new applications of communications technologies.

Mobile devices make communicating easier and more frequent, and they serve as the conduit for social negotiation across time and physical spaces. "With their inherent possibilities of linking and filtering information," writes Christiane Paul, "digital technologies are providing new tools for networking and contextualizing physical locations and social interactions, thereby creating referential frameworks for understanding cultures."[61] New skills are emerging and learned, such as content and social management on devices, in our systems, and in person. This comes with the territory of having the Internet accessible in persistent and myriad ways. danah boyd considers the implied always-open invitation to connect, being "always-on" – or being "always connected to the network" – and thinks about its effects on lifestyle and evaluating connection through context, referring to this awareness as being "procontext." Context is based on social and cultural values, and not always on age groups, contrary to popular belief. "Being always-on works best when the people around you are always-on, and the networks of always-on-ers are defined more by values and lifestyle than by generation. In essence, being always-on started as a subcultural practice, and while it is gaining momentum, it is by no means universal."[62] Being always-on involves a personal negotiation influenced by the context of one's surroundings, communities, and personal experiences, and is managed accordingly.

Participatory culture involves a combination of giving and taking: contributing and receiving, producing and spectating, and ultimately new ways of interacting with media and ideas that do not require special access or authority. At the launch of Web 2.0, "participatory culture was the buzzword that connoted the Web's potential to nurture connections, build, communities, and advance democracy."[63] Talk of democracy and participation in the web is often informed by critical theorist Jürgen Habermas's observations of the emergence of the public sphere in eighteenth-century Europe, which he describes as a forum in which individuals could form a public to engage in discussion and debate.[64] The web became the transformative (virtual) public sphere of the twenty-first century. Like its predecessor, access and some literacy are required to participate, but it is intended to be open to anyone who engages. However, despite the many permissions the web allows, there are issues of ownership, censorship, technical limitations, and social antagonisms to contend with. Likewise, the finer points of Habermas's argument are often overlooked in favor of more idealized interpretations of what a public sphere can achieve for everyday participants. He stresses that "the public sphere is a question of its members' command of resources (property, intellectual skills) by its members."[65] The savviness of participants translates to some elements of political economy of media, and it can be most effectively displayed in the forms of social status and social currency. Moreover, given the web's digital nature, comparisons to public forums in material space have their limits.[66]

The intricate ties between on- and off-line spaces and the ways we spend our time, not necessarily alternating between them but rather overlapping through and within them, demonstrate that identities – individual and collective – are shaped by online communications, activities, and creative efforts across them. "If dynamic data spaces," writes Paul, "from networked data sets to social media, are the 'landscape' of contemporary culture, they also have to be seen as a context in which we construct our identity and define ourselves in virtual as well as networked physical space."[67] Especially in the mid-1990s, when the World Wide Web was first publicly released, web users openly experimented with the affordances of semi-anonymity and personae-formation. "With no limit to the number of names which can be used," Sadie Plant writes, "one individual can become a population explosion on the Net: many sexes, many species,"[68] and numerous identities could be forged. This affordance speaks to the original idea of making the web a democratic medium in which users can freely express themselves. Zizi Papacharissi considers the realities and potential of communication technologies that have expressive power: "Not all technologies are democratizing or democracy-related. Most technology has little to do with the condition of democracy. Yet, technologies that afford expressive capabilities, like the radio, television, the Internet, and related media, tend to trigger narratives of emancipation, autonomy, and freedom in public imagination."[69] This freedom relates to civic engagement as well as individual expression and experimenting with identity.

Data Bodies and Representation

Digital objects allow users the freedom to create, share, and interact with other data and users regardless of space and time, and in the process, users create multiple digital selves across platforms. Before most people had access to personal computers and the Internet was still private, Turkle reflected on the potential for personal reflection and experimentation with new identities: "A relationship with a computer can influence people's conceptions of themselves, their jobs, their relationships with other people, and with their ways of thinking about social processes."[70] Because digital objects are intangible, they function very much like virtual bodies, the virtual counterparts to our physical selves. "On the one hand, our physical bodies are still individual, physical 'objects;' on the other hand, our virtual being can be described as a multiple self of mediated realities."[71] Indeed, virtual bodies are especially complicated by the disarrangement and apparent collapse of linear time and geographic space. We experience a multidimensional world at the touch of our fingertips and on screens, perceptually flattening spaces in ways that mutilate the complexity of distance and temporality. The weight of this realization incites arguments about how the mind-body relationship is affected by increased experiences with real-time, remote interactions, including debates over whether eSports, competitions using video games, should be considered physical activity. However, as Paul argues, "The relation of these two states can hardly be understood as a simple dichotomy."[72]

Mind-body relations are part of how users organize, manage, access, coordinate, and negotiate digital realms. At the intersection of the mind-body relationship are questions about how time, effort, creativity, and personhood are understood and shaped by the interplay between and intermingling of virtual and physical bodies. N. Katherine Hayles warns of the dangers of suggesting a hierarchy between virtual information and the physical, especially the human, body, because doing so promotes the preservation of the former while disposing of the latter, meaning "because we are essentially information, we can do away with the body." Such attitudes encourage fantasies that, for Hayles, dismiss the fundamental connection between the human mind and body. "Central to this argument," writes Hayles, "is a conceptualization that sees information and materiality as distinct entities. This separation allows the construction of a hierarchy in which information is given the dominant position and materiality runs a distant second."[73] Paul echoes this concern:

> On one end of the spectrum, there has been fully immersive virtual reality, which constitutes a psychology of disincarnation, promising the possibility of leaving the obsolete body behind and inhabiting the

datascape as a cyborg. The ultimate dream of virtual reality is a mind independent of the biology of bodies, thus oscillating between a celebration of the Cartesian separation of mind and body and the "I think, therefore I am" metaphysics of philosopher Descartes.[74]

A ranking system between material and virtual disregards the interplay and interdependency between them, including how we physically interact with digital content. "One cannot afford," writes Paul, "to ignore the materiality of the interfaces that are being created or the effect of these interfaces on our bodies, and one has to pose the question of how far the human body has already become an extension of the machine."[75] McLuhan framed this idea in a slightly different way in 1964, inverting the argument to suggest that media are extensions of (hu)man(s). If the machine or medium refers to the Internet and web, both views seem fitting. Unlike previous technologies and communication devices, the Internet and the World Wide Web operate and serve as extensions of important human senses and behaviors: sight, sound, memory, interpersonal communication, imagination, and more. In turn, users are situated as extensions of the web through collective participation, interaction, and digital contributions. This is a unique and expanding affordance of the twenty-first century.

Networked communication enables remote interactions between nodes, and our bodies are not required to physically change locations to produce actions across geographic points simultaneously.[76] Except for basic digital inputs, our bodies are thus momentarily suspended from being physically exertive, enabling the so-called embodied aspect of human-machine interaction. This does not make the body obsolete, rather produces a kind of digital surrogate or virtual stand-in, that acts on the user's behalf through digital objects like avatars, profile pictures, or other personally designed icons. Digital surrogates can also be text-based, and "often mimic the functionalities of codices and other material formats, ostensibly to reproduce the experience of handling the originals while taking advantage of the vastly different cognitive and representational possibilities afforded by the new medium."[77] Digital objects imitate and remediate many of their material counterparts, building on the basic principle of facilitating communication with ease and efficiency across distances, communicating essentially premised on absence,[78] and in turn accepting and ultimately encouraging absence as a condition of everyday communication.

As such, digital objects and their predecessors work toward strengthening relations between material objects and information. "*Virtuality,*" writes Hayles, "*is the cultural perception that material objects are interpenetrated by information patterns. This definition plays off the duality at the heart of the condition of virtuality* – materiality on the one hand, information on the other."[79] Like the digital surrogates that serve as our virtual proxy, "every act of copying creates an effigy: a likeness, portrait or image that lacks the character of the original yet stands in for our pursuit of it."[80] Our web-based engagements thus foster interactions based on perception and copies.

Consequently, the physical/digital dichotomy does not go far enough to encapsulate the significance of its implications on users' experiences. "The tension between embodiment/disembodiment," writes Paul, "cannot be constructed as a choice of 'either/or' but rather has to be understood as a reality of 'both/and.'"[81] This is relevant particularly in terms of how we negotiate and organize our physical bodies in both physical and virtual space and time, summoning the perceptual collapse of being here *and* there, with *and* without. Autonomy, agency, and identity formation come together in this management of information, socialization, input, and output. In networked environments "the audience and the performer," writes Erika Pearson, "are disembodied and electronically re-embodied through signs they choose to represent themselves."[82]

Representation via digital objects allows for quite a bit of visual (and sometimes audio-visual) latitude, fostering self-expression and self-presentation. The selfie is a popular way for users to enlist facets of their physical bodies in creating digital content that graphically reveals, experiments with, or challenges aspects of identity, character, or other individual qualities. Unlike a self-portrait, a selfie is a "type of digital self-portrait [that] is taken with a mobile phone and characterized by its ubiquity." Hashtags often accompany posted selfies allowing users to self-select and identify with certain ideas while also potentially increasing traffic to their content. "Fascinated by the promise of pluripotentiality," writes Brooke Wendt, "we create numerous selfies with many different looks that can be hashtagged to theoretically unlimited and virtual locations."[83] Because a version of the self is literally at the center of these images, and they are produced in ever increasing quantities, selfies are often criticized for being products of narcissistic tendencies. Others argue the opposite. "Both in terms of content and of what happens to them, selfies may represent a more socialized and less individually focused activity than traditional photography – almost the opposite of what is commonly claimed." In addition to group selfies, deviations from the portrait-oriented selfie include attempts at more casual or less seemingly staged images. "One common version of the selfie is the foot photo, or 'footie,' almost always taken in a lounging position while watching television or playing a video game."[84] Context and environment serve as identifying or expressive information for the user and broaden the means through which personalization takes place. When shared, selfies and their variations also provide a template for others to modify accordingly and contribute their own version. In this sense, the personal is potentially communal, forming and identifying groups by suggestion and association, and repetition and variation.

Creativity, Play, and Digital Objects

Building on the idea of repetition and variation, digital objects and spaces encourage users and inhabitants to express themselves using memes. Coined in 1976 by evolutionary biologist Richard Dawkins, who studied memetics, or gene-based replication, a meme refers to a pattern of cultural, not biological, replication. "Dawkins observes," writes Limor Shifman, "that humans have devised small *cultural* units of transmission that, like genes, spread from person to person through imitation. These units – which evolve and propagate much faster than genes do – follow the same basic principles of variation, competition, selection, and retention." Given the rapid and simple creation, replication, spread, and evolution of digital content through text, images, video, and their combinations, Dawkins's term was quickly adopted by Internet users to refer to this cultural phenomenon and its similarities to Dawkins's pre-Internet observations of cultural production and exchange. However, as Shifman argues, the affordances and limitations of the web shape these factors considerably, especially in terms of scale, transformation, transparency, structure, and of course speed. "Dawkins's initial framing highlighted three qualities that enhanced memes' success: longevity (survival over time), fecundity (the number of copies produced within a time unit), and copying fidelity (accuracy)," which argues that the Internet "affords broad, quick, and accurate meme propagation."[85]

Web users have tools to transform content to personalize or adjust messages, along with readily available audience streams through social media platforms, video sharing sites, personal blogs, and others for uploading and disseminating content. A well-known recent example is the series of memes involving "Grumpy Cat," a cat born with feline dwarfism whose face appears as though she is in a bad mood. Memes were created by appropriating images of the cat and attaching a funny caption about her alleged anger or judgment about something culturally relevant or recognizable. Participants thus produced a plethora of memes that zigzag through cultural history, content, and geographic space. This format morphed, too, and images of the cat were transposed on culturally significant imagery, such as Leonardo's *Mona Lisa* and the promotional poster for the blockbuster film *Titanic*. Eventually, copycat felines mixed in other grumpy-looking felines to expand on the initial idea. The intensity and saturation of this kind of meme generation is long-lived in terms of Internet behavior but short-lived by other cultural standards. The mention of a meme after its trendiness has expired does not generate the enthusiasm or recognition it once did, making it culturally (and digitally) passé.[86]

Because memes are closely associated with cultural groups and participants who are joined by a mutual understanding, their content, meanings, and relevance greatly vary and are often misunderstood by outsiders.

Quantities, in terms of copies and reach, are extremely valuable measures of success to online communities and may appear in a different cultural context and across media. If a news agency, television show, or other cultural entity references a meme, it changes and expands the cultural dynamic around it. Memes can also return in other cultural contexts. Consider *What Do You Meme?*, a tabletop, adult card game conceived in 2016 via a Kickstarter crowdfunding campaign that involves matching pre-printed captions with images from popular Internet memes and voting for the funniest combination. In this game, digital experiences and content are literally lifted from the web and transformed to analog (material) objects and exchanges, creating new experiences and meanings for users and embodying content that was primarily conceived digitally.

Virality and Popularity as Means of Flow

Digital content that spreads like a virus, or "goes viral," requires extensive replication and dissemination across networked environments. Like memes, viral events are neither new nor specific to the web. "Before the Internet, there are plenty of examples of fast-moving information flows that reached many people and happened as a result of people sharing – the key elements of virality." Examples include times of crises, such as the organization of activities and protest in support of the Civil Rights Movement in 1950s' America, as well as situations of political commentary, like the use of poetry in eighteenth-century Europe to widely share and spread ideas between common people. People have long used social networks and available means of communication to spread information. What changes with every iteration of communications technology are the scale, pace, and frequency of dissemination of content. "Viral events are not new. What *is* new is that a viral video, news story, or a photo can reach 40,000 people in hours, or even minutes, instead of days."[87]

Our networks are primed and ready for message dissemination and retrieval, increasing the possibility for a viral event, but what is it exactly? According to Karine Nahon and Jeff Hemsley, "Viral events are a naturally occurring, emergent phenomenon facilitated by the interwoven collection of websites that allow users to host and share content (YouTube, Instagram, Flickr), connect with friends and people with similar interests (Facebook, Twitter), and share their knowledge (Wikipedia, blogs)."[88] Both virality and meme generation refer to various flows of information. Another term with origins deeply embedded in the past and within numerous contexts, flow is a useful way of thinking about how information travels through communications systems. Sandra Braman writes, "What remains the same, across time, cultures, disciplines, genres, and uses, is that flow – the exchange of information – is essential to the existence of systems."[89]

Not all flows of information are created equally, and neither are the reception, attention, or adoption of content within these streams. "Viral content is what stands out as *remarkable* in a sea of content."[90] Unlike memes, however, viral content is not propagated alongside creative differences and variations to the original text, rather it travels far and wide while remaining intact. Marketing and similar measures to push content far and wide by businesses and individuals to monetize influence differ from memes but are sometimes part of a campaign with the intention of going viral. Individuals and advertisers contribute content to the same streams and often share tricks toward increasing attention and visibility. For individuals, the *currency* or reward is not necessarily monetary, though efforts can indirectly lead to financial gain, but rather social status. Alice E. Marwick studies the ways that people use social media to compete for social benefits. "To boost social status, young professionals adopt self-consciously constructed personas and market themselves, like brands or celebrities, to an audience or fan base. These personas are highly edited, controlled, and monitored, conforming to commercial ideals that dictate 'safe-for-work' self-presentation."[91] These kinds of digital contributions stand apart from other amateur content and are more consistent with professional marketing, which helps increase their visibility.

Unwanted Manipulation of Digital Objects

Users experiment with personae and self-presentation for a range of purposes. Social media sites have standardized requirements for sharing, such as preliminary registration to verify authenticity and ties to identities in the physical world, to thwart nefarious activities conducted under anonymous, semi-anonymous, or pseudonymous identities. Additionally, users' personal accounts are password protected, increasingly with multi-step factor authentication, to help ward off unwanted access. Yet, since the web has been a populated system of information exchange, there have been disruptions in information flows produced by hackers, Internet trolls, griefers, bugs, and viruses. The term *hacker* and the act of *hacking* are often associated with malicious intent, but their origins denote something far more earnest, in part because these terms were coined by the community that hacking is purported to perniciously injure. Originally, hackers were associated simply with developments and innovations among computer scientists. "In the 1950s," writes Gabriella Coleman, "a small group of MIT-based computer enthusiasts, many of them model train builders/tinkerers, adopted the term *hacker* to differentiate their freewheeling attitude from those of their peers."[92] Turkle adds to the notion of hacking's modest beginnings by defining computer hackers as "members of the artificial intelligence community, and the first generation of people who owned computers."[93] Initially, the term referred to activities of dabbling and disruption, in an area of understanding that was once completely niche, for the benefit of innovation and advancement. "To hack is to seek quality and excellence in technological production."[94]

A so-called hacker ethic was afoot. "Hackers believe," writes Steven Levy, "that essential lessons can be learned about the systems – about the world – from taking things apart, from seeing how they work, and using this knowledge to create new and even more interesting things."[95] Such inquiry into and tinkering with systems processes carries a great deal of power. McKenzie Wark reflects on this, referring to hackers as a kind of elite social class. "We produce new concepts, new perceptions, new sensations, hacked out of raw data. Whatever code we hack, be it programming language, poetic language, math or music, curves or colorings, we are the abstracters of new worlds."[96] Hacking is a power of manipulation that allows for a new model of organization, a new or altered system of abstract thinking, and thus creates a disruption or rerouting of information. This sentiment suggests an outsider quality shared by computer hackers, and a sense of pride that accompanies it. "Whatever the label, these are people for whom computers have become ... a way of life."[97]

The power of expertise in the wrong hands can have damaging results, but many hackers see their work as revolutionary and prosocial, like the Anonymous collective that "had established itself as a social, political force with a series of ops" that range in scale and scope from a "digital direct action by launching a distributed denial of service (DDoS) campaign" to street protests in support of social and political issues. Maintaining anonymity allows a different kind of power to manifest in networked environments, as it protects individuals' identities and thus hampers accountability. Anonymity fosters the ability to make choices and change course without the influences of a sounding board or critics. "Beyond a foundational commitment to the maintenance of anonymity and a broad dedication to the free flow of information, Anonymous has no consistent philosophy or political program. While increasingly recognized for its digital dissent and direct action, Anonymous has never displayed a predictable trajectory."[98] Those who act anonymously are empowered to remain capricious, acting in their own self-interest. On the other end of the spectrum is the Electronic Disturbance Theater (EDT) group, formed by performance artist Ricardo Dominguez in 1997 to protest issues of social and political importance through acts of civil disobedience in digital and non-digital arenas. The most relevant is FloodNet, a webjamming tool designed to target specific websites and disrupt the flow of web traffic as a form of protest, a kind of virtual sit-in. It was designed to get the attention of powerful corporate and government entities and raise awareness among the public of important issues.

There are other, less demanding ways to disrupt networked flows of information with malicious intent. Internet trolls aim to maliciously disrupt information flows as well as the personal experience of other web users. "Trolling is the multifarious activity that flourishes online and boasts a range of tight-knit associations (such as the Patriotic Nigras, Bantown, Team Roomba, Rustle League), a variety of genres (differentiated mostly by target – for example, griefers target gamers, RIP trolls target the families and friends of the recently deceased), and a small pantheon of famed individuals (*Violentacrez, Jameth*)."[99] Trolling behavior can be difficult to detect at first, as it is often "experienced and disguised as play," luring and appealing to web users before launching more aggressive and harassing behaviors that can sometimes drive users off-line altogether.[100]

Bugs and viruses disrupt and rearrange flows of information in software and networked environments. Basic programming, nefarious hacking, and replicating and spreading infected information can introduce bugs and viruses into a system. Bugs are usually unintentional, human errors performed during programming that can impair or block proper or seamless functioning of a computer program. What seems like a redundancy in communication is a negotiation between abstract ideas and concrete machine systems. It is at this intersection in computer programming that mistakes are likely to be made. "When you're learning the concepts of computer programming, it's never too early to get acquainted with *bugs*. When you're coding – particularly in machine code – it's very easy to make mistakes."[101] Computer programming involves different languages, and like spoken language or writing, the programmer has a great deal of authority to wield it. "Programmers learn to think about what ails their products without recourse to the formula 'the program is wrong.' The program is basically sound. It just needs to be debugged."[102] Debugging, or addressing errors, involves first identifying then removing or repairing them, like conducting a thorough copyedit. From an end user's standpoint, however, bugs can be a nuisance, sometimes requiring additional work to resolve them. A patch might be created to address bugs and other vulnerabilities in already released software, a metaphorical bandage to repair the disruption in information flow.

Computer viruses differ in that they are intentional, one method in a toolbox of options for computer hackers to make trouble for web users. The computer jargon for nefarious activities is robust: virus, malware, spyware, worm, phishing, spam, botnet, trojan, DDoS, and many more. Consider this short excerpt from Coleman:

> A computer most often becomes a member of a botnet by getting infected by malware. This can happen through a number of different methods – that hilarious cat video you downloaded, the malicious link in an email from your aunt, a phishing attack you didn't even know about, or a virus piggybacking on some software you downloaded from the Internet. Once infected, the computer runs a small program, usually hidden in the process table so it is not easily found, which mediates its involvement in the botnet.[103]

Viruses can be arranged into botnets to infect more efficiently. Botnets are "a collection of computers connected to the Internet, allowing a single entity extra processing power or network connections toward the performance of various tasks including (but not limited to) DDoSing and spam bombing." The person in charge of the botnet is a *herder*,[104] given their special objective of wrangling unsuspecting computers and their users. Additionally, viruses of this sort spread like a virus but do not infect the host like a virus.

Despite the extreme online behaviors and vicious activities concealed by anonymous identities, for the most part the web identities users construct and maintain are arguably no different from the identities users construct and maintain in person-to-person, physical social realms.[105] However, context, social conditions, and each medium bring specific circumstances to shape behaviors, socialization, and activities, as Innis's and McLuhan's arguments demonstrate. As more objects are networked and advancements in ubiquitous computing continue, our attention increasingly shifts to the convergence of those information flows: what we can do with the data we are collecting about our bodies, our cities, and our homes.

Networking Physical Objects

At the surface level, we relate to physical objects via networked communications amounts that we can see and touch. "The introduction and convergence of technologies like Bluetooth, Wi-Fi, and GPS allow for more accurate contextual and geographical detections, leading us into the REAL."[106] Ubiquitous computing, or the application of computation everywhere and in everything, marks a clear integration between data, systems, bodies, physical space, and physical objects. "Ordinary objects, from coffee cups to raincoats to the paint on the walls, would be considered as sites for the sensing and processing of information." More importantly, "people would interact with these systems fluently and naturally, barely noticing the powerful informatics they were engaging."[107] Computer scientists working toward ubiquitous computing imagine a world in which so-called smart objects are everywhere – at home, school, work – and are optimized to interact with each other on our behalf. The visible aspect of computing itself disappears and is instead embedded in everyday objects, including wearables.

We refer to the effects of ubiquitous computing as the Internet of Things (IoT), meaning things are networked to the Internet and to one another and can be manipulated remotely via mobile applications, extending teleaction to include objects of everyday life. The current design of the web and the behaviors, activities, and expectations that users have developed lend themselves to this additional application of the technologies, laying the groundwork for increased connection. "Today every connected device receives an IP address, and every address allows every device to connect to other devices, including smartphones, tablet computers, gaming consoles, automobiles, refrigerators, washing machines, lighting systems, front door locks, electronic toll devices in vehicles."[108]

Convenience, popularity among users, and compatibility between devices are driving the integration of more physical objects into this networked system. "Commands, functions and coding that would have once required an army of developers with an intimate knowledge of a programming language now take place at the tap of a finger or the utterance of a spoken word." Many of these devices and smart objects are well-known and common, such as wearable activity trackers, home automation devices (thermostats, smoke detectors, alarms, etc.), remote health monitors (for conditions such as heart disease, diabetes, etc.), and voice-enabled digital assistants. Additionally, "RFID [radio-frequency identification] technology has matured, sensor technology has leapt forward, miniaturization has accelerated, and computer software has taken a giant leap forward."[109] More features and other devices continue to appear on the market as technologies advance and beta testers help improve subsequent offerings.

Apart from having the ability to remotely adjust a connected device, like the temperature in your home or the timer for a lawn sprinkler system, IoT devices also collect and store data. Users can study collected data to determine patterns, behaviors, and activities associated with the device, such as frequency of use, time(s) of day, location(s), and more. Fitness trackers, for example, collect new data but also analyze incoming information by relying on individual inputs by the user, such as age, weight, height, and location. Using sensors and customized data collection software, the trackers determine patterns of activities and suggest improvements or changes, bridging digital objects and information with physical bodies. On a small scale, this interaction works effectively toward the user's curiosity and end goals. On a larger scale, however, these now common data collections raise important questions about users' ownership, privacy, and authority over data.

Because IoT systems rely on cloud computing, home and personal devices may be hacked, especially if security protocols are weak or unfamiliar to users. But even if precautions are taken, there are still questions about data collection and ownership. Seemingly innocuous activities, such as exercise, can lead to potentially invasive data collection and exploitation of users by platform developers. By now we expect this from Facebook and similar services, and we would be remiss to overlook data collection of all Internet-connected offerings. Peloton is an Internet-enabled home exercise bike that offers on-demand and live-streamed group classes with its monthly membership. Like fitness tracking devices, it requires personal user inputs, but it also collects, stores, and shares other user data that seemingly have nothing to do with a user's fitness or physical makeup. Their privacy policy states:

We may collect certain information automatically through our Services or other methods of web analysis, such as your Internet protocol (IP) address, cookie identifiers, mobile carrier, mobile advertising identifiers, MAC address, IMEI, Advertiser ID, and other device identifiers that are automatically assigned to your computer or device when you access the Internet, browser type and language, geo-location information, hardware type, operating system, Internet service provider, pages that you visit before and after using the Services, the date and time of your visit, the amount of time you spend on each page, information about the links you click and pages you view within the Services, and other actions taken through use of the Services such as preferences.[110]

Upon signing onto their services, users agree to allow Peloton access to and use of any information submitted by the user "including any ideas, inventions, concepts, techniques, or know-how disclosed as part of that content, for any purpose including developing, manufacturing and/or marketing goods or Services." Peloton is not unique in outlining these terms and conditions in their privacy policy, and it is common for users to overlook these details prior to registration, but we are continuing to learn from these mistakes as users and developers of these systems. "At the very least, the Internet of Things will deliver new challenges and problems revolving around security, privacy, and how we go about living our digital lives."[111]

Connectivity between systems exists outside the mindset of the IoT, in part because so many of our activities take place in networked, especially social media, environments. As such, the seamless integration between these systems has been sought and achieved in other ways. "Plug-ins and apps are continuously invented to interconnect platforms and align their operability, even if they are incompatible."[112] This helps improve the management of data across platforms – especially with capabilities like photo sharing and music streaming – as well as increase user presence in these domains, in the interest of boosting contributions as well as audiences. "Expressions in networked publics would be persistent (recorded, archived), replicable, scalable and searchable. Audiences in these publics would often be invisible, social contexts collapsed and the boundary between public and private would often blur."[113]

This relates to the glass bedroom metaphor enlisted by many web theorists to describe networked exchanges and the contested distinctions between public and private spaces, conditions, and/or content across them. Personal privacy and the shared public of networked environments inevitably creep into each other, eventually becoming difficult or impossible to fully separate. By default, one becomes at least somewhat public while operating within networked environments, digital publics that vary in scope between platforms, and communities of users. Pearson describes the glass bedroom as "a bridge between public and private, constructed online through signs and language."[114] Over time, patterns of behavior determine the meaning and intent of signs and language, but given their shifting contexts, even these are not fixed. Moreover, the conditions for what is appropriate for a public audience and a private one is culturally determined but constantly in flux, and individual privacy is subjectively defined. One person's boundary is another's comfort zone. Networked environments, geographic locations, personal experiences, disparate cultures, and more converge with different ideas about suitability and conduct. Different platforms promote different behaviors through different affordances and limitations, and communities of users and their behaviors adjust accordingly. However, one could argue that the web, overall, is designed to be more open and less private. Personal (private) and public are merged. Some of the same features that help platform owners track users' activities (for practical purposes and otherwise) also aid in users tracking other users. Time stamps, counters, endorsements, and geolocation data are increasingly openly displayed in the user interfaces of most social media platforms and other websites, and quantify visitors' physical and virtual locations and activities, further blurring any boundaries between on- and off-line presence.

Conclusion

Digital objects are at the core of our present communications environment. They are selected, organized, disseminated, accessed, and stored through many cultural, economic, structural, and habitual systems that are expanding every day. Though they are immaterial in form, digital objects are deeply tethered to and integrated with material life, from desktop computers and mobile devices to fiber optics cables and storage servers to everyday objects from our homes and daily lives. The intricacies of the World Wide Web are largely hidden from view, but their impact and integration in daily life demonstrate the ways that material and digital objects are bound to one another and are mutually persuasive. Our bodies are also key to the ways that we create and share digital objects that serve as a proxy, representing or recreating facets of our identities, performing truths and fantasies of our imaginations, and allowing for teleaction across geographic time and space. Organization of digital objects and flows of data in networked environments take place in diverse ways: through personal social media feeds; by stealthy acquisition through third-party collectors; in fits and starts by way of computer bugs; at a standstill courtesy of a computer virus; and more. Web 2.0 design encourages and depends on contributions by everyday users: Google's search engine improves with each user search; social media platforms operate through the participation of users; and cloud computing hovers over our networked activities as an invisible storage system containing digital objects from millions of users. The landscape of digital objects is vast.

Understanding their physical and virtual relations to daily life and how systems are designed, used, and change over time helps situate the digital world we helped create, currently inhabit, and continuously influence. As our dependence on the Internet and web persist, new ways of curating, protecting, and sharing data will also evolve.

Notes

1. Benjamin Peters, "Digital," in Benjamin Peters, ed., *Digital Keywords* (Princeton: Princeton University Press, 2016), 94.
2. Marcello Vitali-Rosati, *On Editorialization: Structuring Space and Authority in the Digital Age* (Amsterdam: Institute of Network Cultures, 2018), 33.
3. Lev Manovich, *The Language of New Media* (Cambridge: MIT Press, 2001), 11.
4. George Mason University. "History of Computing." George Mason University (2010). http://mason.gmu.edu/~montecin/computer-hist-web.htm.
5. Manovich, *The Language of New Media*, 64.
6. Ibid, 14.
7. Ibid, 20.
8. Ibid, 28.
9. "Timeline of Computer History: Memory and Storage." Computer History Museum (2018). www.computerhistory.org/timeline/memory-storage/.
10. Ibid.
11. Sadie Plant, *Zeros + Ones* (London: Fourth Estate, 1998), 34.
12. Charles Seife, *Zero: The Biography of a Dangerous Idea* (New York: Penguin, 2000), 66.
13. Manovich, *The Language of New Media*, 21, 22.
14. Thomas Streeter, "Internet," in Benjamin Peters, ed., *Digital Keywords* (Princeton: Princeton University Press, 2016), 184.
15. Peters, "Digital," 94.
16. Streeter, "Internet."
17. Christiane Paul, "Contextual Networks: Data, Identity, and Collective Production" in Margot Lovejoy, Christiane Paul, and Victoria Vesna, eds., *Context Providers: Conditions of Meaning in Media Arts* (Bristol: Intellect, 2011), 107.
18. Manovich, *The Language of New Media*, 166, 167.
19. Yuk Hui, *On the Existence of Digital Objects* (Minneapolis: University of Minnesota Press, 2016), 48.
20. Alexander Galloway, *Gaming: Essays on Algorithmic Culture* (Minneapolis: University of Minnesota Press, 2006) 2, 3.
21. Tung-Hui Hu, *A Prehistory of the Cloud* (Cambridge: MIT Press, 2016), 4.

22. Paul, "Contextual Networks: Data, Identity, and Collective Production," 109.
23. Plant, *Zeros + Ones*, 49.
24. Paul, "Contextual Networks: Data, Identity, and Collective Production," 110.
25. Plant, *Zeros + Ones*, 47.
26. Vitali-Rosati, *On Editorialization*, 7.
27. Ibid.
28. Ibid, 36, 40.
29. Manuel Castells, *The Rise of the Network Society* (Oxford: Blackwell, 1996), 471.
30. Don Tapscott and Anthony D. Williams, *Wikinomics: How Mass Collaboration Changes Everything* (New York: Portfolio, 2008), 11, 13.
31. Ágnes Veszelski, "#time, #truth, #tradition: An Image-Text Relationship on Instagram: Photo and Hashtag," in András Benedek and Ágnes Veszelszki, eds., *In the Beginning Was the Image: The Omnipresence of Pictures* (Frankfurt: Peter Lang, 2016), 139.
32. Jeffrey Pomerantz, *Metadata* (Cambridge: MIT Press, 2015), 1.
33. Andreas Kaplan and Michael Haenlein, "Users of the World, Unite! The Challenges and Opportunities of Social Media," *Business Horizons* 53 (2010): 61.
34. Tim O'Reilly, "What is Web 2.0? Design Patterns and Business Models for the Next Generation of Software," in Michael Mandiberg, ed., *The Social Media Reader* (New York: New York University Press, 2012), 35, 37.
35. Harold Innis, *The Bias of Communication* (Toronto: University of Toronto Press, 2008 [1951]), 33.
36. Marshall McLuhan, *Understanding Media: The Extensions of Man* (Cambridge: MIT Press, 2004 [1964]), 9.
37. O'Reilly, "What is Web 2.0?" 38.
38. Ibid.
39. Castells, *The Rise of the Network Society*, 470.
40. For up-to-date information on the overall size of the indexed web, see https://www.worldwidewebsize.com/.
41. Paul, "Contextual Networks: Data, Identity, and Collective Production," 108.
42. Tom Standage, *The Victorian Internet* (New York: Walker, 1998), 11.
43. Pew Research Center. "Social Media Fact Sheet, February 5, 2018." www.pewinternet.org/fact-sheet/social-media/.
44. Ibid.
45. Jose van Dijck, *The Culture of Connectivity: A Critical History of Social Media* (New York: Oxford University Press, 2013), 4.
46. Ibid, 46–47.
47. Ibid, 47.
48. Theodor Nelson, "A File Structure for the Complex, the Changing, and the Indeterminate," in Noah Wardrip-Fruin and Nick Montfort, eds., *The New Media Reader* (Cambridge: MIT Press, 2003 [1965]), 138.

49. Plant, *Zeros + Ones*, 48.
50. Vannevar Bush, "As We May Think," in Noah Wardrip-Fruin and Nick Montfort, eds., *The New Media Reader* (Cambridge: MIT Press, 2003 [1945]), 45.
51. "Web Tracking: What You Should Know about Your Privacy Online." Free Code Camp. (April 23, 2018). https://bit.ly/3IGROPF.
52. "The Murky World of Third Party Web Tracking." *Technology Review* (September 12, 2014). https://bit.ly/3lTxMrn.
53. Ibid.
54. Christian Fuchs, *Social Media: A Critical Introduction* (London: Sage, 2014), 156–57.
55. Ibid, 108.
56. Henry Jenkins, Sam Ford, and Joshua Green, *Spreadable Media: Creating Value and Meaning in a Networked Culture* (New York: New York University Press, 2003), 2.
57. Paul, "Contextual Networks: Data, Identity, and Collective Production," 103.
58. Sherry Turkle, *Alone Together: Why We Expect More from Technology and Less from Each Other* (New York: Basic Books, 2011), 15, 17.
59. Standage, *The Victorian Internet*, 14.
60. Manovich, *The Language of New Media*, 165.
61. Paul, "Contextual Networks: Data, Identity, and Collective Production," 103.
62. danah boyd, "Participating in the Always-On Lifestyle," in Michael Mandiberg, ed., *The Social Media Reader* (New York: New York University Press, 2012), 72.
63. Van Dijck, *The Culture of Connectivity*, 4.
64. See Jürgen Habermas, *The Structural Transformation of the Public Sphere* (Cambridge: MIT Press, 1991).
65. Fuchs, *Social Media*, 183.
66. Paul, "Contextual Networks: Data, Identity, and Collective Production," 109.
67. Ibid.
68. Plant, *Zeros + Ones*, 46.
69. Zizi Papacharissi, *A Private Sphere: Democracy in a Digital Age* (Cambridge: Polity Press, 2010), 3.
70. Sherry Turkle, *The Second Self: Computers and the Human Spirit* (Cambridge: MIT Press, 2005 [1984]), 156.
71. Paul, "Contextual Networks: Data, Identity, and Collective Production," 110.
72. Ibid.
73. N. Katherine Hayles, *How We Became Posthuman* (Chicago: University of Chicago Press, 1999), 12.
74. Paul, "Contextual Networks: Data, Identity, and Collective Production," 111.

75. Ibid.
76. Ibid.
77. Jeffrey Drouin, "Surrogate," in Benjamin Peters, ed., *Digital Keywords* (Princeton: Princeton University Press, 2016), 278.
78. For information about how absence relates to communication and meaning in both the written word and speech, see Jacques Derrida, *On Grammatology*, trans. Gayatari Spivak (Baltimore: Johns Hopkins University Press, 1976).
79. Hayles, *How We Became Posthuman*, 13, 14.
80. Drouin, "Surrogate," 282.
81. Paul, "Contextual Networks: Data, Identity, and Collective Production," 111.
82. Erika Pearson, "All the World Wide Web's a Stage: The Performance of Identity in Online Social Networks," *First Monday* 14, no. 3 (2 March 2009). https://bit.ly/3IO48Om.
83. Brooke Wendt, *The Allure of the Selfie: Instagram and the New Self-Portrait* (Amsterdam: Institute of Network Cultures, 2014), 7.
84. Daniel Miller, Elisabetta Costa, Nell Haynes, Tom McDonald, Razvan Nicolescu, Jolynna Sinanan, Juliano Spyer, and Shriram Venkatraman, *How the World Changed Social Media* (London: UCL Press, 2016), 158, 164.
85. Limor Shifman, "Meme," in Benjamin Peters, ed., *Digital Keywords* (Princeton: Princeton University Press, 2016), 197–98, 199.
86. At the time of this writing, Tardar Sauce recently made news in the forms of obituary and eulogy, death being one circumstance that temporarily reinvigorates interest in the culturally passé.
87. Karine Nahon and Jeff Hemsley, *Going Viral* (Cambridge: Polity Press, 2013), 1.
88. Ibid, 2.
89. Sandra Braman, "Flow," in Benjamin Peters, ed., *Digital Keywords* (Princeton: Princeton University Press, 2016), 118–9.
90. Nahon and Hemsley, *Going Viral*, 2.
91. Alice E. Marwick, *Status Update: Celebrity, Publicity, & Branding in the Social Media Age* (New Haven: Yale University Press, 2013), 5.
92. Gabriella Coleman, *Hacker, Hoaxer, Whistleblower, Spy: The Many Faces of Anonymous* (London: Verso, 2014), 158.
93. Turkle, *The Second Self*, 23.
94. Coleman, *Hacker, Hoaxer, Whistleblower, Spy*, 162.
95. Steven Levy, *Hackers: Heroes of the Computer Revolution* (Sebastopol: O'Reilly Media, 2010), 28.
96. McKenzie Wark, *A Hacker Manifesto* (Cambridge: Harvard University Press, 2004), 002.
97. Turkle, *The Second Self*, 186.
98. Coleman, *Hacker, Hoaxer, Whistleblower, Spy*, 3.
99. Ibid, 19.

100. Ibid, 20.
101. Charles Petzold, *Code: The Hidden Language of Computer Hardware and Software* (Redmond: Microsoft Press, 2000), 236.
102. Turkle, *The Second Self*, 150.
103. Coleman, *Hacker, Hoaxer, Whistleblower, Spy*, 93.
104. Ibid, 92–93.
105. For additional information about self-presentation, see Erving Goffman, *The Presentation of Self in Everyday Life* (New York: Anchor Books, 1959).
106. Hui, *On the Existence of Digital Objects*, 48.
107. Adam Greenfield, *Everyware: The Dawning Age of Ubiquitous Computing* (Berkeley: New Riders, 2006), 11.
108. Samuel Greengard, *The Internet of Things* (Cambridge: MIT Press, 2015), 10–11.
109. Ibid, 11, xiii.
110. "Peloton Privacy Policy." Peloton (September 30, 2019). www.onepeloton.com/privacy-policy.
111. Greengard, *The Internet of Things*, 137.
112. Van Dijck, *The Culture of Connectivity*, 156.
113. Fuchs, *Social Media*, 187.
114. Pearson, "All the World Wide Web's a Stage."

25

Boundaries and Borderlands, Inclusion and Holism

Political and Relevant Material Culture Studies

Lu Ann De Cunzo and Catharine Dann Roeber

> I'm interested in the moment when two objects collide and generate a third. The third object is where the interesting work is.
>
> Bruce Mau
>
> Take away a nation's heritage, and they are more easily persuaded.
>
> Karl Marx

We have three objectives as we leave you to pursue your own practice of material culture study: (1) to review the common threads in contemporary material culture research that our authors explored; (2) to assess approaches and perspectives that offer the greatest potential for future developments in material culture studies; and (3) to define material culture and to position the practice for the future.

Material Culture Research

In the introductory chapter we identified three main themes that link the twenty-three diverse chapters comprising this handbook: materiality and immateriality, lived experience, and politics. Within these themes, authors addressed the scope, foci, and structures of contemporary material culture scholarship. In doing so, they consistently raised topics as broad as inclusion and holism, globalism, transformation, and conceptual frameworks.

First, on inclusion and holism: Material culture scholars embrace holistic approaches and the inclusion of diverse voices. They acknowledge the role of interlocutors' standpoints – emergent from lived experience – in defining research topics, questions, analyses, and interpretations. Holism has several dimensions. It refers to richly textured and nuanced object studies imbued with the technical, economic, social, political, and ideological. It involves object biographical and life cycle studies encompassing abstracted design processes; production chains; exchange processes and values; object work and mobility – doing, representing, sensing, and meaning – and its attendant mending, adapting, and remodeling; and abandonment and decay. And this list is by necessity incomplete and unsuitably linear. Holism centers relationships of objects in assemblages, with living beings, and in processual systems. It encompasses the material – the matter – of objects and the abstract and conceptual – the imagined and the immaterial. In sum, the principles of holism and inclusion provoke material culture studies that are critical, reflective, comparative, contextual, and evidence based. Gretchen Sorin captures its essence concisely: "It means breaking open the usual canon and changing it, which requires new scholarship as well as an open mind."

Second, on the global scope of material culture scholarship and practice: Holistic global scholarship engages object lives, biographies, mobilities, and histories. Ann Stahl has maintained that the goal is understanding the material histories of global entanglements – object approaches to nationalist and imperialist political discourses and hierarchical relationships, and the creative adaptability and mutability of objects in motion, in new cultural contexts.[1] Moreover, consideration is given to the ways that objects work as instruments and expressions of identity. Especially in imperialist and capitalist settings, the obsession with possession and ownership as means to and representations of power also receive critical attention. Material culture studies as a global practice implicates scholarly perspectives, and embraces Indigenous, Global South, and other nonwestern ways of thinking and doing. One important intervention with great consequences for material studies involves rupturing and/or reuniting the innumerable oppositions structuring Western dichotomous thinking, such as subject/object, nature/culture, time/space, object/representation, material/immaterial, and male/female. Piercing these binaries enables intellectual freedom and space for those who have not yet participated in these discussions.

Third, on transformations of matter: Scholars of material transformations examine sources of creativity and inspirations for innovation in developing mechanical, chemical, electronic, and genetic tools and processes that change materials, objects, bodies, and ideas. Much of this research is politically charged, centering on human manipulation of matter and interventions that set processes of transformation in motion, and the nature and scope of the consequences.

Fourth, on frameworks: As scholars engage with, analyze, and interpret material culture, we deploy diverse frameworks. This volume's contributors have introduced readers to several organizing frameworks, including narrative, system and network, performance, expressed cognitive geometries, and lived experience. Each framework has a distinctive core agent or instrument, in these instances, story and plot, structure, purposive action, mind, and body respectively. For some theorists, these frameworks are mutually exclusive; many others imagine a complex construct of interpenetrating structures. To cite but one example, understanding the mortification, constraint, satiety, pain, pleasure, sorrow, joy, and sensation of lived experience demands internal and external gazes at a unified mind-body in motion through time and across space, acting with and acted upon by material things and forces.

Approaches and Perspectives for the Future

Looking to the future, let us begin with the question with which we opened this volume, what is material culture? Past practice has demonstrated the value of maintaining an openness, fluidity, and dynamism to the category material culture. Do not police the borders too closely; here the greatest innovation has and will continue to occur. In scope, it may suffice to "define" material culture as means and forms of human (debatable) expression integral to reproductive, political, and social action. Veronica Strang warned us that the links between identity, power, and agency depend to a great extent on "who gets to decide what the categories ... should be, what these will mean, and how categorical boundaries will be maintained." In the world of art, for example, Timothy Carroll suggests that those with "the capacity to capture the imagination and drive forward a group of people via the actions to 'create art – destroy the world' instrumentalizes, and weaponizes, aesthetics." No longer is material culture practice limited to studies of physical things valued for their function or aesthetics.

Recent paradigm shifts such as the "new materialism" and posthuman discourses reinforce our understanding of their political (broadly defined) contingency. Cutting edge and ethically debatable work on new technologies that alter the sensory, intellectual, and emotional experiences of humans and other beings will surely captivate us for years to come. So too will "advances" in AI and forays into other posthuman, including digital, materialities. The value and potential of these alternative forms of materialization depends on one's standpoint; exposing and assessing these processes of valuation and application will remain a challenging and fascinating endeavor.

Global mobilities is another matter of great urgency. Raw materials and commodities are moving around the globe at an unprecedented rate. As I write this in early 2020, news agencies are reporting a 200-billion-dollar trade deal between China and the USA that will set astounding quantities of agricultural and manufacturing products in motion. From a transcultural perspective, we may gain great insight from these goods and materials as they are transformed in physical form, meaning, and value through their travels, inspiring cross-cultural understanding, creativity, innovation, and conflict. These insights, however, may come at great cost as global trade amplifies the energy and environmental crises. Countering these massive mobilizations of goods and people are "slow" and "tiny" movements. "Slow food" proponents, recognizing the "strong connections between plate and planet," advocate eco-gastronomy for environmental and personal well-being.[2] An architectural and social movement advocates living simply in "tiny houses" as a means to achieve "financial prudence, economically safe, shared community experiences, and a shift in consumerism-driven mindsets."[3] Material culture scholars are already considering if and how humans can disentangle the deeply rooted interpenetration of material appropriation, possession, accumulation, and the value of a human life.[4]

Such political and moral economies are implicated in the ethics of our practice. John Law and Ruth Benschop incite us to expose the "ontological politics" of material culture. Their argument is compelling and poetic:

> To represent is to perform division. To represent is to generate distributions. Distributions between painter and observer, between a depicting surface and object depicted, between places located on a surface, between that which is depicted and that which is not. To represent is to narrate, or to refuse to narrate. It is to perform, or to refuse to perform, a world of spatial assumptions populated by subjects and objects. To represent thus renders other possibilities impossible, unimaginable. It is, in other words, to perform a politics. A politics of ontology.[5]

Post-disciplinary and "after ethics" scholars and advocates seek to dismantle the ontological politics that have generated the "asymmetrical relation between disciplinary knowledge ... and local, indigenous and subaltern knowledge." Their goal is to decolonize knowledge and embrace "alternative and rival regimes of care."[6] In doing so, material culture becomes energized and challenged by new voices and experiences that were previously silenced.

Material Culture Studies and Disciplinarity: After Disciplines

We conclude with a return to the matter of disciplinarity raised in the volume's introductory chapter. How might material culture studies best be structured to achieve the greatest insight and impact in the future? Many authors echo Fredrik Fahlander and Terje Oestigaard's concern that disciplinary boundaries have "become more structures of dominance and weapons of exclusion" than arenas of intellectual excitement and openness.[7] Having witnessed and experienced this exclusion, we are attracted by the opportunity to position material culture studies as an inter-discipline, intervention between disciplines, perhaps even post-discipline or un-discipline and infused with postcolonial, queer, and anarchic thinking and perspectives. Power and politics are central dynamics: they inspire and infuse contemporary imaginaries and critique the traditions of dominance, science, and hierarchical structures. Schweitzer and Frey represent many scholars' position when they write that by animating all objects, "new materialism" offers the potential to "disrupt the power hierarchies that privilege human subjects over animals, environments, objects, and other entities that decenter human agency." New materialists challenge our concepts of "being," acknowledge and explore the "vital materiality" that runs through and across all bodies, granting things the capacity not only to disrupt or obstruct human designs, "but also to act as ... forces with trajectories, propensities, or tendencies of their own ... These material powers ... can aid or destroy, enrich or disable, ennoble or degrade us."[8] Agents of this survivalist, political and post-humanitarian (materialitarian, perhaps) project for environmental and social justice interrogate the history and consequences of settler colonialism and capitalism. Heritage and memory studies contribute their focus on relationships and conflicts among past, present, and imagined futures in all forms of material expression. In doing so, scholars of heritage negotiate multiple notions of heritage and associated beliefs surrounding preservation, conservation, and decay rooted in culturally and historically contingent values.

We briefly revisit the arguments that advocates of each have presented, leaving readers to probe the complexities. Positioning material culture studies as an "intervention between disciplines" enables us to critically engage with all forms and conceptions of materiality.[9] Post-disciplinarity models inclusion, uniting scholars from diverse backgrounds around common research interests, promoting the sharing of good ideas and productive approaches.[10] By unhinging material culture studies from disciplines, Alejandro Haber and Nick Shepherd envision practitioners engaging "body and soul" to pursue every disarticulated and disjointed lead, whatever the language, textuality, or form of expression. In doing so, we are better situated to expose the histories that disciplinary practices have repressed and reveal the "spectral presences" of the past influencing the present.[11] Whether the authors directly reject disciplines or embrace aspects of these scholarly traditions is not the point. Each of the essays in this volume contributes valuable perspectives to the practice of material culture. They also model the disjunctions that make the volume as a whole, and inter-, post-, and un-disciplinary material culture studies writ large, a vibrant intellectual space deeply engaged with the world. This freedom of expression stands squarely on the foundation of postcolonial approaches.

Post–World War II postcolonial approaches have informed all these critiques of disciplinarity. Postcolonial studies do not constitute a coherent project, but rather encompass many trajectories with a common goal to understand and critique global power relationships from self-reflexive, political points of view. Queer theory represents one of these nonlinear, emergent trajectories. We take a moment to introduce it here not because material culture scholars have ignored it, indeed it is an important and valuable standpoint, but because it does not figure strongly in any of this volume's essays.[12] Originally, queer theorists concentrated on a critique of non-heteronormative, nonbinary sex and gender ascriptions. Noreen Giffney captures how much more expansive and inclusive queer theory has become: "Queer loosely describes a diverse, often conflicting set of interdisciplinary approaches to desire, subjectivity, identity, relationality, ethics and norms ... with an unremitting emphasis ... on fluidity, über-inclusivity, indeterminacy, indefinability, unknowability, the preposterous, impossibility, unthinkability, unintelligibility, meaninglessness and that which is unrepresentable or uncommunicable."[13]

Anarchist theory has a longer but similarly disrupting history in American thought, at least back to philosopher William James' 1907 claim that his pragmatist philosophical theory was a kind of anarchism.[14] Lewis Borck and Matthew Sanger report that the "Western philosophical tradition of anarchism was born out of an interest in how individuals could form cooperative social groups without coercion."[15] It promotes "free association" among theorists and practitioners in multiple disciplines, a form of reflective collaboration exploring the processes "by which states and hegemonic ideals influence the production of knowledge ... which manifests ... in the ways in which we classify artifacts ... [and] people."[16] In contemporary practice, it is a trajectory of postcolonialism, challenging normative values based on colonial epistemologies.[17] Anarchic archaeologists have found it especially illuminating regarding the histories of Indigenous populations, but these are not the only groups who have found productive space in rejection of traditional power differentials.

Anarchic archaeologists inspired by punk rock created a powerful, if short-lived experiment. Despite a devotion to hipsterism we many not all share, their manifesto is quite familiar in the context of this chapter. Michael Laughy explains in their signature publication, *Punk Archaeology*. punk archaeologists share with punk rockers "a desire to express and accept the complexity and contradictions of the human experience, an embrace of physicality, a rejection of the hegemony of the Truth, and a belief that our work is conducted on behalf of the world, to be shared with the world."[18] The radical openness suggested here and by others pushes against and tests disciplines and finds a somewhat comfortable home in the slightly misfit umbrella of material culture. Perhaps this is one of the most important roles for material culture studies, a collective of approaches to understanding the world, a space for innovative and provocative scholarship that straddles humanities, social sciences, and much more.

We assembled this handbook during an extraordinary historical moment that encompassed the Trump presidency in the USA and parallel conservative governments in locations around the world, dire predictions of a sixth mass extinction, devastating fires and hurricanes, and a global pandemic that crossed species and killed more than 3,025,000 by mid-2021.[19]

Newscasters and media pundits have ratcheted up apocalyptic rhetoric in their reporting. Former US president Trump threatened to bomb cultural heritage sites in Iran and committed almost nineteen billion dollars to materialize and further weaponize the US border with Mexico. His administration ended in January 2021 with an unprecedented assault on the US Capitol. The UN Convention on Biological Diversity drafted an agreement on nature to combat what scientists have portended as the sixth mass extinction event in earth's history that would result in a drastic loss of biodiversity. The 2030 deadline for conserving and restoring ecosystems and wildlife that perform crucial services for humans reflects the urgency, even as it remains anthropocentric. In Australia conflagrations fueled by record high temperatures incinerated more than twenty-five million acres. One ecologist estimated that more than one billion animals, excluding insects, fish, and some amphibians died. Amid this annihilation of plant and animal life, at least a dozen animal species face extinction.

The Australian government dropped thousands of pounds of food for survivors, and New Zealanders stitched joey pouches and bat wraps.[20] And then there were those quilters in the Netherlands who made mittens for koalas with burned paws. Quilter Jeltje van Essen explained that ordinary mittens made in factories would not do because they contain plastic. The koalas' burnt feet and hands are too fragile and so the quilters sewed cotton mittens, which are "soft and will prevent infections."[21]

Increases in the number and intensity of hurricanes, cyclones, and typhoons and the flooding they precipitated in Asia, Africa, the Americas, and the Caribbean destroyed innumerable homes and habitats.[22] Coupled with climate change, storms and flooding in southern Africa left fifty million people facing food insecurity.[23] Civil war in Syria and Yemen caused more than 75 percent of these countries' populations to need humanitarian aid.

And then came COVID-19, still evolving as of this writing. The true extent of our loss from this pandemic may be beyond our abilities to calculate.

We have been inspired by the tenacity and resilience of health care professionals and voluntary caregivers working at great personal risk. Flavia Brunetti, Italian aid worker in Libya, returned home to help her family just before COVID hit Italy. "In the end, it was China who sent more than 30 metric tonnes of emergency supplies and a nine-member aid team to help us contain the outbreak. When emergencies crop up, whether thrown at us from nature or man-made, will we make the connection in our minds that there is no such thing as them versus us?"[24] We do not have to be immersed in materiality theory or self-identify as a "new materialist" to do good. Richard Hutchings's accusation of the academy's complicity, my professional home, in creating this environmental crisis, hurts "body and soul." Things are changing. Scholars working "after the discipline" are building strong, increasingly deep intellectual traditions.

Notes

1. Ann B. Stahl, "Material Histories," in Dan Hicks and Mary Beaudry, eds., *Oxford Handbook of Material Culture Studies* (Oxford: Oxford University Press, 2010), 157–60.
2. Slow Food. www.slowfood.com/about-us/slow-food-terminology.
3. "Tiny House Movement." https://en.wikipedia.org/wiki/Tiny_house_movement.
4. Ian Hodder, *Entangled: An Archaeology of the Relationship between Humans and Things* (Hoboken: John Wiley, 2012).
5. John Law and Ruth Benschop, "Resisting Pictures: Representation, Distribution, and Ontological Politics," *The Sociological Review*, 45, no. 1 (May 1998), 58.
6. Alejandro Haber and Nick Shepherd, "After Ethics: Ancestral Voices and Post-disciplinary Worlds in Archaeology: An Introduction," in Alejandro Haber and Nick Shepherd, eds., *After Ethics: Ancestral Voices and Post-disciplinary Worlds in Archaeology* (Springer, 2015), 5, 7.
7. Fredrik Fahlander and Terje Oestigaard, "Introduction: Material Culture and Post-disciplinary Sciences," in Fredrik Fahlander and Terje Oestigaard, eds., *Material Culture and Other Things: Post-disciplinary Studies in the Twenty-First Century* (Lindome: Bricoleur Press, 2004), 7–8.
8. Jane Bennett, *Vibrant Matter: A Political Ecology of Things* (Durham: Duke University Press, 2010).
9. Victor Buchli, "Introduction," in Victor Buchli, ed., *Material Culture Reader* (Oxford: Berg, 2002), 13.
10. Christopher Tilley, ed., *Reading Material Culture: Structuralism, Hermeneutics, and Post-structuralism* (Oxford: Basil Blackwell, 1990); Christopher Tilley, Webb Keane, Susanne Küchler, Michael Rowlands, and Patricia Spyer, eds., *Handbook of Material Culture* (London: SAGE, 2006).
11. Haber and Shepherd, "After Ethics," 3–5. See also Jane Lydon and Uzma Z. Rizvi, "Introduction: Postcolonialism and Archaeology," in Jane Lydon and Uzma Z. Rizvi, eds., *Handbook of Postcolonial Archaeology*,

World Archaeological Congress Research Handbooks in Archaeology, Volume 3 (Walnut Creek: Left Coast Press, 2010), 19.

12. See, for example, Donald Morton, ed., *The Material Queer: A LesBiGay Cultural Studies Reader* (Boulder: Westview Press, 1996); Kevin Ohi, *Dead Letters Sent: Queer Literary Transmission* (Minneapolis: University of Minnesota Press, 2015); Kath Browne, Jason Lim, and Gavin Brown, eds., *Geographies of Sexualities: Theory, Practices, and Politics* (Aldershot: Ashgate, 2007).

13. Noreen Giffney, "Introduction: The 'q' Word," in Noreen Giffney and Michael O'Rourke, eds., *The Ashgate Research Companion to Queer Theory* (Farnham: Ashgate: 2009).

14. Andrew Fiala, "Anarchism," in Edward N. Zalta, ed., *The Stanford Encyclopedia of Philosophy*. Online (Stanford: Stanford University Press, Spring 2018). https://stanford.io/3rUVrM3. See also Johnathan Purkis and James Bowen, eds., *Changing Anarchism: Anarchist Theory and Practice in a Global Age* (Manchester: Manchester University Press, 2004). Mike Sell, *Avant-garde Performance and Material Exchange: Vectors of the Radical* (New York: Palgrave Macmillan, 2011).

15. Lewis Borck and Matthew C. Sanger, "An Introduction to Anarchism in Archaeology," *SAA Archaeological Record*, 17, no. 1 (January 2017), 9.

16. Ibid, 10.

17. Edward R. Henry, Bill Angelback, and Uzma Z. Rizvi, "Against Typology: A Critical Approach to Archaeological Order," Anarchy and Archaeology. *SAA Archaeological Record* 17, no. 1 (Jan. 2017), 28.

18. Michael H. Laughy, Jr., "Confessions of a Punk Rock Archaeologist," William Caraher et al., eds., *Punk Archaeology*. Online (Grand Forks: University of North Dakota, 2014), 73. https://bit.ly/3BQWTSw.

19. World Health Organization, "WHO Coronavirus (COVID-19) Dashboard." June 14, 2021. https://covid19.who.int/.

20. Jopie Witzand, "Dutch Quilters Make Exquisite Mittens for Aussie Koalas." *SBS Dutch*, November 26, 2019. https://bit.ly/3lVFPnQ.

21. Livia Albeck-Ripka, "Koala Mittens and Baby Bottles: Saving Australia's Animals after Fires." *New York Times*. January 8, 2000. https://nyti.ms/3dHakcp.

22. Andrea Thompson, "A Running List of Record-Breaking Natural Disasters in 2020." *Scientific American*. December 22, 2020. https://bit.ly/3IGvJB1; Kaia Hubbard, "Here Are 10 of the Deadliest Natural Disasters in 2020." *U.S. News & World Report*. December 22, 2020. https://bit.ly/3DKBKZI.

23. Chris Huber, "6 of the Worst Disasters in 2019." *World Vision*. November 26, 2019. https://bit.ly/3GvEWKq.

24. Flavia Brunetti, "From Italy to Libya, and the World, With Love." *The New Humanitarian*. March 23, 2020. https://bit.ly/3dGrya0.

Bibliography

"Babybot," *Discover* 19, no. 12 (1998), 18.
"Celebrate Emancipation Day." *Oxford Public Ledger*. January 7, 1910 .
"Contract for Oxford Confederate Monument Awarded." *Charlotte Observer*. March 13, 1909.
"Current Modes for Children: Novelties in Fancy Dresses," *Myra's Journal* 4 (April 1, 1889), 4.
"Digital Assistants: Losing Face," *The Economist* 426, no. 9073 (2018), 57–8.
"Not Your Momma's History." https://bit.ly/3tWlnbl.
"The History of Zero: Discovery of the Number 0 by Ancient India." BBC's Story of Maths. www.youtube.com/watch?v=LQEuywkWa2U.
"represent, v.1," OED Online, Oxford University Press, August 2018.
"representation, n.1," OED Online, Oxford University Press, August 2018.
Acheraiou, Amar. *Questioning Hybridity, Postcolonialism and Globalization*. Basingstoke: Palgrave Macmillan, 2011.
Aczel, Amir D. *Finding Zero: A Mathematician's Odyssey to Uncover the Origins of Numbers*. New York: St. Martin's Griffin, 2015.
Adair, Bill, Filene Benjamin, and Laura Koloski, eds., *Letting Go? Sharing Authority in a User-Generated World*. Philadelphia: The Pew Center for Arts & Heritage, 2011.
Adler, Matthew D. "Well-Being and Academic Achievement." In Matthew White, Gavin R. Slemp, and A. Simon Murray, eds., *Future Directions in Well-Being: Education, Organizations and Policy*. New York: Springer, 2017, 203–8.
Advisory Committee for Indigenous Repatriation. "National Resting Place Consultation Report." Canberra: Commonwealth of Australia, 2014. https://bit.ly/3azcl9j.
Agamben, Giorgio. *Remnants of Auschwitz: The Witness and the Archive*, Daniel Heller-Roazen, trans. New York: Zone Books, 1999.
Ahmad, Yahaya. "The Scope and Definitions of Heritage: From Tangible to Intangible." *International Journal of Heritage Studies* 12, no. 3 (2006), 292–300.

Ahmed, Sara. *The Cultural Politics of Emotion.* London: Routledge, 2004.
　Queer Phenomenology: Orientations, Objects, Others. Durham: Duke University Press, 2006.
Ajmar, Marta. "Mechanical Disegno." *RIHA Journal* 84 (2014). https://doi.org/10.11588/riha.2014.1.69962.
　"The Renaissance in Material Culture: Material Mimesis as Force and Evidence of Globalization." In Tamar Hodos, ed., *The Routledge Handbook of Globalization and Archaeology.* London and New York: Routledge, 2016, 669–86.
Akrich, Madeleine. "The De-Scription of Technical Objects." In Wiebe E. Bijker and John Law, eds., *Shaping Technology/Building Society: Studies in Sociotechnical Change.* Cambridge, MA and London: The MIT Press, 1992, 205–24.
Alaimo, Stacy. *Bodily Natures: Science, Environment, and the Material Self.* Bloomington: University of Indiana Press, 2010.
Al-Ali, Nadje, and Khalid Koser, eds., *New Approaches to Migration? Transnational Communities and the Transformation of Home.* London: Routledge, 2002.
Albeck-Ripka, Livia. "Koala Mittens and Baby Bottles: Saving Australia's Animals after Fires." *New York Times.* January 8, 2020. https://nyti.ms/3mRmRhV.
Albera, Dionigi, and John Eade. *International Perspectives on Pilgrimage Studies: Itineraries, Gaps, and Obstacles.* London and New York: Routledge, 2015.
Albera, Dionigi, and John Eade, eds., *New Pathways in Pilgrimage Studies.* London and New York: Routledge, 2017.
Albrecht, Glenn A. "Public Heritage in the Symbiocene." In Angela M. Labrador and Neal Asher Silberman, eds., *The Oxford Handbook of Public Heritage Theory and Practice.* Oxford: Oxford University Press, 2018, 355–67.
Albrecht, Glenn A., Gina-Maree Sartore, Linda Connor, Nick Higginbotham, Sonia Freeman, Brian Kelly, Helen Stain, Anne Tonna, and Georgia Pollard. "Solastalgia: The Distress Caused by Environmental Change." *Australasian Psychiatry*, 15 (2007), special supplement 95–8.
Alcoff, Linda, and Eduardo Mendieta. *Identities: Race, Class, Gender and Nationality.* Oxford: Blackwell, 2003.
Alderman, Derek H. "Martin Luther King Jr. Streets in the South: A New Landscape of Memory." *Southern Cultures* 14, no. 3 (Fall, 2008), 88–105.
Alexander, Bruce. *The Globalization of Addiction: A Study in Poverty of the Spirit.* Oxford: Oxford University Press, 2008.
Alexander, Jeffrey, Ron Eyerman, Bernard Giesen, Neil J. Smelser, and Piotr Sztompka. *Cultural Trauma and Collective Identity.* Berkeley and Los Angeles: University of California Press, 2004.
Alexandre, Sandy. "'[The] Things What Happened with Our Family': Property and Inheritance in August Wilson's *The Piano Lesson*." *Modern Drama* 52, no. 1 (2009), 73–98.

Allen, Thomas, and Jennifer Blair, eds. *Material Cultures in Canada*. Waterloo: Wilfrid Laurier University Press, 2015.

"Material Cultures in Canada, Material Cultures Now." In Thomas Allen and Jennifer Blair, eds., *Material Cultures in Canada*. Waterloo: Wilfrid Laurier University Press, 2015, 1–22.

Allmond, Gillian. "'The Outer Darkness of Madness': The Edwardian Winter Garden at Purdysburn Public Asylum for the Insane." In Marion Dowd and Robert Hensey, eds., *The Archaeology of Darkness*. Barnsley: Oxbow Books, 2016, 117–28.

"Light and Darkness in an Edwardian Institution for the Insane Poor: Illuminating the Material Practices of the Asylum Age." *International Journal of Historical Archaeology* 20, no. 1 (2015), 1–22.

Alva, Walter, and Christopher B. Donnan. *Royal Tombs of Sipán*. Los Angeles: Fowler Museum of Cultural History, 1993.

Ames, Michael. *Cannibal Tours and Glass Boxes: The Anthropology of Museums*. Vancouver: University of British Columbia Press, 1992.

Anderson, Benedict. *Imagined Communities: Reflections on the Origin and Spread of Nationalism*. London: Verso, 2016 [1983].

Anderson, Dag T. "Trusted Vagueness: The Language of Things and the Order of Incompleteness." In Bjørnar Olsen and Þóra Pétursdóttir, eds., *Ruin Memories: Materiality, Aesthetics and the Archaeology of the Recent Past*. New York: Routledge, 2014, 33–40.

Anderson, Jennifer. *Mahogany: The Costs of Luxury in Early America*. Cambridge, MA: Harvard University Press, 2012.

Andrade, Tonio. "Cannibals with Cannons: The Sino-Portuguese Clashes of 1521–22 and the Early Chinese Adoption of Western Guns." *Journal of Early Modern History* 19, no. 4 (2015), 311–36.

Andrews, Cecile. *Slow is Beautiful: New Visions of Community, Leisure and Joie de Vivre*. Gabriola: New Society, 2006.

Anthes, Bill. *Native Moderns: American Indian Painting, 1940–1960*. Durham: Duke University Press, 2006.

Anzaldúa, Gloria. *Borderlands/La Frontera: The New Mestiza*. San Francisco: Spinsters/Aunt Lute, 1987.

Appadurai, Arjun. *Modernity at Large: Cultural Dimensions of Globalization*. Minneapolis and London: University of Minnesota Press, 1996.

The Social Life of Things: Commodities in Cultural Perspective. Cambridge: Cambridge University Press, 1986.

Arcand, Bernard. *The Last of the Cuiva*. Documentary Film, 1991.

Arendt, Hannah. *The Human Condition*. Chicago and London: University of Chicago Press, 1998 [1958].

Arese, Nicholas S. "Seeing like a City-State: Behavioral Planning and Governance in Egypt's First Affordable Gated Community." *International Journal of Urban and Regional Research* 42, no. 3 (2018), 461–82.

Arguedas, José María. *Señores e Indios: Acerca de la Cultura Quechua*. Angel Rama, ed. Buenos Aires: Arca Editorial, 1976.

Aria, Mrs. Eliza Davis. *Costume: Fanciful, Historical and Theatrical*. London and New York: Macmillan and Co, 1906.

Armitage, Natalie. "Vodou Material Culture in the Museum: Reflections on the Complexities of Demonstrating Material Culture of Assemblage and Accumulation in a Traditional Museum Environment." *Material Religion* 14, no. 2 (2018), 218–34.

Arrom, José Juan. "The Creation Myths of the Taíno." In Fatima Bercht, Estrellita Brodsky, John Alan Farmer, and Dicey Taylor, eds., *Taíno: Precolumbian Art and Culture from the Caribbean*. New York: Monacelli Press, 1997, 68–79.

Arroyo, Jossianna. "Transculturation, Syncretism, and Hybridity." In Miguel Y. Martínez-San, B. Sifuentes-Jáuregui, and M. Belausteguigoitia, eds., *Critical Terms in Caribbean and Latin American Thought: New Directions in Latino American Cultures*. New York: Palgrave Macmillan, 2016, 133–44.

Arthur, Linda B., ed. *Religion, Dress, and the Body*. Oxford: Berg, 1999.

Undressing Religion: Commitment and Conversion from a Cross-Cultural Perspective. Oxford: Berg, 2000.

Artstuffmatters. https://bit.ly/33Lq2Se.

Arweck, Elizabeth, and William Keenan, eds., *Materializing Religion: Expression, Performance, and Ritual*. London: Routledge, 2006.

arXiv. "The Murky World of Third Party Web Tracking." September 12, 2014. https://bit.ly/3lTxMrn.

Asad, Talal. *Genealogies of Religion: Discipline and Reasons of Power in Christianity and Islam*. Baltimore: Johns Hopkins University Press, 1993.

Asch, Timothy, and Napoleon A. Chagnon. *The Feast*. Documentary Film. Watertown: Center for Documentary Anthropology, 1970.

Asimov, Isaac, *The Caves of Steel*. New York: Bantam Books, 1991 [1954].

Assembly of First Nations and Canadian Museums Association. "Turning the Page: Forging New Partnerships between Museums and First Peoples." 3rd ed., 1994. https://bit.ly/3FhT8WH.

Astor-Aguilera, Miguel. *The Maya World of Communicating Objects: Quadripartite Crosses, Trees & Stones*. Albuquerque: University of New Mexico Press, 2010.

Astuti, Rita. "'It's a Boy!', 'It's a Girl!', Reflections on Sex and Gender in Madagascar and Beyond." In A. Strathern and M. Lambek, eds., *Bodies and Persons: Comparative Perspectives from Africa and Melanesia*. Cambridge: Cambridge University Press, 1998, 29–52.

Attfield, Judy. "Design as a Practice of Modernity: A Case for the Study of the Coffee Table in the Mid-century Domestic Interior." *Journal of Material Culture* 2, no. 3 (1997), 267–89.

"The Empty Cocktail Cabinet: Display in the Mid-Century British Domestic Interior." In Tim Putnam and Charles Newton, eds., *Household Choices*. London: Futures Publication, 1990, 84–8.

Wild Things: The Material Culture of Everyday Life. Oxford, NY: Berg, 2000.

Audouze, Françoise. "Leroi-Gourhan, a Philosopher of Technique and Evolution." *Journal of Archaeological Research* 10, no. 4 (2002), 227–306.

Auerbach, Erich. *Mimesis: The Representation of Reality in Western Thought*. Princeton: Princeton University Press, 2003 [1953].

Auld, Danica, Tracey Ireland, and Heather Burke. "Affective Aprons: Object Biographies from the Ladies' Cottage, Royal Derwent Hospital New Norfolk, Tasmania." *International Journal of Historical Archaeology*, 23, no. 2 (2018) 1–19.

Auschwitz-Birkenau Memorial and Museum. Auschwitz Report, 2013. News-Main Page. http://auschwitz.org/en/.

"Memorial and Museum Auschwitz-Birkenau: Former German Nazi Concentration and Extermination Camp/Conservation of vegetation." http://auschwitz.org/en/museum/preservation/vegetation.

Australian Bureau of Statistics. Census Quickstats. Barunga. 2016. https://bit.ly/2ZRm3Cc.

Census: Younger Australians More Likely to Make a Move, 2017. https://bit.ly/32d9jH0.

Australian Supreme Court. *Milirrpum v. Nabalco Pty Ltd*, (April 27, 1971) Supreme Court (NT).

Bae, Kyoungjin. "Around the Globe: The Material Culture of Cantonese Round Tables in High-Qing China." In Anna Grasskamp and Monica Juneja, eds., *EurAsian Matters: China, Europe, and the Transcultural Object, 1600–1800*. Cham: Springer, 2018, 37–55.

Bae, Kyoungjin. "Joints of Utility, Crafts of Knowledge: The Material Culture of the Sino-British Furniture Trade during the Long Eighteenth Century." Ph.D. dissertation, Columbia University, 2016.

Bakan, Joel. *Childhood Under Siege: How Big Business Callously Targets Children*. London: Penguin, 2006.

The Corporation: The Pathological Pursuit of Profit and Power. London: Penguin, 2004.

Bákula, Cecilia. "The Art of the Incas." In Laura Laurencich-Minelli, ed., *The Inca World: The Development of Pre-Columbian Peru, AD 1000–1534*. Norman: University of Oklahoma Press, 2000, 218–22.

Balfet, Hélène, ed. *Observer l'action technique: Des chaînes opératoires, pour quoi faire?* Paris: Éditions du CNRS, 1991.

Balint, Peter J., Ronald E. Stewart, Anand Desai, and Lawrence C. Walters. *Wicked Environmental Problems: Managing Uncertainty and Conflict*. Covelo and London: Island Press, 2011.

Bandle, Anne Laurel, Raphael Contel, and Marc-André Renold. "Case Auschwitz Suitcase–Pierre Lévi Heirs and Auschwitz-Birkenau State Museum Oświęcim and Shoah Memorial Museum Paris," Platform ArThemis (Art-Law Centre, University of Geneva). http://unige.ch/art-adr.

Barad, Karen. *Meeting the Universe Halfway: Quantum Physics and the Entanglement of Matter and Meaning*. Durham, NC: Duke University Press, 2007.

Barbieri, Donatella. *Costume in Performance: Materiality, Costume, and the Body.* London: Bloomsbury, 2017.

Barkan, Elliott R., ed. *Immigration, Incorporation and Transnationalism.* New York: Routledge, 2017.

Barnett, Elizabeth, and Michele Casper. "A Definition of 'Social Environment'." *American Journal of Public Health* 91, no. 3 (2001), 465.

Barrow, John, D. *The Book of Nothing: Vacuums, Voids and the Latest Ideas About the Origins of the Universe.* New York: Vintage Books, 2000.

Barthes, Roland. *Camera Lucida: Reflections on Photography.* London: Vintage, 1993.

"Myth Today." *Mythologies.* New York: Hill and Wang, 1972.

"The Kitchen of Meaning." *The Semiotic Challenge.* Berkeley: The University of California Press, 1994, 157–9.

"The Reality Effect." In Richard Howard, trans. *The Rustle of Language.* Oakland: University of California Press, 1989, 141.

Basu, Paul, and Simon Coleman. "Introduction: Migrant Worlds, Material Cultures." *Mobilities* 3, no. 3 (2008), 313–30.

Bateson, Gregory. *Mind and Nature: A Necessary Unity.* New York: EP Dutton, 1979.

Steps to an Ecology of Mind: Collected Essays in Anthropology, Psychiatry, Evolution, and Epistemology. Chicago: University of Chicago Press, 1972.

"Style, Grace, and Information in Primitive Art." In Anthony Forge, ed., *Primitive Art and Society.* London and Oxford: Ely House, Oxford University Press, 1973, 235–55.

Battiste, Marie. "You Can't Be the Global Doctor if You're the Colonial Disease." In Peggy Tripp and Linda Muzzin, eds., *Teaching as Activism: Equity Meets Environmentalism.* Montreal: McGill-Queen's Press, 2005, 120–33.

Baudrillard, Jean. *For a Critique of the Political Economy of the Sign.* St. Louis: Telos Press, 1981.

The System of Objects. New York: Verso, 1996 [1968].

Baugher, Sherene. "At the Top of the Hierarchy of Charity: The Life of Retired Seamen at Sailors' Snug Harbor, Staten Island, New York." *Northeast Anthropology* 73 (2009), 59–86.

"Historical Overview of the Archaeology of Institutional Life." In April Beisaw and James Gibb, eds., *The Archaeology of Institutional Life.* Tuscaloosa: University of Alabama Press, 2009, 5–13.

"Landscapes of Power: Middle Class and Lower Class Power Dynamics in a New York Charitable Institution." *International Journal of Historical Archaeology* 14, no. 4 (2010), 475–97.

Baumgarten, Alexander Gottlieb. *Theoretische Ästhetik: die Grundlegenden Abschnitte aus der 'Aesthetica' (1750/58): Lateinisch-Deutsch.* Hans Rudolf Schweizer, trans. Hamburg: Meiner, 1983 [1750].

Beck, Wendy, and Margaret Somerville. "Conversations between Disciplines: Historical Archaeology and Oral History at Yarrawarra." *World Archaeology* 37, no. 3 (2007), 468–83.

Becker, Howard. *Art Worlds*. Berkeley: University of California Press, 1982.

Behar, Katherine, *Object Oriented Feminism*. Minneapolis: Minnesota University Press, 2016.

Beisaw, April M. "Constructing Institution-Specific Site Formation Models." In April Beisaw and James Gibb, eds., *The Archaeology of Institutional Life*. Tuscaloosa: University of Alabama Press, 2009, 49–68.

Beisaw, April M., and James G. Gibb, eds., *The Archaeology of Institutional Life*. Tuscaloosa: University of Alabama Press, 2009.

Belk, Russell. "Moving Possessions: An Analysis Based on Personal Documents from the 1847–1869 Mormon Migration." *Journal of Consumer Research* 19 (1992), 339–61.

Bell, Clive. *Art*. New York: Frederick A. Stokes, 1914.

Bell, Florence. *Fairy Tales and How to Act Them*. London, New York, and Bombay: Longmans, Green, 1896.

Bell, Joshua A., Briel Kobak, Joel Kuipers, and Amanda Kemble. "Unseen Connections: The Materiality of Cell Phones." *Anthropological Quarterly* 91, no. 2 (2018), 465–84.

Bell, Lee Anne. "Theoretical Foundations for Social Justice Education." In Maurianne Adams and Lee Anne Bell, with Diane J. Goodman and Khyati Y. Joshi, eds., *Teaching for Diversity and Social Justice*, 3rd ed. London: Routledge, 2016, 3–26.

Belting, Hans. "Iconic Presence: Images in Religious Tradition." *Material Religion* 12, no. 2 (June 2016), 235–7.

Likeness and Presence: A History of the Image before the Era of Art. Chicago: University of Chicago Press, 1997.

Bender, Barbara, and Margot Winer, eds., *Contested Landscapes: Movement, Exile and Place*. Oxford and New York: Berg, 2001.

Benfer Jr., Robert A. "Monumental Architecture Arising from an Early Astronomical-Religious Complex in Perú, 2200–1750 BC." In Richard L. Burger and Robert M. Rosenswig, eds., *Early New World Monumentality*. Gainesville: University Press of Florida, 2012, 313–63.

Benjamin, Walter. "On the Concept of History." In Howard Eiland and Michael W. Jennings, eds., *Walter Benjamin: Selected Writings, Vol. 4 (1938–40)*, trans. Edmund Jephcott (Cambridge, MA: Belknap Press, 2003), 392.

Selected Writings, Howard Eiland and Michael W. Jennings, eds., 4 Vols. Cambridge, MA: Belknap Press, 2002.

Selected Writings Volume 3, 1935–1938. Cambridge, MA: Belknap Press, 2002.

The Arcades Project, Cambridge, MA: Harvard University Press, 1999. "The Work of Art in the Age of its Technological Reproducibility."

The Work of Art in the Age of its Technological Reproducibility. Michael W. Jennings, Brigid Doherty, and Thomas Y. Levin, eds.; Edmund Jephcott, Rodney Livingstone, Howard Eiland, et al., trans. Cambridge, MA: The Belknap Press of Harvard University Press, 2008.

Bennett, Jane. *Vibrant Matter: A Political Ecology of Things*. Durham: Duke University Press, 2010.

Bennett, Tony, and Patrick Joyce, eds. *Material Powers: Cultural Studies, History and the Material Turn*. London: Routledge, 2010.

Benson, Elizabeth P. *The Worlds of the Moche on the North Coast of Peru*. Austin: University of Texas Press, 2012.

Benterrak, Krim, Stephen Muecke, and Paddy Roe. *Reading the Country: An Introduction to Nomadology*. Liverpool: Liverpool University Press, 1996.

Bentham, Jeremy. *The Works of Jeremy Bentham, Published Under the Superintendence of His Executor, John Bowring*. Edinburgh: William Tait, 1838.

Berg, Lawrence D., Edward H. Huijbens, and Henrik Gutson Larsen, "Producing Anxiety in the Neoliberal University." *The Canadian Geographer* 60 (2016), 168–80.

Berg, Maxine, ed. *Goods from the East, 1600–1800: Trading Eurasia, Europe's Asian Centuries*. Basingstoke: Palgrave Macmillan, 2015.

Berger, John, and Jean Mohr. *A Seventh Man*. London: Verso, 1975.

Berger, John, and Michael Dibb. *Ways of Seeing*. London: BBC Enterprises, 1972.

Berger, Peter L. *The Desecularization of the World: Resurgent Religion and World Politics*. Grand Rapids: Wm. B. Eerdmans, 1999.

Bergeron, Anne, and Beth Tuttle. *Magnetic: The Art and Science of Engagement*. Washington, DC: The AAM Press, 2013.

Berlinger, Gabrielle. *Framing Sukkot: Tradition and Transformation in Jewish Vernacular Architecture*. Bloomington: Indiana University Press, 2017.

Berlo, Janet C., and Ruth B. Phillips. *Native North American Art*. 2nd ed. Oxford: Oxford University Press, 2015.

Bernstein, Robin. "Dances with Things: Material Culture and the Performance of Race." *Social Text* 27, no. 4 (2009), 67–94.

Racial Innocence: Performing American Childhood from Slavery to Civil Rights. New York: New York University Press, 2011.

Best, Susan. "Rethinking Visual Pleasure: Aesthetics and Affect." *Theory & Psychology* 17, no. 4 (2007), 505–14.

"The Trace and the Body." *First Liverpool Biennial of International Contemporary Art: Trace*. Liverpool: Tate Gallery, 1999, 172–7.

Betcher, Talia, and Ann Garry. "Transgender Studies and Feminism: Theory, Politics, and Gendered Realities." *Hypatia* 24, no. 3 (2009), 1–10.

Biedermann, Zoltan, Anne Gerritsen, and Giorgio Riello, eds. *Global Gifts: The Material Culture of Diplomacy in Early Modern Eurasia*. Cambridge and New York: Cambridge University Press, 2017.

Bijker, Wiebe E. "How is Technology Made? That is the Question!" *Cambridge Journal of Economics* no. 34 (2010), 63–76.

"The Social Construction of Bakelite: Towards a Theory of Invention." In Wiebe E. Bijker, Thomas Hughes, and Trevor J. Pinch, eds., *The Social Construction of Technological Systems*. Cambridge, MA and London: The MIT Press, 1987, 159–87.

Bijker, Wiebe E., and John Law. eds. *Shaping Technology/Building Society: Studies in Sociotechnical Change*. Cambridge, MA and London: The MIT Press,1992.

Bijker, Wiebe E., Thomas P. Hughes, and Trevor J. Pinch, eds. *The Social Construction of Technological Systems: New Directions in the Sociology and History of Technology*. Cambridge, MA: The MIT Press, 2012 [1987].

Bilecen, Başak. "Home-making Practices and Social Protection across Borders: An Example of Turkish Migrants Living in Germany." *Journal of Housing and the Built Environment* 32, no. 1 (2017), 77–90.

Blackwood, Beatrice. *The Technology of a Modern Stone Age People in New Guinea*. Occasional Papers on Technology 3. Oxford: Pitt Rivers Museum of Oxford, 1950.

Blake, Janet. "Seven Years of Implementing UNESCO's 2003 Intangible Heritage Convention: Honeymoon Period of the 'Seven Year Itch'?" *International Journal of Cultural Property* 21 (2014), 291–304.

Blakely, Edward J. "In Gated Communities, such as Where Trayvon Martin Died, a Dangerous Mind-Set," *Washington Post*, April 6 2012 .

Blakely, Edward J., and Mary G. Synder. *Fortress America: Gated Communities in the United States*. Washington, DC: Brookings Institution Press, 1999.

Bleichmar, Daniela, and Meredith Martin, eds. *Objects in Motion in the Early Modern World*, special issue *Art History* 38, no.4 (2015).

Bloch, Maurice, ed. *Marxist Analyses and Social Anthropology*. London, Melbourne and Toronto: Malaby Press, 1975.

Boardman, John. *The World of Ancient Art*. London: Thames & Hudson, 2006.

Boas, Franz. *Primitive Art*. Toronto: Dover, 1955 [1927].

Bodei, Remo. *The Life of Things, The Love of Things*. Murtha Baca, trans. New York: Fordham University Press, 2015.

Bodenhamer, David J., John Corrigan, and Trevor M. Harris, eds. *The Spatial Humanities: GIS and the Future of Humanities Scholarship*. Bloomington: Indiana University Press, 2010.

Bodley, John H. *Anthropology and Contemporary Human Problems*. 6th ed. Lanham: AltaMira Press, 2012.

Victims of Progress, 5th ed., Lanham: AltaMira Press, 2012.

Boivin, Nicole. "Mind over Matter? Collapsing the Mind-Matter Dichotomy in Material Culture Studies." In Elizabeth DeMarrais, Chris Gosden, and A. Colin Renfrew, eds., *Rethinking Materiality: The Engagement of Mind with the Material World*. Cambridge, UK: McDonald Institute for Archaeological Research, 2004, 63–71.

Borck, Lewis, and Matthew C. Sanger. "An Introduction to Anarchism in Archaeology," Anarchy and Archaeology. *SAA Archaeological Record* 17, no. 1 (January 2017), 9–16.

Borneman, Elizabeth. "Cartographic Anomalies: How Map Projections Have Shaped Our Perceptions of the World." February 25, 2014. https://bit.ly/34VcN1O.

Boros, L. "But Some are Less Equal: Spatial Exclusion in Szeged." In C. Kovács, ed., *From Villages to Cyberspace – Falvaktól a Kibertérig*. Szeged: University of Szeged, Department of Economic and Human Geography, 2007, 151–60.

Boström, Magnus, Rolf Lidskog, and Ylva Uggla. "A Reflexive Look at Reflexivity in Environmental Sociology." *Environmental Sociology*, 3 (2017), 6–16.

Bourdieu, Pierre. *Distinction: A Social Critique of the Judgement of Taste*. Cambridge, MA: Harvard University Press, 1984.

Homo Academicus, Peter Collier, trans. Stanford: Stanford University Press, 1980.

Outline of a Theory of Practice. New York: Cambridge University Press, 1977.

Bourget, Steve, and Kimberly L. Jones. *The Art and Archaeology of the Moche: An Ancient Society of the Peruvian North Coast*. Austin: University of Texas Press, 2008.

Bowechop, Janine, and Patricia Pierce Erikson. "Forging Indigenous Methodologies on Cape Flattery: The Makah Museum as a Center of Collaborative Research." *The American Indian Quarterly* 29 no. 1–2 (Winter/Spring 2005), 263–73.

Bowen, Cyril. *Practical Hints on Stage Costume*. London and New York: Samuel French, 1881.

Boyd, Candice P., and Christian Edwardes. "Creative Practice and the Non-Representational." In Candice P. Boyd and Christian Edwardes, eds., *Non-Representational Theory and the Creative Arts*. Palgrave Macmillan, 2019, 1–15.

Braidotti, Rosi. *Patterns of Dissonance: A Study of Women in Contemporary Philosophy*. New York: Routledge, 1991.

The Posthuman. London: Polity Press, 2013.

Brail, Richard K., ed. *Transnational Ties: Cities, Migrations, and Identities*. New York: Routledge, 2017.

Braman, Sandra. "Flow." In Benjamin Peters, ed., *Digital Keywords*. Princeton: Princeton University Press, 2016, 118–31.

Brändli, Bárbara. *Curare*. Documentary film. 1970.

Bray, Francesca. *Technology and Gender: Fabrics of Power in Late Imperial China*. Berkeley, Los Angeles and London: University of California Press, 1997.

Brettell, Caroline. "Theorizing Migration in Anthropology: The Social Construction of Networks, Identities, Communities and Globalscapes." In Caroline Brettell and James Hollifield, eds., *Migration Theory: Talking across Disciplines*. New York and London: Routledge, 2000, 97–136.

Brickell, Katherine, and Ayona Datta, eds. *Translocal Geographies: Spaces, Places, Connections*. Aldershot: Ashgate, 2011.

Briggs, Jen, Anna Lacy, and Psyche Williams-Forson. "What Did They Eat? Where Did They Stay? Black Boardinghouses and the Colored Conventions Movement." Omeka RSS. 2016. https://bit.ly/33SmIVe.

Brisbane, Mark, and John Wood. *A Future for our Past*. London: English Heritage, 1996.

British Museum. "The British Museum (@britishmuseum)." https://sketchfab.com/britishmuseum.

Brooks, Bradley. "Clarity, Contrasts, and Simplicity: Changes in American Interiors, 1880–1930." In Jessica H. Foy and Karal Ann Marling, eds., *The Arts and the American Home, 1890–1930*. Knoxville: University of Tennessee Press, 1994, 14–43.

Brown, Bill. *A Sense of Things: The Object Matter of American Literature*. Chicago: University of Chicago Press, 2004.

Other Things. Chicago: University of Chicago Press, 2016.

The Material Unconscious: American Amusement, Stephen Crane, and the Economies of Play. Cambridge, MA: Harvard University Press, 1996.

"Thing Theory," *Critical Inquiry* 28, no. 1 (Autumn 2001), 1–22.

Brown, Bill, ed. "Things." *Critical Inquiry* 28, 2010.

Brown, Michael F., and Margaret M. Bruchac. "NAGPRA from the Middle Distance." In John Henry Merryman, ed., *Imperialism, Art and Restitution*. Cambridge: Cambridge University Press, 2006, 193–217.

Browne, Kath, Jason Lim, and Gavin Brown, eds. *Geographies of Sexualities: Theory, Practices, and Politics*. Aldershot: Ashgate, 2007.

Bruchac, Margaret. "Lost and Found: NAGPRA, Scattered Relics, and Restorative Methodologies." *Museum Anthropology* 33, no. 2 (2010), 137–56.

Brummitt, D. G. "Address of Acceptance by D. G. Brummitt" *Cornerstone of Confederate Monument Laid*. Oxford: Orphanage Press, 1910, 15.

Brundage, W. Fitzhugh. *The Southern Past: A Clash of Race and Memory*. Cambridge, MA: Belknap Press, 2008.

Brunetti, Flavia. "From Italy to Libya, and the World, With Love." *The New Humanitarian*. March 23, 2020. https://bit.ly/3dGrya0.

Bryden, Inga. "All Dressed Up: Revivalism and the Fashion for Arthur in Victorian Culture." *Arthuriana, Arthurian Revival in the Nineteenth Century* 12, no. 2 Special Issue (Summer 2011), 28–41.

Buchanan, Brenda. *Gunpowder Plots: A Celebration of 400 Years of Bonfire Night*. London: Penguin, 2005.

Buchli, Victor. *An Archaeology of The Immaterial*. New York: Routledge: 2016.

"Introduction." In Victor Buchli, ed., *Material Culture Reader*. Oxford: Berg, 2002, 1–22.

Buchli, Victor, ed. *Material Culture Reader*. Oxford: Berg, 2002.

Buck-Morss, Susan. "Aesthetics and Anaesthetics: Walter Benjamin's Artwork Essay Reconsidered." *October* 62 (1992), 3–41.

Buggeln, Gretchen. *The Suburban Church: Modernism and Community in Postwar America*. Minneapolis: University of Minnesota Press, 2015.

Buggeln, Gretchen, and Barbara Franco, eds. *Interpreting Religion at Museums and Historic Sites*. Lanham, MA: Rowman & Littlefield and the American Association of State and Local History, 2018.

Buggeln, Gretchen, Crispin Paine, and S. Brent Plate, eds. *Religion in Museums: Global and Interdisciplinary Perspectives.* London: Bloomsbury Academic, 2017.

Bunch, Lonnie G. III. *Call the Lost Dream Back: Essays on History, Race and Museums.* Washington, DC: The AAM Press, 2010.

Bunn-Marcuse, Kathryn. "Textualizing Intangible Cultural Heritage: Querying the Methods of Art History." *Panorama: The Online Journal of American Art* 4, no. 2 (Fall 2018). https://bit.ly/3Cjotq7.

Burger, Richard L. *Chavin and the Origins of Andean Civilization.* London: Thames and Hudson, 1992.

Burke, Heather D. *Meaning and Ideology in Historical Archaeology.* New York: Springer, 1999.

Burke, Heather D., Bryce Barker, Noelene Cole, Lynley A. Wallis, Elizabeth Hatte, Iain Davidson, and Kelsey Lowe. "The Queensland Native Police and Strategies of Recruitment on the Queensland Frontier, 1849–1901." *Journal of Australian Studies* 42, no. 3 (2018), 297–313.

Burra Charter. *The Burra Charter: The Australia ICOMS Charter for Places of Cultural Significance.* Australia ICOMOS Incorporated: Burwood, 2013.

Burrell, Kathy. "Materializing the Border: Spaces of Mobility and Material Culture in Migration from Post-Socialist Poland." *Mobilities* 3, no. 3 (2008), 353–73.

"The Objects of Christmas: The Politics of Festive Materiality in the Lives of Polish Immigrants." In Maruška Svašek, ed., *Moving Subjects, Moving Objects: Transnationalism, Cultural Production and Emotions.* New York: Berghahn, 2012, 55–74.

Burström, Mats, and Bernhard Gelderblom. "Dealing with Difficult Heritage: The Case of Bückeberg, Site of the Third Reich Harvest Festival." *Journal of Social Archaeology* 11, no. 3 (2011), 266–82.

Bush, David R. "Interpreting the Latrines of the Johnson's Island Civil War Military Prison." *Historical Archaeology* 34, no. 1 (2000), 62–78.

Bush, Vannevar. "As We May Think." In Noah Wardrip-Fruin and Nick Montfort, eds., *The New Media Reader.* Cambridge, MA: The MIT Press, 1945/2003, 35–47.

Bushnell, Geoffrey H. S. *Ancient Arts of the Americas.* New York: Frederick A. Praeger, 1965.

Butler, Judith. *Bodies that Matter: On the Discursive Limits of "Sex."* New York: Routledge, 1993.

Gender Trouble: Feminism and the Subversion of Identity. London: Routledge, 1990/1999.

Undoing Gender. New York: Routledge, 2004.

Butler, Beverly, and al-Nammari, Fatima. "We Palestinian Refugees – Heritage Rites and/as the Clothing of Bare Life: Reconfiguring Paradox, Obligation, and Imperative in Palestinian Refugee Camps in Jordan." *Journal of Contemporary Archaeology* 3, no. 2 (2016), 147–59.

Butler, Kelly J. *Australian Stories: History, Testimony, and Memory in Contemporary Culture*. New York: Routledge, 2017.
Bynum, William F. "The Rise of Science in Medicine, 1850–1913." In *The Western Medical Tradition, 1800 to 2000*. Cambridge: Cambridge University Press, 2006, 111–239.
Cabot, Heath. "The Governance of Things: Documenting Limbo in the Greek Asylum Procedures." *Political and Legal Anthropology Review* 35, no. 1 (2012), 11–29.
Cabranes Grant, Leo. *From Scenarios to Networks: Performing the Intercultural in Colonial Mexico*. Chicago: Northwestern University Press, 2016.
Callon, Michel. "The Role of Hybrid Communities and the Socio-Technical Arrangements in the Participatory Design." *Journal of the Center for Information Studies* 5, no. 3 (2004), 3–10.
Camp, Stacey L. *The Archaeology of Citizenship*. Gainesville: University of Florida Press, 2013.
  "Commentary: Excavating the Intimate." *Historical Archaeology* 52, no. 3 (2018), 600–7.
Campbell, Shirley. *The Art of Kula*. Oxford: Berg, 2002.
Canning, Charlotte. "Feminist Performance as Feminist Historiography." *Theatre Survey* 45, no. 2 (2004), 227–33.
Cant, Alanna. *The Art of Indigeneity: Aesthetics and Competition in Mexican Economies of Culture*. Austin: University of Texas Press, 2019.
  The Value of Aesthetics: Oaxacan Woodcarvers in Global Economies of Culture. Austin: University of Texas Press, 2019.
Cardinal, Lewis. "What is an Indigenous Perspective?" *Canadian Journal of Native Education* 25, no. 2 (2001), 180–82.
Carlyle, Thomas. *Sartor Resartus*, serialized in *Fraser's Magazine* (1833–34).
Carman, John. *Archaeological Resource Management: An International Perspective*. Cambridge: Cambridge University Press, 2015.
Carriger, Michelle Liu. "No 'Thing to Wear': A Brief History of Kimono and Inappropriation from Japonisme to Kimono Protests." *Theatre Research International* 43, no. 2 (July 2018), 165–84.
Carrington, Christopher. *No Place Like Home*. Chicago: University of Chicago Press, 1999.
Carrington, Damian. "Humanity Has Wiped Out 60% of Animal Populations since 1970, Report Finds." *Guardian*, October 30, 2018. https://bit.ly/3FCvkg4.
Carroll, Timothy. "Axis of Incoherence: Engagement and Failure between Two Material Regimes of Christianity." In Timothy Carroll, David Jeevendrampillai, Aaron Parkhurst, and Julie Shackelford, eds., *Material Culture of Failure: When Things Do Wrong*. London: Bloomsbury Press, 2017, 157–78.
  Orthodox Christian Material Culture: Of People and Things in the Making of Heaven. London: Routledge, 2018.

Carroll, Timothy, Antonia Walford, and Shireen Walton. "Introduction." In Timothy Carroll, Antonia Walford, and Shireen Walton, eds., *Lineages and Advancements in Material Culture Studies: Perspectives from UCL Anthropology*. London: Routledge, 2020, 1–16.

Carter, Paul. *The Road to Botany Bay: An Essay in Spatial History*. London and Boston: Faber and Faber, 1987.

Carter, Thomas. *Building Zion: The Material World of Mormon Settlement*. Minneapolis: University of Minnesota Press, 2015.

Cartmill, Matt. *A View to a Death in the Morning: Hunting and Nature through History*. Cambridge, MA: Harvard University Press, 1993.

Caruth, Cathy. *Unclaimed Experience: Trauma, Narrative and History*. Baltimore: Johns Hopkins University Press, 2016.

Carver, Martin. "On Archaeological Value." *Antiquity* 70 (1996), 45–56.

Casella, Eleanor C. *The Archaeology of Institutional Confinement*. Tallahassee: University Press of Florida, 2007.

  Archaeology of the Ross Female Factory: Female Incarceration in Van Diemen's Land, Australia. Launceston: Queen Victoria Museum and Art Gallery, 2002.

  "'Doing Trade': A Sexual Economy of Nineteenth-Century Australian Female Convict Prisons." *World Archaeology* 32, no. 2 (2000), 209–21.

  "Little Bastard Felons: Childhood, Affect, and Labor in the Penal Colonies of Nineteenth-century Australia." In Barbara Voss, ed., *The Archaeology of Colonialism: Intimate Encounters and Sexual Effects*. Cambridge: Cambridge University Press, 2011, 31–48.

  "Lockdown: On the Materiality of Confinement." In Adrian Myers and Gabriel Moshenska, eds., *Archaeologies of Internment*. New York: Springer, 2011, 285–95.

Casey, Edward S. *The Fate of Place: A Philosophical History*. Berkeley: University of California Press, 1997.

Casid, Jill H. *Sowing Empire: Landscape and Colonization*. Minneapolis: University of Minnesota Press, 2005.

Cassidy, Tony. *Environmental Psychology: Behavior and Experience in Context*. Hove: Psychology Press, 1997.

Cassidy-Geiger, Maureen. "Changing Attitudes towards Ethnographic Material: Rediscovering the Soapstone Collection of Augustus the Strong." *Abhandlungen und Berichte des Staatlichen Museums für Völkerkunde Dresden* 48 (1994), 26–31.

  "Forgotten Sources for Early Meissen Figures: Rediscovering the Chinese Carved Soapstone and Dutch Red Earthenware Figures from the Japanese Palace of Augustus Strong." *American Ceramic Circle* 10 (1997), 55–72.

Castells, Manuel. *The Rise of the Network Society*. Oxford: Blackwell, 1996.

Chagnon, Napoleon A. *Yanomamo*. 6th ed. New York: Harcourt Brace College Publishers, 2013.

Chakrabarty, Dipesh. *Provincializing Europe: Postcolonial Thought and Historical Difference*. Princeton: Princeton University Press, 2000.

Chamorro, Graciela. *Cuerpo Social: Historia y Etnografía de la Organización Social en los Pueblos Guaraní*. Asunción: Tiempo de Historia, 2017.

Chan, Libby Lai-Pik, and Nina Lai-Na Wan, eds., *The Silver Age: Origins and Trade of Chinese Export Silver*. Hong Kong: Hong Kong Maritime Museum, 2017.

Chandler, David. *Semiotics: The Basics*. London and NY: Routledge, 2002.

Chang Sheng-Ching. *Dongfang Qimeng Xifang: Shiba Shiji Deguo Wolizi (Wörlitz) Ziran Fengjing Yuanlin Zhi Zhongguo Yuansu [The East Enlightening the West: Chinese Elements in the Eighteenth-Century Landscape Gardens of Wörlitz in Germany]*. Taipei: Furendaxue chubanshe, 2015.

Charlton, William, trans. *Aristotle: Physics, Books I and II*. Oxford: Clarendon Press, 1970.

Chen, Kaijun. "Transcultural Lenses: Wrapping the Foreignness for Sale in the History of Lenses China." In Anna Grasskamp and Monica Juneja, eds., *EurAsian Matters: China, Europe, and the Transcultural Object, 1600–1800*. Cham: Springer, 2018, 77–98.

Chen, Mel Y. *Animacies: Biopolitics, Racial Mattering and Queer Affect*. Durham: Duke University Press, 2012.

Chen, Xiangming, Anthony M. Orum, and Krista E. Paulsen. "Introduction." *Cities: How Place and Space Shape Human Experience*. 2nd ed. Oxford: Wiley Blackwell, 2018.

Cherniavsky, Felix. *Maud Allan and Her Art*. Toronto: Dance Collection Danse, 1998.

Chidester, David. "Material Terms for the Study of Religion." *Journal of the American Academy of Religion* 68, no. 2 (June 2000), 367–80.

Religion: Material Dynamics. Berkeley: University of California Press, 2018.

Chidester, David, and Edward T. Linenthal. *American Sacred Space*. Bloomington: Indiana University Press, 1995.

Childs, Adrienne. "Sugarboxes and Blackamoors: Ornamental Blackness in Early Meissen Porcelain." In Michael Yonen and Alden Cavenaugh, eds., *The Cultural Aesthetics of Eighteenth-Century Porcelain*. Farnham: Ashgate 2010.

Chilton, Elizabeth S. "The Archaeology of Immateriality." *Archaeologies* 8, no. 3 (December 2012), 225–35.

Chiu Che-Bing. "Vegetal Travel: Western European Plants in the Garden of the Emperor of China." In Petra ten-Doeschatte Chu and Ning Ding, eds., *Qing Encounters: Artistic Exchanges between China and the West*. Los Angeles: Getty Publications, 2015, 95–110.

Yuanming Yuan: Le Jardin de la Clarté Parfaite. Besançon: Les Editions de l' Imprimeur, 2000.

Chong, Kimberley. *Best Practice: Management Consulting and the Ethics of Financialization in China*. Durham: Duke University Press, 2018.

Christen, Kimberly. "Archival Challenges and Digital Solutions in Aboriginal Australia." *The SAA Archeological Record* 9, no. 2 (March 2008), 21–4.

Christianson, Scott. *With Liberty for Some: 500 years of Imprisonment in America*. Boston: Northwestern University Press, 1998.

Christie, Maria. *Kitchenscape: Women, Fiestas and Everyday Life in Central Mexico*. Austin: University of Texas Press, 2008.

Chu, Petra ten-Doesschate and Ning Ding, eds., *Qing Encounters: Artistic Exchanges between China and the West*. Los Angeles: Getty Publications, 2015.

Clark, Andy. *Natural Born Cyborgs: Minds, Technologies, and the Future of Human Intelligence*. Oxford: Oxford University Press, 2003.

Clark, Kathleen. *Defining Moments: African American Commemoration & Political Culture in the South, 1863–1913*. Chapel Hill: University of North Carolina Press, 2005.

Clark, Kenneth. *Civilization: A Personal View by Lord Clark*. The Complete Series. Box Set. Kenneth Clark, actor, Michael Gill, director, Peter Montagnon, director. BBC Video. DVD. June27, 2006 . https://amzn.to/3GJCSz7. Full episodes online at www.bbc.co.uk/programmes/b00dtjbv/episodes/guide.

Classen, Constance. *The Deepest Sense: A Cultural History of Touch*. Studies in Sensory History. Urbana: University of Illinois Press, 2012.

Clavir, Miriam. *Preserving What is Valued: Museums, Conservation, and First Nations*. Vancouver: University of British Columbia Press, 2002.

Clayton, Michelle. "Touring History: Tortola Valencia between Europe and the Americas." *Dance Research Journal* 44, no. 1 (Summer 2012), 30–49.

Clemmer, Donald R. *The Prison Community*. Boston: Christopher Publishing House, 1940.

Clifford, James. "Quai Branly in Process." *October* 120 (2007), 3–23.

"The Museum as Contact Zone." In *Routes: Travel and Translation in the Twentieth Century*. Cambridge, MA: Harvard University Press, 1997, 188–219.

The Predicament of Culture: Twentieth-Century Ethnography, Literature and Art. Cambridge, MA: Harvard University Press, 1988.

Clunas, Craig. *Chinese Carving*. Singapore: Sun Tree, 1996.

"Connected Material Histories: A Response." *Modern Asian Studies* 50 (2016), 61–74.

"Oriental Antiquities/Far Eastern Art." *positions* 2, no. 2 (1994), 318–55.

"Precious Stones and Ming Culture, 1400–1450." In Craig Clunas et al., eds., *Ming: Courts and Contacts*. London: The British Museum, 2016, 236–44.

Coates, John. *Ecology and Social Work: Towards a New Paradigm*. Halifax: Fernwood, 2003.

Coe, Michael D., and Stephen Houston. *The Maya*. 9th ed. New York: Thames & Hudson, 2015.

Cohen, Lizabeth. "Embellishing a Life of Labor: An Interpretation of the Material Culture of American Working-Class Homes, 1885–1915." *Journal of American Culture* 3, no. 4 (Winter 1980), 752–75.

Cohen, William A., and Johnson, Ryan eds. *Filth: Dirt, Disgust, and Modern Life*. Minneapolis, Minnesota University Press, 2004.

Cole, Douglas. *Captured Heritage: The Scramble for Northwest Coast Artifacts*. Seattle: University of Washington Press, 1985.

Coleman, Gabriella. *Hacker, Hoaxer, Whistleblower, Spy: The Many Faces of Anonymous*. London: Verso, 2014.

Coleman, Laura-Edythe. *Understanding and Implementing Inclusion in Museums*. New York: Roman and Littlefield, 2018.

Colwell, Chip. *Plundered Skulls and Stolen Spirits: Inside the Fight to Reclaim Native America's Culture*. Chicago: University of Chicago Press, 2017.

Computer History Museum. "Timeline of Computer History." (2018) www.computerhistory.org/timeline/memory-storage/.

Conkey, Margaret. "Style, Design and Function." In Chris Tilley, Webb Keane, Susanne Kuechler, Michael Rowlands, and Patricia Spyer, eds., *Handbook of Material Culture*. London: Sage, 2006, 355–72.

Connerton, Paul. *How Modernity Forgets*. Cambridge: Cambridge University Press, 2009.

Cook, Harold. *Matters of Exchange: Commerce, Medicine, and Science in the Dutch Golden Age*. New Haven: Yale University Press, 2007.

Coole, Diana. "New Materialism: The Ontology and Politics of Materialization." In Susanne Witzgall and Kerstin Stakemeier, eds., *Power of Material/Politics of Materiality*. Chicago: Diaphanes, distributed by University of Chicago Press, 2017, 27–41.

Coole, Diana, and Samantha Frost. *New Materialism: Ontology, Agency, and Politics*. Durham: Duke University Press, 2010.

Cooper, Cynthia. *Magnificent Entertainments: Fancy Dress Balls of Canada's Governors General, 1876–1898*. Fredericton: Goose Lane Editions, 1997.

Cooper, Karen Coody. *Spirited Encounters: American Indians Protest Museums Policies and Practices*. Lanham: AltaMira Press, 2008.

Cooper, Rachel. "Wellbeing and the Environment: An Overview." In Rachel Cooper, Elizabeth Burton, and Cary L. Cooper, eds., Vol. II. *Wellbeing and the Environment: A Complete Reference Guide*. New Jersey: John Wiley, 2014, 1–19.

Coote, Jeremy. "Marvels of Everyday Vision: The Anthropology of Aesthetics and the Cattle Keeping Nilotes." In Jeremy Coote and Anthony Shelton, eds., *Anthropology, Art & Aesthetics*. Oxford: Oxford University Press, 1992, 245–74.

Cordell, Ryan. "'Q i-jtb the Raven': Taking Dirty OCR Seriously." *Book History* 20 (2017), 188–225.

Cotter, John L., Roger Moss, Bruce Gill, and Jiyul Kim. *The Walnut Street Prison Workshop: A Test Study in Historical Archaeology Based on Field*

Investigation in the Garden Area of the Athenaeum of Philadelphia. Watkins Glen: Athenaeum of Philadelphia, 1988.

Coupaye, Ludovic. "At the Power Plant's Switchboard: Controlling (Fertile) Energy amongst the Abulës-Speakers of Papua New Guinea." In Thomas Galoppin and Cécile Guillaume-Pey, eds., *Ce Que Peuvent Les Pierres: Vie et Puissance des Matériaux Lithiques Entre Rites et Savoirs*. Liège: Presses universitaires de Liège, 2020, 87–107.

"Chaîne Opératoire, Transects et Théories: Quelques Réflexions et Suggestions Sur Le Parcours D'une Méthode Classique." In Philippe Soulier, ed., *André Leroi-Gourhan "L'homme Tout Simplement."* Paris: Éditions de Boccard – Travaux de la MAE – Maison de l'Archéologie et de l'Ethnologie, René-Ginouvès, 2015, 69–84.

Growing Artifacts, Displaying Relationships: Yams, Art and Technology amongst the Nyamikum Abelam of Papua New Guinea. Oxford and New York: Berghahn Books, 2013.

"Making 'Technology' Visible: Technical Activities and the Chaîne Opératoire." In Maja Hojer Bruun and Ayo Wahlberg, eds., *The Anthropology of Technology: A Handbook*. New York: Palgrave Handbooks, in press.

"Things Ain't the Same Anymore": Towards an Anthropology of Technical Objects (or 'When Simondon meets MVC')." In Timothy Carroll, Antonia Walford, and Shireen Walton, eds., *Lineages and Advancements in the Anthropology of Material Culture*. London: Routledge, 2020, 46–60.

"'Yams Have No Ears!': Tekhne, Life and Images in Oceania." *Oceania* 88, no. 1 (2018), 13–30.

Coupaye, Ludovic, and Perig Pitrou. "Introduction: The Interweaving of Vital and Technical Processes in Oceania." *Oceania* 88, no. 1 (2018), 2–12.

Cox, Karen L. *Dixie's Daughters: The United Daughters of the Confederacy and the Preservation of Confederate Culture*. Gainesville: University Press of Florida, 2003.

Cox, Lindsay Kolowich. "The Engagement Ring Story: How De Beers Created a Multi-Billion Dollar Industry from the Ground Up," June 13, 2014. https://bit.ly/3nEz7Dy.

Craps, Stef, Rick Crownshaw, Jennifer Wenzel, Rosanne Kennedy, Claire Colebrook, and Vin Nardizzi. "Memory Studies and the Anthropocene: A Roundtable." *Memory Studies* 11, no 4. (2018), 498–515.

Crawford, Kate, and Vladan Joler. "Anatomy of an AI System: The Amazon Echo as an Anatomical Map of Human Labor." AI Now Institute and Share Lab (September 7, 2018). www.anatomyof.ai.

Cremona, Vicky Ann. *Carnival and Power: Play and Politics in a Crown Colony*. Basingstoke: Palgrave Macmillan, 2018.

Cresswell, Robert. "Of Mills and Waterwheels." In Pierre Lemonnier, ed., *Technological Choices: Transformation in Material Culture since the Neolithic*. London and New York: Routledge, 1993, 181–213.

Cresswell, Tim. "Landscape and the Obliteration of Practice." In Kay Anderson, Mona Domosh, Steve Pile, and Nigel Thrift, eds., *Handbook of Cultural Geography*. London: Sage, 2003, 269–82.

Cressy, David. *Coming Over: Migration and Communication between England and New England in the Seventeenth Century*. Cambridge: Cambridge University Press, 1987.

Cronon, William. "The Trouble with Wilderness; or, Getting Back to the Wrong Nature." In William Cronon, ed., *Uncommon Ground: Rethinking the Human Place in Nature*. New York: W. W. Norton, 1995, 69–90.

Crosby, Denise. "Civil War Reenactments: Cultural Insensitivity of Living History Lessons?" *Chicago Tribune* (June 27, 2019). https://bit.ly/3GDJWx3.

Crossland, Zoe. "Forensic Archaeology and the Disappeared in Argentina." *Archaeological Dialogues* 7, no. 2 (2000), 146–59.

"Of Clues and Signs: The Dead Body and Its Evidential Traces." *American Anthropologist* 111, no. 1 (2009), 69–80.

"The Archaeology of Contemporary Conflict." In Timothy Insoll, ed., *The Oxford Handbook of the Archaeology of Ritual and Religion*. Oxford: Oxford University Press, 2011.

Cummins, Tom. "The Felicitous Legacy of the Lanzón." In William J. Conklin and Jeffrey Quilter, eds., *Chavín: Art, Architecture and Culture*. Los Angeles: Cotsen Institute of Archaeology, 2008, 239–59.

Curtis, Emily Byrne. "A Plan of the Emperor's Glassworks." *Arts Asiatiques* 56 (2001), 81–90.

Glass Exchange between Europe and China, 1550–1800: Diplomatic, Mercantile and Technological Interactions. Farnham and Burlington: Ashgate, 2009.

"Poem of the Glass Bowl." In Emily Byrne Curtis, ed., *Pure Brightness Shines Everywhere*. Farnham and Burlington: Ashgate, 2004, 49–58.

Curtis, Neil G. W. "Universal Museums, Museum Objects and Repatriation: The Tangled Stories of Things." *Museum Management and Curatorship* 21, no. 2 (2006), 117–27.

Cywiński, Piotr M. A. Undated. Auschwitz Birkenau Foundation. www.foundation.auschwitz.org/ (accessed July 2019)

D'Arcens, Louise. "'The Last Thing One Might Expect': The Medieval Court at the 1866 Melbourne Intercolonial Exhibition." *The La Trobe Journal* 81 (2008), 26–39.

D'Harnoncourt, René, and Frederic Douglas. "Indian Art for Modern Living." In *Indian Art of the United States*, Reprint. New York: Arno Press for the Museum of Modern Art, 1969 [1941].

Daes, Erica-Irene. *Protección del Patrimonio de los Pueblos Indígenas*. New York: United Nations, 1999.

Dalakoglou, Dimitris. "Migrating-remitting-'building'-dwelling: House-Making as 'Proxy' Presence in Postsocialist Albania." *Journal of the Royal Anthropological Institute* 16, no. 4 (2010), 761–77.

Dalipaj, Gerda. "Migration, Residential Investment and the Experience of 'Transition': Tracing Transnational Practices of Albanian Migrants in Athens." *Focaal* 76 (2008), 85–98.

Danforth, Loring, and Alexander Tsiaras. *The Death Rituals of Rural Greece*. Princeton: Princeton University Press, 1982.

Dant, Tim. *Materiality and Society*. Maidenhead: Open University Press, 2005.

Danto, Arthur. "Artifact and Art." In Suzanne Vogel, ed., *Art/Artifact: African Art in Anthropology Collections*. New York: Center for African Art and Preston Verlog, 1988, 18–32.

Danto, Arthur. "The Artworld." *Journal of Philosophy* 61 (1964), 571–84.

Darwin City Council. Darwin City Council By-Laws – Reg 103 Camping or Sleeping in Public Place, 2019.

Data Center Knowledge. "Google Data Center FAQ." (March 16, 2017). https://bit.ly/3pHZPvj.

Davey, Steven, and Sarah Gordon. "Definitions of Social Inclusion and Social Exclusion: The Invisibility of Mental Illness and the Social Conditions of Participation." *International Journal of Culture and Mental Health* 10, no. 3 (2017), 229–37.

Davies, Peter, Penny Crook, and Tim Murray. *An Archaeology of Institutional Confinement: The Hyde Park Barracks, 1848–1886*. Sydney: Sydney University Press, 2013.

Davis, Kinglsey. "Social Science Approaches to International Migration." *Population and Development Review* 14 (1988), 245–61.

Davy, John (Jack). "Miniaturization: A Study of a Material Culture Practice among the Indigenous Peoples of the Pacific Northwest." Ph.D. dissertation. University College London, 2016.

"The 'Idiot Sticks': Kwakwaka'wakw Carving and Cultural Resistance in Commercial Art Production on the Northwest Coast." *American Indian Culture and Research Journal* 42, no. 3 (2018), 27–46.

Davy, John, and Charlotte Dixon, eds. *Worlds in Miniature: Contemplating Miniaturization in Global Material Culture*. London: University College London Press, 2019.

Dawdy, Shannon L. *Patina: A Profane Archaeology*. Chicago: University of Chicago Press, 2016.

Dawn, Leslie. *National Visions, National Blindness: Canadian National Art and Identities in the 1920s*. Vancouver: University of British Columbia Press, 2006.

De Certeau, Michel. *The Practice of Everyday Life*. Steven F. Rendall, trans. Berkeley: University of California Press, 1984.

De Cunzo, Lu Ann. "On Reforming the 'Fallen' and Beyond: Transforming Continuity at the Magdalen Society of Philadelphia, 1845–1916." *International Journal of Historical Archaeology* 5, no. 1 (2001), 19–43.

"Reform, Respite, Ritual: An Archaeology of Institutions; the Magdalen Society of Philadelphia, 1800–1850." *Historical Archaeology* 29, no. 3 (1995), 1–168.

de la Fuente, Eduardo. "On the Promise of a Sociological Aesthetics: From Georg Simmel to Michel Maffesoli." *Distinktion: Journal of Social Theory* 8, no. 2 (2007), 91–110.

De Leiuen, Cherrie. "'Corporal Punishment and the Grace of God': The Archaeology of a Nineteenth-Century Girls' Reformatory in South Australia." *Archaeology in Oceania* 50, no. 3 (2015), 145–52.

De León, Jason. "'Better to Be Hot than Caught': Excavating the Conflicting Roles of Migrant Material Culture." *American Anthropologist* 114, no. 3 (2012), 477–95.

The Land of Open Graves: Living and Dying on the Migrant Trail. Oakland: University of California Press, 2015.

"Undocumented Migration, Use Wear, and the Materiality of Habitual Suffering in the Sonoran Desert." *Journal of Material Culture* 18, no. 4 (2013), 321–45.

Deleuze, Gilles, and Félix Guattari. *A Thousand Plateaus*. Minneapolis: University of Minnesota Press, 1987 [1980].

de Moraes, Carlos N. "A Refiguração da Tava Miri São Miguel na Memória Coletiva dos Mbyá-Guarani nas Missões/RS, Brasil." Ph.D. Dissertation, Universidade Federal do Rio Grande do Sul, Porto Alegre, 2010.

de Souza, Jose C., and Jose C. Morinico. "Fantasmas das Brenhas Ressurgem nas Ruínas: Mbyá-Guaranis Relatam sua Versão Sobre as Missões e Depois Delas." In Arno Kern, Maria dos Santos, and Tau Golin, eds., *História Geral do Rio Grande do Sul. Volume 5, Povos Indígenas*. Passo Fundo: Méritos, 2009, 301–30.

de Tocqueville, Alexis. *De la Démocratie en Amérique. Democracy in America*. London: Saunders and Otley, 1832.

De Vos, (Rien), Marius. "Migration Memories." https://bit.ly/3qLvcad.

DeBoer, Warren R. "Report of Archaeological Excavations on the Río Shahuaya: A Western Tributary of the Upper Ucayali, Peru." M. A. thesis. Berkeley: University of California, 1970.

Debord, Guy, and Asger Jorn. *The Naked City*. New Haven: Beinecke Rare Book and Manuscript Library, Yale University, 1957.

DeCelles, Katherine A., and Michael I. Norton. "Physical and Situational Inequality on Airplanes Predicts Air Rage." *Proceedings of the National Academy of Sciences (PNAS)* 113, no. 2 (2016), 5588–91.

DeFrantz, Thomas F., and Gustavo Furtado, "Call for Papers" via email, October 10, 2016, for The Future of Reenactment conference at Duke University (April 20–21, 2017).

Deger, Jennifer. "Review: Bad Aboriginal Art: Tradition, Media and Technological Horizons by Eric Michaels." *Oceania* 66, no. 4 (1996), 332–3.

Shimmering Screens: Making Media in an Aboriginal Community. Minneapolis: University of Minnesota Press, 2006.

"Thick Photography." *Journal of Material Culture* 21, no. 10 (2016), 111–32.

Delson, Susan, ed. *Ai Weiwei: Circle of Animals*. New York: Prestel, 2011.

Descola, Phillipe. *Beyond Nature and Culture*. Janet Lloyd, trans. Chicago: University of Chicago Press, 2013.
  In the Society of Nature: A Native Ecology in Amazonia. Cambridge: Cambridge University Press, 1994 [1986].
DeSilvey, Caitlin. *Curated Decay: Heritage Beyond Saving*. Minneapolis: University of Minnesota Press, 2017.
Di Noto, Paula M., Leorra Newman, Shelley Wall, and Gillian Einstein. "The Hermunculus: What Is Known about the Representation of the Female Body in the Brain?" *Cerebral Cortex* 23, no. 5 (May 1, 2013), 1005. https://bit.ly/33PDkwS.
Díaz, Marcela. *Implicaciones Patrimoniales: La Declaratoria del Qhapaq Ñan como Patrimonio Mundial*. Buenos Aires: Ediciones del Signo, 2017.
Dickie, George. *Art and Aesthetic: An Institutional Analysis*. Ithaca: Cornell University Press, 1975.
Dickinson, Emily, Marta L. Werner, and Jen Bervin, eds. *The Gorgeous Nothings*. New York: New Directions, 2013.
Diehl, Richard A. *The Olmecs: America's First Civilization*. London: Thames & Hudson, 2004.
Dillon, Elizabeth Maddock. *New World Drama: The Performative Commons in the Atlantic World, 1649–1849*. Durham: Duke University Press, 2014.
Dillon, Grace. "Introduction." In Grace Dillon, ed., *Walking the Clouds: An Anthology of Indigenous Science Fiction*. Tucson: University of Arizona Press, 2012.
Diner, Hasia. *Hungering for America: Italian, Irish, and Jewish Foodways in the Age of Migration*. Oxford: Oxford University Press, 1991.
Dobrès, Marcia-Anne. "Technology's Links and Chaînes: The Processual Unfolding of Techniques and Technician." In Marcia-Anne Dobrès and Christopher R. Hoffman, eds., *The Social Dynamics of Technology*. Washington and London: Smithsonian Institution Press, 1999, 124–46.
Doherty, Thomas J., and Susan Clayton. "The Psychological Impacts of Global Climate Change." *American Psychologist*, 66 (2011), 265–76.
Douglas, Mary. *Purity and Danger: An Analysis of Concepts of Pollution and Taboo*. London: Routledge, 2002 [1996].
Douny, Laurence. *Living in a Landscape of Scarcity: Materiality and Cosmology in West Africa*. London: Left Coast Press, 2014.
Douny, Laurence, and Myriem Naji. "Making and Doing: Editorial." *Journal of Material Culture* 14, no. 4 (2009), 411–32.
Dousset, Laurent. *Australian Aboriginal Kinship: An Introductory Handbook with Particular Emphasis on the Western Desert*. Marseille: Pacific-credo Publications, 2011.
Dreiser, Theodore. *Sister Carrie*. New York: Penguin Books, 1981 [1900].
Droogan, Julian. *Religion, Material Culture, and Archaeology*. London: Bloomsbury, 2013.
Drouin, Jeffrey. "Surrogate." In Benjamin Peters, ed., *Digital Keywords*. Princeton: Princeton University Press, 2016, 278–85.

Du Crest, Sabine. *L'Art de Vivre Ensemble: Objets Frontière de la Renaissance au XXIe Siècle*. Rome: Gangemi, 2017.

Dunne, Anthony and Fiona Raby. *Speculative Everything: Design, Fiction and Social Dreaming*. Cambridge, MA: The MIT Press, 2013.

Durkheim, Emil. *The Elementary Forms of Religious Life*. 1912; reprint Oxford: Oxford University Press, 2008.

The Rules of Sociological Method, S. A. Solovay and H. H. Mueller, trans. New York: Free Press 1966 [1894].

Dwyer, Claire. "Spiritualizing the Suburbs: New Religious Architecture in Suburban London and Vancouver." In Victoria Hegner and Peter Jan Margry, eds., *Spiritualizing the City* (London: Routledge, 2017), 115–29.

"Why Does Religion Matter for Cultural Geographers?" *Social and Cultural Geography* 17, no. 6 (2016), 758–62. www.tandfonline.com/doi/full/10.1080/14649365.2016.1163728.

Eagleton, Terry. *Literary Theory: An Introduction*. 2nd ed. Minneapolis: University of Minnesota Press, 1996.

The Ideology of an Aesthetic. London: Wiley-Blackwell, 1990.

Eck, Diana. *Darsan: Seeing the Divine Image in India*. New York: Columbia University Press, 1998.

Eco, Umberto. *Semiotics and the Philosophy of Language*. London: Macmillan, 1984.

A Theory of Semiotics. Bloomington: Indiana University Press, 1976.

Edwards, Elizabeth, and Janice Hart. "Absent Histories and Absent Images: Photographs, Museums and the Colonial Past." *Museums and Society* 11, no. 1 (2013), 19–38.

Edwards, Elizabeth, and Janice Hart, eds. *Photographs, Objects, Histories: On the Materiality of Images*. London and New York: Routledge, 2004.

Eglash, Ron. "Technology as Material Culture." In Chris Tilley et al., eds., *Handbook of Material Culture*. London: Sage, 2006, 327–40.

Ehrenreich, Robert, Carole Crumley, and Janet Levy, eds., *Heterarchy and the Analysis of Complex Societies*. Archaeological Papers of the American Anthropological Association, 1995.

Ehrkamp, Patricia. "Placing Identities: Transnational Practices and Local Attachments of Turkish Immigrants in Germany." *Journal of Ethnic and Migration Studies* 31 (2005), 345–64.

Ekblom, Paul, ed. *Design Against Crime: Crime Proofing Everyday Objects*. Boulder: Lynne Rienner, 2012.

Elera, Carlos G. "The Face Behind the Mask." In Victor Pimentel, ed., *Peru: Kingdoms of the Sun and the Moon*. Montreal: Montreal Museum of Fine Arts, 2013, 96–107.

Eliade, Mircea. *Shamanism, or Archaic Techniques of Ecstasy*. Princeton: Princeton University Press, 1974.

Ellul, Jacques. *The Technological Society*. New York: Vintage Books, 1964 [1954].

Emory Libraries Manuscript, Archives, and Rare Books Archive. "The Digital Archives of Salman Rushdie Help Sheet." https://bit.ly/304ZHgm.

Engelhardt, Elizabeth. "Beating the Biscuits in Appalachia." In Sherrie A. Inness, ed., *Cooking Lessons: The Politics of Gender and Food*. Lanham: Rowman & Littlefield: 2001, 151–68.

Epstein, Julia. *Altered Conditions: Disease, Medicine, and Storytelling*. London: Routledge, 1995.

Equipo Argentino De Antropología Forense (EAAF). Argentine Forensic Anthropology Team. 2017. www.eaaf.org/.

Erikson, Patricia Pierce, with Helma Ward and Kirk Wachendorf. *Voices of a Thousand People: The Makah Cultural and Research Center*. Lincoln: University of Nebraska Press, 2002.

Evans, Jessica. "Introduction: Nation and Representation." In Jessica Evans and David Boswell, eds., *Representing the Nation: A Reader: Histories, Heritage and Museums*. Routledge: London, 1999, 1–8.

Evans, Raymond and Robert Ørsted-Jensen. "'I Cannot Say the Numbers that Were Killed': Assessing Violent Mortality on the Queensland Frontier." 2014. https://ssrn.com/abstract=2467836.

Evans, Robin. *The Fabrication of Virtue: English Prison Architecture, 1750–1840*. Cambridge: Cambridge University Press, 1982.

Evans Pritchard, Edward E., and Eva Gillies. *Witchcraft, Oracles and Magic among the Azande*. Abridged ed. Oxford: Clarendon Press, 1976.

Fabian, Johannes. *Time and the Other: How Anthropology Makes its Object*. New York: Columbia University Press, 1983.

Fahlander, Fredrik, and Terje Oestigaard. "Introduction: Material Culture and Post-disciplinary Sciences." In Fredrik Fahlander and Terje Oestigaard, eds., *Material Culture and Other Things: Post-Disciplinary Studies in the Twenty-First Century*. Lindome: Bricoleur Press, 2004, 1–18.

Farris Thomson, Robert. "The Aesthetics of the Cool." *African Arts* 7, no. 1 (1973), 40–91.

"Yoruba Artistic Criticism." In Howard Morphy and Morgan Perkins, eds., *The Anthropology of Art: A Reader*. Oxford: Blackwell Publishing, 2006 [1973], 242–69.

Farris, Jonathan Andrew. *Enclave to Urbanity: Canton, Foreigners, and Architecture from the Late Eighteenth to the Early Twentieth Centuries*. Hong Kong: Hong Kong University Press, 2016.

"Thirteen Factories of Canton: An Architecture of Sino-Western Collaboration and Confrontation." *Buildings and Landscapes: Journal of the Vernacular Architecture Forum* 14 (2007), 66–83.

Fash, Barbara W. *The Copan Sculpture Museum: Ancient Maya Artistry in Stucco & Stone*. Cambridge, MA: Peabody Museum Press, 2011.

Fassbinder, Samuel Day. "The Literature of the Anthropocene: Four Reviews." *Capitalism Nature Socialism* 28 (2017), 139–48.

Faure, Bernard. *The Rhetoric of Immediacy. A Cultural Critique of Chan/Zen Buddhism*. Princeton: Princeton University Press, 1991.

Feagin, Susan. "Roger Fry (1866–1934) and Clive Bell (1881–1964)." In Alessandro Giovannelli, ed., *Aesthetics: The Key Thinkers*. New York: Continuum, 2012, 113–25.

Feenberg, Andrew. *Critical Theory of Technology*. Oxford and New York: Oxford University Press: 1991.

Questioning Technology. London and New York: Routledge, 1999.

Transforming Technology: A Critical Theory Revisited. Oxford: Oxford University Press, 2002.

Feister, Lois. "The Orphanage at Schuyler Mansion." *Northeast Historical Archaeology* 20, no. 1 (1991), 27–36.

Fennelly, Katherine. *An Archaeology of Lunacy: Managing Madness in Early Nineteenth-Century Asylums*. Manchester: Manchester University Press, 2019.

"Out of Sound, Out of Mind: Noise Control in Early Nineteenth-Century Lunatic Asylums in England and Ireland." *World Archaeology* 46, no. 3 (2014), 416–30.

Ferrari, Giovanni R. F., ed. *Plato. The Republic*. Tom Griffith, trans. Cambridge: Cambridge University Press, 2000.

Ferreira, Patricia, Ariel Ortega, Vincent Carelli, and Ernesto de Carvalho. *Tava, a Casa de Pedra*. Recife: Vídeo nas Aldeias, 2012.

Ferret, Carole. "Towards an Anthropology of Action: From Pastoral Techniques to Modes of Action." *Journal of Material Culture* 9, no. 3 (2014), 279–302.

Ferro, Shanacy. "A More Accurate World Map Wins Prestigious Japanese Design Award." October 31, 2016. https://bit.ly/3KnIKjz.

Fiala, Andrew. "Anarchism." In Edward N. Zalta, ed., *The Stanford Encyclopedia of Philosophy*. Online.Stanford: Stanford University Press, 2018. https://stanford.io/3rUVrM3.

Finkel, Alicia. *Romantic Stages: Set and Costume Design in Victorian England*. Jefferson and London: McFarland, 1996.

Finlay, Robert. *The Pilgrim Art: Cultures of Porcelain in World History*. Berkeley and Los Angeles: University of California Press, 2010.

Finn, Christine. Leave Stay Home. www.leavehomestay.com/.

Fischer, A. M. "Resolving the Theoretical Ambiguities of Social Exclusion with Reference to Polarization and Conflict." Working paper, Development Studies Institute, London School of Economics and Political Science, 2008. www.lse.ac.uk/internationalDevelopment/pdf/WP/WP90.pdf.

Fiske, John. *Introduction to Communication Studies*. 2nd ed. New York: Routledge, 1990.

Fitzsimmons Frey, Heather Marie. Interview with Evelyn and McLovin. August 23, 2019.

Interview with Lynne. August 22, 2019.

"Victorian Girls and At-Home Theatricals: Performing and Playing with Possible Futures." Ph.D. dissertation, University of Toronto, 2015.

Fleisher, Mark S. *Warehousing Violence*. Newbury Park: Sage, 1989.

Fleming, Benjamin J., and Richard D. Mann, eds. *Material Culture and Asian Religions*. London: Routledge, 2014.

Flexner, James L. "An Institution That was a Village: Archaeology and Social Life in the Hansen's Disease Settlement at Kalawao, Moloka 'i, Hawaii." *International Journal of Historical Archaeology* 16, no. 1 (2012), 135–63.

Flood, Catherine, and Gavin Grindon, eds. *Disobedient Objects*. London: Victoria and Albert Museum, 2014.

Flood, Finbarr B. *Objects of Translation: Material Culture and Medieval "Hindu-Muslim" Encounter*. Princeton: Princeton University Press, 2009.

Flores, Alberto. *Buscando un Inca: Identidad y Utopía en los Andes*. Lima: Sur, 1987.

Forberg, Corinna, and Philipp W. Stockhammer, eds. *The Transformative Power of the Copy: A Transcultural and Interdisciplinary Approach*. Heidelberg: Heidelberg University Press, 2017.

Forde, C. Daryll. *Habitat, Economy and Society*. London: Methuen, 1934.

Foreman, Dave. "The Arrogance of Resourcism." *Around the Campfire* 5, 2007. www.rewilding.org/pdf/campfiremarch107.pdf.

Foreman, P. Gabrielle. *Activist Sentiments: Reading Black Women in the Nineteenth Century*. Urbana: University of Illinois Press, 2009.

Forrer, Matthi. "From Optical Prints to Ukie and Ukiyoe: The Adoption and Adaptation of Western Linear Perspective in Japan." In Michael North and Thomas DaCosta Kaufmann, eds., *Mediating Netherlandish Art and Material Culture in Asia, Amsterdam Studies in the Dutch Golden Age*. Amsterdam: Amsterdam University Press, 2014, 245–66.

Foster, Burk, Ron Wikburg, and Wilbert Rideau, eds. *The Wall is Strong: Corrections in Louisiana*. Lafayette: Centre for Louisiana Studies, University of Southwestern Louisiana, 1977.

Foster, Hal, ed. *The Anti-Aesthetic: Essays on Postmodern Culture*. Port Townsend: Bay Press, 1983.

Foster, John Bellamy, Brett Clark, and Richard York. *The Ecological Rift: Capitalism's War on the Earth*. New York: Monthly Review, 2010.

Foucault, Michel. "Des Espaces Autres (Of Other Spaces: Utopias and Heterotopias)." *Diacritics* 16, no. 1 (1986), 22–27.

Discipline and Punish: The Birth of the Prison. New York: Pantheon Books, 1977.

"Technologies of the Self." In Luther H. Martin, Huck Gutman, and Pattrick H. Hutton, eds., *Technologies of the Self*. Amherst: University of Massachusetts Press, 1988, 6–49.

Foy, Jessica, and Karal Ann Marling, eds. *The Arts and the American Home 1890–1930*. Knoxville: University of Tennessee Press, 1994.

Franco, Barbara. "Decentralizing Culture: Public History and Communities." In James B. Gardner and Paula Hamilton, eds., *The Oxford Handbook of Public History*. Oxford: Oxford University Press, 2017, 69–86.

Fraresso, Carole. "The Sweat of the Sun and the Tears of the Moon: Gold and Silver in Ancient Peru." In Victor Pimentel, ed., *Peru: Kingdoms of the Sun and the Moon*. Montreal: Montreal Museum of Fine Arts, 2013, 142–55.

Frazer, Sir James George. *The Golden Bough*. Abridged. New York and London: Penguin Books, 1922.

Free Code Camp. "Web Tracking: What You Should Know About Your Privacy Online." (April 23, 2018). https://bit.ly/3Ae9ZbK.

Freedberg, David. *The Power of Images: Studies in the History and Theory of Response*. Chicago: University of Chicago Press, 1989.

Freedgood, Elaine. *The Ideas in Things: Fugitive Meaning in the Victorian Novel*. Chicago, University of Chicago Press, 2006.

Freud, Sigmund. "Fetishism" (1927). In *Miscellaneous Papers, 1888–1938*, Vol. 5 of *Collected Papers*, 198–204. London: Hogarth and Institute of Psycho-Analysis, 1924–1950.

Frick, Patricia. "Die Lackkunst und ihr Weg nach Europa." In Annette Kanzenbach and Daniel Suebsman, eds., *Made in China: Porzellan und Teekultur im Nordwesten im 18. Jahrhundert. Ein Kapitel Handelsgeschichte*. Emden: Isensee, 2015, 64–73.

Friedlander, Saul. *Memory, History and the Extermination of the Jews of Europe*. Bloomington: Indiana University Press, 1993.

Friedrich, Mona, and Tony Johnston. "Beauty versus Tragedy: Thanatourism and the Memorialization of the 1994 Rwandan Genocide." *Journal of Tourism and Cultural Change* 11, no. 4 (2013), 302–20.

Fry, Hannah. "The Story of Zero: Getting Something from Nothing." Animation. April 13, 2016. www.youtube.com/watch?v=9Y7gAzTMdMA.

Fuchs, Christian. *Social Media: A Critical Introduction*. London: Sage, 2014.

Fuentes, Agustín, and Mark Kissel. "Semiosis in the Pleistocene." *Cambridge Archaeological Journal* 27, no. 3 (2017), 397–412. https://bit.ly/31Bxo9P.

Fulton Suri, Jane. *Thoughtless Acts?: Observations on Intuitive Design*. San Francisco: Chronicle Books, 2005.

Fur, Gunlög, Magdalena Naum, and Jonas M. Nordin. "Intersecting Worlds: New Sweden's Transatlantic Entanglements." *The Journal of American Transnational Studies* 7, no. 1 (2016), 1–22.

Galey, Alan. "The Enkindling Reciter: E-Books in the Bibliographical Imagination." *Book History* 15, no. 1 (2012), 210–47.

Gallagher, Kathleen. "Theatre Pedagogy and Performed Research: Respectful Forgeries and Faithful Betrayals." *Theatre Research in Canada* 28, no. 2 (2007), 105–19.

Galliot, Sébastien. "Ritual Efficacy in the Making." *Journal of Material Culture* 20, no. 2 (2015), 101–25.

Galloway, Alexander. *Gaming: Essays on Algorithmic Culture*. Minneapolis: University of Minnesota Press, 2006.

Galt, John M. *The Annual Report of the Physician and Superintendent of the Eastern Asylum, in the City of Williamsburg, Virginia, for 1842*. Richmond: Shepherd and Colin, 1843.

Gamber, Wendy. *The Boarding House in Nineteenth-Century America*. Baltimore: Johns Hopkins University Press, 2007.

Gamman, Loraine and Adam Thorpe. "What is 'Socially Responsive Design and Innovation'?" In Fiona Fisher and Penny Sparke, eds., *Routledge Companion to Design Studies*. London: Routledge, 2016, 317–29.

Gapps, Stephen. "Mobile Monuments: A View of Historical Re-enactment and Authenticity from the Costume Cupboard of History." *Rethinking History: The Journal of Theory and Practice* 13, no. 3 (2009), 395–409.

Garland, David. *Punishment and Modern Society*. Oxford: Clarendon Press, 1989.

Garman, James C. *Detention Castles of Stone and Steel: Landscape, Labor, and the Urban Penitentiary*. Knoxville: University of Tennessee Press, 2005.

Gaskell, Ivan. "Sacred to Profane and Back Again." In Andrew McClellan, ed., *Art and Its Publics: Museum Studies at the Millennium*. Malden: Blackwell, 2003, 149–62.

Gatto, John Taylor. *The Underground History of American Education: An Intimate Investigation into the Prison of Modern Schooling*. New York: Oxford Village Press, 2001.

Weapons of Mass Instruction: A Schoolteacher's Journey through the Dark World of Compulsory Education. Gabriola: New Society, 2010.

Geertz, Clifford. *Negara: The Theatre State in Nineteenth-Century Bali*. Princeton: Princeton University Press, 1980.

The Interpretation of Culture. New York: Basic Books, 1973.

Gell, Alfred. *Art and Agency: An Anthropological Theory*. Oxford: Oxford University Press, 1998.

"On Coote's 'Marvels of Everyday Vision'," *Social Analysis* 38 (1995), 18–30.

"Technology and Magic." *Anthropology Today* 4, no. 2 (1988), 6–9.

"The Network of Standard Stoppages (c.1985)." In Liana Chua and Mark Elliot, eds., *Distributed Objects: Meaning and Mattering after Alfred Gell*. Oxford: Berghahn, 2013, 88–113.

"The Technology of Enchantment and the Enchantment of Technology." In Jeremy Coote and Anthony Shelton, eds., *Anthropology, Art and Aesthetics*. Oxford: Clarendon, 1992, 40–63.

"Vogel's Net: Traps as Artworks and Artworks as Traps." *Journal of Material Culture* 1, no. 1 (1996), 15–38.

George Mason University. "History of Computing." (2010). http://mason.gmu.edu/~montecin/computer-hist-web.htm.

George, Andrew. *The Epic of Gilgamesh: The Babylonian Epic Poem and Other Texts in Akkadian and Sumerian*. London: The Folio Society, 2010.

George, Gerald. "Historic House Museum Malaise: A Conference Considers What's Wrong." *History News* 57, no. 4 (Autumn 2002).

Gerritsen, Anne. "Domesticating Goods from Overseas: Global Material Culture in the Early Modern Netherlands." *Journal of Design History* 29 (2016), 228–44.

"'Soja, Zoals die uit Oost-Indien Komt'; de Vroege Geschiedenis van Sojasaus in Nederland." *Aziatische Kunst* 45, no. (2015), 24–33.

"The Global Life of a Soya Bottle." Inaugural lecture, Leiden University, December 12, 2014. https://bit.ly/3qHFCqV.

Gerritsen, Anne, and Riello, Giorgio, eds. *The Global Lives of Things: The Material Culture of Connections in the Early Modern World*. Basingstoke: Routledge, 2016.

Ghosh, Pallab. "Net Pioneer Warns of Data Dark Age." BBC News: Science & Environment. (February 13, 2015). www.bbc.com/news/science-environment-31450389.

Gibb, Andrew. "'On the [Historical] Sublime': J. R. Planché's *King John* and the Romantic Ideal of the Past." *Theatre Symposium* 26 (2018), 127–40.

Gibb, James G. "Introduction." In April Beisaw and James Gibb, eds., *The Archaeology of Institutional Life*. Tuscaloosa: University of Alabama Press, 2009, 1–4.

Gibson, James J. *The Ecological Approach to Perception*. Hillsdale: Lawrence Erlbaum, 1986.

Gielis, Ruben. "A Global Sense of Migrant Places: Towards a Place Perspective in the Study of Migrant Transnationalism. *Global Networks* 9 (2009), 271–87.

Giffney, Noreen. "Introduction: The 'q' Word." In Noreen Giffney and Michael O'Rourke, eds., *The Ashgate Research Companion to Queer Theory*. Online. Farnham: Ashgate, 2009.

Gilchrist, Roberta. "Christian Bodies and Souls: The Archaeology of Life and Death in Later Medieval Hospitals." In Steven Bassett, ed., *Death in Towns: Urban Responses to the Dying and the Dead, 100–1600*. Leicester: Leicester University Press, 1992, 100–18.

Gender and Material Culture: The Archaeology of Religious Women. London: Routledge, 1994.

Gille, Bertrand. *The History of Techniques*. 2 vols. New York: Gordon and Breach Science Publishers, 1986 [1978].

"La Notion de Système Technique (Essai D'épistémologie Technique)" *Technique & Cultures*, no. 1 (1979), 8–18.

Gillespie, Marie, Souad Osseiran, and Margie Cheesman. "Syrian Refugees and the Digital Passage to Europe: Smartphone Infrastructures and Affordances." *Social Media + Society* (2018), 1–12.

Glahn, Richard von. "Economic Depression and the Silver Question in Nineteenth-Century China." In Manuel Perez Garcia and Lucio De Sousa, eds., *Global History and New Polycentric Approaches. Palgrave Studies in Comparative Global History*. Singapore: Palgrave Macmillan, 2018, 81–118.

Glass, Aaron. "Indigenous Ontologies, Digital Futures: Plural Provenances and the KwakwaKa'Wakw Collection in Berlin and Beyond." In Raymond Aaron Silverman, ed., *Museum as Process: Translating Local and Global Knowledges*. London and New York: Routledge, 2015.

Glassie, Henry. *Folk Housing in Middle Virginia: A Structural Analysis of Historic Artifacts*. Knoxville: University of Tennessee Press, 1976.
Pattern in the Material Folk Culture of the Eastern United States. Philadelphia: University of Pennsylvania Press, 1971.
Gleixner, Ulrike. "Unlesbare Schriften. Bestände von Weltensammlern des 18. Jahrhunderts in der Herzog August Bibliothek." In Birgit Neumann, ed., *Präsenz und Evidenz fremder Dinge im Europa des 18. Jahrhunderts*. Göttingen: Wallstein Verlag 2015, 203–17.
Glick Schiller, Nina, Linda G. Basch, and Cristina Blanc-Szanton, eds. *Towards a Transnational Perspective on Migration: Race, Class, Ethnicity, and Nationalism Reconsidered*. New York: New York Academy of Sciences, 1992.
Glob, Peter. *The Bog People: Iron-Age Man Preserved*. New York: New York Review of Books, 2004.
Gnecco, Cristóbal. "A World Full of Adjectives: Sustainable Archaeology and Soothing Rhetoric." *Antiquity* 93 (2019), 1664–5.
"An Entanglement of Sorts: Archaeology, Ethics, Praxis, Multiculturalism." In Cristóbal Gnecco and Dorothy Lippert, eds., *Ethics and Archaeological Praxis*. New York: Springer, 2015, 1–17.
"Development and Disciplinary Complicity: Contract Archaeology in South America under the Critical Gaze." *Annual Review of Anthropology* 47 (2018), 279–93.
Gnecco, Cristóbal, and Patricia Ayala. "Introduction" In Cristóbal Gnecco and Patricia Ayala, eds., *Indigenous Peoples and Archaeology in Latin America*. Walnut Creek: Left Coast Press, 2011, 11–27.
Godelier, Maurice. *The Making of Great Men: Male Domination and Power among the New Guinea Baruya*. Cambridge: Cambridge University Press, 1986 [1982].
Godfrey, Marian and Barbara Silberman. Model for Historic House Museums, Pew Charitable Trust, 2008. https://bit.ly/3D3sX5q.
Goffman, Erving. *Asylums: Essays on the Social Situation of Mental Patients and Other Inmates*. New York: Anchor Books, 1961.
The Presentation of Self in Everyday Life. Garden City: Doubleday, 1959.
Gojak, Denis, and Nadia Iacono. "The Archaeology and History of the Sydney Sailors Home, the Rocks, Sydney." *The Bulletin of the Australian Institute for Maritime Archaeology* 17, no. 1 (1993), 27–32.
Goldman, Nick, Paul Bertone, Siyuan Chen, Christophe Dessimoz, Emily M. LeProust, Botond Sipos, and Ewan Birney. "Towards Practical, High-Capacity, Low-Maintenance Information Storage in Synthesized DNA." *Nature* 494, no. 7435 (2013), 77–80.
Goldthorpe, Caroline. *From Queen to Empress: Victorian Dress 1837–1877*. New York: The Metropolitan Museum of Art, 1989.
Gombrich, Ernst. "Review of David Freedberg, *The Power of Images: Studies in the History and Theory of Response*." *New York Review of Books* 15 (1990), 6–9.

Gomez-Temesio, Veronica. "Home is Claiming for Rights: The Moral Economy of Water Provision in Rural Senegal." In Franz Krause and Veronica Strang, eds., *Thinking Relationships Through Water, Special Issue, Society and Natural Resources*. 29, no. 6 (2016), 654–67.

Gonzáles-Ruibal, Alfredo. "Ruins of the South." In Laura McAtackney and Krysta Ryzewski, eds., *Contemporary Archaeology and the City: Creativity, Ruination and Political Action*. Oxford: Oxford University Press, 2017, 149–67.

Gosepath, Stefan. "Equality." In Edward N. Zalta, ed., *The Stanford Encyclopedia of Philosophy* (Spring 2011 ed.). https://plato.stanford.edu/archives/spr2011/entries/equality/. Accessed January 5, 2019.

Gosselain, Olivier. "Mother Bella Was Not a Bella: Inherited and Transformed Traditions in Southwestern Niger." In Miriam T. Stark, Brenda J. Bowser, and Lee Horne, eds., *Cultural Transmission and Material Culture: Breaking Down Boundaries* (Tucson: University of Arizona Press, 2008, 150–77.

Göttler, Christine. "Extraordinary Things: 'Idols from India' and the Visual Discernment of Space." In Christine Göttler and Mia Mochizuki, eds., *The Nomadic Object: The Challenge of World for Early Modern Religious Art*. Leiden: Brill, 2017, 37–73.

Göttler, Christine, and Mia Mochizuki, eds. *The Nomadic Object: The Challenge of World for Early Modern Religious Art*. Leiden: Brill, 2017.

Goulding, Maria. "Migration Memories." https://bit.ly/3FFmmPN.

Graham, Brian, and Sara McDowell. "Meaning in the Maze: The Heritage of Long Kesh," *Cultural Geographies* 14, no. 3 (2007), 343–68.

Graham, Martha, and Nell Murphy. "NAGPRA at 20: Museum Collections and Reconnections." *Museum Anthropology* 33, no. 2 (2010), 105–24.

Graham, Ruth. "The Great Historic House Museum Debate." *The Boston Globe*, August 10, 2014.

Graham-Davies, Sharon. *Challenging Gender Norms: Five Genders Among Bugis in Indonesia*. Belmont: Thomson Wadsworth, 2007.

Grant, Anne. "Adonai/Adidas T-shirt." MAVCOR, Yale University. https://bit.ly/3ozqpax.

Grant, Lyndsay, and Glen O'Hara. "'The Spirit Level' by Richard Wilkinson and Kate Pickett." *Geography* 95, no. 3 (2010), 149–53.

Grasskamp, Anna. "Branches and Bones: The Transformative Matter of Coral in Ming Dynasty China." In Michael Bycroft and Sven Dupré, eds., *Gems in the Early Modern World: Materials, Knowledge, and Global Trade, 1450–1800, Europe's Asian Centuries*. Basingstoke: Palgrave Macmillan, 2018, 118–47.

"EurAsian Layers: Netherlandish Surfaces and Early Modern Chinese Artifact." *The Rijksmuseum Bulletin* 63, no. 4 (2015), 363–98.

"Frames of Appropriation: Foreign Artifacts on Display in Early Modern Europe and China." In Petra ten-Doeschatte Chu and Ning Ding, eds., *Qing Encounters: Artistic Exchanges between China and the West*. Los Angeles: Getty Publications, 2015, 29–42.

    Objects in Frames: Displaying Foreign Collectibles in Early Modern China and Europe. Berlin: Reimer, 2019.

    "Spirals and Shells: Breasted Vessels in Sixteenth-Century Nuremberg." *Res: Anthropology and Aesthetics* 67, no. 68 (2016/17), 146–63.

    "The Frames of Reflection: 'Indian' Shell Surfaces and European Collecting, 1550–1650." In Sabine du Crest, ed., *Exogenèses: Objets Frontière dans l'Art Européen*. Paris: Boccard, 2018, 69–83.

    "Unpacking Foreign Ingenuity: The German Conquest of 'Artful' Objects with 'Indian' Provenance." In Richard Oosterhoff, José R. Marcaida, and Alexander Marr, eds., *Ingenuity in the Making: Matter and Technique in Early Modern Art and Science* (Pittsburgh: Pittsburgh University Press, 2021), 213–28.

Grasskamp, Anna, and Monica Juneja, eds. *EurAsian Matters: China, Europe, and the Transcultural Object, 1600–1800, Transcultural Research – Heidelberg Studies on Asia and Europe in a Global Context*. Cham: Springer, 2018.

Grasskamp, Anna, and Wen-ting Wu, "We Call Them 'Ginger Jars': European Re-framings of Chinese Ceramic Containers." *Vormen uit Vuur* 232, no. 3 (2016), 64–71.

Greenfield, Adam. *Everyware: The Dawning Age of Ubiquitous Computing*. Berkeley: New Riders, 2006.

Greengard, Samuel. *The Internet of Things*. Cambridge, MA: The MIT Press, 2015.

Grier, Katherine. *Culture and Comfort: Parlor Making and Middle-Class Identity, 1850–1930*. Washington: DC: Smithsonian Books, 2010.

Grieser, Alexandra, and Jay Johnston. *Aesthetics of Religion*. Berlin: De Gruyter, 2017.

Griffith, Vive. "You Are What You Eat." December 1, 1999. https://perma.cc/ZT75-SDA8.

Grimes, Sara M., and Andrew Feenberg. "Critical Theory of Technology." In Sara Price, Carey Jewitt, and Barry Brown, eds., *The SAGE Handbook of Digital Technology Research*. Los Angeles, London, New Dehli, Singapore and Washington, DC: Sage, 2013, 121–29.

Grisar, P. J. "Remembering Else Ury, Famed Children's Writer and Victim of the Holocaust," *Forward*. 17 July, 2019. https://bit.ly/3fBH7Re.

Griswold, Susan C. "Appendices." In Fatima Bercht, Estrellita Brodsky, John Alan Farmer, and Dicey Taylor, eds., *Taíno: Precolumbian Art and Culture from the Caribbean*. New York: Monacelli Press, 1997, 164–69.

Grossmann, Ulrich G., ed. *Die Frucht der Verheißung: Zitrusfrüchte in Kunst und Kultur*. Nuremberg: Germanisches Nationalmuseum Nürnberg, 2011.

Grunebaum, Heidi. *Memorializing the Past: Everyday Life in South Africa After the Truth and Reconciliation Commission*. New York: Routledge, 2011.

Guarino, Mark. "Time for Civil War Reenactments to Die Out?" *Washington Post*, August 25, 2017. https://wapo.st/3FKGbVj.

Guldi, Jo. What is the Spatial Turn? Charlottesville, Virginia: Scholars Lab, University of Virginia Library, 2012. https://bit.ly/3r7Ak8K.

Gumbrecht, Hans Ulrich. *Production of Presence: What Meaning Cannot Convey.* Stanford: Stanford University Press, 2004.

Gunn, Geoffrey. *First Globalization: The Eurasian Exchange, 1500–1800.* Lanham: Rowman & Littlefield, 2003.

Guppy, Nicholas. *Wai: Through the Forests North of the Amazon.* London: John Murray, 1958.

Gurney, Joseph J. *Notes on a Visit Made to Some of the Prisons in Scotland and the North of England, in Company with Elizabeth Fry.* London: Constable, 1819.

Guss, David M. *To Weave and To Sing: Art, Symbol, and Narrative in the South American Rain Forest.* Berkeley and Los Angeles: The University of California Press, 1989.

Haakanson, Sven D., and Amy F. Steffian, eds. *Giinaquq: Like a Face: Sugpiaq Masks of the Kodiak Archipelago.* Fairbanks: University of Alaska Press, 2009.

Haber, Alejandro. "Archaeology and Capitalist Development: Lines of Complicity." In Cristóbal Gnecco and Dorothy Lippert, eds., *Ethics and Archaeological Praxis.* New York: Springer, 2015, 95–113.

Haber, Alejandro, and Nick Shepherd. "After Ethics: Ancestral Voices and Post-disciplinary Worlds in Archaeology: An Introduction." In Alejandro Haber and Nick Shepherd, eds., *After Ethics: Ancestral Voices and Post-disciplinary Worlds in Archaeology.* New York: Springer, 2015, 1–10.

Habermas, Jürgen. "Technology and Science as 'Ideology'." In *Toward a Rational Society.* Boston: Beacon Press, 1970, 81–122.

The Structural Transformation of the Public Sphere. Cambridge, MA: The MIT Press, 1991.

Hafstein, Valdimar Tr. "Intangible Heritage as a List: From Masterpieces to Representation." In Laurajane Smith and Natsuko Akagawa, eds., *Intangible Heritage.* London: Routledge, 2009.

Hahn, Thurston, and Susan Wurzburg. *Hard Labor: History and Archaeology at the Old Louisiana State Penitentiary, Baton Rouge, Louisiana.* Fort Worth: General Services Administration, 1991.

Hainhofer, Philipp. *Der Briefwechsel zwischen Philipp Hainhofer und Herzog August d. J. von Braunschweig-Lüneburg.* Berlin: Deutscher Kunstverlag, 1983.

Hakken, David. *Cyborgs@Cyberspace: An Anthropologist Looks to the Future.* Routledge: New York, 1999.

Halbwach, Maurice. *On Collective Memory.* London: University of Chicago Press, 1992 [1925].

Hall, David D. *Lived Religion in America: Toward a History of Practice.* Princeton: Princeton University Press, 1998.

Hall, Loura. "3D Printer Headed to Space Station." Text. (2016). www.nasa.gov/content/3d-printer-headed-to-space-station.

Hall, Stuart. "Whose Heritage? Un-settling "The Heritage". Re-imagining the Post-nation." *Third Text* 49 (2000), 3–13.

Halsberghe, Nicole "The Resemblances and Differences of the Construction of Ferdinand Verbiest's Astronomical Instruments, as Compared with Those of Tycho Brahe." In John Witek, ed., *Ferdinand Verbiest, S.J. (1623–1688), Jesuit Missionary, Scientist, Engineer and Diplomat.* Nettetal: Steyler, 1994, 85–92.

Hamilakis, Yannis. "Archaeologies of Forced and Undocumented Migration." *Journal of Contemporary Archaeology* 3, no. 2 (2016), 121–39.

Hann, Rachel. "Debating Critical Costume: Negotiating Ideologies of Appearance, Performance and Disciplinarity." *Studies in Theatre and Performance* 39, no. 1 (2019), 2–15.

Hansell, Mike. *Built by Animals: The Natural History of Animal Architecture.* Oxford: Oxford University Press, 2009.

Haraway, Donna. *Simians, Cyborgs, and Women: The Reinvention of Nature.* New York: Routledge, 1991.

Staying with the Trouble: Making Kin in the Chthulucene. Durham: Duke University Press, 2016.

The Companion Species Manifesto. Chicago: Prickly Paradigm Press, 2003.

When Species Meet. Minneapolis: University of Minnesota Press, 2008.

Harley, J. B. "Deconstructing the Map." *Cartographica* 26, no. 2 (Spring 1989), 1–20.

Harman, Graham. *Tool-Being: Heidegger and the Metaphysics of Objects.* Chicago and La Salle: Open Court, 2002.

Harney, Nicholas. "Precarity, Affect and Problem Solving with Mobile Phones by Asylum Seekers, Refugees and Migrants in Naples, Italy." *Journal of Refugee Studies* 26, no. 4 (2013), 541–57.

Harper, Ken. *Give Me My Father's Body: The Life of Minik, The New York Eskimo.* Iqaluit: Blacklead Books, 1986.

Harris, Diane, and D. Fairchild Ruggles. *Sites Unseen: Landscape and Vision.* Pittsburgh: University of Pittsburgh Press, 2007.

Harris, Donna Ann. *New Solutions for House Museums: Ensuring the Long Term Preservation of America's Houses.* New York: AltaMira Press, 2007.

Harrison, Rodney. *Heritage: Critical Approaches.* London: Routledge, 2013.

Hart, Keith. "Forward." In Roy Rappaport, ed., *Rituals and Religion in the Making of Humanity.* Cambridge: Cambridge University Press, 1999, xiv–xix.

Hartington Jr., John. *Aesop's Anthropology: A Multispecies Approach.* Minneapolis: University of Minnesota Press, 2014.

Hartman, Saidiya. "Venus in Two Acts." *Small Axe* 12, no. 2 (2008), 1–14.

Harvey, David. *A Brief History of Neoliberalism.* Oxford: Oxford University Press, 2005.

"A History of Heritage." In Brian Graham and Peter Howard, eds., *Research Companion to Heritage and Identity.* Basingstoke: Ashgate, 2008, 19–36.

"Heritage Pasts and Heritage Presents: Temporality, Meaning and the Scope of Heritage Studies," *International Journal of Heritage Studies* 7, no. 4 (2001), 319–39.

Harvey, Penny, and Hannah Knox. "The Enchantments of Infrastructure." *Mobilities* 7, no. 4 (2015), 521–36.

Haudricourt, André-George. "Domestication of Animals, Cultivation of Plants and Human Relations." *Social Science Information* 8, no. 3 (1969 [1962]), 163–72.

Hayes, Dennis, and Robin Wynyard, eds. *The McDonaldization of Higher Education*. Westport: Praeger, 2002.

Hayles, N. Katherine. *How We Became Posthuman*. Chicago: University of Chicago Press, 1999.

Writing Machines. Cambridge, MA: The MIT Press, 2002.

Hays, Samuel P. *Conservation and the Gospel of Efficiency: The Progressive Conservation Movement 1890–1920*. New York: Athenaeum, 1979.

Hazard, Sonia. "The Material Turn in the Study of Religion." *Religion and Society: Advances in Research* 4 (2013), 58–71.

Hebdige, Dick. "Object as Image: The Italian Scooter Cycle." In *Hiding in the Light: On Images and Things*. London and New York: Routledge, 2001, 77–115.

Heckenberger, Michael J. "Amazonian Mosaics: Identity, Interaction, and Integration in the Tropical Forest." In Helaine Silverman and William H. Isbell, eds., *Handbook of South American Archaeology*. New York: Springer, 2008, 941–61.

Heckman, Andrea M. *Woven Stories; Andean Textiles and Rituals*. Albuquerque: University of New Mexico Press, 2003.

Hegedűs, Gabor. "Features of Gated Communities in the Most Populous Hungarian Cities." In Christian Smiegel, ed., *Forum IfL: Gated and Guarded Housing in Eastern Europe*. Leipzig: Institut für Länderkunde, 2009, 91–9.

Heidegger, Martin. *Being and Time*. Joan Stambaugh, trans.; Dennis J. Schmidt, rev. Albany: SUNY Press, 2010.

The Question Concerning Technology and Other Essays. New York: Harper and Row, 1977 [1954].

What is a Thing? W. B. Barton Jr., Vera Deutsch, and Eugene T. Gendlin, trans. Chicago: Gateway/Henry Regnery, 1970.

Heimerl, Florian, Steffen Lohmann, Simon Lange, and Thomas Ertl. "Word Cloud Explorer: Text Analytics Based on Word Clouds." 47th Hawaii International Conference on System Sciences, January 6–9, 2014.

Heisler, Barbara Schmitter. "The Future of Immigrant Incorporation: Which Models? Which Concepts?" *International Migration Review* 26, no. 2 (1992), 623–45.

"The Sociology of Immigration: From Assimilation to Segmented Integration, from the American Experience to the Global Arena." In Caroline Brettell and James Hollifield, eds., *Migration Theory: Talking across Disciplines*. New York, London: Routledge, 2000, 77–96.

Helland, Janice, Beverly Lemire, and Alena Buis, eds. *Craft, Community and the Material Culture of Place and Politics, Nineteenth–Twentieth Century*. Burlington: Ashgate 2014.

Heller, Henry. *The Capitalist University: The Transformations of Higher Education in the United States since 1945*. London: Pluto Press, 2016.

Hening, William Waller, ed. *The Statutes at Large*, 2, 481–82, June 1680 "An Act for preventing Negroes Insurrections."

Henry, Edward R., Bill Angelback, and Uzma Z. Rizvi. "Against Typology: A Critical Approach to Archaeological Order." Anarchy and Archaeology. *SAA Archaeological Record* 17, no. 1 (January 2017), 28–31.

Herman, Bernard L. *The Stolen House*. Charlottesville: University of Virginia Press, 1992.

Herren, Madeleine, Martin Rüesch, and Christiane Sibille, eds. *Transcultural History: Theories, Methods, Sources*. Cham: Springer, 2012.

Hevia, James. "Plunder, Markets, and Museums: The Biographies of Chinese Imperial Objects in Europe and North America." In Jan Mrazek and Morgan Pitelka, eds., *What's the Use of Art. Asian Visual and Material Culture in Context*. Honolulu: University of Hawai'i Press, 2008, 129–41.

Hewison, Robert. *The Heritage Industry: Britain in a Climate of Decline*. Methuen: London, 1987.

Hicks, Dan. *The Brutish Museums: The Benin Bronzes, Colonial Violence and Cultural Restitution*. London: Pluto Press, 2020.

"The Material-Cultural Turn: Event and Effect." In Dan Hicks and Mary Beaudry, eds., *Oxford Handbook of Material Culture Studies*. Oxford: Oxford University Press, 2010, 26–98.

Hicks, Dan, and Mary Beaudry. "Introduction. Material Culture Studies: A Reactionary View." In Dan Hicks and Mary Beaudry, eds., *Oxford Handbook of Material Culture Studies*. Oxford: Oxford University Press, 2010, 1–21.

Hicks, Dan, and Mary C. Beaudry, eds. *The Oxford Handbook of Material Culture Studies*. Oxford: Oxford University Press, 2010.

Hobsbawm, Eric, and Terence Ranger. *The Invention of Tradition*. Cambridge: Cambridge University Press, 1983.

Hocart, Arthur M. "The Purpose of Ritual." *Folklore* 46, no. 4 (1935), 343–9.

Hodder, Ian. *Entangled: An Archaeology of the Relationships between Humans and Things*. Oxford: Wiley Blackwell, 2012.

Reading the Past. Cambridge: Cambridge University Press, 1986.

Högberg, Anders, Cornelius Holtorf, Sarah May, and Gustav Wollentz. "No Future in Archaeological Heritage Management?" *World Archaeology* 49 (2017), 639–47.

Hølleland, Herdis, and Joar Skrede, "What's Wrong with Heritage Experts?" *International Journal of Heritage Studies* 25 (2019), 825–36.

Holler, Jan, Vlasios Tsiatsis, Catherine Mulligan, Stamatis Karnouskos, Stefan Avesand, and David Boyle. *From Machine-To-Machine to the Internet of Things: Introduction to a New Age of Intelligence*. Waltham: Elsevier, 2014.

Hollinger, Eric, Edwell John, Jr., Harold Jacobs, Lora Moran-Collins, Carolyn Thome, Jonathan Zastrow, Adam Metallo, Gunter Waibel, and Vince Rossi. "Tlingit-Smithsonian Collaborations with 3D Digitization of Cultural Objects." *Museum Anthropology Review* 7 no.1–2 (Spring-Fall 2013), 201–43.

Holt, Ardern. *Fancy Dresses Described: or, What to Wear at Fancy Balls*. London: Debenham and Freebody: Wyman and Sons, 1887.

Holtorf, Cornelius. *Archaeology is a Brand! The Meaning of Archaeology in Contemporary Popular Culture*. New York: Routledge, 2007.

"Can Less be More? Heritage in the Age of Terrorism." *Public Archaeology* 5, no. 2 (2006), 101–9.

Honour, Hugh. *Chinoiserie: The Vision of Cathay*. London: J. Murray, 1961.

Hoover, Stewart M. *Religion in the Media Age*. London: Routledge, 2006.

Hopkins, Pauline. *Contending Forces: A Romance Illustrative of Negro Life North and South*. New York: Oxford University Press, 1991 [1900].

Horkheimer, Max, and Theodor W. Adorno. *Dialectic of Enlightenment*. London: Verso, 1979 [1944].

Horňák, Marcel, and Alena Rochovská. "Do Mesta Čoraz Ďalej: Dopravné Vylúčenie Obyvateľov Vidieckych obcí Gemera." *Geographia Cassoviensis* 8, no. 2 (2014), 141–49.

Horowitz, Tony. *Confederates in the Attic: Dispatches from the Unfinished Civil War*. New York: Vintage Books, 1998.

Horst, van der, Hilje. "Dwellings in Transnational Lives: A Biographical Perspective on 'Turkish-Dutch' Houses in Turkey." *Journal of Ethnic and Migration Studies* 36, no. 7 (2010), 1175–92.

Houghton, David. "What is Virtual Repatriation?" museumsandtheweb.com, April 30, 2010. www.museumsandtheweb.com/forum/what_virtual_repatriation.html.

Houlbrook, Ceri, and Natalie Armitage, eds. *The Materiality of Magic*. Oxford: Oxford University Press, 2015.

Houtman, Dick, and Birgit Meyer, eds. *Things: Religion and the Question of Materiality*. New York: Fordham University Press, 2012.

Howard, David Sanctuary. *Chinese Armorial Porcelain*. London: Heirloom & Howard, 2003.

Howe, Adrian. *Punish and Critique: Towards a Feminist Analysis of Penality*. London: Routledge, 1991.

Hsieh, Ming-Liang. *Taoci Shouji* [Handbook of Ceramics]. Taipei: Shitou, 2008.

Hu, Tung-Hui. *A Prehistory of the Cloud*. Cambridge, MA: The MIT Press, 2015. https://bit.ly/3KoiKom.

Huang, Xingzeng. *Xiyang Chaogong Dianlu* [Records of Tributes from the Western Ocean Countries], 1520. Minguo 54 [1965].

Huber, Chris. "6 of the Worst Disasters in 2019." *World Vision*. November 26, 2019. https://bit.ly/3GvEWKq.

Hubbard, Kaia. "Here Are 10 of the Deadliest Natural Disasters in 2020." *US News & World Report*. December 22, 2020.

Huey, Paul. "The Almshouse in Dutch and English Colonial North America and its Precedent in the Old World: Historical and Archaeological Evidence." *International Journal of Historical Archaeology* 5, no. 2 (2001), 123–54.

HuffPost. "STARS Student Group Takes a Stand Against Racist Costumes." October 24, 2011 . https://bit.ly/3qGswu0.

Hughes, Amanda Millay, and Carolyn H. Wood. *A Place for Meaning: Art, Faith, and Museum Culture*. Chapel Hill: University of North Carolina Press, 2009.

Hughes, Barry. "'Infant Orphan Asylum Hall' Crockery from Eagle Pond, Snaresbrook." *London Archaeologist* 6, no. 14 (1992), 382–87.

Hughes, Thomas P. *Networks of Power: Electrification in Western Society, 1880–1930*. Baltimore and London: The John Hopkins University Press, 1983.

"The Seamless Web: Technology, Science, Etcetera, Etcetera." *Social Studies of Science* 6, no. 2 (1986), 281–92.

Hui, Yuk. *On the Existence of Digital Objects*. Minneapolis: University of Minnesota Press, 2016.

"What is a Digital Object?" *Metaphilosophy* 43, no. 2 (2012), 379–95.

Humle, Tatyana. "Material Culture in Primates." In Dan Hicks and Mary C. Beaudry, eds., *The Oxford Handbook of Material Culture Studies*. Oxford: Oxford University Press, 2010, 406–21.

Hutchings, Richard M. "Archaeology as State Heritage Crime." *Archaeologies* 13 (2017), 66–87.

"Like a Chicken Talking to a Duck about a Kettle of Fish." *Antiquity* 93 (2019), 1672–5.

Maritime Heritage in Crisis: Indigenous Landscapes and Global Ecological Breakdown. London: Routledge, 2017.

"Meeting the Shadow: Resource Management and the McDonaldization of Heritage Stewardship." In Jeremy C. Wells and Barry L. Stiefel, eds., *Human-Centered Built Environment Heritage Preservation: Theory and Evidence-Based Practice*. London: Routledge, 2019, 67–87.

"Sustainable Archaeology: Soothing Rhetoric for an Anxious Institution." *Antiquity* 93 (2019), 1653–60.

"Why Archaeologists Misrepresent their Practice: A North American Perspective." *Journal of Contemporary Archaeology* 2 (2015), S11–17.

Hutchings, Richard M., and Joshua Dent. "Archaeology and the Late Modern State: Introduction to the Special Issue." *Archaeologies* 13 (2017), 1–25.

Hutchings, Richard M., and Marina La Salle. "Archaeology as Disaster Capitalism." *International Journal of Historical Archaeology* 19, no. 4 (2015), 699–720.

Hutchings, Tim, and Joanne McKenzie, eds. *Materiality and the Study of Religion: The Stuff of the Sacred*. London: Routledge, 2016.

Hutchins, Edwin. *Cognition in the Wild*. Cambridge, MA and London: The MIT Press, 1995.

Huxley, Francis. *Affable Savages: An Anthropologist Among the Urubu Indians of Brazil*. New York: Capricorn Books, 1956.

ICOMOS Australia. The Burra Charter: The Australian ICOMOS Charter for Places of Cultural Significance. 2013. https://bit.ly/3rwG0I5.

Idema, Wilt. "Cannon, Clocks and Clever Monkeys: Europeana, Europeans and Europe in some Eighteenth-Century Chinese Novels." In W. J. J. Schipper, W. L. Idema, and H. M. Leyten, eds., *White and Black: Imagination and Cultural Confrontations, Bulletin of the Royal Tropical Institute 320*. Amsterdam: Koninklijk Instituut voor de Tropen, 1990, 54–82.

Ignatieff, Michael. *A Just Measure of Pain: The Penitentiary in the Industrial Revolution, 1750–1850*. London: Macmillan, 1978.

Ihde, Don. *Expanding Hermeneutics: Visualism in Science*. Evanston: Northwestern University Press, 1998.

Impey, Oliver. *Chinoiserie: The Impact of Oriental Styles on Western Art and Decoration*. New York: Scribner, 1977.

Ingold, Tim. "Eight Themes in the Anthropology of Technology." *Social Analysis* 41, no. 1 (1997), 106–38.

"Footprints Through the Weather-World: Walking, Breathing, Knowing." *Journal of the Royal Anthropological Institute*, Special Issue 2010, S121–39.

"Foreword." In Marcia-Anne Dobrès and Christopher R. Hoffman, eds., *The Social Dynamics of Technology*. Washington and London: Smithsonian Institution Press, 1999, vii–xi.

Making: Anthropology, Archaeology, Art, and Architecture. London: Routledge, 2013.

"Materials against Materiality." *Archaeological Dialogues* 14, no. 1 (2007), 1–16.

The Life of Lines. London: Routledge, 2015.

Innis, Harold. *The Bias of Communication*. Toronto: University of Toronto Press, 1951/2008.

Insoll, Timothy. *Archaeology, Ritual, Religion*. London: Routledge, 2004.

International Labour Organization. "Indigenous and Tribal Peoples Convention." No. 169. 1989.

Interview with Judge and Ellie Chavis by James Eddie (James Edward) McCoy. May 5, 1981. Q-0121, in the Southern Oral History Program Collection #4007, Southern Historical Collection, Wilson Library, University of North Carolina at Chapel Hill.

Jacknis, Ira. "Franz Boas and Exhibits." In George W. Stocking, Jr., ed., *Objects and Others: Essays on Museum and Material Culture*. Madison: University of Wisconsin Press, 1985, 75–101.

The Storage Box of Tradition: Kwakiutl Art, Anthropologists, and Museums. Washington, DC: Smithsonian Institution Press, 2002.

Jackson, Anthony, and Jenny Kidd. *Performing Heritage: Research, Practice, and Innovation in Museum Theatre and Live Interpretation*. Manchester: Manchester University Press, 2010.

Jackson, John Brinckerhoff. "The Word Itself." In John Brinckerhoff Jackson, ed., *Discovering the Vernacular Landscape*. New Haven: Yale University Press, 1986, 108.

Jackson, Peter. "Rematerializing Social and Cultural Geography." *Social and Cultural Geography* 1, no. 1 (2000), 9–14.

Jacobs, Courtney, Kevin O'Sullivan, and Marsha McIntosh. "3Dhotbed" (2018). www.3dhotbed.info/.

Jacobus, Mary. *Romantic Things: A Tree, A Rock, A Cloud*. Chicago: University of Chicago Press, 2012.

Jafri, Beenash. "Intellectuals Outside the Academy: Conversations with Leanne Simpson, Steven Salaita, and Alexis Pauline Gumbs." *Social Justice* 44 (2017), 119–31.

Jakelić, Slavica, and Jessica Starling. "Religious Studies: A Bibliographical Essay." *Journal of the American Academy of Religion* 74, no. 1 (March 2006), 194–211.

Jallade, Sébastien. "La Réinvention des Routes Incas: Représentations et Construction de la Mémoire au Pérou (2001–11)." *Droit et Culture* 62 (2011), 119–37.

James, Oliver. *Affluenza: How to be Successful and Stay Sane*. London: Vermillion, 2007.

Jameson, Fredric. *Archaeologies of the Future: The Desire Called Utopia and Other Science Fictions*. New York: Verso, 2005.

Postmodernism or, the Cultural Logic of Late Capitalism. London: Verso, 1991.

Jami, Catherine. "Western Devices for Time and Space Measurement: Clocks and Euclidian Geometry in Late Ming and Ch'ing China." In Chün-chieh Huang and Erik Zürcher, eds., *Time and Space in Chinese Culture*. Leiden: Brill 1995, 169–200.

Jankauskas, Rimantas. "Forensic Anthropology and Mortuary Archaeology in Lithuania." *Anthropologischer Anzeiger* 67, no. 4 (2009), 391–405.

Jansen, Yvonne, Pierre Dragicevic, Petra Isenberg, Jason Alexander, Abhijit Karnik, Johan Kildal, Sriram Subramanian, and Kasper Hornbæk. "Opportunities and Challenges for Data Physicalization." *Proceedings of the 33rd Annual ACM Conference on Human Factors in Computing Systems – CHI '15*. Seoul: ACM Press, 2015, 3227–36.

Jeffries, Nigel, Tim Braybrooke, and Jacqui Pearce. "Development of the Former Radcliffe Infirmary, Oxford, 1770–1900." *Post-Medieval Archaeology* 49, no. 2 (2015), 238–68.

Jenkins, Henry, Sam Ford, and Joshua Green. *Spreadable Media: Creating Value and Meaning in a Networked Culture*. New York: New York University Press, 2013.

Jessiman, Stacey R. "The Repatriation of the G'psgolox Totem Pole: A Study of Its Context, Process and Outcome." *International Journal of Cultural Property* 18, no. 3 (August 2011), 365–91.

João Ferreira, Maria. "Chinese Textiles in Portuguese Sacred Interiors During Early Modern Age." In Sabine du Crest, ed., *Exogenèses: Objets Frontière dans l'Art Européen*. Paris: Boccard, 2018, 72–87.
Jofré, Carina. "Arqueología de Contrato, Megaminería y Patrimonialización en Argentina." In Cristóbal Gnecco and Adriana Dias, eds., *Crítica de la Razón Arqueológica: Arqueología de Contrato y Capitalismo*. Bogotá: Instituto Colombiano de Antropología e Historia, 2017, 123–41.
"Una Mirada Crítica de los Contextos de Patrimonialización en el Contexto Megaminero." In Roberto Pellini, ed., *Arqueología Comercial: Dinero, Alienación y Anestesia*. Madrid: JAS Arqueología, 2017, 143–75.
Johnson, Amandus, ed. *The Instruction for Johan Printz, Governor of New Sweden*. Philadelphia: The Swedish Colonial Society, 1930.
Johnson, Vivian. "Especially Good Aboriginal Art." *Third Text* 56 (2001), 33–50.
Jones, David M. *The Everyday Life of the Ancient Incas: Art, Architecture, Religion, Everyday Life, Culture*. London: Hermes House, 2010.
Jones, Owen. *The Grammar of Ornament: Illustrated by Examples from Various Styles of Ornament*. London: Day and Son, 1856.
Jones, Siân. "Negotiating Authentic Objects and Authentic Selves: Beyond the Deconstruction of Authenticity." *Journal of Material Culture* 15, no. 2 (2010), 181–203.
Juneja, Monica, and Anna Grasskamp. "EurAsian Matters: An Introduction." In Anna Grasskamp and Monica Juneja, eds., *EurAsian Matters: China, Europe, and the Transcultural Object, 1600–1800*. Cham: Springer, 2018, 3–33.
Jungblut, Marie-Paule, and Rosmarie Beier-DeHaan, eds. *Museums and Faith*. Luxembourg: ICOM and Musee d'Historie de la Ville de Luxembourg, 2010.
Kachun, Mitchell. *Festivals of Freedom: Memory and Meaning in African American Emancipation Celebrations, 1808–1915*. Amherst: University of Massachusetts Press, 2003.
Kahan, Dan M., Hank Jenkins-Smith, and Donald Braman. "Cultural Cognition of Scientific Consensus." *Journal of Risk Research*, 14 (2011), 147–74.
Kalff, F. E., M. P. Rebergen, E. Fahrenfort, J. Girovsky, R. Toskovic, J. L. Lado, J. Fernández-Rossier, and A. F. Otte. "A Kilobyte Rewritable Atomic Memory." *Nature Nanotechnology* 11, no. 11 (2016), 926–9.
Kansteiner, Wulf. "Finding Meaning in Memory: A Methodological Critique of Collective Memory Studies." *History and Theory* 41 (May 2002), 179–97.
Kant, Immanuel. *Anthropology from a Pragmatic Point of View*. Robert B. Louden, ed. Cambridge: Cambridge University Press, 2006 [1798].
The Critique of Judgement. Nicholas Walker, ed., and James Creed Meredith, trans. Revised ed. Oxford: Oxford University Press, 2007 [1790].

Kantor, Tadeusz. "Klisze przyszłości," *Metamorfozy. Teksty o latach 1934–1974,* w *Pisma* vol. 1, Krzysztof Pleśniarowicz, ed. Warsaw and Krakov: Księgarnia Akademicka, 2005.

Kanzenbach, Annette, and Daniel Suebsman, eds. *Made in China: Porzellan und Teekultur im Nordwesten im 18. Jahrhundert. Ein Kapitel Handelsgeschichte.* Emden: Isensee, 2015.

Kaplan, Andreas, and Michael Haenlein. "Users of the World, Unite! The Challenges and Opportunities of Social Media." *Business Horizons* 53 (2010), 59–68.

Karlsson, Håkan. "Review of Maritime Heritage in Crisis: Indigenous Landscapes and Global Ecological Breakdown." *Norwegian Archaeological Review* 50 (2017), 174–76.

Karp, Ivan, and Steven D. Lavine, eds. *Exhibiting Cultures: The Poetics and Politics of Museum Display.* Washington, DC: Smithsonian Institution Press, 1991.

Kasser, Tim. "Materialistic Values and Goals." *Annual Review of Psychology,* 67 (2016), 489–51.

Kaufman, Ned. "Resistance to Research: Diagnosis and Treatment of a Disciplinary Ailment." In Jeremy C. Wells and Barry L. Stiefel, eds., *Human-Centered Built Environment Heritage Preservation: Theory and Evidence-Based Practice.* London: Routledge, 2019, 309–16.

"The Social Sciences: What Role in Conservation?" In Angela M. Labrador and Niel Asher Silberman, eds., *The Oxford Handbook of Public Heritage Theory and Practice.* Oxford: Oxford University Press, 2018, 281–94.

Kaufmann, Thomas DaCosta. "Scratching the Surface: On the Impact of the Dutch on Artistic and Material Culture in Taiwan and China." In Michael North and Thomas DaCosta Kaufman, eds., *Mediating Netherlandish Art and Material Culture in Asia, Amsterdam Studies in the Dutch Golden Age.* Amsterdam: Amsterdam University Press, 2014, 205–38.

Kaul, Adam. "The Village That Wasn't There: Appropriation, Domination and Resistance." In Veronica Strang and Mark Busse, eds., *Ownership and Appropriation,* ASA Monograph, 239–60. Oxford and New York: Berg, 2010.

Kay, Edwina. "Containment of 'Wayward' Females: The Buildings of Abbotsford Convent, Victoria." *Archaeology in Oceania* 50, no. 3 (2015), 153–61.

Keating, Jessica. *Animating Empire: Automata, the Holy Roman Empire, and the Early Modern World.* University Park: Penn State University Press, 2018.

Keller Charles M., and Janet Dixon Keller. *Cognition and Tool Use: The Blacksmith at Work.* Cambridge: Cambridge University Press, 1996.

Kensinger, Kenneth M. "Feathers Make Us Beautiful: The Meaning of Cashinahua Feather Headdresses." In Ruben E. Reina and Kenneth M. Kensinger, eds., *The Gift of Birds: Featherwork of Native South American Peoples.* Philadelphia: The University Museum of Archaeology and Anthropology, 1991, 40–49.

Khosravani, Andrew. *The Story of Zero – Getting Something from Nothing.* Royal Institution, animater; Andrew Khosravani, director, illustrator, animator; Ed Proser, writer, sound designer and producer; Hannah Fry, narrator; Music: Kevin Macleod, music composer. 2016. https://vimeo.com/161757232.

Kidd, Jenny and Joanne Sayner. "Intersections of Silence and Empathy in Heritage Practice." *International Journal of Heritage Studies* 25 (2019), 1–4.

Kidron, Carol. "Breaching the Wall of Traumatic Silence: Holocaust Survivor and Descendant Person-Object Relations and the Material Transmission of the Genocidal Past." *Journal of Material Culture* 17 (2012), 3–21.

Kieschnick, John. "Material Culture." In John Corrigan, ed., *The Oxford Handbook of Religion and Emotion.* Oxford: Oxford University Press, September 2009. https://bit.ly/31Hz01G.

The Impact of Buddhism on Chinese Material Culture. Princeton: Princeton University Press, 2003.

Kimmelman, Michael. "A Heart of Darkness in the City of Light." *New York Times*, July 2, 2006.

King, Anthony D. "The Politics of Vision." In Paul Groth and Todd Bressi, eds., *Understanding Ordinary Landscapes.* New Haven: Yale University Press, 1997, 134–44.

King, Tom F. *Cultural Resource Laws and Practice.* Lanham: AltaMira Press, 1998.

Whitewashing the Destruction of Our Natural and Cultural Heritage, Walnut Creek: Left Coast Press, 2009.

Kirksey, Eben S., ed. *The Multispecies Salon.* Durham: Duke University Press, 2014.

Kirksey, Eben S., and Stefan Helmreich. "The Emergence of Multispecies Ethnography." *Cultural Anthropology* 25, no. 4 (2010), 545–76.

Kirschenbaum, Matthew. *Mechanisms: New Media and the Forensic Imagination.* Cambridge, MA: The MIT Press, 2008.

"Software, It's a Thing." (2014). https://bit.ly/3oyVxqp.

Kleutghen, Kristina. *Imperial Illusions: Crossing Pictorial Boundaries in the Qing Palaces.* Seattle and London: University of Washington Press, 2015.

Knappett, Carl. "The Affordances of Things: A Post Gibsonian Perspective on the Relationality of Mind and Matter." In Elizabeth DeMarrais, Chris Gosden, and A. Colin Renfrew, eds., *Rethinking Materiality: The Engagement of Mind with the Material World.* Cambridge, UK: McDonald Institute for Archaeological Research, 2004, 43–51.

Kniffen, Fred B. "Folk Housing: Key to Diffusion." *Annals of the Association of American Geographers* 55, no. 4 (December 1965), 549–77.

"Louisiana House Types." *Annals of the Association of American Geographers* 26, no. 4 (December 1936), 179–93.

Knight, Kim A. Brillante. "Wearable Interfaces, Networked Bodies, and Feminist Interfaces." In Jentery Sayers, ed., *The Routledge Companion* to *Media Studies and Digital Humanities*. London: Routledge, 2018, 204–13.

Knott, Kim. "Religion, Space, and Place: The Spatial Turn in Research and Religion." *Religion and Society: Advances in Research* 1 (2010), 29–43.

Koerner, Joseph. *The Reformation of the Image*. London: Reaktion, 2004.

Kolowich, Lindsay. "The Engagement Ring Story: How De Beers Created a Multi-Billion Dollar Industry from the Ground Up." https://bit.ly/3nEz7Dy.

Kopplin, Monika. "Chrysanthemen am Ostzaun und Andere Ostasiatische Motive in der Dresdner Lackmalerei." *Jahrbuch der Staatlichen Kunstsammlungen Dresden* 28 (2000), 47–55.

"Sakesen Gongting Qijiang. Madung Shunier Yu Dongya De Genyuan [Laquer Production at the Court of Saxony: Martins Schnell and his East Asian Sources]." *Gugong Wenwu Yuekan* 320 (2009), 90–105.

Schwartz Porcelain: Die Leidenschaft für Lack und ihre Wirkung auf das europäische Porzellan. Munster: Museum für Lackkunst, 2003.

Kopplin, Monika, and Gisela Haase, eds., *"Sächßisch Lacquirte Sachen": Lackkunst in Dresden unter August dem Starken*. Munster: Museum für Lackkunst, 1998.

Kopytoff, Igor. "The Cultural Biography of Things: Commoditization as a Process." In Arjun Appadurai, ed., *The Social Life of Things: Commodities in Cultural Perspective*. Cambridge: Cambridge University Press, 1986, 64–91.

Koritz, Amy. "Dancing the Orient for England: Maud Allan's 'The Vision of Salome.'" *Theatre Journal* 46, no. 1 (March 1994), 63–78.

Kovacs, Alexandra (Sasha). "Beyond Shame and Blame in Pauline Johnson's Performance Histories." In Heather Davis-Fisch, ed., *Canadian Performance Histories and Historiographies*. Toronto: Playwrights Canada Press, 2017, 33–51.

Krämer, Sybille. *Medium, Messenger, Translation: An Approach to Media Philosophy*. Amsterdam: Amsterdam University Press, 2015.

Kremer, Brigitte. "Kunstfertigkeit und Glockenklang: Mechanische Uhren und Automaten für die Kaiser von China." In Renate Eikelmann, ed., *Die Wittelsbacher und das Reich der Mitte: 400 Jahre China und Bayern*. Munich: Hirmer, 2009, 130–39.

Kristeva, Julia. *Power of Horror: An Essay on Abjection*. New York: Columbia University Press, 1982.

Krueger, Alan B. "Inequality, Too Much of a Good Thing." In David Grusky and Szonja Szelénya, eds., *The Inequality Reader: Contemporary and Foundational Readings in Race, Class and Gender*. New York: Routledge, 2018, 25–35.

Kubler, George. *The Shape of Time*. New Haven: Yale University Press, 1962.

Küchler, Susanne. "Materials: The Story of Use." In Adam Drazin and Susanne Küchler, eds., *The Social Life of Materials*. London: Bloomsbury, 2015, 267–82.

"Threads of Thought: Reflections on Art and Agency." In Liana Chua and Mark Elliot, eds., *Distributed Objects: Meaning and Mattering after Alfred Gell*. Oxford: Berghahn, 2013, 25–38.

Küchler, Susanne, and Timothy Carroll. *A Return to the Object: Alfred Gell, Art, and Social Theory*. London: Routledge, 2021.

Kuglitsch, Linnea. "Materia Medica, Materia Moral: An Archaeology of Asylum Management and Moral Treatment in the United States, 1840–1914." Ph.D. dissertation. University of Manchester, 2019.

Labrador, Angela M., and Neil Asher Silberman, eds. *The Oxford Handbook of Public Heritage Theory and Practice*. Oxford: Oxford University Press, 2018.

Lacey, Pippa. "The Coral Network: The Trade of Red Coral to the Qing Imperial Court in the Eighteenth Century." In Anne Gerritsen and Giorgio Riello, eds., *The Global Lives of Things: The Material Culture of Connections in the Early Modern World*. London: Routledge, 2015, 81–102.

Lagerqvist, M. "Reverberations of a Crisis: The Practical and Ideological Reworkings of Irish State Heritage in Economic Crisis and Austerity." *Heritage & Society* 9, no. 1 (2016), 57–75.

Lakoff, George, and Mark Johnson. *Metaphors We Live By*. Chicago: University of Chicago Press, 1980.

Lamar, Cynthia Chavez. "Collaborative Exhibit Development at the Smithsonian's National Museum of the American Indian." In Amy Lonetree and Amanda J. Cobb, eds., *National Museum of the American Indian: Critical Conversations*. Lincoln: University of Nebraska Press, 2008, 144–64.

Lamb, Daniel S. *A History of the United States Army Medical Museum*. Washington, DC, 1917. https://bit.ly/3nir8fr.

Lane, Dorothy. "Effective Fancy Dresses." *Hearth and Home* 138 (1896), 274.

Langhout, Regina Day, Francine Rosselli, and Jonathan Feinstein. "Assessing Classism in Academic Settings." *The Review of Higher Education* 30, no. 2 (2007), 145–84.

Lansing, J. Stephen. *Priests and Programmers: Technologies of Power in the Engineered Landscape of Bali*. Princeton: Princeton University Press, 1991.

Larkin, Brian. "The Politics and Poetics of Infrastructure." *Annual Review of Anthropology* no. 42 (2013), 327–43.

Lata, Lutfun N. "Counter-space: A Study of the Spatial Politics of The Urban Poor in the Megacity of Dhaka." Ph.D. dissertation. Queensland: University of Queensland, 2018.

Lathrap, Donald W. "Jaws: The Control of Power in the Early Nuclear American Ceremonial Center." In Christopher B. Donnan, ed., *Early Ceremonial Architecture in the Andes*. Washington, DC: Dumbarton Oaks, 1985, 241–67.

Latour, Bruno. *Aramis, or the Love of Technology*. Cambridge, MA: Harvard University Press, 1996 [1991].
"Factures / fractures." *Res* 36 (1999), 21–31.
"From Realpolitik to DingPolitik." In Bruno Latour and Peter Weibel, eds., *Making Things Public: Atmospheres of Democracy*. Cambridge, MA: The MIT Press, 2005, 14–41.
On the Modern Cult of the Factish Gods. Catherine Porter and Heather MacLean, trans. Durham: Duke University Press, 2010.
Pandora's Hope: Essays on the Reality of Science Studies. Catherine Porter, trans. Cambridge, MA: Harvard University Press, 1999.
Reassembling the Social: An Introduction to Actor-Network-Theory. Oxford and New York: Oxford University Press, 2005.
"Technical does not Mean Material." *HAU: Journal of Ethnographic Theory* 4, no. 1(2014), 507–10.
"Technology is Society Made Durable." In John Law, ed., *A Sociology of Monsters? Essays on Power, Technology and Domination*. London: Routledge, 1991, 103–31.
"The Berlin Key or How to Do Words with Things." In Paul Graves-Brown, ed., *Matter, Materiality and Modern Culture*. London: Routledge, 2000, 10–21.
We Have Never Been Modern. Catherine Porter, trans. Cambridge, MA: Harvard University Press, 1993.
Latour, Bruno, Philippe Mauguin, and Genevieve Teil. "A Note on Socio-Technical Graphs." *Social Studies of Science*, no. 22 (1992), 33–58, 91–94.
Lau, Chrissy Yee. "Loving Luxury: The Cultural Economy of the Japanese American Home, 1920s." Ph.D. dissertation. University of California, Santa Barbara, 2013. https://bit.ly/31SfGiA.
Laughy, Michael H., Jr. "Confessions of a Punk Rock Archaeologist." In William Caraher et al., eds., *Punk Archaeology*. Grand Forks: University of North Dakota, 2014, 71–3.
Lave, Jean, and Etienne Wenger. *Situated Learning. Legitimate Peripheral Participation*. Cambridge: Cambridge University Press, 1991.
Law, John. *After Method: Mess in Social Research*. London: Routledge, 2004.
"Objects and Spaces." *Theory, Culture, and Society* 19 nos. 5–6 (2002), 91–105.
"Technology and Heterogeneous Engineering: The Case of Portuguese Expansion." In Wiebe E. Bijker, Thomas P. Hughes, and Trevor J. Pinch, eds., *The Social Construction of Technological Systems: New Directions in the Sociology and History of Technology*. Cambridge, MA: The MIT Press, 2012 [1987], 111–34.
Law, John, and John Hassard, eds. *Actor Network Theory and After*. Oxford: Blackwell, 1999.
Law, John, and Ruth Benschop. "Resisting Pictures: Representation, Distribution, and Ontological Politics." *The Sociological Review* 45, no. 1 (May 1998), 58–182.

Layton, Robert. "Structuralism and Semiotics." In Dan Hicks and Mary C. Beaudry, eds., *The Oxford Handbook of Material Culture Studies*. Oxford: Oxford University Press, 2010, 29–42.

Lazarus, Richard J. "Super Wicked Problems and Climate Change: Restraining the Present to Liberate the Future." *Cornell Law Review* 94 (2009), 1153–234.

Lea, Sian. "Five Ways Human Rights Help the Fight for Social Justice," Human Rights News, Views, News & Info. 2017. https://bit.ly/33PrKBW.

Leach, Sir Edmund. "Magical Hair." *Man* 88 (1958), 147–64.

Lechtman, Heather. "Pre-Columbian Surface Metallurgy." *Scientific American* 250, no. 6 (1984), 56–63.

Ledderose, Lothar. *Ten Thousand Things: Module and Mass Production in Chinese Art*. Princeton: Princeton University Press, 2000.

Lee, Everett. "A Theory of Migration." *Demography* 3, no. 1 (1966), 47–57.

Lee, Yen Nee. "The World Is Scrambling Now That China Is Refusing to Be a Trash Dumping Ground." CNBC (April 16, 2018). https://cnb.cx/3m7t2ij.

Leiss, William. *The Domination of Nature*. Montreal and Kingston: McGill-Queen's University Press, 1994. Originally published 1972 by George Braziller.

Lemonnier, Pierre. "A Propos de Bertrand Gille: La Notion de 'Système Technique.'" *L'Homme* 23, no. 2 (1983), 109–15.

Elements for an Anthropology of Technology. Ann Arbor: University of Michigan Press, 1992.

"L'étude des Systèmes Techniques: Une Urgence en Technologie Culturelle." *Techniques & Culture*, no. 54–55 (2010 [1976]), 46–67.

Mundane Objects: Materiality and Non-Verbal Communication. Walnut Creek, CA: Left Coast Press, 2012.

"The Study of Material Culture Today: Toward an Anthropology of Technical Systems." *Journal of Anthropological Archaeology* 5, no. 2 (1986), 147–86.

Lemonnier, Pierre, ed. *Technological Choices: Transformation in Material Culture since the Neolithic*. London and New York: Routledge, 1993.

Lennon, John, and Malcolm Foley. *Dark Tourism: The Attraction of Death and Disaster*. London: Thomson Learning, 2000.

Editorial: Heart of Darkness. *International Journal of Heritage Studies*. 2, no 4 (1996), 195–7.

Leone, Mark P. "Interpreting Ideology in Historical Archaeology: The William Paca Garden in Annapolis, Maryland." In Daniel Miller and Christopher Tilley, eds., *Ideology, Power and Prehistory*. Cambridge: Cambridge University Press, 1984, 25–36.

"The Role of Primitive Technology in Nineteenth-Century American Utopias." In Heather Lechtman and Robert Merrill, eds., *Material

Culture: Styles, Organization, and Dynamics of Technology. St. Paul: West Publishing Company, 1977, 87–107.

Leone, Mark P., Parker Potter, and Paul Shackel. "Toward a Critical Archaeology." *Current Anthropology* 28, no. 3 (1987), 283–302.

Leroi-Gourhan, André. *Évolution et Techniques I: L'Homme et la Matière*. Paris: Albin Michel, 1971 [1943].

— *Évolution et Techniques II: Milieu et Techniques*. Paris: Albin Michel, 1973 [1945].

— *Gesture and Speech*. Cambridge, MA and London: The MIT Press, 1993 [1964].

Lesko, Nancy. *Act Your Age! A Cultural Construction of Adolescence*. 2nd ed. London: Routledge, 2012.

Lesnick-Oberstein, Karín et al. (126 signatories). "Let UK Universities Do What They Do Best: Teaching and Research." *Guardian*, July 6, 2015. https://bit.ly/3nE5Toa.

Leurs, Koen. "Communication Rights from the Margins: Politicizing Young Refugees' Smartphone Pocket Archives." *The International Communication Gazette* 79 (2017), 674–98.

Levi, Primo. *The Complete Works of Primo Levi*. London: Penguin Classics, 2015.

Lévi-Strauss, Claude. *Structural Anthropology I*. New York: Basic Books, 1963 [1958].

— *The Savage Mind*. Chicago: University of Chicago Press, 1966.

Levitt, Peggy, and Nina Glick Schiller. "Conceptualizing Simultaneity: A Transnational Social Field Perspective on Society." *International Migration Review* 38, no. 3 (2004), 1002–39.

Levy, Steven. *Hackers*. Sebastopol, CA: O'Reilly Media, 2010.

Lezra, Jacques. "On the Nature of Marx's Things." In Jacques Lezra and Liza Blake, eds., *Lucretius and Modernity*. New York: Palgrave Macmillan, 2016, 125–43.

Lindauer, Owen. *Historical Archaeology of the United States Industrial Indian School at Phoenix: Investigations of a Turn of the Century Trash Dump*. Tempe: Arizona State University, Office of Cultural Resource Management, Dept. of Anthropology, 1996.

— "Individual Struggles and Institutional Goals: Small Voices from the Phoenix Indian School Track Site." In April Beisaw and James Gibb, eds., *The Archaeology of Institutional Life*. Tuscaloosa: University of Alabama Press, 2009, 86–104.

— *Not for School, but for Life: Lessons from the Historical Archaeology of the Phoenix Indian School*. Tempe: Arizona State University, Office of Cultural Resource Management, Dept. of Anthropology, 1997.

Lindorff, Joyce. "Missionaries, Keyboards and Musical Exchange in the Ming and Qing Courts." *Early Music* 32, no. 3 (2004), 405–14.

Link, Carol. "Japanese Cabinetmaking: A Dynamic System of Decisions and Interactions in a Technical Context." Ph.D. dissertation. Urbana-Champaign: University of Illinois, 1975.

Linn, John B., and William H. Eagle, eds. *Pennsylvania Archives*, 2 series, vol. 5. Harrisburg: Clarence M. Busch, 1896.

Linton, Ralph. *The Material Culture of the Marquesas Islands*. Honolulu: Memoirs of the Bishop Museum VIII, no 5, 1923.

Liu, Alan. "Imagining the New Media Encounter." In Susan Schreibman, Ray Siemens, and John Unsworth, eds., *Companion to Digital Literary Studies*, Blackwell, 2008. https://bit.ly/33OYMlZ.

Liu, Lihong. "Pyrotechnic Profusion: Fireworks, Spectacles, and Automata in Time." *Journal 18: A Journal of Eighteenth-Century Art and Culture* 3 (2017). www.journal18.org/1550.

"Vitreous Views: Materiality and Mediality of Glass in Qing China through a Transcultural Prism." *Getty Research Journal* 8, no. 8 (2016), 17–38.

Liu, Xinru. *Ancient India and Ancient China: Trade and Religious Exchanges, AD 1–600*. Delhi: Oxford University Press, 1988.

Lloyd, David. "Race Under Representation." *Oxford Literary Review* 13, no. 1/2 (1991), 62–94.

Lobel, Cindy. "The Institution of the Household: Domesticity and Consumption in Antebellum New York City." Paper presented at the American Studies Association Annual Meeting, Washington, DC 2014, 11–28. http://citation.allacademic.com/meta/p318141_index.html.

Löfgren, Orvar. "Containing the Past, the Present and the Future: Packing a Suitcase." *NU* 53, no. 1 (2016), 59–74.

Lofton, Kathryn. *Consuming Religion*. Chicago: University of Chicago Press, 2017.

Logan, William. "Globalizing Heritage: World Heritage as a Manifestation of Modernism and Challenges from the Periphery." In *Twentieth Century Heritage: Our Recent Cultural Legacy: Proceedings of the Australia ICOMOS National Conference 2001, 28 November–December1 2001*. University of Adelaide, Adelaide, SA, 2010, 51–7.

Logan, William, and Keir Reeves, eds. *Places of Pain and Shame: Dealing with "Difficult Heritage."* London: Routledge, 2008.

Lome, Jordan Kass. "The Creative Empowerment of Body Positivity in the Cosplay Community." *Transformative Works and Cultures* no. 22, (2016). http://dx.doi.org/10.3983/twc.2016.0712.

Lonetree, Amy. *Decolonizing Museums: Representing Native America in National and Tribal Museums*. Durham: University of North Carolina Press, 2012.

Longhurst, Peta. "Institutional Non-correspondence: Materiality and Ideology in the Mental Institutions of New South Wales." *Post-Medieval Archaeology* 49, no. 2 (2015), 220–37.

Loren, Diana D. "Bodily Protection: Dress, Health, and Anxiety in Colonial New England." In Jeffrey Fleischer and Neil Norman, eds., *The*

Archaeology of Anxiety: The Materiality of Anxiousness, Worry and Fear. New York: Springer, 2016, 141–56.

Loring Brace, Charles. *Race is a Four-Letter Word.* Oxford and New York: Oxford University Press, 2005.

Losche, Diane. "The Sepik Gaze: Iconographic Interpretation of Abelam Form." *Social Analysis* 38 (1995), 47–60.

Losson, Pierre. "The Inscription of Qhapaq Ñan on UNESCO's World Heritage List: A Comparative Perspective from the Daily Press in Six Latin American Countries." *International Journal of Heritage Studies* 23, no. 6 (2017), 521–37.

Low, Setha. *Behind the Gates: Life, Security, and the Pursuit of Happiness in Fortress America.* New York: Routledge, 2004.

"The Edge and the Center: Gated Communities and the Discourse of Urban Fear." *American Anthropologist* 103, no. 1 (2001), 45–59.

Lowe, Kelsey M., Noelene Cole, Heather Burke, Lee Anne Wallis, Bryce Barker and Elizabeth Hatte. "The Archaeological Signature of 'Ant Bed' Mound Floors in the Northern Tropics of Australia: Case Study on the Lower Laura (Boralga) Native Mounted Police Camp, Cape York Peninsula." *Journal of Archaeological Science: Reports* 19 (2018), 686–700.

Lowenthal, David. *The Heritage Crusade and the Spoils of History.* Washington, DC: Free Press, 1996.

The Past is a Foreign Country. Cambridge: Cambridge University Press, 1985.

Lozanovska, Mirjana. "Diaspora, Return and Migrant Architectures." *International Journal of Diversity in Organizations, Communities and Nations* 7, no. 2 (2007), 239–50.

Lucas, Gavin. "Archaeology and Contemporaneity." *Archaeological Dialogues* 22, no. 1 (2015), 1–15.

Lucic, Karen, and Bruce Bernstein. "In Pursuit of the Ceremonial: The Laboratory of Anthropology's 'Master Collection' of Zuni Pottery." *Journal of the Southwest* 50, no. 1 (2008), 1–102.

Lukács, György, "Narrate or Describe?" In Arthur Kahn, ed. and trans., *Writer and Critic and Other Essays.* London: Merlin Press, 1970.

Lumbreras, Luís G., C. González, and B. Lietaer. "Acerca de la Función del Sistema Hidráulico de Chavín," *Investigaciones de Campo No. 2.* Lima: Museo Nacional de Antropología y Arqueología, 1976.

Lunsingh Scheurleer, D. F. *Chinese Export Porcelain: Chine de Commande.* London: Faber and Faber, 1974.

Lydon, Jane. *Fantastic Dreaming: The Archaeology of an Aboriginal Mission.* Walnut Creek: AltaMira Press, 2009.

Lydon, Jane, and Uzma Z. Rizvi. "Introduction: Postcolonialism and Archaeology." In Jane Lydon and Uzma Z. Rizvi, eds., *Handbook of Postcolonial Archaeology*, World Archaeological Congress Research

Handbooks in Archaeology, Volume 3. Walnut Creek: Left Coast Press, 2010, 17–34.

Lyon, Margot L. "The Material Body, Social Process and Emotion: 'Techniques of the Body' Revisited." *Body & Society* 3, no. 1 (1997), 83–101.

Lyotard, Jean François, Keith Crome, and James Williams. *The Lyotard Reader and Guide*. Edinburgh: Edinburgh University Press, 2006.

Macdonald, Sharon. *Difficult Heritage: Negotiating the Nazi Past in Nuremburg and Beyond*. London: Routledge, 2010.

Macintyre, Stuart and Anna Clark. *The History Wars*. Carlton: Melbourne University Publishing, 2003.

MacKenzie, Donald. *Inventing Accuracy: A Historical Sociology of Ballistic Missile Guidance*. Cambridge, MA: The MIT Press, 1990.

MacLaurin, Ali, and Aoife Monks. *Costume: Readings in Theatre Practice*. Palgrave Macmillan, 2015.

MacLean, Paul D. "Triune Brain." In Louis N. Irwin, ed., *Comparative Neuroscience and Neurobiology: Readings from the Encyclopedia of Neuroscience*. Boston: Birkhäuser, 1988, 126–28. https://bit.ly/3nHAG3o.

Maddock Dillon, Elizabeth. *New World Drama: The Performative Commons in the Atlantic World, 1649–1849*. Durham: Duke University Press, 2014.

Magdoff, Fred, and John Bellamy Foster. *What Every Environmentalist Needs to Know about Capitalism*. New York: Monthly Review Press, 2011.

Magelssen, Scott. *Simming: Participatory Performance and the Making of Meaning*. Ann Arbor: University of Michigan Press, 2014.

Magritte, Rene. "The Treachery of Images." 1929. www.renemagritte.org/the-treachery-of-images.jsp.

Maike Hamann, Kevin Berry, Tomas Chaigneau, Tracie Curry, Robert Heilmayr, Patrik J. G. Henriksson, Jonas Hentati-Sundberg, Amir Jina, Emilie Lindkvist, Yolanda Lopez-Maldonado, Emmi Nieminen, Matías Piaggio, Jiangxiao Qiu, Juan C. Rocha, Caroline Schill, Alon Shepon, Andrew R. Tilman, Inge van den Bijgaart, and Tong Wu. "Inequality and the Biosphere." *Annual Review of Environment and Resource* 43 (2018), 61–83.

Malafouris, Lambros. *How Things Shape the Mind: A Theory of Material Engagement*. Cambridge, MA: The MIT Press, 2016.

Malinowski, Bronislaw. *Coral Gardens and their Magic: A Study of the Methods of Tilling the Soil and of Agricultural Rites in the Trobriand Islands*. New York: Dover Publication, 1978 [1935].

Magic, Science and Religion. New York: Doubleday, 1954.

Malpas, Jeff. "New Media, Cultural Heritage, and the Sense of Place: Mapping the Conceptual Ground." *International Journal of Heritage Studies* 14, no. 3 (May 2008), 197–209.

Malpass, Matt. *Critical Design in Context: History, Theory, and Practice*. London: Bloomsbury, 2017.

Mann, Steve. "Cyborg Seeks Community." *Technology Review* (May–June 1999), 36–42.

Manoff, Marlene. "The Materiality of Digital Collections: Theoretical and Historical Perspectives." *Portal: Libraries and the Academy* 6, no. 3 (2006), 311–25.

Manovich, Lev. *The Language of New Media*. Cambridge, MA: The MIT Press, 2001.

Manzini, Ezio. *Design, When Everybody Designs: An Introduction to Design for Social Innovation*. Cambridge, MA: The MIT Press, 2015.

Marchand, Trevor H. J. "Muscles, Morals and Mind: Craft Apprenticeship and the Formation of Person." *British Journal of Educational Studies* 56, no. 3 (2008), 245–71.

Marcoux, Jéan-Sebastian. "The Refurbishment of Memory." In Daniel Miller, ed., *Home Possessions: Material Culture Behind Closed Doors*. Oxford: Berg, 2001, 69–86.

Marcus, George E., and Michael M. J. Fischer. *Anthropology as Cultural Critique: An Experimental Moment in the Human Sciences*. 2nd ed. Chicago and London: The University of Chicago Press, 1999.

Marcuse, Herbert. *One-Dimensional Man*. Boston: Beacon Press, 1964.

Marsden, Jonathan. *Victoria & Albert: Art and Love*, London: Royal Collection Trust, 2010.

Marshall, Kate. "Thing Theory at Expanded Scale." In *Thing Theory in Literary Studies* (2018). https://stanford.io/3ECsTdh.

Martinón-Torres, Marcos. "Chaîne Opératoire: The Concept and Its Application Within the Study of Technology." *Gallaecia* no. 21 (2002), 29–43.

Marvin, Garry. "Research, Representations and Responsibilities: An Anthropologist in the Contested World of Foxhunting." In Sarah Pink, ed.,*Applications of Anthropology*. London and New York: Berghahn, 2006, 191–208.

Marwick, Alice. E. *Status Update: Celebrity, Publicity, and Branding in the Social Media Age*. New Haven: Yale University Press, 2013.

Marx, Karl, *Capital: A Critique of Political Economy*. Volume 1. London: Penguin, 1990 [1976].

Das Kapital. In Robert C. Tucker, ed., *The Marx-Engels Reader*. 2nd ed. New York: W. W. Norton, 1978.

Marx, Leo. *The Machine in the Garden: Technology and the Pastoral Ideal*. Oxford: Oxford University Press, 1964.

"'Technology': The Emergence of a Hazardous Concept." *Technology and Culture* 51, no. 3(2010 [1997], 561–677.

Marzoni, Andrew. "Academia is a Cult." *Washington Post*, November 1, 2018. https://wapo.st/3rq7XkQ.

Mascia-Lees, Frances. "Aesthetics: Aesthetic Embodiment and Commodity Capitalism." In Frances Mascia-Lees, ed., *A Companion to the Anthropology of the Body and Embodiment*. London: Wiley Blackwell, 2011, 3–23.

Mason, Randy. "Assessing Values in Conservation Planning: Methodological Issues and Choices." In Graham Fairclough, Rodney Harrison, John H. Jameson Jr, and John Schofield, eds., *The Heritage Reader*. London: Routledge, 2008, 99–125.

Matthewman, Steve. *Technology and Social Theory*. New York: Palgrave Macmillan, 2011.

Mauss, Marcel. *Manual of Ethnography*. New York and Oxford: Berghahn Books, 2007 [1967].

On Prayer. New York and Oxford: Durkheim Press/Berghahn Books, 2003 [1909].

"Techniques of the Body." *Economy and Society* 2, no. 1(1973 [1935]), 70–88.

Maxwell, Richard, and Toby Miller. *Greening the Media*. New York: Oxford University Press USA – OSO, 2012.

McAtackney, Laura. *An Archaeology of the Troubles: The Dark Heritage of Long Kesh/Maze*. Oxford: Oxford University Press, 2014.

"Materials and Memory: Archaeology and Heritage as Tools of Transitional Justice at a Former Magdalen Laundry," *Éire-Ireland* 55, nos. 1+2 (2020), 221–44.

McClellan, Jennifer. "Moana Actress Says It's OK for Kids to Dress Up as Her Disney Character for Halloween." *USA Today*, October 25, 2018 .

McCracken, Grant. "The Evocative Power of Things." *Culture and Consumption: New Approaches to the Symbolic Character of Consumer Good and Activities*. Bloomington: Indiana University Press 1988, 104–10.

McLuhan, Marshall. *Understanding Media: The Extension of Man*. Cambridge, MA: The MIT Press, 1995 [1964].

McConachie, Bruce. *Engaging the Audience: A Cognitive Approach to Spectating in the Theatre*. Palgrave Macmillan, 2008.

McCrave, Conor. "30 Cultural Practices Given Official State Recognition to 'Protect and Preserve' for Future Generations," Thejournal.ie. (July 18, 2019). https://bit.ly/3KiRoQm.

McDannell, Colleen. *Material Christianity: Religion and Popular Culture in America*. New Haven: Yale University Press, 1995.

McDonough, Jerome P., Robert Olendorf, Matthew Kirschenbaum, Kari Kraus, Doug Reside, Rachel Donahue, Andrew Phelps, Christopher Egert, Henry Lowood, and Susan Rojo. "Preserving Virtual Worlds Final Report." (2010). www.ideals.illinois.edu/handle/2142/17097.

McEvilley, Thomas. "Doctor, Lawyer, Indian Chief: 'Primitivism' in Twentieth-Century Art at the Museum of Modern Art in 1984." *ArtForum* 23 (November 1984), 54–61.

McLuhan, Marshall. *The Gutenberg Galaxy*. Reprint. Toronto: University of Toronto Press, 2011.

Understanding Media: The Extensions of Man. Cambridge, MA: The MIT Press, 1964/2004.

McMahon, Marci R. *Domestic Negotiations: Gender, Nation, and Self-Fashioning in United States Mexicana and Chicana Literature and Art*. New Brunswick: Rutgers University Press, 2013.

McMillan, Uri. "Objecthood, Avatars, and the Limits of the Human." *GLQ: A Journal of Lesbian and Gay Studies* 21, 2–3 (2015), 209–48.

Medhora, Shalaila. "Remote Communities are 'Lifestyle Choices', Says Tony Abbott," *Guardian*, March 10, 2015. https://bit.ly/31x3UtK.

Media Archaeology Lab. "What." (2018). https://mediaarchaeologylab.com/about/what/.

Medvetz, Thomas. "Bourdieu and the Sociology of Intellectual Life." In Thomas Medvetz and Jeffrey J. Sallaz, eds., *The Oxford Handbook of Pierre Bourdieu*. Oxford: Oxford University Press, 2018, 454–80.

Mehta, Raj, and Russell Belk. "Artifacts, Identity, and Transition: Favorite Possessions of Indians and Indian Immigrants to the United States." *Journal of Consumer Research* 17, no. 4 (1991), 398–411.

Meillassoux, Claude. *Anthropologie Economique des Gouro de Côte d'Ivoire: De l'Economie de Subsistance à l'Agriculture Commerciale*. The Hague: Mouton, 1964.

Meneley, Anne. "Consumerism." *Annual Review of Anthropology* 47 (2018), 117–32.

Mercier, Charles A. *The Attendant's Companion: A Manual of the Duties of Attendants in Lunatic Asylums*. London: J. and A. Churchill, 1898.

Merlan, Francesca. "Land, Language and Social Identity in Aboriginal Australia." *The Australian Journal of Anthropology* 13, no. 2 (1981), 133–48.

Merleau-Ponty, Maurice. *The Phenomenology of Perception*. London: Routledge, 2007 [1962].

Merriman, Peter, George Revill, Tim Cresswell, Hayden Lorimer, David Matless, Gillian Rose, and John Wylie. "Landscape, Mobility, Practice." *Social & Cultural Geography* 9, no. 2. (2008), 191–212.

Merry, Sally. "Spatial Governmentality and the New Urban Social Order: Controlling Gender Violence through Law." *American Anthropologist* 103, no. 1 (2008), 16–29.

Mesic, Julie. Migration memories. https://bit.ly/30vv58h.

Meskell, Lynn. "Negative Heritage and Past Mastering in Archaeology." *Anthropological Quarterly* 75, no. 3 (2002), 557–74.

"UNESCO's World Heritage Convention at 40: Challenging the Economic and Political Order of International Heritage Conservation." *Current Anthropology* 54, no. 4 (2013), 483–94.

Metz, Cade. "Google Reincarnates Dead Paper Mill as Data Center of Future." WIRED (January 26, 2012). www.wired.com/2012/01/google-finland/.

Meyer, Birgit, David Morgan, Crispin Paine, and S. Brent Plate. "Material Religion's First Decade." *Material Religion* 10, no. 1 (March 2014).

Meyer, Birgit, and Terje Stordalen, eds., *Figurations and Sensations of the Unseen in Judaism, Christianity, and Islam*. London: Bloomsbury Academic, 2019.

Michaels, Eric. *Bad Aboriginal Art: Tradition, Media, and Technological Horizons*. Minneapolis: University of Minnesota Press, 1993.

Mihesuah, Devon A. *Repatriation Reader: Who Owns American Indian Remains?* Lincoln: University of Nebraska Press, 2000.

Miho, Olia. "Concrete Cathedrals: Reinterpreting, Reoccupying, and Representing the Albanian Bunkers." Electronic Thesis or Dissertation. University of Cincinnati, 2012. https://etd.ohiolink.edu/.

Miklós, Attila. "Environmental Attitudes and Ecological Anthropocentrism: A New Challenge in Environmental Higher Education." *Ethics* 1 (2014), 28–40.

Miller, Daniel. *A Theory of Shopping*. Cambridge and Oxford: Polity Press, 1998.

Acknowledging Consumption: A Review of New Studies. New York: Routledge, 1995.

"Consumption." In Chris Tilley, Webb Keane, Susanne Küchler, Mike Rowlands, and Patricia Spyer, eds., *Handbook of Material Culture*. London: Sage, 2006, 341–54.

"Designing Ourselves" In A. Clarke, ed., *Design Anthropology*. New York: Springer, 2010, 88–99.

"Materiality: An Introduction." In Daniel Miller, ed., *Materiality*. Durham: Duke University Press: 2005.

Material Culture and Mass Consumption. New York: B. Blackwell, 1987.

"Migration, Material Culture and Tragedy: Four Moments in Caribbean Migration." *Mobilities* 3, no. 3 (2008), 397–413.

"Social Networking Sites." In Hans Horst and Daniel Miller, eds., *Digital Anthropology*. Oxford: Berg, 2012, 156–61.

Stuff. Cambridge and Oxford: Polity Press, 2009.

The Comfort of Things. Cambridge: Polity Press, 2008.

Miller, Daniel, ed., *Home Possessions*. Oxford: Berg, 2001.

Miller, Daniel, ed., *Materiality* Durham: Duke University Press, 2005.

Miller, Daniel, Elisabetta Costa, Nell Haynes, Tom McDonald, Razvan Nicolescu, Jolynna Sinanan, Juliano Spyer, and Shriram Venkatraman. *How the World Changed Social Media*. London: University College London Press, 2016.

Miller, Klancy. "Overlooked No More: Georgia Gilmore, Who Fed and Funded the Montgomery Bus Boycott." *New York Times* (July 31, 2019). https://nyti.ms/34YRfkR.

Miller, Phil. "No Resurrection for St Peter's: New Report Urges 'Curated Decay' for Modernist Masterpiece." *Herald* (June 28, 2019). https://bit.ly/3AhTP1c.

Mills, Amy. *Streets of Memory: Landscape, Tolerance, and National Identity in Istanbul*. Athens: University of Georgia Press, 2010.

Mills, Simon. "FCJ-127 Concrete Software: Simondon's Mechanology and the Techno-social." *The Fiberculture Journal* (2011). Open access. https://bit.ly/3ra4NTY.
Milton, Kay. *Loving Nature: Towards an Ecology of Emotion*. London and New York: Routledge, 2002.
Mitcham, Carl. *Thinking Through Technology: The Path between Engineering and Philosophy*, Chicago and London: The University of Chicago Press, 1994.
Mitcham, Carl, and Robert Mackey, eds., *Philosophy and Technology: Readings in the Philosophical Problems of Technology*. New York: Free Press, 1972.
Mitchell River Watershed Catchment Management Group. Overview. 2018. www.mitchell-river.com.au/.
Mitchell, W. J. T. "Imperial Landscape." In W. J. T Mitchell, ed., *Landscape and Power*. Chicago: University of Chicago Press, 1994, 5–34.
Mochizuki, Mia. "The Movable Center: The Netherlandish Map in Japan." In Michael North, ed., *Artistic and Cultural Exchanges between Europe and Asia, 1400–1900: Rethinking Markets, Workshops and Collections*. Farnham: Ashgate, 2010, 109–33.
  The Netherlandish Image after Iconoclasm, 1576–1672: Material Religion in the Dutch Golden Age. London and Burlington: Ashgate, 2008.
Mochizuki, Mia, and Claire Smith. *Global Social Archaeologies: Making a Difference in a World of Strangers*. London: Routledge, 2019.
Mochizuki, Mia, and Yoriko Kobayashi-Sato. "Perspective and Its Discontents or St. Lucy's Eyes." In Dana Leibsohn and Jeanette Favrot Peterson, eds., *Seeing Across Cultures in the Early Modern Period*. Farnham: Ashgate, 2012, 21–48.
Moghaddam, Fathali M. *The Specialized Society: The Plight of the Individual in an Age of Individualism*. Westport: Praeger, 1997.
Mohan, Urmila, and Laurence Douny, eds., *The Material Subject: Rethinking Bodies and Objects in Motion*. London: Bloomsbury, 2020.
Moore, Emily. "Propatriation: Possibilities for Art After NAGPRA." *Museum Anthropology* 33, no. 2 (Fall 2010), 125–36.
Moore, Henrietta. *A Passion for Difference: Essays in Anthropology and Gender*. Cambridge: Polity Press, 1994.
  "In the Face of Climate Change, Ranking States by Prosperity Invites Disaster." *Guardian*, December 5, 2018. https://bit.ly/3GIhkms.
Morgan, David. *Protestants and Pictures: Religion, Visual Culture, and the Age of Mass Production*. Oxford: Oxford University Press, 1999.
  "Religion and Embodiment in the Study of Material Culture." *Oxford Research Encyclopedia of Religion*. March 2015. https://bit.ly/3oygLVn.
  The Embodied Eye: Religious Visual Culture and The Social Life of Seeing. Berkeley: University of California Press, 2012.
  Visual Piety: A History and Theory of Popular Religious Images. Berkeley: University of California Press, 1999.
Morgan, David, ed.*Icons of American Protestantism: The Art of Warner Sallman*. New Haven: Yale University Press, 1996.

Morgan, David, ed. *Religion and Material Culture: The Matter of Belief*. London: Routledge, 2010.

Morgan, David, and Sally M. Promey, eds. *The Visual Cultures of American Religions*. Berkeley: University of California Press, 2001.

Morgan, Lewis H. *Ancient Society*. Tucson: University of Arizona Press, 1985 [1877].

Mosko, Mark S., and Fred H. Damon, eds., *On the Order of Chaos: Social Anthropology and the Science of Chaos*. New York & Oxford: Berghahn Books, 2005.

Morphy, Frances. "Invisible to the State: Kinship and the Yolngu Moral Order." Conference Paper, *Negotiating the Sacred V: Governing the Family*, Monash University, 14-August 15, 2008.

The Macquarie Atlas of Aboriginal Australia. Canberra: Australian National University, 2017.

Morphy, Howard. *Ancestral Connections: Art and an Aboriginal System of Knowledge*. Chicago: University of Chicago Press, 1991.

"'Not Just Pretty Pictures': Relative Autonomy and the Articulations of Yolngu Art in its Context." In Veronica Strang and M. Busse, eds., *Ownership and Appropriation*, ASA Monograph.Oxford, New York: Berg, 2010, 261–87.

Morphy, Howard, and Frances Morphy. "Tasting the Waters: Discriminating Identities in the Waters of Blue Mud Bay." *Journal of Material Culture* 11, nos. 1/2 (2006), 67–85.

Morrison, Ann Katherine. "Canadian Art and Cultural Appropriation: Emily Carr and the 1927 Exhibition of Canadian West Coast Art." MA thesis. University of British Columbia, 1991.

Morrison, Michael, Darlene McNaughton, and Claire Keating. "'Their God is their Belly': Moravian Missionaries at the Weipa Mission (1898–1932), Cape York Peninsula." *Archaeology in Oceania* 50, no. 2 (2015), 85–104.

Morrissey, Kris, and Gretchen Sorin, eds., "What is Race?" *Museums and Social Issues* 2, no. 1 (Spring 2007).

Morton, Donald, ed., *The Material Queer: A LesBiGay Cultural Studies Reader*. Boulder: Westview Press, 1996.

Morton, John. "The Effectiveness of Totemism: Increase Rituals and Resource Control in Central Australia." *Man* 22 (1987), 453–74.

Morton, Timothy. *Ecology without Nature: Rethinking Environmental Aesthetics*. Cambridge, MA: Harvard University Press, 2007.

Hyperobjects. Minneapolis: University of Minnesota Press, 2013.

The Ecological Thought. Cambridge, MA: Harvard University Press, 2010.

Moseley, Michael E. *The Incas and their Ancestors*. London and New York: Thames and Hudson, 2001.

Mosko, Mark S., and Fred H. Damon, eds., *On the Order of Chaos: Social Anthropology and the Science of Chaos*. New York and Oxford: Berghahn Books, 2005.

Motz, Marilyn, and Pat Browne. *Middle-Class Women and Domestic Material Culture, 1840–1940*. Bowling Green: Bowling Green State University Popular Press, 1988.

Mullins, Paul R. "Race and the Genteel Consumer: Class and African-American Consumption, 1850–1930." *Historical Archaeology* 33, no. 1 (1999), 22–38.

Mullaly, Bob. *Challenging Oppression and Confronting Privilege*. Oxford: Oxford University Press, 2010.

Mullins, Matthew. *Postmodernism in Pieces: Materializing the Social in US Fiction*. New York: Oxford University Press, 2016.

Mumford, Lewis. *The Myth of the Machine*. 2 vols. San Diego: Harcourt, Brace, Jovanovich, 1967 and 1970.

Technics and Civilization. Chicago: University of Chicago Press, 2004 [1934].

Noble, David F. *America by Design: Science, Technology, and the Rise of Corporate Capitalism*. New York: Knopf, 1977.

Munn, Nancy. *Walbiri Iconography: Graphic Representation and Cultural Symbolism in Central Australian Society*. Ithaca: Cornell University Press, 1973.

Murphy, Sean V., and Anthony Atala. "3D Bioprinting of Tissues and Organs." *Nature Biotechnology* 32, no. 8 (2014), 773–85. https://doi.org/10.1038/nbt.2958.

Museum of Modern Art. "Met's Thingiverse Profile." www.thingiverse.com/met.

Myers, Fred. "Beyond the Intentional Fallacy: Art Criticism and the Ethnography of Aboriginal Acrylic Painting." *Visual Anthropology Review* 10, no. 1 (1994), 10–43.

Painting Culture. The Making of an Aboriginal High Art. Durham: Duke University Press, 2002.

Pintupi Country, Pintupi Self: Sentiment, Place and Politics among Western Desert Aborigines. Canberra, Washington and London: Smithsonian Institute and Australian Institute of Aboriginal Studies. 1986.

Nafte, Miriam. *Flesh and Bone: An Introduction to Forensic Anthropology*. Durham: Carolina Academic Press, 2016.

Nahon, Karine, and Jeff Hemsley. *Going Viral*. Cambridge: Polity Press, 2013.

Nara Document. "Nara Document on Authenticity," ICOMOS, 1994.

Narukawa, Hajime. A Wall Map made of AuthaGraph. size: W841 mm, H594 mm, color: full color and silver print, language: English and Japanese. http://narukawa-lab.jp/archives/authagraph-map/.

National Palace Museum, ed., *Story of a Brand Name: The Collection and Packaging Aesthetics of Emperor Qianlong in the Eighteenth Century*. Taipei: National Palace Museum, 2018.

Naum, Magdalena. "Migration, Identity and Material Culture: Hanseatic Translocality in Medieval Baltic Sea." In Hakon Glørstad, Lene Melheim, and Zanette Glørstad, eds., *Comparative Perspectives on Past Colonisation, Maritime Interaction and Cultural Integration*. London: Equinox, 2016, 129–48.

"Premodern Translocals: Hanseatic Merchant Diaspora between Kalmar and Northern German Towns (ca 1250–1500)." *International Journal for Historical Archaeology* 17, no. 2 (2013), 376–400.

"The Malady of Emigrants: Homesickness and Longing in the Colony of New Sweden." In Mary Beaudry and Travis Parno, eds., *Archaeologies of Movement*. New York: Springer, 2013, 165–77.

Neal, Lynn S. "The Ideal Democratic Apparel: T-shirts, Religious Intolerance, and the Clothing of Democracy." *Material Religion* 10, no. 2 (2014), 182–207.

Needham, Joseph, Wang Ling and Derek J. De Solla Price. *Heavenly Clockwork: The Great Astronomical Clocks of Medieval China*. Cambridge: Cambridge University Press, 1960.

Nelson, Louis P. *The Beauty of Holiness: Anglicanism and Architecture in Colonial South Carolina*. Chapel Hill: University of North Carolina Press, 2009.

Nelson, Louis P., ed. *American Sanctuary: Understanding Sacred Spaces*. Bloomington: Indiana University Press, 2006.

Nelson, Ted. "A File Structure for the Complex, the Changing, and the Indeterminate." In Noah Wardrip-Fruin and Nick Montfort, eds., *The New Media*. Cambridge, MA: The MIT Press, 1965/2003, 133–45.

Neumann, Eduardo. *Letra de Indios*. São Bernardo do Campo: Nhanduti, 2015.

Newey, Katherine. "Embodied History: Reflections on the Jane Scott Project." *Nineteenth Century Theatre and Film* 29 no. 2 (2002), 66–70.

Newman, Conor. "In the Way of Development: Tara, The M3 and the Celtic Tiger." In Rosie Meade and Fiona Dukelow, eds., *Defining Events: Power, Resistance and Identity in Twenty-first Century Ireland*. Manchester: Manchester University Press, 2015, 32–50.

Niles, Daniel. "Agricultural Heritage and Conservation." In Angela M. Labrador and Neil Asher Silberman, eds., *The Oxford Handbook of Public Heritage Theory and Practice*. Oxford: Oxford University Press, 2018, 339–54.

Nizima. "I am not a Balija." In Julie Mertus, Jasmina Tesanovic, Habiba Metikos, and Rada Boric, eds., *The Suitcase: Refugee Voices from Bosnia and Croatia*. Berkeley: University of California Press, 1997, 31–34.

Noël Hume, Ivor. *Here Lies Virginia: An Archaeologist's View of Colonial Life and History*. New York: Alfred A. Knopf, 1963.

"Public Hospital ER 2200 & ER 2299 Field Notes." Colonial Williamsburg Department of Architectural and Archaeological Research, Williamsburg, 1980.

The Virginia Adventure: Roanoke to Jamestown. Charlottesville: University of Virginia Press, 1994.

Noël Hume, Ivor, and Audrey Noël Hume. *The Archaeology of Martin's Hundred*. Philadelphia: University of Pennsylvania Museum of Archaeology and Anthropology, 2001.

Nora, Pierre. "Between Memory and History: Les Lieux de Mémoire." *Representations* 26 (1989), 7–24.
Norberg-Schulz, Christian. *Genius Loci: Towards a Phenomenology of Architecture.* New York: Rizzoli, 1980.
Norcia, Megan A. *X Marks the Spot: Women Writers Map the Empire for British Children, 1790–1895.* Athens: Ohio University Press, 2010.
Norman, Donald. *Design of Everyday Things.* Revised and expanded ed. New York: Basic Books, 2013.
   Emotional Design: Why We Love (Or Hate) Everyday Things. New York: Basic Books, 2004.
North, Michael, and Thomas DaCosta Kaufmann, eds. *Mediating Netherlandish Art and Material Culture in Asia.* Amsterdam: Amsterdam University Press, 2014.
Nuñez, César. *Macao's Church of Saint Paul, A Glimmer of the Baroque in China.* Hong Kong: Hong Kong University Press, 2009.
   Portrait of a Jesuit: Matteo Ricci. Macau: Macau Ricci Institute, 2010.
Nussbaum, Felicity. *Rival Queens: Actresses, Performance, and the Eighteenth-Century British Theatre.* Philadelphia: University of Pennsylvania Press, 2010.
Nyong'o, Tavia. "Racial Kitsch and Black Performance." *The Yale Journal of Criticism* 15, no. 2 (2002), 371–91.
O'Brien, Jodi. *Encyclopedia of Gender and Society.* London: Sage, 2009.
Odell, Dawn. "Delftware and the Domestication of Chinese Porcelain." In Anna Grasskamp and Monica Juneja, eds., *EurAsian Matters: China, Europe, and the Transcultural Object, 1600–1800.* Cham: Springer, 2018, 175–202.
Office for National Statistics, UK. 2018. www.ons.gov.uk/.
Ohi, Kevin. *Dead Letters Sent: Queer Literary Transmission.* Online. Minneapolis: University of Minnesota Press, 2015.
Oldenziel, Ruth. *Making Technology Masculine: Men, Women, and Modern Machines in America, 1870–1945.* Amsterdam: Amsterdam University Press, 1999.
Oleksy, Victoria. "Conformity and Resistance in the Victorian Penal System: Archaeological Investigations at Parliament House, Edinburgh." *Post-Medieval Archaeology* 42, no. 2 (2008), 276–303.
Olesiuk, Danuta. "Obuwie więźniarskie w zbiorach Państwowego Muzeum w Majdanku." *Zeszyty Majdanka* XXIV (2008), 235–62.
Olivier, Laurent. *The Dark Abyss of Time: Archaeology and Memory.* New York: AltaMira Press, 2011.
Olsen, Bjørnar. *In Defense of Things: Archaeology and the Ontology of Objects.* Lanham: AltaMira Press, 2010.
Olsen, Bjørnar, and Þora Pétursdóttir. *Ruin Memories: Materialities, Aesthetics and the Archaeology of the Recent Past.* London: Routledge, 2014. https://doi.org/10.4324/9781315778211.

"Unruly Heritage: Tracing Legacies in the Anthropocene." *Arkæologisk Forum* 35 (2016), 38–45.

Olsen, Bjørnar, Michael Shanks, Timothy Webmoor, and Christopher Witmore. *Archaeology: The Discipline of Things.* Berkeley: University of California Press, 2012.

Opas, Minna, and Anna Haapalainen, eds. *Christianity and the Limits of Materiality.* Bloomsbury Academic, 2017.

Ornstein, Allan C. "Social Justice: History, Purpose and Meaning," *Society* 54, no. 6 (2017), 541–48.

Orser, Charles E. Jr., ed. *Encyclopedia of Historical Archaeology.* London: Routledge, 2002.

Orsi, Robert. *The Madonna of 115th Street: Faith and Community in Italian Harlem.* New Haven: Yale University Press, 1985.

OSWER US EPA. "Basic Information about Electronics Stewardship [Overviews and Factsheets]. (September 3, 2015). https://bit.ly/3InW45T.

Otten, Charlotte, ed. *Art and Aesthetics: Readings in Cross-cultural Aesthetics.* New York: Doubleday, 1971.

Owen, Barbara A. *In the Mix: Struggle and Survival in a Women's Prison.* Albany: State University of New York Press, 1998.

Oxford Living Dictionaries. "Social Exclusion." 2019. https://en.oxforddictionaries.com/definition/social_exclusion.

"Social Justice." 2019. https://en.oxforddictionaries.com/definition/social_justice.

Paine, Crispin. *Godly Things: Museums, Objects, and Religion.* Leicester: Leicester University Press, 2009.

Gods and Rollercoasters: Religion in Theme Parks Worldwide. London: Bloomsbury Academic: 2019.

Religious Objects in Museums: Private Lives and Public Duties. London: Bloomsbury Academic, 2012.

"Religious Theme Parks." *Material Religion* 12, no. 3 (2016), 402–3.

Palmer, Christine, and Mervyn Tano. "Mokomokai: Commercialization and Desacralization." Report for the International Institute of Indigenous Resource Management, 2004. https://bit.ly/3ovstyZ.

Papacharissi, Zizi. *A Private Sphere: Democracy in a Digital Age.* Cambridge: Polity Press, 2010.

Parikka, Jussi. "Turf instead of Turf Wars." *Machinology* (August 30, 2012). https://bit.ly/3GJjDp7.

Parker, Laura and Kennedy Elliott. "Plastic Recycling Is Broken: Here's How to Fix It." National Geographic News (June 20, 2018). https://on.natgeo.com/3EDUkDU.

Parkin, David. "Mementoes as Transitional Objects in Human Displacement." *Journal of Material Culture* 4 (1991), 303–20.

Parkin, David, and Lionel Caplan, eds. *The Politics of Cultural Performance.* Providence: Berghahn Books, 1996.

Parrott, Fiona. "Materiality, Memories and Emotions: A View on Migration from a Street in South London." In Maruška Svašek, ed., *Moving Subjects, Moving Objects: Transnationalism, Cultural Production and Emotions*. New York: Berghahn, 2012, 41–54.

Paul, Christiane. ", Identity, and Collective Production." In Margot Lovejoy, Christiane Paul, and Victoria Vesna, eds., *Context Providers: Conditions of Meaning in Media Arts*. Bristol: Intellect, 2011, 103–21.

Peace, Robin. "Social Exclusion: A Concept in Need of a Definition?" *Social Policy Journal of New Zealand* 16 (2001), 17–36.

Peak Experience Lab. Blogpost, "Museums, Can We Stop Letting Objects Control the Narrative?" https://bit.ly/3FKdDeq.

Pearsall, Sarah. *Atlantic Families: Lives and Letters in the Later Eighteenth Century*. Oxford: Oxford University Press, 2008.

Pearson, Erika. "All the World Wide Web's a Stage: The Performance of Identity in Online Social Networks," *First Monday* 14, no. 3 (March 2, 2009). https://bit.ly/3IO48Om.

Pearson, Maria D. "Give Me Back My People's Bones: Repatriation and Reburial of American Indian Skeletal Remains in Iowa." *Journal of the Iowa Archeological Society* 52, no. 1 (2005), 7–12.

Pearson, Thomas. "A Daughter's Disability and a Father's Awakening," *Sapiens*, 2019. www.sapiens.org/culture/down-syndrome baby.

Pechurina, Anna. *Material Cultures, Migrations, and Identities: What the Eye Cannot See*. London: Palgrave Macmillan, 2015.

Peck, Amelia, ed. *Interwoven Globe: The World-wide Textile Trade, 1500–1800*. New York: Metropolitan Museum of Art, 2013.

Peers, Laura. *Playing Ourselves: Interpreting Native Histories at Historic Reconstructions*. Lanham: AltaMira Press, 2007.

Peirce, Charles Sanders. In Charles Hartshorne and Paul Weiss, eds., *Charles Peirce Sanders, Collected Papers*. Volume 1. Cambridge, MA: Harvard University Press, 1931.

Peluso, Nancy Lee, and Michael Watts, eds. *Violent Environments*. Ithaca: Cornell University Press, 2001.

Penfield, Wilder, and Edwin Boldrey. "Somatic Motor and Sensory Representation in the Cerebral Cortex of Man as Studied by Electrical Stimulation." *Brain* 60, no. 4 (December 1, 1937), 389–443. https://doi.org/10.1093/brain/60.4.389.

Perec, Georges. *Species of Spaces and Other Pieces*. John Sturrock, ed. and trans. London: Penguin Books, 1999.

Perez, Elizabeth. *Religion in the Kitchen: Cooking, Talking, and the Making of Black Atlantic Traditions*. New York: New York University Press, 2016.

Perry, Gill. *Spectacular Flirtations: Viewing the Actress in British Art and Theater, 1768–1820*. New Haven: Yale University Press, 2008.

Peter, Kadonde B. "Transnational Family Ties, Remittance Motives, and Social Death among Congolese Migrants: A Socio-Anthropological Analysis," *Journal of Comparative Family Studies* 41, no. 2 (2010), 225–43.

Peters, Benjamin. "Digital." In Benjamin Peters, ed., *Digital Keywords*. Princeton: Princeton University Press, 2016, 93–108.

Petersen, William. "A General Typology of Migration." *American Sociological Review* 23, no. 3 (1958), 256–66.

Pétursdóttir, Þóra. "Concrete Matters: Ruins of Modernity and the Things Called Heritage," *Journal of Social Archaeology* 13, no. 1 (2013), 31–53.

Pétursdóttir, Þóra, and Bjørnar Olsen. "Imaging Modern Decay: The Aesthetics of Ruin Photography." *Journal of Contemporary Archaeology* 1, no. 1 (2014), 7–56.

Petzold, Charles. *Code: The Hidden Language of Computer Hardware and Software*. Redmond: Microsoft Press, 2000.

Pew Research Center. "Social media fact sheet, February 5, 2018." www.pewinternet.org/fact-sheet/social-media/.

Pfaffenberger, Bryan. "Social Anthropology of Technology." *Annual Review of Anthropology*, no. 21 (1992), 491–516.

—— "Technological Drama." *Science, Technology and Human Values* 17, no. 3 (1992), 282–312.

—— "The Social Meaning of the Personal Computer: Or, Why the Personal Computer Revolution Was No Revolution." *Anthropological Quarterly* 6, no. 1 (1992), 39–47.

Phillips, Ruth. *Museum Pieces: Toward the Indigenization of Canadian Museums*. Montreal: McGill-Queen's University Press, 2011.

—— "Re-placing Objects: Historical Practices for the Second Museum Age." *Canadian Historical Review* 86, no. 1 (2005), 83–110.

—— *Trading Identities: The Souvenir in Native North American Art from the Northeast, 1700–1900*. Montreal: McGill's Queen's University Press, 1998.

Piddock, Susan. *A Space of Their Own: The Archaeology of Nineteenth-Century Lunatic Asylums in Britain, South Australia and Tasmania*. New York: Springer, 2007.

—— "To Each a Space: Class, Classification, and Gender in Colonial South Australian Institutions." *Historical Archaeology* 45, no. 3 (2011), 89–105.

Pierson, Stacey. "The Movement of Chinese Ceramics: Appropriation in Global History." *Journal of World History* 23, no. 1 (2012), 9–39.

Pietz, William. "How to Grow Oranges in Norway." In Patricia Spyer, ed., *Border Fetishisms: Material Objects in Unstable Spaces*, 245–51. New York: Routledge, 1998.

—— "The Problem of the Fetish, II." *Res* 13 (1987), 23–45.

—— "The Problem of the Fetish, IIIa." *Res* 16 (1988), 105–24.

Pinch, Trevor J., and Wiebe E. Bijker. "The Social Construction of Facts and Artifacts: Or How the Sociology of Science and the Sociology of Technology Might Benefit Each Other." In Wiebe E. Bijker, Thomas Hughes, and Trevor J. Pinch, eds., *The Social Construction of Technological Systems*. Cambridge, MA and London: The MIT Press 1987, 17–50.

Pincock, Christopher. *Mathematics and Scientific Representation.* Oxford: Oxford University Press, 2012.

Pinney, Christopher. "Creole Europe: The Reflection of a Reflection." *Journal of New Zealand Literature* 20 (2020), 125–60.

— *Photos of the Gods: The Printed Image and Political Struggle in India.* London: Reaktion Books, 2003.

— "Things Happen: Or, From Which Moment Does That Object Come?" In Daniel Miller, ed., *Materiality.* Durham: Duke University Press, 2005, 256–72.

Piore, Adam. "Friend for Life: Robots Can Already Vacuum Your House and Drive Your Car, Soon, They Will Be Your Companion." *Popular Science* 235, no 5. (2014), 38–44, 83.

Pirazzoli-t'Serstevens, Michele. *Le Yuanmingyuan: Jeux d'Eau et Palais Européens du XVIIIe Siecle a la Cour de Chine.* Paris: Editions Recherche sur les Civilisations, 1987.

Pistrick, Eckhard, and Florian Bachmeier. "Empty Migrant Rooms: An Anthropology of Absence through the Camera Lens." *Journal of Contemporary Archaeology* 3, no. 2 (2016), 205–15.

Pitrou, Perig. "Life as a Process of Making in the Mixe Highlands (Oaxaca, Mexico): Towards a 'General Pragmatics' of Life." *Journal of the Royal Anthropological Institute* 21, no. 1 (2015), 86–105.

Pitt-Rivers, Augustus Henry Lane Fox. *The Evolution of Culture and Other Essays.* Oxford: Clarendon Press, 1906.

Plant, Sadie. *Zeros + Ones.* London: Fourth Estate Limited, 1998.

Plate, S. Brent. *A History of Religion in 5½ Objects: Bringing the Spiritual to its Senses.* Boston: Beacon Press, 2014.

— *Key Terms in Material Religion.* London: Bloomsbury, 2015.

Platter, Thomas. *Beschreibung der Reisen durch Frankreich, Spanien, England und die Niederlande, 1595–1600.* Rut Keiser, ed., Basel and Stuttgart: Schwabe, 1968.

Plotz, John, *Portable Property: Victorian Culture on the Move.* Princeton: Princeton University Press, 2008.

Polanska, Dominika V. "The Emergence of Gated Communities in Post-Communist Urban Context: And the Reasons for Their Increasing Popularity." *Journal of Housing and the Built Environment* 25, no. 3 (2010), 295–312.

Politis, Gustavo. "Reflections on Contemporary Ethnoarchaeology." *Pyrenae* 46, no. 1 (2014), 41–83.

Pollard, Kellie. *Archaeology in the Long Grass: Aboriginal Fringe Camps in Darwin, Northern Territory, Australia.* Ph.D. dissertation. South Australia: Flinders University, 2019.

Pomerantz, Jeffrey. *Metadata.* Cambridge, MA: The MIT Press, 2015.

Pommeranz, Kenneth. *The Great Divergence: China, Europe, and the Making of the Modern World Economy.* Princeton: Princeton University Press, 2000.

Pope John Paul II. "Peace with God the Creator, Peace with All of Creation. Message of His Holiness Pope John Paul II for the Celebration of the World Day of Peace, 01 January 1990." https://bit.ly/3w7ZNQ7.

Portes, Alejandro, Luis E. Guarnizo, and Patricia Landolt. "The Study of Transnationalism: Pitfalls and Promise of an Emergent Research Field." *Ethnic and Racial Studies* 22 (1999), 217–37.

Posen, David. *Is Work Killing You? A Doctor's Prescription for Treating Workplace Stress*, Toronto: Anansi, 2013.

Price, David, and Alison Liebling. *The Prison Officer*. London: Prison Service, 2001.

Price, Sally. *Paris Primitive: Jacques Chirac's Museum on the Quai Branly*. Chicago: University of Chicago Press, 2007.

Primitive Art in Civilized Places. Chicago: University of Chicago Press, 1989.

Proctor, Robert. *Building the Modern Church: Roman Catholic Church Architecture in Britain, 1955 to 1975*. London: Routledge, 2014.

Promey, Sally M. *Spiritual Spectacles: Vision and Image in Mid Nineteenth-Century Shakerism*. Bloomington: Indiana University Press, 1993.

Promey, Sally M., ed. *Sensational Religion: Sensory Cultures in Material Practice*. New Haven: Yale University Press, 2014.

Prown, Jules David. "Mind in Matter: An Introduction to Material Culture Theory and Method." *Winterthur Portfolio* 17, no. 1 (1982), 1–19.

Public Religion Research Institute. "Race, Religion and Political Affiliation of Americans' Core Social Networks." https://bit.ly/3wxjwca.

Purkis, Johnathan, and James Bowen, eds. *Changing Anarchism: Anarchist Theory and Practice in a Global Age*. Manchester: Manchester University Press, 2004.

Pyburn, Anne. "Archaeology as Activism. In H. Silverman and D. Fairchild Ruggles, eds., *Cultural Heritage and Human Rights*. New York: Springer, 2007, 172–83.

Quilter, Jeffrey. *The Moche of Ancient Peru: Media and Messages*. Cambridge, MA: Peabody Museum Press, 2010.

Quinn, Frances, Jérémy Castéra and Pierre Clément. "Teachers' Conceptions of the Environment: Anthropocentrism, Non-Anthropocentrism, Anthropomorphism and the Place of Nature," *Environmental Education Research* 22 (2015), 893–917.

Rado, Mei. "Encountering Magnificence: European Silks at the Qing Court during the Eighteenth Century." In Petra ten-Doeschatte Chu and Ning Ding, eds., *Qing Encounters: Artistic Exchanges between China and the West*. Los Angeles: Getty Publications, 2015, 8–78.

Radstone, Susannah. "Memory Studies: For and Against." *Memory Studies* 1, no. 1 (2008), 31–39.

Rahman, Osmond, Liu Wing Sun, and Brittany Heim-man Cheung. "Cosplay: Imaginative Self and Performing Identity." *Fashion Theory: Journal of Dress, Body and Culture* 16, no. 33 (2012), 317–42.

Rajko, Jessica, Michael Krzyzaniak, Jacqueline Wernimont, Eileen Standley, and Stjepan Rajko. "Touching Data Through

Personal Devices: Engaging Somatic Practice and Haptic Design in Felt Experiences of Personal Data." *Proceedings of the 3rd International Symposium on Movement and Computing.* New York: ACM, 2016, 16:1–16:8.

Ralph, Jordan, and Claire Smith. "'We've Got Better Things to Do Than Worry About Whitefella Politics': Contemporary Indigenous Graffiti and Recent Government Interventions in Jawoyn Country." *Australian Archaeology* 78 (2014), 75–83.

Rao, Seema. Brilliant Ideas Studio, https://bit.ly/3c0JD1G.

Rappaport, Roy. *Pigs for the Ancestors: Ritual in the Ecology of a New Guinea People.* New Haven and London: Yale University Press, 1968.

Ritual and Religion in the Making of Humanity. Cambridge: Cambridge University Press, 1999.

Ravenstein, Ernst. "The Laws of Migration." *Journal of the Royal Statistical Society* 48, no. 2 (1885), 167–235.

"The Laws of Migration." *Journal of the Royal Statistical Society* 52, no. 2 (1889), 241–305.

Raveux, Olivier. "Du Corail de Méditerranée pour l'Asie : Les Ventes du Marchand Marseillais François Garnier à Smyrne vers 1680." In Xavier Daumalin, Daniel Faget, and Olivier Raveux, eds., *La Mer en Partage : Sociétés Littorales et Économies Maritimes (Xvi^e-Xix^e Siècle).* Aix-en-Provence: Presses universitaires de Provence, 2016, 343–59.

Rawls, John. *A Theory of Justice.* Revised ed. Cambridge, MA: Belknap Press, 2009.

Raymond, J. Scott, Warren R. DeBoer, and Peter G. Roe. *Cumancaya: A Peruvian Ceramic Tradition.* Calgary: University of Calgary, 1975.

Regan, Paulette. *Unsettling the Settler Within: Indian Residential Schools, Truth Telling and Reconciliation in Canada.* Vancouver: University of British Columbia Press, 2010.

Reichel-Dolmatoff, Gerardo. "Cosmology as Ecological Analysis: A View from the Rain Forest." *Man* 11 (1976), 307–18.

"Desana Animal Categories, Food Restrictions, and the Concept of Color Energies." *Journal of Latin American Lore* 4 (1978), 243–91.

Reinarz, Jonathan. *Past Scents: Historical Perspectives on Smell.* Studies in Sensory History. Urbana: University of Illinois Press, 2014.

Renfrew, Colin, and Iain Morley, eds. *Becoming Human: Innovation in Prehistoric Material and Spiritual Culture.* Cambridge: Cambridge University Press, 2009.

Revolon, Sandra. "Iridescence as Affordance: On Artefacts and Light Interference in the Renewal of Life Among the Owa (Eastern Solomon Islands)." *Oceania*, 88, no.1 (2018), 31–40.

Reynolds, Henry. *The Law of the Land.* London and New York: Penguin, 1987.

Richter, Amy. *At Home in Nineteenth-Century America: A Documentary History.* New York: New York University Press, 2015.

Rico, Trinidad. "Negative Heritage: The Place of Conflict in World Heritage." *Conservation and Management of Archaeological Sites* 10, no. 4 (2008), 344–52.

Rinehart, James W. *The Tyranny of Work: Alienation and the Labour Process.* New York: Harcourt Brace, 1996.

Ritzer, George. "The McDonaldization Thesis: is Expansion Inevitable?" *International Sociology* 11 (1996), 291–308.

The McDonaldization of Society: An Investigation into the Changing Character of American Life. Thousand Oaks and London: Pine Forge Press, 1993.

Robbins, Richard H. *Global Problems and the Culture of Capitalism.* 7th ed. New York: Pearson, 2018.

Roberts, Les, ed. *Mapping Cultures: Place, Practice, Performance.* London: Palgrave Macmillan, 2015.

Roberts, Catherine, and Philip R. Stone. "Dark Tourism and Dark Heritage: Emergent Themes, Issues and Consequences." In Ian Convery, Gerard Corsane, and Peter Davis, eds., *Displaced Heritage: Responses to Disaster, Trauma and Loss.* Woodbridge: Boydell Press, 2014, 9–18.

Robinson, Danielle. "Simpler Times? Exploring Heritage Weekends in Ontario." Playing with History: A Performance-Based Historiography Symposium, Toronto, October 12–13, 2018.

Rochovská, Alena, and Jurina Rusnáková. "Poverty, Segregation and Social Exclusion of Roma Communities in Slovakia." *Bulletin of Geography: Socio-Economic Series* 42 (2018), 195–210.

Rochovská, Alena, and Miriam Miláčková. "Gated Communities: A New Form of Residential Areas in a Post-Socialist City." *Geographia Cassoviensis* 6 (2012), 165–75.

Roe, Peter G. "A Grammatical Analysis of Cedrosan Saladoid Vessel Form Categories and Surface Decoration: Aesthetic and Technical Styles in Early Antillean Ceramics." In Peter E. Siegel, ed., *Early Ceramic Population Lifeways and Adaptive Strategies in the Caribbean.* Oxford: British Archaeological Reports International Series, 1989, 267–382.

"Art and Residence Among the Shipibo Indians of Peru: A Study in Microacculturation," *American Anthropologist* 82 (1980), 42–71.

Arts of the Amazon. Barbara Braun, ed. London and New York: Thames & Hudson, 1995.

"At Play in the Fields of Symmetry: Design Structure and Shamanic Therapy in the Upper Amazon." In Dorothy Washburn and Donald W. Crowe, eds., *Symmetry Comes of Age.* Seattle: University of Washington Press, 2004, 215–303.

"How to Build a Raptor: Why the Dumbarton Oaks 'Scaled Cayman' Callango Textile is Really a Jaguaroid Harpy Eagle." In William J. Conklin and Jeffrey Quilter, eds., *Chavín: Art, Architecture and Culture.* Los Angeles: University of California, 2008, 181–216.

"Mythic Substitution and the Stars: Aspects of Shipibo and Quechua Ethnoastronomy Compared." In Von del Chamberlain, John

B. Carlson and M. Jane Young, eds., *Songs from the Sky: Indigenous Astronomical and Cosmological Traditions of the World*. Washington, DC: Smithsonian Institution, 2005, 193–227.

"Of Rainbow Dragons and the Origins of Designs: The Waiwai *Urufiri* and the Shipibo Ronin *ëhua*," *Latin American Indian Literatures Journal* 5, no. 1 (1989), 1–67.

"Paragon or Peril? The Jaguar in Amazonian Indian Society." In Nicholas J. Saunders, ed., *Icons of Power: Feline Symbolism in the Americas*. London and New York: Routledge, 1998, 171–202.

"Rivers of Stone, Rivers Within Stone: Rock Art in Ancient Puerto Rico." In Peter E. Siegel, ed., *Ancient Borinquen: Archaeology and Ethnohistory of Native Puerto Rico*. Tuscaloosa: The University of Alabama Press, 2005, 285–336.

"Style, Society, Myth and Structure." In Christopher Carr and Jill E. Neitzel, eds., *Style, Society, and Person*. New York: Plenum Publishing Corporation, 1995, 27–76.

"The Ghost in the Machine: Symmetry and Representation in Ancient Antillean Art." In Dorothy Washburn, ed., *Embedded Symmetries: Natural and Cultural*. Albuquerque: University of New Mexico Press, 2004, 95–143.

"The Language of the Plumes: 'Implicit Mythology' in Shipibo, Cashinahua and Waiwai Feather Adornments." In Mary H. Preuss, ed., *L.A.I.L. Speaks! Selected Papers from the Seventh International Symposium, Albuquerque, 1989*. Culver City: Labyrinthos Press, 1990, 105–36.

"Walking Upside-Down and Backwards: Art and Religion in the Ancient Caribbean." In Timothy Insoll, ed., *Oxford Handbook of the Archaeology of Ritual and Religion*. Oxford: Oxford University Press, 2011, 518–39.

The Cosmic Zygote: Cosmology in the Amazon Basin. New Brunswick: Rutgers University Press, 1982.

Roe, Peter G., and Amy W. Roe. "Jungle Religion: Enduring Mythemes and Mythic Substitution in Amazonian and Andean Cosmology." In Lynea Sundstrom and Warren DeBoer, eds., *Enduring Motives: The Archaeology of Tradition and Religion in Native America*. Tuscaloosa: University of Alabama Press, 2012, 84–128.

Roe, Peter G., Juan González Colón, and Amy W. Roe. "To Feed the Dead: The Fine Ware from the Monserrate Site of San Lorenzo, Puerto Rico." *Proceedings of the 27th Congress of the International Association for Caribbean Archaeology*. St. Croix, USVI, 2019.

Roell, Craig. "The Piano in the American Home." In Jessica H. Foy and Karal Ann Marling, eds., *The Arts and the American Home 1890–1930*. Knoxville: University of Tennessee Press, 1994, 85–110.

Romańska, Magdalena. *The Post-traumatic Theatre of Grotowski and Kantor: History and the Holocaust in "Acropolis" and "The Dead Class."* Kathleen Cioffi, foreword. London: Anthem Press, 2014.

Romey, Kristin M. "Diving the Maya Underworld: An Adventure in the Sacrificial Sinkholes of the Yucatán Jungle," *Archaeology* 57, no 3. (2004), 16–23.

Rosales, Harmonia. "The Creation of God." Oil on Linen. 48"h x 60"w. B.I.T.C.H. Black Imaginary to Counter Hegemony: Art Series. (2017) https://bit.ly/32hk37o.

Rosenzweig, Roy. "Scarcity or Abundance? Preserving the Past in a Digital Era." *American Historical Review* 108, no. 3 (2003), 28.

Rothberg, Michael. *Multidirectional Memory: Remembering the Holocaust in the Age of Decolonialization*. Stanford: Stanford University Press, 2009.

Rothman, David J. *The Discovery of the Asylum*. Piscataway: Transaction Publishers, 1971.

Rothstein, Richard. *The Color of Law*. New York: Liveright, 2017.

Rotman, Deborah L. "Rural Education and Community Social Relations: Historical Archaeology of the Wea View Schoolhouse No. 8, Wabash Township, Tippecanoe County, Indiana." In April Beisaw and James Gibb, eds., *The Archaeology of Institutional Life*. Tuscaloosa: University of Alabama Press, 2009, 70–85.

Rowlands, Michael, and Jean-Pierre Warnier. "The Magical Production of Iron in the Cameroon Grassfield." In Thurstan Shaw, Paul Sinclair, Bassey Andah, and Alex Okpoko, eds., *The Archaeology of Africa: Food, Metals and Towns*. London: Routledge, One World Archaeology, 20 (1995), 512–50.

Roy Rosenzweig Center for History and New Media. "Histories of the National Mall." (2018). http://mallhistory.org/.

Royal Trust Collection, "Queen Victoria and Prince Albert at the Bal Costume of 12 May 1842." https://bit.ly/3Ks1ONO.

Różewicz, Tadeusz. "The Professor's Knife." In *Sobbing Superpower*, Joanna Trzeciak, trans.; Edward Hirsch, foreword. New York and London: W. W. Norton, 2011, 219–37.

Rubin, William. *Primitivism in Twentieth Century Art*. New York: Museum of Modern Art, 1984.

Rudolf, Karl. "Exotica bei Karl V., Philipp II. und in der Kunstkammer Rudolfs II." In Helmut Trnek and Sabine Haag, eds., *Exotica: Portugals Entdeckungen im Spiegel fürstlicher Kunst- und Wunderkammern der Renaissance, Jahrbuch des Kunsthistorischen Museums Wien 3*. Mainz: Philipp von Zabern, 2001, 173–203.

Rushing, W. Jackson. *Native American Art and the New York Avant-Garde: A History of Cultural Primitivism*. Austin: University of Texas, 1995.

Ruuska, Toni. "Reproduction of Capitalism in the 21st Century: Higher Education and Ecological Crisis." Ph.D. dissertation, School of Business, Aalto University, Helsinki, 2017.

Ryan-Saha, Eleanor. "Repossessions. Material Absences, Affective Presences, and the Life-Resumption Labors of Bosnians in Britain." *Social Analysis* 59, no. 1 (2015), 96–112.

Rydell, Robert. *All the World's a Fair: Visions of Empire at American International Expositions, 1876–1916*. Chicago: University of Chicago Press, 1984.

Saggs, H. W. F. *The Babylonians: A Survey of the Ancient Civilization of the Tigris-Euphrates Valley*. London: The Folio Society, 1988.

Said, Edward. *Orientalism*. London and Henley: Routledge, 1978.

Sana, Mariana, and Douglas S. Massey. "Household Composition, Family Migration, and Community Context: Migrant Remittances in Four Countries." *Social Science Quarterly* 86, no. 2 (2005), 509–28.

Sanchez Navarro de Pintado, Beatriz. *Marfiles Cristianos Del Oriente En México*. Mexico: Fomento Cultural Banamex, 1986.

Sandkühler, Hans-Georg. *Transculturality: Epistemology, Ethics, and Politics*. Frankfurt: Lang, 2004.

Sansi, Roger. *Art, Anthropology and the Gift*. London: Bloomsbury, 2014.

Sather-Wagstaff, Joy. *Heritage that Hurts: Tourists in Memoryscapes of September 11*. New York: Routledge, 2016.

Sautchuk, Carlos Emanuel. "The Pirarucu Net: Artifact, Animism and the Technical Object." *Journal of Material Culture* 24, no. 2, (2019), 176–93.

Savaş, Özlem. "Taste Diaspora: The Aesthetic and Material Practice of Belonging." *Journal of Material Culture* 19, no. 2 (2014), 185–208.

Sayeau, Michael. "Realism and the Novel." In Eric Bulson, ed., *The Cambridge Companion to the Novel*. New York: Cambridge University Press, 2018, 91–103.

Scandura, Jani. *Down in the Dumps: Place, Modernity, American Depression*. Durham: Duke University Press, 2008.

Scarry, Elaine. *The Body in Pain: Making and Unmaking the World*. Oxford: Oxford University Press, 1985.

Schaefer, Richard. ed. *Encyclopedia of Race, Ethnicity, and Society*. London: Sage, 2008.

Schaefer, Stacy B. "The Loom as a Sacred Power Object in Huichol Culture." In Richard L. Anderson and Karen L. Field, eds., *Art in Small-Scale Societies: A Contemporary Reader*. Englewood Cliffs: Prentice-Hall, 1993, 118–30.

Schaniel, William C. "New Technology and Cultural Change in Traditional Societies." *Journal of Economic Issues*, no. 22, 1988, 493–98.

Schatzberg, Eric. "Technik Comes to America: Changing Meanings of Technology before 1930." *Technology and Culture* 47, no. 3 (2006), 486–512.

Technology: Critical History of a Concept. Chicago and London: The University of Chicago Press, 2018.

Schechner, Richard and Willa Appel, eds. *By Means of Performance: Intercultural Studies of Theatre and Ritual*. New York: Cambridge University Press, 1991.

Schele, Linda, and David Freidel. *A Forest of Kings*. New York: Quill William Morrow, 1990.

Schellekens, Elisabeth. "Immanuel Kant (1724–1804)." In Alessandro Giovannelli, ed., *Aesthetics: The Key Thinkers*. New York: Continuum, 2012, 61–74.

Schiffer, Michael B., ed. *Anthropological Perspectives on Technology*. Albuquerque: University of New Mexico Press, 2001.

Schiller, Nina Glick, Linda Basch, and Cristina Blanc-Szanton, eds. *Towards a Transnational Perspective on Migration: Race, Class, Ethnicity, and Nationalism Reconsidered*. New York: New York Academy of Sciences, 1992.

Schlanger, Nathan. "The Chaîne Opératoire." In Colin Renfrew and Paul Bahn, eds., *Archaeology: The Key Concepts*. London and New York: Routledge, 2005, 25–31.

Schlereth, Thomas J. compiler and ed. *Material Culture Studies in America*. Nashville: American Association of State and Local History, 1982.

Schmidt, Conrad. *Workers of the World Relax: The Simple Economics of Less Industrial Work*. Vancouver: Conrad Schmidt, 2006.

Schmidt, Leigh Eric. *Consumer Rites: The Buying and Selling of American Holidays*. Princeton: Princeton University Press, 1997.

Schmitt, Thomas. "Jemaa al Fna Square in Marrakech: Changes to a Social Space and a UNESCO Masterpiece of the Oral and Intangible Heritage of Humanity as a Result of Global Influences." *The Arab World Geographer* 8, no. 4 (2005), 173–95.

Schneider, Andrea. *Die Handelsgeschichte der Seide: Historische und kulturgeschichtliche Aspekte*. Munich: GRIN Verlag, 2007.

Schneider, Arnd. "On 'Appropriation': A Critical Reappraisal of the Concept and Its Application in Global Art Practices." *Social Anthropology* 11, no. 2 (2003), 215–29.

Schneider, Rebecca. "New Materialisms and Performance Studies," *The Drama Review* 59, no. 4 (Winter 2015), 7–17.

Performing Remains: Art and War in Times of Theatrical Reenactment. New York: Routledge, 2011.

"That the Past May Have Yet Another Future: Gesture in the Times of Hands Up," *Theatre Journal* 70, no. 3 (2018), 285–306.

Schoch, Richard W. *Shakespeare's Victorian Stage: Performing History in the Theatre of Charles Kean*. Cambridge: Cambridge University Press, 1998.

Schweitzer, Marlis. "'Nothing but a String of Beads': Maud Allan's Salome Costume as a 'Choreographic Thing.'" In Marlis Schweitzer and Joanne Zerdy, eds., *Performing Objects and Theatrical Things*. Basingstoke: Palgrave Macmillan, 2014, 81–104.

Schweitzer, Marlis, and Joanne Zerdy, eds. *Performing Objects and Theatrical Things*. Basingstoke: Palgrave Macmillan, 2014.

Sciorra, Joseph. *Built with Faith: Italian American Imagination and Catholic Material Culture in New York City*. Knoxville: University of Tennessee Press, 2015.

Screech, Timon. *The Lens within the Heart: The Western Scientific Gaze and Popular Imagery in Later Edo Japan*. Richmond: Curzon, 2002.

Seal, Andrew. "How the University became Neoliberal." *Chronicle of Higher Education*, June 22, 2018. www.chronicle.com/article/How-the-University-Became/243622.

Sears, David. "Symbolic Racism." In Phyllis A. Katz and Dalmas A. Taylor, eds., *Eliminating Racism*, Perspectives in Social Psychology Series. Boston: Springer, 1988, 53–84.

Schüll, Natasha Dow. *Addiction by Design: Machine Gambling in Las Vegas*. Princeton and Oxford: Princeton University Press, 2012.

Segato, Rita L. *La Nación y sus Otros : Raza, Etnicidad y Diversidad Religiosa en Tiempos de Políticas de la Identidad*. Buenos Aires: Prometeo, 2007.

Seife, Charles. *Zero: The Biography of a Dangerous Idea*. New York: Penguin, 2000.

Seitsonen, Ouva I., Vesa-Pekka Herva, and Mika Kunnari. "Abandoned Refugee Vehicles 'In the Middle of Nowhere': Reflections on the Global Refugee Crisis from the Northern Margins of Europe." *Journal of Contemporary Archaeology* 3, no. 2 (2016), 244–60.

Sell, Mike. *Avant-garde Performance and Material Exchange: Vectors of the Radical*. New York: Palgrave Macmillan, 2011.

Semple, Janet. *Bentham's Prison: A Study of the Panopticon Penitentiary: A Study of the Panopticon Penitentiary*. Oxford: Clarendon Press, 1993.

Sen, Tansen. *Buddhism, Diplomacy and Trade: The Realignment of Sino-Indian Relations, 600–1400*. Honolulu: University of Hawai'i, 2003.

Senel, Aslihan. "Mapping as Performing Place." *disClosure: A Journal of Social Theory* 23, no. 8 (2014). https://bit.ly/3qIjKf8.

Seremetakis, Nadia. *The Last Word: Women, Death, and Divination in Inner Mani*. Chicago: University of Chicago Press, 1991.

Serres, Michel. *Biogea*. Randolph Burks, trans. Minneapolis: Univocal, 2012.

The Birth of Physics, Jack Hawkes, trans. Manchester: The Clinamen Press, 2000.

The Parasite. Lawrence R. Schehr, trans. [1982]. Minneapolis: University of Minnesota Press, 2007.

The Troubadour of Knowledge. Sheila Faria Glaser with William Paulson, trans. Ann Arbor: The University of Michigan Press, 1997.

Serres, Michel, with Bruno Latour. *Conversations on Science, Culture, and Time*. Roxanne Lapidus, trans. Ann Arbor: The University of Michigan Press, 1990.

Shallcross, Bożena. *The Holocaust Object in Polish and Polish-Jewish Culture*. Bloomington: Indiana University Press, 2011.

Sharf, Robert S. "Introduction: Prolegomenon to the Study of Japanese Buddhist Icons." In Robert Sharf and Elizabeth Horton Sharf, eds., *Living Images: Japanese Buddhist Icons in Context*. Stanford: Stanford University Press, 2001, 1–19.

Sharman, Russell. "The Anthropology of Aesthetics: A Cross-Cultural Approach." *Journal of the Anthropological Society of Oxford* 28, no. 2 (1997), 177–92.

Sharpe, Christina. *In the Wake: On Blackness and Being*. Durham: Duke University Press, 2016.

Shaw, Rosalind. "Provocation: Futurizing Memory," *Fieldsights*, September 5, 2013. https://culanth.org/fieldsights/provocation-futurizing-memory.

Sheets, Connor. "New Confederate Memorial Unveiled in Alabama," *AL.com*, August 27, 2017. https://bit.ly/2ZlUikI.

Shifman, Limor. "Meme." In Benjamin Peters, ed., *Digital Keywords*. Princeton: Princeton University Press, 2016, 197–205.

Shih, Ching-fei. *Riyue guanghua: Qinggong huafalang [Radiant Luminance: The Painted Enamelware of the Qing Imperial Court]*. Taipei: National Palace Museum, 2012.

——— "Shiba Shiji Dongxi Jiaoliu De Jianzheng: Qinggong Huafalang Zhizuo Zai Kangxi Chao De Jianli [Evidence of East-West Exchange in the Eighteenth Century: The Establishment of Painted Enamel Art at the Qing Court in the Reign of Emperor Kangxi]." *Gugong Xueshu Jikan* 24, no. 3 (2007), 45–95.

——— "The Wooden Hundred-layered Goblet from the Western Ocean." *Orientations* 48, no. 4 (2015), 60–64.

——— "'Xuanzi' ji 'Zhuanyi': Quanqiushi Shiye Xia De 'Xiyang' Duo Ceng Mu Tao Bei [Global Visual Studies Perspectives on Multi-Layered Wooden Cups from the "Western Ocean"]. *Yishuxue Yanjiu* 21 (2017), 1–76.

——— "Unknown Transcultural Objects: Turned Ivory Works by the European Rose Engine Lathe in the Eighteenth-Century Qing Court." In Anna Grasskamp and Monica Juneja, eds., *EurAsian Matters: China, Europe, and the Transcultural Object, 1600–1800*. Cham: Springer, 2018, 57–76.

——— "Xiangya Qiu Suojian Zhi Gongyi Jishu Jiaoliu-Guangdong, Qinggong Yu Shensheng Luoma Diguo [Concentric Ivory Spheres and the Exchange of Craft Techniques: Canton, the Q'ing Court and the Holy Roman Empire]." *Gugong Xueshu Jikan* 25, no. 2 (2007), 87–93.

Shove, Elizabeth, Matthew Watson, Martin Hand, and Jack Ingram. *The Design of Everyday Life: Cultures of Consumption Series*. London: Berg, 2007.

Shukla, Pravina. *Costume: Performing Identities through Dress*. Bloomington: Indiana University Press, 2015.

Siebenhüner, Kim. *Die Spur der Juwelen: Materielle Kultur und transnationale Verbindungen*. Vienna, Cologne, and Weimar: Böhlau, 2018.

Sigaut, François. "La formule de Mauss." *Techniques & Culture* 40 (2003), 153–68.

——— "More (and enough) on Technology!" *History and Technology*, no. 2 (1985), 115–32.

——— "Technology." In Tim Ingold, ed., *Companion Encyclopedia of Anthropology*. London: Routledge, 2002 [1994], 420–59.

Silliman, Stephen. "Archaeologies of Survivance and Residence: Reflections on the Historical Archaeology of Indigenous People." In Neal Ferris, Rodney Harrison, and Michael Wilcox, eds., *Rethinking Colonial Pasts through Archaeology*. Oxford: Oxford University Press, 2014.

Simmel, Georg. *Rembrandt: An Essay in the Philosophy of Art*. Alan Scott and Helmut Staubmann, trans. London: Routledge, 2005 [1916].

Simondon, Gilbert. *On the Mode of Existence of Technical Objects*. Minneapolis: Univocal Publishing, 2017 [1958].

Simonson, Mary. "'The Call of Salome': American Adaptations and Re-creations of the Female Body in the Early Twentieth Century" *Women and Music* 11 (2007), 1–16.

Simsek Caglar, Ayse. "A Table in Two Hands." In Deniz Kandiyoti, Ayşe Saktanber, and Sencer Ayata, eds., *Fragments of Culture: The Everyday of Modern Turkey*. London: Tauris, 2002, 294–307.

Sloane, Hans. "Hans Sloane Describes a 'China Cabinet'." In Susan Pearce and Ken Arnold, eds., *The Collector's Voice: Critical readings in the History of Collecting, Volume II: The Early Voices*. Farnham: Ashgate, 2001, 106–09.

Sloboda, Stacey. *Chinoiserie: Commerce and Critical Ornament in Eighteenth-Century Britain*. Manchester: Manchester University Press, 2014.

Slow Food. www.slowfood.com/about-us/slow-food-terminology.

Smentek, Kristel. "Chinoiseries for the Qing: A French Gift of Tapestries to the Qianlong Emperor." *Journal of Early Modern History* 20, no. 1 (2016), 87–109.

"Global Circulations, Local Transformations: Objects and Cultural Encounter in the Eighteenth Century." In Petra ten-Doeschatte Chu and Ning Ding, eds., *Qing Encounters: Artistic Exchanges between China and the West*. Los Angeles: Getty Publications, 2015, 43–57.

Rococo Exotic: French Mounted Porcelains and the Allure of the East. New York: Frick Collection, 2007.

Smith, Claire and Anna Glew. "How Ukraine's personal, grassroots memorials honour individual citizens who fought for their nation." *The Conversation*, 22 March 2022. https://theconversation.com/how-ukraines-personal-grassroots-memorials-honour-individual-citizens-who-fought-for-their-nation-178899.

Smith, Claire, and H. Martin Wobst. "The Next Step: An Archaeology for Social Justice." In Claire Smith and H. Martin Wobst, eds., *Indigenous Archaeologies: Decolonising Theory and Practice*. London: Routledge, 2005, 369–71.

Smith, Claire, Jordan Ralph, and Kellie Pollard. "The Markers of Everyday Racism in Australia." The Conversation (2017). https://bit.ly/3H0WJKG.

Smith, Claire, and H. Martin Wobst, eds. *Indigenous Archaeologies: Decolonising Theory and Practice*. London: Routledge, 2005.

Smith, Ian, and Jessie Garland. "Archaeology of St. Bathans Cottage Hospital, Central Otago, New Zealand." *Australasian Historical Archaeology* 30 (2012), 52–62.

Smith, Jonathan Z. *To Take Place: Toward Theory in Ritual*. Chicago: University of Chicago Press, 1987.

Smith, Laurajane. *Archaeological Theory and the Politics of Cultural Heritage*. London: Routledge, 2004.

—— *Uses of Heritage*. London: Routledge, 2006

Smith, Mark J. *Social Science in Question*. London: Sage, 1998.

Smith, Pam. "Frontier Conflict: Ways of Remembering Contested Landscapes." *Journal of Australian Studies* 31, no. 91 (2007), 9–23.

Smith, Pam, ed. *Entangled Itineraries: Materials, Practices, and Knowledge across Eurasia*. Pittsburgh: University of Pittsburgh Press, 2019.

Smithsonian Institution. "3d.Si.Edu." https://3d.si.edu/.

Smithsonian Museum of Natural History. "Skin and Bones: Mobile Augmented Reality App for NMNH's Hall of Bones." https://naturalhistory.si.edu/exhibits/bone-hall/.

Smyth, John. *The Toxic University: Zombie Leadership, Academic Rock Stars and Neoliberal Ideology*. London: Palgrave Macmillan, 2017.

Snow, Edgar. "Amerykanin i Anglik o Majdanku." *Rzeczpospolita, Amerykanin i Anglik o Majdanku* 27, 29 VIII (1944).

Society for Creative Anachronism. https://sca.org.

Soressi, Marie, and Jean-Michel Geneste. "The History and Efficacy of the Chaîne Opératoire Approach to Lithic Analysis: Studying Techniques to Reveal Past Societies in an Evolutionary Perspective." *PaleoAnthropology*, no. 63 (2011), 334–50.

Spallanzani, Marco. *Ceramiche alla Corte der Medici nel Cinquecento*. Modena: Franco Cosimo Panim, 1994.

—— *Ceramiche orientali a Firenze nel Rinascinto*. Florence: Chiari, 1978.

Spencer-Wood, Suzanne. "Feminist Theoretical Perspectives on the Archaeology of Poverty: Gendering Institutional Lifeways in the Northeastern United States from the Eighteenth Century through the Nineteenth Century," *Historical Archaeology* 44, no. 4 (2010), 110–35.

Spencer-Wood, Suzanne, and Sherene Baugher. "Introduction and Historical Context for the Archaeology of Institutions of Reform. Part I: Asylums." *International Journal of Historical Archaeology* 5, no. 1 (2001), 3–17.

—— "Introduction to the Historical Archaeology of Powered Cultural Landscapes," *International Journal of Historical Archaeology* 14, no. 4 (2010), 463–74.

Spring, Joel. *Global Impacts of the Western School Model: Corporatization, Alienation, Consumerism*. London: Routledge, 2019.

Spring, Joel, John Eric Frankson, Corie A. McCallum, and Diane Price Banks, eds., *The Business of Education: Networks of Power and Wealth in America*. London: Routledge, 2017.

Stahl, Ann. B. "Material Histories." In Dan Hicks and Mary Beaudry, eds., *Oxford Handbook of Material Culture Studies*. Oxford: Oxford University Press, 2010, 150–72.

Stallybrass, Peter. "Marx's Coat." In Patricia Spyer, ed., *Border Fetishisms: Material Objects in Unstable Spaces*. New York: Routledge, 1998, 183–207.

Standage, Tom. *The Victorian Internet*. New York: Walker Publishing Company, 1998.

Starosielski, Nicole. *The Undersea Network*. Durham: Duke University Press, 2015.

Starr, Fiona. "Convict Artifacts from the Civil Hospital Privy on Norfolk Island." *Australasian Historical Archaeology* 19 (2001), 39–47.

Stebbins Craig, Peter, and Kim-Eric Williams, eds., *Colonial Records of the Swedish Churches in Pennsylvania*. Volume 1. Philadelphia: Swedish Colonial Society, 2006.

Stiegler, Bernard. *Technics and Time, 1: The Fault of Epimetheus*. Stanford: Stanford University Press, 1998.

"Teleologics of the Snail: The Errant Self Wired to a WiMax Network." *Theory, Culture & Society* 26, nos. 2–3 (2009), 23–45.

Stewart, Julian. *Theory of Culture Change: The Methodology of Multilinear Evolution*. Urbana: University of Illinois Press, 1955.

Stewart, Susan. *On Longing: Narratives of the Miniature, the Gigantic, the Souvenir, the Collection*. Durham: Duke University Press, 1993.

Stiles, Emily. "Narrative, Object, Witness: The Story of the Holocaust as Told by the Imperial War Museum, London." Ph.D. dissertation. University of Winchester, 2016.

Stokoe, Elizabeth. "Public Intimacy in Neighbour Relationships and Complaints." *Sociology Online*, 11, no. 3 (2006). www.socresonline.org.uk/11/3/stokoe.html.

Stovel, Herb. "Origins and Influences of the Nara Document on Authenticity." *APT Bulletin* 39, no. 2/3 (2008), 9–17.

Strang, Veronica. "Familiar Forms: Homologues, Culture and Gender in Northern Australia." *Journal of the Royal Anthropological Society* 5, no. 1 (1999), 75–95.

Gardening the World: Agency, Identity, and the Ownership of Water. Oxford and New York: Berghahn Publishers, 2009.

"Of Human Bondage: The Breaking in of Stockmen in Northern Australia." *Oceania* 72 (2001), 53–78.

"Raising the Dead: Reflecting on Native Title Process." In S. Toussaint, ed., *Crossing Boundaries: Cultural, Legal, Historical and Practice Issues in Native Title*. Melbourne: Melbourne University Press, 2004, 9–23.

"The Strong Arm of the Law: Aboriginal Rangers and Anthropology." *Australian Archaeology* 47 (1998), 20–29.

Uncommon Ground: Cultural Landscapes and Environmental Values. Oxford, New York: Berg, 1997.

Strang, Veronica, and Mark Busse. "Introduction: Ownership and Appropriation." In Veronica Strang and Marke Busse, eds., *Ownership and Appropriation*, ASA Monograph 47. New York: Berg, 2011, 1–19.

Strang, Veronica, and Mark Busse, eds., *Ownership and Appropriation*. ASA Monographs 47. New York: Berg, 2011.

Strang, Veronica, Tim Edensor, and Joanna Puckering, eds. *From the Lighthouse: Interdisciplinary Reflections on Light*. London: Routledge, 2018.

Strasser, Susan. *Waste and Want: A Social History of Trash*. New York: Henry Holt, 1999.

Strathern, Marilyn. "Cutting the Network." *The Journal of the Royal Anthropological Institute* 2, no. 3 (1996), 517–35.

"Reflections." In Raminder Kaur and Parul Dave-Mukherji, eds., *Arts and Aesthetics in a Globalizing World*. London: Bloomsbury, 2014, 259–64.

"The Aesthetics of Substance." In *Property, Substance and Effect: Anthropological Essays on Persons and Things*. London: Athlone Press, 1999.

The Gender of the Gift: Problems with Women and Problems with Society in Melanesia. Berkeley: University of California Press, 1988.

Streeter, Thomas. "Internet." In Benjamin Peters, ed., *Digital Keywords*. Princeton: Princeton University Press, 2016, 184–96.

Stryker, Susan, and Stephen Whittle, eds. *The Transgender Studies Reader*. New York: Routledge, 2006.

Stumpe, Lynn Heidi. "Restitution or Repatriation? The Story of Some New Zealand Māori Human Remains." *Journal of Museum Ethnography* no. 17, Pacific Ethnography, Politics and Museums (2005), 130–40.

Sturtevant, William Curtis. "Does Anthropology need Museums?" *Proceedings of the Biology Society of Washington* 82 (1969), 22.

Sullivan, Lawrence, and Alison Edwards, eds. *Stewards of the Sacred*. Washington, DC: American Association of Museums, 2004.

Surface-Evans, Sarah L. "A Landscape of Assimilation and Resistance: The Mount Pleasant Indian Industrial Boarding School." *International Journal of Historical Archaeology* 20, no. 3 (2016), 574–88.

Sutton, John. *Philosophy and Memory Traces: Descartes to Connectionism*. Cambridge: Cambridge University Press, 1998.

Svašek, Maruška, ed. *Moving Subjects, Moving Objects: Transnationalism, Cultural Production and Emotions*. New York: Berghahn, 2012.

Taavitsainen, Jussi-Pekka. "Burial Archaeology and the Soviet Era." In Claire Smith, ed., *Encyclopedia of Global Archaeology*. New York: Springer, 2014, 1048–52.

Tallbear, Kim. "An Indigenous Reflection on Working Beyond the Human/Not Human." *GLQ: A Journal of Lesbian and Gay Studies* 21, no. 2–3 (June 2015), 230–35.

Tambiah, Stanley J. *Magic, Science, Religion, and the Scope of Rationality.* Cambridge: Cambridge University Press, 1990.

Tanner, Jeremy. "Portraits and Agency: A Comparative View." In Robin Osborne and Jeremy Tanner, eds., *Art's Agency and Art History.* Malden and Oxford: Blackwell, 2007, 70–94.

Tapscott, Don, and Anthony Williams. *Wikinomics: How Mass Collaboration Changes Everything.* New York: Portfolio, 2008.

Tapsell, Paul. "Ko Tawa: Where are the Glass Cabinets?" In Raymond A. Silverman, ed., *Museum as Process: Translating Local and Global Knowledges.* London and New York: Routledge, 2015.

Tarlow, Sarah. *The Archaeology of Improvement in Britain, 1750–1850.* Cambridge: Cambridge University Press, 2007.

Tate, Claudia. *Domestic Allegories of Political Desire: The Black Heroine's Text at the Turn of the Century.* New York: Oxford University Press, 1992.

Taussig, Michael. *My Cocaine Museum.* Chicago: University of Chicago Press, 2004.

The Nervous System. New York: Routledge, 1992.

Taylor, Paul, Linda Alcoff, and Luvell Anderson, eds. *The Routledge Companion to Philosophy of Race.* London: Routledge, 2017.

Tenen, Dennis. *Plain Text: The Poetics of Computation,* Stanford: Stanford University Press, 2017. www.sup.org/books/title/?id=26821.

The Merriam-Webster New Book of Word Histories. Springfield: Merriam-Webster, 1991.

Thomas, Greg. "Chinoiserie and Intercultural Dialogue at Brighton Pavilion." In Petra ten-Doeschatte Chu and Ning Ding, eds., *Qing Encounters: Artistic Exchanges between China and the West.* Los Angeles: Getty Publications, 2015, 232–47.

"Yuanming Yuan/Versailles: Intercultural Interactions between Chinese and European Palace Cultures." *Art History* 32 (2009), 115–43.

Thomas, Nicholas. *Entangled Objects: Exchange, Material Culture, and Colonialism in the Pacific.* Cambridge, MA: Harvard University Press, 1991.

Thompson, Andrea. "A Running List of Record-Breaking Natural Disasters in 2020." *Scientific American.* December 22, 2020. https://bit.ly/3IGvJB1.

Thorburn, Nicholas. "Communist Objects and the Values of Printed Matter." *Social Text* 103, 28, no. 2 (2010), 1–32.

Thrift, Nigel. *Non-representational Theory: Space, Politics, Affect.* International Library of Sociology. London and New York: Routledge, 2007.

Tickamyer, Julie. "Space Matters! Spatial Inequality in Future Sociology," *Contemporary Sociology* 29, no. 6 (2000), 805–13.

Tilley, Christopher, ed. *Reading Material Culture: Structuralism, Hermeneutics, and Post-structuralism.* Oxford: Basil Blackwell, 1990.

Tilley, Christopher, Webb Keane, Susanne Küchler, Michael Rowlands, and Patricia Spyer, eds., *Handbook of Material Culture*. London: Sage, 2006.

"Tiny House Movement." https://en.wikipedia.org/wiki/Tiny_house_movement.

Tobias, Ronald B. "Theodore Roosevelt's Last Hunt: How to Reconcile the President's Protection of Nature with His Seeming Desire to Destroy It?" *Natural History* 127, no. 3 (2019), 34–9.

Tóibín, Colm. *On Elizabeth Bishop*. Princeton: Princeton University Press, 2015.

Tolia-Kelly, Divya. "A Journey through the Material Geographies of Diaspora Cultures: Four Modes of Environmental Memory." In Kathy Burrell and Panakos Panayi, eds., *Histories and Memories: Migrants and their History in Britain*. London: I. B. Tauris, 2006, 149–70.

"Locating Processes of Identification: Studying the Precipitates of Re-memory through Artifacts in the British Asian Home." *Transactions of the Institute of British Geographers* 29 (2004), 314–29.

"(Postcolonial) Museum: Presencing the Affective Politics of 'Race' and Culture." *Sociology* 50, no. 5 (2016), 876–912.

Tomkins, Silvan. *Affect Imagery Consciousness: Vol. 1. The Positive Affects*. New York: Springer, 1962.

Affect Imagery Consciousness: Vol. 2. The Negative Affects. New York: Springer, 1963.

Affect Imagery Consciousness: Vol. 3. The Negative Affects: Anger and Fear. New York: Springer, 1991.

Townsend, Richard F., ed. *The Ancient Americas: Art from Sacred Landscapes*. Chicago and Munich: The Art Institute and Prestel-Verlag, 1992.

Townsend-Gault, Charlotte. "Circulating Aboriginality." *Journal of Material Culture* 9, no. 2 (2004), 183–202.

"Northwest Coast Art: The Culture of the Land Claims." *American Indian Quarterly* 18, no. 4 (1994), 445–67.

Trennart, Robert A. *The Phoenix Indian School: Forced Assimilation in Arizona, 1891–1935*. Norman: University of Oklahoma Press, 1988.

Trigger, David, and Gareth Griffiths, eds. *Disputed Territories: Land, Culture and Identity in Settler Societies*. Hong Kong: Hong Kong University Press, 2003.

Trope, Jack F., and Walter R. Echo-Hawk. "NAGPRA: Background and Legislative History." In Devon A. Mihesuah, ed., *Repatriation Reader: Who Owns American Indian Remains?* Lincoln: University of Nebraska Press, 2000.

Tsing, Anna. "Worlding the Matsutake Diaspora: Or, Can Actor–Network Theory Experiment with Holism?" In Ton Otto and Nils Bubandt, eds., *Experiments in Holism: Theory and Practice in Contemporary Anthropology*. Oxford: Wiley-Blackwell, 2010, 47–66.

Tuan, Yi Fu. *Place and Space: The Perspective of Experience*. Minneapolis: University of Minnesota Press, 1977.

Tunbridge, J. E. and G. F. Ashworth. *Dissonant Heritage: The Management of the Past as a Resource in Conflict*. Chichester: Wiley, 1996.

Turkle, Sherry. *Alone Together: Why We Expect More from Technology and Less from Each Other*. New York: Basic, 2001.

The Second Self: Computers and the Human Spirit. Cambridge, MA: The MIT Press, 1984/2005.

Turner, Victor. *From Ritual to Theatre: The Human Seriousness of Play*. New York: Performing Arts Journal Publications, 1982.

Tweed, Thomas A. *America's Church: The National Shrine and Catholic Presence in the Nation's Capital, 1917–1997*. Oxford: Oxford University Press, 2011.

Crossing and Dwelling: A Theory of Religion. Cambridge, MA: Harvard University Press, 2008.

Our Lady of the Exile: Diasporic Religion at a Cuban Catholic Shrine in Miami. Oxford: Oxford University Press, 1997.

Tweedie, Ann. *Drawing Back Culture: The Makah Struggle for Repatriation*. Seattle: University of Washington Press, 2002.

Tylor, Sir Edward Burnett. "Religion in Primitive Culture." *Primitive Culture Part II*,. New York: Harper & Row Publishers, 1958.

Tyrikos-Ergas, George. "Orange Life Jackets: Materiality and Narration in Lesvos, One Year after the Eruption of the 'Refugee Crisis.'" *Journal of Contemporary Archaeology* 3, no. 2 (2016), 227–32.

Tyson, Timothy. *Blood Done Sign My Name: A True Story*. New York: Crown Publishers, 2004.

Tythacott, Louise. *Surrealism and the Exotic*. London: Routledge, 2003.

Ucko, Peter. "Penis Sheaths: A Comparative Study." *Proceedings of the RAI*, no. 1969 (1969), 24–67.

Uitzinger, Ellen. "For the Man Who Has Everything: Western-Style Exotica in Birthday Celebrations at the Court of Ch'ien-lung." In Leonard Blusse and Erik Zürcher, eds., *Conflict and Accommodation in Early Modern East Asia*. Leiden: Brill, 1993, 216–39.

Ukrainian Independent Information Agency (UNIAN). "Heavenly Hundred Heroes Honored in Kyiv," February 19, 2018. https://bit.ly/2ZP7y19.

United Nations. Resolution adopted by the General Assembly on 26 November 2007. 62/10. World Day of Social Justice. http://undocs.org/A/RES/62/10.

World Day of Social Justice, February 20, 2019. www.un.org/en/events/socialjusticeday.

UNESCO. "About World Heritage/Ireland." https://whc.unesco.org/en/statesparties/ie.

"Convention for the Safeguarding of the Intangible Culture Heritage." 2003 (2018). https://ich.unesco.org/en/convention.

Guidelines for the Establishment of National "Living Human Treasures" Systems. Paris: UNESCO, n.d.

"The Hague Convention for the Protection of Cultural Heritage in the Event of Armed Conflict," 1954. https://bit.ly/3LREV6U.

"World Heritage." http://whc.unesco.org/en/about/.

United Daughters of the Confederacy. Granville Grays Chapter (Oxford, NC). *Cornerstone of Confederate Monument Laid*. Oxford, North Carolina: Orphanage Press, 1910. In the North Carolina Collection, Wilson Library, University of North Carolina at Chapel Hill.

United States Census Bureau. (2018). www.census.gov/.

Upton, Dell. *Holy Things and Profane: Anglican Parish Churches in Colonial Virginia*. Cambridge, MA: The MIT Press, 1986.

"Sound as Landscape." *Landscape Journal* 26 no. 1 (2007), 24–35.

Uzzell, David L. "The Hot Interpretation of War and Conflict." In David L. Uzzell, ed., *Heritage Interpretation: Volume 1: The Natural and Built Environment*. London: Belhaven Press, 1989, 33–47.

Uzzell, David L., and Roy Ballantyne. "Heritage that Hurts: Interpretation in a Post-Modern World." In David Uzzel and Roy Ballantyne, eds., *Contemporary Issues in Heritage and Environmental Interpretation: Problems and Prospects*. Norwich: The Stationery Office, 1998, 152–71.

Vaillancourt, Jean-Guy. "Environment." In Robert Paehlke, ed., *Conservation and Environmentalism*. New York: Garland, 1995, 217–18.

van Campen, Jan, and Ebltje Hartkamp-Jonxis. *Asian Splendour: Company Art in the Rijksmuseum*. Zutphen: Walburg, 2011.

Van den Dekker, Annemarie. "Review of 'My Headscarf' Exhibition at Amsterdam Historical Museum." *Material Religion* 2, no. 3 (2006), 399–401.

Van der Leeuw, Sander E. "Giving the Potter a Choice: Conceptual Aspects of Pottery Techniques." In Pierre Lemonnier, ed., *Technological Choices: Transformation in Material Culture since the Neolithic*. London and New York: Routledge, 1993, 238–88.

van Dijck, Jose. *The Culture of Connectivity: A Critical History of Social Media*. New York: Oxford University Press, 2013.

van Eck, Caroline. "Living Statues: Alfred Gell's Art and Agency, Living Presence Response and the Sublime." *Art History* 33, no. 4 (2010), 643–59.

Van Gennep, Arnold. *The Rites of Passage*. Chicago: Chicago University Press, 1960.

van Noord, Willemijn, and Thijs Weststeijn. "The Global Trajectory of Nicolaas Witsen's Chinese Mirror." *The Rijksmuseum Bulletin* 4 (2015), 325–61.

Vanni, Ilaria. "Oggetti Spaesati, Unhomely Belongings. Objects, Migrations and Cultural Apocalypses." *Cultural Studies Review* 19, no. 2 (2013), 150–74.

Varnede, Kirk. "Preface." In William Rubin, ed., *"Primitivism" in Twentieth-Century Art: Affinity of the Tribal and the Modern*. Volume 1. New York: Museum of Modern Art, New York Graphic Society Books, 1984.

Vasquez, Manuel A. *More than Belief: A Materialist Theory of Religion*. Oxford: Oxford University Press, 2010.

Veblen, Thorstein. *The Engineers and the Price System*. New York: B. W. Huebsch, 1921.

von Bertalanffy, Ludwig. *General System Theory: Foundations, Developments, Applications*. New York: George Braziller, 1968.

Verano, John W. "Communality and Diversity in Moche Human Sacrifice." In Steve Brändli and Kimberly L. Jones, eds., *The Art and Archaeology of the Moche: An Ancient Society of the Peruvian North Coast*. Austin: University of Texas Press, 2008, 195–213.

Vergo, Peter, ed. *The New Museology*. London: Reaktion Books, 1989.

Vertovec, Steven. "Migrants, Transnationalism, and Modes of Transformation." *International Migration Review* 38 (2004), 970–1001.

Transnationalism. London: Routledge, 2009.

"Transnationalism and Identity." *Journal of Ethnic and Migration Studies* 27 (2001), 573–82.

Vesselinov, Elena, Matthew Cazessus, and William Falk. "Gated Communities and Spatial Inequality." *Journal of Urban Affairs* 29, no. 2 (2007), 109–27.

Veszelski, Ágnes. "#time, #truth, #tradition. An Image-Text Relationship on Instagram: Photo and Hashtag." In András Benedek and Ágnes Veszelszki, eds., *In the Beginning Was the Image: The Omnipresence of Pictures* (Frankfurt: Peter Lang, 2016), 139.

Virgil. *Eclogues, Georgics, Aeneid*. H. Rushton Fairclough and Rev. G. P. Goold, trans. Loeb Classical Library 64. Cambridge, MA: Harvard University Press, 1999–2000.

Vitali-Rosati, Marcello. *On Editorialization: Structuring Space and Authority in the Digital Age*. Amsterdam: Institute of Network Cultures, 2018.

Vlach, John Michael. "Fred B. Kniffen's Milestones in American Folklife Study." *The Journal of American Folklore* 108 no. 429 (Summer 1995), 328–33.

Vogel, Susan, and Francine N'Diaye. *African Masterpieces from the Musée de l'Homme*. New York: Center for African Art and Harry N. Abrams, 1985.

Vogel, Susan, ed. *Art/Artifact: African Art in Anthropology Collections*. New York: Center for African Art and Preston Verlag, 1988.

Vries, Alex de. "Bitcoin's Growing Energy Problem." *Joule* 2, no. 5 (2018), 801–5.

Vyshka, Klea. "Postbllok – Checkpoint – Communist Isolation." 2019. www.spottedbylocals.com/tirana/postbllok-checkpoint/.

Wade, Lizzie. "The City at the Beginning of the World: The Only Maya City with an Urban Grid May Embody an Ancient Creation Myth." *Archaeology* 71, no. 4 (2018), 26–31.

Wajcman, Judy. *Feminism Confronts Technology*. Cambridge: Polity Press, 1991.

TechnoFeminism. Cambridge: Polity Press, 2004.

Waldron, Lawrence. "Whiskers, Claws and Prehensile Tails: Land Mammal Imagery in Saladoid Ceramics." In Samantha A. Rebovich, ed., *Proceedings of the XXIII Congress of the International Association for Caribbean Archaeology (IACA)*. English Harbour: Dockyard Museum, 2011, 556–76.

Waley-Cohen, Joanna. "Diplomats, Jesuits, and Foreign Curiosities." In Evelyn Rawski and Jessica Rawson, eds., *The Three Emperors: Art and Power in Qing Dynasty China*. London: Royal Academy of Arts, 2005, 178–207.

Walkowitz, Judith R. "The 'Vision of Salome': Cosmopolitanism and Erotic Dancing in Central London, 1908–1918." *American Historical Review* 108, no. 2 (April 2003), 337–76.

Wallinger, Hanna. *Pauline E. Hopkins: A Literary Biography*. Athens: University of Georgia Press, 2005.

Walls, Matthew. "Making as a Didactic Process: Situated Cognition and the Chaîne Opératoire." *Quaternary International*, no. 405 (2015), 21–30.

Wang, Cangbai, ed. "'The Material Turn' in Migration Studies," *Modern Languages Open*. Special Issue, September 26, 2016. http://doi.org/10.3828/mlo.v0i0.88.

Wang, Lianming. "From La Flèche to Beijing: The Transcultural Moment of Jesuit Garden Spaces." In Anna Grasskamp and Monica Juneja, eds., *EurAsian Matters: China, Europe, and the Transcultural Object, 1600–1800*. Cham: Springer, 2018, 101–23.

Wang Su-chin, and Liu Yi-chang. "Shiqi Shijie Qianhou Taiwan Boli Zhushi Yu Yancao, Yan Dou De Shuru Wanglu: Yi Ge Xin De Jiaohuan Jieduan [The Import Networks of Tobacco, Tobacco Pipes, and Glass Bead Ornaments into Taiwan Circa the Seventeenth Century: A New Phase of Exchange]." *Guoli Taiwan Daxue Meishushi Yanjiu Jikan* 22 (2007), 51–90.

Wappenschmidt, Friederike. *Chinesische Tapeten für Europa: Vom Rollbild zur Bildtapete*. Berlin: Deutscher Verlag für Kunstwissenschaft, 1989.

"Object Commentary 1955 (1854)" and "Object Commentary 1725 (1617)." In Willibald Sauerländer and Peter Diemer et al., eds., *Die Münchner Kunstkammer*. Munich: C. H. Beck, 2008, 2, 538, 600.

Wark, McKenzie. *A Hacker Manifesto*. Cambridge, MA: Harvard University Press, 2004.

Warnier, Jean-Pierre. "A Praxeological Approach to Subjectivation in a Material World." *Journal of Material Culture* 6, no. 1 (2001), 5–24.

"Technology as Efficacious Action on Objects ... and Subjects." *Journal of Material Culture* 14, no. 4 (2009), 459–70.

The Pot-King: The Body and Technologies of Power. Leiden and Boston: Brill, 2007.

White, Lynn, Jr. *Medieval Technology and Social Change*. (Oxford: Oxford University Press, 1962.

Watson, James E. M., Oscar Venter, Jasmine Lee, Kendall R. Jones, John G. Robinson, Hugh P. Possingham, and James R. Allan. "Protect the Last of the Wild." *Nature* 563 (2018), 27–30.

Webmoor, Timothy. "STS, Symmetry, Archaeology." In Paul Graves-Brown, Rodney Harrison and Angela Piccini, eds., *The Oxford Handbook of the Archaeology of the Contemporary World*. Oxford: Oxford University Press, 2012.

Webster, Chris, Georg Glasze, and Klaus Frantz. "Guest Editorial." *Environment and Planning B: Planning and Design* 29 (2002), 315–20.

Webster, Gloria Cranmer. "The Potlatch Collection Repatriation." *UBC Law Review* 137 (1995), 137–41.

Weil, Stephen E. *Rethinking the Museum and Other Meditations*. Washington: Smithsonian Institution Press, 1990.

Weiner, Isaac. *Religion Out Loud: Religious Sound, Public Space, and American Pluralism*. New York: New York University Press, 2013.

Weiner, James, ed. "Aesthetics is a Cross-Cultural Category." *Group for Debate in Anthropological Theory No. 6*, Department of Social Anthropology. University of Manchester, 1996.

Weissberg, Liliane. "In Plain Sight." In Barbie Zelizer, ed. and preface. *Visual Culture and the Holocaust*. New Brunswick: Rutgers University Press, 2001, 13–27.

Welch, John R. "The White Mountain Apache Tribe Heritage Program: Origins, Operations, and Challenges." In Kurt E. Dongoske et al., eds., *Working Together: Native Americans and Archaeologists*. Washington, DC: Society for American Archeology, 2000, 67–83.

Wells, Jeremy C. "Bridging the Gap between Built Heritage Conservation Practice and Critical Heritage Studies." In Jeremy C. Wells and Barry L. Stiefel, eds., *Human-Centered Built Environment Heritage Preservation: Theory and Evidence-Based Practice*. London: Routledge, 2019, 33–44.

Wells, Jeremy C., and Barry L. Stiefel. "Conclusion: A Human-Centered Way Forward." In Jeremy C. Wells and Barry L. Stiefel, eds., *Human-Centered Built Environment Heritage Preservation: Theory and Evidence-Based Practice*. London: Routledge, 2019, 317–31.

Wells, Jeremy C., and Barry L. Stiefel, "Introduction: Moving Past Conflicts to Foster an Evidence-Based, Human-Centric Built Heritage Conservation Practice." In Jeremy C. Wells and Barry L. Stiefel, eds., *Human-Centered Built Environment Heritage Preservation: Theory and Evidence-Based Practice*. London: Routledge, 2019, 1–30.

Wells, Jeremy C., and Barry L. Stiefel, eds.*Human-Centered Built Environment Heritage Preservation: Theory and Evidence-Based Practice*. London: Routledge, 2019.

Wendt, Brooke. *The Allure of the Selfie: Instagram and the New Self-Portrait.* Amsterdam: Institute of Network Cultures, 2014.

Wernimont, Jacqueline. "Hearing Eugenics" (July 18, 2016). https://soundstudiesblog.com/2016/07/18/hearing-eugenics/.

Weßels, Bernhard. "Political Representation and Democracy." In Russell J. Dalton and Hans-Dieter Klingemann, eds., *The Oxford Handbook of Political Behavior.* Oxford, Oxford University Press, 2007, 833–49.

Wharton, Annabel Jane. *Selling Jerusalem: Relics, Replicas, Theme Parks.* Chicago: University of Chicago Press, 2006.

Whatmore, Sarah, and Steve Hinchcliffe. "Ecological Landscapes." In Dan Hicks and Mary Beaudry, eds., *Oxford Handbook of Material Culture Studies.* Oxford: Oxford University Press, 2010, 440–58.

White, Lynn Jr. "The Historical Roots of Our Ecological Crisis." *Science* 155, no. 3767 (1967), 1203–07.

Whitehead, Harriet. "The Bow and the Burden Strap: A New Look at Institutionalized Homosexuality in Native North America." In Sherry Ortner and Harriet Whitehead, eds., *Sexual Meanings: The Cultural Construction of Gender and Sexuality.* Cambridge: Cambridge University Press, 1981, 80–115.

Wickstrom, Maurya. *Performing Consumers: Global Capital and Its Theatrical Seductions.* London: Routledge, 2006.

Wiessner, Polly. "Style and Social Information in Kalahari San Projectile Points." *American Antiquity* 48, no. 2 (April 1983), 253–76.

Wilde, Guillermo. *Religión y Poder en las Misiones de Guaraníes.* Buenos Aires: Editorial SB, 2009.

Wilford, Justin. *Sacred Subdivisions: The Posturban Transformation of American Evangelicalism.* New York: New York University Press, 2012.

Wilkinson, Richard, and Kate Pickett. *The Inner Level: How More Equal Societies Reduce Stress, Restore Sanity and Improve Everyone's Wellbeing.* London: Penguin, 2018.

The Spirit Level: Why More Equal Societies Almost Always Do Better. London: Penguin, 2009.

Williams, Brett. "Why Migrant Women Feed Their Husbands Tamales: Foodways as a Basis for a Revisionist View of Tejano Family Life." In Linda Brown and Kay Mussell, eds., *Ethnic and Regional Foodways in the United States: The Performance of Group Identity.* Knoxville: University of Tennessee Press, 1984, 113–26.

Williams, Clare. *Thomas Platter's Travels in England 1599.* London: Jonathan Cape, 1937.

Williams, Raymond. *Keywords: A Vocabulary of Culture and Society.* New York: Oxford University Press, 1976.

Williamson, Ashley. "How to Act Like a Viking: The New Role of Performance in Experimental Archaeology." Playing with History: A Performance-Based Historiography Symposium, Toronto, ON, October 12–13, 2018.

Wilson, Thomas, and Hastings Donnan. *A Companion to Border Studies*. Chichester: Wiley, 2012.

Winfield, Pamela D. and Steven Heine, eds. *Zen and Material Culture*. Oxford: Oxford University Press, 2017.

Winner, Langdon. *Autonomous Technology: Technics-Out-of-Control as a Theme in Political Thought*. Cambridge, MA: The MIT Press, 1985 [1977].

"Do Artifacts Have Politics?" In *The Whale and the Reactor*. Chicago: University of Chicago Press, 1986, 19–39.

Winner, Lauren. *A Cheerful and Comfortable Faith: Anglican Religious Practices in the Elite Households of Eighteenth-Century Virginia*. New Haven: Yale University Press, 2010.

Winthrop, John. *History of New England, 1630–1649*. James K. Hosmer, ed., New York: Charles Scribner's Son, 1908.

Wittgenstein, Ludwig. *Wittgenstein's Lectures: Cambridge 1932–35* (Oxford: Blackwell, 1979).

Witmore, Christopher. "Archaeology and the New Materialisms." *Journal of Contemporary Archaeology* 1, no. 2 (2014), 203–46.

Wittman, Hannah. "Domination of Nature." In P. Robbins, ed., *Encyclopedia of Environment and Society*. Thousand Oaks: Sage, 2007. 480–2.

Witzand, Jopie. "Dutch Quilters Make Exquisite Mittens for Aussie Koalas." SBS Dutch. November 26, 2019. https://bit.ly/3lVFPnQ.

Witzgall, Susanne, and Kerstin Stakemeier. "Introduction." In Susanne Witzgall and Kerstin Stakemeier, eds., *Power of Material/Politics of Materiality*. Chicago: Diaphanes, 2017, 1–10.

Wolff, Janet. *Aesthetics and the Sociology of Art*. 2nd ed. London: Macmillan, 1993.

Wood, Charles H. "Equilibrium and Historical-Structural Perspectives on Migration." *International Migration Review* 16, no. 2 (1982), 298–319.

World Health Organization. "The Social Determinants of Health: Social Exclusion." 2019. www.who.int/social_determinants/themes/socialexclusion/en/.

Worstall, Tim. "Poverty and Inequality are Not the Same Thing So Let's Try Not to Confuse Them." *Forbes*, March 19, 2015. www.forbes.com/sites/timworstall/2015/03/19/.

Wright, Conrad Edick and Katheryn P. Viens, eds. *The Future of History: Historians, Historical Organizations, and the Prospects for the Field*. Boston: Massachusetts Historical Society, 2017.

Wright, Robert. *The Evolution of God*. New York: Little, Brown, 2009.

Wrobel, Gabriel, Christophe Helmke, Sherry Gibbs, George Micheletti, Norbert Stanchly, and Terry Powis. "Two Trophy Skulls from Pacbitun, Belize." *Latin American Antiquity* 30, no. 1 (2019), 218–23.

Wu Hung. "Emperor's Masquerade: Costume Portraits of Yongzheng and Qianlong." *Orientations* 26, no. 7 (1995), 25–41.

Wurst, LouAnn. "Should Archaeology have a Future?" *Journal of Contemporary Archaeology* 6, (2019), 168–81.

Yanni, Carla. *The Architecture of Madness: Insane Asylums in the United States*. Minneapolis: University of Minnesota Press, 2007.

Yarborough, Richard. "Introduction." In Pauline Hopkins, *Contending Forces*, Schomburg ed. New York: Oxford University Press, 1991.

Yogev, Gedalia. *Diamonds and Coral: Anglo-Dutch Jews and Eighteenth-Century Trade*. London: Leicester University Press, 1978.

Yonge, Charlotte. "The Mice at Play – The Apple of Discord – The Strayed Falcon." *Historical Dramas*. London: Groomsbridge and Sons, 1864.

Youngberry, April, and Jonathan Prangnell. "Fences, Boats and Teas: Engendering Patient Lives at Peel Island Lazaret." *International Journal of Historical Archaeology* 17, no. 3 (2013), 445–64.

Young-Sánchez, Margaret, and Denise P. Schaan. *Marajó: Ancient Ceramics from the Mouth of the Amazon*. Denver: Denver Art Museum, 2011.

Zent, Egleé L. "Unfurling Western Notions of Nature and Amerindian Alternatives." *Ethics in Science and Environmental Politics* 15 (2015), 1–19.

Zhang, Baichun. "The Importation of European Clock and Watch Technology into China and the Questions Related during the late Ming and Qing Dynasties (1580–1911)." *Journal of Dialectics of Nature* 17, no. 2 (1995), 38–46.

Zhang Pu, and Guo Fuxiang. *L'art de L'horlogerie Occidental et la Chine*. Beijing: China Intercontinental Press, 2005.

Zheng, Yangwen. *China on the Sea: How the Maritime World Shaped Modern China*. Leiden: Brill, 2012.

Zimerman, Heinrich. "Urkunden, Acten und Regesten aus dem Archiv des Ministeriums des Innern Herausgegeben." *Jahrbuch der kunsthistorischen Sammlungen des allerhöchsten Kaiserhauses* 7, no. II (1888), 226–313.

Ziter, Edward. *The Orient on the Victorian Stage*. Cambridge: Cambridge University Press, 2003.

Zolberg, Aristide R. "The Next Wave: Migration Theory for a Changing World." *International Migration Review* 23, no. 3 (1989), 403–30.

Zou, Hui. *A Jesuit Garden in Beijing and Early Modern Chinese Culture*. West Lafayette: Purdue University Press, 2011.

Zuidema, R. Tom. "The Lion in the City: Royal Symbols of Transition in Cuzco." In Gary Urton, ed., *Animal Myths and Metaphors*. Salt Lake City: University of Utah Press, 1985, 183–250.

Index

"Perception of an Object Costs", 57–58
"Photographic Plates of the Future", 151–52
"The Work of Art in the Age of its Technological Reproducibility", 148–49
#MuseumsAreNot Neutral, 191
"Pessimism v Progress," *The Economist*, 436
"The Fate of Jews of France" exhibition, 158
3D printing, 570, 583–84

abduction, 390–91
  of agency, 386
Aboriginal, Australia, 122, *See also* Indigenous
  ancestors, 328–29
  homelessness, 111–13
  land, 333–36
  repatriation, 248–49
  segregation, 109–10
Aboriginal, Canada, 245–46, 247–48, *See also* Indigenous
acculturation, 240, 241, 276
accumulation, 137
activism, 119, 243, 505
adornment, 410
  religious, 522, 547
Aeschylus, *The Persians*, 210
aesthetics, 271–72, 278–80, 476
  as moral, 382, *See also* ethics
  definition, 381, 382
  emotion, 385–86
  four schools of use, 380
  indigenous, 241, 385, 387
  judgment, 382
affect, 386, 403
affordance, 153, 314, 448, 590, 596, 600
African American, 194–95, 224–25, 479–81, 482–83, 493–94, 504, 507, 509, 520, *See also* Black
After Ethics: Ancestral Voices and Post-disciplinary Worlds in Archaeology, 626
agency, 288–89, 338–41, 344–49
  mythic, 406
  object, 371–72
  social, 406

Ahmed, Sara, 31, 222
Ai Weiwei, 282
Akkadia, 403
Alaska, 251, 253–54
Albania, 116, 317
Alcatraz Island
  occupation of, 243
alchemist, 274
alienation, 311, 314
almshouse, 514
alterization, 128
Amazon, 412, 421–23, 445
America
  Central, 201
  North, 219
  South, 119, 128
  United States of, 190–99, 200–3, 478, 493–94
American Indian Movement (AIM), 243
American studies, 501
Amerindian, 402–11, 414–17, *See also* Native American
analytical tool, 287, 381, 451
anarchy, 628–29
Anderson, Jennifer, 201
Andes, 413, 421
animacy, 236, 426
animal, 407
animism, 37, *See also* fetishism
anthropology, 383
  salvage, 240
anthropomorphization, 405, 407
Antilles, 402
  Greater, 407
  Lesser, 420
Aotearoa, 237, 246, *See also* New Zealand
Apache, 242
apocalypse, 258
apprentice, 274, 441
Arch of Titus (Rome), 149
archaeology, 80, 90
  contemporary, 181
  historical, 513
  prehistoric, 402

architecture, 528
  religious, 549–52
  shingle style, 190
Arctic, 243
Aristotle, 33, 57
Arizona, 242
  Phoenix, 551
Armageddon
  ecological, 405
art, 150, 151–52, 179, 240–42, 245–46, 278–80, 288–89, 339, 364–65, 366–67, 370, 376, 382–86, 388–91, 392–93
  corporeal, 402
  decorative, 201
  fine, 240
  mechanical, 438
  modern, 241
  primitive, 240, 389
art history, 542
artisan, 274, 280
Asia
  Southeast, 278
Asimov, Isaac, 70–72
assemblage, 44–45
Assembly of First Nations, Canada, 244
assimilation, 523–25, See also acculturation
Astuti, Rita, 331
asylum, 521
  lunatic, 527–29
Attfield, Judy, 361, 370, 376
Auckland Museum, 248, 252
Auerbach, Erich, 59
augmented reality, 583
August the Strong, 273
aura, 149
Auschwitz-Birkenau, 160, 174–75
Australia, 109–11, 248–49
  Arnhem Land, 328
  Canberra, 249
  Cape York, 328, 332, 334, 339, 341
  Far North Queensland, 328, 345
  language groups, 328, 330
  Melbourne, 521
  Queensland, 344, 527
  Sydney, 522
Australian Aboriginal art, 383–84
Austria, 304, 307, 311, 541
AuthaGraph world map, 368–69
authentic, 128, 147, 148–49, 150–51, 156, 160–61, 177–78, 224, 385
authority, 90, 130, 133, 140, 143, 344, 348
  shared, 252
authorized heritage discourse, 169, 171–72
automation, 447, 592, 594, 615
automaton, 284
Autry, LaTanya S., 191

Babylon, 403
backpack, 313
bacteria, 41, 47
Baha'i, 403
band, 405
Barbieri, Donatella, 208, See also costuming
Baroque, 148, 201, 289

Barrow, John, 365
Barthes, Roland, 61, 357
basket, 418–19
Bateson, Gregory, 391–92, 395–96
Baudrillard, Jean, 62, 375
Baumgarten, Alexander Gottlieb, 381–82
bead, 281, 410, 412, 416
Beaudry, Mary, 5, 6
Beck, Harry, 368
behavior, 104–5, 359, 454, 501
belief, 538–39
belief system, 330, 365, 402, 541
Bell, Clive, 385
Benjamin, Walter, 141, 148–49
Bennett, Jane, 44, 155, 289
Bentham, Jeremy, 515–16
Berger, John, 307–11, 366
Bernstein, Robin, 65, 207–8, 226,
  See also whiteness
Best, Susan, 386
bias, 118, 171, 195, 203, 364, 557
  communication, 598–99
Bible, 59, 540
  King James version, 404
binary opposition, 408
biocentric, 403
biodiversity, 344, 345, 348, 629
biography, 35, 287
biomedia studies, 48
biophilosophy, 19
biosphere, 413
Bishop, Elizabeth, 66–68
Black, 64–66, 192–95, 364–65, 479–81, 482–84, 495–96, 505, See also people of color
blood, 329–31, 416, 422–23, 426
Boas, Franz, 240, 243
Bodei, Remo, 33
body, 209, 227, 245, 362, 413, 440–42, 606–7,
  See also embodiment
body techniques, 440–41, 443, 457
Boldrey, Edwin, 363
bone, 177, 236, 285, 327, 517, 518
Böttger, Johann Friedrich, 274, 278
boundaries
  knowledge, 338
  social, 337
Bourdieu, Pierre, 62, 81–82, 383, 472
Braidotti, Rosi, 44, 331
Brazil, 119, 129, 133, 421
Brilliant Ideas Studio, 191
Britain. See United Kingdom
British Columbia, 251, 385, See also Canada
Brown, Bill, 60, 63–64, 208, See also thing theory
Buchli, Victor, 238
Buck-Morss, Susan, 383
Buddhism, 403, 553
building. See architecture
Bureau of Indian Affairs (BIA), 244
burial, 118, 243, 246, 247, 413
Burra Charter (1979), 168, 177–78
Butler, Judith, 18, 331

Caddo, 246, 250
Caglar, Simsek, 361

California, 245, 508, 555, 581, 585
Canada, 102, 237-38, 244, 245-46, 256
    Ottawa, 238, 241, 246
Canada Indian Act (1884), 237, 256
canon, 132, 365, 624
Cant, Alanna, 384-85
capital, 62, 107, 387
capitalism, 37-40, 77, 79-80, 81-82, 86, 88, 91-93, 302, 437, 627
Caribbean, 201, 403, 423
Cartesian, 42, 366, 383, 607
Casella, Eleanor, 518
categories, 33, 41, 331, 395, 438, 441, 453, 591
Caves of Steel, The, 70, *See also* Asimov, Isaac
ceramics, 274, 277, 278-79, 289, 415-16, 521, 583
Cézanne, Paul, 55
Chaîne Opératoire, 443-44
Chavín (Peru), 402, 406, 421-24, 425
chest, 305
    high, 201
chiefdom, 405, 424, 426
chieftain, 406
China, 269-90, 575-76
    Beijing, 281, 284, 285
    Guangzhou (Canton), 282, 285
    Jingdezhen, 270, 272, 274, 278
chinoiserie, 280, 281
Christen, Kimberly, 255
Christianity, 394, 403, 404, 538, 540, 553
Chuk, Natasha, 374, 569, 570, 572, 577
citizenship, 290, 335, 494-95, 504, 508
civic-ceremonial center, 402, 419
civil rights, 335, 505, 610
civil war, 629
    American, 224-25, 526
clans, 328, 334
Clark, Kenneth, 366
class, 104, 107, 120, 333, 493, 494, 495-504, 507-10, 612
    middle, 108, 172, 225, 438, 493
Classen, Constance, 18
classification, 240, 257, 445, 515, 516, 595
clay, 274, 285, 412, 415, 518, 524
Clifford, James, 244
climate, 46
    change, 69, 80, 86, 184, 344, 404, 436, 629
clinamen, 42-43
clock, 284
Coe, Michael, 425
coercion, 483, 628
cognition, 359, 381, 387, 442
    rational, 380
collections, 236, 529, 545-46, 573-74, 615
    museum, 64, 171, 191-92, 199-200, 202, 244, 254
Colombia, 130, 411, 414
colonialism, 40, 94, 131, 170, 225, 236, 237, 241, 252, 258, 275, 341, 477
colonization, 237, 239, 243, 258, 334, 476
colony, 135, 194, 213, 215-16, 280, 289, 304, 316, 339, 476, 518, 540, 552, *See also* settler-colonial
color, 162, 385, 408

Colored American Magazine, 495
Colored Conventions Movement, 504-5
Colwell, Chip, 252
comfort, 302, 304, 305, 316, 499
commodification, 137, 282
commodity, 35, 38-40, 54, 62, 138, 273, 287, 333, 358, 496, 625, *See also* Marx, Karl
communication, 329, 348, 590, 598-99, 603, 607
Communist, 116, 118, 148, 282
community, 82, 106-11
    gated, 106-9
complicity, 40, 80-81, 92-94
concentration camp, 153-54, 174-75
Confederate States of America
    memorialization of, 12, 115, 479
confinement, 515, 522, 530
connoisseurship, 6
conquest, 130, 131, 139, 478
Conquest of Nature, 404
consensus, 132, 173, 495
conservation, 161, 175, 177-78, 183, 250
consumption, 62, 82, 86, 190, 359, 361, 362, 496
contact zone, 29, 244
contingency, 625
Coole, Diana, 207, *See also* new materialism
Coote, Jeremy, 392
copper, 282, 410, 518
coral, 286, 287
Cordell, Ryan, 374
corset. *See* costuming
cosmology, 412, 425
costuming, 207-30, *See also* critical costume studies
    corset, 205-7, 229-30
costume accuracy, 215, 223, 224
    culturally specific, 226, 410, 416
    historical, 206
craft, 285, 313, 441
creolization, 276
crime, 107, 373, 513, 517, 520
critical costume studies, 208-9
critical heritage studies, 90, 168-69, 181
critical race studies, 65
critique, 103, 181, 244, 257, 349, 364, 366, 404, 438, 474, 477, 478, 483, 484, 555, 585
cross-cultural, 226, 275, 287, 328, 338, 381, 387, 552, 626
cultural center, 236, 254, 258, *See also* museum
    Makah Cultural and Research Center, 256-57
    U'mista Cultural Centre, 256
cultural patrimony, 247, 248, 249
cultural relativism, 240
cultural resource management, 77, 90-92
cultural studies, 54, 208
curate, 62, 159, 161, 191, 200, 202, 252, 524, 552
curiosity cabinets, 237
Custer Died for Your Sins: An Indian Manifesto, 244
cyborg, 44, 405, 573, 585, 607

Danto, Arthur, 393
dark tourism, 174
data center, 567-68, 569, 593
data physicalization, 585
de Certeau, Michel, 361, 474

De Cunzo, Lu Ann, 521
De Leiuen, Cherrie, 522
death, 134, 404, 406, 411, 424, 543
Debord, Guy, 368
decay, 156, 161, 163, 182, 407, 579
Declaration on the Rights of Indigenous Peoples, 251, *See also* United Nations
decolonization, 236, 252, 258, 626
decorating, 271, 279, 283, 305, 333, 406, 411, 413, 419, 422, 425, 497–98
decorative arts, 65, 190, *See also* art history
DeFrantz, Tommy, 206
DeLillo, Don, 69
Deloria, Vine, Jr., 244
democracy, 120, 196, 197, 365, 455, 605
denial of coevalness, 129
Denmark, 171
department store, 60
deprivation, 103, 514, 516, 518, 520
Descartes, René, 34, 607
description, 41, 42, 44, 61, 62, 391
desert, 404, 421
design, 105, 106, 214, 281, 282, 288, 370–73, 418, 527–28, 571–72
deviant, 513, 516, 520
Di Noto, Paula, 364
dialectical images, 141–42
diaspora, 302, 320
Dickinson, Emily, 59
digital, 586, 617–18
  artifacts, 574, 579, 582
  preservation, 581
Dillon, Grace, 258
dining, 282, 501
  room, 497, 499–500
diorama, 240, 245
diplomatic, 272, 273, 284, 287
disciplinary complicity, 80–81, 87, 93
displace, 55, 147, 301, 305, 312, 313, 314, 320, 346
dispossession, 94, 130, 136, 137, 141, 146, 237, 240, 320, 335
diversity, 107, 195, 302, 439, 539, 545
domestication, 278, 503
domesticity, 305–6, 493, 510–11, 521, 530
domination, 82, 87, 167, 244, 302, 405, 442, 455, 476
dominion, 404
Douglas, Mary, 338
Dreamtime, 328
Dreiser, Theodore, 60
dress
  Muslim hijab (headscarf), 547
  religious, 547–48, *See also* adornment: religious
dualism
dual-triadic, 408
dyadic, 408
Duchamp, Marcel, 389–90
Dulcinea (1911), 389
Dunne, Anthony, 372–73
Dutch, 197, 272, 273, 276, 280, 281, 282, 285, 308, 334
dynamism, 314, 625

Eco, Umberto, 358, 391
ecology, 20, 85, 88, 274, 337, 342, 345, 407, 445
economy, 79, 103, 107, 146, 180, 190, 272, 280, 333, 346, 347
education, 81, 82, 228, 522
Edwards, Elizabeth, 339
eighteenth century, 66, 201, 211, 274, 279, 280, 281, 283, 284, 289, 316, 476, 513, 515, 530, 605, 610
elite, 107, 214, 237, 272, 273, 280, 383, 496, 500, 508, 612
embodiment, 34, 100, 116, 317, 331, 413, 440, 472
empirical, 30, 104, 438, 444, 446, 447, 454
enamel, 284, 306
energy, 31, 513, 575
  color, 408, 410
  vital, 402
England. *See* United Kingdom
Enlightenment, 36, 167
enslavement, 65, 66, 114, 194, 198, 341, 494, 520, *See also* slavery
environment, 69, 72, 78–80, 333, 335, 488, 515, 530, 555, 576, 582, 608
  anthropocentric, 403
  cost, 575
  crisis, 87, 94
  social, 78, 90, 94, 333
  theocentric, 403
epistemology, 257, 392
equality, 104, 121, 335, *See also* inequality
Erikson, Patricia Pierce, 257
ethics, 41, 88, 93, 225, 403, 478, 626
ethnic, 65, 107, 202, 227, 302, 385, 411, 450, 507, 508
ethnographic present, 240
ethnography, 108, 237, 239, 415, 437, 440, 505, *See also* aesthetics
ethology, 402, 419
EurAsian, 270, 278, 285, 286, 288–89
Eurocentric, 167, 177, 179, 275, 380, 387, 440, 457
everyday life, 32, 311, 314, 341, 362, 478, 595
  place, 474
  evolution, 129
  social, 239, 597
Evolutions et Techniques, 445
exceptionalism, 493, 501
exclusion, 68, 100, 103–4, 105, 109, 113, 120, 302, 341, 479, 507, 626
exhibition, 191, 198, 200, 213, 252, 275, 552
  Exhibition of Canadian West Coast Art – Native and Modern (1927), 241
  Indian Art of the United States, 1941, 241
  Ko Tawa – Taoanga from our ancestral landscapes, 253
  Primitivism in 20th Century Art: Affinity of the Tribal and the Modern, 1984, 241
  The Spirit Sings, 245, 247
  World's Fair, 219, 239
exotic, 105, 129, 143, 193, 276, 284, 289
experience
  lived, 109, 114, 138, 206, 210, 517, 623
  sensory, 530, 548

exploitation, 46, 273, 280, 320, 576, 615
extinction, 87, 404, 407
extraction, 405, 407, 453, 577

factish, 40–41, *See also* Latour, Bruno
Farris Thompson, Robert, 388, 389, 392, 393
feminism, 493, 517, 585
fetish, 35–41, 136, *See also* Latour, Bruno, *See also* Marx, Karl
Finland, 567
First Nations. *See* Indigenous, *See* Aboriginal Canada
Flood, Catherine, 373
food, 112–13, 280–81, 329, 348, 413, 415, 495, 501, 503, 505, 506–7, 526, 626
forensic, 40, 117, 578
  digital, 577–78
forgetting, 172, 174, 176, 184
form
  strength of, 388
Fort Edmonton Park, 228
Foucault, Michel, 142, 472, 515, 517
framework, 94, 101, 108, 207, 246, 247, 270, 271, 275, 280, 281, 357, 383, 387, 390, 392, 446, 475, 477, 525, 529, 585, 604, 623, 624–25
France, 107, 147, 158–59, 160, 173, 251, 284
Franco, Barbara, 20
Freud, Sigmund, 36, 37
Frost, Samantha, 207, *See also* new materialism
Fry, Hannah, 365
functionalism, 388
funerary objects, 247, 250, 413–14
furnishings, 495, 497, 508, 549
furniture, 196, 201–2, 281–82, 283, 304, 305, 371–72, 496, 498
Furtado, Gustavo, 206
future, 69–72, 90, 117, 121, 128, 170, 183, 207, 213, 258, 303–4, 479, 557, 574, 578, 625, 626
futurisms
  Indigenous, 258

garden, 197, 284, 333, 417, 422, 443, 450, 451, 495, 506
Garden of Eden, 403, 404
Garland, Jessie, 525
Garman, James, 519
Geertz, Clifford, 412
Gell, Alfred, 386, 389–91, 392–93, 400
gender, 68, 227, 302, 305–7, 331–32, 343, 420, 506, 507, 522, 523–25, 527
genealogy, 36, 37, 328, 471, 476, 477
genocide, 116, 131, 159, 161, 175–76, 177, 236, 252, 334, 335, 341
geography, 471
  material culture and, 487
Germany, 148, 176–77, 272, 285, 543
Gibb, Andrew, 211, 212
gift, 253, 272, 273, 284, 285, 287, 288, 314, 316
Gilchrist, Roberta, 525
Global South, 128, 167, 168, 180, 275, 302, 575, 624
global warning. *See* climate change
globalization, 82, 280
Gnecco, Cristóbal, 80, 336

god, 134, 277, 288, 367, 392, 404, 417, 421, 423, 424, 425, 426, 542, 556
Goffman, Erving, 362, 513, 516
Google, 567–68, 569, 598, 600
Great Lakes Research Alliance for the Study of Aboriginal Cultures (GRASAC), 254
Great Migration, 194, 480
Greece
  Mani Peninsula, 394
  Mount Athos, 394
Greenland, 243, 367
Grier, Katherine, 498–99
Grindon, Gavin, 373
Guarani, 119, 129, 130–35
Guatemala, 425
Gumbrecht, Hans, 370
Guyana, 402, 418

habitus, 441, 442
hackers, 455, 595, 611–12, 613
Hague Convention for the Protection of Cultural Property in the Event of Armed Conflict (1954), 150
Handbook of Material Culture, 88
Hann, Rachel, 206, 208, 216, 221, 229, *See also* costuming
Haraway, Donna, 44, 46
Harman, Graham, 32
Hartman, Saidiya, 66
Harvey, David, 137, 171, 473
hashtag, 597, 608
Haudenosaunee, 245, *See also* Iroquois Confederacy
Hawaii, 527
  Kalaupapa, 527
Hebdige, Dick, 361
Hegel, Wilhelm, 33
hegemony, 142, 275, 404, 439, 494, 628
Heidegger, Martin, 32, 33, 63, 395
heritage, 128–32, 134, 135, 137–38, 139–43, 167–84, 627
  cultural, 167, 179, 336, 349, 580
  dark, 174, 176
  definition, 169–70
  intangible, 29, 178
  material, 336
  national, 170, 171, 282
  natural, 167
  tangible, 29, 90
hermunculus, 364
heterarchy, 517, 518
heterotopia, 142–43
Heye, George Gustav, 238, 242
Hicks, Dan, 40
Hidatsa, 243
hierarchy, 29, 102, 103, 105, 136, 137, 226, 344, 364, 521, 606
Hinduism, 403, 553, 556
historical sublime, 211–12, *See also* Gibb, Andrew
Hodges, Christopher, 384
holism, 623–24
Holocaust, 153–62, 173, 176–77
Holy Roman Empire, 271, 276

home, 103, 111, 196, 305, 307, 311, 317, 318, 319, 333, 361–62, 493–511
home place, 329
homunculus, 362–64
Honduras, 424
Hopi, 242
hospital, 513, 525–27
housekeeping, 68, 493, 494, 501
Hrdlicka, Ales, 243
human remains, 175–76, 236, 237, 243, 246, 247, 248, 250–51, 327
    skull, 237, 425
    toi moko, 237, 246, 248
    unaffiliated, 250
humanism, 131, 132, 472, 475, 577
humanities, 44, 173, 301, 578, 629
hybrid, 42, 43, 271, 276, 289, 553, 596
hygiene, 526
hyper-animacy, 408, 410
hyperlink, 569, 599, 601, 603

icon, 128, 132, 288, 358, 376, 394, 416, 425, 426, 515, 543, 555, 607
identity, 116, 172, 210, 225, 227, 228, 301, 305, 327–50, 494, 506, 507, 513, 516, 547
    formation, 545, 603, 608
    individual, 330
ideology, 80, 82, 86, 87, 88, 90, 91, 92, 118, 239, 349, 375, 493, 494, 515, 521, 524, 525
imaginary, 20, 132, 170, 173, 472, 479, 591
immateriality, 28, 38, 474, *See also* materiality
immigrants. *See* migration
improvement, 453, 503, 515, 520, 521, 526, 528
    social, 501
inanimate, 33, 34, 150, 426
Inca, 130, 141, 142, 413, 425
inclusion, 100, 103–4, 120, 195, 241, 623–24, 627
index, 88–89, 142, 358, 359, 376
India, 281, 285, 287, 365
Indigenous, 39, 114, 119–20, 137, 139–40, 168, 207, 219, 228–29, 236–58, 328–29, 334–37, 339–40, 341–44, 345, 346, 348–49, 383–84, 385, 404, 443, 446, 451, 478, 503, 520, 523, 551, 624, 626, 628
Indigenous archaeologies
    using material culture to promote social justice for, 119–20
Indigenous culture, 180, 240
industrial, 91, 138, 361, 438, 452, 513, 515, 523
inequality, 82, 100, 104–5, 108, 114, 120, 121, 302, 421, *See also* equality
Infant Orphan Asylum Hall (London), 523
information, 41, 163, 301, 364, 365, 368, 374–75, 501, 526, 548, 567, 585, 592, 593–94, 595, 597, 598–99, 600–3, 604, 606, 607–8, 610–11, 612–16
    exchange, 591, 611
    storage, 592
Information Age, 590
information technology, 254, 574, *See also* technology
infrastructure, 32, 34, 41, 48, 109, 137, 147, 334, 444, 452, 456, 568
Ingold, Tim, 44, 288, 438

innovation, 373, 385, 437, 450, 453, 611, 624, 625
institution, 94, 101, 191, 202, 256, 302, 513–31, 553
    carceral, 514, 520
    charitable, 522
    total, 513, 516
institutionalize, 78, 119, 170
interdisciplinary, 208, 258, 471, 472, 473, 510, 539, 627
Internet, 255, 568–69, 592, 593–94, 599, 605, 606, 607
Internet of Things, the, 570, 591, 614–16
intervention, 66, 110, 156, 161, 167, 182, 245, 472, 476, 514, 581, 585, 624, 627
intimacy, 210, 216, 221, 282, 349, 550
Inuit, 243, 413
Iowa, 246
Ireland, 174, 179–80, 182, 183, 528, 575
Iroquois Confederacy, 243, 245
irrigation, 342, 345, 403, 421, 423
Isaac Bell House (Newport), 190–91
Islam, 367, 403, 538, 548, 553
Italy, 276, 306, 307, 308
ivory, 285

Jackson, Nathan, 253
Jainism, 403
Jameson, Fredric, 69, 139
Japan, 280, 426
Japanese, 177
Japanese American, 508
jars
    effigy, 414, 415
Jesuit, 129, 130–34, 135, 142, 274, 282, 284, 286, 288
Judaism, 403, 553
jungle, 405, 406–7, 408, 416, 422, 425

Kant, Immanuel, 380, 382–83, 384, 387, 389, 393
Kantor, Tadeusz, 151–52
kendi, 269, 270–74, 275, 277–78, 280, 289
Kennewick Man, 250–51
Kopytoff, Igor, 35, 46
Kuglitsch, Linnea, 528, 551

labor, 34, 38, 258, 420, 495, 505–6, 507, 513, 519–20, 522, 523, 576
lacquer, 274, 281, 283, 288
landscape, 337, 345, 348, 349, 471, 474–79, 488, 513, 515, 516, 522, 527, 531, 617
    definition, 476
    sacred, 402, 419
    visual culture, 477
Lanzón, 422
Latina, 506
Latour, Bruno, 40–41, 42–45, 370, 444, *See also* theory: actor network (ANT)
law, 113, 150, 159, 194–95, 247, 301, 328
    humanitarian, 150
legacy, 336, 477
legal. *See* law
Lemonnier, Pierre, 451, 453
Leroi-Gourhan, André, 445–47

lesbigay, 505-6
life of things
  global, 269, 287, 289
  social, 287, 289, 446
Lindaeur, Owen, 523
Lloyd, David, 66
logic, 66, 119, 225, 256, 312, 313, 362, 381, 390, 443, 444, 448
Lonetree, Amy, 252
Louisiana, 198, 520
love, 214, 306, 360, 366
Lubicon Lake Cree First Nation, 245
Lucretius, 43
Lukács, György, 61, 63
Lumbreras, Luis G., 421
Luna, James, 245
luxury, 272, 508
Lyotard, Jean Francois, 375-76

machine, 285, 347, 405, 426, 446, 573, 575, 577, 580, 591, 607, 613
machine learning, 439
macrocosm, 410, 416, 423
magico-religious, 403, 442
Magritte, Rene, 370, 376, 438
making, 40, 41, 42, 43, 272, 333, 334, 391, 472, 549, 551
Manovich, Lev, 592, 593, 594, 596
  new media object, 592
manufacture, 29, 30, 36, 201, 278, 414
Māori, 237, 244, 246, 248, 252-53, 256
mapping, 367-69, 370, 472, 551, 583
maps, 334, 349, 368, 471, 583
marginalized, 64, 130, 172, 178, 195, 225, 243, 479, 495
Marx, Karl, 36, 37-39, 40, 41, 54, 302, 357, 375, 450
Marx, Leo, 438
Mason, Otis, 239
Massachusetts Bay Colony, 525
material living standards, 100, 109, 114
material religion, 538-57
  definitions, 540
materialism, 84, 146, 190
materiality, 27-31, 37, 46, 57, 58, 128, 142, 143, 147, 160, 163, 174, 206, 303, 318, 331, 332, 339, 360, 368, 471, 472, 475, 515, 530, 543, 545, 569, 570, 573, 577, 578, 579, 582
  and place, 475
  vital, 207, 269, 289
Mauss, Marcel, 440-41, 442, 444, 449, 450, 451, 453
Maya, 406, 410, 424-25
  Classic, 406
  Zinacanteco, 406
medium, 362, 375, 556, 586, 594, 598-99
meme, 609-11
memorialization, 175, 184, 472, 481
memorials, 115-17, 121, 156, 162, 481, 488
memory, 15, 138, 160, 162, 172-73, 175, 176, 184, 302, 303, 338, 573, 579, 592
  operational, 442
memory studies, 169, 172-73, 627
Merleau-Ponty, Maurice, 387, 395

Meskell, Lynn, 173, 175
Mesoamerica, 403, 406, 423, 424
metadata, 594, 597-98, 602
metallurgy, 410, 443, 451
metaphor, 390, 412, 446
methodology, 209, 557
Mexico, 384-85, 402, 418, 423, 425
Mexican, 424, 506-7
Michaels, Eric, 383
Michel, Serres, 41-46
microcosm, 409, 410, 423
migration, 194, 301-20, 484
  escape, 318
  food, 311, 317
  homesickness, 307, 314, 320
  labor, 302
  out-of-placeness, 311, 320
  packing for, 303-14, 316
  remittance, 314, 316
  sense of belonging, 311, 313, 495
  trans-Atlantic, 303, 304
  translocality, 314
migration studies, 301, 314, 318
  affective turn, 302
  Marxism, 302
  material turn, 302
  push and pull model, 301
Miller, Daniel, 318, 362, 473, 475
Mimesis, 59, 275, 278, 289, 388
mind, 59, 381, 389, 390, 391-92, 395, 396, 442, 527, 529, 530, 606-7
mineral, 345, 347, 574, 575
Ming dynasty, 276, 284
missions, 129, 130-35, 139, 142-43
Mitchell River, 334, 347
  watershed management, 341-44
mobility, 114, 194, 280, 301, 303, 318, 319, 327, 333, 341, 412, 441, 478, 479, 513, 624
Moche, 406, 410, 413, 415, 416
modernity, 61, 131, 132, 135, 138, 140, 239, 240, 361, 438, 439, 476, 477, 486, 487, 488, 500, 539
moieties, 334
Monks, Aoife, 208, *See also* costuming
Moore, Henrietta, 331
Moriori, 248, *See also* New Zealand
Mormon (Latter Day Saints), 305
morphology, 402, 419
Morphy, Howard, 339
multicultural, 275, 551
  neoliberalism, 139
multidisciplinary, 472, 488, 515, 549
Munn, Nancy, 390
museum, 40, 147, 160, 161, 162, 169, 170-71, 190-94, 195-203, 236-58, 289-90, 312, 317, 552-55, 583, *See also* exhibition, anthropology
  ethnographic, 237, 238, 240, 245
  fine art, 240-42, 245
  living history, 213, 228
  tribal, 255, 257
  universal, 167, 171
Myers, Fred, 384
myth, 134, 305, 405, 406-7, 417-26, 574

Nara Document (1994), 177
narrative, 69, 132, 171, 176, 200, 206, 243, 258, 269, 290, 302, 333, 383, 479, 514, 567
  archaeological, 129
Narukawa, Hajime, 368-69
nation, 64, 116, 128, 131, 132, 170-72, 250, 256, 282, 330, 334, 504
National Resting Place (Australia), 249
Native. *See* Indigenous
Native American, 197, 198, 402, 403, 479, 503, 523, 524, 525, 552, 555, *See also* Indigenous
Native American Graves Protection and Repatriation Act (NAGPRA), 171, 247, 249-51, 253, 555
nature
  attitudes toward, 403
  definitions of, 72, 404
  material, 175, 180, 183
Nazism, 118, 173, 176-77, 383
network
  definition of, 449, 572
  digital, 570, 595
  global, 287, 569, 595, 599
  social, 109, 195, 374, 597, 610
networking
  social, 600
new materialism, 41, 43, 44, 61, 65, 169, 181, 183, 207-8, 221, 625, 627, 630
new media, 374, 567-68, 586, 593
new museology, 171, 244
New World, 388, 403, 404, 424
New York, 198, 199, 243
New Zealand, 104, 244, 248, 252-53, 318, 526, *See also* Aotearoa
nineteenth century, 60, 61, 63, 65, 68, 112, 129, 134, 170, 192, 205, 206, 208, 209, 210, 212, 214, 219, 221, 223, 225, 226, 229-30, 237-39, 250, 281, 285, 416, 498, 515, 517, 520, 523, 528, 538, 576, 593
nodes, 454, 569, 591, 595, 600, 607
North Carolina, 481-87, 552
nostalgia, 138-39, 160, 182
nothing, 365

object
  biography, 46
obsolescence, 576, 580, 581
Oklahoma, 250
Old World, 402, 424
Olmec, 406, 423-24, 425
Olsen, Bjørnar, 169, 181
Onandaga Nation, 243, *See also* Iroquois Confederacy
ontology, 41, 43, 62, 129, 130, 134, 135, 137-38, 139, 143, 151, 155, 156, 163, 319, 443, 444, 448, 452, 453, 626
oppression, 114, 201, 225, 318, 506
orientalism, 275
Orientalism (1978), 244
Other, 128, 129, 132, 134, 138, 143, 172, 219, 241, 289, 341, 477
Otherness, 227, 338
ownership, 66, 136, 148, 157, 159, 160, 214, 249, 256, 317, 333, 345, 478, 555, 605, 615, 624

land, 335
Native Title Act, 345

paradigm, 302, 541, 625
paternalism, 109, 244, 256
patina, 154, 162, 182
pattern, 114, 150, 163, 288, 343, 344, 367, 391, 392, 395, 415, 418, 420, 449, 502, 503, 600, 609, 615, 616
Paul, Christiane, 594, 595, 603, 604, 605, 606-7, 608
peace, 120, 146, 150, 183, 483
Pearson, Maria, 246
Peirce, Charles Sanders, 358-59, 390, 542
Penfield, Wilder, 362-64
people of color, 115, 195
perception, 58, 65, 72, 149, 161, 163, 335, 364, 368, 374, 381, 392, 395, 545, 549, 573, 608
Perec, Georges, 31-33, 34-35, 47
performance
  gender, 331
  history of, 208, 210, 215
  ritual, 501
  studies, 65, 207
perspective
  anthropological, 443, 457
  art historical, 545
  disciplinary, 87, 474
  interdisciplinary, 14
  transcultural, 625
  Western, 366
Peru, 411, 416, 419, 423
Peruvian, 421
PET, 358-59
Pétursdóttir, Þóra, 169, 181-82
phenomenology, 27, 32, 41, 387, 440
Phillips, Ruth, 252
photographs, 64, 65, 117, 152, 251, 255, 311, 312, 313, 318, 320, 339, 608
physical, 57, 104, 116, 194, 209, 236, 303, 316, 317, 318, 331, 333, 363, 370, 472, 488, 499, 527, 545, 556, 572, 577, 582, 586, 594-95, 606, 608
physicality, 28, 147, 303, 628
Pietz, William, 36-37, 39, *See also* fetishism
Pinney, Christopher, 30, 289
pipe, 370, 518, 522, 524
  tobacco, 281, 523, 525, 531
place
  and space, 473, 546, 551
  definitions of, 177
  making of, 333-34
  materiality of, 471-88
  of origin, 160, 290, 302, 317
  performance of, 367
  sacred, 140
plant, 197, 284, 347, 425, 476
Plant, Sadie, 602, 605
Plato, 56-57, 58, 72
Poland, 108, 148, 150-52, 154, 161, 306-7, 316-17
political economy, 450, 605
politics
  identity, 346, 557

material culture studies, 19-21
  of art production, 383
  of authority, 128-43
  of heritage, 171
  of naming, 136
  of possession and dispossession, 136
  of representation, 368
  of value, 183
  ontological, 626
pollution, 87, 338, 405, 450
Porębski, Jerzy, 155
Porębski, Mieczyslaw, 153-55
Portugal, 129, 135
  Portuguese, 36, 272, 273, 282
possession, 105, 138, 140, 158, 290, 301, 302, 304, 305, 319, 496, 518, 624
postcolonial, 66, 134, 170, 172, 244, 254, 280, 627
post-disciplinary, 100, 121, 258, 626, 627
posthuman, 181, 183, 184, 446, 625
postmodernity, 241, 243, 387
potlatch, 237-38, 256
Potlatch Collection, 238, 256
power
  labor, 137
  material, 627
  relations, 135
  structures of, 539
  transformative, 278
practice
  aesthetic, 270, 278
  craft, 285
  ethical, 225
  heritage, 168, 174, 178, 180, 183
  material, 302, 476, 517, 541, 551
  material culture, 471, 488, 625
  religious, 247, 249, 539, 540, 541, 546, 547, 548, 551, 552, 554
  social, 380, 515
  traditional, 504
practice-centered design, 370, 372
preservation, 147, 156, 161, 174-76, 182, 581, 627
primitive, 132, 135, 239
privacy, 603, 616-17
private, 105-8, 147, 312, 316, 371, 493-94, 496, 502, 504, 506, 507, 509, 538, 603
process
  cultural, 275, 302
  heritage, 131, 141
  of making, 29, 39, 40
  political, 91, 333
  social, 597, 606
  technical, 445, 449, 451, 455, 457
  transformation, 516, 530
professional, 91, 191-92, 199, 200, 210, 338, 340, 506, 553, 600, 611
progress, 87, 91, 136, 149, 237, 238, 246, 405, 438, 439, 487, 553
Progressive Era, 500-1
prototype, 390, 425, 601
provenance, 149, 152-53, 155, 157, 158, 161, 163, 248-49, 250, 281
  Indigenous, 254

Prown, Jules David, 62-63
public spaces, 105, 106, 111, 112, 113, 115, 191, 210, 284, 371, 479, 502, 585
public sphere, 66, 371, 493, 497, 500, 605
punk rock, 628-29
pyramid, 414, 421-23, 424, 425

Qhapaq Ñan, 130, 135-41, 142, *See also* Colombia
Qing dynasty, 276, 281, 284
quality, 44, 108, 148, 149, 152, 156, 223, 272, 273, 316, 342, 343, 365, 382, 385, 388, 389, 603, 612
Quechua, 137, 404

Raby, Fiona, 372-73
race, 65, 111, 114, 239, 328, 331, 334, 481, 494, 501, 509, *See also* species
race and material culture studies, 65
racial inferiority, 237, 238
racism, 114, 228, 243, 509
radical, 40, 65, 69, 94, 140, 160, 387, 407, 515, 572, 585, 628
realism, 60-61, 240
reason, 382, 387, 389, 390, 391
reconciliation, 116, 148, 248, 485
recontextualize, 376, 486
recreation, 213, 273, 337, 345, 516, 527, 529
reenactment, 206-7, 209-10
  history of, 211-30
  politics of, 229
reflective, 360
reform, 136, 349, 495, 501, 513-23, 528, 530, 541
refugee, 304, 312, 313, 480
  Africa, 319
  Bosnia, 304, 312, 320
  Central America, 313
  Palestine, 312-13, 319
  Syria, 308-9, 314
regulation, 101, 105-6, 111, 115, 121, 133, 140, 338, 345, 447, 455, 514, 516, 518, 530
relation
  subject/object, 34
relevance, 88, 90, 128, 199, 600
reliance, 155, 494, 572, 600
religion
  and the senses, 548
  definition of, 541
  evangelical, 405, 551
  museum of, 553
  Orthodox, 394-95, 543, 555
  Protestant, 543, 549-50
  space and place, 551
  Vodou, 554
Renaissance, 205, 211, 274, 289, 584
renaming, 334, 341
repatriation, 171, 236, 243, 246-54, 256, 282, 555
  3D printing, 254
  virtual, 254-55
representation
  digital, 591
  historical, 212
  Indigenous, 240
  material, 487

representation (cont.)
    modes of, 376
    negative, 370
    of reality, 59, 366–70
    self, 362
    symbolic, 273
    traditions of, 367
resistance, 251, 364, 367, 373, 382, 393, 442, 453, 476, 487, 505, 506, 517, 520, 531
resource management, 77, 80, 90–92
resources
    archeological, 236
rhetoric, 132, 133, 138, 143, 151, 271, 289, 348, 483
Rhode Island, 190, 519
rhythm, 386–87
ritual, 318, 339–40, 391, 394, 406, 501, 521, 549
    baptism, 330, 348
    increase, 329, 348
robot, 70, 405, 426
Rosales, Harmonia, 364–65
Rowlands, Michael, 451
ruin, 129, 130–35, 138, 142, 143, 146, 147–48, 181, 182, 184
Rwanda, 175, 177

sacred, 242, 245, 246, 247, 248–49, 255, 256, 281, 328, 329, 334, 339–40, 345, 348, 349, 403, 404, 409, 411, 422, 424, 538, 540, 543, 547, 551, *See also* religion
    devolution, 406
Saïd, Edward, 244
savage, 239, 411, 412, 425, 504
Schneider, Rebecca, 206, 210, 212, 222, 224
science and technology studies (STS), 30, 41, 42, 447
science fiction, 69–72
Scotland, 184, 518
scriptive thing, 207–8, *See also* thing theory
sculpture, 198, 241, 282, 285, 288, 405, 415, 421, 423–25
    kinetic, 416
security, 105–6, 111, 120, 150, 305, 452, 455, 456, 570, 615, 616
segregated communities
    impacts of extreme spatial segregation, 113–14
    rural areas, 109
selfie, 608
semiotics, 41, 357, 374, *See also* symbolism
Şenel, Aslıhan, 367–68
sensation, 148, 381, 382, 393, 407, 542, 573, 612, 625
sense, 29, 381–82, 387
sensory, 31, 58, 337, 358, 392, 516, 518, 528, 541, 546, 548, 554, 555, 556
separate spheres, 493
Seremetakis, Nadia, 395
settlement movement, 503
settler-colonialism, 210, 214
sexuality, 364
shamanism, 402, 406
sharing
    Facebook, 600–1

Sharpe, Christina, 40
Shepherd, Nick, 627
Shipibo, 402, 407, 411–12, 416–18, 422, 423, 425
sign value, 375
Silk Road, 272
Simmel, Georg, 393
simulacrum, 156, 403, 408
Sino-European, 278, 284, 287, 289
Sioux, 246
Sister Carrie, 60, *See also* Dresier, Theodore
slavery, 66, 190, 193, 195, 225, 334, 335, 479, 554
Smith, Laurajane, 168–69, 171, 181, 183
Social Construction of Technology (SCOT), 447
social exclusion
    association with material inequalities, 105
    definition of, 103
    role of memorials, 115–17
social justice, 122
    definition, 102
    empathy as driver of, 113
    individual versus collective action, 100–1, 102
    major approaches, 102
social science, 301, 370, 439
sociology, 373, 545
software, 254, 439, 447, 568, 577–82
soundscapes, 528, *See also* sensory
Southeast Asia, 271, 275, 277–78, 404
sovereignty, 42, 140, 244, 250
space, regulation of
    temporary living spaces of homeless people, 111–13
Spain, 129, 135, 281
spatial theory
    disciplinary turns, 472–75
species, 47, 79, 87, 402, 410, 446
Spencer-Wood, Suzanne, 516
Stallybrass, Peter, 38, 39
Stewart, Susan, 59, 63
storage
    capacity, 592
story, 61, 140, 200, 201, 209, 625
Strasser, Susan, 68
Strathern, Marilyn, 331
style, 59, 170, 190, 201, 205, 223, 372, 380, 390, 391, 393, 411, 499, 500, 502
    technological, 410
substance, 28, 29, 38, 155, 161, 277, 280, 288, 330, 332, 441
Sumer, 403, 404
Suri, Jane Fulton, 370–71, 373
surveillance, 320, 436, 515, 530, 603
survive, 113, 142, 146, 154, 240, 359
Sweden, 316
symbol, 54, 278, 314, 358, 390, 420, 479, 487, 497, 507, 521, 542, 591
system
    aesthetic, 279
    computer, 581
    economic, 82, 118, 120, 365
    kinship, 330, 334, 450
    knowledge, 256
    operating, 580, 591
    philosophical, 33
    political, 82, 365, 455

religious, 405
social, 103, 115, 121, 603
technical, 389, 447, 451–56
thought, 6
value, 34, 36–37, 119

Taiwan, 281, 282
Tapsell, Paul, 253
Task Force on Museums and First Peoples (Canada), 246, 247
Tasmania, 518, 528, *See also* Australia
taste, 65, 107, 193, 269, 272, 279, 280, 311–12, 316, 383, 386, 499, 500
technical process, 439, 443–44
technics, 444–53, 456
technique, 284, 313, 367, 418, 438, 439, 440–43, 451, 476, 528, 530, 578
technocracy, 455, 456
technology
  philosophy of, 373
  wearable, 585–86
temporality, 31, 141, 149, 317, 320, 372, 443, 474, 478, 606, *See also* time
terminology, 45, 168, 171, 173, 174, 175, 249, 275, 276, 277, 280, 289
territory, 107, 250, 334, 443, 479
text
  electronic, 578, 586
  literary, 64
  sacred, 548
  social policy, 103
textiles, 284, 411–12, 418, 499
The Epic of Gilgamesh, 403
The Professor's Knife, 154
theory
  actor network (ANT), 41, 373
  aesthetic, 392
  anarchist, 628
  materiality, 630
  medium, 590, 598–99
  non-representational, 370, 373
  political, 373
  postcolonial, 244
  queer, 331, 628
  secularization, 539
  social, 42, 380
  spatial, 477
  system, 452
thing, 63, 69, 208
thing theory
  thing-ness, 208
Thrift, Nigel, 370
time
  and labor, 41
  cultural, 45
  linear, 606
  non-linear, 45
  prehistoric, 420
timeless, 142, 499
time-space, 210, 222
time-travel, 45, 222
Tlingit, 250, 253–54
Tomkins, Silvan, 386
tool

communication, 314
digital, 578
political, 9
weaving, 239
totem, 132, 241, 251, 253–54, 328, 329, 330, 339, 508
touch time, 206, 209, 224, 227, *See also* Schneider, Rebecca
tradition
  cultural, 113, 251, 270
  design, 112
  heritage, 169, 183
  intellectual, 630
  knowledge, 349
  philosophical, 380, 387, 628
  religious, 545, 546, 551, 556
  spiritual, 524, 554
  western, 475
transcultural, 269–72, 275–78, 282–84, 287, 289, 404
transform, 28, 40, 64, 136, 138, 173, 211, 319, 339, 361, 393, 406, 408, 437, 488, 515, 516, 543, 592, 605, 624
transhumanism, 456, 557
translocality, 314
trash, 68
trauma, 116–117, 146–48, 155, 157, 163, 173, 308, 333
Treaty of Waitangi, 244, 248
tribe, 245, 247–51, 253, 404, 478, 555
truth, 33, 58, 93, 102, 116, 134, 183, 362, 364, 373, 376, 382, 455, 496, 538, 541, 554
Turkey, 311
Turkle, Sherry, 603–4, 606, 611, *See also* hacker
twentieth century, 62, 65, 70, 149, 193, 198, 240–42, 245, 282, 334, 387, 450, 484, 485, 495, 496, 499, 500, 504, 509, 514, 539, 551
twenty-first century, 69, 132, 193, 201, 210, 223–24, 226, 498, 539, 570, 572, 573, 576, 586, 605, 607

un-disciplinary, 627
UNESCO, 29, 129–30, 132, 136, 177–79, 251
  World Heritage, 129–32, 140, 178–80
United, 583
United Kingdom, 212, 215
  London, 211, 213, 219, 246, 281, 284, 318, 368, 523, 551
  Oxford, 526
United Nations, 120
United States, 82, 107, 115, 118, 162, 190, 193, 194–95, 197, 198
Utah, 305, 403
utilitarian, 91, 305, 361, 415, 416, 439, 484

value
  aesthetic, 393
  class, 503, 509
  economic, 270, 272
  emotional, 311
  exchange, 38, 39, 132, 155
  heritage, 138, 139, 142
  historic, 156
  Indigenous, 258

value (cont.)
  instrument, 403
  intrinsic, 403
  moral, 493
  political, 142, 447
  relational, 375
  social, 36–37, 272, 273, 441, 442
  spiritual, 87
  symbolic, 157, 283
  use, 147, 153, 155, 375
Venezuela, 406, 408
vernacular, 439–43, 448, 451–52, 455, 474, 476, 477, 495, 552
Victorian, 205, 213, 216–19, 222, 305, 495–99, 508, 509, 518, 540, 577
video games, 580, 606
violence, 40, 42, 64–66, 92, 114, 131–32, 137, 150, 157–58, 174, 312, 318, 319, 442, 480, 484
viral, 610–11
Virginia, 194, 196, 528, 540, 552
virtual, 314, 570, 591, 595, 602, 605
  bodies, 606
  connections, 590
  environment, 576
  objects, 593
  reality, 583, 604, 606
virtuosity, 387, 390

Waiwai, 402, 406, 407, 408, 409–10, 413, 415, 417–20, 425, *See also* Guyana
wartime, 146–63
Warumungu, 255, *See also* Australia
Washington, 162, 255, 256
water
  bottle, 313, 359, 373
  environmental issues, 80
  holy, 271, 330
  identity, 329–30
  ownership, 345
wealth, 118, 190–91, 195, 196–98, 412, 487
Web 2.0, 595, 598–602, 604, 617
Weil, Stephen, 199
Western, 35, 46, 78, 81–87, 90, 94, 119, 135, 236–37, 239–40, 241–42, 243–45, 247, 252, 256, 257–58, 275, 279, 280, 282, 284, 288, 333, 366–67, 402, 405, 408, 411–12, 416, 426, 440, 477, 508, 515, 530–31, 538, 554, 624, 628
White, Lynn, 404
whiteness
  kimono, 226–27
  Students Teaching Against Racism in Society (STARS), 226
wilderness, 349, 403
womanhood, 481, 509
World Trade Center (New York), 173, 175
World War II, 146–48, 150, 172, 173, 176, 304, 306, 437, 628
writing, 47
women's, 68

Ye'cuana, 406, 407, 411, 418–21, *See also* Brazila, Venezuela
Yongzheng, 281, 284, *See also* China
Yoruba 1, 388
Yuanming Yuan (Old Summer Palace), 281, 282

Zent, Eglee, 403, 408
Zuni, 246

Milton Keynes UK
Ingram Content Group UK Ltd.
UKHW050001091124
450523UK00037B/177